Psychobiology

BPS Textbooks in Psychology

BPS Wiley presents a comprehensive and authoritative series covering everything a student needs in order to complete an undergraduate degree in psychology. Refreshingly written to consider more than North American research, this series is the first to give a truly international perspective. Written by the very best names in the field, the series offers an extensive range of titles from introductory level through to final year optional modules, and every text fully complies with the BPS syllabus in the topic. No other series bears the BPS seal of approval!

Many of the books are supported by a companion website, featuring additional resource materials for both instructors and students, designed to encourage critical thinking, and providing for all your course lecturing and testing needs.

For other titles in this series, please go to
http://psychsource.bps.org.uk

Psychobiology

CHRIS CHANDLER

The British Psychological Society

WILEY

Copyright © 2015 John Wiley & Sons Ltd

All efforts have been made to trace and acknowledge ownership of copyright. The Publisher would be glad to hear from any copyright holders whom it has not been possible to contact.

Cover illustratuion credit: Henrik5000/iStockphoto

Registered office
John Wiley & Sons Ltd, The Atrium, Southern Gate, Chichester, West Sussex, PO19 8SQ, United Kingdom

For details of our global editorial offices, for customer services and for information about how to apply for permission to reuse the copyright material in this book please see our website at **www.wiley.com**.

The right of Chris Chandler to be identified as the author of this work has been asserted in accordance with the Copyright, Designs and Patents Act 1988.

All rights reserved. No part of this publication may be reproduced, stored in a retrieval system, or transmitted, in any form or by any means, electronic, mechanical, photocopying, recording or otherwise, except as permitted by the UK Copyright, Designs and Patents Act 1988, without the prior permission of the publisher.

Wiley publishes in a variety of print and electronic formats and by print-on-demand. Some material included with standard print versions of this book may not be included in e-books or in print-on-demand. If this book refers to media such as a CD or DVD that is not included in the version you purchased, you may download this material at **http://booksupport.wiley.com**. For more information about Wiley products, visit **www.wiley.com**.

Designations used by companies to distinguish their products are often claimed as trademarks. All brand names and product names used in this book are trade names, service marks, trademarks or registered trademarks of their respective owners. The publisher is not associated with any product or vendor mentioned in this book. This publication is designed to provide accurate and authoritative information in regard to the subject matter covered. It is sold on the understanding that the publisher is not engaged in rendering professional services. If professional advice or other expert assistance is required, the services of a competent professional should be sought.

Library of Congress Cataloging-in-Publication Data
Chandler, Chris, 1966-
 Psychobiology/Chris Chandler.
   pages cm. – (Bps textbooks in psychology)
 Includes bibliographical references and index.
 ISBN 978-1-4051-8743-5 (paperback)
1. Psychobiology. I. Title.
 QP360.C44 2015
 612.8–dc23
                                2015027990

ISBN: 9781405187435 (pbk)
ISBN: 9781119069249 (ebk)
ISBN: 9781119068976 (ebk)

A catalogue record for this book is available from the British Library.
Set in 11/12.5pt Dante MT by Thomson Digital, India
Printed in Italy by Printer Trento Srl.

The British Psychological Society's free Research Digest e-mail service rounds up the latest research and relates it to your syllabus in a user-friendly way. To subscribe go to **www.researchdigest.org.uk** or send a blank e-mail to **subscribe-rd@lists.bps.org.uk**.

For Diane, Max and Guy

Brief Contents

Preface		xix
Acknowledgements		xx
PART I	**IN THE BEGINNING**	**1**
CHAPTER 1	Introduction to Psychobiology	3
CHAPTER 2	Genetics and Evolution	23
CHAPTER 3	Neural Development	61
CHAPTER 4	The Neuron, The Endocrine System and Communication	83
CHAPTER 5	Neuroanatomy and The Nervous System	117
CHAPTER 6	Psychobiology and Neuroscience Methods	153
CHAPTER 7	Psychopharmacology	173
CHAPTER 8	Animal Learning	203
CHAPTER 9	Drugs and Behaviour: Behaviour and Drugs	227
PART II	**PSYCHOBIOLOGY: BRINGING BIOLOGY AND BEHAVIOUR TOGETHER**	**249**
CHAPTER 10	Perceptual Systems	251
CHAPTER 11	Motor Behaviour and Control	293
CHAPTER 12	Executive Functions	315
CHAPTER 13	Neural Plasticity and Memory	343
CHAPTER 14	Sex	359
CHAPTER 15	The Neural Regulation of Homeostasis: Feeding and Drinking	391
CHAPTER 16	Motivation	409
CHAPTER 17	Emotion	435
CHAPTER 18	Sleep and Consciousness	463
CHAPTER 19	Lateralization and Language	483

PART III	THE PSYCHOBIOLOGY OF PSYCHOPATHOLOGY	499
CHAPTER 20	Developmental Disorders	503
CHAPTER 21	Schizophrenia Spectrum and Other Psychotic Disorders	523
CHAPTER 22	Affective Disorders	541
CHAPTER 23	Stress and Anxiety	559
CHAPTER 24	Neurodegeneration	583
CHAPTER 25	Psychobiology: Implications for the Brave New World	603
Glossary		613
Index		633

References (Visit the website to download the references - www.wiley.com/college/chandler)

Contents

Preface	xix
Acknowledgements	xx

PART I IN THE BEGINNING — 1

CHAPTER 1 Introduction to Psychobiology — 3

Introduction	4
What is Psychobiology?	4
Reductionism	4
History of Neuroscience	6
Psychobiology: Essential Collaboration	9
Points of View in Psychobiology	9
Physiological Psychology	9
Psychophysiology	9
Psychopharmacology	10
Neuropsychology	10
Cognitive Neuroscience	10
Social/Affective Neuroscience	10
Comparative Psychology	10
Behavioural Genetics	11
Computational Neuroscience	11
Ethics: Bioethics and Neuroethics	12
Animal Research	13
Experiments in the USA	14
Beyond the USA and UK	15
Professional Bodies: British Psychological Society (BPS) and American Psychological Association (APA)	15
Beyond the Ethics of Animal Research: The Validity of Animal Models of Behaviour	16
Good Science Versus Junk In – Junk Out	20
Summary	20

CHAPTER 2 Genetics and Evolution — 23

Introduction	24
In The Beginning – Evolution	24
Darwin's Revolutionary Theory – The Theory of Evolution	25
Evidence: The Case in Support of the Theory of Evolution	25
The Organism and the Environment	26
The Evolution of Humans	27
Evolutionary Psychology	29
From Evolution to Genetics	29
Mendelian Genetics	35
Mendelian Genetics and Eye Colour	36
Mendelian Inheritance: Huntington's Disease – Dominant Allele in Action	37

Mendelian Inheritance: PKU – A Recessive Allele in Action	39
Chromosomes and Inheritance	39
DNA	42
What is DNA?	43
What is the Function of DNA?	44
Genetic Variation	47
Variable Number Tandem Repeats	47
Epigenetics	50
Behavioural Genetics: The Complex Interplay of Psychology and Genetics	50
DNA and Psychology	55
Beyond Mendelian Inheritance: The Endophenotype	56
Molecular Biotechnology and Psychology	56
The Human Genome Project	57
Summary	59

CHAPTER 3 Neural Development — 61

Introduction	62
General Development	62
Neural Development over the Lifespan	62
Neural Development	64
Developmental Changes in the Brain	64
Development of The Peripheral Nervous System (PNS)	71
Development of The Autonomic Nervous System (ANS)	71
Male and Female Brains	71
Adolescent Development	71
Adult Development	75
Critical Periods	76
Teratology	78
Summary	80

CHAPTER 4 The Neuron, The Endocrine System and Communication — 83

Introduction	84
Neurons	84
Inside the Cell: Atoms at the Heart of Life	84
Neurons: Structure and Function	84
Support Cells	89
Glial Cells	89
Types of Neurons	90
Signalling and Communication Within the Neuron	90
Electrical Communication	90
Signalling and Communication between Neurons: Synaptic Transmission	99
Neurotransmitters	101
Receptors	102
Synaptic and Cellular Regulation	104
Retrograde Signalling	107
Signalling and Communication between Neurons: Gap Junctions	108
Endocrinology: Studying Long-Distance Communication	109
Action of Hormones at Their Target	113
Regulation	114
Summary	114

CHAPTER 5   Neuroanatomy and The Nervous System   117

- Introduction   118
- The Nervous Systems   118
  - *The Peripheral Nervous System (PNS)*   *118*
  - *The Autonomic Nervous System (ANS)*   *120*
  - *The Central Nervous System (CNS)*   *126*
- Neuroanatomy   130
  - *White and Grey Matter*   *131*
  - *Spatial Relationships of the Brain and Spinal Cord*   *132*
- Brain Regions   132
  - *Forebrain: Telencephalon and Diencephalon*   *132*
  - *The Limbic System (and Hippocampus)*   *141*
  - *The Basal Ganglia*   *143*
  - *Midbrain: Mesencephalon*   *143*
  - *Hindbrain: Metencephalon and Myelencephalon*   *143*
- The Ins and Outs of Blood Supply to the Brain   145
  - *Arterial Supply of Oxygenated Blood*   *147*
  - *The Cerebral Arterial Circle: The Circle of Willis*   *149*
- Sinuses   149
- Endocrine System   150
  - *The Pituitary Gland*   *150*
- Summary   150

CHAPTER 6   Psychobiology and Neuroscience Methods   153

- Introduction   154
- Physiological Psychology   154
- Neuropsycho-Pharmacology   157
  - *Unilateral and Bilateral Lesions*   *158*
- Psychophysiology   158
  - *The Electroencephalogram*   *158*
  - *Magnetoencephalography (MEG)*   *158*
  - *Event-related Potentials*   *159*
  - *Beyond the Brain*   *160*
- Brain Imaging   161
  - *Nuclear Imaging Using Radioactivity and Radioactive Isotopes*   *161*
  - *Magnetic Resonance Imaging*   *164*
- Optical Imaging of the Brain   166
- Neuroimaging is not the Ultimate Evidence   166
- Neuroimaging Maps of the Mind   168
- Psychophysiology and Neuroimaging Combined   168
- Virtual Lesions – Transcranial Magnetic Stimulation   169
- Summary   169

CHAPTER 7   Psychopharmacology   173

- Introduction   174
- Drug Classification   174
- Drug Action   177
  - *Pharmacokinetics*   *177*
  - *Pharmacodynamics*   *185*

Types of Drugs	193
Stimulants	*194*
Depressants	*194*
Mind-Altering Drugs	*196*
Antidepressants	*197*
Antipsychotics	*197*
Psychopharmacology – The Dark Side	197
Clinical Trials	199
Summary	201

CHAPTER 8 Animal Learning — 203

Introduction	204
Learning Theory: Adaptations and Associations	205
Habituation	205
Reflexes	207
Classical Conditioning	208
Measuring the Conditioned Response	*209*
Acquisition	*209*
Extinction	*209*
Spontaneous Recovery	*209*
Stimulus Generalization and Stimulus Discrimination	*210*
Is the Conditioned Response Identical to the Unconditioned Response?	*210*
The Relationship between the Conditioned Stimulus and the Unconditioned Stimulus	*211*
Delay Conditioning	*212*
Simultaneous Conditioning	*212*
Backward Conditioning	*213*
Trace Conditioning	*214*
Temporal Conditioning	*214*
Latent Inhibition	*215*
Blocking	*215*
The Rescorla–Wagner Model	*215*
Applications of Classical Conditioning: From Bench to Bedside	*215*
Operant Conditioning	216
The Law of Effect	*217*
Behaviourism	*217*
Acquisition	*221*
Shaping and Conditioning by Successive Approximations	*221*
Extinction	*221*
Spontaneous Recovery	*221*
Discrimination and Generalization	*221*
Interoceptive and Exteroceptive Stimuli	*221*
Applications of Operant Conditioning: From Bench to Bedside	*224*
Cognition in Animals	224
Summary	225

CHAPTER 9 Drugs and Behaviour: Behaviour and Drugs — 227

Introduction	228
Schedules as Fundamental Determinants of Drug-Elicited Behaviour	228
Tolerance	230

Sensitization	233
The Placebo	233
Conscious Processes	*238*
Unconscious Processes	*241*
Summary	243

PART II PSYCHOBIOLOGY: BRINGING BIOLOGY AND BEHAVIOUR TOGETHER — 249

CHAPTER 10 Perceptual Systems — 251

Introduction	252
The Sensory Modalities	252
Vision and Visual Perception	252
The Eye	*253*
The Sclera and Cornea	*253*
Aqueous Humour	*255*
The Iris and Pupil	*255*
The Lens	*255*
Vitreous Humour	*255*
The Retina	*255*
The Optic Nerve	*261*
Lateral Geniculate Nucleus	*261*
The Visual Cortex	*263*
Colour Perception	*266*
Binocular Vision: Two Eyes and Two Hemispheres	*270*
A Summary of Visual Perception	*271*
Hearing and Auditory Perception	272
The Ear	*273*
The Auditory Nerve and Cortex	*274*
Smelling and Olfactory Perception	275
The Nasal Membrane	*275*
Tasting and the Gustatory System	276
The Tongue and Mouth	*276*
The Vestibular System	277
Feeling and Somatosensation	279
The Skin	*279*
The Transmission of Tactile Stimuli to the Brain	*279*
Nociception and the Perception of Pain	279
Why Pain?	*281*
Components of Pain	*281*
Receptors	*281*
Pain Fibres	*281*
Pathways	*282*
Descending Pathways	*284*
Endogenous Analgesia	*286*
Pain Control	*286*
Masochism	*290*
The Hard Question	*291*
Sensory Integration	291
Summary	291

CHAPTER 11 — Motor Behaviour and Control — 293

- Introduction — 294
- Regions of the Brain — 294
  - *The Motor Cortex* — 294
  - *The Premotor Cortex* — 295
  - *Supplementary Motor Area (SMA)* — 297
  - *Presupplementary Motor Area (Pre-SMA)* — 297
  - *Cingulate Motor Area* — 297
  - *Broca's Area* — 297
  - *Frontal Eye Fields* — 297
  - *The Basal Ganglia* — 298
  - *The Cerebellum* — 301
  - *Brainstem* — 302
- Descending Pathways — 302
  - *The Pyramidal System* — 305
  - *The Extrapyramidal System* — 305
- Passage of Information to Muscles — 305
  - *The Skeleton* — 306
  - *The Muscles* — 306
  - *Neurochemical Activation of the Muscles* — 307
- Feedback — 309
- Control and Agency — 309
- Summary — 309

CHAPTER 12 — Executive Functions — 315

- Introduction — 316
- Frontal Lobes, Evolution and the Localization of Humanity — 316
- Lesions And Imaging — 317
- The Frontal Lobes: Damage and the Dysexecutive Syndrome — 322
  - *Thinking* — 322
  - *Rule Learning, Planning and Problem Solving* — 323
  - *Error Utilization* — 327
  - *Attention* — 327
- Theories Describing Frontal Lobe Function — 328
  - *Theory of Mind: Mind Reading (or Knowing Me, Knowing You (Aha!))* — 328
  - *Just Say No – The Case of Free Won't* — 329
- Summary — 339

CHAPTER 13 — Neural Plasticity and Memory — 343

- Introduction — 344
- Memory: What is it and Where is it? — 344
- Amnesia — 345
- The Neural Basis of Memory — 353
- What Happens at the Neural Level? — 353
  - *The Neural Bases of Learning: Long-Term Potentiation (LTP) and Long-Term Depression (LTD)* — 353
- Neuroplasticity — 355
- Summary — 356

CHAPTER 14   Sex   359

Introduction   360
Evolution of Sex and the Sexes   360
Differentiation of the Sexes   361
    Female Genitalia   *361*
    Male Genitalia   *365*
Sex Hormones   368
Menstrual Cycle and Ovulation   369
Sexual Development   373
    The Male and Female Brain   *373*
What Regions of the Brain are Different in the Sexes?   377
What Happens During Sexual Arousal?   380
Evolution of Pleasure   386
Sexual orientation   386
Summary   388

CHAPTER 15   The Neural Regulation of Homeostasis: Feeding and Drinking   391

Introduction   392
Feeding Behaviour   392
    Brain Mechanisms for Eating   *397*
    Eating Disorders   *401*
    Psychological Factors which Influence Eating   *405*
Drinking and Thirst   406
    Brain Mechanisms in Thirst   *406*
Summary   406

CHAPTER 16   Motivation   409

Introduction   410
Drug Addiction: The Triumph of Motivation Over Reason   410
What is Addiction?   412
A Reward Pathway: A Common Denominator in Addiction and Motivation   413
    Intracranial Self-stimulation   *413*
    Drug Self-administration   *416*
Amphetamine, Cocaine and Nicotine   416
Natural Reinforcers   419
Theories of Addiction – Theories of Motivation   419
    Positive Reinforcement   *421*
    Sensitization   *421*
    Physical Dependence Theories and Negative Reinforcement   *423*
    Just Say No   *427*
    Motivation, Addiction and Learning   *429*
Which Theory is Correct?   430
Summary   431

CHAPTER 17   Emotion   435

Introduction   436
What is Emotion?   436
Facial Expression   438

Physiological/Psychological Theories of Emotion — 443
   James–Lange Theory of Emotion — 443
   Cannon–Bard Theory of Emotion — 443
   Schachter's Cognitive Labelling Theory of Emotion — 446
The Emotional Brain — 447
   Papez Circuit — 447
   The Temporal Lobe and Limbic System in Emotion — 447
   The Amygdala — 448
   The Hippocampus and Fear — 450
   Fear or Fear Conditioning — 450
Beyond Fear — 452
Conceptual Act Model of Emotion — 452
Rolls' Reinforcement Model of Emotion — 454
The Somatic Marker Hypothesis of Emotion — 456
Emotion: What's Love Got To Do With It? — 456
   Love is the Drug — 457
Aggression and Violence — 458
   Neural Mechanisms and Aggression — 458
   Hormones and Aggression — 459
Stress — 459
Emotion and Music: Beyond Emotion as an Evolutionary Adaptation (Or Not) — 459
Summary — 461

CHAPTER 18   Sleep and Consciousness — 463

Introduction — 464
Circadian Rhythms — 464
Sleep — 465
Sleep Architecture — 465
   The Stages of Sleep — 465
   The Neural Mechanisms of Sleep — 468
   Neurotransmitters and Sleep — 468
   Dreams — 469
Theories of Sleep — 470
   Why Do We Need to Sleep? — 470
   Sleep Disorders and Mental Health — 470
Consciousness — 472
   Who are We and What Do We feel? What is It to Think? — 472
   Free Will — 474
Summary — 481

CHAPTER 19   Lateralization and Language — 483

Introduction — 484
Lateralization: Neuroanatomy — 484
Functional Lateralization — 486
   Asymmetry and Sex — 489
   Is Functional Lateralization Fixed? — 490
   Split Brains — 490
Summary — 496

PART III THE PSYCHOBIOLOGY OF PSYCHOPATHOLOGY — 499

CHAPTER 20 Developmental Disorders — 503

Introduction — 504
Attention Deficit Hyperactivity Disorder — 504
- *Diagnostic Criteria* — 504
- *Structural Changes in the Brain* — 506
- *Functional Neuroimaging of ADHD* — 506
- *Psychophysiological Studies* — 506
- *Frontostriatal Circuits* — 507
- *Pharmacology and Efficacy of Psychostimulants used in treating ADHD* — 507
- *Psychopharmacology: From Treatment to Theory* — 509
- *Barkley's Neuropsychological Account – Behavioural Inhibition* — 511
- *Working Memory* — 513

Autism Spectrum Disorder — 515
- *Diagnostic Criteria* — 515
- *The Genetics of ASD* — 515
- *Structural Neuroimaging in the Brain* — 518
- *Functional Neuroimaging of ASD* — 518
- *Neurochemistry and Psychopharmacology of ASD* — 519
- *Theories of ASD* — 519

Summary — 520

CHAPTER 21 Schizophrenia Spectrum and Other Psychotic Disorders — 523

Introduction — 524
Genetics of Schizophrenia — 525
Neurochemistry of Schizophrenia — 529
- *Typical and Atypical Antipsychotics* — 532

Neurobiological Theories — 534
Neuropsychological Theories — 535
Limitations of Many Studies in Schizophrenia — 537
Summary — 537

CHAPTER 22 Affective Disorders — 541

Introduction — 542
- *What causes depression?* — 545

Genetics of Depression — 545
Neurochemistry of Depression — 548
- *Noradrenergic Hypothesis of Depression* — 548
- *Serotonin Hypothesis of Depression* — 550

Treatments for Depression — 552
- *Selective Serotonin Reuptake Inhibitors* — 552
- *Atypical Antidepressants* — 552
- *Selective Noradrenergic Reuptake Inhibitors* — 552
- *Dual Action Antidepressants* — 552
- *Electroconvulsive Therapy* — 553
- *Lithium* — 553

Neuroanatomy of Depression — 553
Is there a Common Denominator in all the Treatments for Depression? — 554
Summary — 556

CHAPTER 23 Stress and Anxiety — 559

Introduction — 560
Stress — 560
    What is Stress? — 561
    The Stress Response — 563
    Input of the Stress Response — 564
    Sympathetic-adrenomedullary axis (SAM) — 565
    Hypothalamic-pituitary-adrenocortical axis — 566
    Homeostasis Versus Allostasis (Acute Versus Chronic Stress) — 569
Anxiety — 571
    Neurobiology — 576
    GABA and Anxiety — 576
    Barbiturates — 576
    Benzodiazepines — 578
    Noradrenaline — 580
    Serotonin — 580
    A Neuropsychological Theory of Anxiety — 581
Summary — 582

CHAPTER 24 Neurodegeneration — 583

Introduction — 584
Subcortical Neurodegeneration: Parkinson's Disease — 584
    Neuropathology — 586
    Neuropharmacology — 586
    Neuropsychology — 589
Cortical Neurodegeneration: Alzheimer's Disease — 593
    Neuropathology — 594
    Neuropharmacology — 596
    Neuropsychology — 598
Summary — 600

CHAPTER 25 Psychobiology: Implications for the Brave New World — 603

Introduction — 604
Policy — 604
Diagnosis — 606
Treatment — 606
Education — 607
Law — 608
Summary — 610

Glossary — 613

Index — 633

References (Visit the website to download the references - www.wiley.com/college/chandler)

Preface

Another psychobiology book! But I hope it isn't 'just another psychobiology book'. Why?

My mission was to provide adequate coverage of the BPS syllabus for psychobiology. That is easy. The hard part is 325,000 words. A vast number of words but simply not enough. To address the shortfall in words, I have provided an evidence-based approach to psychobiology. What this means is a well-referenced textbook that will guide you to other sources to complement your reading; a book that will guide you to the original studies that have shaped the discipline. Another advantage of this approach is that it provides the student of psychology with an example (I hope a good example) of how to cite work. Apart from the slavish adherence to the APA style of writing (which is somewhat tedious), the list of authors provides an example of how to acknowledge sources. This can sometimes make for a little clumsy reading, but might provide an intermediate stage from the general psychology textbook to the more detailed research and review papers.

Psychobiology is not about facts but the subject matter might feel closer to a fact than some other subdisciplines of psychology. It might feel more tangible. The reality is there is still much argument about how the brain works. We are much closer to understanding the brain that we were decades ago and this brings moral responsibility in which society and neuroscience interact. Throughout the text, I have wanted to provide a view of psychobiology that extends beyond the laboratory.

On the whole, I have tried to provide examples that are illuminating and appealing (and sometimes examples that just entertained me). I have also provided clinical discussion and reviews of diagnostics and symptoms. These are important to understand as they offer limitations to the psychobiological routes of mental illness.

I understand why students see this as hard. The thought going through the average first-year student's head is 'If I had wanted to do stats and biology, I would have chosen them'. Never has there been a time when stats and biology were so closely related. Computational neuroscience and brain imaging bring the two together, but what frightens most students is the language; the seemingly impenetrable language, the big words, the words that are not natural and are too close to their original Latin. On the whole, the words are just names. Names of molecules, brain regions and processes. Biopsychologists have to be academically multilingual.

I have learned a lot during the construction of this book. I use the word 'construction' carefully as it is more than just writing (the publishers refer to my part in the process as being 'to provide content'). I have learned that I need to give more time to my tasks, I have learned more about psychobiology during the process and it has rekindled my passion for the subject. I have learned that we know a lot about the brain, but we do not know enough. I hope that you will be able to learn from this book and associated website and that you will gain some appreciation for psychobiology, even if it is your least favourite subdiscipline.

Acknowledgements

Thanks to everyone at Wiley - especially Claire Jardine, Deborah Egleton, Ellie Wilson, Juliet Booker and Andrew McAleer for their patience and support. Thanks to all involved in creating the final product for their work of alchemy, especially Joyce Poh, Joanna Tester and Holly Regan-Jones; they really turned my base manuscript into something I hoped it would be. I am in their debt.

Thanks also go to Jo Lusher, Sharon Cox, Anita Andrews, Lynn Taurah and Sam Banbury for their help in keeping me going throughout the process; to Liz Charman and Robin Iwanek for somehow managing me; and to Graham Davey for his encouragement, guidance and support.

Special thanks to all the authors who provided me with copies of their work; and to the early reviewers - especially those who waived their right to anonymity. Their critically encouraging words were extremely valuable.

Thanks to Carl Bate for beers and never talking about this book. And thanks to the Prince Albert in Brighton - an oasis, sanctuary and refuge.

Finally, and above all others, so much thanks and love to Diane, Max and Guy for putting up with the process, for providing cups of tea and distractions, and providing the reason for being.

Part I
In the Beginning

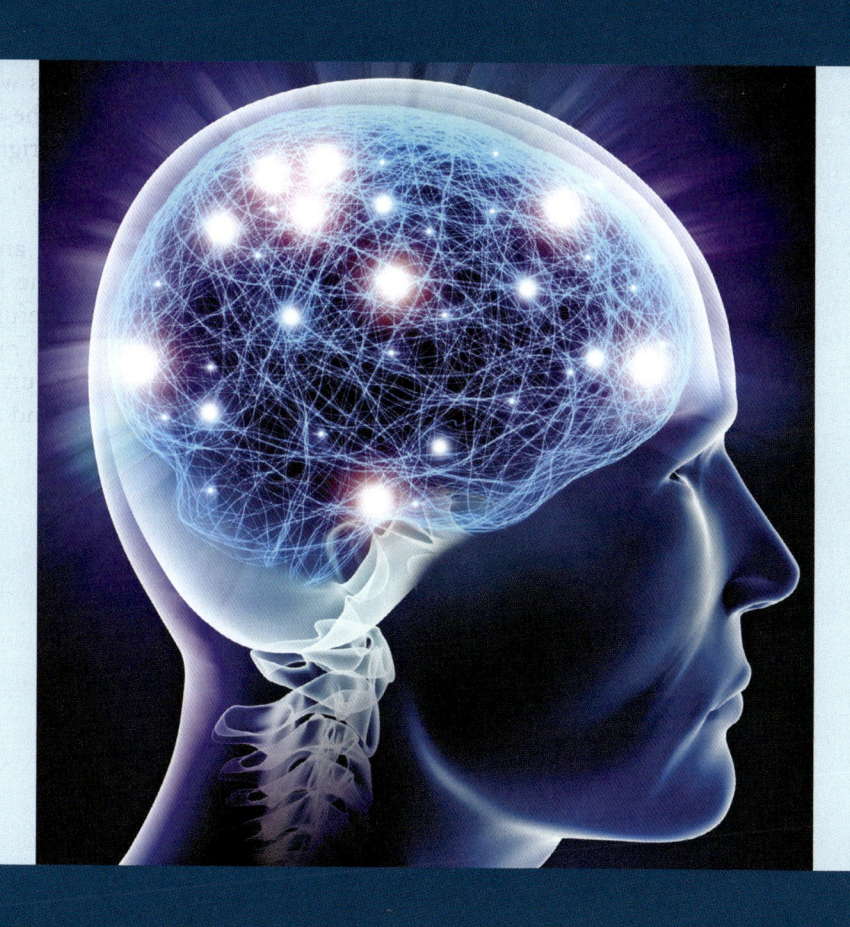

1. Introduction to Psychobiology
2. Genetics and Evolution
3. Neural Development
4. The Neuron, the Endocrine System and Communication
5. Neuroanatomy and the Nervous System
6. Psychobiology and Neuroscience Methods
7. Psychopharmacology
8. Animal Learning
9. Drugs and Behaviour: Behaviour and Drugs

This section is about the basic elements in psychobiology. Without understanding these basic mechanisms, the applications to behaviours in Part II and the psychopathologies in Part III will be hard to comprehend. Whilst the basic principles of genetics and neurobiology might seem ancient, do not be fooled by the historical antecedents of psychobiology. Psychobiology and neuroscience are dynamic and ever changing. New ideas, new technologies and communication within the scientific community allow for progress to be made. Time will tell us if our knowledge was correct or not. Hindsight possesses 20:20 vision; we know the earth is round and not flat, but that was news to people centuries ago. Knowledge changes and arguments advance.

This section addresses the key components of psychobiology. Starting with the philosophical stance and methodology, psychobiology strives to understand the biological bases of behaviour. The basic elements of life in molecular genetics are becoming increasing accessible to the psychobiologist – no more pure reliance on twin studies.

From the joining of maternal and paternal genes, the most fantastic organism develops. The human brain develops throughout gestation and continues to develop for decades and if we turn the power up on our psychobiological microscope, we can see the basic elements of the brain and how they are influenced by experience. The psychobiological microscope comes in many forms. Animals have been influential in shaping our understanding, allowing access to otherwise hidden processes. More recently, neuroimaging and molecular genetics, helped by biotechnology, have allowed a greater insight into real humans.

Using animals is a complex process and we have to be critically aware of their limitations, but also the insights gained. Animals were the first tools in our understanding of everything psychobiological (second is the undergraduate student!). The laws of learning have helped us understand how animals behave in differing environments. Although often pilloried, drugs both legal and illegal have also helped the search for the causal routes of behaviour but, as seen in Chapter 9, a drug response is mediated not just by its pharmacology but also by the state of the organism and the organism's expectations.

Psychobiology is not just about the effect of biology on behaviour, it is also about how experience and environments influence biology. And in turn, biology influences behaviour, which influences biology again, and thus the circle of events continues until the very end.

1 Introduction to Psychobiology

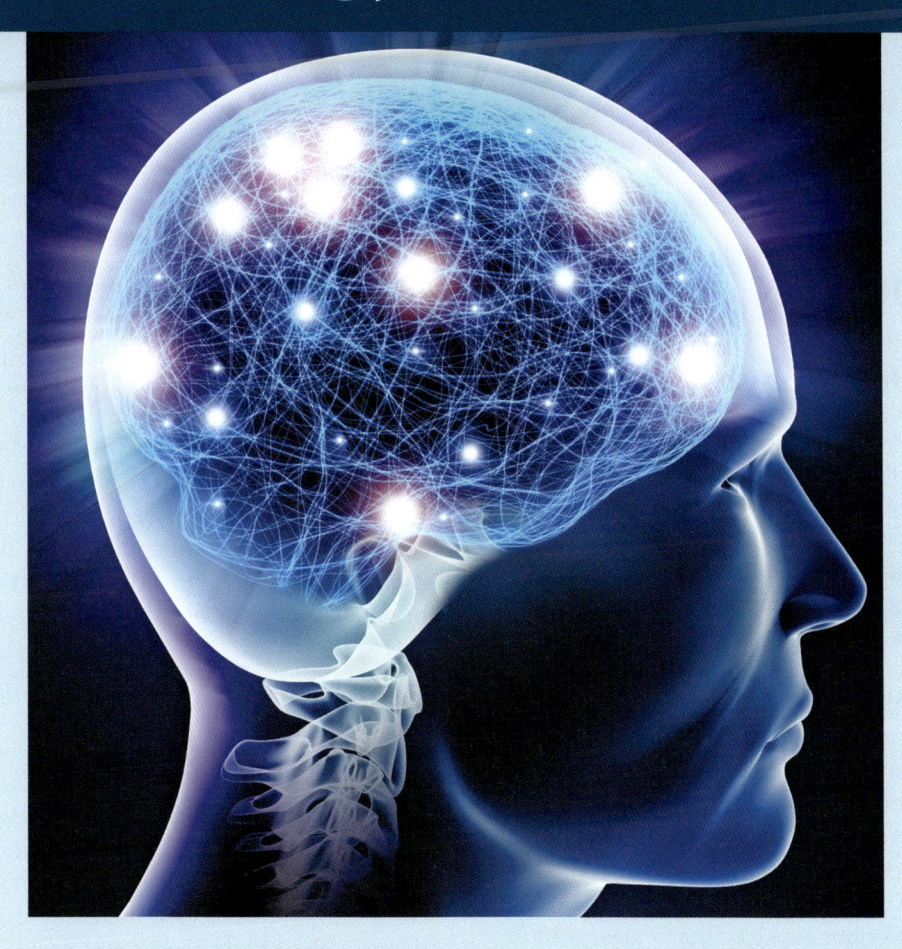

ANATOMY OF THE CHAPTER

This chapter will highlight the following.
- What is **psychobiology**?
- Philosophical background to psychobiology.
- History of psychobiology and neuroscience.
- Ethics and research.
- The use of animals in psychobiology.

INTRODUCTION   4

HISTORY OF NEUROSCIENCE   6

PSYCHOBIOLOGY: ESSENTIAL COLLABORATION   9

POINTS OF VIEW IN PSYCHOBIOLOGY   9

ETHICS: BIOETHICS AND NEUROETHICS   12

ANIMAL RESEARCH   13

GOOD SCIENCE VERSUS JUNK IN – JUNK OUT   20

SUMMARY   20

LEARNING OUTCOMES

1. To know what psychobiology and its subdivisions aim to achieve.
2. To understand the development of neuroscience from a historical and philosophical viewpoint.
3. To appreciate the methods of study in psychobiology.
4. To be able to evaluate the scientific utilization of animals in psychobiology.

INTRODUCTION

What is Psychobiology?

Psychobiology is a subdiscipline of psychology that seeks to explain behaviour in terms of biological mechanisms. Psychobiology is also known as biopsychology, biological psychology and behavioural **neuroscience**. I would argue that neuroscience is the main home for psychobiology rather than biology, which is perhaps too broad. Neuroscience is a truly multidisciplinary study of the nervous system. As we shall see, all behaviour has a neuroscientific underpinning. Such is the importance of neuroscience to the understanding of behaviour that there has been a proliferation of subdivisions, e.g. **social neuroscience**, **cognitive neuroscience** and clinical neuroscience. I like this quote from Arjun Sahgal (1993) defining behavioural neuroscience as 'the study of the neural basis of behaviour, but this colourless definition does not do justice to the wealth of scientific expertise that it incorporates'.

It is often assumed that because the brain is at the centre of behaviour, it is also the cause of all behaviour. Indeed, many courses have a module entitled 'the biological bases of behaviour'. This title is a misnomer because it suggests that the biological influences on behaviour are unidirectional: that biology affects behaviour. This assumption is partially correct but the truth is far more complex. In fact, an organism's behaviour, its interaction with an **environment**, and the environment itself can in turn influence its biology. Then the biology influences the environment. We eventually end up in a circular argument – a tautology. In the whole system, one part cannot be considered without the other: the environment provides the input, the brain processes it and forms an output, which in turn alters the environment, and thus the circle continues.

The term 'environment' in the current context refers to everything outside the organism from the environment *in utero* to the environment of the world in its largest conceivable instance. An obvious example of the environmental influence is presented in Chapter 2 in which during the process of evolution, species respond to external pressures of a harsh environment, albeit over a long period of time.

If we wish to have a causal model of behaviour or a causal model of **psychopathology**, we ultimately have to investigate how the basic elements such as genes and the environment are assimilated into the end-product behaviour/disorder. In Figure 1.1 we can see that genes and environment converge on the black box. It is what happens in this black box that leads to behaviour or clinical disorders. What we need to do is look inside the black box and unpack its contents. When we do this, we can see the brain is the key organ mediating the interaction of genes and environment to affect behaviour.

Reductionism

The circular argument of biology–behaviour–environment–biology (BBEB) is too difficult to fully understand in the whole system. Fortunately, psychobiological accounts of behaviour lend themselves to the philosophical stance of **reductionism**. Reductionism is reducing the complexities, in this case the complexities of behaviour, down to their basic constituent parts (Figure 1.2), which are comparatively simple, easy to investigate and identify.

Within psychobiology, there are different levels of investigation. Investigation can start with large regions of the brain (e.g. the temporal lobes and memory

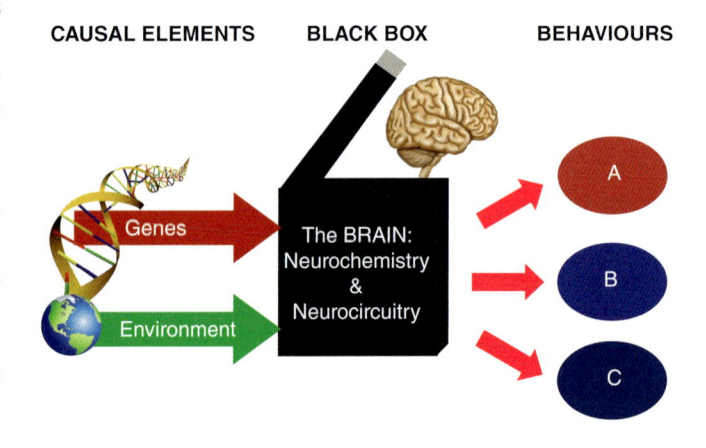

FIGURE 1.1 *Causal model of behaviour. Genes and environment interact to produce morphological and functional changes in the brain that lead to observable behaviours.*

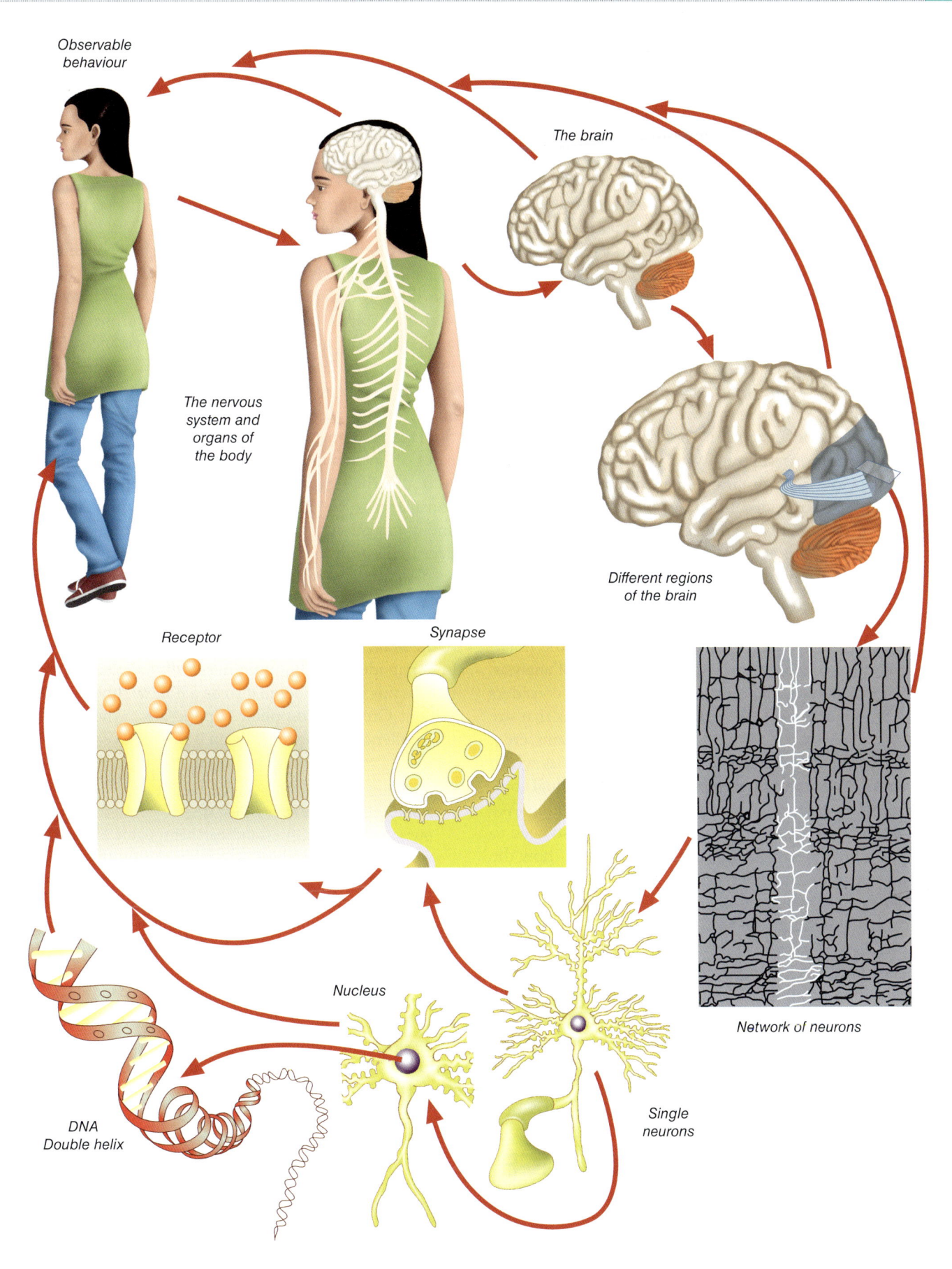

FIGURE 1.2 *Levels of analysis. Psychobiology can be reduced to more basic elements, from biological systems to regions of the brain, then to individual cells and finally the individual genes.*

(Milner, 1970)) and then move to smaller identifiable groups of nerves (e.g. the hippocampus and memory (Zola-Morgan & Squire, 1986)) and then to the individual neurons (e.g. memory consolidation and long-term potentiation (Bliss & Collingridge, 1993)). Although there are limitations in using reductionism, we would be lost without it! Reductionism helps answer the hard question: the question of consciousness (see Chapter 18). When I ask the question 'What does the brain do?' I tend to get a variety of responses that can be summed up as 'the brain does everything' but this is not a satisfactory answer. We need more precise questions, otherwise we get unsatisfactory answers. We have a long way to go in neuroscience. After all, Dr Lyall Watson said, 'If the brain were so simple we could understand it, we would be so simple we couldn't'. We need simple questions that have informed answers. By reducing the big questions to smaller elements, we can ask more specific questions, such as 'What does the hippocampus do?' or 'How does glutamate make memories?'. This is a much more manageable (but not an easy) question, which means that we can give a more precise answer.

What we have to be careful about when considering a reductionistic perspective on behaviour is that while understanding how the basic elements work is important, behaviours are a product of these elements working in unison at different levels of complexity, from the micro (molecular) to the macro (system/brain) level of analysis.

Opposite to reductionism is **holism**, which considers the whole organism. We are whole organisms that are clearly made up of components (genes, cells, brains, etc.), but from these basic elements emerge properties which are reflections of the systems rather than individual components. In essence, we need to have both accounts. We need to understand the components but we also need to understand the nature of emergent properties – how the elements interact. Understanding how the systems work will be of great benefit to the behavioural sciences (e.g. Zorumski & Rubin, 2011).

Reductionism is seen at the finest level when looking at genes. Technological advancement has made such exploration possible (Plomin, 2002; Plomin et al., 2013). Behavioural analysis can now take place at the molecular level: the question now is 'What genes are responsible for what behaviours? And then how do they interact within systems and with the environment?'.

HISTORY OF NEUROSCIENCE

Recent advances in technology have led to a rapid proliferation of neuroscientific knowledge which gives us the idea that neuroscience is a new discipline. Perhaps in name it is, but humanity's interest in behaviour can be traced back to ancient civilizations.

It is impossible to know exactly when neuroscience really first started, and of course it was not called neuroscience back then. Around 4000 BC, early Sumerian notes alluded to the euphoric highs gained from poppy seeds. The seed of the poppy, more specifically the opium poppy, can be refined to make heroin – the dawn of **psychopharmacology**. More recently, South American skulls from 2500 BC show evidence of trepanning, which was the process of drilling a hole in the skull in order to release the behaviours associated with bad spirits, or more likely brain dysfunction. The ancient Egyptians around 1600 BC left evidence of their interest in the brain. In what is known as the *Surgical Papyrus*, an account of the cranial structures, the brain surface and what was to become known as cerebrospinal fluid was presented. This papyrus also describes clinical cases of head injury and their behavioural consequence. Although the Egyptians identified the brain, they did not consider it to be the most important organ in the body and it was often discarded during mummification of the deceased's body.

If we move forward in time to ancient Greece and the period of 500 BC, the philosopher Alcmaeon of Croton claimed that the optic nerve carried sensory information to the brain and that it was the site of sensation. However, understanding of the optic nerve was somewhat rudimentary as he considered it to be a hollow tube. Another ancient Greek philosopher, Hippocrates, who took on the challenge of mind and brain is quoted as saying:

> Men ought to know that from the brain, and from the brain alone, arise our pleasures, joys, laughter and jests, as well as our sorrows, pains, griefs and tears. Through it, in particular, we think, see, hear and distinguish the ugly from the beautiful, the bad from the good, the pleasant from the unpleasant . . . I hold that the brain is the most powerful organ of the human body . . . wherefore I assert that the brain is the interpreter of consciousness . . . (Prioreschi, 1996, p.277)

Plato was also a philosopher who saw the brain as the location of mental life. With all this enlightenment about the brain, Aristotle (384–322 BC) asserted the heart as the organ of thought, perception and feeling. However, he did consider the brain as the organ that could 'cool the Passion of the heart'. Centuries later, such ideas have been refined and we see that the brain is the controller of behaviour; the prefrontal cortex manages the brain's impulses – it cools our wants and desires. Herophilus (335–280 BC), who ventured into the world of anatomy, identified and described the spinal cord as the source from which nerves came and also identified the cerebrum as the site from which voluntary movement stems.

He also considered the fluid-filled ventricles of the brain the area in which human intelligence was based.

During the Roman Empire, Galen (130–200 AD) also considered the ventricles to be of great importance. He proposed aspects of the body called humours which were fluid filled and could be mapped on to seasons and eventually personality characteristics.

- Blood was associated with courageous, hopeful and amorous behaviours and the ancient name of this humour was sanguine.
- Yellow bile coming from the spleen was called choleric and was associated with the characteristics of being bad tempered and volatile.
- Black bile from the gallbladder was considered melancholic with the characteristics of being despondent, irritable and sleepless. We still use the term melancholic to describe some of the symptoms of depression.
- Phlegm in the brain and lungs gave rise to the phlegmatic personality of being calm and unemotional.

Nemesius (320 AD) took Galen's ideas a little further. Against the backdrop of religion and the soul, he claimed that the mind, not the soul, could be localized in the ventricles. The first ventricle was associated with common sense, the second ventricle with reasoning, thinking and wisdom. The third ventricle was where memories resided.

Leonardo da Vinci (1452–1519), when not capturing the enigmatic smile of the Mona Lisa, was also a scientist. Da Vinci was particularly interested in anatomy and engaged in human dissection. He injected the blood vessels and the ventricles with wax to preserve them. Such techniques are still used today (see Pevsner, 2002). His anatomical drawings are informative and of outstanding beauty.

Andreas Vesalius (1514–1564) was also involved in human dissection. He was able to correct numerous mistakes of Galen, whose doctrine continued to reign, and published detailed drawings of the human brain.

Perhaps the most important philosophical stance within neuroscience was that of René Descartes (1596–1650). Descartes describes the brain as a hydraulic system in its control of behaviour. He argued that the mind and body are separate entities, but entities that interact at the pineal gland. He considered that animal spirits operate the muscles and tendons that initiate movements. Cartesian dualism, as it is known, is still an important concept in modern neuroscience, most notably in neurophilosophy.

Thomas Willis (1621–1675) was a professor of natural philosophy at Oxford University. He published the first brain atlas called *Cerebri Anatome* in which he described the functional units of the brain. He is also credited with introducing the term *neurology*.

The idea that animal spirits travel down a hollow tube to effect responses was put to rest by the experiments of Luigi Galvani (1737–1798). Galvani discovered the electrical nature of neural conduction (see Chapter 4).

Luigi Rolando (1773–1831) used electricity to stimulate the brain and discovered that actions were under the control of the cortex in animals. Voluntary action was under the control of the cerebrum, whereas involuntary actions were under the control of the cerebellum. Rolando pioneered the idea that brain functions could be differentiated and located in specific areas of the brain and discovered the fixed pattern of cerebral convolutions, highlighting motor and sensory gyri (see Caputi et al., 1995).

Johannes Purkinje (1787–1869) was the first to describe a nerve cell in detail. He studied sensory experiences after stimulation, for example of the eyeball. He discovered large nerve cells in the cerebellum, now known as Purkinje cells, with characteristic branches (dendrites).

In 1806, the German physicist Franz Joseph Gall (1758–1858) presented a view of the brain which ascribed different regions to different functions. He considered the brain to be an organ not unlike a muscle; the more use an area has, the bigger it would get. The increase in size would manifest itself by protrusions of the skull which could be seen or felt. This is the reading of bumps on the head that is called phrenology. It was, of course, completely wrong.

Marie Jean-Pierre Flourens (1794–1867) rejected Gall's view of cortical localization after experimentation with animals (see Pearce, 2009). Again this was the wrong view, but at least he tried! However, John Baptiste Bouillaud (1796–1881) was in favour of cerebral localization. He presented cases of loss of speech as a result of damage to the anterior lobes of the brain. From this perspective he also considered the frontal lobes to be the location of higher mental functions (executive functions; see Chapter 12) that differentiate humans from animals.

The frontal lobe was also the focus of attention in the famous neuropsychological case study of Phineas Gage (1848). Gage was a railroad worker who suffered brain damage as a result of an iron rod being projected through his skull and destroying part of his frontal lobe. Remarkably, Gage lived to tell the tale but his behaviour was somewhat different after the accident. He was unreliable, he was no longer interested in going to church and was constantly drinking and gambling. He was sexually inappropriate and used offensive language constantly. Ultimately the damage to the frontal lobe had removed his inhibitory faculties – the ability to monitor himself.

The English neurologist John Hughlings Jackson (1835–1911) discovered that epilepsy stems from abnormal electrical activity of the temporal lobe. He also identified that those who had seizures emanating from the left frontal lobe had associated speech difficulties. He considered the nervous system to have three levels of organization: pre-frontal, frontal and spinal/brainstem regions.

The localization of language in the brain gained much credibility with the work of Paul Broca (1824–1880). Paul Broca had been at a meeting with Pierre Gratiolet, who had a dominant position opposing localization of function, and heard Ernest Auburtin put out a call to anybody who could find evidence for functional specificity in the brain. Broca shortly after presented evidence for functional localization by demonstrating that the lesions in patients who could not speak but could still understand language were located in the left frontal lobe. This region is today known as Broca's area. Continuing with language, Carl Wernicke (1848–1904) presented further evidence of cortical localization in a patient similar to Broca's but in this case the patient could speak but made no sense. The damage in the brain of this patient was in the posterior part of the left hemisphere, now known as Wernicke's area (see Chapter 19).

Continuing support for cortical localization of function, Gustav Fritsch (1838–1907) and Eduard Hitzig (1838–1927) investigated motor behaviour by stimulating the surface of dogs' brains. Using this method, particular regions were associated with movement.

Theodor Schwann (1810–1882) described the myelin sheath that is wrapped round nerves and was the first to suggest that the body is made of individual cells. He perhaps did not realize quite how many, but his name was given to the Schwann cell (see Chapter 4).

Korbinian Brodmann (1868–1918), on the basis of cellular structure, was able to divide the human cortex into 52 discrete areas, thus supporting cortical localization. These Brodmann areas are mapped onto specific functions, e.g. the motor cortex is area 4 and areas 41 and 42 are the auditory cortex (see Chapter 12).

Camillo Golgi (1843–1956) developed a silver stain that allowed visualization of a neuron and Santiago Ramón Y Cajal (1852–1934) discovered that neurons were discrete unitary entities. He established the *neuron doctrine*, which is the fundamental organizational and functional principle of the nervous system. The neuron doctrine stated that the neuron is the anatomical, physiological, genetic and metabolic unit of the nervous system and that neurons are discrete and autonomous cells that can interact with each other. The interaction occurs at the synapses, which are the gaps that separate neurons. Information is transmitted unidirectionally from dendrites to the axon. Charles Scott Sherrington (1857–1952) identified and described the gaps between neurons and named them synapses.

We can now see that the study of the brain moved from lone philosophers and physicians to teams of researchers. This is a trend that continues to this day with many important research papers having multiple authors in excess of 10 or 20 people.

In 1940 Henry Dale was able to isolate acetylcholine, the first neurotransmitter – a breakthrough in biochemistry.

Some studies are pioneering and adventurous. A great debt is owed to the brave participants. Wilder Penfield (1891–1976), in quite stunning experiments in which he stimulated different sections of the cortex of epileptic patients during neurosurgery, found that activating multiple cells would produce specific results. What is amazing is that the patients were awake and fully conscious during the brain surgery and were able to verbalize the effects of stimulation.

These landmark studies have taken place over many years and they show neuroscience evolving. In the last 50–60 years there has been huge growth in the understanding of the brain. The scientists of the last few decades have contributed to where we are now and are no less important than their predecessors mentioned above.

In 1953 Brenda Milner described patient HM who had undergone surgery to contain epilepsy. This landmark study, and its continuation for many years, shaped our understanding of memory and amnesia (see Chapter 13). The understanding of memory continues at a micro-level with the description by Bliss and Lomo (1973) of long-term potentiation (LTP) which is thought to underlie memory.

In a series of experiments in the late 1950s and early 1960s, Hubel and Wiesel gained huge insight into visual perception with the discovery of simple and complex cells of the visual cortex (Hubel & Wiesel, 1959, 1960, 1961, 1962, 1963b; Wiesel & Hubel, 1963) (see Chapter 10).

A challenge to our understanding of free will and the philosophy of consciousness came in the 1980s from Benjamin Libet, who suggested that our brains initiate motor acts before we are consciously aware of them (Libet et al., 1982; Libet, Gleason et al., 1983; Libet, Wright et al., 1983), thus questioning the fact that we are in control of our actions.

In modern times there is a whole new world of discovery in neuroscience, especially with the advent of imaging technology and biotechnology. When does the quest for understanding how our brain works end? The answer surely is 'never'. When not being the first man to run a mile under 4 minutes, Sir Roger Bannister, a neurologist, in an interview described neurology as '… one of the most demanding vocations in medicine. Where do you stop, after all, with the brain? How does it function? What are its limits? The work seems unending' (McRae, 2004). Indeed, it remains unending.

PSYCHOBIOLOGY: ESSENTIAL COLLABORATION

It is important to be aware of the dynamic, ever-changing nature of psychobiology. The volume of information is astonishing, coming from many areas of expertise. Indeed, there is so much information it is hard for the mere mortal to assimilate it all. Do not be surprised when you come to the realization that you are studying more than psychology.

You will need to assimilate information from

- **genetics** – Chapter 2;
- **neuroanatomy** – Chapter 5;
- **endocrinology** – Chapters 4 and 14;
- **pharmacology** – Chapters 7 and 9;
- **pathology** – Chapters 20–24;
- **chemistry** – Chapter 4;
- **physiology** – Chapter 4;
- **psychiatry** – Chapters 20–24;
- **ethology** – Chapter 2; and
- **physics** – Chapter 6.

The list could go on, but I will leave it at that.

With new information coming at us from many directions, we have to be prepared to adapt and change any previously accepted ideas regarding the biological mechanisms underlying behaviour. We have to be able to account for behaviour within new theoretical contexts and test these theories rigorously via experimentation.

Similarly, other areas of psychology also benefit from psychobiological investigation. Freud's view of **psychosexual development** can now be placed in a psychobiological context where the id, exerting its primitive demands, can be seen in the old brain (e.g. hypothalamus). The ego can be placed in the limbic system with motivation as the driving force to satisfy the id. On top of all this impulse satisfaction is the superego which can be seen as emanating from the frontal lobe.

Developmental psychologists benefit from charting neurodevelopment, with more recent accounts of adolescence focusing on the brain rather than hormones (which are also important, which may explain some adolescent behaviours). Social psychologists might wish to understand how social constructs such as morality are realized in biological terms (see Chapter 25).

POINTS OF VIEW IN PSYCHOBIOLOGY

Psychobiologists have different perspectives for investigating behaviour. The geneticist is clearly interested in genes, but the psychobiologist who is interested in **behavioural genetics** may look at genes and use methods outside the laboratory (e.g. twin studies; see Chapter 2). These areas are strongly represented in the **British Psychological Society's** view of important areas within psychobiology.

- **Physiological psychology**
- Psychopharmacology
- **Neuropsychology**
- **Psychophysiology**
- Comparative psychology
- Cognitive neuroscience
- Affective/social neuroscience
- Behavioural genetics
- **Computational neuroscience**

Physiological Psychology

Physiological psychologists study the neural mechanism underlying specific behaviours. Essentially they study the nerves. They do this in controlled experiments which often use **lesions** (destruction) of a specific region of the brain in order to determine what its function is. They can perform such lesions highly specifically using electricity to burn out the neuron, chemicals to poison the neuron or mechanically with a scalpel (see Chapter 6). It is probably clear to you that these experiments are not conducted on humans. Medical experiments in humans are carefully monitored in terms of ethics and safety (see later). Such experiments are conducted in animals. Many species are used but most commonly rats (animal experiments are discussed further in this chapter and throughout this book).

Psychophysiology

Psychophysiology is not to be confused with physiological psychology. Such confusion is common when learning about psychobiology. The psychophysiologist studies the relationship between the physiological activity of the brain and psychological processes. They achieve this by studying how the body responds to a particular stimulus or how the brain's electrical activity differs during certain parts of a task. An example of this is a lie detector test which measures the body's reaction during answers to probing questions. The essence here is that when someone tells a lie, their body will indicate that they have lied because it is stressful to do so (e.g. heart rate may increase or they may sweat). These changes may not be detectable to the human eye but are detected by scientific instruments. In Chapter 6 we shall see how these techniques are used and what they tell us and in Chapter 18 will see them in action as they are critical for the evaluation of sleep states and consciousness.

Psychopharmacology

Psychopharmacology is all about the drugs. This subdiscipline seeks to understand behaviour and its neural basis by examining how drugs modify the brain and consequently behaviour. For a psychopharmacologist, drugs are tools for investigating the brain rather than being primarily for treating people, or indeed for recreational purposes. Drugs are the search engines of neurotransmitter systems. It is often the case that a drug is used in treating a particular psychological disorder without a full understanding of how it works. Some drugs are deployed off label, which means they are used in a different way from what they are licensed for. This new use can lead to new insights into the psychopathology of the condition. Psychopharmacological studies can take place in either animals or humans. Clinical trials are an example of a psychopharmacological study in which a new drug is evaluated for its potential use in treating a disorder. Before a drug gets to clinical trial, it will have been evaluated in animals, more of which later.

Psychopharmacology is more than just evaluating drugs, it is about trying to understand the brain and its function by tracing the actions of drugs in the brain.

Neuropsychology

Neuropsychology is the study of the consequences of brain damage. We cannot perform direct experiments on humans that involve destruction of the brain for the purpose of acquiring knowledge – that would be unethical. However, people do suffer from brain damage through a variety of reasons, e.g. accidents and neurosurgery. Occasionally people suffer brain damage as a result of infections, e.g. the encephalitis epidemic that was famously written about by Oliver Sacks in *Awakenings* (later made into a film with Robert de Niro and Robin Williams). In general, neuropsychology deals with case studies. The very nature of brain damage often means that the damage is unique to that individual. Occasionally it can be quasi-experimental with groups of patients who have a common area of damage (e.g. alcoholics with Korsakoff's syndrome). Perhaps the two most famous cases are those of HM and Phineas Gage that lead to a greater understanding of memory and executive functioning respectively.

The effects of brain damage are assessed by neuropsychological tests. There are numerous tests that probe different aspects of cognition. This can give a profile of function and the neuropsychologist may make certain assumptions about the underlying damage that leads to that profile. More recently, neuroimaging has allowed the neuropsychologist to actually see which part of the brain is damaged and the extent of the damage, which increases the precision of neuropsychological accounts of behaviour.

Cognitive Neuroscience

Cognitive neuroscience embraces cognitive psychology and biopsychology. In this marriage cognitive processes are investigated within a neuroscience context. A cognitive neuroscientist will probe cognitive functioning using brain-imaging techniques. This is not dissimilar to the neuropsychologist but there is no need for brain damage here. The cognitive neuroscientist can look at the normal brain, or perhaps a better phrase would be the intact brain, and see how active it is during certain cognitive tasks.

Social/Affective Neuroscience

It would appear that we can put any subdiscipline of psychology in front of the word 'neuroscience' and create a new subdiscipline. In social or **affective neuroscience**, the neural processing of emotional information can be evaluated in the same way cognitive processes are evaluated by the cognitive neuroscientist.

Comparative Psychology

As the name suggests, comparative psychologists compare human behaviour with that of animals. Central to this account is Darwin's theory of evolution (see Chapter 2). Behaviour across species is examined to try and understand the evolutionary and adaptive nature of a particular behaviour. Evaluation of behaviour (note that we are not using experimental approaches here) could take place in a laboratory but more often than not it happens in the field. Where better to study animal behaviour than in their natural habitat? This is called ethological research. The comparative psychologist's exploration of behaviour can sit alongside an evolutionary explanation of behaviour, which leads us to evolutionary psychology. Evolutionary psychologists seek to understand our current behaviours as adaptations of behaviours from our ancestry. The questions they ask include why is a particular behaviour prevalent and how is it adaptive? It may be surprising to think that there are evolutionary accounts of the adaptive nature of many psychiatric disorders, e.g. schizophrenia, depression and attention deficit hyperactivity disorder (ADHD) (see Chapter 2); there are also evolutionary accounts of the dark side of our behaviour, e.g. murder and rape.

Behavioural Genetics

I consider behavioural genetics to be separate from **comparative psychology**. However, behavioural genetics may be theory led in a similar way to evolutionary psychology. The goal for behavioural genetics is to understand the genetic basis of a behaviour, characteristic or disorder. Traditionally, behavioural geneticists have tried to establish hereditary patterns in behaviour. To do this, they have taken advantage of the genetic similarity of families and especially twins. More recently, the behavioural geneticist has used the advances in biotechnology to investigate the very structure of our genes, the DNA, in relation to behaviour. Quite clearly, this can be conducted in human participants but animals can also be used to understand how genes influence behaviour. We can modify the genes of an animal and see what the effects are within a very short timeframe.

Computational Neuroscience

Modelling human behaviour and the underlying neural activity in the animal is one thing, but trying to do it in a computer or a machine is an entirely different proposition. The basic elements for a brain circuit have been proposed by Markram (2006) and are depicted in Figure 1.3. At the

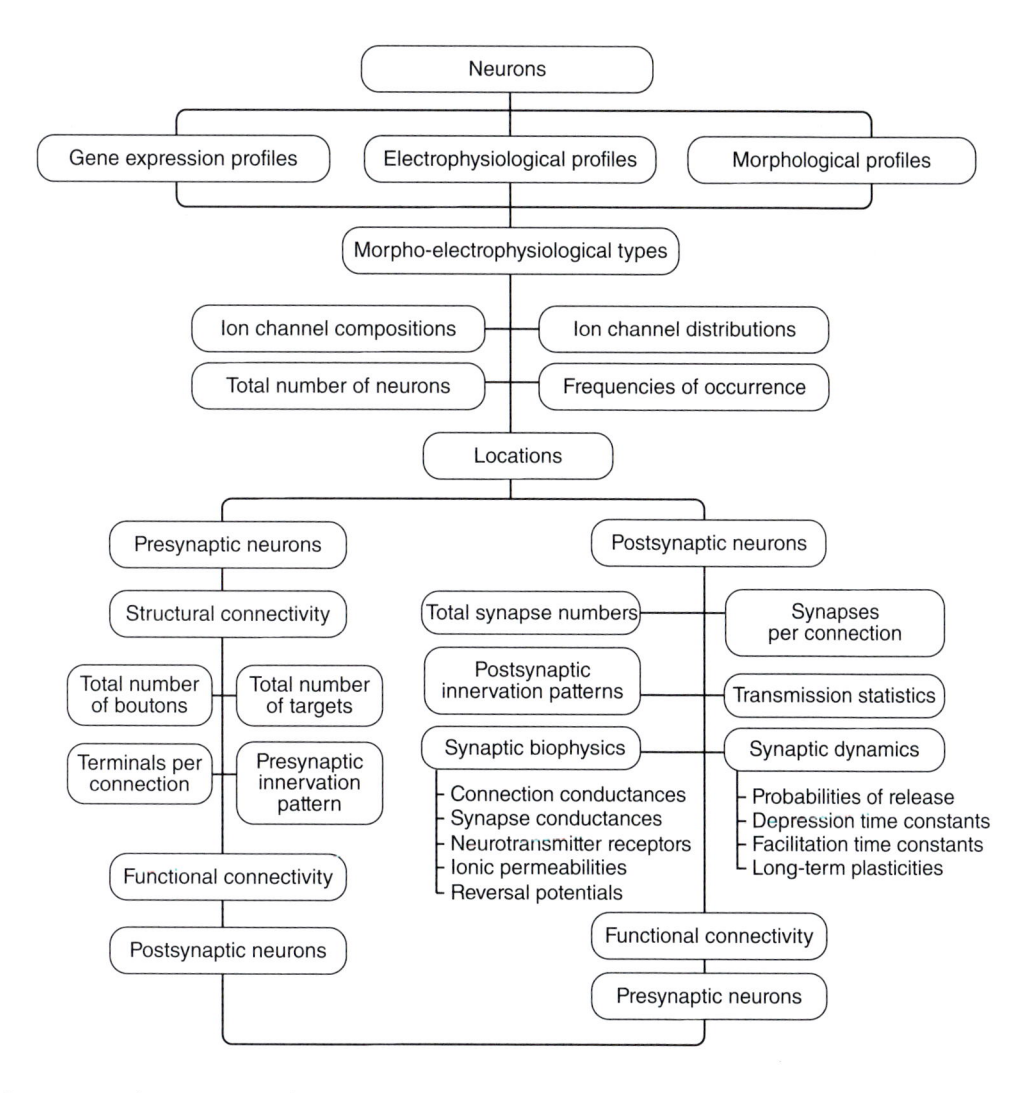

FIGURE 1.3 *Computational neuroscience. The minimal requirement for building a microcircuit of the brain.*
Source: Reprinted by permission from Macmillan Publishers Ltd: Markram, H. (2006). The Blue Brain Project. *Nature Reviews Neuroscience, 7*, 153–160, copyright 2006.

end of the book you should revisit this and see how all the components need to be understood for a small micro-circuit to come even close to modelling the brain.

In 2013 the Human Brain Project was announced in which a 10-year programme of research and scientific endeavour was set up to simulate the human brain in a supercomputer. To quote the Human Brain Project's vision:

> The goal of the Human Brain Project is to build a completely new information computing technology infrastructure for neuroscience and for brain-related research in medicine and computing, catalysing a global collaborative effort to understand the human brain and its diseases and ultimately to emulate its computational capabilities. (www.humanbrainproject.eu/discover/the-project/overview)

The benefits of such a project are outstanding, but how we deploy this new information and technology will have to be carefully monitored (see the *Terminator* movies).

All of the subdisciplines *try* to bring scientific rigour to the study of behaviour (*try* being the keyword – this is not always the case). However, human behaviour does not always obey true scientific rules. In physics and chemistry there are absolutes – the freezing point of water is 0°C and the boiling point is 100°C. In the behavioural sciences there are no such absolutes. When conducting an experiment in chemistry, if you follow exactly the same procedure you will get the same results. In behavioural sciences this is not always the case. People (and animals) have all sorts of different experiences and histories that can affect their behaviour. One person will not necessarily react in the same way as another person, even when the experimental conditions are the same.

ETHICS: BIOETHICS AND NEUROETHICS

To understand behaviour one has to engage in research; that is, controlled experiments or studies. Experiments in psychobiology need to be carefully considered because of the damage that could occur.

It is clear that if you wish to understand human behaviour then you need to investigate humans. Indeed, many experiments are conducted each year that use humans to investigate the relationship between biology and behaviour. These experiments are published only if they fulfil all the requirements of an ethically acceptable procedure. A full account of the ethical guidelines is provided by the British Psychological Society (BPS) for experimental conduct. However, the BPS's jurisdiction only extends to its members and there may be different standards outside the UK.

To summarize the BPS position on research, the areas of concern include multiple relationships where there might be a conflict of interests. This could be the case if the scientist is being funded by a drug company whose drug is involved in a clinical trial or is receiving funding from industry to talk about treating a disorder with the emphasis on their pharmaceuticals.

The BPS requires competence in research and to avoid excessive or misleading claims, in which conclusions are overstretched from what the data are saying. Another problem is where there are inadequate safeguards and/or monitoring of the study. Again, for the psychobiologist this may be an even bigger issue to address as they may well be working with behaviour-changing agents such as drugs. This aspect is expanded upon when we look at clinical trials.

Perhaps the biggest research sin, although all of them are bad, is falsifying data. This may appear outrageous; why would someone do such a thing? In this cut-throat, economics-driven world, people's motivation may be less than honourable. There are fortunately few media reports of such instances, but they do occur. Why do they occur? Career progression, conflict of interest, personal gain, etc. Universities, academia and research come under scrutiny and evaluation in a process that was once called the research assessment exercise (RAE) and is now the research excellence framework (REF). This is when academics have to stand up and be counted in terms of research. The pressure from universities to be excellent in research and thus reward those who contribute to that excellence may unwittingly encourage academics to 'come up with the goods'. There is a lot of money at stake.

The BPS ethics code is based on four core ethical principles:

- respect;
- competence;
- responsibility; and
- integrity.

Research using human participants can answer only some questions. Others remain unanswered because of the ethical and moral restrictions placed on human research. Such restrictions are essential to protect participants and especially vulnerable populations. Such vulnerabilities extend beyond psychological disorders and include those who are economically vulnerable and those in prison who have had their freedom restricted. Hopefully, we are very aware of the moral and ethical issues of human participation. The advancement of genetic engineering, its potential use and misuse, is a high-profile case in the media, as is the debate surrounding it. Genetic engineering has been considered for many decades. The concept of a utopian human race and cloned humans is scientifically plausible, but it remains ethically unacceptable to *most* people, but we should not become complacent in our position of enlightened superiority. The emphasis on 'most' is deliberate. There are numerous instances of inhumanity in the name of science. For example, just over half a century ago in Nazi Germany evolutionary theory was used as the justification for eugenics (Brune, 2001, 2008) and to further scientific knowledge (Shevell & Peiffer, 2001). Sadly, history has a habit of repeating itself and we hear reports of ethnic cleansing in which particular groups or religions are considered undesirable. **Bioethics** is a relatively new area of philosophy that addresses such weighty questions and it is joined by **neuroethics** that focuses on the neural basis of life.

This may appear to be somewhat academic, but the principles of free will and personal agency have been challenged by neuroscientists (see Libet et al., 1983a, and Chapter 18) and could have profound ramifications on the legal system and how we lead our lives (Chapter 25), but here is a taste to provide food for thought when considering the implications of psychobiology. Many claims have been made for *diminished responsibility* on neuropsychological grounds, for example the case of a man convicted of paedophilia. This man had what the doctors referred to as acquired paedophilia which was the consequence of a tumour on the right orbitofrontal cortex. Removal of the tumour resulted in him being considered safe again. The tumour grew again and so did the sexual behaviour (Burns & Swerdlow, 2003). The question is, how accountable was he for his behaviour? In the UK, premenstrual syndrome (PMS) has been used as a mitigating plea in some legal cases, including murder! In 1980–1981, two British women escaped murder convictions by arguing that PMS resulted in diminished responsibility (Boorse, 1987). How can this happen? The answer lies in the philosophical and legal view of being in control.

In law at the core of jurisprudence is the M'Naghten Rule which has the following features.

1. The presumption that the defendant is sane and *responsible* for their criminal acts.
2. That the defendant must have been suffering 'under a defect of reason' or 'from disease of the mind' to be found *not guilty*.
3. That the defendant must 'not know the nature and quality of the act he was doing, or if he did know it that he did not know what he was doing was wrong'.

You can see from this rule that any changes to our understanding of personal responsibility are far reaching and the closing chapter revisits these important themes.

ANIMAL RESEARCH

Psychology (like the other contributory disciplines) uses animals. Studies of animals and their behaviour have been instrumental in shaping theories and advancing our understanding of the biological mechanisms that underlie human behaviour.

Research is vital to increasing our understanding of behaviour. Only by experimental investigation can we begin to unlock the mysteries of the brain. When human participation is unacceptable, animal studies are useful in trying to resolve questions that could not otherwise be answered. Ultimately we, as humans, are animals. We are highly sophisticated and socialized animals, but we are still animals. Humans have evolved but still share many similarities with other species (see Chapter 2). It is this connection and a shared biology that scientists exploit with animals. Scientists can lesion part of a rat's brain but they cannot do the same to a human for the advancement of knowledge (although it can be done for treatment, as in the case study of HM – see Chapter 13). The rat is the most researched animal on the planet. However, rats are not the only animals used by scientists. Many species have been used, ranging from snails to mice and pigeons to chimpanzees. Which animal is used depends on the question asked, and whether the animal is in a position to provide an answer.

Animal research is an area charged with moral, ethical and emotional debate, which we will not go too far into here. If you wish to investigate the arguments surrounding vivisection, then the British Union for the Abolition of Vivisection (BUAV) and Research Defence Society (RDS) provide coherent and contrasting accounts.

The antivivisection movement (of which some scientists are members) has two main objections to experiments with animals. First, it considers it unethical to experiment with animals. The basis of this view is that such procedures are cruel to the animal, inducing unnecessary suffering to an animal that has no choice. Second, the scientific validity of experimentation is called into question: how can an animal provide us with insights into human behaviour? Those who support the use of animals have challenged this view with statements of the advantages, to animals and man, of such animal experimentation. All groups would agree that unnecessary suffering should never occur. Perhaps the biggest point of contention is the definition of what *is* necessary. That question is the subject for another book. However, past and present legislators consider animal experimentation necessary to answer some questions and thereby sanction their use.

If we are going to use animals, we need to know a little more about the use and the context in which such experiments occur. There is so much misinformation about animal experiments that we need to get closer to the facts. Whilst this might appear legalistic, it does place animal studies in context. To do this, we must start by placing animal experimentation within the context of the United Kingdom and the European Union (EU).

In 1986, the Council of the European Communities issued a Council Directive to eliminate the differences in animal protection laws within its jurisdiction. The Directive includes reduction in the number of animals used in experiments, including unnecessary duplication of studies, and the implementation of care guidelines. It seeks to remove unnecessary pain or suffering. It is left to each EU nation to decide how the Directive will be operationalized.

In the UK, the Home Office implement the **Animals (Scientific Procedures) Act (1986)** which is the legislation for the licensing of scientific procedures carried out on any vertebrate (note that not every form of life is included). This Act covers procedures on animals from a simple blood sample to major surgery; it also includes genetic modification and breeding which has given rise to increased numbers of animals being involved in experiments in the UK.

At the heart of the act is the **3Rs**: reducing the number of animals used, refining procedures to minimize pain and suffering, and replacing animal experiments with alternatives where possible.

Three licences are needed from the Home Office before animal experiments can commence.

1. An establishment licence is required for the institute where the experiment is conducted, ensuring a high quality of care and a suitable environment for the animal.
2. A project licence is required for the set of experiments. This permits only certain procedures to be carried out on the animal. A scientist cannot just do anything he or she wants. The issue of a project licence is dependent on several factors underpinning the 3Rs. There has to be justification of cost and benefit from the experiments which includes information and consideration of the number of animals and what species will be used, the specific product (e.g. a drug) or the important knowledge that will be gained. Additionally, the severity of the procedures involved will be assessed with an aim to minimize pain and suffering.
3. A personal licence is given to a particular individual to conduct the experiment. This is granted only if the applicant has received appropriate training and demonstrated sufficient competence in animal welfare.

This is enforced by the Home Office who sends out inspectors and veterinarians, without prior notice, to visit establishments to check that the rules are being maintained. Heavy fines and a custodial sentence may result from successful prosecution of those failing to adhere to the rules governing animal experiments.

Despite the 3Rs, animal experiments have increased in recent years. In 2012, 4.11 million experiments were started which was an increase from the previous year. The rise was mainly attributable to a 22% increase in the breeding of genetically modified animals and involved mainly mice.

Experiments in the USA

The USA has similar legislation to that of the UK and EU. Given that a large amount of research stems from the USA, it is worth describing its systems.

The US legislation has evolved over time. The first law regulating animal research was the Laboratory Animal Welfare Act (AWA) (1966) which covered dogs, cats, non-human primates, guinea pigs, hamsters and rabbits (you will note that these are common pets, and the Act was intended to stop pet theft and the sale to laboratories). The Act is enforced by the Animal and Plant Health Inspection Service (APHIS) of the US Department of Agriculture (USDA). Similar to the UK Act, the USA is concerned about training, prevention of unintended duplication of animal experimentation and improved methods of animal experimentation, to reduce or replace animal use or to minimize pain and suffering. Research facilities have to register with the USDA and establish an Institutional Animal Care and Use Committee (IACUC) to review all experiments with 'live, warm-blooded animals'. That's reptiles out of the equation!

Bizarrely, the AWA does not cover rats, mice and birds but this is because it does not have the resources to inspect all research facilities using these species. However, rats, mice and birds are afforded some protection under public health service policy if the institute receives federal funding.

Laboratory animals are covered by the Public Health Service Policy on Humane Care and Use of Laboratory Animals (PHS Policy). PHS Policy is based on the Health Research Extension Act (1985) which applies to any research facility that receives PHS funds (again it is about the money).

An IACUC has to be established at each research facility and experiments are to be scrutinized. This includes a justification for using animals, the species and the number of animals involved. The IACUC inspects animal facilities twice a year to ensure compliance with policy.

Complications emerge when we compare US federal and state law. Individual states may regulate the care and use of animals for research even further although federal law sets a baseline of protection.

Beyond the USA and UK

Japan, Australia, New Zealand and most recently Brazil all have legislation to protect animals used in research, most adopting the 3R principles. Increased regulations for animal testing in the USA and Europe have led to outsourcing of animal testing to Asia where neither governments nor researchers provide documentation to the same extent as in the EU or USA. With antivivisection groups taking direct action on companies and their employees, they may go outside the EU or USA to experiment. China has become a centre for animal testing as there is scarce implementation and regulation of its animal laws.

Professional Bodies: British Psychological Society (BPS) and American Psychological Association (APA)

Both the **British Psychological Society** (BPS) and the **American Psychological Association** (APA) have drawn up guidelines that address the ethics of animal experimentation. Not surprisingly, they follow the law of their lands.

The BPS *Guidelines for Psychologists Working with Animals* (2012) goes a little beyond the legal framework and includes animals used in teaching and by therapists. It states at 'undergraduate level, it may be appropriate to include some work involving live animals, although the use of animals for demonstrations of known facts using regulated procedures is prohibited' (p.12). However:

> ... students who have career aspirations in professional psychology ... may wish to carry out final year experimental projects involving animals. If such projects may involve pain or suffering, they are only legally permissible if they form part of an ongoing programme of research, and where the study would otherwise have been conducted by the supervisor or his/her research team as work approved under an existing *Project Licence*. (p.13)

Whilst animals that are used in a therapeutic manner fall outside the Scientific Procedures Act (Animals) 1986, the BPS passes comment on their use.

> In all these cases, considerations concerning the general care and welfare of therapeutic animals are similar to those outlined for experimental animals. In addition ... a number of specific considerations can be noted. The individual temperament and training of such animals should be appropriate for the planned task ... Care should also be taken that contact between the therapeutic animal and client/patient is monitored at all times. Therapeutic interactions, especially with children, can be very demanding and tiring for an animal. Animals should, therefore, have the opportunity to retreat from stressful situations or interactions, should they arise. Although such use of animals will not, in general, require a specific licence, it is covered by the broad provisions of the Animal Welfare Act (2006). Psychologists involved in such treatment programmes should ensure that they are familiar with the legislation. (p.14)

The APA is a little more detailed in its requirements (APA, 2012) which are summarized below.

> Research should be undertaken with a clear scientific purpose. Research will:
>
> - increase knowledge.
> - increase understanding of the studied species.
> - provide results that potentially benefit humans or other animals.
>
> The scientific purpose of the research should be of sufficient significance as to justify the use of animals. If animals are to be used, the species chosen for the study should be the best suited to answer the questions posed.

The APA comments on experimental procedures as follows.

> 1. Observational and other non-invasive forms of behavioural studies that involve no aversive stimulation to, or elicit no sign of distress from the animal are acceptable.
> 2. Whenever possible behavioural procedures should be used that minimize discomfort to the animal. Psychologists should adjust the parameters of

aversive stimulation to the minimal levels compatible with the aims of the research. Whenever reasonable, psychologists are encouraged to first test the painful stimuli to be used on non-human animal subjects on themselves.

3. Procedures involving more than brief or slight aversive stimulation should be undertaken only when the objectives of the research cannot be achieved by other methods.

4. Experimental procedures that require prolonged aversive conditions or produce tissue damage or metabolic disturbances require greater justification and surveillance by the psychologist and IACUC.

5. Surgical procedures require aseptic methods that minimize risks of infection and postoperative care.

Multiple research questions that can be answered in an individual animal should be considered in order to reduce the number of animals used. However, there must be sound scientific justification.

To ensure their humane treatment and well-being, laboratory animals generally may not be released from institutional facilities. Non-human animals reared in the laboratory must not be released into the wild because, in most cases, they cannot survive or they may survive by disrupting the natural ecology. Return of any wild-caught animal to the field also carries risks, both to the formerly captive animals and to the ecosystem. http://www.apa.org/science/leadership/care/care-animal-guidelines.pdf

Beyond the Ethics of Animal Research: The Validity of Animal Models of Behaviour

Almost all countries have their own legislation to enforce; however, the scientist has to do more than simply adhere to legislation. Part of the legal process in experiment licensing is justification. The scientist needs to be clear that the questions asked of an animal in an experiment can actually be answered. We need to make sure that the animal can answer the question we have, not simply that we cannot ask a human the question. When it comes to psychology, such questions are complex, making the answers themselves complex. Essentially, we need to make sure that if we have to use animals, they are used wisely, that their participation is informative.

Animals are used in many ways within psychobiology and neuroscience disciplines, but these ways fall into three key domains (Willner, 1984, 1986, 1991; Willner & Mitchell, 2002).

- **Screening tests.** Simply put, these are deployed to find out if a procedure or drug is going to be useful. They are favoured early on in drug development by pharmaceutical companies.

- **Behavioural bioassays.** These aim to mimic or model a *physiological* mechanism in the whole animal. Willner (1991) points out that there are good reasons for looking at the behavioural consequences of a physiological event. Behaviour is the result of the integration of many brain mechanisms. Unlike pure physiology, we can see how the whole system works to influence behaviour.

- **Simulations.** These are the most important to the psychobiologist, as the true animal model or simulation of behaviour. More often than not, these are simulations of abnormal behaviour. However, it is not always the case that simulations look at abnormal behaviour. There have been attempts to model what one would think is a unique human experience – laughter – in an animal; ultrasonic vocalizations are attributed to different emotional states (Panksepp, 2007). Rats can laugh! These types of studies seek to tell us more than just whether a drug or intervention works or not.

The question is whether we can be sure we are asking the right questions. Early criteria for what an animal model should comprise were put forward by McKinney and Bunney (1969). The criteria stated that there should be a comparison between the animal model and the human condition along the following directions: aetiology, symptomatology, similarity in the physiological basis of the disorder and the model, and finally a similarity in the physiological bases of efficacious treatment. These criteria are idealistic and, I would argue, unachievable. Symptomatology and the mapping onto animal behaviours are to some extent straightforward, but aetiology is somewhat harder. Indeed, it is the aetiology that is often the goal of the model. In most psychological disorders, we do not know what the aetiology is and therefore we would fall at the first hurdle. In a similar vein the physiological basis is also one of the goals of an animal model. So where does that leave us? We have to investigate further. Fortunately others have contributed to this quest and have provided scientific rigour to animal experimentation.

According to Willner (1991):

[M]odels are tools. As such, they have no intrinsic value; the value of a tool derives entirely from the work one can do with it. Conclusions arising from the use of a simulation of abnormal behaviour are essentially hypotheses, that must eventually be tested against the clinical state. An assessment of the validity of a simulation gives no more than an indication of the degree of confidence that we can place in the hypothesis arising from its use. (p.7)

Using the concepts behind the development of psychometric testing and questionnaire design, Willner (1984) proposed that animal models should be validated. He developed the appraisal of an animal model for psychopharmacology, but it can be extended to other aspects of psychobiology.

Three sets of validity are differentiated: **predictive validity**, **face validity** and **construct validity**. When assessing the utilization of animals, these criteria provide a useful structure.

Predictive validity

This is similar to a screening test, but goes beyond the straightforward detection of potential therapeutic agents. One should be able to predict how interventions manifest in the animal model. All efficacious drugs for a particular condition should work in the animal model. It should not be limited to a particular chemical class or type of drug. For example, if you wish to have an animal model of schizophrenia, then the many types of antipsychotic medication in the clinic should also work in the model. Furthermore, you should be able to exacerbate symptoms in the animal in the same way you can in the human. This gives symmetry to the interventions: can we make the condition better, but also can we make the condition worse? To continue with the example, schizophrenia experiments in which patients have been given amphetamine have shown some deterioration in their symptoms (van Kammen et al., 1982) (see Chapters 9 and 21). Similarly, if you give a rat amphetamine, its behaviour becomes disorganized (Ellinwood & Escalante, 1977). Within the classification of predictive validity, there should be a correlation with potency, in which the doses used in a clinical setting map onto the animal model.

Face validity

This is the degree to which there is a similarity between the model and the behaviour to be modelled. For example, can the symptoms of schizophrenia be modelled in the animal? Are the symptoms that are modelled in the animal significant in schizophrenia and schizophrenia alone? If the answer is no, there may be problems with the animal model because one cannot be sure it is actually modelling schizophrenia. Additionally, with face validity new research findings need to be accounted for in the model. Thus, a model of behaviour may have face validity one day but not the next, after new knowledge is assimilated. Perhaps the first place for assessing face validity is to look at the diagnostic criteria used. A considerable amount of research uses the APA's guidelines, the *Diagnostic and Statistical Manual* (DSM), to characterize psychiatric disturbances. This provides a list from which one can extract behaviours to apply to the animal model. Over the years of the DSM's existence, there has been a substantial increase in the size of the manuals. We now have DSM5 and no doubt there will be revisions in the near future. Looking at DSM5, you will also note that symptoms can be widespread across disorders. Given the overlap, the scientists have to make sure that the symptoms being modelled are truly reflective of the disorder and are not secondary concerns.

Construct validity

A limitation with face validity is that the different species of animals have different overt behaviour. Willner (1991) uses the example of maternal behaviour to demonstrate this point. Maternal behaviour is evident across all species. However, it is expressed differently. The rat keeps her litter close and retrieves strays with her mouth. The rat mother does not change nappies, warm milk or go to rat playgroups, while the human mother, in general, performs some if not all of these behaviours.

The observable behaviours are different. However, they are regarded as homologous – arising from the same physiological substrate and theoretical construct.

Construct validity refers to the theoretical rationale behind the behaviour. If experimentation supports the theory then the model has a degree of construct validity. Construct validity is therefore the theoretical underpinning of the model that uses our current knowledge and view of a neuropsychiatric condition. When it comes to psychiatry and psychology, as we have already noted, aetiology is elusive and we are therefore working in the realms of theoretical conjecture. To continue the case of schizophrenia, there are many theories of schizophrenia that extend from sociocultural causality to genetic and neural causality. Whilst we know a lot about schizophrenia, we do not know everything and we certainly do not know causality. Thus, construct validity for the animal models of schizophrenia is open to scientific debate. It has been argued that some models of schizophrenia score more highly than others for construct validity (Ellenbroek & Cools, 1990).

A clear example of construct validity being harder to achieve can be seen for animal models of addiction. People voluntarily consume drugs such as heroin and cocaine. This is a great concern to policymakers and scientists because of the damaging effects these drugs can have. In order to understand this, animal models have been deployed but because the theories behind drug misuse do not have a single theoretical rationale, it is hard to claim construct validity for the animal model. The most common animal model of addiction is drug self-administration (see Chapter 9) in which the animal presses a lever in order to get a drug. Animals will readily do this but the reason why they do it is open to debate. Some scientists argue that drug addiction is due to the pleasant actions of a drug, while others claim it is motivated by the urge to avoid unpleasant withdrawal symptoms (see Goudie, 1991). In order to have construct validity, one has to identify the variable being measured, assess the degree of homology and the significance of that variable to the clinical picture.

Others have modified Willner's set of criteria and expanded upon it (Belzung & Lemoine, 2011). Figure 1.4 shows how a model maps onto the human condition.

External validity

In addition to Willner's three criteria, other components have been added to the assessment of animal models. **External validity** is an assessment of the generalizability of the findings using an animal model to that of other species and across populations (Mace, 1996). For example, are the same results obtained from the animal model when animals are reared and housed differently?

Reliability and replicability

Reliability tells us how consistent the model is under the same conditions whereas a study that is replicable is one that produces similar results in an independent laboratory. When you read the research literature, you will see that animal models are used by many groups across many laboratories and if they all find they have similar data then one can assume that the model is reliable (Garner, 2005).

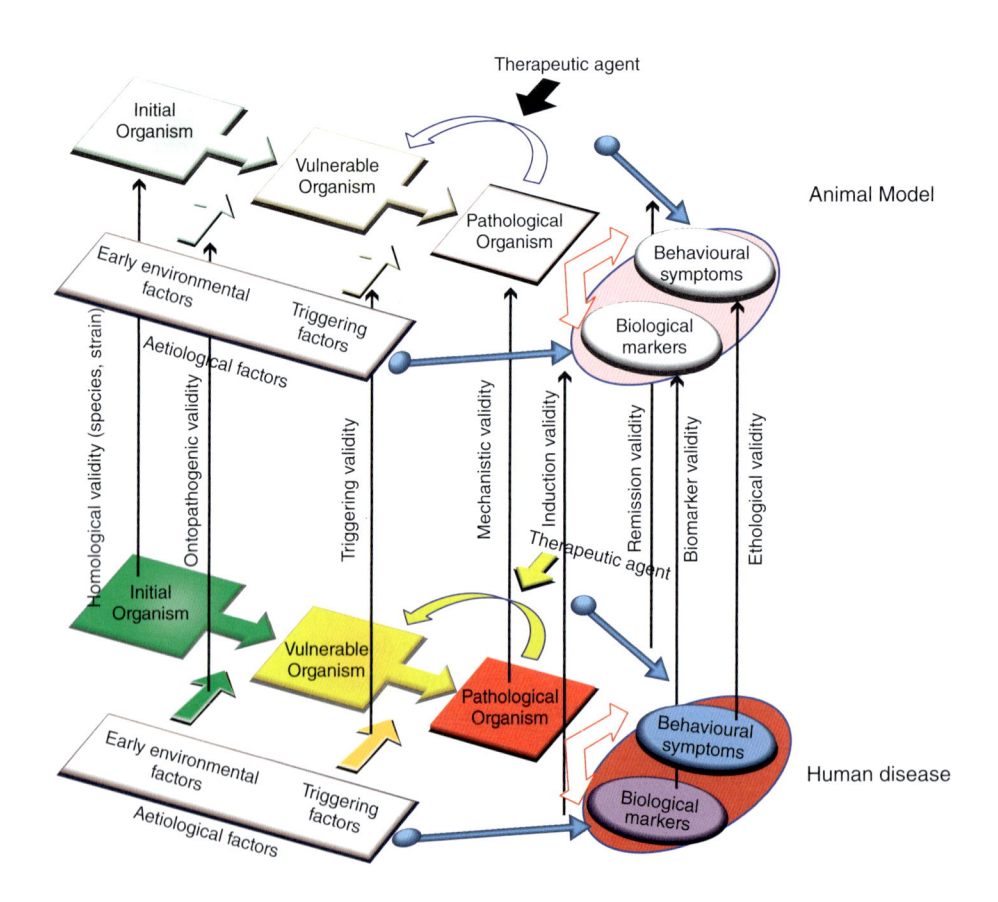

FIGURE 1.4 *Comparative validity between animal models and human disease. Different aspects of validity can be mapped onto the animal model in order to determine the overall similarity between human disease and animal models.*
Source: Belzung, C., & Lemoine, M. (2011). Criteria of validity for animal models of psychiatric disorders: focus on anxiety disorders and depression. *Biology of Mood and Anxiety Disorders, 1*(1), 9.

Internal validity

High reliability and replicability provide internal validity. **Internal validity** is about the integrity of the experiment itself, whether it has been suitably controlled and conducted. If it has not then conjecture stemming from the data is limited to the extent of being near pointless.

Taking the validity criteria and combining them with ethical criteria, van der Staay et al. (2009) have presented a flow diagram of ethical and scientific assurance (Figure 1.5). These principles go some way to providing confidence in the data obtained from animals. Combining them with human data, perhaps gained via neuroimaging or genetics, we can piece together parts of the jigsaw so we can see a more complete picture of behaviour.

The validity of animal models is a recurrent theme throughout this book.

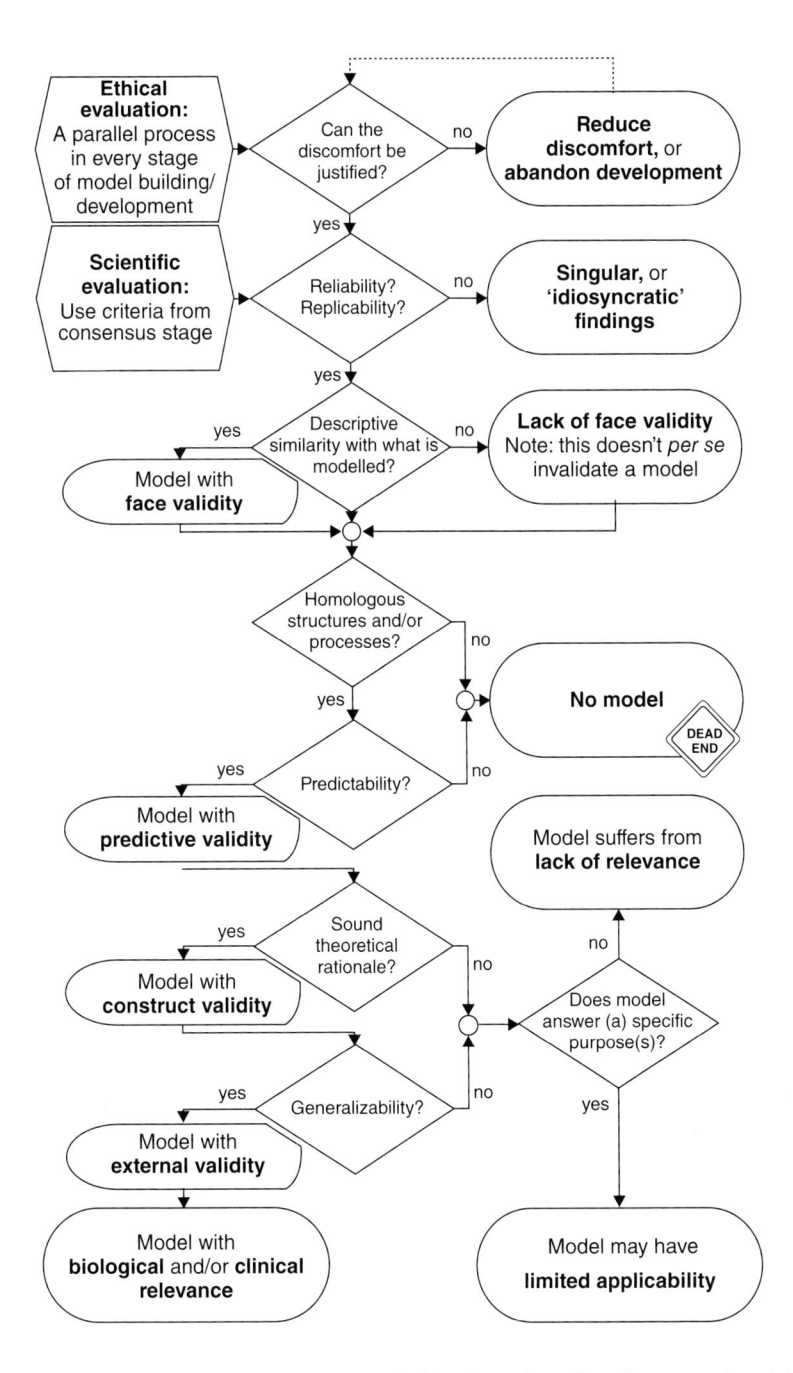

FIGURE 1.5 *Flow chart for animal models in psychobiology. Using the flowchart, the utility of an animal model can be assessed.*
Source: Van Der Staay, F. J., Arndt, S. S., & Nordquist, R. E. (2009). Evaluation of animal models of neurobehavioral disorders. *Behavioural and Brain Functions*, 5, 11.

GOOD SCIENCE VERSUS JUNK IN–JUNK OUT

Technological advances have made understanding brain activity and how that relates to behaviour a more manageable quest. However, we must be careful not to be seduced by what this new technology can offer. To use an American phrase: junk in–junk out. No amount of technology, for example neuroimaging, can make a poorly controlled experiment good. An experiment is only as good as its research methodology. Research methodology is critical to good science and clinical trials (see Chapter 7). Research methodology is all about the design of the study and is critical to answering questions correctly, and therefore critical in forwarding our understanding of psychobiology with any degree of confidence. There are numerous research methodologies that can be deployed and interested readers are directed to Freeman and Tyrer (2006) for a more detailed account. The subdivisions of psychobiology use differing methodologies in their quest for new knowledge.

The media's portrayal of science is often misleading. Most scientific papers are difficult to read, as the language that they use is often turgid and technical. It is common to have to read them several times! Scientific papers are often cautious accounts of what the data suggest and in the behavioural sciences rarely (if ever) prove anything as a fact. The media often cover science-related information, but the journalists who report on scientific publications have to turn the turgid and technical language into an interesting and entertaining story. Good journalism is valuable and informative, bringing complex ideas to a non-expert audience. Bad journalism is often ignorant and full of misinterpretation and prejudice – which in turn may appeal to the reader's own prejudices. Thus the media can sometimes be guilty of sensationalizing research in a non-critical yet authoritative way. Be wary of headlines stating that 'A gene has been found for X, Y or Z' or 'This is the brain region for X, Y or Z'. A recent example is the reporting of the MMR vaccine and its so-called link to autism, in which the poor science was broadcast via the media without critical awareness. The fact it got published in the first place is worrying – it should never have got that far. Furthermore, the impartiality of the scientists had also been queried as they received funding from pharmaceutical companies that they failed to disclose. Thus, there was the smell of corruption. This is a problem as the companies have a financial interest in the direction of the results. It is commonplace for scientists to disclose information about potential conflicts of interest, e.g. a hypothetical cigarette company may not wish the results of a study they fund, to link nicotine with addiction – this bias is not conducive to good science.

Practising *good science* is not only important for evaluating new drugs or treatments, it is also important for evaluating theoretical psychobiological accounts of behaviour. Theories of psychiatric/psychological disorders are designed to be thought provoking and have power to explain the symptoms. A theory is not a fact. Psychiatric disorders have many theoretical accounts of the symptoms and very few hard facts. Experimentation can either support or refute theories. A publication bias in the literature often means that people try to prove that a theory or hypothesis is correct; the philosopher Karl Popper states that one should try to refute rather than prove the theory. If one fails to refute the theory then there may well be some credibility to it (see Popper, 2002); if you cannot knock the theory down then there must be some strength to it. Unfortunately, there is a publication bias in favour of positive results, where the hypothesis is upheld. Publishers, editors and funding bodies are not interested in experiments that do not show a difference, despite these studies being of equal importance if they are conducted correctly (is it possible editors misinterpret non-significant (i.e. *no effect*) to mean insignificant (*not important*)?) Scientists are like other members of society and are interested in extending old ideas to new subjects in what the philosopher Kuhn calls extending the paradigm. Furthermore, a political agenda and cultural expectation exert an influence over what science is funded, that in turn can determine the direction of the results that are found and eventually published.

SUMMARY

Psychobiology has a long history and can be divided into many subdisciplines. The psychobiologist investigates behaviour in humans and animals. The use of animals is especially important and one has to use them wisely.

The large volume of literature in psychobiology can be daunting. The use of scientific methods is the only way in which we can unravel the complexities of the brain, but even science is subject to prejudices and bias.

LEARNING OUTCOME QUESTIONS

You should be able to answer the following questions.
- What are the subdisciplines of psychobiology?
- What other areas of science contribute to psychobiological research?
- How can we determine the scientific value of an animal model of behaviour?

FURTHER READING

Bennet, M. R., & Hacker, P. M. S. (2003). *Philosophical foundations of neuroscience*. Oxford, UK: Blackwell Publishing.
Farahany, N. A. (Ed.). (2009). *The impact of behavioural sciences on criminal law*. Oxford, UK: Oxford University Press.
Finger, S. (2001). *Origins of neuroscience: A history of explorations into brain function*. Oxford, UK: Oxford University Press.
Glickstein, M. (2014). *Neuroscience: A historical introduction*. Cambridge, MA: MIT Press.
Illes, J., & Sahakian, B. J. (Eds.). (2011). *The Oxford handbook of neuroethics*. Oxford, UK: Oxford University Press.
Steinbock, B. (Ed.). (2007). *The Oxford handbook of bioethics*. Oxford, UK: Oxford University Press.
Van Der Staay, F. J., Arndt, S. S., & Nordquist, R. E. (2009). Evaluation of animal models of neurobehavioral disorders. *Behavioral and Brain Functions*, 5, 11.
Willner, P. (Ed.). (1991). *Behavioural models in psychopharmacology: Theoretical, industrial and clinical perspectives*. Cambridge, UK: Cambridge University Press.
Zeki, S., & Goodenough, O. R. (2004). *Law and the brain*. Oxford, UK: Oxford University Press.

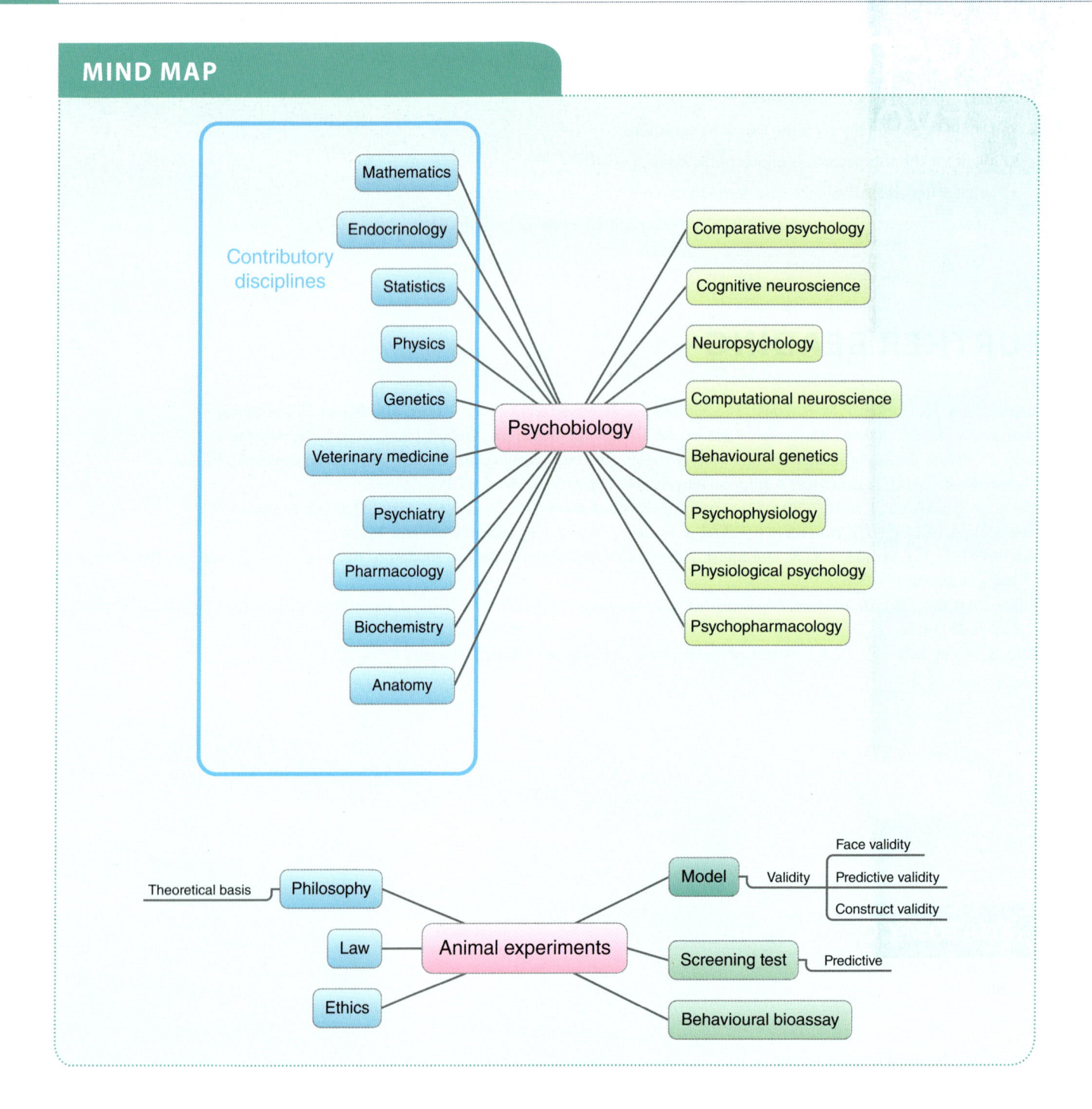

PSYCHOBIOLOGY

MIND MAP

Contributory disciplines → Psychobiology:
- Mathematics
- Endocrinology
- Statistics
- Physics
- Genetics
- Veterinary medicine
- Psychiatry
- Pharmacology
- Biochemistry
- Anatomy

Psychobiology →
- Comparative psychology
- Cognitive neuroscience
- Neuropsychology
- Computational neuroscience
- Behavioural genetics
- Psychophysiology
- Physiological psychology
- Psychopharmacology

Animal experiments:
- Philosophy — Theoretical basis
- Law
- Ethics
- Model — Validity
  - Face validity
  - Predictive validity
  - Construct validity
- Screening test — Predictive
- Behavioural bioassay

2 Genetics and Evolution

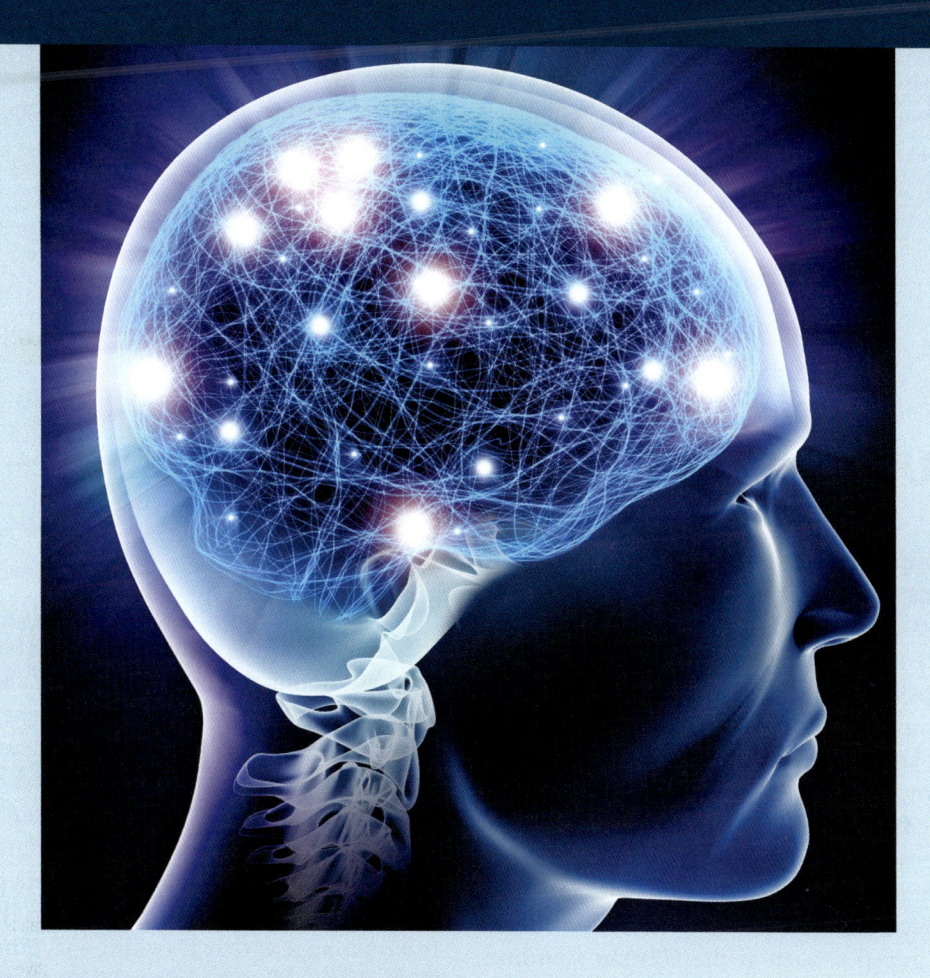

ANATOMY OF THE CHAPTER

This chapter will highlight the following.
- Evolution.
- Mechanisms of heritable traits.
- Molecular genetics: DNA.
- Behavioural genetics.

INTRODUCTION 24

IN THE BEGINNING – EVOLUTION 24

THE EVOLUTION OF HUMANS 27

EVOLUTIONARY PSYCHOLOGY 29

FROM EVOLUTION TO GENETICS 29

DNA 42

EPIGENETICS 50

BEHAVIOURAL GENETICS: THE COMPLEX INTERPLAY OF PSYCHOLOGY AND GENETICS 50

THE HUMAN GENOME PROJECT 57

SUMMARY 59

LEARNING OUTCOMES

1. To understand the importance of evolutionary theory.
2. To understand how characteristics are passed from one generation to another.
3. To have an understanding of molecular genetics.
4. To have an understanding of the methodologies of behavioural genetics and their limitations.
5. To be able to ethically evaluate genetic research and potential.

INTRODUCTION

Genetics is an important and rapidly advancing branch of science, which potentially offers humanity a chance to understand its origins and to put right illnesses and disorders. We frequently see in news reports and television bulletins that a gene has been found for some aspect of the human condition. Sadly this information, whilst often important and informative, gives rise to false optimism (perhaps more a result of media hyperbole rather than sound scientific discourse). We know so much more than we ever have about genetics, but there is still a lot more to understand, and this is especially so in the behavioural sciences.

Advances in genetics, such as the **Human Genome Project**, which has mapped human genes (see http://www.ornl.gov/sci/techresources/Human_Genome/home.shtml), and Dolly the cloned sheep (Campbell et al., 1996), have focused on the molecular structure of genes (e.g. the DNA), but the study of genetics has a much longer history than these relatively recent headline-grabbing developments. The history of genetics has shaped, and misshaped, as is the case with the eugenic policies of various misguided political regimes, our present view of genetics. Our current view of genetics requires close scrutiny, not only by scientists but also philosophers of ethics and policy makers in governments. The power of genetics needs to be addressed coherently and carefully and has given rise to a new branch of philosophy – bioethics. Once the reader has understood the mechanics of genetics, then the next step is to evaluate the far-reaching consequences that this new knowledge, and the resultant new technologies, can bring to humankind.

IN THE BEGINNING – EVOLUTION

Physicists have the big questions about understanding the creation of the universe: the big bang. Then, biologists ask about the creation of life: about the diversity and adaptability of life. Whilst science endeavours to provide answers to these questions, such questions and answers do not remain unchallenged. Religious beliefs about the creation of life are presented as argument against the current scientific explanations. God as the creator has been challenged by science, particularly by the evangelical geneticist Professor Richard Dawkins. It would appear that Dawkins and others face a similar challenge to that experienced by Charles Darwin, the godfather of **evolution**, who wrote about the origins of species against a backdrop of **pro-creationism**.

The idea that species change and evolve over time is now a well-established *fact* in science (and not in religion). The use of the word 'fact' in science is rare; science is a world of theories. Stephen J. Gould sums it up in a paper entitled 'Evolution as fact and theory' with the quote, 'Facts are the world's data. Theories are structures of ideas that explain and interpret facts. Facts do not go away when scientists debate rival theories to explain them' (Gould, 1981). Evidence is paramount in any theory; a theory without evidence is just a story!

Whilst Darwin was not the first to take an evolutionary perspective, he was certainly the most influential. Darwin initiated the evolutionary account of life on earth and published *The origin of species* (1859) at a time when Christianity stated that God had created all species from scratch. Darwin's account of evolution was inspiring and thought provoking at the time, and brought about a change in perspective and dared to be different. His account was convincing to biologists because he used evidence to support his theory – an evidence-based approach in which the facts fit into an explanatory framework. Like all good science, solid evidence is required, speculation without support gains little acceptance and without this supporting evidence his theory would have attracted far less attention. However, one must also be aware that some views remain solid even when there is little evidence to support them.

Darwin's Revolutionary Theory – The Theory of Evolution

Darwin proposed that all organisms are related and share a common ancestor. His theory of descent with modification encapsulated how modern organisms are (successful) adaptations of previous generations. These modifications occur in the process of what he referred to as **natural selection**. Certain characteristics of the organism are more beneficial within a particular environment. In a difficult, demanding and sometimes hostile environment, some characteristics will be to the organism's advantage, others might be a disadvantage. Therefore those organisms that possess beneficial characteristics are more likely to survive and reproduce. It is at this point that Dawkins (1991–2) asserts that the transmission of genetic material is the meaning of life:

> We are machines built by DNA whose purpose is to make more copies of the same DNA ... This is exactly what we are for. We are machines for propagating DNA, and the propagation of DNA is a self-sustaining process. It is every living object's sole reason for living.

Via **reproduction**, these characteristics are passed to the next generation. Organisms that are not ideally equipped to interact with their environment stand a smaller chance of being able to adapt to that environment, thus limiting their opportunity to survive and reproduce. The phrase often used for this is '**survival of the fittest**'; this means that those organisms that '*fit*' into' their environment are more successful at survival (note that the word 'fittest' as used here does not necessarily have anything to do with physical fitness, it may mean behavioural or cognitive fit). Those characteristics that do not fit well with the environment are less likely to exist in successive generations because those who possess them are less likely to survive and breed, so the characteristic is not passed on.

A comparison can be made between natural selection, traditional **selective breeding** and the more recent advances in genetic modification. Natural selection is distinct from selective breeding programmes. With natural selection, there is no specific plan, the environment is the influence and evolution is a relatively slow process. The selective breeding of animals is a specific, and intentional, act that produces offspring with particular characteristics that were present in the parental generation (as in the case of the thoroughbred racehorse, specific breeds of dogs or cows that produce high yields of milk) and is comparatively quick. Genetic modification is an even quicker form of selection (although the science and technology have taken a long time) in which genes are added or deleted for the benefit of the organism or, if not the recipient organism, then at least mankind.

Evidence: The Case in Support of the Theory of Evolution

Much evidence has to be amassed to support a theory (or indeed refute a theory, although this is often easier with one piece of damning evidence). Darwin (and others since) presented a great deal of evidence to support the theory of evolution via natural selection. The supporting evidence derives from the following general features.

- *Biogeography*. Why are some organisms indigenous to particular environments and not others? The obvious environmental difference is that of temperature: deserts are very different environments from those at the north and south poles of the planet. Organisms are the best fit for their unique environment (think of lizards and penguins and how they are adapted to their unique environments). Clearly, biogeography is a very hard area to study because it takes so long – it spans many years. However, what we do have access to are some rapid changes, changes in plants and changes in animals which are brought about by selective breeding. For example, we can see in the Galapagos Islands that the native bird, the finch, changed in response to its environment. During a drought only large seeds exist on the island. The seeds were too big for finches with small beaks but those that had a large beak were able to survive because they had sufficient beak size to eat these large seeds. Thus, they lived to tell the tale and were also able to breed successfully, as they were well nourished, and the characteristic of a large beak was passed to their offspring.

- *Fossil records*. Sedimentary rock formations allow us to chart the time course of evolution.

Sedimentary rocks are formed after eroded materials are deposited downstream and settle. This is on a time scale of thousands and millions of years. Early layers of rock are overlaid by recent layers; thus a time signature is associated with each layer – top layers are recent, bottom layers are older. In these layers are the imprints of animals of a particular era. Looking at different geological layers reveals changing fossils and these changes permit the palaeontologist to chart the evolution of species. For example, the change in the size and shape of the skull is important in tracing our ancestors. As new fossils are found, established views are challenged and our understanding of evolution advances. We can see this even with the human skull. Over the last few years new skulls have been discovered that provide evidence of the missing link between humans and our predecessors.

- *Structural similarity*. Across species there are comparative similarities. Arms, paws, flippers and wings all have similar skeletal structures but serve different functions (although the same construct – movement) (see Figure 2.1). In evolutionary terms, these have developed from a common ancestor. Due to the environmental pressures prevailing, this progenitor organism evolves into a whale, a dog and even humans.
- *Embryology*. By comparing the development of embryos, it was revealed that there are similar stages *in utero* across species. Campbell et al. (1999) point out that both human and fish embryos go through a phase of possessing gills. Often this is considered to be an evolutionary artefact of early life in water. This notion was prevalent in the mid-19th century suggesting that ontogeny was a recapitulation of phylogeny. Ernest Haeckel presented the ontogeny recapitulates phylogeny (ORP) theory as he supported Darwin's theories in Germany. The essence of the ORP theory is that during development, every organism goes through every stage of its evolutionary past. As the embryo develops, these similarities are reduced and the embryo takes on the unique characteristics of their species. Please note that this does not mean that we as individuals started our life as fish (see Chapter 3).
- *Molecular biology*. Darwin did not have the benefit of modern science and our knowledge of DNA. However, molecular biology – the discipline that looks at the actual elements of genes – supports Darwin's account of evolution and the evidence he originally presented. This adds further credibility to the theory of evolution; to use a legal metaphor, this is the forensic evidence of modern molecular genetics that supports Darwin's circumstantial evidence of fossils, etc. Ultimately, we share common strands of genetic material with other organisms, and some are closer than others (see Figure 2.2). Closer than we might realize.

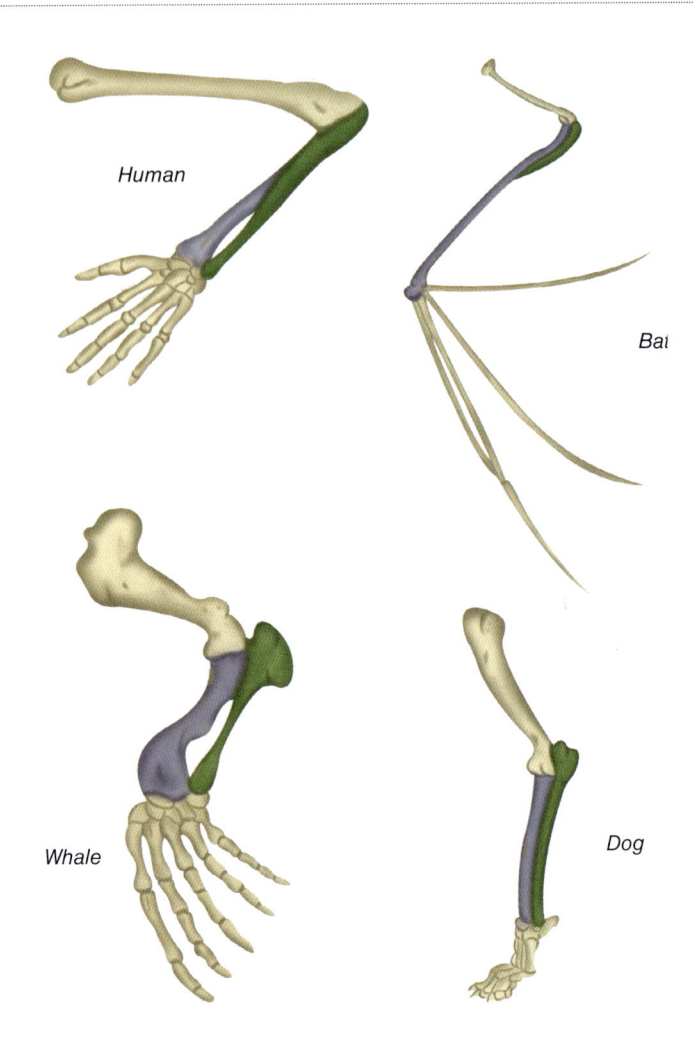

FIGURE 2.1 *Comparative anatomy of four species. The coloured bones represent similar anatomical purposes.*
Source: Davey, G. (Ed.) (2008). *Complete psychology*. London: Hodder Education, p.61.

The Organism and the Environment

One can be forgiven for thinking that we are just slaves to our biology and ultimately our molecular biology. The idea that genes influence behaviour, and not the other way around, can be a persuasive argument. That we are a product of our genes is at the core of our concepts of self, free will and agency. Genetics is at the heart of the age-old dilemma in psychology, that of nature versus nurture, or genes versus experience. The **Darwinian** account is a very good example of how the environment changes biology and behaviour, albeit over an extended period of

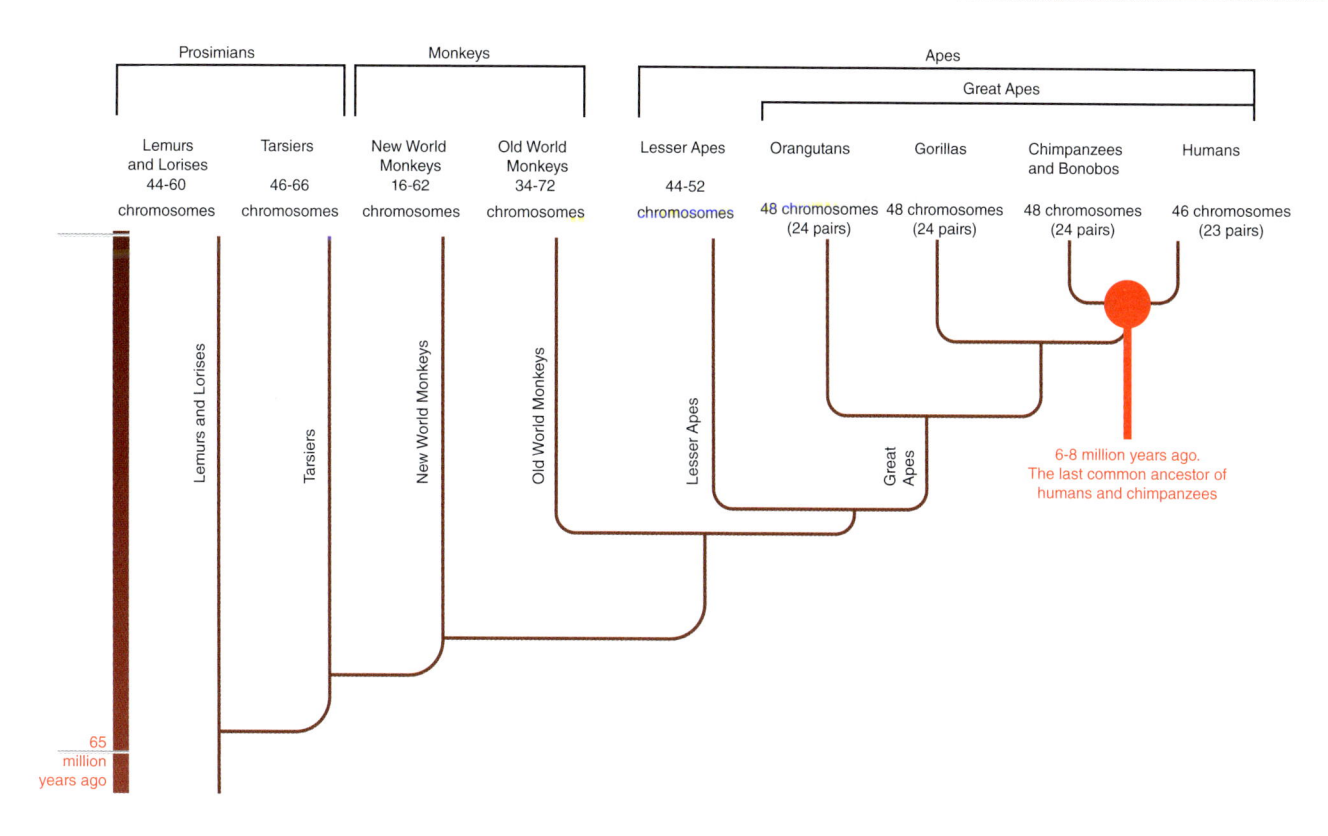

FIGURE 2.2 *The connection of humans with our closest relatives.*

time. In psychology we are interested in how our experiences and environments influence the expression of our genes. Many have suggested a complex interplay between genes and environment, most notably when one critiques the aetiological accounts of psychopathologies. Johnston and Edwards (2002) provide an integrative model of the development of behaviour, and have acknowledged the importance of the environment. They consider the development of behaviour to be a product of interactions between genetics, the environment and perception. Essentially behaviour will be determined not purely by genetic make-up but also by experiences, interpretations and perceptions of the environment. Not only is the environment important, it is also subject to individual differences due to the interpretation and perception of that environment; the environment is not an absolute.

THE EVOLUTION OF HUMANS

From an evolutionary perspective, humankind has evolved from its progenitor species. The question remains – who/what were our ancestors? It is this study of human evolution that gives rise to all sorts of debates and flies in the face of many religions. If we accept the evolutionary theory, and in this context, we should, we have to accept that humans are a recent development in evolutionary history. We separated from our animal relatives and became humans, and this is something we should not forget with our superior species status. Our history spans hundreds of millions of years. The history and evolution of humankind encapsulate the history of life on Earth. It really does go that far back.

So where did we start? After the Earth was created about 600 million years ago, the first signs of life appeared, arising from complex water-dwelling organisms. Then 150 million years later organisms with nerves were evident. Surrounding these new nerves were bone structures. These bone structures with vertebrae would subsequently be known as the spine (the spine came before the brain; see Chapter 3). Life in the water was hard and some of these first incarnations of fish ventured onto the land. This was an evolutionary step in the development of **amphibians**. Those animals that ventured onto the land gained access to life-sustaining fresh water and new food sources. Clearly, from an evolutionary perspective this is good news; with fresh food and water, these animals would survive; if they survive they are able to reproduce, and their offspring should have those valuable characteristics for survival. Eventually the fins and gills characteristic of water-borne creatures developed, or should we say evolved, into legs and lungs. We can see the step of evolution today in the form of frogs and toads that are well adapted to life in the water and on land.

Amphibians were subject to further evolutionary adaptations. Reptiles, such as lizards and snakes, are an evolutionary branch arising from amphibians. Reptiles lay shell-covered embryos (eggs) and are covered in dry scaly skin. The importance of these new developments in egg laying and the possession of dry skin is that it allowed the reptiles to further adapt to life on land. The water-based environment of the lakes and ponds of 300 million years ago is now replaced by the more local fluid environment of within the shell and its associated life-supporting contents. The dry scaly skin meant that the animals could live further away from water as the skin prevented substantial water loss. The need to be close to a source of water for a quick dip was no longer important.

Mammals evolved from reptiles about 180 million years ago. Mammals were able to feed their offspring using mammary glands (breastfeeding). They continued to evolve and developed the ability to produce an internal environment suitable for the protection and development of their offspring – pregnancy. Across different species this takes different lengths of time; for example, humans have an average gestation period of 40 weeks. In humans 40 weeks after conception the mother will give birth to a child or sometimes children (see twins later in this chapter). In other animals the timing is different and multiple births are more commonplace. What were the evolutionary pressures that allow for this to occur? Again in evolutionary terms, it is all about survival; the pond and the egg are subject to the pressures and dangers of a harsh environment. The development *in utero* (in the uterus) of a new living organism permits greater safety and protection from those harsh environments. That is not to say life *in utero* is free from danger – there are many challenges to the **foetus**, for example alcohol is a well-known teratogen (an agent, such as a virus, a drug, or radiation, that causes malformation of an embryo or foetus) and can cause foetal alcohol syndrome (see Chapter 3).

In the category of mammals, humans are exceptional and are arguably the most advanced form of life coming from the order of primates. Included in the primates are the apes, including gibbons, orang-utans, gorillas and chimpanzees. The chimpanzee is incredibly similar to humans when we look further at the genetic make-up of both species. But let's be clear that we haven't come from chimpanzees. Chimpanzees are distant relatives from our past; our immediate ancestors are most probably long extinct (Jaeger & Marivaux, 2005).

Of the numerous families of primates, humans are members of the family Hominines. Within this family are two genera: *Australopithecus* and *Homo*. We come from the Homo group – humans are **Homo sapiens**. Humans have a relative, *Homo erectus*, that is now extinct. *Homo* species emerged about 2 million years ago and are thought to have come from one species of Australopithecus (Asfaw et al., 1999). Early *Homo* species have a larger space for a brain – that is the cavity within the skull. The cavity is bigger than its predecessors, but not as big as our modern human brain.

Where did this all happen? It is suggested that *Homo sapiens* can all be traced back to Africa; the limited fossil record supports this notion. About 200,000 years ago *Homo sapiens* appeared and about 50,000 years ago modern humans began to migrate out of Africa. This is the **'Out of Africa' hypothesis** (see Meredith, 2011). If we go back far enough in time we will discover that our ancestors were African. If we go back even further, more recent work has suggested that the Africans descend from species that hailed from Asia (Chaimanee et al., 2012). Remember that the planet looked different all those years ago and people moved from the African plains in search of resources. The environmental pressures have therefore shaped modern humans but while we look different and come from different environments, we are all the same species.

The increase in brain volume happened before the *Homo* genus arrived, possibly driven by the increased use of tools (Conroy et al., 2000). Furthermore, metopic sutures (joints in the top of the skull) were seen to differ from *Australopithecus*, in which fusion of metopic sutures was evident early in development compared to the late postpartum fusion seen in great apes and humans. This has lead Falk et al. (2012) to suggest that selective pressures favouring delayed fusion might have developed from the difficulty of giving birth to large-headed neonates, high early postnatal brain growth rates, and reorganization and expansion of the frontal cortex.

What makes us different from the chimpanzees? Human genes are not that different from those of our close relatives the chimpanzee (The Chimpanzee Sequencing and Analysis Consortium, 2005; Kehrer-Sawatzki & Cooper, 2007) and the bonobo (Prufer et al., 2012). Clearly, humans are different, and it has been argued that this is due to changes in transcription and translation of the genetic codes (Kim & Hahn, 2012; Sakate et al., 2007). Humans can walk upright, but so can chimpanzees. We both have opposable thumbs, but ours are more useful for manipulating objects. But perhaps the biggest and most important difference is the brain. The human brain has evolved over tens of millions of years to be the most powerful organ in the natural world and now we can look at its genetic basis. There are important changes in the **protein** sequences in the human **genome**, together with **duplication** and deletion of genes, and further changes in non-coding regions of the genome that are involved in gene expression (Vallender et al., 2008). For example, humans have lost some genes for olfactory receptors during our primate-to-human evolution. In humans, of all the genes for olfactory receptors, only 40% have intact coding whereas in the great apes it is up to 72% (Gilad et al., 2003). Smell is a very important sense and in Chapters 10 and 17 we will note that smell is the only sense that does not need to go via the thalamus to be processed and is very important in the animal's perception of danger – another adaptation for survival. Fear promoted the flight or fight response. As humans we have become less reliant on smell and more reliant on vision.

When it comes to the human brain, we have already mentioned that size was important, but size is not the whole of the story. Other animals have big brains but they are nowhere near as complex as the human brain (think of elephants, they have big brains but they did not invent iPads!) (Figure 2.3). Furthermore, given that we consider ourselves the most intelligent species on the planet then perhaps those of our species that are more intelligent have bigger brains? It is a nice idea, but that is all it is, an idea and an idea that is now refuted. Einstein, who was clearly an intelligent man, left his brain to science. Those who were lucky enough to analyse his brain also found it to be generally unremarkable (Diamond et al., 1985; Witelson et al., 1999). Size is not everything, and when it comes to brain evolution and brain development, it is better to look at regional differences rather than the brain overall.

The brain itself is an evolutionary development of the vertebrate's spine (see Chapter 3). The brainstem, which is comparatively old, regulates many activities that are important for sustaining life, and the brainstem is similar across many species. The big difference in brains comes when we look at the more recent adaptations of the brain, most notably the cerebrum. In terms of evolution, the cerebrum is the most developed part of the human brain and is more developed when compared to other species. The human cerebrum has increased in size and when we look at the morphology of the cortex, we see that the human brain has more convolutions (sulci), thus conferring a greater volume to the cortex. In terms of being human, the cortex is the main brain difference; the neurons are the same, the communication is the same, but the architecture and function of the cortex are uniquely human.

EVOLUTIONARY PSYCHOLOGY

Comparative psychologists look at the behaviour of animals and try to understand human behaviour in terms of comparison with other species. From an evolutionary standpoint, we can see that this may make some sense as we are descended from a common species but have separated from other animals during evolution. In recent years evolutionary psychologists have been attempting to understand human behaviour from an evolutionary perspective, one that tries to address how certain pressures in the environment give rise to certain characteristics of human behaviour. Essentially, the questions are: why is a particular behaviour adaptive and still in the behavioural repertoire, or why is this maladaptive behaviour still present, what was its original reason for being? Unlike biologists, evolutionary psychologists do not have access to hard evidence from the past; for example, the fossil records do not give us a full understanding of the behaviour of the organism, only clues to the physical adaptations. There is a tendency for **evolutionary psychology** to be more theoretical, sometimes leading to great controversy when applied to human behaviour. Throughout this book there will be examples of evolutionary accounts of both normal and abnormal behaviour.

FROM EVOLUTION TO GENETICS

Darwin's theory of evolution, whilst extremely influential in shaping our modern thinking, did not have access to some very important evidence. Darwin did not know how species differed or how they were similar. He did not know how particular characteristics, whether anatomical or behavioural, were passed on to the next generation. Essentially Darwin did not have access to the mechanics of evolution. It was many years later that a detailed understanding of such mechanisms was developed. It is clearly important to understand the mechanisms underlying evolution and therefore underlying our species. Such an understanding has evolved over time, starting with Gregor Mendel's account and taking us to modern genetics and the future as yet unknown.

In behavioural genetics there are two subtypes of heritable characteristics or traits: qualitative and quantitative. **Qualitative traits** are often influenced by a single gene and follow a simple pattern of inheritance (such as

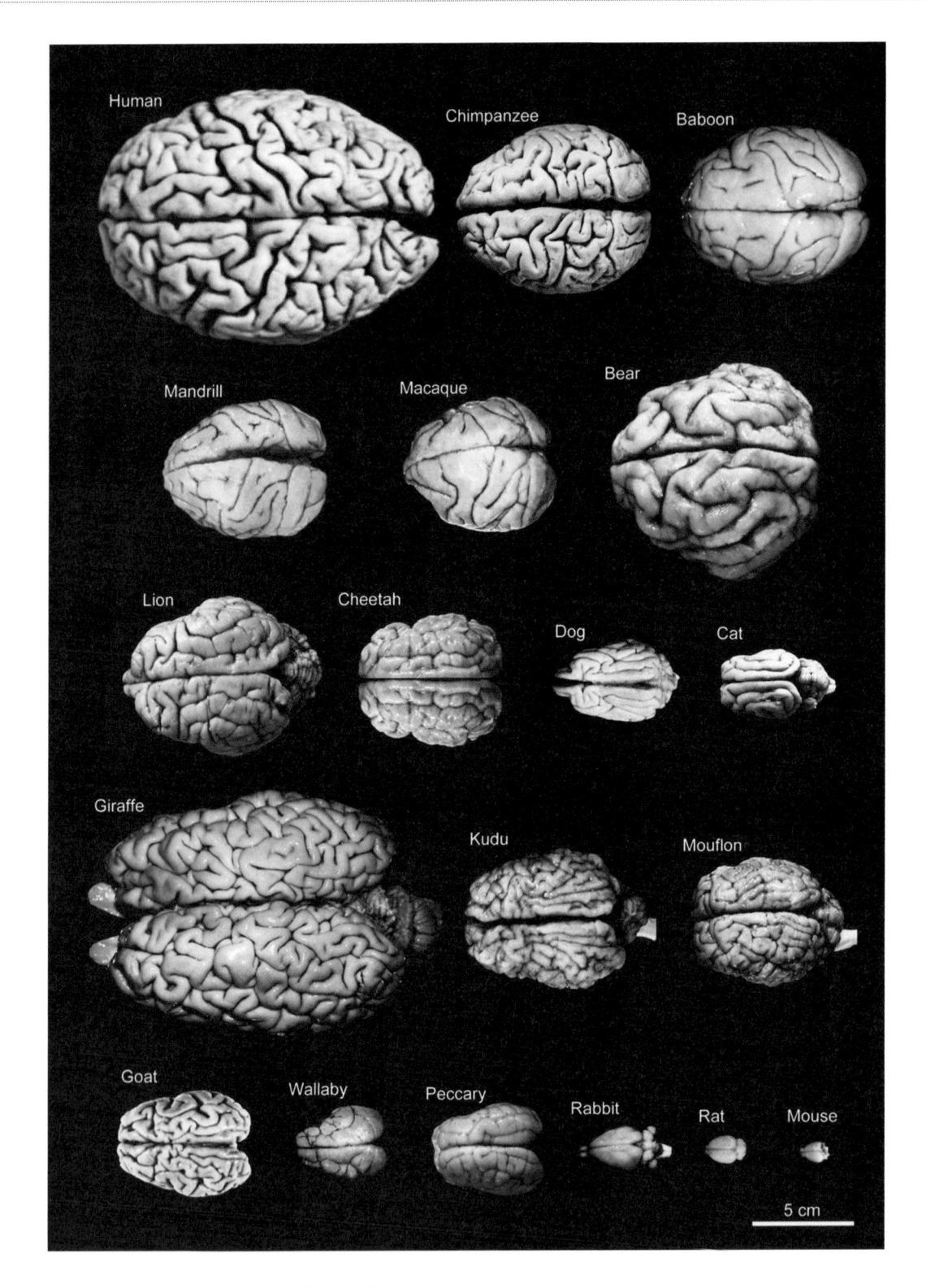

FIGURE 2.3 *The human brain compared to the brains of other species.*
Source: DeFelipe, J. (2011). The evolution of the brain, the human nature of cortical circuits, and intellectual creativity. *Frontiers in Neuroanatomy*, 5, 29.

Mendelian inheritance). Phenotypes are qualitatively different; that is, either a presence or absence of disease. A qualitative trait is typically unaffected by environmental factors. Huntington's disease is an example of a qualitative trait. Just because the single gene disorders appear to obey straightforward rules of genetics, it does not mean that the whole process is straightforward. There are several factors that may alter the pattern of inheritance of the characteristic or disorder. Genetic heterogeneity describes an eventuality where clinically similar disorders are caused by mutations in different genes, or where mutations in the same gene result in diverse conditions. In some cases individuals who have inherited disease-associated alleles do not always express the disease completely or partially. This is referred to as penetrance – an **allele** which does not always lead to the disorder is said to have low penetrance. Even if one has the alleles contributing to a disease state, the severity can be subject to differential expression. In this case the genes may be modifying agents. **Mosaicism** is when not all of the cells in the body are genetically identical. This may come about via atypical cellular divisions during early development, such as in **Turner's syndrome** where there is a deletion of the X chromosome from the normal XX genotype in some but not all of the cells (see Box 2.1).

Up until now we have only really considered genetic abnormalities; however, environmental factors, especially those *in utero*, can give rise to disorders that are similar to those of genetic origin. These are called **phenocopies** (copies of the phenotype – see below). An example of this is the rubella virus that can cause deafness as can a number of genetic defects.

Given that the qualitative traits started out as being comparatively easy to understand, although we added a layer of complexity, one can imagine the **polygenetic disorders** will be immensely complex. In contrast, multiple genes, some of only modest contribution, influence a **quantitative trait**. Quantitative traits do not follow simple patterns of inheritance. They are more variable and less predictable than their qualitative counterparts. With a quantitative trait, the phenotype is not an all-or-none phenomenon, it is expressed along a continuum. For example, ADHD is a quantitative trait with individuals expressing various degrees of symptom severity along a continuum, such as attention with a continuum of inattentive to overattentive (see Box 2.2). Phenotypic expression of a quantitative trait, unlike the qualitative traits, is subject to alteration and mitigation by environmental factors. Many, but not all, of our psychological phenomena and our psychological disorders are quantitative traits. Indeed, many of our disorders

BOX 2.1: TURNER'S SYNDROME

Turner's syndrome is a chromosomal condition that affects development in females. Most cases are not inherited. The chromosomal abnormality occurs at random during the formation of **gametes**.

Turner's syndrome is related to the X chromosome in which women typically have two X chromosomes (XX) in each cell (males have one X chromosome and one Y chromosome therefore they are the ones that determine the sex of the child). In Turner's syndrome one X chromosome is missing (XO) (see Figure 2.1.1). This is **monosomy** (contrast with **trisomy** in Box 2.5). The missing genetic material affects development before and after birth; remember that genes do not all come into action at once, some are timed to express themselves later in life.

Some women with Turner's syndrome have a chromosomal change in only some of their cells – mosaic Turner's syndrome. This tends to be caused by errors occurring during mitosis.

Some facts about Turner's syndrome.

- 1 out of 2000 live births, but more common among non-surviving pregnancies that end via miscarriages or stillbirth.
- Absent or incomplete development at puberty, including sparse pubic hair and small breasts.
- Broad, flat chest shaped like a shield.
- Drooping eyelids/dry eyes.
- Short stature.
- Absence of menstrual period.
- Produce little oestrogen.
- Sterile.
- Extra skin on neck.

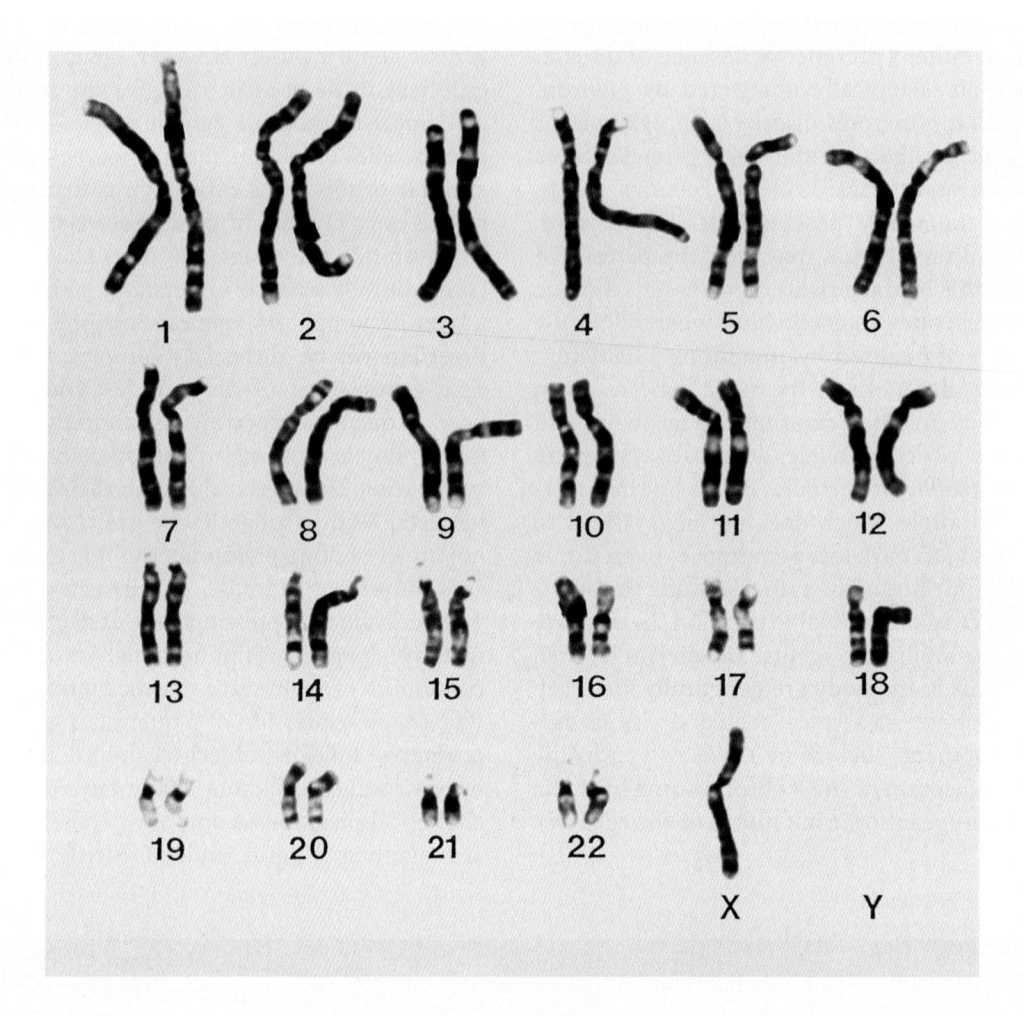

FIGURE 2.1.1 Turner's syndrome karyotype. Note the absence of a sex chromosome.
Source: Dept. of Clinical Cytogenetics, Addenbrooke's Hospital/Science Photo Library.

BOX 2.2: THE EVOLUTION OF A DISORDER: THE CASE OF ATTENTION DEFICIT HYPERACTIVITY DISORDER (ADHD)

Attention deficit hyperactivity disorder (ADHD) is a neurodevelopmental disorder that affects 5% of the paediatric population (Chandler, 2010). The main symptoms are extreme impulsivity, hyperactivity and lack of attention. Whilst it is considered a childhood disorder, it is also seen in adulthood, with DSM 5 recognizing it as such (see Chandler, 2010 for review). A lot of research time and money has been spent on understanding the aetiology and pathogenesis of ADHD, revealing that it runs in families and is most likely to be genetic, although the evidence cannot be regarded as conclusive because there are also potential environmental factors. Psychopharmacological studies suggest that ADHD symptoms arise because of an imbalance of the neurotransmitter dopamine.

Darwin's theory of evolution would suggest that if there is inheritance of an ADHD gene or genes, and these genes are behaviourally maladaptive, then why hasn't it been weeded out of the human genome? The question which remains in evolutionary psychology is: to what extent is ADHD maladaptive? Evolutionary accounts have attempted to explain that a gene may confer a beneficial set of behaviours in our ancestry (Bradshaw & Sheppard, 2000). When it comes to breeding, people with ADHD are more likely to have children at a younger age and with more partners (Barkley et al., 2006), thus perpetuating the transmission of ADHD genes; in evolutionary terms and for the selfish gene, that's job done! However, how can the symptoms of ADHD be beneficial to the individual, the species and the social group?

The notion of an evolutionary advantage of psychiatric disorders is not new and dates back to the late 1960s (Hammer & Zubin, 1968), with more recent accounts placing evolution and psychiatry in a sociopolitical context (Fabrega, 2004). Such accounts are not restricted to ADHD (see Bradshaw & Sheppard (2000) for a review).

Initially it was suggested that ADHD may have served an adaptive function and have been selected by the environment for survival, i.e. best fit (Shelley-Tremblay & Rosen, 1996), in particular as the hunter rather than farmer (Hartmann, 1997, 2003). Jensen et al. (1997) argue that hyperactivity is useful for exploration, especially when food is scarce. Rapidly shifting attention (or as we have come to describe it – inattention) is a form of hypervigilance that is beneficial for monitoring threat or danger in the environment, and impulsivity is a negative term used to describe rapid reflex actions to stimuli, without apparent thought. Clearly, a modern urban environment that is technological and requires co-operation does not value such characteristics. However, if we go back to when we had to hunt for food in a hostile environment, the view might be somewhat different. The symptoms of ADHD would increase the likelihood of survival and as such, we should not refer to them as symptoms. The hunter needs to have stamina, energy and physical prowess in order to catch his prey and have food. The hunter may also become the hunted and therefore needs to pay attention to any changes in the environment and orient to them rapidly – failure to do so may result in their demise. Sustained focused attention, as required in school, is not necessary. Finally, the hunter does not have time to think of the alternatives when confronted by hostile predators but needs to react instinctively and reflexively to increase the chance of survival. Planning and evaluating the outcomes of several options of behaviour is too slow; by the time a plan is put into action, it may be just too late.

In modern urban societies, these behaviours are no longer advantageous. It has been suggested that evolutionary changes in the dopamine genes selected to increase cognitive and behavioural flexibility (of benefit to hunters) may now be associated with attention problems and ADHD (Campbell & Eisenberg, 2007). The goodness of fit that may be conveyed by ADHD symptoms works well in some environments, but now those same characteristics are seen as maladaptive (Crawford & Salmon, 2002). This is really just theoretical conjecture that places a positive spin on ADHD symptoms; however, there has been a relative lack of evidence to support evolutionary accounts of ADHD. This position has somewhat changed using genetic studies, most notably those looking at dopamine genes; Arcos-Burgos and Acosta (2007) have found support for the evolutionary hypothesis. They argue that the ADHD child's hunter gene has been 'rewarded by natural selection over millions of years of human evolution. However, the fast revolution of human society during the past two centuries brought new challenges rewarding planning, design and attention while limiting behaviours associated with ADHD' (Arcos-Burgos & Acosta, 2007, p.237). Such a role is supported by the evolutionary function of the dopamine systems and a mismatch with current environments (Pani, 2000). Evolution is a slow process while changes in society, especially over the last five decades, have been rapid. Human genetics has not been able to keep up with the fast pace of modern life.

ADHD is no stranger to controversy, most notably on its very existence but also on its treatment with a well-known drug methylphenidate (Ritalin). The evolutionary accounts of ADHD are also controversial as not everyone agrees with the evolutionary adaptiveness of ADHD. Evolutionary accounts of behaviour are constantly called into question and are a rich and fertile area for debate.

Barkley (2005) takes a strong view on the evolution of executive functions, which he considers to be the central problem in ADHD. Executive functions (see Chapter 12) are higher-order cognitive processes that manage our behaviour and our thinking. He claims that the development of executive functions through our ancestors has 'the ultimate utility function of conveying an enhanced survival and reproductive advantage to individuals and the species at large. In contrast, ADHD should be found to reduce the survival and reproductive advantage conveyed by the executive functions and self-regulation when observed to operate over substantial time periods of an evolutionary scale' (p.304).

Brody (2001) takes exception to the hunter's traditional qualities and claims that waiting, planning, co-operation and rehearsal are important traits for the hunter. These traits are not highly demonstrated in ADHD so ADHD may be maladaptive and not of functional benefit at any time during our ancestry (Andrews et al., 2002; Baird et al., 2000; Brody, 2001; Matejcek, 2003). The argument continues but does not necessarily explain how disorders such as ADHD remain, although those with ADHD are good at perpetuating their gene pool.

So how do these behaviours continue to flourish? In order to answer this question, we need to step back from Darwinian and Mendelian genetics. The behaviours associated with ADHD have been referred to as spandrels (Andrews et al., 2002). Spandrels are not adaptations and are not reproductively beneficial in early human evolution. Spandrels occur and evolve because they are genetically linked to other advantageous adaptations such as language (Baird et al., 2000) – these behaviours were not in themselves advantageous but have come along for the ride.

One of the features of the evolutionary literature is how language is used to describe the symptoms of ADHD. The accounts that see ADHD as having some adaptive function view the symptoms positively, and some argue that they still have some benefit today with particular occupations being favoured by those with ADHD (Klimkeit & Bradshaw, 2007). Those who see it as maladaptive often cite evidence of how ADHD children behave in today's western world (e.g. Matejcek, 2003). I am not convinced that using behaviours in a 21st-century context provides strong evidence for a maladaptive case; it could be a maladaptive society, as some have suggested (see Timimi & Leo, 2009). Clearly, evolutionary accounts of behaviour describe how environments shape the selection of traits and we come back to the perennial problem of deciding if ADHD is real or merely a social label that is more informative about our intolerance of certain behaviours. Thus, evolutionary accounts of behaviour have an important role in the determination of the disorder and are not just the fanciful ideas of a few scientists. The impact of such a philosophical stance can have real and tangible effects. As Klimkeit and Bradshaw (2007) put it, 'while the prevalence of ADHD genetically may not have changed, what we might be witnessing is the decline in the capacity of western culture to cope with and raise these children' (p.472). However, from a different view on its evolutionary significance, Matejcek states that ADHD would have been an even greater burden on the family and society than it is today, but falls short of saying that it should have died out (Matejcek, 2003).

Goldstein and Barkley (1998) are scathing about those who use evolutionary accounts and state:

> The community of advocates for ADHD that would encourage such practices must take care because they cannot have it both ways. They cannot on the one hand argue that ADHD needs to be taken seriously as a legitimate developmental disability. Then on the other hand simultaneously sing its praises as a once successful adaptation that leads to higher intelligence, greater creativity, and heightened sensory awareness, but that now results in suffering due to an over-ADHD, controlled, linear-focused, and intolerant culture. All such claims fly in the face of available scientific evidence. (p.4)

Goldstein and Barkley continue: '… it is also time for us to acknowledge and accept ADHD as a condition that can be significantly impairing to those so affected in our society. This is neither to pathologize, patronize, nor demonize those with ADHD. It is to say that having ADHD is no picnic' (p.4). Although the behaviours associated with ADHD might once have been of some benefit, the important point is how best to accommodate the needs of those with ADHD and reduce any suffering that they have.

The use of modern genetics may help support or refute some of the evolutionary arguments. The dopamine receptor gene, DRD4, has been associated with ADHD, most notably a type of variation in the gene called the 7R variant that some argue may confer an advantage in conflict resolution (see Swanson et al., (2002)).

The DRD4/7R gene is increased in nomadic tribes compared to settled tribes (Chen et al., 1999; Eisenberg et al., 2008). Research in Kenya has concluded that individuals with the DRD4/7R gene who still live a nomadic life are better fit for their environment, but those who have adopted a more urban life show reduced fit. One can now see the similarities with ADHD. Those with the DRD4/7R gene who were still nomads were better nourished than those without the gene. This led to the widespread media coverage suggesting that the ADHD-related gene may encourage behaviour that is beneficial for a nomadic lifestyle. The chances are that more than the DRD4 gene is involved in ADHD (Faraone et al., 2005); the changes that occur in the brain and influence behaviour are most likely to be many and add to the complexity of the disorder (Bittner & Friedman, 2000).

The debate continues about the benefit to the individual but what about groups or societies? Williams and Taylor (2006) claim that ADHD-like symptoms are of value to the group when they exist only in a minority. More specifically, during group exploration tasks unpredictable behaviour by some of the group optimizes the overall group result, whilst risk taking is confined to a minority and information sharing is enhanced. Thus, those with ADHD can explore the possibilities of an environment without the whole group placing itself in danger; the group can then learn from the valuable experiences of the person with ADHD (Williams & Taylor, 2006). From this perspective the person with ADHD is hunter, explorer, risk taker, teacher and altruist!

Can Mendelian genetics be extrapolated to ADHD? No, it is much more complicated than that. Because ADHD does not follow Mendelian transmission, it is considered a complex disorder (Lander & Schork, 1994) in comparison to phenylketonuria (PKU), for example, which does have a simple genetic basis following Mendelian principles.

> There would appear to be a number of genes that are now associated with ADHD (Gizer et al., 2009).
>
> In trying to understand the genetics of complex disorders such as ADHD, Waldman and Gizer (2006) have summarized the challenges that lie ahead:
>
> - multiple genetic and environmental factors will be involved;
> - the multiple genes involved will only have a small role in the overall picture;
> - there is likely to be genetic heterogeneity in as much as the same gene can have different effects, and the same effect can be derived from different genes;
> - there are likely to be phenocopies, that is, disorders that look genetic but are in fact purely environmental;
> - the genes involved are likely to have low penetrance which means that there is a low chance of having ADHD if you have the gene (Waldman & Rhee, 2002); and
> - environmental factors are more likely to play a prominent role in ADHD. Despite technological advances that can identify individual genes, all of these factors make the genetic analysis of ADHD extremely difficult.

are polygenetic. In the case of a polygenetic characteristic or disorder, the term **quantitative trait loci** (QTL) describes how multiple genes at different locations on the chromosome contribute to the quantitative trait. And using **linkage** analysis (see later in the chapter), geneticists can investigate QTLs looking for common occurrences in individuals who have a particular characteristic or disorder.

Mendelian Genetics

Gregor Mendel (1822–1884) was a monk who was working on inheritance at the same time as Darwin was explaining evolution. Mendel was able to account for differences in **conspecifics** (members of the same species) and for the inheritance of behavioural as well as physiological and anatomical characteristics. If you thought animal experiments were hard to extrapolate to the human condition, then Mendel's evidence derived from his experiments with pea plants may be a step too far. Fortunately, we can extrapolate his work with peas to human inheritance. His experiments were critical to our understanding of patterns of inheritance in humans.

Mendel studied seven different observable characteristics of peas, such as seed colour and flower colour. Regardless of the characteristic he looked at, the principles he uncovered remained the same.

He examined **dichotomous traits**; that is, characteristics that are in one form or another. One dichotomous trait he observed in the pea plants was whether the seed was coloured yellow or green (this also follows to some extent with eye colour, as we shall see later). This variant in colour is called a *trait*. If a yellow-seeded plant (called here Y1) is inbred with another yellow-seeded plant (Y2) then the next generation of offspring is also a yellow-seeded plant and possesses both Y1 and Y2 factors from the parental generation (Y1:Y2). The same pattern applies to the green-seeded plants; g1 and g2 parents give rise to a generation of g1 and g2 factor possessing plants (g1:g2). These plants are true breeding lines and produce the same trait in subsequent generations (yellow seeds or green seeds), because they always have the two factors for seed colour (Figure 2.4).

What happens if a true breeding yellow-seeded plant is crossed with a true breeding green-seeded plant and the yellow and green factors are mixed up? As shown in Figure 2.4, the result is a first generation of yellow-seeded plants. No green seeds can be observed. Mendel then took this first generation of yellow-seeded plants and crossed them with each another. In the second-generation pea plants, 75% had yellow seeds and 25% had green seeds. Despite the parental generation all being yellow seeded, some of the subsequent generation had the observable trait of green seeds. How can this be explained?

Mendel noted that only one trait appeared in the first-generation cross – this is referred to as the **dominant trait** (yellow seeds, in this case either Y1 or Y2). The **recessive trait** (green seeds, as with g1 and g2) was not expressed because it was overridden by the yellow seed trait (in a Y1:g1 seed, the Y1 factor is expressed and the g1 factor is suppressed). In the second generation, green-seeded pea plants were produced (g1:g2) despite not being observed in the first-generation plants; the recessive trait was passed on to the second generation (as with our Y1:g1 plant). The first-generation plants were *carriers* of the recessive trait (g1), but because it was combined with a dominant trait (Y1) it was not observable. Thus, there is a difference between observed traits and genetic traits. What is observed is called the **phenotype** and what is transmitted genetically is the **genotype**. What you see is the phenotype and what you get underneath in the

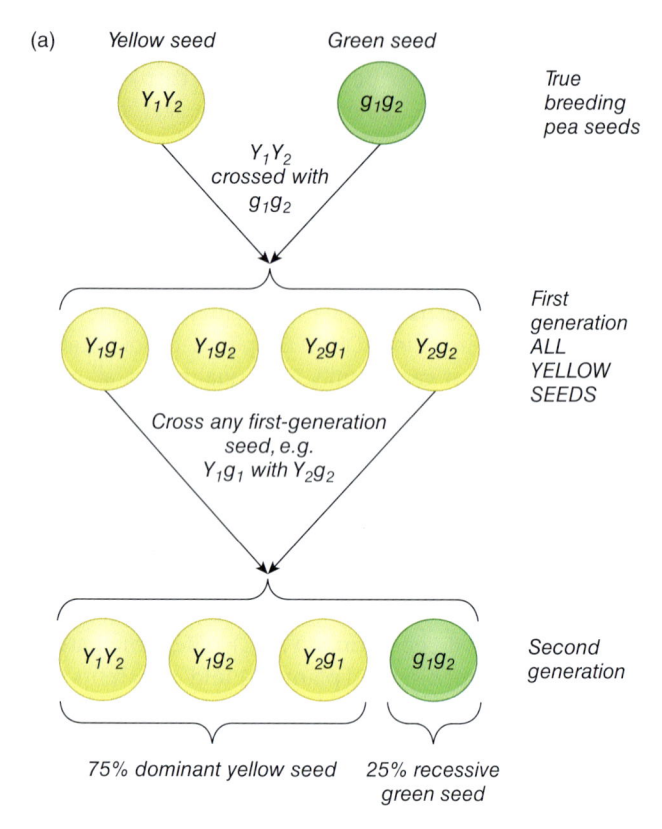

FIGURE 2.4 Mendel's principle of inheritance. (a) The true breeding lines produced seeds that were cross-fertilized to produce a first generation; when the first generation were crossed they produced a second generation. By combining yellow seed factors (Y) and green seed factors (g), different combinations were obtained in the genotype and the phenotype. (b) The principles of Mendelian inheritance can be applied to eye colour in which there is a brown eye factor (B) and a blue eye factor (b). Brown is a dominant allele and blue is a recessive allele.

mechanisms of inheritance is the genotype and these can be different from the observed trait.

Mendel's observations can be expressed in the language of modern genetics. The fact that there are dichotomous traits for pea characteristics means that there is a gene for yellow and a gene for green seeds. Each successive generation inherits two of these genes, one from mother and one from father, or in the case of the peas one from a yellow-seeded plant and one from a green-seeded plant. If the two genes are controlling the same trait (e.g. seed colour or eye colour), they are referred to as alleles (a yellow allele and a green allele). The random inheritance of alleles permits a number of combinations.

Mendelian Genetics and Eye Colour

How can these Mendelian principles of inheritance apply to humans? An obvious example is eye colour which varies in humans. Some of us have blue eyes, some brown, some grey and some green (see Box 2.3). And some even have one eye different from the other! In general, eye colour is similar to the pea plants and adopts a Mendelian pattern of inheritance. Let us consider the example of a blue eye factor and a brown eye factor. A mother and a father can both carry a factor for blue eyes (*b*) and brown eyes (B). When the gametes (**ovum** and **sperm**) are formed, they can only carry one factor, either B or *b*. The combination of eye colour factors is depicted in Figure 2.4. In the example above, B is dominant and *b* is recessive. This means that all offspring with B factor will have brown eyes, regardless of whether they have a blue allele. However, if the combination of sperm and ovum at fertilization results in a combination of *bb* then the offspring will have blue eyes; *b* being recessive, it will only ever be expressed in the company of another recessive *b* allele.

What about people who have one eye blue and one eye brown? This is a question students often ask. The answer takes us off topic, but here is a brief explanation. In the case of a person having different colour eyes, this could be due to either **heterochromia iridium** (two different-coloured eyes within a single individual) or **heterochromia iridis** (a variety of colour within a single iris). Brown eyes are rich in melanin, whereas blue eyes indicate a lack of melanin (melanin is a pigment that gives colour to the iris of the eye). Two of the genes that control eye colour, EYCL3, found on chromosome 15 (15q11–15q21), which codes for brown/blue eye colour (BEY), and EYCL1, found on chromosome 19 (19p13.1–19q13.11) (Sturm & Frudakis, 2004), which codes for green/blue eye colour (GEY), may not be the problem, i.e. it is not inherited. In heterochromia iridium it may be the *reading* of the genetic code that is at fault, i.e. the code is fine but the utilization of the code contains an error. Alternatively, heterochromia iridium could be the outcome of trauma (as is reported in the case of David Bowie). Thus providing the example that the environment or other conditions beyond the basic gene itself can influence a gene's expression or act as phenocopies.

BOX 2.3: LOVE IN THE EYES

My wife the love rat with sex-mad monk

Dear Auntie Agony,

I have been married to my wife for 17 years (you get less for murder!). We have two children aged 12 and 15 years old. The problem is, I think I might not be the father of the youngest child. Their mother and I both have dark brown eyes. So does our 15 year old. However, the 12 year old has blue eyes. I do not understand how this can happen. My best friend and best man at my wedding has blue eyes and has always been close.

Once I got the nerve to ask her about this, she said it was Mendel. Well, Mendel is not my best man! I thought I might track him down on the internet and troll him; my wife, well, she just laughs at me. I am even thinking of confrontation and lie detector on any day-time TV show that will have me! She says that I am the father and it is all in our genes. But how can he have blue eyes when we both have brown eyes?

Yours,
Cheated from Brighton

Dear Cheated from Brighton,

Your wife is not a cheat, at least not for this reason. Your children are just obeying Mendelian genetics. This is nothing to do with what is in Mendel's jeans – he is dead! It is all about genetics. I suggest you have a beer with your blue-eyed mate and laugh about your own stupidity!

Auntie Agony

Mendelian Inheritance: Huntington's Disease – Dominant Allele in Action

The principles of Mendelian genetics can be applied to **Huntington's disease** (HD). HD is a case of a dominant allele (like Mendel's yellow seeds or our example of brown eyes) having debilitating effects. HD is a progressive disorder that is characterized by motor disturbances and a subsequent cognitive decline. Behavioural changes are often the first symptoms to appear, including:

- a lack of emotions and not recognizing the needs of others in the family;
- alternating periods of aggression, excitement, depression, apathy, antisocial behaviour and anger;
- difficulty concentrating on more than one task, which causes irritability;
- short-term memory lapses; and
- problems with orientation.

Huntington's disease patients exhibit slight, uncontrollable movements of the face, and jerking, flicking or fidgety movements of the limbs and body. These move from one area of the body to another and can cause the person to lurch and stumble. As the disease progresses, the uncontrollable movements are more frequent and extreme. This may change over time so that movements become slow and muscles more rigid.

The manifestation of symptoms occurs between the ages of 30 and 45. The significance of this late onset is that reproduction will most likely have occurred prior to the symptoms appearing, so HD is passed on to their offspring. An early onset would minimize the opportunity to reproduce and the transmission of the HD gene. This is where genetic counselling comes to the fore, offering guidance about future planning. Furthermore, this indicates that individuals can have an aberrant gene but it is only switched on at specified times. Similar properties of genetics have been associated with psychiatric disorders such as schizophrenia.

The reason someone contracts HD is because of a dominant allele for HD (H). When this dominant allele is combined with a recessive allele (h), the person will develop HD. A parent who has an Hh genotype will pass on either the H or the h allele to the offspring. In Figure 2.5 it can be seen that each parent has two alleles. These are divided for reproduction into the egg or sperm. For example, if the father has a genotype of Hh then the sperms produced will either be H or h carriers. When this is combined with an hh mother (the eggs contain the recessive allele h), there is a 50% chance of the dominant H allele being expressed in the offspring. This is a population statistic and considers averages in groups. The reality for one family may be different from the statistical average. We will revisit HD when we look at molecular genetics (see Box 2.4).

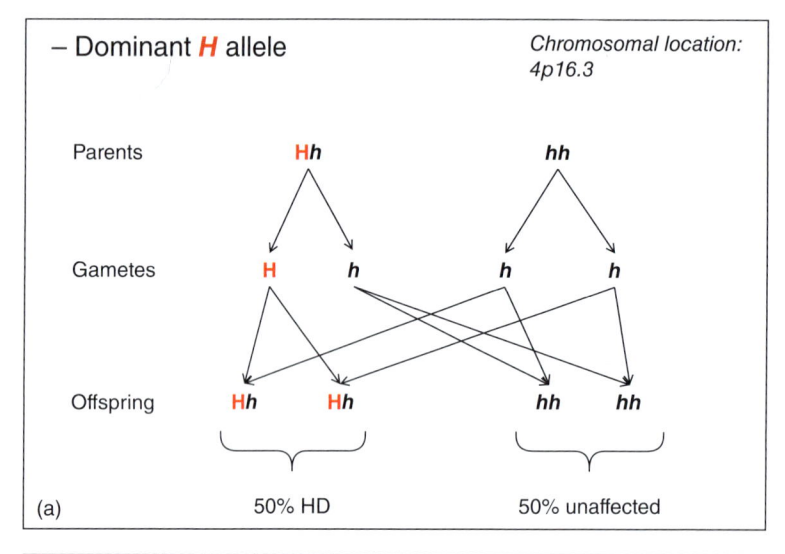

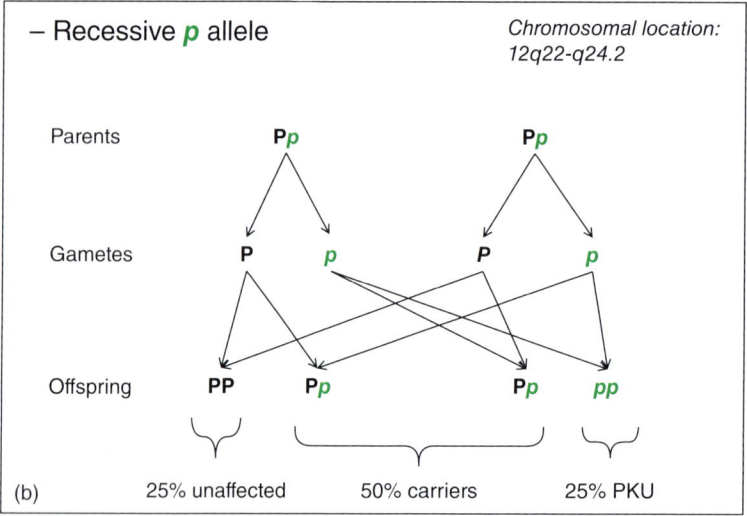

FIGURE 2.5 *Mendelian transmission of Huntington's disease and PKU. (a) Those with a dominant H allele will have Huntington's disease. (b) Those with a recessive p allele will have PKU.*
Source: Plomin, R., DeFries, J. C., & McClean, G. E. (1990). *Behavioral genetics* (2nd edn). New York: W.H. Freeman.

BOX 2.4: HUNTINGTON'S DISEASE: MOLECULAR GENETICS OF AN AUTOSOMAL DOMINANT DISORDER

It is a mutation in the HTT gene on chromosome 4p 16.3 that causes Huntington's disease. The HTT gene codes for the protein **huntingtin**. The mutation involves the DNA segment CAG (**cytosine, adenine** and **guanine**). In unaffected individuals the CAG segment is repeated 10–35 times but in those affected with HD, the segment is repeated 36–120 times. People with 40 or more repeats nearly always develop the disorder (MacDonald et al., 1993).

The HTT mutation leads to the production of an abnormally long version of the huntingtin protein which is cut into smaller, toxic fragments that bind together and accumulate in neurons, disrupting the normal functions of these cells, leading to cell death in certain areas of the brain.

This condition is inherited, as seen in Figure 2.5. As the altered HTT gene is passed from generation to generation, the size of the CAG repeat often increases. Individuals who have 27–35 CAG repeats in the HTT gene do not develop HD but they are at risk of having children who will develop the disorder and as the gene is passed from parent to child, the size of the CAG repeat may lengthen into the range associated with Huntington's disease (40 repeats or more).

Mendelian Inheritance: PKU – A Recessive Allele in Action

Phenylketonuria (PKU) is a form of delayed cognitive maturation and is due to a recessive allele. PKU patients are missing the enzyme phenylalanine hydroxylase, which is needed to break down an essential **amino acid** called phenylalanine (which is found in food). Without the enzyme, levels of phenylalanine and two closely related substances build up in the body. These substances are harmful to the central nervous system and cause brain damage. The symptoms of PKU are delayed mental and social skills, head size significantly below normal, hyperactivity, jerking movements of the arms or legs, mental impairment, seizures, skin rashes, tremors and unusual positioning of hands.

If a recessive allele is to be expressed, there has to be two copies of it (similar to Mendel's second-generation green pea plants were expressed only when the genotype was g1:g2). With the pea plants there is no dominant factor to override the recessive factor. Similarly, with PKU, the disorder is only expressed when there is no dominant allele (P) to override the recessive trait (p). Therefore only 25% of offspring will have the disorder and 50% will be carriers of PKU but will not contract the disorder (see Figure 2.5). Here again is an example of the genotype being very different from the phenotype. A person can be a carrier of PKU but not express PKU.

Chromosomes and Inheritance

The process of inheritance described by Mendel has a clear biological basis, not that Mendel knew of this basis. The examples of HD and PKU demonstrate that the genes (alleles) that each parent has are not expressed in every gamete (sperm/egg) because the genes are divided. In the mid to late 1800s the discovery of chromosomes was able to support Mendel's views. The discovery of chromosomes by Waldeyer, a German cytologist, placed chromosomes in the nuclei of cells.

Genes are located on **chromosomes**. Chromosomes are constructed from the strands of the DNA molecule. On each chromosome there are millions of base pairs. Chromosomes come in matched pairs; humans have 23 pairs (the diploid number; 46 individual **chromatids**). The alleles for a particular trait (e.g. HD or PKU) are found in the same location on a chromosome (see Figure 2.6). We inherit one-half of our chromosomes from our mother and the other half from out father. Thus 23 chromosomes are present in both the egg and the sperm. The 23 pairs are referred to as a **diploid** set of chromosomes. In contrast, **haploid** refers to when a cell has only one set of chromosomes (not paired), and this is the case for the gametes (the egg and the sperm). When the egg is fertilized by the sperm, the two haploid sets of chromosomes combine, resulting in 46 chromosomes (23 matched pairs – a diploid set of chromosomes).

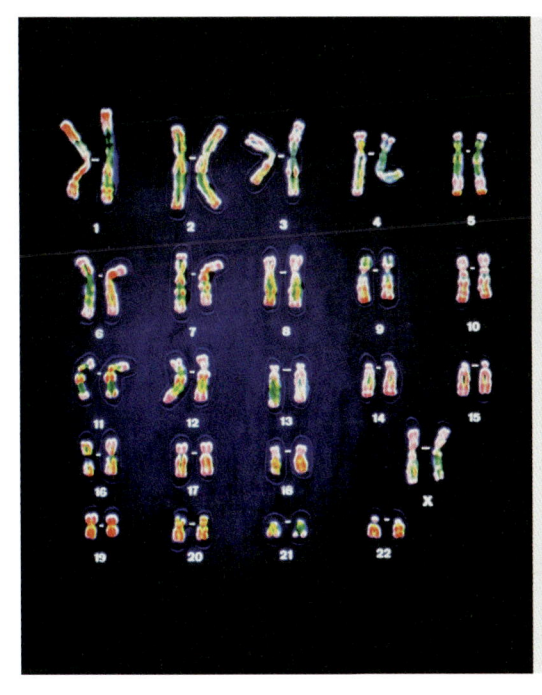

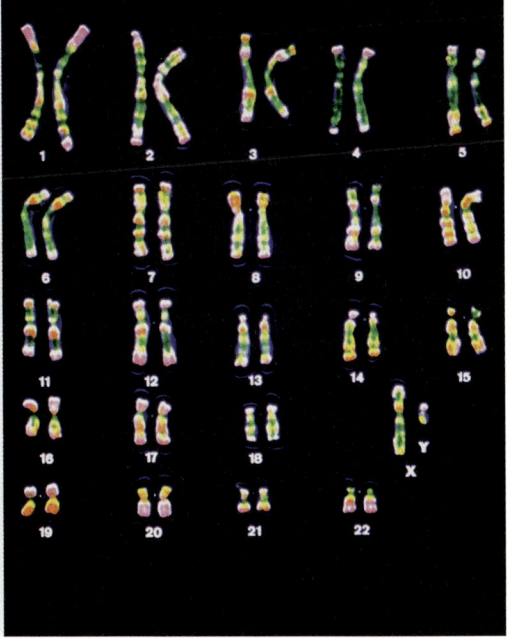

FIGURE 2.6 *The human karyotype. Chromosomes can be organized into 23 pairs, with the female haploid having X chromosomes (left) and the male haploid having a Y chromosome (right).* Source: CNRI/Science Photo Library.

The chromosomes are categorized according to size, with chromosome 1 being the largest and chromosome 21 being the smallest; notice that it was originally considered to be chromosome 22. The first 22 chromosomes are referred to as **autosomes**; these do not differ between the sexes. The 23rd pair of chromosomes is the **sex chromosomes** and they are the exception to the rule. The sex chromosomes are called the X and Y chromosome. Females typically have two X chromosomes (XX), and males typically have an X and a Y chromosome (XY). I use the word 'typically' advisedly, as the difference between the sexes is not always that clear-cut and the genetics can be subject to variation.

The complete set of chromosomes can be viewed as a **karyotype** (see Figure 2.6). The architecture of the chromosomes on the karyotype allows each chromosome to be identified and in some cases abnormalities in number and structure can also be identified (see Box 2.4).

In Figure 2.7 we can see the architecture of a chromosome. At the junction of the chromosome is an anchor point from which the short and long arms of the chromosome emanate. This is called the **centromere** and it does not contain any genetic information. The centromere is an important part of the chromosome's cellular division. The branches or arms that span from the centromere are referred to as p or q. The short arm is the p arm (for petite or small), whilst the long arm is the q arm. The **telomeres** are repeated genetic sequences at the very end of the arms.

If we use staining techniques that allow us to look in more detail at the chromosomes, we can see that stripes appear. The stripes are referred to as **cytogenetic bands**. Using the cytogenetic and structural architecture of the chromosomes, one can identify and locate genes. In Figure 2.5 we can see the location or co-ordinates for the genes involved in Huntington's disease and PKU.

How a complete organism inherits from both mother and father requires further description. After all, our cells contain 46 pairs of chromosomes so how do these get divided in the gametes? The answer is found in cellular division. The 23 pairs of chromosomes are divided into the haploid number in the gametes by cellular division called **meiosis** (see Figure 2.8). Each gamete has half the full complement of chromosomes. Thus meiosis reduces the chromosomes from the diploid number (46) to the haploid number (23) of unpaired single chromosomes. With a sperm and an egg each having 23 unpaired chromosomes, fertilization allows them to pair up and form a **zygote** – a foetus – and a human.

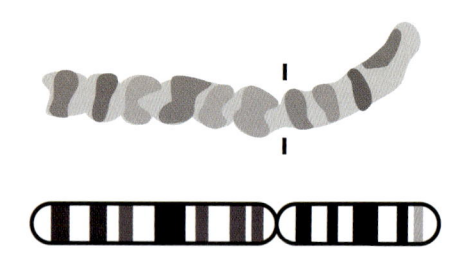

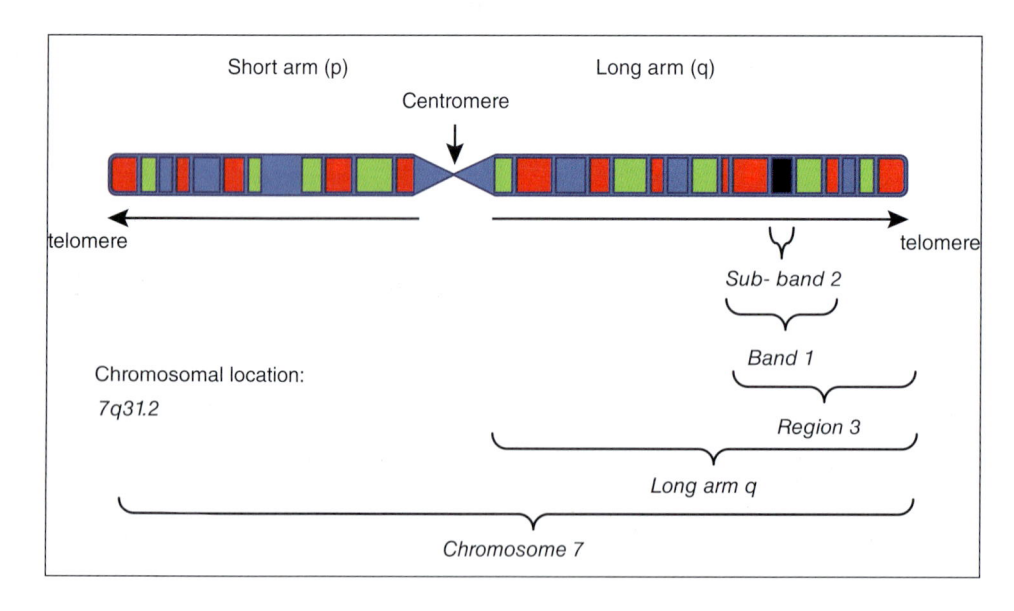

FIGURE 2.7 *Features of a single chromosome. The cytogenetic bands provide co-ordinates for genes on the chromosome.*

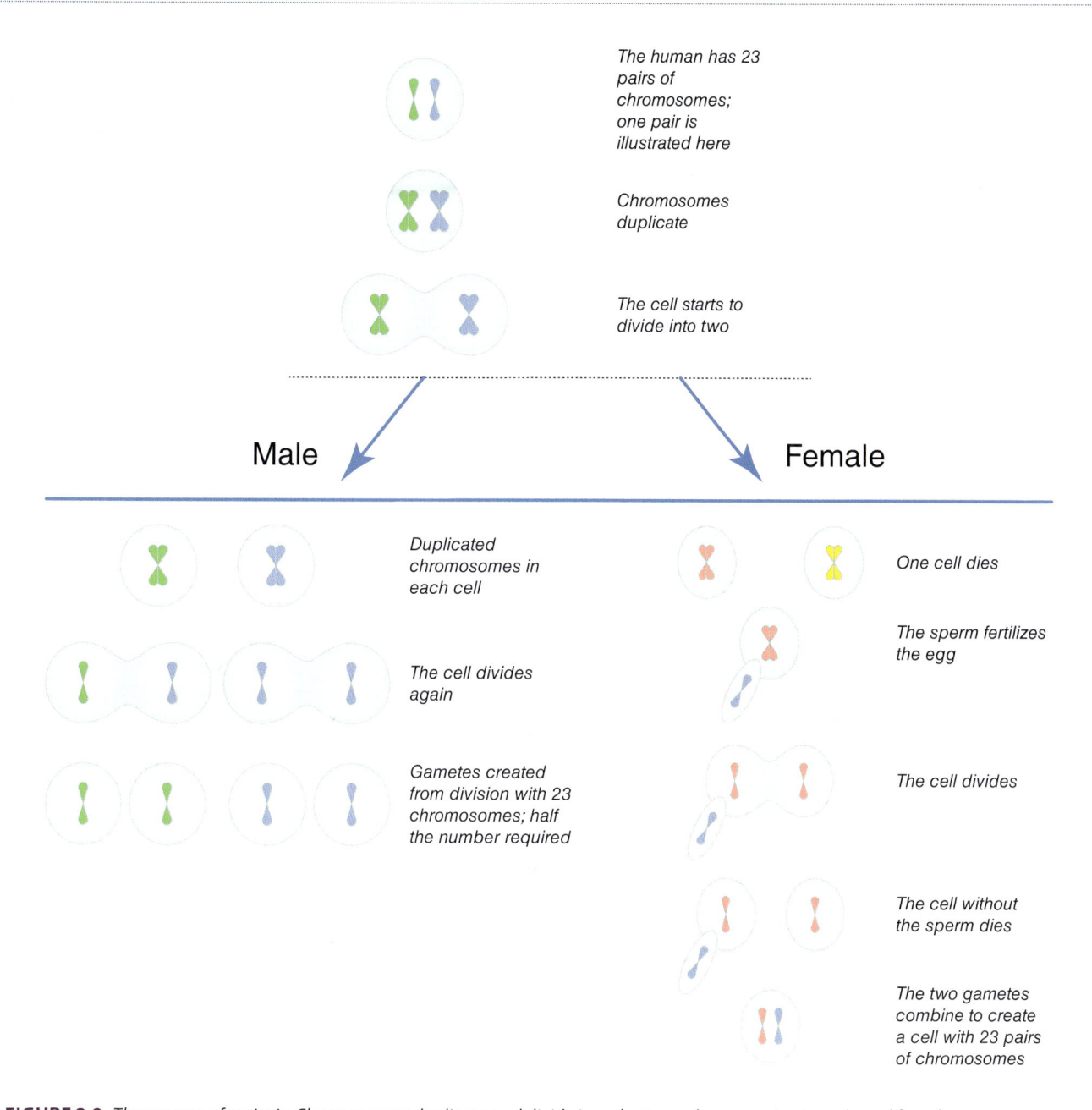

FIGURE 2.8 *The process of meiosis. Chromosomes duplicate and divide in order to produce gametes in male and female.*

A different path of meiotic cell division occurs in sperm and eggs. The pathway for the meiosis of sperm is as follows: as we have established, the human has 23 pairs of chromosomes and these chromosomes are duplicated. Once duplicated, the cell starts to divide into two and the duplicated chromosomes reside in separate cells. The next stage in meiosis sees the chromosomes separate, so instead of a pair they are now individual chromosomes. The cell then divides again, leaving one chromosome in each cell (note not a pair); this is the haploid number of 23 unpaired single chromosomes. The gametes, in this case the sperm, after meiotic cellular division now have half the number of required chromosomes for a complete organism (haploid number). Meiosis takes a different pathway when it comes to egg production. From where we have left off with creating the sperm, we can now follow the pathway leading to the egg. Following chromosome duplication and the first set of cell divisions, one of the cells dies. If the remaining cell is fertilized by the sperm, it divides, giving two haploid daughter cells. The daughter cell without the sperm also dies. The surviving sperm and egg fuse to produce a complete zygote. That is, the cell has the full complement of chromosomes – the diploid number, 23 pairs.

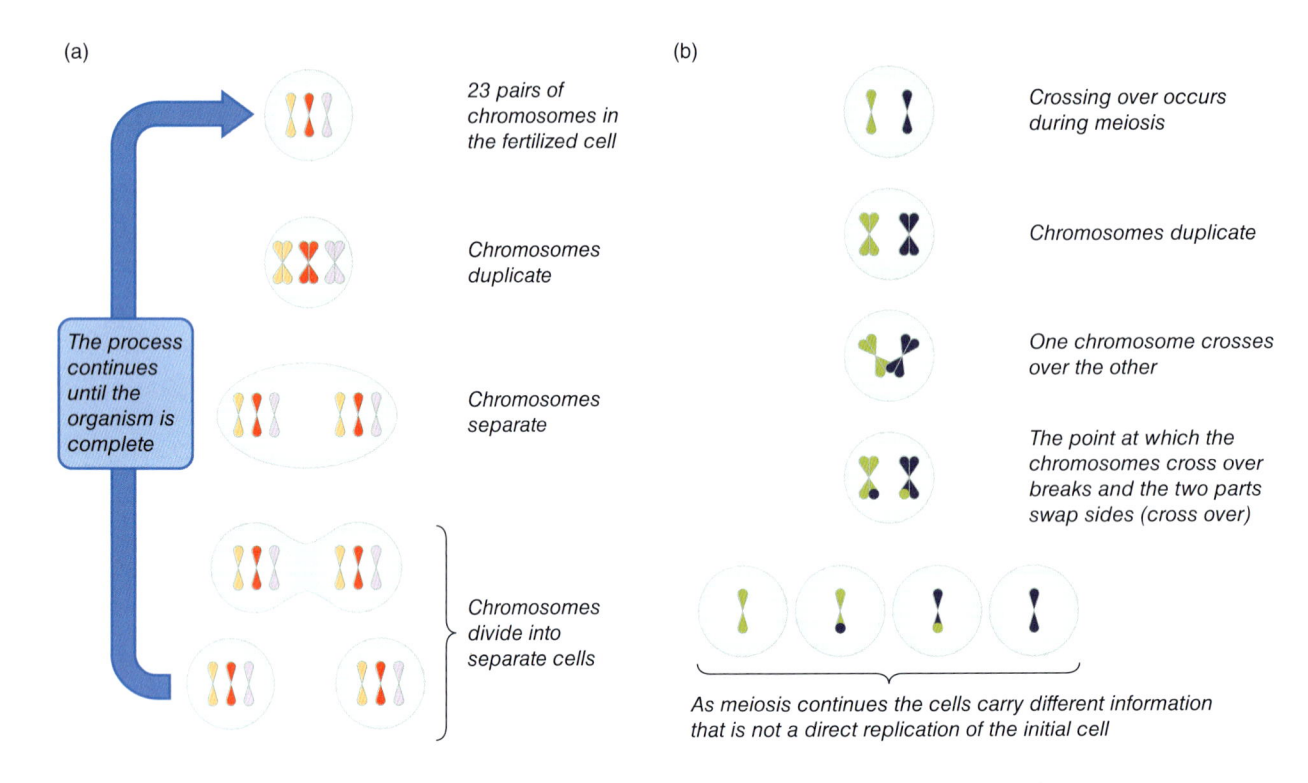

FIGURE 2.9 Mitosis. (a) Cellular division occurs after fertilization in order to complete the organism. (b) An example of the basis of variation. During mitosis the chromosomes can cross over, break and rejoin, producing new variations in the genetic code.

Of course, at this moment we have a very simple cell and obviously we are composed of many more cells. How does this happen? The answer is further cellular division (see Chapter 3 for detail on embryonic development).

To obtain a multicellular organism, the cellular division that takes place is an ongoing process, called **mitosis**. Once created, a zygote grows through cellular division. During mitosis the cell doubles its chromosomes before subsequent division (see Figure 2.9). This doubling permits the new cells to have a full complement of chromosomes. Mitotic division occurs until the organism is complete. During mitosis the 23 pairs of chromosomes in the fertilized cell are duplicated, the chromosomes then separate and divide into separate cells. Our ever-changing bodies make use of this process to repair damaged or dying cells. The production of two identical daughter cells is key to multicellular organisms. Interestingly, neurons stop dividing when the development of the nervous system is complete but skin cells divide throughout our lives (just think of dandruff).

The process of meiosis and mitosis would give us the idea that genetic information is transferred from cell to cell in an identical fashion. However, there is greater variance in genetic transmission than this process suggests. One source of genetic variation is in the process of **crossing over**. Crossing over occurs during meiosis in which the chromosomes duplicate but in doing so the chromatids cross over each other; at the point at which they cross over, they sometimes break and the two parts swap sites, that is, they cross over. As you can see in Figure 2.9(b), we now have different genetic information on the chromatids.

Linkage is a tendency for certain characteristics or alleles to be inherited together as they are located close by on the chromosome. Genes that are located closely on the same chromosome are more likely to be inherited. However, linkage does not obey strict Mendelian rules, as there is variation in the transmission of genetic information. To account for partial linkage from chance (50%) to full linkage (100%), Morgan (1911) suggested crossing over. With the occurrence of crossing over it is unlikely that intact chromosomes will be passed on to the next generation. This process ensures the genetic diversity of a species.

DNA

You will be familiar with the term **DNA (deoxyribonucleic acid)** and its label as the 'building block of life' or its role in forensic investigations, but what is it and what does it do?

DNA has two functions. Firstly, it replicates itself to make new cells and, secondly, it eventually makes proteins and determines the function of the cell. Proteins are extremely important and constitute 50% of the dry weight of a cell (see Campbell et al., 1999). There are many thousands of proteins that are used in a variety of ways. It is beyond the scope of this chapter to provide an exhaustive account of proteins, but it is worth highlighting one example. In Chapter 4 we shall see how cells communicate with each other in the nervous system. This is achieved by a transmitter molecule (a sequence of amino acids that make up polypeptides and proteins) interacting with a receptor protein.

What is DNA?

Each chromosome is made up of two strands of DNA. If we unravel a chromosome we can see strands of DNA stretched out (Figure 2.10). The DNA molecule is along the length of each chromosome. In chromosome 1 DNA is physically about 8 cm long but when packed into the chromosome it is only 8 μm in length. This is done by DNA winding itself into a series of coils that can be seen in Figure 2.10. The nucleic acid is a large molecule made up of smaller components, the most important of which are the nucleotides. DNA is made up of carbon, sugar (ribose), nitrogenous base (of which there are four) and a phosphate group. The nitrogenous bases that make up the characteristic of the nucleotide are adenine, cytosine, guanine and **thymine**. Due to their molecular structure, adenine and guanine always combine. Similarly, cytosine and thymine combine with each other. The **nucleotide bases** are attached to a sugar phosphate support, or backbone.

The two strands of DNA are held together by a mutual attraction of the nucleotides using a carbon bond

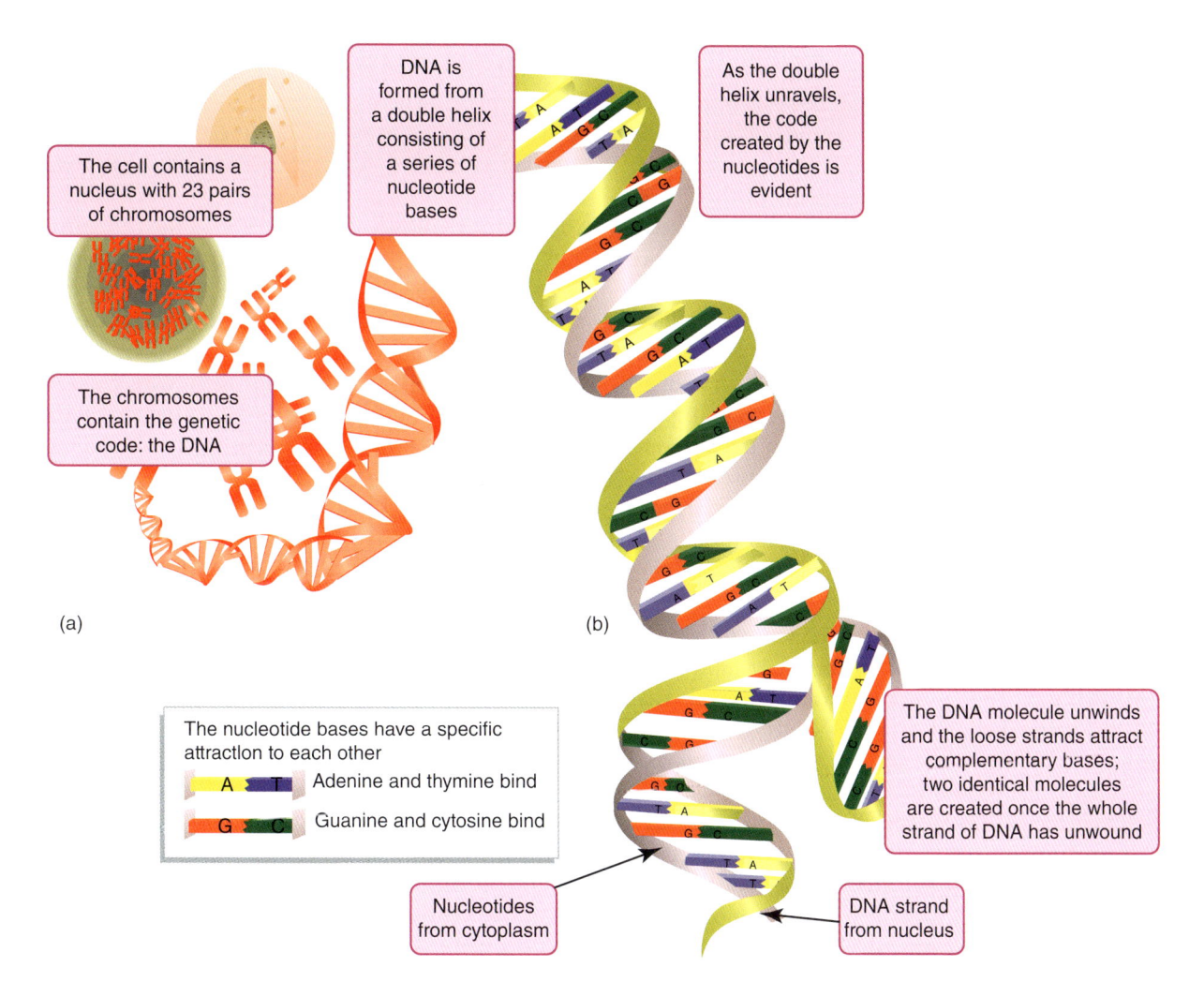

FIGURE 2.10 DNA. (a) The chromosomes can be pulled apart to reveal the double helix. Strands of DNA are connected by the different nucleotide bases. (b) Replication: the strands of DNA unwind and the loose ends are joined by nucleotides from within the cytoplasm, thus making a copy.

as the glue. This double-stranded structure is the famous **double helix** (Watson & Crick, 1953). The attraction of nucleotides can be seen in Figure 2.10. This pattern of bonding means that each strand of DNA is the complement of the other – the base pairs. The resultant long chain of nucleotides consists of one end labelled **three prime** (3′) and the other end labelled **five prime** (5′). When we look at the double-stranded DNA, we can see that the 3′ end connects to the 5′ end and vice versa. In a single strand of DNA or chromosome there are 40 million bases. That is a lot of information.

What is the Function of DNA?

Now that we have a basic knowledge of DNA, we need to find out what it does in more detail. The two functions of DNA are **replication** and protein synthesis.

Replication

Looking more closely at mitotic cell division, here DNA replicates itself before another cell can be created. During DNA replication, the two strands of nucleotide bases unravel. The exposure of the unravelled nucleotide bases attracts their complement from unattached bases in the nucleus. The unravelled strand now has a full complement of attached nucleotide bases and is therefore identical to the original.

This process sounds simple but errors in the replication can occur. Such errors are called mutations. Most mutations disappear through evolution and survival of the fittest. Some mutations remain, such as those responsible for HD and PKU. Mutations result in the different alleles that are responsible for HD being expressed (see Box 2.4). Mutations are rarely beneficial but if they are, then they are passed on to successive generations.

Protein synthesis

The nucleotide bases are the basic elements of a code. This is where the notion of DNA being the *building blocks of life* stems from. The nucleotide bases are a code that permits the construction of amino acids. A series of amino acids can then make up enzymes, proteins and polypeptides (small proteins).

The code for an amino acid is based on sequences of three nucleotides (see Figure 2.11). These triplets of nucleotides are referred to as a **codon**. The code is a little bit like grammar in which there is a start codon at the beginning (not unlike the capital letter at the beginning of a sentence), and then there are the amino acid coding codons and instruction. At the end is a stop codon (again not unlike the full stop indicating the end of a sentence). The code from DNA has to be transported outside the nucleus before the amino acid sequence can be formed. The process of reading the DNA code is called **transcription**. During transcription, a strand of DNA acts as a template for the creation of **messenger ribonucleic acid (mRNA)** which carries the code from the nucleus to the **cytoplasm** of the cell. Unlike the replication of DNA during mitotic cell division, mRNA is not an exact copy. In the case of mRNA, **uracil** substitutes for thymine. The three-nucleotide bases on the strand of mRNA are specifying an amino acid. If this process goes wrong then the wrong amino acid is used, which can have serious effects as illustrated by the case of **sickle cell disease** (Figure 2.12).

Looking closely at transcription and the message coded in the DNA, we can see areas within the sequence which are called **exons** and **introns**. Exons refer to base sequences that code for proteins, whereas introns are non-coding sequences. The primary transcript RNA reads the DNA, including the introns (Figure 2.13). However, the mRNA splices the exons together, removing the introns. The mRNA is then transported out of the nucleus into the cytoplasm where translation is going to occur.

The next step in protein synthesis is to translate the message contained in the strand of mRNA. **Ribosomes** are the translators of the sequence of nucleotide bases contained in mRNA. Ribosomes read the sequence and add amino acids as the codons instruct. The translation starts with a start codon and then the amino acids are taken to the ribosome by **transfer ribonucleic acid (tRNA)**. As the ribosome reads the codons, each specific tRNA molecule adds amino acid after amino acid. Eventually the ribosome reaches a codon that indicates that the protein is complete – the stop codon. Thus the sequence on the DNA strand is translated into a sequence of amino acids that goes on to make proteins, etc.

The construction of a protein is similar to the production of a building. In the beginning, the building starts out as a plan. An architectural plan from which everybody works is essentially the DNA. I know the architect is the creator of the building; do not think for one minute that I am referring to creationism with regard to DNA – as we have seen, this is down to the big bang and evolution. The plan has to be read and interpreted – this is what the builder does. The mRNA in this scenario is the builder. The builder sees what is needed for the building – the steels, the bricks and the glass. These other subcomponents of the building are not dissimilar to the amino acids that make up the proteins. The building materials have to be assembled in order to construct the building. This is the process of tRNA – the building materials are taken and assembled into a protein. The protein is the finished work, the building if you like.

CHAPTER 2 GENETICS AND EVOLUTION 45

1. The DNA molecule unravels for transcription

2. mRNA is transcribed from the unravelled DNA; the mRNA carries the DNA code to the cytoplasm of the cell

mRNA

DNA

3. A ribosome reads the code and each codon translates into an amino acids; transfer RNA (tRNA) collects the amino acids and forms a protien

Ribosome

Completed protein

4. At the end of the mRNA strand there is a codon that signals that the protein is complete

tRNA

Translation: From DNA to protein

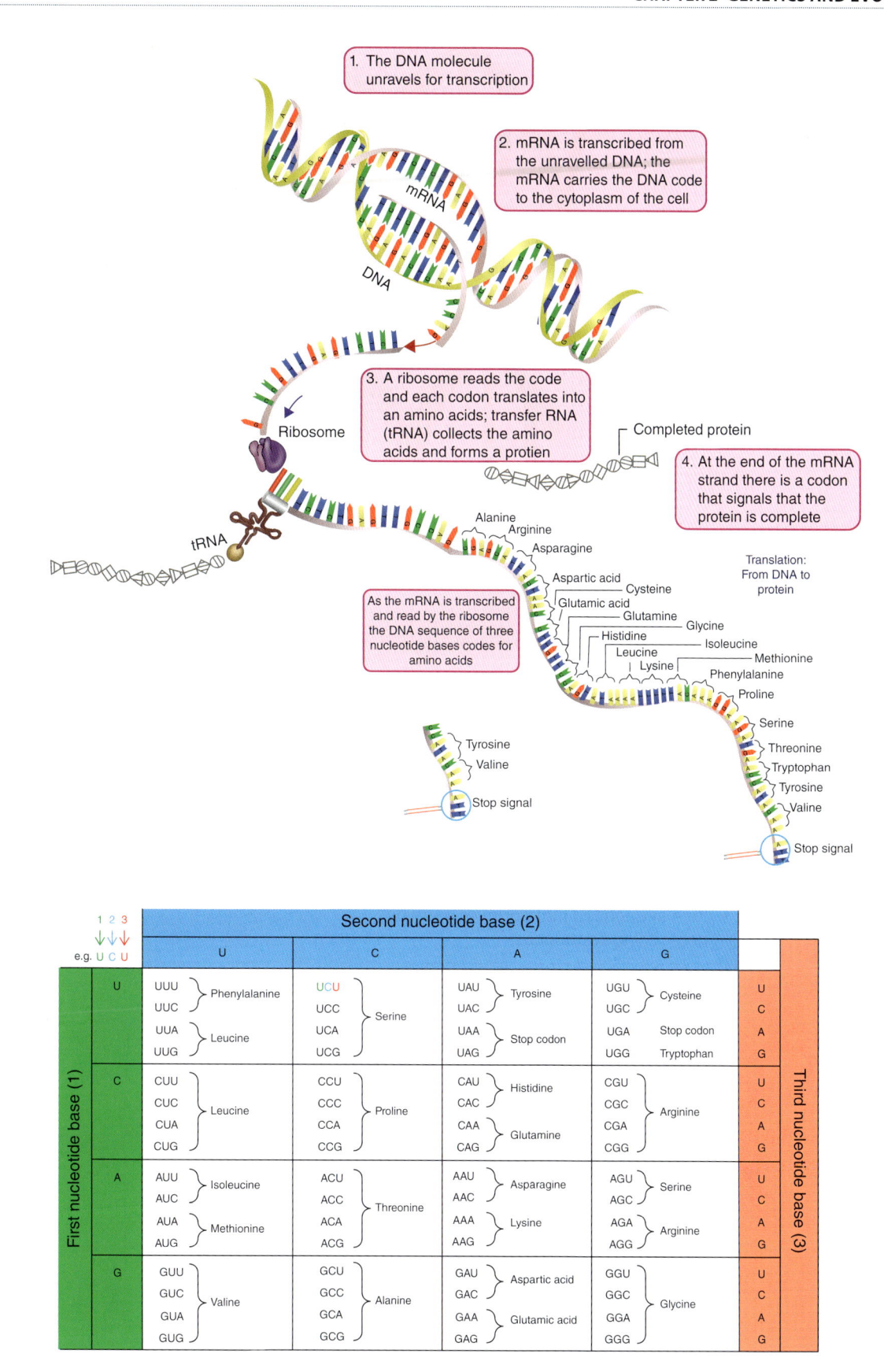

As the mRNA is transcribed and read by the ribosome the DNA sequence of three nucleotide bases codes for amino acids

Alanine
Arginine
Asparagine
Aspartic acid
Cysteine
Glutamic acid
Glutamine
Glycine
Histidine
Isoleucine
Leucine
Lysine
Methionine
Phenylalanine
Proline
Serine
Threonine
Tryptophan
Tyrosine
Valine
Stop signal

Tyrosine
Valine
Stop signal

		Second nucleotide base (2)				
1 2 3 ↓↓↓ e.g. U C U		U	C	A	G	
First nucleotide base (1)	U	UUU, UUC } Phenylalanine UUA, UUG } Leucine	UCU, UCC, UCA, UCG } Serine	UAU, UAC } Tyrosine UAA, UAG } Stop codon	UGU, UGC } Cysteine UGA Stop codon UGG Tryptophan	U C A G	Third nucleotide base (3)
	C	CUU, CUC, CUA, CUG } Leucine	CCU, CCC, CCA, CCG } Proline	CAU, CAC } Histidine CAA, CAG } Glutamine	CGU, CGC, CGA, CGG } Arginine	U C A G	
	A	AUU, AUC } Isoleucine AUA AUG } Methionine	ACU, ACC, ACA, ACG } Threonine	AAU, AAC } Asparagine AAA, AAG } Lysine	AGU, AGC } Serine AGA, AGG } Arginine	U C A G	
	G	GUU, GUC, GUA, GUG } Valine	GCU, GCC, GCA, GCG } Alanine	GAU, GAC } Aspartic acid GAA, GAG } Glutamic acid	GGU, GGC, GGA, GGG } Glycine	U C A G	

FIGURE 2.11 *Translation mRNA. Messenger RNA reads the genetic code. Each three nucleotides are a codon. Each codon provides the code for an amino acid.*

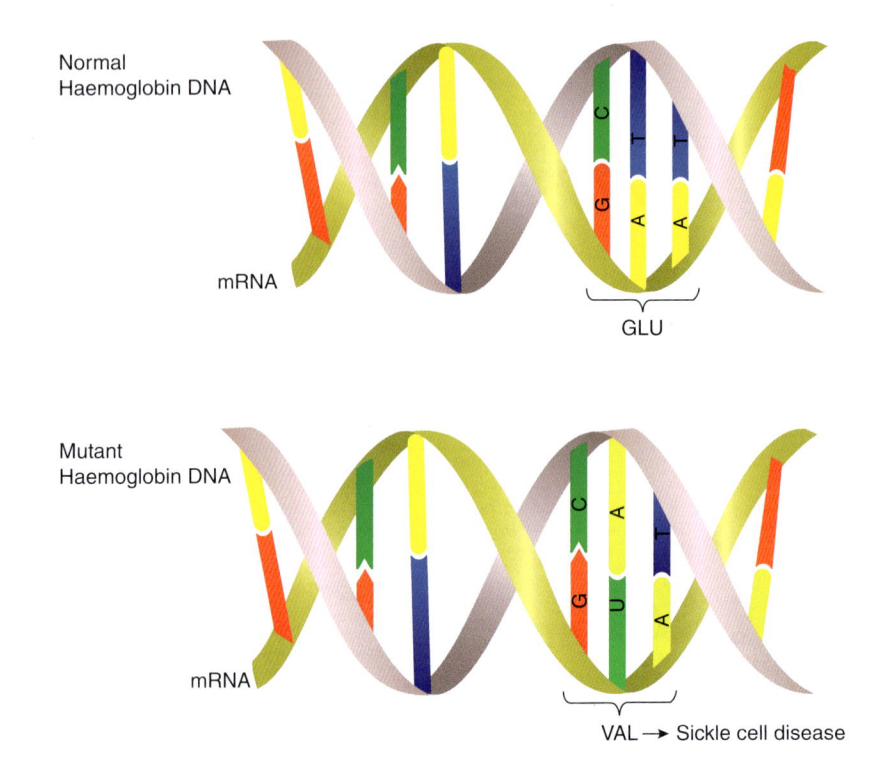

FIGURE 2.12 *Sickle cell disease. Sickle cell disease is the result of a polymorphism in haemoglobin DNA which gets read wrongly by messenger RNA, thus coding for a different amino acid.*

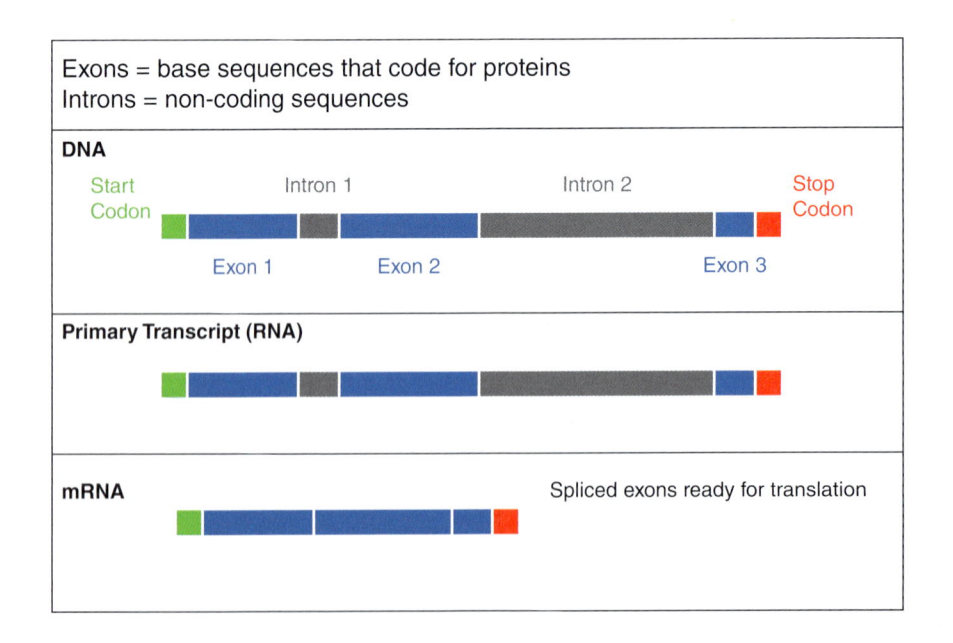

FIGURE 2.13 *Introns and exons. The DNA contains non-coding regions called introns. Messenger RNA does not contain the introns but keeps the coding exon regions.*

Genetic Variation

With the complexity of genetics, it is not surprising that sometimes it goes wrong. What perhaps is more surprising is how often it goes right. One of the preoccupations of geneticists, psychiatrists, psychologists and other scientists is to understand how disorders arise. If we take a purely reductionist viewpoint, this is the true aetiology of a disorder. However, as is so often the case, the aetiology of the disorder is the unknown Holy Grail. We know lots about the underlying pathology of many disorders, but we do not know what causes them.

When things go right you have the genes that are beneficial. Sources of variation in the species that allow for evolution to occur include recombination, in which new combinations of genes in the offspring use a characteristic that was not found in either parent. A particular type of variation, which is often referred to in the context of the genetics of disease and disorder, is the **polymorphism**. Polymorphisms are the differences in DNA sequences among individuals that are present at a frequency greater than 1% of the population. They have a weak effect, or sometimes no effect at all. A polymorphism involves variants of a particular DNA sequence, the most common of which involves variations at a single base pair of nucleotides. Polymorphisms that are larger and have long stretches of DNA are called **single nucleotide polymorphisms** (SNPs). Each SNP represents a difference in a single nucleotide, e.g. cytosine (C) replaces thymine (T) in a particular sequence of DNA. Many SNPs exist in the non-coding sequences of a gene (the introns) and can act as markers for abnormal phenotypes (including disorders). The use of SNPs has facilitated the search of the human genome looking for correlations with atypical phenotypes, such as schizophrenia, personality traits, etc.

Unlike a polymorphism, a **mutation** is a change in a single gene that is rare, random and often independent of the needs of the organism. To compare the mutation with a polymorphism, the mutation directly leads to disorder and often follows a Mendelian pattern of inheritance, e.g. PKU and HD. In contrast, the polymorphism is a gene that confers an increased risk of the disorder but does not directly cause the disorder itself. It provides a vulnerability factor. With a polymorphism, there is no clear pattern of inheritance. It is hard to find, like the proverbial needle in a haystack.

When things go wrong, they can have serious consequences. For example, we have SNPs where one nucleotide is replaced with another, thereby giving rise to an incorrect amino acid. Sickle cell disease is a blood disorder characterized by abnormal **haemoglobin** (the red protein that carries oxygen in blood) that changes red blood cells. These red blood cells are said to be sickle in shape and break down prematurely. The symptoms are anaemia, repetitive infections and pain. It affects certain members of the population, most notably those of African descent. The sickle cell disease is due to an SNP in the HBB gene and decreases the efficiency of haemoglobin to transport oxygen. There are multiple sequence variations that can change the HBB gene and lead to sickle cell disease. The most common SNP is the substitution of adenosine for thymine. In the sequence in Figure 2.12, normal HBB is seen as a codon of CTT, the sickle cell version is CAT. When transcribed, the normal transcription is GAA in the mRNA, which codes for the amino acid glutamic acid. However, the SNP in sickle cell disease results in transcription of CAT into GUA which codes for the amino acid valine (see Figure 2.12).

Variable Number Tandem Repeats

Large parts of non-coding DNA are organized in repeated sequences which vary from individual to individual and can be used for genetic fingerprinting. A **tandem repeat** (or satellite DNA) is the repeated duplication of a core DNA sequence consisting of short, repeated base pair sequences combined together, e.g. GATAGATAGATAGATAGATA is a tandem repeat consisting of five repeats of tandem 'GA' and 'TA'. These can be thousands in number. In addition to satellite DNA, there are microsatellites (about 10–100 base pairs) or **minisatellites** (mostly 2–4 base pairs), which are tandem repeats that are often present in high levels with inter- and intraspecific polymorphisms.

There are also deletions or **insertions**, that is, the loss or addition of one or more nucleotides, and, more dramatically, changes in the chromosome number.

Problems with the large structure of the chromosomes exist. Faithful replication is not always evident. There can be deletions which occur during cell division, especially meiosis. This is where a piece of a chromosome breaks off, resulting in the chromosome not having the full complement of DNA. An example of this is the neurodevelopmental disorder **Williams–Beuren syndrome** that is the result of a deletion on chromosome 7 (7q11.23) (see Merla et al., 2010; Schubert, 2009).

There are also **inversions** where segments of the chromosome are turned round by 180° – it is the same gene but in the opposite direction. Unlike deletions, inversions do not change the overall amount of the genetic material (just the order), thus inversions generally show no phenotypic abnormalities.

Translocations refer to the movement of a chromosome segment from one chromosome to a non-homologous chromosome. There are two types of translocation: balanced, in which equal parts of the two chromosomes are exchanged, and unbalanced, which involves unequal portions of chromosome and leads to extra or missing genes. Duplication is when there is a doubling or enlarging of the chromosome segment because of attaching a broken piece from a homologous chromosome or by unequal crossing over. These are associated with some leukaemias.

However, the most notable problem with chromosomes is that of their number. Monosomy is when there is only one particular type of chromosome; an example of this is Turner's syndrome (see Box 2.1). Trisomy is where there are three chromosomes, i.e. one extra. Trisomy 21 or Down's syndrome is an example of an extra chromatid being present on chromosome 21 (see Box 2.5). **Polyploidy** is having more than two sets of chromosomes; examples are triploidy, in which there are three of each type of chromosome, and tetraploidy with four of each type of chromosome. This is often fatal and results in miscarriage, as the foetus is not viable.

BOX 2.5: DOWN'S SYNDROME

Down's syndrome (Figure 2.5.1) occurs in about 1 in 830 newborns. The symptoms of Down's syndrome are

- decreased muscle tone at birth;
- excess skin at the nape of the neck;
- flattened nose;
- separated joints between the bones of the skull (sutures);
- single crease in the palm of the hand;
- small ears/small mouth;
- upward-slanting eyes;
- wide, short hands with short fingers;
- impulsive behaviour;
- poor judgement;
- short attention span; and
- slow learning.

Down's syndrome is also called **trisomy 21** as there is an extra chromosome in the 21st chromosome (Figure 1(a)). This chromosomal abnormality occurs at random during the formation of gametes in the parent, more often than not in egg cells, but it sometimes happens in sperm cells. Down's syndrome is caused by non-disjunction of the 21st chromosome during meiosis (Figure 2.5.1(b)). Occasionally trisomy 21 occurs when part of chromosome 21 becomes translocated to another chromosome during making of the gametes. Affected people have two regular copies of chromosome 21 plus extra genetic material from chromosome 21 attached to another chromosome; thus there are three copies of genetic material from chromosome 21. A very small minority of affected people have an extra copy of chromosome 21 in only *some* of the body's cells; this is mosaic Down's syndrome.

There is no cure for trisomy 21, although in the laboratory there is some success in manipulating the extra

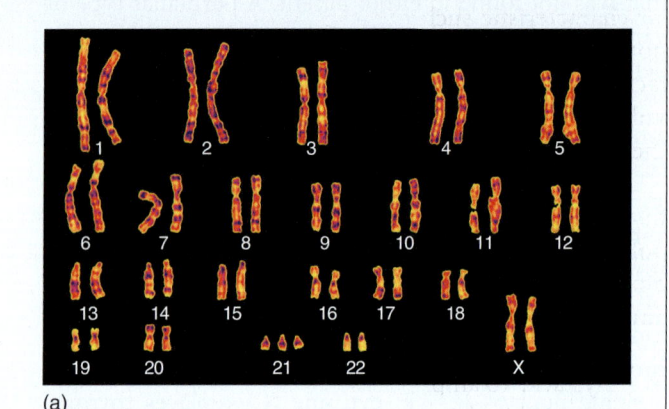

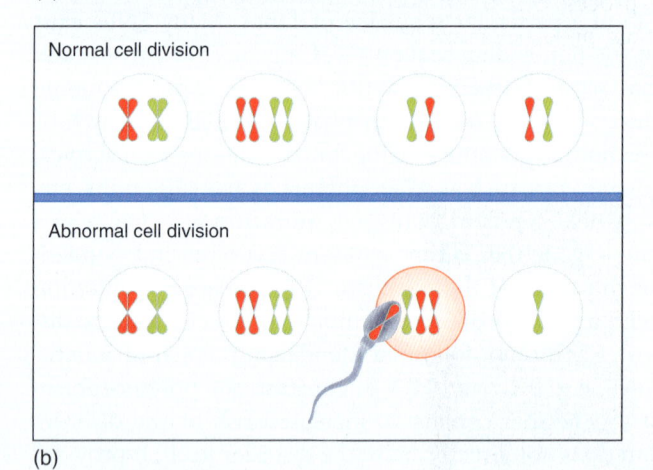

FIGURE 2.5.1 *The karyotype for trisomy 21 and the addition of an extra chromosome. (a) The karyotype with the addition of an extra 21st chromosome. (b) The normal process of cellular division and below the line trisomy 21.*
Source: (a) LOOK AT SCIENCES/Science Photo Library

chromosome. In one laboratory, stem cells were successfully deleted off the extra chromosome through a process of spontaneous loss and enhanced survival of disomic cells (Li et al., 2012). However, this process of spontaneous loss lacks scientific control. A more recent attempt to address trisomy takes a different perspective in which one mimics the natural process that silences one of the two X chromosomes in females. The X chromosomes contain a X-inactivation gene (XIST) and when activated, RNA covers the surface of a chromosome, thereby stopping other genes being expressed. This feature of the XIST gene was exploited by Jiang et al. (2013) who put a XIST gene into one of the three copies of chromosome 21. Furthermore, they were able to provide a 'switch' that could turn on the XIST gene. The results revealed a reduced expression of individual genes on chromosome 21.

Genetic variation is used for mapping genes. SNPs are frequently used as genetic markers to identify genes that may be responsible for disease susceptibility or a particular characteristic such as personality. Remember this is not an absolute; the genes are conferring a vulnerability factor. Just because we have a gene that makes us more vulnerable to a disorder or disease does not mean that the gene has to play out that way.

There are a lot of SNPs. Trying to find them is like finding a needle in a haystack. In order to actually find polymorphisms, we are dependent upon the use of biotechnology. Biotechnologists have created ways of amplifying the DNA signal so that it can actually be seen. It is somewhat like trying to find a large box of needles in a haystack. To amplify this DNA, we take advantage of a process called the **polymerase chain reaction (PCR)**. This process copies a known sequence of DNA and allows multiple copies to be made and thus there is more to be seen.

Once the PCR has established a sufficient amount of DNA to be visualized, the next stage is to put it through a process called **electrophoresis**. In electrophoresis the geneticist uses an **agarose gel block** that has microscopic pores in it. DNA is negatively charged and therefore attracted to the positive charge put through the agarose gel block. The attraction means that the DNA travels through this block towards the positive charge and the amplification of the DNA makes it visible. Large amounts of DNA travel slowly and leave markers or bands early on in the agarose block. In Figure 2.14 we can see the example of polymorphisms in Huntington's disease where there are a number of CAG repeats: cytosine (C), adenine (A) and guanine (G). Those affected with the HD gene have large DNA segments that do not travel far through the block.

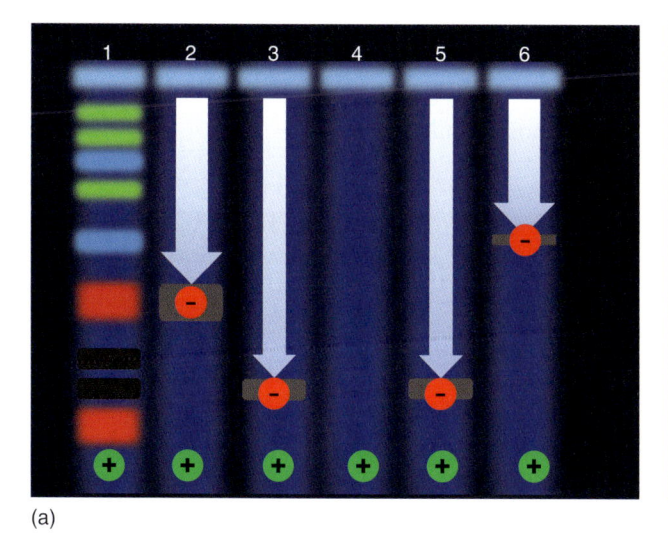

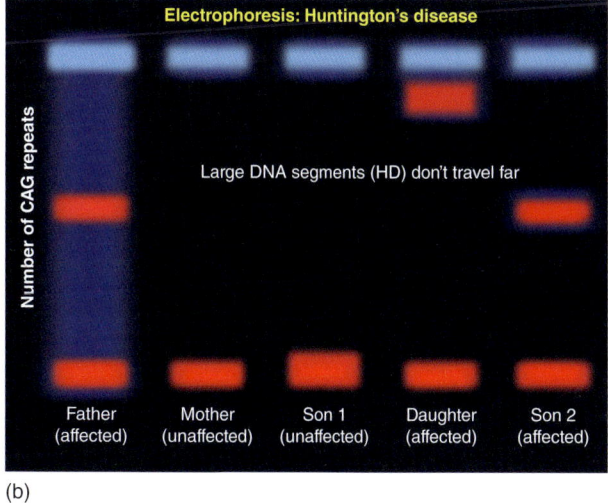

FIGURE 2.14 *The polymerase chain reaction and electrophoresis. (a) Amplified genetic material travels through a gel block at different rates. (b) The affected father has a large number of CAG repeats as does son number 2.*

EPIGENETICS

Epigenetics refers to functional modifications of the genome that do not involve a change in the DNA sequence. Phenotypical changes have been observed to occur in response to environmental exposures, e.g. to food, drugs, radiation, etc. Epigenetics involves genetic control by factors other than an individual's DNA sequence. Epigenetic changes can switch genes on or off and determine which proteins are transcribed. Whilst **monozygotic (MZ) twins** are genetically identical, their phenotype may have differences which can be explained by epigenetics (Wong et al., 2005). In one study of young MZ twins and older MZ twins, it was found that they were indistinguishable during their early years, but the older twins had remarkable differences in the overall content and distribution within the genome (Fraga et al., 2005; Poulsen et al., 2007). Thus, phenotypic discordance between MZ twins is, at least to some extent, due to epigenetic factors that change over the lifetime and can be responsible for behavioural traits and disease (Javierre et al., 2010).

BEHAVIOURAL GENETICS: THE COMPLEX INTERPLAY OF PSYCHOLOGY AND GENETICS

Genetics is clearly a biological science. Psychology is a behavioural science. Married together, genetics and psychology produce behavioural genetics with the aim of understanding the genetic contributions to behaviour.

The understanding that there is a genetic component to behaviour has been central to psychological discourse and in particular the **nature–nurture debate**. The nature–nurture debate has been a long-established argument about the relative contribution of our biology (nature) and the environment (nurture) to behaviour.

Behaviourists such as John Watson surprisingly found no place for genetics, and is often quoted as saying:

> Give me a dozen healthy infants, well-formed, and my own specific world to bring them up in and I'll guarantee to take any one at random and train him to become any type of specialist I might select – a doctor, lawyer, artist, merchant-chief and, yes, even beggar-man and thief, regardless of his talents, penchants, tendencies, abilities, vocations and race of his ancestors. (Watson, 1930)

Clearly, as students of psychobiology, we should take exception to this and suggest that there is indeed a biological and inherited component to our behaviours.

Often the dialogue between students of psychology regarding nature and nurture adopts polarized points of view – it is either one or the other. Are we intelligent because we have inherited the genes for intelligence or have we learned to be intelligent? Another example of the nature–nurture debate is presented in Box 2.6. A more accurate explanation is that nature and nurture interact.

One way in which psychologists have sought to understand the genetic and environmental input to behaviour is to look at the hereditary nature of a behaviour. This can be done by looking at families, twins and adoptees. Numerous **twin studies** have investigated various behaviours and they remain important lines of investigation.

Francis Galton (1822–1911) was half cousin to Charles Darwin and the godfather of behavioural genetics. He suggested the major methods of human behavioural genetics and was the first to conduct systematic studies of families to see if behavioural characteristics would run in those families.

BOX 2.6: THE NATURE–NURTURE DEBATE: A SERIES OF CASE STUDIES

The nature–nurture debate has been discussed in many areas of psychology, most notably in intelligence and personality. One can get a little bogged down by the very nature of intelligence and personality and lose sight of the genetic and environmental contributions to these psychological constructs.

In order to emphasize how nature and nurture can give rise to certain behaviours, I choose to look at the trivial world of superheroes. We have been brought up with cartoons and films of individuals with powers beyond the norm. What is interesting about these superheroes is the cause of their superpowers; causality can be ascribed to nature or nurture and possibly a complex interaction between the two. The use of superheroes also enables us to illustrate to some extent the science of genetics and behavioural genetics. If we take family inheritance first and look at the family transmission of superhero powers, we can take *The Incredibles* as an example. We have co-segregation within families; there is clearly a familial superhero gene that has been passed from mother and father down to their offspring. However, these superheroes have different powers, some fast, some clever, some agile, etc. What we may see here is that the gene is passed on but it is not for a particular power but rather confers a general superpower factor; in fact, this is most probably polygenetic. How those powers manifest may be subject to the pressures of the environmental conditions that the superheroes find themselves in. Clearly, as a group of people, each of their individual qualities is valuable to the group.

When it comes to *Superman*, we may have a fairly straightforward case of Mendelian genetics. Hailing from the planet Krypton, Superman was the product of two Kryptonites, the mother and father. The powers of the mother and father were bestowed upon Superman a.k.a. Clark Kent. What would be interesting here is to use modern molecular biology to thoroughly investigate the genetic structure of Superman. What would we find? Would there be DNA that is similar to our own human DNA or is Superman's DNA of an alien variety? We could use modern technology to create, rather than a human genome, a Superman genome. Clearly, Superman exists firmly on the nature side of the nature–nurture debate.

Peter Parker was a normal student (if there is such a thing) until he visited a laboratory and was bitten by a mutant spider. From this point on Peter Parker was *Spiderman*. This is not a case of nature and Mendelian genetics, but rather genetic engineering. Genes from the spider were taken into the nucleus of Peter Parker's DNA and merged with his own. This is the human arachnid equivalent of the **transgenic mouse**. One might think that this is a case of nature, but when we look at the direction of his powers we can certainly see a case of experience in environment taking a hold on his behaviour. In the early days he used his powers for good but after the trauma of seeing his uncle die, he turned to the dark side and used his powers for objectives other than honourable. Clearly, this is a case of having a particular genetic make-up but the expression of that genetic make-up is mediated by experience and environment.

We are not a slave to our genes; there is a lot we can do to offset their impact. For example, if there was a gene for heart disease would that necessarily mean that we would have to die of a heart attack? The answer is clearly 'no' as there is plenty we can do to minimize the impact of such a gene; for example, we could moderate alcohol intake, stop smoking, eat healthy food and take exercise. Such health behaviours could change the outcome of the genes. Of course, if we were to adopt a sedentary lifestyle, smoke heavily and drink heavily and enjoy the delights of a full English breakfast then we are going to increase the chance that that gene that conveys vulnerability to heart disease will fulfil its potential.

In a similar scenario, David Banner was exposed to high levels of radiation. Such high levels of radiation interfere with the genetic material. Again this is a case of genetic engineering. However, when David Banner was subject to stress and annoyance he would undergo morphological changes and psychological changes that would turn him into the *Incredible Hulk*. This clearly demonstrates how the expression of a gene can be manipulated by the environmental context. David Banner is clearly a man in need of anger management and Cognitive Behavioural Therapy (CBT).

Batman is a completely different case. Bruce Wayne was the victim of childhood trauma upon witnessing the death of his parents. Bruce Wayne is not a genetic manipulation. He is a product of the environmental context; these superpowers have been brought about by technology. Indeed, there may well be a genetic heritage here, as clearly advanced intelligence is required to create the devices he uses as Batman for the greater good. In this case, there really is no room for nature, this is all nurture.

It may not have escaped your attention that all the superheroes discussed so far are male. Could it be that superhero powers are transmitted via the Y chromosome? The answer to this can only be found using genetic analysis. But there is one notable exception from the 1970s. Wonder Woman had several powers that were derived from her Amazonian training, but to quote: 'the only thing that can surpass super-strength is the power of the brain'. Clearly Wonder Woman was a far more cerebral superhero who used the full faculty of her brain. The remainder of this book primarily focuses on how the brain processes incoming information and guides behaviour.

The idea that there is a genetic basis to behaviour comes from **familial studies** of behavioural genetics, the hereditary nature of behavioural characteristics – behaviours that run in families. **Heritability** is a statistical estimate of the contribution of genetic differences to phenotypic differences in traits, e.g. intelligence or personality, and is a proportion of the entire variation that can be explained by genetics and ranges between 0 and 1. A heritability of 1 would mean that all of the variation is entirely attributable to genetics; a heritability of 0 would mean that all the variability is caused by environmental factors. Commonly, there is a heritability estimate of 0.5 which means that about half of the variation seen in a population can be explained by genes and the other half can be explained by different environments. It is not suggesting that in any one individual, behaviour or a disorder, schizophrenia for example, is 75% (0.75) genetic and 25% (0.25) environmental. To place the data in context, height is highly heritable (0.88) as demonstrated in one study (Brown et al., 2003). What this states is that the variance of height in a population is attributable to genes. It is a population statistic and *not* a commentary on an individual.

Familial studies are not actually concerned with a specific gene, they are more concerned with patterns of inheritance, e.g. does a particular characteristic run in a family? The argument is that if it runs in the family then there is a higher chance that it is due to a genetic basis. For example, if you are born to alcoholic parents there is a high chance that you too will be alcoholic. Alcoholism could be due to genetics – a rogue gene that makes people alcoholic. However, familial studies clearly do not give us such conclusive data; they just give us an *idea* of whether something is inherited. If the child of an alcoholic turns out to be an alcoholic, the question remains, was it genetic or was it environmental? There may well be a gene for alcoholism, as has been suggested by many, but the child will be brought up in an environment that is run by alcoholics. This alcoholic environment may also confer a risk factor for subsequent alcoholism. Lest we forget, religion runs in families and we do not suggest that religions, such as Christianity or Islam, are genetic.

In an attempt to address the shortcomings of familial studies and tease apart the genetic and environmental factors involved in the behaviour, behavioural geneticists have looked at a special group of people – twins. In Figure 2.15 we can see the percentage of genetic material that is shared between relatives within a family. Twin studies seek to exploit the close degree of genetic similarity between offspring, siblings and parents.

The rationale behind twin studies is to do with the degree of genetic similarity in twins. There are two types

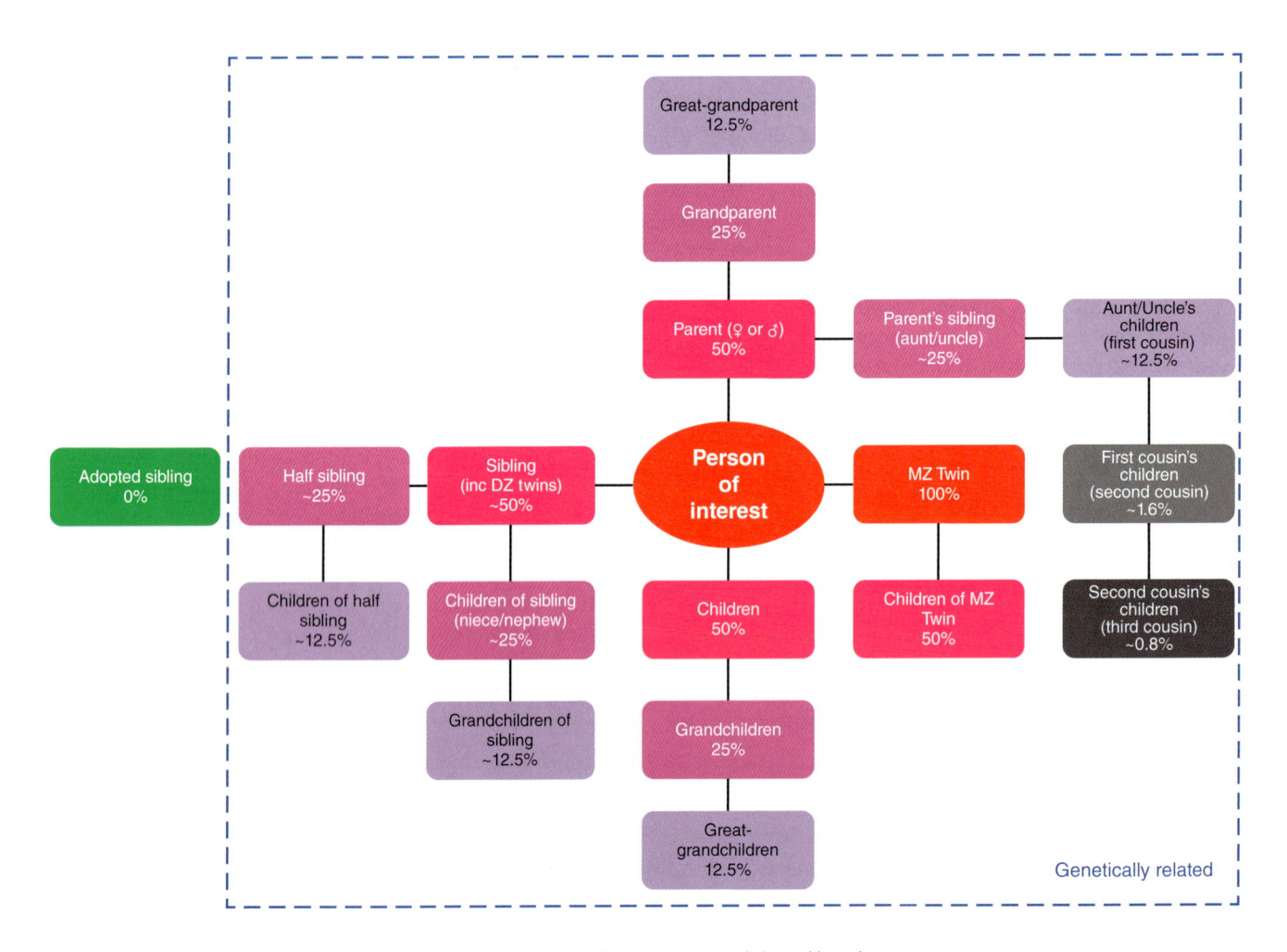

FIGURE 2.15 *Degrees of relatedness. The average percentage of genetic material shared by relatives.*

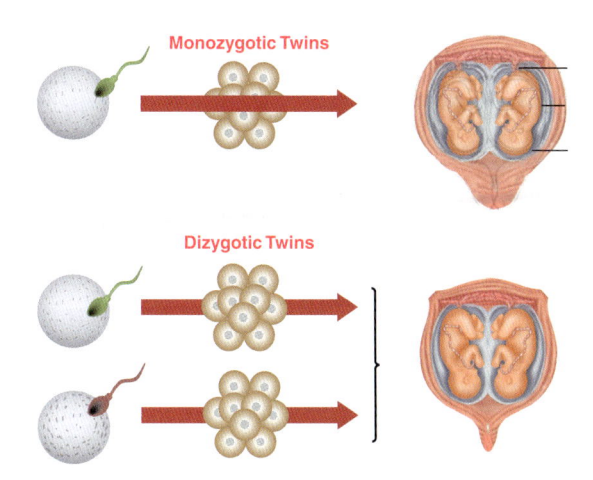

FIGURE 2.16 *Monozygotic or dizygotic twins. Monozygotic twins are derived from one sperm and one egg whereas dizygotic twins are derived from two eggs and two sperms.*

of twins: monozygotic twins (MZ) (from one zygote) and **dizygotic twins** (DZ) (from two zygotes). MZ twins are genetically identical because they are formed by a single sperm fertilizing a single egg that subsequently splits to form two separate embryos; they share 100% of their genes. DZ or fraternal twins share 50% of their genes as they are a result of two separate eggs being fertilized. DZ twins are like other siblings born separately (see Figure 2.16).

As MZ twins are genetically identical, logic dictates they should both be more closely associated with a characteristic (such as IQ or ADHD) compared to DZ twins. The evidence suggests that this is the case for many dimensions of behaviour (Ebstein et al., 2010). However, if the characteristic/behaviour is environmentally mediated, there should be no difference between MZ and DZ. Such studies present a heritability estimate, where 1 is entirely genetic and 0 entirely non-genetic. One would expect MZ twins to have a higher heritability estimate than DZ twins.

It is critical to acknowledge that despite a high heritability estimate, there are environmental factors also involved, e.g. with height the availability of a good diet will influence final height attained. The environmental influences can be categorized into shared and non-shared. The shared environmental influences are the features within an environment or a family that all members share, for example the house they live in, the school they go to and the food they eat. The shared environment comprises all those features of family life that the members of the family experience, whether they are MZ or DZ twins or regular siblings. The non-shared environment refers to the environmental influences that are unique to the individuals within family, e.g. different friends, accidents that one has and possibly schoolteachers. The non-shared environment relates equally to MZ, DZ and regular siblings. The shared and non-shared environmental factors can influence hereditary estimates. A high **concordance rate** is expected in a simple single-gene disorder, e.g. HD. Unrelated individuals have 0% of shared genetic material, DZ twins have on average 50% shared genetic material, whereas MZ twins have 100% of the same genes. The effects of the non-shared environment result in lower concordance rates for both types of twins; unrelated individuals still maintain 0% concordance rate. The shared environment reduces the concordance rate between the siblings. However, the shared experience raises concordance rates between siblings as well as for unrelated individuals, because they are raised together in the shared environment.

The question still remains over how much of the variation in the population is due to genetics or environment. Now we have the addition of shared and non-shared environments. Plomin and Daniels (1987), who coined the phrase 'non-shared environment', found there was a substantial amount of variability in behavioural characteristics that could not be explained by genes or shared environmental influences. According to Plomin and Rende (1991):

> [W]hat runs in families is DNA, not experiences shared in the home. However, *environmental factors are very important even though experiences shared by siblings are not*. The significant environmental variation lies in experiences *not* shared by siblings. (p.180)

Turkheimer (2000), who states 'the nature–nurture debate is over' (p.160), continues to suggest that there are three laws of behavioural genetics.

1. All human behavioural traits are heritable.
2. The effect of being raised in the same family is smaller than the effect of genes.
3. A substantial portion of the variation in complex human behavioural traits is not accounted for by the effects of genes or families.

This alone does not help untangle the nature–nurture issues. The question still remains on the nature of interactions between genetics and environment, whether that environment is shared or non-shared. Understanding how genes influence behaviour and how environments influence behaviour is crucial to answering the many questions. Once we have the answers to those questions, we can start to address the complex interactions of genes and environments.

Behavioural sciences have placed great faith in the twin study method as a means of unravelling the complex interplay between genes and environments. However, the twin study method is not without criticism. Joseph (2000) provides an important and thought-provoking critique of the use of behavioural genetics. None of the twin studies, according to Joseph, have looked at twins reared apart. The assumption of twin studies is that the environment remains equal (the **Equal Environment Assumption** **[EEA]** according to Joseph) for both twins. That is, each twin (or sibling for that matter) shares the same environment. Thus, the greater association seen in MZ compared to DZ twins must be attributed to genes. Such an assumption has been questioned (Pam et al., 1996). The evidence for MZ and DZ twins differing in genes only is not supported. Joseph (2009) has reviewed the literature and states that MZ twins are more likely to spend time together, have close emotional bonds, have the same friends and be treated the same by others, and perhaps as a consequence of these features they are more likely to have identity confusion. Thus, the environment of MZ twins is different for the very reason they are MZ twins – to put it in legal terms, twin studies might be regarded as circumstantial evidence in behavioural genetics.

With the criticisms noted, twin studies still remain useful but they are limited by their theoretical assumptions.

What about assessing those people who have been reared apart? Would this help untangle the genetic–experiential contributions to behaviour? Under such studies the genes are the same but the environment is different. Again, if there is a higher rate across MZ twins, the case for genes is greater. This is the premise of **adoption studies**; ideally we could look at MZ twins in this way. Adoption studies therefore work on the basis that adopted children share the genes but not the environment with their biological parents so similarities between the child and the biological parent are attributed to genes. Conversely, adopted children share the environment and not their genetics with the adoptive parents. If the child shows similarities with their biological parents, then the assumption is that it is down to genes. If the child shows similarities with their adoptive parents this is due to environmental factors, e.g. child-rearing practices.

Joseph is also critical of adoption studies. Such studies have failed to look at the biological parents of the adoptive child, thus limiting the conclusions that can be drawn (Joseph, 2000, 2009). Indeed, many studies have indicated that environmental adversity is also a big factor in psychopathology (see Chapter 3). Furthermore, Joseph points out that the adoptive families are different by the very virtue of the act upon which they are engaged – adoption. Adoptive families are screened for mental health as part of the process of adoption and therefore less likely to have adverse environments. The adoptive family is carefully chosen for their health whereas the biological family is not; thus we have two very different groups to compare, again limiting the conclusions of a genetic basis (Joseph, 2000, 2009).

It is worth noting that there are other types of twins that can be studied. Nancy Segal (2010) has referred to the twin studies as 'the finest natural experiment'. She also highlights the use of virtual twins; this is not a computer-generated idea. Virtual twins are same age yet unrelated siblings who are raised together. They do not have a genetic link but share the same rearing practices. Such twins provide an estimate of environmental factors on any particular measure. The Fullerton Virtual Twin Study indicated modest shared environmental influences on intelligence (Segal et al., 2012, 2013), but the non-shared environment is still a factor.

Where virtual twins know they are different, DZ and MZ twins who are switched at birth do not. They are brought up by parents who think they are real twins (Segal & Blandon-Gitlin, 2010). Such switches happen in hospitals by accident and are fortunately very rare. Such occurrences represent case studies rather than providing population data as obtained with numerous twins. In a case study of switched twins in the Canary Islands, Segal (2013) provides an account of how the twins were reunited after two years. In this scenario there were MZ twins reared apart, with one of the MZ twins being reared with her biological parents and an unrelated female (although at the time thought to be her twin sister) and the other MZ being reared by a non-biological family (although they all thought they were biologically related). The two women who were inadvertently raised as twins never *felt* like twins, whereas the two actual MZ twins had that *special* connection. Clearly these cases, and those like it, are interesting but have yet to contribute to the untangling of the nature–nurture debate.

It is of great importance that the study of behavioural genetics is rigorous in its methodology in order to have any confidence in its ability to tease apart the factors involved in the variation of a characteristic or a disease. Lest we forget, we are dealing with extremely complicated organisms within complex environments. This is summed up in the following quote which also alludes to the societal impact of science.

> Although developmentalists may be disappointed that a substantial portion of human development remains too complex, too interactive, and too resistant to controlled investigation and straightforward statistical methods to yield to systematic scientific analysis as we currently understand it, it must be remembered that the alternative – a world in which human behavior could be understood all the way down in terms of correlations between difference scores – would present its own gloomy prospects in the ethical evaluation of human agency. The limitations of our existing social scientific methodologies ought not to provoke us to wish that human behavior were simpler than we know it to be; instead they should provoke us to search for methodologies that are adequate to the task of understanding the exquisite complexity of human development. (Turkheimer & Waldron, 2000, p.93)

DNA and Psychology

Once the only method for investigating genetics of psychological characteristics was the use of family studies and specialist cases of twins. There is much more available now.

Advances in biotechnology have permitted a more detailed analysis of genetics. The twin studies have looked at the phenotype with some speculation about the genotype. Now it is possible to look at the actual individual genes themselves. Increasingly, the modern techniques of molecular biology are telling us about the specific genetic basis of disorders such as Alzheimer's disease (Larner & du Plessis, 2003), schizophrenia (McDonald & Murphy, 2003) and drug addiction (Li et al., 1997). While understanding the underlying genetics of disorders is unquestionably important, behavioural geneticists have also looked at personality traits, e.g. aggression in children (Schmidt et al., 2002).

The study of behavioural genetics can be approached at different levels of analysis, e.g. the macro level of family studies or the genetic detail of the chromosomes. On those chromosomes we can look at **candidate genes** and from those candidate genes, we can look at the gene sequences and subsequent mutations that lead to diseases and disorders.

This is all very important work that may one day unravel the genetic basis of our behaviours. However, we have to proceed with caution. We could be forgiven for thinking that we have found a gene for many of our disorders but the truth is not so grand. The popular press and media often talk about finding 'a gene for this' and 'a gene for that', when the reality is far less precise; very few disorders or behaviours can be pinpointed to one gene. Our complex arrays of behaviours are the result of a multifaceted interplay between many genes and a wide and varied, forever changing environment.

The search for an understanding of the genetics of personality is an ongoing quest, but some headway has been made; one personality trait that has received a lot of attention is **sensation seeking**. The possibility that there is a gene for sensation seeking, and the methodological limitations of some studies, are addressed in Box 2.7.

BOX 2.7: ADRENALINE JUNKY: THE GENETICS OF SENSATION SEEKING

The search for genes and a genetic basis of personality is a well-told story. Clearly understanding the genetics of personality requires the understanding of personality first. However, to simplify the search one must focus on specific aspects of personality. The idea that there is a gene for novelty or sensation seeking (SS) has been investigated (Ebstein et al., 1996). The early search for a gene for SS focused on the gene coding for the dopamine D4 receptor (DRD4).

Dopamine is a neurotransmitter that has numerous associations with numerous behaviours, one of which is the notion that it underlies SS. After the initial finding that there is a gene for SS, a number of other studies have been conducted. This is an important gene and SS is an important concept. SS has been cited as a personality type that is involved in several psychopathologies, e.g. severity of addiction (Lusher et al., 2000) and ADHD (see Chandler, 2010, for review).

With the scientific rigour of molecular biology, one would assume a consistent methodology across laboratories. A review by Lusher et al. (2001) pointed out that there are many methodological inconsistencies.

- *Ethnic differences.* Different ethnic groups have been used. There are genetic variants across ethnic groups. Therefore an SS gene may be different in one group from another.
- *Age.* Studies that have not found an association between the DRD4 gene and SS in some cases have used older participants. SS declines with age.
- *Measures of personality.* There are a number of scales used to assess SS. The reports used different scales.
- *Sex.* Some studies used only males while others used only females.

The overall position at present is that the DRD4 gene is not associated with SS (Strobel et al., 2003). The search continues for a gene for SS and to find out what the DRD4 gene does. The DRD4 gene has been linked with severity of addiction (Lusher et al., 2000), fear (Falzone et al., 2002), nicotine craving (Hutchison et al., 2002), attention deficit hyperactivity disorder (Tovo-Rodrigues et al., 2012), gambling (Comings et al., 2001) and many more behaviours. But as usual there are also studies that demonstrate no effect or partial effects (e.g. Nederhof et al., 2011).

Beyond Mendelian Inheritance: The Endophenotype

Not all disorders have simple Mendelian transmission; in fact, many or even most are complex polygenetic disorders. This complexity in a polygenetic disorder/behaviour makes understanding how genes operate even more difficult. From the comparatively straightforward examples of Huntington's disease and PKU, with their serious and multiple symptoms, one can begin to appreciate how difficult it is to find genes in polygenetic disorders.

Look at the symptoms list of DSM5; it is not hard to imagine that these psychiatric disturbances will have a multitude of genes involved, and sometimes with a gene providing only a small contribution. However, together these genes influence behaviour, and behaviour can then alter the expression of the genes. It might be too big a gap to bridge when trying to find the genes for the vast array of symptoms in disorders such as schizophrenia. The question as to which gene is responsible for a disorder may well be too big a question. We need to simplify the question; for example, what gene or genes are responsible for just one particular symptom or behaviour?

An **endophenotype** is an intermediate account of genes and environment that 'was adapted for filling the gap between available descriptors and between the gene and the elusive disease processes' (Gottesman & Gould, 2003). Thus, between the genes that are likely to cause a disorder (e.g. ADHD) and the symptoms (e.g. impulsivity) is a theoretical account of the disorder (e.g. faulty **behavioural inhibition**) that links the physical (gene/brain) to the behavioural.

Criteria have been suggested for the identification of endophenotypes (Gottesman & Gould, 2003).

- The endophenotype is associated with illness in the population.
- The endophenotype is heritable.
- The endophenotype is primarily state independent, i.e. it will manifest itself in an individual whether or not they are symptomatic.
- Within families the endophenotype and the disorder co-occur.
- The endophenotype found in affected family members is found in non-affected family members at a higher rate than in the general population.

Molecular Biotechnology and Psychology

In order to investigate and experiment with DNA, numerous copies have to be made (you need enough DNA to work with). This is gene cloning. The PCR described earlier is one way to amplify (clone) a specific strand of DNA; during a PCR, the DNA is replicated many times by an enzyme. Once the DNA has been isolated, numerous studies can be conducted. Southern blots look for a particular sequence of DNA; this is important for evolutionary psychologists as we can see the degree of relatedness between species. Northern blots confirm which cells are using a specific gene.

As a species, the human breeding cycle is comparatively slow. Sexual maturation is in early adolescence and due to societal pressure and the laws of the land, reproduction is usually left until early adulthood. Even then, after conception, 40 weeks are required to produce offspring, often just one child as twins and multiple births are comparatively rare in humans. From this perspective, studying genetics in the human population and manipulating it experimentally is going to be very slow. To speed the process up, we can look at animals, such as rats, which reach sexual maturation very early and produce large litters. The biggest increase in the use of animals in experimentation is for genetics, especially with mice. The manipulation of genes in animals is somewhat similar to selective breeding, but in this case the actual genes are being manipulated by the scientist directly.

The use of transgenic models allows geneticists to look at the impact of sequences of DNA. **Transgenic mice** (see Carter & Murphy, 1999) can be manipulated to produce either **knock-in** or **knock-out models**. With knock-in models, a segment of DNA or a whole gene from another animal can be inserted and incorporated into a mouse zygote; the mouse then codes for this new gene. In contrast, in knock-outs a particular gene is deleted or knocked out. These transgenic animals are usually compared to their normal counterparts or wild types. By doing this, the geneticist can see what the effects of genetic regulation are on the phenotype.

THE HUMAN GENOME PROJECT

The Human Genome Project is a collaborative venture set up to determine the sequence of each human gene. Two of the primary purposes of the project are to identify all the genes in human DNA, and to determine the sequences of the chemical base pairs that make up human DNA. In 2001 a multi-authored pair of draft papers appeared in the prestigious journals *Nature* (where Crick and Watson published their paper on the double helix) (Lander et al., 2001) and *Science* (Venter et al., 2001). Finally in 2004 came the completion paper (International Human Genome Sequencing Consortium, 2004) with its 14 pages of supplementary material naming the authors. Clearly, the Human Genome Project is a big endeavour. Upon its completion, it involved 15 million separate PCR reactions from many collaborating institutions.

The Human Genome Project has provided us with much information.

- The human genome contains 3.2 billion chemical nucleotide base pairs (A, C, T and G).
- There were some surprises for the scientific community, especially with regard to size. There are only an estimated 20,000–25,000 protein coding genes (http://www.ornl.gov/sci/techresources/Human_Genome/faq/genenumber.shtml), which is surprisingly low for such a complex species (Stein, 2004). Many had thought the number would be in the region of 80,000–140,000 genes.
- The human genome sequence is almost the same (99.9%) in all people – it is the 0.1% that is going to be most interesting.
- About 2% of the genome encodes instructions for the synthesis of proteins.
- About 50% of sequences do not code for proteins.
- The human genome's gene-dense regions are mainly composed of the nucleotides G and C, whereas gene-poor regions are rich in A and T. The GC- and AT-rich regions can be seen as the light and dark bands on chromosomes.
- Genes appear to be concentrated in random areas along the genome, with vast expanses of non-coding DNA between.

Frequent reports in the media identifying the location of a gene responsible for some disorder or disease are inescapable. Genetics is being incorporated into forensic science, diagnosis, gene therapy (see Box 2.8) and pharmaceutical design. Since the 19th century, when Darwin and Mendel presented their theories of evolution and inheritance, our understanding of genetics has increased enormously, but even in the 21st century it is still an ongoing area of exploration. The optimism about genetics is typified by the quotes of the behavioural geneticist Professor Robert Plomin. In 1990 Plomin et al. stated: 'During the past decade, advances in molecular genetics have led to the dawn of a new era for behavioral genetic research . . . these techniques are already beginning to revolutionize behavioral genetic research in some areas, especially psychopathology'. However, in 2003 Plomin and McGuffin stated that: 'progress . . . towards finding genes . . . has nonetheless been slower than some had originally anticipated'.

The case is that we are not quite there yet, and we should approach with a great deal of caution the media reports that state that a gene has been found for (insert any characteristic/disorder/disease/behaviour).

BOX 2.8: GENE THERAPY

'Gene therapy trial "cures children"' was the headline on the BBC news website on 11 July 2013.

Metachromatic leukodystrophy (MLD) is a disorder inherited in an autosomal recessive pattern. It results in an accumulation of sulfatides (fats) in the cells of the nervous system that produce myelin. This causes destruction of white matter. The behavioural consequences are as follows:

- deterioration of intellectual functions;
- deterioration of motor skills;
- loss of sensation in the extremities (peripheral neuropathy);
- incontinence;
- seizures;
- paralysis;
- an inability to speak;
- blindness; and
- hearing loss.

Eventually patients lose awareness of their surroundings and become unresponsive.

Metachromatic leukodystrophy usually appears in the second year of life and children lose any speech they have acquired and develop problems with walking.

The gene responsible is the ARSA gene, which results in a decreased ability to break down sulfatides. Sulfatides are toxic to the nervous system. This is clearly a terrible disorder and in need of a treatment.

Gene therapy has recently been used successfully in MLD. The aim of gene therapy is to modify the genetic material of living cells for therapeutic purposes (Amado & Chen, 1999). Gene therapy involves the insertion of a functional gene into a cell to correct the genetic abnormality and ultimately achieve a therapeutic outcome. The gene in this case is not unlike a drug in its mission to treat disease and disorder. This is achieved by harnessing viruses. Viruses have specialized molecular mechanisms to efficiently transport their genomes inside the cells they

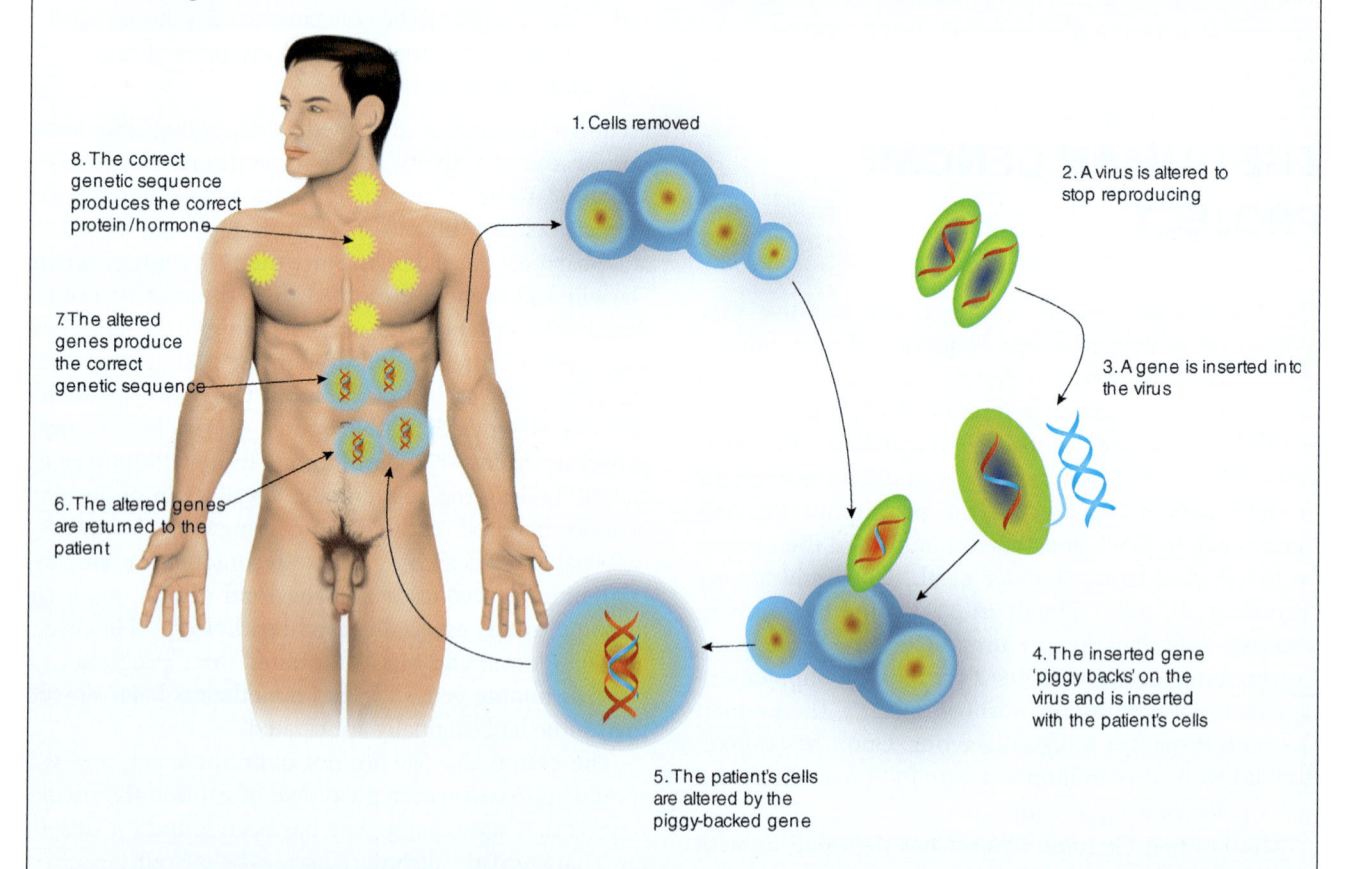

FIGURE 2.8.1 *Gene therapy: how a retrovirus works. Malfunctioning genes are a potential target for treatment. Using a retrovirus, new genes can piggy-back into the genome.*

infect (think of HIV). The type of virus used is called a retrovirus as it contains a reverse transcriptase that allows genetic integration into the host's genes by generating complementary DNA from RNA. This process is called reverse transcription – transcription in the other direction. Reverse transcription is needed for the replication of retroviruses (e.g. HIV). Obviously, retroviruses can have dramatic negative effects, as in HIV, but they can be used in a beneficial way (see Figure 2.8.1).

In the report using gene therapy for MLD, the scientists used lentiviral vectors which are a type of retrovirus that can infect cells because they can get through the membrane of the nucleus of the target cell and change the expression of their target cell's gene. In the case of MLD three presymptomatic paediatric patients who showed genetic, biochemical and neurophysiological evidence of late infantile MLD received this gene therapy targeting the dysfunctional ARSA gene. The report concluded that 'notably, the disease did not manifest or progress in the three patients 7 to 21 months beyond the predicted age of symptom onset. These findings indicate that extensive genetic engineering . . . may offer therapeutic benefit for MLD patients' (Biffi et al., 2013). Or to put it in plain language, Dr Biffi told the BBC: 'The outcome has been very positive, they're all in very good condition, with a normal life and going to kindergarten at an age when their siblings were unable to talk' (http://www.bbc.co.uk/news/health-23269778).

SUMMARY

Genetics is an expanding discipline in which the psychobiologist takes advantage of new technology allowing research into the genetic basis of behaviours. Humans are the most recent in a long line of ancestors that has evolved over millions of years. The basis of all our genetic understanding stems from the work of Charles Darwin. Since then the mechanisms of genetics have been identified and they allow for the exploitation of science in genetic engineering and the misuse of science.

LEARNING OUTCOME QUESTIONS

You should be able to answer the following questions.
- How are characteristics inherited?
- Evaluate the methods of the behavioural geneticist.
- Describe the use of the endophenotype.
- Describe the process of evolution.

FURTHER READING

Barrett, L., Dunbar, R., & Lycett, J. (2002). *Human evolutionary psychology*. Basingstoke, UK: Palgrave.
Brune, M. (2008). *Textbook of evolutionary psychiatry: The origins of psychopathology*. Oxford, UK: Oxford University Press.
Dawkins, R. (2006). *The Selfish Gene* (3rd edn). Oxford, UK: Oxford University Press.
Dunbar, R., & Barrett, L. (Eds.) (2007). *Oxford handbook of evolutionary psychology*. Oxford, UK: Oxford University Press.
Kelsoe, J. R. (2004). Genomics and the Human Genome Project: implications for psychiatry. *International Review of Psychiatry, 16*(4), 294–300.
Rutter, M. (2005). *Genes and behaviour: Nature–nurture interplay explained*. Oxford, UK: Blackwell.

MIND MAP

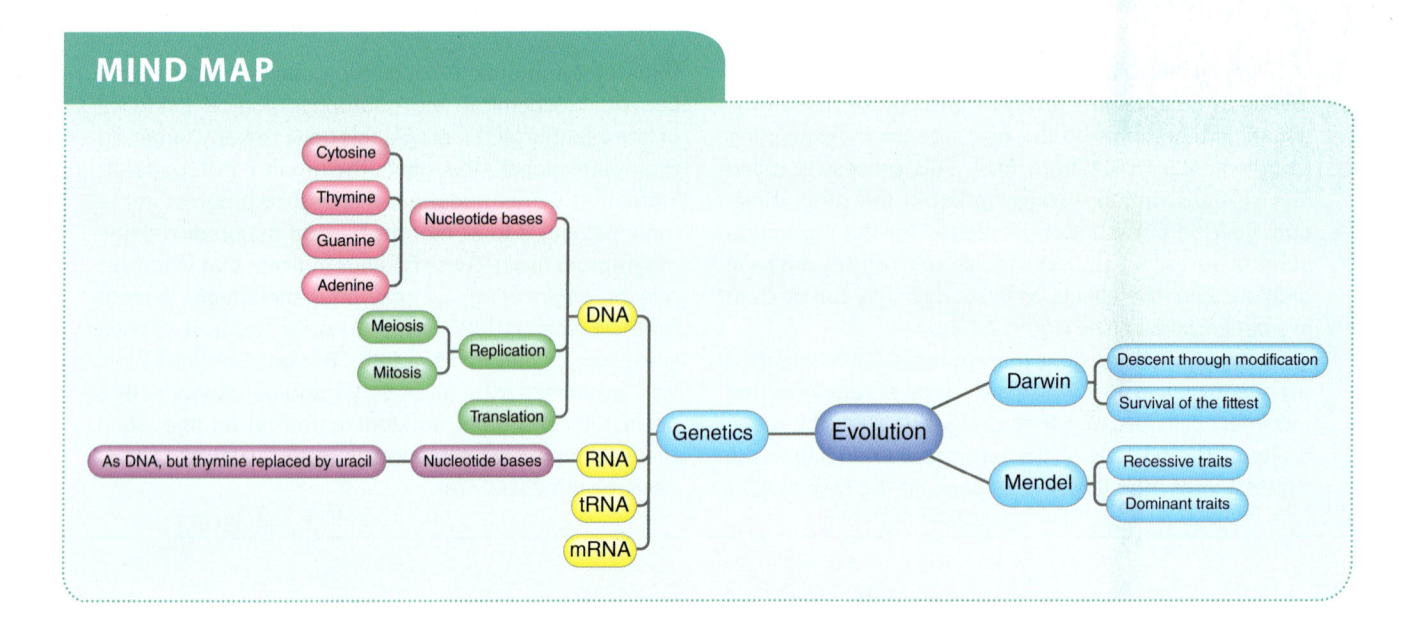

- **Genetics**
  - **DNA**
    - Nucleotide bases
      - Cytosine
      - Thymine
      - Guanine
      - Adenine
    - Replication
      - Meiosis
      - Mitosis
    - Translation
  - **RNA**
    - Nucleotide bases: As DNA, but thymine replaced by uracil
  - **tRNA**
  - **mRNA**

- **Evolution**
  - **Darwin**
    - Descent through modification
    - Survival of the fittest
  - **Mendel**
    - Recessive traits
    - Dominant traits

3 Neural Development

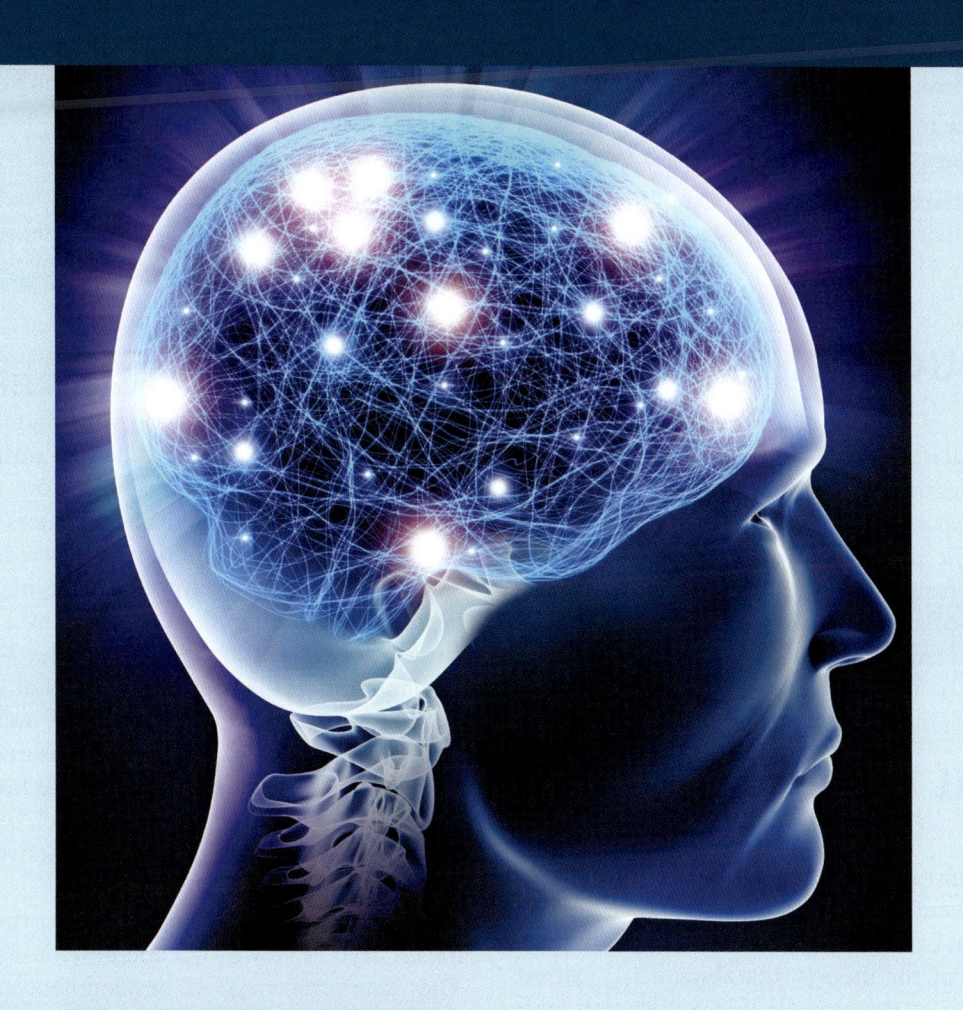

ANATOMY OF THE CHAPTER

This chapter will highlight the following.
- General embryological development.
- Neural development *in utero*.
- Neural development in adolescence and adulthood.
- **Teratology**.

INTRODUCTION   62

GENERAL DEVELOPMENT   62

NEURAL DEVELOPMENT OVER THE LIFESPAN   62

NEURAL DEVELOPMENT   64

DEVELOPMENT OF THE PERIPHERAL NERVOUS SYSTEM (PNS)   71

DEVELOPMENT OF THE AUTONOMIC NERVOUS SYSTEM (ANS)   71

MALE AND FEMALE BRAINS   71

ADOLESCENT DEVELOPMENT   71

ADULT DEVELOPMENT   75

CRITICAL PERIODS   76

SUMMARY   80

LEARNING OUTCOMES

1. To understand the elements of neural development *in utero*.
2. To understand the processes of neural development throughout the lifespan.
3. To appreciate the potential impact of neural development on policy.
4. To have knowledge about the critical/**sensitive periods** of neural development and how toxic agents and adverse environments can influence development.

INTRODUCTION

Genetic material is assembled in the cell and meiotic cell division produces the gametes that are the progenitors of new life. The making of a brain, arguably the most complex organ in the universe, all starts with a sperm and an egg (ovum) fusing. In order to get a more complete understanding of development *in utero*, this chapter will first address embryological development in general.

GENERAL DEVELOPMENT

After **ejaculation**, sperms make their way through the acidic environment of the vagina to the more hospitable environment of the **uterus**. About 200 sperms arrive at the **ampulla** of the uterine tube (Figure 3.1) (Moore et al., 2012). It is at the ampulla that fertilization takes place over a 24-hour period. The sperm and the egg have to fuse and do so after proceeding through a number of stages (see Figure 3.2). The sperm has to traverse the layers surrounding the ovum (the **corona radiata** and **zona pellucida**). At the tip of the sperm is the **acrosome** that contains enzymes to break down the outer layers of the ovum. Once past these barriers, the sperm leaves behind its plasma membrane and enters the cytoplasm of the ovum. The ovum that is now containing the nuclei of the female and male is called an **ootid** and has the haploid number of chromosomes from the sperm and ovum. The fusion of the nuclei produces a diploid number of chromosomes and then is referred to as a zygote. The single cell of the zygote, or the **blastomere**, then begins a series of mitotic divisions in a process called cleavage, thus creating new cells. After 4–6 days, before implantation in the uterus, this mass of cells is called a **blastocyst**. The blastocyst consists of an inner cell mass (embryoblast) which are the **progenitor cells** of the final human – these are the **stem cells** (see Box 3.1). In addition, there is an outer cell mass, which becomes part of the placenta. By the end of the second week, the blastocyst implants into the uterus.

After successful implantation into the uterine wall, the embryo rapidly grows and develops (see Figure 3.3). The embryonic stage of development ends on day 56 when the foetal period begins. The embryo is now called a foetus and remains as such until birth. During the foetal period, growth and differentiation of the embryonic cells occur.

NEURAL DEVELOPMENT OVER THE LIFESPAN

Many biopsychology textbooks focus on the very early changes of development *in utero*. Furthermore, the student often sees developmental psychology as referring to *child* development. However, the development of the brain goes beyond the embryological stage and the immediate postnatal periods and stretches into adulthood. The brain undergoes many changes during its life, from conception to death, but a good place to start is

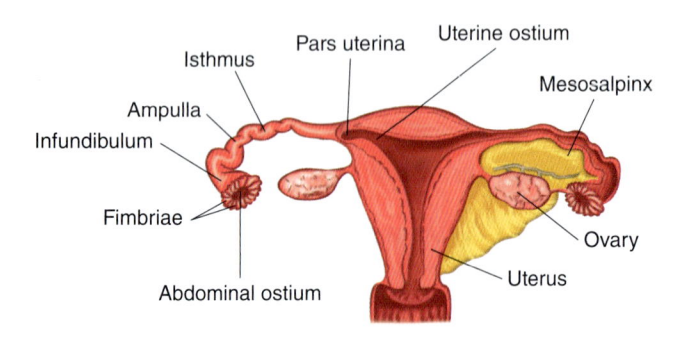

FIGURE 3.1 *The female reproductive system.*

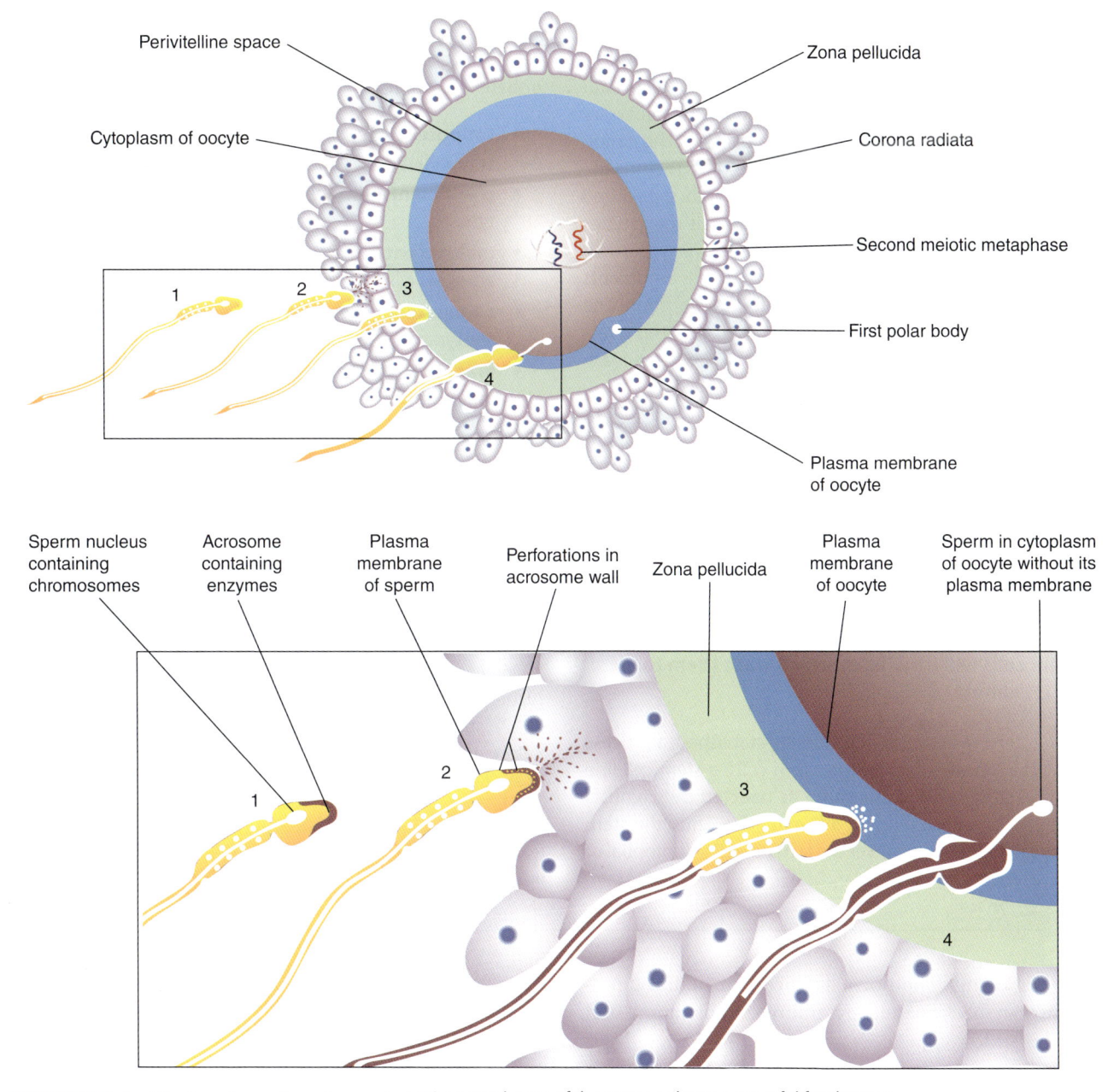

FIGURE 3.2 *Fertilization.* Sperm have to penetrate the outer layers of the egg to achieve successful fertilization.

BOX 3.1: STEM CELLS

Stem cells are undifferentiated cells that can replicate and are able to turn into specialized cells.

There are two main sources of stem cells:

- **embryonic stem cells**;
- adult stem cells.

Embryonic stem cells

Embryonic stem cells come from a 4–5-day-old embryo (the blastocyst phase of development). The embryos are created during *in vitro* **fertilization** (IVF) treatment where several eggs are fertilized in a test tube, but only one is implanted into a woman – for want of a better phrase, these are spare embryos. The stem cells from the blastocyst are put into a culture dish containing the necessary ingredients for survival. As the stem cells lack the conditions to differentiate in the natural setting, they divide and replicate. As they have not turned into specialized cells yet, they can become any cell type. It is these types of stem cells that have caused much controversy, particularly in the Bible Belt of the USA where similar arguments about life are presented in the context of abortion. The big question is about when human life starts – this question is too big for us to address here but interested readers should see Steinbock (2007).

Adult stem cells

Adult stem cells exist throughout the body and importantly for the psychobiologist, they are found in the brain. Adult stem cells remain in a quiescent state until activated by disease or tissue injury when they are mobilized to deal with the condition.

Stem cells will be whatever you want them to be . . . almost

Once stem cell cultures have been established, a process that is easier with embryonic stem cells, a stem cell line can be stimulated to specialize as directed by scientists in a process called *directed differentiation*. Thus, the stem cells can become whatever cell is needed. The potential of this science is immense.

Stem cells are categorized by their potency to differentiate into other types of cells and can be:

- **totipotent** – the ability to differentiate into *all* possible cell types;
- **pluripotent** – the ability to differentiate into *most* cell types;
- **multipotent** – the ability to differentiate into *related* types of cells;
- **oligopotent** – the ability to differentiate into a *limited few* types of cells;
- **unipotent** – the ability to produce cells of *only* their *own* type (but can self-renew).

Stem cells – the future

Stem cells have the potential to treat serious and debilitating diseases. Pluripotent stem cells offer the possibility of growing replacement cells to treat, for example, Parkinson's disease or spinal cord injury. There are numerous experiments looking at their preclinical and clinical applications in Parkinson's disease (Badger et al., 2014; Kearns et al., 2006; Martinez-Morales & Liste, 2012; Moriyasu et al., 2006), Alzheimer's disease (Abdel-Salam, 2011; Young & Goldstein, 2012), strokes (Banerjee et al., 2011; Hassani et al., 2012; Katare et al., 2013; Zhou, 2011), multiple sclerosis (Martino et al., 2010) and spinal injuries (Sabelstrom et al., 2013).

For information on clinical trials in the USA and UK go to: http://www.nhs.uk/Conditions/clinical-trials/Pages/introduction.aspx
http://clinicaltrials.gov

---

at the beginning. The normal process of neural development can be impaired by trauma, deprivation and **teratogens** (Box 3.2).

NEURAL DEVELOPMENT

During the **gastrulation** phase of embryonic development, the embryo begins to take its multicellular form in a process called **invagination** in which the infolding of embryonic cells produces three cell layers:

- **ectoderm** (outer layer);
- **mesoderm** (the middle layer); and
- **endoderm** (inner layer).

As a result of gastrulation, there is the formation of a cylinder-like structure in the mesoderm called the **notochord** which arises from an area called the **primitive streak**. The primitive streak establishes bilateral symmetry of the embryo and eventually the body.

All parts of the nervous system develop from an area of the embryonic ectoderm called the **neural plate** (Figure 3.4). The neural plate goes on to form the **neural tube** and the **neural crest**. The neural tube will eventually become the brain and spinal cord, whereas the neural crest becomes the peripheral nervous system and the autonomic nervous system.

Developmental Changes in the Brain

There are several stages in the development of the brain and each stage is critically important for a normal outcome.

Induction of the neural plate

Neurulation – the formation of the neural tube – starts about 22 days after conception (Figure 3.5). The neural

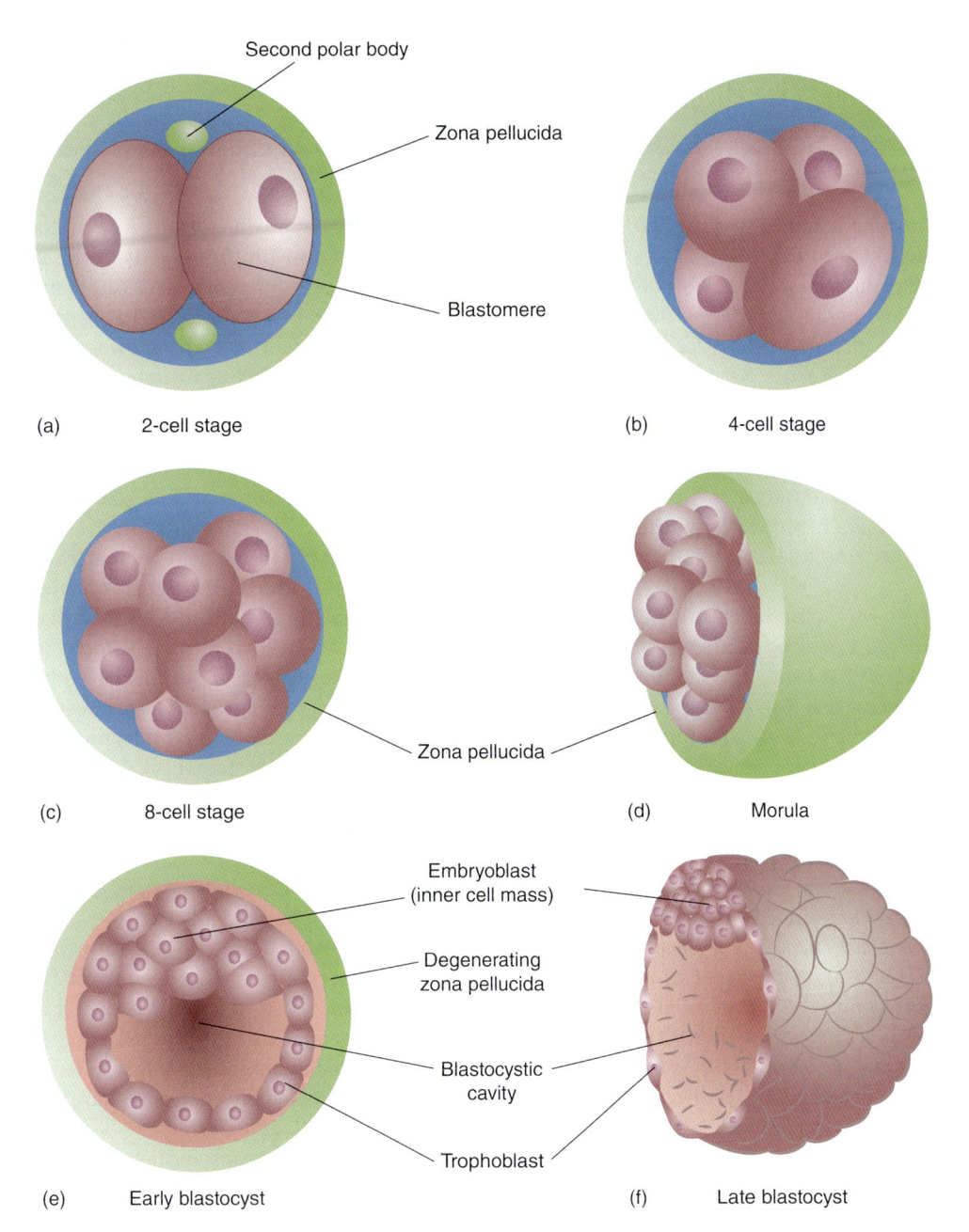

FIGURE 3.3 *The development of the zygote.*

plate at around day 20 begins to fold along the midline. This produces a groove along the plate called the neural groove that will become the neural tube. As this process happens, the neural crest also develops from the neural groove. As the neural plate folds in along the neural groove, it eventually folds in on itself and fuses. This is now the neural tube. On either side of the neural tube is a thickening of mesodermic cells called **somites** which give rise to skeletal muscle, etc. The part of the neural tube that is next to the somites becomes the progenitor cells of the spine. The anterior part of the neural tube – the anterior neural fold – continues to expand and becomes the brain. The fluid-filled cavity of the neural tube becomes the central canal of the spinal cord and the ventricles of the brain that contain **cerebrospinal fluid** (CSF) (Figure 3.6).

If neural development goes wrong, this can have pronounced effects. The most common neural tube defect is **spina bifida**, which is a failure of the lower spinal neural tube to close. Individuals affected with spina bifida may suffer from motor and sensory defects in the legs, incontinence, vertebral curvature and increased CSF pressure in the brain (Copp et al., 2003). As is often the case, the study of abnormalities has provided great insight, not

BOX 3.2: BIRTH TRAUMA AND TERATOGENS IN ADHD

In the quest to understand the aetiology of attention deficit hyperactivity disorder (ADHD), investigators have looked at birth complications and teratogens. When one is looking for causality in a syndrome that is characterized by behaviour disturbances, it is perhaps impossible to determine one single cause. Behaviours could arise for a number of reasons as a consequence of alteration in neural substrates. ADHD is a common paediatric diagnosis affecting approximately 5% of the population, and now being recognized in the adult. This is a large number of people who are functionally impaired and understanding the source or indeed the variety of sources is important.

Some studies have found an effect of complications such has eclampsia or those needing assisted delivery (Claycomb et al., 2004; Hartsough & Lambert, 1985) but not all studies have found such a link (Barkley, Dupaul et al., 1990; St Sauver et al., 2004). When assessing the functional impact of assisted births such as forceps delivery or Ventouse, which have been associated with developmental delays (Pauc & Young, 2006), we have to remember that the mere fact that assistance is required indicates that there are already problems with the delivery – so which is the causal factor? The assisted delivery or the need for assisted delivery? Birth complications, especially hypoxia, may lead to neural damage (Ben Amor et al., 2005; Milberger et al., 1997).

The studies looking at birth trauma and interventions do not account for a single cause of ADHD; not everyone who has ADHD has had complications *in utero* or at birth, and conversely not everyone with birth complications has ADHD. Indeed, birth complications are associated with numerous outcomes, not just ADHD (Pauc & Young, 2006).

When the mother is pregnant there are some obvious behaviours she should avoid; smoking and drinking alcohol are the two most notable. Smoking during pregnancy is a risk factor for many adverse outcomes (Ernst et al., 2001) and has been associated with a greater risk of ADHD symptoms (Linnet et al., 2005; Mick et al., 2002, Milberger et al., 1996, 1998; Obel et al., 2009; Thapar et al., 2003).

Whilst there are other variables that may be linked to maternal smoking during pregnancy, e.g. mother's age and educational level, the question remains: is it smoking or is it the nicotine that is the main culprit? When smoking a cigarette, one is inhaling some 4000 chemicals, one of which is nicotine – the one that is addictive. Smoking has many effects on the unborn child, including hypoxia (Haustein, 1999). Hypoxia has been suggested as a possible factor in causing ADHD (Lou, 1996) and has been linked with the regions of the brain that are thought to be dysfunctional in ADHD (Toft, 1999). There are few studies that have looked at hypoxia in humans and they have not found strong evidence (Rennie et al., 2007). To understand this further, experimental studies of animals have found some support for hypoxia in the manifestation of symptoms associated with ADHD and the neurochemistry/neuroanatomy of ADHD (Decker and Rye, 2002; Decker et al., 2003, 2005; Oorschot et al., 2007).

If hypoxia is not the culprit then that leaves us with nicotine. In human studies, it is generally impossible to disentangle smoking and nicotine – although now there are many ways of delivering nicotine without smoke. Animal studies are able to address the role of nicotine experimentally. Prenatal exposure to nicotine has been demonstrated to increase hyperactivity in rat offspring (Newman et al., 1999; Paz et al., 2007; Thomas et al., 2000; Tizabi et al., 1997, 2000), to cause cognitive deficits (Vaglenova et al., 2004, 2008) and increase impulsivity (Sobrian et al., 2003). How prenatal exposure achieves such changes is still subject to scrutiny, but prenatal exposure does alter nicotine receptors in the brain dependent upon the stage of development (Mansvelder & Role, 2006). Furthermore, prenatal exposure to nicotine has effects on developing dopaminergic **neurons** which one might expect if ADHD was all down to dopamine (see Chapter 19), but the effect of nicotine is far greater on noradrenergic systems and this has been argued to possibly contribute to ADHD symptomatology (Leslie et al., 2006).

Maternal alcohol consumption and foetal exposure have been associated with a number of adverse outcomes in offspring (see Box 3.5). As far as a role for alcohol in ADHD is concerned, the findings have been contradictory (Linnet et al., 2003). The studies that have looked at alcohol have often studied large amounts of alcohol consumption and have been confounded by smoking. Studies have found links between parental alcoholism and ADHD (e.g. Knopik et al., 2006), whereas low doses of alcohol did not cause ADHD-like symptoms once smoking was taken out of the equation (Rodriguez et al., 2009). With high levels of alcohol exposure, a link to ADHD emerges (Fryer et al., 2007). In a review of the literature surrounding foetal alcohol syndrome, it was noted that these children also demonstrated higher levels of ADHD-I subtype (O'Malley & Nanson, 2002).

When looking for environmental or teratogenic risk factors in ADHD, the obvious candidates of trauma, smoking and drinking have gained varying degrees of support. However, two other variables are frequently associated with ADHD: low birth weight and sex.

Low birth weight has been associated with the symptoms and prevalence of ADHD (Botting et al., 1997; Hack et al., 2009, Hultman et al., 2007). Low birth weight is implicated either directly or indirectly as a consequence of smoking, for example. It is necessary to determine if low birth weight itself or the cause of low birth weight is the important factor; low birth weight might be associated with another problem.

It is not surprising that being male is a risk factor, after all, the epidemiological data support that. However, in the context of risk factors, males may be more vulnerable to all the above-mentioned variables.

In an article entitled 'The fragile male', Kraemer reviews the literature that points to males being more vulnerable from conception (Kraemer, 2000). The male embryo is more vulnerable to insult and trauma with more resultant deaths (Mizuno, 2000). At birth, the female child is 4–6 weeks more physiologically advanced than her male counterpart (Gualtieri & Hicks, 1985). However, a direct effect of the intrauterine environment with ADHD has not been supported (Flannery & Liederman, 1994).

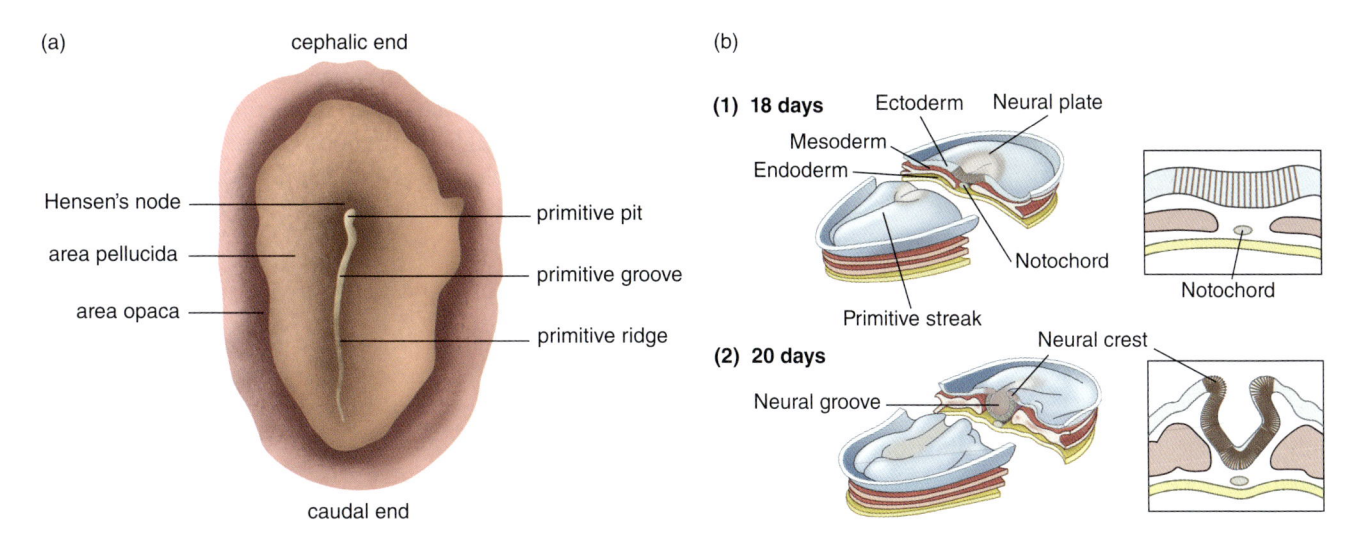

FIGURE 3.4 *The neural plate. (a) The primitive bridge can be clearly seen. (b) A schematic representation of the structure of the neural plate.*

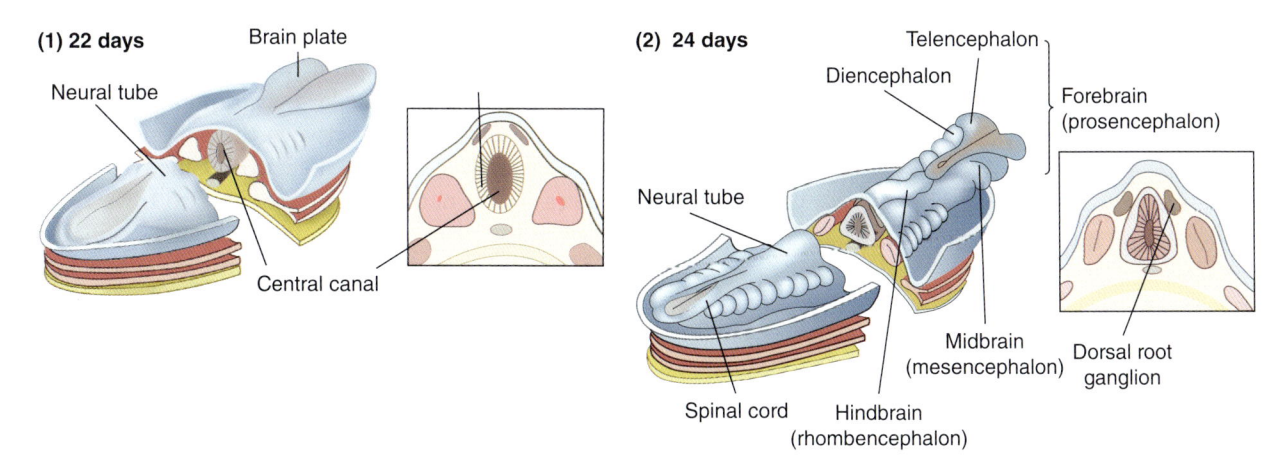

FIGURE 3.5 *The development of the neural plate at 22 and 24 days.*

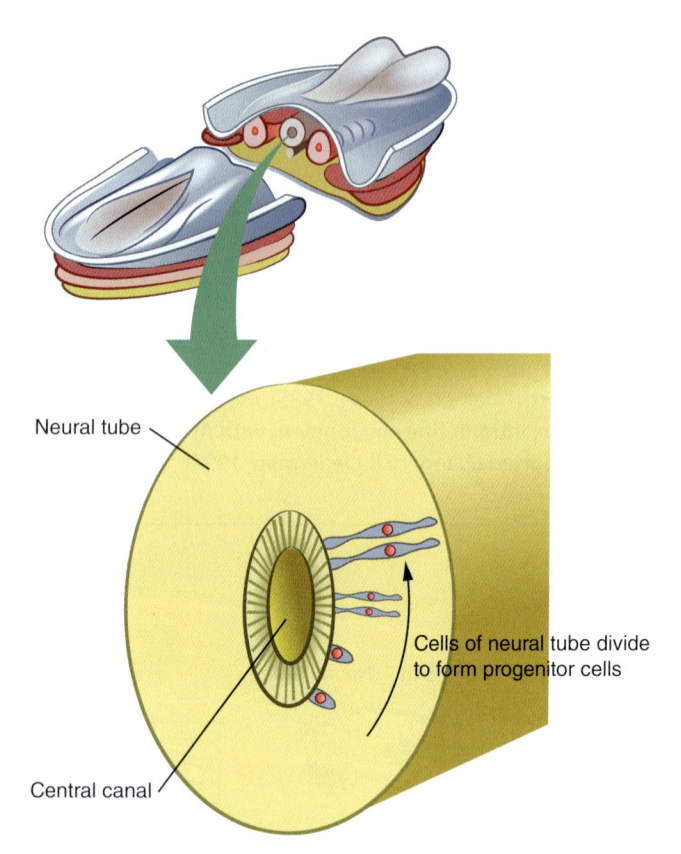

FIGURE 3.6 The development of the neural tube. As the neural plate folds, a neural tube is created.

only into defects such as spina bifida but also the normal processes of development itself (Greene et al., 2009). One wonderfully named yet critical protein gene that is involved in signalling neural tube development is the **sonic hedgehog gene** (Briscoe & Therond, 2013).

Neural proliferation

Neural proliferation is the phase in brain development in which new cells are generated. Early in development, cells lining the ventricles divide, some of which become stem cells and continue to divide, while others become neurons or glial cells. At the height of proliferation it is thought that 250,000 neurons are created per minute (Cowan, 1979). As the anterior end of the neural tube increases in size, the preliminary structures of the brain can be seen:

- **prosencephalon** (forebrain);
- **mesencephalon** (midbrain); and
- **rhombencephalon** (hindbrain).

Migration

The cells of the brain arrive at their specific locations during a process called migration. The migrating neurons are immature and lack dendrites and once they are in position, they align themselves with the cells at their destination and form the structures of the brain. The genetic code provides each cell with its location. Their journey to a particular destination is facilitated by **radial glia** (Figure 3.7). Radial glia provide a network of guidewires and support structures that the migrating neuron wraps around and follows to its destination (Rakic, 1985). Once in place, the formation of the dendrites gives the neuron its shape. Clearly, the brain comprises many specialized cells and the neural stem cells become differentiated, taking on their shape and chemical composition depending on their location within the brain.

Myelination

Glia also have another function within the developing nervous system, providing **myelin** around some neurons that increases the speed of neurotransmission (Figure 3.8). **Myelination** starts in the spinal cord and progresses through the regions of the brain. It is not restricted to embryonic development and continues into the first and second years of life (Paus, 2010; Paus et al., 1999).

Arborization

As the neuron differentiates and becomes its eventual cell, the dendrites grow and form connections in a process called **arborization**. Arborization permits the neurons to receive and integrate the input of neural messages from other neurons. The number of dendrites is related to the volume and frequency of incoming signals. Such signals are dependent upon experience (Perry, 2002). The neurons are now ready to make connections.

Synaptogenesis and apoptosis

With the rapid increase in the number of neural cells and their placement within particular regions of the brain, they have to be able to communicate with each other. Communication between the billions of neurons is achieved by chemical mediators called neurotransmitters. These neurotransmitters have to traverse a gap between the neurons called the synapse. The final stage of development is the formation of the synapses in a process called **synaptogenesis** (Figure 3.9). Synaptogenesis is an ongoing process throughout life but is much slower in old age.

The synapses are overproduced – there are more than are actually needed in the average 1 year old. Whilst almost all the neurons are formed prenatally, there are few synaptic connections. Synapses are dependent upon experiences and interactions with an environment – it is at the synapse where learning takes place (see Chapter 13).

CHAPTER 3 NEURAL DEVELOPMENT 69

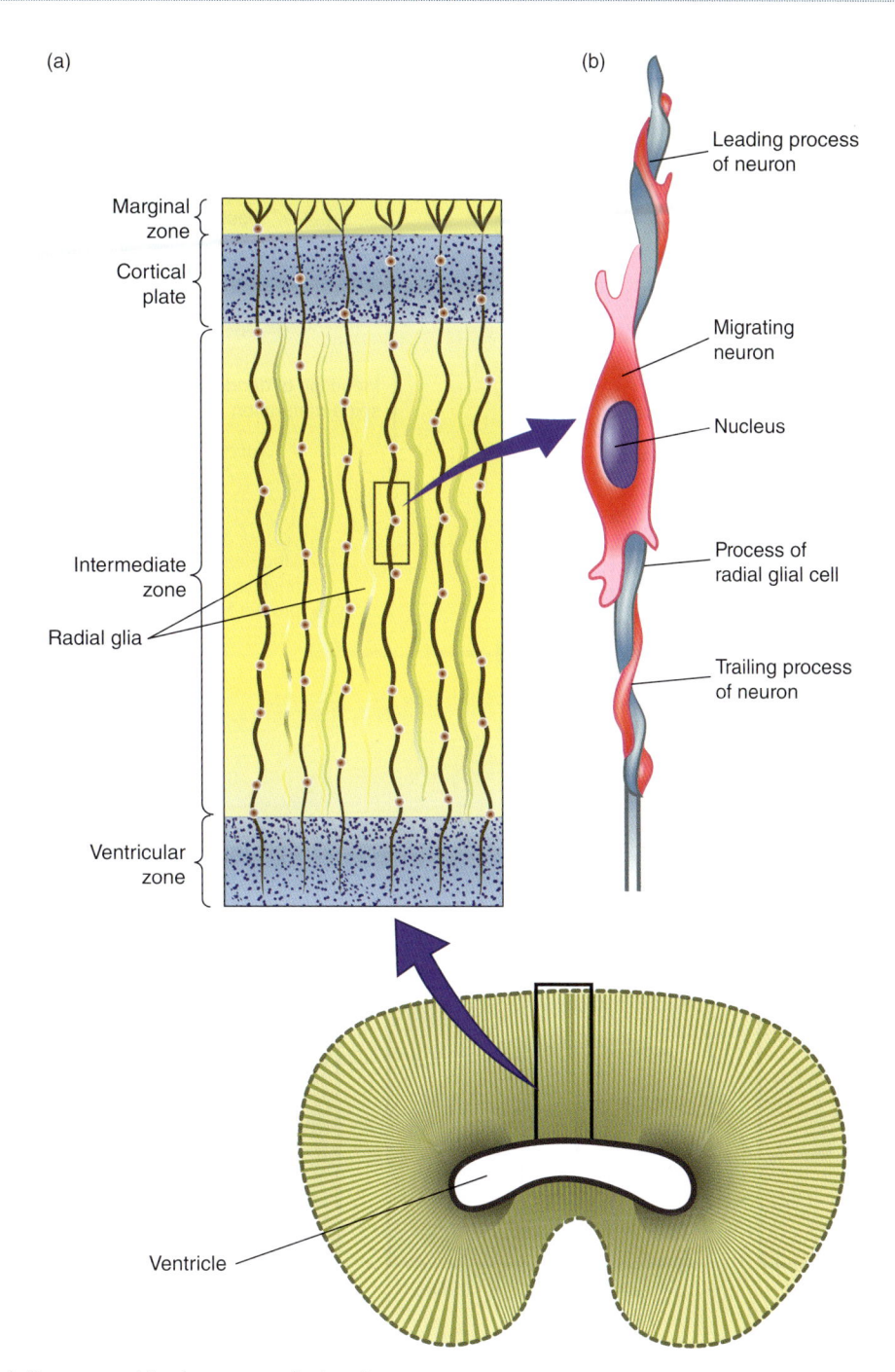

FIGURE 3.7 *Radial glia act as guidewires to neural migration.*

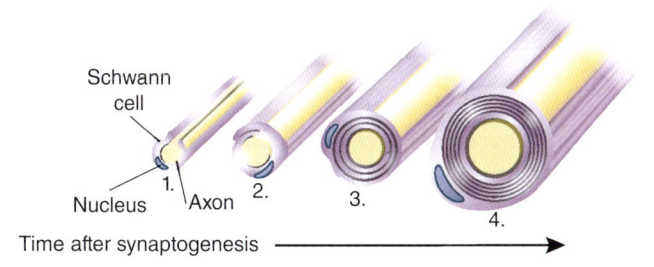

FIGURE 3.8 *Myelinated neurons. Schwann cells wrap the axons of neurons in myelin which acts as insulation and speeds neurotransmission.*

A large amount of dendritic growth and the connections between synapses occur after birth.

The overproduction of synapses is addressed by the process of pruning. During pruning, the synapses that are being used a lot become stronger and those that are not used are pruned away. During childhood, pruning reduces the volume of **grey matter** in the cortex, and there is substantial loss in the **frontal lobes** of teenagers. The essence of pruning is similar to muscle development: if we work out with weights in the gym, we strengthen our muscles and they get bigger; similarly,

(a) **Synaptogenesis**

stabilization of contacts between neurons

Recruitment of specific presynaptic proteins

Adhesion molecules

Recruitment of specific postsynaptic proteins

Signalling to actin cytoskeleton

Induction of dendritic spine maturation

(b) **Mature synapse**

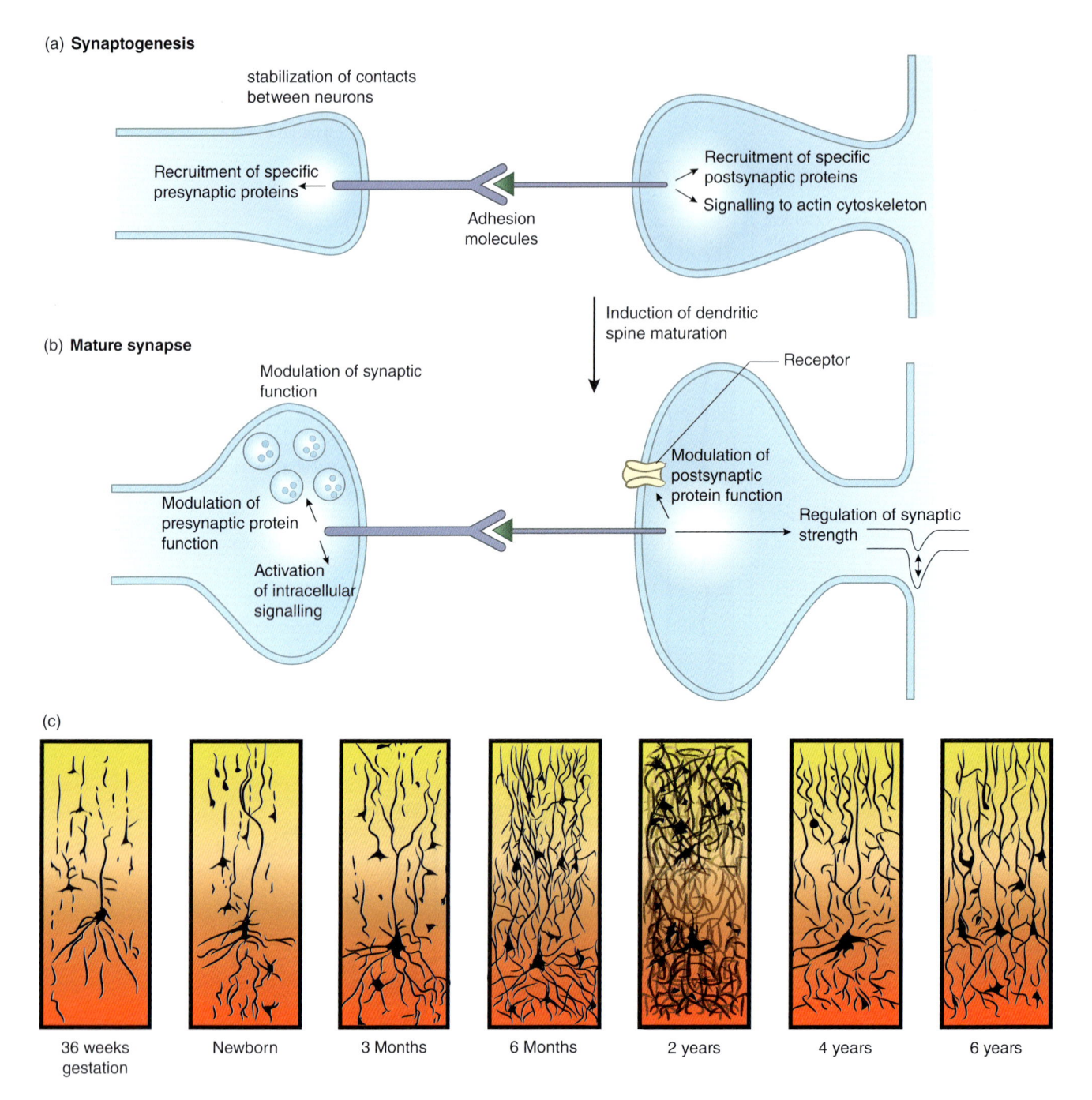

Modulation of synaptic function

Receptor

Modulation of presynaptic protein function

Modulation of postsynaptic protein function

Activation of intracellular signalling

Regulation of synaptic strength

(c)

36 weeks gestation | Newborn | 3 Months | 6 Months | 2 years | 4 years | 6 years

FIGURE 3.9 *Synaptogenesis. (a) Synapses in a developing circuit. (b) Mature synapses. (c) Synaptic density from newborn to adult.*
Source: (a) & (b) Dalva, M. B., McClelland, A. C., & Kayser, M. S. (2007). Cell adhesion molecules: signalling functions at the synapse. *Nature Reviews Neuroscience*, 8(3), 206–220.

if we exercise our brain, those neurons remain and become stronger.

After migration, many neurons will die in a process called **apoptosis** (cell death). Neurotrophins promote the growth and survival of the neuron and stimulate synaptogenesis. Neurons die because they failed to compete for such chemicals at their target site. Synaptogenesis is assisted by **nerve growth factor** (**NGF**), which is a protein that promotes the survival of only certain neurons (Levi-Montalcini, 1982). This competition has been referred to as *neural Darwinism* in which the successful neurons connect and strengthen.

DEVELOPMENT OF THE PERIPHERAL NERVOUS SYSTEM (PNS)

The peripheral nervous system develops from cells that make up the neural crest. The PNS consists of cranial, spinal and visceral nerves and ganglia. All the sensory cells that we have are derived from the neural crest cells. The sensory cells are not a development of the central nervous system, but are located outside. The exception to this is the ganglion of the cochlear and the vestibulocochlear nerve. The peripheral sensory cells start as bipolar but when the two nerves from the sensory cells and the central nervous system meet, they become unipolar cells. The peripheral end of the cell is linked to the sensory end of the cell and the central process enters the spinal cord and the brain. Neural crest cells therefore migrate to their sensory ganglia. The neural crest cells also give rise to a type of Schwann cell called satellite glial cells. Satellite glial cells wrap around the neurons and control the microenvironment of the neuron (Hanani, 2010).

In addition to the sensory afferents, the PNS has motor nerves (efferents). These arise from cells in the basal plates of the developing spinal cord and form bundles connecting to the developing limbs. The cranial nerves begin to develop around the fifth week. There are 12 cranial nerves that can be divided into three groups according to their embryological origins (see Chapter 5):

- somatic efferent cranial nerves;
- nerves of pharyngeal arches; and
- special sensory nerves.

Somatic efferent cranial nerves include the hypoglossal nerve (innervating the tongue), the abducent nerve (innervating the muscles of the eye in order to have them looking forward), the trochlear nerve (innervating another muscle of the eye and interpreting neural signals to move eyes up and down and outwards) and the oculomotor nerve (also innervating the eye and controlling the muscles that permit visual tracking and fixation by the eye and papillary light reflexes).

The nerves of the pharyngeal arches are the trigeminal nerve, the facial nerve, the glossopharyngeal nerve, the vagus nerve and the accessory nerve (see Chapter 5).

The three cranial nerves that make up the special sensory nerves are the olfactory nerve, the optic nerve and the vestibulocochlear nerve. These sensory nerves deliver messages regarding smell, vision, sound and position.

DEVELOPMENT OF THE AUTONOMIC NERVOUS SYSTEM (ANS)

The autonomic nervous system comprises sympathetic and parasympathetic divisions (see Chapter 5). Cells of the ANS arise from neural crest cells in the thoracic region. The sympathetic ganglia are connected and form sympathetic trunks. Once the sympathetic trunks have formed, axons located in the lateral horn of the spinal cord connect with other neurons or ascend or descend in the sympathetic trunk to synapses at different levels (see pain mechanisms in Chapter 10). Parasympathetic nervous system fibres arise from neurons from nuclei in the brainstem or the sacral region of the spinal cord. Recently, it has been suggested that the source of some parasympathetic neurons is cranial Schwann cells (Dyachuk et al., 2014; Espinosa-Medina et al., 2014). The fibres from the brainstem exit as the oculomotor, facial, vagus and glossopharyngeal cranial nerves. These parasympathetic nerves connect with peripheral ganglia of the structure being innervated.

MALE AND FEMALE BRAINS

Much has been said about the differences between male and female brains. Sometimes those differences are greatly exaggerated but nevertheless there are differences – and this is a case where size does not matter. How they differ is a result of genetics – X and Y chromosomes and their effect on hormones *in utero*. Imaging studies have shown that female brains reach their peak volume at a younger age than males (Lenroot & Giedd, 2010). One must remember that the differences between the sexes alter across the lifespan, with the effects of ageing being more prominent in some regions of the male brain (Coffey et al., 1998). Chapter 14 addresses the sex difference issue in more detail, but at this point we should note that the brain is organized in a sex-appropriate manner in a process controlled by the sex hormones (Arnold & Breedlove, 1985).

ADOLESCENT DEVELOPMENT

The behaviour of adolescents is a source of concern for most parents and often attributed to the hormone surge during puberty. This is clearly something that is happening

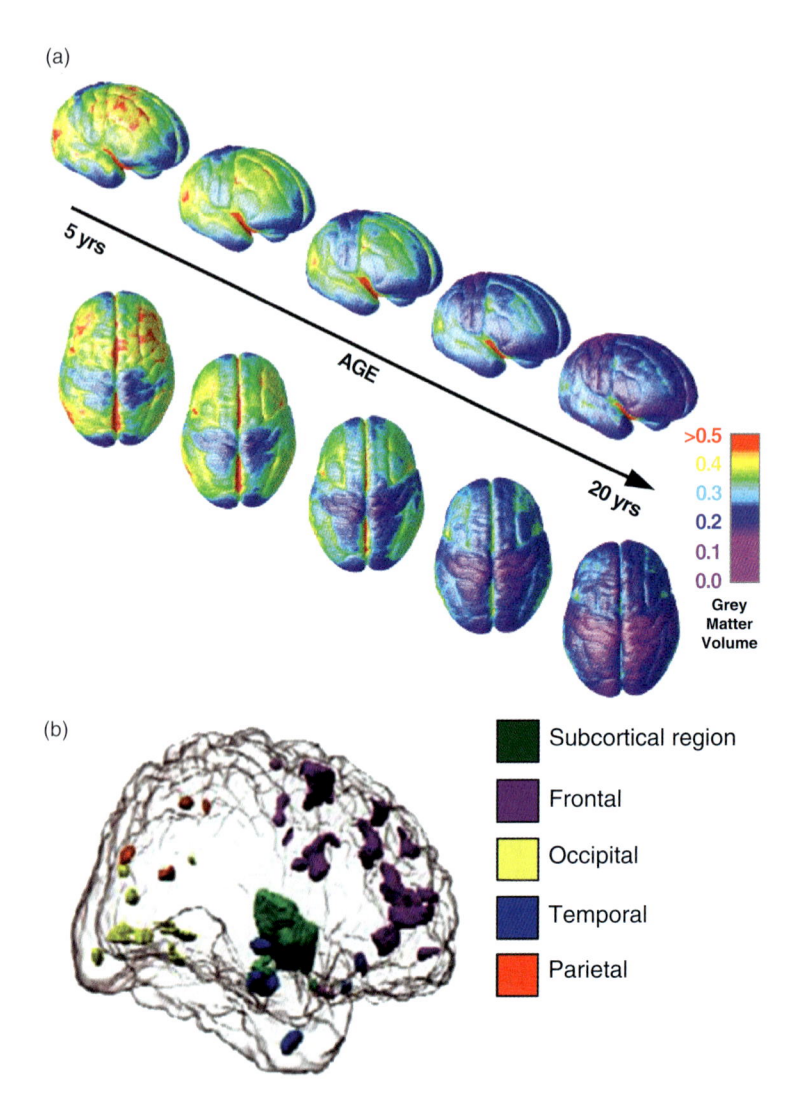

FIGURE 3.10 Cortical development in grey matter from 5 to 20 years. (a) The brain changes throughout childhood. (b) Maturation changes in the cortex from adolescence to adulthood. The coloured areas represent significant changes in the brain from adolescence to adulthood.
Source: Reprinted by permission of Macmillan Publishers Ltd from Sowell, E. R., Peterson, B. S., Thompson, P. M., Welcome, S. E., Henkenius, A. L., & Toga, A. W. (2003). Mapping cortical change across the human life span. *Nature Neuroscience, 6*(3), 309–315, copyright 2003.

(see Chapter 14), but the brain is still very much a work in progress. The rise of neuroimaging has provided access to the otherwise unseen adolescent human brain *in situ*.

When one looks at the adolescent brain, when compared to a younger child, it can be seen that amounts of grey matter in the frontal and parietal cortices are reduced whereas there is a higher volume of **white matter** (Sowell, Thompson, Holmes, Batth et al., 1999). In a **longitudinal study**, the volume of grey matter in the frontal cortex was shown to increase in childhood and early **adolescence** and then reduce during the remainder of adolescence (Lenroot & Giedd, 2006) (see Figure 3.10); a similar effect was found in the **temporal lobe** but when the children were older (Giedd et al., 1999). Elizabeth Sowell and colleagues noted that the decreasing grey matter was accompanied by an increase in white matter, which continues to the age of 30 (Sowell, Thompson et al., 2001). Why age 30? Simply because that was the age of the oldest participant in this study. However, in a subsequent study, this increase was demonstrated up to the age of 60, and the age range of participants in this study went up to 87 (Sowell et al., 2003). These changes may reflect the synaptic reorganization of the brain during adolescence and even into the 20s (Petanjek et al., 2011). It is known that there is a proliferation of synapses which are subsequently eliminated on a selective basis (Changeux & Danchin, 1976). This elimination or pruning may be manifest in the reduction of grey matter during adolescence (Giedd et al., 1999, Sowell, Thompson et al., 2001).

Using magnetic resonance imaging (MRI), Sowell, Thompson, Holmes, Jernigan et al. (1999) were able to see the changes in brain development from adolescence to adulthood. They generated a statistical parametric map of the brain's grey matter, thus demonstrating that the frontal lobes and some subcortical regions go through substantial changes.

Looking at the functional aspects of brain activity rather than purely the structural reveals interesting features of the adolescent brain. It is the functional development of the adolescent's brain that is thought to underlie many of the age-typical behaviours (Blakemore & Choudhury, 2006). Adolescents are not known for their ability to control themselves and are often seen as hedonistic pleasure seekers who act impulsively.

There may be a strong neurobiological reason for this. Adolescents have been shown to have reduced activity in the **orbitofrontal cortex** and an increase in **mesolimbic** areas that mediate rewards (Ernst et al., 2005; Galvan et al., 2006). The **amygdala** was seen to be more active in the adolescent during emotional tasks (Hare et al., 2008) which may go some way to explain the emotional life of your average adolescent (Casey et al., 2008).

Only when the frontal lobe is fully developed is complete control of one's impulses achieved. However, the nature of synaptic proliferation and pruning works on a 'use it or lose it' basis. It becomes critical for the future adult that the brain is put to good use. Risk taking is one of the features of adolescence and this can manifest in experimenting with drugs (see Box 3.3).

BOX 3.3: THE ADOLESCENT BRAIN AND VULNERABILITY TO ADDICTION

Data from the Crime Survey of England and Wales 2011–2012 indicate that illicit drug users commence their drug-taking lives in their late teens and early 20s (see Figure 3.3.1). This is consistent with data from the USA and includes tobacco and alcohol (Wagner & Anthony, 2002a, 2002b). In a longitudinal study in Finland, the average age at which drinking alcohol commenced was 15 years old (Pitkanen et al., 2005). The rates of lifetime dependence were more than 40% if they started drinking at 14 years or younger. This dropped to 10% if they started at 20 years and older, so an early onset age was a predictor of subsequent dependence problems (Grant & Dawson, 1997, 1998).

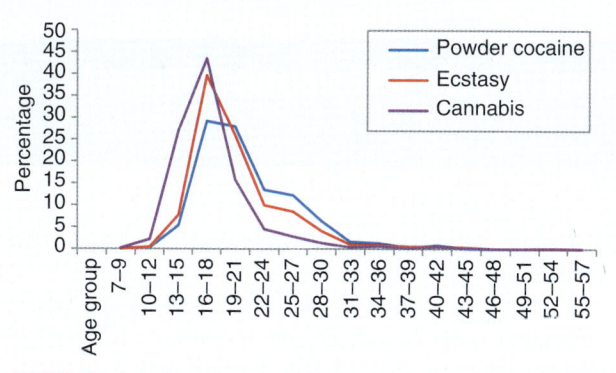

FIGURE 3.3.1 *Age of onset of drug taking.*

The initiation into drug consumption in the late teens and early 20s corresponds with one of the critical periods in brain reorganization and development. During this time the new circuitry of motivation is undergoing substantial change which could make the individual vulnerable to **addiction** (Chambers et al., 2003).

It is not just drugs of addiction that may be of concern; drugs used clinically to treat the likes of depression or ADHD may also have effects on the developing brain (Andersen, 2003, Andersen & Navalta, 2004). One clear example of this is methylphenidate which has a similar pharmacology to cocaine. Methylphenidate is given to children with ADHD (or narcolepsy) to manage their symptoms. It is a long-term medication and is only effective whilst it is present in the brain. One of the worries that people have about such medication is that because it is like cocaine, it is changing the brain during adolescence and may make users more vulnerable to subsequent addiction (Chandler, 2007).

Clearly it is not ethical to perform experiments on children in order to find out what the effects of various drugs are on the developing adolescent brain. Such controlled experiments can only take place in the animal. Studies using animals have found that the balance between the rewarding and aversive effects of drugs during adolescence has a far greater weight on the reward mechanisms (Galvan, 2010; Schramm-Sapyta et al., 2009). Alongside this is the development of cortical regions, especially the frontal lobe (Crews et al., 2007). The adolescent brain is therefore sensitive to reward but has yet to develop the controlling influence of the frontal lobe to manage the desire for reward (Bava & Tapert, 2010) (Figure 3.3.2).

Most of the studies have focused on alcohol consumption due to its ease of access. Binge drinking

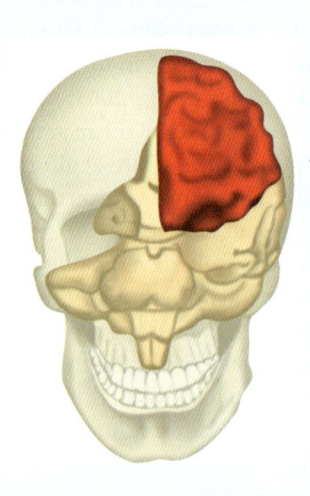

- Planning
- Attention
- Judgement
- Reflection
- Prioritizing
- Self-control
- Strategizing
- Sequencing
- Anticipation
- Organization
- Impulse control
- Second thought
- Working memory
- Modulating mood
- Response flexibility
- Goal-directed behaviour
- Foresee consequences

FIGURE 3.3.2 *Executive functioning. Deviations by drug consumption may affect the above behaviours.*

during adolescence has been shown to compromise white matter development (Bava et al., 2013; McQueeny et al., 2009).

In adolescence the developing brain operates on a 'use it or lose it' basis. How it is used will be critical to its development and future behaviours. Early onset of drug consumption, as we have see, is a predictor of future drug problems. If during adolescence the brain is exposed to alcohol or other drugs, this may strengthen the neurons involved in addiction and reduce the likelihood of cortical development that would manage behaviour. In this sense, the brain is like a muscle; if you expose the developing brain to alcohol, you may be strengthening the alcoholic substrate of the brain.

With the transition from child to adult, adolescence is a stressful time. Adolescents have the aspirations of adulthood and the pressure of school and achievement – perhaps more so now than ever. Therefore, stress is a problem for children and adolescents and has been suggested to be a contributory factor for later mental health problems (see Chapter 20 and Romeo (2010) for a review). In a mouse model of **schizophrenia** (Jaaro-Peled et al., 2013), activation of **glucocorticoids** in adolescence by stressors impacted upon the adult regulation of dopaminergic neurons and subsequent behaviours (Niwa et al., 2013). Stress may alter the pathways of the brain that are being reorganized during adolescence.

If all goes to plan, we become adults with fully functional and fully developed brains. The question is – when is adulthood? There is no biological date; adulthood is a social construct. There are different ages at which we are considered adult (or old enough to understand our actions and their consequences) and the ages change, e.g. formal schooling in the UK is now required until the age of 18. In the UK you can purchase alcohol at the age of 18, whereas in the USA the age is 21. The age to become an MP was reduced from 21 to 18, but you could go to war for your country at the age of 16. The age of sexual consent in the UK is 16, in France it is 15. As you can see, there is a substantial amount of variability, but it can have important ramifications for one's life (see Box 3.4).

BOX 3.4: ADOLESCENT BRAINS AND PUNISHMENT: THE NEUROSCIENTIFIC INFLUENCE ON POLICY

Teenagers are not known for their self-control and thoughtfulness. They often do things that the adult fails to fully understand with their mature rational brains. As a consequence of their behaviour, teenagers can find themselves in trouble with the police and in front of the courts. Whilst never desirable, the consequences of being found guilty in the USA can be fatal. In the USA several states execute offenders of capital crimes (murder – homicide). Crucial in law is the notion that one is in control of one's actions. Those who are children are treated differently in law, as are those with pronounced learning difficulties and psychiatric conditions that impair their judgement.

Given the current knowledge on the brain, where does that leave the adolescent, whose brain is a work in progress and who has not fully matured yet?

In the case of *Roper v. Simmons* in which Christopher Simmons was found guilty of murder when he was 17 and tried when he was 18 and sentenced to death, the US Supreme Court overruled the decision to execute and stated that it was unconstitutional to use the death penalty for individuals under the age of 18 years.

> Beckman (2004) quotes law professor Steven Drizin as stating, 'Juveniles function very much like the mentally retarded. The biggest similarity is their cognitive deficit. [Teens] may be highly functioning, but that doesn't make them capable of making good decisions' (p.599).
>
> In a review of capital cases, it was noted that 'the Court drew on scientific studies of the adolescent brain in concluding that adolescents, by virtue of their inherent psychological and neurobiological immaturity, are not as responsible for their behaviour as adults' (Steinberg, 2013, p.513).
>
> In his review of science in justice, Steinberg (2013, p.516) quotes court papers:
>
> ... as one attorney stated during oral arguments in *Roper [v. Simmons]*, 'I'm not just talking about social science here, but the important neurobiological science'.
>
> This clearly indicates the importance of psychobiology... just in case you were in any doubt!

ADULT DEVELOPMENT

As we noted earlier, developmental psychology is often concerned with the child but, with an increasingly elderly population, old age has become a growth industry. Research reveals that the brain undergoes substantial changes not only prenatally but also during the first few years of life and again during the period of adolescence. But what of old age? Is it all downhill for the brain from the age of 25?

A great deal of research is being conducted to determine the effects of time on the brain. It is well supported by most people's real-life experience that cognitive functions change with age. Such age-related cognitive deficits need to be evaluated against neural changes in the healthy population. This will help us compare normality against pathology. If we know what is normal, we might have some chance of understanding what is abnormal. However, it is noteworthy that the chief scientist of a well-known drug company reported that their new drug was suitable for treating 'age-related memory deficits'. I mention this report because it highlights some of the ethical issues that surround neuroscience and ageing. The question is, do we treat normal ageing as pathological and therefore treatable?

From a more pragmatic perspective, understanding normal ageing will help us with understanding diseases such as Alzheimer's disease which has received considerable attention, with many changes in the brain being evident (see Chapter 24) (Wenk, 2003).

Early studies on postmortem brain slices have shown that ageing affects the cortical regions differently and that the main change is shrinkage rather than the loss of large neurons (Terry et al., 1987). Alongside that, there is an increase in the numbers of small neurons, resulting in constant neuronal density and diminished cortical volume, indicating that the small amount of neuronal loss with age 'is of much lesser magnitude than previously supposed' (Terry et al., 1987, p.530).

Research into the ageing process has proliferated in the past two decades as neuroimaging permits the evaluation of the changing brain in the living human. The increased resolution of imaging technologies means that understanding the ageing process in the brain is no longer restricted to postmortem samples. Generally, two types of methodologies are deployed when studying the ageing brain: cross-sectional and longitudinal. Cross-sectional methodologies provide a relatively quick answer to our questions regarding ageing as they evaluate groups of people at different ages. Thus, age differences rather than age changes can be measured. Longitudinal studies have the advantage of assessing individuals at many time points in their lifespan. Answers are slower to obtain but they do allow for individual differences to be determined. Another problem with the longitudinal study is maintaining co-operation of participants albeit for reasons beyond their control. However, despite the differing methodologies the data obtained regarding the ageing process are similar (Sowell et al., 2003a).

In a review of the age-related changes in the brain, Fjell and Walhovd (2010) report that there is a consistent reduction in grey matter with age. They also note that different areas of the brain change at different rates in the adult. White matter volume grows to about 40–50 years and after that volume reductions occur (Sowell et al., 2003a). However, there is a great deal of variability across the studies which gives rise to diverging data on the ageing brain (Fjell & Walhovd, 2010). Furthermore, understanding age-related changes in the brain is complicated by the fact that such changes progress in a non-linear manner (Fjell et al., 2013). In a review of 56 longitudinal MRI studies, Hedman et al. (2012) reported that from the age of 35, there is a reduction in volume of about 0.2% per year which accelerates to 0.5% per year at the age of 60. After 60, there is a steady volume loss of more than 0.5%.

Readers may be interested to note that those who spend more years in education show fewer signs of reduction in brain tissue (Arenaza-Urquijo et al., 2013; Coffey et al., 1999), and associated cognitive functions (Farfel et al., 2013) which may delay the onset of dementia (Wang et al., 2012). This effect of education is said to enhance the cognitive or brain reserve of the individual. One definition of **cognitive reserve** is where 'the brain is actively attempting to cope with or compensate for pathology' or 'the amount of damage that can be sustained before reaching a threshold for clinical expression' (Stern, 2002, p.449). Thus, your education is building up your brain/cognitive reserve that will be able to compensate, to some extent, for age-related changes in your declining years. So your course may have **neuroprotective** outcomes in the long term! However, a longitudinal study spanning an average 5–6 years did not find any evidence for a protective effect of education (Raz et al., 2005) but this is a relatively short time and raises the question of what really can be considered longitudinal.

Why do we age and what causes ageing? These questions can be looked at from the genetic, evolutionary and neural perspectives. Given that ageing is a universal phenomenon and does not fit with a Darwinian account of survival of the species, it is somewhat difficult to find a rationale for it. The challenge of answering such questions was taken up independently by Medawar (1952), Williams (2001) and Haldane (1941) who contributed three factors to the explanation (Flatt & Schmidt, 2009).

- That the world is dangerous and because of such dangers, organisms rarely grow old.
- The force of selection declines with age; older individuals are at greater risk of death than younger individuals.
- The decline in selection is unable to negate the effects of old age, e.g. genes that express themselves in old age continue in the human genome because they manifest themselves after reproduction (see Chapter 2).

In evolutionary terms, humans after their reproductive age are past their sell-by date (males and females). As humans, we have the longest life of any mammal (Finch, 1994). The main reason for this increase in life expectancy is thought to be the increase in brain size and the subsequent reduction in environmental risk which arises from increased cognitive abilities and social living (Kirkwood, 1997). Human brains have created environments that are safe and have developed medicine to treat our ailments, thus increase longevity.

With an evolutionary account of ageing, one might expect to find the genetic mechanisms responsible. As is often the case with genetics, this may be a search for a needle in a haystack. However, just because it is difficult to do does not mean that it should not be attempted. Definitive conclusions on the genetics of ageing are limited but chromosomes have been identified in human genome-wide scans that are linked to longevity (Beekman et al., 2013). The logical next step in the process is to look at the mechanisms that affect the ageing brain.

One of the main changes seen in the brain is a reduction in **neural plasticity** that subserves cognitive functions (Burke & Barnes, 2006). Neural plasticity is the subject of Chapter 13. There are many changes in the ageing brain, some of which are accentuated in dementia (Anderton, 2002). However, it is comparatively easy to correlate changes with age but it is somewhat harder to determine how these changes may cause ageing. There are two other notable functional changes which highlight the effect of reduced expression of mitochondrial genes: a reduction in the function of **mitochondria** is associated with a reduced lifespan and impairment of health (Bratic & Trifunovic, 2010; Trifunovic et al., 2004) and genes involved in the stress response alter mitochondria and ageing (Haigis & Yankner, 2010; Yankner et al., 2008).

It is noteworthy that a reduced **calorie** intake enhances the chances of survival and longevity (Bishop et al., 2010) and is beneficial to cognitive processes (Dal-Pan et al., 2011; Witte et al., 2009). A restricted diet 'augments stress resistance in many species by altering cellular metabolism and mobilizing protective stress responses' (Haigis & Yankner, 2010). With western populations growing in size and obesity at epidemic proportions, this may have a greater impact than expected. It has been suggested that genes that are strongly conserved (that is, remain essentially unchanged throughout evolution) are associated with age-dependent expression changes (Bishop et al., 2010). It is clear that we age and die and during ageing there is a cognitive decline; the mechanisms responsible are being unravelled but there is still a long way to go.

CRITICAL PERIODS

It is not surprising given the complexity of neurodevelopment that there might be certain times in the process that are more important for normal development (Figure 3.11). These critical or sensitive periods are often observed in response to toxic assault *in utero*. However, as we have seen with adolescent development, the critical periods extend beyond gestation and can be seen at certain times in the developing human.

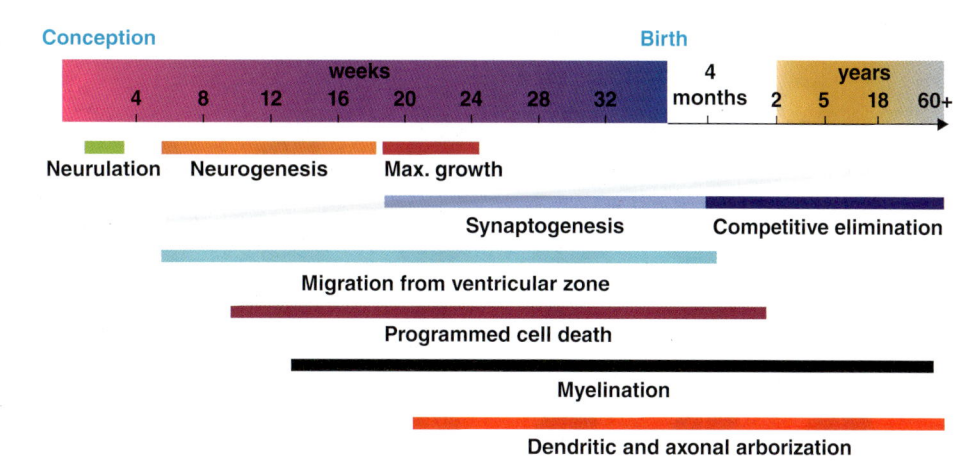

FIGURE 3.11 *The time course of critical events in human brain morphometric development. From conception to old age there are certain time periods during which neural events occur.*

According to Rice and Barone (2000), 'It is important to recognize that the nervous system continues to remodel and change not just early in development but throughout the entire period of development (and even during adulthood) in response to environmental influences as well as genetically programmed events' (p.519).

Thomas and Johnson (2008) note that sensitive periods end with reduced plasticity. Plasticity is the term given to neurons that are adaptable or mouldable – they have the qualities of plastic. Thomas and Johnson claim that there are three types of explanation for this.

1. Termination of plasticity due to maturation. This is where changes in the neurochemistry may increase the rate of pruning and hardwire remaining patterns of functional connectivity.

2. Self-termination of learning is where the very act of learning produces changes that reduce plasticity.

3. Stabilization of constraints on plasticity, which is when the onset of stability in a constraining factor is responsible for reducing plasticity rather than a reduction in plasticity itself. The example the authors use to illustrate this is the distance between an infant's eyes, which increases during development. This change in distance creates changes or instability in the information that is presented to the visual cortex. Once the distance between the eyes is stable, the inputs to the cortex also become stable. This plasticity may be hidden rather than absent.

The mechanisms of action underlying plasticity and learning during the sensitive periods have been linked to cognitive and behavioural processes (Knudsen, 2004). Three processes can change the architecture of the neuronal networks.

1. **Axonal elaboration** is when arborization takes place and learning increases dendritic innervation.

2. **Synaptic elimination** is the pruning of neurons in which non-selective synapses become highly selective through activation after the sensitive period.

3. **Synaptic consolidation** is a mechanism strengthening the synapses with **cell adhesion molecules (CAMs)** that can insert into synapses that have become functionally strong (Benson et al., 2000; Bukalo, 2008; Dityatev et al., 2008; Ehlers, 2003; Tanaka et al., 2000). CAMs are stable molecules that can cross-link pre- and postsynaptic membranes; they act like scaffolding around the synapse (Knudsen, 2004).

It has already been noted that stress affects the adolescent brain, but stress affects the brain throughout the lifespan; from conception to the end of the critical periods are particular points of vulnerability (Lupien et al., 2009). Much of the work on critical periods has been done on experimental animals and sensory systems. Typically, such experiments involve some sort of sensory deprivation in which the impact is measured later. Obviously, human data cannot be derived in such an experimental way but there are cases in which the consequences of deprivation and abuse can be measured (see Perry (2002) for review). A notable set of studies from Professor Sir Michael Rutter and colleagues have evaluated such occurrences in Romanian orphans (Castle et al., 1999; Rutter, 1998; Rutter et al., 1999).

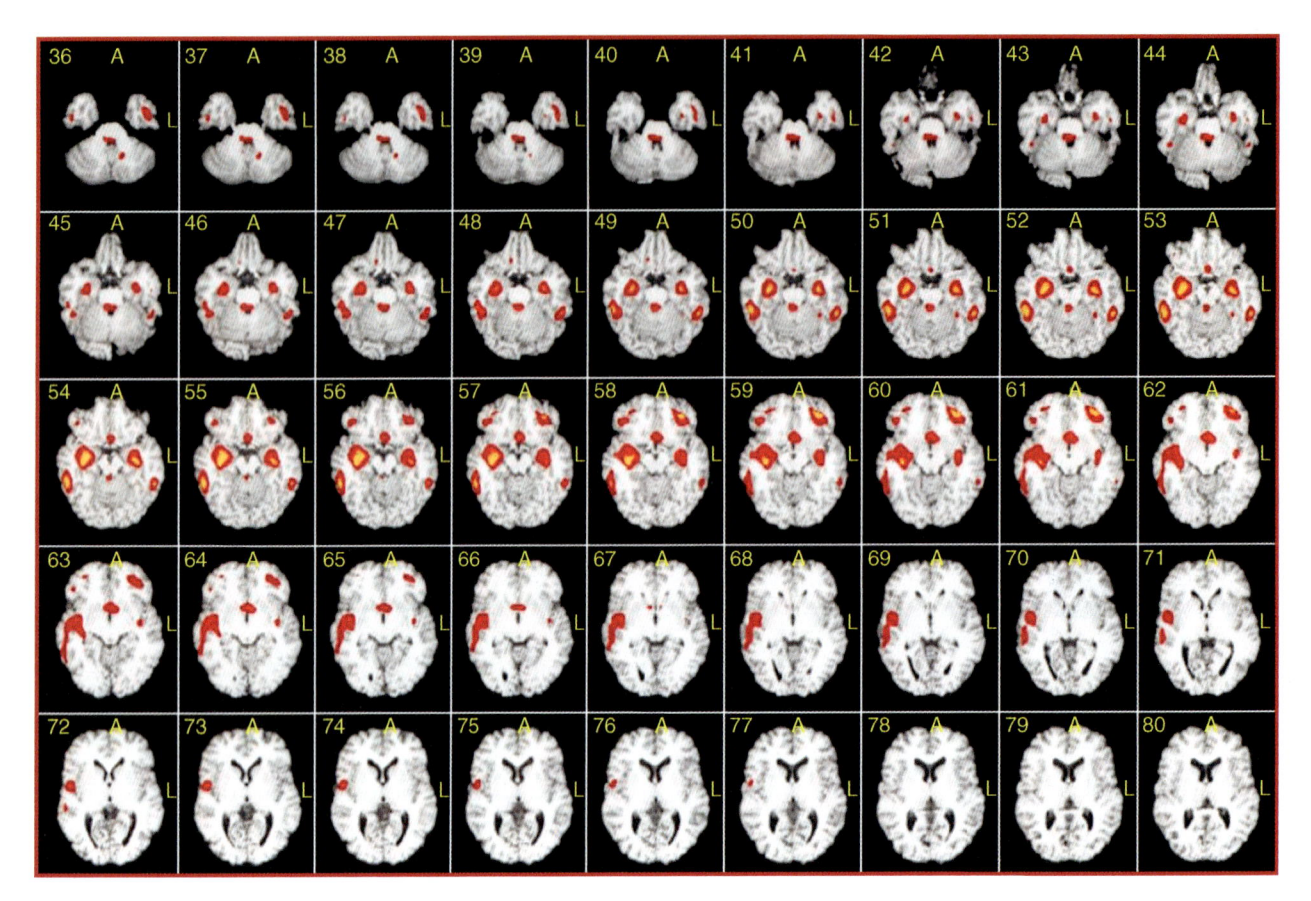

FIGURE 3.12 *Neuroimaging maps showing regions with lower glucose metabolism in the Romanian orphan group in comparison to the adult control group superimposed onto a representative MRI scan in standardized space. The left side of the image represents the right side of the brain. Regions in red and yellow represent significant (P , 0.05) decreases of activity in the Romanian orphan group in comparison to the adult controls.*
Source: Chugani, H. T., Behen, M. E., Muzik, O., Juhasz, C., Nagy, F. & Chugani, D. C. (2001). Local brain functional activity following early deprivation: a study of postinstitutionalized Romanian orphans. *Neuroimage, 14,* 1290-1301.

Just looking at the gross anatomy of the 3-year-old children revealed pronounced changes in their brains (Perry & Pollard, 1997). When looking at the brains of those coming from orphanages, there was significantly decreased activity in the orbital frontal cortex, the prefrontal cortex, temporal cortex and brainstem (Chugani et al., 2001, see Figure 3.12). Structurally there were reductions of cortical thickness (McLaughlin et al., 2014). Furthermore, children who experienced socio-emotional deprivation had structural changes in the left **uncinate fasciculus** that connects temporal and frontal structures that partly may underlie the cognitive, socioemotional and behavioural difficulties seen in these children (Eluvathingal et al., 2006). Interestingly not all regions of the brain showed reductions. Despite reductions in grey and white matter, the amygdala was reported to be larger in comparison to the rest of the brain in children coming from institutional care (Mehta et al., 2009; Tottenham et al., 2010). In functional terms, the amygdala was more active in such children when they were required to perform in a emotional processing experiment (Tottenham et al., 2011). The good news is that there can be some recovery, as those children who went to an improved environment showed increased white matter (Sheridan et al., 2012).

Teratology

The continual development of the brain, which includes growth and death of brain cells at critical periods, means that neural structures are more vulnerable to toxicological or environmental insult – a problem more acute in males than females (Kraemer, 2000). **Teratology** is the study of abnormal development and often concerns itself with the action of teratogens. Teratogens are often thought to be compounds such as drugs, but a teratogen can be more than just a drug; it could be a virus or radiation, for example. The term 'teratogen' has been avoided in a review by Obican and Scialli (2011) in favour of the phrase 'teratogenic exposure' because they consider that time of exposure and level of exposure are important features that are not considered in the all-or-none phrase 'teratogen'. What they mean by teratogenic exposure is that there is an increased risk of abnormal development.

The most notable teratogen that has received widespread media attention is **thalidomide**. Thalidomide was a drug used in the 1950s and 1960s to treat morning sickness in pregnancy. Morning sickness is common in early pregnancy and usually stops by the second **trimester**. Although referred to as morning sickness, it isn't just restricted to the morning and therefore can be a very unpleasant experience for the expectant mother. Thalidomide was therefore given during the first trimester – a key critical period. The consequences of thalidomide were that it dramatically affected the development of the limbs (Kim & Scialli, 2011).

There are many toxins that can affect the foetus physically, but there are also functional/psychological consequences. The consumption of alcohol during pregnancy is not advisable as it can lead to malformation of the child's brain. This is called foetal alcohol syndrome (FAS) (see Box 3.5).

BOX 3.5: FOETAL ALCOHOL SYNDROME

Maternal consumption of large amounts of alcohol during pregnancy can give rise to pronounced physical and psychological changes in the child (Lemione et al., 1968). Effects of alcohol on the unborn foetus exist along a continuum with FAS at one extreme. There are three main characteristics of FAS: facial abnormalities, growth impairment and mental retardation (Hanson et al., 1976; Jones & Smith, 1973).

In a review of the cognitive impact of FAS, Davis et al. (2013) highlight the following:

- impaired intellectual functioning;
- impaired attention;
- impaired executive functioning;
- impaired reasoning;
- impaired social cognition; and
- impaired learning and memory.

A longitudinal study of heavy drinking during pregnancy has shown that the brain's development and maturation are affected by alcohol (Lebel et al., 2012). The brains of those with FAS look different (see Figure 3.5.1). Early postmortem studies have generally been confirmed by using more recent neuroimaging techniques. There are now numerous studies looking at the effects of exposure to large quantities of alcohol. Imaging studies indicate a decrease in the size of the brain (Roebuck et al., 1998). MRI studies show that the basal ganglia are reduced in volume in children with FAS (Mattson et al., 1994, 1996). The **corpus callosum** was found to have abnormalities ranging from thinning to complete absence (Roebuck et al., 1998; Sowell, Mattson et al., 2001; Yang et al., 2012). The volume of the **cerebellum** was reduced (Archibald et al., 2001). These findings partially replicate previous reports of reduced cerebellar size in FAS and children exposed to alcohol prenatally (Sowell et al., 1996). Furthermore, an MRI study reported asymmetries in the **hippocampus**, with the left temporal lobe smaller than the right (Riikonen et al., 1999).

Sowell and colleagues (Sowell, Mattson et al., 2001; Sowell et al., 2002; Sowell, Johnson et al., 2008; Sowell, Mattson et al., 2008) have shown that individuals exposed to alcohol have relatively more grey matter and less white matter in the temporal and **parietal lobes** and greater cortical thickness over large areas of lateral temporal, parietal, frontal and **occipital lobes**.

How does alcohol do this? Alcohol readily crosses the placental barrier and interacts with the foetus. Alcohol has many effects on the brain. It acts on glutamate and GABAergic transmitter systems. The mechanisms in the developing brain include (Alfonso-Loeches & Guerri, 2011):

- alterations in gene expression and regulation;
- interference with mitosis and growth;
- disturbances in the molecules that mediate cell–cell interactions;
- dysregulation of cell survival; and
- derangements in glial proliferation, differentiation and functioning.

The question one might ask is, how much alcohol is dangerous? Given that FAS is now referred to as foetal alcohol *spectrum* disorder (FASD), the answer will not be easy to determine. Alcohol will have effects on the brain at all doses. There are no solid definitions of mild, moderate or heavy drinkers. Furthermore, the unit system used in the UK is not based on solid scientific data, but rather is a political and policy-driven ideology.

The answer to the question of how much alcohol can be safely consumed is easy – none.

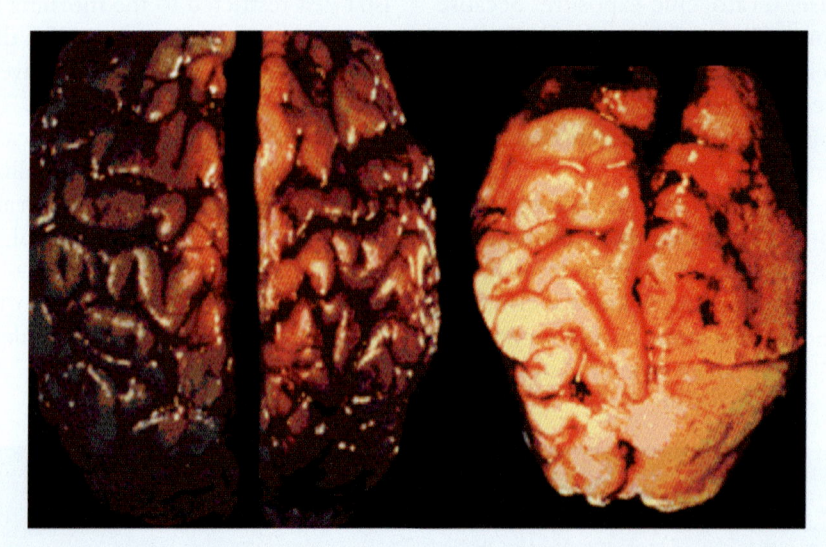

FIGURE 3.5.1 *Foetal alcohol syndrome. The left-hand brain is from the normal child which is distinctly different in structure from the right-hand brain from a child born with FAS (ignore the colour of the brains).*
Source: Courtesy of Prof Sterling K. Clarren.

SUMMARY

The brain is an amazingly plastic organ that develops and changes throughout life. Understanding brain development and its functional consequences is really only just beginning. New technologies are permitting us to look at both normal and abnormal development in humans, even prenatally (Miller et al., 2014).

LEARNING OUTCOME QUESTIONS

You should be able to answer the following questions:
- Describe how the CNS develops after conception.
- Neural development is sensitive at specific developmental stages. Discuss.
- How can neural development be damaged?

FURTHER READING

Martin, R. P., & Dombrowski, S. C. (2008). *Prenatal exposures: Psychological and educational consequences for children.* New York: Springer.
Miller, M. W. (2006). *Brain development: Normal process and the effects of alcohol and nicotine.* New York: Oxford University Press.
Moore, K. L., Persaud, T. V. N., & Torchia, M. G. (2012). *The developing human: Clinically oriented embryology.* Philadelphia, PA: Saunders.
Rice, D., & Barone, S. Jr. (2000). Critical periods of vulnerability for the developing nervous system: evidence from humans and animal models. *Environmental Health Perspectives, 108*(Suppl 3), 511–533.
Romer, D., & Walker, E. F. (2007). *Adolescent psychopathology and the developing brain: Integrating brain and prevention science.* New York: Oxford University Press.
Stiles, J., & Jernigan, T. L. (2010). The basics of brain development. *Neuropsychology Review, 20*(4), 327–348. doi: 10.1007/s11065-010-9148-4
Striedter, G. F. (2005). *Principles of brain evolution.* Sunderland, MA: Sinauer Associates.

MIND MAP

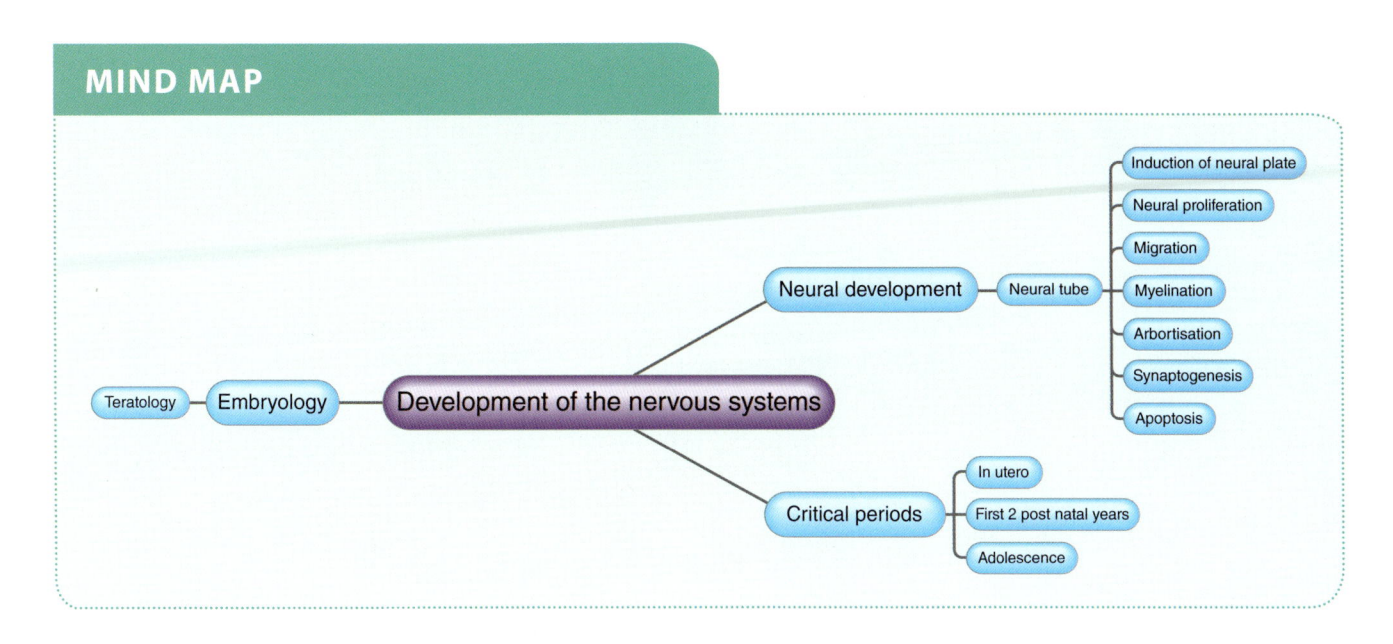

Development of the nervous systems

- Embryology
  - Teratology
- Neural development
  - Neural tube
    - Induction of neural plate
    - Neural proliferation
    - Migration
    - Myelination
    - Arbortisation
    - Synaptogenesis
    - Apoptosis
- Critical periods
  - In utero
  - First 2 post natal years
  - Adolescence

4 The Neuron, The Endocrine System and Communication

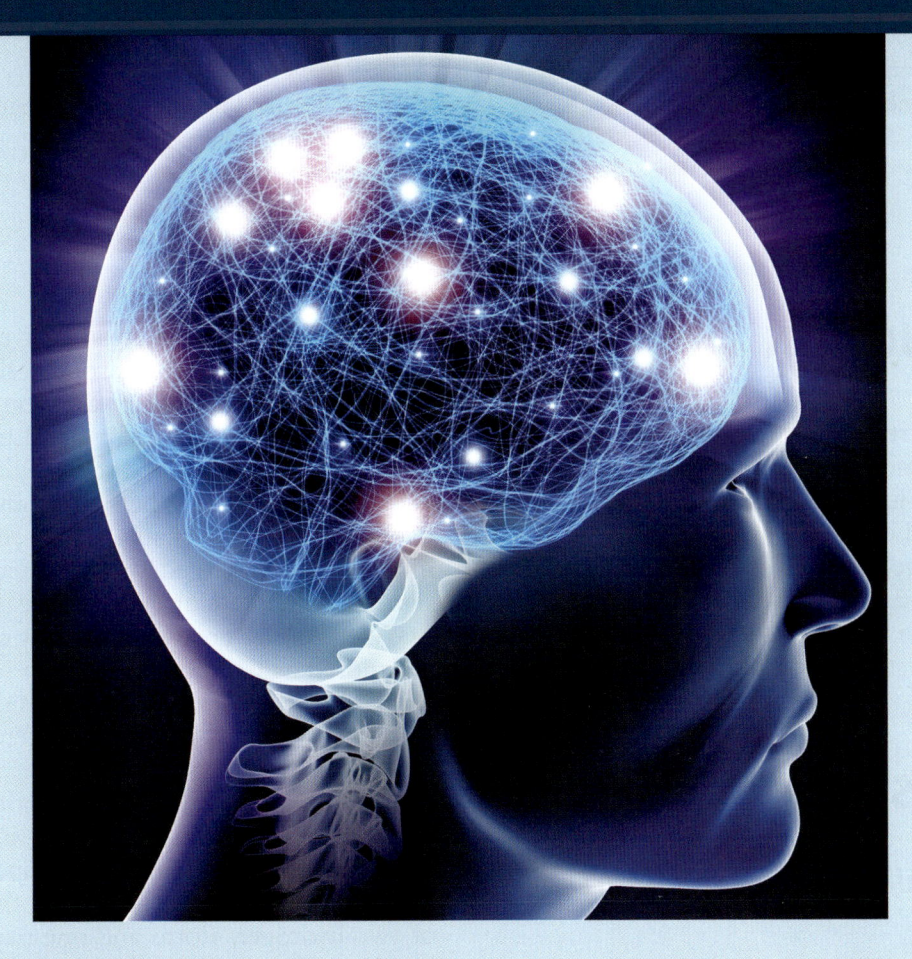

ANATOMY OF THE CHAPTER

This chapter will highlight the following.

- The architecture and apparatus of the neuron.
- Electrical signalling within the neuron.
- Synaptic communication between neurons.
- Non-synaptic communication between neurons.
- Long-range communication of hormones.

INTRODUCTION 84

NEURONS 84

SUPPORT CELLS 89

TYPES OF NEURONS 90

SIGNALLING AND COMMUNICATION WITHIN THE NEURON 90

SIGNALLING AND COMMUNICATION BETWEEN NEURONS: SYNAPTIC TRANSMISSION 99

SIGNALLING AND COMMUNICATION BETWEEN NEURONS: GAP JUNCTIONS 108

ENDOCRINOLOGY: STUDYING LONG-DISTANCE COMMUNICATION 109

SUMMARY 114

LEARNING OUTCOMES

1. To understand the composition of neurons.
2. To understand how impulses are transmitted within the neuron.
3. To understand how neurons communicate with each other.
4. To understand the nature of endocrines system of communication.

INTRODUCTION

The nervous system, as described in Chapter 5, is made up of numerous specialized cells that all contribute to behaviour. The key element of the nervous systems is the nerve – or, to be more accurate, the neuron. If we consider DNA to be the blueprint or architectural drawing, then neurons and the supporting cells are the bricks and mortar (or more likely today, the steels and glass).

NEURONS

Inside the Cell: Atoms at the Heart of Life

Within the cell are very small particles. However, despite their size their importance is immeasurable. Alterations in these cells affect behaviour and normal functioning. The apparatus within a cell makes proteins from the DNA code. What type of cell it is depends upon the proteins. Proteins are made of molecules and molecules are made of **atoms**.

About 10 elements, such as hydrogen, carbon, oxygen, sodium and potassium, make up most of the cell (see Figure 4.1). Oxygen, carbon and hydrogen are the main elements of the cell's composition. There are two particularly important elements, sodium (NA^+) and potassium (K^+), involved in the communication of an impulse within the neuron. A full account of all the elements is in the periodic table together with their atomic weights.

The elements are made up of atoms. An atom is a **nucleus** containing both **neutrons** and **protons**. Neutrons are neutrally charged particles, e.g. neither positively nor *negatively charged*, and protons are *positively charged* atoms. Atoms have particles called **electrons**, which orbit around them. Electrons are negatively charged. If an atom deviates from an equal number of positive and negative charges then it can be considered to be either positively or negatively charged. When an atom is either negatively or positively charged, it is referred to as an **ion**. Positively charged ions are denoted with a plus sign, such as potassium K^+. If there is the removal of two electrons to create a positively charged ion, this is denoted as $Ca2^+$ or Ca^{++}. If an ion is negatively charged, e.g. chlorine which takes on an additional electron above and beyond the normal balance, this is denoted as follows: Cl^-.

A molecule is created when atoms are bound together and make up a substance, e.g. water, hydrogen or oxygen. Looking at the composition of a molecule, e.g. water, H_2O, this tells us that it is made up of two hydrogen atoms and one oxygen atom. The human body contains a large percentage of water. The hydrogen atoms of the water molecule can also bind together: the hydrogen bond. This hydrogen bond leads to features of water such as strong cohesion, i.e. we see water as a substance such as a drop. This is all rather complicated physics but serves to tell us about the very basic elements of the nervous system and how electrical charges are derived.

Neurons: Structure and Function

Neurons are cells that communicate with each other using electrochemical signals. Neurons come in different shapes and sizes, but all share a similar anatomy (Figure 4.2). Surrounding the cell is the **cell membrane** which consists of two **lipids** (fat molecules) and phosphorus heads, making up a phospholipid. The phosphorus head is attracted to water whereas the lipid tails are not, so the

(a)

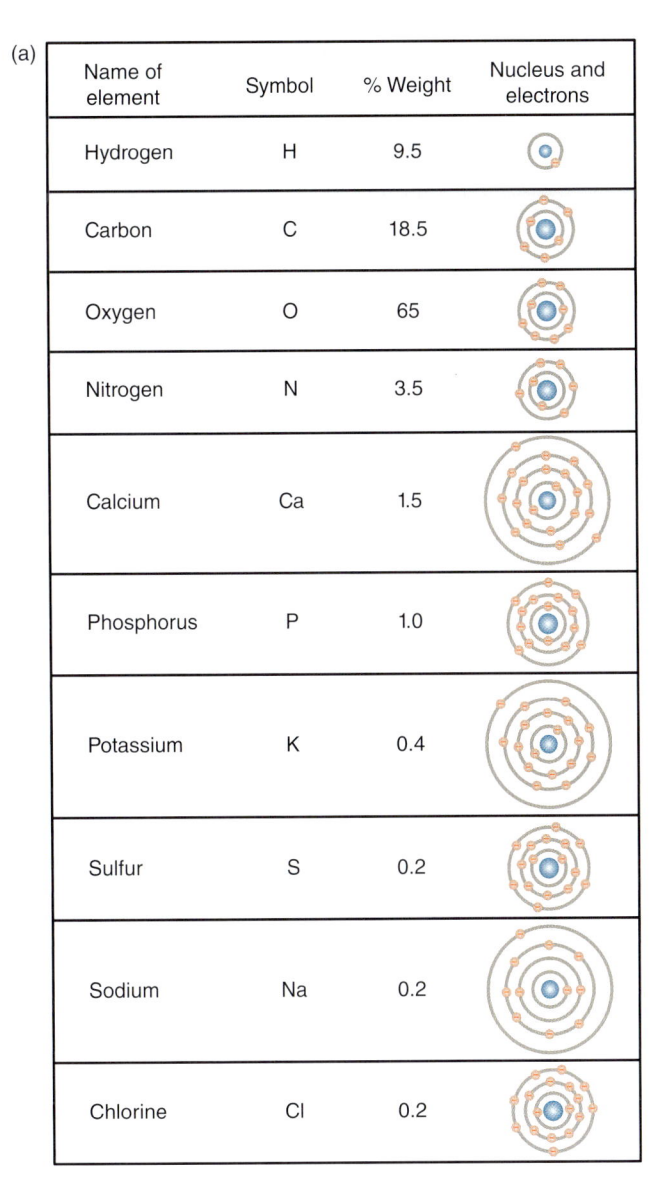

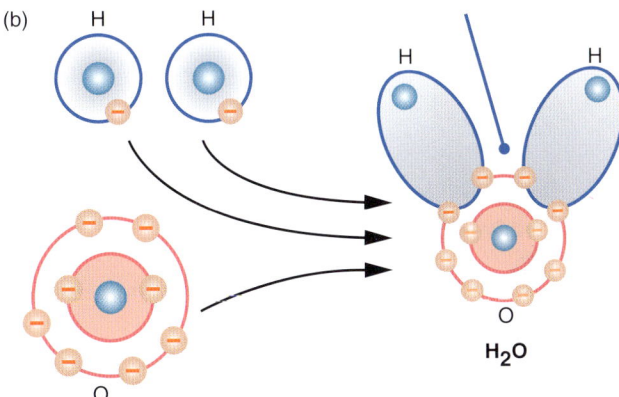

Name of element	Symbol	% Weight	Nucleus and electrons
Hydrogen	H	9.5	
Carbon	C	18.5	
Oxygen	O	65	
Nitrogen	N	3.5	
Calcium	Ca	1.5	
Phosphorus	P	1.0	
Potassium	K	0.4	
Sulfur	S	0.2	
Sodium	Na	0.2	
Chlorine	Cl	0.2	

FIGURE 4.1 *The atomic structure of the brain. (a) Atoms are made up of neutrons and protons surrounded by electrons. The organization of protons and electrons determines the atomic structure of the common elements of the brain. (b) The atomic structure of water. Hydrogen and oxygen are negatively and positively charged respectively, giving their mutual attraction.*

membrane looks like tadpoles swimming away from each other. The **phospholipid layers** have protein channels in them that allow certain molecules to pass from inside the cell (**intracellular**) to outside the cell (**extracellular**), or vice versa. There are also receptor proteins that receive information. The importance of both types of proteins will become clear later. Suffice to say that the function of the cell membrane is to separate the internal components of the cell world from the immediate external environment of the cell (this is the intracellular and extracellular environment).

Neurons are the simplest unit of the nervous system and consist of three components: the **soma**, the **axon** and the **dendrites** (see Figure 4.2). The soma or cell body contains the **nucleus** and mitochondria. Groups of neuronal cell bodies are called nuclei or a nucleus. This nucleus is not to be confused with the other nucleus that contains the genetic code. Neurons, like all other cells, are **eukaryote cells,** because they possess a clearly defined nucleus. The nucleus of the cell contains all the genetic information that has been transmitted from parents to offspring (see Chapter 2). One of the purposes of the genetic code is to provide instruction for the creation of proteins from a series of amino acids.

Around the nucleus is the **endoplasmic reticulum** comprising folded layers of membrane where protein manufacturing takes place. The endoplasmic reticulum is covered with ribosomes that are involved in protein assembly (see Chapter 2).

The **Golgi apparatus** is another part of the protein manufacturing and utilization machinery within the cell. Golgi bodies are membrane-like structures that package some of the cell's protein molecules for transport. The packaging process involves wrapping proteins with a membrane and providing them with information somewhat like an address. They are then attached to motor molecules that transport them along the microtubules to their eventual destination (perhaps at the end of the cell to provide structure and communication molecules, e.g. **neurotransmitters**).

Mitochondria provide the energy that the cell needs by generating large quantities of energy in the chemical form of **adenosine triphosphate (ATP)** (Ly & Verstreken, 2006; Nicholls & Ferguson, 1992). ATP are energy-carrying molecules and capture the chemical energy obtained from the breakdown of food molecules and use it to fuel other cellular processes such as metabolic activity, transporting required substances across membranes and mechanical work, e.g. moving muscles. ATP is mobilized from storage and delivers energy to places within the cell where energy is required (see Nicholls & Budd (2000) for review). Mitochondria have their own genetic sequence and **mitochondrial DNA** contains 37 genes, 13 of which are used for ATP. Mitochondrial DNA is thought to be the oldest of our evolutionary genetic pathways as it is seen in simple molecules such as bacteria. Mitochondrial DNA is usually inherited from the mother (Schon et al., 2012). Mitochondria are also involved in Ca^{2+} regulation and therefore can affect synaptic signalling (Ly & Verstreken, 2006). There are a number of mitochondrial diseases such as myoclonic epilepsy, Kearns–Sayre syndrome, which affects the eyes, and some cancers (DiMauro, 2004) and psychiatric disorders (Manji et al., 2012) (see Box 4.1).

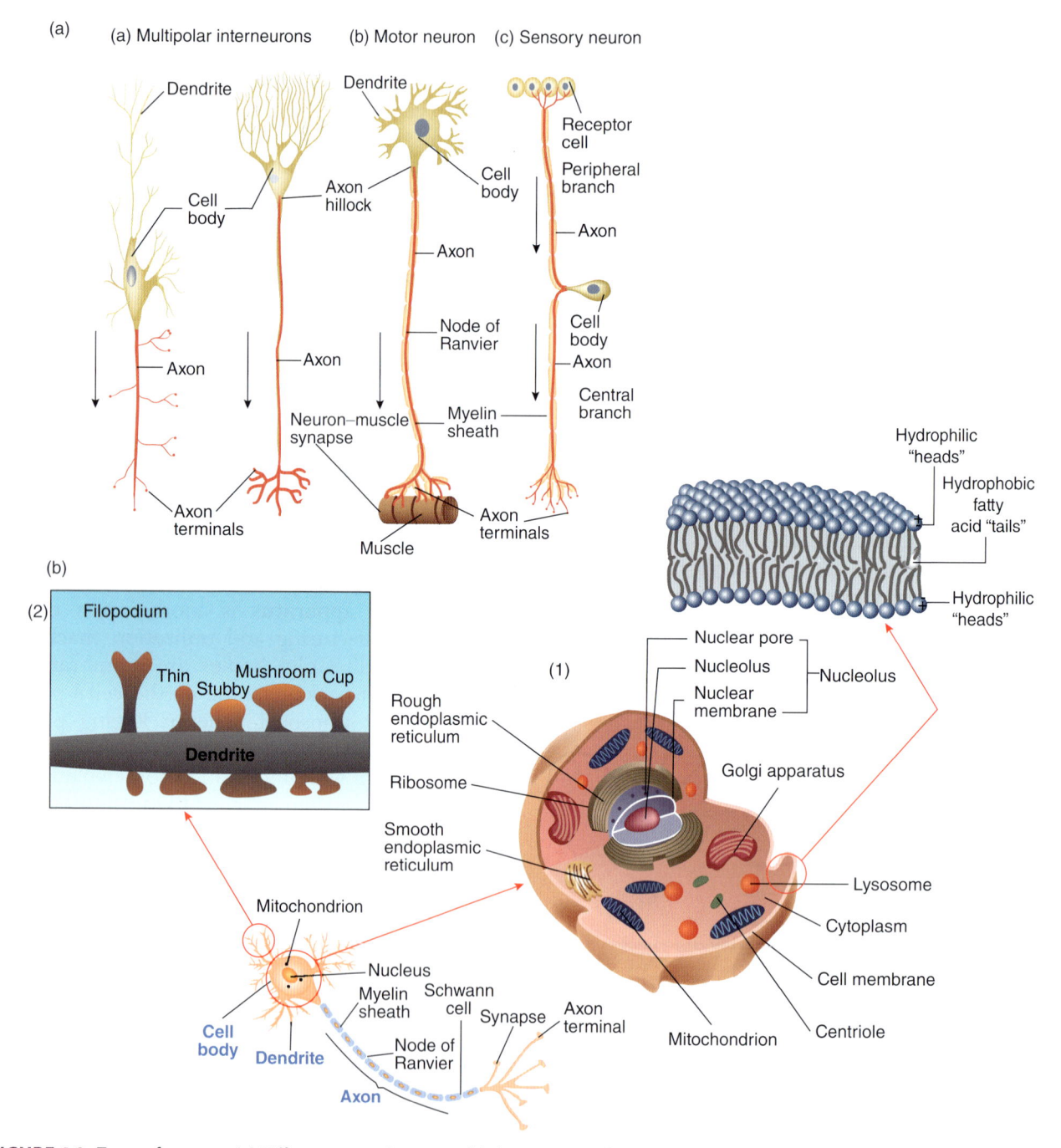

FIGURE 4.2 *Types of neurons. (a) Different types of neurons. (b) The structure of a typical neuron. 1. The cell body with nucleus, mitochondria and endoplasmic reticulum. 2. Dendrites.*

BOX 4.1: MITOCHONDRIA, DISEASE AND AGEING

Mitochondria are crucial for providing the cell's energy but also have a role in apoptosis (cell death). Clearly a defect in mitochondria would have a pronounced effect on any cell. This is the case for a number of mitochondrial disorders (MCDs), which can have devastating effects.

Mitochondrial disorders (MCDs) include (Finsterer, 2006):

- mitochondrial encephalomyopathy, lactic acidosis and stroke-like episode syndrome (MELAS) which results from several genetic mutations (Hilton, 1995). Symptoms include: muscle weakness and pain, recurrent headaches, loss of appetite, vomiting, seizures, stroke-like episodes which result in changes in consciousness, vision and possible brain damage leading to problems with movement and cognitive decline;
- Friedreich's ataxia, which is an autosomal recessive degenerative disorder caused by a GAA triplet expansion in the *FRDA* (9q13) with a deficit in ATP production (Lodi et al., 1999). Symptoms include: onset before 25 years of age, progressive gait and limb ataxia, absence of deep tendon reflexes, extensor plantar responses, and loss of position and vibration sense in the lower limbs;
- Kearns–Sayre syndrome, which is caused by mtDNA deletions removing 12 mitochondrial genes. Whilst this is a genetic disease, it is not inherited (Zeviani et al., 1988). Symptoms include: ophthalmoplegia (weakness/paralysis of the eye muscles impairing ocular movement), pigmentary retinopathy (loss of vision and changes in pigment), ataxia, high levels of protein in the **cerebrospinal fluid (CSF)**; and
- Leigh syndrome, which is a genetic disorder involving mutation of mtDNA (Rahman et al., 1996). Within the brain there are lesions in the basal ganglia, cerebellum and brainstem. There is also demyelination. Symptoms include: onset in infancy, hypotonia, dystonia and ataxia, peripheral neuropathy, optic atrophy.

In addition to the MCDs, a number of other diseases have now been associated with mitochondrial abnormalities. Changes in mitochondrial DNA (mtDNA) are the main reason for malfunctioning mitochondria, but also to a lesser extent changes in the nuclear DNA (Schapira, 2012). The inheritance pattern of mtDNA is down the maternal line. Defective mitochondria can reduce ATP synthesis which will 'reduce membrane potential and the threshold for apoptotic cell death' (Schapira, 2012). Abnormalities in mitochondrial genes have been demonstrated in **Parkinson's disease, Alzheimer's disease** (Schapira, 2008) and even depression (Gardner & Boles, 2011). With the discovery that mitochondria may be dysfunctional in neurodegenerative diseases and psychological disorders, there is a potential for new avenues of treatment with or without traditional interventions.

Whilst neurodegenerative diseases such as Parkinson's show clear abnormalities in neural and mitochondrial functioning, ageing can also be seen as a degenerative process. The most common form of cell death in neurodegeneration is through the mitochondrial apoptotic pathway (DiMauro & Schon, 2008).

According to Lee and Wei (2012):

> Aging is a degenerative process that is characterized by a time-dependent decline in physiological function and an increase in the chance of disease and death. The deleterious changes with time occur in all organisms that are believed to be associated with the metabolic activity and are influenced by genetic and environmental factors.

The role of mitochondria in ageing is thought to be because of a progressive accumulation of somatic mutations in mtDNA throughout the lifespan, which causes a decline in mitochondrial function. Furthermore, it has been said that 'decreasing mitochondrial reserves and function as documented in aged human and mouse tissues . . . might also explain the cumulative and precipitative nature of ageing symptoms observed late in life' (Sahin & Depinho, 2010). The brain has a notable loss of mitochondrial action (Loerch et al., 2008) which may be related to cognitive deficits seen with ageing (Bishop et al., 2010).

Not only is there a potential to treat disease and disorder, there is also the potential to treat the normal process of ageing and what one pharmaceutical executive referred to as treating age-related cognitive impairments. Clearly, ageing is a normal process but perhaps some members of the pharmaceutical industry would rather see it as a pathological process for which a new market could be developed. Obviously there is a demand for such medication as there is already a large industry trying to minimize the physical impact of ageing – cosmetics and cosmetic surgery. Perhaps in the near future we will see demands to reduce the cognitive impact of ageing.

PSYCHOBIOLOGY

If mitochondria are the energy-producing power stations, then energy leads to waste products. **Lysosomes** are vesicular structures that contain **enzymes** which can break down and metabolize many biomolecules. Lysosomes degrade material taken up from outside the cell and digest obsolete components of the cell itself, thus providing a homeostatic balance in the cell (Luzio et al., 2007).

The purpose of the neuron is to receive and send information from and to other neurons. The dendrites are the main recipients of information from other neurons. The dendrites can be seen as the branches extending from the cell body, reaching deep into the networks of the brain to receive incoming information. The branching of dendrites is referred to as **arborization**. Dendrites can either be long or short and some contain spines which provide sites of contact with other neurons (Nimchinsky et al., 2002) (Figure 4.2). The dendrites pass on their messages to the axon hillock. The communication from the dendrites to the cell body is electrical in nature and the result of changes in the ionic concentration of positive and negative charges on either side of the cell membrane (see later in this chapter).

Incoming information from the dendrites is integrated at an area known as the **axon hillock** (see Bender & Trussell (2012) for review). Extending from the axon hillock is the axon and an electrical message is passed down the axon to the terminal buttons. The axon is like a wire that carries electricity (see Debanne et al. (2011) for review). Generally, neurons only have one axon but it can divide into several branches called axon collaterals, which permit a large mosaic of communication of one neuron with many others. At the end of the axon is the **presynaptic terminal**. This is the endpoint; from here communication with another neuron tends to be chemical in nature, traversing the synapse. The axon not only sends messages to the presynaptic terminal, but it also transports various materials to the terminal region, e.g. neurotransmitter substances. The axon also transports material from the presynaptic terminal region to the cell body, e.g. for recycling. The axonal transport of material is slow in comparison to the transmission of the neural information.

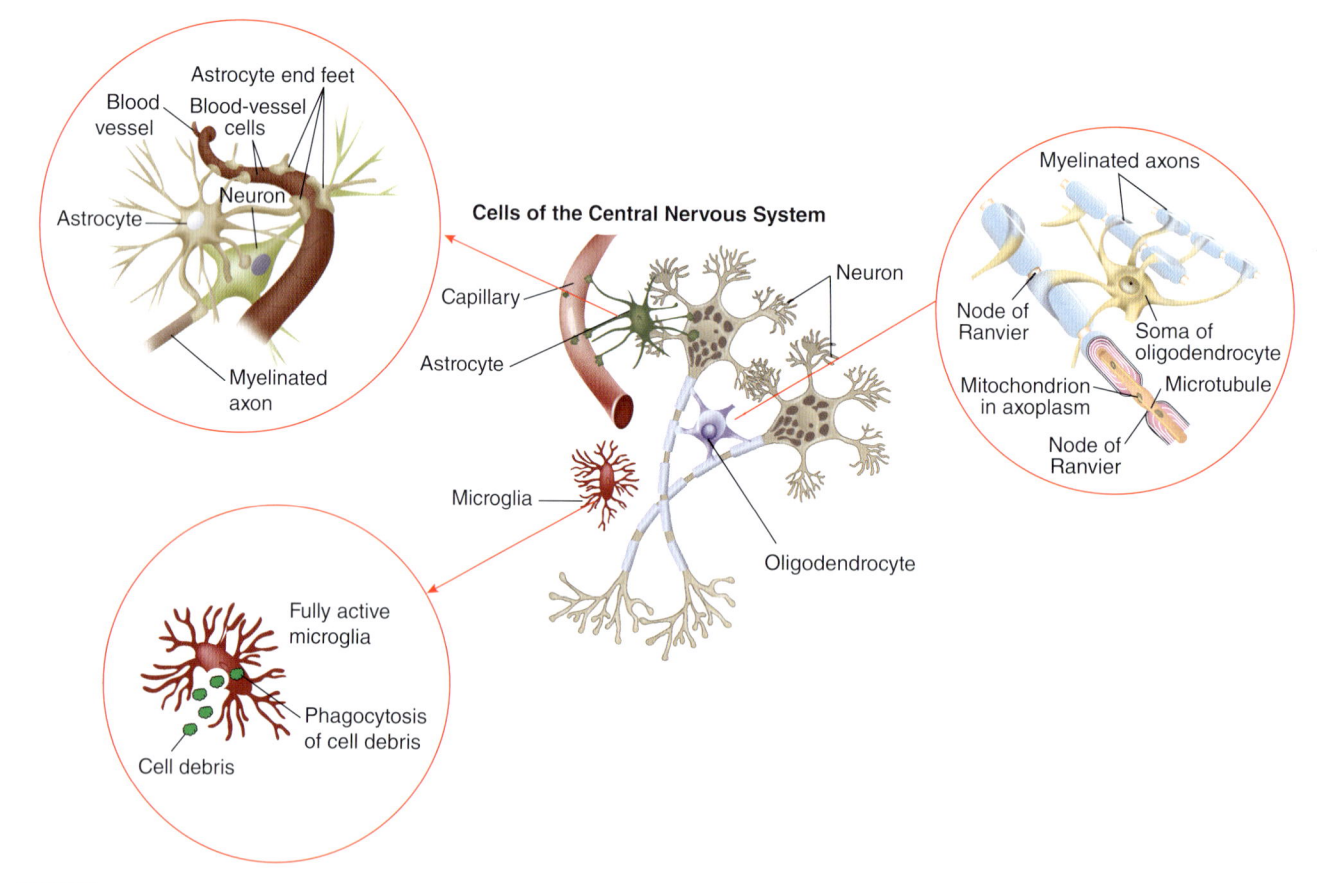

FIGURE 4.3 *Astrocytes, microglia and oligodendrocytes.*

SUPPORT CELLS

Glial Cells

The neurons are the main actors in the nervous system but they require support. Satellite cells in the peripheral nervous system and **glial cells** in the central nervous system provide this. As steel girders provide support and structure in a building, support cells provide the infrastructure to hold together and maintain the integrity of the complex matrix of neural circuits. Radial glial cells are progenitor cells that manage the development of the CNS (Barry et al., 2014).

Whilst it was traditionally considered that glial cells were without communicative function, that position is now no longer upheld (Araque & Navarrete, 2010). Glial cells communicate not only with each other but also with neurons. There are five main types of glial cells:

- astrocytes
- microglia
- ependymal cells
- oligodendrocytes
- Schwann cells (in the PNS).

Astrocytes are multifunctioning cells (Ransom et al., 2003). They control the extracellular environment of the neuron and have contact with capillaries, cerebrospinal fluid and the neurons themselves. Astrocytes therefore maintain neuronal **homeostasis**, which is necessary because neurons are sensitive to extracellular changes in ions and neurotransmitters. The brain cannot expand too much and therefore needs to control water expansion via osmotic processes. Astrocytes have extensive projections which allow for movement of nutrients between blood vessels and neurons (Allaman et al., 2011). The astrocytes form the densely packed protective layer between blood vessels and the brain called the **blood–brain barrier**. They also allow the capillaries to dilate at times when there is an increased need for energy by the neurons; thus they allow more oxygen- and glucose-carrying blood to get through. Astrocytes are involved in the uptake and release of transmitters, modulate synaptic transmission and are involved in repair of the nervous system (Clarke & Barres, 2013).

Microglia are, as the name suggests, small. They originate in the mesoderm and are converted from monocytes originating in the bone marrow during embryological development and then are transformed into microglial cells once in the nervous system. They are considerably important after injury. Microglia are thought to be in constant activity checking on their immediate environment for injury or debris indicative of cellular damage (Eric Thomas, 1992). They work by releasing inflammatory agents and help clear up foreign or dead material (Aloisi, 2001). Because they deal with cell damage, they have also been indicated in pain in which microglial cells in the spinal cord are activated when there has been nerve damage (see Chapter 10) (Tsuda et al., 2005).

Ependymal cells produce and secrete cerebrospinal fluid. They form the epithelial lining of the fluid-filled cerebral ventricles (see Chapter 5). CSF provides protection to the brain from physical movement/shock and is a substrate via which waste products can be eliminated (Bruni, 1998). The ependymal cells also have hair-like structures called cilia which beat in a co-ordinated pattern, influencing the direction of flow of CSF, bringing nutrients to neurons and filtering out potentially harmful molecules (Del Bigio, 2010).

Oligodendrocytes and **Schwann cells** can be taken together as they serve the same function of providing a myelin sheath around the axon; however, they do this in the CNS and the PNS respectively. Whilst they have the same job, they perform it differently. Schwann cells wrap around only one axon whereas oligodendrocytes can provide a myelin sheath for several axons (Baumann & Pham-Dinh, 2001; Bruska & Wozniak, 1999). Schwann cells also aid the regrowth of axons in the PNS (Bunge, 1993).

The myelin sheath is like the insulating wrapper on the axon (Baumann & Pham-Dinh, 2001). The purpose of the myelin sheath is to reduce the loss of electrical current to the extracellular fluid, although there have been suggestions that myelin serves additional functions such as providing energy (Morelli et al., 2011; Yamazaki et al., 2010). The myelin sheath is made of many layers of cell membrane. These layers occur via the cell wrapping itself a number of times; think of wrapping insulating tape around a wire. Myelin is whitish in colour and the term 'white matter' refers to regions that are high in myelinated neurons. Conversely, grey matter consists of cell bodies and dendrites where there is no myelin. Myelination of the neurons starts *in utero* and continues for some time after birth (see Chapter 3).

The myelin sheath is not a continuous, unbroken layer of insulation; it is interrupted by gaps called **nodes of Ranvier**. The nodes of Ranvier are not evenly distributed along the axon; there may be long stretches of unmyelinated axon (Tomassy et al., 2014). Nodes of Ranvier exist because each glial cell lies along the course of the axon and therefore only provides insulation on a segmental basis. At the node of Ranvier, there is obviously no insulation – no myelin. It is at this point that ionic exchange can occur across the cell membrane of the axon. The nodes of Ranvier act as repeaters in the neural circuitry. This ionic exchange is fundamentally important to neural communication (see below). Not all axons are myelinated. Those that do not have myelin are much slower in their rate of communication. Myelin is particularly prominent in the pathogenesis of **multiple sclerosis** (Box 4.2).

TYPES OF NEURONS

Most neurons are multipolar which means they have many dendrites converging on the cell body and being integrated at the axon hillock before being transmitted down the axon to the presynaptic terminal region. There are also **bipolar neurons** that have a single dendrite connected to the cell body and a single axon (see Chapter 10 for numerous bipolar neurons within the sensory systems). **Unipolar neurons** or monopolar neurons are composed of dendrites converging into an axon-like structure before connecting with the cell body and then sending information down the axon to the presynaptic terminal.

Neurons can be divided further according to their functional properties. Some will be motor neurons which are involved in sending out neural information to effect behaviour; this will occur along **efferent pathways** (efferent = effector, i.e. they produce an effect). Sensory information comes along the sensory neurons or **afferent pathways**. Thus the brain has input and output although it is far more complicated than that! However, not all neurons are projecting neurons such as the motor and sensory neurons. In the extensive neuronal networks of the brain, most of the neurons are interneurons in that they pass information from one neuron to another (Figure 4.4). Projection neurons travel longer distances whereas interneurons are far smaller and have a shorter distance to communicate.

The different shapes the neurons take are due to cytoskeletal specialization. Within the cell bodies and axons and dendrites are thread-like structures called **neurofilaments** which collectively make up the cytoskeleton (the cell's skeleton) (Yuan et al., 2012). The neurofilaments are also important in axonal transport of material around the neurons (Yuan et al., 2012).

With the structure and some of the functions of the neuron and the immediately surrounding cells accounted for, it is now time to address the all-important process of neural communication. Neural communication is composed of electrochemical signalling: within the neuron communication is electrical and between neurons communication is chemical or synaptic.

SIGNALLING AND COMMUNICATION WITHIN THE NEURON

Electrical Communication

Electricity is about the movement of electrons from a region of higher charge to a region of lower charge. The basis of the charge is the electron. Regions with higher numbers of electrons are negatively charged in comparison to another area that has fewer electrons and is therefore comparatively positively charged. The difference between the positive and negative charge is referred to as the potential and this is what we measure in volts. The flow of electrons is referred to as a current. In the current, the electrons pass from the negative to the positive side.

Much of our knowledge regarding the electrical charge and action of a neuron is derived from the giant axon of the squid (Box 4.3). The reason why the axon of the squid is studied is because it is comparatively large compared to other species – approximately 1 mm which is big in the world of axons. The use of the oscilloscope, which is sensitive to electricity and can measure the current in volts, has allowed us to probe the function of the squid's axon with relative ease. In addition to the oscilloscope, microelectrodes can be placed either on the surface or inside the axon; this means that they are placed either side of the cell membrane and/or myelin sheath. When placed on the outside, the electrode can measure the extracellular

BOX 4.2: MULTIPLE SCLEROSIS AND DEMYELINATION

Multiple sclerosis (MS) is an autoimmune inflammatory neurological disorder. The disease process in MS attacks the myelin of axons. A loss of myelin gives rise to neurological symptoms. There is considerable variability in the level of demyelination in MS which makes the progression and presentation of symptoms varied and unpredictable. Symptoms include:

- extreme tiredness (fatigue);
- numbness and tingling;
- blurring of vision;
- problems with mobility and balance; and
- muscle weakness and tightness.

Whilst the cause of MS is not fully known, it would appear to be a mixture of genetic vulnerability in the presence of environmental trigger mechanisms (Gourraud et al., 2012).

Patients with MS can be grouped into four major categories based upon the disease course (Goldenberg, 2012):

- relapsing/remitting MS: in which there are periods of flare-ups and remission;
- secondary progressive MS: in which the disease worsens and in some cases without periods of remission;
- primary progressive MS: in which there are no relapses or omissions and the disease progresses from the very beginning; and
- progressive relapsing MS: is progressive from the beginning but does have intermittent flare-ups or worsening of the symptoms without periods of remission.

How the disease presents depends upon the part of the brain affected, e.g demyelination within the hippocampus has been associated with cognitive symptoms (Dutta et al., 2011). Loss of myelin around the axons will have a pronounced effect on the speed with which neural impulses are conducted. However, the exact mechanism by which demyelination occurs and the functional impact is yet to be determined. Attempts to remyelinate have not been successful (Franklin, 2002).

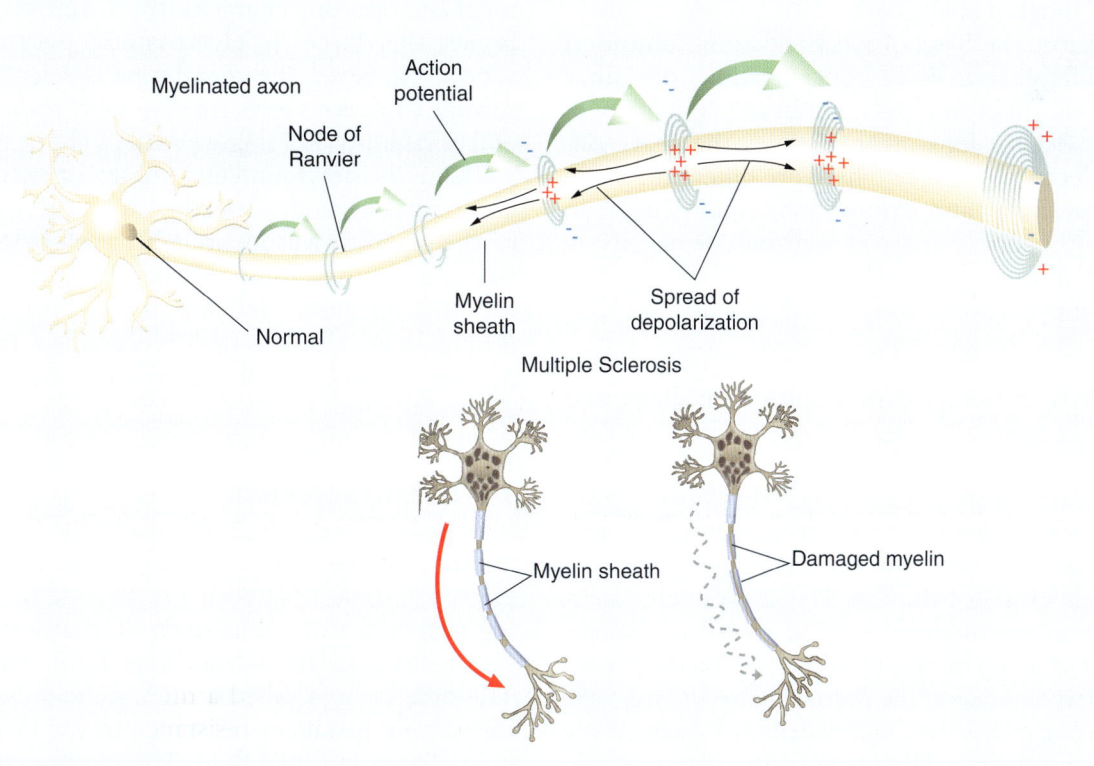

FIGURE 4.2.1 *Demyelination in multiple sclerosis. Damage to the myelin makes neurotransmission slower in multiple sclerosis.*

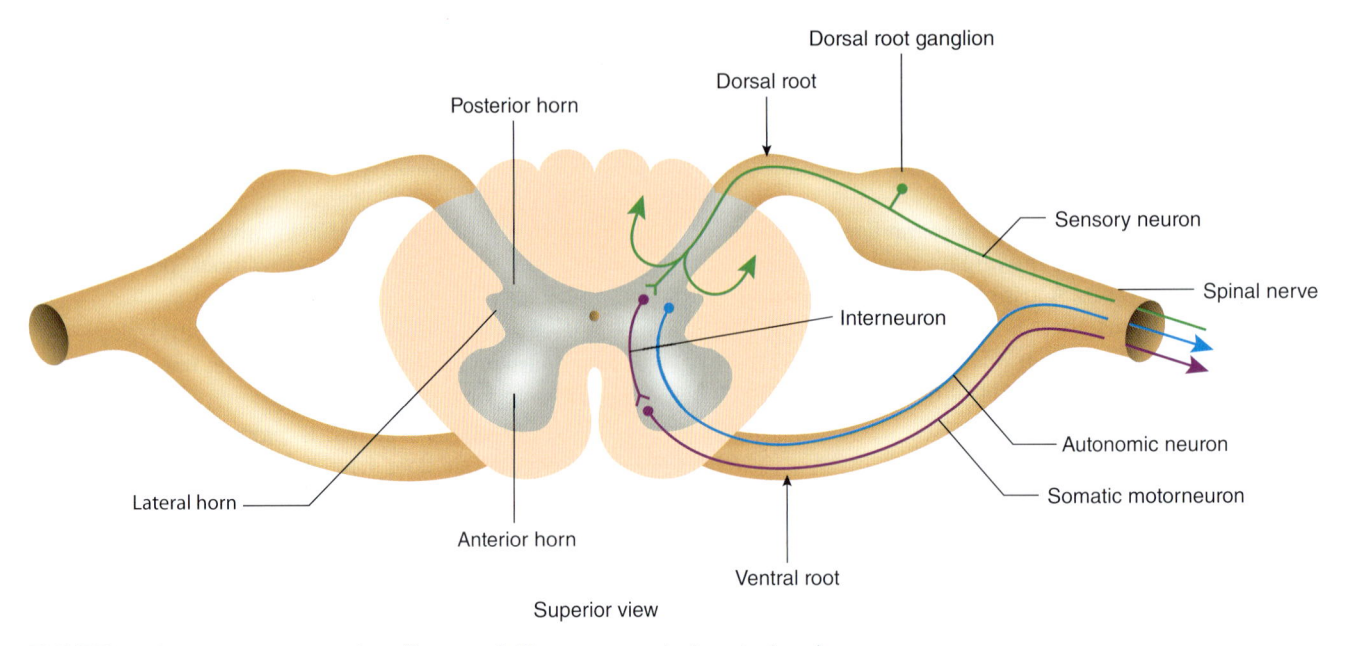

FIGURE 4.4 *Interneurons connecting afferent and efferent neurons in the spinal cord.*

electrical current at the point of the electrode tip. When placed inside, it can measure the intracellular electrical current. The difference between the two is the measure of voltage across the cell membrane (Hodgkin et al., 1952).

Therefore the basis of electrical communication is the difference in ionic concentrations on either side of the neuron's cell membrane (Hodgkin & Huxley, 1952b). Ions are molecules that have different electrical charges. There are different ions in the intracellular and extracellular fluid. They can be either positively charged (**cations**) or negatively charged (**anion**s).

The movement of ions in and out of the cell is mediated by the following processes:

- diffusion along a **concentration gradient**; and
- electrostatic pressure.

Diffusion is the process in which the moving molecules go from areas of high concentration to low concentration along a concentration gradient until there is an even distribution. This is somewhat similar to the action of sugar in tea. If you place a spoon of sugar in a cup of tea, there is an initial high concentration of sugar at the bottom. Give the tea a stir and the sugar dissolves and distributes itself evenly throughout the tea. The term 'concentration gradient' refers to the concentration of molecules within our solution in two different cellular locations. Thus, an area of high concentration moves down the concentration gradient towards an area of low concentration.

Due to the fact that ions are electrically charged, an electrical force exists between ions: like charges repel and opposite charges attract. Across the membrane, this force or **electrostatic pressure** is in action. However, the membrane is selectively permeable to various ions, most notably sodium (NA^+) and potassium (K^+) (Figure 4.5).

Using the newfound technology of oscilloscopes and microelectrodes together with the giant axon of the squid, it was identified that electrical potential was in either a state of rest or a state of action: the **resting potential** and the **action potential** (Hodgkin & Huxley, 1945). When we talk about a neuron firing or spiking, we are referring to the action potential.

The resting potential

If we place one electrode inside the neuron and another outside, we can measure the difference in electrical charge between the two sides. The resting potential is a comparison of charges from the extracellular to the intracellular fluid (Figure 4.6). The difference is called a membrane potential; the membrane produces resistance to the normal passage of ions within a fluid. The membrane is semipermeable and allows only certain ions to pass through when at rest. When there are no influences impinging on the neuron, it is said to be at rest, thus

BOX 4.3 SQUID AXON

Without the squid and its giant axon we would know very little about neurons. The squid themselves are not giant – it is just their axons. The size of their axons permits researchers to investigate the electrical properties with comparative ease. The first report identifying the potential (no pun intended) of the giant axon of the squid was by John Young (1939). The advantages of the squid axon can be seen in Figure 4.3.1. It was Hodgkin and Huxley who identified the electrical nature of neural communication in a series of experiments using the giant axon (Hodgkin & Huxley, 1952a, 1952c, 1952d, 1952e, 1953; Hodgkin et al., 1952). One hopes they had an appetite for the calamari.

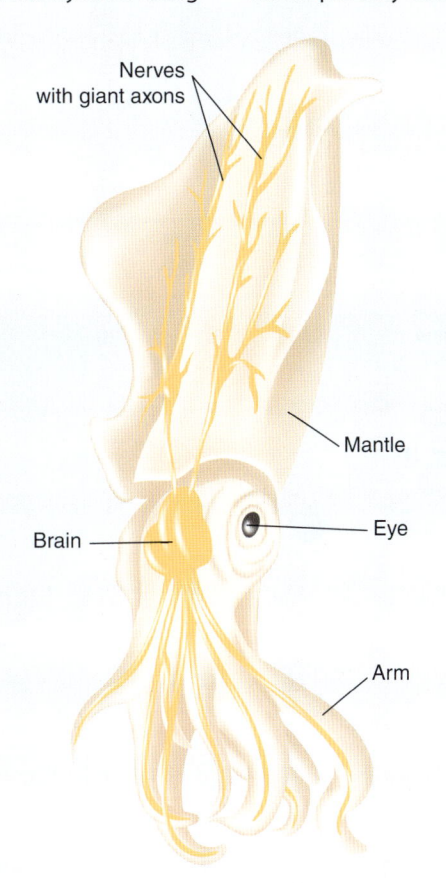

FIGURE 4.3.1 *The giant axon of the squid.*
Source: CAMPELL, NEILA.; REECE, JANE B., *BIOLOGY*, 8th, ©2008, p.1048. Reprinted by permission of Pearson Education, INC., New York, New York.

the 'resting potential'. The resting potential in neurons is about −70 mV. The number −70 mV refers to the fact that the inside of the cell has a negative charge. Whilst −70 mV is a somewhat magic number in physiological textbooks, it ranges from −52 to −80 mV, but we will adhere to −70 mV.

There are four main ions that contribute to the resting potential: **sodium** (NA^+), **potassium** (K^+), chloride (Cl^-) and some negatively charged proteins. **Calcium** (Ca^{++}) is also involved, but more so at the synapse. These ions are not equally distributed across the cell membrane. There are two reasons for this uneven distribution. The first is that the membrane is semi-permeable and permits certain molecules to pass through it. The site at which an ion can gain passage to either side is called the **ion channel**. The ion channels are proteins that are configured to allow only certain ions through.

K^+ channels remain open and allow K^+ to cross either side of the membrane. The movement of K^+ follows that of diffusion and the concentration gradient and also electrostatic pressure.

The second mechanism responsible for this distribution is the sodium—potassium pump (see

94 PSYCHOBIOLOGY

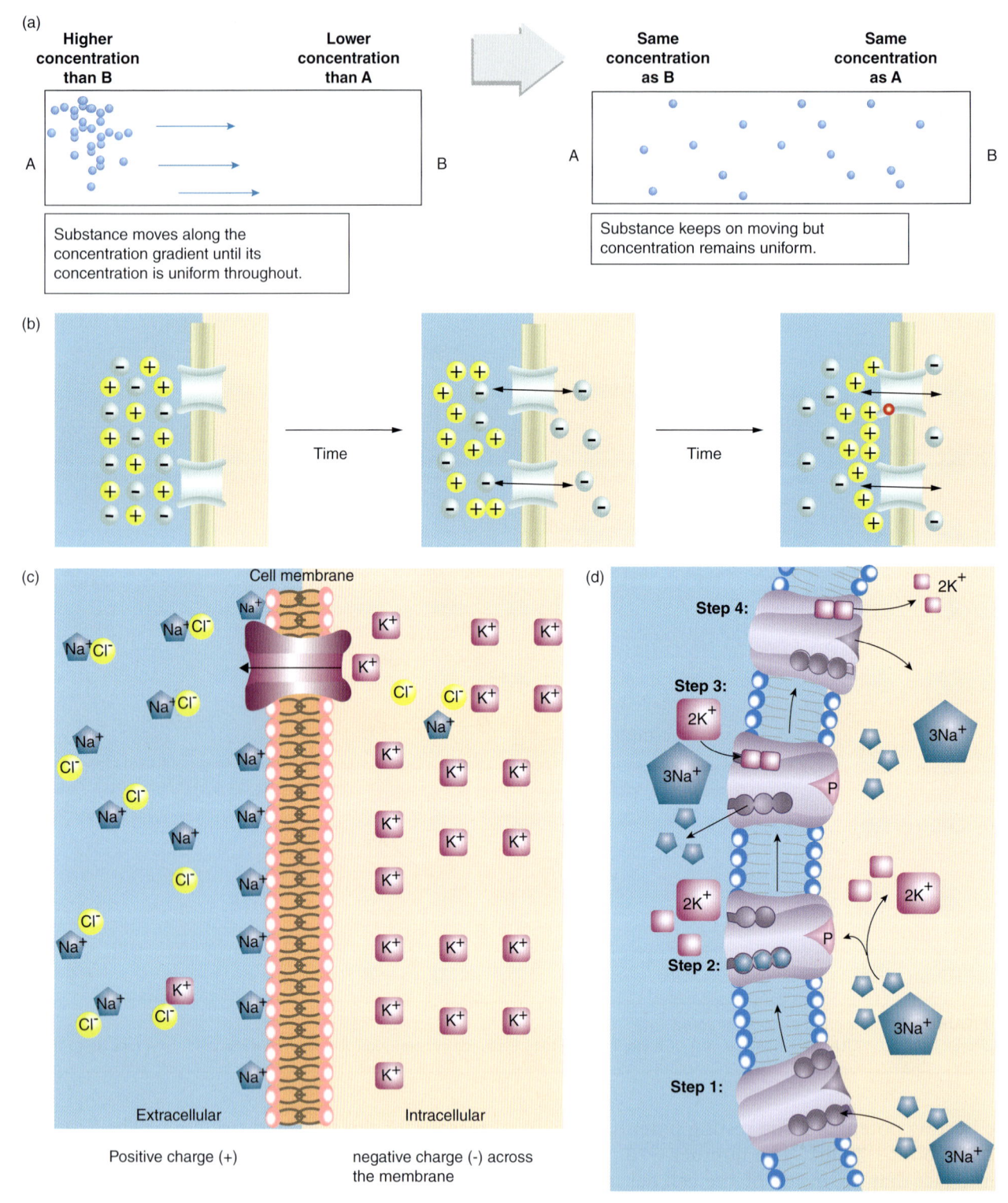

FIGURE 4.5 *Concentration gradient and electrostatic pressure. (a) Diffusion along the concentration gradient, high to low. (b) Electrostatic pressure – positive and negative ions are mixed together on one side of a semi-permeable membrane. After a period of time, negatively charged ions pass through the channels in the membrane. The negative ions pass back to the other side because of the attraction to a positive charge. And the process continues back and forth. (c) Ions cross the membrane along their ionic concentration gradients. (d) The sodium–potassium pump.*

1. *3 Na+ molecules are taken up …*
2. *and pumped out.*
3. *Two potassium molecules are taken in …*
4. *and pumped into the cell.*

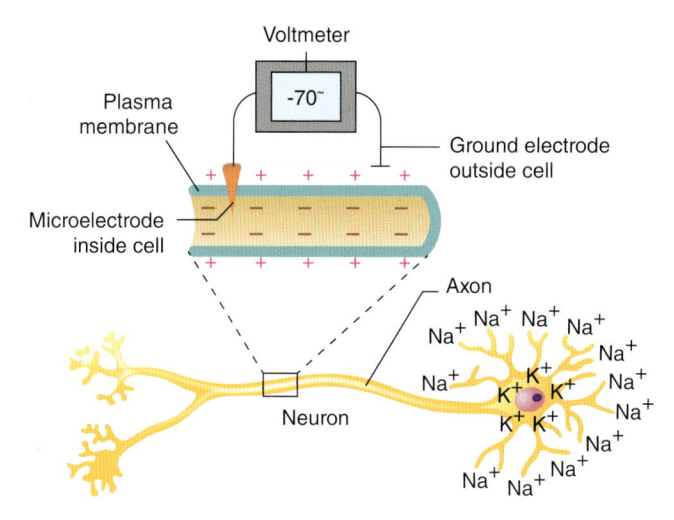

CHAPTER 4 THE NEURON, THE ENDOCRINE SYSTEM AND COMMUNICATION

FIGURE 4.6 *A neuron at rest. The ionic status of a neuron at rest with an intracellular and extracellular electrode.*

Figure 4.5) which is an energy-consuming mechanism (a protein molecule in the cell membrane), which pumps Na$^+$ out and K$^+$ in. It does this in a three-for-two manner: three Na$^+$ ions for two K$^+$ ions. The **sodium–potassium pump** is expensive to run, requiring large amounts of energy. It causes a build-up of K$^+$ within the cell but because the membrane is semi-permeable and allows K$^+$ to move, K$^+$ leaves the inside of the cell along the concentration gradient. This leaves a build-up of Na$^+$ and a negative charge within the cell. Electrostatic pressure builds up as a result of the increase in the negative charge and the pressure pulls K$^+$ back in again. There are opposing forces of the concentration gradient and electrostatic pressure. The sodium–potassium pump is there to counteract the seepage of Na$^+$ into the cell via the semi-permeable membrane. Na$^+$ attempts to gain entry because of the concentration gradient and electrostatic pressure. When all these forces are in action and equilibrium has been reached, we are measuring the resting potential. Due to the differences at rest, the neuron is polarized – that is, the two sides of the neuronal membrane are differentially charged.

The action potential

When a neuron is activated (or fires), it produces an action potential. Action potentials are the neural impulses involved in communication. An action potential is a rapid reversal of the membrane potential and is graphically depicted in Figures 4.7 and 4.8. The change in membrane potential permits an exchange of ions. During the resting potential, the neuron is polarized; an action potential reduces the polarity and is **depolarizing** (or hypopolarizing). Conversely, **hyperpolarization** is when the neuron becomes even more polarized than when it is at rest.

The sequence of events during an action potential

The initiation of the action potential occurs because of the axon hillock (see Figure 4.7) which has a large number of voltage-sensitive channels. An action potential is achieved if the combination of inhibitory and excitatory inputs on the cell body membrane reaches a sufficient level to depolarize the membrane at the axon hillock. The dendrites acquire information in the form of neural impulses which are either excitatory or inhibitory and, depending on their relative strengths, will initiate the action potential at the axon hillock (see below for excitatory and inhibitory postsynaptic potentials).

In the case of an action potential, there is depolarization caused by an excitation. An action potential can be induced artificially with electrodes. If an electrical stimulus is of sufficient strength, it reaches the threshold of excitation which is the point at which an action potential can occur. The action potential is an **all-or-nothing event**. Action potentials either happen or they do not. A big stimulus does not produce a bigger action potential. The action potential is always the same size.

The process of an action potential starts with the opening of Na$^+$ channels. When the channels open, Na$^+$ enters the cell, causing a change in membrane potential. In response, K$^+$ channels open and K$^+$ exits the cell. Na$^+$ channels close but K$^+$ ions are still exiting, producing a repolarization of the cell. K$^+$ channels close slowly and an overshoot occurs, which results in hyperpolarization. Once all channels are closed, the membrane returns to the resting potential. All this happens in the space of 3–4 milliseconds. It is the action potential that electroencephalogram (EEG) and event-related potentials (ERP) recordings aggregate to provide a measure of electrical activity in the brain (see Chapter 6).

After the start of an action potential, there is a period of time in which another one cannot occur. There are two preventative periods of an action potential: the **absolute refractory period**, which is followed by the **relative refractory period**. The latter requires greater stimulation to obtain an action potential. Thus, if a stimulus is of sufficient intensity, it will produce an action potential during the relative refractory period. The refractory periods emerge due to the way the voltage-sensitive channels open and close allowing Na$^+$ and potassium to traverse the membrane. Na$^+$ channels have two

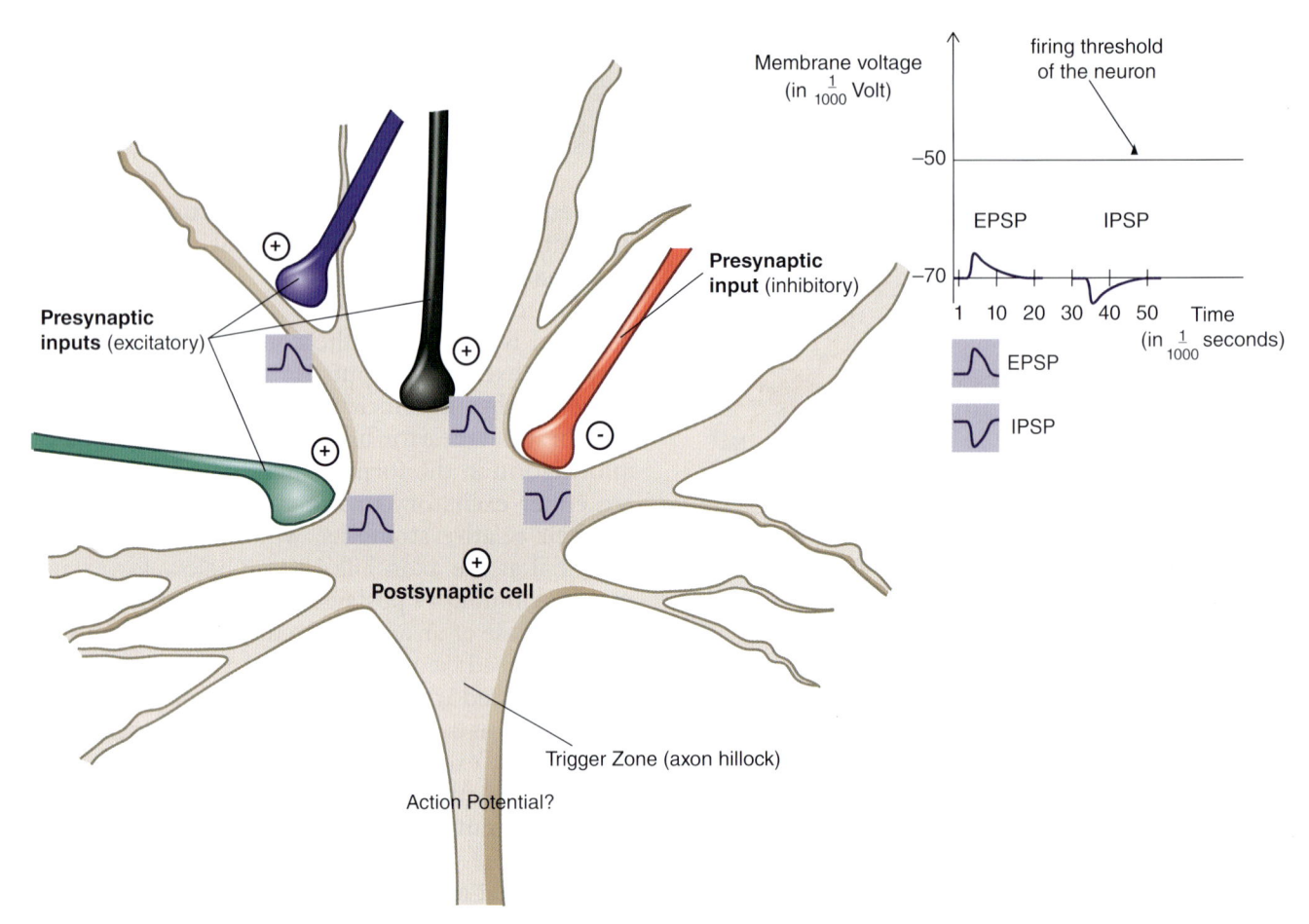

FIGURE 4.7 *Initiation of the action potential at the axon hillock. Inputs from excitatory and inhibitory neurons are integrated at the axon hillock and determine whether an action potential is generated.*

gates whereas potassium channels only have one gate. The Na⁺ channel gates are either voltage sensitive or they are not. Starting at rest on the outside of the membrane, the gates for Na⁺ and K⁺ (both of which are voltage sensitive) are closed, whereas on the inside only the Na⁺ channel has a gate and that is open and not voltage sensitive. During depolarization, the voltage-sensitive changes open the Na⁺ channel gate on the outside of the cell membrane. This allows Na⁺ to enter the cell. Once the outside gate opens, very soon afterwards the internal gate closes on the Na⁺ channel. When the internal gate is closed, no more action potentials can be initiated (the absolute refractory period). The gates of the Na⁺ channel then return to their resting state. K⁺ channels respond by opening and allowing potassium to exit the cell. The K⁺ gates close slowly in comparison to the Na⁺ gates which results in K⁺ still exiting the cell. This hyperpolarization cell is the relative refractory period in which an action potential is inhibited but still possible. The membrane then returns to the resting potential.

Propagation of the action potential From the axon hillock the action potential moves down the axon. The initial part of the axon is unmyelinated (Kole & Stuart, 2012) and varies in length depending upon the region of the brain (Tomassy et al., 2014). The exchange of ions at any one point influences the neighbouring section of the axon; depolarization destabilizes its next-door neighbour. To clarify this concept, think of the axon as a set of dominoes laid out ready to topple over. If you are the electrical stimulus and knock over one domino, the next one falls over too. Eventually, all the dominoes fall without you having to touch each one. Each domino falling represents the sequence of events during action potential: one point on the axon influences the other.

Whilst most of the discussion within this chapter is about the transmission of the action potential down the one-way street of the axon, it is also important to remember that under certain conditions (e.g. during sleep) the direction of the action potential can change which may be important in

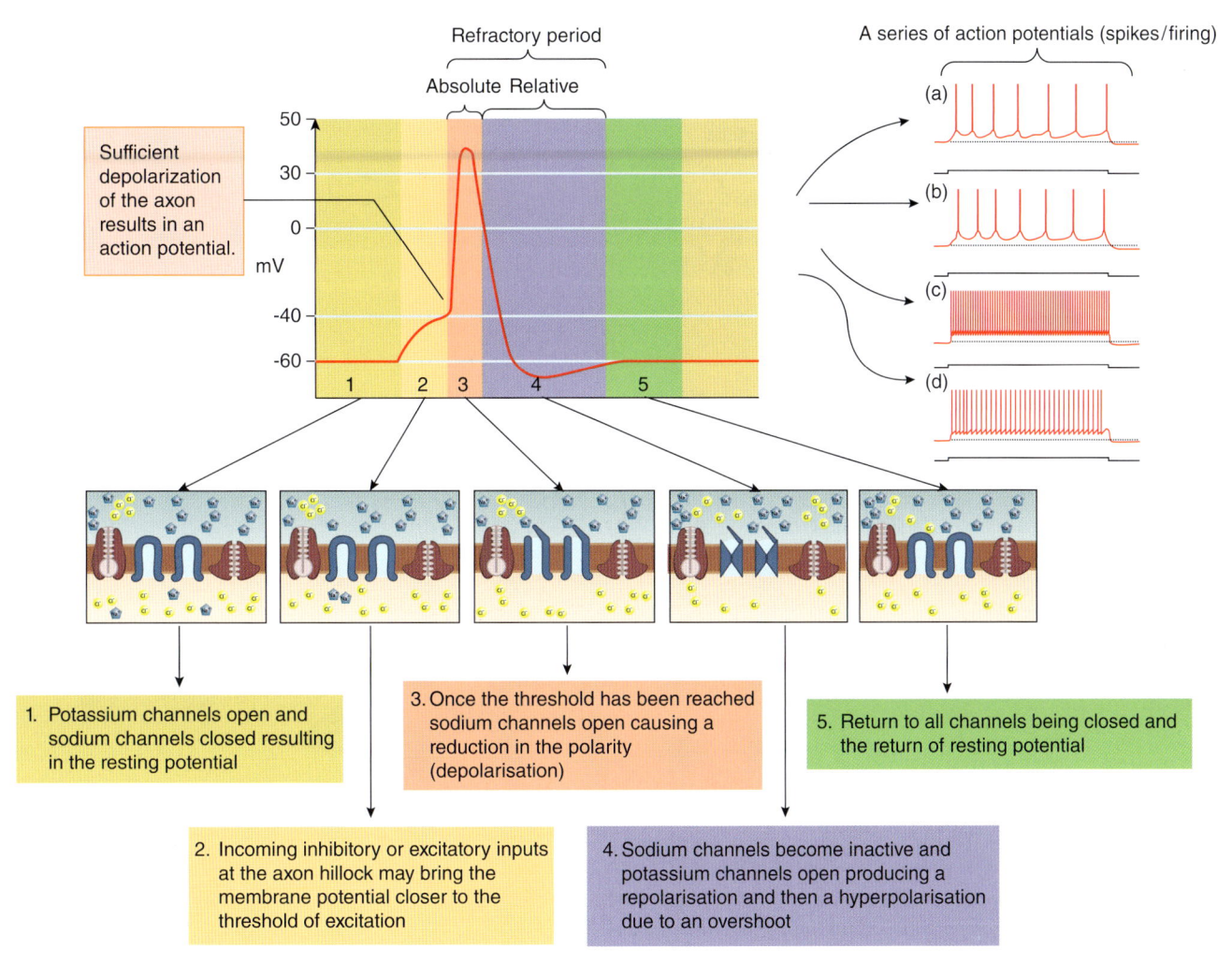

FIGURE 4.8 *The sequence of events in an action potential. (a) Regular-spiking neuron with depolarizing after potential. (b) Intrinsically burst-spiking cell. (c) Fast-spiking neuron. (d) Regular-spiking non-pyramidal cell.*

synaptic plasticity (see Chapter 13) (Bukalo et al., 2013).

The speed of propagation depends on the size of axon; large axons are faster than smaller ones. The speed is increased in myelinated neurons. The signal produced by the action potential passes along the sheathed area passively. The electrical impulse along the myelinated axon is diminished. However, in the myelin sheath there are gaps, as we have seen, called nodes of Ranvier where the cell membrane is densely populated with sodium channels (Ritchie & Rogart, 1977). The diminished electrical signal is sufficient for an action potential to occur at these gaps. Thus, the action potential appears to jump from node to node in a process called **saltatory conduction** (see Figure 4.9).

Myelinated neurons send information at great speed. The importance of myelin can be seen in patients with MS. In MS the neurons are there but an immune response attacks and destroys the myelin (Hallpike, 1972) (see Box 4.2). This has profound effects on sufferers, who experience motor and sensory difficulties. Deficiencies in myelin have also been hypothesized to account for the symptoms of disorders such as ADHD (Russell et al., 2006), **cerebral palsy** (Yin et al., 2000), stroke (Kelley, 2006) and Alzheimer's disease (Bartzokis, 2011).

The neuron transmits information as action potentials on an all-or-none basis. However, we intuitively know that some sensations are stronger than others, e.g. some light is brighter than other light or a touch is harder than another touch. This information is conveyed via a frequency code which is integration of synaptic input. If synaptic input is sustained and strong enough to produce

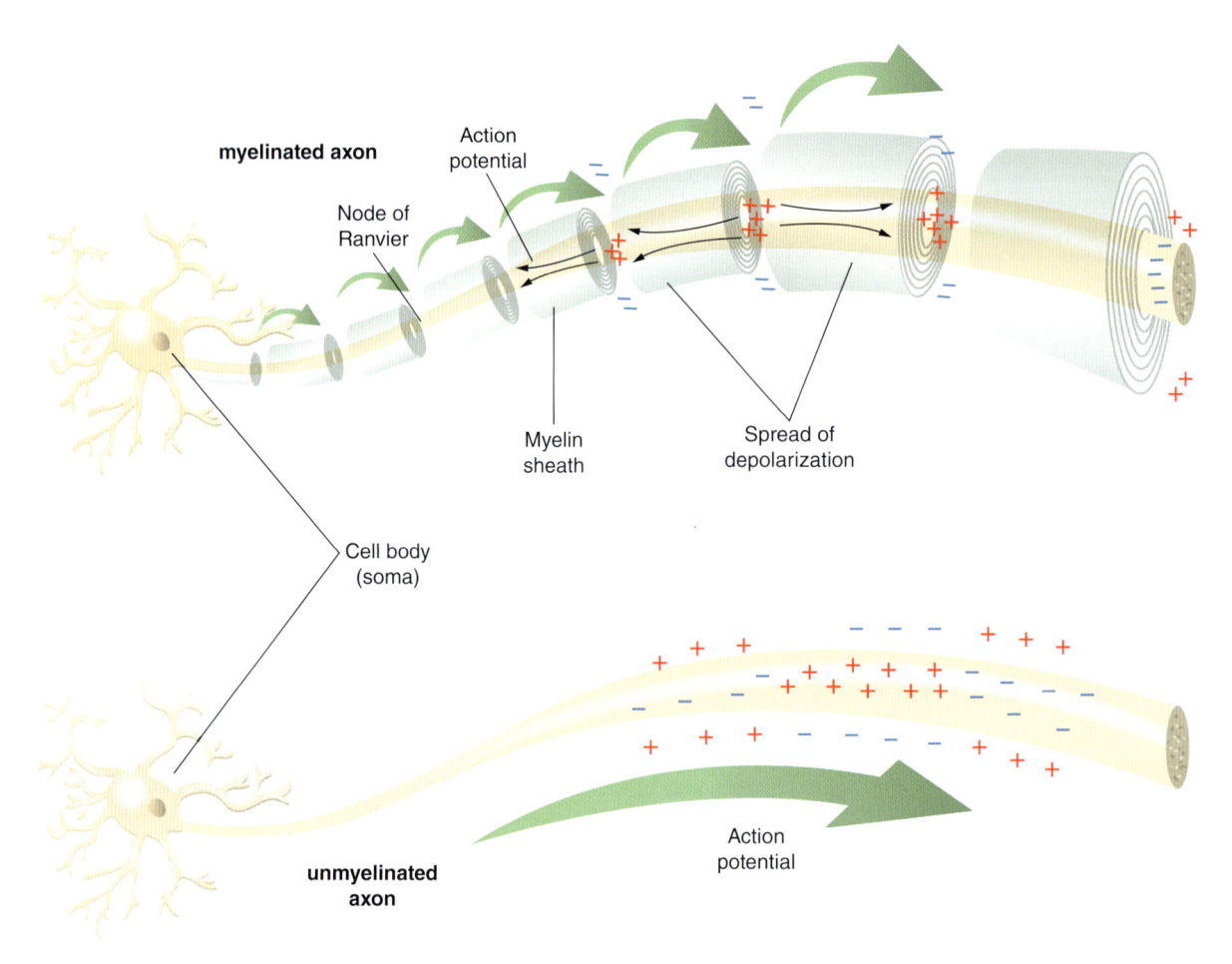

FIGURE 4.9 *Saltatory conduction. The top axon is myelinated and the action potential jumps from node to node. The bottom axon is unmyelinated and the action potential occurs throughout the length of the axon.*

depolarization, then there will be several action potentials in a row. Stronger depolarization results in shorter times being required to reach the threshold for each subsequent action potential. More information is conveyed in the firing pattern of the neuron. Some neurons may have bursts of activity followed by a pause before another burst, whereas other neurons may be single spike neurons that produce action potentials at regular intervals.

Postsynaptic potentials

During synaptic transmission, the presynaptic neuron (the neuron sending the message) releases a chemical called a neurotransmitter, which crosses the synapse. Neurotransmitters interact with **receptors** on another neuron (the **postsynaptic neuron**). The neuron that receives the message transforms the message into an action potential which travels down to the axon and releases a neurotransmitter into another synapse.

Incoming signals from other neurons are received by receptors on the dendrites and soma. If the message that is received depolarizes the receptor, it produces an **excitatory postsynaptic potential** (**EPSP**). An inhibitory input produces a hyperpolarization called an **inhibitory postsynaptic potential** (**IPSP**). Both types of input vary according to the intensity of the signal received. An EPSP increases the probability that an action potential will occur and an IPSP decreases that probability.

Excitatory postsynaptic potentials and IPSPs are integrated at the axon hillock which acts like a funnel, collecting all the information before passing it down the axon. Depending on the balance of incoming information (EPSPs and IPSPs), a depolarization of the axon may occur (Figure 4.7).

The integration of information at the axon hillock accounts for the location and timing of inputs (Figure 4.10). In **spatial summation** there is integration of information coming in from different sites.

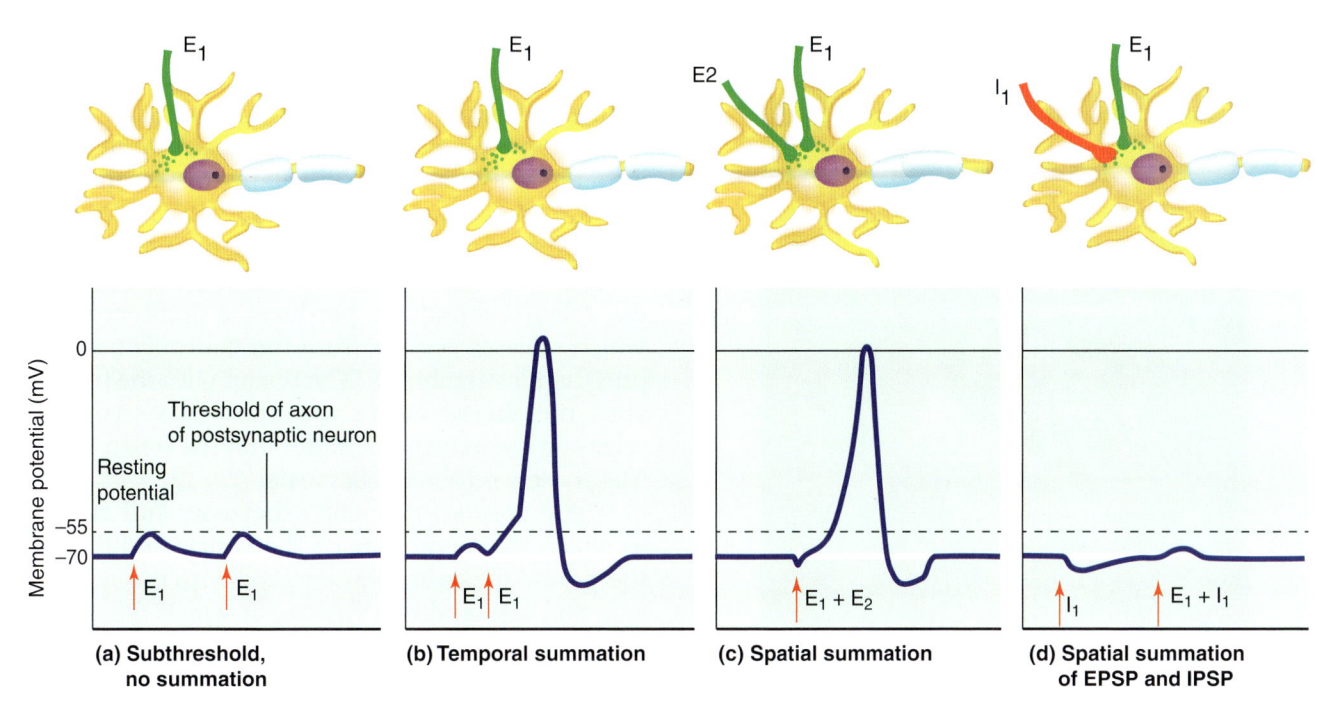

FIGURE 4.10 *Temporal and spatial summation.*

With **temporal summation**, if the incoming information is close together in time there is an increased change of response in a particular direction. In the case of a barrage of EPSPs, an action potential will be initiated.

Sensory signals travel via afferent neurons to the brain. Sensory input has to be converted into neural impulses (see Chapter 10) or action potentials, e.g. photoreceptors in the eye convert light into neural messages for visual perception to take place. Similarly, mechanical receptors in the skin respond to touch. Motor signals produced via efferent neurons communicate with target muscles via synapses at the endplate region, i.e. where the axon meets the muscle, and release transmitter substance to bring about an effect in the muscle (see Chapter 11). Obviously, what goes on is more complex than Cartesian dualism would allow. The majority of the chapters in this book are concerned not with input or output, but rather how the brain processes and makes sense of the world and how it acts upon it.

As is becoming clear, electrical communication is only one part of the complex process of neural communication. In order to connect with other neurons (mainly interneurons), they must do so via a chemical exchange (although there is electrical exchange at electrical **gap junctions** – see later).

SIGNALLING AND COMMUNICATION BETWEEN NEURONS: SYNAPTIC TRANSMISSION

Moving away from the physics of the resting and action potentials, we now have to consider the biochemistry of the synapses. The bridging of the gap between neurons (the **synapse**) is achieved in a process called synaptic transmission. Synaptic transmission involves neurotransmitters that can traverse the synaptic gap and interact with the postsynaptic neuron. There are many neurotransmitters within the nervous system, and with advances in biochemistry the list of chemicals that act as neurotransmitters is sure to grow. Before we consider the neurotransmitters, we can look at the processes of synaptic communication that they all share.

If we look at the schematic representation of the synapses (Figure 4.11), a number of structures are visible. At the end of the axon are the **microtubules** that deliver the material from manufacturing neurotransmitters. They also send down the material for making the packaging of the neurotransmitters – the **vesicles**. The vesicles are spherical structures that contain the neurotransmitter ready

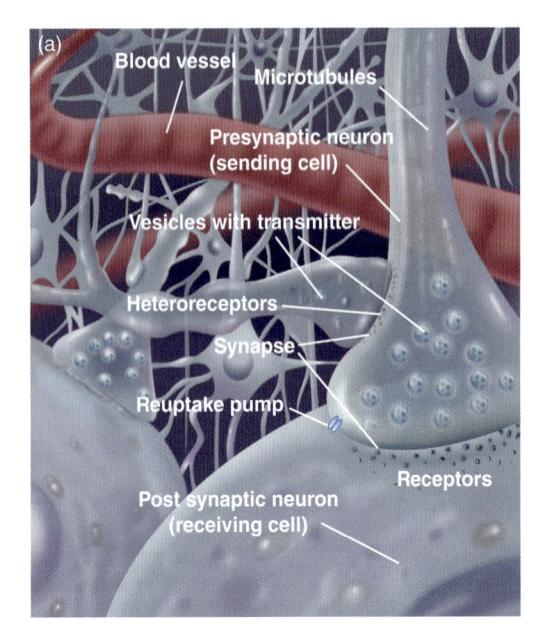

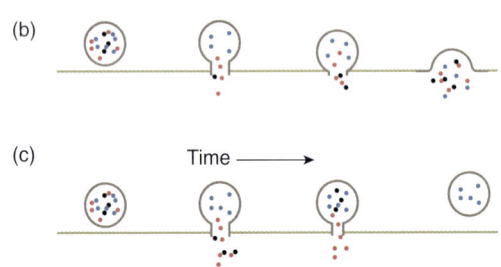

FIGURE 4.11 The synapse. (a) Neurons communicate across a synapse, using neurotransmitters during exocytosis. (b) Exocytosis: full fusion where the vesicle collapses. (c) Exocytosis: kiss-and-run fusion where the vesicle releases its contents and is recycled.

for deployment in the synapse. Looking around the edge of the presynaptic terminal, we can see the cell membrane within which are voltage-gated calcium channels, autoreceptors and transporters. We may also see **heteroreceptors** which receive input from other neurons using a different neurotransmitter as a messenger. The figure shows a small gap before the **postsynaptic membrane** of the next neuron, known as the synaptic gap or cleft. On the postsynaptic membrane are also receptors that are configured to accept a particular neurotransmitter. It is a neurotransmitter interacting with these receptors on the postsynaptic membrane that initiates either EPSPs or IPSPs. And so the cycle continues.

Like the action potential, synaptic transmission involves a sequence of events. To begin with, the action potential travels down the axon and arrives at the end terminal (the presynaptic terminal, the terminal before the synapses). The depolarization brought by the travelling action potential at the presynaptic terminal opens calcium channels in the presynaptic membrane which allows calcium to travel into the presynaptic terminal region of the cell. Calcium interacts with the synaptic vesicles, causing them to fuse with the presynaptic membrane. The interaction of calcium with an intermediate chemical called calmodulin produces a joint complex which releases vesicles from the neurofilaments or presynaptic membrane. The fusion with the presynaptic membrane means that the vesicles rupture, releasing the neurotransmitter into the synapse gap: this process is called **exocytosis**.

There are two types of exocytosis: **full fusion**, in which the membrane of the vesicle and the cell merge and the entire contents spill into the synaptic gap, and **kiss-and-run fusion**, in which the vesicle releases the transmitter through a transient fusion pore in the cell membrane and retains its shape, preventing full integration into the cell membrane (see Figure 4.11) (Alabi & Tsien, 2013).

The recycling of cellular membrane is referred to as **endocytosis** (see Doherty & McMahon (2009) for review) although endocytosis refers more generally to the cell's ability to absorb molecules, in particular those that cannot pass through the cell membrane. Calcium is thought to determine which process is in action, full fusion or kiss-and-run (Wang et al., 2003), with the calcium acting as an intermediate stage providing an actin coating around the vesicle (Miklavc et al., 2009). **Actin** is a protein that has many functions, one of which is vesicular movement. The transient nature of kiss-and-run fusion means that the entire contents of the vesicle may not be released; this process is dependent upon another protein called myosin which determines how long the vesicle is open (Aoki et al., 2010). Kiss-and-run fusion permits the vesicle to be reused more readily because there is some integrity remaining in the vesicle. With full fusion release, the integrity of the vesicle is lost and new vesicles have to be made from the increased area of cell membrane and vesicle membrane. Full fusion requires about 20 seconds before the vesicle is regenerated (Heuser & Reese, 1973) whereas kiss-and-run takes approximately 1–2 seconds (Richards et al., 2005; von Gersdorff & Matthews, 1994). However, in the mouse hippocampus an ultrafast version of endocytosis has been found, operating within 50–100 ms (Watanabe et al., 2013). After prolonged exocytosis, there is a process of bulk endocytosis that retrieves a large amount of membrane (Heuser & Reese, 1973).

Once in the synapses, neurotransmitters interact with various receptors on the pre- and postsynaptic membrane. It is the interaction with receptors on the postsynaptic membrane that leads to an opening of ion channels. This allows ions to enter, creating EPSPs or IPSPs in the postsynaptic neuron.

In terms of the neurotransmitter's function, that is job done. However, the neurotransmitter does not remain active within the synapse but becomes inactivated or removed. Enzymes (see below for metabolism) can now degrade the neurotransmitter. Alternatively, they are retrieved by the presynaptic neuron via the **transporter proteins** in the presynaptic membrane. The neurotransmitter can be then degraded further by enzymes within the presynaptic cytoplasm or repackaged into the vesicles.

The neurotransmitter also interacts with presynaptic receptors which are called autoreceptors and reside within the presynaptic cell membrane. The autoreceptors help to regulate the synaptic environment by providing negative feedback to the presynaptic neuron. Too much transmitter in the synapses sends back messages that there is a lot of transmitter available and that production and release should be reduced. Similarly, too little neurotransmitter in the synapses is relayed to the presynaptic neuron which responds by releasing transmitter.

Neurotransmitters

There are many neurotransmitters within the nervous system. The neurotransmitters already identified have undergone extensive investigation. Research has provided detailed accounts of neurotransmission in general and the application of this knowledge to various disorders. Many neurotransmitters are classified into groups or families (see Figure 4.12). The group a neurotransmitter belongs in depends on its chemical structure.

There are a number of principles by which a chemical can lay claim to being a neurotransmitter:

- the chemical must be synthesized in the neuron, or at least be present within it;
- the chemical must be released and produce a functional change in the target cell;
- the same response should occur when the chemical is directly placed on the target in physiological experiments; and
- there must be some retrieval mechanism to remove the chemical from the site of action.

The first neurotransmitter to be identified was **acetylcholine** (ACh) which is a small molecule transmitter. The main components of these transmitters are obtained from food. Other small molecule transmitters include **dopamine,**

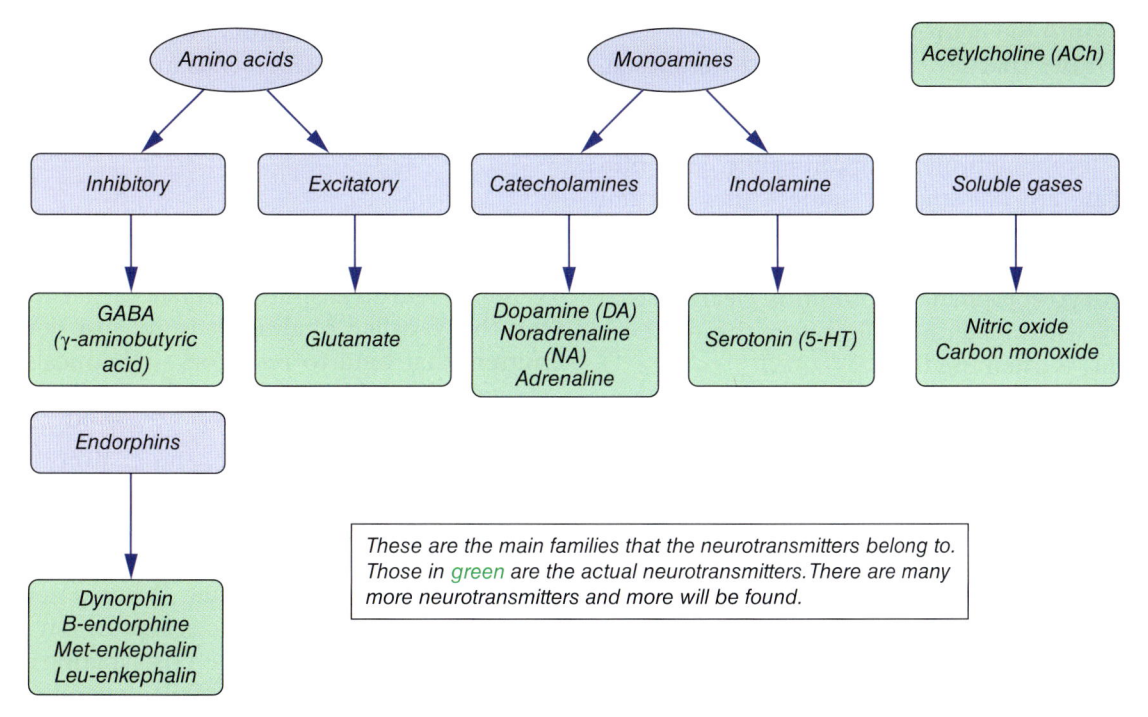

FIGURE 4.12 *Classes of neurotransmitters.*

noradrenaline, adrenaline, serotonin, glutamate, gamma-aminobutyric acid (GABA), **glycine** and **histamine**.

There are also peptide neurotransmitters or **neuropeptides**. Perhaps the most well-known of the neuropeptides are **enkephalins** and **endorphins** which are endogenous pain management chemicals (see Chapter 10). The receptors for the endorphins are also the target of what some might consider our most dangerous drug – heroin (see Chapters 7 and 16).

There are also **soluble gases** that act as neurotransmitters, e.g. **nitric oxide** (NO) and **carbon monoxide** (CO). The soluble gases are not stored like traditional neurotransmitters but are synthesized when required. To illustrate the importance of the soluble gases, Viagra is an NO agent.

Neurotransmitters are made – they do not just appear, they have to be synthesized (see Figure 4.13). Synthesis of a neurotransmitter is like a recipe: all the ingredients must be added before the meal is ready. The synthesis of a neurotransmitter takes place in the soma or the presynaptic terminal. The newly made neurotransmitter in the cell body is packaged into the vesicles. The vesicles are then transported down microtubules to the presynaptic terminal. They stay there until they are released into the synapse. Alternatively, in the presynaptic terminal neurotransmitters can be manufactured from precursor chemicals that are absorbed from the blood supply by the transporter mechanisms. Axonal mitochondria provide the energy to synthesize the precursor chemicals into the neurotransmitter.

Please note that for adrenaline and noradrenaline, there are differences across the literature. In the USA, adrenaline is called epinephrine and noradrenaline is norepinephrine. Noradrenaline and norepinephrine are one and the same – they are not different (adrenaline and epinephrine are also the same). In addition, the chemical name for serotonin is 5-hydroxytryptophan. Serotonin is clearly easier to say, but when reading the literature the abbreviation '5-HT' is often used.

Particular neurons release particular neurotransmitters. A neuron that releases dopamine (DA) is referred to as a dopaminergic neuron. Neurons that release glutamate are glutamatergic neurons. This convention can be applied to many neurotransmitters. To use the example of a telephone conversation, each neurotransmitter can be considered a particular language. A dopaminergic neuron speaks the language of DA, etc. Thus, the different neurotransmitters of the nervous system can be considered as the different languages of our world. An example of excitatory and inhibitory messages can be seen in Chapter 12 with Parkinson's disease, in which the balance of glutamate and GABA (excitatory and inhibitory amino acids respectively) has wide-ranging effects on different neural targets.

Now that the neurotransmitter is in the synapse, its job is to communicate with the postsynaptic neuron (the neuron at the other side of the gap). The postsynaptic neuron requires a means of receiving the message. In order to receive the message, the postsynaptic membrane of the neuron has specialized receptors. These are proteins that are configured so that only certain neurotransmitters can talk to certain receptors, e.g. 5-HT with 5-HT receptors (see Table 4.1).

Similarly, if we are to understand a message on the telephone, we have to be able to interpret the language being spoken. Our ears are like the receptors for neurotransmitters. We need our ears to hear the other person on the telephone. However, if that person speaks a language we do not understand, the message cannot be conveyed to us. People who understand only English can act only on a message in English. They cannot interpret a message, for example, in German. However, neurons can be multilingual and can understand other languages (e.g. some DA neurons can understand a message sent by ACh). The language can be further extended to account for inhibitory and excitatory actions of the transmitter. Glutamate and GABA are amino acids but they are either excitatory or inhibitory. That is, glutamate sends excitatory messages that are activating whereas GABA sends out inhibitory messages that essentially put the brakes on their contact neuron.

Receptors

When a neurotransmitter attaches itself to a receptor, this is called binding. It is not just neurotransmitters that bind to receptors – chemicals bind to receptors too. Chemicals that bind to receptors are called **ligands**.

There are two types of receptors: **ionotropic** and **metabotropic** (see Figure 4.14). These two types of receptors respond to neurochemical messages in different ways. The ionotropic receptor responds quickly to a neurotransmitter. When a neurotransmitter acts at an ionotropic receptor, ion channels are activated. Ions enter the postsynaptic cell. This induces either an EPSP or IPSP, depending on the ion that enters.

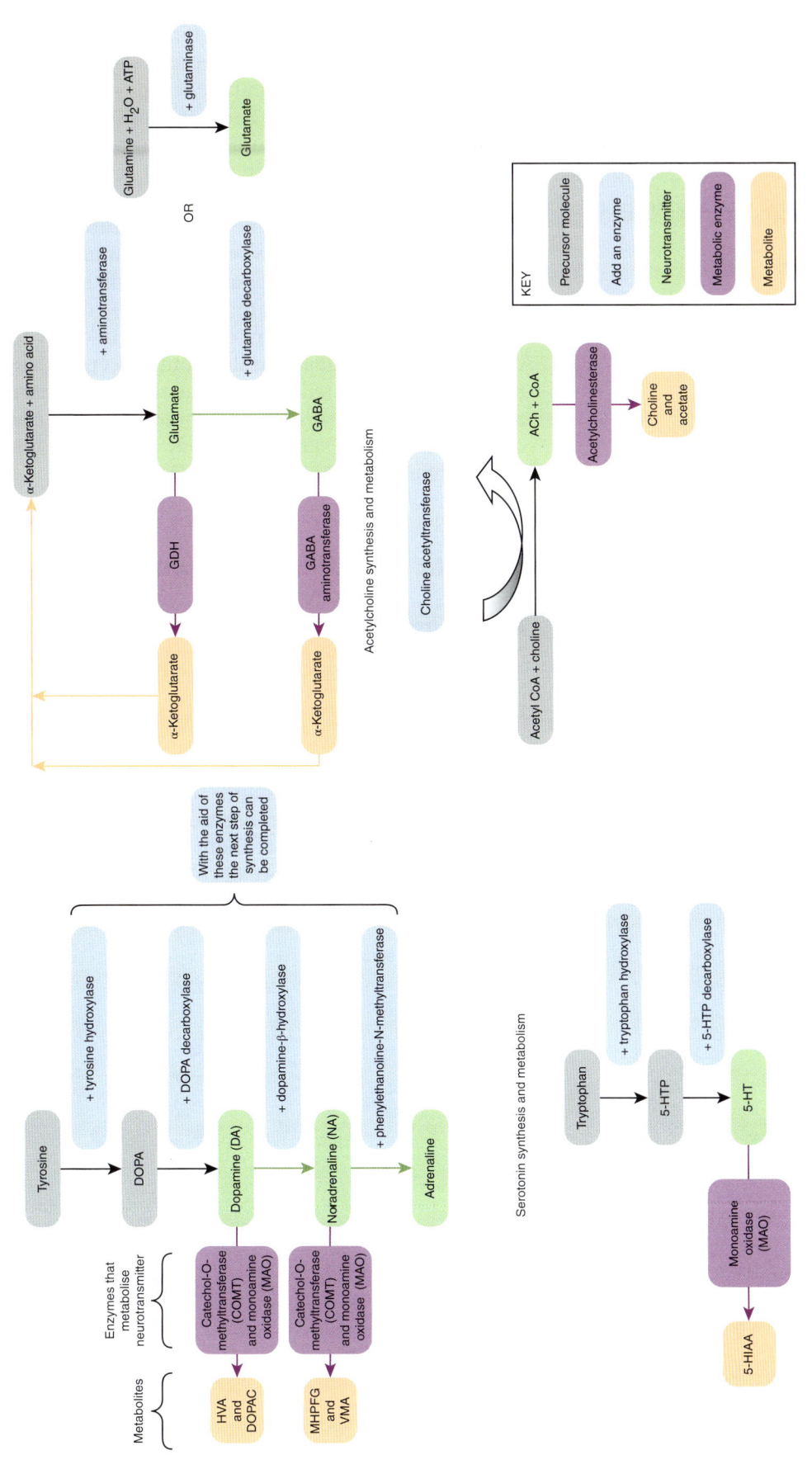

CHAPTER 4 THE NEURON, THE ENDOCRINE SYSTEM AND COMMUNICATION

FIGURE 4.13 *Synthesis and metabolism of the main neurotransmitters.*

TABLE 4.1 Neurotransmitters and receptors

Neurotransmitter (not an exhaustive list)	Example receptors (more subdivisions may apply)
Serotonin (5-HT)	5-HT1, 5-HT2, 5-HT3, 5-HT4, etc.
Dopamine (DA)	D1, D2, D3, D4, D5
Adrenaline/noradrenaline (NA)	α1, α2, β1, β2, etc., adrenoceptors
GABA	GABA A, GABA B
Endorphins	μ, κ, δ (mu, kappa and delta)
Acetylcholine (ACh)	Nicotinic and muscarinic receptors
Glutamate	NMDA, AMPA, mGluR1, etc.
Histamine	H1, H2, etc.
Cannabinoids	CB1, CB2

Metabotropic receptors respond to ligands with an intermediate step. The metabotropic receptor activates **G-proteins**. More often than not, the G-proteins activate another chemical called a second messenger which takes the signal to an enzyme that alters ion channel activity. G-proteins bind **guanosine diphosphate** (GDP) and **guanosine triphosphate** (GTP). Once the G-protein has been activated, it either directly or indirectly, via stimulation of another internal chemical signal, interacts with the ion channel. The intermediate chemical is a second messenger, for example cyclic adenosine monophosphate (cyclic AMP). If an ionotropic receptor is a straight race, the metabotropic receptor is a relay race. The activation of the second messenger has been used to differentiate receptor subtypes, e.g. dopamine D1 and D2 receptors (Kebabian & Calne, 1979). There are numerous receptors in the brain for DA, imaginatively called D1, D2, D3, D4 and D5. The differences between these receptors can be traced to the molecular structure; however, DA receptors fit into two broad families: the D1-like family (ionotropic) and the D2-like family (metabotropic) (Kebabian & Calne, 1979). The differences are still the subject of research in order to understand their behavioural output. Receptors are not evenly distributed throughout the brain; there are clusters of D3 receptors in some areas and not others, whilst the D4 receptors may appear in completely different regions from the D3 receptors.

Synaptic and Cellular Regulation

Metabolism

Neurotransmitters are rapidly broken down and deactivated once they have been released into the synapses. This process is known as enzymatic degradation. It is analogous to the way in which enzymes in biological washing powder break down those stubborn organic stains. The enzymes such as **monoamine oxidase** degrade dopamine and noradrenaline and convert them into **metabolites**. The metabolites for DA are HVA and DOPAC. The

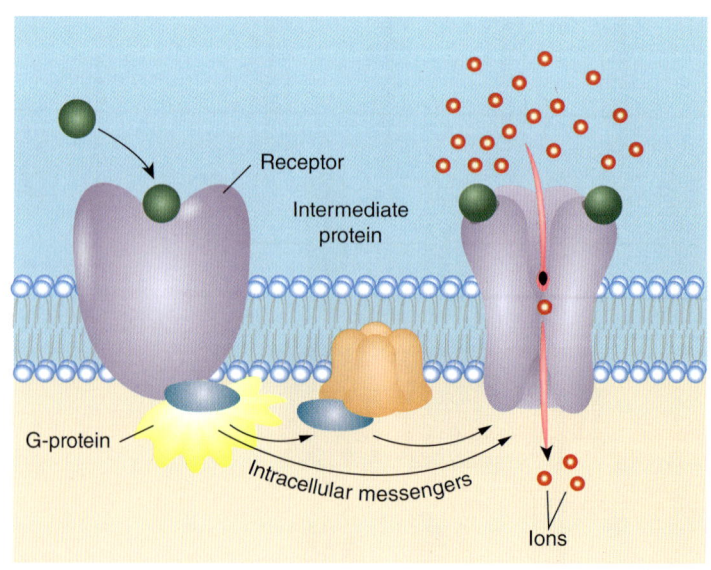

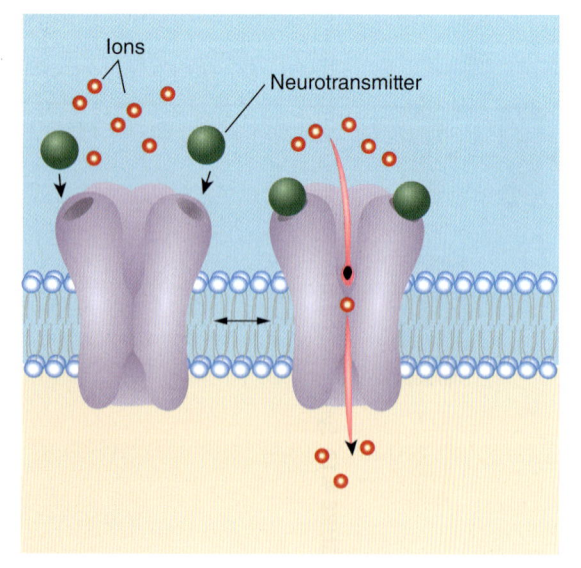

FIGURE 4.14 (a) Ionotropic and (b) metabotropic receptors.

metabolites can then be removed from the body and sometimes are used as an index of activity when they can be measured in the CSF (via lumbar puncture), urine and blood. However, peripheral measures of metabolites are not necessarily reflective of activity within the brain; they may be more representative of neurotransmitter activity elsewhere in the body.

Autoreceptor regulation

The released neurotransmitter is monitored by the presynaptic neuron. It does this by using receptors for the neurotransmitter that are located on the presynaptic membrane. These receptors are called **autoreceptors** (see Figure 4.15). They act a bit like a thermostat on a central heating system. If you set the thermostat to 18°C and the temperature in the room rises over 18°C, the heating cuts out. Conversely, if it falls below the temperature, the heating comes on. We can apply this principle to DA. For example, if there is too much DA in the synapse, the autoreceptor relays the message to the neuron and it shuts down the production and release of DA. If there is too little DA, the neuron increases production and release. The neuron therefore uses feedback derived from the autoreceptor to regulate release of the neurotransmitter.

Reuptake

Reuptake also stops the action of a neurotransmitter by reclaiming it from the synapse. This is commonly seen in noradrenergic, dopaminergic and serotonergic neurons. The presynaptic neuron can have another set of receptors called transporters which reclaim the neurotransmitter from the synapse and repackage it for further use. This is the site of action of many drugs that are used for recreational purposes (e.g. cocaine) or in treatment (e.g. Prozac) (see Chapter 7) (Figure 4.16).

Endocytosis

Earlier it was noted that endocytosis was involved in the recycling of the cell membrane to form vesicles. Endocytosis is also involved in the retrieval of material within the synapses that the cell needs. This process retrieves material that generally cannot pass through the active reuptake channels.

There are a number of types of endocytosis in action (Figure 4.17):

- pinocytosis;
- phagocytosis; and
- receptor-mediated endocytosis.

Pinocytosis involves small particles being brought into the cell via a process of invagination – namely liquid molecules. The cell membrane surrounds and engulfs extracellular substances, collecting them into vesicles contained within the cell, and pinches off to form a vesicle in the cytoplasm.

Phagocytosis is a process in which solids are internalized into the cell. The microglia gather up debris and are involved in inflammation that could be potentially damaging to the nervous system (Gehrmann et al., 1995). The importance of microglia in maintaining homeostasis within the network of the brain's neurons is clearly demonstrated in their mediated inflammatory response which may be an important component in neurodegenerative diseases such as Alzheimer's disease (Mrak & Griffin, 2005).

Receptor-mediated endocytosis (sometimes referred to as clathrin-dependent endocytosis; clathrin is another protein involved in the formation of vesicles) is where specific molecules are ingested by the cell. As the name suggests, membrane receptors receive information which initiates the process of invagination of the extracellular substance and subsequent inclusion within the cell (Besterman & Low, 1983).

Heteroreceptors

Heteroreceptors are another type of presynaptic receptor, which modulate synaptic transmission. However, they are different from autoreceptors as they receive messages from other neurons. Heteroreceptors on a neuron are responsive to different neurotransmitters. Received signals are either excitatory or inhibitory, and can increase or decrease the likelihood of neurotransmitter release. The neuron can understand other neurotransmitters' messages.

Types of synapses

There are a number of types of synapses. What we have considered so far is the axodendritic **synapse**; however, there are others (Figure 4.18).

- In **axodendritic synapses**, the axon synapses on the postsynaptic dendrites of another neuron.
- In **dendrodendritic synapses**, the dendrites send messages to each other.
- In **axosomatic synapses**, the presynaptic terminal synapses on the cell body of another neuron.

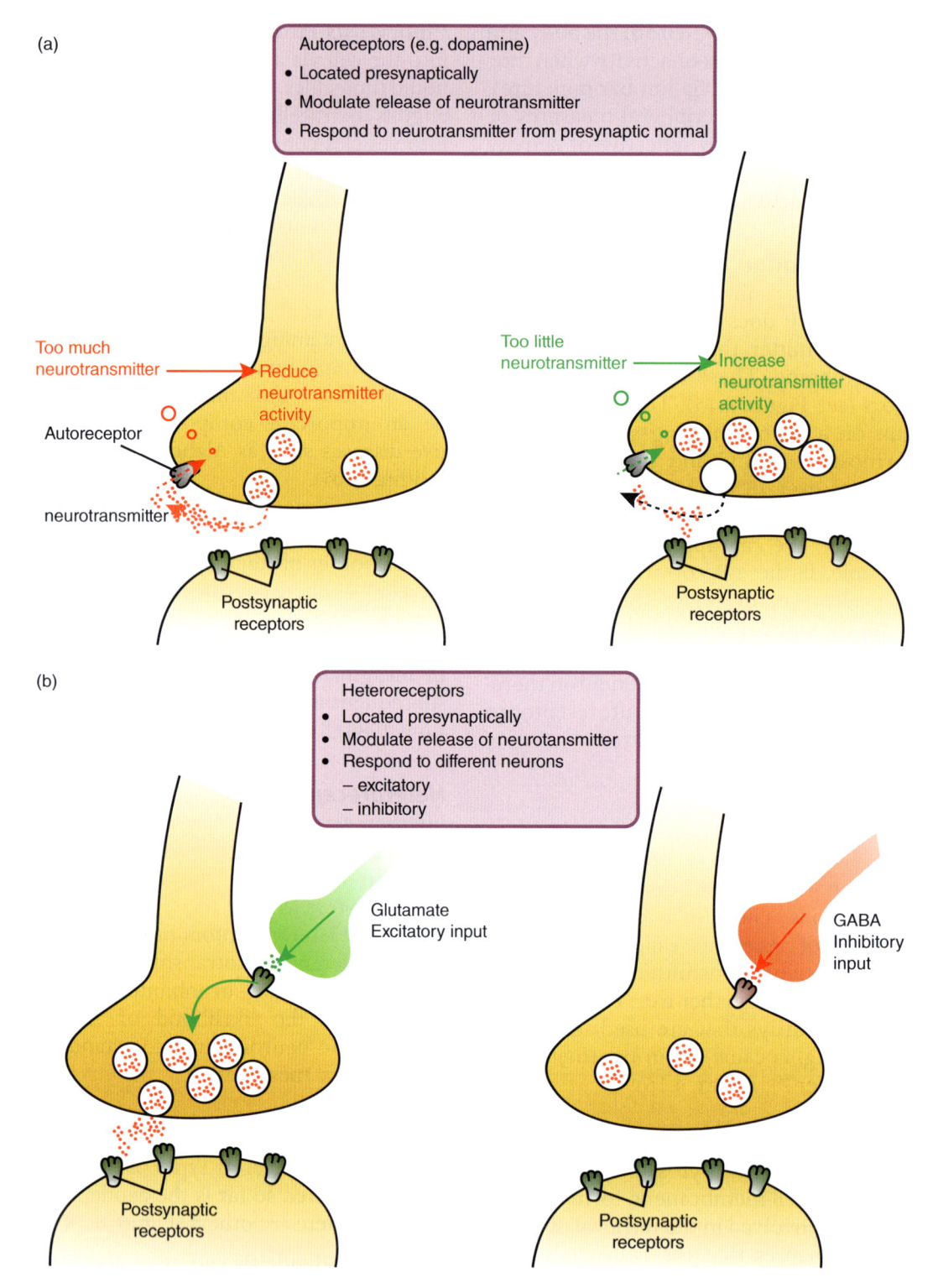

FIGURE 4.15 *Autoreceptor regulation and heteroreceptors. (a) Autoreceptors respond to the synaptic environment. (b) Heteroreceptors receive presynaptic input from other neurons. (Left) Glutamate is an excitatory amino acid that facilitates the release of dopamine from this dopaminergic neuron. (Right) GABA is an inhibitory amino acid and stops the release of dopamine from this neuron.*

CHAPTER 4 THE NEURON, THE ENDOCRINE SYSTEM AND COMMUNICATION

With all these connections in the billions of neurons within the brain, the complex network of neuronal interaction means that the neuroscientist's work will be never-ending.

Retrograde Signalling

Up until this point we have dealt with a presynaptic cell communicating with a postsynaptic cell and not a postsynaptic cell communicating with a presynaptic cell. It is now accepted that the latter case is possible (see Alger, 2002). In **retrograde signalling**, the postsynaptic neuron communicates with the presynaptic neuron which may inhibit further release (but not always). Three forms of retrograde signals have been identified (Fitzsimonds & Poo, 1998) (see Figure 4.19):

- membrane-permeant factors: the fusible factors such as nitric oxide fuse from the postsynaptic membrane to the presynaptic neuron;

- membrane-bound factors: when modulation is achieved by receptors on the postsynaptic membrane being physically linked with receptors on the presynaptic membrane; and

- secreted factors: a chemical messenger is released from the postsynaptic cell and interacts with the presynaptic cell.

All of these have been implicated in both developing and mature synapses (Tao & Poo, 2001). Much of

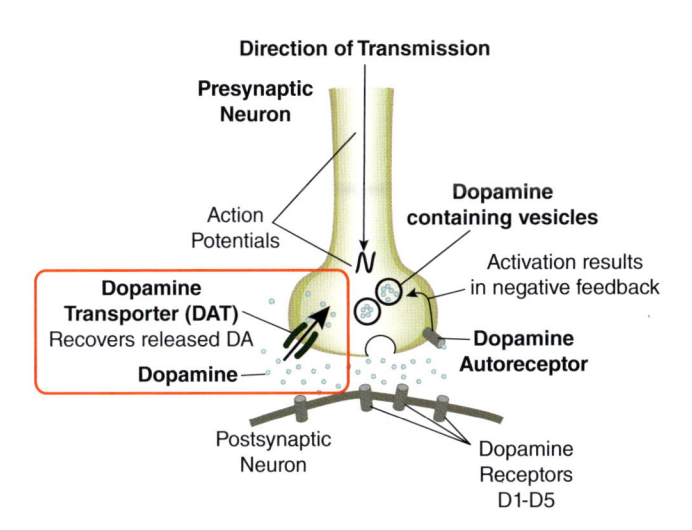

FIGURE 4.16 *Reuptake.*
Source: Chandler, C. (2010) *The Science of ADHD*, p151.
Reproduced by permission of John Wiley & Sons Ltd.

- In **axoaxonic synapses**, the presynaptic terminal synapses onto the axon of another neuron.

- In **axosynaptic synapses**, the presynaptic terminal of one axon synapses with the presynaptic terminal of another neuron. The interaction of these two neurons can include, for example, the GABA being released from one presynaptic terminal and interacting with a heteroreceptor on a dopaminergic presynaptic terminal. The actions in this case will be to inhibit the release of dopamine from the dopaminergic presynaptic terminal because GABA is an inhibitory amino acid.

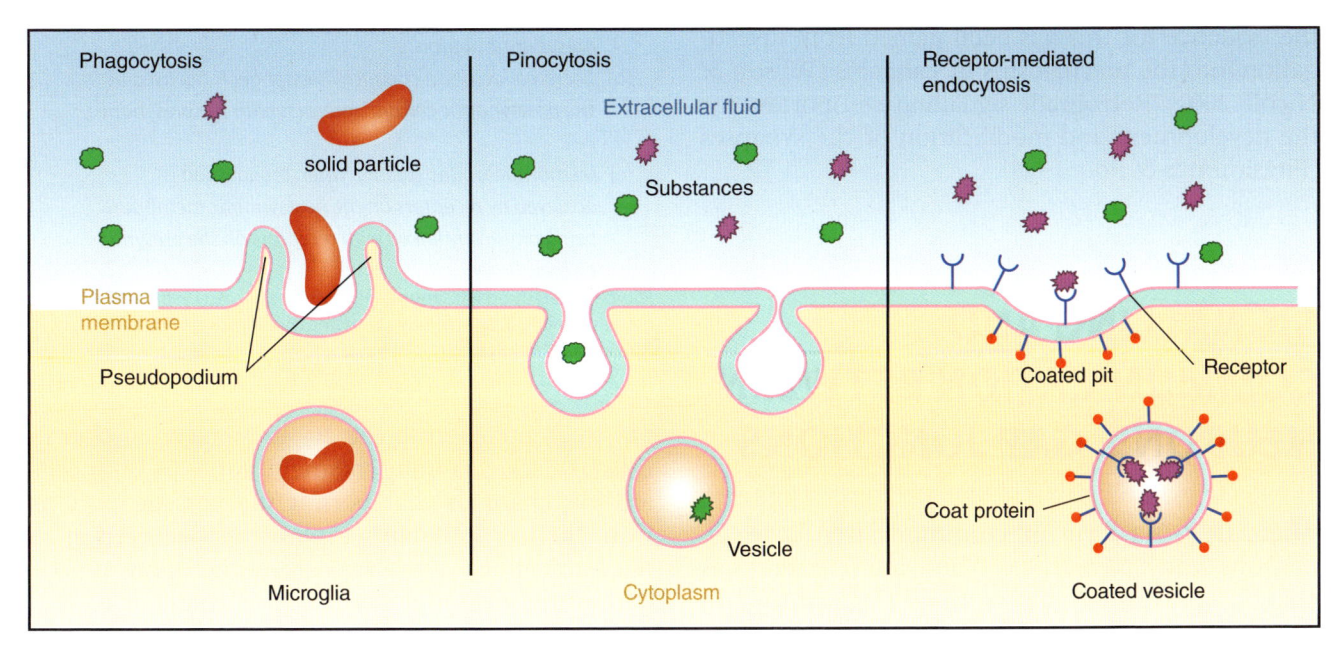

FIGURE 4.17 *Endocytosis.*

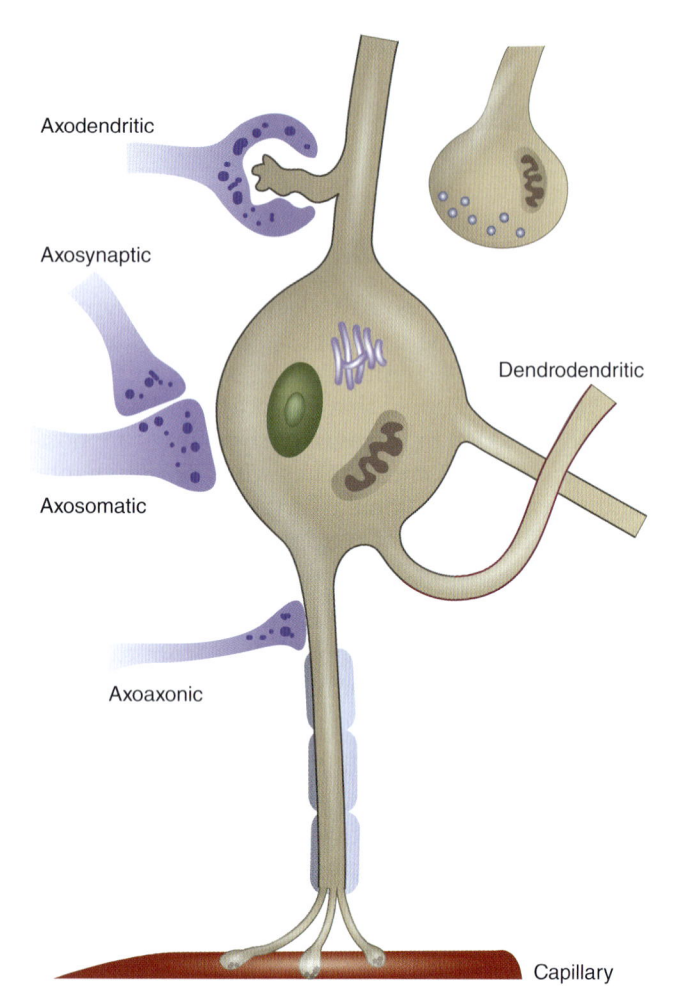

FIGURE 4.18 Synaptic connections and their locations.

the evidence for this has been gained from investigation into the mechanisms of cannabis (Wilson & Nicoll, 2001). Retrograde signalling is important for the development and modification of the synapses (Fitzsimonds & Poo, 1998).

SIGNALLING AND COMMUNICATION BETWEEN NEURONS: GAP JUNCTIONS

There is also a form of communication between neurons which is electrical. These are referred to as electrical synapses or gap junctions (Figure 4.20). In a gap junction, the gap between the pre- and postsynaptic membrane is extremely small, for example 2–4

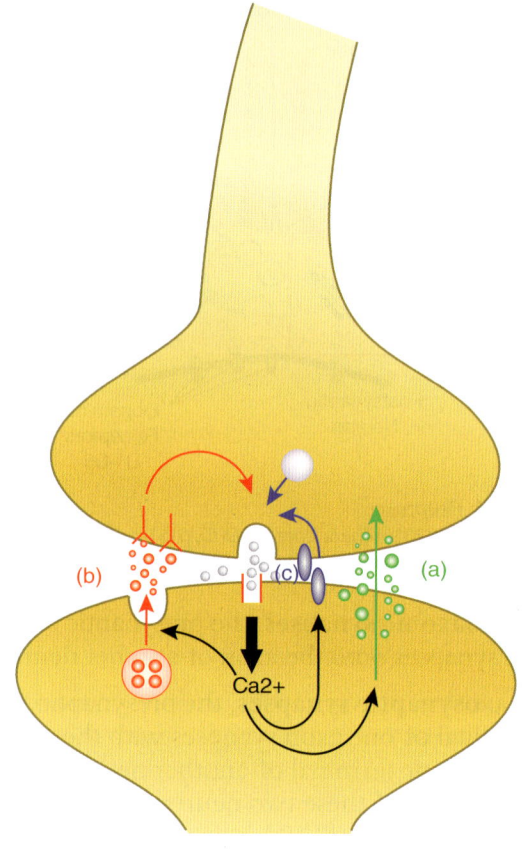

FIGURE 4.19 *Retrograde signalling. Using cannabis as a research tool has led to an increased understanding of neurotransmission in which neurochemicals can be released from precursor molecules on the postsynaptic membrane, thereby modulating neurotransmitter release by interacting with calcium (Ca^{2+}).*

(a) *Membrane-permeant factors: the fusible factors such as nitric oxide fuse from the postsynaptic membrane to the presynaptic neuron.*
(b) *Secreted factors: a chemical messenger is released from the postsynaptic cell and interacts with the presynaptic cell.*
(c) *Membrane-bound factors: when modulation is achieved by receptors on the postsynaptic membrane being physically linked with receptors on the presynaptic membrane.*

Source: Based upon Fitzsimonds, R. M., & Poo, M.-M. (1998). Retrograde signaling in the development and modification of synapses. *Physiological Reviews, 78*(1), 143-170.

nm in comparison to the 20–40 nm seen in chemical synapses. Spanning the membranes of both cells are ion channels that permit the passage of ions from the intracellular cytoplasm of one neuron to the intracellular cytoplasm of another neuron. The communication in a gap junction is similar to that of the action potential (see Connors & Long (2004) for reviews; Meier & Dermietzel, 2006). The speed

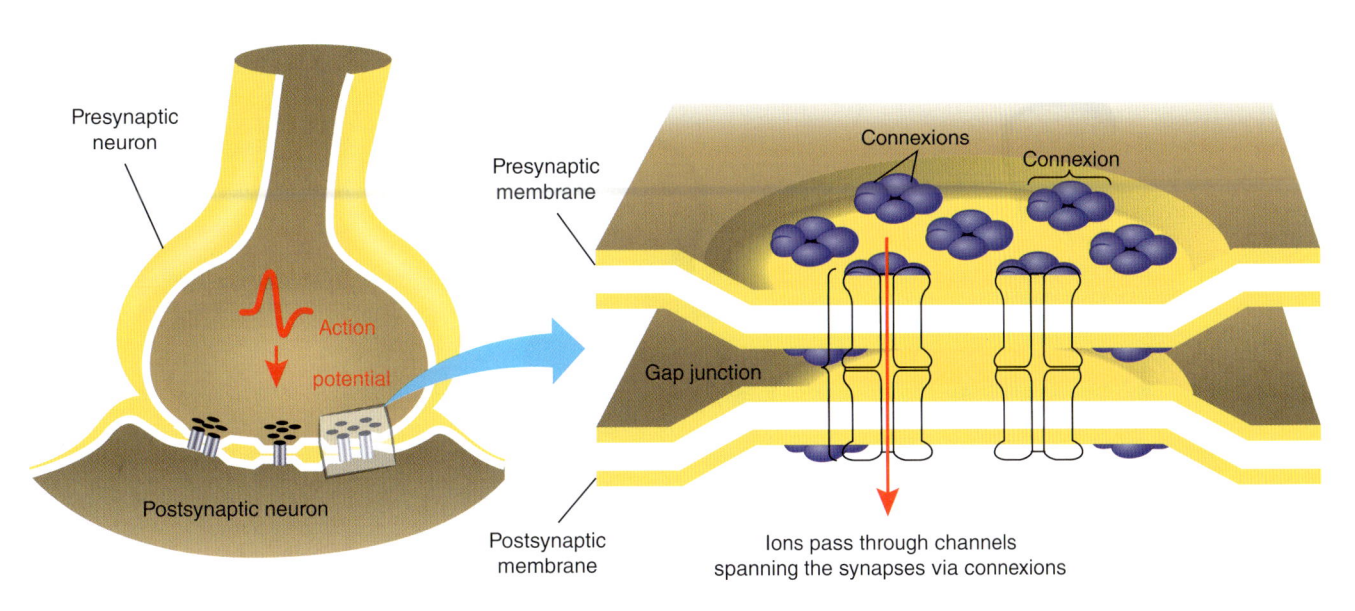

FIGURE 4.20 *Gap junctions. Electrical synapses exist in the tightly connected gap junction.*

at which communication occurs in a gap junction is therefore considerably quicker than a chemical synapse. Pereda (2014) emphasized that we should consider chemical and electrical synapses as working together rather than being separate chemical or electrical synapses. Electrical synapses are thought to be important in developmental processes (Dere & Zlomuzica, 2012), perception (Sohl et al., 2005) and also in disease processes such as autistic spectrum disorder and Alzheimer's disease (Van Spronsen & Hoogenraad, 2010).

ENDOCRINOLOGY: STUDYING LONG-DISTANCE COMMUNICATION

Electrical and synaptic communication are very localized forms of communication in which entities converse with each other over short distances. However, there is another mechanism by which information can be transmitted throughout the body. This mechanism occurs via the secretion of **hormones** into the bloodstream and is the subject of endocrinology. Hormones are chemical substances formed in specialized glands or cells and affect targets often some distance away (Figure 4.21). They are distinct from neurotransmitters by virtue of the distance that they have to travel.

Hormones are chemicals that can be lipids (e.g. steroid such as **testosterone**), peptides/proteins (e.g. vasopressin) or amine molecules (e.g. adrenaline). Note that adrenaline is also listed as a neurotransmitter. Adrenaline and noradrenaline can both be considered neurotransmitters and hormones, depending upon their site of action. As a neurotransmitter, adrenaline and noradrenaline only have a short distance in which they traverse the synapse but as a hormone they have far greater distances to travel once they are released from the **adrenal gland**. As Neave (2008) points out, finding a precise definition of a hormone has not been easy as some classifications have been overinclusive or restrictive.

Amino acid hormones are modified from amino acids and include the **catecholamines**, the **indolamines** and **thyroid hormones**. The catecholamines and indolamines have been discussed earlier and can be seen in Figure 4.12. The thyroid hormones are known as thyroxine and tri-iodothyronine. Many may be familiar with thyroxine as this is the substitute given to people with **hypothyroidism** (see Box 4.4).

Peptide hormones consist of chains of amino acids that are differentiated by size. **Oxytocin** and **vasopressin** typify the small peptide hormones, whereas glucagon and adrenocorticotrophic hormone are representative of the large peptide group. Polypeptides include insulin (see Chapter 15) and growth hormone.

The **steroid hormones** are typified by the sex hormones such as testosterone and oestrogen (see

110 PSYCHOBIOLOGY

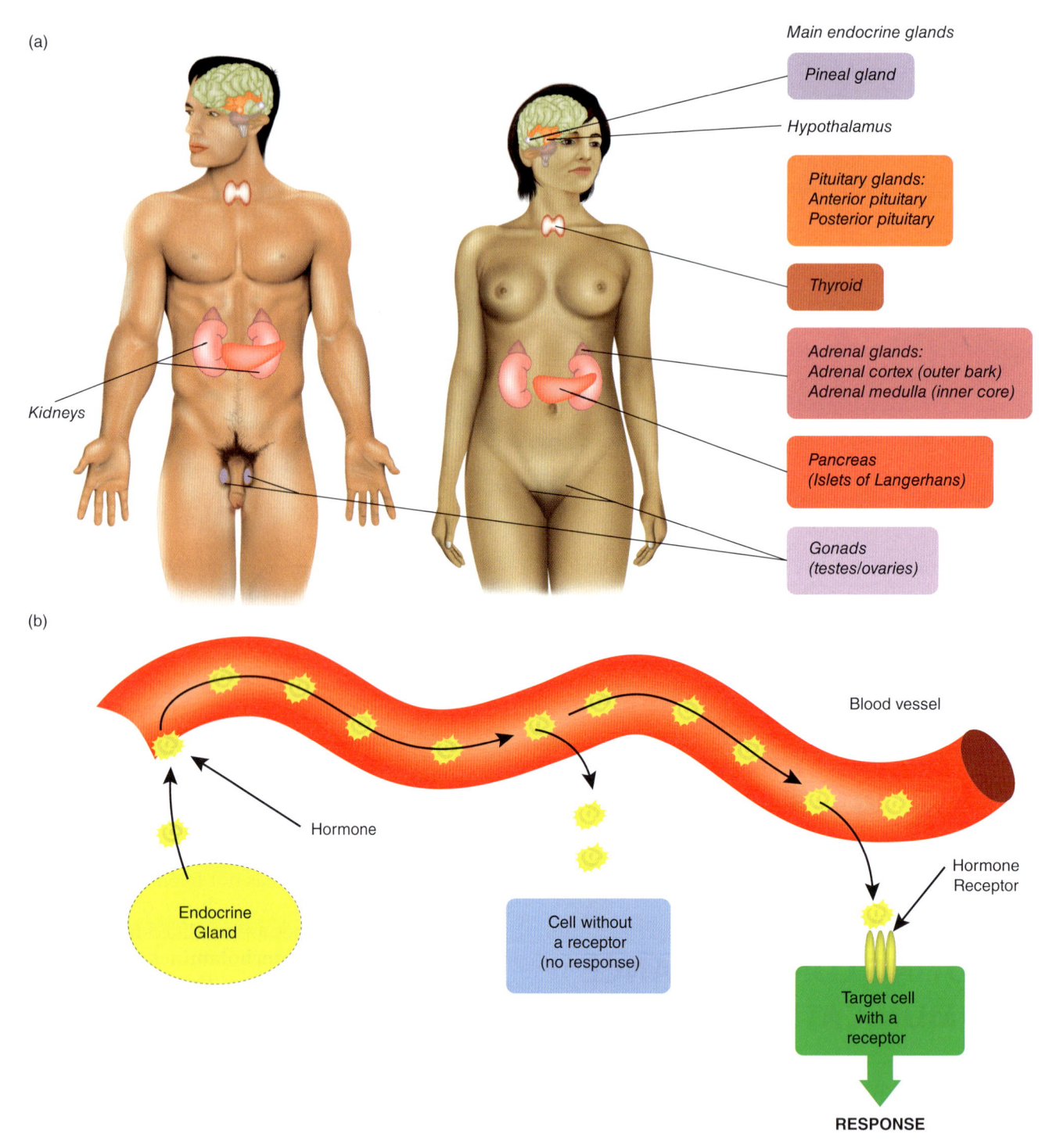

FIGURE 4.21 The endocrine glands. (a) The endocrine glands in male and female. (b) Hormones are released from endocrine cells into the bloodstream and travel some distance until they find a target cell with a hormone receptor and produce a response.

Chapter 14). The male sex hormones are referred to as **androgen**s and the main one is testosterone, but they also include **dehydroepiandrosterone** (DHEA) and **dihydrotestosterone** (DHT). The effects of male hormones were noted in the late 19th century when Brown-Séquard (1889) injected a liquid obtained from the testes of dogs and guinea pigs. Surprisingly, he found the effects to be beneficial with a general feeling of well-being. I am not convinced that anyone knowing that they had

BOX 4.4: HYPO- AND HYPERTHYROIDISM

The thyroid gland can be either overactive or underactive in 1–5% of the population (Vanderpump, 2011).

The symptoms of hypothyroidism are similar to other disorders and can lead to physical and psychological changes. The onset is insidious and may not be detected until the symptoms are well established and become problematic. Hypothyroidism is a result of an underactive thyroid not producing enough thyroxine (T4). The most common cause of an underactive thyroid gland is an autoimmune response in which the immune system attacks the thyroid gland (Stathatos & Daniels, 2012).

Common symptoms in the psychological domain include:

- tiredness;
- being sensitive to cold;
- weight gain;
- depression;
- slow movements;
- slow thoughts;
- loss of libido;
- pain, numbness and a tingling sensation in the hand and fingers (carpal tunnel syndrome); and
- irregular or heavy periods (I include this due to the hormonal influences on behaviour).

Hyperthyroidism is when there is an increase in thyroid gland activity and therefore too much thyroxine or tri-iodothyronine. The most common cause of hyperthyroidism is Graves' disease which is an autoimmune disorder in which the autoimmune attack increases thyroid hormones (Brent, 2008; Weetman, 2000) with 100–200 cases per 100,000 population per year in the UK (Tunbridge et al., 1977).

The symptoms of hyperthyroidism include:

- hyperactivity;
- anxiety, irritability and nervousness;
- insomnia;
- fatigue;
- muscle weakness;
- dysmenorrhoea or amenorrhoea; and
- loss of libido.

A group of drugs known as thionamides can inhibit the excess amounts of thyroid hormones, thus alleviating the symptoms of hyperthyroidism.

The symptoms of both hyper- and hypothyroidism overlap not only with each other but also other psychological conditions. It is therefore crucial to engage in differential diagnosis in which one should eliminate abnormal thyroid activity as a suspect before continuing with a psychiatric diagnosis.

---

received extract of dog testes would feel the same benefit – nausea and revulsion might well be the predominant emotional reaction.

Despite the high concentrations of testosterone in males, it is not restricted to males. Females also have androgens, but not in the same quantities as males. And of course, in the female androgens are not derived from testes but instead from ovaries and the adrenal gland; levels change with age (Davison et al., 2005) and the menstrual cycle (Judd & Yen, 1973).

Oestrogen and progesterone are the female sex hormones that are released by the ovaries and are critically involved in pregnancy. Levels of these hormones are influenced by pregnancy and also the menstrual cycle (Norman & Litwack, 1997).

Glucocorticoids are another type of hormone that are manufactured and liberated by the adrenal glands. These have a wide range of affects, most notably because of the actions of **corticosterone** and **cortisol**. The glucocorticoids are important in mediating our stress response, in particular along the **hypothalamic-pituitary-adrenal axis** (see Chapter 23).

The adrenal gland is one of the many endocrine glands that we have (see Figure 4.21). The main endocrine glands are:

- **pineal gland**;
- **hypothalamus**;
- **pituitary gland**;
- **thyroid gland**;
- **pancreas**;
- **ovaries**; and
- **testes**.

TABLE 4.2 Hormones and their function

Hormone	Function
Follicle-stimulating hormone (FSH)	Ovaries: stimulates development of eggs and follicles
	Testes: stimulates production of sperm
Luteinizing hormone (LH)	Females: stimulates ovulation and corpus luteum to secrete progesterone and oestrogen
	Males: stimulates interstitial cells of testes to secrete testosterone
Thyroid-stimulating hormone (TSH)	Stimulates growth of gland and secretion of thyroid hormone (TH)
Adrenocorticotrophic hormone (ACTH)	Regulates response to stress, stimulates adrenal cortex to secrete corticosteroids that regulate glucose, fat and protein metabolism
Prolactin (PRL)	Female: milk synthesis after delivery
	Male: increases LH sensitivity, thus increasing testosterone secretion
Growth hormone (GH)	Promotes tissue growth

The function of the **endocrine system** is to maintain internal homeostasis, support cell growth, **co-ordinate** development and reproduction and facilitate responses to the external environment. Hormones have diverse effects. In the brain, they can alter neuronal responsiveness or the activity of genes within the cell. The effects of hormones are set out in greater detail in Chapter 14 in which we see that the sex hormones are extremely important in the developing brain. Hormone secretion is generally restricted to the endocrine glands and it is therefore pertinent to discuss them within the context of communication. In the process of endocrine regulation, the hormones that are released are regulated by other hormones which are referred to as releasing hormones.

The pineal gland produces **melatonin**, levels of which fall and rise according to the time of day; during the night melatonin is released and during daylight it is reduced (Wurtman et al., 1963). Melatonin is synthesized from serotonin and is thought to control our sleep patterns (Brzezinski, 1997) (see Chapter 18).

Although it is difficult to pinpoint the most important of the endocrine glands, if there were such a position available, the hypothalamus and pituitary gland are rivals for it. The hypothalamus and the pituitary gland are intimately connected. The hypothalamus synthesizes and releases via the **periventricular nucleus** (PVN) of the hypothalamus **corticotrophin-releasing hormone** (CRH or corticotrophin-releasing factor (CRF)). CRH then goes on to stimulate the secretion of **adrenocorticotrophic hormone** (ACTH). **Gonadotrophin-releasing hormone** is made in the anterior hypothalamus and controls the release of **luteinizing hormone** (LH) and follicle-stimulating hormone (FSH) (see Table 4.2). Growth hormone-releasing hormone is released from the ventro/medial nucleus (VMA) and the arcuate nucleus of the hypothalamus.

Thyrotrophin-releasing hormone comes from the PVN which stimulates the anterior pituitary gland, enabling it to release TSH.

The target of many of these hypothalamic hormones is the pituitary gland which is divided into anterior and posterior sections (see Figure 4.22). The pituitary gland is sometimes known as the master gland. Table 4.2 lists hormones secreted by the anterior pituitary gland and their primary functions. The posterior pituitary gland releases oxytocin and vasopressin (which is an antidiuretic hormone). Vasopressin targets the kidneys to increase water retention and therefore reduce urination (Schrier, 2006). Oxytocin has many functions including the transport of sperm to the **fallopian tubes** (Kunz et al., 2007), the control of labour contractions during birth (Fuchs et al., 1982) and lactation for feeding after the birth (Soloff et al., 1979).

The thyroid gland releases thyroid hormones but its main function is to regulate metabolism and the development of the brain and nervous system and guide sexual maturation. The pancreas is an important gland, especially for feeding and drinking (see Chapter 15) as it secretes glucagon and insulin (Adrian et al., 1978).

The adrenal gland sits above the kidneys and is divided into the adrenal cortex and the adrenal medulla. The adrenal cortex secretes corticosteroids, mineralocorticoids and glucocorticoids. **Aldosterone** is the main mineralocorticoid which responds to changes in blood volume or pressure

CHAPTER 4 THE NEURON, THE ENDOCRINE SYSTEM AND COMMUNICATION

Action of Hormones at Their Target

The amine and peptide hormones interact with a hormone receptor in the cell membrane in a somewhat similar way as neurotransmitters interact with the metabotropic receptor (Catt & Dufau, 1977). The resultant change in the receptor upon the attachment of a hormone results in second messengers being activated (Bohm et al., 1997). These hormones are relatively quick in their activation, i.e. from a number of seconds to a few minutes.

Steroid hormones are slower to act than the peptide hormones and can take a number of hours before the effects occur. The target of steroid hormones is somewhat different from that of the peptide hormones in as much as the receptor is inside the cell, not spanning the cell membrane (Figure 4.23). Steroid hormones can pass in and

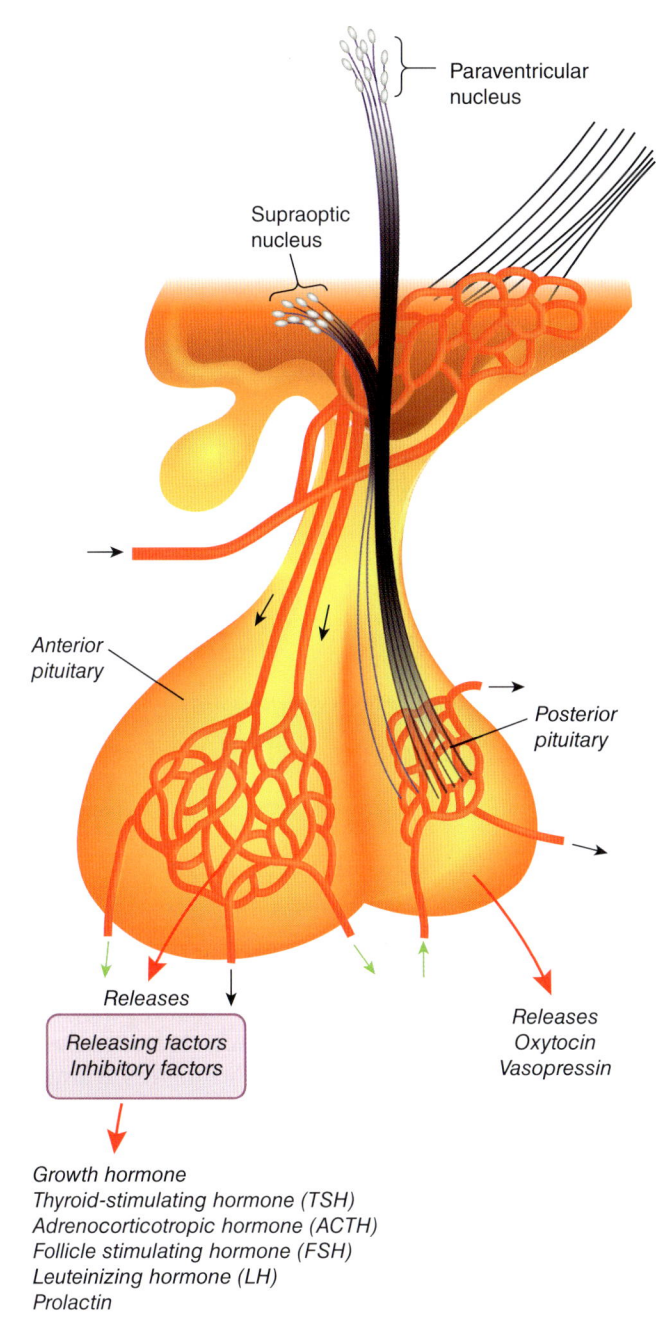

FIGURE 4.22 *The anterior and posterior pituitary gland.*

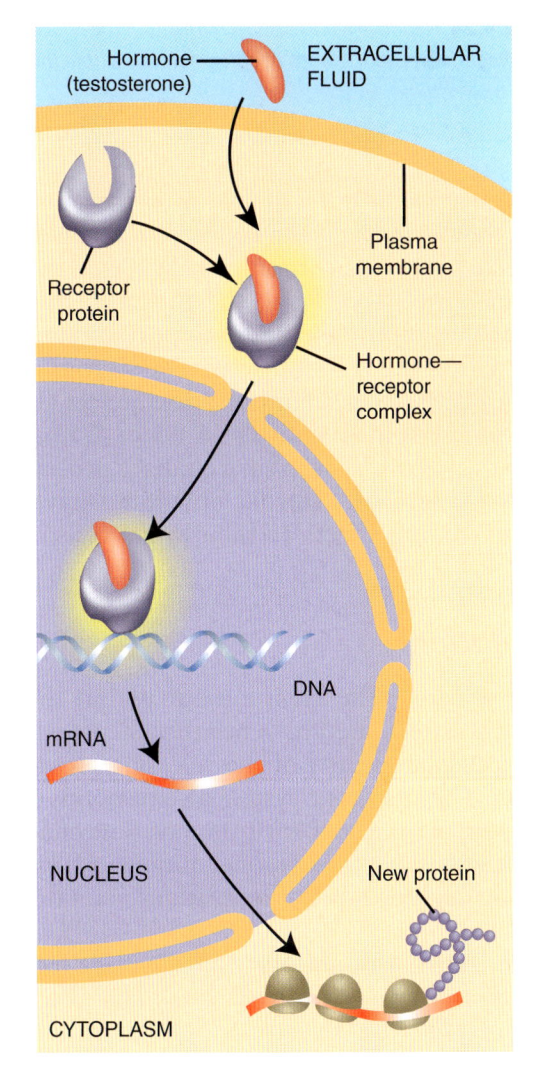

FIGURE 4.23 *Steroid hormone receptor interaction.*

by increasing sodium and water retention. Cortisol is also released by the adrenal cortex and more detail can be found in Chapter 23. It is important in how we deal with stressful situations, but it is also involved in numerous other homeostatic functions and regulators of cardiovascular, metabolic and immunological systems (Abraham et al., 2013; Brenner et al., 1998; Whitworth et al., 2005).

The ovaries and testes have already been mentioned in relation to the sex hormones and a full review can be found in Chapter 14.

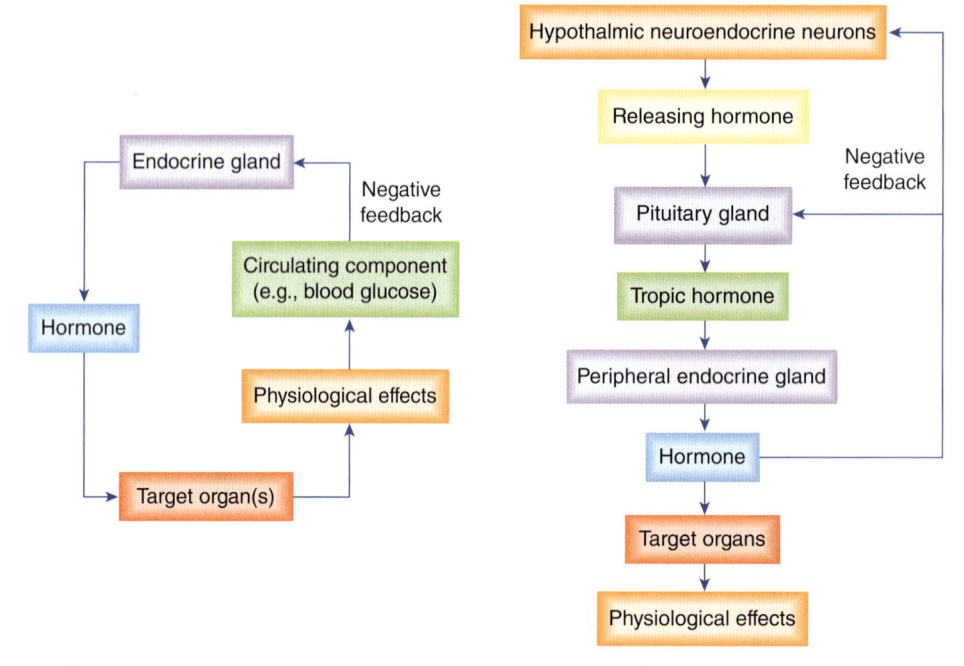

FIGURE 4.24 Negative feedback mechanisms of the endocrine system. (Left) Negative feedback loop to the general system. (Right) Negative feedback loops at different levels within the system.

out of many cells but will only produce a response when they come across a cell with a receptor that is selected for the hormone inside. Once the steroid hormone is bound to the receptor, this steroid–receptor complex binds to specific regions of DNA within the cell's nucleus. The steroid–receptor complex acts as a transcription factor, altering the expression of specific DNA codes (Yamamoto & Alberts, 1976). This in turn changes protein production. Therefore, steroid hormones have slow yet long-lasting effects on their target cells.

Regulation

In the synapse, the environment within the synaptic gap is regulated by a number of processes in the immediate vicinity of the releasing presynaptic neuron. The endocrine system also responds to feed back from the external environment. The endocrine system is sensitive to hormonal output and responds to either high or low concentrations via a negative feedback loop.

The most straightforward negative feedback loop is **autocrine feedback** in which the endocrine glands that release a particular hormone respond to feedback from the circulating hormone (Figure 4.24). Feedback loops can be elaborate and include feedback from the target cell, in which the endocrine gland releases a hormone and the resultant interaction with the target cell where its response is monitored by the endocrine gland. The response of the target cell is also monitored by higher regions of the brain in which feedback is received by the hypothalamus. Within this framework, we can also add in the anterior pituitary gland which is also sensitive to the output of the endocrine glands and, together with the hypothalamus, will either increase or decrease the secretion of releasing factors.

SUMMARY

Despite the implication of the resting potential, the intact brain is never at rest. The brain is actively communicating via a number of methods. Intracellular communication involves electrical signals via which the neuron is depolarized and an action potential occurs. Communication between neurons happens via both chemical effects at the synapses and at electrical synapse or gap junctions. The neuron is the main protagonist in the brain, but requires considerable support from other cells and structures within

CHAPTER 4 THE NEURON, THE ENDOCRINE SYSTEM AND COMMUNICATION

itself. Neurons communicate within the small vicinity of their local neighbourhood; the endocrine system also communicates with the brain (and body) but does so by travelling far greater distances. To use a London Underground analogy, synaptic communication is all in zone 1 (the central area), while endocrine communication takes one out to suburban zone 6.

LEARNING OUTCOME QUESTIONS

You should be able to answer the following questions.
- Describe the infrastructure of a neuron.
- How is a neural impulse propagated from the dendrite to the synapse?
- What do hormones do?

FURTHER READING

Brodal, P. (2010). *The central nervous system: Structure and function*. Oxford, UK: Oxford University Press.

Carpenter, R., & Reddi, B. (2012). *Neurophysiology: A conceptual approach*. Boca Raton, FL: CRC Press.

Neave, N. (2008). *Hormones and behaviour: A psychological approach*. Cambridge, UK: Cambridge University Press.

MIND MAP

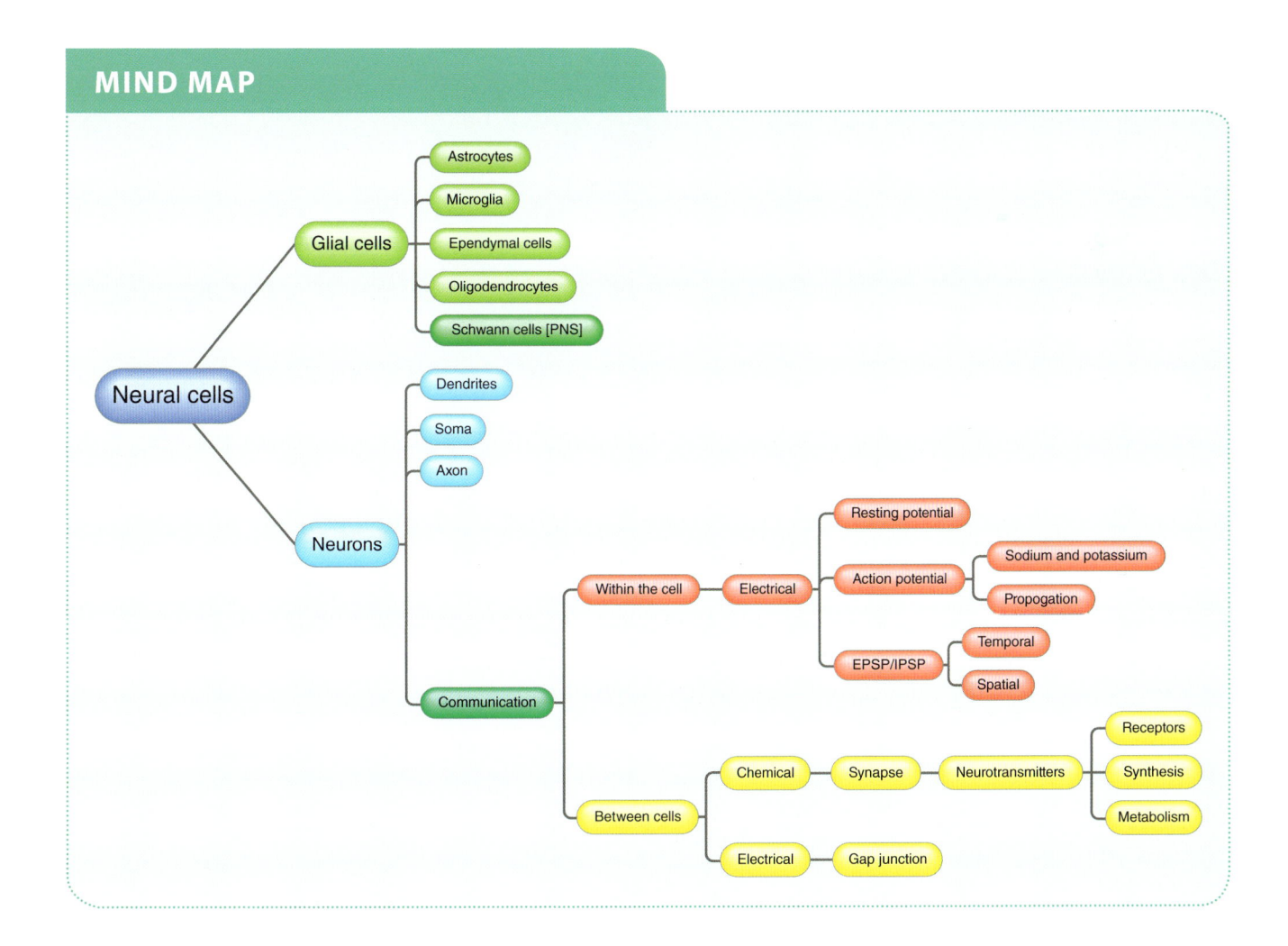

- **Neural cells**
  - **Glial cells**
    - Astrocytes
    - Microglia
    - Ependymal cells
    - Oligodendrocytes
    - Schwann cells [PNS]
  - **Neurons**
    - Dendrites
    - Soma
    - Axon
    - **Communication**
      - Within the cell
        - Electrical
          - Resting potential
          - Action potential
            - Sodium and potassium
            - Propogation
          - EPSP/IPSP
            - Temporal
            - Spatial
      - Between cells
        - Chemical — Synapse — Neurotransmitters
          - Receptors
          - Synthesis
          - Metabolism
        - Electrical — Gap junction

5 Neuroanatomy and the Nervous System

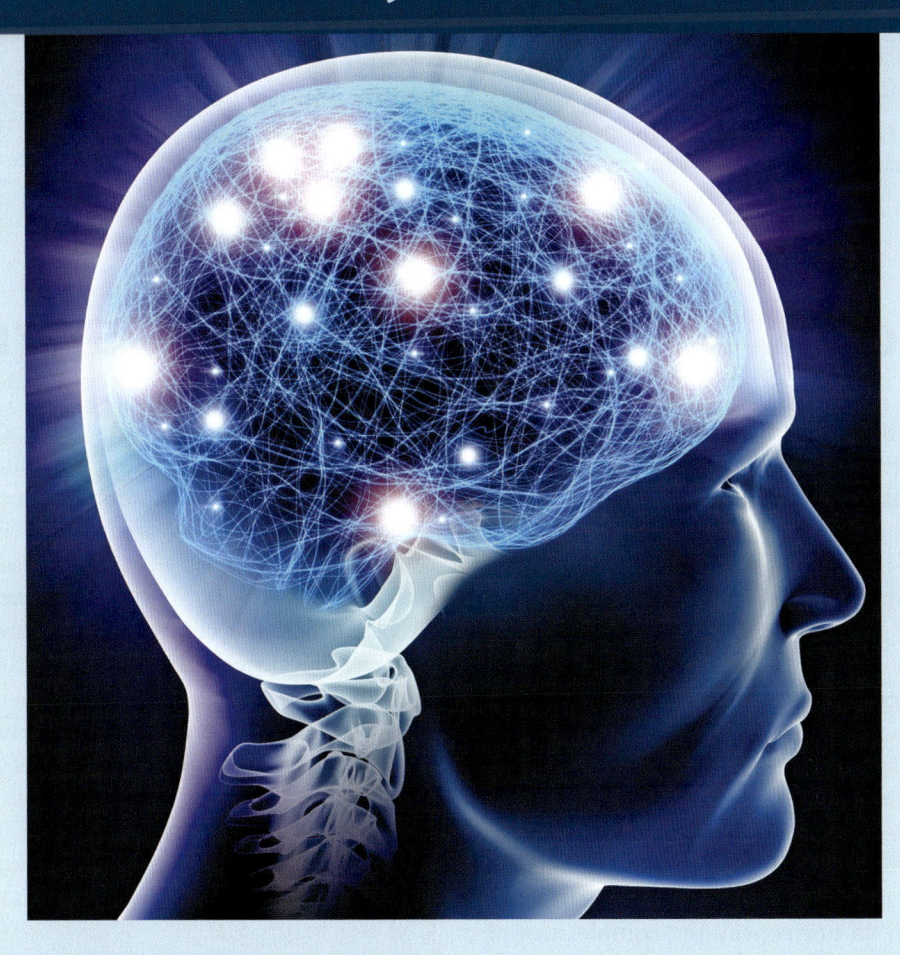

ANATOMY OF THE CHAPTER

This chapter will highlight the following.

- The different nervous system components and their functional role.
- Divisions of the brain and their functional neuroanatomy.
- Communication between the nervous and endocrine systems.
- Afferent (input) and efferent (output) connections.
- The vascular supply of the brain.

INTRODUCTION 118

THE NERVOUS SYSTEM 118

NEUROANATOMY 130

BRAIN REGIONS 132

THE INS AND OUTS OF BLOOD SUPPLY TO THE BRAIN 145

SINUSES 149

ENDOCRINE SYSTEM 150

SUMMARY 150

LEARNING OUTCOMES

1. To understand the differences between the components and divisions of the nervous system and their functional significance.
2. To be able to differentiate regions of the brain on different levels and identify their functions.
3. To understand how the brain processes afferent and efferent projections.
4. To appreciate the interconnections of neuro-anatomical regions and nervous systems.

INTRODUCTION

The cells of the body are divided into systems that perform particular functions. The hepatic system comprises the liver and processes nutrients and toxins, the cardiovascular system comprises a heart that pumps blood through the body. The nervous system comprises neurons and support cells. In this chapter attention is focused on the organization of the nervous systems and their functional role. In addition, the brain will be dissected into its component parts and the functional architecture evaluated. It is these components that often receive media attention suggesting that scientists have found the region of the brain responsible for either a particular behaviour or a disorder. Often these reports are misleading in that they offer conclusive evidence for the role of the brain region in a particular behaviour. Such reports often do not convey the complexities of the brain and how specific regions of the brain communicate internally. The brain is a huge network of billions of neurons that are in constant communication. It is somewhat simplistic to consider a particular region in isolation from other regions of the brain. However, because of the complexities of the brain, such reductionistic techniques make a rather complicated system a little easier to understand. I take no pride but also have no shame in adhering to similar reductionistic techniques.

The nervous system, including the brain, is composed of the functional units – neurons (see Chapter 4). When considered *en masse*, neurons within the brain make up specific regions. The specific regions of the brain can be identified by both structural and functional architecture. When one considers the nervous system and the brain, it has to be remembered that the focus of our microscope can be directed at either gross anatomy or very specific anatomy with an increase in optical power.

THE NERVOUS SYSTEM

When discussing the **nervous system**, one starts off with the most gross resolution of neuroanatomy. However, as we get more precise and zoom in to the finer detail, it can be seen that there are many subdivisions of the nervous system (see Figure 5.1). At low resolution the microscope detects that the nervous system can be split into two branches: the **central nervous system** (CNS) and the **peripheral nervous system** (PNS). Much attention is given to the CNS as it is contained within the skull and spine. The CNS is composed of the brain and the spinal cord. Although we have a brain-centric view of ourselves, it should be remembered that the brain has evolved as an outgrowth from the spinal cord (see Chapter 3).

The PNS is on the outside of the skull and spine, thus communicating with the regions of the body outside the CNS (see Figure 5.2).

The Peripheral Nervous System (PNS)

The PNS is composed of a dense network of nerves. Nerves are merely bundles of axons. The PNS is further subdivided into the **somatic nervous system** (SNS) and the **autonomic nervous system** (ANS).

The somatic nervous system (SNS)

The SNS interacts with the external environment. It receives sensory information along **afferent nerves** (e.g. signals from eyes, skin, muscles, etc.) and relays the information to the CNS. The CNS processes this incoming information and sends motor signals via **efferent nerves** to the skeletal muscles (e.g. your hand grips a pen). Therefore, afferent nerves carry sensory information and efferent nerves send out motor commands. The SNS is involved with voluntary action, whereas the ANS controls the actions of the internal organs (e.g. a heart).

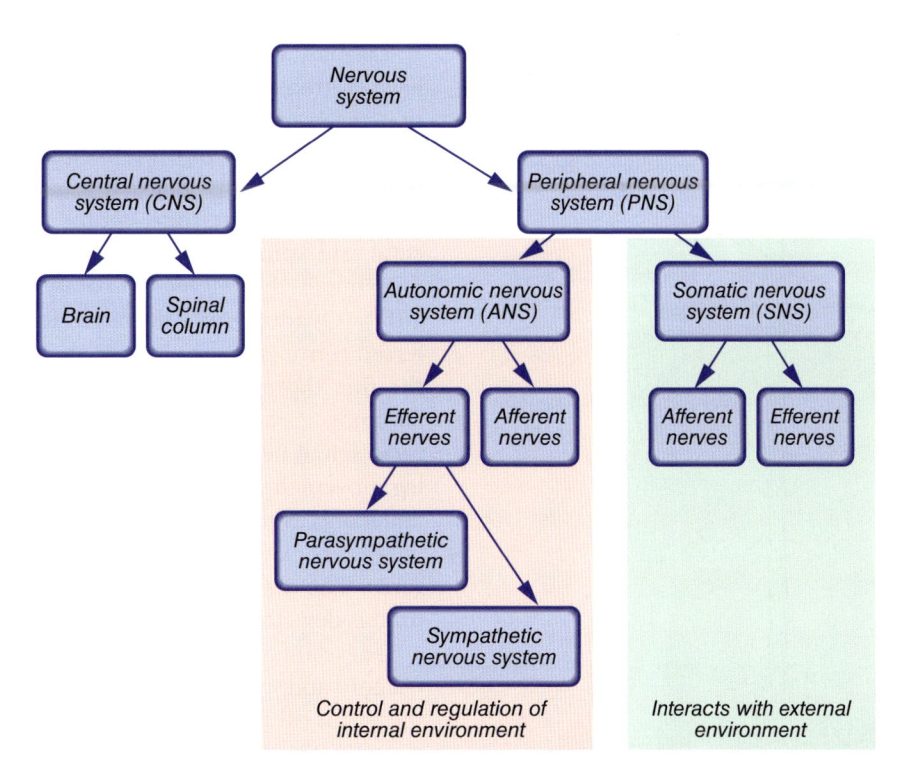

FIGURE 5.1 *Divisions of the nervous system.*

The SNS can be divided into two further components: the cranial nerves and the spinal nerves.

Cranial nerves

There are 12 pairs of **cranial nerves** serving left and right sides of the head and neck (cranial nerves numbered I–XII). The 12 pairs are either sensory or motor nerves or both. The cranial nerves leave the CNS at the level of the brainstem. However, two of the cranial nerves providing sensory input, the olfactory and optic nerves, enter the CNS directly at the forebrain. Olfactory information has been important throughout evolution and is essential for providing the organism with a detailed account of the environment. Olfactory information can pass directly to the amygdala (processing fear, see Chapter 17) and somatosensory cortices without passing through the thalamus (see Chapter 10). The cranial nerves pass either through the foramina, which are little holes in the skull, or through canals within the bone of the skull. The accessory nerve is the only cranial nerve which exits via the spinal cord and not the brain.

The cranial nerves and their broad functions are as follows.

I	Olfactory	Sensory
II	Optic	Sensory
III	Oculomotor	Motor
IV	Trochlear	Motor
V	Trigeminal	Sensory/motor
VI	Abducens	Motor
VII	Facial	Sensory/motor
VIII	Vestibulocochlear	Sensory
IX	Glossopharyngeal	Sensory/motor
X	Vagus	Sensory/motor
XI	Spinal accessory	Motor
XII	Hypoglossal	Sensory/motor

The role of the cranial nerves can be seen in Figure 5.3. With such important information passing through the cranial nerves, damage to one or more of them could have pronounced effects (see Box 5.1).

The spinal nerves

While the cranial nerves interact with the head and neck, the spinal nerves emanate from the length of the spinal cord. There are 31 pairs of **spinal nerves** that exit the spine on each side of the vertebral column. The spinal nerves are composed of two roots, which serve different functions: the dorsal root, which transmits sensory information to the CNS, and the ventral root, which consists of motor projections to effector organs. The spinal nerves are grouped into the regions of the spinal column – cervical, thoracic, lumbar, sacral and coccygeal

Lesions, or breaks, in the spinal column therefore have a tremendous impact on the sensory information received and also on the ability to send messages to the extremities in order to initiate movement – this is seen as paralysis. Below the site of the lesion there is a loss of muscle tone, motor function, reflexes, visceral and somatic sensation. Where the lesion occurs determines the degree of paralysis (Kirshblum et al., 2011). Quadriplegia, although tetraplegia is the preferred term, is when the spinal cord is damaged above the first thoracic vertebra. This results in paralysis of all limbs. Paraplegia occurs with lesions below the thoracic spinal nerve and results in varied impairments of leg movement. The paraplegic has full use of their arms and hands as the lesion is below the site at which the spinal nerves exit the spinal column to innervate the upper torso. The mapping of the body parts to the spinal column is depicted in Figure 5.4.

There are numerous disorders and diseases of the spinal cord and spinal nerves. **Brown-Séquard syndrome** is the result of a hemi-section of the spinal cord and produces disassociation between conscious proprioception (knowing where your body is) and the sensations of pain and temperature. The loss of proprioception and the disassociation from sensation occur due to the lesion influencing proprioception on the ipsilateral (same) side and sensation on the **contralateral** (opposite) side (Brody & Wilkins, 1968).

Amyotrophic lateral sclerosis (ALS) or Lou Gehrig's disease is a degenerative disease of upper and lower motor neurons. The disease manifests itself early on in the hands or arms as simple tasks become difficult to execute (Walling, 1999). **Multiple sclerosis**, which is demyelination of neurons, results in numerous symptoms including motor and sensory symptoms (see Chapter 4).

The Autonomic Nervous System (ANS)

The ANS regulates the internal organs of the body. This is achieved via **autonomic ganglia** which are collections of neurons. Thus, the ANS interacts with the internal environment to maintain homeostasis (however, some have disputed that homeostasis is required and it is allostasis that is important – see Chapters 15 and 16 (Sterling, 2003)). **Homeostasis** is where equilibrium is maintained by bringing deviations back to a set point. **Allostasis** is similar in nature but it refers to setting new average set points (McEwen & Wingfield, 2003). The ANS regulates all the involuntary functions of the body and not those brought about by conscious decision making (i.e. it is autonomous).

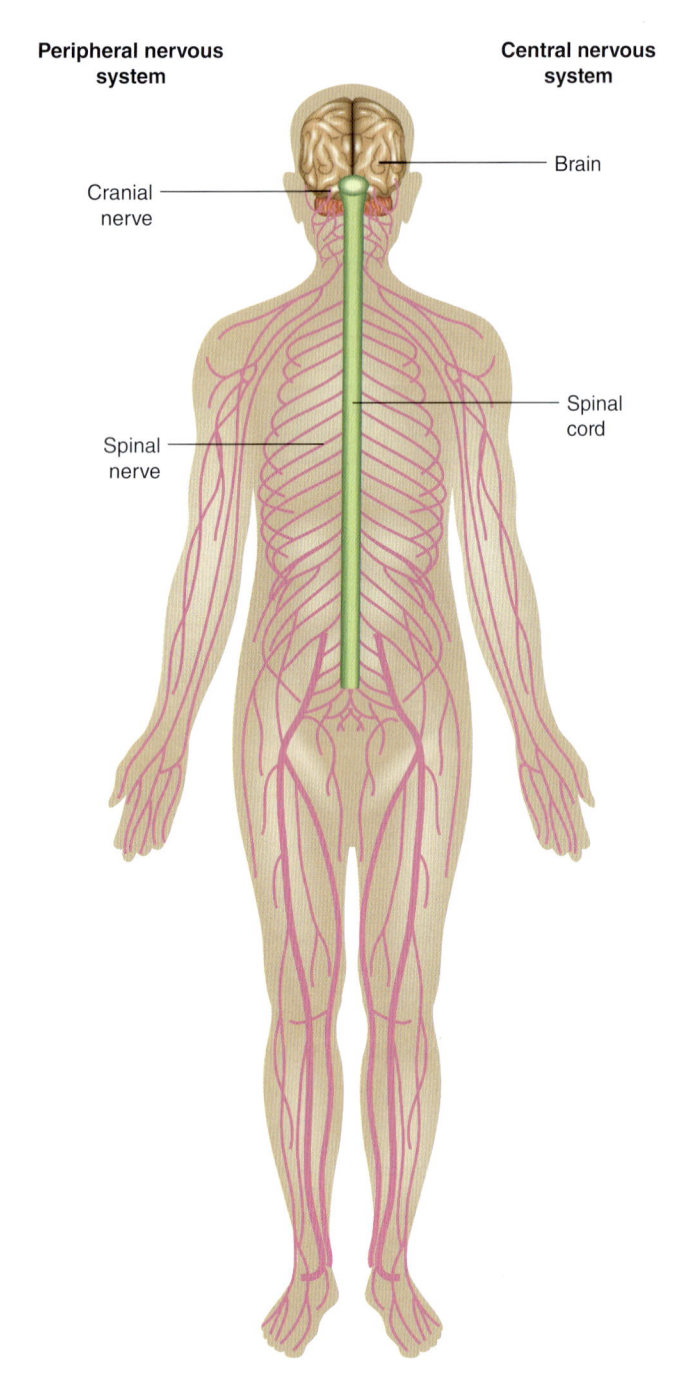

FIGURE 5.2 *The central nervous system and the peripheral nervous system.*

regions (see Figure 5.4). There are eight pairs of cervical nerves, 12 pairs of thoracic nerves, five pairs of lumbar nerves, five pairs of sacral nerves and one pair of coccygeal nerves. The spinal nerves leave the spinal column through gaps in the vertebrae (intervertebral foramina). The importance of the spinal nerves and how they operate is illustrated elegantly in the study of pain mechanisms (see Chapter 10).

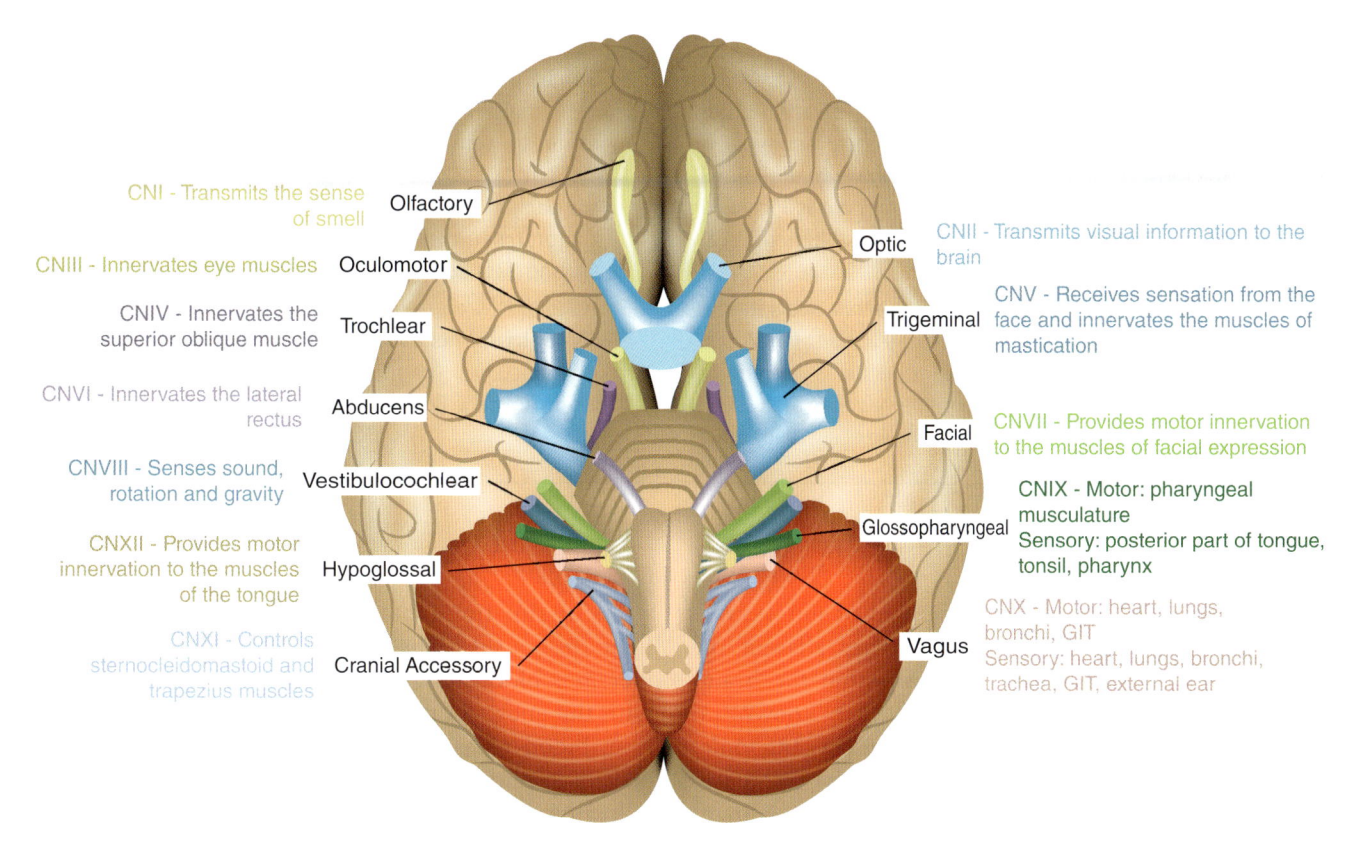

CNI - Transmits the sense of smell — Olfactory
CNII - Transmits visual information to the brain — Optic
CNIII - Innervates eye muscles — Oculomotor
CNIV - Innervates the superior oblique muscle — Trochlear
CNV - Receives sensation from the face and innervates the muscles of mastication — Trigeminal
CNVI - Innervates the lateral rectus — Abducens
CNVII - Provides motor innervation to the muscles of facial expression — Facial
CNVIII - Senses sound, rotation and gravity — Vestibulocochlear
CNIX - Motor: pharyngeal musculature; Sensory: posterior part of tongue, tonsil, pharynx — Glossopharyngeal
CNXII - Provides motor innervation to the muscles of the tongue — Hypoglossal
CNXI - Controls sternocleidomastoid and trapezius muscles — Cranial Accessory
CNX - Motor: heart, lungs, bronchi, GIT; Sensory: heart, lungs, bronchi, trachea, GIT, external ear — Vagus

FIGURE 5.3 *The cranial nerves. GIT, gastrointestinal tract.*

BOX 5.1: DISORDERS OF THE CRANIAL NERVES

Given the connections of the cranial nerves, it is not surprising that disorders and disease or dysfunction of the cranial nerves can have notable behavioural effects. Some of the problems are listed below.

- **Olfactory nerve (CN I)**. Anosmia (loss of the sense of smell), hyposmia (a decreased sense of smell), parosmia (inability to identify a smell) or cacosmia (imagining an offensive odour that does not exist). Problems with olfaction have been considered to be important in neurodegeneration and ageing (Kovács, 2004).
- **Optic nerve (CN II)**. Immediate monocular blindness (partial or complete), visual field deficits, blurring, scotomata (permanent blindspot) and monocular diplopia (double vision) (Quigley et al., 1982).
- **Oculomotor nerve (CN III)**. Oculomotor nerve palsy (paralysis) (Rush & Younge, 1981).
- **Trochlear nerve (CN IV)**. Vertical diplopia on looking downward (Burger et al., 1970).
- **Abducens nerve (CN VI)**. The eye is turned medially inward, diplopia (Geçirilmesi, 2008).
- **Trigeminal nerve (CN V)**. Corneal drying, abrasions, decreased salivation and, especially, loss of facial sensation, e.g. the forehead, eyebrow and nose. Trigeminal neuralgia is the most notable disease characterized by intense pain in the face (Kumar et al., 2013).
- **Facial nerve (CN VII)**. Complete or partial paralysis of the face, hyperacusis and/or an unusual or impaired sense of taste. The most notable disease is Bell's palsy which is a paralysis of one side of the face. Patients with Bell's palsy have one side of their face that droops down (Gilden, 2004).
- **Vestibulocochlear nerve (CN VIII)**. Positional vertigo, tinnitus, hearing loss and deafness (Jannetta, 1980).

- **Glossopharyngeal nerve (CN IX).** Loss of taste and dysphagia (impaired swallowing) and dysarthria (difficulties with speech). Glossopharyngeal neuralgia is the most common disorder and is similar to trigeminal neuralgia except that the unilateral pain is localized to the root of the tongue and throat (Blumenfeld & Nikolskaya, 2013).
- **Vagus nerve (CN X).** Dysphagia, dysarthria and aphonia (loss of voice) or weak/hoarse voice (Kandan et al., 2010). Locked-in syndrome, in which a person is cognitively able but the body is not responsive, has been associated with damage to the vagus nerve (Haig et al., 1996).
- **Spinal accessory nerve (CN XI).** Spinal accessory nerve palsy. Complete lesion of the accessory nerve results in weakness of the sternocleidomastoid muscle (in the neck) and upper part of the trapezius (down the back of the neck to midway down the spine). The symptoms include reduced muscle mass, paralysis and fasciculation (twitching muscles) (Wiater & Bigliani, 1999).
- **Hypoglossal nerve (CN XII).** Dysarthria and swallowing difficulties. Tongue points to the direction of the lesion (Castling & Hicks, 1995).

Like the SNS, the ANS is composed of autonomic ganglia outside the CNS that are either afferent or efferent nerves. Autonomic neurons within the brain innervate the autonomic ganglia and are known as preganglionic autonomic neurons. The preganglionic autonomic neurons synapse with neurons that will connect and innervate effector organs of the body, known as postganglionic neurons. The ANS has efferent nerves that can be further subdivided into the **sympathetic nervous system** and the **parasympathetic nervous system**. The difference between these two systems is based on location.

The sympathetic nervous system

The sympathetic nerves project from the CNS in the lumbar and thoracic regions, while the parasympathetic nerves project from the brain and the sacral region (Figure 5.5). With regard to sympathetic outflow via the different nerve fibres, the **preganglionic neurons** in the sympathetic nervous system send axons to an area of the autonomic ganglia running along each side of the spinal column called the **sympathetic chain**. The sympathetic chain consists of groups of ganglia called paravertebral ganglia ('para' meaning adjacent to the vertebrae). From the sympathetic chain postganglionic cells innervate the body parts. Thus, the sympathetic chain is the point of convergence in which preganglionic and postganglionic neurons synapse. The input to output ratio of preganglionic to postganglionic neurons is 1:10 with neural information fanning out into the environment of the body (Snell, 2010). Thus, one preganglionic neuron can have a widespread effect. In the autonomic nervous system preganglionic neurons are myelinated whereas their postganglionic counterparts are unmyelinated.

The sympathetic nervous system is particularly important for our survival. It is activated during stressful situations, preparing the body for flight or fight responses. The sympathetic nervous system increases blood flow to the muscles, providing them with the energy for flight or fight, and increases heart rate, blood pressure and blood sugar levels, thereby providing more energy and dilation of the pupils (allowing more light into the eye and therefore more information).

Afferent nerve fibres are myelinated and pass through the sympathetic ganglia without synapses and reach the posterior root ganglia of corresponding spinal nerves. The input of autonomic afferent nerves to the spinal cord can result in a local reflex arc via an **interneuron** or ascend the spinal **tracts** to the higher regions of the brain.

The parasympathetic nervous system

The parasympathetic nervous system is *Yin* to the sympathetic nervous system's *Yang*; the parasympathetic nervous system relaxes the body and aids recuperation. Neurons of the parasympathetic nervous system arise above and below those of the sympathetic nervous system in the brain and sacral spinal cord (the parasympathetic nervous system comprises the top and the tail only). These parasympathetic neurons travel longer distances before arriving at the parasympathetic ganglia. Parasympathetic ganglia are dispersed throughout the body near or in the organs that are to be affected; they do not have to synapse like sympathetic neurons in the sympathetic chain.

From an evolutionary and functional perspective, the parasympathetic nervous system reduces the demand for energy and decreases heart rate. When activated, it allows for digestion and fuel storage. Whilst we have considered the evolutionary importance of the fight or flight response and the sympathetic nervous system,

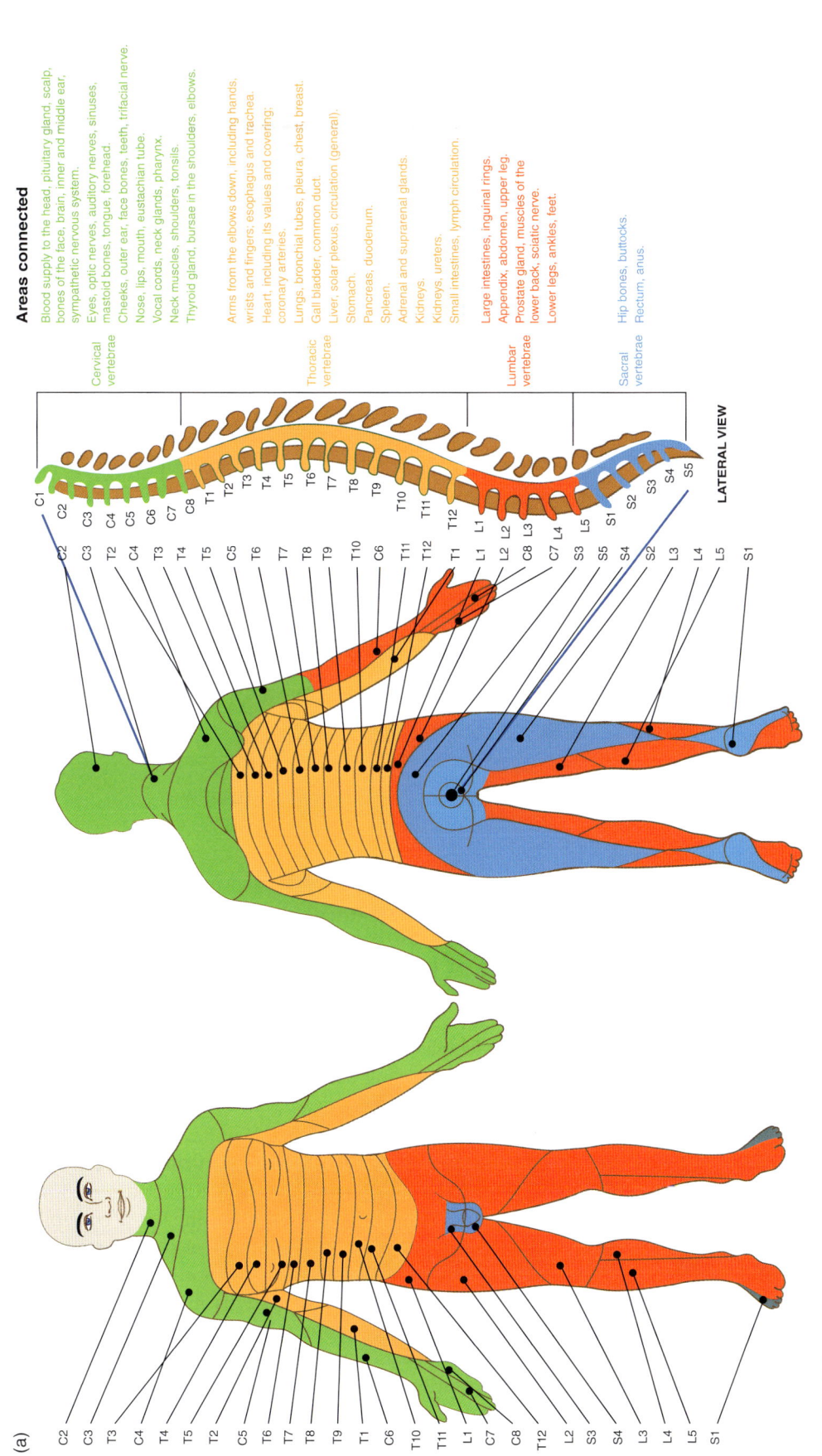

FIGURE 5.4 (a) The regions of the spinal cord. (b) The effects of lesions of the spinal cord.

(b)

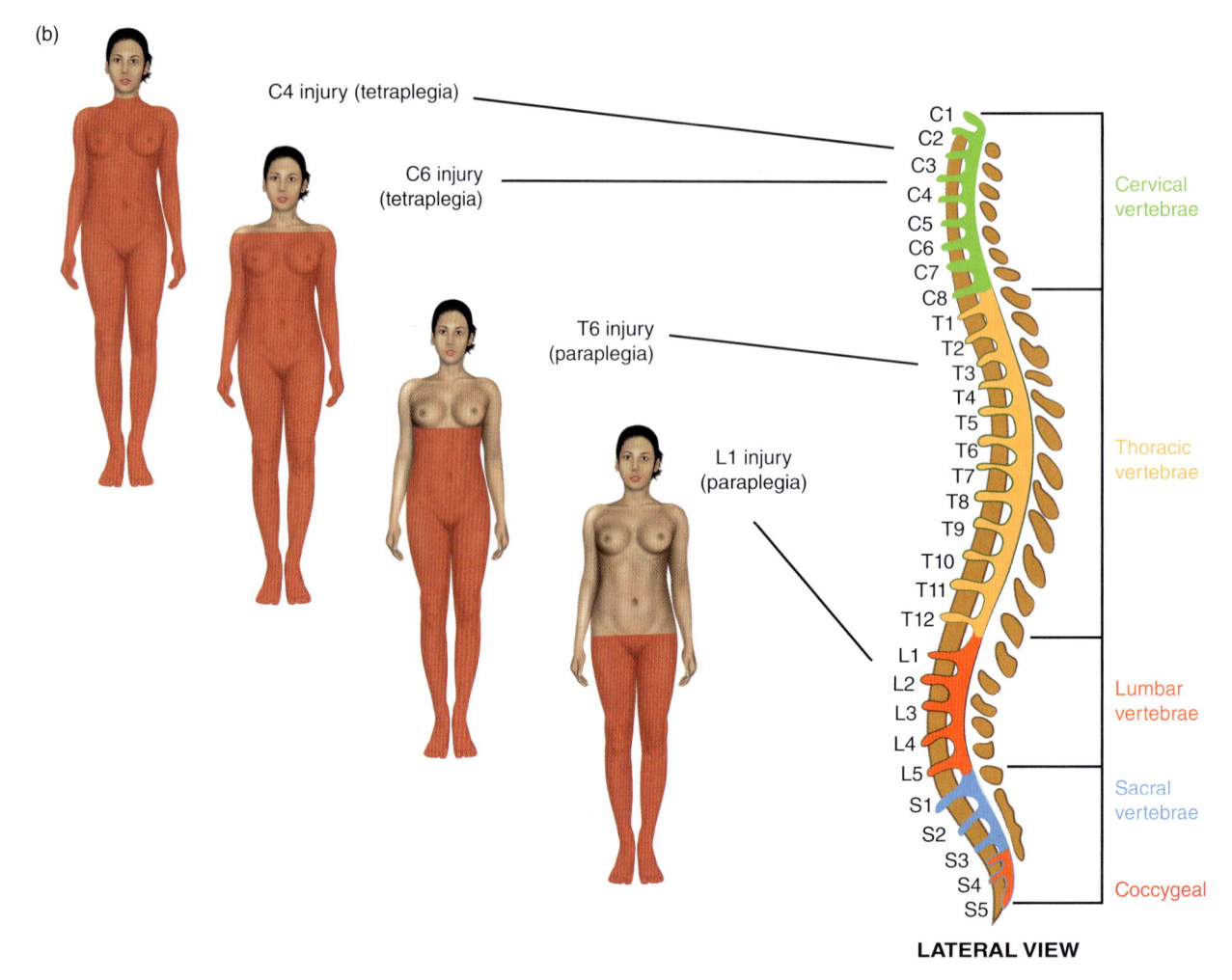

FIGURE 5.4 *continued*

we have yet to consider alternative measures for protecting the organism. Bracha (2004) has added faint alongside freeze, fright, flight and fight to the list of adaptations to acute stress (see Chapter 17 for more details).

The effects of the sympathetic and parasympathetic nervous systems can be seen in Table 5.1.

Sympathetic and parasympathetic nervous systems: a balancing act

In general, when the sympathetic nervous system is activated the person/animal is aroused. Energy resources are mobilized ready for flight or fight – in a threat situation, your heart rate increases and your muscles receive more energy either to run away or stay and fight. (The psychobiology of fear and emotion will be covered in greater depth in Chapter 17.) The amount of stimulation an internal organ receives depends on the input of sympathetic and parasympathetic nerves. Parasympathetic neurons act in the opposite direction to sympathetic neurons and induce relaxation. This is achieved by different neurotransmitters acting at the internal organs. The activation and stimulation produced by sympathetic activity are a result of noradrenergic activity. The parasympathetic system uses acetylcholine (ACh).

The balancing act between the two can be seen in Tables 5.1 and 5.2.

Control of the autonomic nervous system

Although it is not considered until the next section, it is noteworthy that the **hypothalamus** is a controlling neural substrate of the autonomic nervous system. The hypothalamus integrates the autonomic nervous system and the neuroendocrine systems in order to maintain homeostasis (see Chapter 15). The anterior hypothalamus can produce parasympathetic responses whereas the posterior hypothalamic regions produce sympathetic responses.

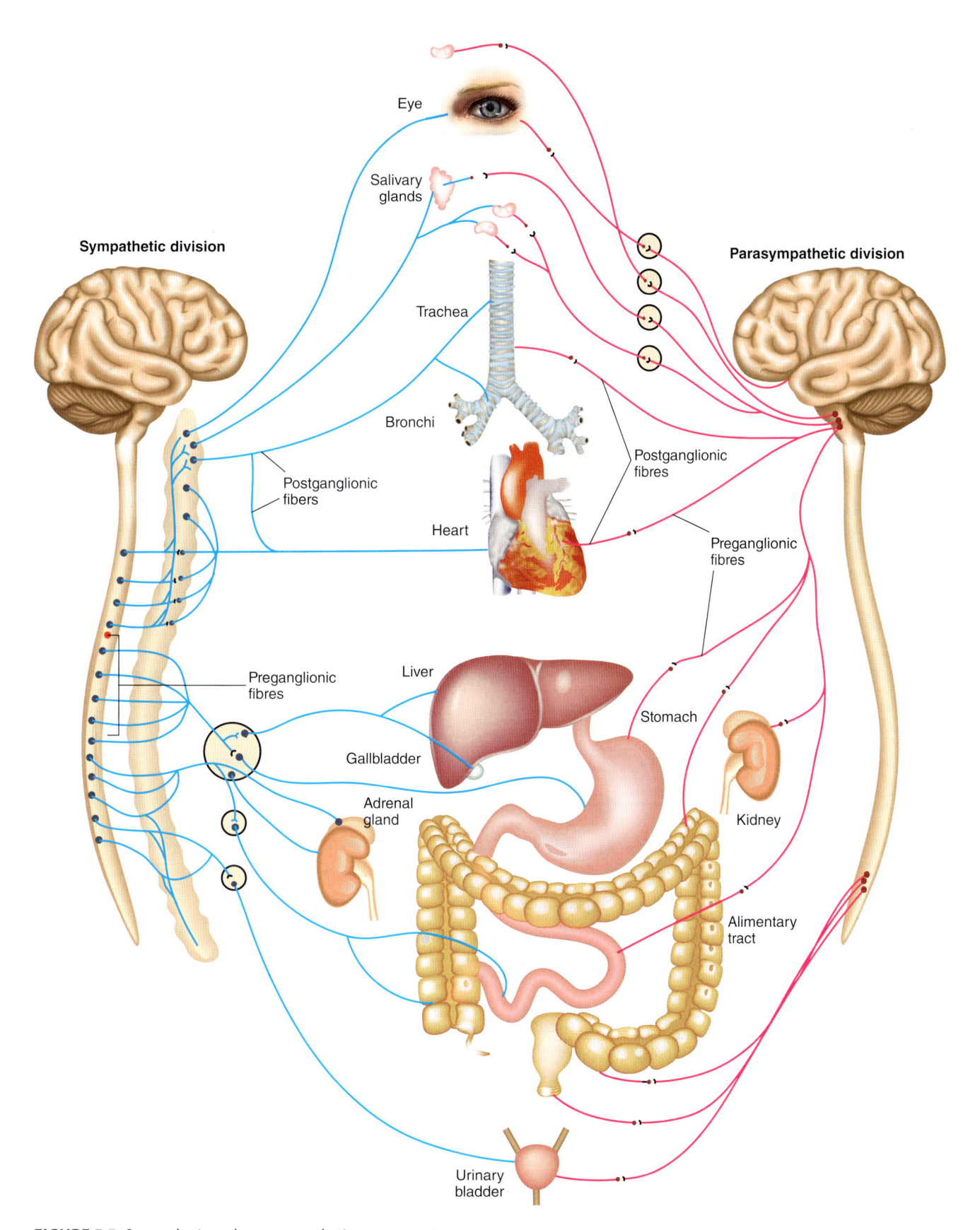

CHAPTER 5 NEUROANATOMY AND THE NERVOUS SYSTEM   125

FIGURE 5.5 *Sympathetic and parasympathetic nervous systems.*

TABLE 5.1 Sympathetic and parasympathetic nervous systems

	Sympathetic	Parasympathetic
Function	Mobilizes body ready for fight or flight	Conserves energy and restores energy
Outflow	T1–L2 (thoracic–lumbar region)	Cranial nerves III, VII, IX and X
		S2–4 (sacral region)
Preganglionic fibres	Myelinated	Myelinated
Ganglia	Paravertebral	Small ganglia close to or in viscera
Ganglia: neurotransmitter	Acetylcholine (ACh)	Acetylcholine (ACh)
Postganglionic fibres	Long and unmyelinated	Short and unmyelinated
Postganglionic: neurotransmitter	Noradrenaline (UK) (norepinephrine (USA))	Acetylcholine (ACh)
Activity	Widespread activity due to the large number of fibres	Discrete activity with few fibres

The Central Nervous System (CNS)

The central nervous system comprises the brain and spinal cord. Such is the importance of the brain and spinal cord to our functioning that both are incredibly well protected. However, despite the protection, the brain can be subject to damage from external forces, e.g. a blow to the head can lead to concussion.

TABLE 5.2 Organs and their sympathetic and parasympathetic actions

Organ	Organ specifics	Sympathetic action	Parasympathetic action	Relevant chapter
Eye	Pupil	Dilation	Constriction	10
	Ciliary muscle	Relaxation	Contraction	
Heart	Cardiac muscle	Increase contractions	Decrease contractions	7
	Coronary arteries	Dilation via beta-receptors, constriction via alpha-receptors		
Lung	Bronchial muscle	Relaxation	Contraction	7
	Bronchial secretion		Increased secretion	
	Bronchial arteries	Constriction	Dilation	
Gastrointestinal tract	Muscles in walls	Decreased peristalsis	Increased peristalsis	15
	Muscles in sphincters	Contraction	Relaxation	
	Glands	Decreased secretion	Increased secretion	
Liver		Relaxation: glycogen breakdown and glucose activation	Contraction: glycogen synthesis	7, 15
Gallbladder		Relaxation: inhibition of bile release	Contraction: releases bile	7, 15
Kidney		Decrease in urine	Increase in urine	7, 15
Urinary bladder	Bladder wall	Relaxation	Contraction	15
	Sphincter	Contraction	Relaxation	
Erectile tissue (penis/clitoris)			Relaxes	14
Penis	Ejaculation	Contraction of smooth muscles		14

The brain's security service

Meninges

The skull is a hard shell, a bit like a hard hat. Just below the skull is the cranial epidural space, which is only a potential space because the dura mater (see below) adheres to bone and is only filled with fluid when things go wrong. Next in line, below the skull are three protective membranes called the **meninges** (see Figure 5.6), made up of fibroblasts and collagen. Fibroblasts are the main cells of

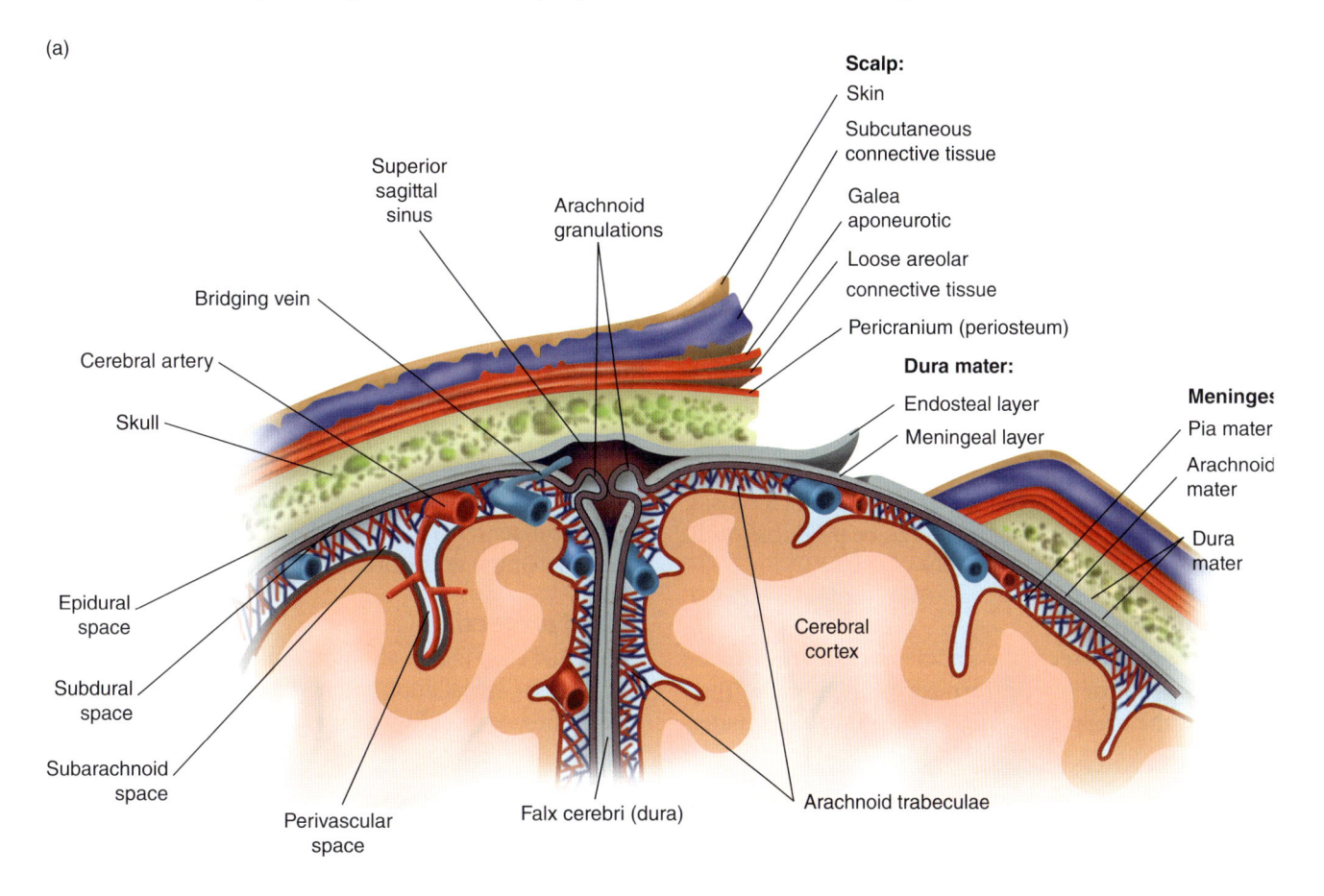

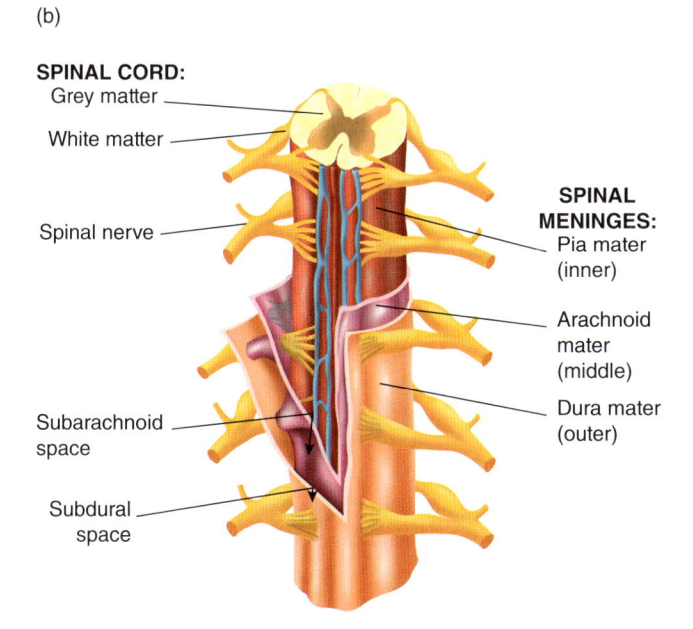

FIGURE 5.6 *The meninges and spinal meninges. (a) Brain protection. (b) Spinal protection.*

connective tissue and collagen is a group of very strong proteins that are present in tendons and ligaments.

Dura mater

The **dura mater** is made up of two layers that are sandwiched together except where they are separate and form the venous sinus (see later). The two layers are the endosteal layer and the meningeal layer. The endosteal layer covers the inner surface of the skull whereas the meningeal layer is the dura mater proper. The meningeal layer is a continuous layer surrounding the brain and spinal cord. The dura has sensory endings which can lead to the perception of pain (e.g. headache). The dura mater also receives a rich blood supply from many arteries. The sensory input from the trigeminal nerve and the first three cervical nerves is responsible for the headache that is experienced due to the swelling of the meninges (see Box 5.2 for an account of **meningitis**). The headache one gets with a hangover is due to the toxic effect of alcohol and acetaldehyde. The meninges shrink as a result of the dehydrating effects of alcohol which causes the headache – a similar headache can be produced with water deprivation (Blau et al., 2004).

Arachnoid mater

The **arachnoid mater** is the middle layer of the meninges, made up of an impermeable membrane that surrounds the brain. It is separated from the dura mater by another potential space called the subdural space that is filled with a thin layer of fluid. The arachnoid layer does not follow the contours of the brain by dipping in and out of the brain's sulci (grooves in the cortex).

In between the arachnoid membrane and the next layer down, which is the pia mater, is the **subarachnoid space**. The subarachnoid space contains all the blood vessels and **cerebrospinal fluid** (CSF). The CSF fills the spinal canal (which runs down the spine) and the cerebral ventricles (see below). Spanning the subarachnoid space are strands of connective tissue called arachnoid trabeculae which start in the arachnoid mater and terminate in the pia mater. Their purpose is to suspend the brain within the meninges. Thus, the brain can move a little without collision with the skull.

Pia mater

The **pia mater** is the innermost membrane of the meninges (see Figure 5.6). It closely hugs the contours of the brain, descending into the fissures and sulci of the brain. The pia mater extends out from the bone and over the cranial nerves. Thus, the cranial nerves are given the same protection as the brain.

Spinal protection

The spinal cord is also afforded similar protection to the brain, by the spinal dura, arachnoid and pia mater. While overall these layers are the same as in the brain, there are

---

BOX 5.2: MENINGITIS

Meningitis is the infection of the meninges, the pia and arachnoid mater. Meningitis can be contracted via bacteria or viruses. Bacterial meningitis is caused by close contact with, for example, streptococcus and listeria. Viral meningitis can be caused by enterovirus, herpes simplex virus or HIV.

The meninges become inflamed in response to the bacteria or virus which are able to cross the blood–brain barrier (Nau & Brück, 2002). The most serious outcome is bacterial meningitis which occurs quickly after contraction, leading to:

- nausea;
- vomiting;
- increased sensitivity to light (photophobia);
- altered mental status (confusion);
- severe headache; and
- long-term consequences such as coma and death if not treated adequately.

According to Nau and Brück (2002), the long-term neurological sequelae and death from bacterial meningitis are caused by:

- the systemic inflammatory response of the host, leading to white blood cell invasion into the subarachnoid space, inflammation of blood vessels, brain **oedema** (a build-up of fluid) and secondary **ischaemia** (restriction of blood supply);
- stimulation of resident microglia within the CNS by bacterial compounds; and
- possible direct toxicity of bacterial compounds on neurons.

some differences. The spinal dura is only a single layer (meningeal layer) and does not have the layer that contacts bone. The spinal epidural is where the venous plexuses (the collection of multiple veins) are located.

The cerebral ventricles and cerebrospinal fluid

There are four **cerebral ventricles** which are chambers within the brain (Figure 5.7). There are two lateral ventricles and a third and fourth ventricle. Each of the lateral ventricles takes the shape of the cerebral hemispheres and can be divided into four principal components: the anterior horn, the body, the posterior horn and the inferior horn. Thus, the lateral ventricles span from the frontal lobe through to the occipital lobe. The lateral ventricles are connected to the third ventricle through small holes called **interventricular foramina**. The third ventricle lines the surfaces of the thalamus and hypothalamus and the fourth ventricle is located posterior to the pons and medulla. In the brains of boxers, the lateral ventricles are enlarged due to deterioration of brain tissue caused by trauma from being punched (Unterharnscheidt, 1994, 1995) and also linked to other contact sports (Stern et al., 2011). Enlarged ventricles are one of the many pathological changes seen in Alzheimer's disease (Soininen et al., 1993).

Cerebrospinal fluid is made by the **choroid plexus**, which is a network of cells within the lateral and third and fourth ventricles. The choroid plexus actively secretes CSF which circulates continuously. There are four main functions of CSF.

- It allows the central nervous system to float in suspension, reducing traction on the nerves and blood vessels connected to the CNS.
- It provides a protective buffer for the effects of trauma.
- It facilitates the removal of metabolites from the CNS.
- It provides a stable ionic environment.

The blood–brain barrier

The brain is also protected by tightly packed blood vessels called the **blood–brain barrier** (**BBB**) (see Abbott et al., 2010) (Figure 5.8). This barrier only allows certain molecules to pass through it. Drugs that exert their effects in the brain cross the BBB (see Chapter 7).

The BBB consists of:

- **endothelial cells** that line the capillary wall with the tight junctions between them that make it difficult for molecules to pass through;
- the processes of astrocytes; and
- the capillary basement membrane outside the endothelial cells.

Whilst the BBB provides a continuous protective layer for the brain, there are some regions within the CNS where the BBB is absent, allowing passage of larger molecules between them and the circulating blood:

- area postrema (sensitive to toxins in the blood and can induce vomiting);
- pineal body (controls sleep and receives sympathetic and parasympathetic innervation);
- subcommissural organ (clearance and maintenance of CSF);

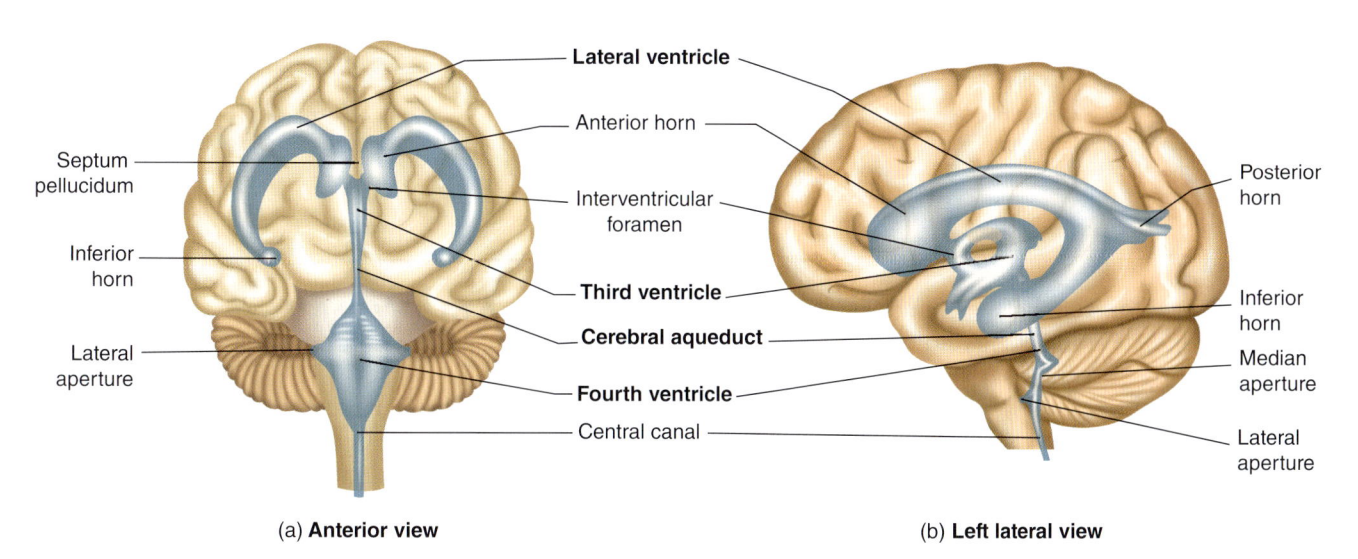

(a) **Anterior view**

(b) **Left lateral view**

FIGURE 5.7 *The ventricles.*

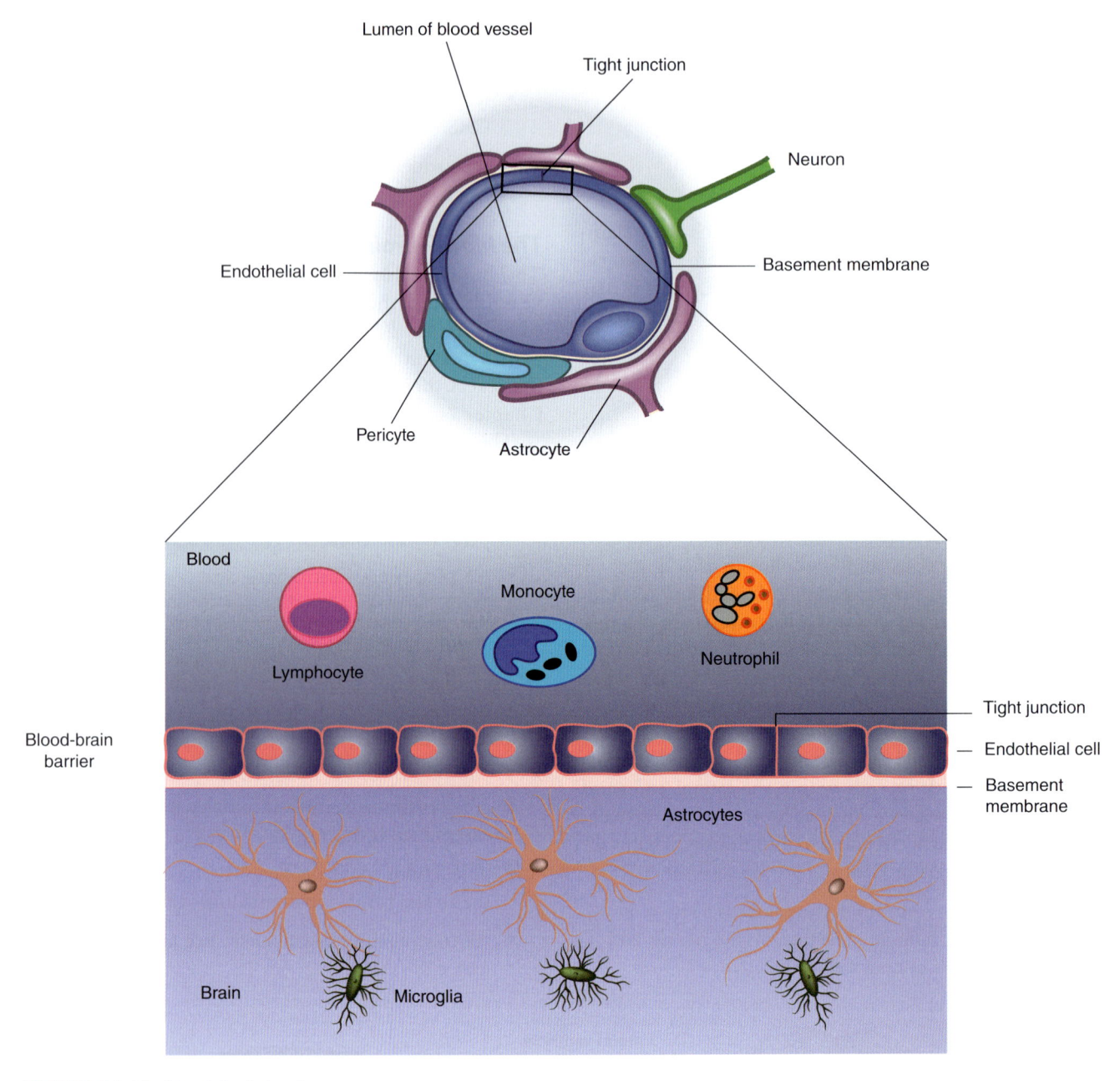

FIGURE 5.8 *The blood–brain barrier.*
Source: Francis, K., van Beek, J., Canova, C., Neal, J.W., & Gasque, P. (2003). Innate immunity and brain inflammation: The key role of complement. Expert Reviews in Molecular Medicine, 5, 1–19. Reproduced with permission.

- subfornical organ (regulates osmosis, the cardiovascular system and energy homeostasis);
- organum vasculorum of laminae terminalis (sensitive to osmotic pressure);
- neurohypophysis (posterior pituitary gland) (regulates hormone secretion); and
- median eminence (involved in hormone secretion).

NEUROANATOMY

During early brain development, the cells become differentiated (see Chapter 3). Cellular differentiation permits the architecture of the brain to be seen. Some features can be seen clearly with the naked eye, others require scientific techniques to visualize them, e.g. staining the cells. Whilst students of psychology are used to differences of opinion, it is somewhat surprising that neuroanatomy does not always use the same names for the same structures and not all textbooks use the same categorization of brain regions. It is beyond the scope of this text to provide a definitive account of all the brain regions, and this is certainly the case as we get down closer to the molecular level of analysis. However, it is possible to provide an overview of the brain that emphasizes its gross structure and some of the fine detail. The origins of understanding the functional role of the different regions of the brainstem from the neuropsychological evaluation of brain damage. More recently, cognitive neuroscience with its imaging technology has enabled a finer level of analysis of the brain's functions.

White and Grey Matter

The first notable feature of the dissected brain that is readily detected by the naked eye is its colour. Depending on the region of the brain being studied, it will appear either white or grey (Figure 5.9). **White matter** consists of myelinated axons. This is because myelin is composed of lipid-based tissue of the glial cells. The freshly cut brain thus appears pink because of the vascular innervation. **Grey matter** refers to the colour of neuronal cell bodies and dendrites (this would also include unmyelinated neurons). The grey matter is most evident in the cortex.

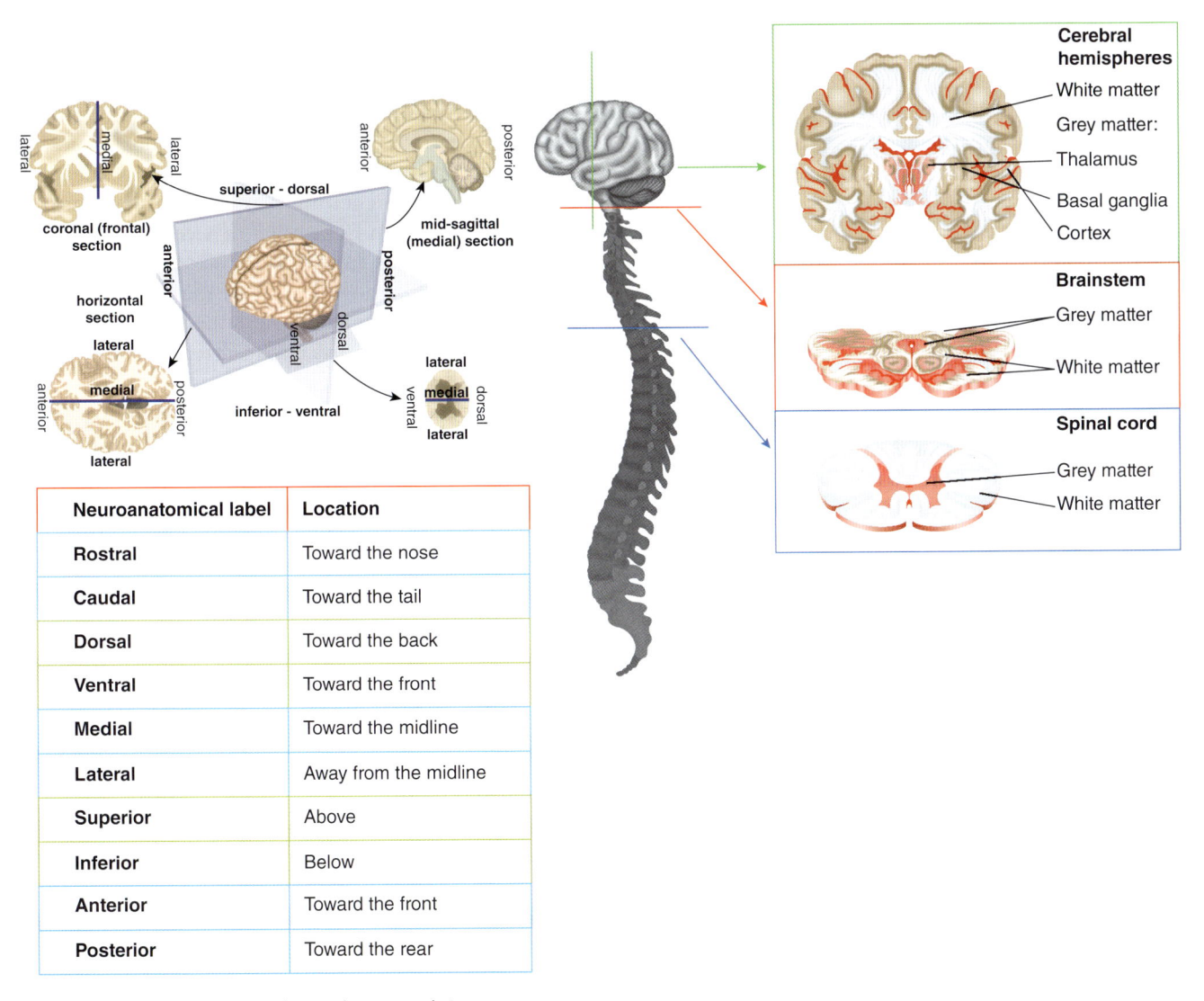

Neuroanatomical label	Location
Rostral	Toward the nose
Caudal	Toward the tail
Dorsal	Toward the back
Ventral	Toward the front
Medial	Toward the midline
Lateral	Away from the midline
Superior	Above
Inferior	Below
Anterior	Toward the front
Posterior	Toward the rear

FIGURE 5.9 *Neuroanatomical co-ordinates and views.*

Spatial Relationships of the Brain and Spinal Cord

The names of the brain regions are hard enough to remember as it is without having to add their neuro-anatomical location. Many regions of the brain can be described in fine detail by referring to their location, e.g. the hypothalamus can be divided into subregions such as the lateral hypothalamus (an area towards the outer edge of the hypothalamus). The prefixes to the brain regions serve as a crude SatNav/GPS for the brain and allow for greater precision in the identification of a particular region.

The brain exists in three dimensions so it can be looked at from three orientations: from the top, from the side and from the front (these are the views that brain scans will generate – see Chapter 6). Looking down on the brain from the top is the **horizontal plane**, from the side is the **sagittal plane** and finally looking face on is the **coronal plane**.

There is a convention to describe where a particular orientation is or where sets of nuclei are situated (see Figure 5.9) along a particular axis of paired terms using the midlines of the brain as a reference point.

- Medial–lateral: medial is towards the middle plane whereas lateral is away from the median line.
- Anterior–posterior: anterior is above the midline towards the front of the brain whereas posterior is towards the back.
- Rostral–caudal: above the midline rostral is towards the front of the brain whereas caudal is towards the back. Below the midline rostral means towards the cortex whereas caudal means towards the sacral lens of the spinal cord.
- Dorsal–ventral: dorsal refers to the back of the brain and ventral to the front.
- Superior–inferior: superior means towards the top of the cortex and inferior means towards the bottom of the spinal cord.

BRAIN REGIONS

Identifying and examining brain regions can occur at the gross surface level and then as we turn the power up on the microscope, at the level of small discrete nuclei ('nuclei' in this context refers to a group of cells rather than the nucleus of the cell).

Forebrain: Telencephalon and Diencephalon

The telencephalon

The **telencephalon** is made up of the two **cerebral hemispheres** containing the cortex, the basal ganglia and the limbic system.

Cerebral hemispheres

If we adopt a viewing position that provides either a horizontal or coronal plane then it is clear that there are two cerebral hemispheres The left and right hemispheres look like mirror images of each other but there are small structural differences between the two that mean they are not identical, e.g. the planum temporale of the temporal cortex (Jansen et al., 2010).

The functional significance of the two hemispheres has long been discussed, with independent roles in behaviour for the left and right hemispheres leading us to statements suggesting that an individual may be more left brain than right brain or vice versa. The difference in the hemispheres is referred to as **cerebral lateralization** and is most notable in the generation and understanding of language where there is a large body of literature that supports a specialized role for the left brain (see Chapter 19).

Looking at the surface features of the **cerebrum** (the cortex), a number of folds can be seen (Figure 5.10). The surface area of the cortex is greatly increased by these folds. The folds or **gyri** (gyrus is the singular) are separated by **fissures** and **sulci**. The fissures and sulci are the grooves in the brain whereas the gyri are the peaks. The difference between fissures and sulci is that the former are deep grooves and the latter are shallow grooves. Using these surface landmarks, the different regions of the cortex have been identified and named. These are the lobes of the cortex, e.g. frontal, parietal, temporal and occipital lobes.

Corpus callosum

The **corpus callosum** is a set of axons which connect the left and right hemispheres (Figure 5.11). Whilst this is the biggest collection of neurons permitting communication between the hemispheres, it is not the only route of information exchange. There is also the anterior commissure and the hippocampal commissure. It is the corpus callosum that is severed in split-brain patients or animals (see Chapter 19).

FIGURE 5.10 *Fissures, Sulci and gyri of the cerebral cortex.*

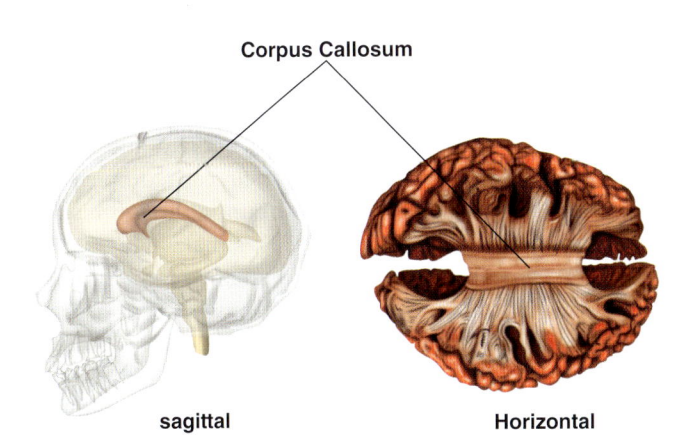

FIGURE 5.11 *The corpus callosum.*

The functions of the different regions of the brain have been associated with different behaviours. Regional function is an area of extensive research and theorizing. However, ascribing a particular function to one region is not simple as all the areas communicate with each other.

The lobes

The lateral and central fissures divide the brain into four lobes: the **frontal**, **occipital**, **temporal** and **parietal lobes** (see Figure 5.12). These areas have been ascribed various functions: the occipital lobe is the area of visual perception (see Chapter 10); the temporal lobe is the focus of many theories of memory (see Chapter 13); and the parietal lobe is associated with visuomotor guidance

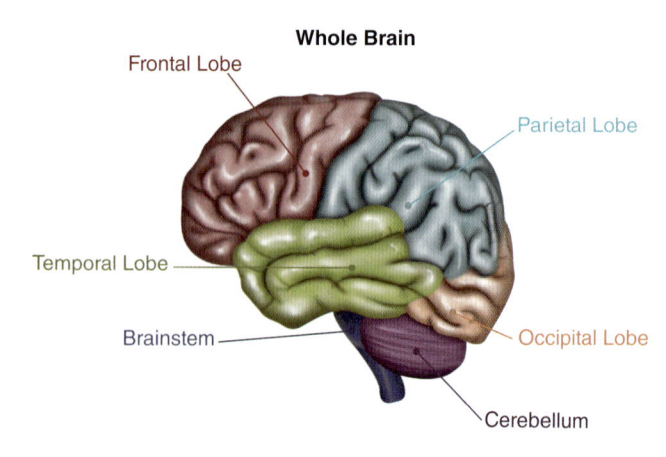

FIGURE 5.12 *Lobes of the brain.*

(see Chapter 11) (see Kolb & Whishaw, 2008). Sometimes the name of the lobes refers to their function, e.g. the occipital lobe is the visual cortex.

Cells of the cortex

The folds of the cerebral cortex can be unfolded and 'the combined area of the two unfolded cortices is about 0.89 m^2... also about eight-ninths of the cortical area lies within the sulci' (James, 1992, p.552).

Within the cortex, neurons are arranged in six layers parallel to the cortical surface. The cortical layers can be visualized because of the similarity of neurons or axons and dendrites within a particular layer. The outer layer (I) has few cell bodies and mainly contains axons and dendrites, which can be clearly differentiated from layer II. Layers II and IV contain **granule cells** (cells with small bodies). The granule cells form what are also referred to as the internal and external granule cell layer. These layers are recipients of information from the thalamus and other cortical regions. Layers III and V contain pyramidal cells. Similarly there is an internal and external pyramidal layer. **Pyramidal cells** have large cell bodies and are the most distinctive of cortical cells because of their shape (Figure 5.13). The pyramidal cells have other distinctive features, e.g. a single axon, a large apical dendrite and multiple basal dendrites. The **apical dendrites** arise from the apex of the pyramidal cell's body and branch several times as the distance from the soma increases. These dendritic projections extend to the outer layers of the cortex. The basal dendrites come from the base of the pyramidal cell's body and extend horizontally. The basal dendritic tree consists of three to five primary dendrites that increasingly branch out as distance from the cell body increases.

Layer VI contains a variety of neurons including pyramidal cells but also spindle-shaped cells, **Martinotti cells** and **Golgi cells**. The cells in the different layers of the cortex are often arranged in columns and mini-columns perpendicular to the layers (see Mountcastle, 1997). Thus, communication between the layers within a column can be seen as a single processing unit (Horton & Adams, 2005) that has been embraced by the world of computing to create neural networks (Alexandre et al., 1991). The mini-column integrates the horizontal and vertical components of the cortex within the same cortical area (Buxhoeveden & Casanova, 2002).

The different layers of the cortex are differentiated not only by their **cytoarchitecture** (their cellular composition) but also by their function. Layer I receives non-specific afferents. Layer II receives signals from cortical afferents whereas layer IV receives thalamic afferents. Layer III contains interhemispheric and cortical association fibres. Layer V contains efferent projections to the neostriatum, brainstem and spinal cord. From layer VI neurons project to the thalamus and others contain short projections within the cortical column.

Brodmann's areas

Using the cytoarchitectural organization of neurons, Brodmann (1909) created a map of the different cortical areas (called **Brodmann's areas**) (see Figure 5.14). Brodmann gave these regions numbers that now also have names. These areas can also be functionally identified (see Table 5.3). Areas of the cortex have been associated with regions of the body in what is called the **homunculus** (Figure 5.15).

Frontal lobe

The **frontal lobes** form the area that is considered to make us unique as humans and sit forward of the central sulcus. For an account of the frontal lobes see Chapters 2, 3 and 12. In evolutionary terms, the cortex is the most recent addition to the brain and also the last to develop, not considered complete until the age of 25 years (Sowell et al., 2003). Damage to the frontal lobe provided the world with one of the most famous case studies in neuropsychology. The case of Phineas Gage demonstrates the importance of the frontal lobe for a wide range of behaviours (see Chapter 12 and Macmillan (2002)). However, some have done well without a complete cortex. A case study of a French civil servant and father of two demonstrates that individuals can compensate for large areas of damage to the brain (although his IQ scores were lower than average). This male had an MRI scan that 'revealed massive enlargement of the lateral, third, and fourth ventricles, a very thin cortical mantle' (Feuillet et al., 2007, p.262).

The frontal cortex can be divided into subregions: the **orbitofrontal cortex**, the **prefrontal cortex**, the **cingulate gyrus** and the **motor cortex**. The functions of the frontal lobe with regard to motor behaviour are discussed in

CHAPTER 5 NEUROANATOMY AND THE NERVOUS SYSTEM

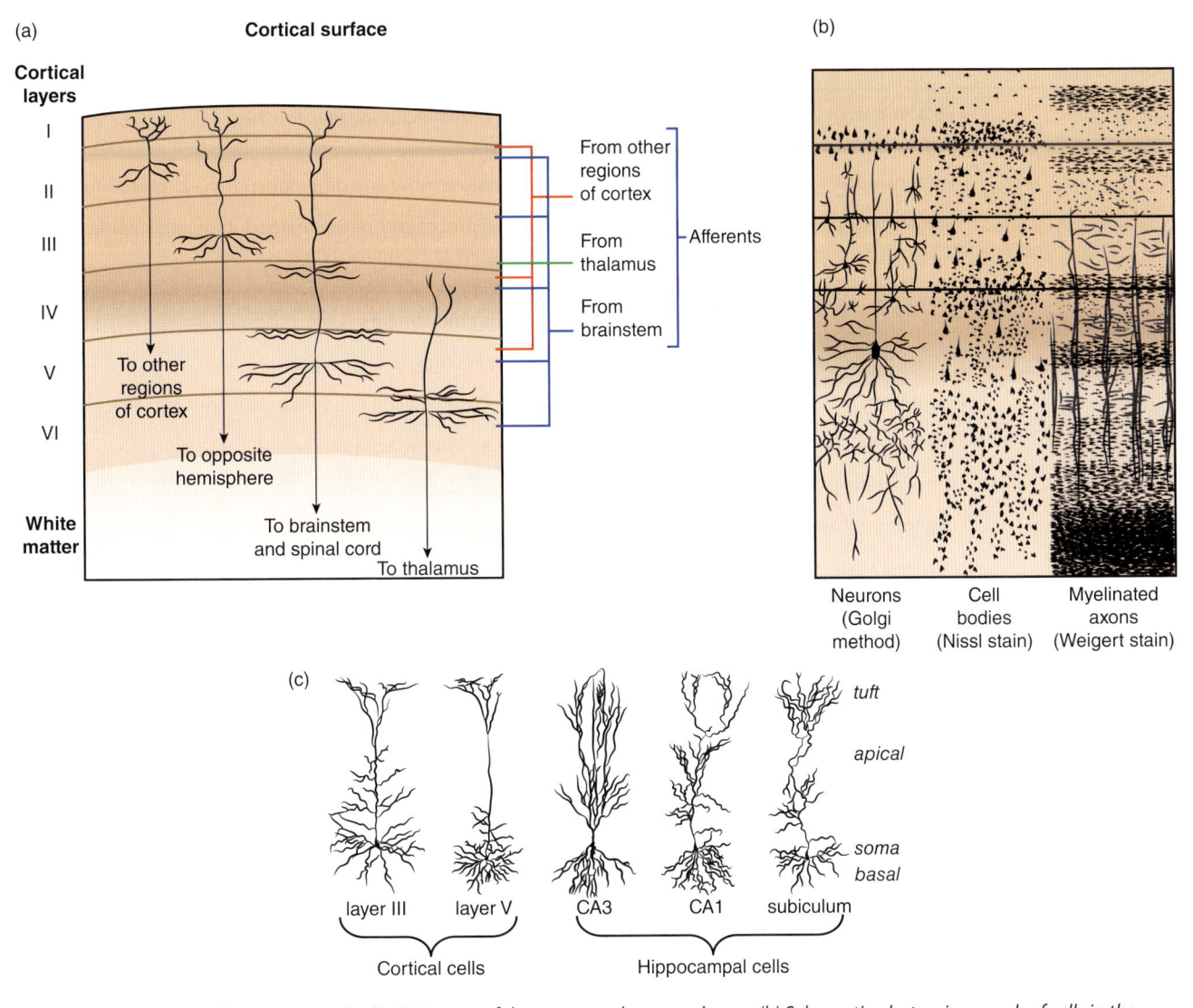

FIGURE 5.13 Layers of the cortex and cells. (a) Layers of the cortex and neuronal span. (b) Schematic photomicrograph of cells in the cortex. (c) Pyramidal cells (pyramidal cells of the cortex, hippocampus (CA and subiculum)).

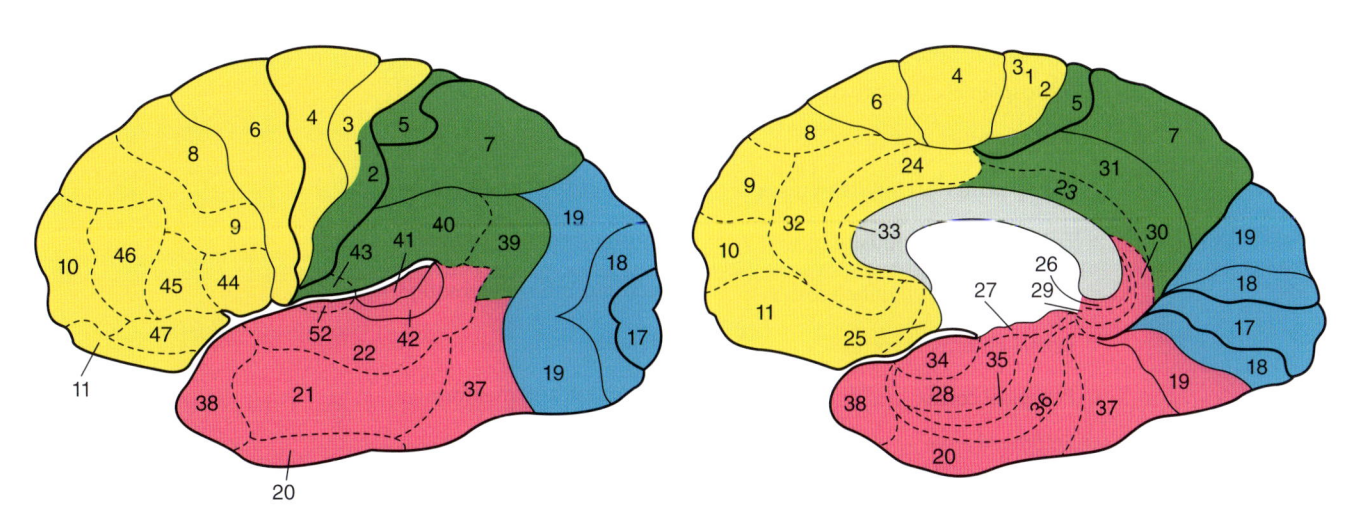

FIGURE 5.14 Brodmann areas. For numbers key see Table 5.3.

TABLE 5.3 *Brodmann areas and their names and functions*

Brodmann area	Name	General functions
1, 2, 3	Postcentral gyrus (primary somatosensory cortex)	Somatosensory perception (e.g. touch)
4	Primary motor cortex	Motor, somatosensory and other functions (e.g. motor memory)
5	Somatosensory association cortex	Visuospatial processing, motor imagery, bimanual manipulation (e.g. two hands performing different actions)
6	Premotor cortex	Diverse functions, the main function being motor sequencing and planning movements
7	Somatosensory association cortex	Spatial processing, e.g. tactile location
8	Frontal eye fields	Motor, language, executive function, memory and attention
9	Dorsolateral prefrontal cortex	Memory, executive functions
10	Anterolateral prefrontal cortex	Memory, executive functions
11, 12	Orbitofrontal area	Sensory integration, reward evaluation
13, 14	Insular cortex	Motor control, homeostasis, emotion
15	Anterior temporal lobe	Memory, language
16	Insular cortex	Motor control, homeostasis, emotion
17	Primary visual cortex	Vision
18	Secondary visual cortex	Vision
19	Associative visual cortex	Vision
20	Inferior temporal gyrus	Language processing
21	Middle temporal gyrus	Language processing
22	Superior temporal gyrus	Language processing
23	Ventral posterior cingulate cortex	Memory and emotion
24	Ventral anterior cingulate cortex	Reward learning, executive functions
25	Subgenual area	Emotion
26	Ectosplenial area	Executive functions
27	Periform cortex	Olfaction
28	Ventral entorhinal cortex	Memory
29	Retrosplenial cingulate cortex	Learning, memory, emotion
30	Part of cingulate cortex	Learning, memory, emotion
31	Dorsal posterior cingulate cortex	Learning, memory, emotion
32	Dorsal anterior cingulate cortex	Learning, memory, emotion, reward
33	Part of anterior cingulate cortex	Learning, memory, emotion, reward
34	Dorsal entorhinal cortex	Memory
35	Perirhinal cortex	Perception and memory
36	Ectorhinal area	Perception and memory
37	Fusiform gyrus	Visual language
38	Temporopolar area	Language, emotion, executive functions and memory
39	Angular gyrus	Reading and arithmetic

TABLE 5.3 (continued)

Brodmann area	Name	General functions
40	Supramarginal gyrus	Language processing
41	Primary auditory cortex	Auditory processing
42	Association auditory cortex	Auditory processing
43	Primary gustatory cortex	Taste perception, multisensory integration
44	Pars opercularis	Broca's area – language
45	Pars triangularis	Broca's area – language
46	Dorsolateral prefrontal cortex	Memory, executive functions
47	Inferior prefrontal gyrus	Language
48	Retrosubicular area	Not included in the map of human cortex
49	Parasubicular area	Not included in the map of human cortex
52	Parainsular area	Not known

Chapter 11 and with regard to executive functioning in Chapter 12.

Parietal lobe

The **parietal lobe** is situated above and forward of the occipital lobe and is involved in the integration of sensory inputs. The parietal lobe contains as subcomponents the **primary somatosensory cortex**, the **secondary somatosensory cortex** and the **somatic association area**. The parietal lobe receives information from numerous thalamic nuclei. In each parietal lobe, the opposite half of the body is represented as inverted (see the human homunculus). Thus, the left parietal lobe receives information about the right-hand side of the body (contralateral, as opposed to **ipsilateral** which is the same side). Whilst the majority of innervation is contralateral, there are some ipsilateral projections from the oral regions of the pharynx, larynx and perineum which go to both sides of the parietal lobe. The association area of the parietal lobe integrates information from other sensory areas of the cortex (Lewis & Van Essen, 2000). Neurons of the parietal lobe have also been shown to be involved in understanding others' intentions from their motor behaviour (Fogassi et al., 2005) and also representation of the body's state, thereby integrating information from different sensory modalities (Wolpert et al., 1998). Thus, we have an understanding of our own sensory input and others' motor output.

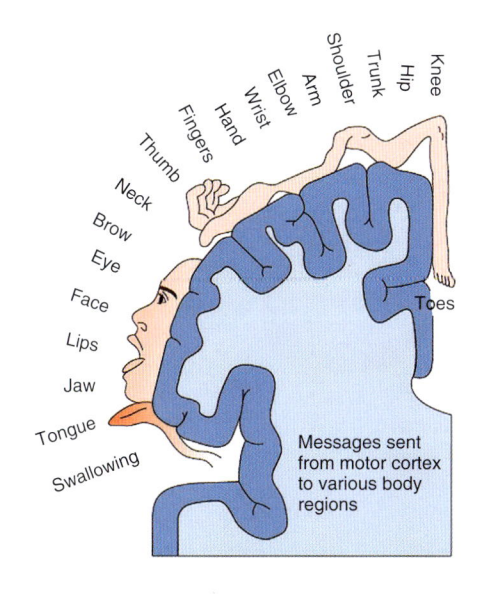

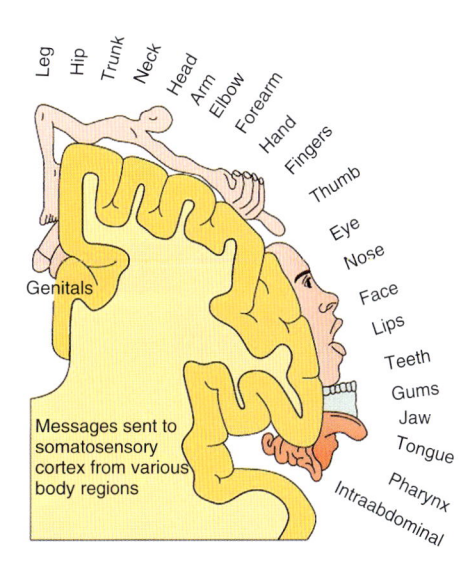

FIGURE 5.15 *Homunculus.*
Source: Comer, R., Gould, E. & Furnham, A. (2013). *Psychology.* Reproduced by permission of John Wiley & Sons Ltd.

Lesions of the parietal lobe can lead to **agnosia** (difficulty or inability to recognize objects) (Warrington & Taylor, 1973) and **apraxia** (the inability to carry out motor actions) (Goldenberg, 2009).

Temporal lobe

The **temporal lobe** is situated below the parietal lobe and forward of the occipital lobe to the side of the brain. The temporal lobe can be functionally identified and has particular importance in auditory processing. The primary auditory area of the temporal lobe receives auditory information from the medial geniculate nucleus of the thalamus. Lesions of the primary auditory area have been associated with deafness (Earnest et al., 1977). A secondary auditory area of the temporal lobe receives input from the primary auditory area and the thalamus and is thought to be crucial for interpretation of sounds and sensory integration (Belin et al., 2002). The temporal lobe will be looked at in greater detail when we consider language and lateralization (see Chapter 19). The story of language concerns the left temporal lobe. Lesions of the temporal lobe have been linked to **prosopagnosia** (impairment of facial recognition) (Evans et al., 1995), deficits in movement perception (where patients cannot differentiate objects that are moving or not moving) (Saygin, 2007) and **acoustic agnosia** (inability to recognize sounds) (Fujii et al., 1990).

Occipital lobe

The **occipital lobe** is the **visual cortex** and is situated at the back of the brain. The occipital lobe has been extensively researched and is crucial for visual processing (see Chapter 10). The occipital lobe can be further divided into its functional components of the primary visual area, the secondary visual area and the **occipital eye field**. The primary visual cortex receives sensory innervation from the **lateral geniculate nucleus** (LGN) of the thalamus. The secondary visual area receives both thalamic and cortical input. The secondary visual cortex integrates the current perceptual input to memories of past visual experiences (Mishkin, 1982). The occipital eye field is involved with moving the eyes and the tracking of an object (Sakata et al., 1983). After lesions of the occipital lobe, patients may suffer from homonymous hemianopia (see below) (Huber, 1962). Damage to the visual cortex can give rise to visual hallucinations because of the activity of neighbouring neurons that they were previously attached to (Anderson & Rizzo, 1994).

The diencephalon

The **diencephalon** is made up of the **thalamus** and **hypothalamus**. The thalamus is a relay station that receives sensory information and sends it to appropriate areas of the brain. The role of the lateral geniculate nuclei of the thalamus is illustrated in Chapter 10. The hypothalamus is below the thalamus (hence the 'hypo' prefix). The hypothalamus is in close communication with the pituitary gland, and has been a key site of investigation for motivational behaviours such as eating (see Chapter 15).

The thalamus

The thalamus is an important egg-shaped region of grey matter that integrates and relays sensory information from the periphery to the cortex. Like many of the regions of the brain, the thalamus can be divided into subcomponents (nuclei), e.g. anterior thalamic nuclei and dorsomedial thalamic nuclei (see Figure 5.16). Thalamic

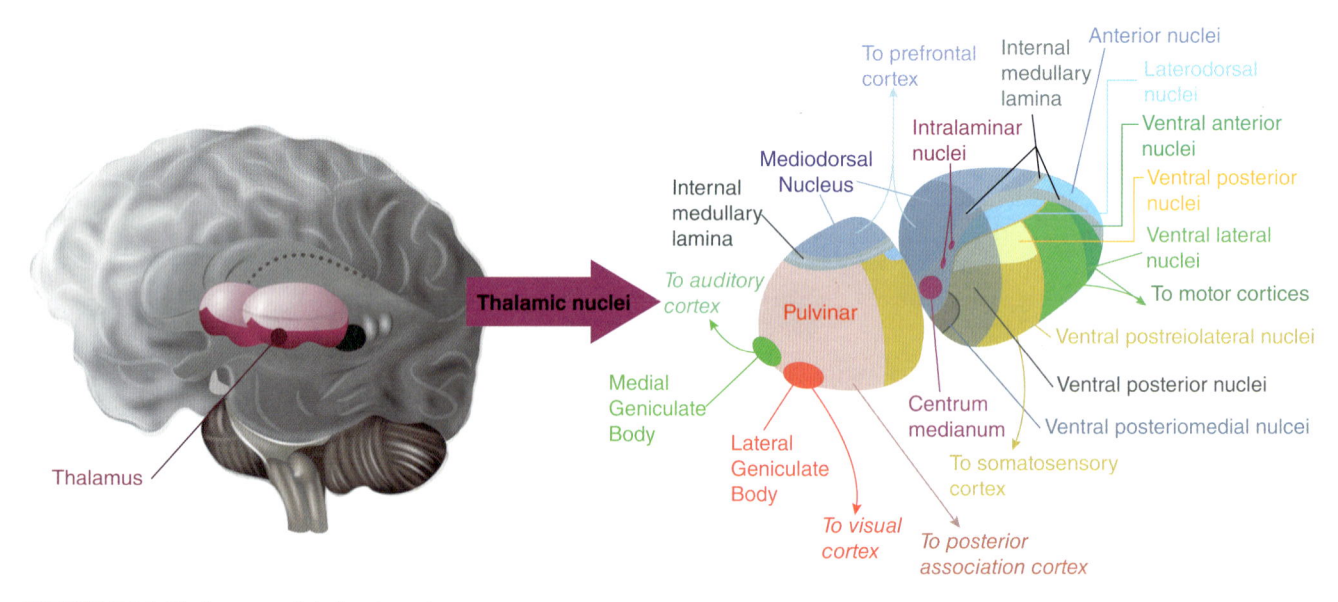

FIGURE 5.16 *Thalamus and thalamic nuclei.*

nuclei can be considered either specific association or non-specific nuclei according to their function.

The specific thalamic nuclei receive specific signals from sensory modalities and project topographically to regions of the cortex. The topographical representation of the sensory modalities within the cortex can be seen in the human homunculus (meaning 'little man'). The cortical homunculus derives from studies by Wilder Penfield and colleagues who used electrical stimulation of the cortex to create a representation of the body within the brain (see Figure 5.15) (Penfield & Rasmussen, 1950). The distorted sensory representations in the homunculus are a reflection of the extensive input to the cortex.

In addition to the specific thalamic nuclei, there are association nuclei that receive little sensory input but do receive neural information from other regions of the brain, e.g. the cortex and basal ganglia. These nuclei are thought to have an integrative function (see Haber and Calzavara (2009) for review).

In addition, there are non-specific thalamic nuclei that project in a diffuse pattern rather than the specific relay of the other nuclei (see Figure 5.16). Non-specific thalamic nuclei also communicate with specific thalamic nuclei, thereby controlling a lot of cortical activity.

The specific thalamic nuclei relay the following somatosensory inputs to the cortex.

- Pain (ventral posterior lateral and ventral posterior medial nuclei of the thalamus)
- Thermal (posterolateral nucleus)
- Auditory (medial geniculate nucleus (MGN))
- Visual (LGN)
- Taste (ventral posterior medial nucleus)
- Vestibular (ventral posterior nuclei)
- Olfactory (olfactory bulb although olfactory information can pass directly to the cortex without having to go via the thalamus)

The thalamic nucleus most often discussed is the lateral geniculate nucleus (LGN) and its involvement in projecting visual information along the optic nerve from the retina to the occipital cortex (see Chapter 10).

Damage to the sensory cortex can manifest as changes within the thalamus via a process of **retrograde thalamic degeneration** (Diamond & Utley, 1963; Matthews, 1973; Ross & Ebner, 1990; Tanaka & Chen, 1974). Lesions of the sensory cortex produce downstream changes in the thalamus that can be clearly identified. For example, a lesion to the occipital lobe of the rhesus monkey results in degeneration of the LGN (Horoupian et al., 1973; Mihailovic et al., 1971). Lesions of the rat's frontal cortex resulted in reduced neurons in the mediodorsal nucleus of the thalamus (Van Eden et al., 1998) and lesions of the somatosensory cortex in mice led to degeneration of the thalamic ventrobasal complex and the medial division of the posterior thalamic nuclei (Ross & Ebner, 1990, p.523). This is not merely a laboratory phenomenon and 'traumatic or stroke-like injuries of the cerebral cortex result in the rapid retrograde degeneration of thalamic relay neurons that project to the damaged area' (Ross & Ebner, 1990). Using a powerful magnet in a functional magnetic resonance imaging (fMRI) scan, Miki et al. (2005) found decreased activation of the visual cortex and LGN on the side of the lesion in patients with homonymous hemianopia. A **homonymous hemianopia** is the loss of part of the visual field on the same side, in both eyes. There was one case in which a 21-year-old woman who had a stroke four years previously experienced sudden onset of a left-sided headache, followed by nausea and vomiting. There was no numbness, weakness or language difficulty. Two days later, she had a computed tomography (CT) scan, which revealed a left occipital stroke. The fMRI revealed that there was activation of the right LGN but activation of the left LGN was not detectable (Miki et al., 2005).

Lesions of the thalamus also have devastating effects. According to Schmahmann (2003), vascular lesions (stroke) destroy thalamic nuclei in different combinations and produce sensorimotor and behavioural syndromes depending on which nuclei are involved. Furthermore, and in contrast to lesion studies, deep brain stimulation of the sensory thalamus has been used to treat chronic pain disorders (Duncan et al., 1998).

The hypothalamus

As has already been mentioned, the hypothalamus is the main controller of the autonomic nervous system. Due to its regulation of the ANS, it has widespread effects on numerous behaviours including feeding, drinking, sex, sleep, circadian rhythms and aggression. Like the thalamus, the hypothalamus is composed of separate nuclei (Figure 5.17). The main nuclei of the hypothalamus are the:

- paraventricular nucleus;
- **ventromedial nucleus**;
- suprachiasmatic nucleus;
- **preoptic nucleus**;
- supraoptic nucleus;
- **dorsomedial nucleus**;
- arcuate nucleus;
- mammillary bodies;
- **anterior nucleus**; and
- **lateral nucleus**.

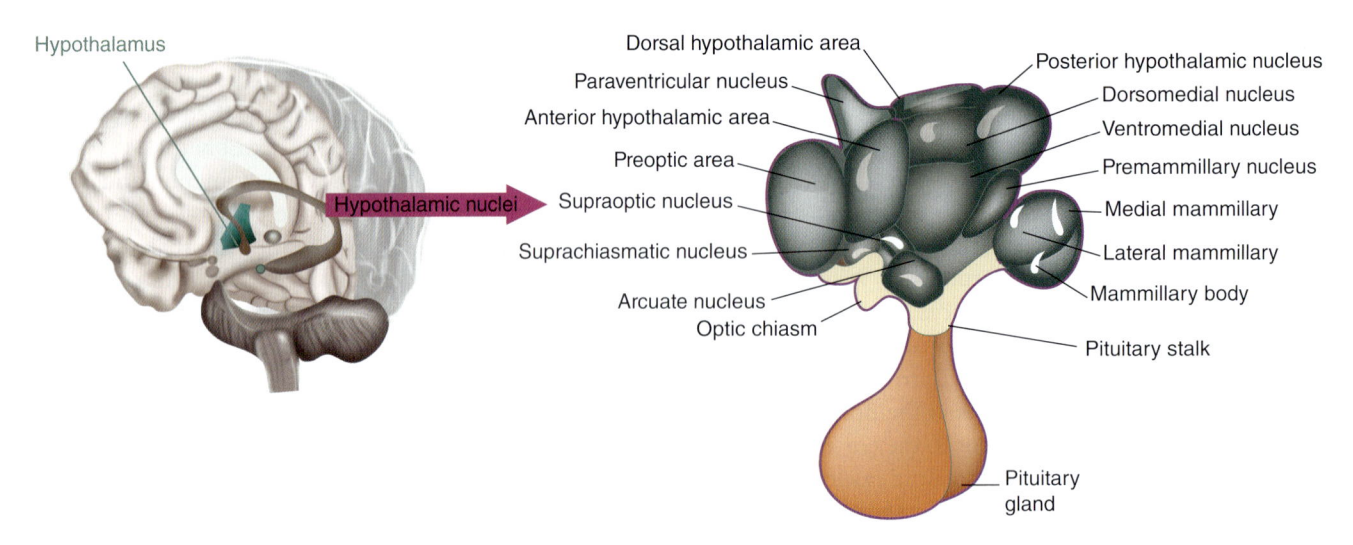

FIGURE 5.17 *Hypothalamus and nuclei.*

The hypothalamus receives information from the body via neural connections, the blood supply and the CSF. Thus, the hypothalamus integrates information on the state of the body and influences the ANS and CNS via mechanisms of control such as the endocrine system. Neural input to the hypothalamus comes from a wide range of structures:

- viscera and somatic structures;
- retina;
- olfactory membrane;
- inner ear;
- frontal lobe;
- hippocampus;
- amygdala; and
- thalamus.

The efferent projections of the hypothalamus arise from the mammillary bodies, the medial hypothalamus and the lateral hypothalamus.

Projections from the **mammillary bodies** via the **mammillothalamic tract** synapse with the anterior thalamic nucleus. Projections from the mammillary bodies also synapse with the midbrain tegmentum via the **mammillotegmental tract**.

The medial hypothalamus connects with the amygdala and midbrain periaqueductal grey (PAG). Fibres emanating from the lateral hypothalamus connect with preoptic areas, the temporal lobe, the hippocampus and the midbrain PAG.

The far-reaching effect of hypothalamic activity is most notable in its communication with the pituitary gland. The paraventricular nucleus and supraoptic nuclei connect the hypothalamus with the pituitary gland. The hypothalamus produces a series of hormones that either release or inhibit hormone secretion from the anterior pituitary gland (see Table 5.4).

The **paraventricular nucleus** and the **supraoptic nucleus** synthesize and release **antidiuretic hormone** (ADH, or **vasopressin**) and **oxytocin** which are released into the bloodstream. ADH increases water absorption in the kidneys (see Chapter 15) and oxytocin is involved in the milk ejection reflex from the mammary glands and produces contractions during birth.

Subthalamus

The **subthalamus** is divided into the subthalamic nucleus and the **zona incerta**. The subthalamic nucleus is involved in motor behaviour and is richly connected with the basal ganglia, in particular the globus pallidus (Parent & Hazrati, 1995). The zona incerta has been considered an area without particular function (see Mitrofanis (2005) for review) but it has been associated with motor behaviour, anxiety and depression (Burrows et al., 2012).

Epithalamus

The **epithalamus** is a series of structures comprising the **habenular** and the pineal gland. The habenular complex can be divided into the lateral and medial nuclei and is involved in many behaviours, e.g. mating and reward (Sutherland, 1982). The **pineal gland** receives input from the sympathetic nervous system (Figure 5.18). The pineal gland is sensitive to light and governs circadian rhythms via the suprachiasmatic nucleus from the retina (see Chapter 18).

TABLE 5.4 *Hormones – effects and functions*

Hypothalamic hormone*	Effect on pituitary hormone	Function
Growth hormone-releasing hormone (GHRH)	↑ Growth hormone (GH)	Stimulates growth
Growth hormone-inhibiting hormone (GHIH) or somatostatin	↓ Growth hormone	Reduces growth
Prolactin-releasing hormone (PRH)	↑ Prolactin	Stimulates lactation
Prolactin-inhibiting hormone	↓ Prolactin	Reduces lactation
Corticotrophin-releasing hormone (CRH)	↑ Adrenocorticotrophic hormone (ACTH)	Activates adrenal gland, producing corticosteroids and sex hormones
Thyrotrophin-releasing hormone (TRH)	↑ Thyroid-stimulating hormone (TSH)	Stimulates thyroid gland, producing thyroxine
Luteinizing hormone-releasing hormone (LHRH)	Luteinizing hormone (LH)	Stimulates ovulation
Follicle-stimulating release hormone (FRH)	Follicle-stimulating hormone (FSH)	Stimulates the growth of ovaries and spermatogenesis

*Sometimes called factors.

The Limbic System (and Hippocampus)

The **limbic system** is not a structure but rather a network of nuclei that are thought to be involved in emotions and learning. The limbic system comprises the **hippocampal formation**, **amygdala** and **septum**. Also included in this network are mamillary bodies of the hypothalamus and the cingulate cortex (see Figure 5.19).

The hippocampal formation consists of the hippocampus, the **dentate gyrus** and the **parahippocampal gyrus** (see Figure 5.19). They are made up of cellular layers, not dissimilar to the cortex:

- external plexiform layer – contains pyramidal axons;
- stratum oriens – contains basal dendrites;
- pyramidal cell layer – contains pyramidal cells;
- stratum radiatum – contains apical dendrites of the pyramidal cells; and
- stratum lacunosum moleculare – contains apical dendrites of the pyramidal cells.

The pyramidal cells of the hippocampus are arranged in a C-shaped loop interlocked with a corresponding loop of the dentate gyrus. The hippocampus is divided into distinct fields called CA1, CA2, CA3 and CA4.

The dentate gyrus is similar to that of the hippocampus but the main cells are granule cells and connect with pyramidal cells in CA3. The parahippocampal gyrus contains a thick pyramidal cell layer that provides a transition between the entorhinal cortex and the hippocampus. The **entorhinal cortex** is a part of the medial temporal lobe and is involved in memory formation (see Chapter 13).

Amygdala

The **amygdala** is an almond-shaped structure made of several distinct nuclei (Figure 5.19c):

- central nucleus;
- medial nucleus;

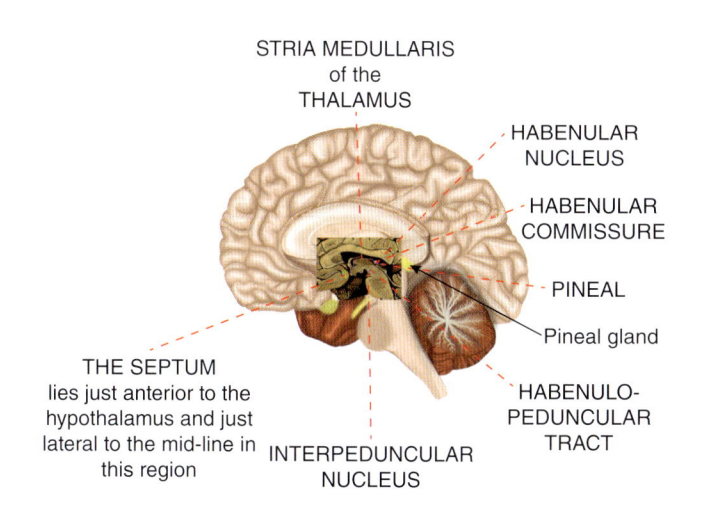

FIGURE 5.18 *Pineal gland.*

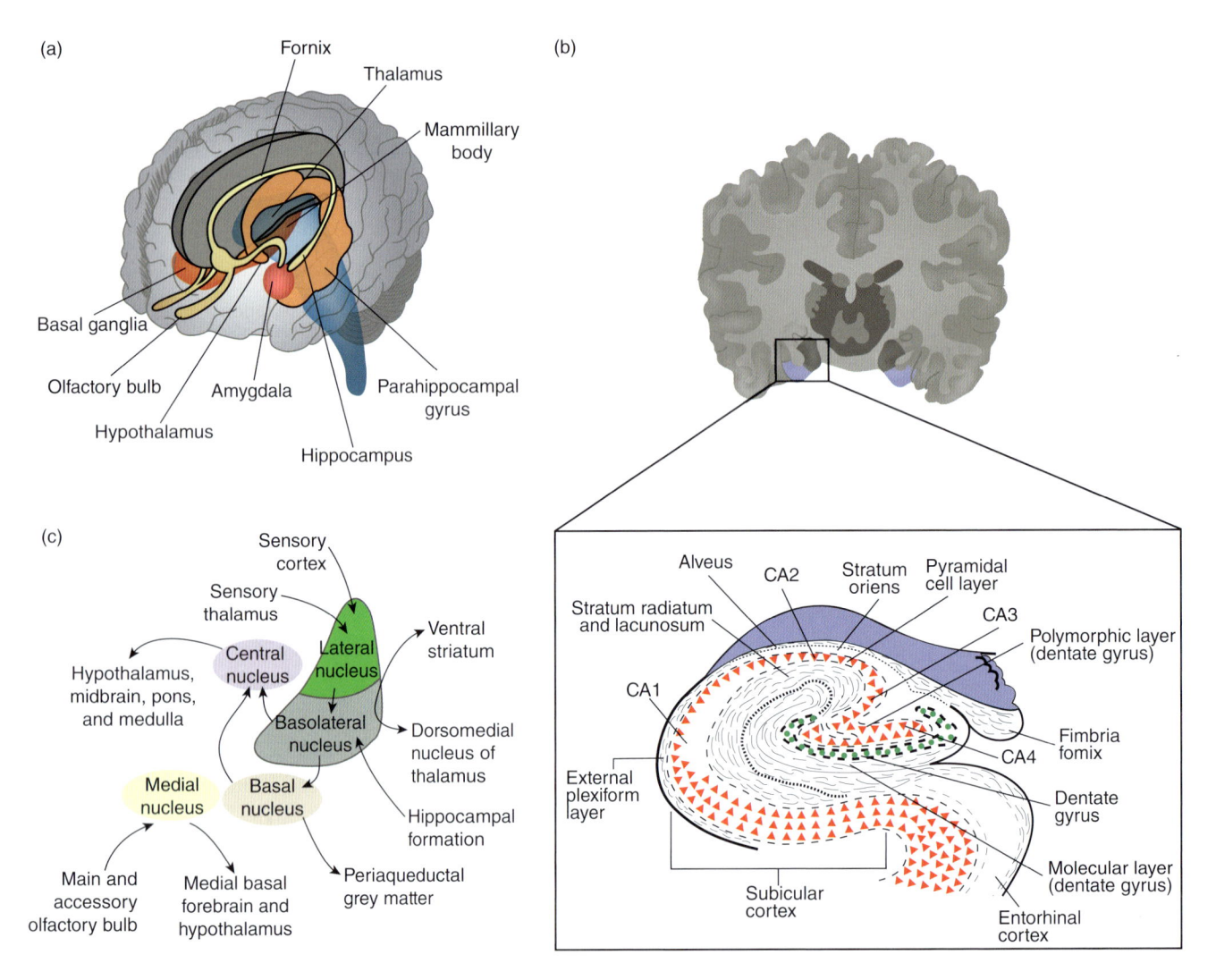

FIGURE 5.19 Limbic system. (a) Regions of the limbic system. (b) The hippocampus in detail (horizontal plane of the hippocampal formation). (c) The amygdala in detail.

- basal nucleus;
- lateral nucleus; and
- accessory basal nucleus.

The amygdala enjoys rich connections with other regions of the brain and is important in fear and emotion (see Chapter 17) (LeDoux, 2000).

The septum

The **septum** or **septal area** reciprocally communicates with the hippocampus and the hypothalamus. There are two regions that are often included within the septal area: (1) the **bed nucleus of the stria terminalis** and (2) the nucleus accumbens, both of which have been implicated in the maintenance of addictive behaviours (Koob & Le Moal, 2006) (see Chapter 16).

The nucleus accumbens

The **nucleus accumbens** comprises a core and a shell (Figure 5.20). The nucleus accumbens receives dopaminergic projections from the **ventral tegmental area (VTA)**, prefrontal cortex and amygdala. The connection to the VTA is referred to as the mesolimbic pathway and it is considered to be the reward pathway which gives rise to addiction (see Chapter 16). The nucleus accumbens communicates with the prefrontal cortex via the **ventral pallidum** (part of the globus pallidus) and the medial dorsal nucleus of the thalamus.

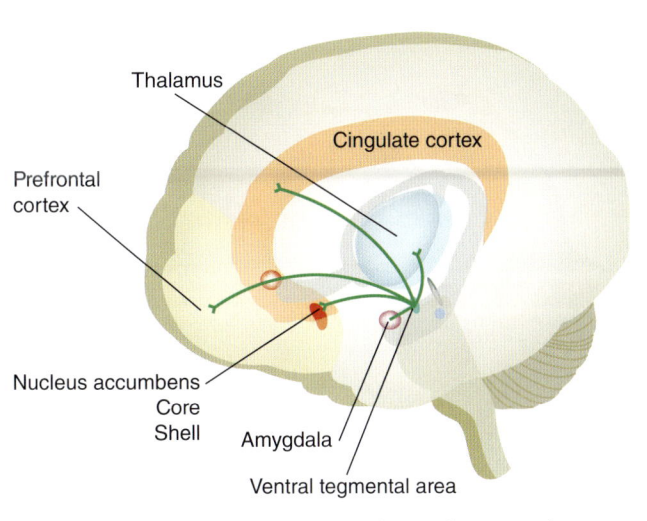

FIGURE 5.20 *Nucleus accumbens and ventral tegmental area.*

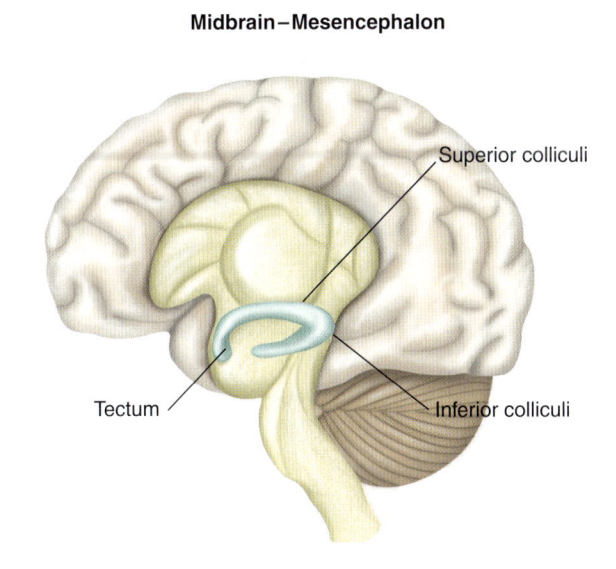

FIGURE 5.22 *Inferior and superior colliculi.*

The Basal Ganglia

In some neuroanatomical classifications, the **basal ganglia** also contain the amygdala. The basal ganglia comprise the **striatum, globus pallidus** and **substantia nigra** (Figure 5.21). The striatum is further subdivided into **caudate nucleus** and **putamen**. The **globus pallidus** has internal and external parts. The substantia nigra divides into two areas called the *pars compacta* and *pars reticulata*. The basal ganglia are connected to the somatosensory cortex, the primary motor cortex of the parietal and frontal lobes. The basal ganglia are extremely important in motor control and it is this area that contains the underlying fault in Parkinson's disease and Huntington's disease (see Chapter 24).

Midbrain: Mesencephalon

The **mesencephalon** is divided into two parts: the **tectum** and **tegmentum**. Again, this division is based on location; the tectum is dorsal and tegmentum is ventral. The tectum comprises the **inferior** and **superior colliculi** (Figure 5.22). These relate to auditory and visual functions respectively (see Chapter 10). The tegmentum comprises the substantia nigra (also part of the basal ganglia – see above) and another motor area called the red nucleus. The mesencephalon also contains the PAG (Figure 5.23), which is tissue around the cerebral aqueduct that connects the third and fourth ventricles. This site is the target of many analgesics. It also contains the **reticular formation** that extends from the spinal cord to the cerebrum, which has been implicated in sleep (see Chapter 18). The reticular formation can be divided into three columns – lateral, medial and median – that can be differentiated by the size of cells. The reticular formation is a recipient of many afferent projections and communicates down the brainstem and spinal cord via the descending pathways. It also communicates with the striatum, cerebellum, red nucleus, substantia nigra, tectum, thalamus, hypothalamus and cortex.

Hindbrain: Metencephalon and Myelencephalon

The **metencephalon** comprises the **brainstem** and the **cerebellum** (see Figure 5.24). The **brainstem** is the term given to a collection of regions comprising the midbrain (see above), pons and medulla oblongata originating from the **myelencephalon**.

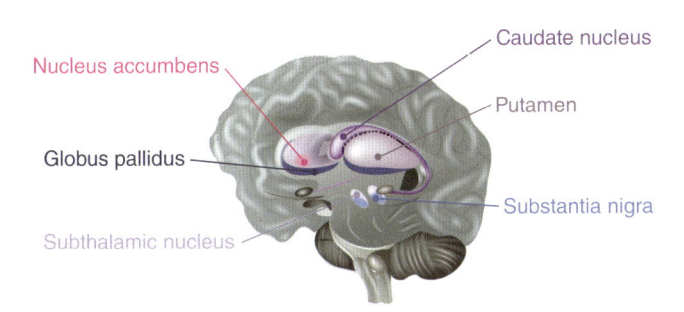

FIGURE 5.21 *The basal ganglia.*

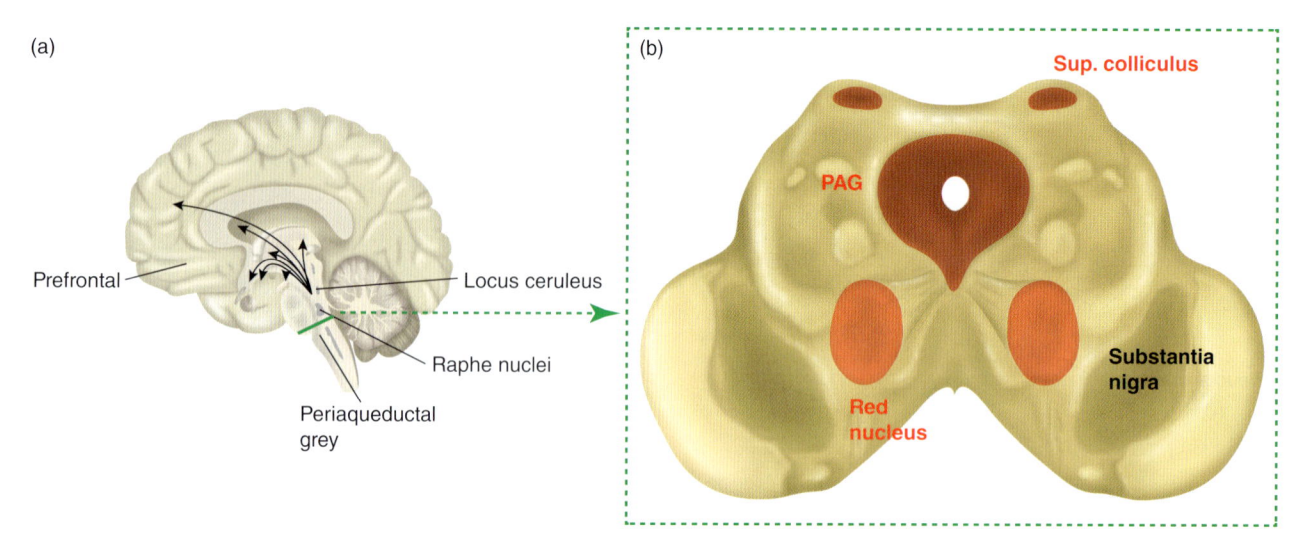

FIGURE 5.23 *Locus coeruleus and red nucleus. (a) Locus coeruleus. (b) Cross-section of midbrain.*

The pons
The pons contains a part of the reticular formation, and descending and ascending neural fibres. The pons is a bridge between the two hemispheres. A number of cranial nerves are present in the pons (e.g. trigeminal nerve and facial nerve) and it is therefore important in relaying afferent and efferent communications. The **medulla oblongata** connects the pons with the spinal cord and is important in mediating the ANS.

The cerebellum
The cerebellum is the coral-like structure seen in MRI images and is involved in motor control. It is composed of grey matter on the outside (cortex) and white matter

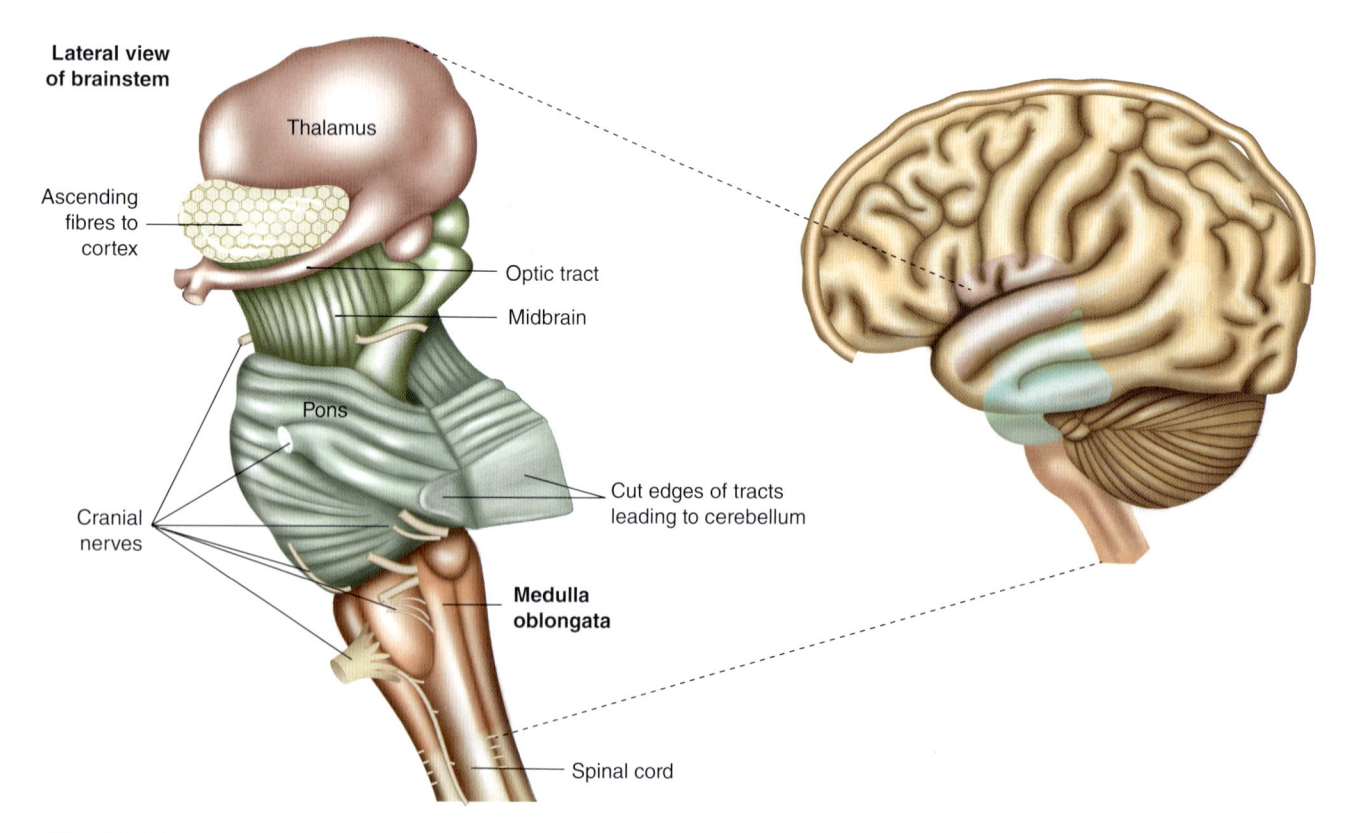

FIGURE 5.24 *Brainstem.*

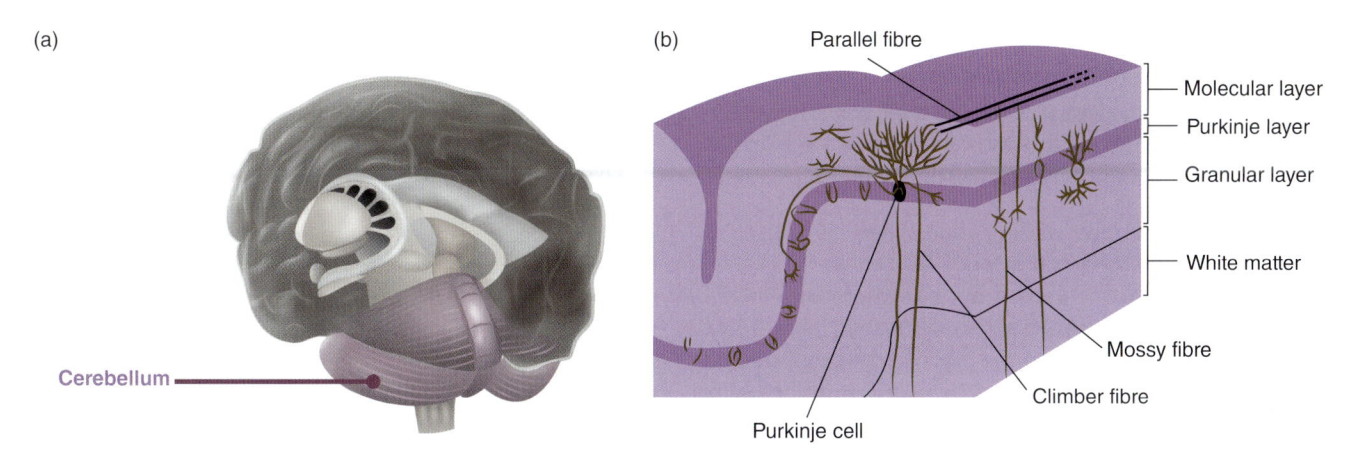

FIGURE 5.25 The cerebellum. (a) Location of the cerebellum. (b) Cortical layers of the cerebellum.

on the inside. The cortex of the cerebellum is made up of three layers (Figure 5.25):

- a molecular layer;
- a **Purkinje cell** layer, which are large GABAergic cells; and
- a granular layer.

The cerebellum receives communications from the cortical lobes and transmits information to the red nucleus, thalamus, vestibular system and reticular formation. The cerebellum is particularly important in voluntary movement (Middleton & Strick, 2000).

THE INS AND OUTS OF BLOOD SUPPLY TO THE BRAIN

The brain is a large consumer of energy. Energy arrives at the brain via the blood supply. It has been known for many years that there is a correlation between blood flow, indicating energy consumption, and cognitive processing (Lennox et al., 1938). Now blood flow is a common measure in cognitive neuroscience as regional cerebral blood flow is used to locate areas of the brain with high energy consumption (see Chapter 6). Dramatic changes in blood flow can give rise to dramatic neurological problems, e.g. **cerebrovascular stroke** (see Box 5.3) and **migraine headache** (Box 5.4).

Blood flow to and from the brain via **arteries** (inflow) and **veins** (outflow) is a dynamically regulated mechanism in which interruption can change the volume of the brain with potentially damaging effects (Roy & Sherrington, 1890). In a typical human at rest, the oxygen-rich blood entering the brain can be compared to that leaving the brain. The blood leaving the brain has reduced levels of oxygen compared to the incoming blood by a factor of 32.1% and an increase in carbon dioxide (Gibbs et al., 1942). The blood supply network is not only important for providing the brain with the energy for its function and survival, it is also the distribution network for the delivery of drugs (see Chapter 7).

BOX 5.3: CEREBROVASCULAR DISEASE: STROKE

Damage to the blood supply to the brain produces profound disability and death. The two most common forms of cerebrovascular disease are stroke and subarachnoid haemorrhage.

Stroke or cerebral ischaemia is when there is a reduced blood supply to the brain that produces effects lasting greater than 24 hours. This has been the subject of public information films using the acronym FAST.

- Face – has the face fallen all along one side? Can the person smile?
- Arms – can they raise their arms and keep them there?

- Speech – is their speech slurred?
- Time – if the answer to the first three points is yes then you need to act fast and call emergency services as time is of the essence to minimize the impact.

If the signs disappear within 24 hours then it is referred to as a **transient ischaemic attack** (TIA).

A stroke can be caused by a haemorrhage, infarction or atherosclerosis (Clarke, 2007) (see Figure 5.3.1). A **haemorrhage** is when the blood vessels rupture and there is a leak from the blood circulation into the brain. An ischaemic stroke is when there is an infarction because the blood vessel becomes blocked, e.g. from an embolism from the heart. Atherosclerosis is narrowing of the blood vessels by fatty deposits. These can also break off and cause an embolism.

The net effect regardless of the cause is injury to the brain (an **infarction**) (Dirnagl et al., 1999).

The loss of blood supply means that oxygen and glucose are not being delivered to the brain. The loss of energy means that the membrane potential is also lost and the neurons and glia depolarize. This results in an increase in the release of glutamate that has a knock-on effect of producing a large influx of sodium and chloride. This influx leads to water moving passively and producing an oedema in the region.

Overactivation of glutamate receptors (NMDA receptors) is involved in ischaemic cell death. Glutamate-induced excitotoxicity can cause immediate and delayed cell death (necrosis and apoptosis respectively).

Due to the depolarization as a result of interrupted energy supply, cells undergo an anoxic depolarization from which they do not recover. However, with increasing levels of glutamate or potassium that can build up in the extracellular fluid, further depolarizations may be possible. Repetitive depolarizations or peri-infarct depolarizations increase in number as the infarcts grow larger.

To add to the difficulties, postischaemic inflammation of the brain exacerbates the damage. The area of impairment due to damage is referred to as the penumbra. As time passes, the damage can increase (see Figure 5.3.1). Thus, a number of neural events arising from the ischaemic attack can result in short- and long-term damage to the brain.

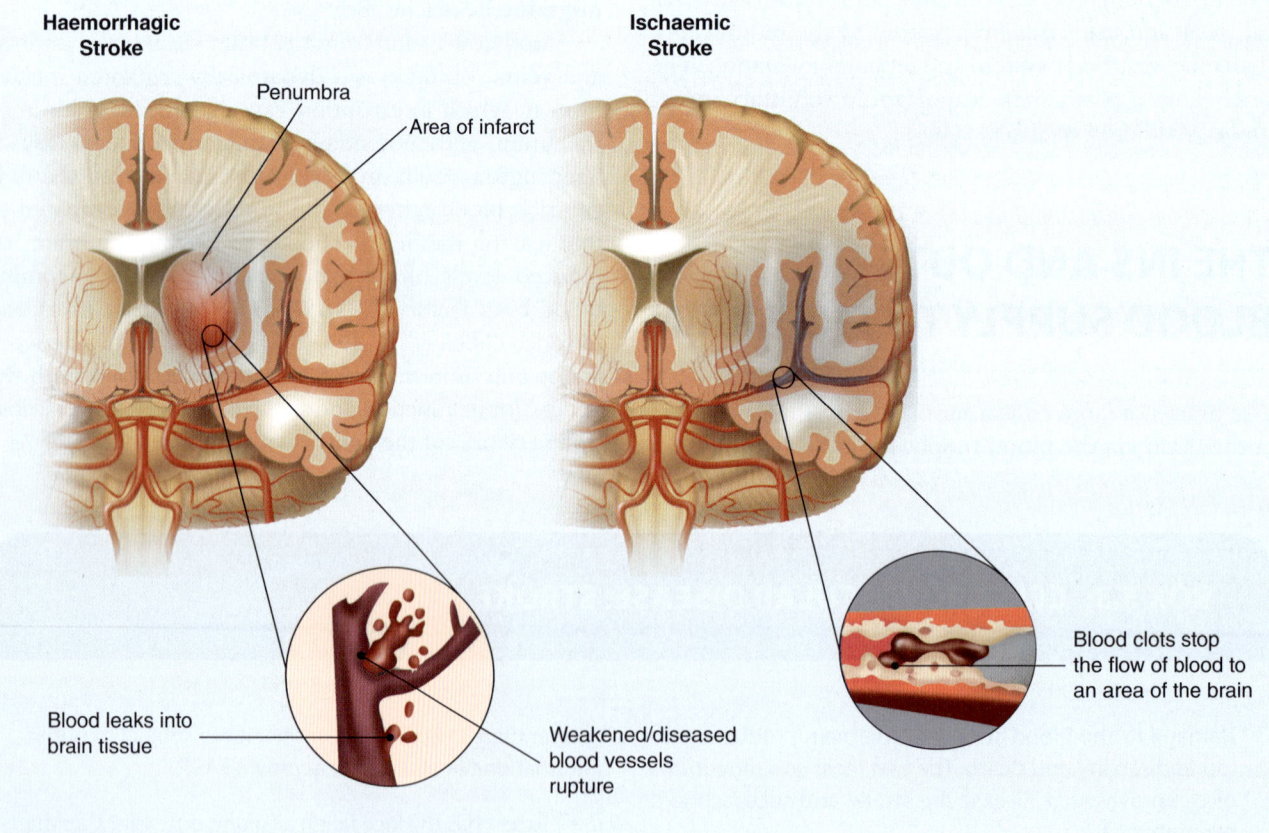

FIGURE 5.3.1 *The different mechanisms of a stroke.*

BOX 5.4: MIGRAINE HEADACHE

Pain is something that we experience if we are lucky. It is there to protect us from damage (see Chapter 10). The brain itself does not have pain receptors but clearly we experience the pain of headaches. We can localize the source of our discomfort to the head.

One of the more debilitating headaches is the migraine which is one of the vascular headaches that also includes cluster headaches. There are four stages of migraine headache (but not all are experienced).

- Prodrome – signs that a migraine is coming, e.g. constipation, depression, hyperactivity, irritability and neck stiffness.
- Aura – visual disturbances such as being sensitive to light.
- Headache – pulsating pain on one or both sides of the head, nausea and vomiting, blurred vision and light-headedness.
- Postdrome – after the migraine attack, lethargy and possible mild euphoria.

Migraine headaches are caused by a primary neuronal dysfunction that results in a sequence of changes that account for the different phases of a migraine headache. The development of a migraine and the sensation of pain depend on nociceptive receptors of the trigeminal nerve that innervate the blood vessels. Two main pain mechanisms have been considered: neurogenic inflammation of the meninges, and peripheral and central trigeminal sensitization (Pietrobon & Striessnig, 2003).

One mechanism involved in the initiation of a migraine is cortical depression that spreads across the cerebral cortex (Goadsby et al., 2009; Pietrobon & Striessnig, 2003). Cortical spreading depression (CSD) causes the migraine aura and activates trigeminal nerve nociceptive afferents, substance P and calcitonin gene-related peptide (CGRP), which produce inflammation of the meninges and dilation of affected cranial blood vessels, which generates the headache (Goadsby et al., 2009). There is also the involvement of serotonin and dopamine as serotonin agonists and dopamine antagonists have been used in the treatment of migraine (Monteith & Goadsby, 2011).

To put the whole process simply, oxygen is taken into the body via the lungs from which it passes into the bloodstream and is pumped around by the heart. The heart beats approximately 72 times a minute and pumps approximately 5 L of blood around the body.

Arterial Supply of Oxygenated Blood

Two arteries supply oxygenated blood to the brain: the internal **carotid artery** and the **vertebral artery** (Figure 5.26).

The carotid artery branches into several sections, ensuring a rich supply of oxygenated blood to the different regions of the brain.

- The ophthalmic artery innervates the eye which leads to the central artery of the retina.
- The posterior communicating artery branching at the optic chiasm which innervates the hypothalamus, thalamus and hippocampus.
- The anterior choroidal artery arises in the optic chiasm and supplies the choroid plexus, hippocampus, globus pallidus and other regions of the thalamus.
- The anterior cerebral artery supplies blood to the medial region of the cerebral hemispheres via a number of branches.
  - The anterior communicating artery supplies blood to the preoptic and suprachiasmatic areas of the hypothalamus.
  - The medial striate artery supplies blood to striatal regions.
    (a) Orbital branches and frontopolar branches supply the frontal lobe.
    (b) The colosomarginal artery supplies the cingulate gyrus.
    (c) The pericolossal artery supplies parts of the parietal lobe.

The middle cerebral artery has several branches to cortical regions.

- The lenticulostriate branches connecting to the striatum.

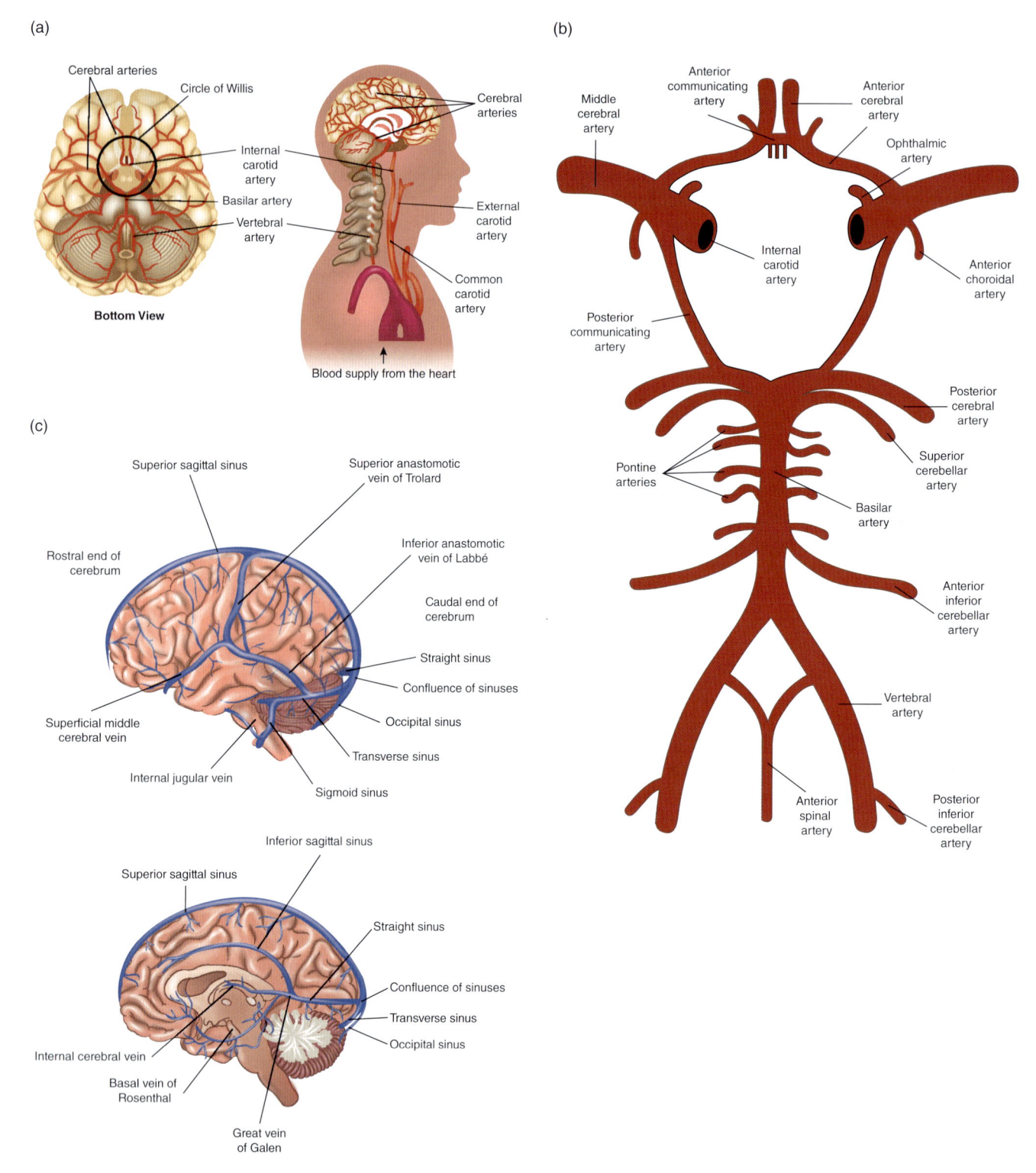

FIGURE 5.26 *The internal carotid artery and the vertebral artery. (a) Overview of arterial blood supply. (b) The circle of Willis. (c) The sinuses (surface-based sinuses and cross-section of sinuses).*

- Orbitofrontal artery, prerolandic and central rolandic supplying the frontal lobe.
- Anterior and posterior parietal arteries supplying the parietal lobe.
- The angular artery supplying the angular gyrus.
- Temporal arteries supplying the temporal lobe and occipital lobe.

The **vertebral artery** enters the brain at the level of the medulla and branches into the:

- anterior spinal artery supplying the medulla;
- posterior inferior cerebral artery supplying other regions of the medulla and the choroid plexus of the fourth ventricle;
- posterior spinal artery supplying the medulla and the vagus nerve;
- meningeal branches that supply bone and dura; and
- medullary arteries supplying the medulla oblongata.

The basilar artery also has several branches innervating different brain regions:

- pontine arteries supply the pons;
- labyrinthine artery supplies blood to the internal ear;
- anterior inferior cerebellar artery supplies the anterior and inferior parts of the cerebellum and also the pons and upper part of the medulla;
- superior cerebellar artery supplies the cerebellum, pons, pineal gland and medulla; and
- posterior cerebellar artery supplies the visual cortex, midbrain, thalamus and subthalamic nucleus.

The Cerebral Arterial Circle: The Circle of Willis

The cerebral arterial circle is formed from branches of the internal carotid artery and vertebral arteries. The connection of these arteries forms a circle (the **circle of Willis**) around the optic chiasm and the pituitary stalk. The circle of Willis allows blood that enters by either the carotid or vertebral arteries to be distributed to any part of the cerebral hemispheres (see Figure 5.26). This provides a safety net for the brain. If there is a blockage in one of the arteries serving the brain then the other arteries that enter the circle of Willis can compensate for the blockage and continue to supply the brain with oxygenated blood.

From the network of arteries serving the brain, the blood enters capillaries at which point the exchange of nutrients and oxygen can occur with the cells of the brain. This exchange is greatest in the grey matter of the brain (the cell bodies). To draw an analogy, the arteries are like the large roads serving a city and the capillaries are the streets that radiate off; many times you will hear traffic reports of arterial roads that supply the lifeblood to a city.

The blood has to leave the brain to be recycled; if not, blood pressure can increase, causing substantial damage. The exit route is via the veins. Unlike the veins in our arms and legs, for example, the veins of the brain do not possess valves. They exit the brain via the subarachnoid space and penetrate the subarachnoid mater and the meningeal layer of the protective dura from where they drain into the sinuses.

The cerebral veins are also divided by location. The superficial cerebral vein can be further divided into three branches:

- the superficial middle cerebral vein – which drains the temporal lobe and empties into the cavernous sinus;
- the superior anastomotic vein drains the parietal lobe into the superior sagittal sinus; and
- the inferior anastomotic vein connects the superficial middle cerebral vein with the transverse sinus and drains from the temporal lobe into the transverse sinus.

The deep cerebral veins can also be divided into three branches:

- the great cerebral vein of Galen which receives blood from the two internal cerebral veins that receive blood from the thalamus, striatum, nucleus accumbens, choroid plexus and hippocampus;
- the basal vein of Rosenthal is an exit route for blood from the frontal lobe and striatum; and
- the internal cerebral vein which empties from the great cerebral vein of Galen.

SINUSES

The veins eventually drain into the cranial venous sinuses which in turn empty into the left and right internal jugular veins. There are several **sinuses** (see Figure 5.26).

- The superior sagittal sinus.
- The inferior sagittal sinus.
- The straight sinus.
- The transverse sinuses.
- The intercavernous sinuses.
- The cavernous sinuses.
- The confluence of the sinuses.
- The occipital sinus.

- The superior petrosal sinus.
- The sphenoparietal sinus.

Whilst the brain is an avid consumer of the body's blood, the spinal cord also receives arterial supplies. It receives oxygenated blood from the posterior spinal arteries, anterior spinal arteries and segmental spinal arteries. The prefixes to the spinal arteries refer to location within the spine (see Figure 5.4). Blood going in also comes out via the spinal veins: anteromedian spinal vein, anterolateral spinal vein, posteromedian spinal vein and posterolateral spinal vein (see Figure 5.26).

ENDOCRINE SYSTEM

The endocrine system is not necessarily a nervous system but that does not mean that it does not have interactions with the nervous system. The endocrine system uses hormones to send messages to distant parts of the body (see Chapter 4 for details). The hypothalamus communicates with the pituitary gland allowing other hormones to be released.

The Pituitary Gland

The **pituitary gland** is often referred to as the master gland as it has the greatest influence on hormones. The pituitary gland sits below the hypothalamus and is connected via the pituitary stalk (see Figure 5.17). It can be divided into anterior and posterior regions. Depending upon the messages received from the hypothalamus (supraoptic nucleus and paraventricular nucleus), the anterior and posterior pituitary gland will release particular hormones. The anterior lobe of the pituitary releases **follicle-stimulating** hormone, luteinizing hormone, **thyroid-stimulating** hormone, adrenocorticotrophic hormone, prolactin and growth hormone (see Table 5.4). The posterior pituitary gland releases antidiuretic hormone and oxytocin.

SUMMARY

By turning up the power of the microscope, we can zoom in on the different regions of the brain. We can identify surface detail but also the brain's cellular organization. It should always be remembered that whilst neuroanatomy often portrays the regions of the brain in isolation or in small networks, all these regions of the brain are richly connected with each other. Lesion studies gave the first insight into functional neuroanatomy which has been confirmed more recently with brain imaging. The advantage of brain imaging techniques over case studies derived from brain injury is that the intact brain can be evaluated for its functional contribution. When a particular task is in operation, e.g. reading this text, then certain regions of the brain will be more busy/active and utilize oxygen supplied via the bloodstream.

The connectivity of brain regions can also be extended to the ANS and endocrine systems in which target organs can be influenced by the brain and its sensory input.

Neuroanatomy is a complicated discipline that sometimes is surprisingly inconsistent. One of the biggest obstacles to overcome with psychobiology is learning the names of the brain regions and the chemicals that permit neural communication. Do not be put off by the names; after all, they are just names like the names of the individuals on your course and in a multicultural society those names are beautifully varied.

LEARNING OUTCOME QUESTIONS

You should be able to answer the following questions:
- How are the nervous systems differentiated?
- What are the different views of the brain?
- How can the brain be subdivided?
- What are the functions of the sympathetic and parasympathetic nervous systems?
- Describe the vascular innervation of the brain.
- What are the cranial nerves?

FURTHER READING

Blumenfeld, H. (2010). *Neural anatomy through clinical cases*. Sunderland, MA: Sinauer Associates.
Richards, D., Clark, T., & Clarke, C. (2007). *The human brain and its disorders*. Oxford, UK: Oxford University Press.
Snell, R. S. (2010). *Clinical neuroanatomy* (7th edn). Baltimore, MD: Lippincott Williams & Wilkins.

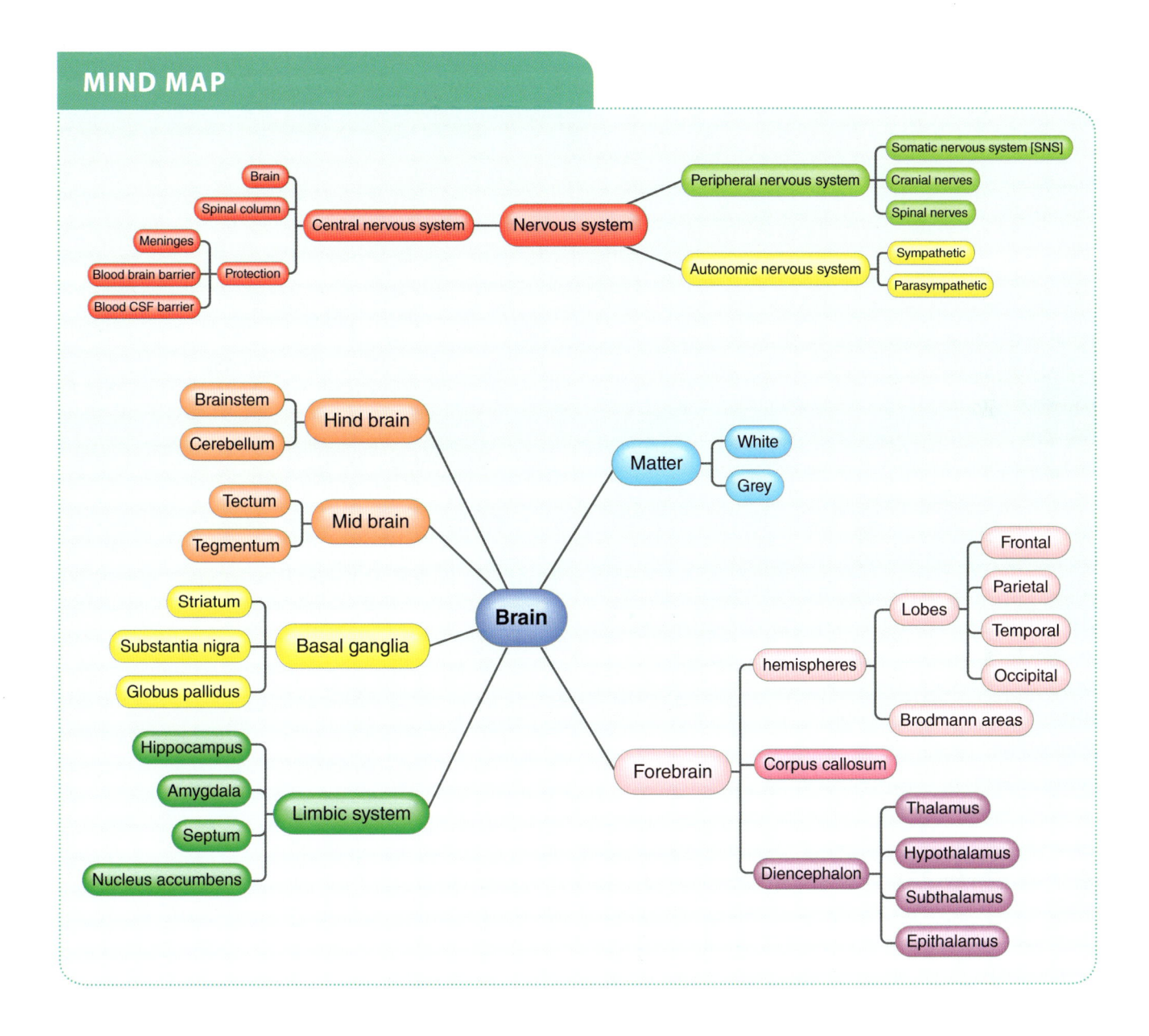

MIND MAP

- Nervous system
  - Central nervous system
    - Brain
    - Spinal column
    - Protection
      - Meninges
      - Blood brain barrier
      - Blood CSF barrier
  - Peripheral nervous system
    - Somatic nervous system [SNS]
    - Cranial nerves
    - Spinal nerves
  - Autonomic nervous system
    - Sympathetic
    - Parasympathetic

- Brain
  - Hind brain
    - Brainstem
    - Cerebellum
  - Mid brain
    - Tectum
    - Tegmentum
  - Basal ganglia
    - Striatum
    - Substantia nigra
    - Globus pallidus
  - Limbic system
    - Hippocampus
    - Amygdala
    - Septum
    - Nucleus accumbens
  - Matter
    - White
    - Grey
  - Forebrain
    - hemispheres
      - Lobes
        - Frontal
        - Parietal
        - Temporal
        - Occipital
      - Brodmann areas
    - Corpus callosum
    - Diencephalon
      - Thalamus
      - Hypothalamus
      - Subthalamus
      - Epithalamus

6 Psychobiology and Neuroscience Methods

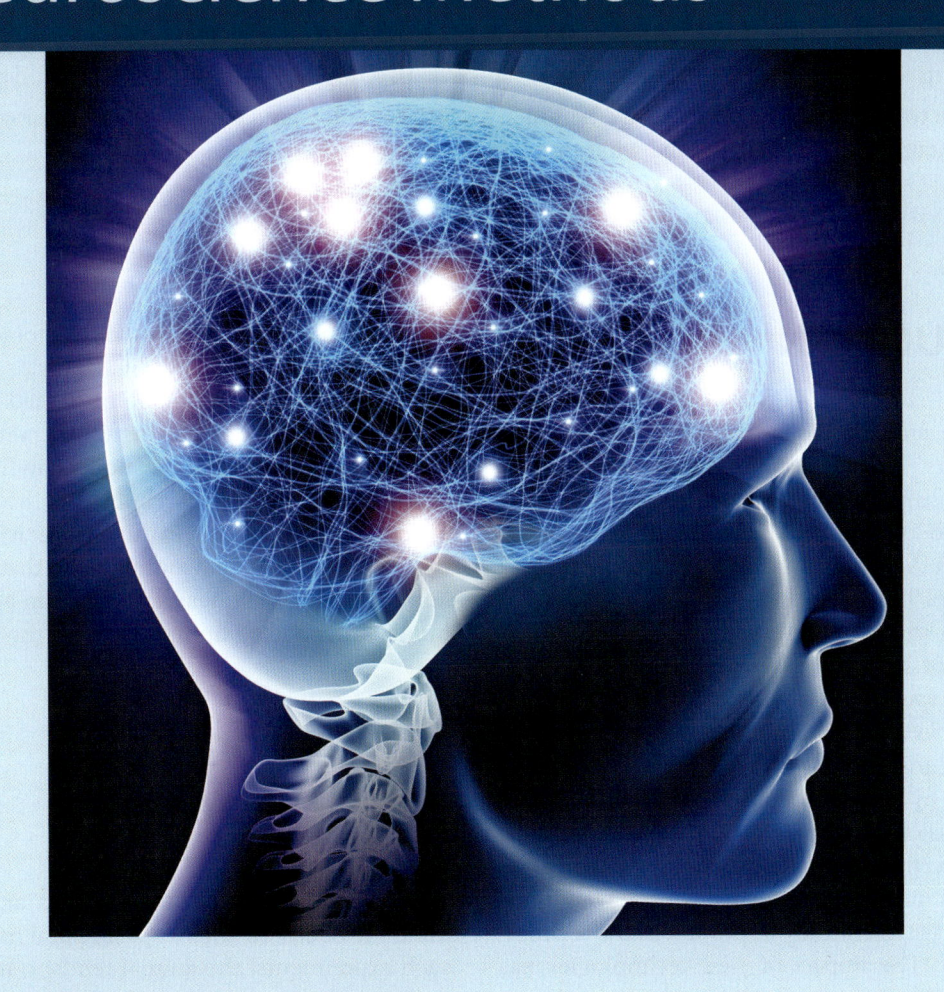

ANATOMY OF THE CHAPTER

This chapter will highlight the following.
- Methods used by physiological psychologists.
- Neuropsychopharmacological methods.
- Psychophysiology.
- Neuroimaging methods including magnetic resonance imaging and positron emission tomography.

INTRODUCTION 154

PHYSIOLOGICAL PSYCHOLOGY 154

NEUROPSYCHOPHARMACOLOGY 157

PSYCHOPHYSIOLOGY 158

BRAIN IMAGING 161

OPTICAL IMAGING OF THE BRAIN 166

NEUROIMAGING IS NOT THE ULTIMATE EVIDENCE 166

NEUROIMAGING MAPS OF THE MIND 168

PSYCHOPHYSIOLOGY AND NEUROIMAGING COMBINED 168

VIRTUAL LESIONS – TRANSCRANIAL MAGNETIC STIMULATION 169

SUMMARY 169

LEARNING OUTCOMES

1. To understand the importance of methodology when using technology and biological methods.
2. To be able to differentiate between the different types of neuroimaging available and what they measure.
3. To understand the limitations of neuroimaging, psychophysiology and physiological psychology.
4. To understand what psychophysiology is measuring.

INTRODUCTION

Psychobiology and neuroscience are fast-moving, dynamic subjects. The vast majority of research in psychobiology focuses on *in vivo* methodologies, as opposed to *in vitro* methodologies used by the biologist (*in vivo* is Latin for 'within the living', *in vitro* is Latin for 'in glass', i.e. the test tube). To understand behaviour, we need living organisms – this puts the *psycho* into *psychobiology*. The rapid pace of advances in research providing an evidence-based perspective on the underlying mechanisms of behaviour is in part due to new technologies allowing the scientist an overview into the brain. It is easy to be side-tracked by the seduction of new technologies. The complexities of neuroimaging and the resultant pictures provide convincing data. However, the psychological tasks that an individual performs whilst having their brain evaluated are as critically important as the technology being used. The impact of new technologies has far-reaching implications, not only for the understanding of human behaviour and disorders, but for how we consider ourselves as free agents in control of our own behaviour (see Chapters 18 and 25).

This chapter is not designed to evaluate the psychological methodology, although chapters within this book will address some of those issues, but rather to provide the reader with a review of neuroscience/psychobiological methods. In Chapter 1, psychobiology was placed in the context of other disciplines, e.g. neurochemistry, and also its own subdivisions, e.g. psychophysiology. These disciplines and subdisciplines utilize different techniques to ask essentially the same questions in their broadest format: what does the brain do? And how does it go about doing it?

Technology has driven our understanding of the basic mechanisms of genetics (see Chapter 2) but is now increasing our understanding of how genes interact with environments to influence cellular structure and ultimately behaviour. The research techniques of molecular biology can now be used by the psychobiologist and have been discussed previously in Chapter 2.

Although not a technique or indeed a methodology, animal studies have been extremely, yet controversially important in furthering our understanding of the brain. The use of animals in psychobiology has been discussed in detail in Chapter 1 but in this chapter it is the techniques rather than the behavioural tasks that are described. Some of the techniques can be used in both animals and humans, depending upon the size of the animal.

PHYSIOLOGICAL PSYCHOLOGY

The physiological psychologist uses animals to determine the effects of their experimental manipulations. In such experiments, the animal tends to undergo surgery to manipulate or measure the brain and its responses. The surgery may involve the animal receiving a lesion to a specific site of the brain or having an electrode placed within a discrete area for subsequent stimulation. In a somewhat more passive manner, the physiological psychologist may wish to record the activity of brain regions in the animal.

The advantage of these methods is that there is a great deal of precision and one can measure the effect of the manipulation in the whole behaving animal. Pure physiology tends to look at the neurons in isolation from the network from which they came.

The experimental nature of physiological psychology requires groups of animals to be studied – experimental groups and control groups. The experimental groups have the invasive surgery that produces the functional change in the animal. In effect, there could be numerous experimental groups in any one study. However, in order to assess the impact of the lesion, etc., the physiological psychologist needs to compare the results obtained from the experimental groups with those from appropriate control groups. The control group would receive the same treatment as the experimental group with the exception of the active ingredient, e.g. the lesion. This control group is often referred to as the sham group or the group which has had sham surgery (i.e. surgery without effect). This is important as the experimenter needs to eliminate extraneous variables that could affect the data, thus making it difficult to determine if it is the lesion that is responsible for any changes subsequently measured.

The process of surgery is complex and involves many stages. Each animal, regardless of whether it is in the experimental or control group, should receive the same attention and handling from the experimenter and technicians. Both groups should receive the same anaesthetic and mechanics of surgery. The groups should undergo the same recovery processes and time scale of events. The only difference between the two groups should be that of the active component of the surgery, e.g. a lesion.

Like humans, the animals need to be anaesthetized before surgery. There are numerous different types of anaesthetic that can be used and these have to be carefully considered in terms of their impact on the intervention and subsequent data.

Once anaesthetized, the animal is placed in a **stereotaxic frame** (Figure 6.1). This frame is not dissimilar to the frames that humans would use when they undergo brain surgery. The stereotaxic frame holds the animal in place and stops the head from moving so that accurate measurements can be made for the surgery. The frame can hold in place an electrode or a cannula (to deliver neurotoxins or other chemicals) that can be moved in three dimensions: left and right, forward and backwards, and up and down. In order to perform the surgery on the correct area of the brain, the experimenter uses an

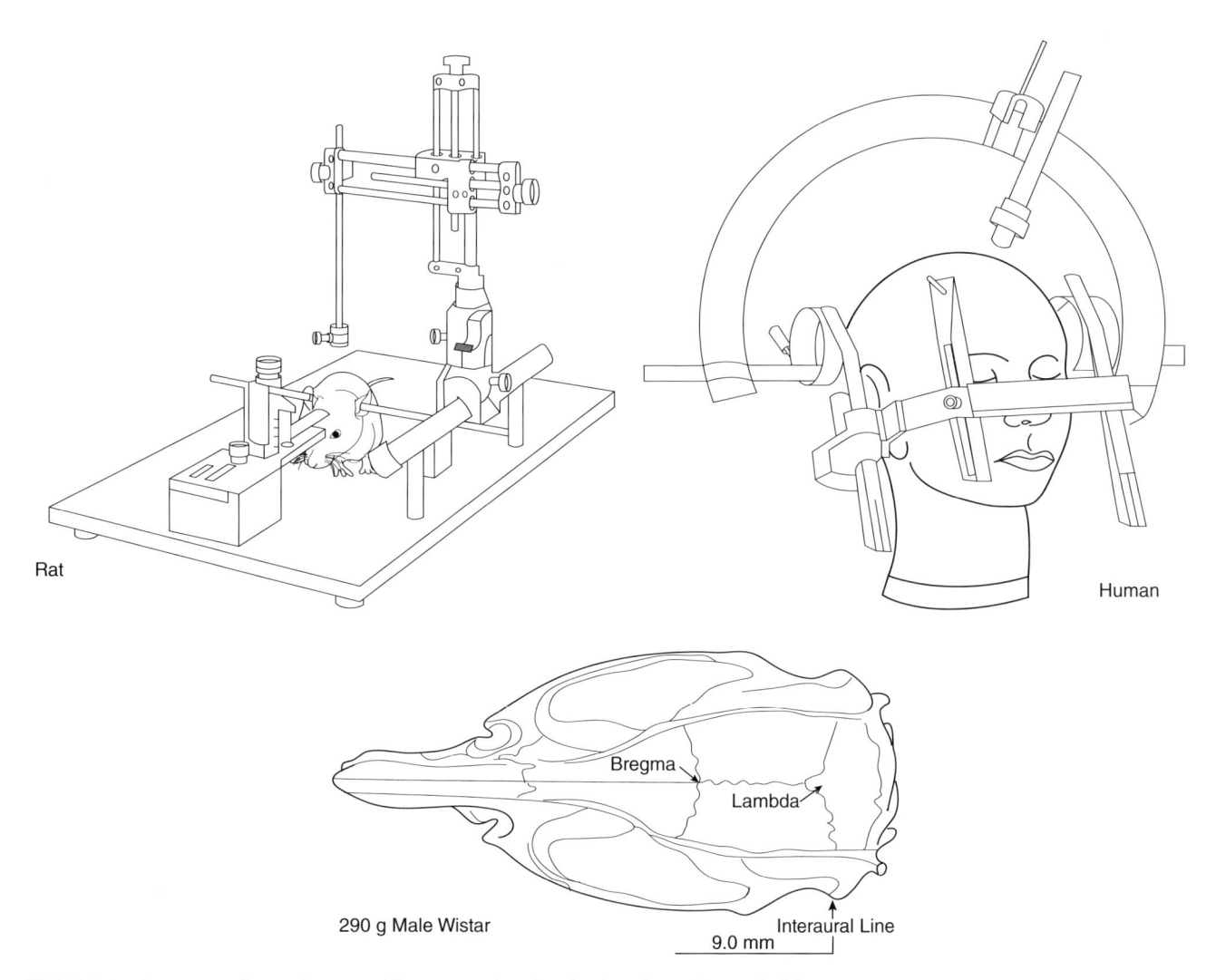

FIGURE 6.1 *Stereotaxic frames for rat and human, and surface landmarks on the rat skull for navigation.*

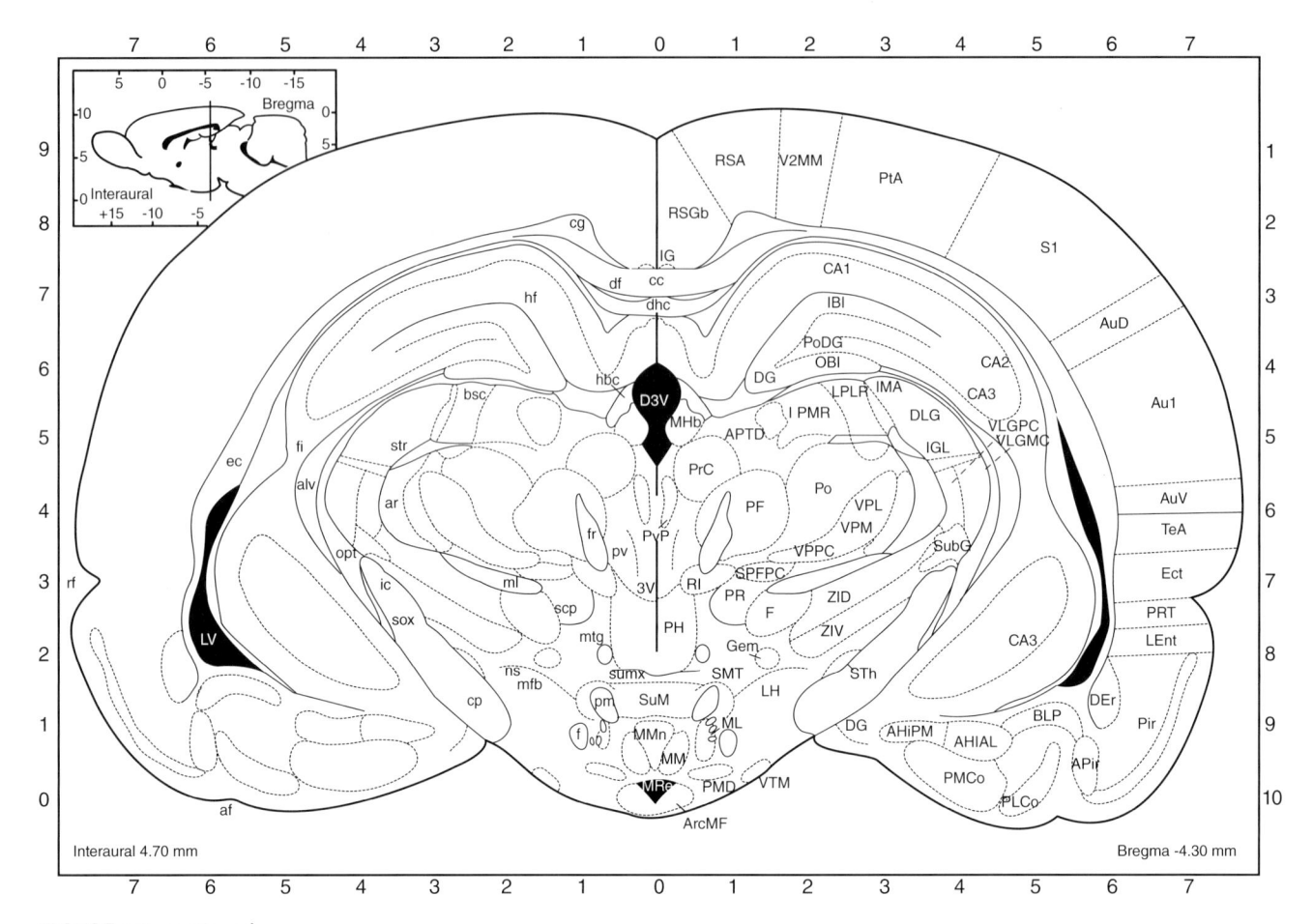

FIGURE 6.1 *continued*

atlas of the rat brain that gives the three-dimensional co-ordinates (e.g. Paxinos & Watson, 2006).

An incision is made into the skin of the animal to reveal the skull. Using the visible architecture of the skull, one can place the electrode/cannula in the correct site according to the stereotaxic atlas. **Bregma** and **lambda** provide reference points so that the experimenter can use the atlas to locate the area of the brain required. Once the area has been identified on the animal, the skull is drilled to provide a small hole through which the electrode/cannula can pass. Using the co-ordinates on the stereotaxic frame, the electrode/cannula can be lowered just far enough to locate the brain region of study.

The physiological psychologist has a choice of lesion methods. Although much neurosurgery involved scalpels in the past, they lack precision. Alternative methods provide a more accurate experimental manipulation. **Aspiration lesions** are often used in which a little bit of the brain is removed by suction. With practice, the physiological psychologist can do this with a great deal of accuracy, preserving the underlying white matter and vascular structure. Alternatively, an electrode is used, the tip being placed in the region of interest. This electrode when turned on produces a high-frequency current that heats up the electrode tip and destroys the brain tissue around it. This is referred to as an **electrolytic lesion**.

Neurotoxic lesions are performed using a chemical that selectively destroys regions of the brain, e.g. 6-hydroxydopamine (6-OHDA) is a selective neurotoxin for dopamine and noradrenaline (Adams & Olivera, 1994). The advantage of neurotoxic lesions is that they target only the neurons for which the neurotoxin is selective. The more specific the neurotoxin, the more accurate the lesion.

Cryogenic lesions involve putting a **cryoprobe** into the brain and reducing the temperature at the tip (Rubinsky, 2000). By keeping the temperature low but not freezing, the neurons remain alive but inactive. Such lesions are reversible as they only cause a temporary loss of function, rather than the permanent damage inflicted by neurotoxic and electrolytic lesions.

The brain is a very complicated organ that comprises many subregions that can be identified postmortem during histological examination. However, those regions are not visible during surgery and the only way of verifying if the correct area of the brain was lesioned is to kill the animal and retrieve their brain. Only those animals that had postmortem verification of accuracy of the manipulation would be included in the final data analysis.

The premise of lesion studies is that particular areas of the brain have particular functions and that removal of these regions will disrupt that function. However, lesions of the brain may produce more widespread cell death and secondary changes in the brain such as receptor supersensitivity that means the histological verification of the lesion needs to extend beyond the region of interest and look at surrounding damage (Block et al., 2005; Schoenfeld & Hamilton, 1977).

Using similar techniques, the physiological psychologist can also measure the activity of specific brain regions. Instead of destroying brain tissue, an electrode can be used to measure electrical activity. Electrodes can be placed within the cell as is the case with intracellular single unit recording which tells the scientist about changes in membrane potential. Extracellular single unit recording measures the action potentials of neurons that line the extracellular space. This sort of recording measures the spikes or neurons firing (a lot of action potentials) (Humphrey & Schmidt, 1990; Lewicki, 1998). Looking at Figure 4.8 in Chapter 4 depicting the action potential, this is what is seen in the figurative output from extracellular unit recording but in a far more compressed manner. Multiple unit recording uses a slightly bigger electrode that can detect electrical changes in several neurons (Buzsáki, 2004).

NEUROPSYCHO-PHARMACOLOGY

Whilst the above methods often involve lesions and the measurement of electrical activity within the brain, the neuropsychopharmacologist can deploy similar methods for the manipulation and measurement of drugs and neurotransmitters within the brain.

Using small cannulas, drugs can be delivered to specific parts of the brain without having to cross the blood–brain barrier. By direct application of the drug to a specific area of the brain, the experimenter can avoid the widespread effect that systemic administrations of drugs cause (see Chapter 7). Whilst this might be considered an advantage, it can also be considered a limitation as it does not determine the bioavailability of the drug and its widespread effects. However, from a purely scientific point of view, as opposed to a clinical point of view, the advantages outweigh the disadvantages.

In vivo **micro-dialysis** involves placing a dialysis probe into a specific region of the brain to collect and sample substances, e.g. neurotransmitters in the interstitial space (the fluid-filled areas around the cell) (Chefer et al., 2009) (Figure 6.2). During micro-dialysis, substances move from an area of higher concentration to an area of lower concentration which is determined by the expertimenter. The dialysis probe delivers dialysate (the fluid delivered

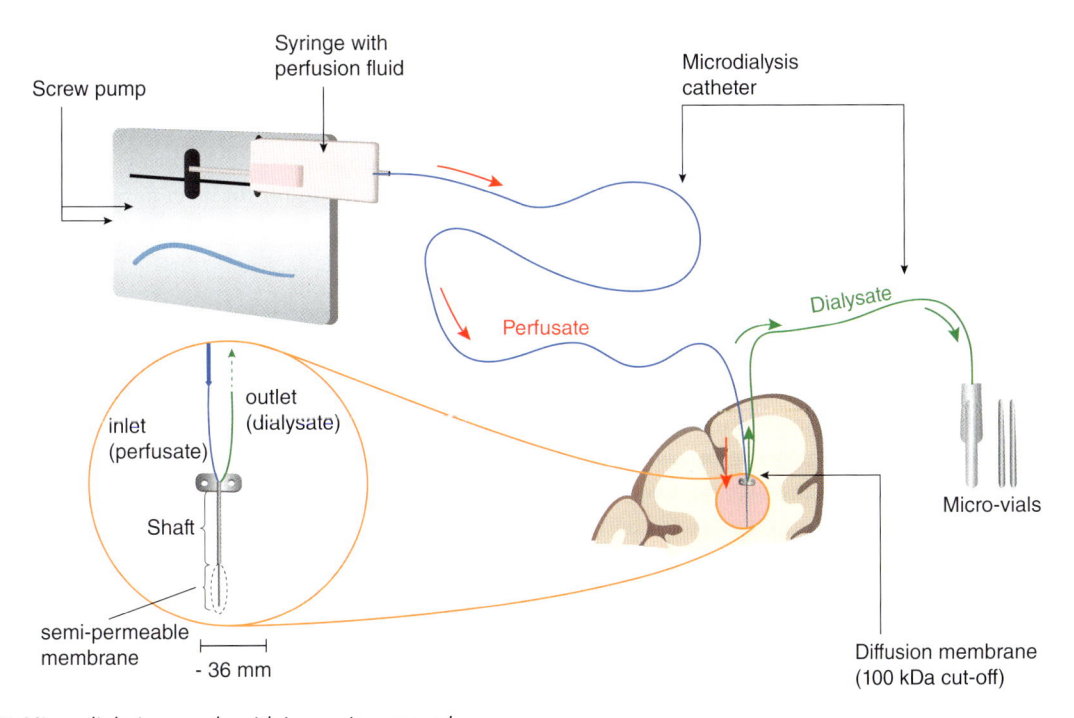

FIGURE 6.2 *Micro-dialysis cannula with inner pin removed.*

by the experimenter) to the brain, which replaces the neurochemical content that can be recovered and measured. The dialysis probe can be used either to sample a substance from an external solution or to deliver a substance to the external solution. An increase in analytical technology has allowed the recovered dialysate to be measured (Darvesh et al., 2011).

Another method that the neuropsychopharmacologist might use to assess brain activity after a task is the consumption of radioactive **2-deoxyglucose** (2-DG) which because of its similarity to glucose (the main energy supplier of the brain) is utilized when a particular part of the brain is busy (Sharp & Kilduff, 1981). Because the 2-DG is made radioactive, it can be measured in the brain of the euthanized animal. The recovered brain can be sliced and assessed for the amount of radioactivity being released from the discrete areas of the brain. This is called **autoradiography**. The living equivalent is similar to the PET scan (see below).

There are numerous *in vitro* methods that can also be used to assess neurochemical activity in the brain; see Martin (1998) and Xiong and Gendelman (2014).

Unilateral and Bilateral Lesions

Lesions and electrode placements can be performed on one side of the brain (unilateral) or on both sides (bilateral), depending on the nature of the experiment. Unilateral lesions will have a behavioural effect on the contralateral side of the body (opposite).

PSYCHOPHYSIOLOGY

Psychophysiology has been defined as 'the study of relations between psychological manipulations and resulting physiological responses, measured in the living organism, to promote understanding of the relation between mental and bodily processes' (Andreassi, 2007, p.2).

Although not strictly neuroimaging as we have come to know it, measuring electrical activity via surface electrodes placed on the scalp has one distinct advantage over magnetic or nuclear imaging: the temporal resolution is excellent. Scans take a measure over relatively long periods, whereas psychophysiology can deal with changes measured in milliseconds. However, the spatial resolution is not as good as with other imaging technologies.

Psychophysiological studies are essentially measuring the action potentials generated in the brain (see Chapter 7). The two types of studies that are frequently used are the **electroenecephalogram** (EEG) and **event-related potentials** (ERPs). The former measures general activity whereas the latter measure activity in response to a stimulus. The EEG is about measuring activity during resting states but of course, the brain is never really at rest. ERP studies look at responses to tasks or stimuli.

The Electroencephalogram

The EEG measures what is referred to as 'brain waves' (Figure 6.3b). It provides frequencies and amplitudes of brain waves from which they can be identified and differentiated. The EEG records the following waves (those in bold are the most common).

- **Alpha waves: rhythmic oscillation of 7.5–12.5 Hz (hertz = cycles per second); 20–60 µV.**
- **Beta waves: irregular waves of 14–30 Hz; 2–20 µV.**
- **Delta waves: low-frequency, 0.5–3.5 Hz; 20–200 µV.**
- **Theta waves: uncommon, rhythm of 4–7 Hz; 20–100 µV.**
- Kappa waves: comparatively rare at 10 Hz.
- **Lambda waves:** recorded in the visual cortex.
- Mu waves: recorded from the fissue of Rolando; 8–13 Hz.
- Gamma waves: rhythmic activity to sensory stimulation. Equivocal data on amplitude and cycle.

A series of electrodes is placed over the scalp to record EEG signals. There is also an electrode attached to an inactive areas such as the earlobe that acts as a reference point to which others can be compared. Figure 6.3 illustrates the electrode placement on the scalp. Electrode placement follows the convention of the 10–20 system and ensures standardization across laboratories. Each electrode site has an identifying letter for its general location.

F – frontal lobe

T – temporal lobe

C – central (the central area)

P – parietal lobe

O – occipital lobe

In addition to the letters, even numbers refer to electrode placements on the right hemisphere and odd numbers refer to the left hemisphere; Z refers to the midline.

Magnetoencephalography (MEG)

Magnetoencephalography is a magnetic equivalent of the EEG. MEG works on the principle that when an electric current flows, it produces a magnetic field in the surrounding

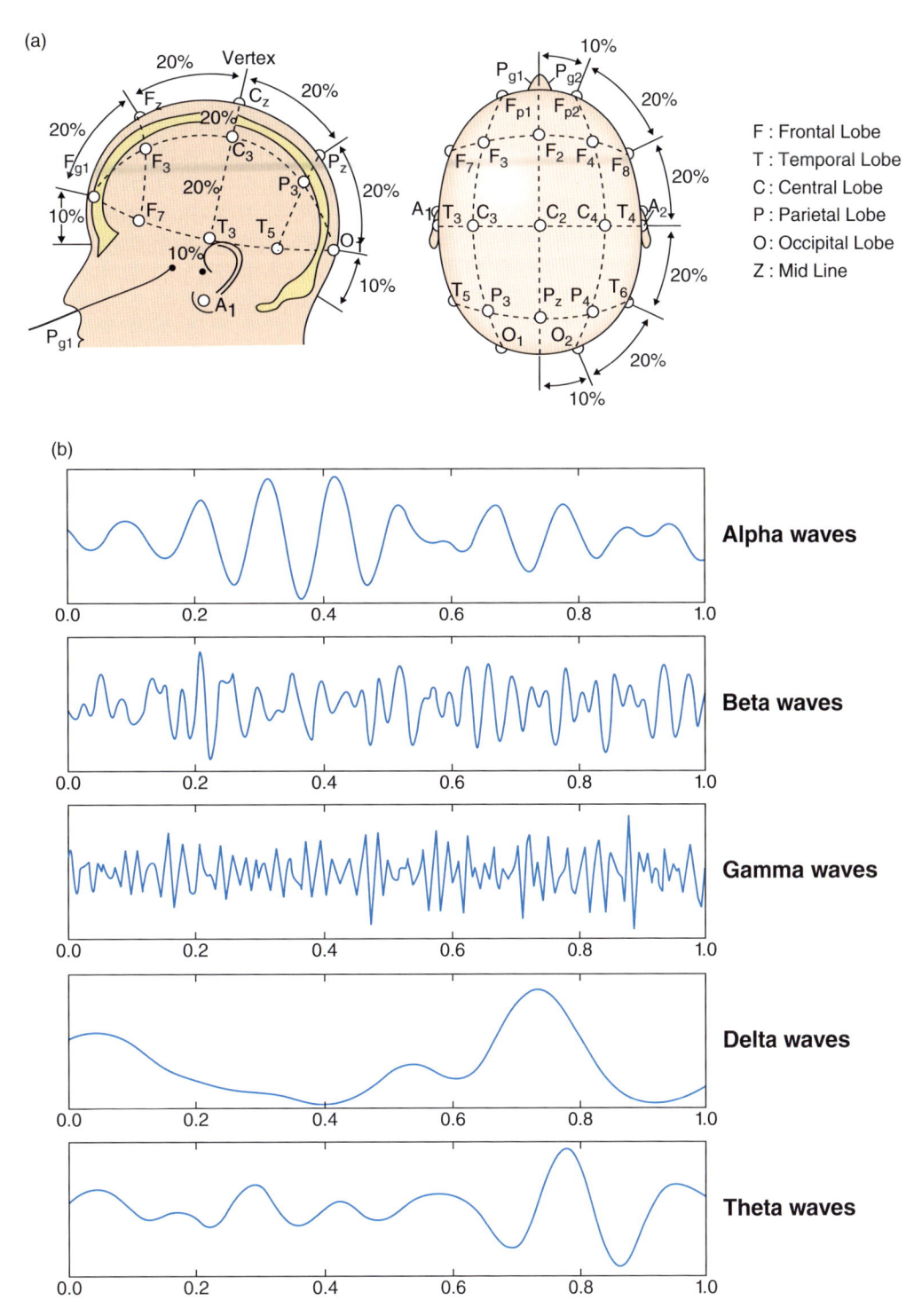

CHAPTER 6 PSYCHOBIOLOGY AND NEUROSCIENCE METHODS 159

FIGURE 6.3 *EEG and brain waves. (a) Electrode placement on surface of the head. (b) Recorded brain waves.*

area, the field being created by the neurons as they are activated. The magnetic field can then be measured.

Event-related Potentials

An ERP is a potential that is measured after a particular event has occurred (Figure 6.4). The temporal resolution of these measures is excellent. An example of the ERP in action is seen in studies measuring the brain's activity using surface electrodes, in which Banaschewski et al. (2004) were able to detect neural events associated with motor preparation, motor response execution and motor response inhibition on a go/no-go task (see Chapter 12). The two ERPs that they specifically looked at are called N2 and P3 which are recorded in response to a stimulus

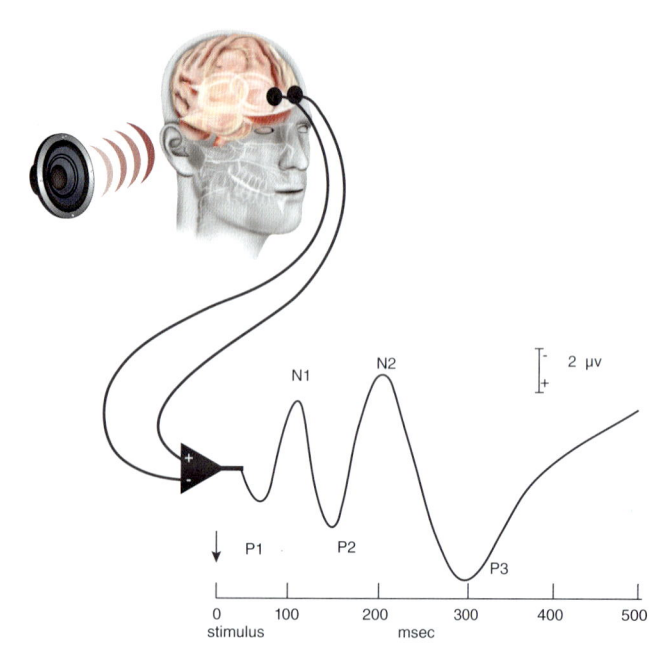

FIGURE 6.4 *Event-related potentials.*

at different sites on the scalp and therefore correspond to different brain regions (see McLoughlin et al. (2005) for review). The N and the P refer to negative or positive potentials, i.e. positive and negative voltage changes. The number following can either refer to the position at which the peak occurs in a sequence, e.g. N1 equals the first peak which is a negative peak or as is the case in P300 (or P3), the positive peak occurs between 250 to 700 ms after the stimulus. The N2 ERP is associated with frontal areas of the brain and with behavioural inhibition, the P3 is associated more with central-frontal regions.

Beyond the Brain

Psychophysiological measures do not have to be focused on the brain. Measurement of autonomic activity can be revealing. Such peripheral measures of activity have been used with varying degrees of success in the lie detector or polygraph.

Cardiovascular measures

Perhaps the most familiar of the psychophysiological measures assesses cardiovascular activity (see Brownley et al., 2000). Heart rate can be recorded easily via an **electrocardiogram** (ECG). Blood pressure changes can also be measured by a **sphygmomanometer**. This measures **diastolic** and **systolic blood pressure**. You will probably be familiar with the convention of systolic over diastolic as a ratio of blood pressure, such as when you watch medical shows and they refer to 130 over 70 (130/70). It is important to have normal blood pressure as increased blood pressure presents a risk factor for ischaemic events (see Chapter 5). The movement of blood in and out of body regions can also be measured using **plethysmography** which takes advantage of two features in order to measure blood flow: the enlargement of the area being examined and also the amount of light absorbed by the tissue from a light source (more light is absorbed where there is more blood). The most obvious example of this measurement is seen in Chapter 14 where blood flow to the penis and clitoris/vagina can be measured during sexual arousal.

Muscle measures

The tension of the muscles can also be measured using **electromyography** (EMG) which can be either surface or intramuscular. EMG can be used on many muscles including the fine muscles of the face which facilitates the measurement of emotion (Dimberg, 1990).

Eye movement

Eye movements are particularly important in psychobiology and can reveal the processes of attention and reading (Bulling et al., 2011). The **electro-oculogram** (EOG) takes advantage of the fact that there is a difference between the front and back of the eyeball in terms of electrical potential. Movement of the eye changes the potential that the electrodes placed around the eye can detect (Figure 6.5). There are several types of eye movements that can be detected with EOG (see Andreassi (2007) for more details).

- **Saccadic eye movements** – the fast movements of the eye from one fixation point to another.

- Smooth pursuit and compensatory eye movements – the movement an eye makes when following an object and the corrective movements of the body or head to maintain an upright view of the visual field.

- Nystagmoid eye movements – oscillations of the eye along the horizontal plane with a quick return to the original position.

- Eye blinking.

Skin conductance

One of the outcomes of being stressed is sweating. This changes **skin conductance**, which is the ability of the skin to conduct electricity. Sweat may be the underlying influence of measures of **electrodermal activity** (EDA) which measures changes in the skin's ability to conduct electricity. The two most common measures of EDA are **skin conductance level** (SCL) and **skin conductance response** (SCR). SCL represents the background or the tonic skin conductance whereas SCR measures the transient changes in skin conductance in response

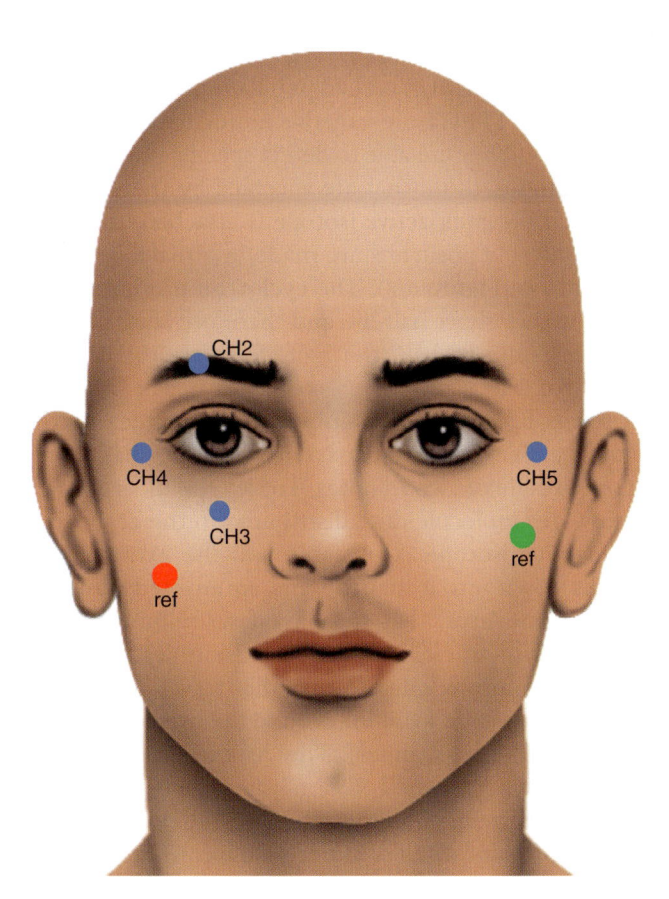

FIGURE 6.5 EOG electrode placement. The difference between channels 2 and 3 shows whether the user is looking up or down. The difference between channels 4 and 5 determines if the user has looked to the left or to the right.

to an event (phasic responses). Typically electrodes are placed on the index and middle fingers.

BRAIN IMAGING

The psychophysiological and physiological psychology methods have been around for many years but for some they have been superseded by the seductive technology of neuroimaging. Neuroimaging is comparatively new and constantly developing. As the resolution increases, the utility improves.

Penfield's early experiments, in which the top of the skull was removed so that he could place electrodes on the surface of the cortex, were stunning not only in terms of the data collected but also the bravery of the participants. Imaging the brain without opening the skull is similar to taking X-rays of bones to determine a fracture. In 1971 Sir Godfrey Hounsfield revolutionized neuroscience by taking X-rays of the brain and plac-

ing them in its three-dimensional space (Raichle, 2009). Hounsfield won the Nobel Prize for physiology or medicine in 1979 for this breakthrough (Hounsfield, 1980). It has been suggested that the development of the commercial CT scan by EMI (as in the record label) was only possible because of the revenue that the Beatles (who were signed to EMI) provided; a story that would appear not to be true (Maizlin & Vos, 2012).

Neuroimaging requires a multidisciplinary team to conduct successful and meaningful scans; medical staff, statisticians, physicists and engineers are all needed (not to mention accountants and financiers – neuroimaging is an expensive business). All these disciplines are required for their own specialisms but the psychobiologist brings one of the most important skills to the scanning room: the behavioural methodology for the scan. Without coherent and methodologically rigorous experimental procedures, the scan is pointless. To emphasize this point further:

> It is important that this collaboration be mutually informed, and that neuroscientists have an understanding of relevant methodological issues rather than regarding data collection and image analysis as a black box: the specific set of methodological and analytical methods employed in any given study have implications in terms of the question that can be addressed, the effect size that can be reliably detected, and the extent to which study results will withstand the test of time. (Pan et al., 2011, p.245)

For the participants, brain imaging can be a stressful event that is exacerbated by the equipment used. Often the image deriving scanner is in close proximity to the head which can result in feelings of claustrophobia. The noise that some scanners make can also be extremely off-putting and increase levels of anxiety.

Currently five main imaging techniques are used. These can be divided into two camps: magnetic imaging and **nuclear imaging**. Many studies in paediatric and female populations use the magnetic imaging technique as it avoids the use of the radioactive substances that are required in nuclear medicine. Too much radioactivity is not a good thing.

Nuclear Imaging Using Radioactivity and Radioactive Isotopes

Nuclear imaging requires the administration of an X-ray or a **radioactive isotope** that will be detected by the scanner. Due to the inherent danger of radiation, nuclear imaging techniques are seldom used in children or women for research purposes (due to the effects of radiation on fertility).

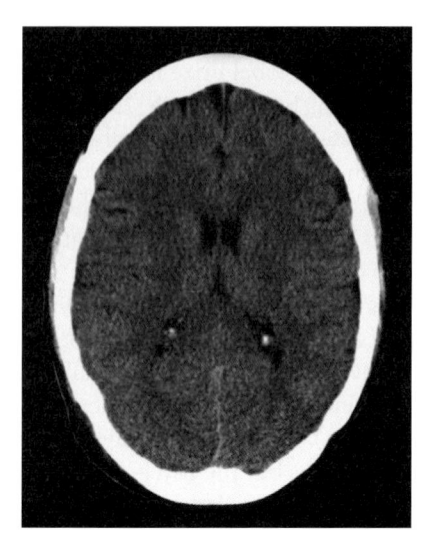

FIGURE 6.6 X-ray CT (or CAT) scan. Limited detail of the brain.
Source: http://en.wikipedia.org/wiki/File:Brain_CT_scan.jpg.
Credit: Aaron G. Filler, MD, PhD, FRCS. Released under Creative Commons Attribution-ShareAlike 3.0 license: http://creativecommons.org/licenses/by-sa/3.0/

X-ray or computed tomography (the CT scan)

The **Computed Tomography** (CT) scan uses X-rays to obtain the data (Figure 6.6). The tissue in the path of the X-ray beam can be transformed via statistical analysis into images of the brain because the X-rays are taken from numerous angles. Certain tissues will have more or less ability to block the X-ray beam; that is what is recorded. The CT scan provides structural information about the brain. Whilst this is important, it does not provide a measure of function, i.e. the 'busyness' of an active brain. Furthermore, X-rays do not provide high-contrast images without the aid of contrast agents such as radioactive dyes. To some extent, CT scans have become near obsolete with the advent of magnetic resonance imaging (MRI – see below), although they are used in patients when they have medical devices fitted such as cardiac pacemakers when an MRI would be dangerous due to the magnetic fields it generates.

Positron emission tomography and single photon emission computed tomography

- Positron: the opposite corresponding particle of an electron.
- Emission: release or discharge of a substance.
- Tomography: detailed pictures (slices) of areas inside the body.

Positron emission tomography (PET) and **single photon emission computed tomography** (SPECT) use low doses of radiation, which are relatively safe, but it is inadvisable to use them in certain populations.

PET and SPECT are valuable in understanding neural activity. They are able to detect specific molecules in the brain, i.e. those that are specified by the chemical to which the radioactive isotope is attached. In a PET scan, unstable positrons are made in a machine called a cyclotron (Figure 6.7). The **cyclotron** produces positrons with a short half-life and therefore they become relatively safe to use (the half-life refers to the time taken for the radioactive isotope to decay by half). In terms of oxygen consumption, as an index of the brain's activity the radioactive isotope [^{15}O] has a very short half-life of two minutes. The [^{15}O] is incorporated into water molecules and distributed to the brain. The radioactive isotope is unstable and the extra proton breaks down into a neutron and an emitted positron. It is this positron that travels a few millimetres and collides with an electron. This collision destroys both particles, emitting gamma rays that travel in opposite directions. A large machine around the head detects the gamma rays (the scanner). The distance that the positrons move before the collision limits the resolution of a PET scan to only millimetres. Whilst that may seem a high resolution, when considering the complexities and the detailed cellular structure of the brain, millimetres are big units. Scans are made up of voxels which are the three-dimensional equivalent of a pixel (e.g. the pixels on a TV screen). The temporal resolution is further limited in PET scans. The time it takes to get the signal means that behavioural tasks cannot be accurately assessed.

Early work on the neural basis of behaviour using PET scans focused on the brain's consumption of glucose using ^{18}F-2-fluoro-2-deoxyglucose (FDG) (Sokoloff et al., 1977) was severely limited by the temporal resolution.

However, an advantage of PET scan technology is that chemicals can be visualized in their locations within the brain. Whereas oxygen consumption can be used as an index of activity, drugs can also be made radioactive so that they can be visualized within the brain. For example, if you see a prefix such as [^{11}C] or [^{15}O] or [^{18}F] prior to a chemical name, this usually means it has been made radioactive. For example, a drug such as cocaine can be made radioactive with a [^{11}C] radioisotope, thus [^{11}C]-cocaine. The radioactivity can then be visualized and measured by the scanner (e.g. Volkow et al., 1995). Small concentrations can be measured and many chemicals can be used, making it possible to study specific systems. The radioactive information can be assembled into a visual image of the brain with 'hot spots' of activity.

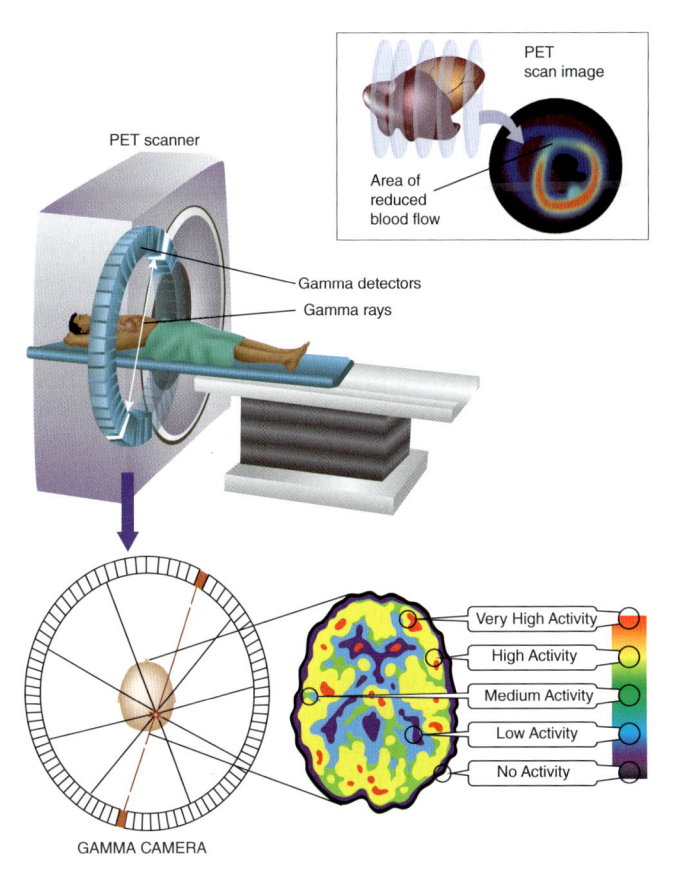

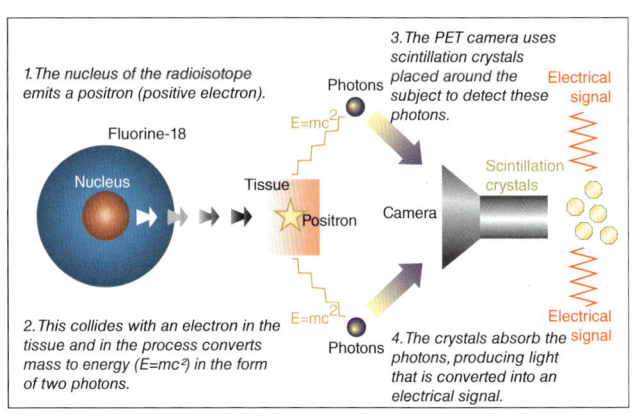

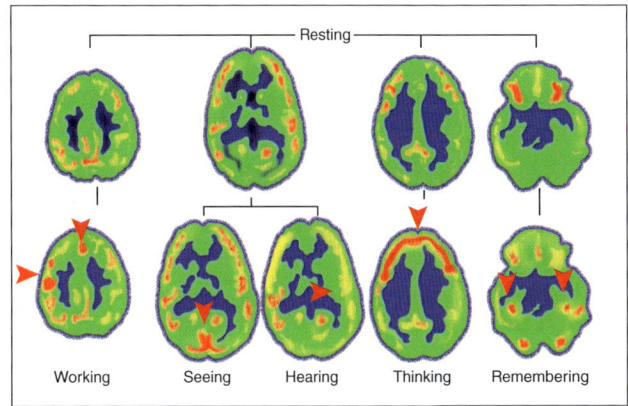

FIGURE 6.7 *PET scan.*
SEEING: shows activation of the visual cortex (arrow) at the back of the brain when a subject observes a simple visual scene.
HEARING: shows activation of the left (horizontal arrow) auditory cortex when a subject is listening to language and music (the mystery story 'The Shadow' with language in the foreground and Brandenburg Concerto in the background). Many other studies were performed to show hemispheric specialization, functions moving from one hemisphere to the other, etc.
THINKING: shows activation of the frontal cortex (arrow) when the subject is performing a task of counting backwards from 100 by 7s, being paid in proportion to how fast and accurate they are.
REMEMBERING: subjects are asked to recall simple objects (animals, house, car, etc.) that were previously memorized. This activates the left and right hippocampus (arrows).
WORKING: subjects are asked to touch their thumb to their fingers on their right hand. This activates the portion of the motor cortex, of the opposite (left) hemisphere, that deals with control of the hand and fingers. In addition, the supplementary motor cortex (vertical arrow) is also activated.
Source: Phelps, M. E., & Mazziotta, J. C. (1985). Positron emission tomography: human brain function and biochemistry. *Science, 228*(4701), 799–809.

Clearly, the PET scan provides us with important information on the neural site of action, but the scan is limited by the specificity of the drug. If the drug has a highly specific target then it can provide us with accurate information. However, if the drug has a broad spectrum of activity or many targets then it becomes somewhat more limited in its utility. Despite these limitations, such techniques have been used in understanding neural systems with a great deal of success, but of course it is somewhat limited in paediatric populations and females.

Single photon emission computed tomography is similar to PET, in that it uses a radioactive tracer. However, SPECT uses a tracer in which the gamma radiation is directly measured (and does not require collision of the positron with the electron). SPECT has a lower spatial resolution than a PET scan but it is cheaper and quicker.

TABLE 6.1 Structural versus functional MRI

Structural MRI	Functional MRI
Studies the spatial relationships of voxels	Studies the temporal relationships of individual voxels
3-D image	3-D image
Temporal dimension collapsed to create a 3-D image with high spatial resolution	Temporal resolution good as short time required to acquire each image

Magnetic Resonance Imaging

- Magnetic: having the properties of a magnet – attraction and repulsion.
- Resonance: vibrations caused by the transfer of energy.
- Imaging: the production of the picture.

A big advantage of **magnetic resonance imaging** (MRI) is that it is non-invasive and does not require radioactive isotopes. Within the domain of magnetic imaging are three different variations: MRI; **functional magnetic resonance imaging** (fMRI); and **magnetic resonance spectroscopy** (MRS). All methods can tell us something different about the brain (see Table 6.1).

Structural MRI

Magnetic resonance imaging is a non-invasive procedure that involves the patient being placed in a narrow cylinder. The MRI image is a visual reconstruction of the different concentrations of water molecules in cells; the shades of grey seen in MRI scans represent the different concentrations (Figure 6.8). How the scanner does all this is complicated. MRI permits a structural analysis of the brain: location, shape and size of subregions. As the name suggests, a large magnet is used. The magnetic field produced by the scan is extremely strong (the unit of measurement for the strength of the magnet is the **tesla** (T)). The magnetic field makes the protons in the water molecules line up in parallel. The stronger the magnet, the greater the anatomical detail. Short bursts of radio waves are sent to knock the protons off their alignment. With the magnetic field still active, the protons try to realign and in doing so they emit radio signals (the resonance) which can be measured. The contrast between the different regions of the brain is a result of the different time course by which the protons within the cells return to their alignment.

Structural MRI scans have been used in many studies to determine the size of different brain regions. Although the differences that have been found are small, they are statistically significant. However, how a statistically significant difference maps onto psychological processes requires further investigation.

Functional MRI

Functional MRI is similar in method to structural MRI. However, fMRI further utilizes the fact that busy parts of the brain have increased oxygen-containing haemoglobin in the red blood cells (Figure 6.9). Blood that is bound with oxygen and blood that is not bound to oxygen have different magnetic resonance signals. The utilization of oxygen is an index of activity within the brain. Increases in neural activity produce changes in the signal emitted during the scan, termed **blood oxygen level dependent** (BOLD). fMRI has good spatial and temporal resolution and is therefore used in behavioural experiments. Regions of activity in the brain are shown in colour, with highly active regions in the red–yellow spectrum (often referred to as hot spots). Such images allow scientists to determine which part of the brain is being used for a particular task – this is the **region of interest** (ROI). There are increasingly large numbers of publications using fMRI to look at cognitive processes or clinical conditions. The impact of fMRI is reviewed by Rosen and Savoy (2012) who state that advances in this technology could have a far-reaching impact upon society (see Chapter 25).

Magnetic resonance spectroscopy

Magnetic resonance spectroscopy looks at particular individual chemicals that can be differentiated by the scanner. It works in a similar manner to MRI, but is selective in detecting particular cell nuclei. Each biochemical or metabolite emits a different frequency. Hydrogen is the most commonly detected nucleus. However, only a few chemicals can be detected using this technique, e.g. glutamate, glutamine and choline, which limits its utility. Some of the big neurotransmitter systems that one would wish to study are beyond the scope of MRS.

Imaging studies have attracted a lot of criticism (Vul et al., 2009) and one should be cautious about overestimating their importance. Adolph and colleagues (2008) have also criticized the time of measuring a phenomenon typically used by developmental researchers, and suggest it may be inadequate to accurately depict the pattern of developmental changes. Thus, we have inaccurate knowledge about normal development, let alone atypical development.

Diffusion tensor imaging

- Diffusion: the movement of molecules.
- Tensor: the mathematics and scaling of molecular movement.

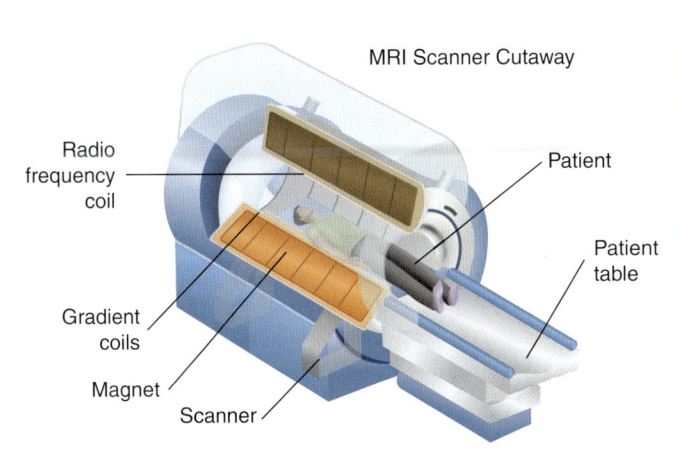

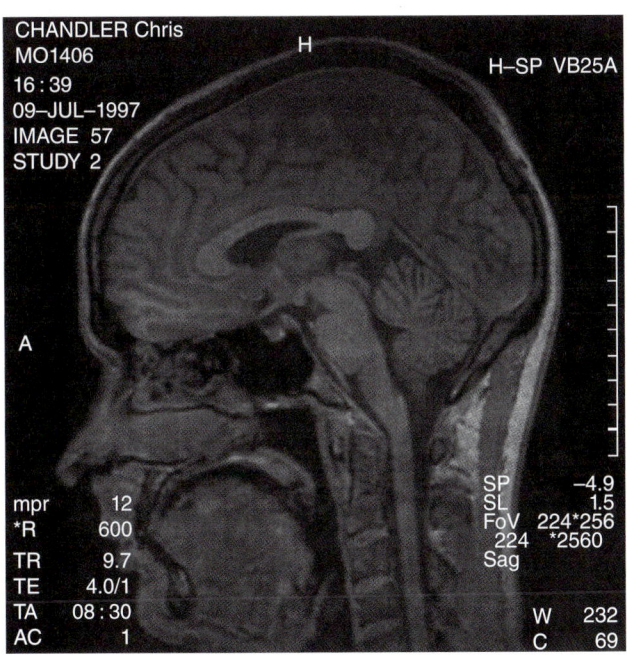

CHAPTER 6 PSYCHOBIOLOGY AND NEUROSCIENCE METHODS   165

MRI Scanner Cutaway

MRI – the physics

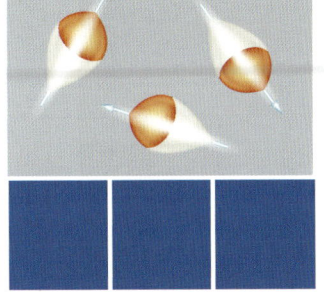

1. Hydrogen protons, positively charged particles in the hydrogen molecule's nucleus, normally spin in random directions

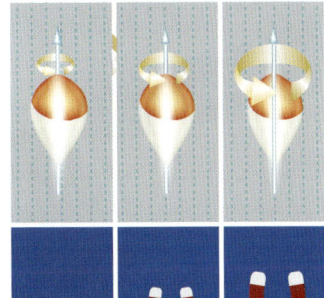

2. Protons wobble in alignment with magnetic fields of varying intensity; frequency of wobble is proportionate to strength of individual magnetic field

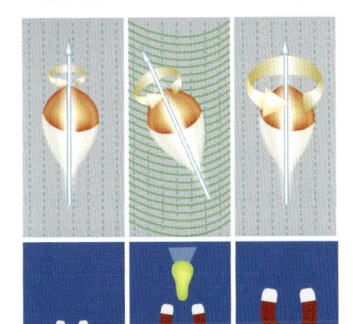

3. A brief radio signal, whose soundwave frequency equals the frequency of wobble of certain protons, knocks those protons out of alignment

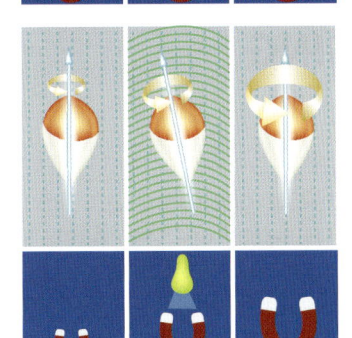

4. When radio signal ceases, protons snap back into alignment with magnetic field, emitting a radio signal of their own, that announces the presence of a specific tissue

FIGURE 6.8 *MRI scans.*

Diffusion tensor imaging (DTI) is a type of MRI scan which allows a map of the diffusion processes (movement) of molecules in the brain to be created (Figure 6.10). These molecules, mainly water, are restricted in their pattern of diffusion, e.g. membranes and fibres. By following the movement of the water molecules, details about the tissue architecture can be established. In DTI, the rate and direction of diffusion can be assessed. A considerable amount of statistical information is then generated to provide information on fibre tracts, etc. The DTI scan can track neural impulses along their pathways. And an extra bonus is the beautiful pictures that can be produced – works of art!

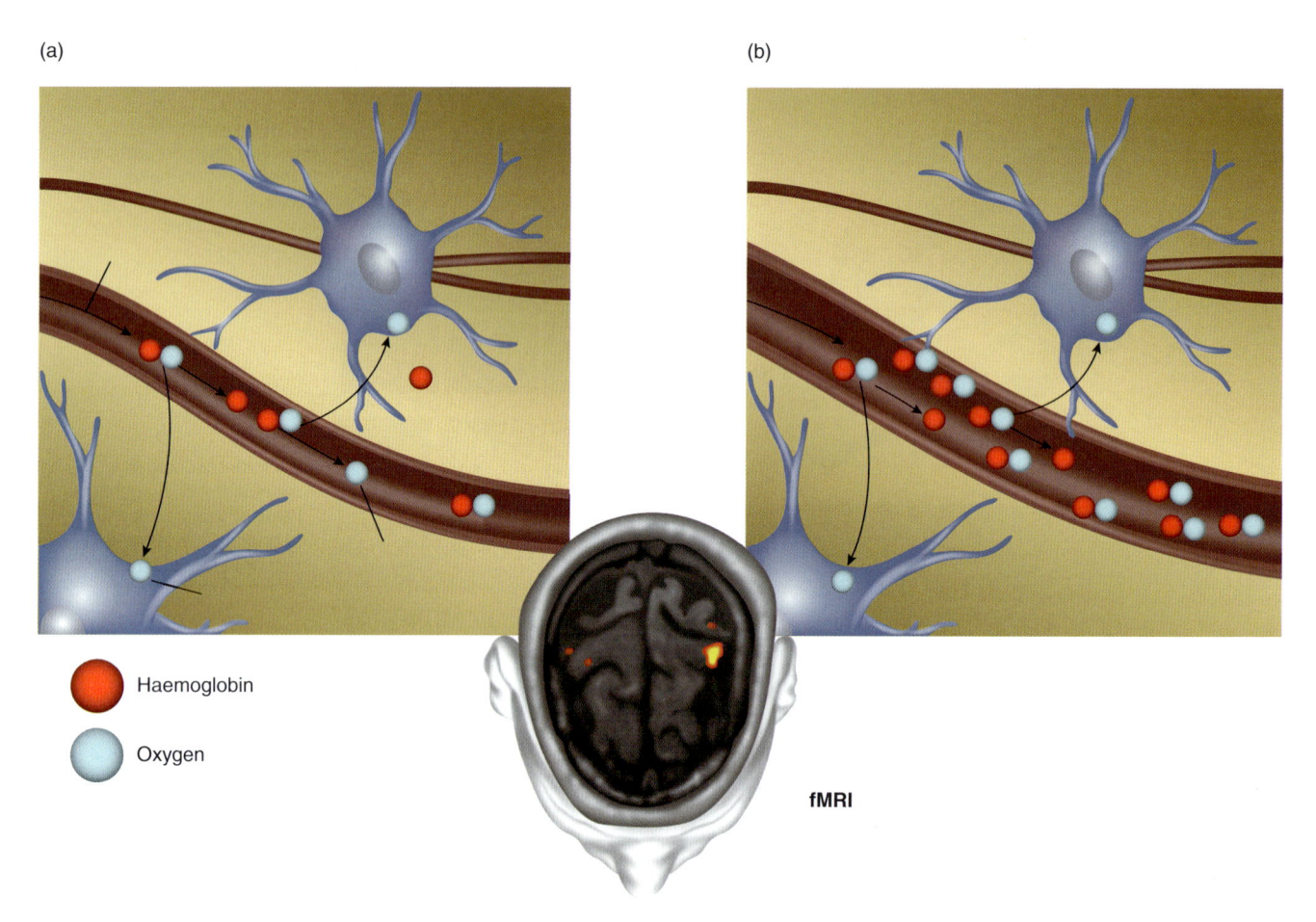

FIGURE 6.9 BOLD activity and fMRI. (a) Neurons increase their firing rates, also increasing the oxygen consumption. (b) Haemodynamic response in a second scale increases the diameter of the vessel close to the activated neurons.

OPTICAL IMAGING OF THE BRAIN

Optical imaging of the brain involves shining a light through the skull and measuring how that light is absorbed and reflected by the tissue below (Figure 6.11). This is analogous to how light is absorbed and reflected through water, for example. In near infrared spectroscopy (NIRS), a light is shone through the skull and detects changes in blood haemoglobin and therefore can measure brain activity in humans and animals (see Hillman (2007) for review). Clearly in the way of optical imaging is the skull; this could be avoided by its removal but obvious limitations arise. More commonly, imaging is done through the skull and is particularly useful for children as their skulls are thinner (Hespos, 2010).

NEUROIMAGING IS NOT THE ULTIMATE EVIDENCE

Neuroimaging is very expensive and this limits its use. On the whole, the small numbers of individuals used in imaging studies make it difficult to generalize findings: 10–20 people is hardly representative of the population. The importance of understanding the limitations of neuroimaging has focused on three main points: what is being measured; the statistical treatment of the data; and the tangibility of the image.

As its name suggests, in neuroimaging we are measuring the neurons themselves. However, the reliance of most of these methods on blood flow suggests that we are making secondary evaluations of neuronal activity

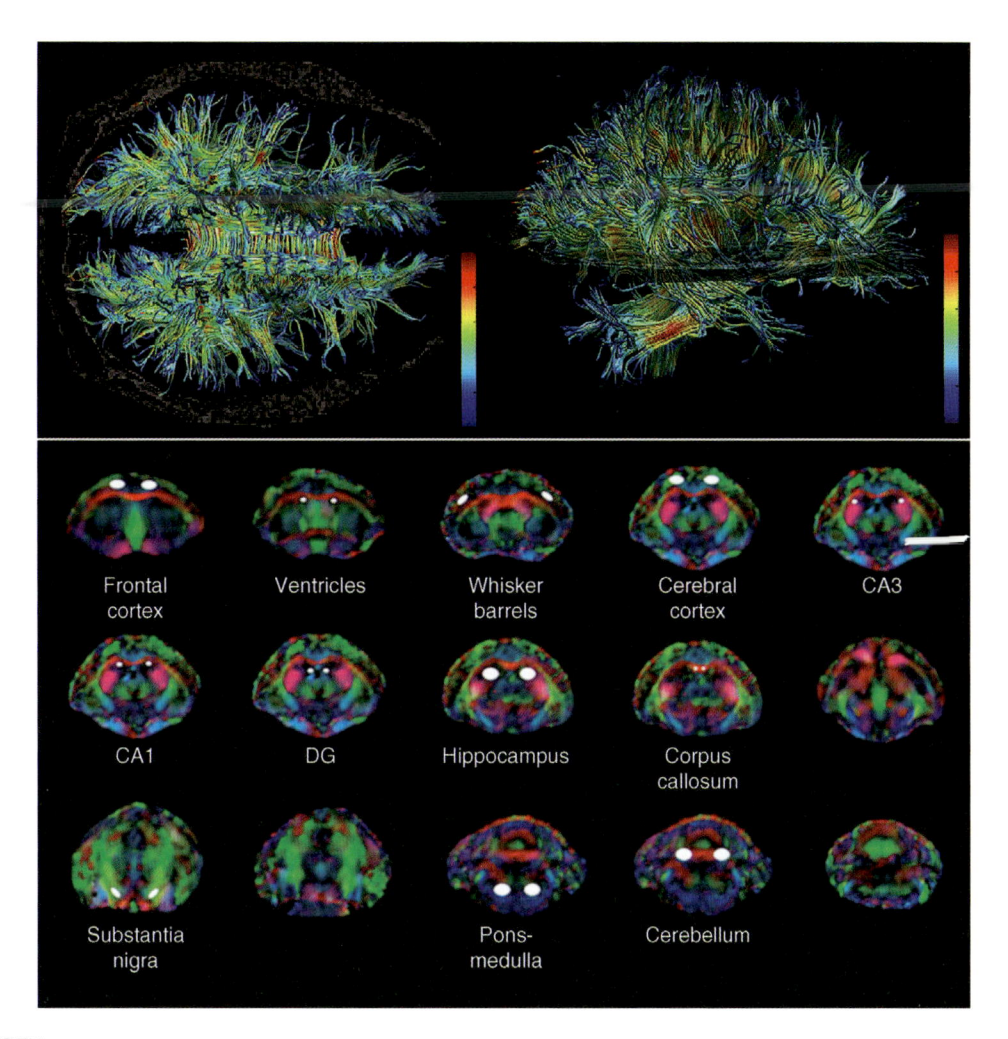

FIGURE 6.10 *DTI images.*
Source: (top) Kubicki, M., McCarley, R., Westin, C. F., Park, H. J., Maier, S., Kikinis, R., Jolesz, F. A. & Shenton, M. E. (2007). A review of diffusion tensor imaging studies in schizophrenia. *Journal of Psychiatric Research, 41*, 15-30. (bottom) Boska, M., Hasan, K., Kibuule, D., et al. (2007). Quantitative diffusion tensor imaging detects dopaminergic neuronal degeneration in a murine model of Parkinson's disease. *Neurobiology of Disease, 26*(3), 590–596.

of the energy consumption indicated by the movement of blood to particular regions of the brain.

The neuroimaging world has been criticized from within, in that high-profile journals have been shown to publish imaging studies that are guilty of statistical crimes (Vul et al., 2009). Vul and Kanwisher (2010) argue that fMRI studies have non-independent errors arising:

> ... when a subset of voxels is selected for subsequent analysis, but the null-hypothesis of the analysis is not independent on the selection criteria used to choose the voxels in the first place. Take the simplest practical case: if one selects only voxels in which condition A produces a greater signal challenge than condition B, and then evaluates whether the signal change for conditions A and B differs in those voxels using the same data, the second analysis is not independent of the selection criteria. The outcome of this non-independent second analysis is statistically guaranteed and thus uninformative (p.2).

The technology of imaging is as much dependent on the correct statistical analysis as any other type of study.

The third limitation refers to the fact that having something as concrete as a picture gives the viewer the impression that the fact is more tangible. Beautiful pictures of glowing areas of the brain would appear to be conclusive evidence and to the layperson, the science of data acquisition and treatment is irrelevant. The seduction of the image could have serious ramifications if neuroimaging is to be used in courts of law. In Chapter 25 the impact of

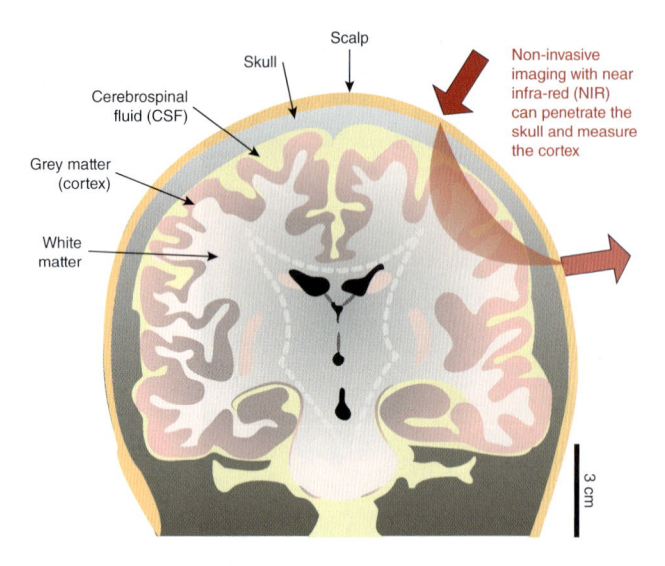

FIGURE 6.11 *Optical imaging.*

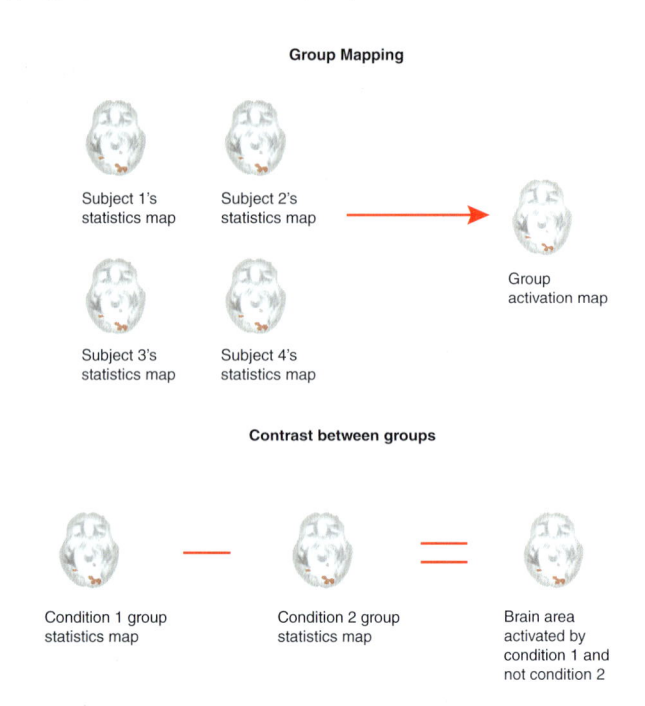

FIGURE 6.12 *Neural maps from neuroimaging.*

neuroimaging on society as a whole, and law in particular, is addressed.

A serious criticism of imaging studies, that can also be levelled at many other studies, is that they often have medication as a confounding variable. Drugs such as cocaine and methylphenidate can have long-lasting effects on the structure and function of the brain (Silveri et al., 2004). Numerous animal studies have shown neural changes in response to medications such as antipsychotics and psychostimulants which block dopamine (DA) receptors or stimulate DA respectively (Hall et al., 1984; Jenner et al., 1983, 1985; Kerwin et al., 1984; Rupniak et al., 1983) which fits with our pharmacological understanding of up- and down-regulation (see Chapter 7) (Creese et al., 1981). Scientists have to be careful that they are not in fact measuring medication effects in neuroimaging studies and reporting them as pathological effects.

conditions where participants performed two or more tasks that can be compared. An example of such experimental design can be seen in cognitive tasks that involve a motor component, e.g. pressing a button in response to seeing a visual stimulus. When one performs a motor response during a cognitive task, the scientist needs to subtract the motor component from the cognitive component. In order to do this, a straightforward motor task would be compared with the motor and cognitive task, e.g. finger tapping versus pressing a button in response to seeing a light flash. When the motor component is subtracted from the overall scan, what remains is hopefully the neural correlate of the cognitive task (see Amaro & Barker, 2006).

NEUROIMAGING MAPS OF THE MIND

An image of one brain could give us considerable information from a clinical perspective. However, case studies are somewhat limiting as they only represent the one individual. Group mapping involves obtaining the statistical maps of the subjects in an experiment and then combining them together to find regions that are common across all the individual participants (Figure 6.12). Alternatively, one might look at a contrast between

PSYCHOPHYSIOLOGY AND NEUROIMAGING COMBINED

Due to the fact that neuroimaging techniques such as fMRI provide good spatial resolution but relatively poor temporal resolution and the EEG provides good temporal resolution but poor spatial resolution, the combination of the two is increasingly being used (Ritter & Villringer, 2006; Rosa et al., 2010).

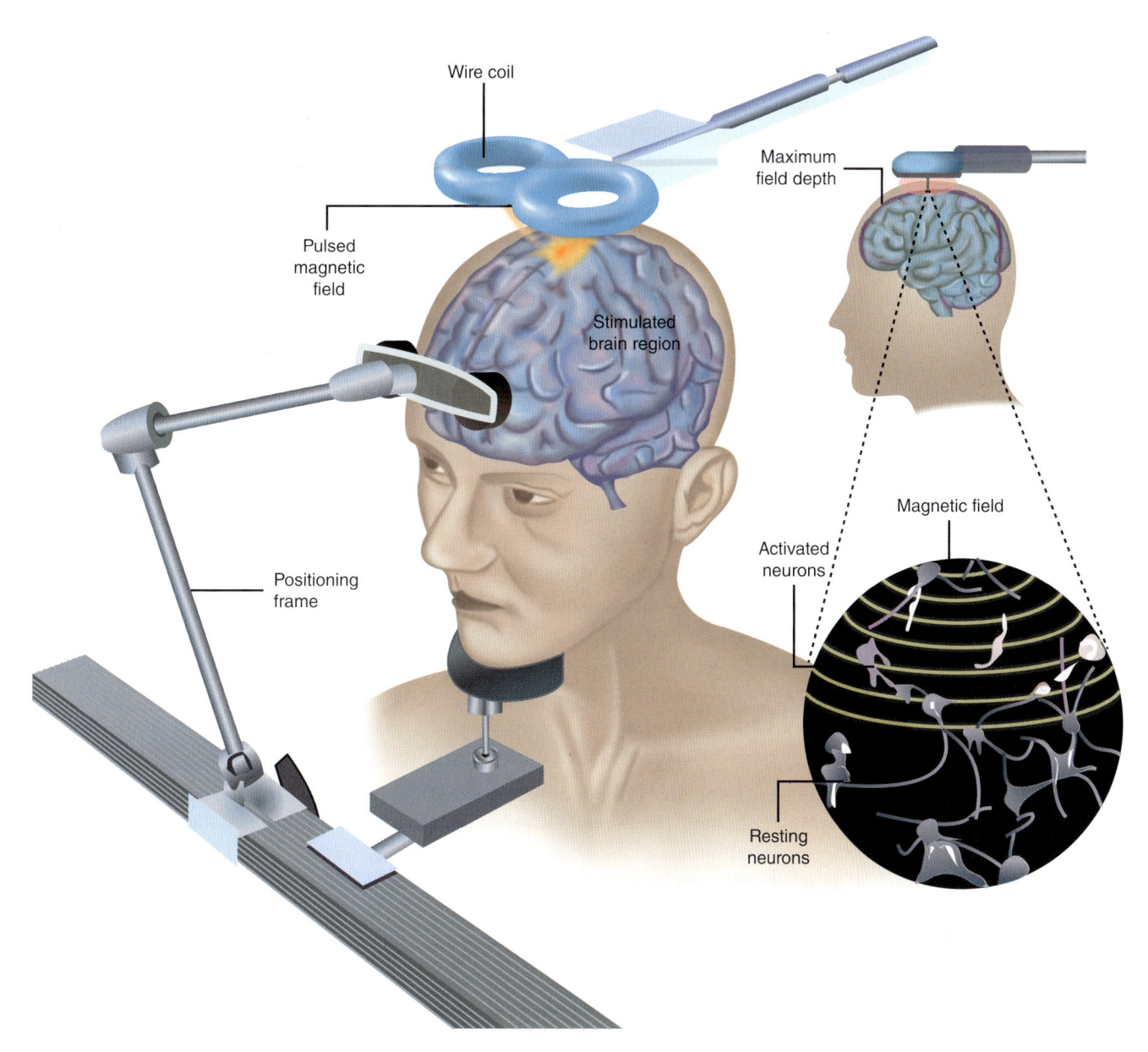

FIGURE 6.13 *Transcranial magnetic stimulation.*

VIRTUAL LESIONS – TRANSCRANIAL MAGNETIC STIMULATION

Magnetic fields can alter neural function and are considered a potential treatment for some psychiatric disorders. Magnetic fields can also be used to disrupt cognitive processing temporarily. This is what **transcranial magnetic stimulation** (TMS) achieves. By placing a strong magnetic field over the scalp, the interaction with the brain below creates a virtual lesion (Figure 6.13). TMS is used clinically for a range of disorders, e.g. depression (Dell'Osso et al., 2011), but also for research purposes (Guse et al., 2010). TMS causes the neurons to depolarize and produce an action potential followed by a period of deactivation, presumably through prolonged inhibitory postsynaptic potentials, thereby producing a virtual lesion (Bolognini & Ro, 2010).

SUMMARY

The seductive nature of neuroimaging, in part due to the pretty pictures that it generates, and the media portrayal of something far more tangible and concrete give us the impression that neuroimaging provides definitive facts. The technology is forever advancing and the resolution of scanners is improving. Imaging the brain at the molecular level has now been made possible with neurotransmitter-sensitive MRI contrast agents that the scanner can detect (Lee et al., 2014). The potential of this technology is considerable and the ramifications for society require careful ethical consideration (see Chapter 25). From the previous section, it is clear that those facts are subject to interpretation and methodological limitations. When it comes to providing evidence in psychobiology, the case for a neurotransmitter or a brain region being involved in a particular behaviour or disorder requires evidence from several different sources before there can be any confidence for functional role. Therefore, all the sub-disciplines of psychobiology using their different methodologies and techniques need to provide evidence that converges on an answer. Alone, they may only provide circumstantial evidence but together they may provide a convincing argument. There is no one damning piece of evidence in neuroscience (not yet).

LEARNING OUTCOME QUESTIONS

You should be able to answer the following questions.

- How can electrical activity of the brain be measured?
- Describe the advantages and disadvantages of the different methods for visualising the brain.
- How can changes in the body be measured and used to inform the psychophysiologist about deception?

FURTHER READING

Andreassi, J. L. (2007). *Psychophysiology: Human behavior and physiological response* (5th edn). New Jersey: Psychology Press.
Cacioppo, J. T., Tassinary, L. G., & Berntson, G. (2000). *Handbook of psychophysiology* (2nd edn). Cambridge, UK: Cambridge University Press.
Cheeran, B., Koch, G., Stagg, C. J., Baig, F., & Teo, J. (2010). Transcranial magnetic stimulation: from neurophysiology to pharmacology, molecular biology and genomics. *Neuroscientist, 16*(3), 210–221.
Lomber, S. G., & Galuske, R. A. (Eds.). (2002). *Virtual lesions: Examining cortical function with reversible deactivation*. Oxford, UK: Oxford University Press.
Malhi, G. S., & Lagopoulos, J. (2008). Making sense of neuroimaging in psychiatry. *Acta Psychiatrica Scandinavica, 117*(2), 100–117.
Martin, R. (1998). *Neuroscience methods: A guide for advanced students*. Amsterdam, Netherlands: CRC Press.
Sahgal, A. (1993). *Behavioural neuroscience: A practical approach* (Vols. 1 & 2). Oxford, UK: IRL Press.

MIND MAP

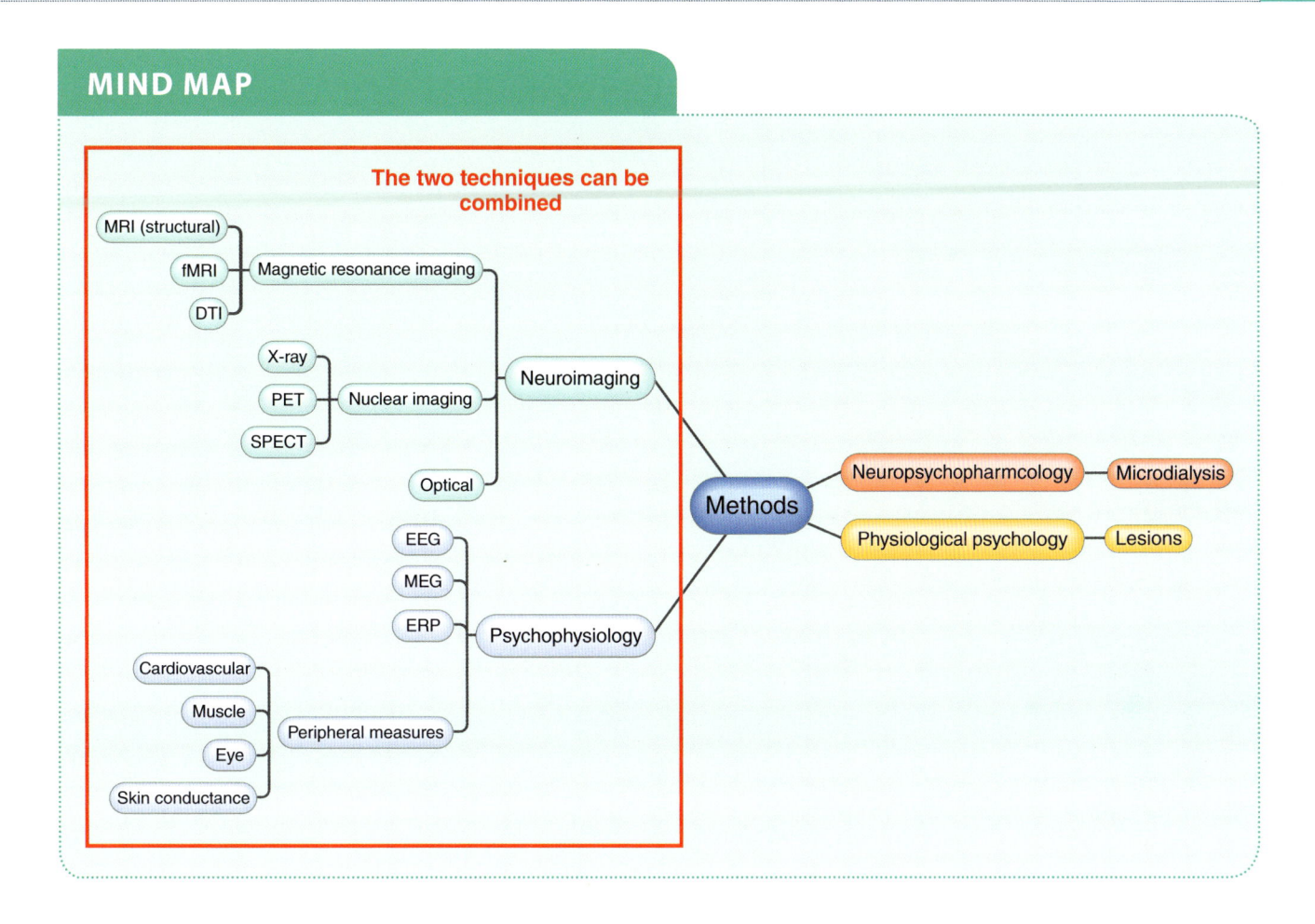

Methods

- Neuroimaging
  - Magnetic resonance imaging
    - MRI (structural)
    - fMRI
    - DTI
  - Nuclear imaging
    - X-ray
    - PET
    - SPECT
  - Optical
- Psychophysiology
  - EEG
  - MEG
  - ERP
- Peripheral measures
  - Cardiovascular
  - Muscle
  - Eye
  - Skin conductance
- Neuropsychopharmcology
  - Microdialysis
- Physiological psychology
  - Lesions

The two techniques can be combined (MRI and Nuclear imaging)

7 Psychopharmacology

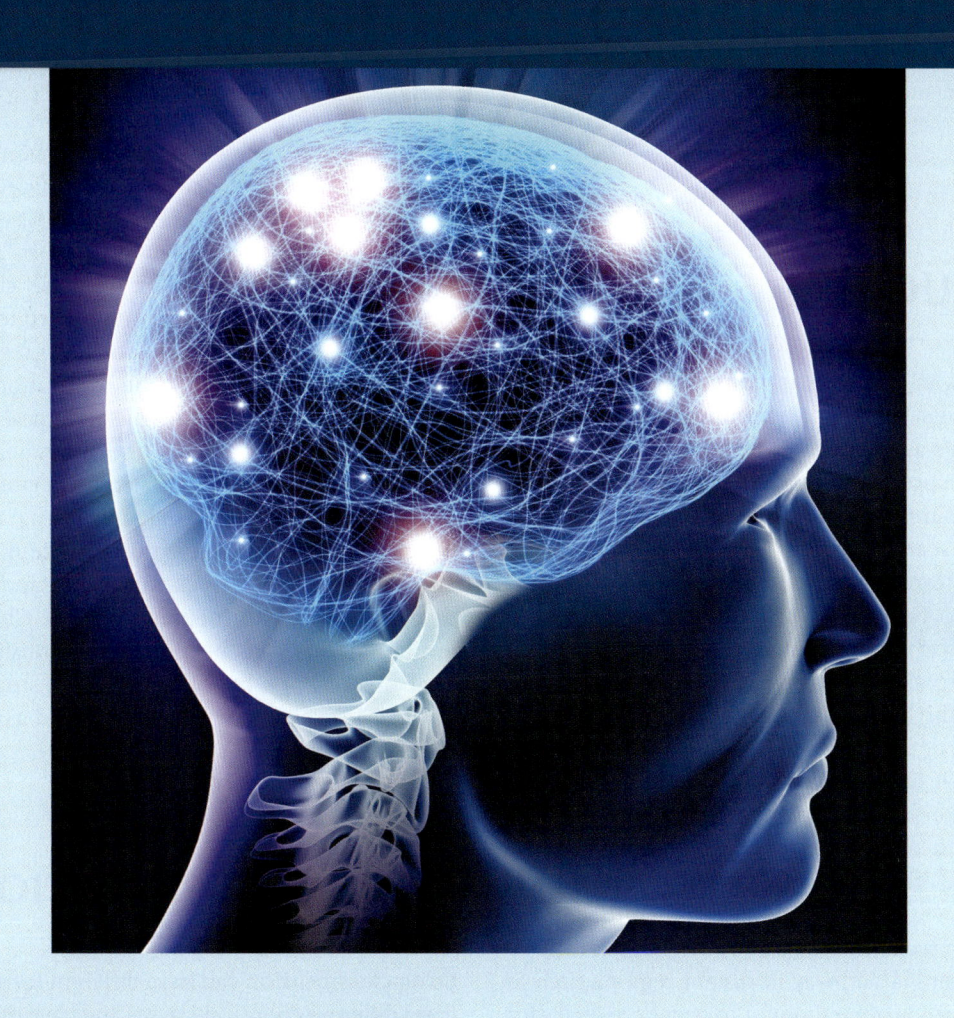

ANATOMY OF THE CHAPTER

This chapter will highlight the following.

- Pharmacokinetics.
- Pharmacodynamics.
- Classification of drugs.
- Clinical trials.

INTRODUCTION   174

DRUG CLASSIFICATION   174

DRUG ACTION   177

TYPES OF DRUGS   193

PSYCHOPHARMACOLOGY – THE DARK SIDE   197

CLINICAL TRIALS   199

SUMMARY   201

LEARNING OUTCOMES

1. To understand the processes which sensory signals are subject to in the brain.

2. To understand the mechanisms by which different types of pain are produced.

INTRODUCTION

Drugs can exert an influence at many points throughout the entire process of neural communication. We tend to think of drugs as clinical agents; however, we can use drugs as tools to probe the functions of the brain. Drugs can be used in a similar way to the key words that are input into an internet search engine. When one is performing a search of the internet, one has to refine the search terms used in order to narrow down output from the search engine. In a similar vein, by using a more precise drug that has a specific target, the psychopharmacologist can refine their search of the brain. However, this approach is only as good as the drug itself. If we have many drugs to use we can look for their common features which may pinpoint the underlying problems. A further problem with using drugs as a search term for causality is that they do not always target the site of origin. Instead they are connected at distant and downstream locations, e.g. the problems of a disorder may arise in the cortex but this has a knock-on effect further along a pathway in distant regions such as the striatum which is often thought to be where drugs for schizophrenia and ADHD work (Chandler, 2010).

Drugs can be used to influence physiology and behaviour in either the short or the long term. Drugs can cause structural changes in the brain, especially after long-term use. Psychopharmacology has helped develop many theories of abnormal behaviour (for example, the dopamine (DA) hypothesis of schizophrenia; see Chapter 21). Most students usually assume that the development of drugs for the treatment of a disorder comes after understanding of the disorder is achieved. However, drug discovery owes a great deal to serendipity, when drugs are used for purposes for which they were not originally intended (off-label prescribing). Thus, if a drug proves to be useful for a disorder or condition then how that drug works can provide some insight into the pathological mechanisms of the disorder. Very rarely would a drug treatment give us insight into the aetiology of a disorder, e.g. depression.

The way in which drugs help inform understanding of behaviour does not just arise from clinical applications and off-label prescribing, but also from recreational drug use. Recreational drug use is a politically charged area, but what people choose to consume has led to a great deal of scientific enquiry which has provided greater understanding of our reward systems and motivational systems (see Chapter 16). Understanding the biological mechanisms of drugs and their behavioural effects has helped inform legislation, such as the level of alcohol permitted in drivers.

Although extremely valuable, drug research is not conclusive and at times it raises more questions than it answers (e.g. in the quest to understand the new pharmacological basis of depression – see Chapter 22). Such limitations need to be noted and considered, but one does not accept a hypothesis on one small piece of evidence. More evidence can be obtained from the different areas of the medical sciences.

DRUG CLASSIFICATION

Drug classification can have different forms. Drugs come from different chemical classes and have different pharmacological actions. The chemist may be interested in the molecular structure of the drug and the pharmacologist will be interested in how the drug interacts with biological systems, neither of which will provide information specifically about the behavioural effects of the drug. For the psychopharmacologist and the psychobiologist, the best way to categorize drugs is by their behavioural function (e.g. stimulants are activating, depressants are calming, antidepressants treat depression and **anxiolytics** relieve anxiety). The doctor's prescribing guide, the *British National Formulary*, is laid out by drug effect. For example, antidepressants come from different chemical classes and have different modes of action, yet are still effective in treating depression (see also Chapter 22). In addition, drugs are not always used specifically for the disorder for which they are intended (Dean, 2011).

Another more pragmatic way of looking at drugs is by their legal status. It is well known that certain drugs are illegal and carry high penalties for use, possession and sale. In the UK there are two legal ways of looking at drugs, either by schedule or by control (see Box 7.1). However, science has challenged the rationale for drug classification, which led to the dismissal of Professor David Nutt as chair of the **Advisory Council on the Misuse of Drugs** (ACMD) (Box 7.2).

Drugs may have a number of names which can sometimes lead to confusion. However, when explained, the process becomes transparent. Initially a drug is synthesized and given a sequence number (like a barcode); the drug also has a chemical name (which is informative of its

BOX 7.1: LEGAL CLASSIFICATION OF DRUGS

Misuse of Drugs Act (1971) and amendments thereafter

Drugs have not always been illegal – heroin, cocaine and amphetamine have all been used and sold for medicinal purposes. Only comparatively recently have drug laws imposed restrictions on their use. The classification of drugs and their legal status are often somewhat confusing. Under the law, drugs fall into the categories of class and/or scheduled.

Class of drugs

The class of a controlled drug is intended to reflect the harm associated with it. Parliament determines the relevant class based on the recommendations of the ACMD. This classification, in turn, determines the penalties that are available to the courts when sentencing.

Class A

Class A drugs are considered by Parliament to be the most harmful. This category includes heroin, methadone, crack cocaine, ecstasy, magic mushrooms and 'crystal meth'. An offence involving a class A substance carries the harshest penalties.

Class B

Class B drugs are considered by Parliament to be less harmful than class A drugs and include amphetamines, barbiturates and dihydrocodeine. Certain class B drugs are reclassified to class A if they have been prepared for injection. These include amphetamines, dihydrocodeine and codeine.

Class C

Class C drugs are considered by Parliament to be the least harmful of the controlled drugs. These include benzodiazepines, steroids and subutex (buprenorphine).

Scheduled drugs

The 2001 Regulations determine in what circumstances it is lawful to possess, supply, produce, export and import controlled drugs. The authorized scope of activity will depend on the schedule to which the controlled drug is assigned. There are five schedules. Schedule 1 contains those drugs that are considered to have little or no therapeutic value and are subjected to the most restrictive control. Schedule 5 contains drugs that are considered to have therapeutic value and are commonly available as over-the-counter medicines.

Schedule 1

Drugs belonging to this schedule are thought to have no therapeutic value and therefore cannot be lawfully possessed or prescribed, e.g. LSD, MDMA (ecstasy) and cannabis.

Schedules 2 and 3

The drugs in these schedules can be prescribed and therefore legally possessed and supplied by pharmacists and doctors. They can also be possessed lawfully by anyone who has a prescription. It is an offence contrary to the 1971 Act to possess any drug belonging to schedule 2 or 3 without prescription or lawful authority. Examples of schedule 2 drugs are methadone and diamorphine (heroin). Schedule 3 drugs include subutex and most of the barbiturate family. The difference between schedule 2 and schedule 3 drugs concerns record keeping and storage requirements.

Schedule 4(i) and (ii)

Schedule 4 was divided into two parts by the 2001 Regulations (as amended by the Misuse of Drugs (Amendment No. 2) Regulations 2012).

Schedule 4(i) controls most of the benzodiazepines. Schedule 4(i) drugs can only be lawfully possessed under prescription. Otherwise, possession is an offence under the 1971 Act.

Schedule 4(ii) drugs can be possessed as long as they are clearly for personal use. Drugs in this schedule can also be imported or exported for personal use where a person himself carries out that importation or exportation. The most common example of a schedule 4(ii) drug is steroids.

Schedule 5

Schedule 5 drugs are sold over the counter and can be legally possessed without a prescription.

In the United States there has been a long history of drug restrictions. The Controlled Substance Act 1970 specifically stated that drugs under the Act were now under federal jurisdiction and dealt with both narcotics and other 'dangerous' drugs. It also dealt with prevention and treatment. The USA treated marijuana differently, creating a separate commission to study this and report in 1972. Continuing the trend started in 1965, and in contrast to earlier acts, this Act was created to control drugs directly, not through taxes, moving enforcement from the jurisdiction of the Treasury to the Justice Department, and establishing the **Drug Enforcement Agency (DEA)**. The Attorney General was in charge of enforcement but the Department of Health, Education, and Welfare (through the Food and Drug Administration) was in charge of defining what needs to be controlled, considering:

- pharmacological actions;
- other scientific knowledge about the drug and related drugs;
- risk to public health;
- dependence (psychological or physiological) potential; and
- whether the drug was a precursor for other drugs listed.

BOX 7.2: POLICY DECISION: PROFESSOR DAVID NUTT VERSUS THE HOME SECRETARY

Professor David Nutt was once chairperson of the Advisory Council on the Misuse of drugs (ACMD). The ACMD's remit is to review drug safety and inform politicians of the science so that they can make policy decisions.

David Nutt crossed swords with the government in 2007 when he wrote 'the current classification system has evolved in an unsystematic way from somewhat arbitrary foundations with seemingly little scientific basis' (Nutt et al., 2007). In the same paper a metric was used to measure the harm of both legal and illegal drugs. This rated heroin and cocaine as the top two but when one goes down the list, there are some surprises; for example, alcohol is number 5 whereas ecstasy is number 18.

Nutt then wrote an editorial in the *Journal of Psychopharmacology*, the in-house journal of the British Association for Psychopharmacology, in which he created a spoof addiction (Nutt, 2009). This spoof addiction was referred to as equasy (not to be confused with the ADHD medication but probably intended to have a similar sound to the drug ecstasy to which he compared it). Equasy is essentially an addiction to horse riding and he outlined the dangers associated with horse riding in comparison to consuming ecstasy (MDMA). This put Nutt at loggerheads with the then Home Secretary Jacqui Smith who demanded an apology (Nutt, 2012). Although Nutt was not trying to play down the effects of MDMA, his purpose was to demonstrate that the current methods for assessing whether or not a drug should be made illegal and controlled were not fit for purpose. All of this got picked up by the media and distorted to some extent – mad Professor type headlines. The ultimate response by the government was to ask for his resignation and when that was not forthcoming, he was dismissed. Upon his departure, he created with other scientists the Independent Scientific Committee on Drugs, now called DrugScience (http://www.drugscience.org.uk/). Its mission statement is as follows.

- The Independent Scientific Committee on Drugs reviews and investigates the scientific evidence relating to drugs, free from political concerns.
- The Committee provides accessible information on drugs to the public and professionals.
- The Committee works in the UK and internationally and addresses issues surrounding drug harms and benefits; regulation and education; prevention, treatment and recovery.

The ISCD published a paper on drug harm in the *Lancet* in 2010 using a new set of criteria in which drugs were scored out of 100 points, and the criteria were weighted to indicate their relative importance (Nutt et al., 2010). This new metric had 16 evaluation criteria regarding the harms of drugs.

In an exceptionally colourful bar chart, the overall harm score put alcohol at number 1 followed by heroin, crack cocaine and methamphetamine. Clearly, this is not a politically popular decision as the drinks industry is a significant part of our economy. David Nutt's stand against government highlights the importance of scientists' independence from politics and policy. The accusation that psychiatry, medicine and psychology can be used for political ends needs to be firmly addressed (Moncrieff, 2010). What is required is an ethical discourse on the legal status of drugs and then some serious consideration of what is popularly known as the 'war on drugs' which has to be conducted without prejudice (this is unlikely to happen any time soon).

structure). If the drug has potential to be useful, it might be given a more memorable generic name and finally once it reaches the market, it has a brand name. A clear example is that of the antidepressant better known as Prozac.

Sequence number:	Lilly 110140 (LY110140)
Chemical name:	3-(p-Trifluoromethylphenoxy)-n-methyl-3-phenylpropylamine
Generic name:	**Fluoxetine**
Brand name:	Prozac

DRUG ACTION

The fate of a drug is determined by two chief characteristics: **pharmacokinetics** and **pharmacodynamics**.

Pharmacokinetics

Pharmacokinetics is about the factors that influence a drug as it travels through the body, i.e. what the body does to the drug. Route of administration, rate of absorption, termination of drug action and elimination of the drug are important pharmacokinetic factors.

The study of the pharmacokinetic properties of the drug allows the psychopharmacologist to determine when the drug starts working and how long the drug is working for. It determines the dose and route of administration for clinical applications.

Route of administration

The route of administration affects how the drug will be absorbed and transported to the brain (Figure 7.1). Absorption is the process by which the drug enters the bloodstream, either via passing through cell membranes or by direct administration to the bloodstream.

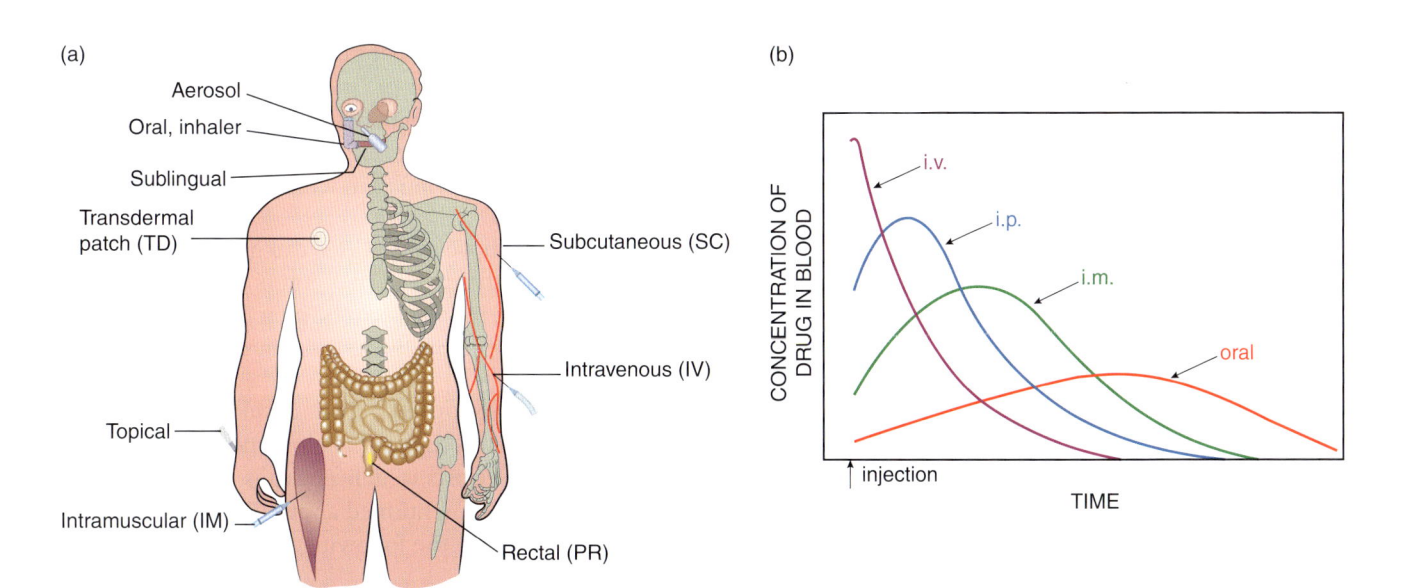

FIGURE 7.1 *Common routes of drug administration. (a) Route of administration. (b) Speed of drug delivery. High concentration almost immediately after IV injection.*

There are several routes of administration that have significant effects on the pharmacokinetic properties of the drug.

- **Oral** (*per os* – PO), taken via the mouth, e.g. swallowing a pill – paracetamol.
- **Rectal** (*per rectum* – PR), administered in the rectum, e.g. a suppository – diazepam post epileptic seizure.
- Inhaled, via the lungs, e.g. tobacco smoking, but also via aerosol sprays.
- **Transdermal** (TD), across the skin, e.g. hormone replacement or nicotine replacement therapies.
- **Transmucosal** (TM) – topical application via the mucous membranes, e.g. through the membranes of the nose with intranasal administration of cocaine, or mouth (sublingual).
- **Parenteral**, an injection, e.g. anaesthetics.

PO (*per os*), by mouth

This is perhaps the most familiar route of drug administration. Drugs that are swallowed have to be soluble and stable within the stomach. Liquids are absorbed more readily than solids, e.g. a pill, because they do not have to go through the process of dissolving within the stomach. The molecules of a drug are absorbed across the intestinal mucosa via passive diffusion. This is similar to the ionic transfer described in Chapter 4 in which ions move along a gradient from high concentration to low concentration. Because the drugs are crossing membranes that are made up of lipids, the drug has to be lipid soluble. The degree of solubility affects the speed of transfer of the drug. The rate of absorption by the oral route is affected by the contents of the stomach. Enzymes within the stomach may break down and deactivate the drug in what is known as first-pass metabolism. Also of significance is food present within the stomach – drugs taken after a meal are more slowly absorbed.

PR (*per rectum*), in the rectum

This is an uncommon route of administration and often reserved for those who are vomiting (and therefore cannot hold down a pill), unconscious (and therefore cannot swallow) or have general difficulties with swallowing. This route is irregular, unpredictable and incomplete (Van Hoogdalem et al., 1991), so for scientific purposes it is avoided. One drug service for opiate users that shall remain anonymous decided to use the PR route to avoid the health risks of intravenous drug use. Whilst this was a noble attempt, it was soon realized that there are a unique set of problems associated with PR administration of opiates (the drug users were helping each other deliver the drug).

Inhaled

This route of administration is favoured by the recreational drug user. Smoking of cannabis, tobacco and crack cocaine ensures speedy delivery of drug molecules to the brain. Smoke taken into the lungs has a large surface area through which the drug can enter the bloodstream. The speed is further increased as the capillaries of the lung carry the drug directly to the heart and from the heart it is pumped to the brain. The effectiveness of smoking over other routes of administration has been confirmed (Cone, 1995). Whilst this is a very quick route to access the brain, there are considerable dangers associated with smoking substances.

TD (transdermal), across the skin

A drug can be administered through the skin via a semi-permeable membrane on a specially constructed plaster (a patch) which allows the drug continuous yet slow access to the bloodstream. A trip to the chemist will reveal numerous devices to aid smoking cessation with nicotine replacement therapy (NRT) taking advantage of transdermal administration with the patch. This is also used for the treatment of deficient hormones with hormone replacement therapy (HRT), depression with selegiline (Bodkin & Amsterdam, 2002) and ADHD (Pelham et al., 2005). To give the reader a further indication of the use of off-label prescribing which can open up new avenues of investigation, children with ADHD were given transdermal nicotine for symptom management (Shytle et al., 2002). However, whilst the theoretical rationale for using nicotine remains, the prohibitive side-effects of NRT meant that it was of little use.

TM (transmucosal), across mucous membranes

Some drugs can be administered via the mucous membranes of the nose (**intranasal**) and mouth (under the tongue – **sublingual**). Perhaps the most notable one is the intranasal administration or 'snorting' of cocaine. Other examples include the sublingual administration of a tablet that sits under the tongue (e.g. buprenorphine for opiate dependence) and chewing gum which releases nicotine.

With all the above routes, one can give a precise dose of the drug but the dosage that enters the blood stream and therefore the brain cannot be guaranteed. The route that allows for more precision is the injection.

Parenteral (injections)

The development of the hypodermic needle (hypo = below, dermal = of the skin) allowed scientists to deliver drugs bypassing many of the membranes mentioned above (Figure 7.2). Types of injections include the following.

- **Intravenous** (IV), where a drug is delivered directly to the bloodstream and is therefore delivered to the brain very quickly.

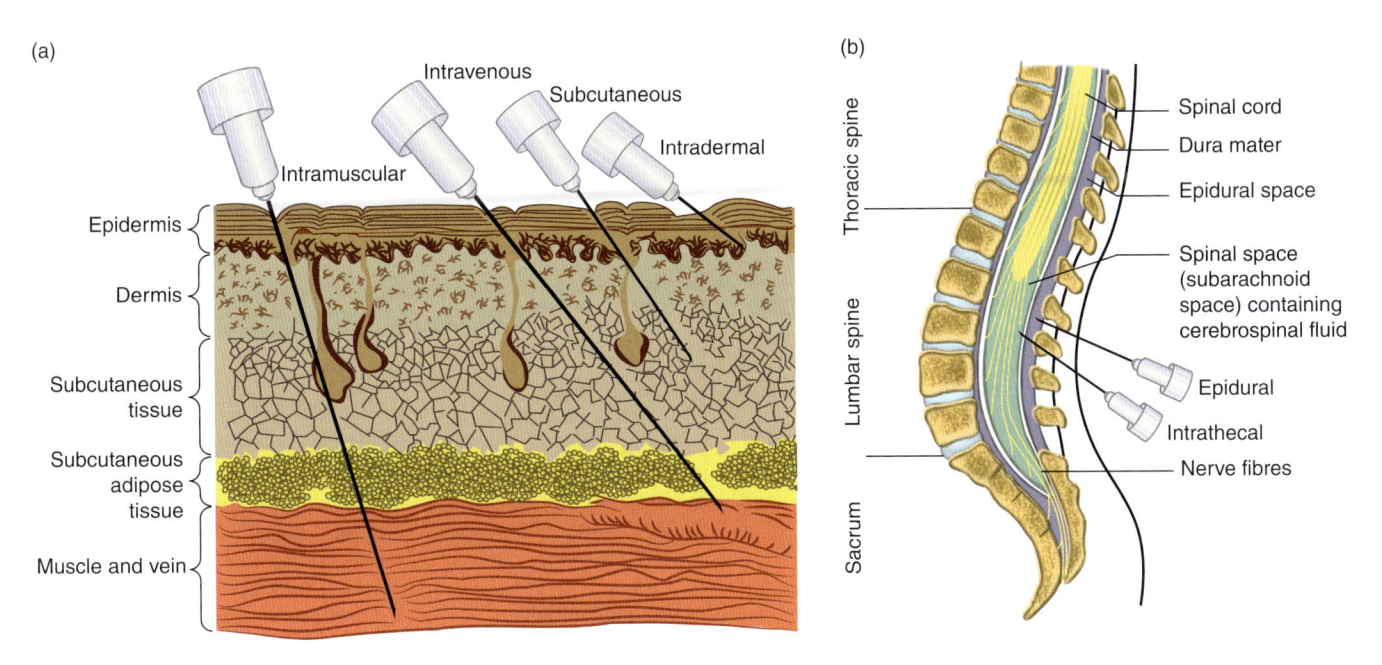

FIGURE 7.2 *Injections. (a) Parenteral. (b) Intrathecal and epidural injection. The intrathecal injection goes deeper into the spine.*

- **Subcutaneous** (SC) is when the drug is delivered just below the skin. Absorption is slow and steady and depends on the blood flow to the area of the injection. In a similar manner, subcutaneous implants can deliver large volumes of drug over a prolonged period of time, e.g. contraceptive implants.
- **Intraperitoneal** (IP) administration is predominantly used in animals. The drug is delivered through the abdominal wall into the peritoneal cavity.
- **Intramuscular** (IM) is when the drug is delivered into the muscle. Such injections provide slower progress to the bloodstream.
- **Intrathecal** (IT) is when a drug is injected into the subarachnoid space of the spinal canal so that it reaches the CSF; this is more commonly used in spinal anaesthesia where a nerve block is required.
- **Intracerebroventricular** (ICV) and intracranial administrations are performed in animals. ICV administration involves the drug being delivered to the ventricles of the brain whereas intracranial is the delivery of drug to discrete areas of the brain.
- **Epidural** is similar to intrathecal and is used in obstetrics as a nerve block to relieve labour pain. It is similar to the spinal anaesthetic but differs by dose and positioning. It is delivered to the epidural space which is the outer part of the spinal column.

Each route has a different speed of entry to the brain and has been shown to have a deterministic effect on whether a drug, e.g. cocaine, is addictive (Box 7.3).

BOX 7.3: ADDICTION IS ABOUT SPEED OF ENTRY

Addictive drugs tend to share a similar underlying mechanism in that they stimulate the release of dopamine from the nucleus accumbens. However, when one looks at the pharmacokinetics of addictive drugs, another common denominator emerges. Nearly all drugs that are addictive (not necessarily abused/misused) enter the body via routes that mean they enter the brain rapidly. The speed by which they enter the brain is considered essential for their addiction potential (Figure 7.3.1).

In a series of studies by Jim Swanson and Nora Volkow, the importance of the speed of entry was emphasized using cocaine and methylphenidate (Swanson & Volkow,

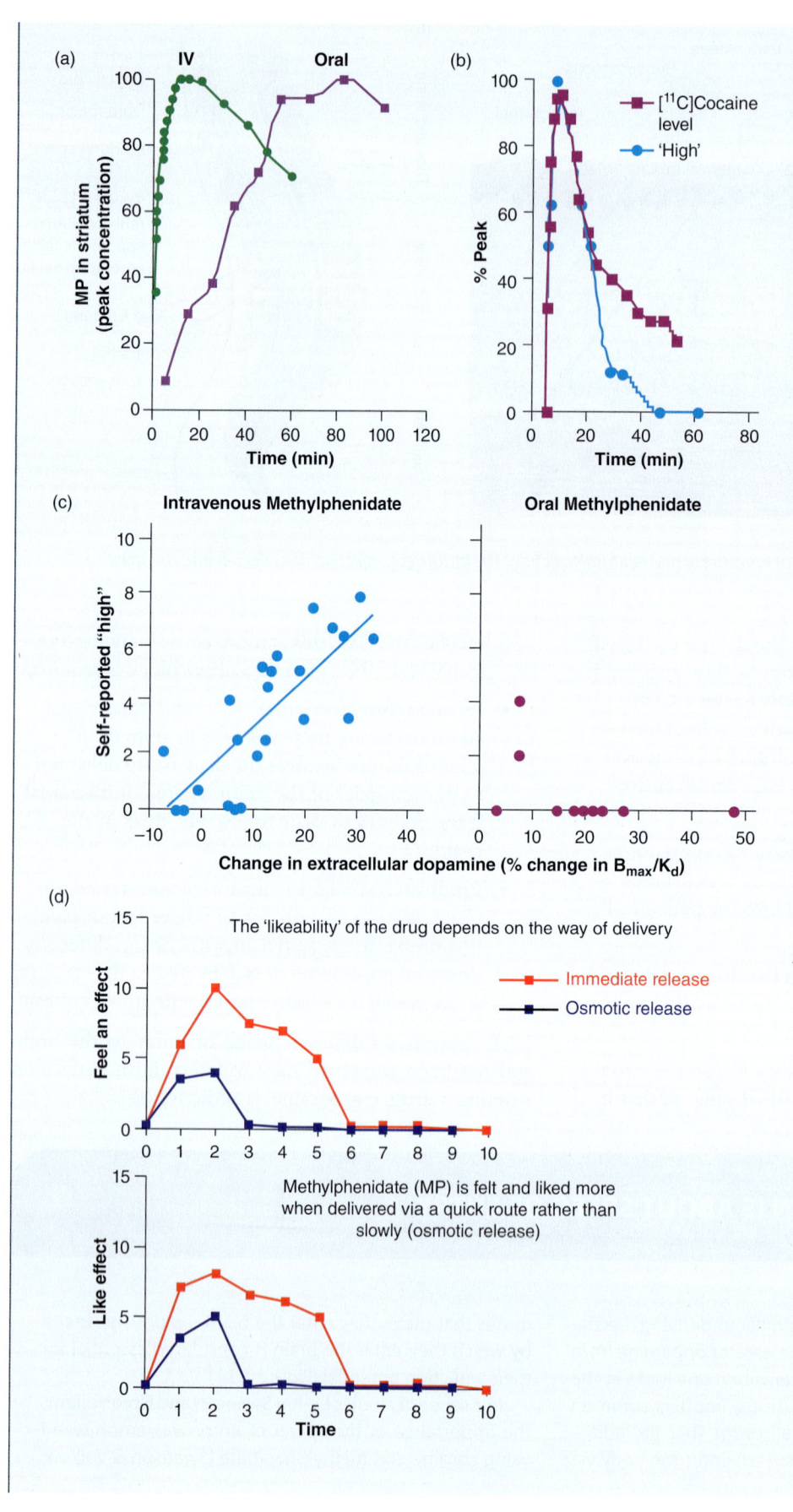

FIGURE 7.3.1 *Speed of entry is critical for the feelings of a drug-induced high. (a) Methylphenidate (MP) reaches a peak concentration quickly via the IV route compared to the oral route. (b) Cocaine's 'high' can be mapped onto the speed of entry of [^{11}C] cocaine. (c) IV MP but not oral MP produces a subjective feeling of a 'high'. (d) Methylphenidate is felt and liked more when delivered via a quick route rather than slowly (osmotic release).*
Sources: (a) Swanson, J. M., & Volkow, N. D. (2003). Serum and brain concentrations of methylphenidate: implications for use and abuse. *Neuroscience and Biobehavioral Reviews, 27*(7), 615–621. (b) and (c) Volkow, N. D., & Swanson, J. M. (2003). Variables that affect the clinical use and abuse of methylphenidate in the treatment of ADHD. *American Journal of Psychiatry, 160*(11), 1909–1918. (d) Spencer, T. J., Biederman, J., Ciccone, P. E., Madras, B. K., Dougherty, D. D., Bonab, A. A., et al. (2006). PET study examining pharmacokinetics, detection and likeability, and dopamine transporter receptor occupancy of short- and longacting oral methylphenidate. *American Journal of Psychiatry, 163*(3), 387–395.

2003; Volkow & Swanson, 2003). Cocaine and methylphenidate share near identical pharmacodynamic properties – they both block the dopamine transporter, thereby increasing dopamine in the synapse. Cocaine and methylphenidate have different pharmacokinetic properties due to the way they are delivered: cocaine is snorted which leads to rapid increases within the brain whereas methylphenidate is taken orally so high concentrations take much longer to achieve.

Intravenous methylphenidate produced a rapid rise in concentrations within the striatum in comparison to oral administration that took approximately 60 minutes to reach the same heights. When looking at cocaine administration, the peak concentration of cocaine was near identical to the subjective self-reported high.

It was also demonstrated that intravenous methylphenidate elevated extracellular dopamine which was correlated with the self-reported high; oral methylphenidate did not correlate with the self-reported high.

Speed of entry to the brain and rate of metabolism are therefore important factors in methylphenidate's abuse potential (Volkow & Swanson, 2003; Volkow et al., 1995, 2002). The therapeutic effects of methylphenidate can be differentiated from the abuse potential (Swanson & Volkow, 2003; Volkow & Swanson, 2003). Using methylphenidate in immediate-release and slow-release forms, Spencer et al. (2006) found that participants were more sensitive to detecting an effect of the drug and liking the drug when they received the quick-acting form. Indeed, this is how many preparations of methylphenidate are marketed (Chandler, 2010).

All drugs are delivered in a vehicle. When one takes a tablet, the drug is included with a number of other normally inactive agents that bind the material together. In an injection, the drug is delivered in water, saline or an oil base. The vehicle will be one factor that determines the release rate of the drug. Oil-based suspensions provide the slowest release. The vehicle should always be used as the comparator or control agent in an experiment (in clinical trials this will be the placebo group – see Chapter 9). In animal experiments, the control animal has to receive the exact same attention and intervention as the experimental animals, the only difference being that the control animal does not receive the active ingredient.

Each tablet has the same amount of drug in it (in the case of paracetamol, 500 mg). However, humans vary in size and body composition and this impacts upon the drug's effect. In a large person, 500 mg would be effectively less than in a small person. It is not practical to calibrate for every individual in a clinical setting, therefore there are only a limited number of differing doses of any drug. In the experimental context, the drug can be calibrated to body weight. The drug in milligrams is calibrated to the weight of the animal/person in kilograms: milligrams per kilogram (mg/kg). Thus, a larger person or rat would receive more drug than one of lower weight. This means every animal receives the exact same dose regardless of their weight and thus the experiment is more controlled.

Drug distribution

Once in the blood, the drug is carried around the body. Blood circulates round the body approximately once every minute, thus ensuring wide distribution of a drug (Figure 7.3). This wide distribution can also account for some of the associated side-effects. Blood in the veins is returning to the heart which pumps it to the lungs where carbon dioxide is removed and oxygen is absorbed. Oxygenated blood is then returned to the heart and pumped to the aorta. The blood then goes to smaller arteries and eventually capillaries where the drugs are able to enter the cell.

In the study of psychopharmacology, we are predominantly interested in the drug entering the brain. Two arteries supply oxygenated blood to the brain: the internal carotid artery and the vertebral artery (see Chapter 5). This complex network of blood supply is indicative of the brain being a big consumer of energy. Interruption of supply can have devastating effects as is seen in the case of stroke. This extensive network of blood vessels also means that psychoactive drugs readily enter the brain. However, the drug still has some obstacles to overcome on its journey to the site of action within the brain – body membranes.

Body membranes

All cells have membranes made of lipids (see Chapter 4) that need to be traversed. Furthermore, there are dense networks of cells that create barriers to protect the brain (or the unborn foetus) from foreign bodies. There are four main barriers that the drug has to overcome: the cell membrane, the walls of the capillaries, the blood–brain barrier and the **placental barrier**.

The cell membrane The drug has to penetrate the **phospholipid cell membrane** and enter the cell. Lipid-soluble drugs readily pass the cell membrane but many drugs are not lipid soluble. Most drugs are weak organic acids or bases, existing in unionized and ionized forms in an aqueous environment. The unionized form is usually

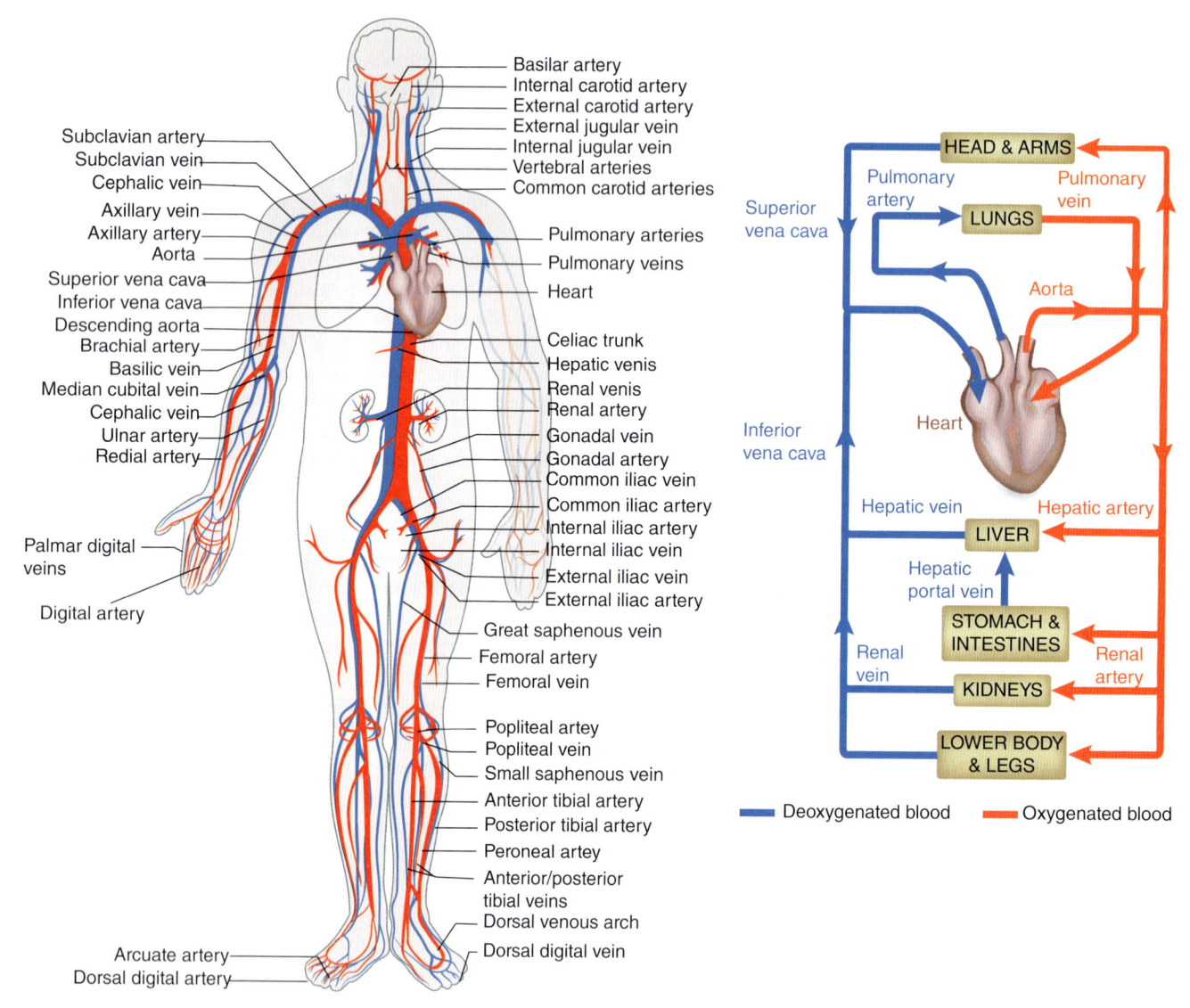

FIGURE 7.3 *Blood circulation takes drugs around the body rapidly.*

lipid soluble (lipophilic) and diffuses readily across cell membranes. Ionized drugs are those drugs that when dissolved in water form two charged ions. The ionized form has low lipid solubility and high electrical resistance and thus cannot penetrate cell membranes easily. For example, sodium chloride (common table salt) has a positive sodium and negative chloride ion. The ionized part of the drug attracts water molecules, thus forming a large complex of molecules, which cannot cross the membranes because they are rendered less lipid soluble. The proportion of the unionized form present (and thus the drug's ability to cross a membrane) is determined by the environmental acidity (pH) and the drug's pH when the concentrations of ionized and unionized forms are equal (pKa). A pH of 7 is neutral; this was an important variable in the experiments of Bill Corrigall and colleagues in their attempts to get rats to self-administer nicotine (Corrigall & Coen, 1989).

The wall of the capillaries

In order to enter the cell, the drug has to leave the capillaries. Capillary walls are thin and formed of a single layer of cells. Between the cells are small holes that allow small molecules to be exchanged.

The blood–brain barrier (BBB)

The BBB has two main components – capillaries and glial cells. In the brain, the capillaries are tightly packed together and covered by a glial sheath created from astrocytes (see Chapter 5). This means that the drug has to pass the capillary wall and the glial sheath. All of our psychoactive drugs are able to traverse the BBB.

The placental barrier The placenta connects the mother and the foetus and is a point of exchange of nutrients and foetal waste. It is also a point where drugs that the mother has consumed can be passed on to the unborn child. Drugs that pass this barrier can have devastating effects upon the developing foetus, e.g. foetal alcohol syndrome (see Chapter 3).

Metabolism and termination of drug action

Drugs have to overcome a number of obstacles on their journey to the brain and site of action. However, at their destination they do not remain active indefinitely. Drugs metabolize into a form that can leave the body, thus terminating their action. The most common exit route is in urine via the kidneys. Other exit routes include via the lung, bile and skin. The most notable use of the lung as the exit route is the breathalyser test used by police forces to detect drunk driving (see Box 7.4).

BOX 7.4: THE BREATHALYSER TEST

Alcohol is not digested upon absorption, nor chemically changed in the bloodstream. As the blood goes through the lungs, some of the alcohol moves across the membranes of the lung's air sacs (**alveoli**) into the air, because alcohol will evaporate from a solution – that is, it is volatile. The concentration of alcohol in the alveolar air is related to the concentration of alcohol in the blood. As the alcohol in the alveolar air is exhaled, it can be detected by the breath alcohol testing device. Instead of having to draw a driver's blood to test his alcohol level, an officer can test the driver's breath on the spot and instantly know if there is a reason to arrest the driver.

Because the alcohol concentration in the breath is related to that in the blood, you can determine the blood alcohol concentration (BAC) by measuring alcohol on the breath. The ratio of breath alcohol to blood alcohol is **2100:1**. This means that 2100 milliliters (mL) of alveolar air will contain the same amount of alcohol as 1 mL of blood.

- Pint of ordinary strength lager (e.g. Carling Black Label, Fosters) — 2 units
- Pint of strong lager (e.g. Stella Artois, Grolsch) — 3 units
- Pint of ordinary bitter (e.g. John Smiths, Boddingtons) — 2 units
- Pint of best bitter (e.g. Fuller's ESB, Young's Special, Harveys Best) — 3 units
- Pint of ordinary strength cider (e.g. Woodpecker) — 2 units
- Pint of strong cider (e.g. Strongbow) — 3 units
- 175 mL glass of wine — ~2 units
- Pub measure of spirits — 1 unit
- Alcopop (e.g. Smirnoff Ice, Bacardi Breezer) — ~1.5 units

How to calculate **alcohol units**:

volume (mL) × ABV (%)/1000

For example, a large glass of wine is 250 mL with a strength of 13.5% ABV.

250 × 13.5/1000 = 3.375 units

One UK unit is 10 mL of pure alcohol – you won't be drinking that! Wine that is labelled 12% ABV means that 12% of the volume of the wine is pure alcohol. 88% is therefore not alcohol and is composed of water and congeners.

Blood alcohol level (%)	Effects
0.02–0.03	Mood elevation. Slight muscle relaxation
0.05–0.06	Relaxation and warmth. Increased reaction time. Decreased fine muscle co-ordination
0.08–0.09	Impaired balance, speech, vision, hearing, muscle co-ordination. Euphoria
0.14–0.15	Gross impairment of physical and mental control
0.20–0.30	Severely intoxicated. Very little control of mind or body
0.40–0.50	Unconscious. Deep coma. Death from respiratory depression

In the UK, 0.08% is the maximum legal blood alcohol concentration for driving. One unit of alcohol is processed per hour, but this depends upon the individual's weight, sex, age, stomach contents and metabolism and if they are taking any medication.

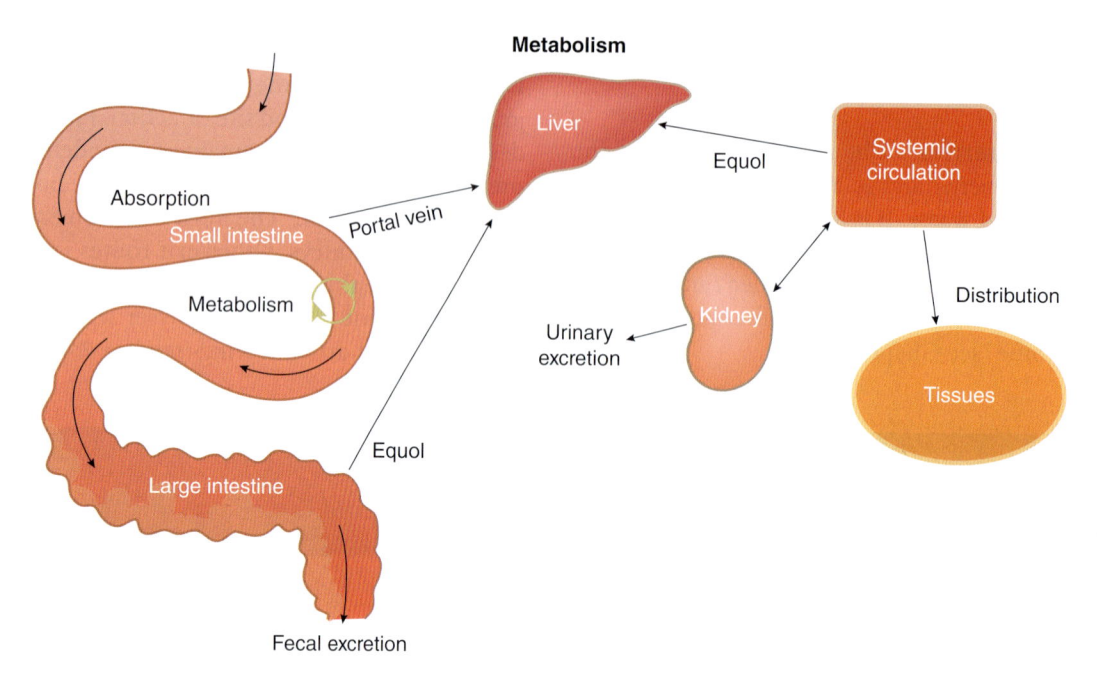

FIGURE 7.4 *Absorption and metabolism.*

Psychoactive drugs need to be converted from their lipid-soluble state into a water-soluble state (**hydrophilic**). The liver metabolically transforms drugs into either active or inactive metabolites which are able to leave the body (see Figure 7.6). The liver is involved in two phases of biotransformation:

Phase 1 involves the oxidation (oxygen being incorporated into the drug molecule) of the drug, converting it into a compound that is less lipid soluble and also less active (but not always the case, e.g. MPTP is a pro-neurotoxin that causes Parkinson's disease which is converted by monoamine oxidase B in the astrocytes to an active metabolite – MPP+; see Chapter 24). Phase 2 biotransformation involves the combination (conjugation) of the drug and a small molecule. Small molecules such as glucuronide, which is important in inactivating the drug, produce a metabolite that is highly ionized and inert. Remember, highly ionized drugs find it extremely difficult to cross lipid membranes and therefore are eliminated by the kidneys. Active metabolites may undergo further biotransformation. The whole process of phase 1 and phase 2 metabolism is referred to as **hepatic metabolism** (pertaining to the liver).

Damage to the liver can occur from acute and chronic alcohol consumption. A blood test can check for three liver enzymes (aspartate aminotransferase (AST), alanine aminotransferase (ALT) and especially gamma glutamyl transferase (GGT)) which are usually elevated by heavy drinking over a short period of time. This type of damage is associated with binge drinking. It is potentially reversible upon cessation of drinking. If the liver is damaged, the enzymes are released into the bloodstream and show up in the blood test – the higher the enzyme count, the greater the liver damage. The most accurate of these tests for alcoholic liver damage is GGT.

The renal system processes hydrophilic drugs and those that have undergone **hepatic biotransformation**. The kidneys excrete most of the waste material via urine (Figure 7.4). In the kidneys waste material is exchanged for water, glucose, sodium, potassium and chloride. This exchange means that there is more water in the tubules of the kidney and many drugs are reabsorbed along the concentration gradient. The ionization in phase 1 hepatic biotransformation reduces the reabsorption because it makes the drug less lipid soluble.

Understanding the pharmacokinetic properties of a drug is important in behavioural studies because it allows one to predict the optimal dose required, how often the drug is required and how quickly it is eliminated. Within the pharmacological literature there is reference to the drug's half-life (Figure 7.5) which is the time required for the drug concentration to fall by 50%. It also allows the researcher/clinician to determine the interdose interval required to reach a steady-state concentration. One does not deliver the next dose of a drug after the first dose has been completely eliminated – one continually tops up the dose.

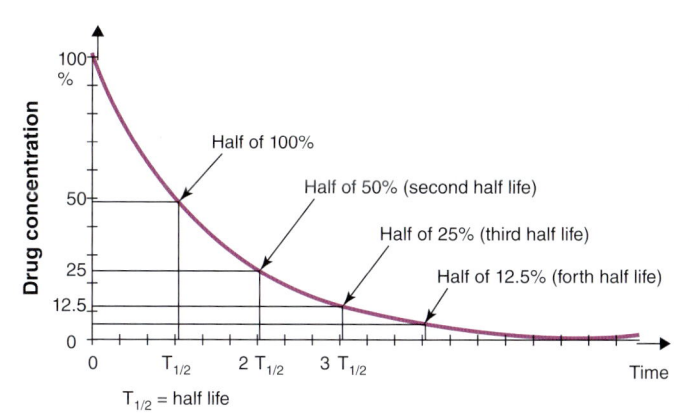

FIGURE 7.5 Drug half-lives. The time it takes to reduce the concentration by half (first half-life) and then half again (second half-life).

Pharmacodynamics

Pharmacodynamics is concerned with what the drug does to the body – what happens when it reaches its destination. Drugs can interact with their target cell in a number of ways, thus bringing about a biochemical and functional change. In Chapter 4 it was noted that receptors on pre- and postsynaptic neurons receive messages from neurotransmitters. This interaction of neurotransmitter with receptor can be extended now to include drugs and the phrase 'receptor ligand' is used as an all-encompassing description.

The basic types of drug action

There are numerous categorizations of drugs. In Box 7.1 we addressed the legal descriptors. Drugs can be looked at in terms of their pharmacological effects. All drugs *bind* to the receptor; that is, they attach themselves to the receptor. Efficacy is the property of a ligand that causes the target cell to change upon binding. However, this property is also subject to interpretation by cells and it is the interaction of drug and cell that results in the observed drug/receptor activity.

Drugs can be divided into four groups depending on what they do at the synapse: **agonists**, antagonists, partial agonists and inverse agonists.

Full agonists facilitate the action at the synapse. An agonist binds to the receptor and produces a response as an endogenous neurotransmitter might. A full agonist produces the full maximal response capability of the cell (in contrast to partial agonists which produce a submaximal response; see Figure 7.6).

Antagonists (or blockers) inhibit the activity of a neurotransmitter at the synapse. The antagonist does not bring about a physiological change but instead just stops the receptor being activated by endogenous ligands or agonists. Antagonists can block receptors by binding to the same site as the endogenous agonist (orthosterically) or by binding to a separate site and changing the conformation of the receptor (allosterically) (Kenakin & Williams, 2014). **Orthosteric antagonism** is where the drug completely blocks the agonist effect without any degree of antagonism (all or none) whereas the **allosteric antagonist** may modulate drug effects without recourse to all-or-none principles. Another way of viewing the antagonist's interaction with the receptor is if it is either **competitive** (orthosteric) or **non-competitive**

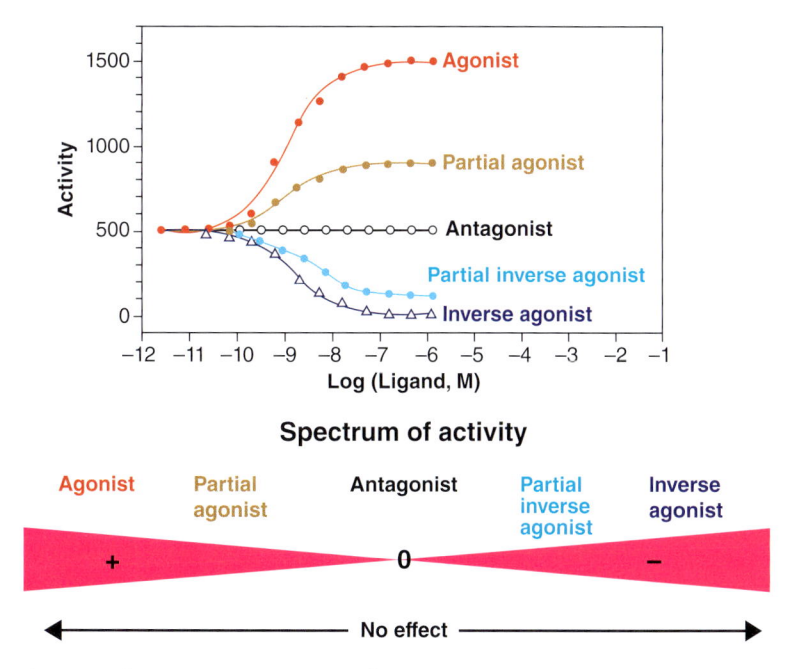

FIGURE 7.6 Activity of agonists, partial agonists, antagonists and inverse agonists.

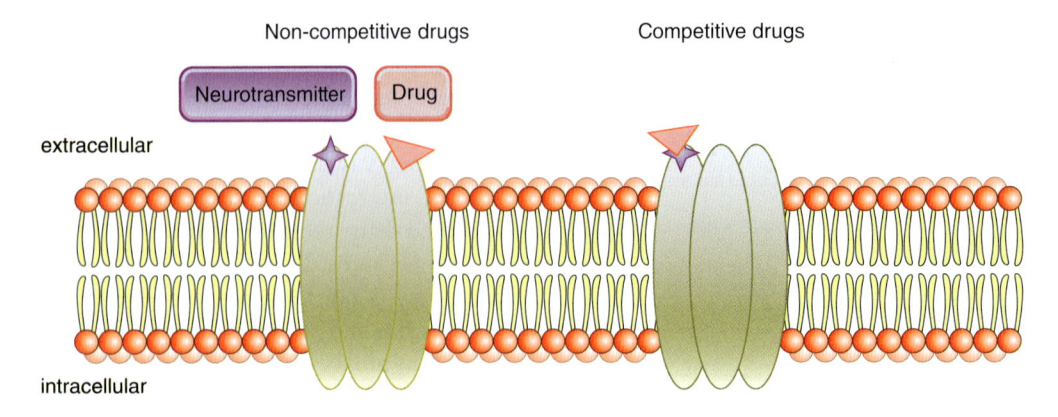

FIGURE 7.7 *Competitive and non-competitive drugs.*

(allosteric) (see Figure 7.7) (see Lambert, 2004). Competitive drugs fight for the same place as the neurotransmitter whereas non-competitive drugs act at a different site on the receptor.

Partial agonists operate somewhere between a full agonist and a full antagonist (see Figure 7.8). The partial agonist binds to the receptor, thus preventing other ligands from binding, but only has reduced efficacy at the receptor to bring about a functional and biochemical change. Partial agonists represent an interesting group of drugs that can be deployed for their therapeutic advantage. Whereas an agonist is a full efficacy ligand and an antagonist is a zero efficacy ligand, the partial agonist sits somewhere in between the two. To draw an analogy with household lights, the agonist is the lights turned on and the antagonist is the lights turned off – an all-or-none experience. However, the partial agonist is more like having a dimmer switch fitted – you can adjust the levels of lighting. The effects of the partial agonist are different depending on the levels of the endogenous neurotransmitter which can be seen behaviourally (see Box 7.5) (Kenakin & Williams, 2014). Partial agonists cause agonism at low doses when there is no other agonist present but antagonism when a full agonist is present.

Inverse agonists produce a response that is in the opposite direction to that of an agonist. Inverse agonists should not be confused with antagonists. Antagonists *inhibit* a response; they do not *produce* a response. If an agonist has a positive effect and an antagonist has zero effect then the inverse agonist has negative effect (Figure 7.9). Inverse agonists are a comparatively recent discovery (Costa et al., 1990) that have challenged the categorization of some antagonists which had been found to exert an effect in the opposite direction (Bond & Ijzerman, 2006). How an inverse agonist operates has been the subject of much speculation. It is considered that the inverse agonist interacts with the metabotropic receptor or, as they are often referred to, G-protein-coupled receptors (GPCR). It has been argued that 'inverse agonism is the property of a ligand to produce a decrease in the basal level of signalling after binding to a receptor' (Parra & Bond, 2007, p.146). Costa and Cotecchia (2005) also consider inverse agonists to be either orthosterically or allosterically modulated.

The clinical significance of inverse agonists is yet to be determined, and in Chapter 23 the significance is more apparent in the generation of fear and anxiety.

Modulation of neurotransmission by drugs

The basic types of drug action have focused on the local effects of the drug at the receptor but drugs can influence neurotransmission at a number of different points that can ultimately influence behaviour (see Figure 7.10).

Precursor preloading drugs
These drugs enhance the synthesis and increase the turnover of a neurotransmitter by acting as a precursor in the neurotransmitter's synthesis. They provide some of the ingredients for a neurotransmitter, e.g. in Parkinson's disease one of the main therapies is to provide patients with the precursor to dopamine – L-DOPA (Birkmayer & Hornykiewicz, 1961).

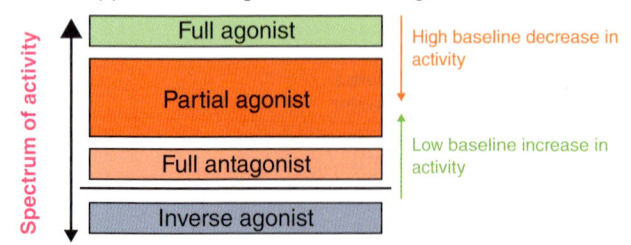

FIGURE 7.8 *Partial agonists.*

BOX 7.5: PARTIAL AGONISTS

Depending upon the state of the system in which it is working, a partial agonist will display itself as either an agonist or an antagonist. When there is low baseline activity, the partial agonist will appear like an agonist whereas during high baseline activity the partial agonist will appear to act a little bit more like an antagonist. The effects of the partial agonist can be seen in mouse behaviour in which mice that are habituated to the test environment and therefore have reduced dopamine levels show an increase in activity in response to the partial agonist CY208243; however, in the naive animal that has never experienced a test environment before, when dopamine levels are presumably high there is no effect of the partial agonist (Chandler et al., 1990) (Figure 7.5.1).

The clinical utility of a partial agonist can be seen in the treatment of nicotine dependence. The partial agonist **varenicline** occupies nicotinic receptors and exerts a limited efficacy whilst preventing nicotine from acting at those receptors (Rollema et al., 2007) (Figure 7.5.2). This means that the person trying to give up smoking has some activation of nicotine receptors, thus avoiding withdrawal, but the drug also prevents any top-up smoking from interacting with nicotine receptors.

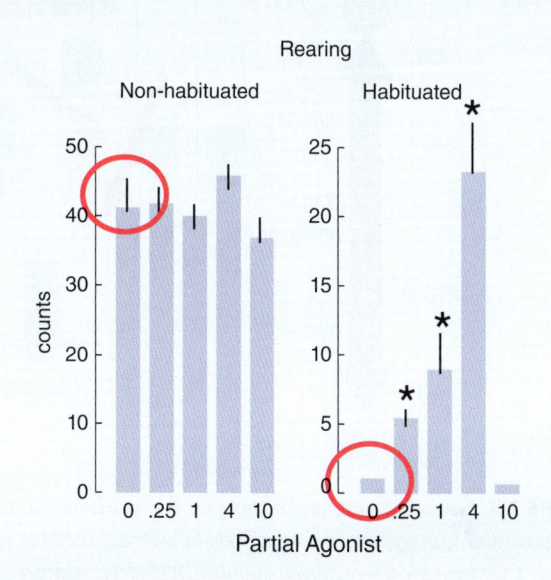

FIGURE 7.5.1 *The effects of habituation on the behavioural effects of a DA receptor partial agonist. The effects of the drug are only seen when the animal has been pre-exposed to the test environment and the baselines of behaviour are low.*

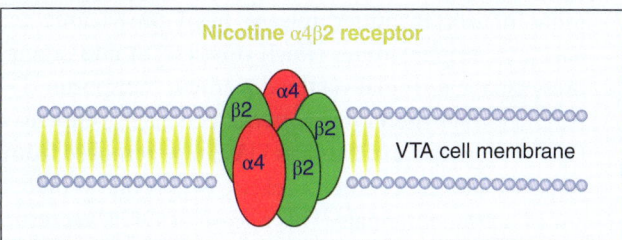

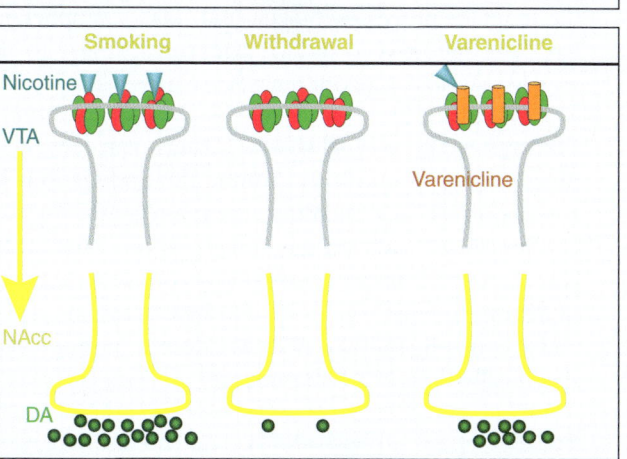

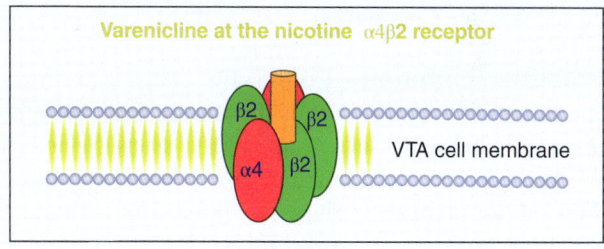

FIGURE 7.5.2 *The effects of varenicline.*

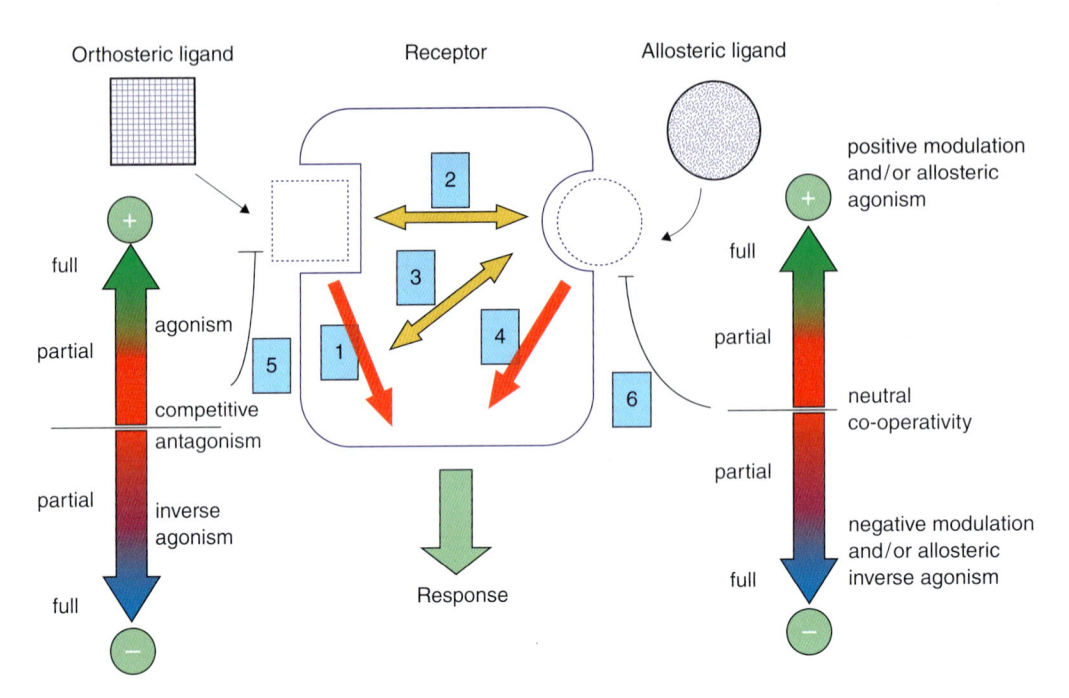

FIGURE 7.9 *Inverse agonists and orthosteric and allosteric modulation. Orthosteric and allosteric ligands bind to distinct sites on a receptor. Both can positively or negatively influence signalling, either on their own or by modulating each other's affinity and/or efficacy. 1. Orthosteric full or partial agonism or inverse agonism. 2. Affinity modulation (positive or negative). 3. Efficacy modulation (positive or negative). 4. Allosteric agonism or inverse agonism. 5. Neutral binding to the orthosteric site – competitive antagonism. 6. Neutral binding to the allosteric site.*
Source: Urwyler, S. (2011). Allosteric modulation of family C G-protein-coupled receptors: From molecular insights to therapeutic perspectives. *Pharmacological Reviews, 63*(1), 59–126. Reproduced by permission of ASPECT.

This method is not always appropriate and has only limited success (see Chapter 24).

Synthesis inhibition Conversely, drugs can interrupt and inhibit synthesis, thus preventing a neurotransmitter from being made (e.g. alpha-MPT stops the action of tyrosine hydroxylase and therefore DA (and noradrenaline) cannot be made). There is limited deployment of such drugs in a clinical setting but they have been used in combination with other drugs, for example in the treatment of depression with metyrapone, a cortisol synthesis inhibitor (Sigalas et al., 2012), which has been found to block the recall of emotional memories in healthy participants (Marin et al., 2011).

Storage prevention Once synthesized, drugs can prevent the neurotransmitter from being stored in the vesicle (e.g. reserpine makes monoamine vesicles 'leaky'). Just as a tea bag allows the flavour to flood out into the water, monoamines flood out into the cytoplasm of the cell. Once in the cytoplasm, the monoamines are metabolized. Reserpine was once used as a treatment for schizophrenia (Bleuler & Stoll, 1955), reducing DA levels, but it has also been used to induce the symptoms of depression in animals (see Skalisz et al., 2002).

Enhance neurotransmitter release Drugs can promote neurotransmitter release from presynaptic terminals, e.g. amphetamine which mimics DA and enters the presynspatic terminal via the dopamine transporter (DAT). Amphetamine therefore has two effects: (1) it competes with DA for reuptake and thus less DA can be removed from the synapse, and (2) it causes a release of DA that is independent of action potentials. This release of DA is via reversing the reuptake processes (Sulzer et al., 2005). Amphetamine has been reported to induce symptoms similar to those seen in paranoid schizophrenia (see Chapter 21).

Postsynaptic stimulation Drugs can act at the postsynaptic receptor and mimic the endogenous neurotransmitters, e.g. nicotine acts at a receptor for acetylcholine (ACh), called a nicotinic receptor. This receptor was discovered using nicotine as a tool to locate its site of action (Luetje et al., 1990). However, nicotine is not an endogenous ligand like ACh; we do not have a receptor specifically designed for smoking.

Postsynaptic antagonism As mentioned earlier, drugs can be antagonists. A drug can act at the postsynaptic receptor to block the action of endogenous neurotransmitters (an antagonist) (e.g. the antipsychotic

Drugs inactivate synthesis
- Stop synthesis and turnover of neurotransmitter e.g. αMPT activation of DOPA dehydroxylase

(Tyrosine hydroxylase) DOPA (DOPA decarboxylase) ← Administer αMPT to stop DA synthesis

Drugs acting as a precursor
- Enhance synthesis and turnover of neurotransmitter e.g. L-DOPA therapy in Parkinson's disease (PD)

Tyrosine → (Tyrosine hydroxylase) DOPA (DOPA decarboxylase) DA ← Administer DOPA to make DA in Parkinson's disease

Drugs block metabolism
- Drugs prevent the neurotransmitter being metabolized e.g. Machobenide (Manerix) Monoamine oxidase inhibitor (MAO) increases synaptically available aminoamines (NA) which add to the approach of depression

Block MAO with an inhibitor

Drugs preventing storage
- Vesicle cannot contain neurotransmitter e.g. neurone makes vesicle membrane leaky metabolized in exoplasm

DA leaks out of vesicle in response to reserpine administration. Metabolized by MAO

Drugs block reuptake
- Drugs act at the reuptake carrier to prevent the neurotransmitter being removed from the synapse e.g. Cocaine blocks DA receptor

Cocaine ▲

Drugs promoting release
- Neurotransmitter release from presynaptic terminal e.g. amphetamine

DA released in response to amphetamine

Drugs stimulate or block autoreceptors
- Drugs act at the autoreceptors to provide false feedback on synaptic activity

Stop DA release | Increase DA release

microtubules, vesicles, Monoamine oxidase (MAO), neurotransmitter, Postsynaptic receptors, Reuptake carrier, Autoreceptor

Drugs stimulate postsynaptically
- Drugs act at the postsynaptic receptor to mimic endogenous transmitter e.g. Nicotine at ACh receptor

Nicotine ▼ acts directly at the receptor

Drugs block postsynaptically
- Drugs act at the postsynaptic receptor to block the action of endogenous transmitter e.g. Clozapine at DA receptor

Clozapine blocks the receptor

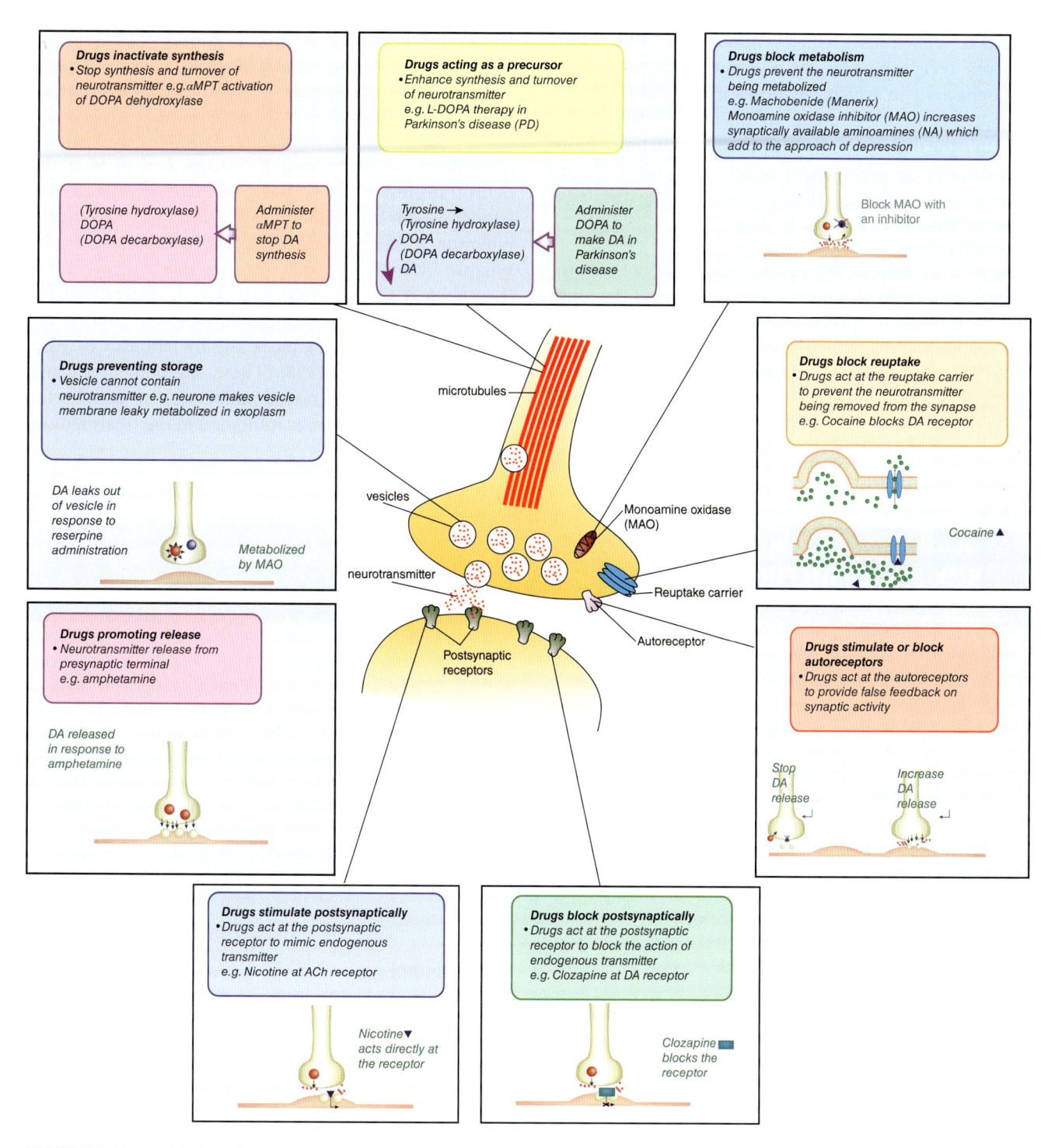

FIGURE 7.10 Modulation of neurotransmission by drugs.

haloperidol blocks DA D2 receptors and thus stops DA interacting with these receptors; see Chapter 21).

Autoreceptor stimulation and antagonism Drugs can act at the autoreceptor to provide false feedback on synaptic activity (e.g. the dopamine receptor agonist apomorphine at low doses stimulates the DA autoreceptor to reduce the release of DA) (Aghajanian & Bunney, 1977). Conversely, the DA antagonist haloperidol increases DA. This would appear counterintuitive, as its task is to stop DA activity and reduce the symptoms of schizophrenia (see above and Chapter 21 for haloperidol's therapeutic target). The selective stimulation of the autoreceptor in low doses of apomorphine has different behavioural effects to higher doses which continue to stimulate postsynaptic receptors. This has been seen in mouse climbing behaviour in which low doses inhibit climbing and high doses increase climbing (Kendler et al., 1982). In this example the dopaminergic autoreceptor is 10 times more sensitive than its postsynaptic counterpart, and therefore at low doses acts preferentially to provide negative feedback via the autoreceptor (White & Wang, 1984).

Drugs that block reuptake The level of neurotransmitter can be elevated by drugs that act at the reuptake transporter to prevent the neurotransmitter being removed from the synapse (blocking the metabolic escape route), e.g. cocaine and methylphenidate (Ritalin) block the DA transporter and thus increase DA in the synapse because it cannot escape and be deactivated (Volkow, Wang, Fowler, Fischman et al., 1999). This is also how the antidepressant fluoxetine (Prozac) initially works, but specifically at 5-HT transporters; hence it is referred to as a selective serotonin reuptake inhibitor (SSRI) (Wong et al., 1974) (see Chapter 22).

Inhibition of metabolism Drugs can prevent the neurotransmitter from being metabolized (e.g. the antidepressant moclobemide is a monoamine oxidase inhibitor (MAOI)). MAOIs increase monoamines in the synapse by inhibiting the enzymes that degrade them (Lecrubier & Guelfi, 1990). The only drugs available for the treatment of Alzheimer's disease (e.g. donepezil) act in a similar way to block the metabolism of ACh (Shintani & Uchida, 1997). These anti-dementia drugs are called anticholinesterase inhibitors. See Box 7.6 for a further use of metabolic inhibition in the treatment of alcoholism.

BOX 7.6: DISULFIRAM

It is very difficult to treat alcoholism. One method is to interfere with the metabolic pathway. Disulfiram (Antabuse) blocks acetaldehyde dehydrogenase which causes an excess build-up of acetaldehyde, leading to a particularly unpleasant reaction (Figure 7.6.1).

- Flushing
- Nausea
- Copious vomiting
- Sweating
- Thirst
- Throbbing in the head and neck
- Throbbing headache
- Respiratory difficulty
- Chest pain
- Palpitations
- Dyspnoea
- Hyperventilation
- Tachycardia
- Hypotension
- Syncope
- Marked uneasiness
- Weakness
- Vertigo
- Blurred vision
- Confusion

The alcoholic therefore avoids drinking alcohol because of this unpleasant reaction. Hopefully, as time goes by, the alcoholic will avoid alcohol altogether – easier said than done. The effect is similar to that experienced by certain Oriental Asians who have a polymorphism at the ALDH2 gene which means they cannot process alcohol and therefore get a similar response. Having such a gene is protective against alcoholism (Couzigou et al., 1994; Muramatsu et al., 1995; Thomasson et al., 1993).

Disulfiram

By blocking acetaldehyde dehydrogenase there is an excess build-up of acetaldehyde

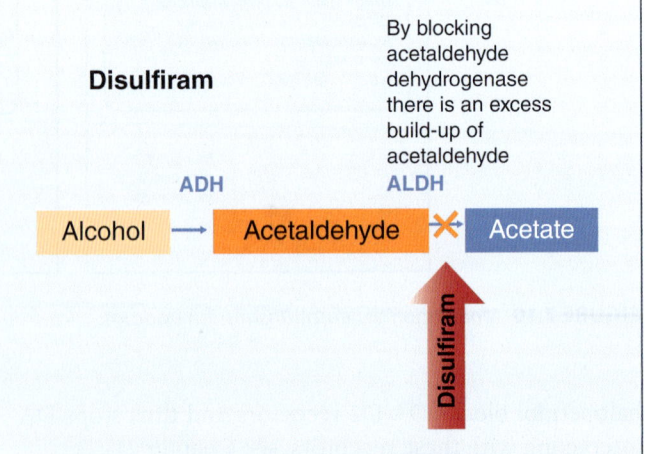

Alcohol —ADH→ Acetaldehyde —✗→ Acetate
↑ Disulfiram (ALDH)

FIGURE 7.6.1 *The metabolic pathway of alcohol and the action of disulfiram to aid alcohol abstinence. ADH, alcohol dehydrogenase; ALDH, aldehyde dehydrogenase.*

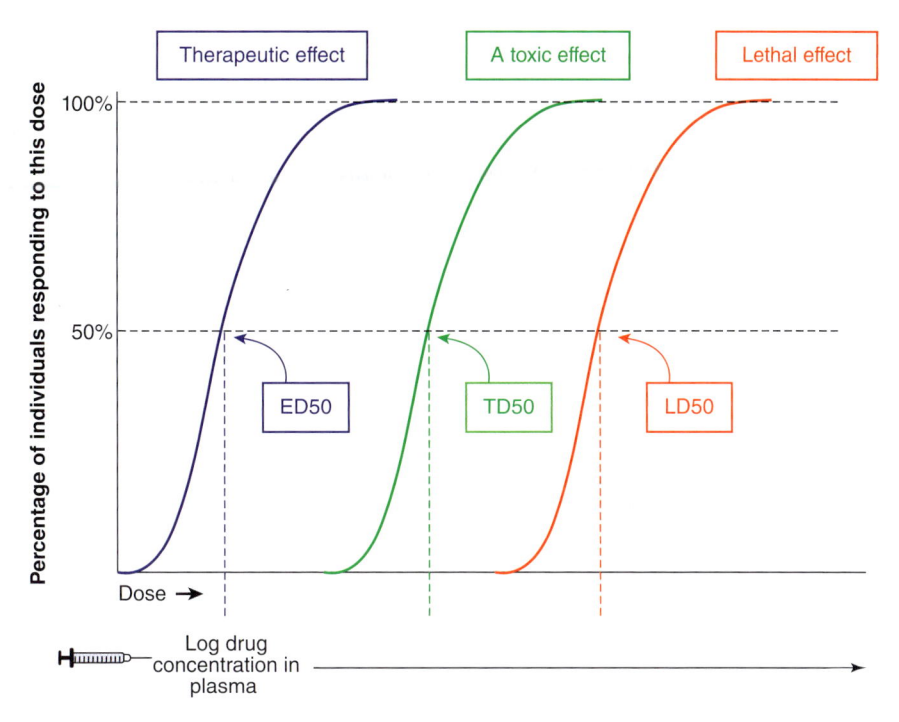

FIGURE 7.11 Dose–response curves.

To evaluate the effect of a drug, the psychopharmacologist will administer different doses. A dose–response curve will be generated which can describe the biological or behavioural effect of the drug. When the dose–response curve is plotted on a log scale, the curve takes an S shape in which low doses have little effect and increasingly high doses do not produce even greater effects as they reach asymptote (in behavioural terms, the maximal effect). It is important to use a dose–response curve because it shows the different behavioural effects that the drug can have at different doses. If just one fixed dose was taken then one might jump to the wrong conclusion about its effect.

Dose–response curves permit the identification of the following (Figure 7.11).

- **Potency** – amount of drug needed to get the effect; compare ED_{50}
- **Efficacy** – the maximum effect – ED_{100}

Traditionally the measures of doses take the form of ED_{50}s.

- **ED_{50}** – the dose that produces half the maximum effect – effective dose, e.g it is effective in half the population.
- **TD_{50}** = the dose which is toxic in 50%.
- **LD_{50}** = the dose which is lethal in 50%. We shall not be considering this in psychobiology.

It is possible to trace where the drug goes and to see how it competes with other drugs for occupancy of the receptor. This is done by labelling a drug or neurotransmitter with a radioactive isotope that can be detected using machines such as PET scanners, e.g. dopamine labelled with the radioactive isotope tritium is [^{3}H]-dopamine. Other radioactive isotopes include [^{14}C] and [^{125}I] (carbon and iodine respectively). Using these radioactive drugs, the scientist can measure the number of receptors (Bmax) and the **affinity** of the receptor (Kd) (see Figure 7.12).

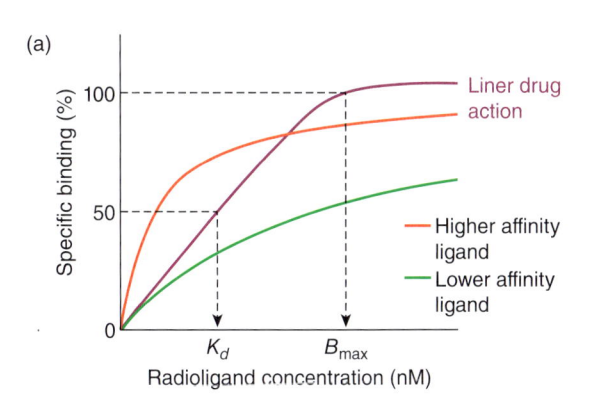

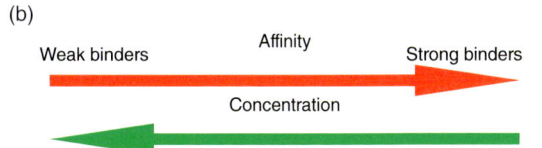

FIGURE 7.12 *Affinity and binding to a receptor. (a) The affinity of a receptor (Kd) is the percentage of maximum amount of binding to receptors (Bmax). (b) Strong binding need less concentration and vice versa.*

Drug–receptor affinity

The chemical structure of a drug may differ only slightly from that of another drug, but this can alter the magnitude of response. A drug exists in two mirror images of itself called stereo-isomers which are labelled with the prefixes *d = dextro* (right) and *l = levo* (left), e.g. *d*-amphetamine is the active isomer of racemic amphetamine. Isomers are the molecules of identical atomic compositions, but with different bonding arrangements of atoms and are mirror images of each other (think of the image generated in a mirror; the same image is seen but it is reversed – a left hand placed at 90° to a mirror looks like a right hand). They are commonly called **enantiomers** (enantio = opposite, morph = form). Single enantiomers have less complex and more selective pharmacodynamic profiles compared to racemic mixtures (both enantiomers). This has important ramifications because the single enantiomers may have reduced adverse drug reactions and improved therapeutic response, e.g. R-thalidomide is sedative while S-thalidomide has known teratogenic effects (Chhabra et al., 2013). Adderall™ is a combination of amphetamine isomers, in which the predominant isomer is *d*-amphetamine with *l*-amphetamine only making up 19% of the drug. Adderall comes in immediate- and extended-release formulations, the latter providing symptom relief for the day. The *d*-isomer of amphetamine is thought to be twice as potent as the *l*-isomer on DA reuptake and release (Holmes & Rutledge, 1976). The *l*-isomer was twice as potent at stimulating NA release in the cortex (Easton et al., 2007b). It was also found to have a more widespread effect in the rat brain, which the authors link to different behavioural effects (Easton et al., 2007a).

Thus, by increasing the pharmacological precision of a drug, the target can be more precise occupancy of receptors in the brain. Not only is this important in terms of clinical efficacy, it also provides the scientist with more refined tools for probing the brain.

The affinity (Kd) of a drug can be measured as the percentage amount of drug that binds to the receptor (Bmax) according to a concentration; thus the steeper the curve in Figure 7.12, the higher the affinity.

Multiple sites of drug action

What the scientist requires is precision tools but sometimes a drug's multiple sites of action may be of therapeutic benefit. Often in discussions about a particular drug's action, one can be forgiven for thinking that the drug has one *modus operandi*. Drugs often act at more than one site. This can lead to increased therapeutic efficacy, e.g. the anti-schizophrenic drug clozapine acts on DA, 5-HT and glutamate systems to be clinically effective (see Chapter 21). Multiple sites may be required for the pharmacotherapy of Alzheimer's disease; because so much goes wrong in the brains of these patients, one target is not sufficient (see Chapter 24). However, multiple sites of action can also contribute to neurotoxicity and adverse effects (Box 7.7). The action of drugs, other than at the desired target, can lead to side-effects. As time passes

---

BOX 7.7: THE AGONY OF ECSTASY: LONG-TERM EFFECTS OF MDMA

There is controversy surrounding the effects of **MDMA** (ecstasy) on the brain. MDMA releases DA and 5-HT (Johnson et al., 1986). The initial release of 5-HT is followed by depletion (Green et al., 1995). The acute behavioural effects of MDMA are well known, e.g. positive mood (Parrott, 2001). MDMA fits the criteria of an abuse drug as it is self-administered (see Schenk (2009) for review), and produces a conditioned place preference (Schechter, 1991), acts as a discriminative stimulus (Schechter, 1988) and induces locomotor sensitization (Kalivas et al., 1998). However, it is the long-term neurotoxicity of MDMA that is the main cause for concern. Controversy surrounds this area and highlights the need for high levels of organization in the manufacturing laboratory.

In 2002 in the prestigious journal *Science*, George Ricaurte and colleagues published their findings indicating dopaminergic neurotoxicity after MDMA. The paper linked ecstasy with a potential for inducing Parkinson's disease. Understandably, this received a large amount of media attention – users were putting themselves at potential risk of brain damage. This view was queried in the same journal (Mithoefer et al., 2003). In response, Ricaurte provided a retraction of the original paper, suggesting that the bottles of MDMA had been mixed up with methamphetamine which is known to be a dopaminergic neurotoxin (Ricaurte et al., 2003). Such mistakes can be damaging to the public perception of science and also play into the hands of the conspiracy theorists suggesting that scientists are not independent from political forces.

However, no such controversy surrounds the serotonergic neurotoxicity of MDMA (Benningfield & Cowan, 2013; Parrott, 2013). In a series of studies by Ricaurte et al. with the correct drug (Finnegan et al., 1988; Ricaurte et al., 1988), it was demonstrated that MDMA administration results in neurodegeneration of 5-HT terminals. Using PET scans in humans, McCann et al. (1994) found a decreased global and regional reduction in 5-HT transporters in the brain. Reports on the behavioural consequences of MDMA neurotoxicity have been published. Serotonin is implicated in sexual activity, sleep, pain, circadian and seasonal rhythms, affective behaviours, motor activity and body temperature. It is particularly linked to depression (see Chapter 22). Studies have demonstrated that MDMA users had lower scores on measures of impulsivity and indirect hostility (McCann et al., 1994) and memory (Parrott et al., 1998). They also had low mood problems after drug use (Curran & Travill, 1997) and MDMA use has been linked to depression (Roiser & Sahakian, 2004) which could last up to one year (Taurah et al., 2014). Brain imaging studies have also supported a role of serotonergic dysfunction in depression and MDMA users (Salomon & Cowan, 2013).

Whilst the studies on dopamine were founded on a false premise, dopamine does have a role in neurotoxicity. Blockade of dopamine prevented MDMA-induced neurotoxicity (Schmidt et al., 1990) and dopamine agonists (L-dopa) enhanced serotonergic deficits (Johnson et al., 1991; Schmidt et al., 1991). Thus, the interaction of dopamine with serotonergic mechanisms increases the likelihood of neurotoxicity.

There are methodological problems associated with studying the consequences of MDMA use. Most users do not take just MDMA; they may take other drugs such as ketamine or cannabis. However, many studies account for the polydrug use and still find a long-term psychological effect of MDMA (Roiser & Sahakian, 2004; Taurah & Chandler, 2003; Taurah et al., 2014). MDMA is illegal, therefore the recruitment of participants is difficult. Those who volunteer may be different in some way from those who do not wish to participate. The illegal nature of MDMA means that one cannot determine accurate details of drug taking. People do not know how much of the drug they are taking and what other drugs it may be combined with (e.g. amphetamine). Ethical considerations mean that controlled studies are not permitted in the human population. Of course, this is not unique to MDMA. Research into the effects of other illegal drugs is limited by such variables.

A conclusive answer accounting for the long-term effects of MDMA is yet to be found. In the rat the effects of MDMA persist for some time after discontinuation of the drug (Mayerhofer et al., 2001). In a human case study it was found that even after seven years of abstinence there were neuropsychological problems evident after MDMA use (Soar et al., 2004) which can be extended to a large cohort study of MDMA and polydrug users (Taurah et al., 2014).

and MDMA users grow older, the effects may start to become increasingly apparent. These reports allude to a future danger. The high derived from ecstasy may well give way to depression in later years.

Side-effects The side-effects of drugs can sometimes be prohibitive. It may be considered preferable to have the disorder rather than the side-effects attributed to the drugs. One of the quests of the pharmaceutical industry is to find therapeutic drugs (which they already have) with minimal side-effects. By increasing the tolerability of the drugs, the patient is more likely to take them. The blood distribution network leads to those drugs that we consume entering the brain and interacting with many regions (as we have just seen, this can be beneficial). To use military terminology, whilst the therapeutic target is hit by the drug, the drug also produces collateral damage, e.g. it affects other parts of the brain where the effect is undesirable, e.g. the side-effects produced by antipsychotic agents often give rise to motor problems similar to that of Parkinson's disease (see Chapters 21 and 24). Whilst side-effects can be a problem for the clinician and patient, they can be informative to the scientist – they may tell us new facts about the brain.

TYPES OF DRUGS

There are many types of drugs and it is beyond the scope of this book to consider them all. However, there are a number of drugs that serve as good examples of psychopharmacology in action.

Stimulants

Psychostimulants include cocaine, the amphetamines, nicotine and caffeine.

Cocaine is now a controlled substance but was once an ingredient in Coca-Cola. It is a dopamine transporter (DAT) antagonist and requires an action potential to release dopamine before it can be effective (Carboni et al., 1989). Cocaine blocks the DAT, thereby preventing reuptake of dopamine into the synapse; if it cannot be taken up, it stays in the synapse, remaining available to stimulate receptors. A similar mechanism can be seen for the drug used to treat ADHD – methylphenidate (see Chapter 20). Cocaine is a known abused drug that is considered in more detail in Chapter 16.

Like cocaine, amphetamine is a controlled substance but was once freely available and used to treat asthma and as a general stimulant. It is currently used in the treatment of narcolepsy and ADHD, but is also used by the military to keep personnel awake and alert. Amphetamine works by increasing the dopamine release from the presynaptic neuron. Amphetamine mimics DA and enters the presynspatic terminal via the DAT. This has two effects: it competes with DA for reuptake and thus less DA can be removed from the synapse; and it causes a release of DA that is independent of action potentials (Carboni et al., 1989). Further release of DA is via reversing the reuptake processes (Sulzer et al., 2005). Again the net effect is to flood the synapse with dopamine.

Nicotine is also a psychostimulant with a rich history and is the main psychoactive component in tobacco. Nicotine, unlike cocaine and amphetamine, is freely available albeit with some restrictions. Nicotine acts at ACh receptors that have been named nicotine receptors. It is activation of these receptors that underlies the addictive nature of smoking (Stolerman & Jarvis, 1995). Stimulation of nicotine receptors on the ventral tegmental area means that nicotine facilitates the release of dopamine in a similar manner to that of amphetamine (Nisell et al., 1994a, 1994b).

Caffeine is perhaps the most widely consumed psychoactive agent in the world. Nearly every street corner now has a coffee shop. Caffeine has multiple effects which include the blockade of benzodiazepines at GABA A receptors (Shi et al., 2003), the stimulation of calcium release (McPhersonx et al., 1991) and the blockade of adenosine receptors (Daly et al., 1983). Adenosine acts as an inhibitory neurotransmitter in the CNS and caffeine's antagonism accounts for the excitatory actions of coffee (Dunwiddie & Masino, 2001). If one thinks the effects of caffeine are benign because of its availability, study Figure 7.13 which shows the effects of caffeine and other drugs on the integrity of the spider's web; you might

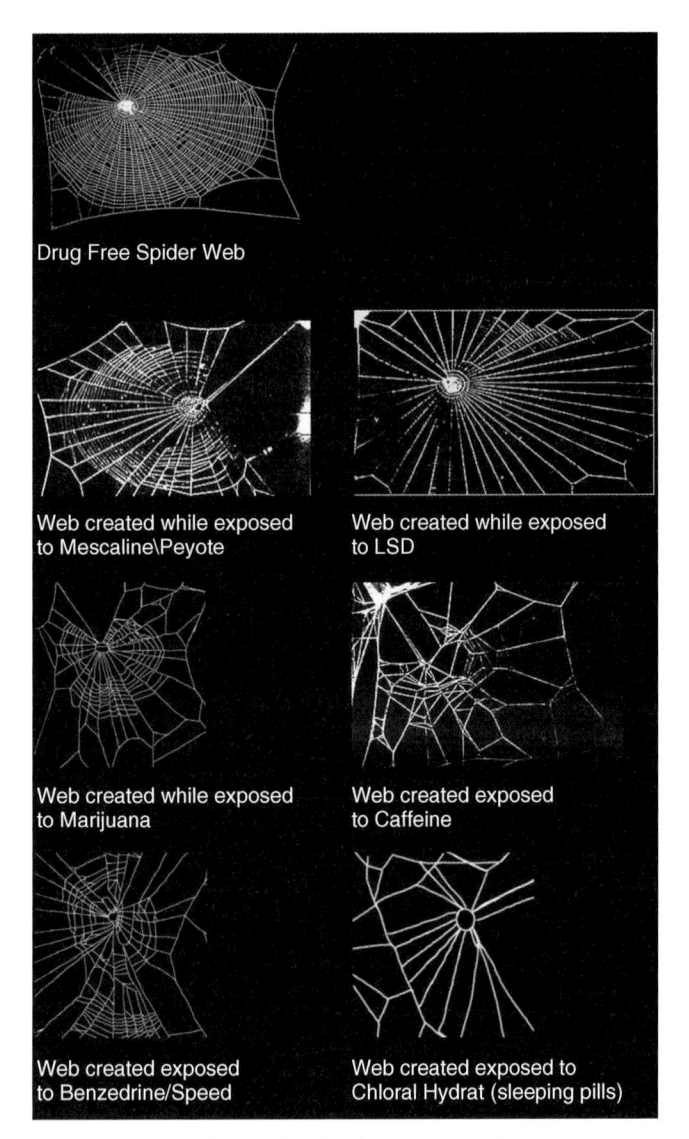

FIGURE 7.13 *Spider's webs after drug consumption.*
Source: Wiit, P. N., & Rovner, J. S. (1982). *Spider communication: Mechanisms and ecological significance*. Princeton, NJ: Princeton University Press. Reprinted by permission of Princeton University Press.

wish to think twice before taking energy drinks prior to an exam.

Depressants

Opioids

Opioids are drugs that interact with endogenous neuropeptides that have evolved to manage pain relief (see Chapter 10). Opiates (derived from the opium poppy) are CNS depressants and produce postsynaptic, axoaxonic and presynaptic inhibition (Waldhoer et al., 2004). Perhaps the most well known of the opiates is **heroin**, but one should not consider this in isolation or simply in the context of addiction. It has also had a long history in which it was used to suppress coughs. Heroin (diacetylmorphine) crosses the blood–brain barrier rapidly (morphine crosses more slowly). Heroin is referred to as a prodrug because it is broken down into an active drug when it is converted to morphine. Heroin makes more **morphine** in the brain thus it is 3–4 times more potent. More detail on opiates and opiate receptors can be seen in Chapter 10.

Alcohol

Alcohol, like nicotine, is readily available but with some restrictions. Alcohol also has a long history and drunkenness and alcoholism are not new phenomena. Alcohol is the centre of many people's social life and is firmly entrenched in western society. To remove it can have serious consequences as America found out during prohibition.

Alcohol is a complex molecule that has a wide spectrum of activity but the net effect is CNS depression. The effects of alcohol are also dose dependent with disinhibition and euphoria being characteristic of low doses and impairment of numerous cognitive and motor functions being prevalent upon consumption of higher doses. Alcohol has widespread effects across many regions of the brain (Oscar-Berman & Marinkovic, 2007) and operates on multiple sites (Vengeliene et al., 2008):

- neuronal membranes;
- ion channels;
- enzymes; and
- receptors.

Alcohol binds directly to numerous receptors including:

- serotonin;
- ACh;
- GABA; and
- glutamate.

The action of alcohol at these different sites leads to different behavioural responses (Table 7.1). At the glutamatergic NMDA receptor, alcohol is an inhibitor, thus reducing excitation, and is linked with physical dependence, withdrawal and behavioural disinhibition. At the GABA A receptor, alcohol facilitates the inhibitory effects of GABA and is associated with developing tolerance. Restoration of the balance between GABA and glutamate underlies the use of the drug acamprosate in the treatment of alcoholism (Boothby & Doering, 2005). The anxiolytic and sedative properties and feeling sick may also be attributed to alcohol's action at 5-HT3 receptors.

TABLE 7.1 Alcohol's psychopharmacology

Subjective experience	Transmitter/receptor
Euphoria/pleasure	Dopamine, opioids
Anxiolytic/ataxia	↑GABA
Sedation/amnesia	↑GABA + ↓NMDA
Nausea	5-HT3
Withdrawal	↑GABA, ↓NMDA

Many of those who drink alcohol will be familiar with the next day effects of excessive consumption (Wiese et al., 2000). The mechanisms by which alcohol causes a hangover the following day are poorly understood but include (Penning et al., 2010):

- dehydration;
- electrolyte imbalance;
- gastrointestinal disturbances;
- low blood sugar;
- sleep disturbances;
- withdrawal;
- immune factors;
- acetaldehyde toxicity as a result of alcohol metabolism; and
- the effects of non-alcohol compounds such as methanol.

The damaging effects of alcohol on the individual and society are both direct and indirect and have led scientists to suggest that if it was introduced to the world today, it would be a prohibited substance.

Anxiolytics

Drugs used to treat anxiety are also CNS depressants. Early drugs such as the barbiturates were shown to have sedative qualities and relaxant properties. However, overdose was a problem and could lead to death. The action of these drugs focuses on the GABA receptor. GABA is an inhibitory amino acid and when activated produces CNS depression via noradrenaline, dopamine, serotonin and ACh. It is the GABA A receptor that mediates the anxiolytic effects of the drugs. Barbiturates potentiate GABA actions but also inhibit the excitatory amino acid glutamate. The net effect is to inhibit excitatory postsynaptic potentials (EPSPs) and enhance inhibitory postsynaptic potentials (IPSPs). In the 1960s a new type of drug, chlordiazepoxide or Librium, was discovered to be useful in anxiety and shortly after, the infamous **diazepam** (Valium) became available. Both these drugs are considered to be benzodiazepine agonists. The **benzodiazepine receptor** complex exists on GABA A receptors.

By interacting with the GABA A receptor, the benzodiazepine receptor can facilitate synaptic inhibition. For a more detailed review see Chapter 23.

Mind-Altering Drugs

Hallucinogens

Hallucinogenic drugs are mind-altering drugs that lead to perceptual and cognitive alterations. **Hallucinogens** are typified by LSD but also include **mescaline** (from the peyote cactus) and **psilocybin** (magic mushrooms). Albert Hofmann synthesized **D-lysergic diethylamide** (LSD) in 1938 (see Hofmann, 2013). Hofmann accidentally took LSD and experienced vertigo, restlessness, optical distortions, dream-like state, feelings akin to drunkenness, kaleidoscope of colours and an exaggerated imagination. All of which was regarded as pleasant. Hofmann continued with the scientific pursuit of LSD and took a larger dose which produced disassociation and hallucinations. He also noted the psychedelic effects of psilocybin (Hofmann et al., 1958). Psilocybin, LSD and mescaline all have serotonergic effects (Haigler & Aghajanian, 1973; Tyls et al., 2014). Interestingly, unlike other drugs that are misused/abused, LSD is not self-administered by the animal in an operant chamber and was considered to be a negative reinforcer, in which operant behaviour organized around avoiding LSD (Hoffmeister, 1975).

The effects of LSD and other hallucinogenics on serotonin systems are extensive and diverse (Nichols, 2004). The main focus of these drugs is on the 5-HT2A receptor (Halberstadt & Geyer, 2011) in which LSD acts as an agonist (Aghajanian & Haigler, 1974). Antagonists of the 5-HT2A receptor, e.g. ritanserin, are able to block the effects of LSD (Colpaert et al., 1985), therefore giving greater credibility to the 5-HT2A hypothesis of LSD and LSD-like drugs.

Another group of psychedelic drugs focus on glutamate as their place of action: **ketamine** and **phencyclidine** (PCP). Both of these drugs were used for their anaesthetic qualities but both have trance-like qualities (Morgan & Curran, 2012; Sioris & Krenzelok, 1978). PCP has been used to generate an animal model of schizophrenia (see Chapter 21) (Jentsch & Roth, 1999). The pharmacological action of both PCP and ketamine is to provide non-competitive antagonism of the glutamatergic NMDA receptor (see Paoletti & Neyton, 2007). Depending upon the dose of ketamine, it was found to either increase glutamate outflow in the prefrontal cortex (PFC) or at high doses decreased glutamate outflow (Moghaddam et al., 1997). An increase in glutamate in response to ketamine was correlated with changes in behaviour (Stone et al., 2012). The NMDA receptor has been a particularly important receptor to study as it has given considerable insight into neural plasticity and learning (see Chapter 13).

Cannabinoids

Cannabis has a long history dating back many centuries, but in recent history has been a political pawn for those who wish to see legislation increased and those who wish to see decriminalization or legalization. The main active constituent of cannabis is the **Cannabinoid-Δ⁹-tetrahydrocannabinol** (THC) (Isbell et al., 1967). THC is the common denominator in many forms of cannabis and its behavioural effects are well documented (Green et al., 2003).

Cannabis has been used to further our understanding of neural mechanisms. The identification of a cannabinoid receptor provided the first insight into the mechanisms of cannabis (Devane et al., 1988). The distribution of cannabis receptors is widespread, involving cortical and subcortical regions, although they are not present in the brainstem nuclei (therefore not lethal in excess) (Herkenham et al., 1990). The question may arise, why have an **endocannabinoid** system? How has evolution shaped its necessity? The answer may lie in the modulation of a number of neurotransmitters (see Chapter 4), thus modifying a number of behaviours such as pain and stress (Di Marzo et al., 2004; Hohmann et al., 2005; Piomelli, 2003). The discovery of endocannabinoids supports the evolutionary importance of the system rather than it being an artefact of drug administration. Two receptors for endocannabinoids have been discovered and are referred to as the CB1 and CB2 receptors (see Pertwee, 2006) (Figure 7.14). Cannabinoid receptors are

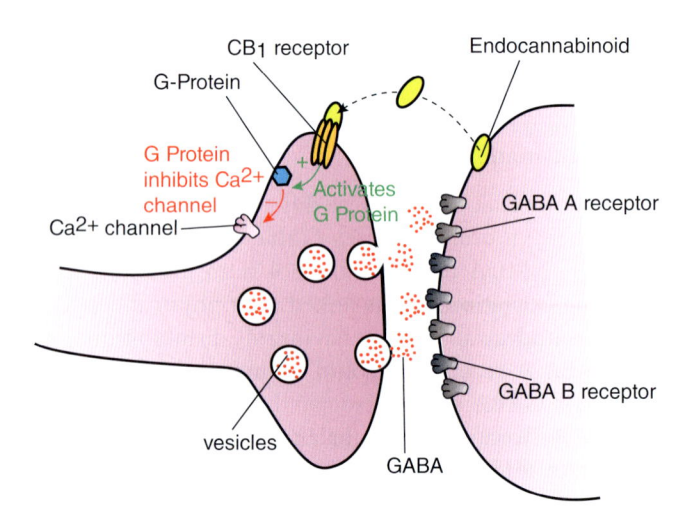

FIGURE 7.14 *Cannabis influences GABA (and glutamate) neurotransmission. ⁹-tetrahydrocannabinol (THC) interacts with the CB1 receptor on a GABA neuron.*

metabotropic receptors linked to G-proteins and second messengers. The CB1 receptor is the main protagonist in behavioural studies (Mechoulam & Parker, 2013).

Antidepressants

Antidepressants typically fall into the following categories:

- **tricyclic antidepressants (TCA);**
- **monoamine oxidase inhibitors (MAOI);**
- **selective serotonin reuptake inhibitors (SSRI); and**
- **selective noradrenergic reuptake inhibitors (SNRI).**

The use of these drugs has been instrumental in understanding depression. However, as demonstrated in Chapter 22, the antidepressants have given rise to multiple hypotheses regarding the pathogenesis of depression and also reveal the complexities of the disorder. In addition to these main types of antidepressants there is also lithium bicarbonate that is used in the treatment of bipolar disorder (formerly known as manic depression).

Antipsychotics

Antipsychotic agents are used to treat schizophrenia and have been essential in the development of a greater understanding of the condition. There are many different types of antipsychotics that are now challenging received wisdom about what goes wrong with the brain in schizophrenia. The predominant view is that all of these drugs have as a common denominator blockade of dopamine receptors. For a more detailed account see Chapter 21.

PSYCHOPHARMACOLOGY – THE DARK SIDE

Psychopharmacology offers hope in the management of clinical disorders but also the posssibility of increasing our understanding of brain mechanisms. However, it is essential to remember that medicine and psychiatry have been guilty of abusing their position. One only has to read the accounts of what happened during World War II, with the Nazi use of medicine to justify their policies, to realize how science and medicine can be severely misused (Lopez-Munoz et al., 2007). Under the Nazi regime, captives and mentally ill patients were forced to participate in studies which ended in their death so their brains could be evaluated. Psychopharmacological studies were conducted using many drugs, e.g. methamphetamine, mescaline and phenobarbital. The significance of these atrocities cannot be overestimated as after the Nuremberg trials of the doctors involved, the **Nuremberg Code** of medical ethics was created (Annas and Grodin, 1992; Shuster, 1997) (Box 7.8). The **Declaration of Helsinki** took

---

BOX 7.8: THE NUREMBERG CODE

1. The voluntary consent of the human subject is absolutely essential. This means that the person involved should have legal capacity to give consent; should be so situated as to be able to exercise free power of choice, without the intervention of any element of force, fraud, deceit, duress, overreaching, or other ulterior form of constraint or coercion; and should have sufficient knowledge and comprehension of the elements of the subject matter involved as to enable him to make an understanding and enlightened decision. This latter element requires that before the acceptance of an affirmative decision by the experimental subject there should be made known to him the nature, duration, and purpose of the experiment; the method and means by which it is to be conducted; all inconveniences and hazards reasonably to be expected; and the effects upon his health or person which may possibly come from his participation in the experiment.

   The duty and responsibility for ascertaining the quality of the consent rests upon each individual who initiates, directs or engages in the experiment. It is a personal duty and responsibility which may not be delegated to another with impunity.

2. The experiment should be such as to yield fruitful results for the good of society, unprocurable by other methods or means of study, and not random and unnecessary in nature.
3. The experiment should be so designed and based on the results of animal experimentation and a knowledge of the natural history of the disease or other problem under study that the anticipated results will justify the performance of the experiment.
4. The experiment should be so conducted as to avoid all unnecessary physical and mental suffering and injury.
5. No experiment should be conducted where there is an *a priori* reason to believe that death or disabling injury will occur; except, perhaps, in those experiments where the experimental physicians also serve as subjects.
6. The degree of risk to be taken should never exceed that determined by the humanitarian importance of the problem to be solved by the experiment.
7. Proper preparations should be made and adequate facilities provided to protect the experimental subject against even remote possibilities of injury, disability, or death.
8. The experiment should be conducted only by scientifically qualified persons. The highest degree of skill and care should be required through all stages of the experiment of those who conduct or engage in the experiment.
9. During the course of the experiment the human subject should be at liberty to bring the experiment to an end if he has reached the physical or mental state where continuation of the experiment seems to him to be impossible.
10. During the course of the experiment the scientist in charge must be prepared to terminate the experiment at any stage, if he has probable cause to believe, in the exercise of the good faith, superior skill, and careful judgment required of him, that a continuation of the experiment is likely to result in injury, disability, or death to the experimental subject.

the original points from the Nuremberg Code to provide guidance for medical ethics. The Declaration of Helsinki has undergone many changes since its first creation in 1964. It has been stated that 'The Nuremberg Code focuses on the human rights of research subjects, the Declaration of Helsinki focuses on the obligations of physician-investigators to research subjects' (Shuster, 1997, p.1440). Such guiding principles are essential for psychiatry and psychopharmacology and at the heart of clinical trials.

The use of psychopharmacology can also be seen in bioterrorism (Box 7.9).

BOX 7.9: NERVE AGENTS AND BIOTERRORISM

The world is an increasingly unstable place to live with each warring faction determined to win.

However, disputes between groups may not use traditional methods of fighting such as guns and tanks. The use of biological agents is not new in war, but bioterrorism is now regarded as a significant threat.

Nerve agents such as **sarin** have the effect of preventing acetylcholine esterase from metabolizing ACh (Khan et al., 2000) (Figure 7.9.1). The net effect of exposure to sarin is an increase in ACh available at the muscarinic and nicotinic receptors (Khan et al., 2000). In the CNS, the behavioural effects are irritability, anxiety, impaired cognition and loss of consciousness (Landauer and Romano, 1984; Sirkka et al., 1990).

The good news is that there are drugs that can negate the effects of nerve agents. Treatment is based on the use of large doses of **atropine** and pralidoxime (Volans, 1996). The bad news is that they need to be delivered quickly to the victim.

Sarin binds to one end of the acetylcholinesterase enzyme, blocking its activity. Pralidoxime is able to attach to the other half (the unblocked, anionic site) of the acetylcholinesterase enzyme. It then binds to the organophosphate, the organophosphate changes conformation and loses its binding to the acetylcholinesterase enzyme. Atropine is a competitive antagonist for the muscarinic acetylcholine receptor.

FIGURE 7.9.1 (a) The effects of sarin on the body. (b) The effects at the neuromuscular junction.

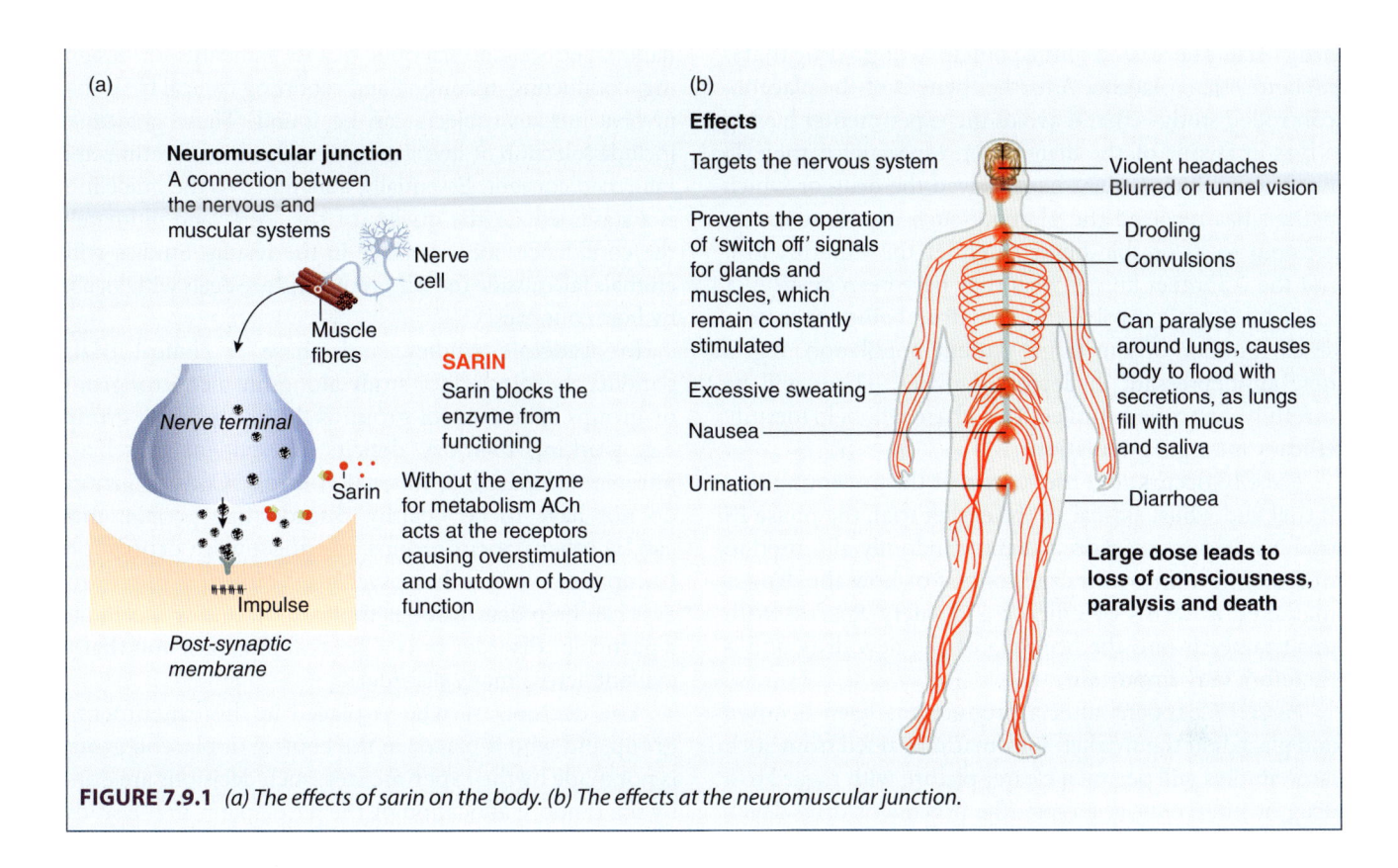

CLINICAL TRIALS

Good science is critical for the understanding of psychobiology; it is also crucial for the development of new treatments. New drugs need testing to ensure they are safe and effective. Before a drug can be used in humans, it has to go through a period of safety evaluation. This can be done in cells that are grown in laboratories and also in live animals.

Once a drug is considered safe enough in incubated cells and animals, it goes to the next stage of development – the clinical trial. **Clinical trials** are divided into four phases (Figure 7.15).

Phase I takes place in a small number of (paid) human volunteers. Small amounts of the novel drug are initially given and if all goes well, the dose is then escalated, and again if all is well then repeated doses can be given. The drug is compared to a placebo, which is an inert substance that does not contain the active ingredients.

Why are placebos used and why are they so important? Placebo effects are complicated and a more detailed account can be obtained elsewhere (see Chapter 9) (Benedetti, 2008b; Crow et al., 1999; Klosterhalfen & Enck, 2006; Price et al., 2008), but essentially the experience of being in a study and receiving attention could have effects in its own right which are quite separate from the

Preclinical	Phase I	Phase II	Phase III	Phase IV
▪ Drug metabolism	▪ First in humans	▪ Initial testing in patients	▪ Testing in wider range of patients	▪ Post-marketing studies
▪ Pharm.	▪ Healthy volunteers	▪ Efficacy	▪ Prove efficacy	▪ Very wide ranging
▪ Toxicology	▪ Safety	▪ Safety	▪ Prove safety	▪ Further evaluation of safety and efficacy
	▪ Tolerability	▪ Dose range		
2 years		6–10 years		
		20 years		

FIGURE 7.15 Phases of a clinical trial. From preclinical to phase IV can take 20 years, which is why drugs are so expensive at first.

drug itself. There is very little point in taking a drug that is no better than placebo. A further benefit of the placebo-controlled study is that it avoids the experimenter having a bias in favour of the drug effect, especially if they do not know which patient has received the drug or which patient has received the placebo (such experiments are referred to as double blind – neither the experimenter nor the volunteer knows what they have been given).

Phase II trials involve the new drug being given to a small number of the target patient population, e.g. a new antidepressant in depressed males. These will be carefully controlled studies. This phase will help identify efficacy in target populations.

Phase III occurs after the success of the previous phase II trial and whilst similar to the earlier trial, the phase III trial involves many more patients randomly allocated to treatment groups within the context of how the drug is marketed in terms of efficacy and safety. Success with this trial feeds into the licensing of the new drug and is therefore very important.

Phase IV happens after a product has been licensed and placed on the market. Information gained from such large studies will permit a clearer picture with regard to a drug or intervention. Despite the process of drug development taking around 12 years, long-term safety is not immediately established in the human population. It is surprisingly difficult to find true long-term evaluations of drug treatment. One of the reasons is that getting people to maintain contact and sustain interest in studies is difficult at the best of times; stretch that out over a number of years and one would have to start off with a very large number of participants to account for natural attrition.

Continuing the collection of drug information in the UK is the *Yellow Card system* which is a process under the auspices of the Medicines and Healthcare products Regulatory Agency (MHRA) which operates a feedback system for drugs that are on the market. The Yellow Card is available for medics and patients to complete and send to the MHRA – and to this extent we are all part of a giant clinical trial if we take a particular drug. One of their aims is to make more information on a particular drug available.

Clinical trials are in the interest of public safety. Given the financial interest of pharmaceutical companies, how can we trust clinical trials? The only way we can trust them is through their publication, demonstrating their good science and replicability. The International Conference on Harmonization of Technical Requirements for Registration of Pharmaceuticals for Human Use (ICH) provides a consensus between European, Japanese and American regulatory authorities on the scientific and technical aspects of drug registration. The ICH lays out what is termed Good Clinical Practice. In a 59-page document, available from the ICH website (http://www.ich.org), details of international ethical and scientific quality standards for designing, conducting, recording and reporting clinical trials that involve human subjects can be found. These guidelines include selection of investigators, trial protocols, ethics and informed consent. Essentially, adherence to the guidelines is a statement of the quality of the work, and ultimately the confidence one can place in the results. Studies with animals fall outside the ICH remit and are dealt with locally by host countries.

In academic studies, and phase II clinical trials, patients are selected for study alongside a control group or groups. The control group is the comparison group, e.g. working memory deficits are evident in schizophrenia compared to normal controls. Control groups do not have to be healthy, disorder-free people; they can be other patient groups, e.g. those with depression. Comparison with other psychiatric groups is important as it can help determine if the result found is specific to a particular disorder or is a general phenomenon that is evident across many disorders.

The decision of who is placed in the experimental group and who is placed in the control or placebo group is not made by the experimenter; such decisions are done by the random allocation of the participants in the study. Hence, we have the **randomized controlled trial** (RCT) that is operated to avoid contamination of experimenter effects of allocation bias, e.g. the most severe cases get the new drug.

Scientists are only human and are open to bias, even when they think they are not. Certain methodological designs aim to minimize such biases. In a **single-blind** experiment, the individual participants do not know what group they are in; they have no prior knowledge or expectation that can influence the data. However, the experimenter is aware of the treatment the participant is to receive and such knowledge can influence the data, albeit unwittingly. In studies that use *good science*, the scientist in direct contact with the participant is unaware of the group to which the participant is assigned. This is common in drug studies where the design of the experiment is said to be **double blind** – neither the experimenter nor participant knows which group they are in. This aspect of scientific work is crucial for the clinical trial or study to be credible. Thus, the **double-blind, randomized, placebo-controlled trial** is the gold standard.

Many studies are multicentre trials which means they take place in many geographically separate locations and the data are pooled at the end; a large number of people are usually involved in such studies.

The success of a clinical trial is somewhat dependent upon the outcome measures. This might appear to be an obvious statement but consider what outcome measures of an asthma drug might be and then consider the outcome measures for heroin addiction. I would imagine for asthma you would have outcome measures such as reducing the number of attacks to zero – this is readily quantified. Considering the heroin user and our knowledge of addiction (see Chapter 16), a noble outcome of treatment might be to stop drug taking; however, the reality is somewhat different. The National Treatment Outcome Research Study (NTORS) looked at changes in drug use, health and criminal behaviour (Gossop et al., 1998). The outcome measures were not about cessation but the reduction in crime, improved health and maintenance in therapy. These were all facets of the addict that could be addressed.

Practising *good science* is not only important for evaluating new drugs or treatments, it is as important for evaluating theoretical accounts of a disorder. Experimentation can either support or refute theories. A publication bias in the literature often means that people try to prove that a theory or hypothesis is correct; the philosopher Karl Popper states that one should always try to refute the theory. If one fails to refute the theory, then there may be some credibility to it (see Popper, 2002). Unfortunately, there is a publication bias in favour of positive results, where the hypothesis is upheld. In fact, when one reads some journal articles, the positive results that seem implicit in the way the article is written are often in stark contrast to the student's experience of finding no effect. Publishers, editors and funding bodies are not interested in experiments that do not show a difference, despite these studies being of equal importance if they are conducted correctly. Scientists are like other members of society and are interested in extending old ideas to new subjects in what the philosopher Kuhn calls extending the paradigm (see Kuhn (2012) for anniversary edition). Furthermore, a political agenda and cultural expectation exert an influence over what science will receive funding, e.g. research into cannabis has only recently started to be funded. Whatever research is funded in turn determines the results that are found and eventually published.

Large amounts of research work can be made into a single sensible account by using meta-analysis. **Meta-analysis** has become more widely used in recent years and consists of an analysis and evaluation of several original research reports; thus it is a study of the studies. Such meta-analyses use many separate research reports to determine if there is an overall effect or not. These are valuable additions on top of the original investigations and make life so much easier in drawing conclusions from the data. Of course, a meta-analysis is only as good as the original studies themselves.

SUMMARY

Drugs can be used to modify behaviour for either clinical reasons or recreational purposes. Acting at the synapse, they can modify neurotransmission that can have a profound effect on all aspects of the individual's psychology: cognitive, perceptual and affective. Whilst taking a drug appears to be a simple activity, underlying it are numerous factors that can affect the drug's fate. Once in the brain and at their target, drugs can modify neurotransmission in a number of ways. Drugs have been important to the scientist as an understanding of the neuropathology of disorders often comes from tracing the mechanisms of action of clinically efficacious drugs (and not vice versa). The rationale is straightforward: if we know how a drug works, then whatever it is correcting is what has gone wrong. However, that rationale is too simplistic. A drug may work in one area of the brain or at a particular target within the brain, but that point in the brain is not necessarily the central mechanism of neuropathology.

In Chapters 20–24 the influence of drugs on the hypotheses of various disorders is evaluated, and often those drugs are effective at a target downstream from the site of origin (I am deliberately avoiding the use of the words 'aetiology' or 'cause' – this still remains an elusive Holy Grail in many cases). This chapter has also taken a standpoint that emphasized the drug's effect on behaviour; Chapter 9 takes the counterposition in which behaviour affects the drug response, especially the tolerance and the placebo effect.

LEARNING OUTCOME QUESTIONS

You should be able to answer the following questions.
- Describe the pharmacokinetic factors that affect the behavioural effects of a drug.
- Explain the modification of neurotransmission via different mechanisms within the synaptic environment.
- Provide an account of how drugs inform psychobiological theory.
- Place psychopharmacology within an ethical context.

FURTHER READING

Advokat, C. D., Comaty, J., & Julien, R. M. (2014). *Julien's primer of drug action* (13th edn). New York: Palgrave Macmillan.
Everitt, B., & Wessley, S. (2004). *Clinical trials in psychiatry*. Oxford, UK: Oxford University Press.
Hintzen, A., & Passie, T. (2010). *The pharmacology of LSD*. Oxford, UK: Oxford University Press.
Iversen, L. L. (2000). *The science of marijuana*. Oxford, UK: Oxford University Press.
Leonard, B. E. (2003). *Fundamentals of psychopharmacology*. Oxford, UK: John Wiley & Sons.
Meyer, J. S., & Quenzer, L. F. (2013). *Psychopharmacology: Drugs, the brain, and behavior* (2nd edn). Sunderland, MA: Sinauer Associates Inc.
Nutt, D. (2012). *Drugs without hot air: minimising the harms of legal and illegal drugs*. Cambridge, UK: UIT Cambridge.
Spiegel, R. (2003). *Psychopharmacology: an introduction* (4th edn). Chichester, UK: John Wiley & Sons.

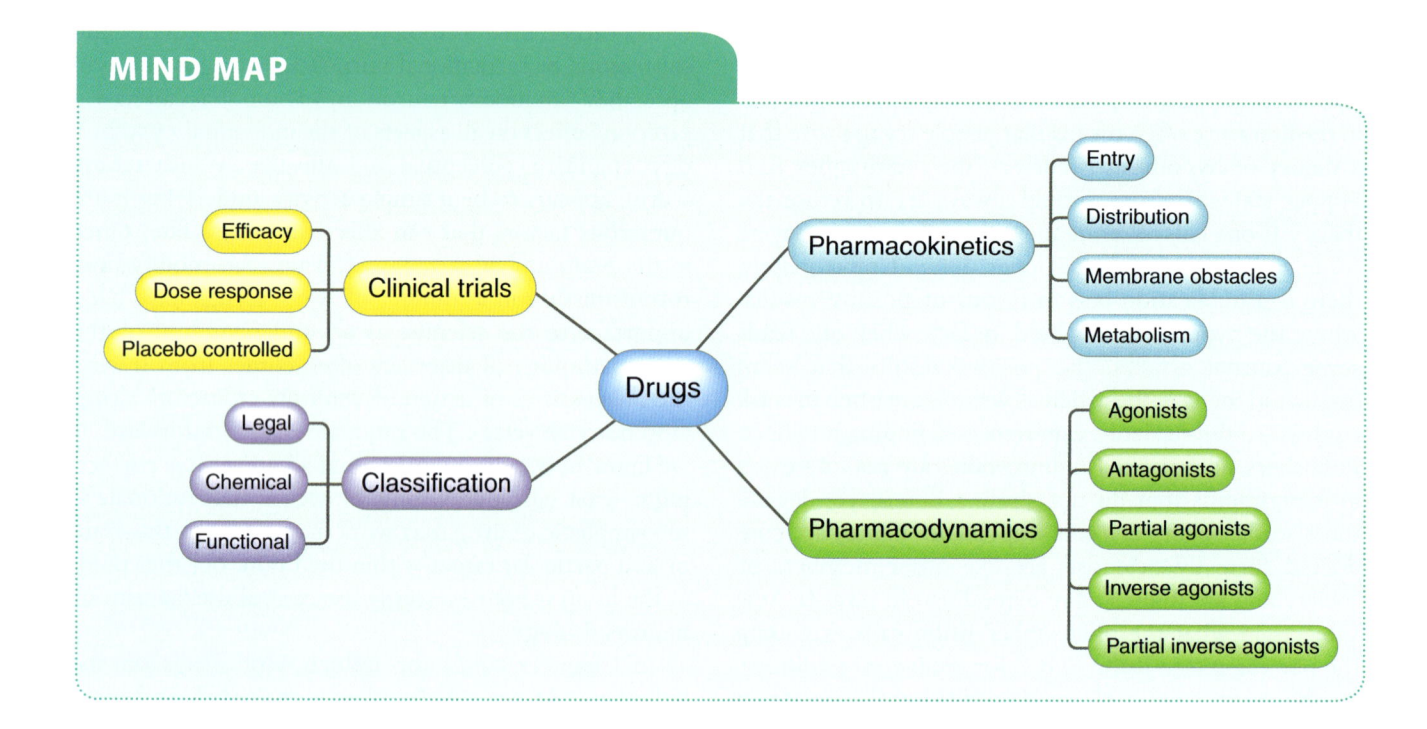

MIND MAP

- **Drugs**
  - **Clinical trials**
    - Efficacy
    - Dose response
    - Placebo controlled
  - **Classification**
    - Legal
    - Chemical
    - Functional
  - **Pharmacokinetics**
    - Entry
    - Distribution
    - Membrane obstacles
    - Metabolism
  - **Pharmacodynamics**
    - Agonists
    - Antagonists
    - Partial agonists
    - Inverse agonists
    - Partial inverse agonists

8 Animal Learning

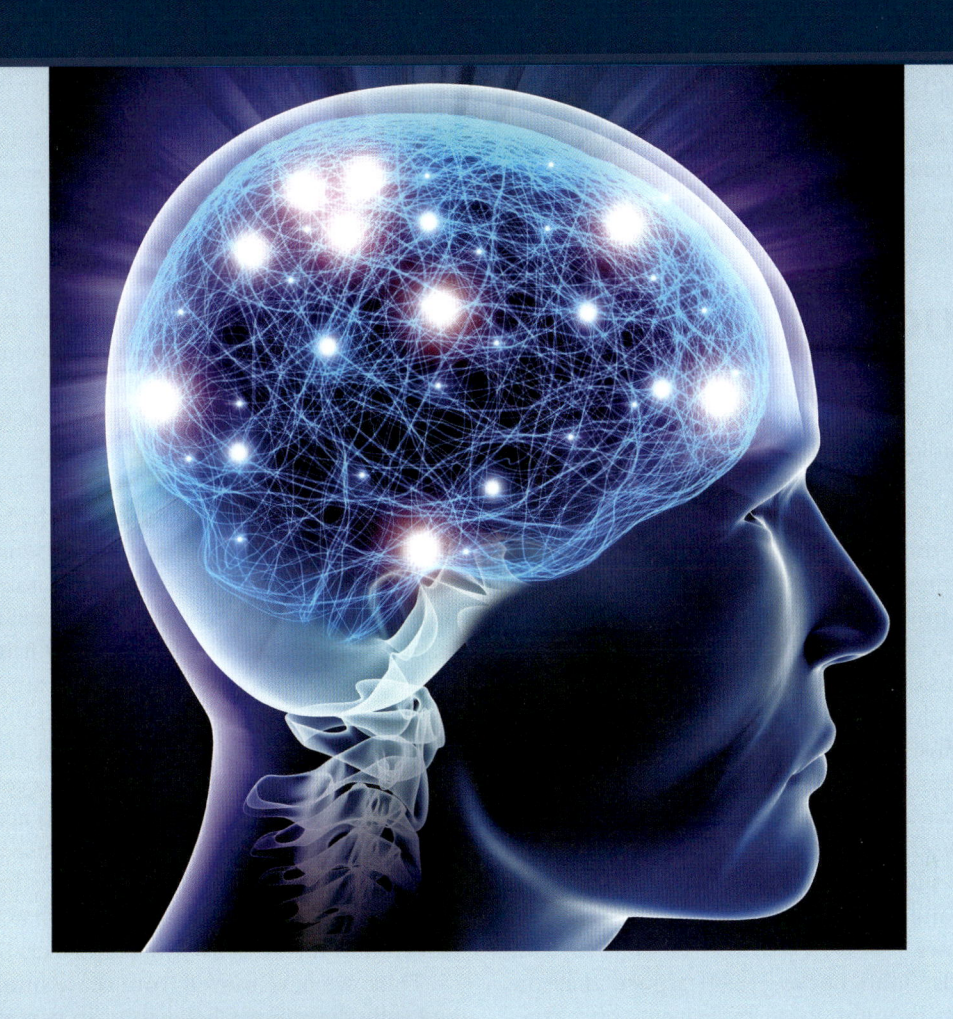

ANATOMY OF THE CHAPTER

This chapter will highlight the following.
- Habituation.
- Classical conditioning.
- Operant conditioning.

INTRODUCTION 204

LEARNING THEORY: ADAPTATIONS AND ASSOCIATIONS 205

HABITUATION 205

REFLEXES 207

CLASSICAL CONDITIONING 208

OPERANT CONDITIONING 216

COGNITION IN ANIMALS 224

SUMMARY 225

LEARNING OUTCOMES

1. To understand the background and philosophical heritage of learning theories.
2. To have a detailed knowledge of the laws of classical conditioning.
3. To have a detailed knowledge of the laws of operant conditioning.
4. To be able to apply the principles of learning theory to practical real-world problems.

INTRODUCTION

Up to this point, we have tended to view behaviour as the result of biological processes: the output of the brain. We have taken the nature stance in the nature–nurture debate. This chapter is concerned with the nurture side of the debate. Here we have the empiricist's position that we are a product of experience. This position predates the dawn of psychological investigation.

Descartes considered behaviour to be either voluntary or involuntary. Voluntary behaviour was a product of the mind whereas involuntary behaviour was mechanical and reflexive. This machine-like account of involuntary action was known as the reflex arc. The reflex arc was according to Descartes the only explanation of animal behaviour. The philosopher Thomas Hobbes differed from Descartes and suggested that the mind was subject to mechanical laws.

The empiricist John Locke (1690) argued that the idea of God was brought about by learning and experience because there was no evidence of it in children or 'savages'. David Hume a Scottish empiricist, argued that humans only have knowledge from what they have experienced through their senses. According to empiricism (aka associationism), the experiences we have can be linked together (associated) if they are repeatedly presented closely in time. It is these associations which give us our notions of cause and effect. The concept of cause and effect is an inference derived from sensory input experience. Cause and effect is therefore beyond simple input. Immanuel Kant continued the empiricist tradition of focusing on experiences but suggested that it is a psychological imperative for people to infer causation. He argued that it is natural for humans to consider cause and effect in the same way people consider objects to be spatially located, e.g. an object is located above, below, behind or in front. Such philosophical debates still continue to provide lively argument on human nature.

Even Charles Darwin invoked the empiricist cause and effect accounts in his theory of evolution. In a chapter entitled 'Darwin was a learning theorist', Garcia Y Robertson and Gracia (1988) provide an interesting view on evolution and emphasize the importance of learning. They highlight the importance of a process known as **conditioned taste aversion** in which animals learn to associate the flavours and other sensory properties of food with either a subsequent nutritional benefit or in some cases a toxic reaction (aversion) (Garcia & Hankins, 1977) (see Box 8.1). Clearly it is important for the animal to learn that certain foods are good and other foods are bad. Knowing what is good food is of benefit to survival and those that survive get to breed and the genes continue. Herbert Spencer was a contemporary of Darwin who claimed that the random activity of an animal becomes associated with the consequences of that behaviour. The action of an animal is based on experience with the environment and it is that experience that determines future behaviours (Spencer, 1885).

Thus, we have moved from the assumption that biology fully determines behaviour. In part it does – we are born with the necessary equipment to learn and adapt, which is called preparedness. It is clearly not economical for an organism to be born with a complete set of programmes for every situation it could encounter – it has to adapt its behaviour for survival. As we have seen, this does not present a challenge to evolutionary theory; rather it is a logical extension of that theory.

An example of preparedness in learning is that of **imprinting** (Lorenz, 1937). In one example, imprinting is when a newly born animal attaches itself to a moving object. In the case of Lorenz's ducks, they followed him rather than their mother. These adaptations and experiences shape future behaviour and also the underlying physiology of behaviour. The organism learns from experience both behaviourally and physiologically. As Skinner (1984) states, 'as evolved processes through which behaviour changes during the lifetime of the individual, imitation and modelling prepare the individual only for behaviour that has already been acquired by the

> ### BOX 8.1: CONDITIONED TASTE AVERSION
>
> Taste aversion learning is when an animal consumes something and becomes ill as a consequence. The animal tends not to consume the food or drink again. Clearly this has evolutionary advantage in that the animal avoids potentially poisonous food.
>
> In the laboratory, conditioned taste aversion (CTA) was investigated in detail by Garcia and Koelling (1966). In a number of studies, they demonstrated that toxins, radiation and certain drugs could act as stimulators that would induce illness. This illness then became associated with particular tastes (Garcia & Koelling, 1967). The typical CTA experiment involves thirsty rats drinking distinctive-tasting water whilst also receiving stigmas to make them ill; the pattern can be seen below.
>
> Unconditioned stimulus (toxin) + Conditioned stimulus (taste) → Unconditioned response (illness)
>
> Conditioned stimulus (taste) → Conditioned response (aversion)
>
> However, unlike normal conditioning experiments in which there is close temporal contiguity between the conditioned stimulus (CS) and unconditioned stimulus (US), in CTA experiments the delay can be between two and 24 hours. Seligman (1970) suggested that animals are biologically prepared to associate stimuli such as taste with subsequent illness.
>
> In most animals, taste aversions are more readily learned when paired with illness than other sensory modalities (Shettleworth, 1983). In a study looking at children who received chemotherapy, Bernstein (1978) found that the children developed taste aversions to food consumed before treatment. This was achieved even when they knew that there was no causal connection.
>
> Familiarity also has an effect in which those tastes that are not familiar are more likely to become taste aversions as another example of the US following a CS (Kurz & Levitsky, 1982).

organisms that model it. Other processes have evolved which bring the individual under the control of environments to which the individual alone is exposed. One is respondent (Pavlovian or classical) conditioning' (p.218).

From an evolutionary perspective, behaviour that favours survival will be selected. Those behaviours that are not useful will not be selected. There are many similarities between the learning theories and evolutionary theories (e.g. adaptation to the environment). The main difference between the two is timescale. Learning is within an organism's lifetime whereas evolution transcends the life of an individual, but both confer the essential survival of Dawkins' selfish gene (Dawkins, 2006).

LEARNING THEORY: ADAPTATIONS AND ASSOCIATIONS

Two notable theorists have dominated the field of animal learning: Ivan Pavlov and B.F. Skinner. The initial learning theories have been adapted, refined and supported by empirical study in both animals and humans. The two main theories – classical conditioning and operant conditioning – are referred to as 'associative learning'; this is because associations are made between stimuli and their responses.

HABITUATION

The example of conditioned taste aversion indicates that much of learning theory has focused on the acquisition of new knowledge (see Box 8.1). However, there is one form of learning that is not about the animal responding; it is about the animal not responding. This is **habituation** which is the simplest and most ubiquitous form of learning. It is when you learn to ignore a stimulus that does not convey any meaning.

Habituation can be seen in many organisms as it has a clear and adaptive function. It can be readily measured in the rat in controlled experiments. If you make a loud noise, the rat behaves as if startled. The rat jumps just like we would. If the rat is repeatedly exposed to the noise, and that noise has no consequence, the magnitude of the startle response diminishes. The classic example of habituation in the human is that of city dwellers no longer responding to or noticing urban noise, e.g. the sirens of emergency vehicles and the traffic in general.

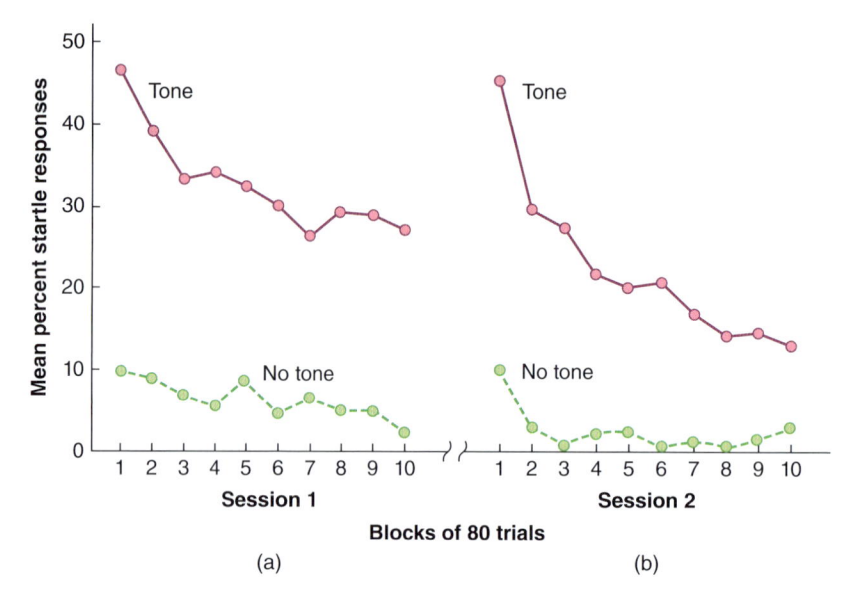

FIGURE 8.1 *Habituation of startle response. (a) The percent of tone presentations that produced a startle response over 800 tone presentations. Control animals received no tones, but their startle responses were measured at the same time in the session that tones were presented to the experimental group. (b) Startle responding a day later. Note the recovery of responding to the tone at the outset of the session.*
Source: After Marlin, N.A. and Miller, R.R. (1981) Associations to contextual stimuli as a determinant of long-term habituation. *Journal of Experimental Psychology: Animal Behavior Processes, 7*(4), 313–333.

It is not that city dwellers have reduced sensory input because when they venture to the country and spend the night there, the small noises of insects and other animals are enough to keep them awake.

From an evolutionary perspective, habituation is an adaptation that aids survival. It makes good sense for the animal to respond to a stimulus that it has never experienced before. A novel stimulus may or may not pose a threat. However, if the stimulus is repeated with no consequences, the animal habituates to it. This enables the animal to get on with the important business of survival. Thus, the only stimuli that are attended to are those that may pose a threat to survival. A rat, then, should habituate to traffic noise in the streets above but not to the predator cat. Humans can also habituate. If we hear a loud noise behind us we respond by trying to locate its source. This is called the orienting response. If we observe that the source of the loud noise is non-threatening (e.g. a builder hammering) and the noise continues, we habituate to the noise. If the sound is indicative of a threat, like gunfire, we locate it and preferably avoid it.

Habituation is a learned response rather than a sensory adaptation or motor fatigue. The outcome may be the same but the underlying processes are different, e.g. a rat may stop responding to an auditory tone because of changes in the neural patterns of its continued presentation or it may stop responding over time because it is too tired from all the previous responding. Or it could be learning – the rat has learned that the auditory tone is of no consequence to it or its environment.

Habituation of the acoustic startle response in the rat shows that the rat develops a habituated response over time (see Figure 8.1) (Marlin & Miller, 1981).

Once the animal has habituated to the stimulus and no longer responds, there are certain conditions in which the original response can return. This is the rather clumsy term **dishabituation** (Figure 8.2). This can occur

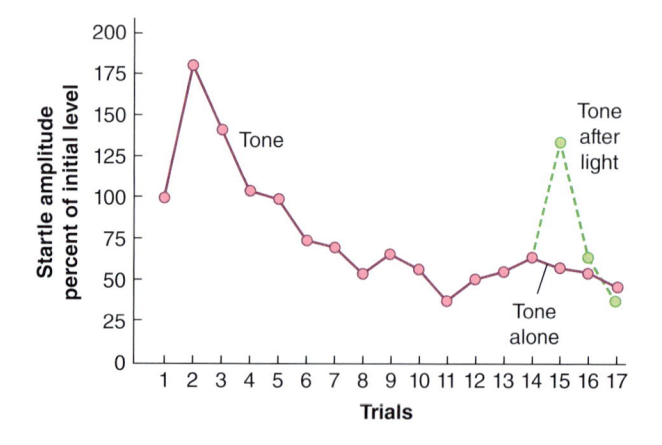

FIGURE 8.2 *Dishabituation of startle responding to a tone. Two groups of rats are given 14 presentations of a tone to produce habituation of the startle response (measured as a percent of the startle amplitude to the tone before habituation training). On trial 15, one group is exposed to a flash of light before the tone and a second group receives no light. Startle responding to the tone is restored following the light flash, but drops back to habituated levels on the next trial.*
Source: After Groves P M & Thompson R F. (1970). Habituation: a dual-process theory. *Psychological Review, 77*, 419–450.

after the animal has had a rest period from the stimulus. If the auditory tone is no longer presented to the animal, the animal no longer has learning trials contributing to the ignoring of that stimulus. However, it is possible to reignite the habituated response without the rest period. Dishabituation can be brought about by (1) presenting a new stimulus together with the habituated stimulus – this new stimulus produces a startle response not only to itself but also to the subsequent presentation of the original stimulus; (2) a change in the habituated stimulus, e.g. if a male rat copulates with a female rat, it does so about seven times before it stops responding; however, if the male rat is given a succession of different females it is able to manage 13 episodes (Fisher, 1962). Clearly variety is the spice of life.

Two broad theories provide an account of habituation: dual process and memory. The dual process theory put forward by Groves and Thompson (1970) describes two distinct processes: (1) habituation, and (2) **sensitization** – increased activity of the animal. These two processes have developed independently but interact to form the response output. These two behaviourally opposing systems can work to produce habituation dependent upon the situation. When an auditory tone is presented to a rat when there is little background noise, habituation develops, but if that same tone is presented to another animal but this time with a lot of background noise, the responding is increased. In the first instance, the habituation pathway is strongest and in the second instance, the overall increase in background noise increases activity and arousal, thereby resulting in sensitization (Figure 8.3) (Davis, 1974).

An alternative account of habituation was presented by Wagner (1976). This model was an information-processing/cognitive view of learning in general. Wagner's theory focused on short-term and long-term memory. If events are already active in short-term memory and the stimulus is presented, it is less likely to evoke a response. If a representation of the events is not active in short-term memory then the presentation of the stimulus will be seen as unexpected or surprising and then the animal will respond. A representation of an event can become active in short-term memory by two processes: via self-generated priming or via retrieval-generated priming. Self-generated priming is when a stimulus causes a memory to be activated whereas retrieval-generated priming is when an event associated with the stimulus activates short-term memory, e.g. environmental contexts activate memory systems.

The dual process theory and information-processing theory both provide accounts of habituation as a learning process, albeit learning to ignore irrelevant stimuli. Whilst habituation is an important learned behaviour, the vast majority of psychological research investigates the production of behaviour rather than the reduction of behaviour. The accounts of habituation can also be used to describe and explain behaviour production.

REFLEXES

Descartes viewed involuntary action as a result of the reflex arc. The response of the organism during habituation is also reflexive. A **reflex** is an automatic response to an external stimulus. That is, you do not think about your response – it happens automatically and is beyond conscious control. An example of this is the leg jerking in response to a tap on the knee area with a tendon hammer or the blinking of an eye in response to a puff of air.

A reflex involves closely related events. For a reflex to occur, an input stimulus is necessary. The input triggers the cellular events of neurotransmission. Stimulus input is via afferent neurons to the spinal column. The afferent neuron communicates with an **interneuron**, a neuron that is neither sensory nor motor but connects the two. The interneuron communicates with an efferent neuron. The efferent neuron activates muscles to execute the reflex.

If you touch something hot, you automatically retract your hand from the source of the heat (the stimulus). You do not think 'That's hot! I must remove my hand before I suffer tissue damage' (or words to that effect). The thermal information is sent along afferent neurons that connect to efferent neurons (via the interneuron) and

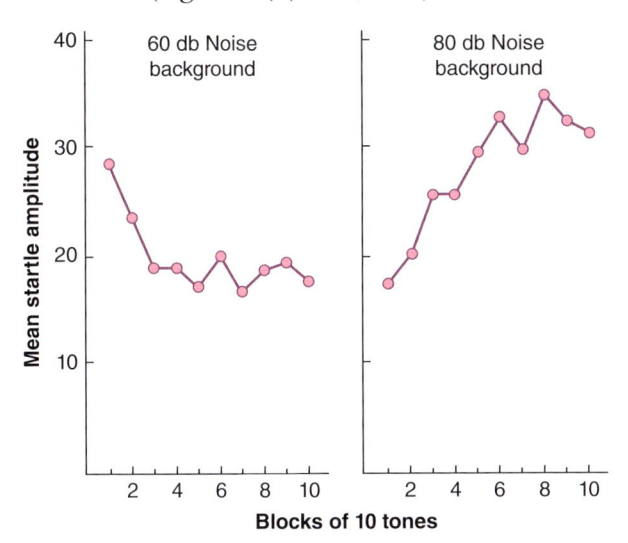

FIGURE 8.3 *Startle responding to a 100 db tone habituates when a 60 db background noise is presented. However, responding becomes sensitized (increases) when the background noise is louder.*
Source: After Davis, M. (1974). Sensitization of the rat startle response by noise. *Journal of Comparative and Physiological Psychology, 87*(3), 571–581.

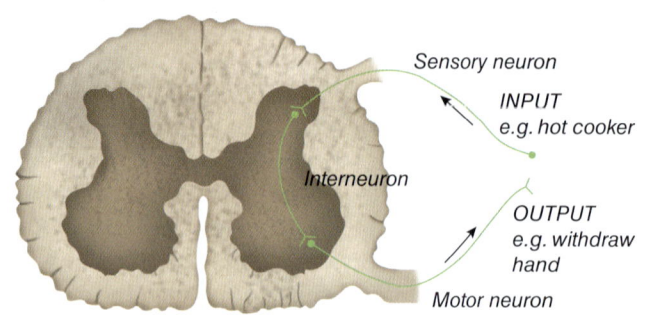

FIGURE 8.4 *A reflex comprises the activation of an afferent nerve connected to an interneuron, which is in turn connected to an efferent neuron.*

the reflex of hand removal is executed (see Figure 8.4). Thus, you avoid getting a serious burn to your hand. Such a reflex obviously has adaptive significance; sustaining tissue damage could result in infection, disease and possibly death.

CLASSICAL CONDITIONING

While they are automatic responses, reflexes can be subject to learning. The reflex is central to Ivan Pavlov's theory of **classical conditioning**. Classical conditioning is when a neutral stimulus becomes associated with a stimulus that is able to produce a reflex. The neutral stimulus, which previously had no effect, becomes able to produce the reflex.

Pavlov was investigating digestion in the dog. Incidental to this, Pavlov and his students noticed that dogs would salivate in response to stimuli that were predictive of feeding time. Like all good scientists, they systematically investigated this phenomenon.

Pavlov put the dogs in a special apparatus that allowed saliva to be collected and measured. When food was put into a dog's mouth, saliva was produced. Saliva contains enzymes that are used in the digestion of food. The saliva-producing response is a reflex to the orosensory stimulus of food in the mouth.

In Pavlovian terms, the food is an **unconditioned stimulus (US)** and the production of saliva is an **unconditioned response (UR)**. A reflex can be described as an unconditioned response to an unconditioned stimulus: US (food) →UR (salivation).

So far, nothing had been learned by the dog in the experiment. During the next stage of the experiment, a tone was introduced (a bell), which accompanied the presentation of food. Initially the tone was a neutral stimulus and did not produce a response. However, after a number of tone/food presentations, the tone was presented alone and, on its own in the absence of food, produced salivation in the dog. This tone is referred to as the **conditioned stimulus (CS)**. The response to the tone, in this case salivation, is called the **conditioned response (CR)**. The dog is said to have acquired an association between the tone and the production of food (see Figure 8.5).

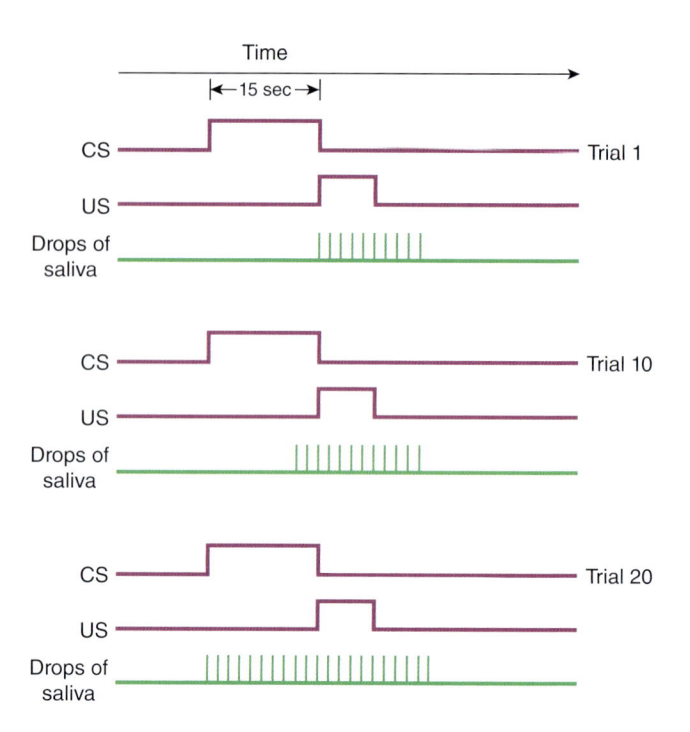

FIGURE 8.5 *In trial 1, the dog salivates (vertical lines) only after food is presented. In trial 10, a few drops of saliva come before the delivery of food. By trial 20, salivation begins at the onset of the CS and continues throughout the trial. CS, conditioned stimulus; US, unconditioned stimulus.*

Thus at the start of the study:

US (food) → UR (salivation)

Then during the learning phase:

CS (tone)/US(food) → UR (salivation)

And finally at the end of the study:

CS (tone) → CR (salivation)

The CR is an anticipatory response allowing the dog to prepare for the arrival of food.

Pavlov's experiments provided the basic premise of classical conditioning. Using this framework, a large number of behaviours can be described. However, at no point are anthropomorphic or mentalistic descriptions made of what the animal is doing, e.g. the dog *knows* food is coming or the dog *thinks* food is coming. The learning theorists are only concerned about input and output and not about the underlying processes of learning. The ramifications of classical conditioning can be seen in the realm of clinical psychology in which phobias can develop; the good news is that classical conditioning also offers a solution. From the basic principles of classical conditioning, we can now build up a more elaborate account of associative learning.

Measuring the Conditioned Response

How do we know we got a conditioned response? The simple answer is that we measure it but measuring a CR is not an all-or-nothing observation. Such a measure would put us in danger of missing the subtleties of the conditioning process. The devil is in the detail! There are three main ways of assessing the strength of a CR.

- **Response amplitude**: how large is the CR? In Pavlov's experiments, how much saliva does the dog produce? The more saliva produced then the stronger the conditioning.
- **Response probability**: how many times does a CR occur in response to a CS? A probability of 0.5 (50%) would indicate responding at the level of chance. A CR probability of 0.9 (or 90%) would indicate that there is a strong association between the CS and US.
- **Response latency**: how long after the CS does the CR appear? The closer in time they occur, the stronger the conditioning. How long does it take for the dog to salivate after hearing the CS?

Acquisition

Learning takes time. Over successive pairings, the CS gradually becomes associated with the US, producing a CR. The more pairings (or trials), the stronger the conditioning (see Figure 8.6). However, numerous CS–US pairings do not result in a continual increase in learning – they reach what is called **asymptote**, a plateau in learning.

Extinction

Once asymptote has been reached and the CS reliably produces a CR then presentation of the CS without the US would eventually decrease the CR. Stop giving a dog food after it hears the tone and it will eventually stop salivating

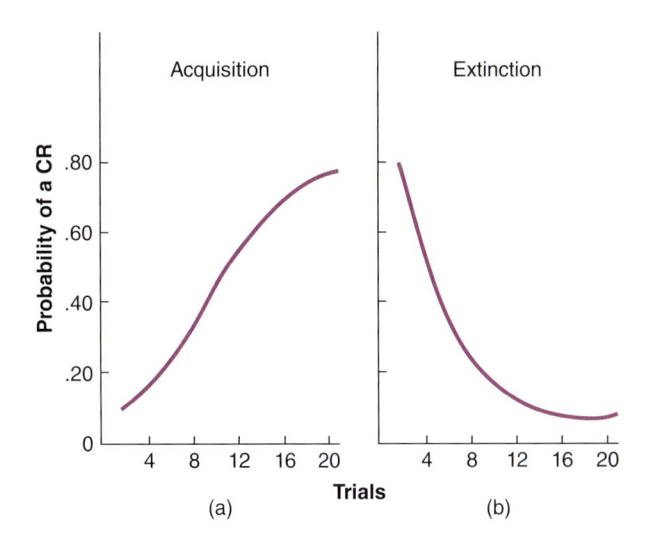

FIGURE 8.6 *Depicted in (a) is the gradual increase in the probability of a CR as CS–US pairings occur. (b) The gradual decrease in probability as CS presentations continue, but without the US.*

to the tone. The absence of a CR after discontinued pairings of the CS and US is called **extinction**. The CR is extinguished gradually as the animal experiences the CS without the US (see Figure 8.6). Although there are many similarities with habituation, e.g. we are looking at a reduction in responding, extinction is different from habituation as no associations have been made with habituation. With extinction, the associations have been weakened considerably by removal of the US.

Spontaneous Recovery

After the extinction of the CR and a period of rest without experimentation, the CR can appear again in response to the CS. Perhaps the word 'extinction' is a misnomer in learning theory, especially given the evolutionary views that extinction leads to the permanent deletion of a species. Extinction in learning theory is not necessarily a permanent removal of the CR forever. The phenomenon of the CR emerging again after successful presentations of the CS and US is known as **spontaneous recovery** (see Figure 8.7). The CR is not as strong as it was during earlier training. If training is restarted, learning the CS–US pairing will be quicker than it was in the initial learning period. Spontaneous recovery can occur after a substantial rest period, indicating the permanence of learning. Thus, extinction is not forgetting, but is similar to proactive interference in which new learning supersedes old (Bouton, 1994; Bouton & Moody, 2004).

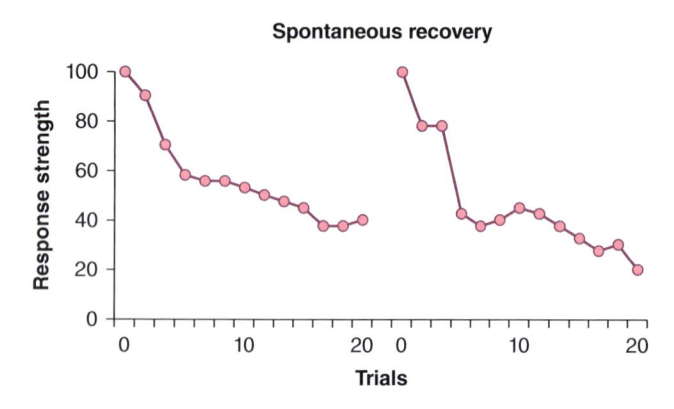

FIGURE 8.7 *Spontaneous recovery.*

Stimulus Generalization and Stimulus Discrimination

Pavlov's experiments used a tone of a particular frequency as the CS. What would happen if another similar, but not identical, tone was used? If the new tone was very similar to the CS then the CR would be strong. If the new tone was somewhat dissimilar to the CS then the CR would be comparatively weak. Similarly, an organism is able to differentiate between stimuli that are similar but not identical to the CS (see Figure 8.8).

Is the Conditioned Response Identical to the Unconditioned Response?

So far, in Pavlov's experiments the CR and UR are both salivation. However, with a more detailed analysis of the saliva, differences in CR and UR are evident. Saliva contains enzymes that are used for digestion. In the CR there are fewer of these enzymes than in the UR, highlighting the importance of detailed measures in behavioural studies. If our measure was as crude as 'present' or 'absent', that would give us important information but if our measure was about how much saliva or the composition of the saliva, we could obtain a finer analysis of the behaviour.

The **conditioned emotional response** (CER) is the basis for a classically conditioned phobia (see Box 8.2)

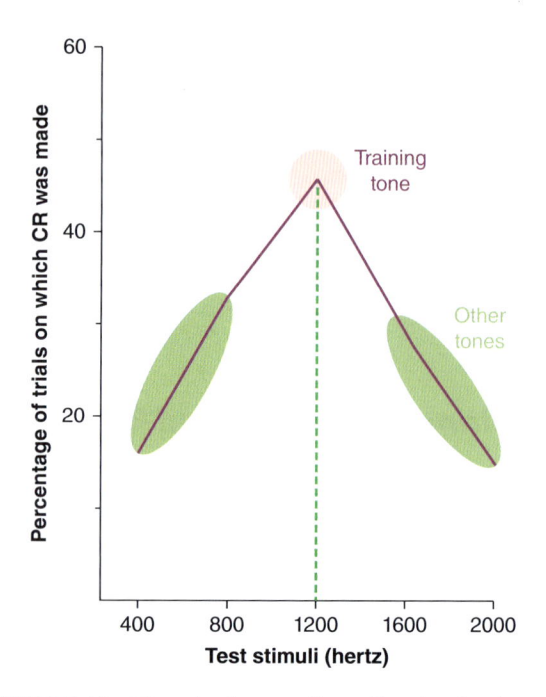

FIGURE 8.8 *The CS can both generalize to like stimuli or be discriminated from other stimuli.*

BOX 8.2: PHOBIAS

Phobias are irrational fears. For example, there is little evolutionary advantage or indeed little point in being frightened of spiders in the UK. However, in other territories such as Australia, there is good reason to be frightened of spiders – they are venomous and potentially their bites are fatal.

The example of a spider phobia (arachnophobia) perhaps does not do justice to the great variety of phobias that exist, some of which do not have an evolutionary adaptive parallel.

Classical conditioning laws have been deployed in an attempt to explain phobias. In an experiment with a young child called Little Albert who was 11 months old (!), Watson and Rayner (1920) paired the presentation of a white lab rat with a loud noise. The loud noise would produce an emotional reaction in the child – crying. The child eventually responded to the sight of the rat with a conditioned emotional reaction of crying. Clearly this was in the days before scientists were required to seek ethical approval for their studies!

US (loud noise) + CS (white rat) → UR (crying/fear)

CS (white rat) → CR (crying)

BOX 8.3: SEXUAL FETISH

A quick search of the internet will show you that people have a wide range of unusual and fabulous sexual attractions. Clearly sex is important for the continuation of the species, but what have the fetishes got to do with that? Sex is pleasurable (no news in that statement!) and from an evolutionary perspective motivates people into the act and as a by-product of the pleasure principle, children are born. It is the pleasure derived from sexual stimulation that lends itself readily to associative learning.

The fetish, the stockings, the underwear and female clothes in general can elicit strong responses. In one memorable lecture on the subject, a well-to-do student stood up in front of a class of 200 and asked 'Chris, can you explain the gas mask fetish?'. With my knowledge of conditioning and a vivid imagination, I was proudly able to offer her an explanation!

There has been some research into the aetiology of fetishes but not as much as with phobias.

Rachman and Hodgson (1968) studied the classic boot fetish – a textbook fetish! They paired knee-length boots with erotic pictures and measured the ability of the boots to elicit a penile erection.

US (erotica) + CS (knee-length boots) → UR (penile erection)

CS (knee-length boots) → CR (penile erection)

(Watson & Morgan, 1917; Watson & Rayner, 1920) and possibly the sexual fetish (Box 8.3).

This clearly was not an ethical study. However, Little Albert did provide some information on the possible aetiology of some phobias. It is not the only explanation of phobias and readers interested in phobias and general psychopathology are directed to Davey (2008).

What happened to Little Albert has become part of the urban myth (see Harris, 2011). Eventually the identity of Little Albert was revealed, albeit with a degree of uncertainty (Beck et al., 2009). Little Albert was actually Douglas Merritte (1919–1925) and hospital records revealed that Douglas was neurologically impaired with 'congenital obstructive hydrocephalus, iatrogenic streptococcal meningitis/ventriculitis, and retinal and optic nerve atrophy' (Fridlund et al., 2012, p.302).

A more detailed study in which pictures of nude females were presented to heterosexual males during masturbation revealed that the stimuli associated with the plateau phase (excitement prior to orgasm) resulted in penile erections, stimuli presented during the refractory phase (immediately post orgasm) produced a decrease in penile erections and during the resolution phase (when sexual arousal goes back to a lower level), the stimuli were devoid of effect (Kantorowitz, 1978). For more detail on sexual responses go to Chapter 14.

In experiments to obtain a CER, rats are trained in an operant chamber (see below for more about operant conditioning) (Estes & Skinner, 1941). In the chamber, the rats press a lever to receive food. Rats are good at this task. Sometimes a tone will sound for 30 seconds. Following the tone, an electric shock is given through the grid floor. As training continues, the rat stops pressing the bar for food when the tone is presented. This is called conditioned suppression or the conditioned emotional response. In studies of conditioned suppression in which ongoing activity is suspended, this can be brought about by positive reinforcement as well as the aversive events such as electroshock (Azrin & Hake, 1969). The CER has been of critical importance for understanding the neural processing of emotion, in particular fear (see Chapter 17).

In the CER experiment in which a rat receives an electric shock, the CR and UR are different. In response to the US (shock), the rat's heart rate increases and it jumps about the chamber. The response to the CS (tone) is different: the rat's heart rate decreases and it remains still. The importance of the CR being different from the UR is exemplified in drug tolerance (see Chapter 9).

The Relationship between the Conditioned Stimulus and the Unconditioned Stimulus

In all these experiments, it is clear that the CS becomes associated with the US. When a CS appears the probability of this being followed by a US is high. The association between CS and US varies in strength depending on the temporal characteristics.

if half the time the US appeared after the CS and half the time it didn't; thus there was no reliable prediction that could be made from the CS being presented. If the probability was 0.8 (80%), then the CS would be associated with the production of a US. If the probability was low (e.g. 0.2, 20%), then the absence of a CS indicates a higher likelihood of a US. The role of contingency has been investigated by Seligman (1975) in the **learned helplessness** model of depression (Box 8.4).

Delay Conditioning

The acquisition of associations is fastest when the CS precedes the onset of the US. Having the CS and US close together in time increases the likelihood that associations will be made. However, in **delay conditioning**, the interval between the onset of the CS and the delivery of the US is increased. During training, the CR under delayed conditioning is evident soon after the CS is presented; however, as training progresses, the onset of the CR is delayed and comes about halfway between onset of the CS and the onset of the US. Thus, the animal learns that the CS is predictive and its temporal relationship. Again, through associative learning the animal does not produce a CR at the onset of the CS, but also learns that it is some time through the CS before the US is present.

Simultaneous Conditioning

Simultaneous conditioning is when both the onset and offset of the CS and US occur at the same time. Interestingly, this kind of pairing does not normally produce conditioning, despite the temporal relationship between stimuli. The reason for the lack of conditioning and a perfect temporal contiguity may be explained by overshadowing. Normally, overshadowing refers to the phenomenon of when two CSs are presented simultaneously, creating a compound CS. If we have two CSs, e.g. CS 1 is light and CS 2 is a tone, and this is followed by the US (shock) then CS 1 may overshadow CS 2, and CS 2 alone may not produce a CR. The more salient CS is associated with the US, in this case CS 1 – light. Similarly, if a CS and US are presented simultaneously, e.g. CS 1 light and US shock, then CS 1 may be overshadowed by the aversive nature of the shock. Because CS 1 and the US are presented simultaneously, CS 1 has no predictive value. By bringing CS 1 forward in time, one can establish conditioning to the US as even a small temporal gap between the two stimuli conveys some information (Figure 8.10).

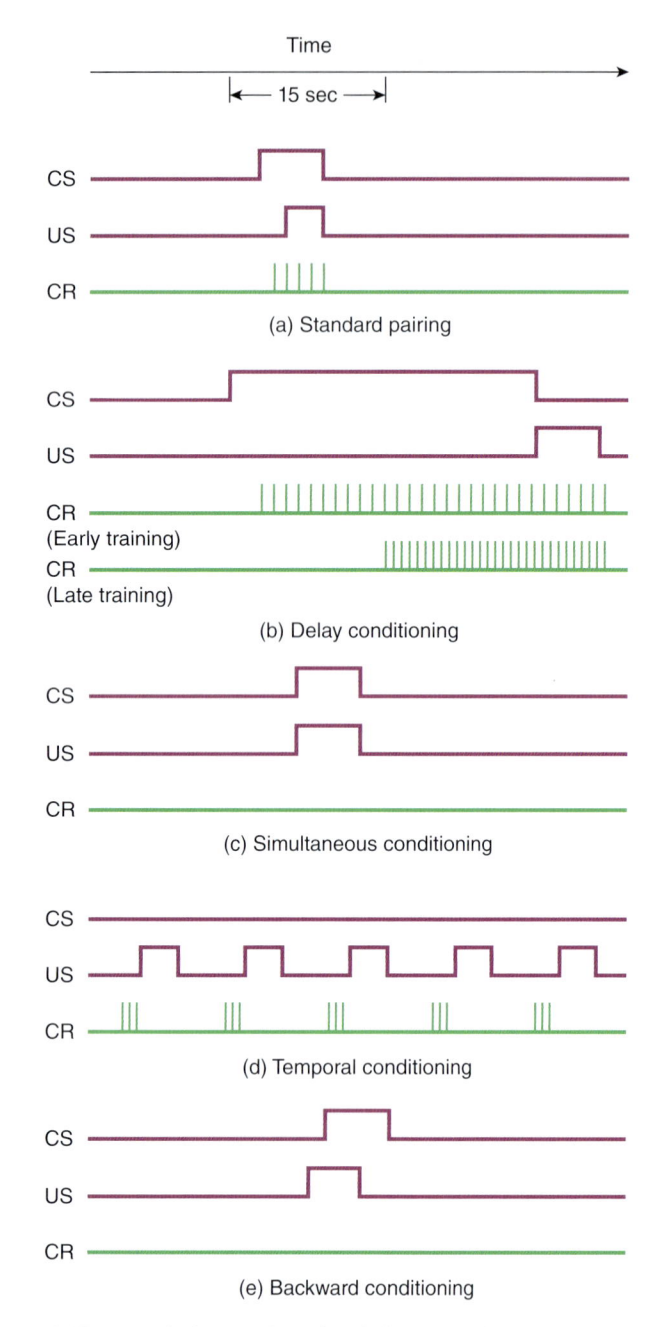

FIGURE 8.9 *The bottom line of each drawing indicates the pattern of conditioned responding typically observed in these procedures. CR, conditioned response; CS, conditioned stimulus; US, unconditioned stimulus.*

The temporal relationship between the CS and the US is important (see Figure 8.9). **Contiguity** is when the CS and US are presented close together in time. Rescorla (1968) suggested that contiguity was necessary but not sufficient for conditioning. Differential **contingency** was also required: this is the likelihood (probability) of a US following a CS. If the probability of a US following a CS was 0.5, then there would be no learning

BOX 8.4: LEARNED HELPLESSNESS AND DEPRESSION

Most of the studies investigating associative learning are looking at response dependence; a response leads to a change in environment. Response dependence is typified by operant conditioning. However, in 1975 Martin Seligman wrote in great detail about response independence. Response independence is that the outcome is not dependent at all times on a response been made. Seligman (1991) referred to the outcome of response independence as learned helplessness. He states that 'helplessness is a psychological state that frequently results when events are uncontrollable' (p.9).

Numerous experiments were conducted by Seligman to evaluate learned helplessness. In a classical conditioning experiment, dogs were placed in a harness to impair mobility and exposed to tone–electric shock pairings. The tone was the CS and the electric shock was the US. The electric shock was of sufficient strength to be painful but not so great that it would cause tissue damage. There was nothing the dogs could do to control the shock. After the animals had been exposed to uncontrollable shock, they were placed in a shuttle box. In a shuttle box, the animals have the option to jump from one side to the other in order to escape an electric shock delivered through the floor. Dogs would normally run, yelp and eventually jump to the other side, resulting in termination of the shock. In successive placements in the shuttle box, the animal quickly learns to jump to the other side. However, dogs that were exposed to uncontrollable electric shock when placed in the shuttle box did not jump to the other side but instead sat and took the shock. The shock was then terminated one minute after it started. This was experimental verification of learned helplessness. Of 150 dogs tested, 100 were helpless. That still leaves 50 that did not succumb to learned helplessness – we shall come back to these.

In order to tease apart shock from the process of learned helplessness, Seligmann performed a number of experiments using a triadic design. The triadic design comprised three groups of animals: (1) naive animals that had not been pre-exposed to electric shock, (2) control-outcome animals that could terminate the shock, and (3) yoked animals that received the same electric shock as the control-outcome animals but could not terminate the shock themselves. Out of the three groups, it was only the yoked animals that performed poorly in the shuttle box. Thus, it was not the shock *per se* that led to helplessness but rather the lack of control.

Seligman continued to suggest that learned helplessness was the fundamental problem in those with depression. He was able to point out many similarities between the features of learned helplessness and depression. There is a great deal of debate as to what psychiatric condition is the fundamental construct of learned helplessness, as anxiety has also been considered.

The learned helplessness theory has been criticized in terms of understanding what the animal has learned. In a series of experiments, Weiss and Glazer (1975) noted that animals that receive shock in the shuttle box become inactive after an initial burst of activity. The termination of the shock after a minute coincides with the immobility, therefore the immobility becomes associated with termination of the shock.

The 50 dogs in Seligman's early experiments that did not succumb to learned helplessness provide an example of studying the phenomenon from a different direction. These 50 animals appeared to be immune to Seligman's experimental procedures. What was it about them that meant they were resistant to learned helplessness? If we can understand that, we may unlock the secret of resilience that health psychologists are interested in pursuing. It is not those that succumb to disorder after provocation that are interesting, but rather those that do not succumb. This is analogous to men (in particular) who expose themselves to HIV by having unprotected sex with infected prostitutes but they themselves do not contract it. Their immune system provides important information about the virus and how to protect against it.

Seligman now champions positive psychology and deals with happiness, excellence and optimal human functioning rather than looking at deficits.

Backward Conditioning

Backward conditioning is essentially when the presentation of the stimulus is reversed, i.e. the US comes before the CS. Unsurprisingly, training using such parameters does not lead to conditioning. One of the important points to note about this set-up is that despite the US and CS being close together in time, temporal contiguity is insufficient on its own to lead to conditioning. However, there are some cases in which backward conditioning can be seen to exist (Shurtleff & Ayres, 1981) which has led to the suggestion that '. . . the failure to recognize backward conditioning as a legitimate phenomenon seems to reflect theoretical biases rather

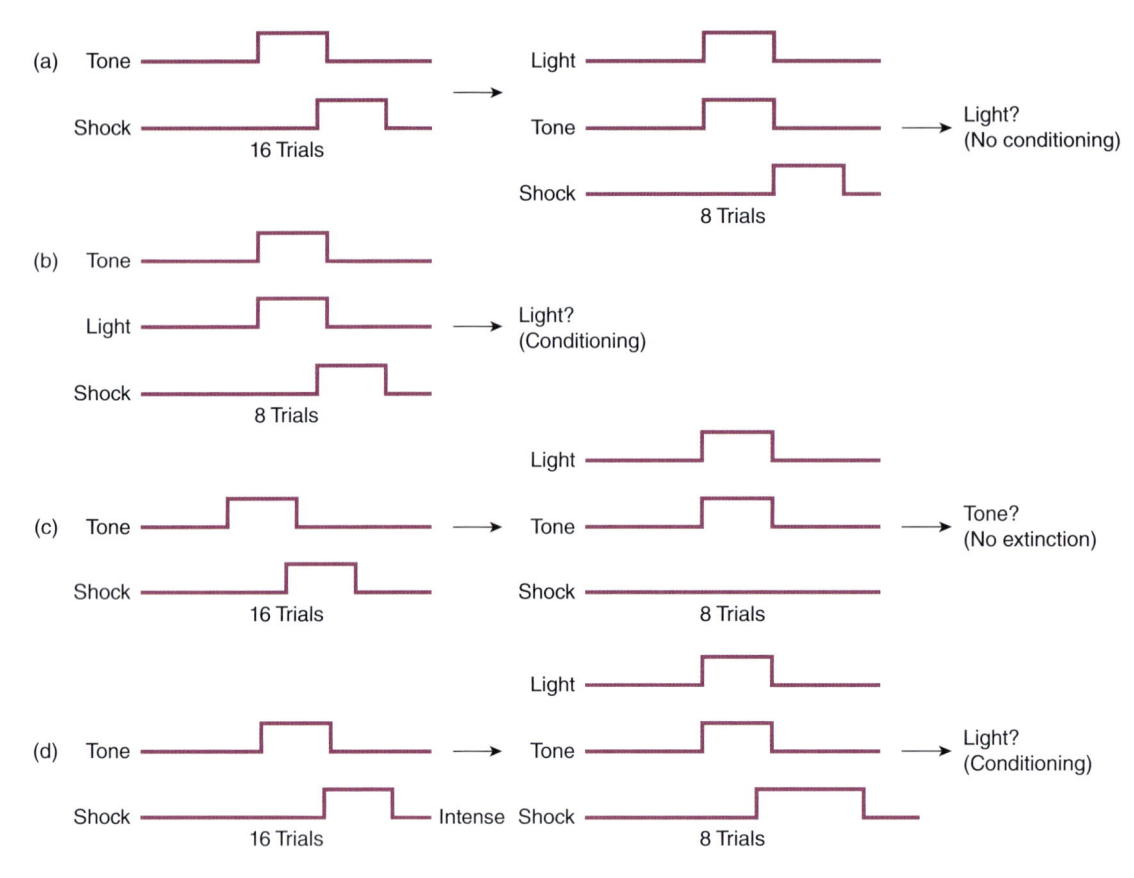

FIGURE 8.10 *Procedures in which the redundancy of light as a CS is varied. In (a), light is redundant (the animal has already learned all there is to be learned); no conditioning occurs. In (b), (c) and (d), light is not redundant; it has effects on behaviour. In (b), since the animal has not learned anything yet, nothing is redundant and nothing is blocked. In (c), light signals no shock, and thus blocks the tone from extinction. Finally, in (d), light is correlated with an increase in shock intensity. Thus, light is not redundant and is not blocked.*

than a paucity of empirical evidence' (Spetch et al., 1981). It has further been suggested that CS–US pairings result in inhibition (Chang et al., 2003, 2004; Hall, 1984; Heth, 1976). In cases of inhibition the CS predicts the termination of the US, thus the CS is inhibitory–there is no need for a response. Clearly, one needs to establish what is learned in backward conditioning and Zeiner and Grings (1968) state that 'the backward conditioning effect was found only with those SS *[subjects]* attributing significance to the CS . . . *[and]* is determined by the way SS perceives or structures the experimental situation' (p.232). Thus, this extends beyond the law-based premise of associative learning.

In studies measuring reflexes in the cat's spine, Durkovic and colleagues suggest that backward and forward conditioning are functionally different and involve different neural pathways (Durkovic & Damianopoulos, 1986; Onifer & Durkovic, 1988). Furthermore, using conditioned taste aversion paradigms, backward conditioning was seen in a single trial in the conditioned response to saccharine laced water and tolerance to the US (an endotoxin that activates immune responses) (Washio et al., 2011). Whilst backward conditioning is not the norm, there are some cases in which it does exist and interested readers are directed to Miller and Barnet (1993).

Trace Conditioning

In delay conditioning, a CS is presented and continued before and during the US. In **trace conditioning**, the CS is presented and then there is a gap in time before the US is presented. The strength of associative learning and trace conditioning is not as great as with delay conditioning.

Temporal Conditioning

If the US is presented repeatedly at constant intervals without any CS, the animal eventually produces a CR (**Temporal conditioning**). The CR occurs just before each US because the fixed passage of time serves the animal as a CS.

Latent Inhibition

If in an experiment the CS is presented without the US on numerous occasions before CS–US pairings then the conditioning that takes place when the two are paired is retarded. This pre-exposure to a CS before learning results in **latent inhibition** (Lubow & Moore, 1959). Latent inhibition has been used as an animal model (Weiner & Arad, 2009) for the deficits of information processing seen in schizophrenia (Braunstein-Bercovitz et al., 2002).

Blocking

The **blocking** effect involves two CSs and a US. If CS 1 and the US have been paired successfully, leading to a CR, then the subsequent addition of a new CS (CS 2) alongside CS 1 does not add any new information. CS 2 alone does not produce a CR; the CS 2–US association has been blocked (Kamin, 1969). If, however, the CR to CS 1 is extinguished, the animal may then start responding to CS 2, thus indicating that the animal had learned the association to CS 2 but it was considerably weaker than the CS 1 response.

The Rescorla–Wagner Model

The description so far of classical conditioning only addresses lawful features derived from pairings of the CS and the US. Conditioning takes place in the wider context with a vast array of potential CSs; learning does not take place in a vacuum even in the highly controlled experiments already discussed. Another component of the theory is that prior to conditioning the subject is 'surprised' by the US, but after conditioning the subject is no longer surprised because the CS predicts the coming of the US – thus there is less to learn about the association.

The **Rescorla–Wagner theory of classical conditioning** is perhaps the most influential explanation of the underlying processes. The heart of the theory is that the learning curve is negatively accelerated (Figure 8.11). That is, early in the learning trials learning strength is greater than in later learning trials (see Box 8.5). As the trials progress and lessons are learned, a plateau is reached, referred to as the asymptote. The theory also explains extinction in which the CS no longer predicts the US – the CS is presented without a US. Given that the once established CS–US contingency was readily predictable, during extinction the absence of the US is a somewhat surprising event. The animal now starts to learn that the CS is independent of the US.

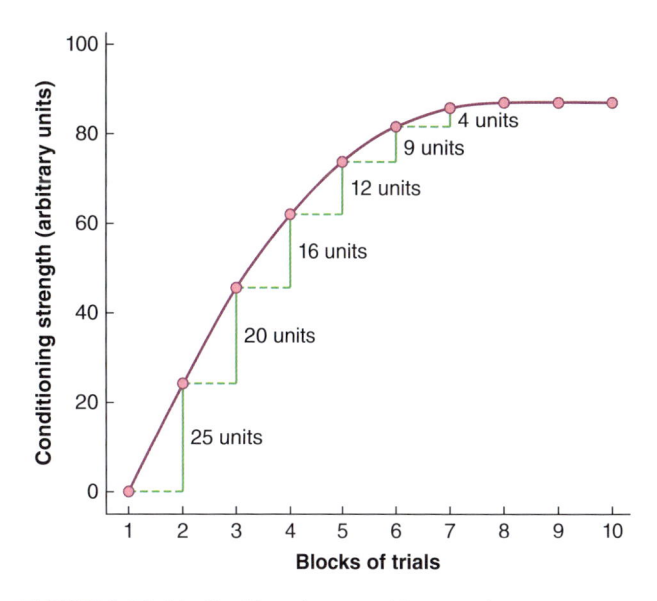

FIGURE 8.11 *Idealized learning curve. The curve is negatively accelerated, which means that the amount of change in conditioning strength (in arbitrary units) gets smaller and smaller with repeated trials.*

The Rescorla–Wagner theory is able to describe classical conditioning mathematically but you will be glad to know that we will not follow this route. Those interested in a full account are directed to the text by Schwartz et al. (2002). Needless to say, the theory could account for compound stimuli, blocking and inhibition, amongst other features.

Applications of Classical Conditioning: From Bench to Bedside

Classical conditioning has been used to explain behaviour such as **phobias** and sexual fetishes (see Boxes 8.2 and 8.3), but there are also treatments that use the laws of conditioning. **Systematic desensitization** involves exposing the individual to the CS gradually. For example, the spider phobic may start with imagining a small spider and progress to different levels of interaction with spiders of increasing size as they begin to get their CR under control. **Flooding** is somewhat similar but instead of a gradual exposure to the CS, participants are thrown in 'at the deep end' and exposed immediately to the CS.

Classical conditioning is also influential in understanding the phenomenon of drug tolerance and overdose (see Chapter 9). Aversive conditioning, as popularized in the book and film *A Clockwork Orange*, can be seen in aversion therapies for the **paraphilias** and is also used in the psychopharmacological treatment of alcoholism. One method is to make the effects of alcohol unpleasant.

BOX 8.5: RESCORLA–WAGNER EQUATION AND ACQUISITION OF CR

The Rescorla–Wagner equation is:

$$\Delta V_n = K(\gamma - \Sigma V_{n-1})$$

V = associative strength (the measure of learning – a theoretical quantity)

K = (range 0–1) salience of the CS and US used; the bigger K, the greater the salience

γ = (≥ 0) reflects the fact that different USs have different asymptote, e.g. the more intense the US, the higher the asymptote, and the higher γ.

The change in associative strength on trial n (ΔV_n) is proportional to the difference between asymptote and the previous associative strength (ΔV_{n-1}). As the trial continues the amount of learning about the CS–US declines (reaches asymptote – the point at which $V = \gamma$ [0]).

The trials below provide a hypothetical example of the Rescorla–Wagner equation used to describe acquisition of learning.

Where	$V = 0$	$K = 0.4$	$\gamma = 80$
Trial 1	0.4 (80–0) = 32		
Trial 2	0.4 (80–32) = 19.2		
Trial 3	0.4 (80–51.2) = 11.28		
Trial 4	0.4 (80–62.48) = 7.008		
Trial 5	0.4 (80–69.488) = 4.2048		
Trial 6	0.4 (80–73.7) = 2.52		
Trial 7	0.4 (80–76.22) = 1.52		
Trial 8	0.4 (80–77.74) = 0.9		
Trial 9	0.4 (80–78.64) = 0.54		
Trial 10	0.4 (80–79.18) = 0.32		

This equation and the result above are represented in Figure 8.11 in which a cumulative graph of learning shows an approach to asymptote, in which conditioning is complete.

The sum of T_1 and T_2, e.g. 32 + 19.2 = 51.2

The amount of learning with each trial declines as there is little new information provided by each successive trial

---

This is called **counter-conditioning** in which the pleasant effects of alcohol are replaced with unpleasant effects (see Schwartz et al., 2002). To achieve counter-conditioning, the pleasant effects of the drug are replaced by nausea and vomiting. This can be induced by another drug called an emetic. **Disulfiram** (Antabuse) is used to produce unpleasant affects if alcohol is consumed. If alcohol is consumed there is a rise in toxic metabolites which produces facial flushing, nausea, vomiting, dizziness and confusion, shortness of breath and changes in heart rate (Peachey, 1981).

Disulfiram can also be placed within a classical conditioning framework. The benefit of disulfiram is that its pharmacological action lasts a number of days. Therefore the process of conditioning can take place outside the clinic.

OPERANT CONDITIONING

In classical conditioning the animal does not make a choice to respond – reflexes are beyond such control. **Operant conditioning** is all about control. Operant conditioning (or instrumental conditioning) is about the organism operating in the environment to produce an outcome. If we do something and the outcome is good, then there is a greater chance we will do it again.

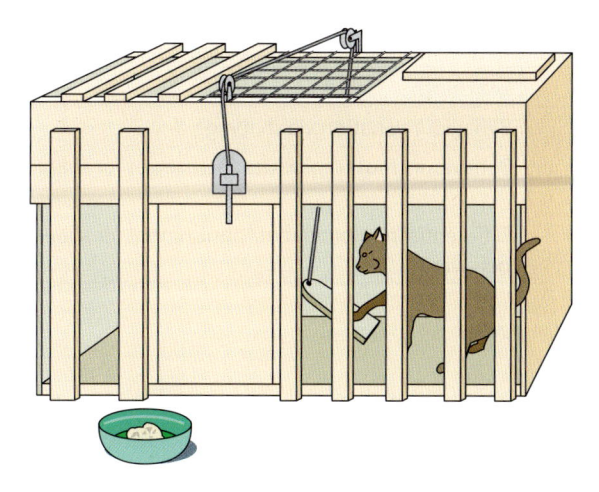

FIGURE 8.12 Thorndike's puzzle box.
Source: Comer, R., Gould, E. & Furnham, A. (2013). *Psychology*. Chichester, UK: Wiley. Reproduced with permission.

In operant conditioning, we are addressing goal-directed behaviour.

The Law of Effect

Thorndike (1898) described learning from his experiments with cats. He put a cat in a cage with a latch on the door. Outside the cage he placed cat food – something the cat was motivated to obtain (Figure 8.12). In the cage, initially the cat engaged in a set of seemingly random behaviours, e.g. scratching, sniffing, circling, etc. Eventually, by accident rather than design, the cat knocked the latch on the door. The door opened; the cat got the food. Successive trials of this nature led the cat to gain access to the food quickly. The behaviour exhibited by the cat was strengthened by its relationship with reward. Thorndike referred to this as the **law of effect**. In essence, the cat learns which of its many behaviours leads to freedom and food. It is a gradual process (see Figure 8.13), which leads to the strengthening of a stimulus–response (S–R) relationship. The acquisition of learning how to operate the environment to access food was a gradual process in which there was no eureka moment in which the cat '*knew*' what to do (I've placed the word '*knew*' in italics because obviously we have no idea what the cat knows – this is just anthropomorphic language that serves as an illustration of the processes and would ideally be avoided).

Behaviourism

B.F. Skinner was instrumental in shaping **behaviourism** and put forward the view that behaviour followed laws. He experimented with pigeons in a box, which became

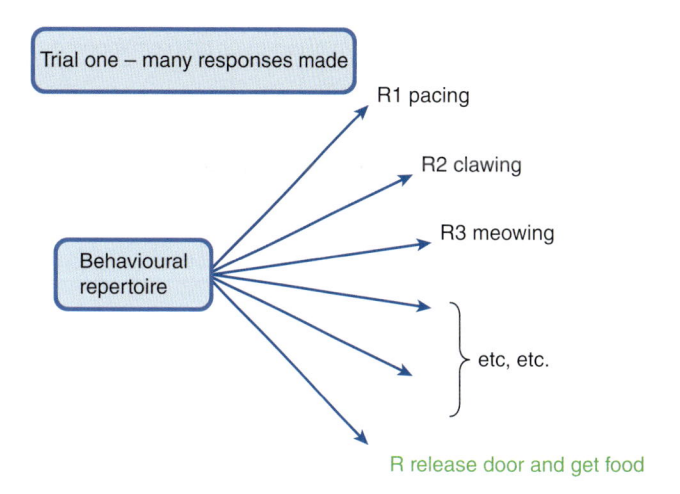

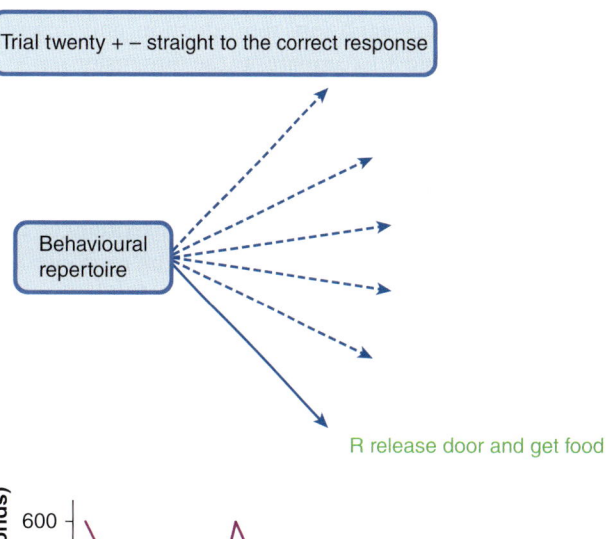

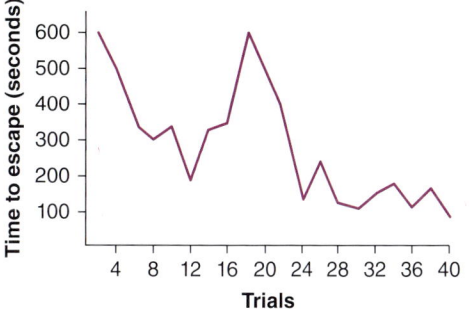

FIGURE 8.13 The law of effect and acquisition of learning.

known as the Skinner box (or operant chamber). Using the laws of behaviourism, rats can be trained to perform complex laboratory tasks and also other activities that are associated more with dogs. The basic premise is the same as the law of effect: S–R associations. In Skinner's view 'operant conditioning is a second kind of selection by consequences' (Skinner, 1981, p.501). Skinner (1984) continues the evolutionary or adaptive nature of operant conditioning: 'The operant response would be an exact duplicate of the phylogenic response, and the strengthening consequences would be the same, contributing to

TABLE 8.1 *The three dimensions of evolution and conditioning*

Dimensions	Evolution	Learning
Variation	Trait variation	Behaviour variation via shaping
Reproduction	Trait variants must reproduce themselves, e.g. inheritance	Behaviours must reproduce themselves for shaping
Differential success	Some variations of a trait are more successful than others (fitness)	Differential reinforcement/ punishment for shaping behaviour

the survival of the individual and hence of the species through both natural selection and an evolved susceptibility to reinforcement' (p.219).

There are parallels on three dimensions of evolution and conditioning: variation, reproduction and differential success. Table 8.1 compares these dimensions.

Reinforcement

Fundamental to operant conditioning is **reinforcement**. For behaviour to be repeated, it has to be reinforced. Reinforcement is when the consequences of a response increase the probability that the response will reoccur. If a rat presses a lever and gets food, it will be more likely to press the lever again. If you work hard for a test and get a good mark, you are more likely to work hard for the next test. The first example uses a **primary reinforcer** (e.g. food, water, shelter and sex). The primary reinforcers are essential for survival. In order for our DNA to be passed on, we have to survive and we have to have sex – the primary reinforcers ensure this happens. Chapter 16 looks in more depth at motivation. A secondary reinforcer is something that does not satisfy a physical need (e.g. money, praise or attention); for example, while the scores in a test are important to us as individuals, they are not directly essential for survival.

Positive and negative reinforcement

Using reinforcement, behaviours can be selected and strengthened. There are two types of reinforcement: positive and negative. **Positive reinforcement** is when a reinforcer is presented after a response and it increases the likelihood of that response recurring. In animal experiments, food is a positive reinforcer. For humans, money and praise (particularly in children) are positive reinforcers. Basically, you get something you want after you have done something (e.g. wages for working, stickers for good behaviour).

An experiment with monkeys demonstrated that they would reject unequal pay conditions. In this experiment, they would not participate in the experiment if they saw another monkey get a better reward for less work (Brosnan & de Waal, 2003) – welcome to the 21st century! Clearly, there is something more complex occurring in these monkeys than just associative learning, but more of that later.

Negative reinforcement also increases the probability of a particular response. However, in this case, it is the removal of an unpleasant event or circumstance that strengthens a response. For example, a pigeon will peck a shape to escape an electric shock (Rachlin, 1969). When a stimulus is indicative of electric shock, the rat will press a lever and thus avoid the shock. Similarly, humans respond to negative reinforcement, e.g. you leave early to make sure you get to your morning exam, thus avoiding the hideous rush-hour traffic and the perils of public transport. The rules of positive and negative reinforcement have been used to account for drug addiction – positive reinforcement for the initial hedonic effects and then later perhaps negative reinforcement in order to avoid withdrawal (see Chapter 10 and Box 8.6).

Punishment

The first point to note about **punishment** is that it is *not* negative reinforcement. The difference between punishment and negative reinforcement focuses on what it does to a particular behaviour. Negative reinforcement *increases* the likelihood of a particular behaviour, whereas punishment *decreases* the likelihood of a particular behaviour. Thus, punishment is used to stop a behaviour whereas reinforcement is used to promote a behaviour.

Punishment can be subdivided into positive and negative punishment. Positive punishment is when behaviour leads to an undesired consequence. In the rat this could be an electric shock. In the human it could be a fine for illegal parking. Negative punishment is when behaviour results in the removal of or failure to obtain a desired reinforcer. In the rat this could be restricted access to food (e.g. Chandler & Stolerman, 1997). In the child it could be the removal of television time.

In order for punishment to be as effective as possible, it should contain three features. First, the

BOX 8.6: REINFORCEMENT STRENGTH OF DRUGS

Addiction is an increasing problem which drives the need to understand it more. One of the ways to do this is to create an animal model of drug addiction. Drug self-administration is one such method. The animal, typically a rat, has an indwelling catheter connected to a pump that will deliver an infusion of a drug when the rat performs a task such as a bar press in an operant chamber.

Using drug self-administration permits a greater understanding of the following features.

- Acquisition (conditions under which drug self-administration can be fostered)
- Extinction (elimination of drug consumption – not an effective treatment!)
- Drug-induced reinstatement (the free priming dose)
- Cue-induced reinstatement (the environmental stimuli associated with drugs)
- Stress-induced reinstatement (the enemy of abstinence)
- Choice of stimulus
- The magnitude of the reinforcement

Drugs can vary in their relative abilities to affect self-administration. One question is how reinforcing is the drug? Progressive ratio (PR) schedules of drug delivery generate an index of a reinforcing efficacy – the break point, the point at which the animal no longer works for the drug (Stafford et al., 1998). Animals on a PR schedule have to work increasingly harder as the session continues. They start with a fixed ratio 1 schedule (FR1, see below) and the ratio is doubled with each response:

FR1 → 2 → 4 → 8 → 16 → 32 → 64, etc., etc.

Cocaine increases the breakpoint in animals (Richardson & Roberts, 1996) and humans (Stoops et al., 2010). In the wonderfully titled paper 'How to make a rat addicted to cocaine', Roberts et al. (2007) illustrate how a rat works for cocaine on a FR1 schedule and then a PR schedule.

There are numerous variations on the self-administration paradigm which allow a more detailed analysis (Banks & Negus, 2012). However, the behavioural economics of drug self-administration can take on a more complicated turn when looking at demand. When demand is measured at different prices, a demand curve is produced which normally follows the law of demand: demand for a drug decreases as its price increases (Bentzley et al., 2013).

Is drug self-administration a good animal model of addiction? On the surface, it appears to be but addiction itself is a complex disorder and in this model we are only measuring consumption and operant behaviour. Drug self-administration in the animal has good predictive and face validity. It is when we get to construct validity that we encounter a fundamental problem (Goudie, 1991). The question remains as to why the animal is performing the behaviour. The first answer is that the drug is a positive reinforcer and that it is an appetitive stimulus. However, there is a second explanation which regards the drug as a negative reinforcer. The animal may continue to press a bar not because they want the drug effect *per se* but because the drug alleviates the unpleasant effects of being without the drug – hence a negative reinforcer. A drug can be both a positive reinforcer and a negative reinforcer at different times in the drug-taking career. As someone starts taking drugs, there are the positive reinforcing effects such as the high but these develop tolerance over time. Negative reinforcement comes into play later in the time course and exerts an influence on consumption to offset the withdrawal symptoms which often present in the absence of the drug in the addict. This has been referred to as the dark side of addiction (Koob, 2013; Koob & Le Moal, 2005).

---

punishment has to come straight after the behaviour; there has to be contiguity between the response and the punishment. Second, the behaviour has to be consistently punished; failure to be consistent means that an association between the behaviour and the punishment is not established. Third, the punishment needs to be sufficiently aversive, but not too aversive. If the punishment is not sufficient then the behaviour may continue. A slap on the wrist for armed robbery is insufficient to stop the criminal reoffending. If the punishment is too aversive then other problems may occur, like high levels of fear and anxiety.

There are also a number of problems with punishment. The first is that the recipient of punishment may, via classical conditioning, come to fear the person giving the punishment rather than the punishment itself.

In such a scenario, there is a failure to modify the undesired behaviour. Additionally, there is a new problem created – fear – which can be very difficult to eliminate (LeDoux, 2000). For example, a dog requires training. During training, the trainer may punish the dog. Consequently, the dog may cower at the sight of its trainer (a CER) and not make the association between behaviour and punishment.

Due to the unpleasant consequences of punishment, a person may seek to escape it. To escape punishment, they may cheat and lie. If escape is not possible, the person may consider aggression and attack. Think of a bank robber – the consequence of punishment is sufficient to make the robber challenge police with violence. If eventually caught, the robber may lie about the crime. The robber will still engage in the activity, but become more devious in order to avoid detection.

Punishment may suppress many behaviours rather than eliminate one. The person may just give up and become apathetic. Finally, the punished may start to imitate the punisher. A child will imitate and learn from its parents. If parents use physical punishment, this is likely to be seen in their children.

Schedules of reinforcement

When a particular behaviour is reinforced every time, it is said to be on a **continuous reinforcement (CRF) schedule**. Behaviourists consider all our actions to be under the control of operant conditioning (see Box 8.6). Clearly we are not on a CRF schedule for all our behaviours, so how is behaviour maintained in the absence of a CRF schedule?

The answer can be found when we consider partial reinforcement. With partial reinforcement the organism is not reinforced every time it responds. There are four **schedules of reinforcement**. The nature of the schedule can influence the response output of the organism (or, as in the examples below, the rat).

Fixed ratio schedules

With a **fixed ratio (FR) schedule**, the rat is reinforced after a number of bar presses. If the schedule is said to be FR10, this means that the rat is reinforced after the 10th response has been made. Similarly on an FR30, schedule the 30th response is reinforced. People on piecework are on FR schedules (i.e. they get paid for, say, every 100 boxes packed).

A rat on an FR schedule will respond (work) rapidly until the reinforcer is delivered. After reinforcement there is a pause, which is followed by another period of rapid responding (see Figure 8.14).

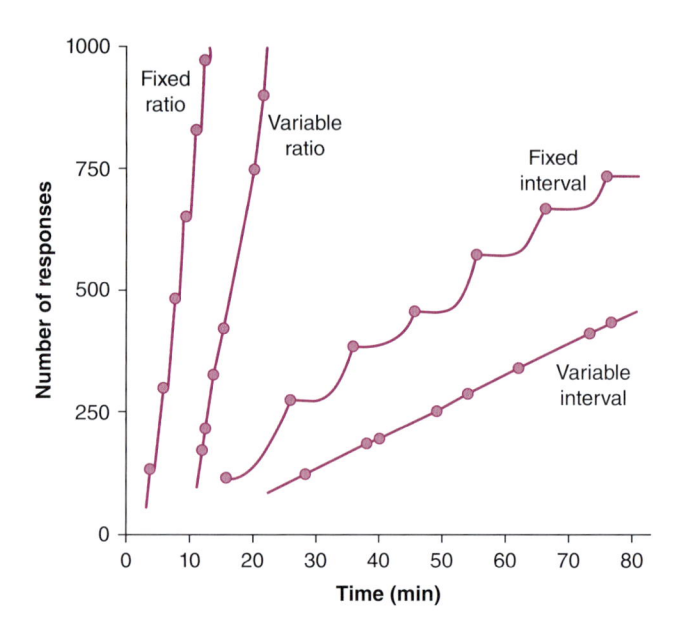

FIGURE 8.14 *Schedules.*

Variable ratio schedules

A **variable ratio (VR) schedule** is similar to the FR schedule, except that reinforcement occurs after a variable amount of responses. If the rat is on a VR10 schedule then it is reinforced *on average* after 10 responses. However, this varies around an average of 10. Sometimes the rat receives reinforcement after five responses and other times after 15. On a VR schedule, the rat does not know exactly when the reinforcement is going to occur. A VR schedule produces a high rate of rapid and constant responding (see Figure 8.14).

The VR schedule is resistant to extinction. This is demonstrated clearly in gamblers. Slot machines are on VR schedules: sometimes you win but many times you do not. A machine is programmed to pay out on a VR schedule. You will get reinforced every so often but you cannot predict the payout. This schedule means you keep putting money in the machine.

Fixed interval schedules

A **fixed interval (FI) schedule** is when, after a specified period of time, the rat receives reinforcement only if it has pressed the bar during that time, e.g. the microwave ready meal requires a specific time to be set before the food is cooked just right – too early and it isn't cooked, too long and it is burnt! A rat on an FI30 schedule receives reinforcement every 30 seconds if it has pressed the bar. The rat may press the bar once or many times in the intervening period between reinforcements. A clear scallop shape is produced in the cumulative response record (see Figure 8.14). This happens because the rat learns not to respond at the beginning of the interval and only starts responding towards the end of the interval.

Variable interval schedules

A rat on a **variable interval (VI) schedule** receives reinforcement after an average period of time only if it has responded correctly, e.g. you may compulsively check your status updates and news feeds on whatever social media you use, but that checking is not rewarded every time – sometimes you get a reward after five minutes, sometimes after 15 minutes. On a VI30 schedule the rat receives reinforcement on average after 30 seconds, but sometimes after 20 seconds and sometimes after 40. This schedule produces slow but consistent responding (see Figure 8.14). Home Office inspectors (see Chapter 1) visit animal laboratories on a VI schedule to spot-check that the law is being adhered to and animal welfare maintained. If they arrived on an FI schedule then the laboratories could predict an inspection and could put on a 'good show' just for the inspectors.

Schedules can change as learning progresses both within and across schedule type. The schedule is an important aspect of studies within behavioural pharmacology. The schedule itself can determine the effect a drug has (see Chapter 9).

Acquisition

Animals, like people, do not learn immediately. A number of learning trials have to be completed before a rat can respond to a stimulus reliably. Many of the experiments you will read about have involved long, and sometimes complex, training regimes. The more complex the task, the longer the training. In the example of rats as drug connoisseurs, Garcha and Stolerman (1989) required up to 90 sessions of 15 minutes' duration for the rat to be a reliable detector of nicotine.

Shaping and Conditioning by Successive Approximations

A complex piece of behaviour cannot be learned overnight. In order to train an animal one must start with simple behaviours, which contribute to the overall goal behaviour. Once acquired, new behaviours can be worked on and refined. This process is called **shaping**. The shaping of the smaller subsets of behaviours is called **conditioning by successive approximations** – that is, one reinforces behaviours that are getting closer to the desired behaviour. Such procedures are used regularly in training animals (dogs in particular).

Extinction

On a CRF the animal stops responding soon after reinforcement stops. Initially a rat presses the lever rapidly (an **extinction burst**), but eventually this diminishes until it stops responding altogether. Partial reinforcement schedules make extinction of a response more difficult (see Figure 8.15).

Spontaneous Recovery

As is the case with classical conditioning, spontaneous recovery can occur. After a period of absence from training, the rat, on reacquaintance with the apparatus, will start responding again.

Discrimination and Generalization

The animal is able to discriminate between stimuli that bring about reinforcement and stimuli that do not. These are called **discriminative stimuli (SD)**. A pigeon will peck an illuminated key for food reinforcement. It will peck any key at first but if reinforcement is made contingent upon pressing a green key (and not a red key), the pigeon learns to discriminate between the two stimuli. The green switch is called S^+ (a stimulus that is contingent with reinforcement). The red key is S^- (a stimulus that is *not* contingent with reinforcement). The colour of the key is a clear SD. Other discriminative stimuli can be subtler. A pigeon may go on to discriminate between shades of green, for instance.

Unlike discriminative learning, generalization refers to the phenomenon where an animal responds to different stimuli. The pigeon that is trained to discriminate between coloured switches initially generalizes to all coloured switches.

Interoceptive and Exteroceptive Stimuli

Up to this point, the animal has produced a response to an SD (a light or a tone). This is an **exteroceptive stimulus** (sometimes called a stimulus cue). The rat detects the SD, presses a lever and gets reinforced.

A rat can also respond to its internal physiological state (an **interoceptive stimulus** or cue). A procedure called **drug discrimination** is used to understand the stimulus properties of drugs. The rat uses the feelings derived from a drug to determine which bar in the operant chamber leads to reinforcement (see Box 8.8).

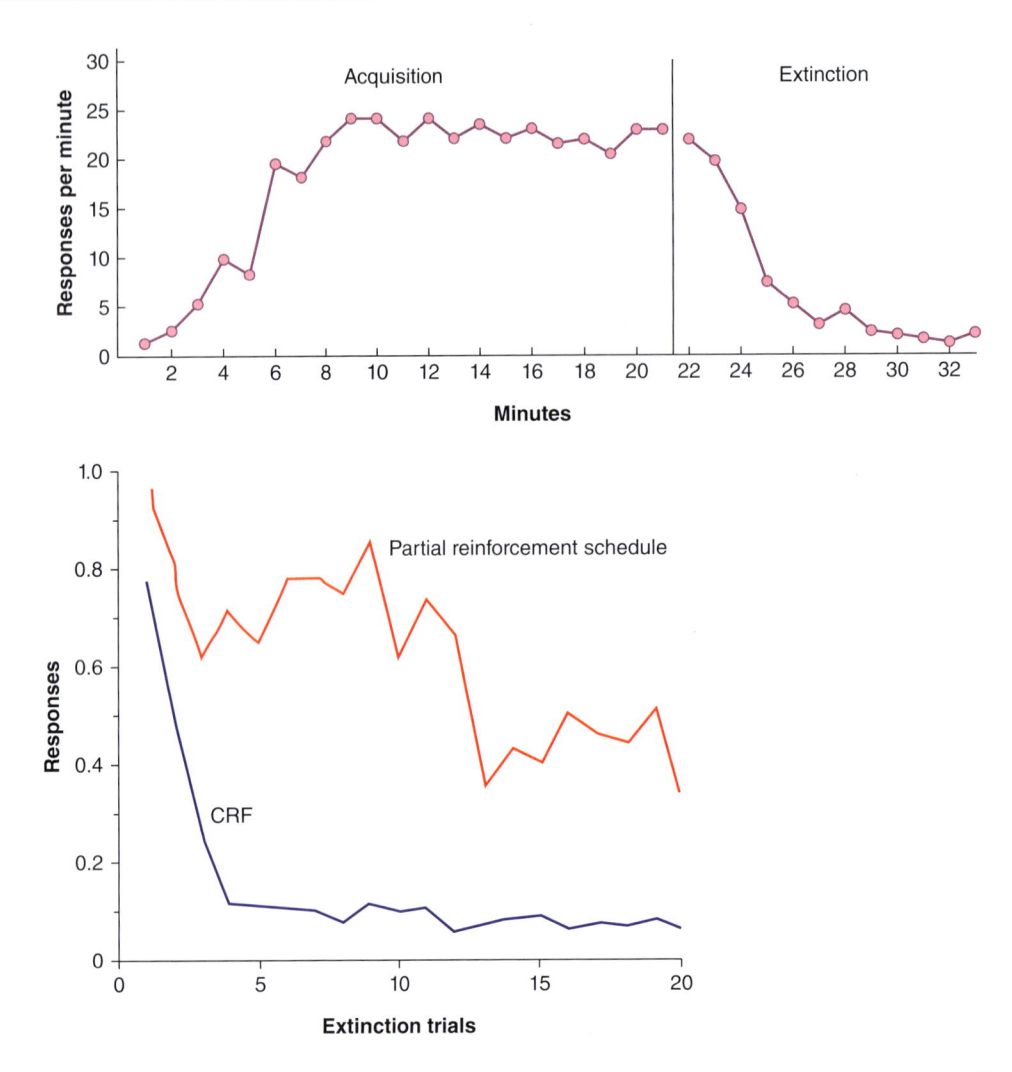

FIGURE 8.15 *Acquisition and extinction of lever pressing. This hypothetical curve depicts the growth in the frequency of lever pressing over time, followed by its extinction when reinforcement is discontinued.*

BOX 8.8: DRUG DISCRIMINATION

In the vast majority of behavioural experiments using operant conditioning, a signal is provided telling the animal that it is time to respond and if it does respond, it may get reinforced. Usually such signals are exteroceptive signals (cues) such as a light or a sound. However, the animal can be trained to respond in the same way as with exteroceptive cues but with interoceptive cues. Why would you do this and why is it interesting?

People take drugs for a number of reasons, but one of those reasons is how a drug makes them feel, e.g. euphoria or alertness. We can access how a drug feels in a human by asking them questions but we do not have that opportunity with animals. We can ask the questions, but the answers have to be in the form of overt behaviour rather than language. The capacity to detect the feelings that the drug creates can be mirrored to some extent in the animal using a procedure called drug discrimination. Nearly all drugs of abuse are readily discriminated by humans but also by animals. If we can understand the mechanisms that bring about the affective components of the drug, we may go some way in understanding why people take certain drugs and how those feelings are processed in the brain.

Animals can be trained to be drug connoisseurs in an operant conditioning process. This can be done by getting the animal to perform a task to obtain food when they have received a drug. Experimental procedures used mazes with the drug acting as a cue for the direction the animal should take. The most common method of drug discrimination is using the operant chamber. Early experiments involved one lever being present in the chamber and reward being contingent upon pressing that lever when the drug is present. There is a methodological problem with this procedure as some drugs increase motor activity in general. In the case of a drug like nicotine, which is a psychostimulant similar to amphetamine, that enhances locomotor activity under certain conditions; the animal may just press the bar because it is very active rather than because it is discriminating when it has or has not had the drug. To avoid such confounding variables of locomotor activity, two bars can be present in the operant chamber; one bar is associated with drug, the other is associated with saline (Morrison & Stephenson, 1969). In such experiments, being able to discriminate having the drug can be teased apart from the drug's effect on locomotor activity. Therefore, we can be more confident that we are measuring the stimulus properties of the drug.

Continuing the example of nicotine, we know people smoke and that nicotine is the prime reason for that behaviour. Rats can also detect the presence of nicotine but we do not do this by inducing the rat to smoke. The rat is given an injection of nicotine approximately 15 minutes before being put in the operant chamber. Obviously the rat has to be trained to use the nicotine cue to direct its behaviour. Training can take a number of months and starts with the animal being acclimatized to the environment. In order to motivate the animal to behave by pressing the lever for food, it has to be placed on a restricted diet, e.g. 80% of the feeding weight (the animal is 20% lighter than it would be if it could eat all the time; this is similar to a rat in the wild which has to forage for its food). Training starts by placing the animal in the operant chamber and teaching it that the clicking sound of the food magazine results in food being available in the hopper. Once that is mastered, one of the retractable bars is placed in the chamber and every time the animal presses it, it receives a reward (FR1). The next day the other bar is presented under the same circumstances. As the rat masters the task, the FR schedule is steadily increased up to FR5, for example. Note that no drug has been given to the animal yet once they have acquired the basic premise of the task, injections of nicotine can commence. In an experiment of this kind, one only needs to use approximately eight rats because they act as their own controls. Four of the rats will receive nicotine and food will be contingent upon pressing the left bar. The other four rats receive the nicotine injection and food will be contingent on pressing the right bar. This is a counterbalance design to avoid any inherent side bias the rat may have. It is important to note that the rat does not press a bar to receive the drug, the drug is given by the experimenters prior to the rat being put in the operant chamber. The experimental paradigm known as drug self-administration is when the animal performs a behaviour to receive the drug as a reinforcer. In drug discrimination studies the drug acts as a cue for food reinforcement. In order to avoid the confounding variable of the injection itself, the rats also receive a saline injection in which they are trained to press the non-nicotine bar.

Training continues so that the rat acquires the association of drug–bar–food. To avoid sequencing effects, the rat will receive saline injections on the other bar on days that it does not receive nicotine.

In order to maintain accuracy and a consistent high level of behaviour in the rat, Stolerman (1993) introduces punishment for an incorrect response. This punishment is not a shock but it is aversive as he resets the FR component, e.g. if the rat is on an FR10 and on the ninth response makes an error, then it has to press 10 more times before it gets a reward. Stolerman also introduces a variable interval component and increases the VI to 60 seconds. This is now a tandem schedule of VI60–FR10. This type of schedule stops the animal from receiving too many reinforcers in a session and also stops it being able to predict reward. Thus, the animal works hard for little pay and in doing so provides a large amount of behaviour to be measured.

Once it has been trained to discriminate nicotine from saline, the nature of the cue can be probed in what are called extinction tests. In an extinction test, both bars are present in the chamber and neither is going to provide reward. The subjects are only put into an extinction test for a short period of time, and together with the tandem schedule during training, they do not realize that they will not be reinforced. The nicotine cue can now be probed fully to determine the mechanisms underlying its stimulus properties. Using nicotinic agonist and antagonists, numerous studies have demonstrated that the stimulus properties of nicotine are mediated via the acetylcholine receptor (Pratt et al., 1983).

Perkins et al. (1994) used a similar behavioural technique in humans rather than experimenter-influenced questionnaires. In these experiments observable behaviour was achieved using an operant task and a cash incentive. Participants delivered nicotine via a nasal spray and depending upon whether the nasal spray had nicotine in it or not, they had to choose either 'A' or 'B'. The nasal spray had to be laced with chilli so that the participants received physical irritation from the spray even when it didn't have nicotine in it because nicotine alone is somewhat unpleasant when sniffed up the nose. Using such experiments in the human, the data of the animal studies are also confirmed (Perkins, 2009). However, the animal studies permit us to probe the brain further than human studies would allow.

Drug discrimination studies demonstrate that our internal state can act like a stimulus cue in much the same way as Skinner's pigeons responded to light and tones.

Applications of Operant Conditioning: From Bench to Bedside

It is a little more obvious how operant conditioning can be applied; after all, as children we were clearly on the receiving end of our carer's reinforcement schedules. The most obvious example is in the classroom where teachers of primary school children reward them with stickers for almost every positive piece of behaviour. These stickers are like crack cocaine for five year olds! They love stickers. These stickers can then be traded for extra playtime or other desirable activities – 'golden time'. Stickers act as tokens that can be exchanged for something more tangible. Money is another token reinforcer – one that can be exchanged for *all* our primary reinforcers!

In schools, at home and in psychiatric services, many behaviour modification interventions use operant conditioning as their basis.

COGNITION IN ANIMALS

Strict behaviourists reject all forms of cognitive explanation that are in opposition to behavioural explanations, but it is possible to conceptualize them in cognitive terms (see Bouton & Moody, 2004) or an interaction of the two (McDonald et al., 2004). More recent theories of animal learning do argue that cognition and cognitive processes underlie learning in animals. Cognition here refers to mental processes that are not subject to direct behavioural observation. In fact, according to Lieberman (2000), the behaviourist view and cognitive view of animal learning have become increasingly similar.

Tolman (1948), who championed the cognitive view, presented the idea of cognitive maps and latent learning. Rats learned to navigate a maze quickly despite an absence of reward. When given rewards, these rats were quick to learn the whereabouts of the reinforcer. Tolman claimed that the rats had a cognitive map of the maze. After receiving reward, the learning of the rat became observable, whereas previously learning was not observable. Behaviourists will account *only* for observable behaviour. Clearly, in Tolman's studies learning had occurred that was not directly observable. This is referred to as **latent learning**.

Tolman argued that behaviour is goal directed and that animals (and humans) act as if they expect certain behaviours to lead to a desired goal (Tolman, 1932, 1959). Dickinson (1989) has further accounted for expectancy in both classical and operant conditioning. His concepts of expectancy involve two types of information.

First, the contiguity between events gives rise to a representation of the associative link between those events. In Pavlov's experiments, the dog developed a representation of the CS and US, which would elicit the CR in response to the CS. That is, the dog developed associative expectations that the bell preceded food and produced salivation in response to the expectation of food.

Second, expectancy involves the belief that a particular behaviour will have a specific effect. In the operant conditioning experiment, the rat presses a bar to get food. That is, there is a *belief* that the behavioural response results in reward. Dickinson (1989) claims that, with increased training, stimulus–response habits emerge that do not involve the expectation that a particular behaviour will lead to reinforcement. Thus, the cognitive phenomenon of expectancy can eventually change into an automatic habit.

The area of animal cognition focuses on how the animal uses experience to form the basis for future behaviour. Of course, how the past affects our behaviour is to do with memory. Cognitive psychologists have demonstrated that there are numerous types of memory (see Chapter 13), but the most common investigated in animals is spatial memory (see Sarter et al., 1992a, 1992b).

The phenomenon of learned helplessness (Seligman, 1975) also points to cognitive learning (see Box 8.4). The animal has to compute the probabilities of affecting the environment and receiving reward. In learned helplessness, a chance level of affecting the environment leads to there being no predictive information about reward contingencies. Underlying the computation of probability are neural mechanisms. Dopamine neurons of the midbrain have been shown to be differentially active on presentation of different probabilities of reward (Fiorillo et al., 2003). Matsumoto et al. (2003) identified the lateral and medial prefrontal cortex (mPFC) as a site that is active when there is anticipation of reward. The mPFC was also identified as the place where responses are selected.

It may not be possible, and it may also be unnecessary, to provide a definitive answer to the cognitive versus associative learning debate. The two forms of learning can co-exist. Cognitive learning involves attention, and concepts of abstraction and expectation. Associative learning may represent automatic processes that are well learned and do not require conscious attention.

SUMMARY

The study of animal learning has provided us with a more thorough understanding of the laws underlying how associations are made. Using associative learning and animals allows us to probe many questions about acquisition of information, biological processes and motivation, memory and other aspects of cognition. Throughout this book, learning theory will be used as a tool to enhance our understanding.

LEARNING OUTCOME QUESTIONS

You should be able to answer the following questions:

- Describe the process of classical conditioning.
- How can the laws of classical conditioning be applied to real-world situations?
- To what extent is behaviour determined by its consequences?
- The use of operant techniques is critically important to understanding behaviour. Discuss.

FURTHER READING

Domjan, M. (2005). Pavlovian conditioning: a functional perspective. *Annual Review of Psychology*, 56, 179–206.
Schwartz, B., Wasserman, E. A., & Robbins, S. J. (2002). *Psychology of Learning and Behavior*. New York: W.W. Norton.
Skinner, B. K. (1971). *Beyond Freedom and Dignity*. Harmondsworth, UK: Penguin.

MIND MAP

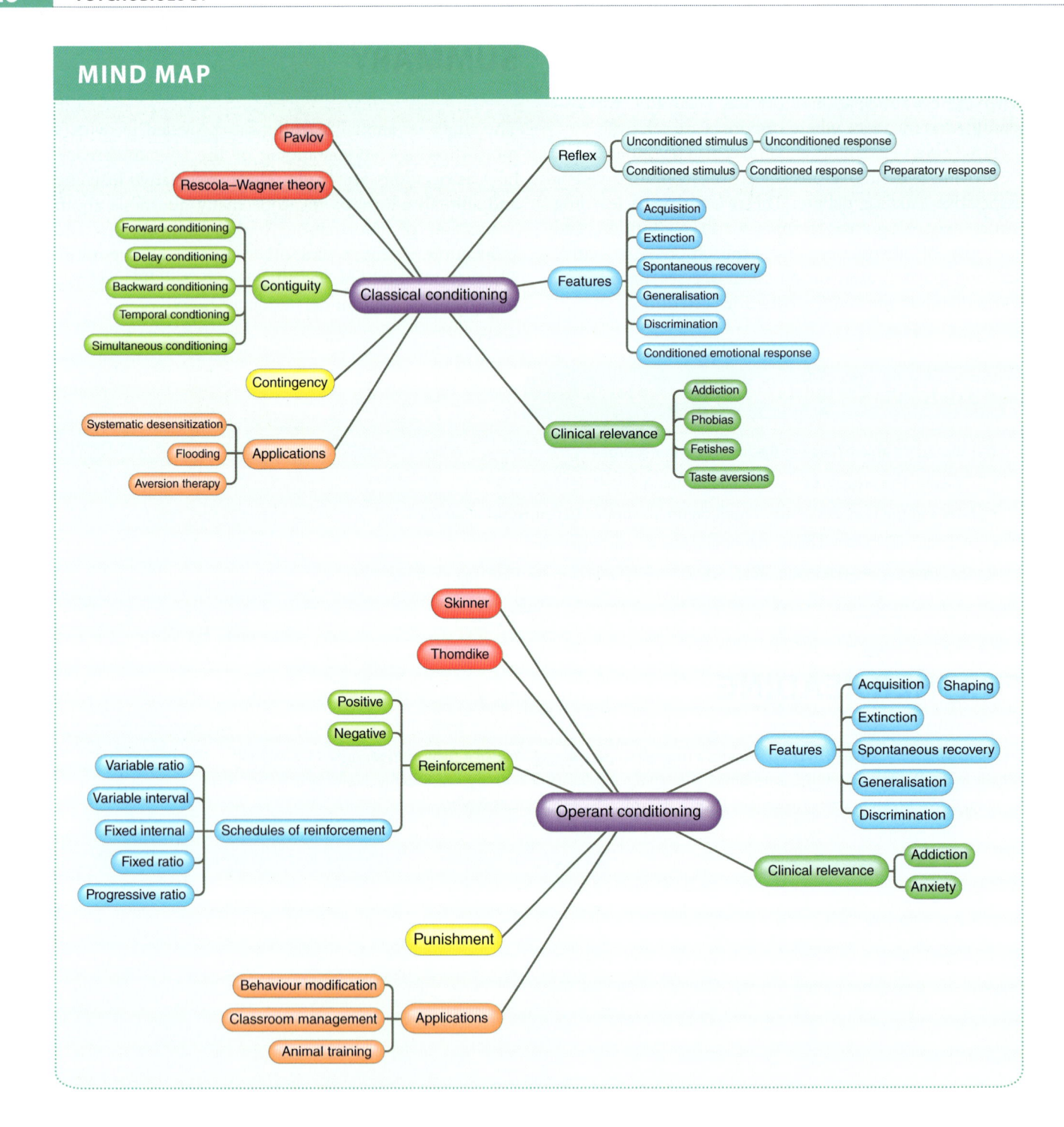

Classical conditioning

- Pavlov
- Rescola–Wagner theory
- Contiguity
  - Forward conditioning
  - Delay conditioning
  - Backward conditioning
  - Temporal condtioning
  - Simultaneous conditioning
- Contingency
- Applications
  - Systematic desensitization
  - Flooding
  - Aversion therapy
- Reflex
  - Unconditioned stimulus — Unconditioned response
  - Conditioned stimulus — Conditioned response — Preparatory response
- Features
  - Acquisition
  - Extinction
  - Spontaneous recovery
  - Generalisation
  - Discrimination
  - Conditioned emotional response
- Clinical relevance
  - Addiction
  - Phobias
  - Fetishes
  - Taste aversions

Operant conditioning

- Skinner
- Thorndike
- Reinforcement
  - Positive
  - Negative
- Schedules of reinforcement
  - Variable ratio
  - Variable interval
  - Fixed internal
  - Fixed ratio
  - Progressive ratio
- Punishment
- Applications
  - Behaviour modification
  - Classroom management
  - Animal training
- Features
  - Acquisition — Shaping
  - Extinction
  - Spontaneous recovery
  - Generalisation
  - Discrimination
- Clinical relevance
  - Addiction
  - Anxiety

9 Drugs and Behaviour: Behaviour and Drugs

(Co-Authored with Semanthi Sagathevan)

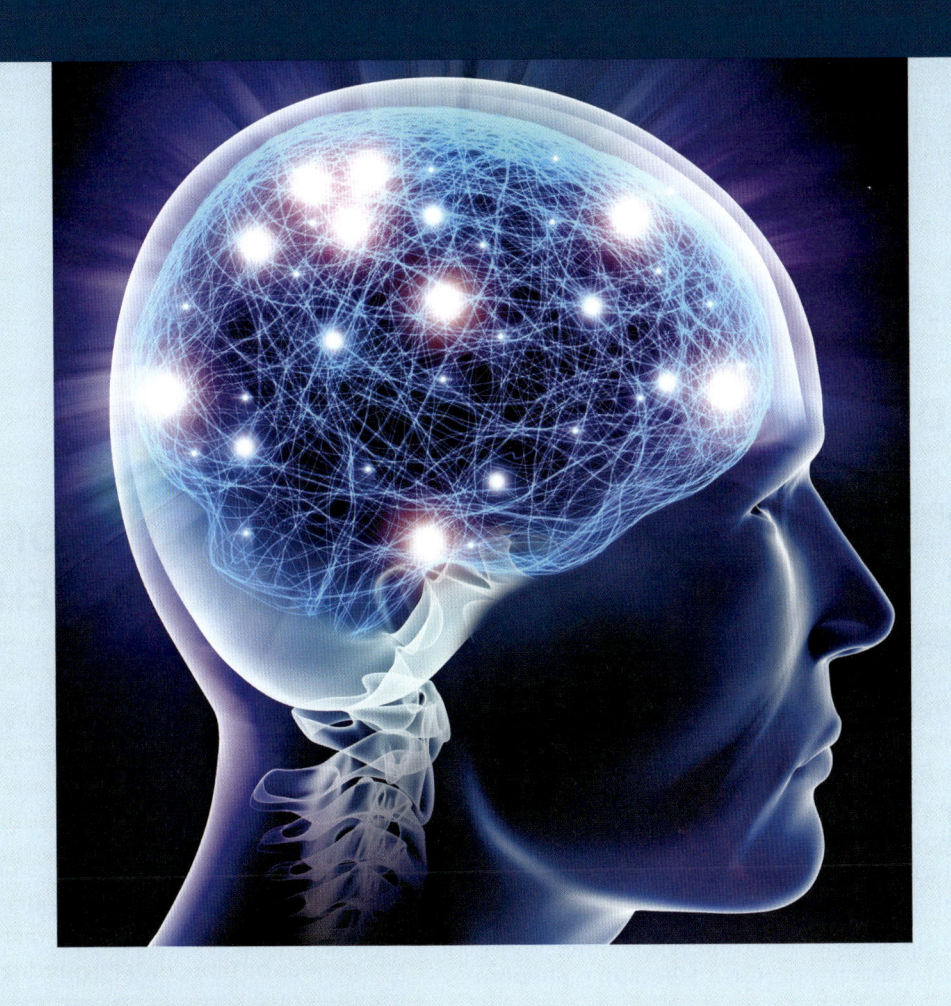

ANATOMY OF THE CHAPTER

This chapter will highlight the following.

- The schedule as a determinant of behavioural response to a drug.
- Tolerance, sensitization and conditioning.
- The placebo effect.

INTRODUCTION 228

SCHEDULES AS FUNDAMENTAL DETERMINANTS OF DRUG-ELICITED BEHAVIOUR 228

TOLERANCE 230

SENSITIZATION 233

THE PLACEBO 233

SUMMARY 243

LEARNING OUTCOMES

1. To understand how behaviour, the environment and learning can affect the response of a drug.

2. To understand the processes by which tolerance and sensitization can occur to a drug and its clinical application.

3. To understand the mechanisms of the placebo response/effect and the ethical implications of its use.

INTRODUCTION

Psychopharmacology has a tendency to portray itself as a discipline in which drugs affect behaviour. Chapter 7 was also guilty of adopting such a perspective. However, the behavioural effect of a drug is determined as much by baseline levels of behaviour as by the pharmacology of the drug itself. In terms of behaviour, the psychopharmacologist needs to be aware that the experimental conditions themselves can determine how the drug behaves. Much of the work that has contributed to our understanding of how behaviour affects a drug response is historical and animal focused. Sadly, many textbooks on psychopharmacology do not address adequately such issues and because of the historic nature they are consigned to the past. Furthermore, it is important to understand that this is not just a laboratory phenomenon seen in a handful of animals; there are practical clinical aspects of understanding how behaviour affects drugs.

Whilst this chapter focuses on drug effect there is another phenomenon that is critically important to understand when evaluating drugs and how drug responses can be formed. This is the area of placebos. Placebos are normally pharmacologically inert substances but by virtue of the context in which they are taken, they can bring about very real effects in the consumer.

To begin with, an understanding of how behaviour affects drug response can be achieved by manipulating behaviour by altering the environment, most notably in the operant chamber or Skinner box.

SCHEDULES AS FUNDAMENTAL DETERMINANTS OF DRUG-ELICITED BEHAVIOUR

Schedules of reinforcement, discussed in Chapter 8, have been used to elucidate the behavioural mechanisms affecting the drug response. Using operant techniques to understand drug effects has become a well-established methodology. Sanger (1987) asserts that there are practical advantages of using operant techniques.

- Schedule-controlled behaviours provide predictable patterns of responding that are stable for long periods of time, thus permitting subjects to act as their own control in before-and-after drug designs.
- Individual animals can be studied in detail.
- The patterns of schedule-controlled responding can be applied across many species.
- Many different reinforcing events can be used to maintain schedule control behaviour, thereby permitting motivational factors to be determined, e.g. appetitive stimuli compared to aversive stimulation.
- Schedule-controlled behaviour is often sensitive to drug effects.

The first study that demonstrated the true importance of schedule-controlled behaviour in relation to

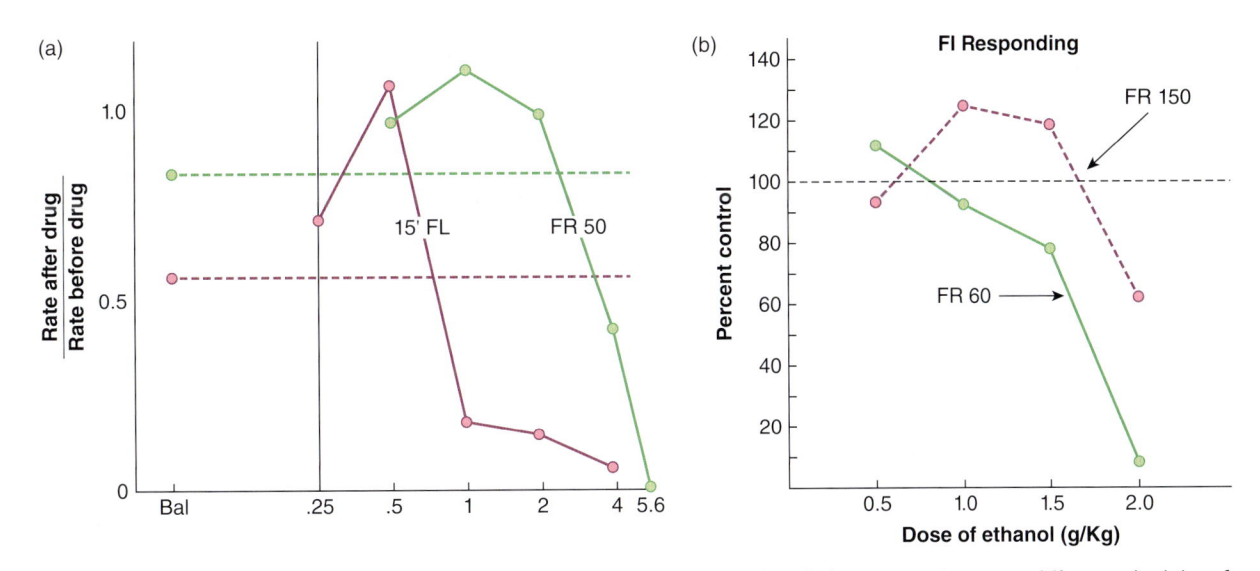

FIGURE 9.1 Schedule-controlled behaviour. (a) The effect of pentobarbital on pecking behaviour in pigeons on different schedules of reinforcement. (b) The effects of different FR schedules on alcohol reduced response rates. Alcohol reduced responding (key pecking by pigeons) on an FR60 schedule to a greater extent than an FR150 schedule.
Source: (a) Dews, P. B. (1955). Studies on behavior. I. Differential sensitivity to pentobarbital of pecking performance in pigeons depending on the schedule of reward. *Journal of Pharmacology and Experimental Therapeutics, 113*(4), 393–401. Reproduced by permission of ASPECT.
Source: (b) Redrawn from Barrett, J. E., & Stanley, J. A. (1980). Effects of ethanol on multiple fixed-interval fixed-ratio schedule performances: Dynamic interactions at different fixed-ratio values. *Journal of the Experimental Analysis of Behavior, 34*(2), 185–198.

drug effects was by Dews (1955). In this study Dews trained four pigeons to peck an illuminated disc for food. Two pigeons were placed on an FR50 (fixed ratio of 50 responses before reinforcement) and the other two were placed on a FI 15 minutes (fixed interval of 15 minutes in which the first response made after the key had been illuminated within 15 minutes was reinforced – premature responding was not rewarded) (Figure 9.1). Once responding was stable, the pigeons then received different doses of the barbiturate pentobarbital which is a CNS depressant acting at the GABA receptor. Dose–response curves were obtained for all the animals under the two schedules of reinforcement. Then the animals were placed on the alternative schedules of reinforcement and again once they were stable, they were administered pentobarbital. In this study, everything was the same except for the schedule of reinforcement.

The effects of pentobarbital can be seen in Figure 9.1. At 1 and 2 mg/kg the effect is strikingly different across the two schedules of reinforcement. Under FR50, 1 and 2 mg/kg produce behavioural activation whereas under FI 15 minutes, pentobarbital reduced response rates. This figure also demonstrates the importance of having a variety of doses because it is only at these two doses that the differential effect is seen. A similar effect was seen with alcohol with a fixed ratio component adjusted on a tandem FR-FI 3 minutes schedule. Under the FR60 component of the tandem schedule, moderate doses of alcohol reduced response rates, whereas on an FR150 schedule responding was increased (see Figure 9.1) (Barrett & Stanley, 1980).

This is not unique to pentobarbital; differential effects are seen with many drugs. A study by Clark and Steele (1966) revealed that amphetamine has different effects on response rates with an FI 4 minute schedule, an FR25 schedule or an extinction schedule. The high rates of responding produced by the FR schedule were reduced by amphetamine whereas the intermediate rates of responding under FI produced a slight increase at low doses; on an extinction schedule amphetamine increased responding (Figure 9.2). This is consistent with numerous studies looking at the effects of amphetamine on many behaviours (Dews & Wegner, 1977) in which amphetamine exhibits stimulatory effects when baseline rates are low and the doses are low. When amphetamine is given at high dose and baseline rates are low, responding is reduced and when it is given when there are high levels of baseline responding, it is seen as a depressant (see Boxes 9.1 and 9.2 for clinical applications). You may

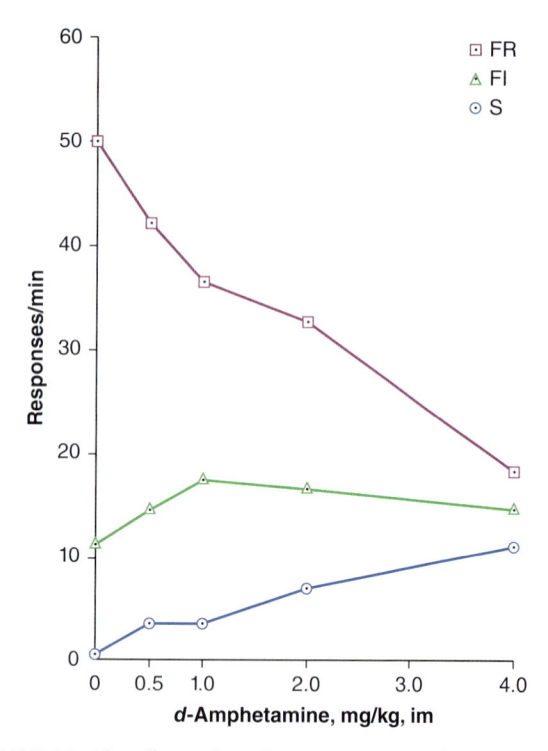

FIGURE 9.2 *The effects of amphetamine on FR and FI schedules. Amphetamine decrease responding in rats on an FR25 schedule. Extinction produced little responding and an FI 4 minute schedule increased responding at low doses of amphetamine but started to decrease with higher doses. S, response rate when not receiving reinforcement.*
Source: Clark, F. C., & Steele, B. J. (1966). Effects of d-amphetamine on performance under a multiple schedule in the rat. *Psychopharmacologia, 9*(2), 157–169. With kind permission from Springer Science and Business Media.

question the fact that under different schedules the animal receives different volumes of reinforcement but such an effect has not been upheld (Sanger & Blackman, 1981).

This is not restricted to positive reinforcement. In an experiment on squirrel monkeys, Kelleher and Morse (1964) altered the schedule of reinforcement (FR30 or FI10) and the reinforcer, which was either escape from a conditioned stimulus (CS) that was linked to shock or the delivery of food which was a positive reinforcer. Under these conditions, amphetamine was administered. The results indicated that the dose–response curves differed between the two schedules. The FR30 schedule was not affected by low doses but an increase was measured at high doses. Under an FI10 schedule increases were seen at low doses and decreases at the highest dose. The shape of the dose–response curve was similar for both positive and negative reinforcers, indicating that it was the schedule that was important rather than the reinforcing itself. However, this was not the case with morphine which decreased food-maintained responding and increased shock-maintained responding (McKearney, 1974) and similar effects were found with alcohol, chlordiazepoxide and pentobarbital (Barrett, 1976). One tentative explanation for this is that food and shock presentations have different durations and engender different types and intensities of elicited behaviours (McKearney & Barrett, 1978).

The behavioural parameters surrounding the effects of the drug extend beyond positive and negative reinforcement and include punishment (McKearney & Barrett, 1978), providing further support for the schedule as a fundamental determinant of behaviour. The effect of behaviour and drug responses extends beyond the immediate demands of the experiment. The behavioural history of an organism can determine subsequent responses to a drug under the experimental conditions that have already been discussed (Barrett & Witkin, 1986).

The work of Peter Dews and others had clearly demonstrated the importance of pre-existing behaviour and the subsequent effects of drugs. Drugs produce effects but those effects are shaped by variables other than the drug itself. The importance of knowing this in psychopharmacology has been highlighted by Sanger who wrote:

> The now well-established observation that drug induced changes in behavior are not immutable properties of particular drugs, but are dependent on aspects of the experimental situation (such as the schedule of reinforcement), can perhaps be thought of as the most fundamental principle in psychopharmacology. (1987, p.222)

TOLERANCE

Repetitive administration of drugs can produce **tolerance** which can be defined as the diminishing effect of the drug as a result of chronic administration. It can be operationalized in dose–response curves as a shift to the right.

The mechanisms that underlie tolerance are:

- metabolic/pharmacokinetic tolerance
- pharmacodynamic tolerance
- behavioural tolerance.

Pharmacokinetic tolerance is focused on the metabolic pathway of the drug. Repetitive consumption results in the more effective metabolism of the drug, therefore deactivating it, e.g. chronic alcohol treatment increases

BOX 9.1 THE RATE-DEPENDENT HYPOTHESIS AND THE EFFECTS OF AMPHETAMINES IN ATTENTION DEFICIT HYPERACTIVITY DISORDER

It is bizarre that a drug with the street name 'speed' should be effective in treating ADHD. One would expect methylphenidate and amphetamine to exacerbate the symptoms of ADHD. However, these drugs have been argued to work differently in those with ADHD. The difference in ADHD is the baseline of activity prior to treatment; when given to someone with high levels of activity, amphetamine will produce a reduction, whereas someone with a low level of activity may exhibit activation. This is called the **rate-dependent hypothesis**.

The rate-dependent hypothesis of drug effects changed our preconceptions of how drugs work. We are familiar with the concept that drugs bring about an effect and that the drug's pharmacology is central to the behaviour. However, the effects of a drug are not exclusively determined by pharmacological factors, but also by environmental and behavioural factors independent of the drug.

When there are low rates of activity, psychostimulants were shown to increase behaviours (in the early studies pigeons were used), whereas when rates of activity were high they reduced the behaviour (Dews, 1958). Similarly, effects were seen in humans (Dews & Morse, 1958). Numerous studies have built on this work and refined the rate-dependent hypothesis. It has been proposed that rate dependency may account for the effects of methylphenidate and amphetamine in ADHD (Green & Warshauer, 1981; Robbins & Sahakian, 1979). There is some evidence to support a rate-dependent effect of ADHD drugs, but these have been in laboratory tasks (DuPaul et al., 1988; Rapport et al., 1985; Weber, 1985). However, comparisons between groups of people with and without ADHD have not provided support for rate dependency, where one might expect to see a suppressant effect in ADHD and an activating effect in those without it (Hicks et al., 1989; Millard and Standish, 1982; Rapoport and Inoff-Germain, 2002; Rapoport et al., 1980; Zahn et al., 1980).

A critic of the rate-dependent hypothesis, Professor Jim Swanson (1988), argues that looking at behaviour between groups of people was not a suitable test of the rate-dependent hypothesis. He suggested that the same people should be measured on both high and low baselines of behaviour. A second criticism of rate-dependent studies when looking at differences between groups is that they are showing a *regression to the mean*. This is when people are measured more than once on a test and show a lower level of responding on the second test. Given that this happens, then the rate-dependent hypothesis needs to show an even stronger effect for it to be considered. In a set of experiments by Teicher et al., these two criticisms were addressed. The rate-dependent effect was seen in response to methylphenidate on some, but not all, measures of attention (Teicher et al., 2003).

An interesting study would be to look at the rate-dependent effect of methylphenidate across the different severities and subtypes of ADHD. One might be able to predict that those with a hyperactive component would benefit most. Although such a study has yet to be conducted, differential effects of methylphenidate have been shown in subgroups with ADHD-C, the most common type, showing that increasing doses of stimulant medication were associated with increased improvement of inattention and hyperactivity symptoms, whereas in those with ADHD-I, symptoms improved with lower doses with less benefit seen at higher doses (Stein et al., 2003).

Finally, methylphenidate is used for sleeping disorders such as narcolepsy. One might consider this to be at the opposite end to ADHD along a hyperactivity continuum. Thus, the effects of these drugs may be dependent upon the activity levels at baseline. But the question remains, 'What is the neurophysiology of these baseline states?'. The neurophysiological changes may be key to this effect and be accounted for by theories such as those proposed by Grace (2001) and Carlsson (2000).

---

alcohol metabolism rates and alcohol dehydrogenase (Israel et al., 1979). The body would become much better at processing the drug which will offset its behavioural actions to some extent. But, do not consider that increasing consumption of the drug will lead to increasing levels of tolerance – there comes a point at which no more tolerance can be gained and the damage to the liver is now well documented.

Pharmacodynamic tolerance is when the drug changes the target cells in the brain. When the target cells are exposed for a long period of time to an agonist, for example, the change that occurs is downregulation of target receptors. They either become fewer in number or their affinity is reduced. However, if receptors have been blocked for some time this leads to compensatory increases in receptor number and affinity. An example

> **BOX 9.2 AMPHETAMINE AND THE POSITIVE AND NEGATIVE SYMPTOMS OF SCHIZOPHRENIA**
>
> Schizophrenia is a debilitating disorder with many hypotheses existing about its cause and underlying pathology (see Chapter 21). One of the main hypotheses is that of excess dopamine. Part of the reason for assuming that schizophrenia is a disorder of excess dopamine comes from the use of antipsychotic agents which block dopamine. However, it is not the only line of evidence that has been used to support dopamine. The use of amphetamine to enhance dopamine has been linked to the symptoms of schizophrenia and for some time there has been an animal model of schizophrenia.
>
> Schizophrenia can be divided into positive and negative symptoms. The positive symptoms, e.g. hallucinations and delusions, refer to behaviours that are in addition to normal ongoing behaviour, e.g. there are extra unusual behaviours. Negative symptoms refer to those symptoms in which there is a deficit in behaviour, e.g. attentional impairments.
>
> Enhancing dopamine is thought to provoke positive symptoms. In a study by van Kammen et al. (1982), the effects of amphetamine in people with schizophrenia were evaluated. This study used 45 drug-free schizophrenic patients who were given either placebo or 20 mg of amphetamine. One might expect that this would make the symptoms of schizophrenia worse but 13 patients improved, 18 got worse and 14 remained unchanged. This at first is somewhat surprising, but when we dig a little deeper an explanation can be found. The most parsimonious explanation is in terms of positive and negative symptoms. If prior to the administration of amphetamine, the patients were demonstrating more positive symptoms then amphetamine exacerbated them. However, if they were exhibiting negative symptoms and perhaps doing very little during their evaluation then the addition of amphetamine with its psychostimulant effects might be seen to be beneficial. In terms of rate dependency, the negative symptoms are indicative of a low rate of behaviour whereas the positive symptoms are indicative of a high rate of behaviour; therefore when amphetamine is given to patients the response is dependent upon baseline rates. Underlying the behavioural changes were different levels of catecholamine activity (van Kammen & Schooler, 1990). Further studies supported the use of amphetamine for the treatment of negative symptoms (Angrist et al., 1982; Sanfilipo et al., 1996; van Kammen & Boronow, 1988). However, when compared to placebo, amphetamine had very little effect on the negative symptoms except for those with the most severe form of negative symptoms in whom there was an improvement in blunted affect (Sanfilipo et al., 1996).

of this can be seen in the work of Peter Jenner and colleagues (Jenner et al., 1985; Kerwin et al., 1984; Rupniak et al., 1984). In these studies rats were given dopamine receptor antagonists for 21 days, after which their brains revealed an increase in the specific receptor target of the drug. Such compensatory actions can change the effectiveness of a drug. This sort of tolerance also demonstrates the plasticity of the nervous system to respond to prolonged events. Another feature of tolerance to a specific drug is that it can cross-generalize to other similar drugs, e.g. alcohol, pentobarbital and chlordiazepoxide (Le et al., 1986).

Both pharmacokinetic and pharmacodynamic tolerance are biological mechanisms. The third type of tolerance, **behavioural tolerance**, is involved in the diminishing effects of a drug by the mechanisms of classical conditioning. Thus, it is behavioural tolerance, i.e. what is learned, that can affect the behavioural fate of a drug.

The importance of behavioural tolerance was first illustrated by Shepherd Siegel (1975) when he investigated tolerance to the analgesic effects of morphine. In these experiments, paw licking in response to being on a hotplate was measured after morphine or placebo. Four groups were used:

- morphine was administered for four days prior to the hotplate test in the test environment (M-HP);
- morphine was administered for four days with a final test on a cold plate (M-CP);
- rats were administered morphine in the home cage for four days and then tested on the hotplate test environment (M-CAGE); and
- saline given to the first four hotplate tests.

The results can be seen in Figure 9.3, in which those animals that had experienced the hotplate and the morphine together showed tolerance over the other groups. In this study the environment became a conditioned stimulus and was predictive of **analgesia**. The compensatory response was similar to that in the CER (see Chapter 8)

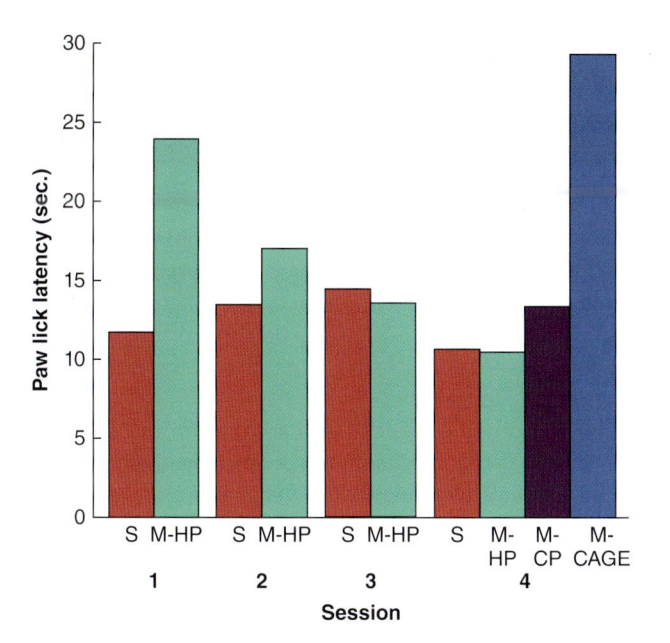

FIGURE 9.3 *Tolerance to the effects of morphine. Paw lick latency as a measure of analgesia was assessed in rats who experienced either morphine (M – green bars) or saline (S – red bars) on a hotplate (HP) or a cold plate (CP). Animals were tested in session 4 in which tolerance was seen in the M-HP group but not the animals that received morphine in the home cage prior to session 4 (M-CAGE).*
Source: Siegel, S. (1975). Evidence from rats that morphine tolerance is a learned response. *Journal of Comparative and Physiological Psychology, 89*(5), 498–506.

in which opponent processes were evoked (Siegel, 1978a, 1978b; Siegel et al., 1978). The phenomenon of behavioural tolerance indicates how classical conditioning and environmental cues are important in determining the drug's effect. The features of behavioural tolerance have immediate clinical application and have been considered critically important in understanding drug overdose (see Box 9.3).

The role of conditioning in mediating a drug response is discussed in further detail in Chapter 16 in which motivation and addiction are addressed.

SENSITIZATION

If tolerance describes the diminishing effects of a drug upon repeated administrations, then **sensitization** is the opposite. Sensitization (also called reverse tolerance) is the increase in an effect after repeated administrations.

The effects of time and repetition can be seen with amphetamine, for example (Figure 9.4) (Anagnostaras & Robinson, 1996). The effects of sensitization are mediated in the same way as those of tolerance. Do not fall into the trap of thinking that a drug can produce either tolerance or sensitization. Any drug can produce both, it depends upon the behaviour being measured, e.g. tolerance to the analgesic effects of morphine (Siegel, 1976) and sensitization to its locomotor activating effects (Contet et al., 2008; Vezina et al., 1987). Like tolerance, cross-sensitization can also occur with heightened responses to drugs that are similar in action to the initial drug.

Sensitization of drug effects has received increasing attention over the last two decades due to its implications in theoretical accounts of addiction in which conditioning and drug actions combine to maintain drug abuse (see Chapter 16) (Robinson & Berridge, 1993).

THE PLACEBO

Placebos are a fascinating area of psychobiology. The study of the **placebo** is the study of the interface of psychology and biology. Placebos could be considered a case of mind over matter. The study of the placebo is not looking at how a drug works but at how the belief that a drug will work can change psychological and physical processes. Placebos are used in clinical practice and in experimental procedures (Box 9.4).

The placebo is an inert treatment, more often than not a drug, but it can be a procedure such as sham surgery. Placebo means 'I shall please' and a placebo is a 'simulation of an active therapy within the psychosocial context' (Price et al., 2008). Placebos have been known about for centuries and may even go back as far as Socrates, in approximately 400 BC. According to Plato, Socrates discussed a headache cure which was 'a kind of leaf, which required to be accompanied by a charm, and if a person would repeat the charm at the same time that he used the cure, he would be made whole; but that without the charm the leaf would be of no avail'. The statement acknowledges that for treatment to be successful, it needs to be shrouded in ritual and associated stimuli. Without the ritual, the drug had little effect – not a good sign for a clinical trial.

When discussing placebos, we can consider two outcomes: the placebo response and the placebo effect. The placebo response is the 'change in a symptom or condition of that individual that occurs as a result of a placebo' (Price et al., 2008, p.567). The placebo effect, on the other hand, is 'the average placebo response in a group of individuals' (Price et al., 2008, p.567).

BOX 9.3 TOLERANCE AND THE PARADOXICAL OVERDOSE

The body likes to maintain homeostasis. That is, it does not like external agents upsetting the balance. Opponent processes compensate for changes in the body to achieve homeostasis. If you take morphine for pain relief, the body compensates for the drug by producing a reaction in the opposite direction, e.g. more pain. After the drug has been given a number of times, its effect weakens. This is tolerance. Tolerance could be seen as a pure biological activity in response to the drug. However, classical conditioning is very important in drug tolerance and can account for the overdose effect to a regular dose (Siegel et al., 1982, 2000).

Using the example of heroin, the drug is a US which produces an UR (euphoria and analgesia). However, drugs are not taken in an environmental vacuum and plenty of stimuli are associated with heroin intake, e.g. syringes, tin foil, etc. These stimuli act as a CS. The CS then produces a CR. The CR is the compensatory response from the body in the opposite direction. The CR produces dysphoria and hyperalgesia. Thus, the compensatory CR negates the effect of the drug. The effect on the person is one of tolerance and the need for greater quantities of the drug to get an effect (Figure 9.3.1).

Classical conditioning can also account for the overdose effect of a regular dose. Most people take their drug in a particular environment. The very nature of heroin use means it has to be taken in a clandestine manner. All the cues in the environment provide the users with a CR. What happens if you take the drug user out of their environment, put them somewhere new and give them their regular dose? They may well die from their regular dose in what looks like an overdose. In the new environment the cues are no longer there to provide the user with a CR. The absence of the compensatory CR means that the intake of

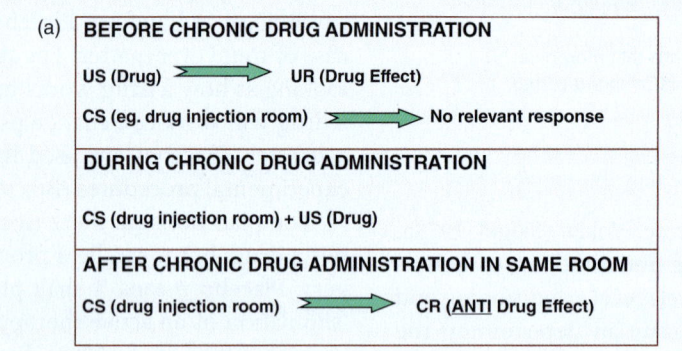

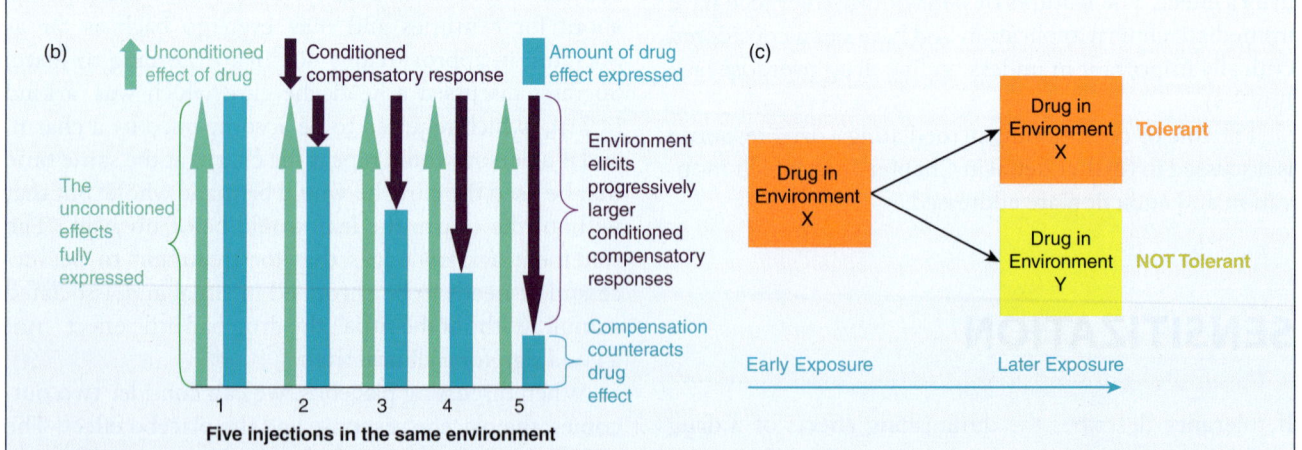

FIGURE 9.3.1 *Drug tolerance. (a) Pavlovian explanation of drug tolerance. (b) Compensatory effects to the drug and CS/CR effects. (c) Tolerance is only effective in the environment in which it develops. CR, conditioned response; CS, conditioned stimulus; UR, unconditioned response; US, unconditioned stimulus.*

their normal dose of heroin has a greater effect because it does not have to account for the CR.

This is an effect that has been systematically studied in the rat under controlled conditions. In this experiment one group of rats was exposed to heroin in the test environment and another group in a different environment. A third control group received neither. The group that received the heroin in a different environment showed the overdose effect whereas the rats that received the same dose in the test environment did not.

The scientific pursuit of the placebo began with Henry Beecher in an article titled 'The powerful placebo' (Beecher, 1955). Beecher identified 50 placebo trials with 1082 patients that were receiving treatment for either pain, nausea, anxiety or a cough. Approximately a third of the patients improved considerably under the placebo regime and Beecher attributed this to the placebo effect. Beecher's study demonstrated the importance of the placebo, but it was not without criticism. Of the 15 trials that made up Beecher's study, 13 did not include a no treatment group – the question remains what would have happened if nothing was done. Kienle and Kiene (1997) state that there are many reasons why Beecher may have found this effect other than the placebo: ' the placebo topic seems to invite sloppy methodological thinking'. In their review of Beecher's original paper, Kienle and Kiene (1997) cite alternative explanations for the results obtained.

- *Spontaneous improvement*: people sometimes just get better as a function of time.
- *Spontaneous fluctuation of symptoms*: in chronic disease symptoms wax and wane and are not consistent throughout the course of the disease.
- *conditional switching of treatment*: this involves 'cherry picking' of participants in which those who are doing well get placed on placebo and those who are not doing well are switched to active treatment and possibly excluded from evaluation.
- *Scaling bias*: the measurement of the placebo effect was augmented because the scales used were only sensitive to improvement.

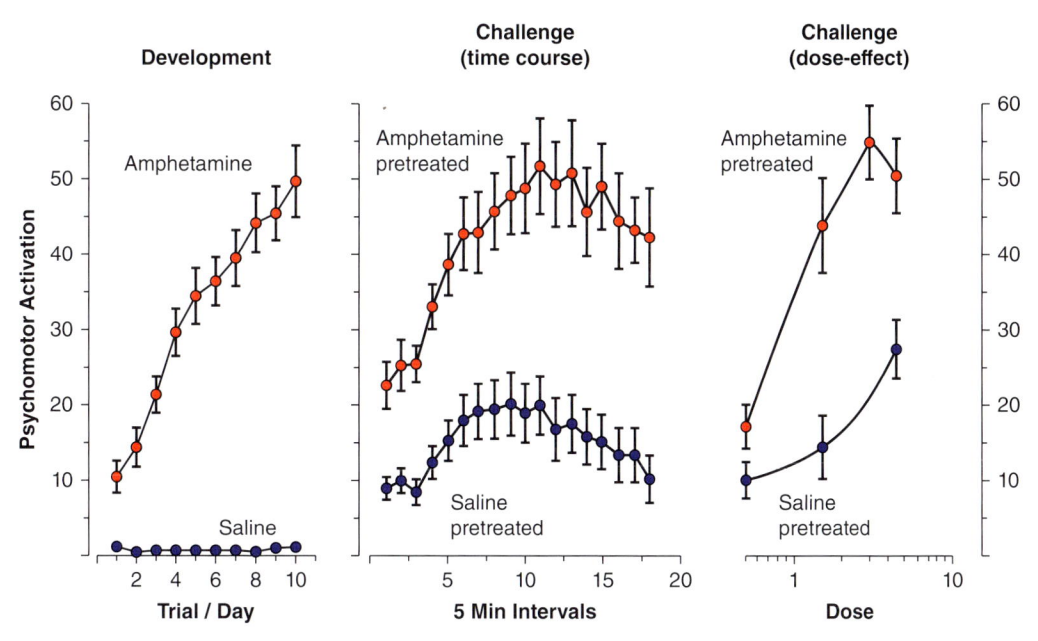

FIGURE 9.4 *Locomotor sensitization to amphetamine in the rat. The effect of a dose of amphetamine (red filled) versus saline (blue filled) increase over sessions (development). A challenge of amphetamine to saline- and amphetamine-pretreated rats produced a sensitized response in amphetamine by time course (challenge – time) and dose (challenge – dose).*
Source: Anagnostaras, S. G., & Robinson, T. E. (1996). Sensitization to the psychomotor stimulant effects of amphetamine: Modulation by associative learning. *Behavioral Neuroscience, 110*(6), 1397–1414.

BOX 9.4 PLACEBO IN CLINICAL TRIALS: DECLARATION OF HELSINKI

The World Medical Association's (WMA) Declaration of Helsinki (1964) has undergone numerous revisions. With respect to paragraph 33 of the 2013 revision (WMA, 2013), it states the following.

Use of placebo

33. The benefits, risks, burdens and effectiveness of a new intervention must be tested against those of the best proven intervention(s), except in the following circumstances:

Where no proven intervention exists, the use of placebo, or no intervention, is acceptable; or

Where for compelling and scientifically sound methodological reasons the use of any intervention less effective than the best proven one, the use of placebo, or no intervention is necessary to determine the efficacy or safety of an intervention.

And the patients who receive any intervention less effective than the best proven one, placebo, or no intervention will not be subject to additional risks of serious or irreversible harm as a result of not receiving the best proven intervention.

Extreme care must be taken to avoid abuse of this option.

Rothman and Michels (1994) are critical of the continuing unethical use of placebos in clinical trials. They cite many studies, one of which was a study on antidepressants in which the authors state that there is effective treatment and they continued to 'assign half the seriously depressed patients in the trial to receive placebo and the other half to receive paroxetine' and that '... placebo controls are commonplace in trials of antidepressant drugs, despite the availability of therapies whose success is acknowledged' (p.395). They suggest that the Food and Drug Administration (FDA) generally requires placebo-controlled trials for the licensing of new drugs. Clearly this leaves everybody in a difficult position.

Emanuel and Miller (2001) refer to two main ethical standpoints on the use of placebos in clinical trials.

1. Placebo orthodoxy it is ethical to conduct clinical trials even in the case of conditions for which there are interventions known to be effective due to the methodological limitations of trials in which active treatment is used as the control, e.g. drug response variability. Rothman and Michels (1994) claim that two ethical arguments are often used to justify placebo-controlled trials: (1) that withholding treatment does not have serious consequences, in which investigators and research ethics panels are the arbitrators of how much pain or discomfort is permissible; and (2) that if patients are fully informed and consenting then that is their choice.

2. Active control orthodoxy is that if an effective intervention exists, it must be used in the control group. The question is not whether a new drug is better than nothing but whether it is better than existing treatments. 'Placebo-controlled trials in which patients receive potentially therapeutic clinical attention test whether an investigational treatment is better than this attention, not whether it is better than nothing' (Emanuel & Miller, 2001).

Dissatisfaction with placebo orthodoxy and active control orthodoxy has led Emanuel and Miller (2001) to a third viewpoint that sits between the two established positions.

3. A middle ground is when placebo-controlled trials are permitted but only when the methodological reasons for their use are compelling. It must be made clear that patients receiving placebo will not be subject to serious harm and any risk is minimized. There is room for differences of opinion in this version.

The debate regarding the ethical use of placebo in controlled trials continues. Arguments focus on the use of words in the Declaration of Helsinki, e.g. what is 'best proven' and what dimension are we attributing 'best' to?

- *Additional treatment*: there are many examples in which the placebo was not the sole treatment and therefore it is difficult to attribute any improvement to the placebo itself.
- *Irrelevant response variables*: changes in behaviour or feeling that the placebo may produce were irrelevant to the actual condition, e.g. the patient may state that they feel better but the condition is still the same.

- *Answer politeness*: a positive reporting bias by patients is possible in order to please the physician.
- *Conditioned answers*: this is related to answer politeness and experimental subordination because the therapeutic setting provides many condition cues on how to behave.
- *Neurotic or psychotic misjudgement*: within the realms of psychiatry and psychology, the placebo

effect needs to be differentiated from the neurotic or psychotic dysfunctional view of reality. These patients might not be the most reliable of informants.

- *Misquotation*: Beecher misquoted 10 of the 15 trials listed in his paper. This highlights the dangers of relying on secondary sources.
- *Everyday symptoms misinterpreted as placebo side-effects*: in which patients identified normal everyday responses with that of the placebo.
- *Habituation*: learning to ignore the symptoms of the condition. Each day represents a learning trial.
- *Poor definition of drug efficacy*: the outcome measures of the treatment are poorly defined.
- *Subsiding toxic effect of previous medication*: many medicines have a carry-over effect and their side-effects take time to diminish; this may coincide with the commencement of placebo administration.

Jakovljevic (2014) recently continued the critique, suggesting that researchers should consider a number of concepts when discussing the placebo.

- *Reactivity*: subjects change their behaviour due to the mere fact of being watched.
- *Hawthorne effect*: changes in behaviour due to attention from superiors, clinicians, etc.
- *John Henry effect*: when a control group compares themselves to the experimental group and by virtue of effort gets the same results.
- *Pygmalion effect*: when there is greater expectation placed upon individuals, they will perform better.
- *Galatea effect*: when people believe in themselves and succeed as a result.
- *Gollum effect*: low expectations lead to poor performance.
- *Halo effect*: behaviour changes as a result of the novelty of the situation.
- *Experimenter effect*: when researchers communicate their expectations to participants, albeit unwittingly, other participants change their behaviour accordingly.

This all could be considered a damning indictment upon placebo research and has led some to consider that 'the so-called placebo effect is a myth borne of misperception, misunderstanding, mystery and hope' (Roberts (1995) cited by Kienle & Kiene (1997), p.1317) or 'an entity with occult-like powers that could mimic potent drugs' (Kaptchuk, 1998). Despite such accusations, placebo research continues both at the theoretical/experimental level and in the practical world of clinical trials.

To avoid the sloppy methodology, one needs to have a design specific for teasing apart placebo effects from either treatment effects or no treatment effects (Figure 9.5).

The definition of the placebo as an inert substance does not do justice to the whole process of treatment. Treatment, regardless of what it is, e.g. pharmacotherapy, surgery or even psychotherapy, takes place within

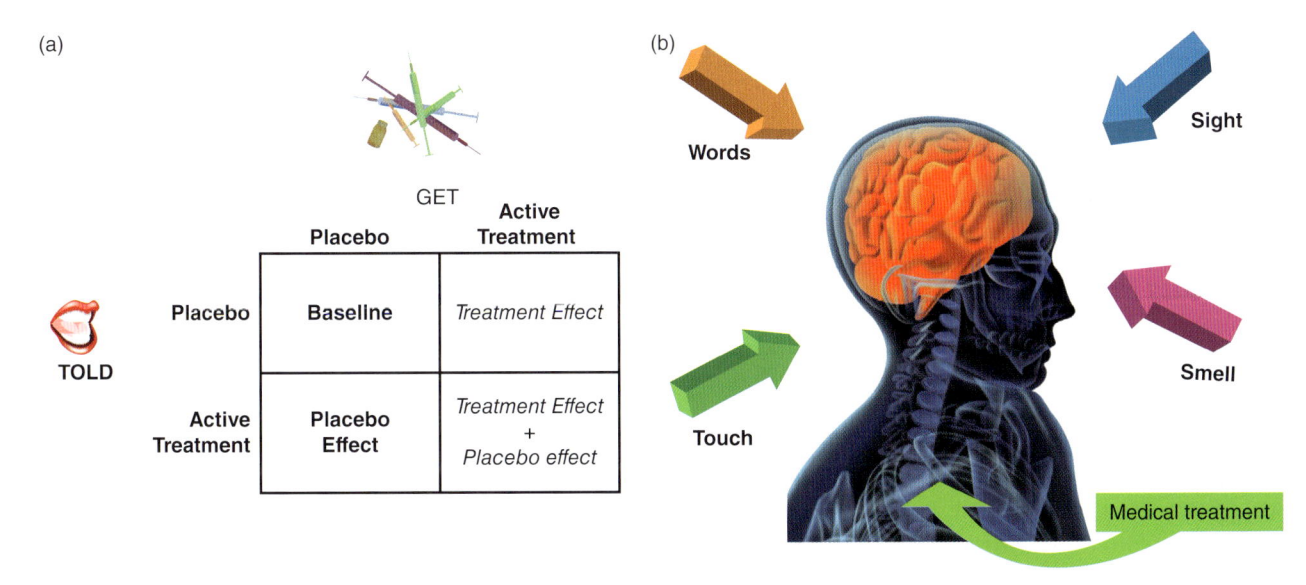

FIGURE 9.5 *The matrix of placebo effect methodology and factors contributing. (a) The methodology of a placebo study. (b) Factors involved in the placebo response.*

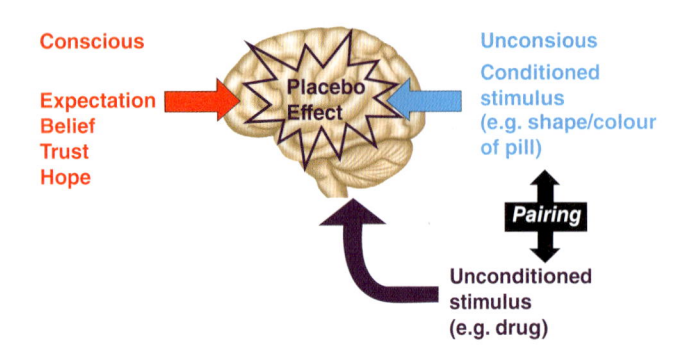

FIGURE 9.6 *Conscious and unconscious mechanisms contribute to the placebo effect.*

a psychosocial context. That psychosocial context provides meaning, taking the substance from a mere inert compound to the simulation of an active therapy (Figure 9.6). That psychosocial context comprises the words spoken or the literature read, the visual properties of the environment and the placebo, the touch and possible examination from physicians and the smell; olfactory mechanisms are particularly adept at steering our behaviour and hospitals and medical establishments often harbour strong, emotionally evocative smells.

The whole environment contributes to the placebo effect but how does that work on the individual? The best answers focus on conscious and unconscious processes – cognition and conditioning respectively.

Within the psychosocial context, conscious or cognitive processes such as expectations, beliefs, trust and hope are all in action. Simultaneously, unconscious processes that involve conditioning are at play. Neutral stimuli such as the shape, size and colour of the pill become conditioned stimuli after successful pairing with the unconditioned stimulus (the real drug). The conditioned stimulus produces a conditioned response, e.g. hormone secretion. There is a considerable body of evidence to support both conscious and unconscious mechanisms in the placebo effect.

Conscious Processes

A pain experiment involving neuroimaging and using the mu-opioid agonist **remifentanil** illustrated that different expectations influenced perception and brain activation (Bingel et al., 2011). All participants were given the analgesic but different groups were told to expect nothing, to expect analgesia or to expect hyperalgesia. Subjective accounts matched expectancy conditions, but more interestingly, positron emission tomography (PET) scans corroborated subjective accounts, showing changes in neural activity in areas of the brain coding for pain intensity: thalamus, posterior insula, midcingulate cortex (MCC) and somatosensory cortex, basal ganglia, brainstem and periaqueductal grey (PAG) (Bingel et al., 2011). Positive and negative expectancy can be differentiated by the activity of the brain.

Knowledge of a treatment plays a key role in emergent placebo effects. Using a hidden–open experimental paradigm, Colloca et al. (2004) demonstrated that in postoperative patients, anxious patients and patients with Parkinson's disease (PD), open treatment with a placebo produced more effective results than hidden treatment with active medical interventions. The design of these studies is somewhat different to traditional drug/placebo experiments. Regular placebo studies use an inert substance combined with a psychosocial context in which expectations about drug (placebo) action are conveyed. Colloca et al. (2004) had a different way of approaching the level of expectation in drug response. This approach used open and hidden treatment in which an active drug was administered with or without the participant knowing (Figure 9.7). This could be achieved by having an intravenous line permanently in place. This experiment involves deception of a different kind. The three groups of patients were given interventions without them knowing it: postoperative patients received morphine, anxiety patients received diazepam and parkinsonian patients received deep brain stimulation of the subthalamic nucleus (STN) – all without knowing it. The results for all three groups revealed that a greater therapeutic response was achieved to the open administration of treatment rather than the hidden treatments, suggesting that knowledge and expectation were key components to successful treatment.

Thus, the knowledge of a treatment is central to generating expectations and triggering the placebo effect. Moreover, there is compelling evidence that expectations, whether negative or positive, activate the reward mechansims in the mesolimbic dopaminergic pathway (see Chapter 16), especially the nucleus accumbens (NAC) (de la Fuente-Fernandez et al., 2004; Enck et al., 2008; Scott et al., 2007).

The evidence for the expectation of the rewarding effects of placebo stems from studies on Parkinson's disease (see Chapter 24). Briefly, Parkinson's disease is a disorder of dopamine, in which there is extensive loss in the substantia nigra and the projection to the striatum – the nigrostriatal pathway. Next-door neighbour of the nigrostriatal pathway is the mesolimbic pathway comprising the ventral tegmental area (VTA) projecting to the NAcc. The main therapy for Parkinson's disease is L-DOPA therapy that enhances the synthesis of dopamine. However, there is a dopamine increase

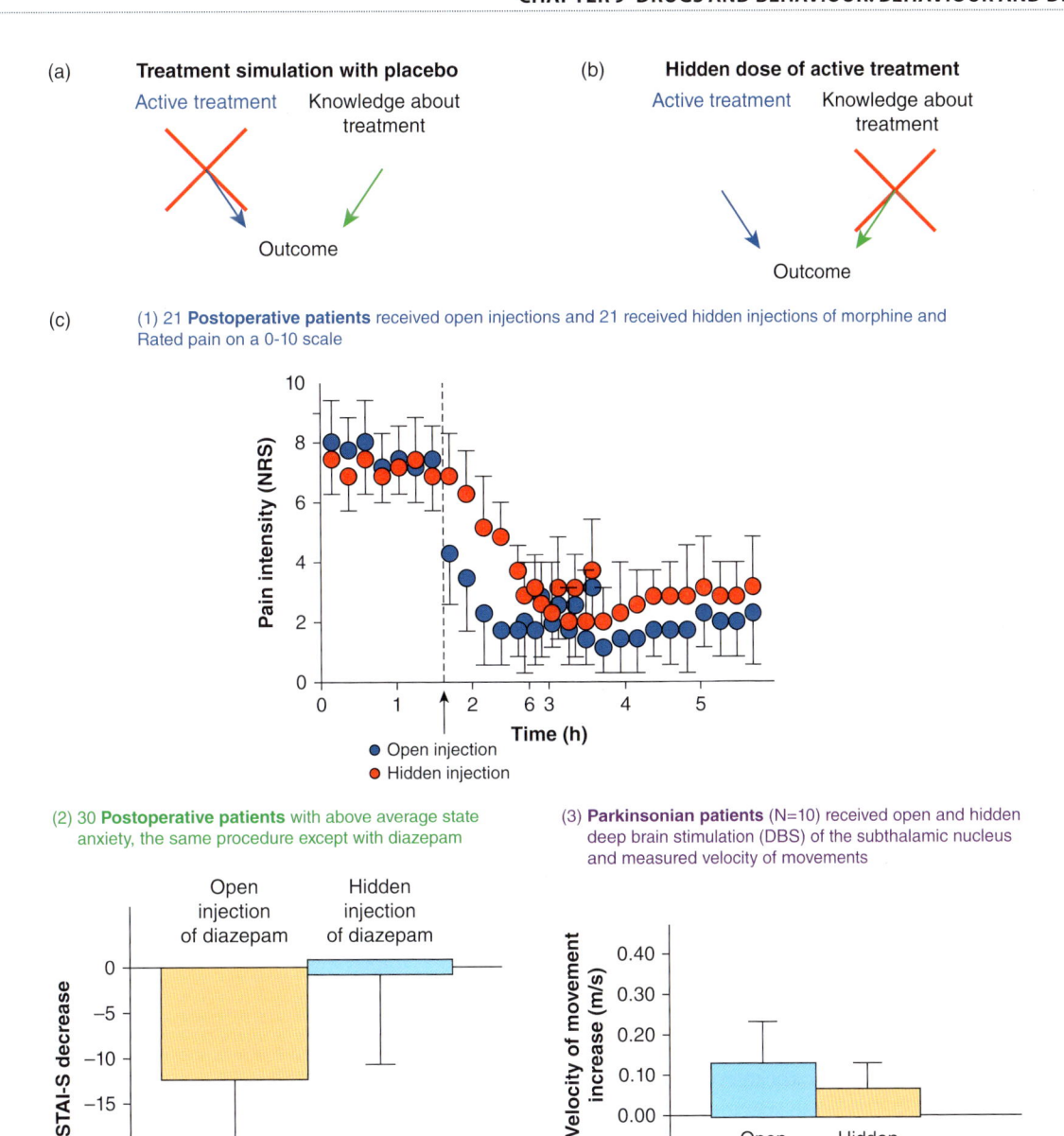

FIGURE 9.7 Colloca et al.'s hidden administration design. (a) The normal placebo design. (b) The hidden administration of a drug. (c) The effects in patients.
Source: Colloca, L., Lopiano, L., Lanotte, M., & Benedetti, F. (2004). Overt versus covert treatment for pain, anxiety, and Parkinson's disease. *Lancet Neurology, 3*(11), 679–684. STAI, State-Trait Anxiety Inventory.

in parkinsonian patients when they are administered placebo and this increasing dopamine is measured in the NAcc, mediating reward and not related to motor improvements required in the treatment of Parkinson's disease (de la Fuente-Fernandez & Stoessl, 2002; de la Fuente-Fernandez et al., 2001, 2004; de la Fuente-Fernandez, Phillips et al., 2002; de la Fuente-Fernandez, Schulzer 2002b, 2004). The PET scans of Parkinson's patients before and after placebo indicate that there is a dopamine increase because it displaces the radioactive isotope [^{11}C] raclopride which binds to dopamine D2 receptors (de la Fuente-Fernandez et al., 2001; Lidstone et al., 2010).

The role of expectation in the placebo-induced dopamine release in Parkinson's disease was found to be specific to the probability of getting a placebo. When patients were told they had a 75% chance of receiving active medication, the dopamine response was greatest; lower and higher probabilities were not as effective (Lidstone et al., 2010). The authors suggest that the

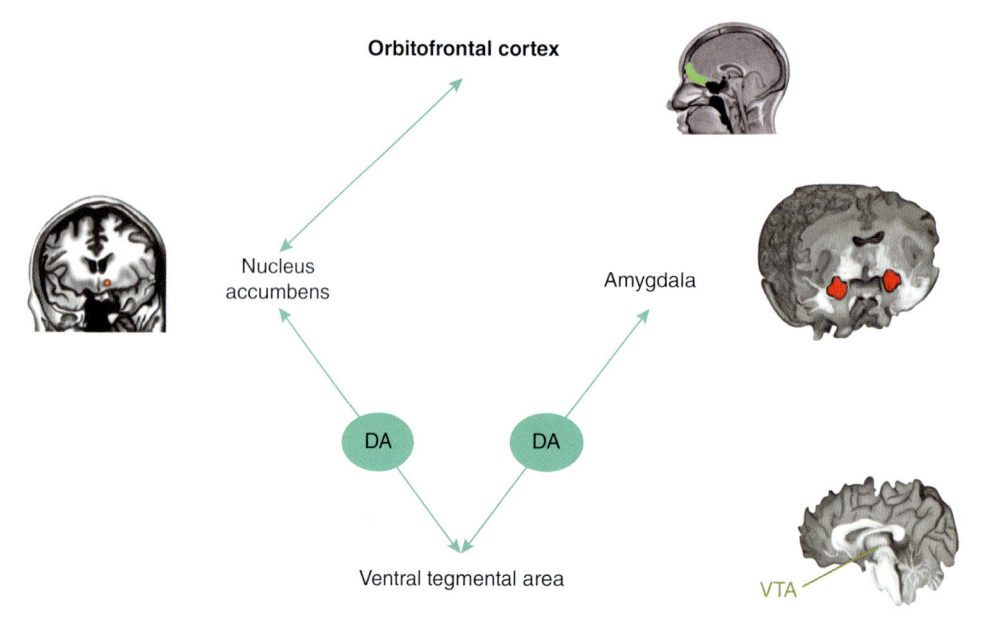

FIGURE 9.8 Reward and expectation. The placebo effect can be mediated by the orbitofrontal cortex (expectation) and the mesolimbic pathway (ventral tegmental area to nucleus accumbens) (reward).

reason why a 75% chance of receiving active treatment was a key number is because dopamine is involved with conditioned learning when reward is likely but not certain (see Chapter 16). Thus, the studies involving Parkinson's disease patients highlight cognitive processes but also associative processes about reward. Lidstone et al. (2005) place the placebo in the context of acting at two levels: (1) at the ventral tegmental area – coding for the rewarding aspects of the placebo; and (2) at the prefrontal cortex (PFC) – cognitive processing of expectation (Figure 9.8). Activation of these cortical and subcortical processes invokes disease-specific mechanisms, e.g. endorphin release with placebo analgesia (Lipman et al., 1990; Zubieta et al., 2005).

The placebo effect is also evident in the reduced firing rate of the STN in Parkinson's disease after false treatment (Benedetti et al., 2004). The studies involving Parkinson's disease are particularly impressive with regard to the placebo effect because they demonstrate not only the importance of the expectation of reward but also that the placebo effect produces a demonstrable change in the brain – a true psychobiological effect.

Expectation and knowledge are essential for emergent placebo effects but evidence underlines the centrality of the PFC specifically in supplying the cognitive engagement required to process psychosocial contextual features into placebo effects (Benedetti, 2010). In a review of the neural mechanisms of the placebo effect, Fabrizio Benedetti (the leading authority on placebos) found evidence in the domains of Alzheimer's disease, analgesia and temporary inactivation of the cortex. Patients with Alzheimer's disease, and consequent deficits in cortical function, do not benefit from placebo administration for analgesic treatment (Benedetti, 2008a, 2010; Levine et al., 1978). Alzheimer's disease is a devastating loss of cortical activity which negates the placebo effect (Benedetti, Arduino et al., 2006). It is important to note that patients with Alzheimer's disease responded to analgesic intervention, therefore the loss of the placebo effect was not due to a loss of pain mechanisms. This implies that due to deficits in their PFC, people with Alzheimer's disease do not have the cognitive skills to process contextual features that generate expectations leading to placebo effects. Further support for the cortex's involvement in analgesia derives from the ability of **naloxone**, an opioid antagonist, to block placebo-induced analgesia via the descending pathways from the dorsolateral PFC (DLPFC) (Levine et al., 1978). What this means is that naloxone was able to block the actions of a pharmacologically inert substance. Therefore, naloxone could be said to be blocking expectation. Another line of evidence supporting the DLPFC stems from the use of regional transcranial magnetic stimulation (rTMS – see Chapter 6 for more details) which transiently disrupts a localized area of the brain. Using a heat pain paradigm, rTMS over the DLPFC resulted in a blockade of placebo-induced analgesia without affecting the pain experience (Krummenacher et al., 2010). All three studies point towards the cortex in the processing of expectation without the concomitant influence on perceptual processes involved in pain (see Chapter 10) (Figure 9.9).

(a)
- Placebo analgesia
  – Blocked by naloxone
    • Blocks analgesia
    • (opioid antagonist)
  – dorsolateral prefrontal cortex (DLPFC)

(b)
- Alzheimer's disease patients
  – reduced Frontal Assessment Battery scores
  – showed reduced placebo component of the analgesic treatment.
- disruption of the placebo response when reduced connectivity of the prefrontal lobes with the rest of the brain

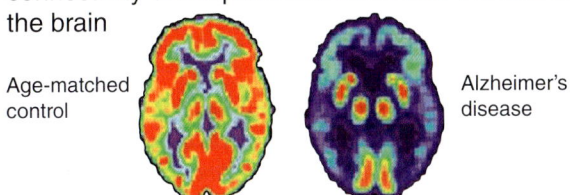

Age-matched control   Alzheimer's disease

(c)
- Transcranial Magnetic Stimulation
  – Disrupts DLPFC
- Heat Pain paradigm

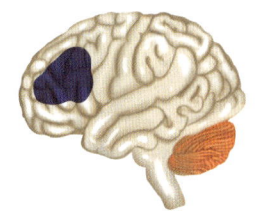

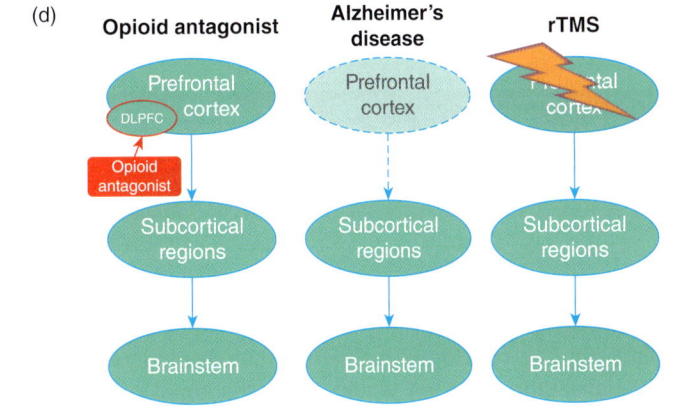

- TMS no effect on pain experience
- Blocked placebo analgesia
- Expectation mediated via DLPFC

(d) Opioid antagonist | Alzheimer's disease | rTMS

Prefrontal cortex (DLPFC) → Subcortical regions → Brainstem
Prefrontal cortex → Subcortical regions → Brainstem
Prefrontal cortex → Subcortical regions → Brainstem

FIGURE 9.9 *The role of the dorsolateral prefrontal cortex (DLPFC) in the placebo effect. (a) Placebo-induced analgesia is blocked by the opiate antagonist naloxone. (b) Reduced cortical activity in Alzheimer's disease reduces placebo-induced analgesia. (c) Transient deactivation of the DLPFC blocks placebo-induced analgesia. (d) The action of all three attributed to the DLPFC.*
Source: (a) Levine, J. D., Gordon, N. C., & Fields, H. L. (1978). The mechanism of placebo analgesia. Lancet, 2(8091), 654–657. (b) Benedetti, F., Arduino, C., Costa, S., Vighetti, S., Tarenzi, L., Rainero, I., & Asteggiano, G. (2006). Loss of expectation-related mechanisms in Alzheimer's disease makes analgesic therapies less effective. Pain, 121(1-2), 133–144. (c) Krummenacher, P., Candia, V., Folkers, G., Schedlowski, M., & Schonbachler, G. (2010). Prefrontal cortex modulates placebo analgesia. Pain, 148(3), 368–374. (d) Benedetti, F. (2010). No prefrontal control, no placebo response. Pain, 148(3), 357–358.

Unconscious Processes

The unconscious processes involve pavlovian conditioning (see Chapter 8). Placebo effects are subject to previous learning where previous administration of effective drugs has been beneficial (Amanzio & Benedetti, 1999). The terminology of conditioning can be used to describe the learning aspects of the therapeutic process (Figure 9.10).

Animal studies which have been used to support conditioning in the placebo effect are typified by conditioned **immunosuppression**. In these types of experiments, a distinct and novel flavour such as a saccharine laced liquid (CS) is paired with an immunosuppressant agent such as **cyclophosphamide** (US), immunosuppression to cyclophosphamide being the UR. After a number of saccharine- cyclophosphamide (CS+UCS) pairings, the saccharine solution alone (CS) decreased the rats' immune response (CR) (Ader & Cohen, 1975).

The learned immune response is now well established and also seen in humans (Schedlowski & Pacheco-Lopez, 2010). With regard to placebo, the learned immune response is central to our evolutionary accounts of the placebo effect (Box 9.5).

In a study using a 5-HT1B/1d receptor agonist to stimulate growth hormone and inhibit cortisol in humans, it was shown that subsequent replacement with a placebo produced a similar response (Benedetti et al., 2003).

In Chapter 8 a number of features of classical conditioning were discussed and some of these apply to the conditioning of the placebo response (Colloca & Miller, 2011a). For example, in a study looking at placebo analgesia, the number of trials in which the CS-US pairings experiment were presented influenced the placebo response, with more trials leading to more effective conditioning and more resistance to extinction (Colloca et al., 2010).

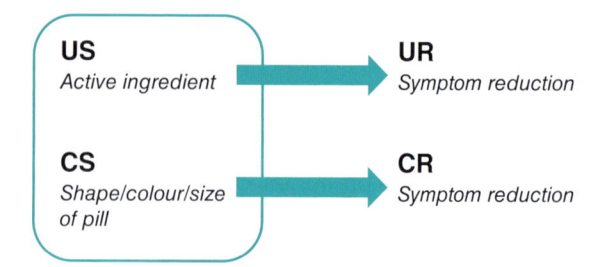

```
US                          UR
Active ingredient           Symptom reduction

CS                          CR
Shape/colour/size           Symptom reduction
of pill
```

FIGURE 9.10 *Application of conditioning to the placebo effect. Unconscious processes are argued to use conditioning principles for the placebo effect. CR, conditioned response; CS, conditioned stimulus; UR, unconditioned response; US, unconditioned stimulus.*

A series of experiments using analgesia sought to clarify whether conditioning to placebos could occur (Voudouris et al., 1985, 1989). These studies investigated the effects of placebo analgesia, but to do this the investigators adjusted the nociceptive stimulus by either increasing or decreasing the pain. Subjects were tested before and after conditioning for a placebo response and it was found that those who had reduced pain (pseudo-analgesia) were strong placebo responders. However, Montgomery & Kirsch (1997) were not convinced that conditioning explanations of the placebo effect can be separated from the role of expectancy. They provided some participants with information

BOX 9.5 EVOLUTION OF THE PLACEBO RESPONSE

The placebo response clearly has some value in promoting self-healing. At some point in human evolution, the brain had developed sufficiently that sick individuals understood that they would recover. An individual's response to a placebo would enhance the probability of wellness and survival of themselves and their offspring. An as yet unknown genetic mechanism has been suggested to underlie the placebo response and in particular polymorphisms will be able to account for individual differences in the placebo response (Bendesky & Sonabend, 2005). Social mechanisms that support or trigger therapeutic responses (e.g. ritual, religions and social support) would enhance the resilience of the 'sick' individual to return to good health, thus enhancing the success of the group (Thompson et al., 2009).

Humphrey (2002) provides an evolutionary account of the placebo effect. He claims that placebos should inhibit self-cure. He talks in terms of a *natural health-care service* (his pun is entirely intended), in which there is a cost of activating the immune system. In general, one needs to conserve resources. However, when a valid medicine is expected, the patient sees this as a sign that recovery is in sight and immune agents can now be mobilized and deployed where needed, as they no longer need to be conserved. In turn, a placebo would also effectively liberate such resources.

The evolution of learned immunosuppression involving immune conditioning and conditioned taste aversion (CTA – see Chapter 8) is a case in point. Conditioning is considered to be the mediator of placebo-evoked immune responses (Vits et al., 2011). Cyclophosphamide is an immunosuppressive agent and can be placed in the following conditioning paradigm:

- US (cyclophosphamide), CS (sweet water)
- UR (nausea/immunosuppression)
- CR (immunosuppression).

The CR of immunosuppression means that resources are saved and not used in the expensive-to-run immune system. Thus, those who suppress the immune response may save immune agents for a more important time. Furthermore, immune agents are greedy and take away resources from other mechanisms.

However, what about immuno-enhancement? After all, the conditioning of the immune system can take place in both directions – suppression and enhancement (Ader & Cohen, 1991). This could be a spandrel. It is the conditioning that is important, not the direction. The question remains: 'Why do behavioural conditioned immune responses exist at all?' (Schedlowski & Pacheco-Lopez, 2010). All would agree that the placebo is beneficial, but how it evolved is still subject to argument.

Evans' (2005) evolutionary account comprises two immune responses: (1) innate (acute); and (2) acquired (adaptive mechanism following innate). Placebos work on the innate immune system, promoting pain, swelling, stomach ulcers, depression and anxiety. Endorphins are released in response to placebo, producing analgesia and immunosuppression of the acute response.

> According to Trimmer et al. (2013):
>
> For conditions where an increased immune response will promote health, a belief that the treatment should enable their immune system to fight more effectively should have positive effects; we have termed this the 'Humphrey effect'. In contrast, a belief that the treatment will cure them, without any need for the immune system to do anything, could have deleterious effect on the patient's health: the 'reverse Humphrey effect'. (p.14)
>
> However, the **nocebo** effect (the opposite of the placebo effect) would suggest that evolution has played a rotten trick. Similar to immune suppression, when considering the placebo and nocebo, we need to remind ourselves that it is the ability to learn and respond that is of evolutionary importance rather than the specific direction in which that learning may take us – there is little point is searching for a placebo gene. The nocebo could be considered as the dark side of evolutionary mechanisms.

about a pretend analgesic called 'trivaricaine' that was intended to impede the formation of placebo expectancies during conditioning trials (they were even told that the experiment would reduce the stimulus) and then assessed their expectancies. Although conditioning trials significantly enhanced placebo responding, this effect was eliminated by adding expectancies to the analysis.

A psychophysiological study of placebo analgesia looked at three groups of participants: (1) verbal suggestion of placebo; (2) conditioning of placebo in which the nociceptive stimuli were surreptitiously reduced (pseudo-analgesia); and (3) a control group told about the real nature of the treatment (Colloca & Benedetti, 2009). By placing electrodes on the scalp of participants to record the electrical activity of the brain, it was found that there was greater brain activity in the conditioning group which was followed by the expectancy group, with no effect in the control group. The authors concluded that the perception of effectiveness of treatment can occur from experience (learning/conditioning) and suggestion. What this reveals is that expectation is also subject to conditioning.

This further led Benedetti and colleagues to suggest that:

> ... placebo responses are mediated by conditioning when unconscious physiological functions such as hormonal secretion are involved, whereas they are mediated by expectation when conscious physiological processes such as pain and motor performance come into play, even though a conditioning procedure is performed. (Benedetti et al., 2003)

It is important to remember that when one considers the conditioning effects of the placebo in which endogenous transmitters and hormones are released, such a release is specific to previous experience and unique to the system being manipulated (Benedetti et al., 2003).

A number of experiments looking at alcohol and the placebo response demonstrated that conditioning does not necessarily have to follow the same direction as the drug it is mimicking. In Chapter 7 the effects of alcohol are documented, and these are subject to conditioning. The effects of placebo alcohol were to produce effects in the opposite direction to that of alcohol – a conditioned compensatory response that was extended to alcohol cues (McCaul et al., 1989; Newlin, 1985, 1986). Such compensatory responses have already been discussed in the previous section on tolerance.

The laws of associative learning dictate that there should be numerous pairings of the CS and US during conditioning of the placebo response. However, learning about the potential benefits of an intervention does not have to involve direct experience. Observational learning also potentiates the placebo response. A study by Colloca and Benedetti (2009) investigated placebo analgesia produced via social observation and found that there were beneficial effects when a demonstrator displayed analgesia to an intervention which was similar to those that had direct experience.

In answer to the question 'Are placebos used by doctors?', the answer is yes (Howick et al., 2013). The same principles have been applied to the opposite of the placebo, which is the nocebo effect (Box 9.6).

SUMMARY

The commonplace view that a drug's influence on behaviour is a one-way process in which the drug affects behaviour is misplaced. Baseline levels of

BOX 9.6 NOCEBO EFFECTS

The nocebo (Latin for 'I shall harm') is widely contextualized as the opposite reaction to the placebo phenomenon. The first western publication on nocebo phenomena was titled '"Voodoo" death' and recounted instances wherein profound fear in an individual, due to perceived preternatural stimulus, led to death (Cannon, 1942). Cannon (1942) suggested that the negative expectation generated by fear ultimately led to the individual's demise. Since 1942, an increasingly large body of literature has suggested that sudden unexpected death can be brought about by stress and catecholamine toxicity (Samuels, 2007). Cannon's fundamental hypotheses have given rise to the nocebo effect (Sternberg, 2002). According to Helen Pilcher (2009), Cannon's characterization of 'voodoo' death may be an extreme version of the nocebo phenomenon. According to Lex (1974):

> The hitherto mysterious, arcane nature of voodoo death is supplanted by a physiologically based interpretation. Suggestion in this context is accomplished by the practitioner's manipulation of the autonomic nervous system through the victim's cognitive apprehension of the meaning of witchcraft. The extreme fright experienced by the individual who has been thus singled out can be as fatal as a dose of poison. (p.822)

However, nocebo effects occur outside voodoo, Pilcher (2009) cites the story of patient DA. Depressed after splitting up with his girlfriend, DA took all his 29 pills from a clinical trial he was participating in. Shortly after, he began to regret it. He went to hospital and was seen to be shaky, pale and drowsy, his blood pressure dropped and his breathing was rapid. The doctors sent off blood samples to toxicology which came back clear. Over the next four hours he received 6 litres of saline with little improvement in his condition. The doctor from the clinical trial was called and revealed that DA was in the control group and not in the treatment group for the antidepressant. The pills he had 'overdosed' on were harmless – placebos. Upon hearing this news, DA was surprised and relieved – and just a little bit emotional. Within 15 minutes he was fully alert, and his blood pressure and heart rate had returned to normal.

Not surprisingly, there is comparatively little research into nocebo phenomena. Of the approximately 10,000 articles on laboratory and clinical trials published each year (Klosterhalfen & Enck, 2008), only 2200 investigated placebo effects in 2011 and many fewer, only 30, investigated nocebo effects (Hauser et al., 2012). This may, in part, be explained by the fact that nocebos often represent an anxiogenic procedure, thus limiting ethical investigation (Enck et al., 2008).

Nevertheless, understanding the nocebo phenomenon is important for three main reasons. Firstly, nocebo effects are related to informed consent in clinical practice, influencing adverse expectations of symptoms and patient experience (Barsky et al., 2002; Cohen, 2014; Colloca & Miller, 2011b; Varelmann et al., 2010; Wells & Kaptchuk, 2012). Secondly, nocebo effects need to be distinguished from medication side-effects, to benefit clinical practice and develop rigorous clinical trial methodology (Colloca & Miller, 2011b; Liccardi et al., 2004; Miller & Colloca, 2011). If improvement of clinical outcomes and quality of life is a research priority, then understanding nocebo effects is crucial, to effectively limit their influence.

Nocebo administration is the reverse of the positive psychosocial context typical of placebo administration, creating a negative psychosocial context, wherein resultant nocebo effects may emerge (Enck et al., 2008). The nocebo effect is, thus, the negative outcome, generated by negative expectation, following the administration of a nocebo (Carlino et al., 2012; Hauser et al., 2012). Whereas placebo administration may be an inactive pill or sham procedure, nocebo administration may include these or be a negative verbal suggestion without the administration of an inert substance (Enck et al., 2008).

The context in which the nocebo is administered is vital. This psychosocial environment transforms the nocebo from an inert intervention to an 'active' one as is seen with the placebo.

Classical conditioning is implicated in the production of unconscious physiological effects such as hormone secretion (de la Fuente-Fernandez & Stoessl, 2002; Price et al., 2008). In this context, the nocebo and its psychosocial context, the CS, leads to a CR: symptom worsening (Amanzio & Benedetti, 1999; Benedetti et al., 2003; Colloca et al., 2008). There is substantial evidence to support classical conditioning as an explanatory mechanism across an array of conditions (Ader, 2003; Ader & Cohen, 1975; Benedetti et al., 2003; Giang et al., 1996; Voudouris et al., 1989).

Despite supporting evidence for classical conditioning, there remain areas of ambiguity. The maintenance of the pairing between the CS and US, in the absence of consolidation, cannot be explained by classical conditioning (Enck et al., 2008). Moreover, effects have been found in participants without previous drug experience, indicating no pairing between the CS and US, suggesting classical conditioning may not be the operating mechanism (Pihl & Altman, 1971). This has led to the argument that 'conditioning' may actually be another form of expectation (de la Fuente-Fernandez & Stoessl, 2002; Stewart-Williams & Podd, 2004).

Negative expectations influence behaviour, along with possible neuroanatomical correlates in the PFC, bilateral anterior cingulate cortex (ACC), left hippocampus, orbitofrontal cortex (OFC), insular cortex, nucleus accumbens (NAC), amygdala, thalamus, perigenual cingulate, somatosensory cortex, head of caudate, cerebellum, contralateral nucleus cuneiformis (nCF) and PAG (Keltner et al., 2006; Kong et al., 2006; Ploghaus et al., 1999, 2001; Rodriguez-Raecke et al., 2010; Scott et al., 2008). However, neuroanatomical findings are not entirely congruent, e.g. with regard to the right parietal operculum, which may only be activated during longer duration nocebo effects (Rodriguez-Raecke et al., 2010).

The study by Bingel et al. (2011) using pure remifentanil highlights the importance of expectation. Negative expectancy was reflected by increased brain activity in the somatosensory cortex, MCC, insula and thalamus (i.e. the brain's pain matrix – see Chapter 10), and increased activation in the hippocampus bordering the amygdala, medial PFC and cerebellum, whereas positive expectancy reflected activation in dorsolateral PFC, ACC, striatum and frontal operculum (Bingel et al., 2011). These data suggest that regulatory brain mechanisms differ as a function of expectancy, but that both positive and negative expectancy use the same key component of the descending pain pathways but in opposite ways (Bingel et al., 2011). Thus, expectation is the driver of changes in the brain.

The neurofunctional correlates of the nocebo effect are not as well mapped as those for placebo, and it is noteworthy that our understanding of the neurobiology of both effects stems largely from neuroimaging studies on pain (Enck et al., 2008; Tracey, 2010). Evidence suggests that negative expectations may result in pain amplification (Koyama et al., 1998), with activation in the ACC, PFC and insula during pain anticipation (Keltner et al., 2006; Koyama et al., 2005; Ploghaus et al., 1999). Specifically, findings were that the expectation of a painful stimulus increased the perception that an innocuous thermal stimulation was unpleasant, with concomitant increased brain activation in the ACC, parietal operculum and posterior insula (Sawamoto et al., 2000). Additionally, as the magnitude of the expected pain grew, activation increased in the thalamus, insula, PFC and ACC, whereas, as the magnitude of expected pain diminished, there was reduced activation in the primary somatosensory cortex, insular cortex and ACC (Koyama et al., 2005). Similarly, further research has determined that expected levels of pain altered perceived levels of pain, confluent with the activation of the ipsilateral caudal ACC, cerebellum and contralateral nCF (Keltner et al., 2006).

Scott and colleagues' (2008) PET imaging study revealed that the placebo response shows activation of opioid transmission in the ACC, OFC, insular cortex, NAC, amygdala and PAG, dopamine activation in the ventral basal ganglia, and mu-opioid activity in the ACC, OFC, anterior insular cortex, mediolateral thalamus, NAC bilaterally and amygdala bilaterally. Conversely, the nocebo response resulted in deactivation of dopamine and endogenous opioid release in these same areas (Scott et al., 2008). Thus, placebo and nocebo effects are associated with opposite responses in dopamine and endogenous opioid transmission in the brain (Scott et al., 2008). This considerable overlap between placebo and nocebo effects suggests that the mechanism engaged is expectation, rather than the directionality of the effect.

Pharmacological studies have also provided insights into the biochemistry of negative expectations and the nocebo effect (Enck et al., 2008). Similar to Scott et al. (2008), Enck et al. echo the hypothesis that opposite systems are activated during opposite expectations of pain, specifically, the endorphin and enkephalin systems with expectations of analgesia, and increases in **cholecystokinine** (CCK) with expectations of hyperalgesia (Benedetti, Amanzio et al., 2006; Benedetti et al., 2007). This is supported by evidence that a weak, non-specific CCK antagonist (proglumide), for both CCK-A and CCK-B receptors, can promote pain relief by blocking the anti-opioid actions of CCK (Benedetti, Amanzio et al., 2006), and mediate nocebo-induced hyperalgesia, strongly suggesting the involvement of CCK in nocebo effects (Benedetti, Amanzio et al., 2006; Benedetti et al., 2011).

The involvement of CCK in nocebo hyperalgesia may be mediated by nocebo-induced anxiety (Benedetti, Amanzio et al., 2006). The proposed mechanism of hyperalgesic nocebo effects is the actuation of two pathways, mediated by nocebo-induced anxiety (Benedetti, Amanzio et al., 2006; Tracey, 2010). Firstly, anxiety activates the hypothalamic-pituitary-adrenal (HPA) axis and increases the release of cortisol. Secondly, anxiety galvanizes the CCK-induced pronociceptive system (Benedetti, Amanzio et al., 2006). Evidence for two pathways has been obtained by the actions of benzodiazepines, which act on both anxiety and HPA axis overstimulation, whilst proglumide acts on anxiety but leaves the HPA axis unaffected, underscoring the existence of two discrete systems (Benedetti, Amanzio et al., 2006).

Because benzodiazepines are GABA agonists, this suggests the involvement of GABA in nocebo effects. Potentiating GABA enhances the placebo effect but reduces the nocebo effect; conversely antagonism (although more likely inverse agonists) of GABA receptors decreases placebo and stimulates nocebo effects (Benedetti, Amanzio et al., 2006; Tuenter, 2012).

Studies in patients with PD supported expectation as a driver of placebo and nocebo responses, in line with the PD clinical profile patients expected of deep brain stimulation (DBS) of the STN (Keitel, Ferrea et al., 2013). Nocebo administration did not show significant effects in this study, perhaps due to the well-documented positive effects of DBS of the STN (Keitel, Ferrea et al., 2013; Keitel, Wojtecki 2013). However, placebo administration showed increased proximal motor performance (placebo effect) and simultaneously, decreased cognitive verbal fluency performance (nocebo effect), in response to a positive suggestion of increased motor performance and sham stimulation (DBS) of the STN (Keitel, Wojtecki et al., 2013). The expected PD clinical profile of DBS of the STN is increased proximal motor function and decreased verbal fluency. Thus, expectations may drive opposing placebo and nocebo effects, even to the same stimulus (Keitel, Wojtecki et al., 2013).

Thus, evidence suggests a complex interaction involving different neurotransmitters, including dopamine, CCK, endogenous opioids and GABA, upon nocebo administration (Enck et al., 2008; Price et al., 2008). No single neurobiological or psychobiological mechanism can explain nocebo phenomena – instead different mechanisms may exist which all contribute to nocebo effects across clinical and experimental situations (Cannon, 1942).

More generally, the methodological demands of nocebo research are considerable (Price et al., 2008). Research needs to differentiate the nocebo effect from the natural history of a condition and account for symptom fluctuation, regression to the mean and response bias (Price et al., 2008; Tracey, 2010). Moreover, research in randomized controlled trials now advocates a three-arm trial and a no treatment group (Colloca & Miller, 2011b), to verify nocebo effects in placebo arms of trials, currently measuring 4–27% (Liccardi et al., 2004; Rief et al., 2006, 2011). Research needs to separate nocebo effects from side-effects in active treatment trials. A meta-analysis of nocebo effects in multiple sclerosis trials found the incidence of nocebo responses to be 74.4% (Papadopoulos & Mitsikostas, 2010), indicative of the magnitude of nocebo effects in clinical research.

Additionally, deception, endemic to nocebo research, is a controversial area of bioethics. While the BPS makes allowances for deception of research participants if the deception is an 'essential design element' (BPS, 2010), it simultaneously requires informed consent and the positioning of participants at the very centre of research. Accomplishing this is difficult, with the consequence that published research in this domain has become less transparent about using deception, with some researchers not telling participants they had been misinformed (Miller & Kaptchuk, 2008).

behaviour are extremely influential in determining the drug's effect. How a drug is perceived, whether it be a stimulant or a depressant, can be different under certain circumstances, e.g. the schedule of reinforcement. Instrumental control of reinforcement and drug effects represents one behavioural influence on the drug. The fact that a drug is consumed or delivered in a particular environment means that repetitive administration is associated with cues. These cues become conditioned stimuli and provoke a conditioned response. The classical conditioning that occurs during repetitive drug administrations contributes to the overall phenomena of tolerance.

The associative learning processes that can determine a drug's effect are also in play with the placebo effect. However, with the placebo effect associative learning processes take second place to cognitive processes of expectancy.

LEARNING OUTCOME QUESTIONS

You should be able to answer the following questions.
- How can schedules of reinforcement influence the drug's response?
- What are the main features of drug tolerance?
- What are the mechanisms of the placebo effect?
- What are the benefits of placebos in medicine and research?

FURTHER READING

Benedetti, F. (2009). *Placebo effects: understanding the mechanisms in health and disease.* New York: Oxford University Press.
Brown, W. A. (2013). *The placebo effect in clinical practice.* Oxford, UK: Oxford University Press.
Colloca, L., Flaten, M. A., & Meissner, K. (2013). *Placebo and pain: from bench to bedside.* London: Academic Press.
Evans, D. (2004). *Placebo: Mind over matter in modern medicine.* Oxford, UK: Oxford University Press.
Goudie, A. J., & Demellweek, C. (1986). Conditioning factors in drug tolerance. In S. R. Goldberg, & I. Stolerman (Eds.), *Behavioral analysis of drug dependence* (pp. 225–285). London: Academic Press.
Robinson, T. E., & Berridge, K. C. (2001). Incentive-sensitization and addiction. *Addiction, 96*(1), 103–114.
Siegel, S., & Ramos, B. M. (2002). Applying laboratory research: drug anticipation and the treatment of drug addiction. *Experimental and Clinical Psychopharmacology, 10*(3), 162–183.

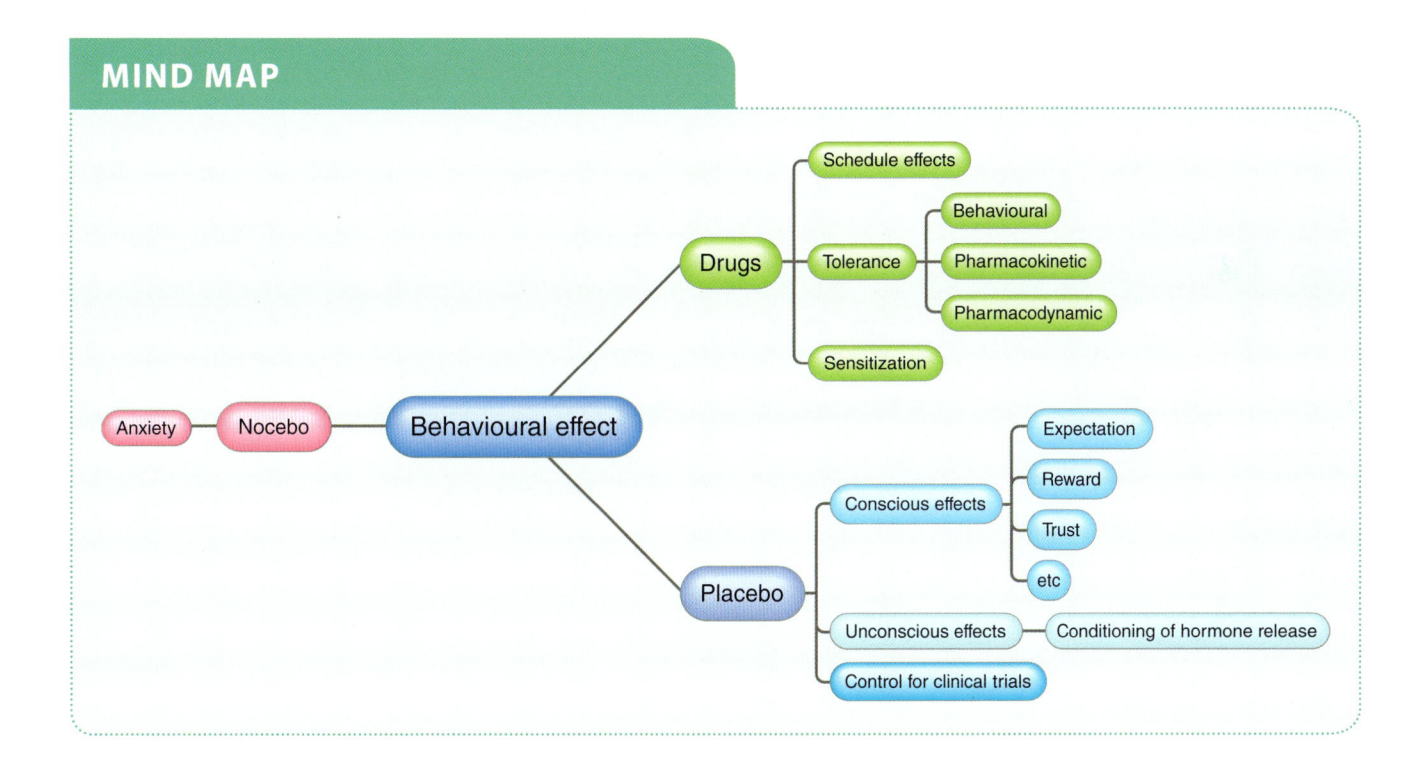

MIND MAP

- Behavioural effect
  - Anxiety — Nocebo
  - Drugs
    - Schedule effects
    - Tolerance
      - Behavioural
      - Pharmacokinetic
      - Pharmacodynamic
    - Sensitization
  - Placebo
    - Conscious effects
      - Expectation
      - Reward
      - Trust
      - etc
    - Unconscious effects — Conditioning of hormone release
    - Control for clinical trials

Part II
Psychobiology: Bringing Biology and Behaviour Together

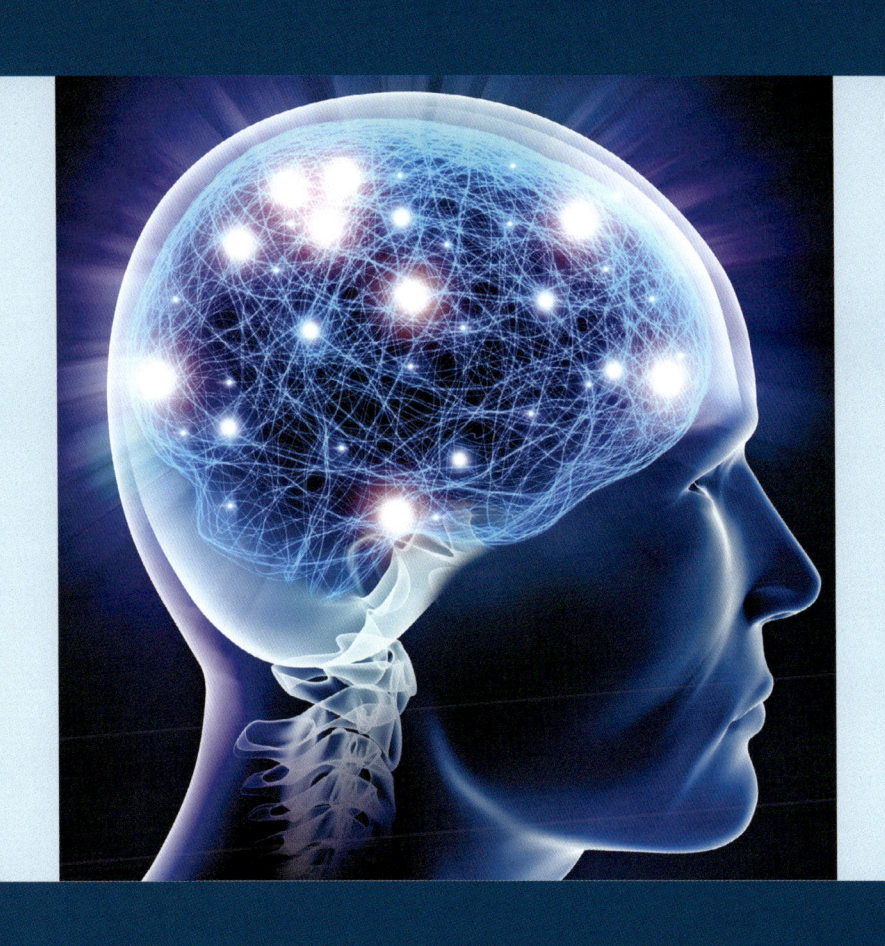

10. Perceptual Systems
11. Motor Behaviour
12. Executive Functioning
13. Neural Plasticity and Memory
14. Sex
15. The Neural Regulation of Homeostasis: Feeding and Drinking
16. Motivation
17. Emotion
18. Sleep and Consciousness
19. Lateralization and Language

Part II takes the basic knowledge from Part I and applies it to behaviour. Many questions can be asked, e.g. what is the basis of seeing or hearing? Why do we eat? Why do we do anything? What is it to be conscious or asleep?

Understanding the mechanisms is not straightforward. It is not always done on the basis of having a search through the brain to find the 'bit' responsible. Often the starting point is about trying to solve a real problem, e.g. why do people behave inappropriately after damage to the frontal lobe? Therefore, there is a type of reverse engineering on abnormalities. Deconstruct the neural basis of a particular problem and we will gain insight, not only into the neuropathology of the problem but also what it should do when not being pathological. Therefore, the chapters in this section will refer to behaviour when it is broken (not the norm) and when it is intact (normal). In this sense we refer to normal as being the average display of behaviour. More often than not, abnormal takes on a qualitatively different meaning, e.g. broken. But abnormal can be when a function/behaviour is better than normal. However, there is no tradition of studying superhumans. Thus, we make attempts to understand normal behaviour by studying abnormal/negative behaviour.

10 Perceptual Systems

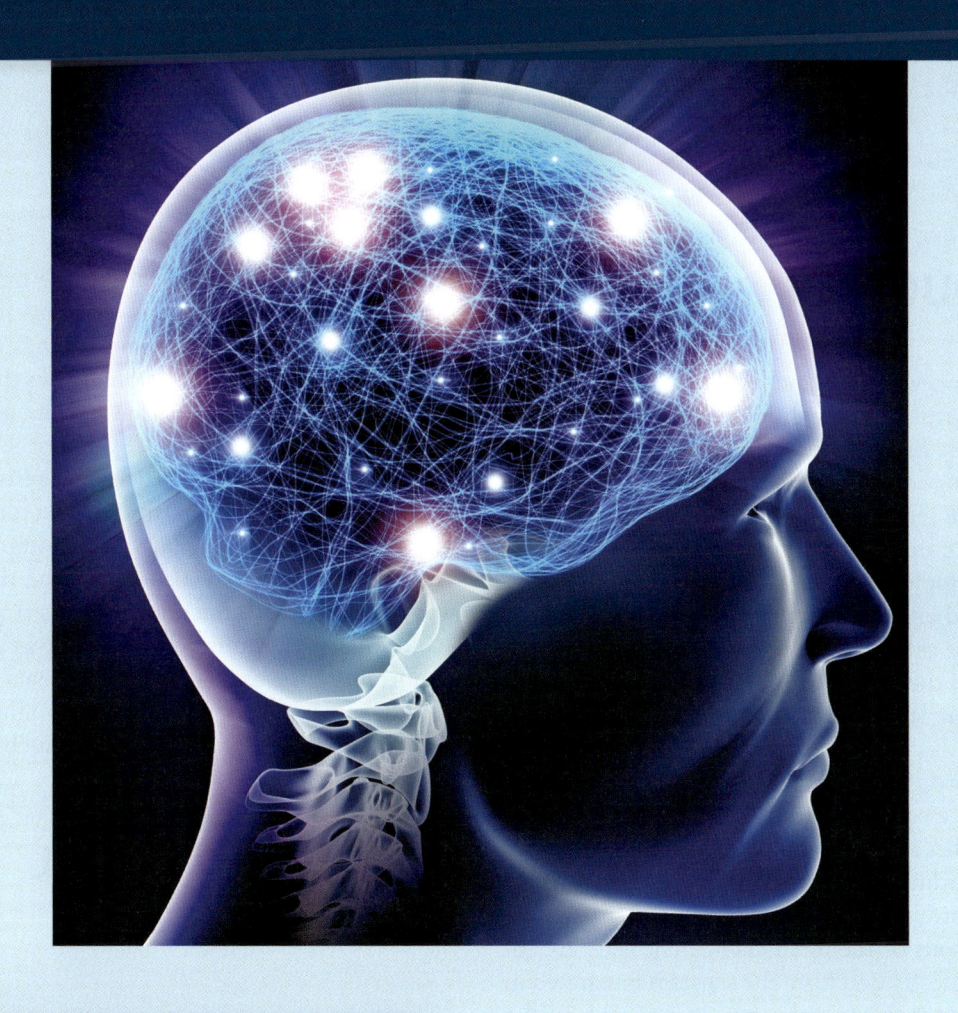

ANATOMY OF THE CHAPTER

This chapter will highlight the following.
- Sensory systems.
- Organization of the sensory brain.
- Mechanisms of pain.

INTRODUCTION 252

THE SENSORY MODALITIES 252

VISION AND VISUAL PERCEPTION 252

HEARING AND AUDITORY PERCEPTION 272

SMELLING AND OLFACTORY PERCEPTION 275

TASTING AND THE GUSTATORY SYSTEM 276

THE VESTIBULAR SYSTEM 277

FEELING AND SOMATOSENSATION 279

NOCICEPTION AND THE PERCEPTION OF PAIN 279

SENSORY INTEGRATION 291

SUMMARY 291

LEARNING OUTCOMES

1 To understand the transmission of sensory signals through the sensory organs.

2 To understand the processes which sensory signals are subject to in the brain.

3 To understand the mechanisms of pain.

INTRODUCTION

We see, we hear, we smell and we feel. Our eyes, ears, nose and skin provide us with information. That information is about light, sound, airborne molecules and stimuli touching our skin. Perception might appear straightforward, inasmuch as we are dealing with input channels. However, perception is so much more than input. It is a complex process whereby sensory information is managed and processed by the brain; often with an output being clear; for example, in the case of pain a person removes their body from the source of that pain. Questions about our conscious awareness are never far away when we discuss perception, e.g. how is the colour red converted into neural signals that result in the concept of RED as a conscious entity (a question that keeps the neuroscientist and philosopher busy).

The bombardment of information on the sensory modalities is converted into neural signals that are sent to the various regions of the brain via afferent neurons. All this incoming information from the senses is integrated in the brain and we are able to make some sort of sense of the world. Perception is not passive; it is the brain that interprets sensory signals. It is the brain that decodes the neural inputs and it is the brain that perceives. It is the brain that sees, hears, tastes, smells and feels pleasure and pain.

THE SENSORY MODALITIES

The **sensory modalities** receive the following information about the environment.

- Visual information
- Auditory information
- Tactile information
- Thermal information
- Olfactory information
- Taste information

Such information is important to the organism and the sense organs are adaptations that have been successful in Darwinian terms. The brain too has evolved to process all the sensory information. It does this via incoming pathways from the senses that usually go via the thalamus before radiating to the specialist sensory cortices. I say 'usually go to the cortices'; there is one exception that can shortcut the thalamus. Olfactory-derived messages can proceed to the amygdala without having to go via the thalamus (they also go via the thalamus on the way to the cortex). Such a mechanism may betray our evolutionary origins in which smell was a dominant and important sense, as it is in many animals still.

In Chapter 17 we address the significance of this in generating life-preserving emotions such as fear.

VISION AND VISUAL PERCEPTION

As humans, we have become reliant on vision more than any other sense. However, other species have different levels of reliance on perceptual systems, e.g. the rat and smell or the bat and sound/echolocation. We might be tempted to think that these animals are very clever to be able to do this, but take a moment and think how clever it is to be able to see.

Humans' anthropocentric nature places an emphasis on visual perception more than any other sensory modality; after all, you are reading this text and looking at the words on these pages. There is more research on vision than any other sense, but is that surprising? Experiments on vision are easier to control than those investigating olfaction.

Vision starts with the eye, which is a complex structure that has evolved for over 500 million years. The eye proved to be a tricky organ for Darwin to come to terms with. Darwin said: 'The eye to this day gives me a cold shudder', and continued:

> To suppose that the eye, with all its inimitable contrivances . . . could have been formed by natural selection,

seems, I freely confess, absurd in the highest possible degree . . . Yet reason tells me, that if numerous gradations from a perfect and complex eye to one very imperfect and simple, each grade being useful to its possessor, can be shown to exist . . .

The eye's challenge to Darwin has since being demystified with numerous studies that have identified gradations of the eye (Albalat, 2012; Lamb, 2013; Lamb et al., 2007). It has been argued that the complexity of the eye evolved in a comparatively short time; 364,000 years for a light-sensitive patch to turn into a simple camera eye (Nilsson & Pelger, 1994). Such estimates are made on the basis of the eye alone and not the infrastructure supporting the processing of the visual information (the brain). As Nilsson and Pelger (1994) suggest, there is little point in an eye on its own!

The evolution of the eye was driven by functional requirements . . . it is useful. As Nilsson (2013) states, 'For each evolutionary transition to a higher class (*of eye*), the rate of information delivered to the nervous system increases by several orders of magnitude. This provides opportunities for more advanced behaviors and requires larger brains' (p.18) (italics my addition).

Not only has the eye and the visual apparatus supporting perception evolved over millions of years, it also develops within the lifespan of the individual. We know that learning changes the functional architecture of the neural systems subserving visual perception.

The Eye

Now that billions of years of evolution of the eye have been clarified in one small paragraph, the business of what the eye actually does can be addressed. The eye is an instrument for collecting light. Light enters the eye as a waveform. It is not my intention to review the physics of light, and those interested in a more detailed exposition should read George Mather's book (Mather, 2009).

The eye sits within the orbit and is made up of a number of interconnected structures (see Figure 10.1) that are adapted to the process of receiving light. Each eye is spherical and about 24 mm in diameter (Stone, 2012).

The eyes are moving constantly in what are called **saccades**. The eye also moves under conscious and unconscious control toward stimuli. To do this, a number of muscles connected to the eye steer the motor movement (see Figure 10.1).

The Sclera and Cornea

When you look at a human eye, you see three principle components differentiated by colour: the white of the eye, the colour of the eye (**iris**) and the black dot at the centre (the **pupil**). The outer layer of the spherical eye is the **sclera**. The sclera is the white of the eye and

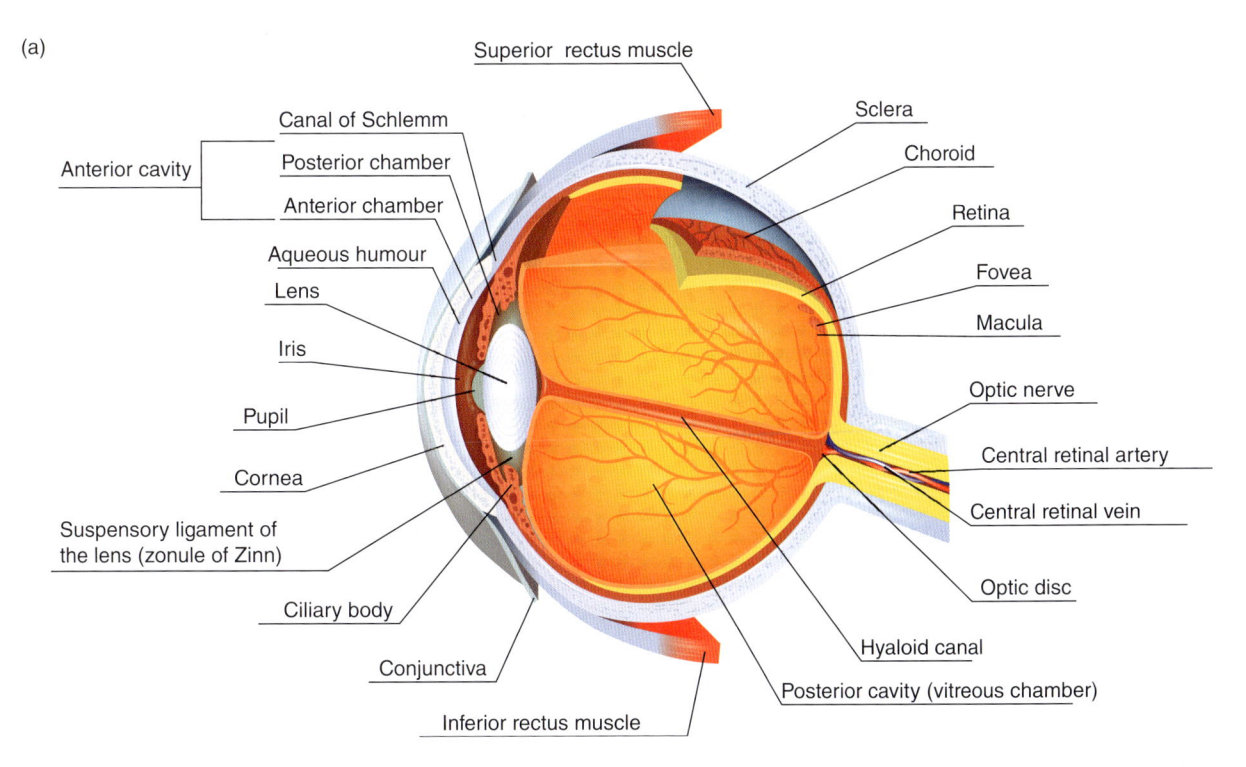

FIGURE 10.1 *Architecture of the eye. (a) The structure of the eye. (b) The muscles and cranial nerves controlling the eye.*

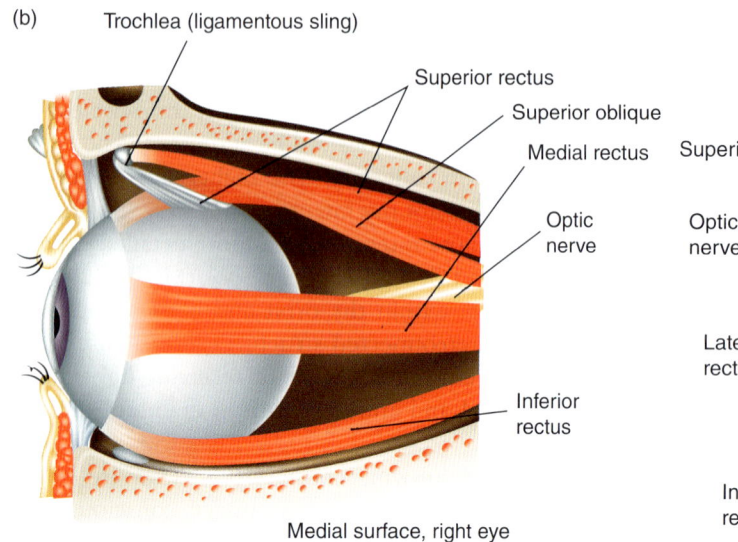

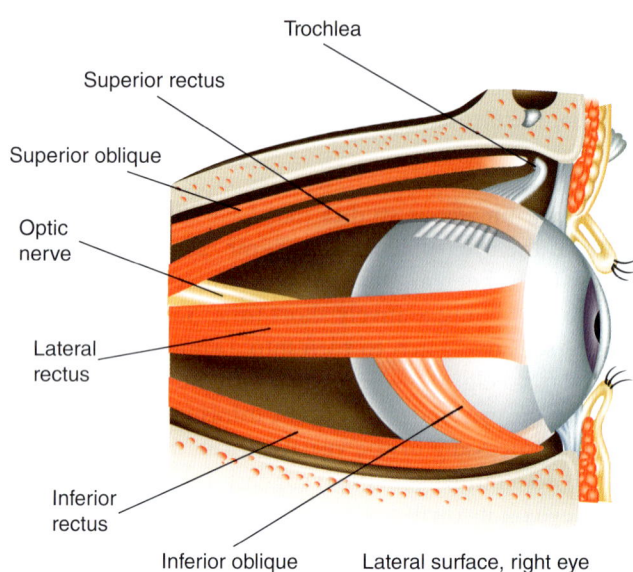

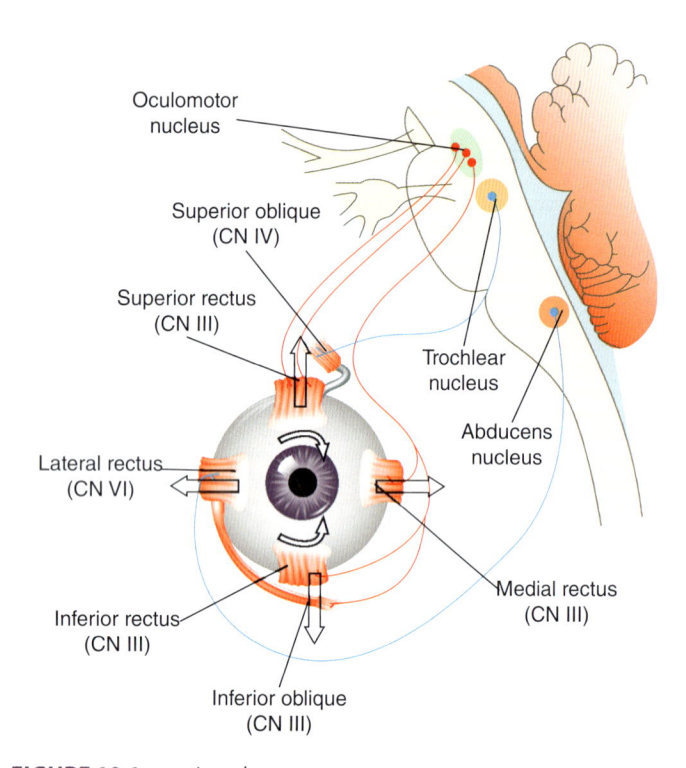

FIGURE 10.1 continued

is a protective layer that develops from neural crest cells (Sellheyer & Spitznas, 1988). The main functions of the sclera are to:

- protect the microstructures of the eye;
- maintain structural shape and dimensions in order to achieve a stable image;
- provide a base for the **ciliary muscles** that are used in adjusting the shape of the lens;
- provide a stable base for the effects of muscles moving the eye; and
- provide a protective route for vascular and neural systems to operate within (McBrien & Gentle, 2003).

The **cornea** of the eye is the clear area that includes the iris and pupil. Unlike the sclera, the cornea is clear and obtains its life support from the **aqueous humour** to its rear. The cornea is therefore transparent, thus allowing light to pass through. The cornea is made up of connective tissue, similar to skin and tendons, in several layers.

- The **epithelium** at the front is a protective layer.
- **Bowman's layer** which is made of collagen (a protein) and has been traditionally devoid of a specific

function in the cornea (Wilson & Hong, 2000), but has since been shown to enhance recovery and protect the layer below it (Lagali et al., 2009).

- The **stroma** is the thickest layer and is also made of overlapping collagen cells.
- **Descemet's membrane** is another protective layer made of a different kind of collagen to that of the stroma.
- The **endothelium** is the innermost layer of the cornea and keeps the cornea clear by pumping fluid out of the stroma after it has entered from the aqueous humour through the process of slow diffusion. Without this pumping the stroma would be opaque.

Aqueous Humour

The **aqueous humour** is a transparent fluid similar to plasma behind the cornea in the anterior chamber of the eye. It serves a number of functions.

- It supplies nutrients and oxygen to the cornea and lens.
- It removes metabolic wastes from the cornea and lens.
- It creates intraocular pressure to maintain the shape of the eye.
- It transports ascorbic acid which serves as an antioxidant.
- It facilitates the local immune responses, thus protecting the eye (To et al., 2002).

The Iris and Pupil

The iris is the coloured part of the eye and derives its name from the Greek goddess who is the personification of rainbows. The iris is made up of two layers of pigmented cells (see Chapter 2, genetics of eye colour). It functions as an adjustable aperture and, unlike the cornea, only allows light through via the pupil. The pupil is not a structure in itself but rather the space at the centre of the iris, which we see as a black dot. In dim light the iris opens, letting more light in, while in bright light it constricts, reducing the amount of light passing through to the retina. With a constricted pupil, the light is limited to the central part of the lens (Gregory, 1998).

The iris is connected to the **ciliary body** which is in turn connected to the sclera. The responsiveness of the pupil is determined by the opposing actions of the dilator and sphincter muscles in the iris which are controlled by sympathetic and parasympathetic nerves (Heller et al., 1990). This is achieved by the photoreceptive retinal ganglion (Gamlin et al., 2007) and retinorecipient olivary nucleus projecting to the Edinger–Westphal nucleus containing the parasympathetic neurons controlling pupilloconstriction (Gamlin et al., 1995).

Whilst the pupil looks black, it is in fact pink. The reason for this is that when we are looking in the eye the head gets in the way of the light where it is needed (Gregory, 1998). When one shines a light into the eye, one can see the infrastructure, and indeed the vascular innervation of the eye and retina can be seen, as in many photographs where 'red eye' is the result of the flash.

The Lens

Behind the iris is the lens which is adjustable and focuses the light onto the retina. Such adjustments in the lens, or accommodation, allow for distant and close vision. The lens is attached to the ciliary body via the **zonules of Zinn** (Davanger, 1975). Contraction of the ciliary muscles relaxes the zonules of Zinn which in turn reduces the pull on the lens, allowing it to become more spherical or fatter. This gives the lens more refractive power, allowing light to be bent more and the image that is close up to be projected clearly onto the retina. The opposite is the case for looking at objects in the distance.

Vitreous Humour

The **vitreous humour** is a large chamber behind the lens filled with fluid similar to the aqueous humour that is in front of the lens. Unlike the aqueous humour, the vitreous humour is a stagnant pool and is not replenished or innervated by any blood vessels. The vitreous humour gives the eye's general shape and form, keeping the retina in place. The fluid that makes up the vitreous humour is predominantly water and is approximately two-thirds of the eye's volume.

The next stop in visual perception is where the real business of converting light into neural impulses takes place – at the retina.

The Retina

The retina is where the light lands. Light is what an image is made of and therefore an image of the environment is projected directly onto the retina. The **retina** is part of the CNS, and comprises several cellular layers that communicate with each other using neurotransmitters. The architecture of the retina is inside out (see Figure 10.2). Light has to pass through the layers of the retina in order

256   **PSYCHOBIOLOGY**

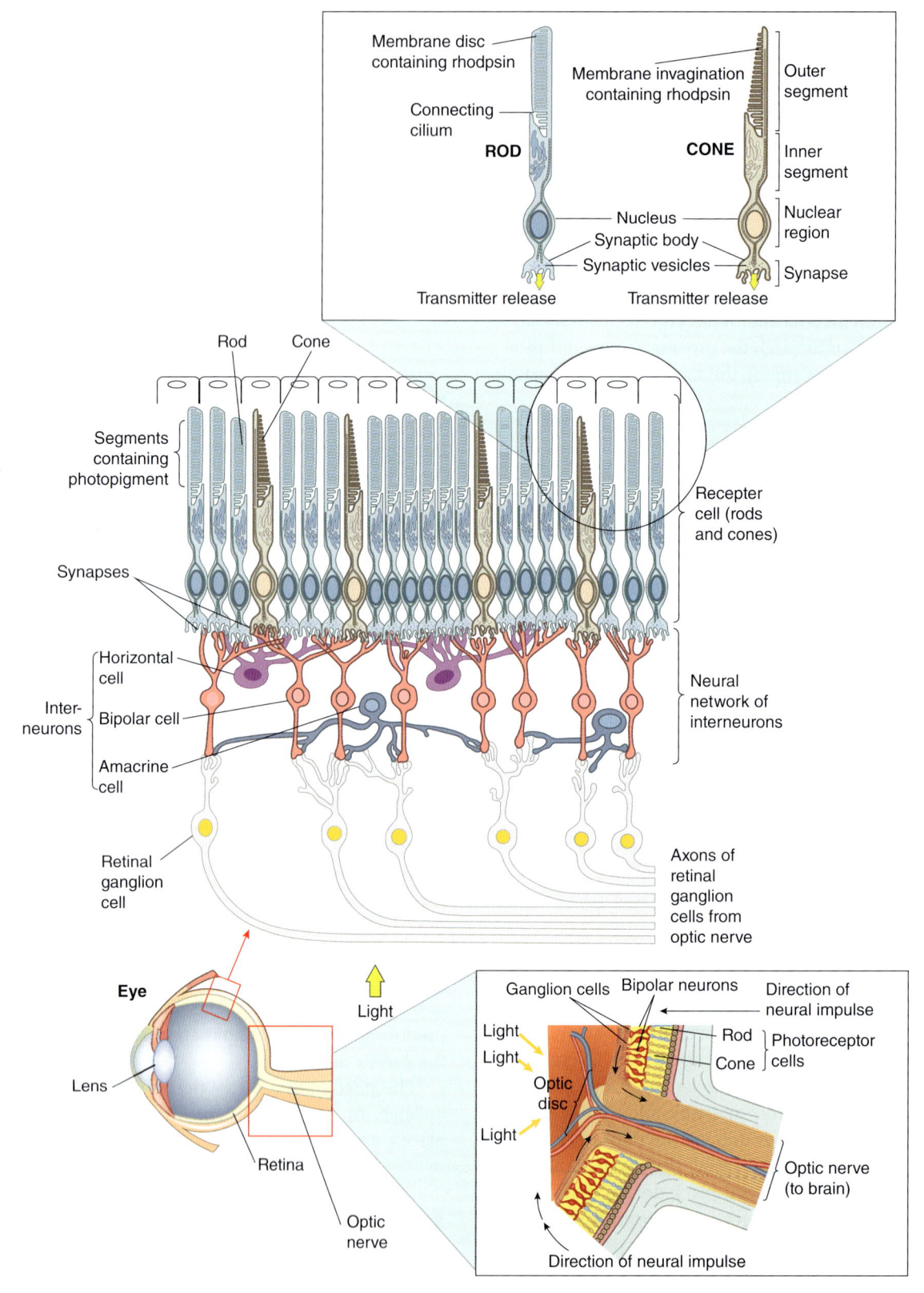

FIGURE 10.2 *The retinal cells.*

to be detected by cells sensitive to light (**photoreceptors**). Remember, evolution does not always produce the perfect design (this fact is used to counter the pro-creationists' argument of intelligent design) (Lamb, 2011). The inside-out arrangement is an artefact of embryological development, and the retina is equipped to deal with it. The development of the eye into optic vesicles from the forebrain and the subsequent invagination (folding in of various parts to form a pocket/tube/sheath; think of a calzone pizza) mean that the photoreceptors are now at the back (Moore et al., 2012). However, this is no problem as the cells preceding the photoreceptors, and in the pathway of light, are thin and transparent.

There are two types of photoreceptor, which have an uneven distribution over the retina: **rods** and **cones**. Rods are very sensitive but do not provide high acuity (fine detail) or colour. They are found in greater numbers on the edges of the retina. Cones, on the other hand, provide high acuity and respond to colour. There is a high density of cones in a central area of the retina called the **fovea**, in which the spacing of the cones corresponds with the resolution (high resolution) (Rossi & Roorda, 2010). In terms of evolutionary biology, the cones existed first, while the rods provided adaptive advantages in low light and are argued to have been subsequently wired in to the existing cone system (Lamb, 2009).

Photoreceptors are connected to interneurons and **ganglion** cells that form the optic nerve. The point at which information funnels out of the retina on its way to the brain (via the optic nerve) is the **blind spot** (see Box 10.1).

When light falls on the rods and cones, they convert the image into a neural impulse. The rods and cones contain visual pigments that are photosensitive, and there are different visual pigments that are made from **opsins** and retinal (Wald, 1964). **Rhodopsin**, usually referred to as the chemical for rods, is now also used to refer to the visual pigments for cones.

Rods

Rods are functionally active in dim light. It is these photoreceptors that give us night vision. When rods are active in dim light it is called **scotopic vision**. In contrast, bright light results in **photopic vision** and when light activates both the rods and cones, this is **mesopic vision**.

In the dark, rods are relatively depolarized – about −35 mV (see Bowmaker, 2002). This is achieved because rhodopsin is not activated. Rhodopsin is G-protein linked (which means it is linked to an intermediate second messenger system; see Chapter 4). A second messenger (**cyclic GMP**) keeps Na$^+$ channels open and Na$^+$ can flow into the rod. To counteract this, K$^+$ flows out. The rod in the dark state releases glutamate. However, light produces a reaction with rhodopsin and it disrupts the second messenger and Na$^+$ is no longer permitted to enter the cell. The rod then becomes hyperpolarized and glutamate release stops. In continuous light, the rod will recalibrate itself to the ambient light (Bowmaker, 2002).

Cones

Cones are considered our colour receptors. They are less sensitive than rods and are abundant in the central area of the retina – the fovea. Often the cones are conceptualized as being either red, green or blue. This is incorrect as these photoreceptors respond to different wavelengths of light. This clearly corresponds with the primary colours and lends itself to the analogy of pixels on a TV. Giving the cones colour names lends one to think that colour is real. However, the information that is received by these photoreceptors is of wavelengths and it is the brain that interprets this input and turns it into our perception and experience of colour. We shall revisit cones when we try to account for colour perception.

According to Stone (2012), there are three reasons why the eye has evolved in humans to respond to a

BOX 10.1: THE BLIND SPOT

The inside-out nature of the retina means that the neurons that are connected to the rods and cones have to exit the eye at the optic disc. The optic disc is an area where images cannot be seen because there are no photoreceptors.

Looking at Figure 10.1.1, close your left eye. Focus on the black star. Maintain your focus and move the book backwards and forwards. There is a point at which the black circle is not visible. You have now found your blind spot.

FIGURE 10.1.1 *The blind spot.*

limited range of light waves, not UV or infrared, and it is all to do with the sun and earth.

- The energy from the sun (our main source of light) is strongest within the visible light range of 400–700 nm.
- The atmosphere blocks short wavelengths and minimizes longer wavelengths because of molecules within the air.
- Because we have evolved out of the sea, seawater is transparent to wavelengths at about 500 nm.

Activation of rods and cones by the different wavelengths of light is the first part of the process of converting sensory input into neural impulses, which leads eventually to the occipital lobe or the visual cortex. The rods and cones connect via a series of intermediate neurons, or interneurons, to the retinal ganglion cells that form the optic nerve.

Bipolar cells and receptive fields

The glutamate released from the photoreceptors differentially reacts with the next cellular layer, the **bipolar cells**. There are a number of types of bipolar cells but in general these cells are divided into two receptive fields: **off-centre cells** and **on-centre cells**. The cells of the visual system have receptive fields that are sensitive to light (see Figure 10.3). When light is shone in the

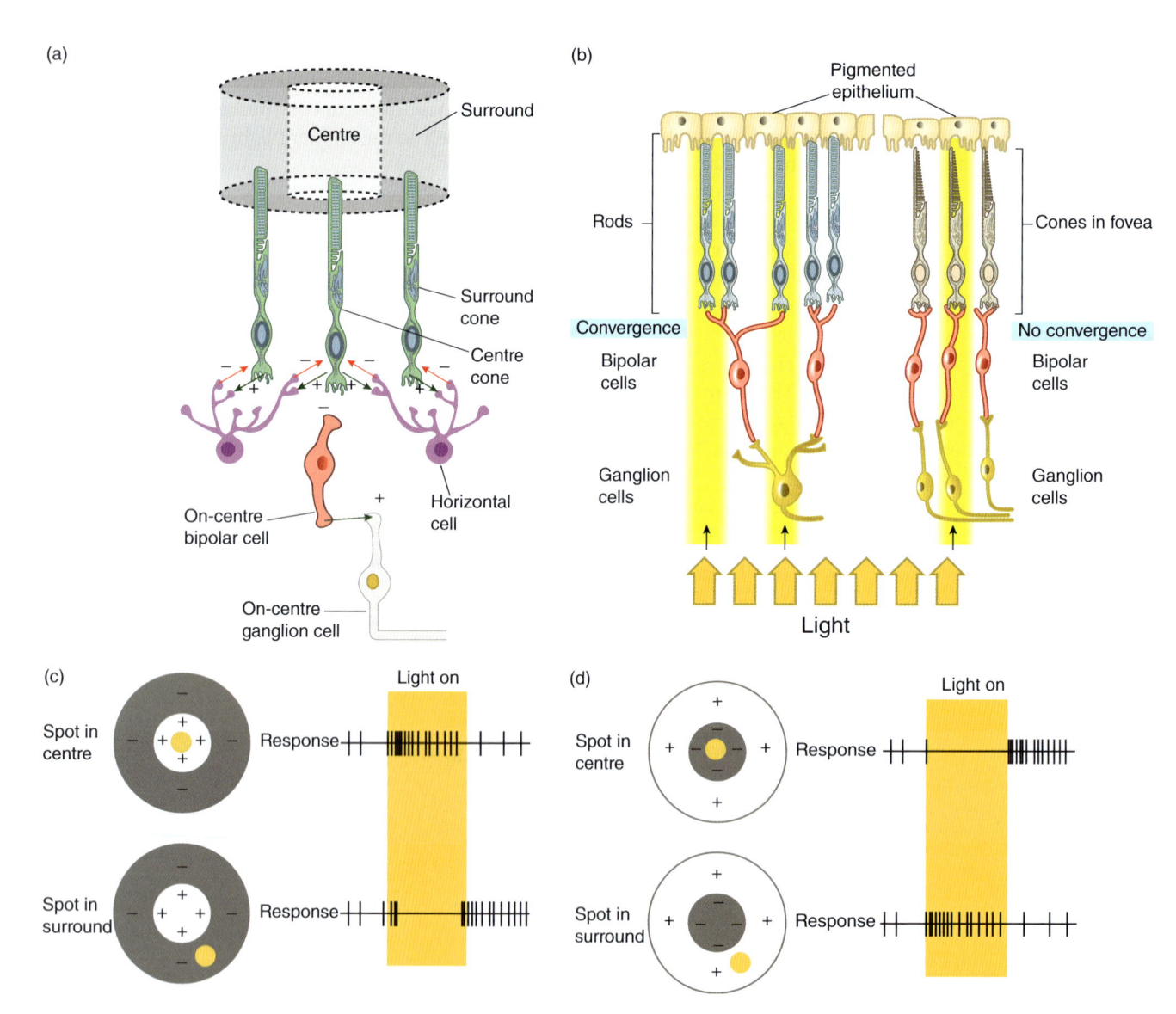

FIGURE 10.3 Receptive field of retinal ganglion cells. (a) Retinal ganglion cells can be divided into light-sensitive regions that either produce action potential (firing) in response to a light in the area (on) or reduce firing in another area (off). Horizontal cells provide lateral inhibition via GABA synthesis and release to neighbouring photoreceptors. (b) Convergence of rods and cones onto bipolar cells and ganglion cells. Rods have high convergence, which means that many rods synapse onto the same bipolar cell. Cones have low or no convergence as they synapse onto separate bipolar cells. (c) On-centre/off-surround receptive fields (+ –). (d) Off-centre/on-surround receptive fields (– +).

CHAPTER 10 PERCEPTUAL SYSTEMS

on-centre area, the cell fires. If a light is shone in the off-centre area it does not fire. Other cells have off-centres and on-surrounds.

The effect of having two receptive fields is that the cell responds best when there is contrast. If both receptive fields of the cell have light on them, the cell does not fire – one field cancels out the other. The consequence of having receptive fields can be seen in Box 10.2.

When the light is off, glutamate is released into the synapse, which depolarizes off-centre bipolar cells. Conversely, in on-centre bipolar cells, the reduction of glutamate in response to the light on photoreceptors results in

BOX 10.2: RECEPTIVE FIELDS

Look at the grid in Figure 10.2.1. You may have to adjust the distance from your eyes to get the full impact. The figure is made up of solid square and white bisecting lines, but is that what you can see? If you are doing it correctly, at the junction of the crossing white line you can see the colour white. However, in the adjacent junctions to the one that you are focusing on, there are light grey dots. If you try to focus on one of the grey dots, it disappears . . . as if by magic.

It isn't magic, but part of what magicians use commonly . . . an illusion. And the illusion can be explained by the appliance of science. The grid is known as a Hermann grid and the reason for this effect is due to **receptive fields** (see Spillmann, 1994).

At the junction there are four inhibitory inputs compared to one excitatory input. Along the white line, there are only two inhibitory inputs compared to one excitatory input. The firing of the cell will be influenced by the ratio of input across the receptive field. Thus, at the white intersection there is more inhibition than at the lines. The information coded by the cell is then passed on to the next set of neurons in the visual pathway.

The reason we see these spots outside the one we are looking at is because the receptive fields in the periphery are larger than those occupying the fovea (Spillmann et al., 1987).

However, others have argued against this relatively straightforward account. Schiller and Carvey (2005) argue that there are seven reasons why the explanation is inadequate.

- The illusion is perceived over a large range of sizes. The retinal ganglion view requires the illusion to be specific to a certain size in bisecting bars. This is not the case.
- Rotation of the grid by 45° reduces the illusion which is not readily accounted for by the retinal ganglion cell theory.
- The illusion can be minimized by manipulations that do not alter the on/off-centre/surround activation of retinal ganglion cells.
- The ratio of square size to the size of the bisecting bars is important to the illusion. When the white bars are the same width as the black square, the illusion diminishes.

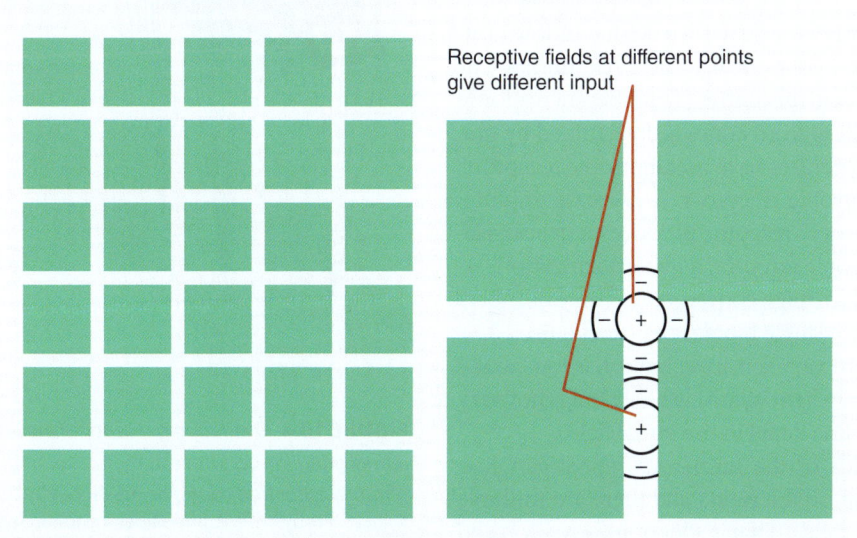

FIGURE 10.2.1 *A Hermann grid and the effect on receptive fields.*

- Enhancing centre/surround antagonism at the intersections of bars does not enhance the illusory effect and the grid should have more inhibitory input, thereby increasing the effect. It does not.
- Changing the contrast and/or colour produces illusory effects not accounted for by the retinal ganglion theory. In Figure 1, those bars that are 'behind' the grey bars yield a stronger effect than if 'in front'. Additionally, when using colour grids where the squares and lines are of similar luminance, the illusion vanishes.
- The spatial arrangement of retinal ganglion cell receptive fields is not what has been assumed by the theory. There are different types of retinal ganglion cells, two of which are midget and parasol cells. The ratio of midget and parasol cells is approximately 9:1 in the central retina and in the peripheral retina it is approximately 1:1. Thus, there is not an even distribution of cells as is assumed by the retinal ganglion theory.

This leaves us with a theory that is somewhat inadequate in explaining the subtle nuances of the Hermann grid illusion. However, Schiller and Carvey (2005) come to the rescue with two general premises: (1) that orientation-selective neurons are crucial to the illusion, and (2) that the perception of lightness and darkness is the product of the relative activity of neurons driven by antagonistic on/off systems. The on/off regions of the cells are centres or surrounds. The perception of lightness and darkness is a result of activity emanating from on/off systems. The perception is produced by simple cells in the cortex that receive selective input from each of the on/off systems.

Thus, Schiller and Carvey (2005) point their theoretical account at the simple cells in the V1 area of the visual cortex and not at the retinal ganglion cells. They claim the illusion is the result of the comparative degree of activity of the ON and OFF simple cells at the bisecting white lines, as compared with activity at non-bisecting parts of the white lines. Because the receptive fields of simple cells are not limited to one size, this can explain why the illusion continues when the size of the grid is varied.

depolarization. Thus, glutamate can influence cells in two different ways, depending on the type of receptive field it has.

When activated, bipolar cells release glutamate, which stimulates the **retinal ganglion cells**. Again, there are two types of ganglion cell: on-centre and off-centre (Kuffler, 1953). The retinal ganglion cells respond to incoming information, and relay the coded messages about light and dark to the brain. The retinal ganglion cells form the optic nerve.

Convergence

Cones feed into the bipolar cells with a degree of low **convergence**; that is, each cone speaks to a small number of bipolar cells (both on- and off-centre). The different response to incoming information from cones is determined by glutamate receptors. On-centres have metabotropic receptors; off-centres have ionotropic receptors. A decrease in glutamate at the metabotropic receptor produces a depolarization and at the ionotropic receptor, a hyperpolarization.

Rods, in contrast, have high convergence. Large numbers of rods synapse on to a single bipolar cell (see Figure 10.3). This makes the system very sensitive, but it has low acuity (i.e. it detects changes in light relatively easily but is not very good at transmitting fine detail in the visual field).

The receptive fields of the numerous retinal ganglion cells cover every point on the retina and there are multiple overlapping receptive fields. That is a lot of information and 'several neurons are conveying information about the same location in the visual image' (Meister & Berry, 1999, p.442). Each photoreceptor can belong to about 10 receptive fields (Figure 10.4).

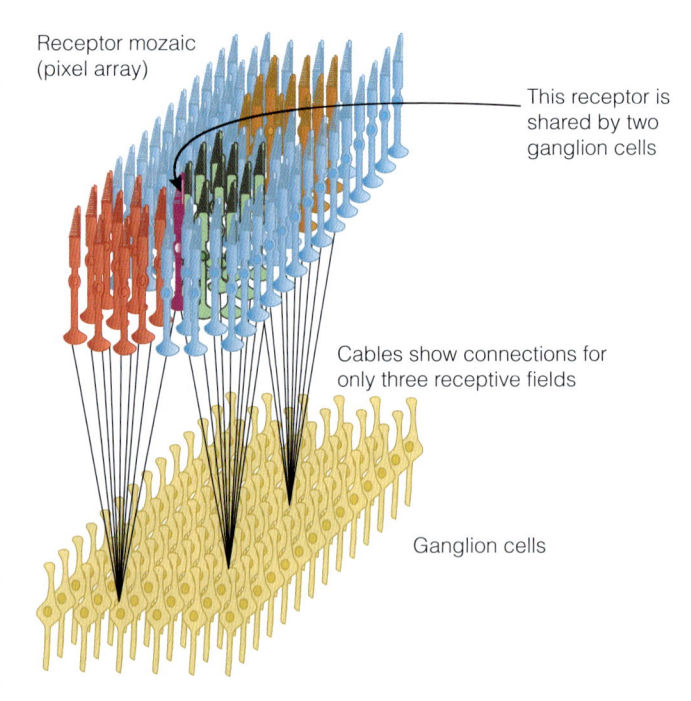

FIGURE 10.4 *Overlapping receptive fields. Receptive fields of retinal ganglion cells have a small amount of overlap with each photoreceptor (rod cones) being shared by two receptive fields.*
Source: Frisby, John P., and James V. Stone., *Seeing, second edition: The Computational Approach to Biological Vision*, figure, page 116, © 2010 Massachusetts Institute of Technology, by permission of The MIT Press.

Horizontal communication within the retina

While it is clear that visual information is transmitted from the eye to the brain, there is also communication between the cells of the retina (horizontal communication). Rather than a simple funnel of information stemming from the rods and cones and extending towards the optic nerve, there is also communication at the level of the rods and cones, via **horizontal cells** and **amacrine cells**. Between the rods and cones are gap junctions (which are electrical synapses – see Chapter 4) (Raviola & Gilula, 1973); although their function in visual processing remains uncertain (Asteriti et al., 2014), the main hypothesis is that they enhance the signal-to-noise ratio in the retina (DeVries et al., 2002). Horizontal cells also have gap junctions which are thought to modulate the firing of neighbouring cells (Sohl et al., 2005).

Look at Figure 10.2 again and you will see a set of cells that communicate across the retinal cells: the amacrine cells and horizontal cells. Horizontal cells synapse with the photoreceptors and provide feedback that is in opposition to the photoreceptor. If a rod stimulates a horizontal cell, it sends a message back saying 'stop it'. Note that horizontal cells synapse with more than one photoreceptor, and horizontal cells are involved in a process called lateral inhibition.

Lateral inhibition

Studies on the horseshoe crab have cast light on the mechanisms of **lateral inhibition** (Hartline et al., 1956). Lateral inhibition is when one neuron inhibits its neighbouring neurons. Light activates a photoreceptor and glutamate release stops. The horizontal cell sends inhibitory messages (using GABA) to all the photoreceptors to which it is connected. The role of GABA in the horizontal cells is more complicated than in typical GABAergic neurons because there is no storage of GABA and the released GABA is synthesized immediately on demand from glutamate (Deniz et al., 2011).

Look at Box 10.3 to see the effects of lateral inhibition. The effect is achieved because the edges of the different contrasting bands are being differentially inhibited. The receptor at the edge of the more intense light fires more than the other receptors receiving the same light input. On the darker side, the receptor at the edge fires less compared to the others in the middle of the band. The middle receptors fire at the same rate because they receive the same amount of stimulation and the same amount of inhibition from the horizontal cell. The receptors at the edge of the light receive the same amount of light input, but receive different levels of inhibition. The bright receptor inhibits the darker receptor. Meanwhile the darker receptor has less inhibitory power on the adjacent bright-sided receptor.

The amacrine cells, which communicate with the bipolar and retinal ganglion cells, achieve a similar process. Depending on the type of incoming information from the bipolar cells, the amacrine cells can inhibit retinal ganglion cells. Furthermore, gap junctions also exist between amacrine cells and bipolar cells which are thought to be important for increasing the sensitivity and spatial resolution of the visual pathway by allowing the amacrine cells to act as a group in low light conditions and in daylight conditions the amacrine cells are uncoupled or ungrouped (Bloomfield et al., 1997).

The Optic Nerve

The **optic nerve** is the collated axons of the retinal ganglion cells. Because we have two eyes, we have two optic nerves. Two eyes mean we receive slightly different images of the same stimulus; this is called **binocular vision**. Look at an object and close one eye. Then close that eye and open the other. You will see that the image of the object is slightly different and appears to move. The information that is transmitted to the brain is sorted according to the visual field.

In Figure 10.5 you can see that the **nasal hemiretina** projects to the opposite side of the brain (contralateral) and the **temporal hemiretina** projects to the same side of the brain (ipsilateral). Information from both eyes is integrated.

The point at which the visual fields cross is called the **optic chiasm**. There are no connections in the optic chiasm; the axons of the optic nerve synapse at the **lateral geniculate nucleus** (**LGN**) of the thalamus.

Lateral Geniculate Nucleus

The LGN is a multilayered structure. Each layer contains a map of the visual field (a **retinotopic map**). There are six layers that can be differentiated into two types, depending on the size of the cell: the **magnocellular layer** and the **parvocellular layer** (see Figure 10.6). Signals from cones tend to innervate the parvocellular layer, and signals from rods innervate the magnocellular layer.

There is a third layer called the **koniocellular layer** which resides at the base of each magnocellular layer and parvocellular layer (Hendry & Reid, 2000). These cells which respond to blue light (or, to be accurate, the wavelength that conveys it) (Dacey & Lee, 1994) have been identified as conferring an evolutionary advantage on those that possess them. The koniocellular pathway projects to diffuse higher cortical stages but also to the **amygdala** via the **superior colliculus**. This connection is relevant as the superior colliculus has a role in responses to events

BOX 10.3: LATERAL INHIBITION

Look at the Mach bands in Figure 10.3.1. What do you see? Within each band, there appears to be a gradient of tone. Now take two pieces of paper and cover all but one of the Mach bands. Now what do you see? I hope that you can see that there is no tonal gradient within a single band. What is actually there and what you see/perceive is different.

Again science can account for this illusion. In this case the horseshoe crab provides the answer with a process called lateral inhibition.

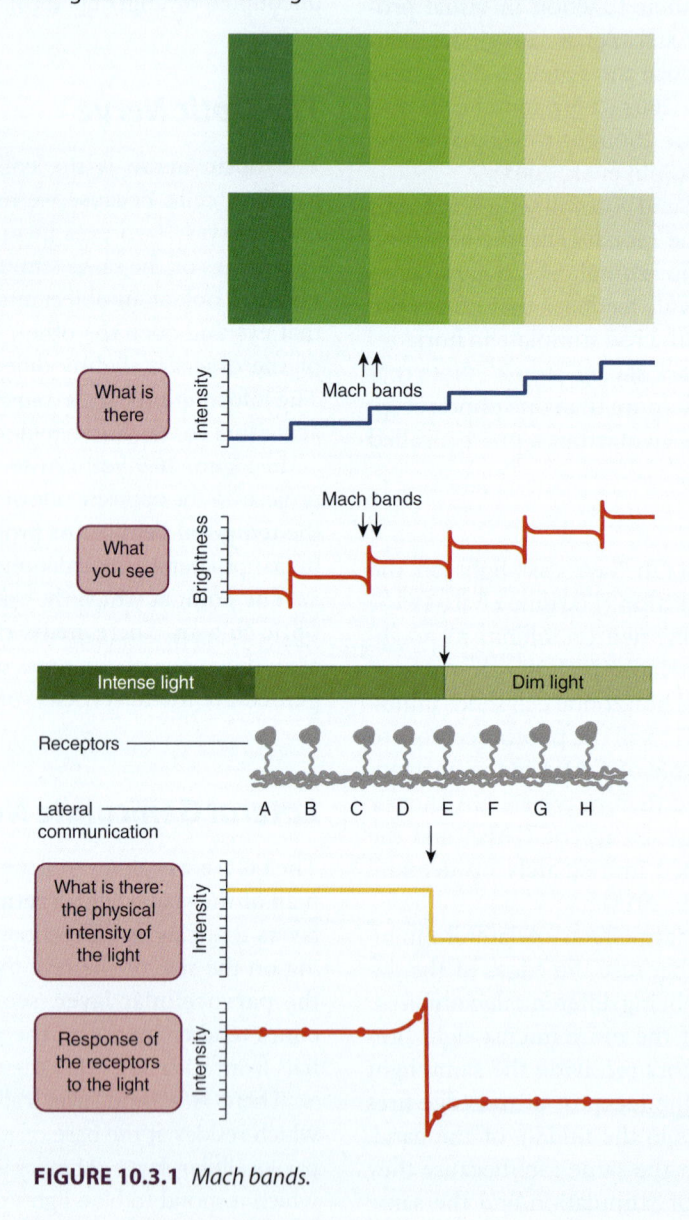

FIGURE 10.3.1 *Mach bands.*

and emergencies and the amygdala is involved in emotional responses (Carvajal et al., 2012; Teftef et al., 2013).

The information from the retina does not appear to be reorganized by the LGN (Derrington, 2002). The receptive fields of the LGN are the same as the retinal inputs. The information at this point may be integrated with other signals before they are passed to the cortex. One of the main inputs to the LGN is from the visual cortex, in a process

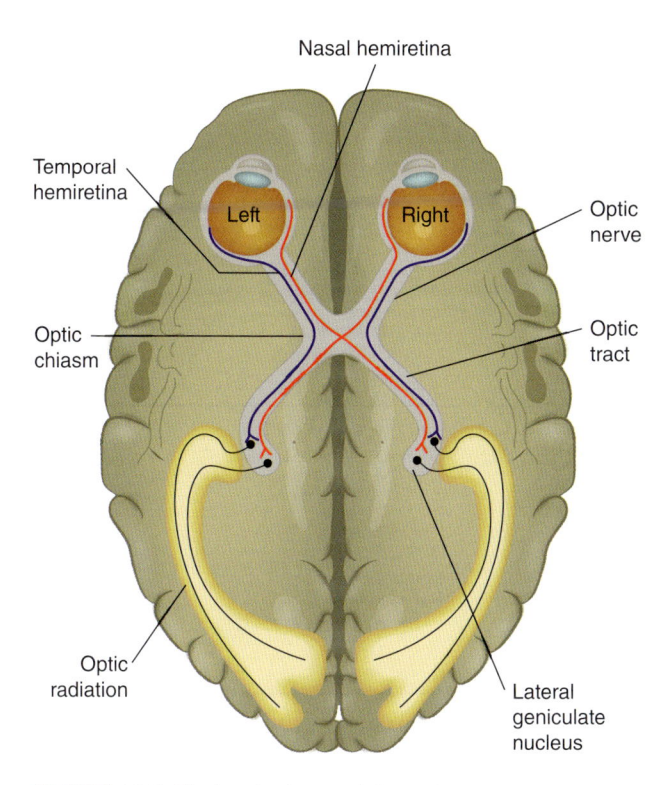

FIGURE 10.5 *The hemiretinas and the optic nerve projection.*

of modulating feedback. This feedback is postulated to change the efficacy of retinal relays of visual information.

The magnocellular, parvocellular and koniocellular layers project to the occipital cortex (visual cortex). It is at the next stage in perception that all this neural information is processed.

The Visual Cortex

The visual cortex (or occipital cortex or striate cortex) interprets the signals received from the retina via the LGN. The visual cortex is made up of layers called V1, V2, V3, etc., with V1 being the first visual (V) area to receive sensory input. The visual cortex has a further type of organization – **retinotopic organization** in which the 'map' of visual input on the retina is represented as a similar 'map' in the visual cortex. Using electrical stimulation directly to the visual cortex, early studies by Penfield and colleagues demonstrated that patients could report images produced by the stimulation (Penfield & Jasper, 1954; Penfield & Rasmussen, 1950). These studies are amazing as the patients were undergoing surgery for epilepsy and were conscious whilst their brains were being manipulated.

Within the visual cortex, there are two types of cell that respond to visual input: simple cells and complex cells. Our understanding of these comes mainly from the early experiments of Hubel and Wiesel, which used animals that had electrodes placed in regions of the visual cortex to record activity. Light was shone on the retina and changes in the firing rate of the cells could be measured.

Hubel and Wiesel (1959, 1962, 1968) discovered that like other cells in the visual system, the ones in the cortex also had receptive fields that could be divided into on/off areas. They also investigated the effects of visual deprivation (Box 10.4). The effects of learning and experience are evident in the case study of a blind skier (Box 10.5).

Simple cells

The **simple cells** of the visual cortex differ from the cells of the rest of the visual pathway as they have visual fields that are divided by straight lines. They respond best when the light falls in a particular orientation. The hypothesized manner by which the LGN projects this information to the simple cells is depicted in Figure 10.7.

Simple cells are elongated structures rather than circular structures as found in the LGN. The elongated receptive fields of the simple cells mean that they are configured to detect lines; they have been referred to as edge detectors and bar detectors. As simple cells are responding to contrasting light that indicates lines or edges, they detect the lines of a particular orientation. The input to simple cells comes from a number of cells in the LGN. Excitatory regions of the simple cell correspond to the on-centre regions of the cells in the LGN and conversely, the inhibitory regions of the simple cells respond to the off-centre regions of cells within the LGN. Thus, the overlapping receptive fields of the LGN relay to the elongated region receptive fields of the simple cells in the cortex (Ferster et al., 1996; Hubel & Wiesel, 1962; Reid & Alonso, 1995).

Complex cells

Complex cells are more numerous than simple cells and respond to straight lines of a particular orientation. Complex cells differ from simple cells in four ways:

- they are large;
- the receptive field cannot divide into on- and off-areas;
- they are binocular, whereas simple cells are monocular (one eye); and
- they respond when the stimulus is moving across the receptive field.

Complex cells respond to stimuli in their entire receptive field (Figure 10.8). The incoming information from simple cells to complex cells is depicted in Figure 10.8(b).

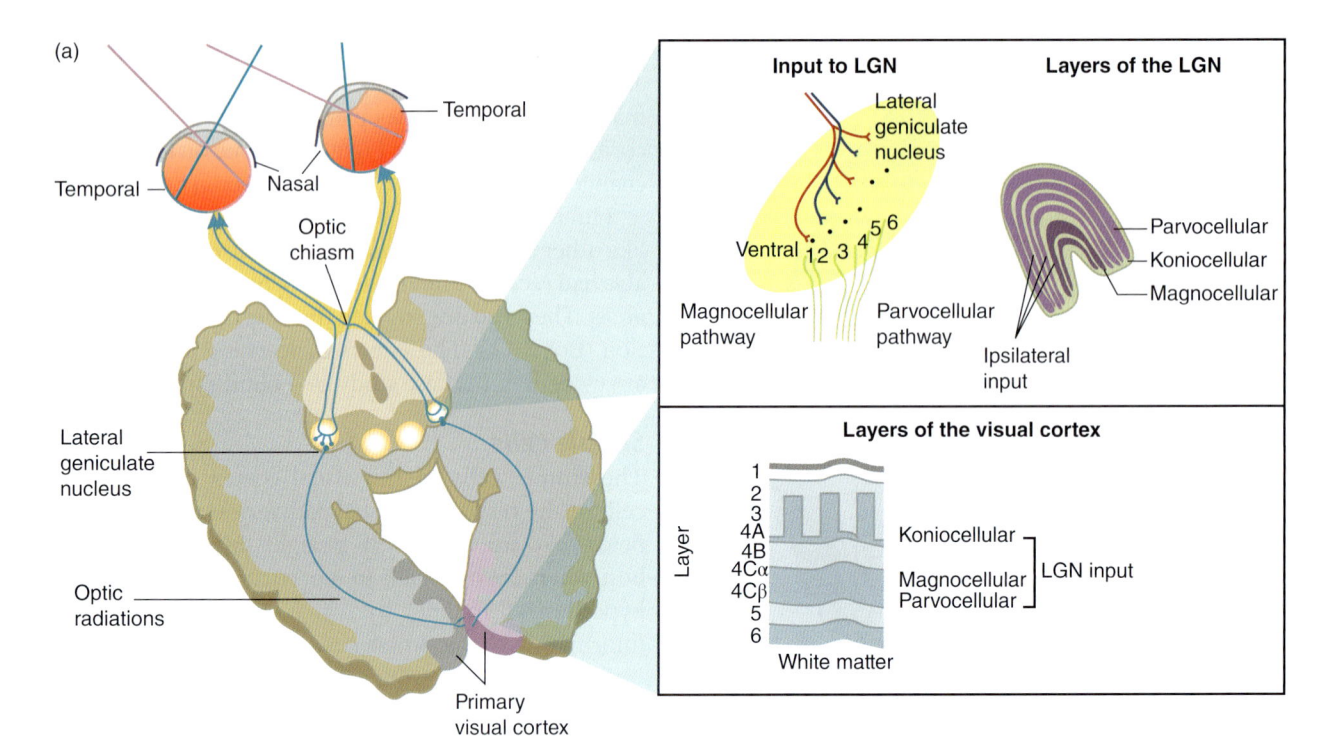

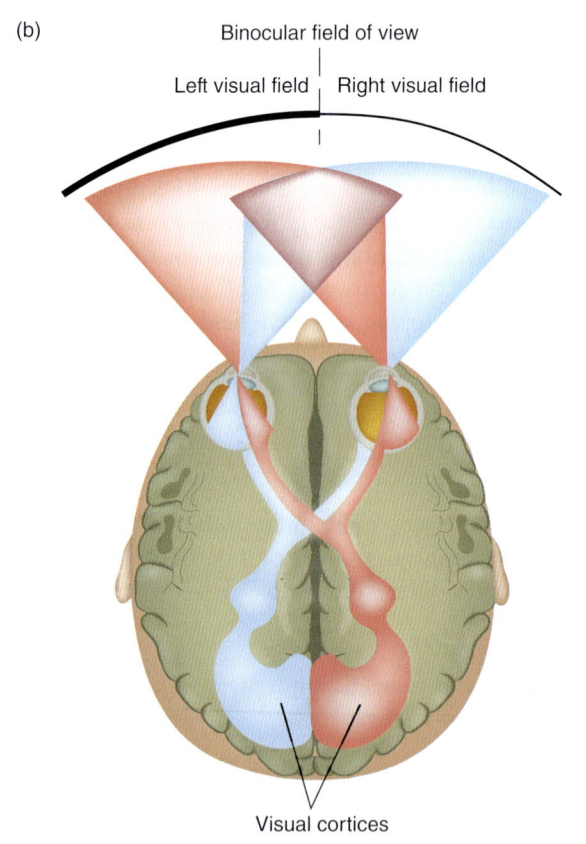

FIGURE 10.6 *The lateral geniculate nucleus (LGN). (a) The LGN receives input into different layers which then project to the visual cortex. (b) Binocular vision.*

BOX 10.4: VISUAL SYSTEM AND DEPRIVATION

Although we are born with a brain and a visual system, postnatal experience of the visual world has profound effects on the perceptual system. A number of experiments were carried out looking at the effects of early visual deprivation on animals. Such experiments typically use methods such as closing the eyelids or restricting visual information such as form, or by inducing a squint in one eye, which produce large changes in the neural architecture of the animal.

In the experiments of Wiesel and Hubel (1963a), cats' eyelids were closed in the first postnatal week and when the eye was opened later on, e.g. at three months, the cat was effectively blind in that eye (Figure 10.4.1). The first thing to check was if the eye was functionally operating, which it was, as were the retinal ganglion cells and LGN (Wiesel & Hubel, 1963b). However, looking at the cortex, the effects of early visual deprivation were clear. The visual cortex did not respond to input from the previously closed eye and any neurons that did respond had abnormal receptive fields (Hubel & Wiesel, 1963a). Such changes are not seen in adult animals (LeVay et al., 1980).

Further experiments by Wiesel and Hubel (1963b) indicate that it is form that is important rather than light *per se* because when light was allowed through but form definition was obscured, the same effects were found as in previous studies. Despite the fact that the LGN was functioning in response to visual input in the deprived eye in a similar manner to that of the non-deprived eye, it was physically different. The LGN corresponding to the deprived eye included cells that were smaller and this was considered a reflection of the arborization process in the cortex (Hubel et al., 1977; Wiesel & Hubel, 1963a). Hubel and Wiesel (1965a) induced a strabismus (where both eyes are not aligned) in their animals by cutting muscles in the eye. This resulted in both eyes having different visual input that could not be integrated into one coherent picture. The results indicated that each eye produced separate changes in the activity measured in the visual cortex.

Whilst these deprivation experiments indicate that a lack of input changes cortical architecture, it is not

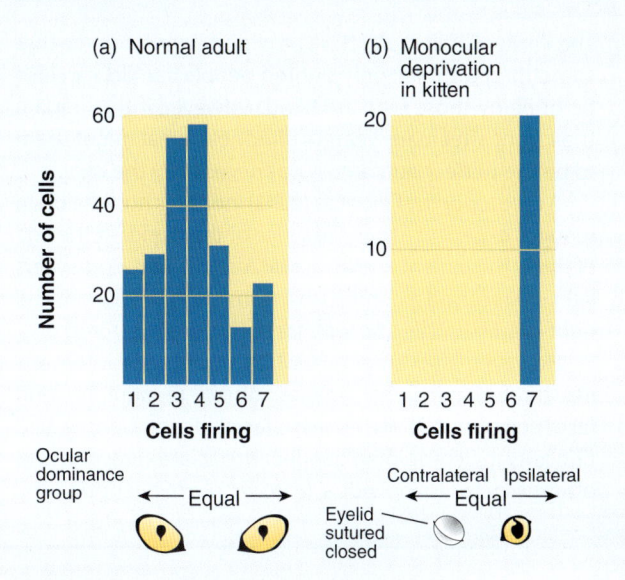

FIGURE 10.4.1 Cell activation after visual deprivation in one eye. Cell firing rate in cats with monocular deprivation. The bottom axis is the amount of firing on contralateral or ipsilateral sides of the deprivation. Normal cats have a dominant eye, those deprived have no cell firing in the newly opened eye.
Source: Hubel, D. H., & Wiesel, T. N. (1964). Effects of Monocular Deprivation in Kittens. *Naunyn-Schmiedebergs Archiv für experimentelle Pathologie und Pharmakologie, 248*, 492–497. With kind permission from Springer Science and Business Media.

a one-way street. If sensory regions of the cortex are damaged or surgical lesions are made, as is the case in animals, then the loss of neurons in the cortex is consequently seen downstream in the thalamus. The cells of the thalamus show signs of degeneration in response to a loss of innervation from the sensory cortex. This process is called **thalamic retrograde degeneration** (Diamond & Utley, 1963; Matthews, 1973; Ross & Ebner, 1990; Tanaka & Chen, 1974). Looking at cellular changes in the LGN after cortical lesions allows a more precise marker for the functional location of that lesion.

Simple cells and complex cells show correlated firing consistent with their synaptic connections and 'were in the direction from the simple cell to the complex cell, most frequently between cells with similar orientation preferences' (Alonso & Martinez, 1998, p.395).

Spatial frequency

The receptive fields of simple and complex cells led to the notion of edge and bar detectors. This somewhat oversimplified account gave way to the **spatial frequency** theory, which states that cells work on the number of

BOX 10.5: THE BLIND SKIER

The Winter Paralympics have provided clear evidence that something we think only sighted people can do, can also be done by those who are blind. However, if they regain their sight after many years of blindness, what might seem to be the perfect outcome is not necessarily the case.

A case report by Fine et al. (2003) indicates how the brain requires experience to make sense of the world. At the age of three, the patient known as MM lost his sight. Forty years later, he received a corneal and stem cell transplant to the right eye. Essentially the tools for seeing were restored.

However, after surgery, MM had trouble in interpreting three-dimensional images, object recognition and face recognition. With regard to facial recognition, he had difficulty in determining gender and facial expression and often resorted to individual features like hair length.

Functional MRI scans indicated that during such recognition tasks, his lingual and fusiform gyri – the brain regions of object and face recognition – were not as active as those of control participants. His occipital lobe (visual cortex) was activated, so he could see, but he could not interpret the image. Here information is getting to the brain, but the brain has had little experience of how to process and make sense of the visual input.

His motion perception was good. When he was blind he was an accomplished skier. After surgery, he would close his eye because he was frightened of a collision. Two years after surgery he was able to ski with sight, but he had to use the shading patterns of the snow to determine the slope; however, on difficult runs he still chose to ski blind.

---

light/dark cycles in a receptive field. If you look at Figure 10.9 you can see high- and low-frequency grids, and how retinal ganglion cells can interpret them. These grids can be described by a sine wave. These sine waves can differ from each other in frequency (width of light/dark cycles), amplitude (the difference between the light and dark parts of the grid) and angle. The complexity of a visual stimulus can be broken down into constituent sine waves by a mathematical process called **Fourier analysis**.

Presentation of sine wave grids, in the same way that Hubel and Wiesel presented light, demonstrates that cortical cells are more responsive to this type of stimulus (De Valois et al., 1979). The cells of the visual cortex are thought to perform a biological version of Fourier analysis on the incoming information. This analysis turns the complex spatial information into its component sine waves. Cortical cells are individually tuned for a particular orientation and frequency. Therefore, different groups of cells will be active depending on the spatial frequency of the visual stimuli. The initial work by Hubel and Wiesel can be accounted for in these terms, as they presented stimuli that could be described by spatial frequency analysis.

Hypercomplex cells

The cells of the visual cortex go from simple to complex and now to **hypercomplex**. Like complex cells, the hypercomplex cells respond to moving stimuli in a particular orientation, the difference being they respond to stimuli of a specific length. This leads to the speculation that they are end stopping detectors (Hubel & Wiesel, 1965b). However, the notion of hypercomplex cells gave way to contrary evidence that simple and complex cells also respond to ends (Gilbert, 1977) which lead to a recapitulation of the theory that now includes end-stop cells (Hubel & Wiesel, 1998).

Hypercolumns

Cortical cells are organized in columns. Proceeding down a column, all the cells have receptive fields in the same visual field. They also respond to stimuli of the same orientation (Hubel et al., 1978). However, if you cut across the columns, the column next in line has a slightly different input from a different location of the visual field, and responds to stimuli of a slightly different orientation. This continues as one navigates the architecture of the cortex until eventually the orientation turns full circle and the cells respond to a stimulus of the same orientation that you started with. Each column has a dominant input from either the left or the right eye. **Hypercolumns** are focused primarily on receiving input from the central areas of the retina, with a relative paucity dedicated to the peripheral regions of the retina (Figure 10.10).

Colour Perception

Up to now we have focused on the structural aspects of vision, e.g. lines and edges. However, our visual

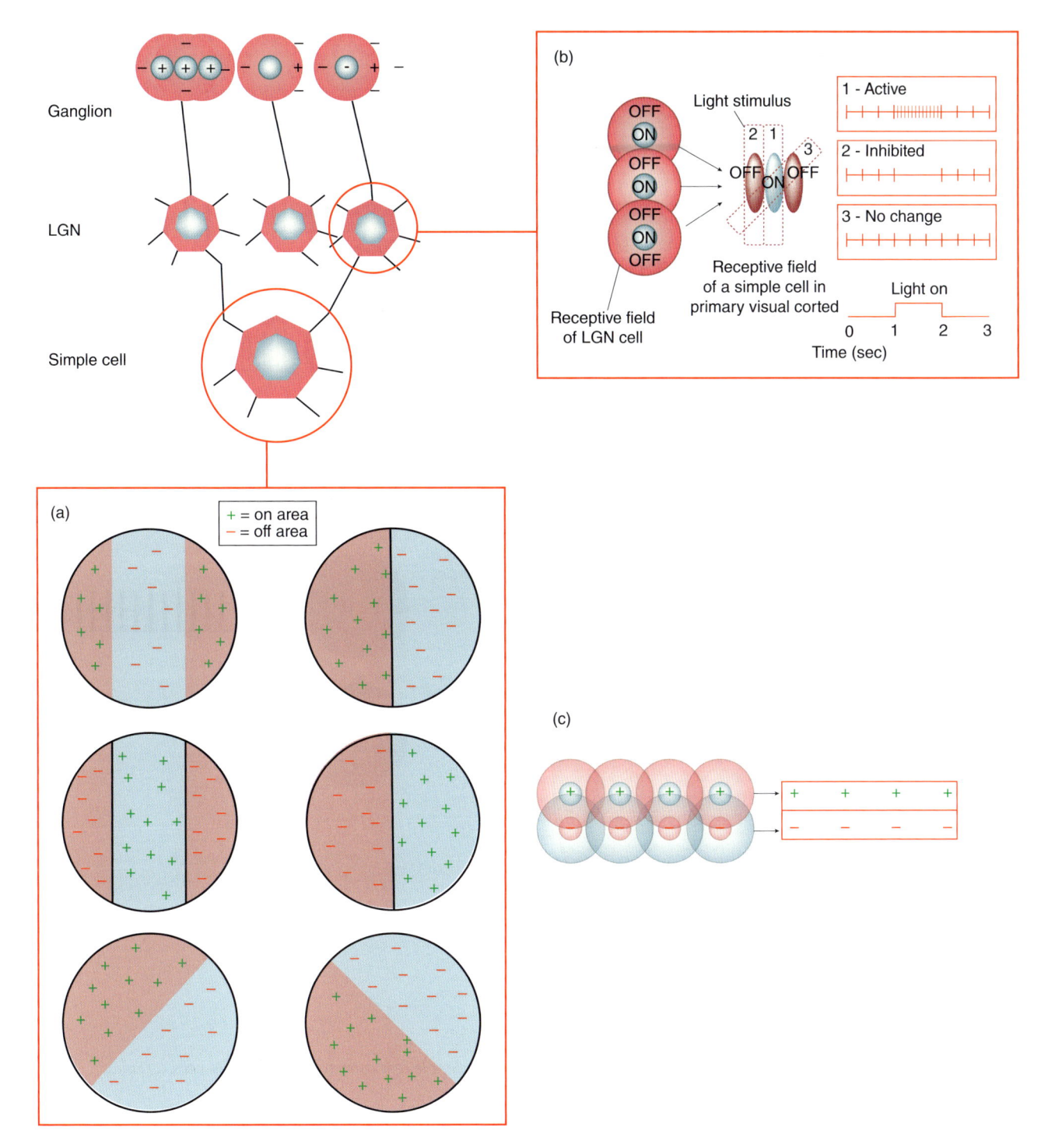

FIGURE 10.7 *Simple cells. (a) Simple cells have receptive fields that detect straight lines. (b) Simple cells respond to lines of a particular orientation (in this case vertical bar detected across the on-centres of the LGN cells). (c) The configuration of an edge detector.*

system perceives colour. There are three aspects of colour perception:

- *brightness*, which varies from dark to light;
- *hue*, which represents what we mean by colour and varies across the spectrum through blue, green, yellow, orange and red; and
- *saturation*, which varies from rich and full colours through to varying shades of colour, and grey in the centre (Figure 10.11).

As already mentioned, the cones are the photoreceptors that mediate colour. What the cones are really sensitive to are different wavelengths of light: short, medium and

268 PSYCHOBIOLOGY

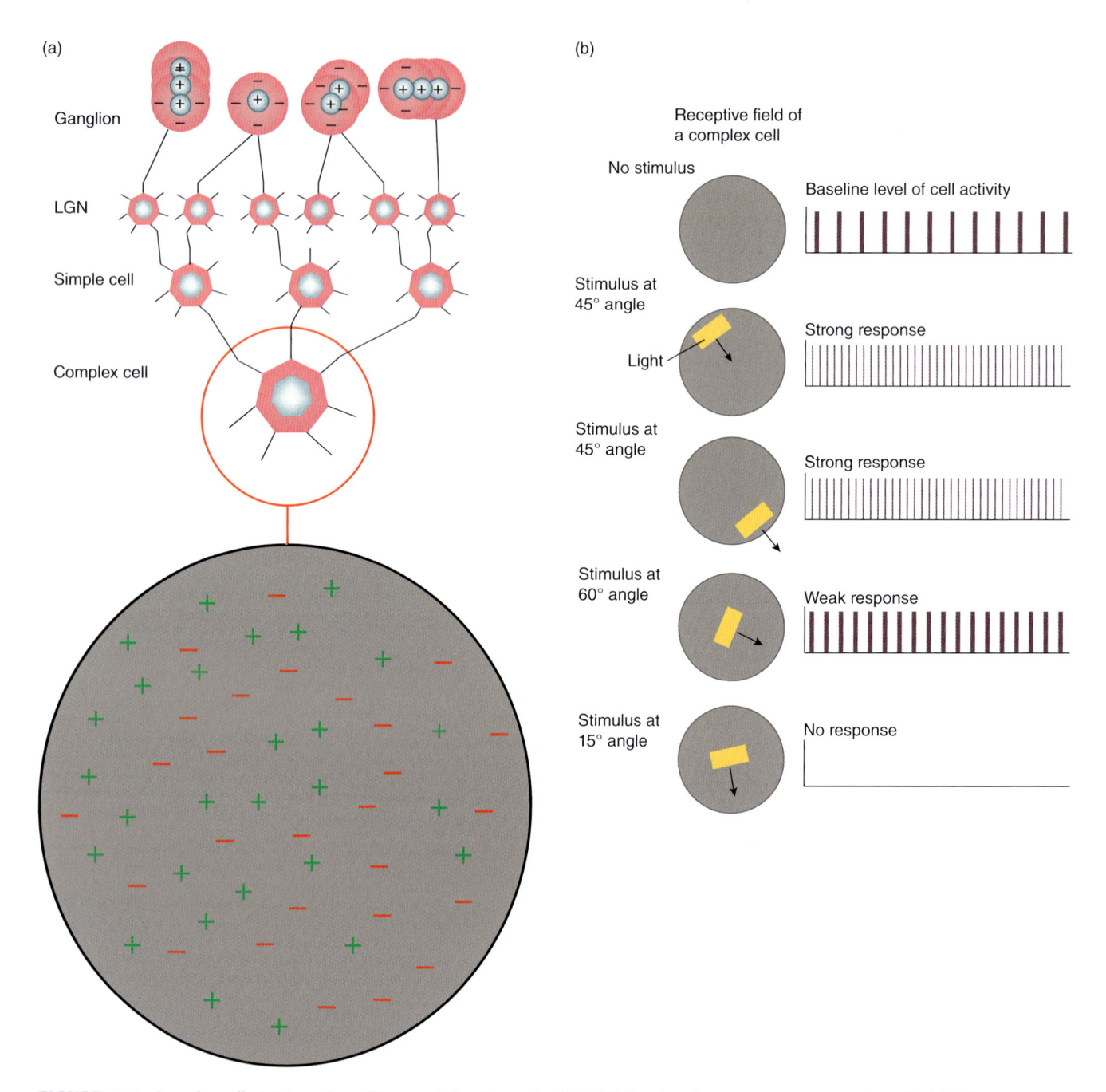

FIGURE 10.8 Complex cells. (a) Complex cell has no defined receptive field. (b) Simple cells converge onto complex cells. (c) Firing pattern in response to moving light.

long waves. The cones are tuned to much of the visual spectrum of light. The short, medium and long waves to some extent correspond with blue, green and red light respectively, but there is considerable overlap. Given that the cones are actually responding to wavelengths, they should be referred to as S, M and L cones rather than blue, green and red but for ease I shall continue to refer to them incorrectly as blue, green and red cones.

Colour vision is enabled by the comparison of signals from the cones; thus we can perceive colours beyond red, green and blue. Our colour system is referred to as trichromatic because it uses these three channels. According to Stone (2012), the wavelengths of green and red are so close together that they should appear to be redundant and the after-effect of looking at red is green and vice versa. Furthermore, Stone argues that despite

(a)

Receptive fields

(b) Square-wave grating

Intensity

Sine waves

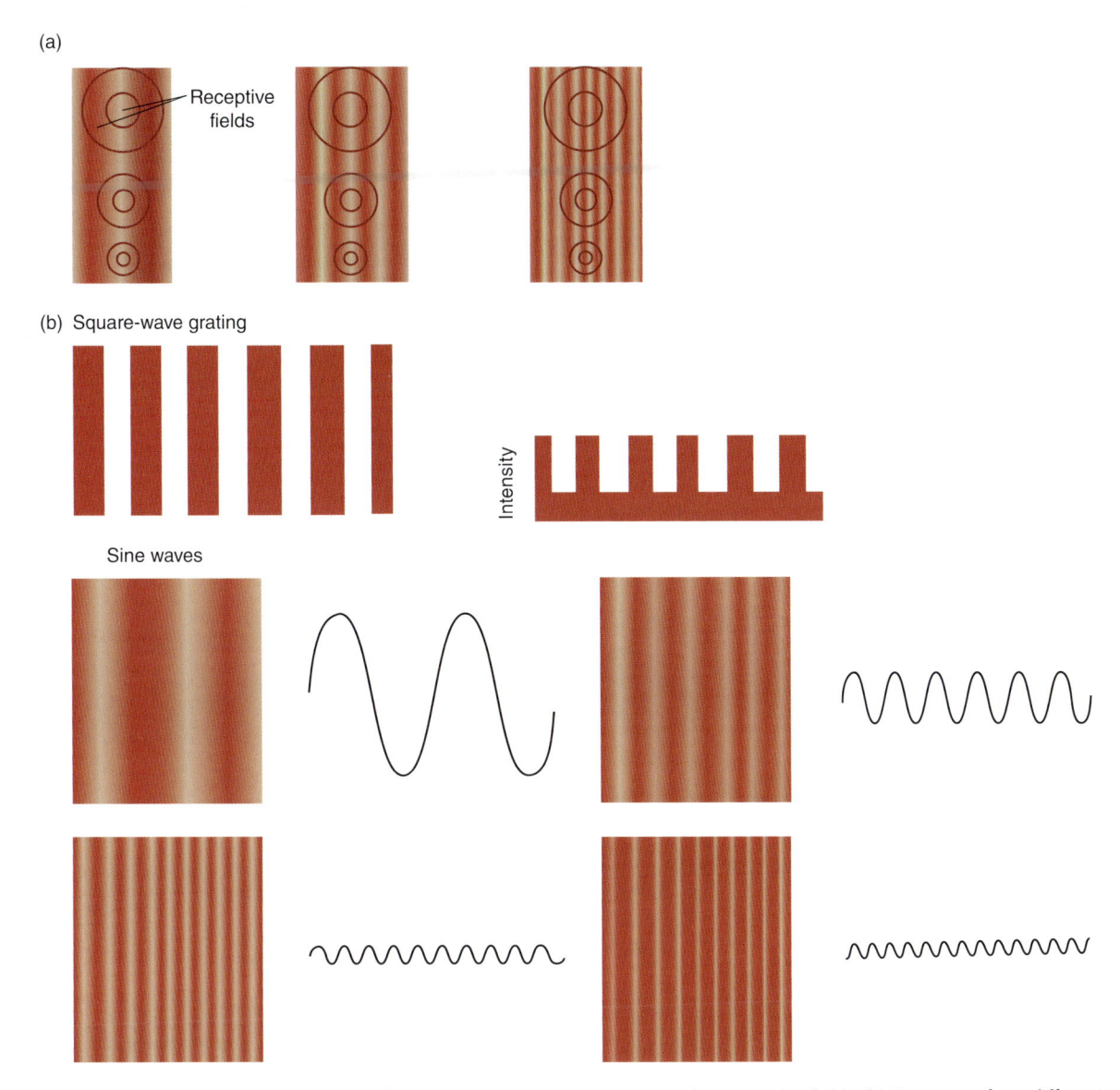

FIGURE 10.9 *Spatial frequency of vision. (a) Different sine wave gratings over ganglion receptive fields. (b) Sine waves from different spatial frequencies.*

there being three primary colours (red, green, blue), the after-effect of blue is yellow and conversely the after-effect of yellow is blue, suggesting that there are indeed four primary colours.

The cones are just the first part of colour perception, like detection of structural features such as edges and lines, information coding colour synapses onto retinal ganglion cells before they are passed on to the LGN and the visual cortex. These intermediate stages of the journey of colour perception are involved in additional processing of the incoming stimuli.

Cone signalling pathways converge antagonistically in the receptive fields of ganglion cells (Dacey, 2000). At the retina and the LGN, two cone opponent pathways are recognized: a 'red-green' pathway, in which red and green cone signals are antagonistic, and a 'blue-yellow' pathway in which blue cones are opposed by combined red and green cone signals (Dacey & Packer, 2003). If light with a wavelength selective for red cones is shone onto the receptive fields of ganglion cells, then green cones will be inhibited, and vice versa. This is mediated by the overlapping excitatory and inhibitory receptive fields from different parts of the visual spectrum (Chatterjee & Callaway, 2003). This is referred to as opponent processing or opponent coding. It is the ratio of activity in the cones that is important, e.g. how much red to green there is or blue to yellow. From this perspective, an increase in firing rate does not change the colour as the ratio between the cones remains the same.

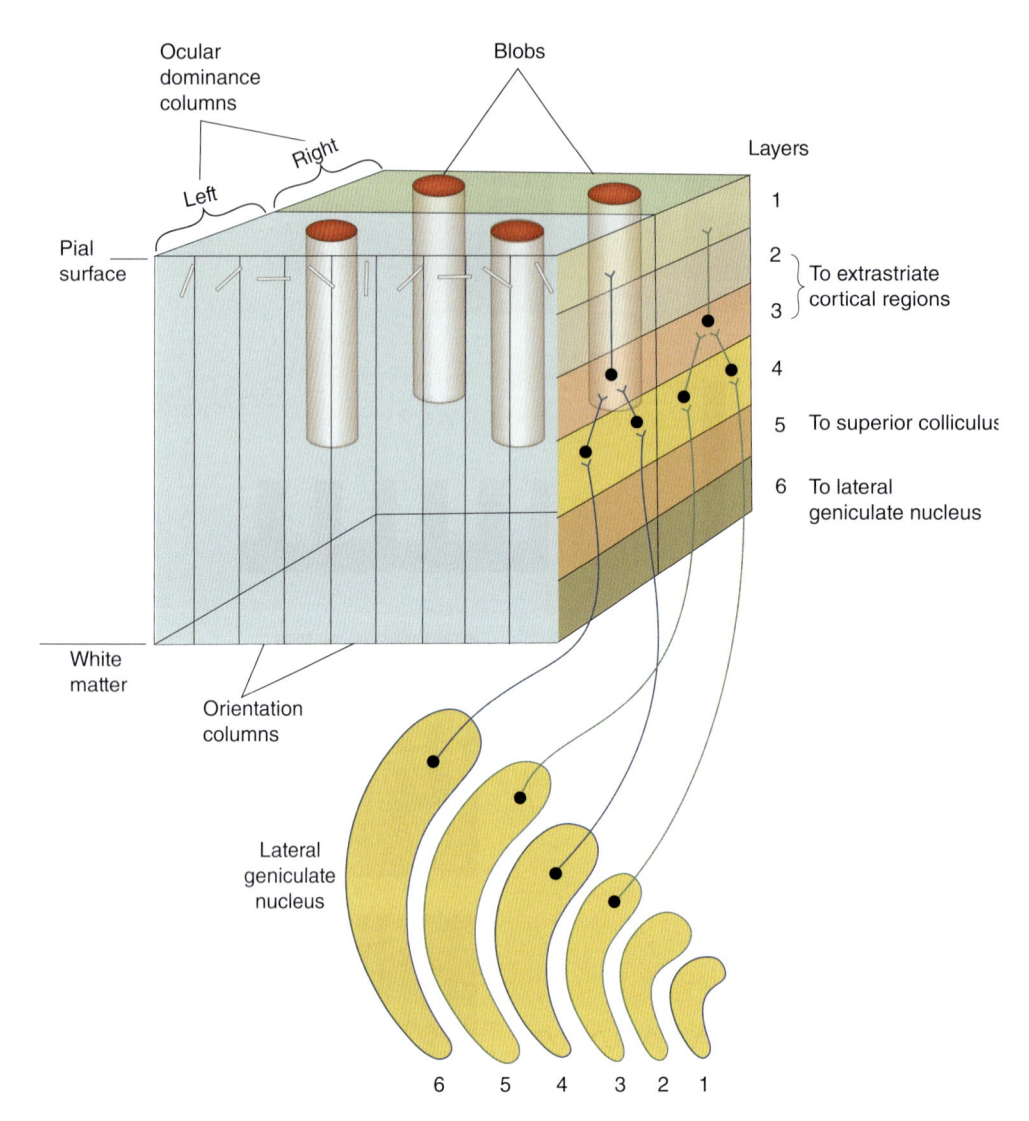

FIGURE 10.10 *Column organization of the visual cortex. Columns of the visual cortex respond to particular orientations and ocular dominance (left/right). Cytochrome oxidase (CO) blobs are features of the column organization thought to be involved in colour perception.*
Source: Adapted from Derrington, A. (2002). From retina to cortex. In D. Roberts (Ed.), *Signals and perception: The fundamentals of human sensation*. Basingstoke, UK: Palgrave Macmillan.

According to Snowden et al. (2012), this leaves three signals:

- a luminance signal, from red and green cones;
- a red-green signal; and
- a blue-yellow signal.

This accounts for colour remaining the same in different levels of brightness.

Once processing has taken place in the retinal level, the signals are relayed to the LGN. Within the LGN, the parvocellular layers carry out the majority of colour processing and in particular the red-green processing (De Monasterio & Gouras, 1975; De Monasterio et al., 1975). The blue-yellow signal takes a different route via the koniocellular pathway (Hendry & Reid, 2000). The route from the LGN can be followed and indicates that the blue-yellow channels terminate in superficial cortical layers, whereas red-green channels project deeper into the visual cortex (Chatterjee & Callaway, 2003).

Binocular Vision: Two Eyes and Two Hemispheres

Images that fall onto the retina are relayed to the visual cortex; however, we have two eyes that provide

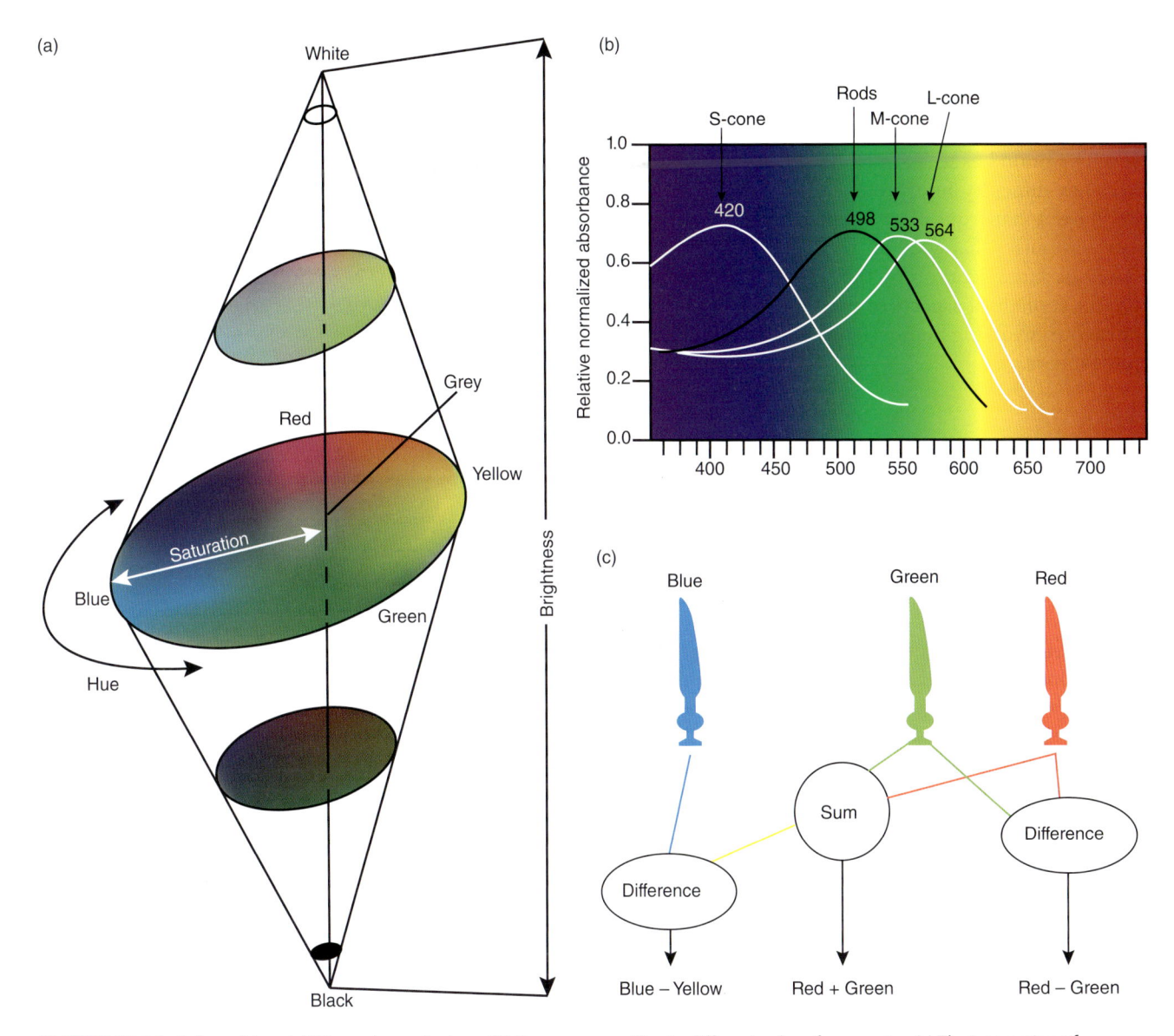

FIGURE 10.11 *Colour vision. (a) Dimensions of colour. (b) Cones are sensitive to different colour frequencies. (c) The interaction of cones of different frequencies.*

two separate yet overlapping images. The visual cortex resides in the separate hemispheres but we do not see two pictures; the brain assimilates and processes the information to make sense of the binocular input. The two hemispheres communicate via the corpus callosum. In a series of experiments by Sperry in humans and animals, it was shown that these fibres that connect the left and right halves of the brain allow information from the left and right visual fields to be integrated (Gavalas & Sperry, 1969; Sperry, 1970; Trevarthen & Sperry, 1973).

Binocular vision and the overlapping visual information give us stereopsis, which means that we can turn a two-dimensional image on the retina into a three-dimensional perception which includes depth (see Blake & Wilson, 2011).

A Summary of Visual Perception

The eye receives the complexities of our visual world and converts the information into neural messages for the brain to interpret. The cells of the brain work on the visual input to allow the person to have some understanding of the visual world. However, the brain does not automatically interpret the signals from the eyes. The brain has to learn to see and without experience, has difficulty interpreting the visual world. We also have a hard question to answer; how do these neural impulses that code for perception turn into our conscious interpretation of the world? To explain the phenomenological aspects of perception is an ongoing endeavour involving neuroscientists, psychologists and philosophers.

HEARING AND AUDITORY PERCEPTION

We hear many sounds that influence our behaviour and colour our emotions; for example, 'dinner music' can increase food intake in patients with dementia (Ragneskog et al., 1996). As with visual perception, auditory stimuli are converted into signals that are sent to the brain. Similar to the visual system, the auditory system responds to experience (see Box 10.6).

BOX 10.6: AUDITORY PLASTICITY

We have already seen the effects of deprivation on the development of visual perception; this is not restricted to the visual modality but is also apparent in audition. One of the driving forces of studying auditory plasticity is the success of cochlear implants which restore hearing in some patients who are deaf because of damage to the hair cells in their cochlea (Dahmen & King, 2007). Cochlear implants do not produce perfect hearing but can improve hearing, leading to the wearer being able to understand speech.

We are constantly exposed to sounds and by four weeks of age, there is an adult-like tonotopic representation of sound (the auditory equivalent of the visual retinotopic map which is a map of the retina in the cortex) in the primary auditory cortex (A1) (Zhang et al., 2001). Animal studies have shown that there are critical periods during which the primary auditory cortex is organized in response to auditory input (Hartley & King, 2010; see Weinberger (2011) for reviews). Syka (2002) states that 'the loss of auditory receptors, the hair cells, results in profound changes in the structure and function of the central auditory system, typically demonstrated by a reorganization of the projection maps in the auditory cortex' (p.601).

In humans, hearing is essential for the development of language (see Kuhl et al., 2005). One can also look at musicians to study the plasticity of the auditory cortex. A question that arises is whether musicians have a different auditory cortex before they start learning their instrument or whether this is a consequence of the learning process. As a learning process this represents neural plasticity. A study looking at children's cortical activity found that after one year of music training, there were slight differences in activity (Schlaug et al., 2005) that were not present before they commenced music training (Norton et al., 2005). The impact of musical training is not restricted to the domain of audition but also extends to motor behaviours, for which there may also be sensitive periods for the development of music-mediated motor learning (Penhune et al., 2005; Watanabe et al., 2007).

However, excessive noise can have detrimental effects on the ear and the brain. Noise can cause hearing loss by a one-time exposure to an intense impulse sound or by steady-state long-term exposure at 75–85 decibels (dB). Indeed, many ageing rock stars now suffer from hearing loss as a result of excessive exposure to high volumes during live performances (the Marshall amplifier turned up to 11). Noise-induced hearing loss results in a loss of hair cells in the cochlea (Moore, 2007) which has a knock-on effect in the auditory cortex. This causes a degeneration of neurons within the auditory cortex (Syka, 2002). More recent studies have found that exposure to even moderate levels of sound (~70 dB) can reduce the activity of the auditory cortex (Pienkowski et al., 2013).

Changes in the auditory cortex as a result of noise exposure have been hypothesized to lead to difficulties in speech perception (Pienkowski & Eggermont, 2012). This begs the question as to what damage can be inflicted by personal music systems. Ever since Sony launched the Walkman in 1979 there have been media reports suggesting that overuse or high volumes lead to hearing loss. Such stories re-emerge in the media with each new technology that delivers music to our ears, most recently with Apple's iPod. One also has to remember that exposure to excessive noise, particularly if it is beyond our control, can lead to other types of health problems (Basner et al., 2014). Think of what your weekend parties are doing to your next-door neighbours!

The Ear

We have two ears, which helps us to locate sounds in space. Just as our two eyes have slightly different images, so our ears receive sounds milliseconds apart, and this difference provides information about the location of the sound.

The part of the ear we can see is only the tip of the iceberg. The ear comprises the outer ear, the middle ear and the inner ear (Figure 10.12). The outer ear is a funnel that collects sound waves and sends them to the middle ear. It consists of the **pinna** and **the auditory canal**.

Sound waves vibrate the structures of the middle ear. The first structure to vibrate is the eardrum (tympanic membrane). The vibrations affect a set of three bones behind the eardrum called **ossicles**: the **hammer (malleus)**, **anvil (incus)** and **stirrup (stapes)**, and vibration affects each one in turn.

The stirrup communicates with the inner ear by vibrating the oval window, which is a thin membrane that covers the inner ear. The vibrations are conducted to the **cochlea**, a fluid-filled tube with a membrane that is receptive to auditory information. This membrane is called the **organ of Corti** and is made up of three

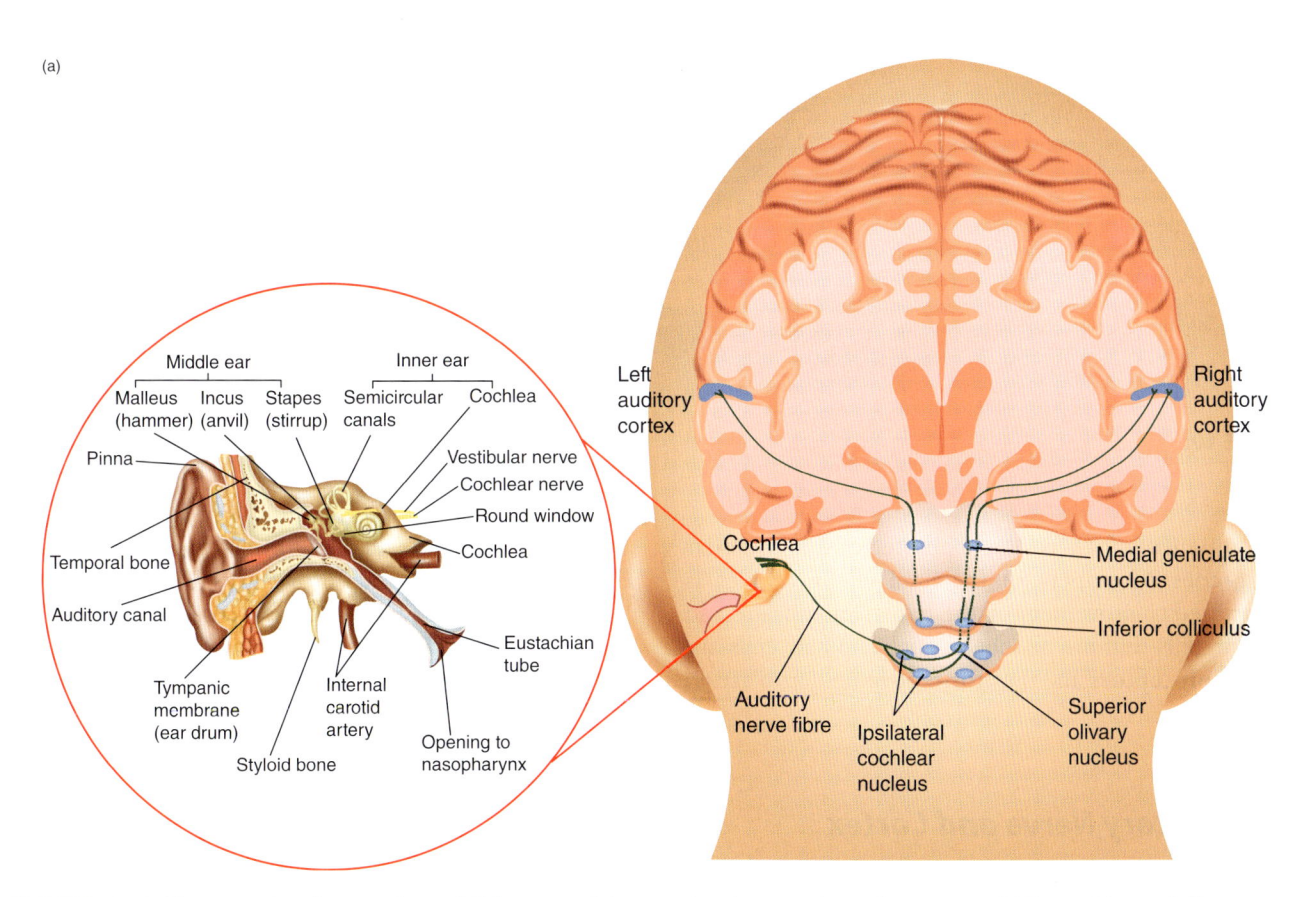

FIGURE 10.12 *The ear and auditory pathway. (a) The ear and the neural pathway to the auditory cortex. (b) The cochlea and cilia. (c) Frequencies of sound detected in the cochlea.*

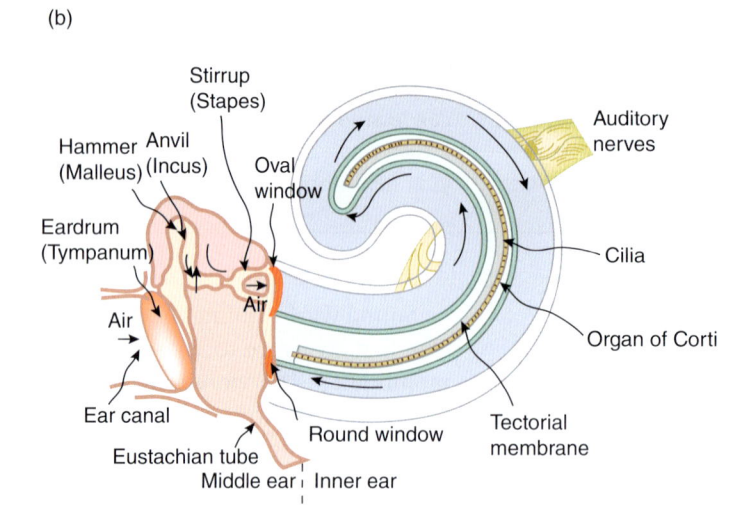

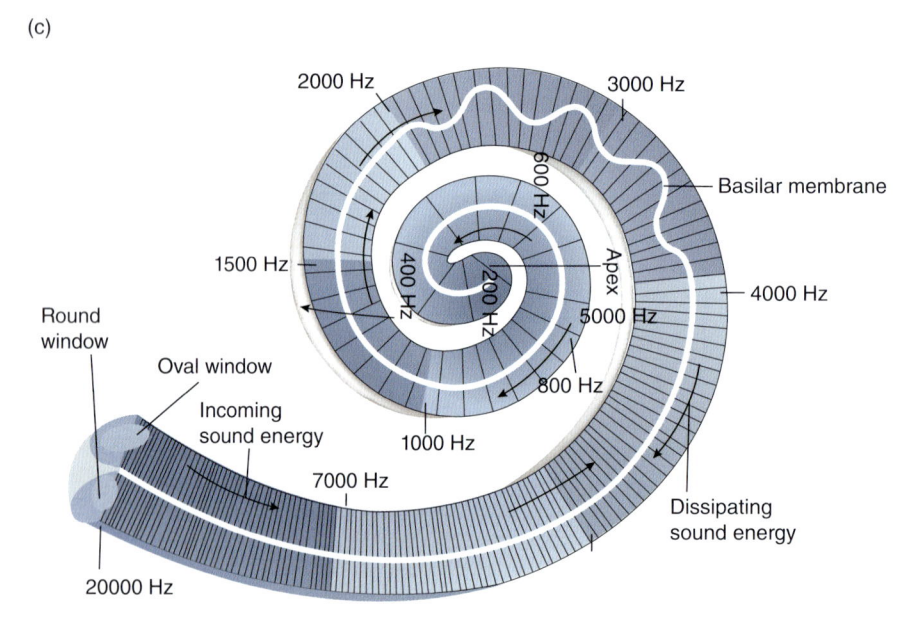

FIGURE 10.12 *continued*

subcomponents: hair cells and the tectoral and basilar membranes. Movement of the fluid in the cochlea is transmitted to movement of the basilar membrane and the hair cells that are attached to it. The hair cells are **mechanoreceptors** and they turn movement into action potential.

The Auditory Nerve and Cortex

The auditory nerve synapses with the hair cells and relays auditory signals to the brain, then enters the brainstem and divides in two. The split input projects to dorsal and lateral cochlear nuclei. The projections of the cochlear nuclei go to the **superior olivary nuclei**. This area receives and integrates signals from both ears and is used in auditory location. Other projections from the cochlear nuclei go to the **inferior colliculus** (see Figure 10.12). The superior olivary nuclei also send messages about location to the inferior colliculus, which connects to the **medial geniculate nucleus** (**MGN**) of the thalamus, and the MGN then projects to the auditory cortex. The cells of the auditory cortex are in columns that respond to similar frequencies.

In a similar way to the visual system, information from the left auditory input goes to the right brain and vice versa. This arrangement can be exploited in experiments using dichotic listening tasks (Kimura, 1967) which present different stimuli independently to each ear (see Chapter 19).

> **BOX 10.7: TINNITUS**
>
> You may have heard the phrase 'phantom limb', and we will be addressing this in Box 10.10, but you may not have heard of phantom auditory perception. **Tinnitus** is one form of phantom auditory perception which affects a large number of people (approximately 10–15% of the adult population (Heller, 2003). Tinnitus is characterized as a chronic ringing in the ears in the absence of a real sound. The main cause of tinnitus is cochlear injury which leads to changes in the auditory pathways, including reorganization of the **tonotopic map**, hyperactivity of the auditory cortex and thalamus, and subcortical auditory nuclei responding (Eggermont & Roberts, 2012). The initial cause is thought to be a change in the balance of excitatory and inhibitory firing of neurons. This may lead to spontaneous neural activity even in the absence of a real sound (Eggermont & Roberts, 2012).
>
> It is obvious that cochlear damage leading to tinnitus would affect the auditory cortex but neuroimaging studies have demonstrated that patients also have activity in the prefrontal cortex, parietal cortex, insula and cingulate gyrus (Langguth et al., 2012). These areas are also involved when one is engaged in attention-demanding tasks, such as thinking and being aware of task structures, and therefore having tinnitus is about the conscious awareness of a ringing sound. The conscious awareness of tinnitus shares similar characteristics with phantom limb pain (De Ridder et al., 2011). Thus, tinnitus is not in the ear – it is in the cortex.

The direction of information flow is bidirectional with ascending fibres relaying input and descending fibres from the auditory cortex to the thalamus and other structures modulating that input. These projections, known as **corticofugal projections**, influence subcortical aspects of auditory perception, e.g. tuning, neural plasticity and also the integration of auditory information with other sensory systems and also with the motor system (He & Yu, 2010). One of these descending pathways, the **corticocollicar pathway** (the auditory cortex to the inferior colliculus), has been shown to be essential for learning to localize sounds (Bajo et al., 2010).

We have already seen that having two eyes permits the two-dimensional retinal image to be processed within the neural architecture to provide the third dimension of depth. We also have two ears, which permit the location of sounds in space by the processing of auditory information that is received at slightly different times (Yin & Kuwada, 2010).

Audition as a perception is most notable in the distressing condition tinnitus (Box 10.7).

SMELLING AND OLFACTORY PERCEPTION

The sense of smell is called **olfaction**. Whilst not the dominant sensory modality in humans (although it is in many other animals), olfactory stimulation has the power to change our behaviour and affect our memories. The perfume and deodorant industries are highly profitable – no one actually wants to smell the human. The increase in sales of aromatherapy products as an alternative medicine highlights the potential of olfactory mechanisms. However, scientific evidence for the effectiveness of aromatherapy is speculative (Martin, 1996). Smells are some of our most emotive stimuli and, as many of you will know, can retrieve vivid memories (LeDoux, 1998). The smell of a hospital is often a potent cue to aid memory of previous visits. Odours can also affect cognitive processing; for example, bergamot reduces visual vigilance (Gould & Martin, 2001).

The Nasal Membrane

The nose has receptors in the **olfactory epithelium**, which is located at the top of the nasal passage. An odour molecule interacts with the **olfactory receptor** and produces a depolarization of the cell membrane. There are numerous receptors for different types of odours. (On a hot tube train at rush hour evolution does not appear to have done us any favours!) The action potential from the depolarization is carried along the olfactory nerve, which then connects to the olfactory bulb, which in turn transmits impulses to the primary olfactory cortex (Figure 10.13).

Olfaction does not have to pass via the thalamus on its way to the cortex. After leaving the primary olfactory cortex, there are two branches the signals can take.

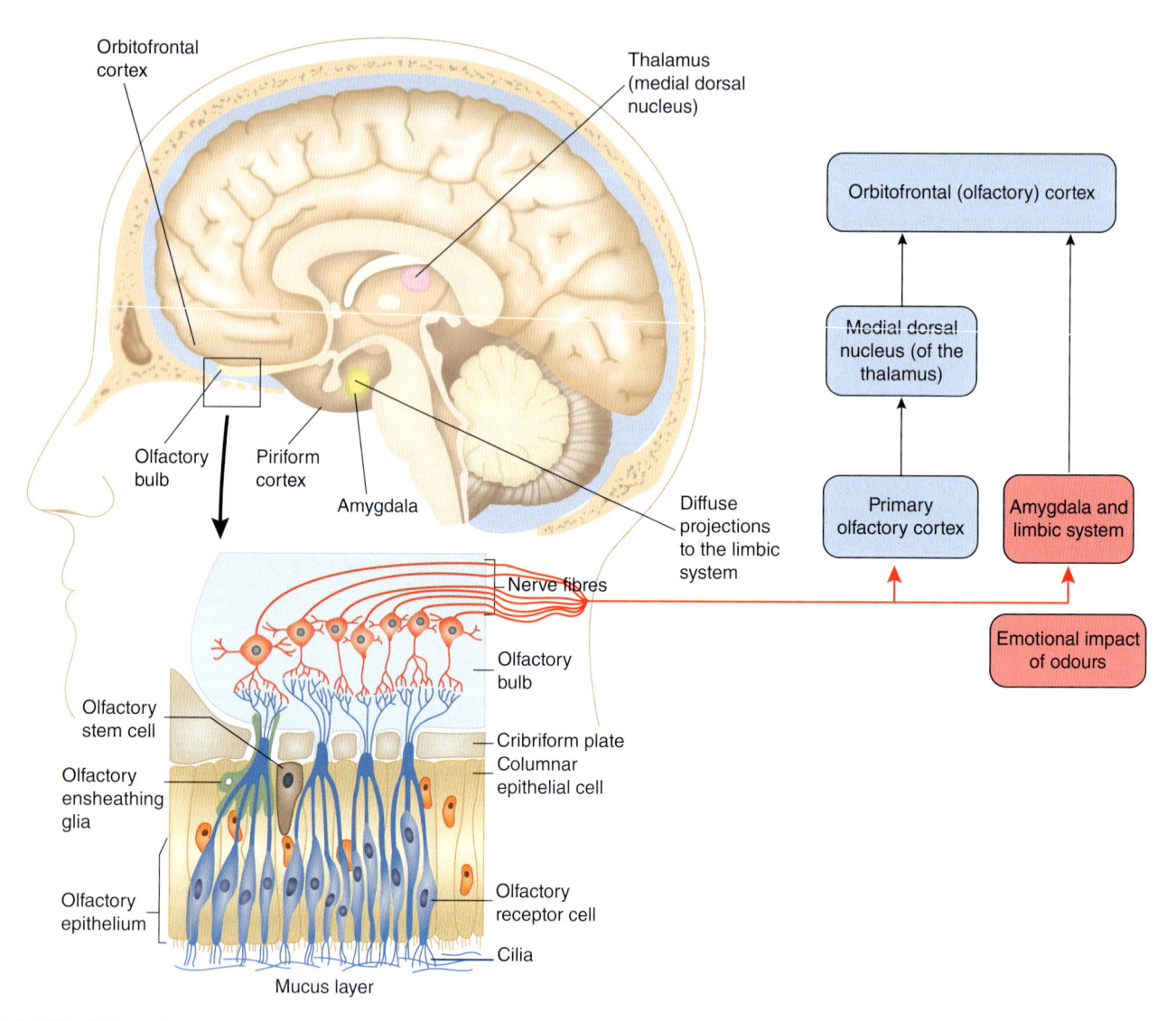

FIGURE 10.13 *Olfactory system.*

The first is via the amygdala, which may give rise to the emotional response to odours. The second branch is to the medial dorsal nuclei of the thalamus, and the signals from the amygdala and thalamus converge on the olfactory (orbitofrontal) cortex. The fact that olfactory signals can circumnavigate the thalamus means that in evolutionary terms of being able to smell, stimulation is important. In Chapter 17, when we discuss emotion, we will see that the amygdala is particularly important in our fear responses. Fear is powerfully motivating and engages our flight or fight responses. Many animals can smell predators from a great distance (and predators can also smell better prey); thus, the animal can take action to avoid becoming dinner. Even in humans, olfactory cues are extremely effective in recalling stressful situations (Wiemers et al., 2014).

TASTING AND THE GUSTATORY SYSTEM

One only has to watch the plethora of celebrity cookery programmes on TV to hear about something 'tickling the taste buds'. It is the gustatory system that mediates the culinary experience.

The Tongue and Mouth

Taste buds are a collection of receptors configured for particular molecules. The receptors are located on **papillae** on the tongue (Figure 10.14).

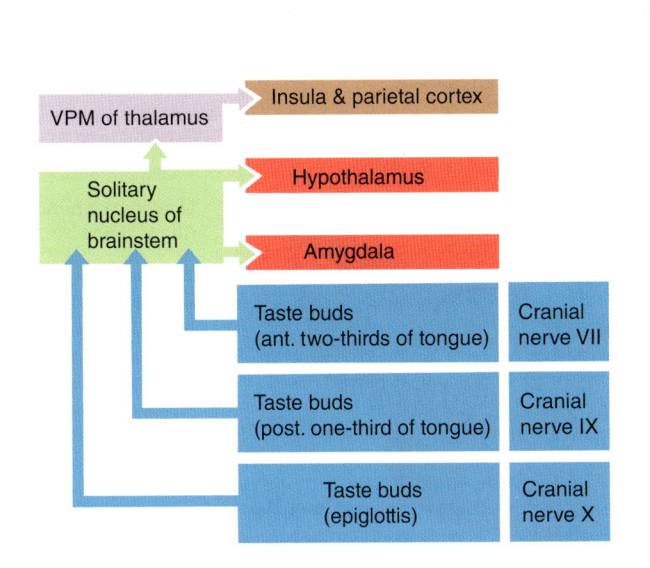

FIGURE 10.14 *The tongue and gustatory sensory pathway.*

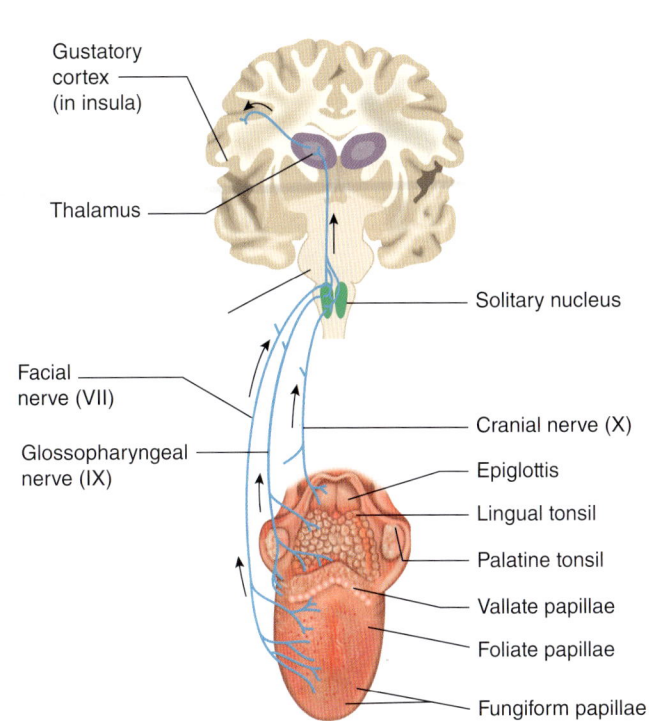

There are four basic tastes that these receptors mediate: salty, sour, sweet and bitter.

- Salt (or Na^+) passes readily through Na^+ channels and depolarizes the cell – thus salt directly activates an action potential.
- Sour tastes are produced by acidic substances which release a hydrogen ion that blocks K^+ channels. Blockade of K^+ channels stops the release of K^+, and the ionic imbalance created leads to depolarization of the cell and an action potential.
- Bitter and sweet tastes are mediated by G-protein linked receptors. On stimulation by a sweet or bitter taste, a second messenger is released before depolarization.

Taste buds have a short existence and are constantly being replaced.

Three cranial nerves carry the signal from the taste buds. The facial nerve carries information from the anterior of the tongue, the glossopharyngeal nerve carries messages from the posterior portion of the tongue and throat, and the vagus nerve carries information from the lower part of the throat. All three cranial nerves project to the **nucleus of the solitary tract**, which passes the information to the ventral posterior medial nucleus of the thalamus. The thalamic nuclei pass the signal on to the primary taste cortex in the frontal lobe.

THE VESTIBULAR SYSTEM

The **vestibular system** is not concerned with sensory processing of the external environment. Instead, it detects changes in the position of the head and changes in gravity. It is located next to the cochlea in the inner ear, and comprises the **utricle**, the **saccule** and three **semicircular canals** (Figure 10.15). These canals provide the sensation of movement and enhance our enjoyment of theme park rides (Box 10.8).

The utricle and saccule respond to static positions of the head, while the semicircular canals, which are at 90° to each other, detect motion. The receptors in the vestibular system, as in the ear, are hairs; movement of fluid acts upon these hairs and produces action potentials.

The vestibular system relays information down part of the auditory nerve and synapses at the vestibular nucleus. Projections from the vestibular nucleus are diffuse and connect with many areas of the brain (e.g. the thalamus, the cortex and other motor areas like those that innervate the eye muscles) (Lopez & Blanke, 2011).

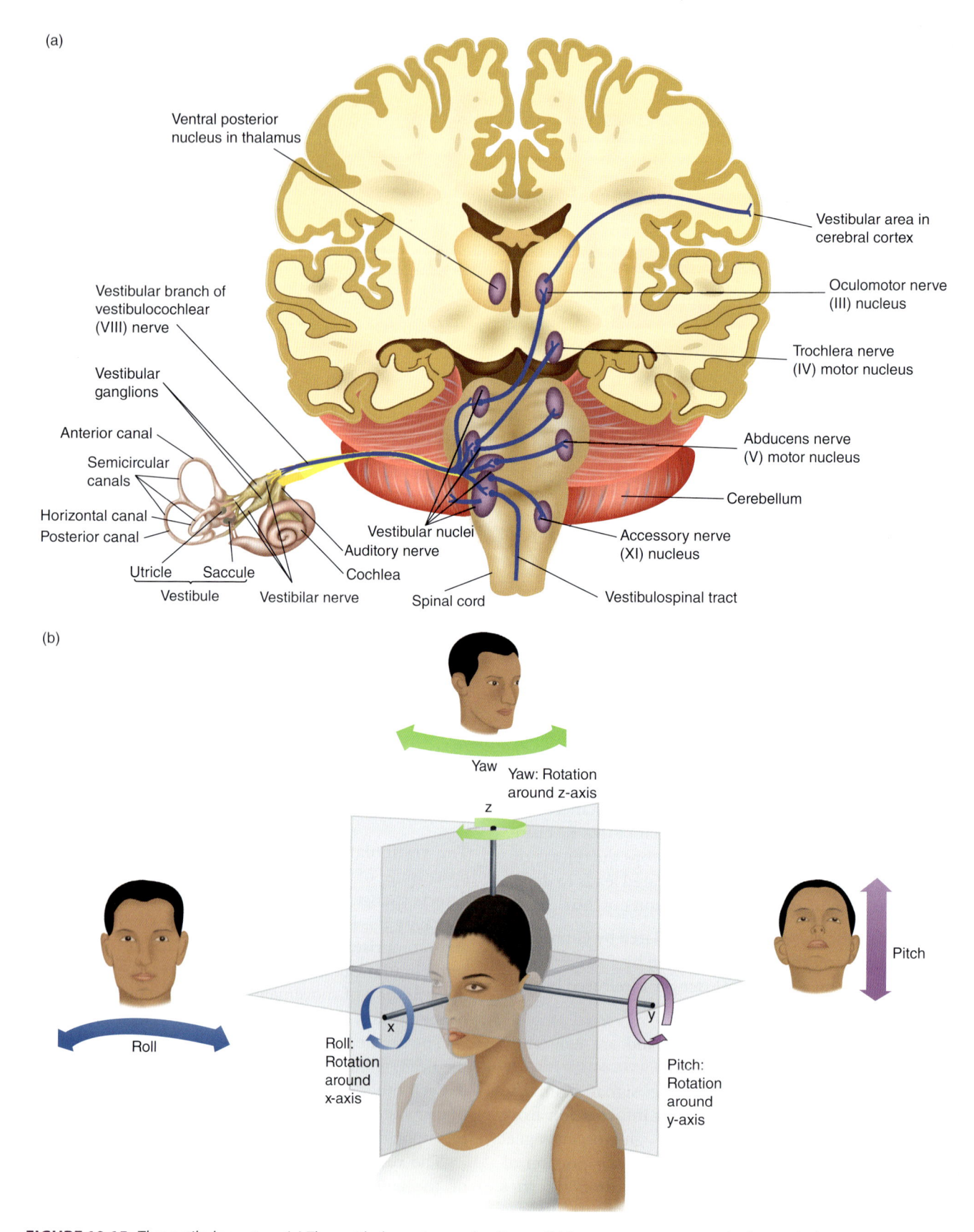

FIGURE 10.15 *The vestibular system. (a) The vestibular system and pathway. (b) Response to movement in the vestibular system.*

> **BOX 10.8: THE VESTIBULAR SYSTEM AND THRILL SEEKING**
>
> Many of us enjoy going to fun parks where we can experience rides that throw us about or accelerate rapidly. Children love playgrounds in which they can spin on roundabouts and swing on the swings. Other people, however, suffer from vertigo and have a fear of heights. In these activities the vestibular system is active and informing us about where our head is in relation to the world around us and the speed at which it is moving. Of course, the vestibular system is not the only perceptual system in operation during these sensations, but it is an important one that receives less attention than some of the other sensory modalities.
>
> The calming effect of rocking is most obvious in young children; we rock the child to sleep or when we take the child out in the pushchair or in a car they fall asleep. A study by Winter et al. (2012) looked at the effects of vestibular stimulating paradigms on mood states. They subjected their participants to different passive rotational and translational vestibular stimulating paradigms in a motion simulator. Passive rotation included yaw, pitch and roll whereas translational activation included heave, sway and surge. The results indicated that yaw rotation was associated with feeling comfortable and roll rotation with being less comfortable. Pitch rotation was associated with being more alert and energetic. Heave translation made the volunteers feel more alert, less relaxed and less comfortable whilst surge translation was only associated with feeling more alert. In another experiment in which participants were spun round, they felt less 'good', 'relaxed', 'comfortable' and 'calm' and reported increased alertness after vestibular stimulation' (Winter et al., 2013). Thus, the vestibular system can change our mood.

FEELING AND SOMATOSENSATION

Somatosensation is the process of communicating information from regions of the body, and messages are sent from the skin, muscles and joints, etc. to areas of the brain.

The somatosensory system can be divided to account for external stimuli, internal influences (**interoception**) and where the body is positioned (**proprioception**).

Clearly the somatosensory system has to integrate a great deal of information, and the remainder of this section will focus solely on the sensation of touch. Touch is a useful mechanism to look at because of its involvement in pain.

The Skin

Touch is mediated through mechanoreceptors responsive to physical changes in the skin. Activation of these mechanoreceptors produces a depolarization and thus an action potential is transmitted.

The Transmission of Tactile Stimuli to the Brain

The action potentials initiated by the mechanoreceptors are sent along the axons of afferent nerves, and enter the **dorsal column of the spinal cord**. The part of the skin that projects to the dorsal column is segregated and called a dermatome. There are two pathways that carry different information to the brain: the anterior lateral system and the dorsal column system. The anterior lateral system carries thermal and **nociceptive** (pain) messages; the dorsal column system sends touch information.

The dorsal column passes through the dorsal column nuclei where the axons cross over to project to the other side of the brain. The neurons pass through the **medial lemniscus** where they synapse at the ventral posterior nucleus of the thalamus. From the thalamus, electrical signals are projected to the **somatosensory cortex** (Figure 10.16).

NOCICEPTION AND THE PERCEPTION OF PAIN

Pain is a sensation of discomfort, distress or indeed agony; pain is an aversive sensation. There are many different ways of categorizing pain, from what it feels like to the length of time we have it. There are also numerous disorders of pain which have far-reaching and damaging effects on the individual (see Box 10.9).

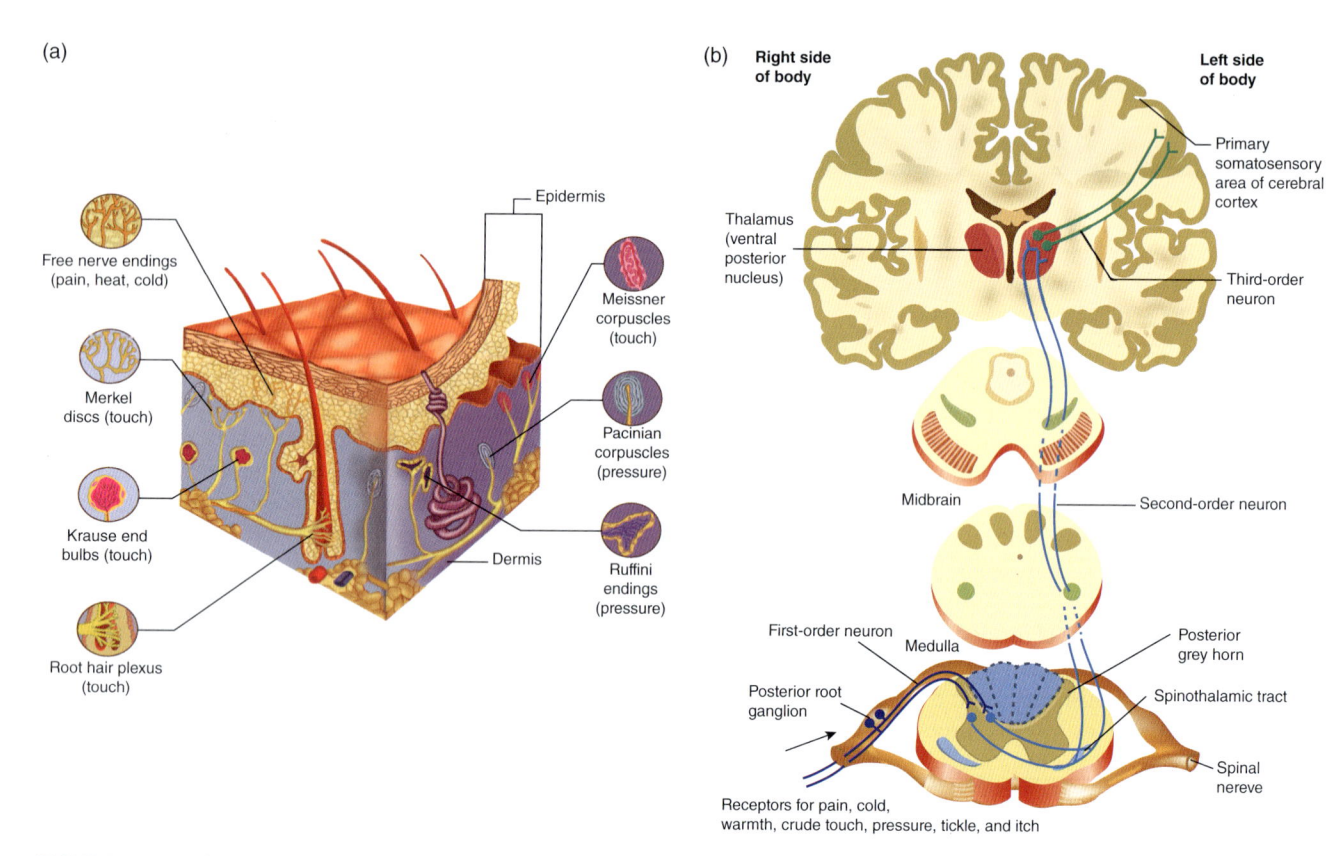

FIGURE 10.16 *The skin and sensory pathway. (a) Receptors in the skin. (b) Somatosensory pathway.*

BOX 10.9: PROBLEMS OF PAIN

A number of interesting conditions associated with pain require further investigation.

Congenital analgesia is where a person is born without the ability to feel pain. A well-known case study of a woman referred to as Miss C, who was a student at McGill University in Montréal, illustrates the severity of congenital analgesia. Miss C was normal in every way but could not experience pain. When she was a child she bit off her tongue and suffered burns after kneeling on a radiator. When she was evaluated for pain perception, it was noted that she could not feel pain even from strong electric shocks or exposure to extreme temperatures. She showed no change in heart rate, blood pressure or respiration in response to these painful stimuli. The function of pain is to protect people and without this protection she was vulnerable. Avoidance of pain and resting in response to pain would not occur because of congenital analgesia. She died at the young age of 29 from this condition, as a failure to recuperate and recover meant that she contracted infections which ultimately killed her.

Pain asymbolia is a condition in which people receive and feel the sensory input but they do not respond as if they are in pain; in fact, they react with amusement and laugh when experimenters try to induce pain in them. With pain asymbolia, they do not have the appropriate affective component (Grahek, 2007). They experience the pain sensation but it is interpreted very differently.

The types of pain we can experience fall into the following categories:

- mechanical pain such as pinching, stabbing or pricking;
- thermal pain such as burning or freezing;
- chemical pain such as stinging and soreness (for example, from an open wound); and
- visceral pain which can be the pain derived from mechanical or chemical changes in the internal organs (e.g. a heart attack).

Pain can also be categorized as acute, chronic or recurrent.

When we consider pain, we are considering two separate but interacting processes: nociception, which is the activation of pain receptors, and then the experience of pain itself which is a result of cortical processing often some distance from the site of pain. Thus, pain is a perception, not a sensation; indeed, we can have pain without nociceptive input. However, pain has effects far reaching from the pain itself and can alter other aspects of cognitive functioning (Neugebauer et al., 2009; Simons et al., 2014).

Why Pain?

In evolutionary terms, pain is essential: no pain, no gain. The gain here is survival. Bizarrely, pain is functional and adds to the chances of the organism surviving. No one likes pain (except for the masochists, more of which later) but under normal circumstances, it is good for us. Pain acts as a signal to tell us that there is danger, e.g. we remove our hands from a hot surface or a flame. This prevents extensive tissue damage, which ultimately could lead to death due to infection. Pain also acts as a signal that there is something wrong and that repair is needed; pain in our joint limits what we can do, therefore we have to take it easy and rest and thus avoid possible permanent damage. It allows the body time to heal and we may guard the affected areas from further trauma. Furthermore, we learn what will induce pain and we are keen to use that learning to avoid pain.

Components of Pain

Pain is a simple four-letter word and we immediately know what it means, but this small word does not betray the complexity of the pain response. Pain involves an emotional-affective component and a behavioural-motor component. The different components that make up pain have prompted Perl (2011) to suggest that:

One difficulty in relating concepts about pain is that the term is used to refer to human and animal reactions ranging from protective spinal reflexes to complex affective behaviors. As a result, the spectrum of 'pain'-related neural organization extends to operation of multiple neuronal arrangements. (p.20)

Receptors

The receptors that we can consider here are **nociceptors** which provide information about the location, intensity and duration of noxious stimuli. Like other receptors, they send neural messages as a result of their activation (Basbaum et al., 2009). Molecular geneticists have found a large number of molecules that are involved in the mediation of pain (Reichling et al., 2013).

Some receptors are sensitive to temperature – thermal receptors (Figure 10.17). These temperature-sensitive receptors react to a range of temperatures ranging from cold to hot. Cold receptors (TRPM8 receptors) are most sensitive to temperatures below 25°C (with a range of 8–40°C). Below 10°C the firing rate increases. Cold receptors synapse onto Aδ fibres. Warm receptors (TRVP3 receptors) respond to temperatures in the region of 35–45°C and connect to C fibres. The firing rate of these receptors increases when exposed to thermal stimuli greater than 45°C.

Mechanical receptors respond to physical touch, but that touch has to be of sufficient pressure to activate them. Pinching and squeezing are examples.

Polymodal receptors are linked to C fibres and are responsive to heat, cold and pinch.

They respond to irritant chemicals such as:

- capsaicin (chilli peppers);
- mustard oil, garlic, horseradish;
- low pH (acids);
- endogenous peptides; and
- environmental irritants and pollutants.

Capsicum (better known as the chilli pepper) can produce pain. The mouth contains receptors that respond to painful stimuli and temperature. Caterina et al. (1997) identified the capsaicin receptor, which is heat activated. The message from these heat-sensitive receptors is transmitted via the trigeminal nerve to the brain and the pain pathways.

Pain Fibres

The nociceptors are attached to first-order neurons in the process of pain transmission and can be differentiated by their physical structure. There are **A fibres** and **C fibres**.

The A-fibres are myelinated and can be further divided into four types according to their size and speed of transmission:

- alpha (α): 13–20 mm, 70–120 m/s
- beta (β): 6–13 mm, 40–70 m/s
- gamma (γ): 3–8 mm, 15–40 m/s
- delta (δ): 1–5 mm, 5–15 m/s.

It is the **Aδ fibres** that transmit information derived from noxious stimuli. The C fibre is slow (0.5–2 m/s), unmyelinated and small.

The pain system sends pain information via the two afferent nerves: C fibres and Aδ fibres (Figure 10.17). The Aδ fibres send fast pain messages, whereas C fibres send slow pain messages ("ouch!" and "ache" respectively). The Aδ fibres mediate the first aspect of pain and produce the sharp prickling pain often familiar with trauma. Second pain comes later, mediated by C fibres, and is duller pain that will last a lot longer than first pain. Aδ fibres and C fibres have different spatial resolutions. The Aδ fibres are able to locate pain with a high degree of accuracy because the receptive fields are narrow. C fibres have diffuse receptive fields, thus making it difficult to locate the precise location of the pain, e.g. the dull ache of a whole limb.

The afferent C fibres terminate in the first **lamina** of the **dorsal horn** of the spinal segment that they enter and the **substantia gelatinosa**. A fibres also terminate in the first lamina but also penetrate further to the fifth lamina of the dorsal horn. At this point, they synapse onto other neurons that continue the pain pathway (Figure 10.18).

Pathways

The anterior lateral system is divided into three pathways: the **spinothalamic pathway**, the **spinoreticular pathway** and the **spinotectal pathway** (Figure 10.19). All these pathways begin at the spine and end up at different locations: the thalamus, the reticular system and the superior colliculus respectively. The spinothalamic pathway and the spinoreticular pathway both project to the thalamus and then to the cortex.

The spinothalamic pathway is divided into anterior and lateral tracts and is the pathway we know the most about.

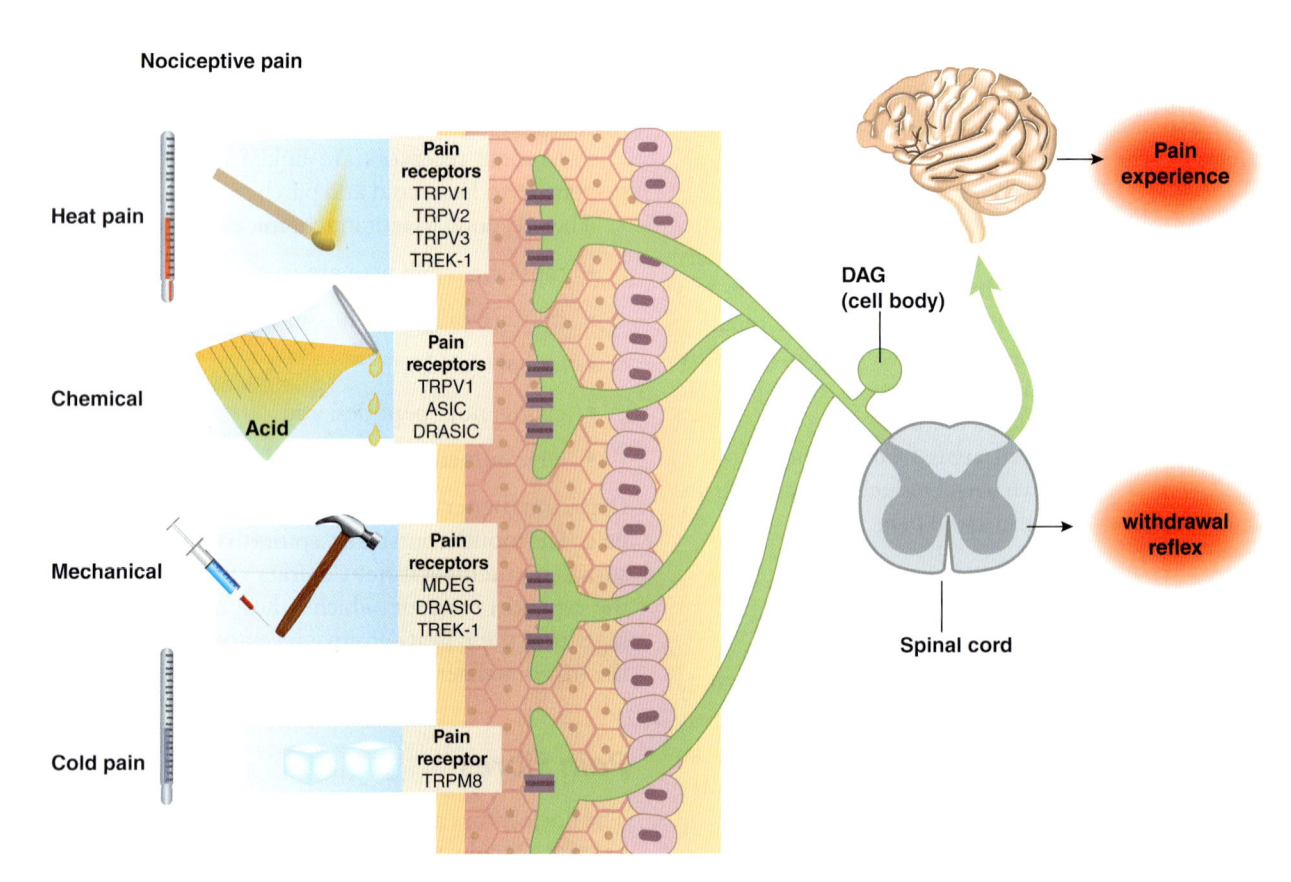

FIGURE 10.17 *Pain receptors and ascending pain pathways*

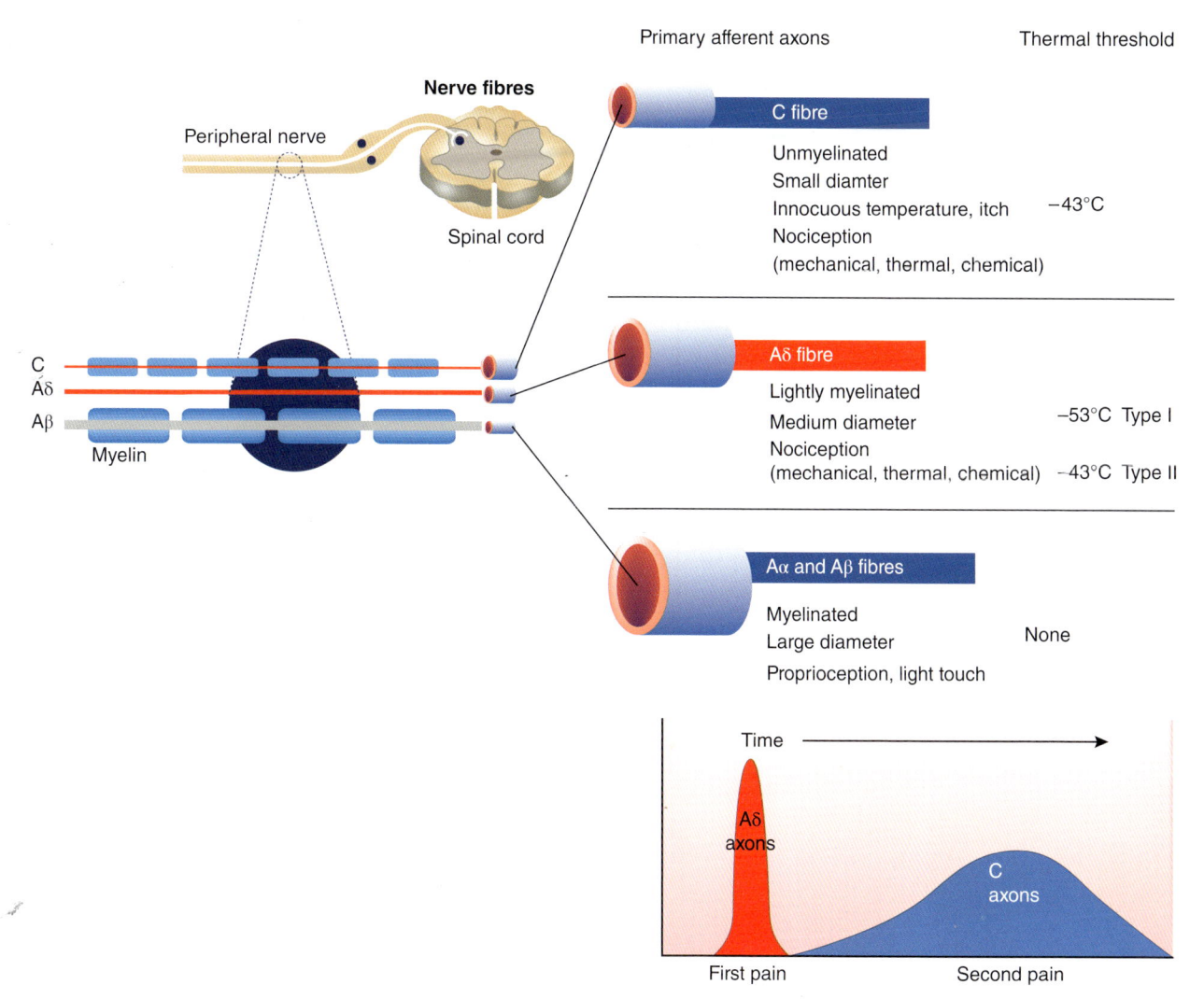

FIGURE 10.17 *continued*

Like much of the brain and its connections to the body, stimulation of pain receptors and activation of pain pathways to the dorsal horn of the spinal column are transferred to the other side of the spine (contralateral). Therefore, as soon as the information enters the spine, it transfers to the other side and ascends to the brain. This is somewhat different from normal sensory input that ascends the spinal column before crossing over the thalamus.

The lateral tract of the spinothalamic pathway originates in cells of lamina 1 of the dorsal horn whereas the anterior tract originates in the cells of laminae 4 and 5. The lateral tract of the spinothalamic pathway processes information from the Adelta fibres, whereas the anterior tract processes information from the C fibres. The lateral tract of the spinothalamic pathway is responsible for mediating the affective and emotional properties of pain. Activation of the lateral spinothalamic tract sends signals up the spine where they terminate in several regions of the thalamus. Messages are then projected to other parts of the brain such as the anterior cingulate gyrus, specific regions of the somatosensory cortex and the dorsal anterior insula (Apkarian et al., 2005). The anterior tract of the spinothalamic pathway originates from deeper layers of the dorsal horn. In this region both Adelta fibres and C fibres relay information that is to ascend the anterior spinothalamic pathway. The anterior pathway fibres ascend the spinothalamic pathway to connect with the ventral posterior lateral thalamus. Some fibres from the thalamus go to the brainstem and reticular formation and others extend to the somatosensory cortices.

The spinoreticular pathway is involved in the increase in arousal as a result of pain. The **spinotectal fibre** terminate in the superior colliculus which mediate reflex actions of turning the body, head and eyes to locate a painful stimulus.

The pain fibres have a diffuse set of projections that can account for perception and reflex actions, and response to pain is mediated via efferent neurons that produce a motor response.

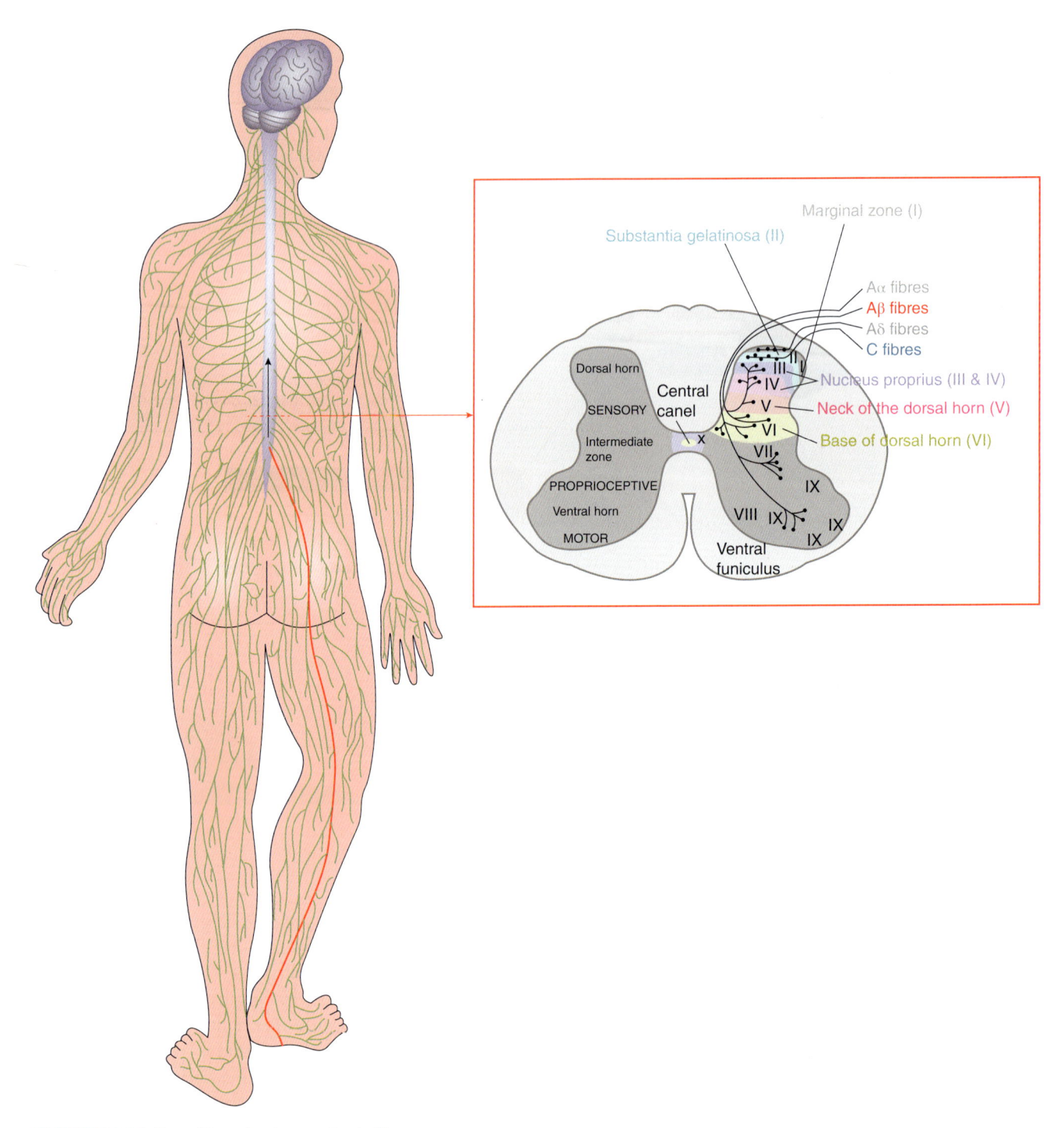

FIGURE 10.18 *Dorsal horn laminae and pain fibres.*

Descending Pathways

Descending pathways send messages down the spine to the dorsal horn regions. There are two main descending systems, the rostral ventral medial medulla and the dorsolateral pontine tegmentum, both of which originate in the **periaqueductal grey** (PAG). Via these pathways, the PAG controls pain and nociceptive neurons. Activation of the PAG has the ability to reduce pain. The PAG receives information from a number of brain regions including the medial prefrontal cortex, hypothalamus, amygdala and locus coeruleus. Thus, the PAG via the

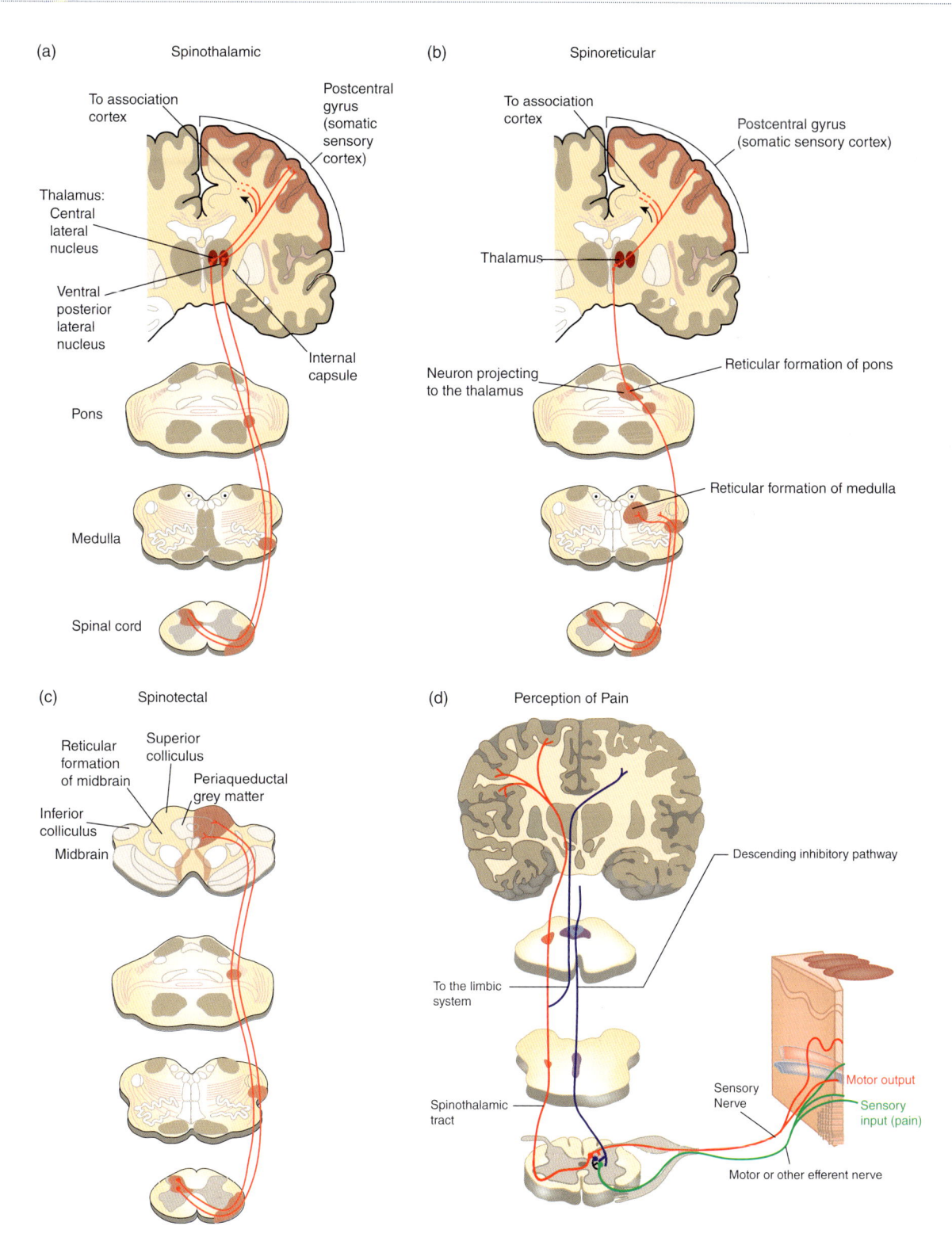

FIGURE 10.19 *Ascending and descending pathways involved in pain. (a) Spinothalamic pathway. (b) Spinoreticular pathway. (c) Spinotectal pathway. (d) Descending pain pathways.*

rostral ventral medial medulla pathway inhibits nociceptive ascending information via C fibres. It does so without interfering with the discriminative information conveyed by the Adelta fibres. The dorsolateral pontine tegmentum pathway operates in a similar way.

Endogenous Analgesia

The descending fibres originating from the PAG can modulate pain and do so within the dorsal horn via receptors for endorphins, which are our natural painkillers (the word 'endorphin' comes from 'endogenous' and 'morphine'). It is within this system that opiate analgesics are effective (Box 10.10).

There is another system that can modulate pain but this has only recently been looked at, the reason being that the drug is cannabis. Cannabis comes fully loaded with a political agenda that has in the past made research somewhat difficult. However, anecdotal evidence and more recent scientific evidence suggest that it has an important role in pain modulation, and one which can be exploited by pharmaceutical companies. One only needs to walk along the seafront of Venice Beach, California, to see that cannabis is being used for medicinal purposes. Cannabinoids can diminish pain via suppression of neural activity in nociceptive neurons in the spinal cord and thalamus (Walker & Hohmann, 2005). They can also suppress C fibre-mediated responses in the dorsal horn (Drew et al., 2000).

We have two mechanisms for modulating pain: the endorphin/enkephalin system and the endogenous cannabis system; it is a shame that both are associated with addiction (see Chapter 16).

Pain Control

Nobody likes pain (except perhaps for masochists), so why should we experience it? Clearly, an evolutionary explanation can account for its existence. Think of what would happen to you if you could not experience pain – it could seriously compromise your chance of survival. However, pain can be modulated from within. Early theories of pain postulated that there was a receptor for every type of stimulus – this is the specificity theory which had its origins in Cartesian dualism. Other theories attributed pain perception to an increase in the intensity of the stimulus – turning the volume up (Moayedi & Davis, 2013).

Melzack and Wall (1965) proposed perhaps the most influential theory with their **gate control theory** of pain. This theory gained much attention in part due to the simplicity of the diagram contained within their

---

BOX 10.10: OPIATE ANALGESIA

One of the greatest painkillers that we have is morphine and morphine-like drugs. These interrupt the pain signal and interact with endogenous pain pathways. Opium has been around for a long time and is obtained from poppy plants from which the resin has to be milked. Opiates are substances derived from opium and an opioid is a substance with morphine-like actions, but not derived directly from the poppy plant.

There are three opiate receptors.

Mu receptors

- Analgesic effects of opioids.
- Major unwanted effects (e.g. respiratory depression, euphoria, sedation and dependence).
- Most of the analgesic opioids are mu receptor agonists.

Delta receptors

More important in the periphery, but may also contribute to analgesia.

Kappa receptors

- Analgesia at the spinal level.
- May elicit sedation and dysphoria.
- Produce relatively few unwanted effects, and do not contribute to dependence.

Each of these receptors responds to its own endogenous compound. Opiate analgesics can act in the brain and the dorsal horn, thereby alleviating pain perception.

paper. Melzack and Wall claimed that cognitive and emotional factors could, via descending brain circuits, mediate the blockade of incoming pain signals. Such descending circuits have been identified, most notably including the PAG where stimulation is analgesic. The PAG also contains endorphin receptors that modulate pain and respond to endorphins, our natural painkillers. It is within this system that opiate analgesics are effective. The PAG projects to the raphe nuclei, which then project down the spinal column where the pain signal is blocked (Basbaum & Fields, 1978).

Melzack and Wall looked at the features of pain and realized that there were a number of cases in which a simple stimulus input theory could not be correct. They suggested that:

- the relationship between injury and pain is highly variable;
- innocuous stimuli can produce pain;
- the location of pain may be different from that of the damage;
- pain can persist after complete healing, e.g. phantom limb pain (Box 10.11);
- the nature and location of pain change over time;
- pain is not a single sensation but multidimensional perception; and
- there is no adequate treatment for some pain.

The preceding sections have established that there are ascending and descending pathways that moderate and mediate pain. The gate control theory takes full advantage of these, albeit without knowing the details of their existence – 1965 was a long time ago.

The gate control theory includes a gate, which is in the dorsal horn (**substantia gelatinosa**), that can be either opened or closed, thus allowing or not allowing the transmission of pain messages. It also includes transmission cells which are linked to the ascending pathways. Activity of nociceptive receptors in the pain pathways actively opens the gate, allowing pain signals to be sent to the transmission cells for processing by the

BOX 10.11: PHANTOM LIMB PAIN

After limb amputation, patients can experience the feeling that the absent limb is present and that there is pain in that limb (Ramachandran & Hirstein, 1998). Clearly, there is no limb present that is sending such signals indicating pain or indeed the presence of the limb. In cases where the limb has been removed because of extreme pain and damage, it has been suggested that there are some memories of that pain that persist post amputation (Katz & Melzack, 1990). There are of course changes in peripheral afferents as a result of amputation that may possibly account for some of the experience of phantom limb pain (Flor et al., 2006). However, this does not account for the phantom experience of those born without the limb. In the spinal cord there might be sensitization of the sensory relay cells after prolonged stimulation from painful stimuli, albeit now removed. There are also changes in the brain, including possible cortical reorganization, especially of the somatosensory cortex (Lotze et al., 2001). Lesions of the somatosensory cortex result in the removal of the phantom limb pain (Appenzeller & Bicknell, 1969).

The view is that a pain memory has been established and that deafferentation of the pain fibres and the activation of neighbouring sensory neurons to the area of the amputation may activate pain-mediating neurons in the spinal and supraspinal structures.

How might one treat phantom limb pain? After all, there isn't actually a site to treat. There are a number of approaches one can take to this conundrum. Pre-emptive analgesia whilst the limb is still attached may prevent pain memories from establishing so that when the limb is removed, the illusion of phantom limb pain is minimized. Opiates are effective in the treatment of phantom limb pain and mediate the effects centrally and in the dorsal horn, far removed from the site of amputation.

However, there are also non-pharmacological treatments that may be helpful. Transcutaneous electrical nerve stimulation (TENS) is sometimes used by women to reduce labour pains during birth. This works via stimulation of those inhibitory pathways from other sensory inputs. TENS has been shown to be effective in helping phantom limb pain (Mulvey et al., 2013).

> The most interesting treatment for phantom limb pain is mirror therapy. In mirror therapy, the patient looks at a recreation of the intact limb in the mirror, which creates the illusion of the missing limb. The argument is that when a person looks at the mirror image of where the amputated limb should be, this activates a group of neurons called mirror neurons. Mirror neurons are activated because there is no inhibitory information to the contrary that would have been generated had the limb not being amputated. If this is indeed the case then activation of mirror neurons may help modulate pain perception in the phantom limb (Kim & Kim, 2012; Seidel et al., 2011). Mirror neurons allow us to simulate the sensations and movements of others which is thought to be an important component in empathy. When other people hurt themselves we often wince and feel their pain, albeit in a rather second-hand fashion – this is the mirror neurons in action. In Chapter 19 the issue of mirror neurons will be elaborated upon.

brain. Other sensory nerves close the gate, thus preventing painful stimuli from being transmitted. Descending messages from the PAG also inhibit pain messages by keeping the gate closed.

The build-up of the gate control theory can be seen in Figure 10.20. Pain stimulation messages are received by the Adelta and C fibres and go to the transmission cells in the dorsal horn. The transmission cells send them off to an action system that activates the reticular and limbic systems, thus providing the effective and behavioural aspects of pain. Melzack and Wall add into the process an excitatory interneuron between the sensory input and the transmission cells to account for the prolonged burst of firing that occurs after stimulation. The transmission cells also receive input from large, low-threshold myelinated afferents which comprise receptors that have a **wide dynamic range** (WDR) and nociceptive specific receptors. In the next stage of building up the gate control theory, Melzack and Wall place an inhibitory interneuron between the transmission cells and the large, low-threshold myelinated afferents. The inhibitory interneuron is in the substantia gelatinosa. This inhibitory interneuron receives further inhibitory input from the midbrain and medulla which leads to inhibitory actions on the transmission cells, thus keeping the gate closed. The WDR receptors which provide input of a general nature and the descending inhibitory inputs from the midbrain account for why the general rubbing of a wounded area is analgesic and why conscious attempts to minimize pain are sometimes effective.

The complete gate control theory is depicted in Figure 10.20 which shows that cognitive information and the central control of higher brain functions can have an effect on pain perception (see Table 10.1).

Since 1965 there has been a large body of literature published looking at pain. That has indicated that not everything the gate control theory postulated was accurate in the detail (Mendell, 2014; Nathan, 1976).

The phenomenon of the **phantom limb** prompted Melzack to present a new theory of pain (Melzack, 1989, 1990, 1999, 2001, 2005). This theory involved a **neuromatrix**. Melzack noted seven features of the phantom limb that needed explanation.

1. The phantom limb feels real.
2. The phantom arm hangs down at the side when resting and appears to swing in time with other arm when walking.
3. The phantom limb sometimes gets stuck in awkward positions.
4. An artificial limb appears to fit like a glove and patients see the artificial limb as part of their body.
5. The phantom limb gives the impression of pressure and pain.
6. If the phantom limb is experienced as spatially detached from the body, it is still felt to belong to the patient.
7. Paraplegic people experience phantom limbs.

This is more than missing something that was once there as:

> A substantial number of children who are born without a limb feel a phantom of the missing part, suggesting that the neural network, or 'neuromatrix', that subserves body sensation has a genetically determined substrate that is modified by sensory experience. (Melzack, 1990, p.88)

Melzack considered that there was an anatomical substrate of the body-self which was made up of loops interconnecting between the thalamus and cortex in the limbic system. These interconnecting systems are the components of the neuromatrix. The neuromatrix receives inputs from cognitive related brain areas that

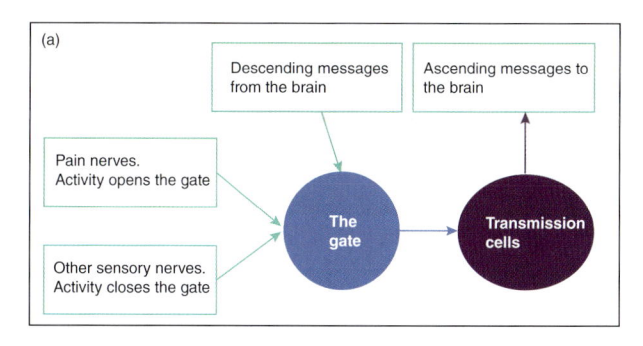

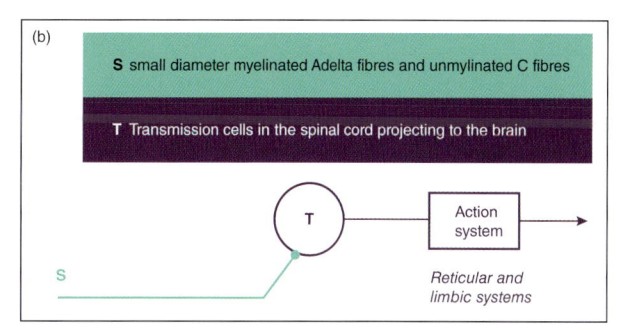

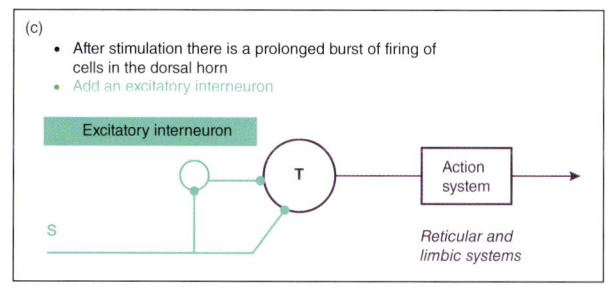

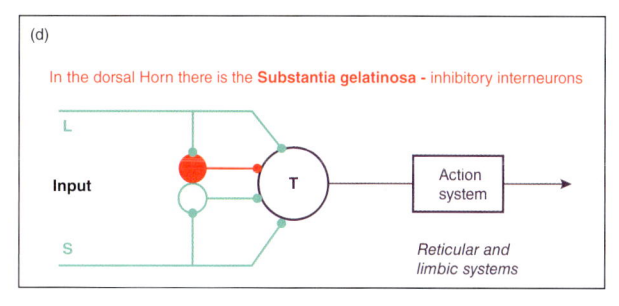

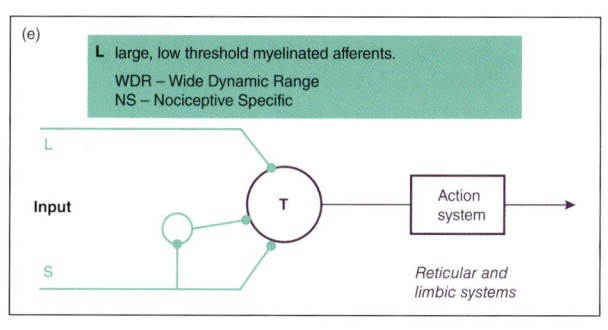

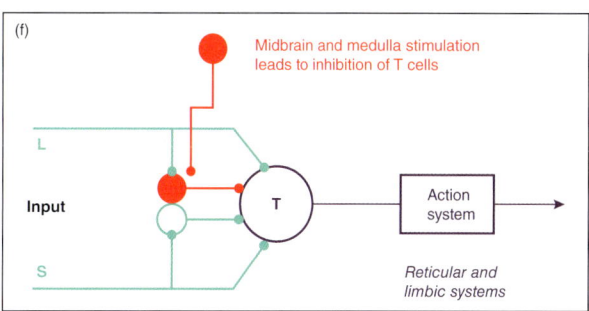

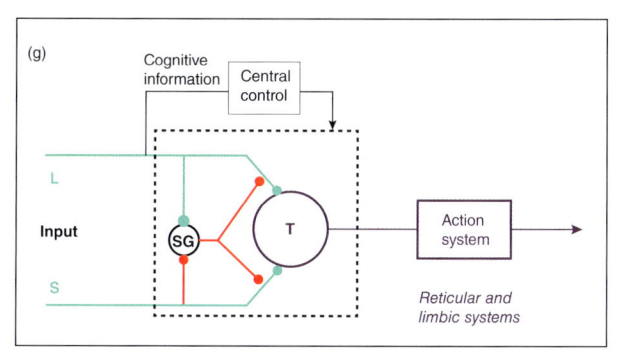

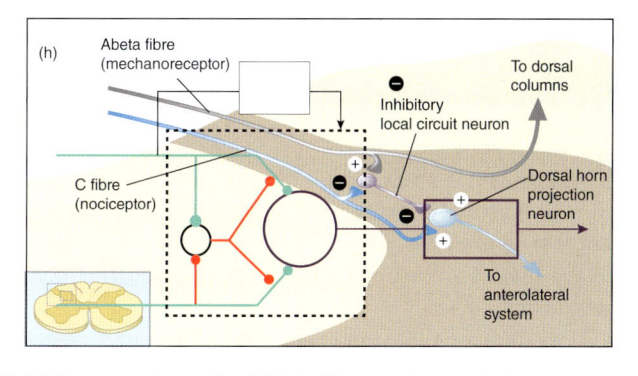

FIGURE 10.20 The gate control theory of pain (Melzack & Wall, 1965). (a) The general premise. (b) Pain fibres and transmission (T) cells. (c) Add in excitatory interneurons. (d) Add large fibre inputs. (e) Add inhibitory interneuron. (f) Add descending pathway. (g) The full conceptualization of the gate control theory (SG, substantia gelotinosa). (h) How the gate looks in the dorsal horn.

mediate memories and attention, etc., sensory signalling systems and emotional affective brain areas. They each have corresponding outputs to other regions of the brain that produce pain perception, action programmes and stress regulation programmes.

A pattern of activity in the neuromatrix as a result of nerve impulses is referred to as the neurosignature. All inputs from the body are processed to produce this neurosignature, with some areas specializing in pain. The neurosignature is therefore an output from the body-self neuromatrix that can project to an area that Melzack refers to as the sentient neural hub. This is a conscious experience. The neuromatrix is modulated by genetic and sensory influences. Thus, in the absence of a recently amputated limb, the brain still maintains a neurosignature of its existence; furthermore, the genetic contribution can account for the phantom limb phenomenon seen in congenital cases.

TABLE 10.1 *Conditions that open or close the gate*

	Conditions that open the gate	Conditions that close the gate
Physical conditions	Extent of the injury Inappropriate activity level	Medication Counterstimulation, e.g. massage
Emotional conditions	Anxiety or worry Tension Depression	Positive emotions Relaxation Rest
Mental conditions	Focusing on the pain Boredom	Intense concentration or distraction Involvement and interest in life activities

The neural circuitry of pain is complex and challenging to the neuroscientist. Many features of pain still require understanding (Box 10.12). In the control of pain, we have seen that we can consciously influence its perception. We can think pain away. It is these thoughts that may underlie the placebo effect which is intimately connected with the study of analgesia and is studied in greater detail in Chapter 9.

Masochism

Pain is a necessary burden and we would usually seek to avoid situations that induce it. However, there are a group of people who like pain – the masochists. Sexual masochists have been known to exist for a long time and find sexual gratification and pain to be intimately entwined. How does this happen? The simple answer is, I do not know. A search of the literature on masochism revealed considerable Freudian speculation about its existence; it did not inform me of a neuropharmacological basis. It would appear that the neuroscientific study of masochism is a field ripe for study. However, we can speculate why this may occur.

It is known that opioids produce hedonic experiences in their own right, and when one is engaged in pleasure-inducing acts there is an increase in endogenous opiate activity, most notably in the nucleus accumbens (see Leknes

BOX 10.12: SYNAESTHESIA

Synaesthesia is a strange condition in which a stimulus in one sensory modality gives rise to an experience in another sensory modality. Such an experience is typified in the title of a book by Cytowic (2003), called *The man who tasted shapes*.

Investigations into numbers evoking colour synaesthesia have suggested that it is a result of cross-wiring in the brain (Hubbard et al., 2005). These authors used a task in which synaesthetes had to identify a particular number (number 2) from an array of digits (the number 5) (see Figure 10.12.1). The colour coding nature of synaesthesia means that the numbers they were searching for jump out of the array. Both colours and numbers are initially processed in the fusiform gyrus, so this type of synaesthesia may be caused by cross-wiring between the colour coding V4 area of the visual cortex and the number appearance area (both within the fusiform). Alternatively, it might be 'between the higher colour area and the number concept area (both in the junction of the temporal, parietal and occipital lobes)' (Ramachandran & Hubbard,

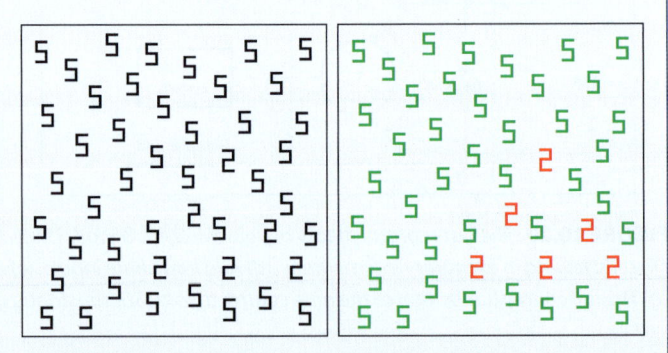

FIGURE 10.12.1 *Synaesthesia test. Finding the number two embedded in many number fives is difficult unless you have synaesthesia and see the number two in a different colour.*
Source: Hubbard, E. M., Arman, A. C., Ramachandran, V. S., & Boynton, G. M. (2005). Individual differences among grapheme-color synesthetes: brain-behavior correlations. *Neuron, 45*(6), 975–985.

2003). Other types of synaesthesia may be due to different wires being crossed in the brain.

& Tracey (2008) for review). There are numerous regions of overlap within the human brain that mediate pleasure and pain. Thus, masochism could be explained as a result of 'cross-wiring' and 'faulty learning'. In a study looking at 'pleasant pain', Leknes et al. (2013) found that participants had increased activity in reward pathways and descending pain pathways. Furthermore, the endocannabinoid system may also be activated when pain is perceived to be positive (Benedetti et al., 2013). Clearly the context in which pain takes place is important and it is tempting to suggest that the sexual masochist voluntarily seeks painful stimuli in order to activate endogenous cannabinoid and opioid systems. However, this is mere speculation and leads to the question, what about the sadists?

The Hard Question

Our external world is made up of tangible entities that can be described in terms of physics, whether it is light, sounds, smells or touch. Undoubtedly, sensory modalities, the apparatus by which we connect with the outside world, receive physical information. But how does this translate into consciousness? Our perception, whether visual, auditory or feelings of pain, is a process which culminates in our conscious awareness of our external world. These neural signals that convey sensory information can be traced from the receptors through to higher cortical areas of the brain. However, what we do not know is how these neural impulses become conscious experiences. This is the hard question, the question that keeps neuroscientists, psychologists and philosophers gainfully employed. The study of consciousness is addressed in more detail in Chapter 18.

SENSORY INTEGRATION

In this chapter we have treated each sense as a separate entity. This is because we have taken a bottom-up approach to perceptual processing in which we start with the input and follow its route to the sensory cortices. However, our interaction with a stimulus in the environment is a multisensory event with information being assimilated from all the senses. Regions such as the superior colliculus and cortical areas (Stein & Stanford, 2008) have been identified as locations of multisensory processing (Bolognini et al., 2007; Meredith & Stein, 1983, 1985, 1986) Multisensory integration involves not only the ascending but also the descending sensory pathways.

Received wisdom dictates that those who have lost one sensory modality, e.g. either blind or deaf, have increased sensitivity in another sensory modality. For example, people who are blind may have more acute hearing or be more sensitive to touch. It was found that parts of the auditory cortex in a deaf cat were reorganized for visual motion detection (Lomber et al., 2010). The condition synaesthesia is associated with sensory modalities getting mixed up in the brain, leading those with the condition to 'hear' the colour red (see Box 10.12).

SUMMARY

Perception and the sensory modalities have evolved to provide the organism with information about the external environment. Perception is an active process that converts neural information into conscious awareness. It is more than simple sensation. Perception involves interpretation and refinement of sensory input. Neural mechanisms have adapted and evolved to enhance the perceptual process, ensuring the survival and continuation of the species.

All the senses are integrated, most notably in thalamic regions projecting to the sensory cortices. A multisensory view of the world is achieved by the neural processing and sharing of sensory information from the various modalities. Adaptation in the perceptual systems is also evident during the lifetime of the organism, e.g. we learn to see. The loss of a sensory system can lead to some compensatory reorganization of the brain.

Perception is the input; the following chapter addresses how we act upon our world in response to the internal and external environments. At the centre of all this activity is the brain – again.

LEARNING OUTCOME QUESTIONS

You should be able to answer the following questions:
- Describe the passage of light from entry to the eye and conversion to a neural impulse extending to the occipital cortex.
- Describe the difference between sensation and perception.
- Pain is an evolutionary necessity. Discuss.
- How can pain be modulated?.

FURTHER READING

Farah, M. J. (2000). *The cognitive neuroscience of vision.* Oxford, UK: Blackwell.

Fuchs, P. (2010). *Oxford handbook of auditory science: The ear.* Oxford, UK: Oxford University Press.

Hadjistavropoulos, T., & Craig, K. D. (2004). *Pain: Psychological perspectives.* Hove, UK: Psychology Press.

Lamb, T. D. (2011). Evolution of the eye. Scientists now have a clear vision of how our notoriously complex eye came to be. *Scientific American, 305*(1), 64–69.

Pickles, J. R. (1988). *Introduction to the physiology of hearing* (2nd edn). New York: Academic Press.

Rees, A., & Palmer, A. R. (2010). *Oxford handbook of auditory science: The auditory brain.* Oxford, UK: Oxford University Press.

Roberts, D. (2002). *Signals and perception: The fundamentals of human sensation.* Basingstoke, UK: Palgrave Macmillan.

Stone, J. V. (2012). *Vision and brain: How we perceive the world.* Cambridge, MA: MIT Press.

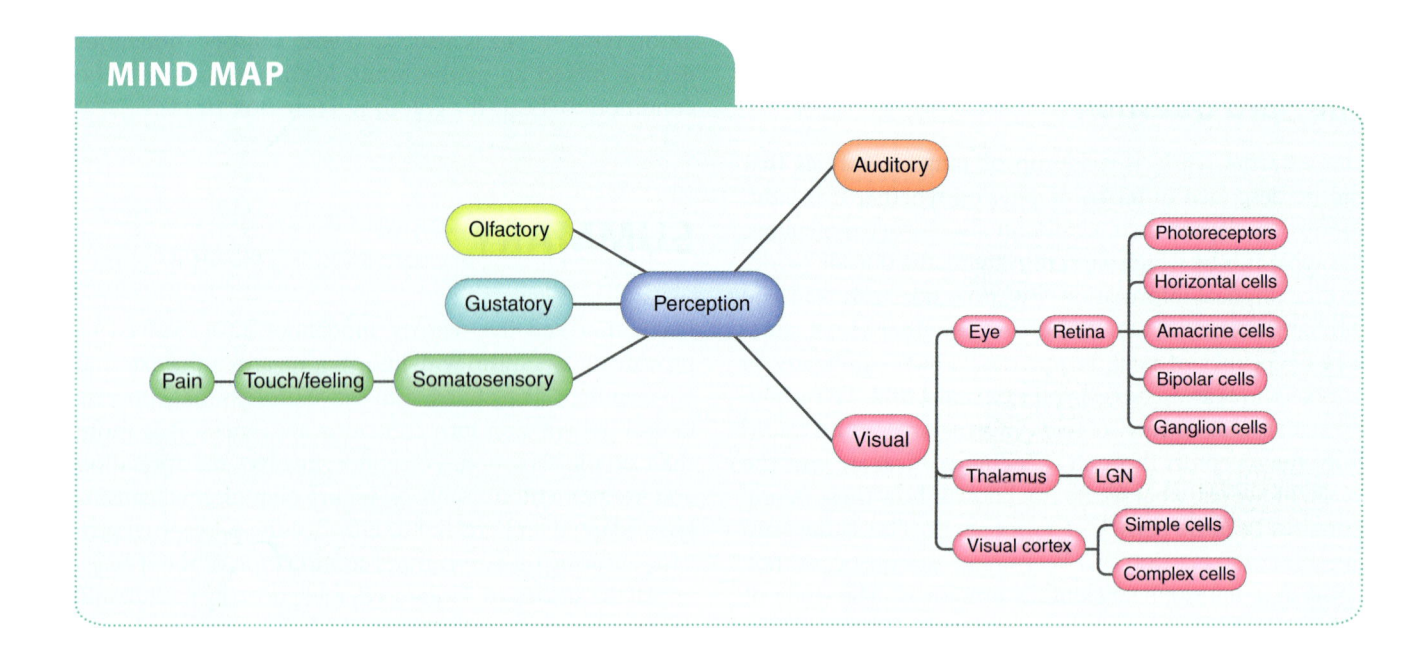

MIND MAP

- Perception
  - Olfactory
  - Gustatory
  - Somatosensory — Touch/feeling — Pain
  - Auditory
  - Visual
    - Eye — Retina
      - Photoreceptors
      - Horizontal cells
      - Amacrine cells
      - Bipolar cells
      - Ganglion cells
    - Thalamus — LGN
    - Visual cortex
      - Simple cells
      - Complex cells

11 Motor Behaviour and Control

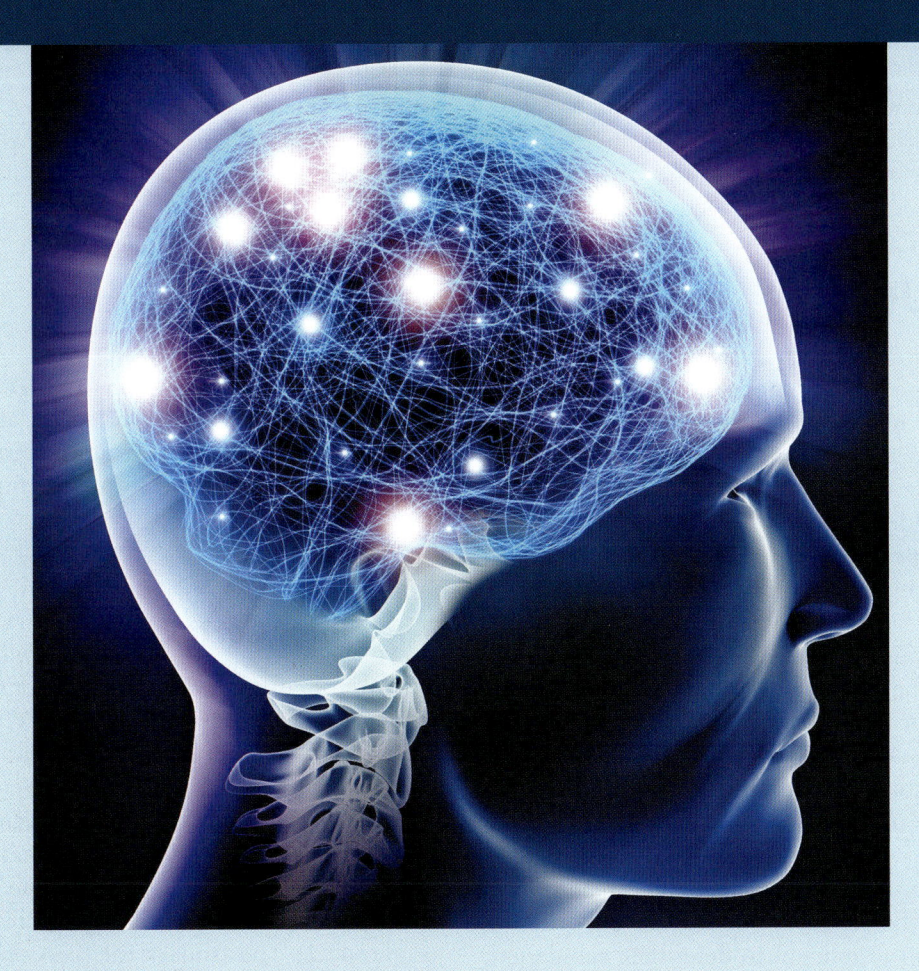

ANATOMY OF THE CHAPTER

This chapter will highlight the following.
- The role of the basal ganglia in motor behaviour.
- The role of the motor cortex (M1) and premotor cortex in motor behaviour.
- The function of the cerebellum.
- The neuromuscular junction.
- Motor feedback mechanisms.

INTRODUCTION   294

REGIONS OF THE BRAIN   294

DESCENDING PATHWAYS   302

PASSAGE OF INFORMATION TO MUSCLES   305

FEEDBACK   309

CONTROL AND AGENCY   309

SUMMARY   309

> **LEARNING OUTCOMES**
>
> 1. To understand the neural circuitry involved in movement.
> 2. To understand how the different regions contribute to the execution of movement.
> 3. To be able to describe the effects of acetylcholine at the neuromuscular junction.
> 4. To be able to describe the effects of degeneration within specific areas of the motor circuitry.

INTRODUCTION

The brain and the sensory modalities are not just passive recipients of incoming signals – the signals that are received are acted upon. We make decisions and perform actions to achieve our goals. All of this involves motor co-ordination and activation. It could be argued that there are two types of motor behaviour, volitional and reflexive. The primary concern of this chapter is with volitional motor behaviour, which requires the involvement of numerous cortical regions. Furthermore, the involvement of the cortex in decision making and acting is at the centre of our understanding of consciousness. Whilst consciousness is addressed in Chapter 18, this chapter investigates the mechanics of movement from the cortex to the muscles. It should also be appreciated that the motor systems are intimately connected with perceptual systems. Therefore perception can be seen as input and motor behaviour is output. The big question is, what happens to the input to determine subsequent output, i.e. how is the brain processing information?

REGIONS OF THE BRAIN

There are many regions of the brain dedicated to motor behaviour.

- Primary motor cortex (M1)
- Premotor cortex
- Supplementary motor area (SMA)
- Presupplementary motor area (pre-SMA)
- Cingulate motor area
- Broca's area (speech only)
- Frontal eye fields
- Basal ganglia
- Cerebellum
- Brainstem

The list above is configured into a hierarchical organization with the primary motor cortex at the top and the brainstem at the bottom. From the brainstem, descending spinal axons connect to the muscles that allow movement.

The Motor Cortex

The motor cortex and adjacent regions are highly interconnected areas of the frontal lobe. The frontal lobe, as discussed in Chapter 12, is involved in the planning and execution of complex voluntary movements.

The **primary motor cortex** (Figure 11.1) contains pyramidal cells in cortical layer 5 that are the primary motor neurons. The axons of the motor neurons descend via the **corticobulbar** and **corticospinal tracts** (Figure 11.2). The axons of the corticobulbar tract terminate in the brainstem and the axons of the corticospinal tract terminate in the spinal cord. The corticobulbar and corticospinal tracts pass through the base of the pons to the medulla and form **medullary pyramids** which are ridges spanning the length of the medulla (extrapyramidal tracts do not cross the medullary pyramids). The corticobulbar tract connects with the trigeminal and hypoglossal cranial nerves. On the way, these tracts connect with the **reticular formation** and the **red nucleus**. The majority of corticospinal axons at the end of the medulla cross over and enter the opposite side of the spinal cord. A small minority remain on the same side. Those that cross over are referred to as the **lateral corticospinal tract** while those that remain on the same side form the **ventral corticospinal tract**.

The primary motor cortex when stimulated with electrodes produces contractions on the contralateral (opposite) side of the body (Fritsch & Hitzig, 1870; see Fritsch & Hitzig (2009) for translation). In 1873 John Hughlings Jackson argued that the motor cortex has a spatial map

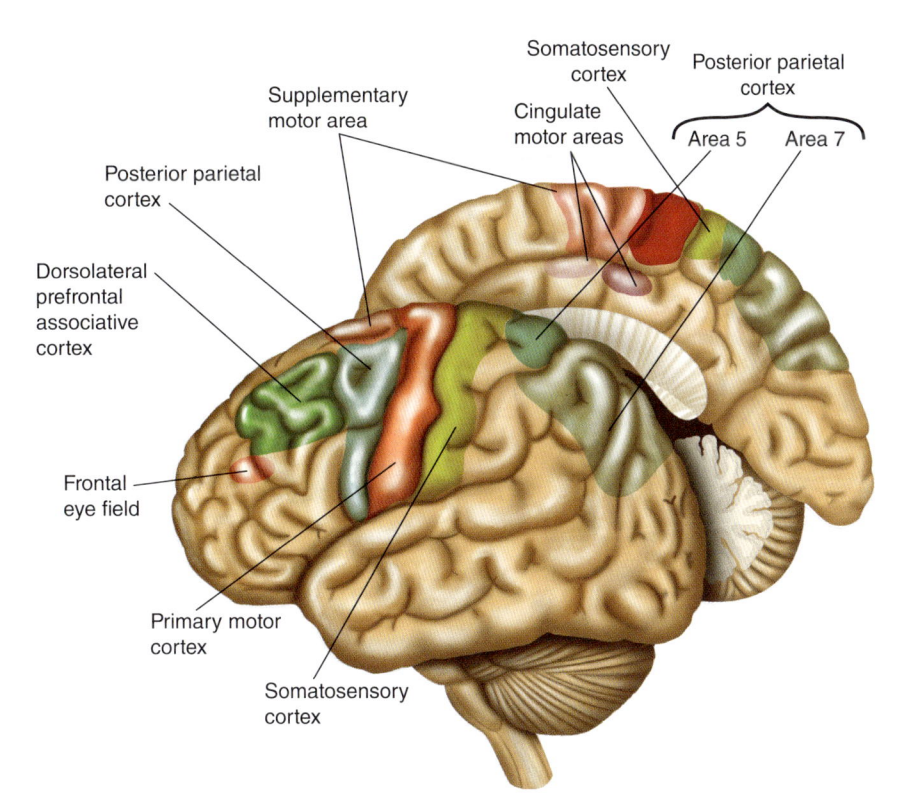

FIGURE 11.1 *The motor cortex.*

of the musculature of the body. Sherrington (1892) confirmed the motor organization of the cortex in great apes by stimulating the cortex with electrodes. Similarly, Penfield and Boldrey (1937) observed in humans both motor and sensory regions of the cortex. This gave rise to the motor and sensory **homunculus** (Penfield & Rasmussen, 1950).

The **somatotopic maps** of the motor cortex are not straightforward one-to-one mapping processes. According to Graziano (2006):

> The somatotopic map in the primary motor cortex is overlapping, intermingled, and fractured, which suggests that it is organized to promote co-ordination among muscles and joints rather than to separate movements into constituent muscles and joints. (p.108)

An alternative view of the somatotopic organization of the motor cortex has been suggested to involve organization based on ecologically relevant categories of motor behaviour (Graziano et al., 2005). Instead of using short electrical pulses that would normally evoke muscle twitches (as used in previous experiments), Graziano and colleagues used longer stimulation durations (half a second) that were selected to approximate the timescale of movements in the monkey's arms and hands. Using these long stimulation times, complex motor behaviours were observed that constituted meaningful behaviours, e.g. hand-to-mouth co-ordination or grasping an object. What was noted was that the categories of movement could be evoked from different regions of the cortex (Figure 11.3). Based on the data, the authors suggest that the primary cortex provides a representation of complex behaviour and not merely a one-to-one map of the body and that behaviours are ecologically organized, e.g. hand movements bringing food to the mouth.

The Premotor Cortex

The **premotor cortex** receives widespread multisensory input from the parietal lobes and motivational input from the prefrontal cortex. The premotor cortex has both direct and indirect effects on motor behaviour. The direct effects proceed via axons projecting to the corticobulbar and corticospinal pathways, and the indirect effects via reciprocal connections with the primary motor cortex. The premotor cortex therefore integrates information from other cortical regions. An example can be seen with the sensorimotor integration within the premotor cortex in which neurons continue to fire in a receptive field even when the object is no longer visible, so that this action allows one to reach for an object even when one cannot see it (Graziano et al., 1997). The premotor cortex is thought to be involved in motor sequences that are responding to external stimuli (Larsson et al., 1996). Graziano (2006)

296 PSYCHOBIOLOGY

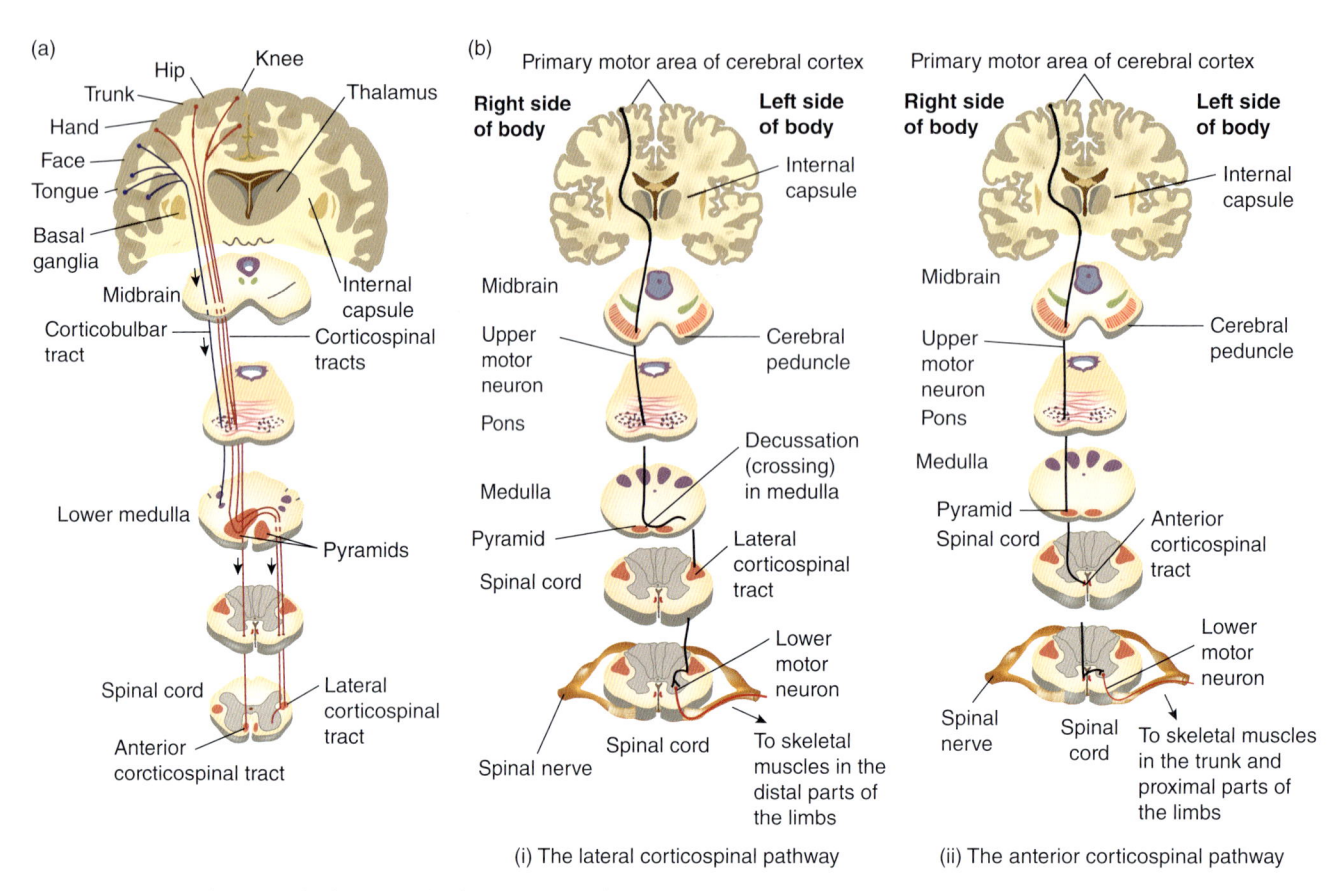

FIGURE 11.2 *(a) The corticobulbar tract. (b) The corticospinal tract.*

argues that the functional distinction between the primary motor cortex and the premotor cortex is blurred because both regions have parallel projections to the spinal cord, therefore making differentiation difficult.

Within the premotor cortex there is an area that has been identified to contain mirror neurons. **Mirror neurons** are activated, for example, when a monkey sees another monkey make a particular movement. These mirror neurons allow a representation of the actor's movement (Fadiga et al., 1995; Rizzolatti et al., 1996). Similar sets of neurons have been found in humans (Buccino et al., 2004). For more detail on mirror neurons see Chapter 20 which discusses their application to autistic spectrum disorder.

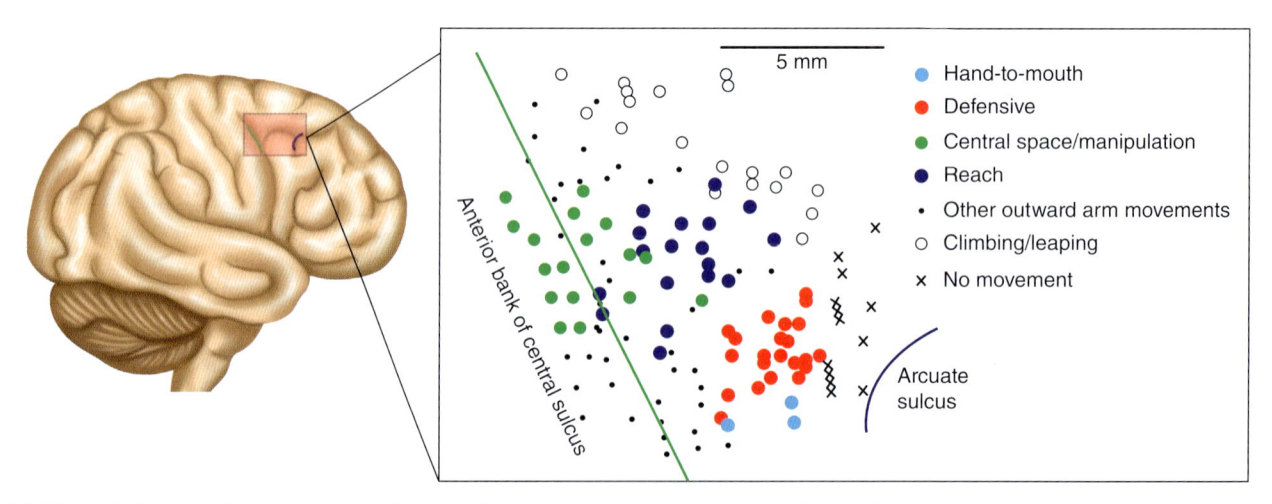

FIGURE 11.3 *Topographic arrangement of stimulation effects in an example monkey. Rectangle shows location of studied cortex, spanning the arm and hand. Sites are colour-coded according to type of complex movement evoked.*
Source: Graziano, M. S. A., Aflalo, T., Cooke, D. F. (2005). Arm movements evoked by electrical stimulation in the motor cortex of monkeys. *Journal of Neurophysiology*, 94, 4209–4223. Reproduced by permission of The American Physiological Society.

Supplementary Motor Area (SMA)

The SMA receives input from the **basal ganglia** (see below) and modulates the primary motor cortex. The SMA has numerous proposed functions, e.g. co-ordination of the sequence of actions (e.g. Gerloff et al., 1997), modulation of the interaction of limbs to form a sequence of behaviour and interhemispheric communication (Serrien et al., 2002), and internally generated movements (Halsband et al., 1994). Just before a motor movement is made, the activity in the SMA (SMA) is terminated, therefore providing a signal of forthcoming activity (Brotchie et al., 1991b).

Presupplementary Motor Area (Pre-SMA)

The **pre-SMA** has extensive connections with the prefrontal cortex (Wang et al., 2005). It is involved in numerous behaviours, including movement recognition (Stephan et al., 1995), learning motor sequences (Hikosaka et al., 1996), voluntary/internally generated action (Frith et al., 1991) and changing motor actions (Matsuzaka & Tanji, 1996). In a case study of a 52-year-old woman who had a tumour removed from her pre-SMA, it was found that she had difficulty inhibiting motor plans even when there were a number of alternative plans (Nachev et al., 2007).

Cingulate Motor Area

The cingulate motor area has been associated with reward information and the selection of motor acts to obtain a goal (Shima & Tanji, 1998). The interaction between motor behaviour, cognition and motivational systems has been regarded as uniquely integrated within the cingulate cortex, thereby translating intentions into actions (Paus, 2001).

Broca's Area

Broca's area is addressed in greater detail in Chapter 19. It is an area associated with the generation of speech. Speech motor control includes approximately 100 muscles of different types with neural information arriving via the cranial nerves (see Box 11.1).

Frontal Eye Fields

Stimulation of the **frontal eye fields** produces saccadic eye movements in monkeys (Robinson & Fuchs, 1969). The frontal eye fields control visual attention and eye movements, permitting orientation to a stimulus (Schall, 2004) and following of a stimulus (Mustari et al., 2009). Therefore, the frontal eye fields allow for visual information to be received by the eye and the input to be processed by the cortex (see Chapter 10).

BOX 11.1 LANGUAGE, MUSCLE AND BRAIN

Motor control of speech involves the respiratory, laryngeal and upper airway muscle systems (Kent, 2005). Many muscles are used in the generation of speech and are capable of precise co-ordination, allowing for the complexities of speech production. Han et al. (1999) noted that the muscles of the vocal fold:

> ... do not contract with a twitch like most muscle fibers, instead, their contractions are prolonged, stable, precisely controlled, and fatigue resistant. The human voice is characterized by a stable sound with a wide frequency spectrum that can be precisely modulated and [these muscles] may contribute to this ability. (p.146)

Speech is fast, accurate and derived from complex interactions and involves more motor fibres than any other motor act (Fink, 1986; Kent, 2004).

The neural control of speech has long been associated with Broca's area but also includes the SMA, insula, premotor cortex, motor cortex, basal ganglia, cerebellum, periaqueductal grey, and the brainstem and cranial nerves (Figure 11.1.1). In Chapter 19, evidence will be presented supporting a view that language is located predominantly in the left hemisphere, but there are also bilateral regions, e.g. SMA activation during language-based tasks.

Jurgens (2009) hypothesized from studies on the squirrel monkey that there are two pathways involved in vocalization. One pathway runs from the anterior cingulate cortex to the periaqueductal grey and then to the reticular formation and from there to motor neurons responsible for vocalization. The anterior cingulate is activated in the voluntary production and initiation of vocalizations.

The other pathway stems from the motor cortex and projects to the reticular formation and motor neurons in which there are two feedback loops, from the basal ganglia and the cerebellum, which provide information for the fine motor commands of speech.

Therefore, the articulation of words into sentences involves a complex array of motor components. This does not convey the whole story of language, as the generation of language expresses consciousness and thought (Bridgeman, 1992).

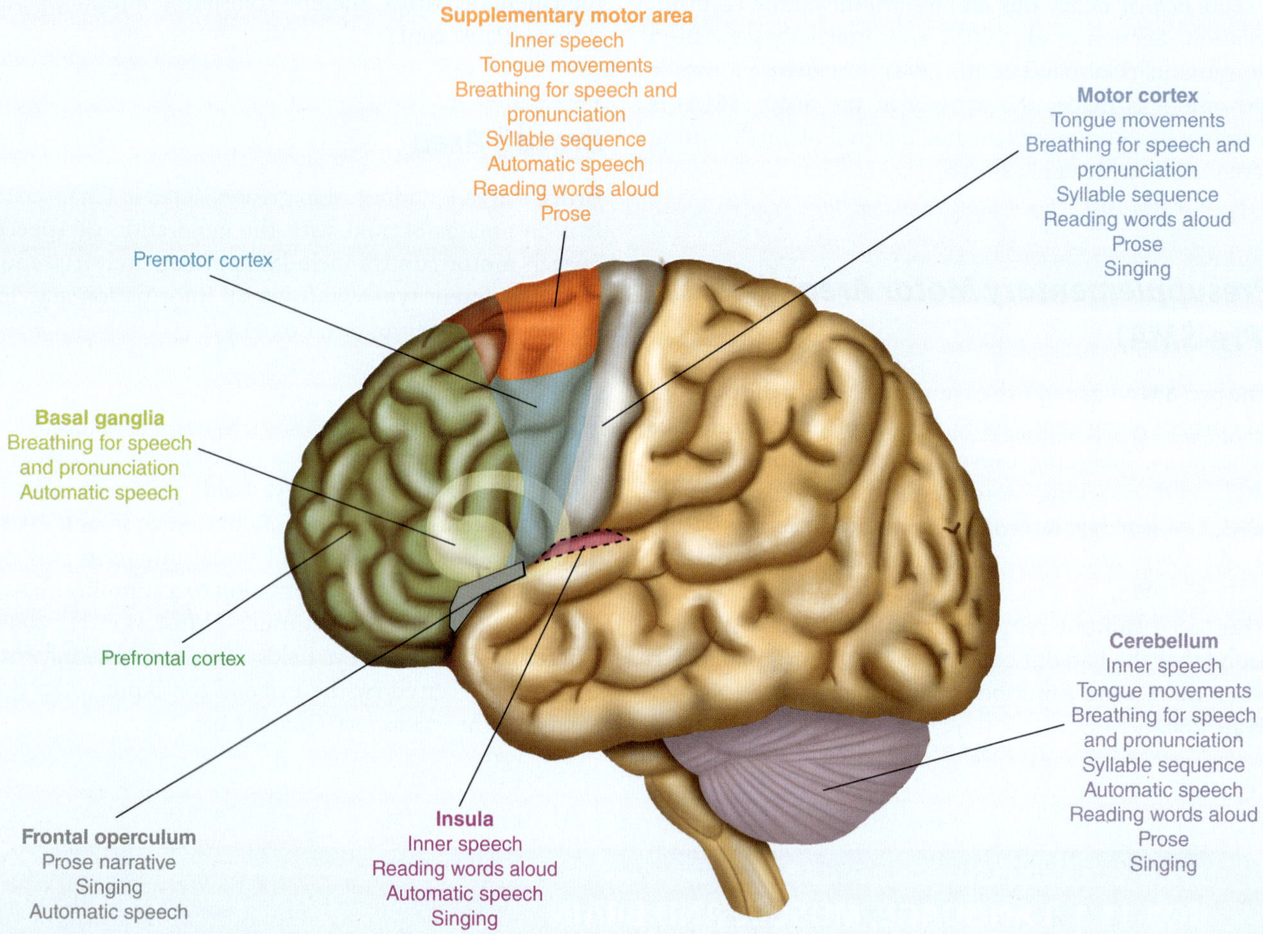

Supplementary motor area
Inner speech
Tongue movements
Breathing for speech and pronunciation
Syllable sequence
Automatic speech
Reading words aloud
Prose

Motor cortex
Tongue movements
Breathing for speech and pronunciation
Syllable sequence
Reading words aloud
Prose
Singing

Premotor cortex

Basal ganglia
Breathing for speech and pronunciation
Automatic speech

Prefrontal cortex

Cerebellum
Inner speech
Tongue movements
Breathing for speech and pronunciation
Syllable sequence
Automatic speech
Reading words aloud
Prose
Singing

Frontal operculum
Prose narrative
Singing
Automatic speech

Insula
Inner speech
Reading words aloud
Automatic speech
Singing

FIGURE 11.1.1 Regions of the brain activated in oral movements or speaking.

The Basal Ganglia

The **basal ganglia** are a group of subcortical structures that receive information from the cortex and loop back to the cortex. There are a number of routes through the basal ganglia, but essentially, they all start at the SMA and go back to the cortex via the thalamus. There is also a route from the **globus pallidus internal segment** (GPi) to the pons. There are no direct outputs to the spinal cord.

The role of the basal ganglia is to modulate the motor programmes of the pyramidal system. The two routes of the basal ganglia are referred to as the direct and indirect pathways (Figure 11.4). The direct pathway provides positive feedback for sustaining or facilitating an ongoing action, in which the GPi and the **substantia nigra pars reticulata** (**SNr**) release the thalamus from tonic inhibition and therefore activate the cortex. The indirect pathway is able to suppress unwanted movements via GABAergic projections to the thalamus.

The **nigrostriatal pathway**, containing dopamine, provides a gating role and differentially affects the direct and indirect pathways; it facilitates activity via the direct pathway and decreases activity in the indirect pathway. Therefore, the basal ganglia can select and inhibit motor programmes. The basal ganglia have been suggested to act as an autopilot controlling, at a subconscious level, different motor

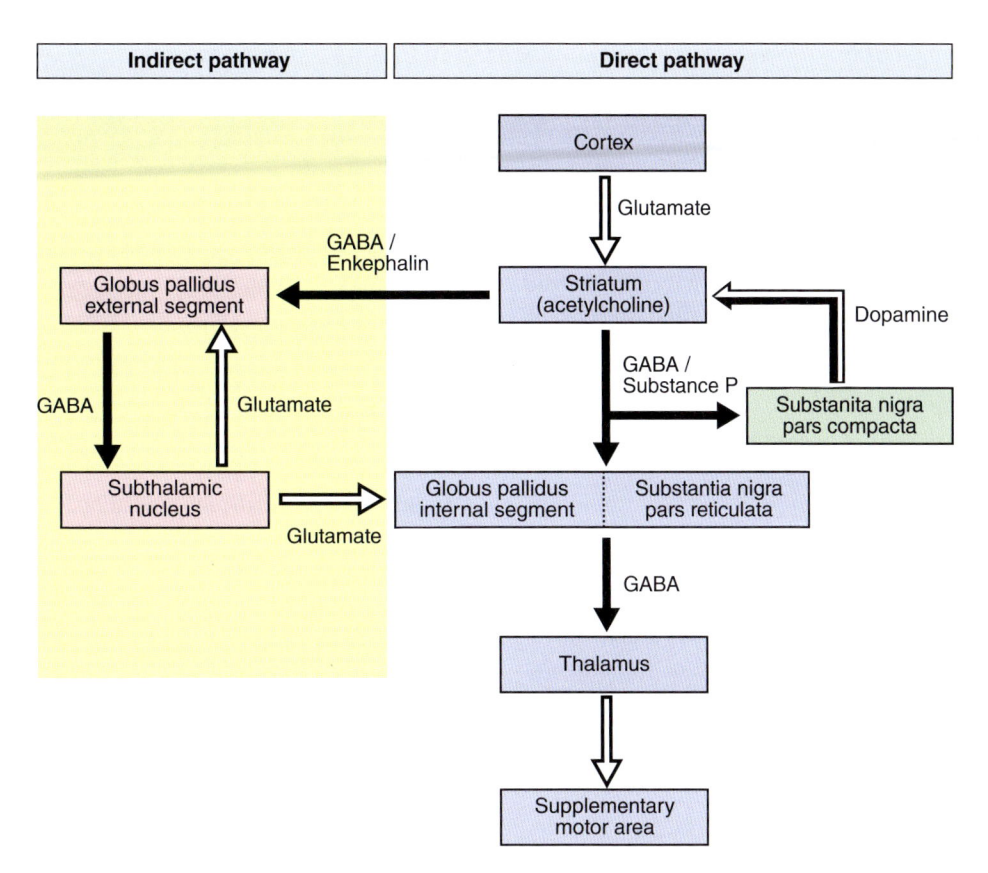

FIGURE 11.4 *Pathways in the basal ganglia.*

programmes selected from higher cortical regions (Steg & Johnels, 1993). Brotchie et al. (1991a) suggested that phasic activity was generated by the basal ganglia in which well learnt internally generated movements provide a cue to signal the switch between components in a motor sequence. Jin et al. (2014) reported an experiment in which they recorded the activity of the direct and indirect pathways in mice. They found that both pathways were activated in a similar manner during the start or the end of a response sequence, but the indirect pathway preferentially was active at the start of the sequence and this was thought to underlie the inhibition of other potential motor responses.

Whilst some support the view that the basal ganglia are involved in monitoring and selection of motor responses (Houk et al., 2007; Humphries & Prescott, 2010), there are alternative perspectives on the function of the basal ganglia. McNab and Klingberg (2008) identified the basal ganglia as a filter for **working memory**. Working memory has a limited capacity and the basal ganglia's activity during working memory tasks was a predictor of working memory capacity. By filtering irrelevant information in working memory, the basal ganglia can be seen to be involved in modulating excitatory and inhibitory responses (which is consistent with the role of indirect and direct pathways, but using a different concept to describe the process).

Others have argued that the basal ganglia are involved in movement directed by motivational factors and also motor learning (Turner & Desmurget, 2010). The basal ganglia regulate the speed and size of movements (movement gain) (Anderson & Horak, 1985; Hallett & Khoshbin, 1980); movement gain is regulated by dopamine in the motivational systems, with the basal ganglia providing the motivational force (or vigour) driving the behaviour (Niv et al., 2007). Another view of the basal ganglia is their involvement in the learning of new skills (but not their retention) (Graybiel, 2008). During learning, the basal ganglia are active, but once the skill has been acquired the memory of that skill is transferred to the cortex. The learning of new skills takes advantage of the plasticity seen in the striatum, but long-term retention of the new skill is transferred to the cortex for future needs (Turner & Desmurget, 2010).

Thus, the basal ganglia have numerous functions, which have been hypothesized to be correct to some degree (Utter & Basso, 2008). Much of our understanding of these putative functions has been gleaned from the study of disorders of the basal ganglia. The implications of a dysfunction of the basal ganglia are clearly evident in Parkinson's disease (Chapter 24) and Huntington's disease which are a result of degeneration of the striatum (Calabresi et al., 2000) and produce abnormal involuntary movements (Box 11.2).

BOX 11.2 HUNTINGTON'S DISEASE

Huntington's disease was first described by George Huntington in 1872 (Huntington, 2003). It is characterized by late onset (40+) with symptoms including (see Walker, 2007):

- a lack of affect;
- oscillating periods of aggression, excitement, depression and apathy;
- attentional difficulties; and
- short-term memory failures.

However, the main symptom of Huntington's disease is the effect on movement. These include uncontrollable movements of the face and jerking movements of the limbs and body with no clear purpose, called choreiform movements.

The motor symptoms change as the disease progresses.

Early stage

- Alterations in co-ordination
- Involuntary movement (e.g. irregular, sudden jerks of limbs)
- Fidgeting
- Restlessness
- Twitching, muscle spasms, tics
- Reduced control over handwriting
- Facial grimaces
- Difficulty with co-ordinated activities, e.g. driving
- Rigidity

Middle stage

- Dystonia (prolonged muscle contractions), often of the face, neck and back
- Increased involuntary movements
- Difficulties with balance and walking
- Chorea, twisting and writhing, jerking
- Staggering, swaying, gait problems
- Speech difficulties, e.g. poor articulation, abnormal speech patterns
- Difficulty swallowing
- Difficulties with tasks involving manual dexterity
- Slow voluntary movements
- Difficulty initiating movement
- Inability to control speed and force of movement
- Slow reaction time
- Overall general weakness

Late stage

- Rigidity
- Bradykinesia (difficulty initiating and continuing movements)
- Severe chorea
- Weight loss
- Inability to walk
- Inability to speak
- Swallowing problems (leading to possible choking)
- Inability to care for oneself

Huntington's disease is referred to as a hyperkinetic movement disorder originating from degeneration of neurons projecting from the **striatum** to the **globus pallidus external segment** (Halliday et al., 1998; Vonsattel, 2008). This loss of striatal innervation occurs within the indirect pathway, having a downstream effect that releases the thalamus from tonic inhibition, thereby increasing cortical excitation (the opposite being the case for Parkinson's disease – see Chapter 24) (Figure 11.2.1). Other areas of the brain that are affected are the substantia nigra, specific cortical layers, hippocampus, parietal lobe, cerebellum, thalamus and hypothalamus (Dierks et al., 1998, 1999; Heinsen et al., 1999; Kremer et al., 1991; Macdonald & Halliday, 2002; Nana et al., 2014; Rub et al., 2013, 2014; Spargo et al., 1993).

Despite our knowledge of the neuropathology, treatment is limited. Although there are numerous drugs targeting different mechanisms and symptoms of Huntington's disease, only one drug is licensed in the USA (Venuto et al., 2012). **Tetrabenazine** is a presynaptic monoamine transporter inhibitor (Login et al., 1982). The **vesicular monoamine transporter** (VMAT) facilitates the packaging of monoamine into vesicles, therefore tetrabenazine depletes the monoamine reserves, in particular dopamine (DA) (Henry et al., 1994) (see Figure 11.2.1(c)). Thus, reducing DA activity in the basal ganglia has a benefit on symptom management of the chorea. Note that it only manages the symptoms; it does not cure or even retard the progress of the disease.

Antipsychotic medication may also be used, but with a preference for atypical antipsychotics due to the reduction of side-effects. Antipsychotic medications generally are antagonists of dopamine receptors and therefore can have a similar outcome to tetrabenazine. However, as will be seen in Chapter 21, antipsychotic medications can sometimes have prohibitive side-effects. The wide spectrum of behaviours affected as Huntington's disease progresses means that numerous drugs may be prescribed to address psychosis, irritability, depression, anxiety and abnormal sleep patterns.

Knowing the genetic code underlying Huntington's disease has not yet given rise to a suitable therapy, but such targets are being explored (Labbadia & Morimoto, 2013; Ross & Tabrizi, 2011).

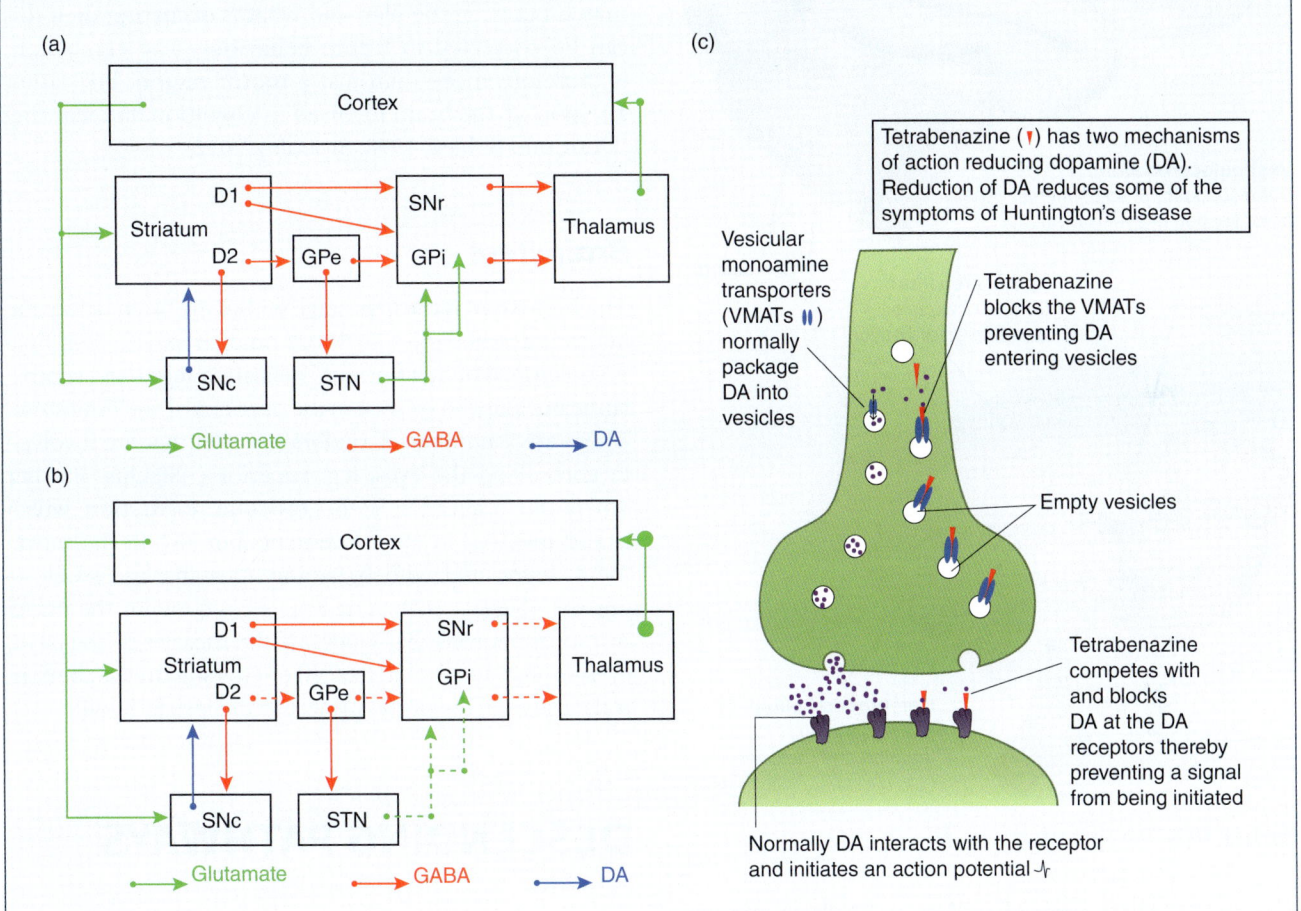

FIGURE 11.2.1 *The direct and indirect pathways of the basal ganglia in Huntington's disease. (a) Normal pathway. (b) Abnormality in the striatum in Huntington's disease has effects throughput the basal ganglia. SNc, substantia nigra pars compacta; SNr, substantia nigra pars reticulata; GPi, globus pallidus internal segment; GPe, globus pallidus external segment; STN, subthalamic nucleus. (c) The action of tetrabenazine.*

The Cerebellum

The **cerebellum** receives sensory input and information from the pyramidal and extrapyramidal systems emanating from the cortex and is important in modifying fine motor movement, posture and the learning of new motor sequences. The cerebellum can be divided into three constituent parts with functional specificity (Figure 11.5).

- *Cerebrocerebellum* – connecting cortical output with the cerebellum and involved in skilled movements.
- *Spinocerebellum* – receives input from the spinal cord and is involved with movements of distal muscles (those further away in the extremities).
- *Vestibulocerebellum* – receives input from the vestibular system and is involved in movements that maintain posture and equilibrium.

Damage to the cerebellum can have numerous effects on motor behaviour (such as **ataxia**, which is the inability to walk in a co-ordinated manner) (see Schmahmann (2004) for review).

Vestibulocerebellum:
Balance, postural adjustments, co-ordination of eye movements

Spinocerebellum:
Control of muscle tone and co-ordination

Cerebellum

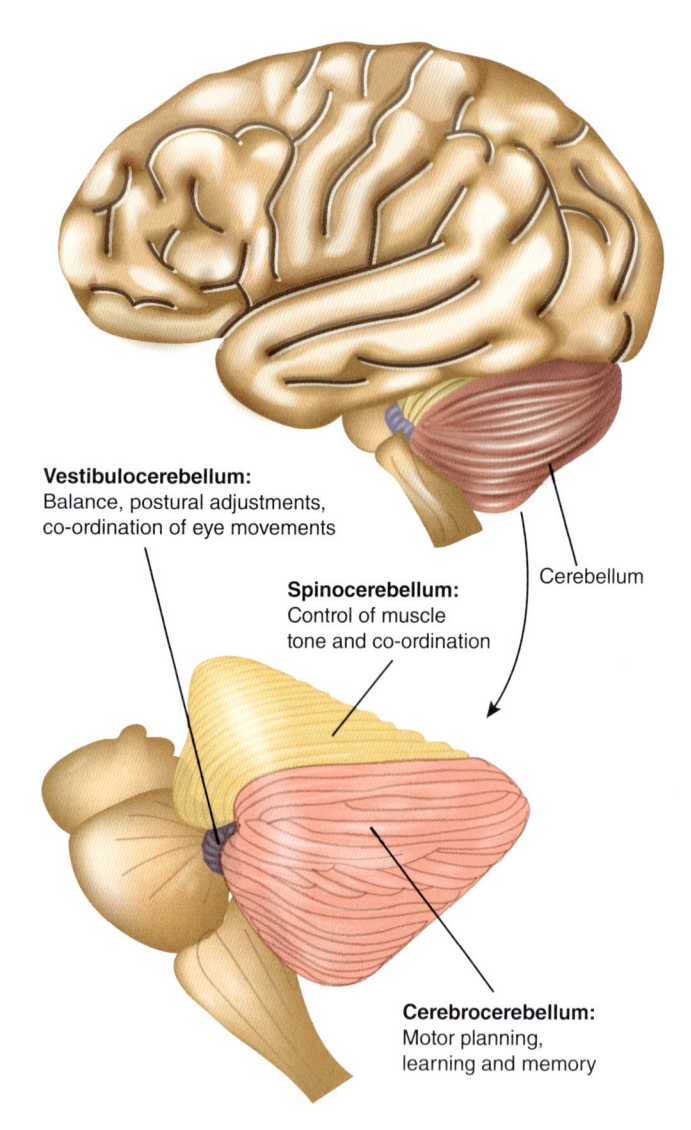

Cerebrocerebellum:
Motor planning, learning and memory

FIGURE 11.5 *The cerebellum.*

The cerebellum projects to deep cerebellar nuclei and vestibular nuclei. These structures project to motor neurons in the brainstem and subthalamic nuclei innervating motor neurons in the motor cortex (and ascending pathways).

As each hemisphere of the cerebellum is connected with the same side of the body (ipsilateral), the output pathway must cross over to the opposite side of the motor cortex which governs the body via contralateral reference. Along the pathway, connections with the **red nucleus**, together with its connection with the **inferior olive**, provide feedback to the cerebellum. These closed-loop systems provide feedback to modulate the activity of the cerebellum, running parallel to open loops that receive diverse inputs and transmit information to the motor cortex.

The spinocerebellar pathways (Figure 11.6) project to the reticular formation and vestibular system and to the thalamic circuits interacting with the motor cortex. Both the spinocerebellar and the cerebrocerebellar pathways provide the cerebellum with information about the muscular activity of complex voluntary movements and also other circuits that have executive control over movement (Bellebaum & Daum, 2007; Strick et al., 2009).

Thus, the cerebellum integrates the plans and intentions of movements with the inputs from sensory systems monitoring those movements, permitting executive control and error monitoring. If there is a mismatch between the plan and what is occurring then this can be corrected in future behaviour. The cerebellum is therefore more than just a motor region, but rather a region of the brain involved in cognition and learning (Desmond & Fiez, 1998; Stoodley, 2012).

Brainstem

The **brainstem** is the final stage within the brain before the neurons descend the spinal cord on their way to their final destination. The red nucleus, substantia nigra and subthalamic nucleus can be seen in the portions of the brainstem. There are a number of midbrain nuclei that are involved in controlling the eyes, e.g. superior colliculus. Further down the brainstem is the **reticular formation** which is also involved in eye movements but also in the movements associated with breathing, chewing and swallowing, etc. (Siegel, 1979). The brainstem contains the nuclei of motor neurons that innervate the muscles of the head, eyes, mouth and throat. Instead of crossing over to the contralateral side, the nuclei project to the ipsilateral side.

DESCENDING PATHWAYS

The descending pathways (or tracts) are myelinated axons that communicate with the skeletal muscles from the following areas (tracts in parentheses):

- cerebral cortex (pyramidal tract);
- red nucleus (rubrospinal tract) (Figure 11.7);
- superior colliculus (tectospinal tract);
- vestibular nuclei (vestibulospinal tract); and
- reticular formation (reticulospinal tract).

There are two regions of the brain that control two motor pathways, with a great deal of communication between the two. The **pyramidal motor system** starts at the primary motor cortex, which is responsible for fine motor programmes. The **extrapyramidal system** projects from a number of brain regions: the cortex, cerebellum, basal ganglia, reticular formation and thalamus.

CHAPTER 11 MOTOR BEHAVIOUR AND CONTROL   303

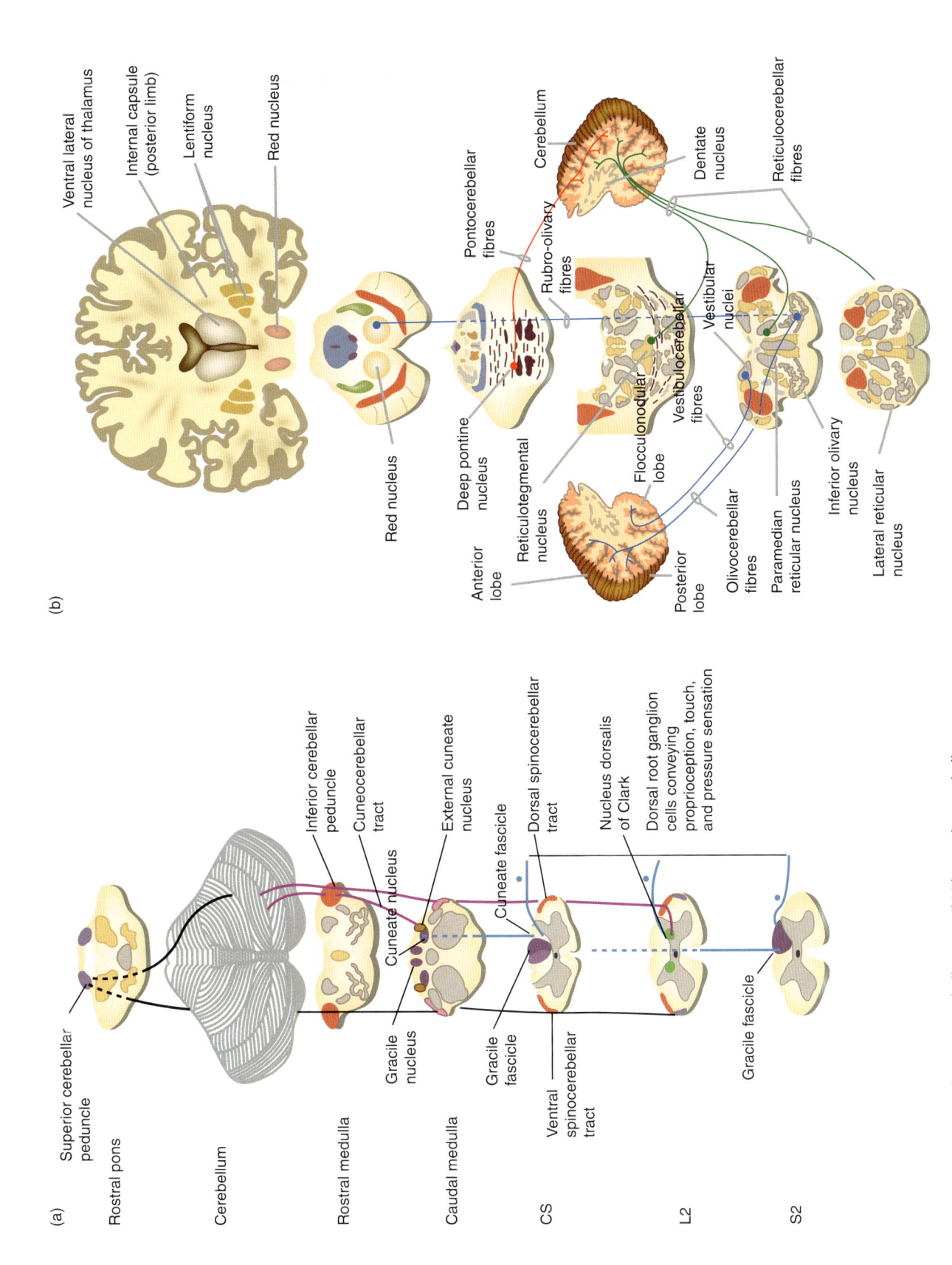

FIGURE 11.6 *(a) The spinocerebellar tract. (b) The cerebrocerebellar tract.*

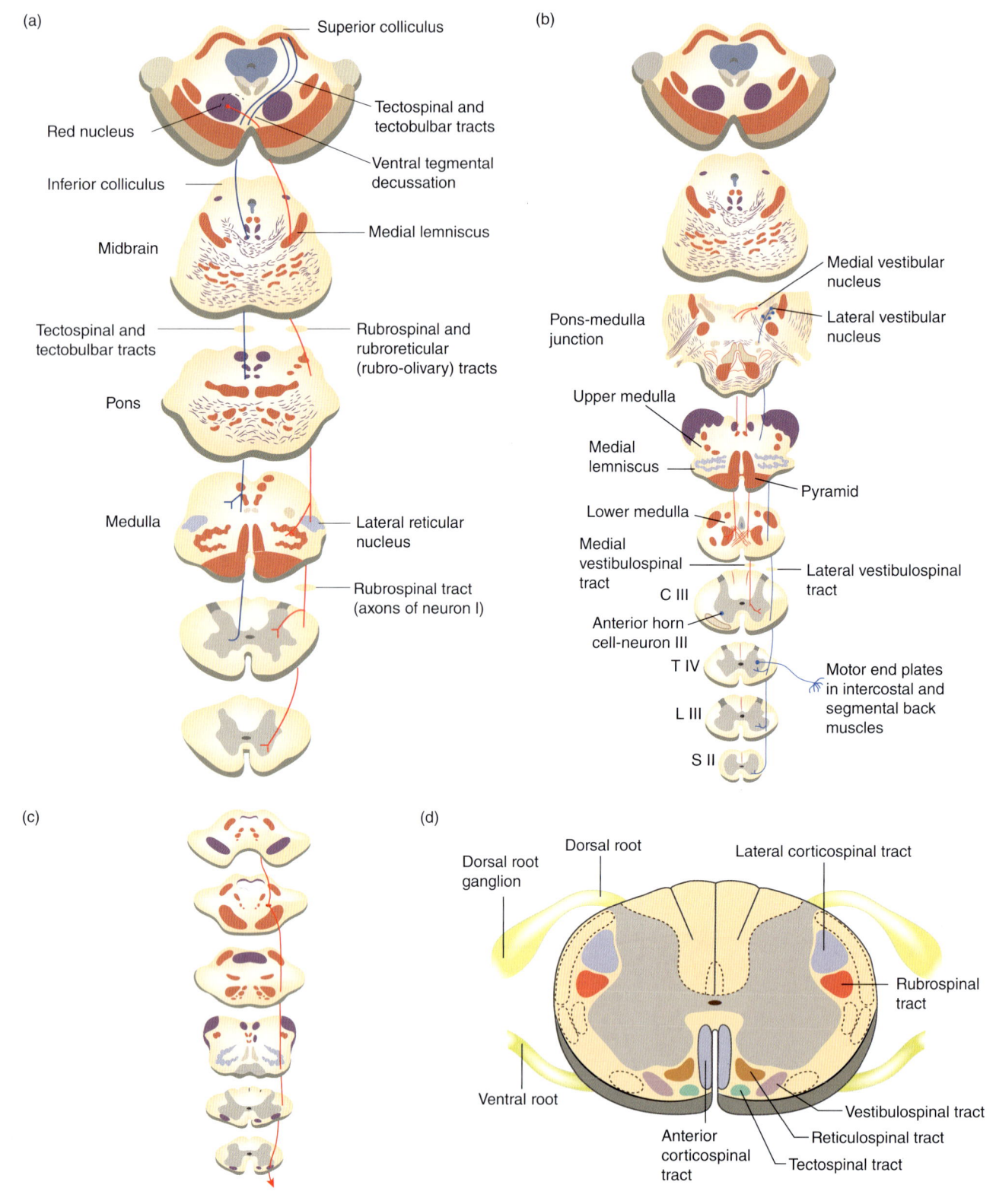

FIGURE 11.7 *(a) Rubrospinal and tectospinal tracts. (b) Vestibulospinal tract. (c) Reticulospinal tract. (d) Cross-section of the spine revealing arrangement of the motor tracts.*

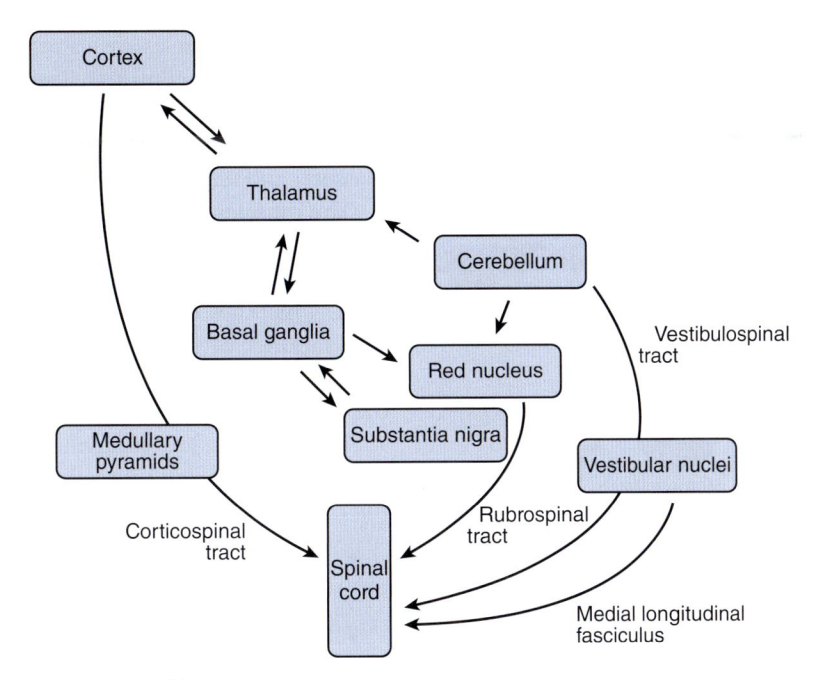

FIGURE 11.8 *Schematic representation of the motor tracts.*

The Pyramidal System

The primary motor cortex (M1) is located in the frontal lobes. It communicates information to the **secondary motor cortex**. The secondary motor cortex comprises the premotor area and the SMA and receives information from the association cortex, which receives sensory inputs.

The primary motor cortex sends messages to the muscles via efferent fibres. The muscles respond, permitting fine motor movement such as writing. The pyramidal tracts can be divided into the corticospinal tract and the corticobulbar tract. The corticospinal tract has axons which project to the spinal cord and when the tract reaches the medulla, numerous axons cross to the contralateral side of the midline (centre line of the brain looking face on). The remainder stay on the same side of the midline (ipsilateral). This crossing over is called **decussation**.

The descending axons have connections with motor neurons that exist in the grey matter of the ventral horns of the spinal cord. Motor neurons are clustered together and innervate a particular skeletal muscle; they are separate from the motor neurons of the muscles.

The Extrapyramidal System

The extrapyramidal system is differentiated from the pyramidal system in that it does not originate from the pyramids of the medulla. The extrapyramidal system receives input from the primary motor cortex and the SMA, and communicates with a diverse set of structures to control gross motor movements. There are two key areas in the extrapyramidal system: the basal ganglia and the cerebellum. They project information via the reticulospinal tract and the rubrospinal tract to the spinal cord.

The rubrospinal tract terminates primarily in the cervical region of the spinal cord, thereby innervating the upper body. The reticulospinal tract innervates the trunk of the body. The vestibulospinal tract projects to the lumbar region of the spine and facilitates the maintenance of balance and upright position. The tectospinal tract descends to the cervical regions of the spinal cord, mediating reflexive responses to sensory input (Figure 11.8).

PASSAGE OF INFORMATION TO MUSCLES

The information, or instructions, from the brain to the descending pathways of the pyramidal and extrapyramidal systems eventually reach their targets – the muscles. However, before we address the communication with the muscles, the superstructure underneath the muscles warrants some attention because this configuration of skeletal joints determines the type of movement that can be produced.

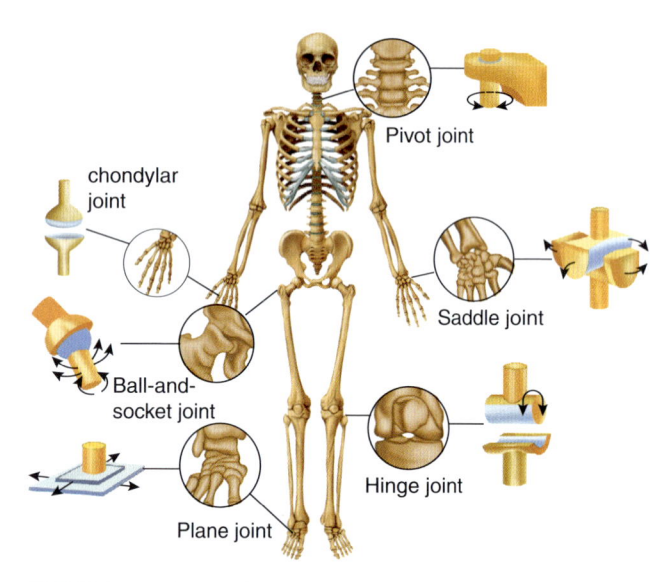

FIGURE 11.9 Synovial joints.

The Skeleton

The human skeleton consists of 206 bones in adulthood and provides support, movement, protection and the production of blood. Between the bones of the skeleton are joints, and the vast majority of joints allow for movement. The joints that allow movement are referred to as **synovial joints**, which hold the bones together whilst allowing for smooth movement without the joints becoming dislocated (under normal circumstances). There are six types of synovial joints in humans (Figure 11.9).

- Hinge joint (e.g. the elbow and knee).
- Pivot joint (e.g. the forearm bones at the elbow).
- Saddle joint (e.g. the metacarpal joint of the thumb).
- Condylar joint (e.g. the knuckles of the hand).
- Plane joint (e.g. the hand and foot).
- Ball and socket joint (e.g. the hip and shoulder).

The joints allow movements in a particular direction and with varying degrees of freedom, i.e. directions of movement (e.g. the ball and socket joint has three degrees of freedom whereas the hinge joint has only one degree of freedom). Allowing these joints to operate are the muscles that are attached to the bones.

The Muscles

There are 600 skeletal muscles varying in size, strength and structure. The muscles are attached to the bone via connective tissue (the **tendons**); the end of the muscle that is attached closest to the midline is called the origin whereas the one furthest from the midline is called the insertion. The muscles are arranged in reciprocal pairings. When one muscle contracts, it stretches the other one and they are therefore antagonistic (e.g. biceps and triceps). Muscles that act together are synergistic (e.g. both the masseter and temporalis muscles work to close the jaw).

The muscles are made up of fibres which run in parallel from the origin to its insertion (Figure 11.10). Muscle fibres are in turn made up of smaller tubes of **myofibrils**, which are chains of proteins (**actin** and **myosin**). The number of fibres depends on the type of muscle, with calf muscles having considerably more fibres than the muscles of the inner ear.

The muscles are controlled by the motor neurons which can be divided into three types differentiated by the muscle fibres that they innervate:

- **alpha (α) motor neurons** – connecting with extrafusal muscle fibres;
- **beta (β) motor neurons** – connecting with extrafusal and intrafusal fibres;
- **gamma (γ) motor neurons** – connecting with intrafusal fibres.

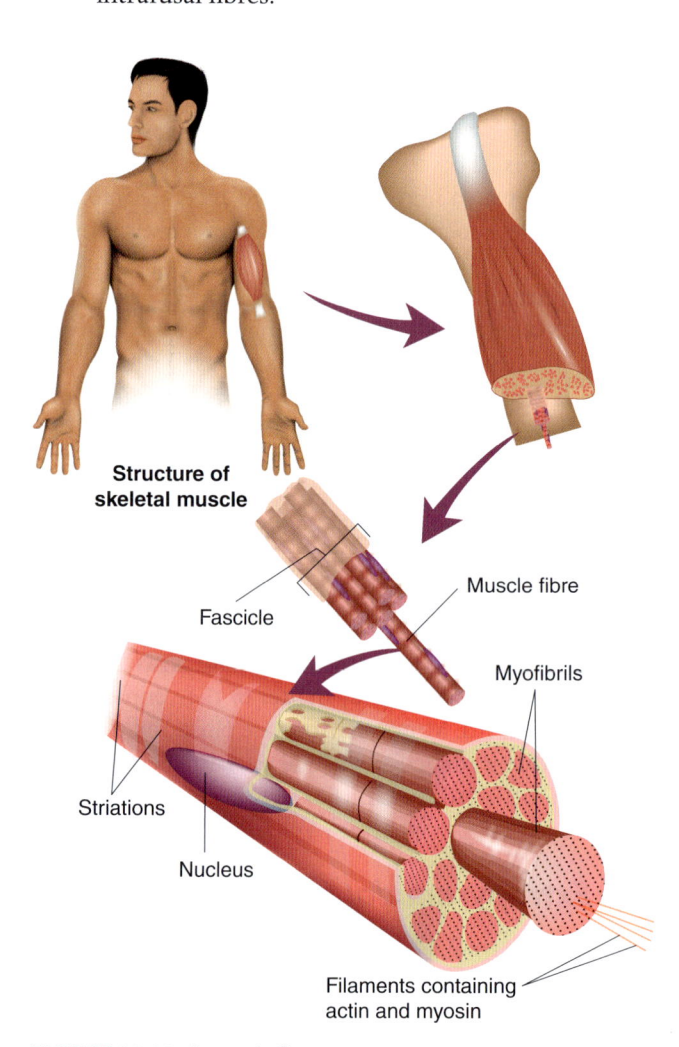

FIGURE 11.10 A muscle fibre.

Intrafusal muscle fibres are muscle spindle fibres found in sensory organs, whereas **extrafusal muscle fibres** are the main skeletal muscles. Each muscle fibre is only innervated by one motor neuron (Figure 11.11).

The alpha motor neurons are divided into three functionally different types:

- S type – slow-contracting motor units;
- FR – fast-contracting, fatigue-resistant motor units;
- FF – fast-contracting, fatiguable motor units.

Neural information is conveyed down the descending tracts of motor neurons by the action potential, the speed of which is greatly increased due to the myelination of these axons. The effect of demyelination is most notable in multiple sclerosis (see Chapter 4). When the action potential reaches the terminal of the neuron, chemical transmission perpetuates the information from the neuron to the muscle.

Neurochemical Activation of the Muscles

Neural messages are communicated at the **neuromuscular junction** (NMJ), where the action potential releases acetylcholine (ACh) (Figure 11.12). The ACh has to traverse the synapses to reach the cell membrane of the muscle cell (called the **sarcolemma**). The sarcolemma increases its surface area by the addition of postjunctional faults or invaginations of the cell membrane. The postjunctional sarcolemma is referred to as the **motor endplate** and includes the ACh receptors. The muscles react to ACh via **nicotinic** and **muscarinic receptors**, producing excitatory postsynaptic potentials. The action potential from the motor neuron terminals therefore produces an action potential in the muscle fibre caused by an influx of Na^+. The propagation of the action potential within the muscle fibre, which is comparatively slow compared to the neuron, initiates the muscle contractions.

Whilst each muscle fibre is only activated by one motor neuron, a single motor neuron can connect to several muscle fibres; this is referred to as a **motor unit**. The number of fibres that are activated by a single motor neuron is referred to as the innervation ratio. This is similar to the convergence seen with rods and cones into the retinal ganglion cells, in which rods have high convergence (many rods converge on one cell) and cones have low convergence (few cones converge on any one cell), thereby allowing a high resolution and detail with the cones. So, a low innervation ratio means that one motor

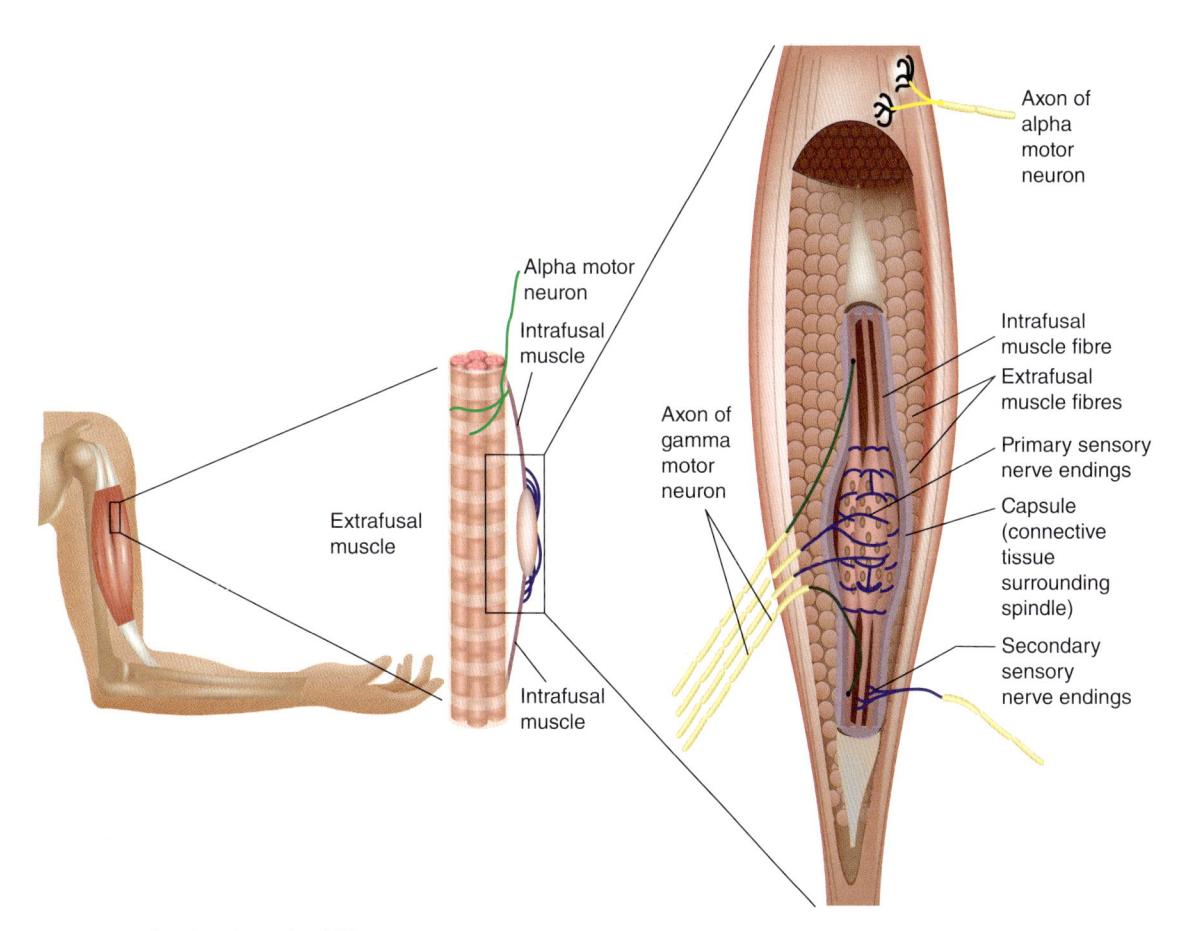

FIGURE 11.11 *Extrafusal and intrafusal fibres.*

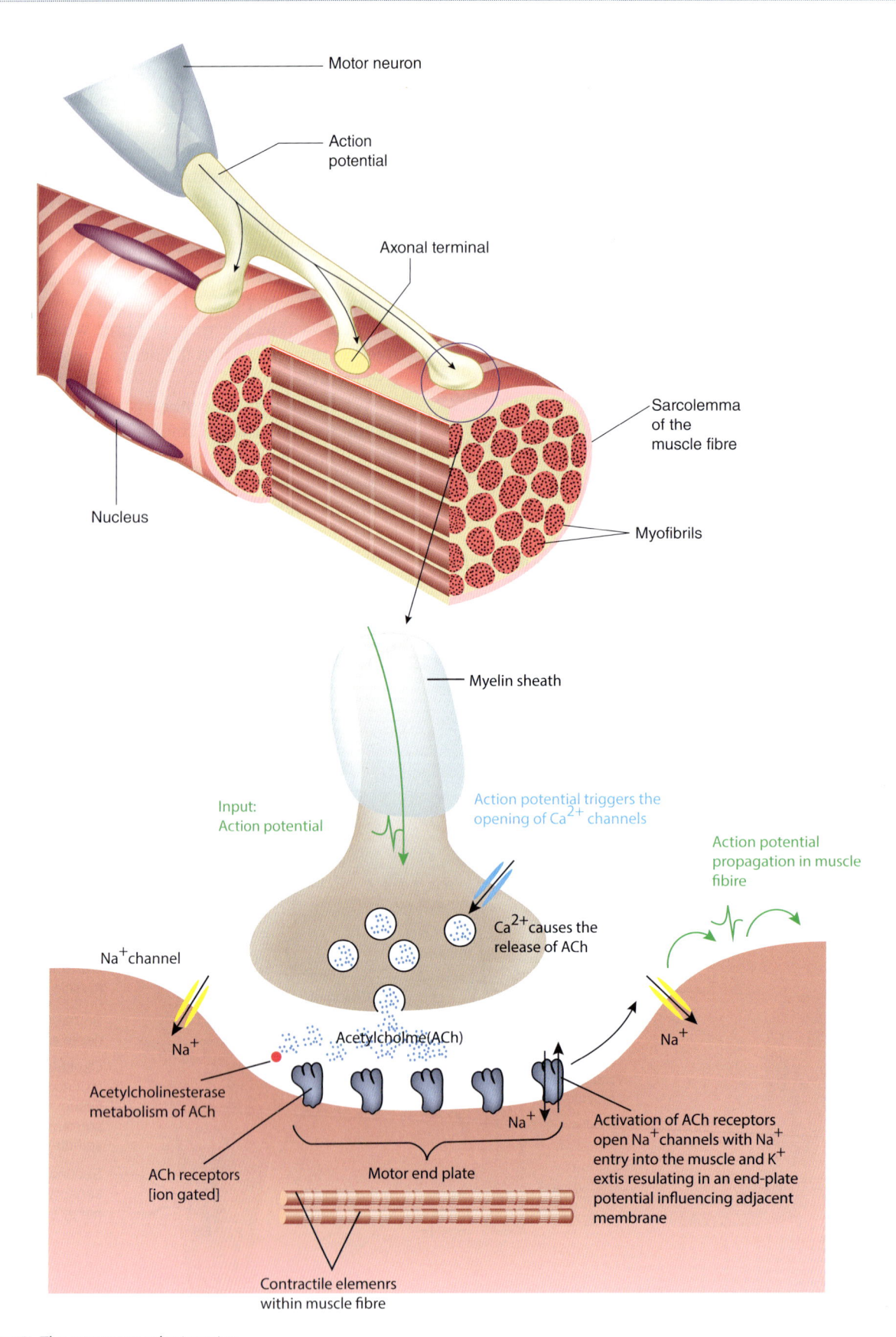

FIGURE 11.12 *The neuromuscular junction.*

neuron connects with only a small number of fibres. This ratio is evident in motor behaviour involving fine and precise movement. A high innervation ratio, in which one motor neuron connects with many muscle fibres simultaneously, allows for more gross movements.

FEEDBACK

The whole process of receiving sensory input and acting upon it is a **sensorimotor loop**. The muscles send back information that helps guide future components of the motor programmes. This information is integrated with other sensory modalities.

Knowing where the body is and what it is doing is essential for successful execution of the motor programme. Being able to perceive where one's body is in space and how the movements are related is called **proprioception**. Sensory information is transported back to the brain by myelinated axons. There are two kinds of proprioceptive sites providing feedback: the muscle spindles and Golgi tendon organs.

The **muscle spindles** are sensory receptors that detect changes in the length of the muscle. There are two types of receptor endings on the muscle spindles: primary sensory endings and secondary sensory endings. The primary sensory ending of the muscle spindle is wrapped around the central region of the intrafusal fibre, whereas the secondary sensory endings are located towards the ends of the fibre. The information from these receptors is integrated and informs the brain about the muscles, e.g. if a load is put on a muscle by picking something up that is heavy then the biceps will stretch and the spindles will trigger action potentials that spread to the spinal cord and the brain. The firing rates of the sensory endings are modulated by changes in muscle length. The primary sensory endings are activated early on in the stretch movement and then slow down. The secondary sensory endings are slower to change during the early phase of activity but are sensitive to prolonged or static muscle activity. The muscle spindles in this latter category need to be about the same length as the muscle itself. In order to maintain a similar length, gamma motor neurons stimulate the spindles to alter their sensitivity, to keep them taut and sensitive to stretch and therefore able to provide feedback.

Golgi tendon organs are receptors located between the muscle and the tendon (Figure 11.13). They respond to muscles operating on large loads that will stretch the tendons. Stretching the Golgi tendon organs increases their firing rate. The Golgi tendon organs also prevent overload, which could result in damage to the muscles, because they inhibit motor neurons that pull on the tendons.

Thus, feedback from the muscles provides the individual with information by which they can modulate their motor behaviour. Furthermore, this proprioceptive information is integrated with input from the sensory modalities and also the higher order plans and intentions.

CONTROL AND AGENCY

This chapter has been about the voluntary control of motor behaviour. It has not been about reflexes (which are mediated via interneurons – see Chapters 8 and 10). It has not been about unconscious movement or movement without intention. Voluntary movement involves a complex sequence of events organized and executed in order to obtain a goal position. We move because we want to and because we want to obtain a certain position that will ultimately achieve our final goal. However, there are individuals who have little control over some of their limbs (see Box 11.3). Being in control means that the motor cortex and associated regions are activated and integrated with executive functions and motivational systems. This subject is considered in more detail in Chapter 18 in which the experiments of Benjamin Libet are discussed further. Libet, Wright et al. (1983) challenge the idea that the decision to move precedes the mechanical processes that allow the movement to happen.

SUMMARY

Being able to move is something most of us take for granted. Our conscious decisions are orchestrated by the motor cortex, cerebellum and basal ganglia to allow the signals governing movement to be sent to the muscles (Figure 11.14).

The regions of the brain involved still require further functional elucidation. The complexities of the systems are becoming more apparent and more functional roles are being ascribed to them. A considerable amount of our understanding of motor behaviour comes from animals, but also those unfortunate enough to suffer from disorders that affect movement, e.g. Huntington's disease and Parkinson's disease. Both these and many other motor diseases have helped us to understand specific parts of the large motor system. However, the majority of these diseases remain in need of not only cure but long-term effective treatments.

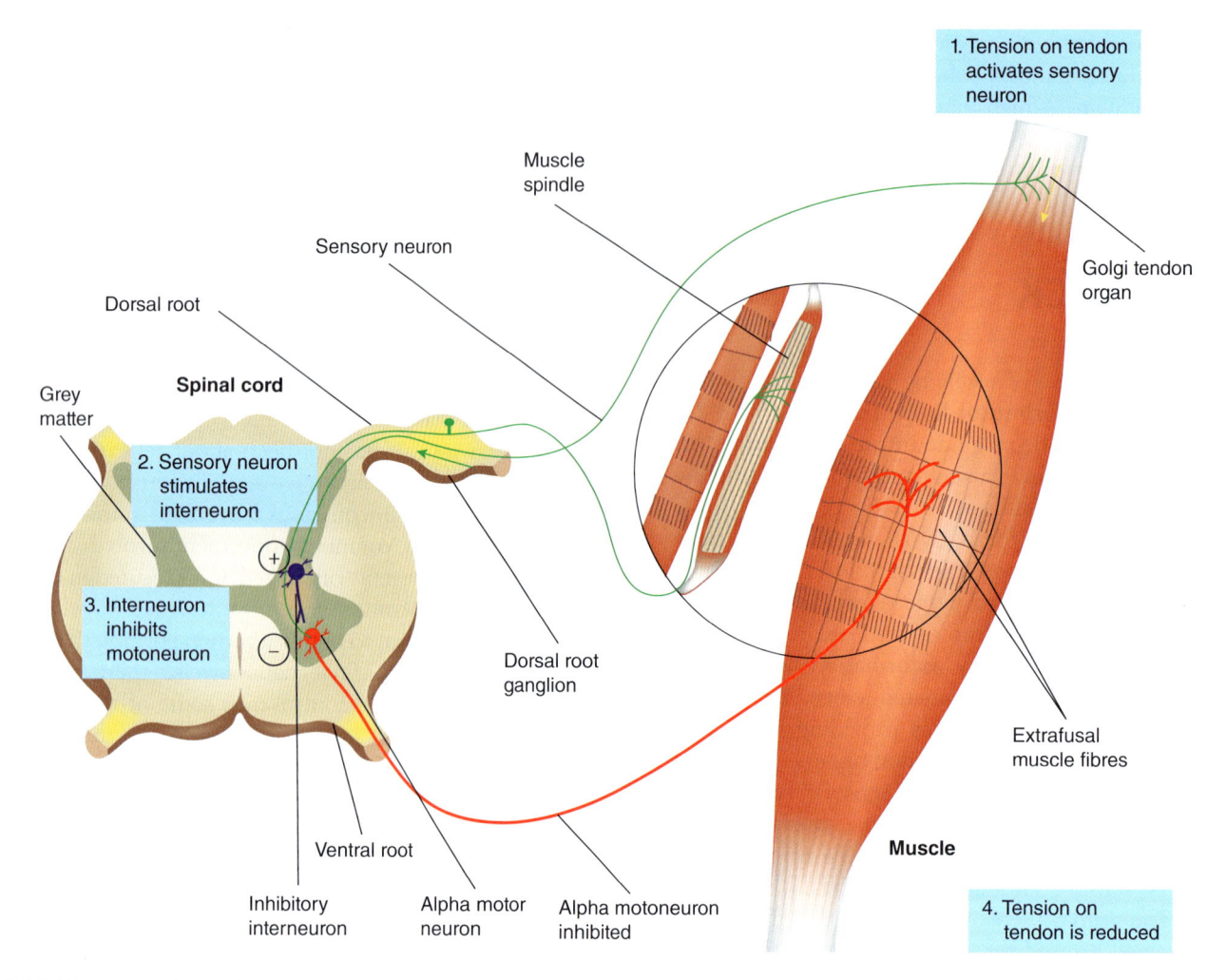

FIGURE 11.13 *Golgi tendon organs.*

BOX 11.3 THE ANARCHIC HAND

Anarchic hand syndrome was first described by Sergio Della Sala and colleagues (1991), although Goldstein in 1908 described something similar, but Della Sala coined its striking name (see Della Sala & Marchetti, 2005). Anarchic hand syndrome can be differentiated from a similar syndrome called alien hand syndrome as anarchic hand syndrome is characterized as an inability to control one's hand, whereas alien hand syndrome is the inability to recognize one's ownership of the hand (Marchetti & Della Sala, 1998). In anarchic hand syndrome, there are complex movements of the arm which are goal directed and well executed but unintended (Della Sala et al., 1994). Della Sala's patients are reported to have no control over the actions of their hand. For example, one patient (patient GP) could not stop her left hand scavenging for fish bones from the leftovers on a plate and putting them in her mouth. In an attempt to prevent the left hand acting, she used the right hand to restrain it (Della Sala et al., 1994). In another patient, the frustration of not being able to control the arm resulted in verbal and physical violence directed at the offending arm (Della Sala et al., 1991).

Although rare, anarchic hand syndrome is interesting on two counts: firstly, its psychobiological underpinnings and secondly, philosophically, with considerations of agency and control. The initial neuropathological

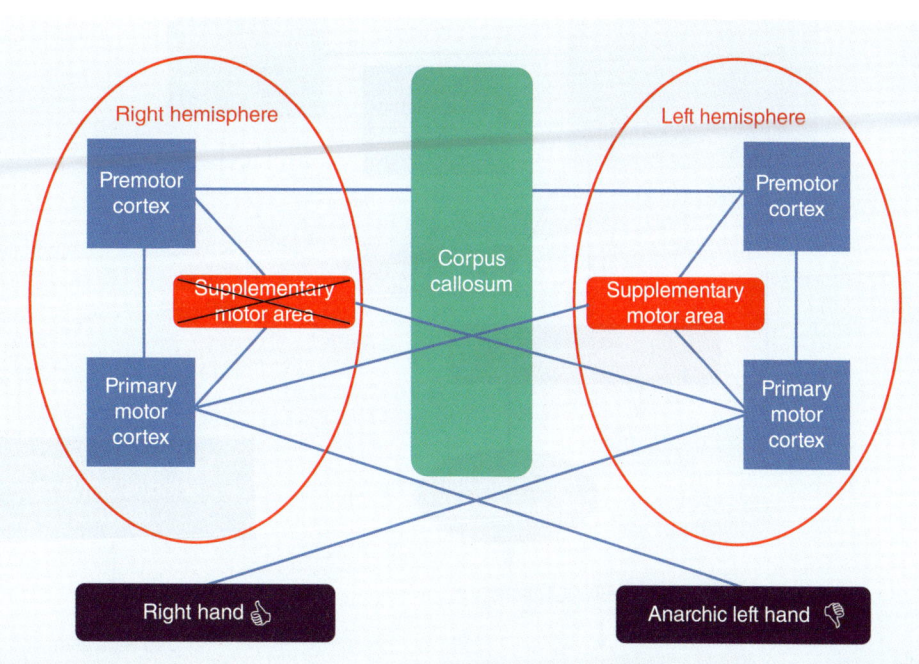

FIGURE 11.3.1 *Mechanisms of anarchic hand after a lesion of the right supplementary motor area.*
Source: Based on Della Sala, S., & Marchetti, C. (2005). Anarchic hand. In H. J. Freund, M. Jeannerod, M. Hallett & R. Leiguarda (Eds.), *Higher-order motor disorders: From neuroanatomy and neurobiology to clinical neurology* (pp. 291–301). Oxford, UK: Oxford University Press.

hypothesis of anarchic hand syndrome centred on the disconnection of the left and right hemispheres through the corpus callosum (see Della Sala & Marchetti, 2005). Della Sala et al. (1994), in a review of 39 cases, noted that the majority had lesions near the medial wall of the frontal lobe centred on the corpus callosum and the SMA contralateral to the anarchic hand with lesions. However, the corpus callosum was intact in a number of patients, thereby casting doubt on its central role in anarchic hand (Della Sala & Marchetti, 2005). It has also been suggested that lesions of the SMA provide an imbalance of activity compared with the premotor cortex (Della Sala & Marchetti, 2005). The SMA is normally responsible for voluntary actions and the inhibition of automated responses, whereas the intact premotor cortex responds to external stimuli. Therefore a lesion of the SMA renders the contralateral hand exclusively responsive to external stimuli which cannot be inhibited as an unwanted behaviour.

When the lesion of the SMA is unilateral, the symptoms of anarchic hand syndrome emerge; however, rare cases of bilateral lesions of the SMA resulted in utilization behaviour in which the patient is responsive to the sensory input of an object, promoting interaction with the object (see Chapter 12; Boccardi et al., 2002). The frontoparietal networks were shown in an fMRI study to be selectively active when there was a mismatch between the observed and performed action in normal participants (Leube et al., 2003). If there are lesions of this network, then mismatches are less likely to be detected.

A defect in agency has been identified in a case of anarchic hand syndrome arising from right hemisphere parietal damage (Jenkinson et al., 2014).

Pacherie (2007) attempts to explain the difference between utilization behaviour patients and anarchic hand syndrome in terms of agency. She argues that patients have lost the capacity to inhibit stimulus-driven actions but the difference between the two disorders is that utilization behaviour patients have lost the capacity to use endogenous intentions, whereas anarchic hand syndrome patients have not lost that capacity because they have retained the ability to evoke willed actions. Therefore utilization behaviour patients:

> . . . have lost the capacity for full-blown agency: they can neither form nor implement willed intentions and the self-agentive awareness is downsized accordingly. Having lost the capacity to will their actions, they have also lost the capacity to experience them as willed. [Anarchic hand syndrome] patients have not lost the capacity to form willed intentions but they have lost the capacity to implement them when they involve movements of the anarchic hand. Their self-agentive awareness reflects their motor impairment: they experience their will as powerless. (Pacherie, 2007, p.216)

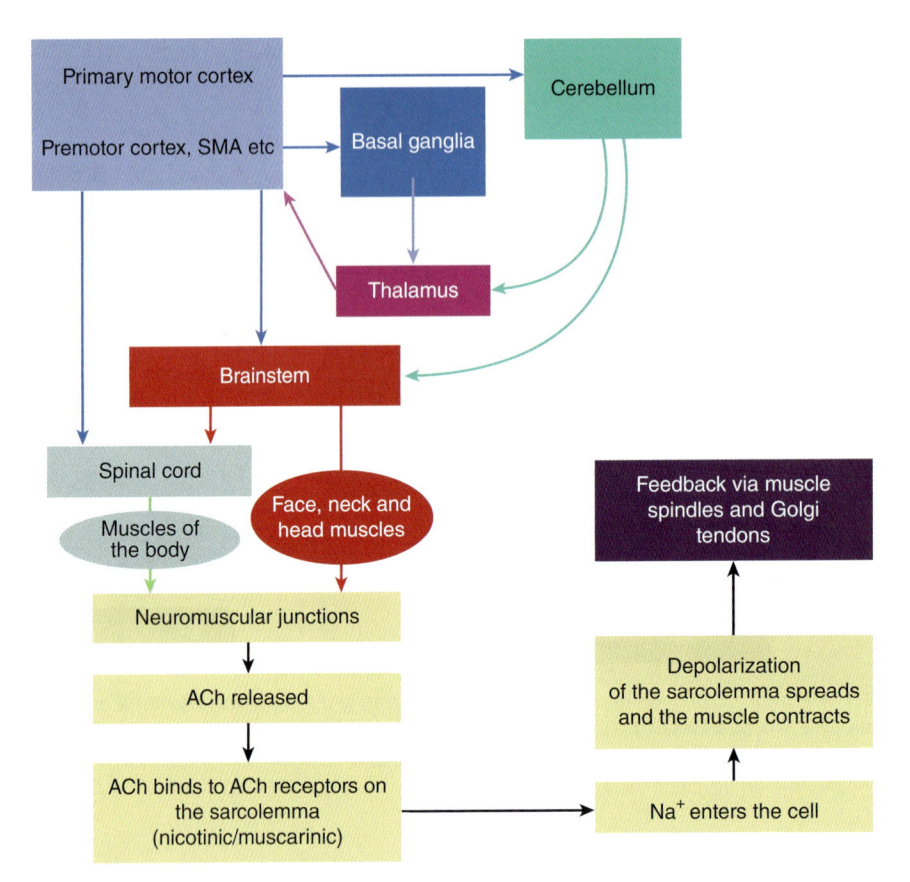

FIGURE 11.14 *Summary of the motor pathway. ACh, acetylcholine.*

In terms of psychology, motor behaviour is often neglected in research methodologies. It is critically important to understand that virtually every experiment involving a response from a participant requires a motor act. In particular, cognitive experiments which require a motor response to be delivered as fast as possible in response to a stimulus need to be free from the contamination of motor artefacts. Even the spoken word involves motor behaviour; indeed, it requires the most complex set of muscle movements and neural innervation. Therefore, in any research methodology one should always account for straightforward motor behaviour.

LEARNING OUTCOME QUESTIONS

You should be able to answer the following questions.
- Describe the process from initiation to execution of a motor act.
- Describe the neuroanatomy and functional neuroanatomy of the basal ganglia.
- What has Huntington's disease told us about motor behaviour?
- What is the importance of proprioception in ongoing motor behaviours?

FURTHER READING

Graziano, M. (2006). The organization of behavioral repertoire in motor cortex. *Annual Review of Neuroscience, 29,* 105–134.

Haggard, P. (2008). Human volition: towards a neuroscience of will. *Nature Reviews Neuroscience, 9*(12), 934–946.

Manuel, M., & Zytnicki, D. (2011). Alpha, beta and gamma motoneurons: functional diversity in the motor system's final pathway. *Journal of Integrated Neuroscience, 10*(3), 243–276.

Nachev, P., Kennard, C., & Husain, M. (2008). Functional role of the supplementary and pre-supplementary motor areas. *Nature Reviews Neuroscience, 9*(11), 856–869.

Paus, T. (2001). Primate anterior cingulate cortex: where motor control, drive and cognition interface. *Nature Reviews Neuroscience, 2*(6), 417–424.

Tresilian, J. (2012). *Sensorimotor control and learning.* Basingstoke UK: Palgrave Macmillan.

Walker, F. O. (2007). Huntington's disease. *Lancet, 369*(9557), 218–228.

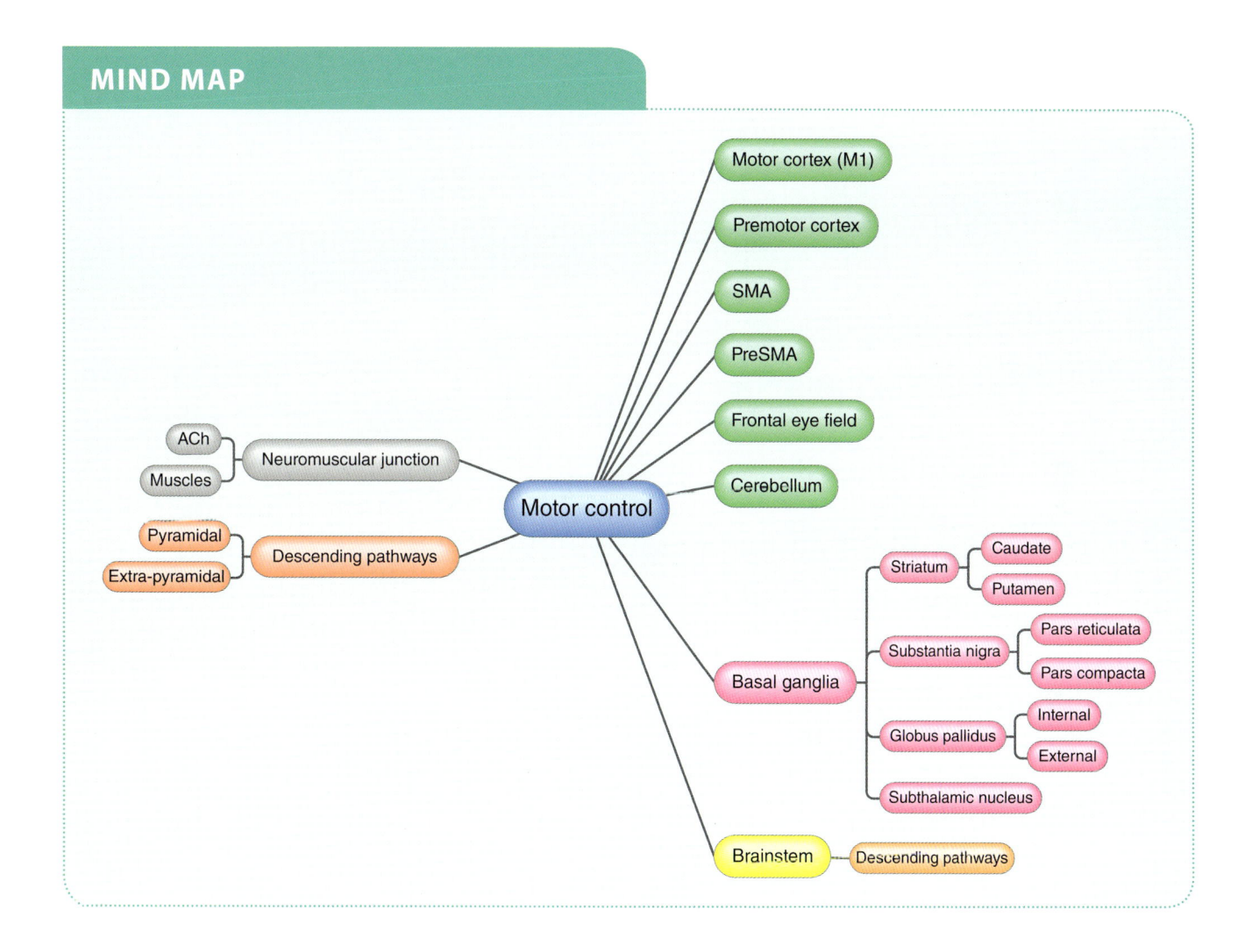

MIND MAP

Motor control
- Neuromuscular junction
  - ACh
  - Muscles
- Descending pathways
  - Pyramidal
  - Extra-pyramidal
- Motor cortex (M1)
- Premotor cortex
- SMA
- PreSMA
- Frontal eye field
- Cerebellum
- Basal ganglia
  - Striatum
    - Caudate
    - Putamen
  - Substantia nigra
    - Pars reticulata
    - Pars compacta
  - Globus pallidus
    - Internal
    - External
  - Subthalamic nucleus
- Brainstem
  - Descending pathways

12 Executive Functions

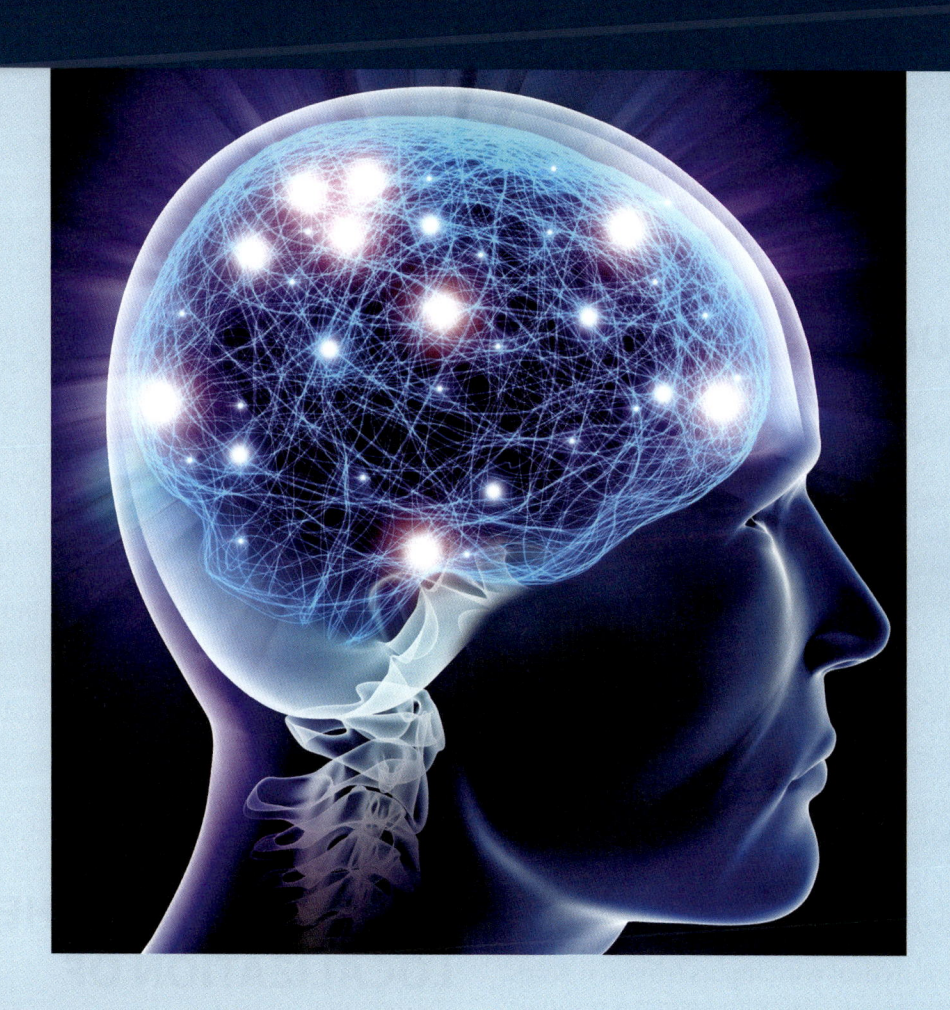

ANATOMY OF THE CHAPTER

This chapter will highlight the following.

- The role of neuropsychological tests in identifying cognitive and social processes.
- The study of brain-damaged patients to determine the role of the frontal lobes.
- The use of neuroimaging to identify regions of the frontal lobe and cortex involved in different processes being measured in neuropsychological tests.
- The role of the frontal lobes in controlling behaviour.
- Theories of the frontal lobe.

INTRODUCTION 316

FRONTAL LOBES, EVOLUTION AND THE LOCALIZATION OF HUMANITY 316

LESIONS AND IMAGING 317

THE FRONTAL LOBES: DAMAGE AND THE DYSEXECUTIVE SYNDROME 322

THEORIES DESCRIBING FRONTAL LOBE FUNCTION 328

SUMMARY 339

LEARNING OUTCOMES

1. To be able to evaluate different theories of frontal lobe function.
2. To understand the function of the frontal lobes.
3. To understand how case studies have informed theories.

INTRODUCTION

Executive functions (**EFs**) are a collection of high-level cognitive processes that control and regulate other lower-level processes; the essence of EFs is that they are the manager of many workers, which together produce a final product (behaviour). The term 'executive function' was introduced by Luria (1966, 1973b, 1980) who distinguished three functional units in the brain:

- *arousal* – limbic and reticular systems (motivation);
- *receiving, processing and storing information* – postrolandic cortical areas (memory); and
- *programming, controlling and verifying activity* – prefrontal cortex (EF).

Executive functions deal with inputs from the world around us, organize the inputs and select a response output (behaviour/symptom). Thus, EFs are sandwiched mysteriously between perception (input; see Chapter 10) and motor control (output; see Chapter 11).

The exact nature of EFs is hard to define. In fact, there are many definitions, but as Jurado and Rosselli (2007) suggest, the common definition of EFs can be divided into four components: goal formation, planning, execution of goal-related plans, and effective performance. Thus, EFs are involved in:

- the identification of what we want/need to do/achieve;
- how we are going to go about achieving the objective;
- putting these plans into a sequence of actions; and
- monitoring performance and correcting mistakes or changing plans when the evidence suggests a plan is faulty.

We are not born with a set of fully formed EFs; they develop throughout childhood, and can decline in old age. The development of EFs in childhood and adolescence is correlated with neural changes in the frontal lobe. These periods of growth occur between birth and two years, then between seven and nine years and finally between 16 and 19 years (see Jurado & Rosselli, 2007). Thus, the neural development at different stages has an impact on behaviour and cognition.

FRONTAL LOBES, EVOLUTION AND THE LOCALIZATION OF HUMANITY

The frontal lobe is the most recent evolutionary development of the brain (see Chapters 3 and 5). Furthermore, its functional development is also the last to reach maturity. Thus, the human has a fully functional frontal lobe by approximately the age of 25 (Sowell et al., 2003). Such is the importance of the frontal lobes in human evolution that Stuss and Benson (1984) quote the assertion of the neurologist Tilney (1928) that 'the entire period of human evolutionary existence could be considered the age of the frontal lobe' (p.4). The skulls from our ancestors demonstrate how the human frontal lobe has evolved, with straight foreheads superseding the earlier brow ridges, allowing for the expansion of the cortex (Figure 12.1).

The evolution of the frontal lobe signifies a departure from subhuman species, in that the brains of

CHAPTER 12 EXECUTIVE FUNCTIONS

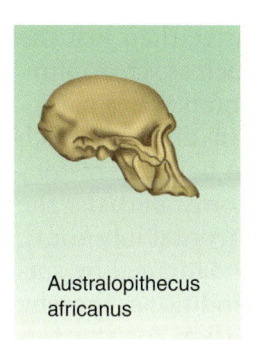

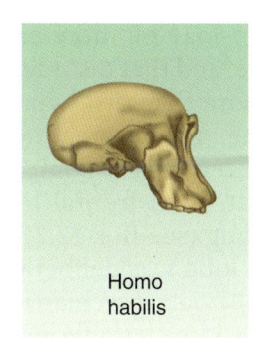

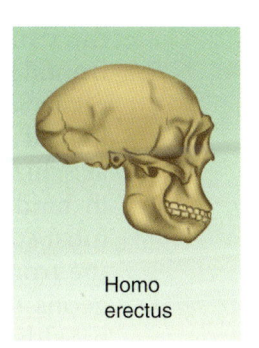

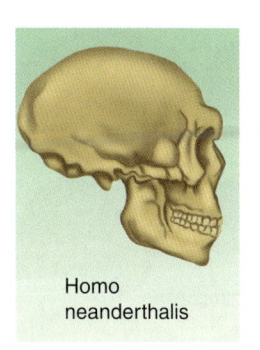

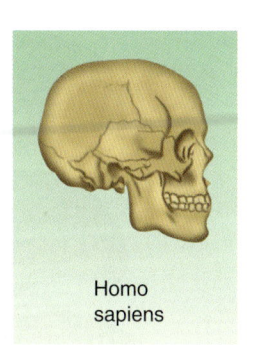

Australopithecus africanus | Homo habilis | Homo erectus | Homo neanderthalis | Homo sapiens

FIGURE 12.1 *The evolution of the human skull. Using the skulls of our ancestors, we can build a picture of the development of the frontal lobes.*

humans are most characteristically different in their architecture within the cortex (Figure 12.2).

Humans have a large brain and therefore a large frontal lobe in comparison to our closest ancestors, the apes (bonobos, chimpanzee, gorillas, orangutans and gibbons) (Figure 12.3) (Semendeferi & Damasio, 2000; Semendeferi et al., 1997). However, the size of the frontal lobe relative to the overall volume of the brain did not differ across humans and apes, suggesting that the frontal lobe did not become larger after humans split from their ancestral line (Semendeferi & Damasio, 2000). That is not to say that other animals are devoid of a cortex, but it is the human cortex, and in particular the frontal lobe, that provides us with our unique humanity.

LESIONS AND IMAGING

The early studies of frontal lobe function were based on case studies of people who had injuries to the brain. Within the neuropsychological literature, there are two famous case studies: HM, providing insight into memory, and the even more notorious Phineas Gage. The case of Phineas Gage highlights numerous aspects of frontal lobe functioning (see Box 12.1). Although Phineas Gage lived many years ago, people still continue to have similar accidents; for example, nail guns produce extensive lesions in the brain as when the nail enters the soft tissue, it rotates, destroying a large pathway of tissue.

Bianchi (1895, 1922) supported the important role of the frontal lobes after lesions in monkeys and dogs prompted him to conclude that 'The frontal lobes are the seat of co-ordination and fusion of the incoming and outgoing products of the several sensory and motor areas of the cortex' (Bianchi, 1922, p.34).

There are also numerous disorders associated with hypofrontality that demonstrate deficits in EF, e.g. schizophrenia, autism and ADHD. When one is considering the case studies and also the clinical cases of hypofrontality, one has to remember that

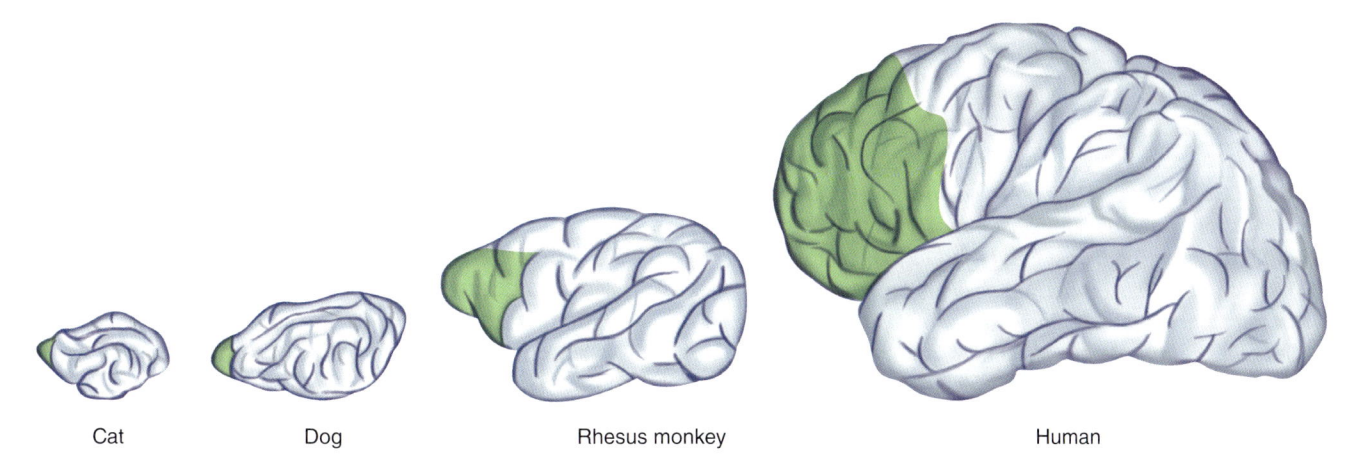

Cat | Dog | Rhesus monkey | Human

FIGURE 12.2 *The frontal lobe (shown in green) in different species.*

the damage may be more extensive than just the frontal lobe, and that disorders such as schizophrenia have more than just hypofrontality as a pathological state. Yet the treatment of disorders such as schizophrenia has a somewhat barbaric history in hindsight, with frontal lobotomy perhaps the most startling (see Box 12.2). In frontal lobotomy, the frontal lobe was deliberately damaged by surgeons to alleviate psychiatric conditions, thereby providing a large sample population for the further investigation of frontal lobe function.

Perhaps the most extensive use of neuroimaging in cognitive neuroscience has been to evaluate EFs in normal populations. Neuroimaging allows for the correlates of neural activity to be mapped on to task performance. The frontal lobe can also be divided into subregions (based on their position, e.g. dorsolateral prefrontal cortex, or their functions, e.g. premotor cortex) with the prefrontal cortex getting a considerable amount of the attention (Figure 12.4). Furthermore, the lobes of the brain are functionally and anatomically lateralized, for example with language being dominant in the left hemisphere (see Chapter 20). One also has to remember that the frontal lobes are also connected to many of the other brain regions and changes in behaviour may be seen downstream. According to Damasio (1985):

> The frontal lobes . . . have diverse anatomical units, each with distinct connections to other cortical and subcortical structures and to each other. Disregard for this heterogeneity has not helped to unravel the so-called riddle of the frontal lobes. As a consequence, attempts to shape the diverse manifestations of frontal lobe dysfunction have been somewhat unsatisfactory. (p.339)

Relevant connections include:

- inputs from association cortex (occipital, parietal, temporal and olfactory areas);
- convergence and integration of higher-order input from all sensory modalities;
- reciprocal connections in which prefrontal processing affects perceptual processing;
- limbic connections (memory/emotion), most notably the orbitofrontal cortex (or the ventromedial prefrontal cortex, to give its neuroanatomical location); and
- input to premotor areas which control/programme behaviour.

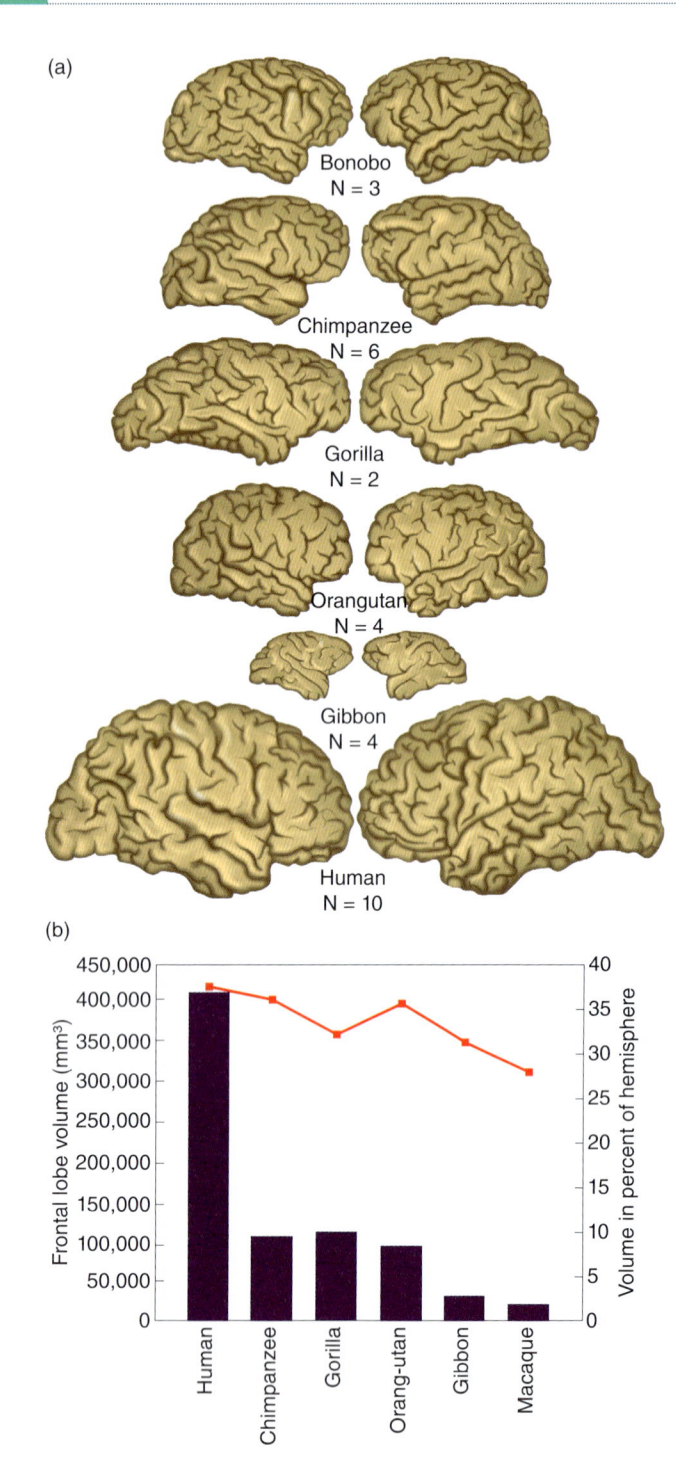

FIGURE 12.3 *The frontal lobes are developed in different hominoids. (a) A three-dimensional reconstruction from an MRI study on several hominoid species, including humans. N = number of animals. (b) The human brain is considerably bigger than that of other hominoids but as a proportion of the whole brain, the frontal lobes differ little across species.*
Sources: Semendeferi, K., & Damasio, H. (2000). The brain and its main anatomical subdivisions in living hominoids using magnetic resonance imaging. *Journal of Human Evolution*, 38(2), 317–332.

BOX 12.1: PHINEAS GAGE

Phineas Gage (aged 25) was a construction worker on the railroad in America. On 13 September 1848 in Cavendish, Vermont, he was packing an explosive charge into rock using a tamping iron. Although there is some debate about the sequence of events, what ultimately happened was that a spark ignited the charge and the iron rod flew through the air like a missile and hit Gage. The rod entered Gage's face below the left eye socket, penetrated his skull and brain and exited through the top of the skull (Figure 12.1.1).

Surprisingly, Gage survived and regained consciousness almost immediately. He was treated by Dr John Harlow who is credited with providing the care that led to his survival (Harlow, 1868). Harlow treated the infection that developed and Gage's condition improved (see Garcia-Molina (2012) for a brief review). Harlow (1848) published a study of the accident and its immediate aftermath under the title 'Passage of an iron rod through the head' with no mention of the neural damage.

Damasio et al. (1994) performed a three-dimensional reconstruction of the lesion site using the skull of Phineas Gage. The reconstruction provided evidence that his prefrontal cortex was damaged and in particular the ventral medial prefrontal area, subsequently thought to be confined to the left frontal lobe (Ratiu et al., 2004). The effects of the lesion should not be seen in isolation as the damage would have a profound effects on cortical connections.

In a computational analysis of brain connectivity, Van Horn et al. (2012) compared data derived from normal right-handed males with a model of the damage suffered by Phineas Gage (Figure 12.1.1(b)). The figures adapted from van Horn's analysis show a rich diversity of connections within the normal group whereas those connections are severely compromised in the model of Gage.

In a follow-up publication discussing Gage's emotional state, Harlow (1868) reported that he was:

> ... fitful, irreverent, indulging at times in the greatest profanity (which was not previously discussed), manifesting but little deference to his fellows, impatient of restraint or advice when it conflicts with his desires, at times pertinaciously obstinate yet capricious and vacillating, devising many plans for future operation which no sooner arranged than they are abandoned in turn for others appearing more feasible.

Perhaps this should not be surprising as recent research has identified the ventromedial prefrontal as an area of the brain whose size is linked to the ability to understand others and interact with large social networks (Lewis et al., 2011).

Included in Harlow's statement are a second set of changes, termed 'intellectual':

- impaired integration of behaviour over time;
- impaired recent memory;
- loss of abstract thinking; and
- inability to plan and follow a course of action through.

Although Gage was more noted for his personality/social changes, it has been argued that the effect of damage to the ventromedial prefrontal cortex in terms of cognitive decrements has been elusive.

Cato et al. (2004) have presented another case study in which there was damage to the same region of the brain as Gage. CD, a 26-year-old man, was involved in a motor accident after a landmine exploded underneath his car. The damage was restricted to the ventromedial prefrontal cortex and was evaluated with a neuropsychological test battery, in which many tests indicated normal cognitive functioning. However, executive functioning tasks that involved multiple steps, e.g. Wisconsin Card Sorting Test have revealed cognitive deficits. Thus the more sophisticated analysis of cognitive deficits indicates that the deficits become more evident with the increase in task complexity and demand.

In a computational model of Gage, loss of the ventromedial prefrontal cortex results in emotionally influenced decision making (Wagar & Thagard, 2004) by disconnecting the nucleus accumbens and the amygdala from the higher cortical region. The disconnection of the amygdala prevents information from being processed via the nucleus accumbens that would normally be able to promote behaviours beneficial to long-term survival. Thus, consideration of decisions is limited and driven by the emotional valence of the trigger stimuli.

Phineas Gage died in 1860 of a seizure. Since 1848 this case study has captivated the minds of scientists and informed multitudes of controlled experiments.

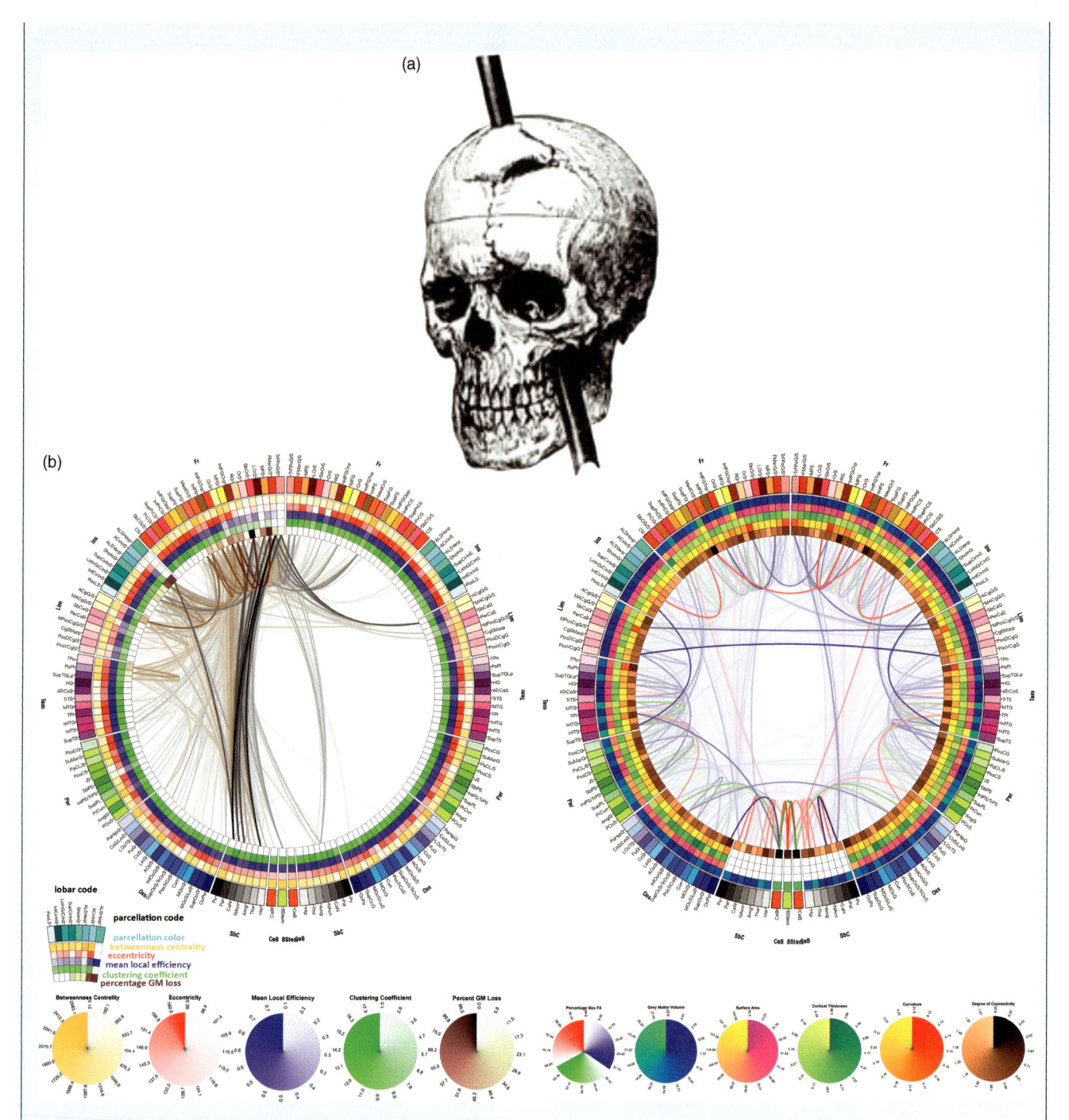

FIGURE 12.1.1 (a) A drawing of Phineas Gage's injury from Harlow's paper. (b) Connections (connectogram) of Phineas Gage's brain (left panel) and normal males (right panel). The outermost ring shows the various brain regions arranged by lobe (fr, frontal; ins, insula; lim, limbic; tem, temporal; par, parietal; occ, occipital; nc, non-cortical; bs, brainstem; CeB, cerebellum) and further ordered anterior to posterior basedupon the centres of mass of these regions. The left half of the connectogram figure represents the left hemisphere of the brain, whereas the right half represents the right hemisphere with the exception of the brainstem, which occurs at the bottom, 6 o'clock position of the graph. The set of five rings (from the outside inward) reflect average (i) regional volume, (ii) cortical thickness, (iii) surface area, and (iv) cortical curvature of each parcellated cortical region. The innermost ring displays the relative degree of connectivity of that region with respect to WM fibres found to emanate from this region, providing a measure of how connected that region is with all other regions in the parcellation scheme. Circular 'colour bars' at the bottom of the figure describe the numeric scale for each regional geometric measurement and its associated colour on that anatomical metric ring of the connectogram.
Source: (b) Van Horn, J. D., Irimia, A., Torgerson, C. M., Chambers, M. C., Kikinis, R., & Toga, A. W. (2012). Mapping connectivity damage in the case of Phineas Gage. *PLoS One, 7*(5), e37454.

BOX 12.2: FRONTAL LOBOTOMY

It seems barbaric now but surgeons would destroy the prefrontal cortex of humans in order to treat various psychological ailments.

As reported by Kotowicz (2005), between 1888 and 1889 Burckhardt performed frontal lobotomy on six patients in an asylum, and was severely criticized. In 1936, Egas Moniz reported the results of operations on 20 patients. He used a leucotome which could be inserted into boreholes in the skull with a plunger (a little bit like the plunger on a syringe) that extended a wire or mental blade which could then be rotated. The rotation cuts the tissue and cores the brain like an apple corer (Figure 12.2.1).

The results revealed that the patients experienced various problems.

- In the first hours postoperatively:
  - drowsy;
  - apathetic;
  - incontinent;
  - akinetic; and
  - mute.
- In the first few days postoperatively:
  - decreased initiative;
  - lack of worry;
  - free from anxiety; and
  - apathetic.
- And weeks to months postoperatively:
  - regained memory and intellect;
  - personality changes;
  - indifferent to the problems of others;
  - no thought about their own conduct;
  - tactless;
  - distractible;
  - socially inept; and
  - euphoria and emotional outbursts.

Despite the poor reception of Moniz's surgery, it was taken up by numerous countries but the vast majority of similar operations were performed in America and Britain. In 1949 Moniz was awarded the Nobel Prize for his work on lobotomies. Freeman and Watts published extensively on the advances of the lobotomy to relieve 'mental pain' (e.g. Freeman & Watts, 1942); they also identified thalamic retrograde degeneration following lobotomies (Freeman & Watts, 1947a) (see Chapter 10). Somewhat more frightening is the use of lobotomy in children diagnosed with schizophrenia (Freeman & Watts, 1947b).

On the basis of limited scientific knowledge, lobotomies were used clinically as a means to understand the frontal lobe, but as represented by McKenzie and Proctor (1946), this understanding is somewhat simplistic.

Freeman and Watts (1939) have a subheading 'Symptoms relieved do not indicate normal functions' and proceed to catalogue some of the difficulties in interpretation of lesions in relation to functions.

Lesion studies have been argued to be limited in their scope because:

- the assumption is that discrete regions deal with different cognitive functions;
- 'superimposing individual lesions to identify the crucial area for a certain function assumes that these functional modules are in the same locations in different individuals' (Rorden & Karnath, 2004, p.814);

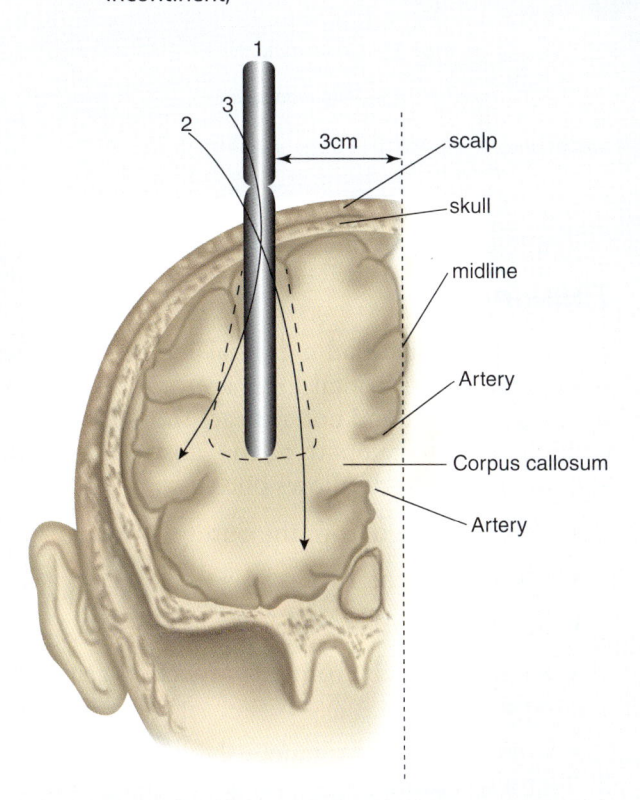

FIGURE 12.2.1 The frontal lobotomy. Entry to the brain is through boreholes in the skull; other routes include through the eye socket and nasal cavity.

- the assumption that the intact regions of the brain function normally is incorrect; and
- regions that appear to be intact may be disconnected from regions downstream that are required for cognitive/affective processing.

The frontal lobotomy continued to be practised until chlorpromazine was introduced by Delay and Deniker (1955). The evaluation of the efficacy of lobotomies was somewhat limited, with mixed results, especially in the long term (Swayze, 1995). The discontinuation of the lobotomy was less about the scientific basis and more to do with the convenience of pharmacotherapy (Braslow, 1999).

Chlorpromazine was later to come under scrutiny. As its nickname suggests, the 'chemical cosh' was the chemical equivalent of being hit over the head with a blunt instrument (or having frontal lobotomy).

Although psychosurgery has been superseded by pharmacotherapy, this does not mean it has been eliminated. The option still remains (Mashour et al., 2005).

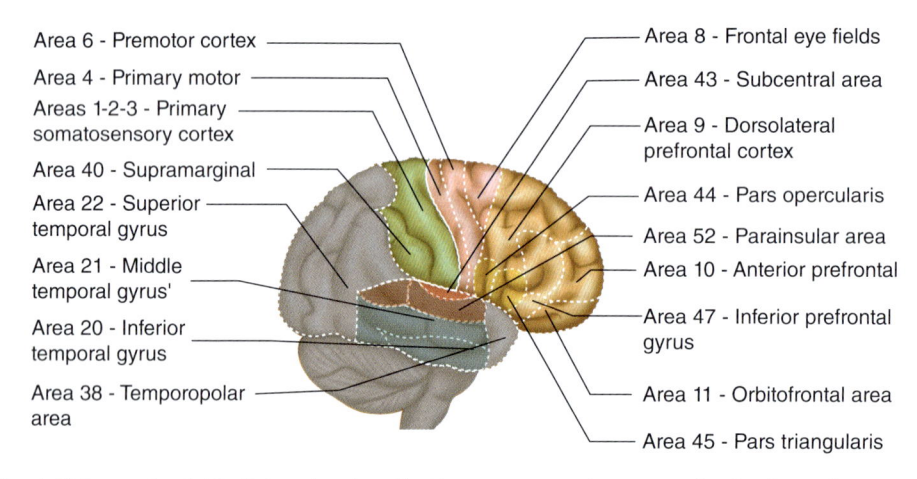

FIGURE 12.4 *The frontal lobe can be divided into subregions that have names and correspond to Brodmann's areas.*

THE FRONTAL LOBES: DAMAGE AND THE DYSEXECUTIVE SYNDROME

Damage to the frontal lobes leads to what is known as the **dysexecutive syndrome** or frontal lobe syndrome – a dysfunction of higher cognitive processes. The frontal lobe syndrome was first characterized by Feuchtwanger (1923) to include personality changes, affective dysregulation and reduced capacity to regulate and integrate other behaviours. The dysexecutive syndrome includes problems in planning, organizing behaviours, disinhibition, perseveration, reduced fluency and initiation (Baddeley, 1986). Furthermore, the frontal lobes are associated with morality and ethical behaviour (see Fumagalli & Priori, 2012).

Thinking

Patients who have had a frontal lobotomy, which is a lesion of the frontal lobe, are only able to use concrete thought and not abstract thought, in what Goldstein (1949) refers to as the 'abstract attitude'. The abstract attitude allows one to:

- detach the ego from the outer world;
- assume a mental set;
- account for acts to oneself;
- shift reflectively from one aspect of a situation to another;
- hold in mind simultaneously various aspects of a situation;
- grasp the essentials of a given whole – decomposition;
- form hierarchical concepts;

- plan ahead; and
- think symbolically.

The prefrontal cortex has been associated in particular with the abstract attitude in which more anterior regions of the prefrontal cortex are involved with more abstract control (Badre, 2008).

Rule Learning, Planning and Problem Solving

Messerli et al. (1979) noted multiple reasons for poor performance on a rule learning task (RGRG; RRGG; RGGRGG). The asymmetrical rule (RGGRGG) was more difficult to follow for frontal lobe patients as they show perseveration of the old rule (they persevere despite being incorrect), perseveration of an erroneous new hypothesis and disregard for a successful hypothesis. Luria (1973a) states that:

> Man not only reacts passively to incoming information, but creates intentions, forms plans and programmes of his actions, inspects their performance and regulates his behaviour so that it conforms to these plans and programmes; finally, he verifies his conscious activity, comparing the original intentions and correcting any mistakes he has made. (pp.79–80)

The Porteus maze (Figure 12.5) requires planning, which is a prerequisite to every intelligent act. A large number of studies demonstrate poor performance in patients with frontal lobe damage (Porteus, 1959). Similarly, in a neuroimaging study, frontal lobe areas were activated during maze tasks (Flitman et al., 1997). In the **Koh Block** design test (which is in the **Wechsler Intelligence Scale**), problems arise from deficits in intention, programming, regulation or verification (Elithorn, 1955; Lezak, 2004; Shallice & Burgess, 1991). Lhermitte et al. (1972) noted that if patients were given instructions as to how to complete the task, then they were able to perform within normal limits. Thus, if someone else provided the requirements of the frontal lobe task, the patient was able to do it. In another visuoconstructive task, the **Figure of Rey** (Figure 12.6), patients with frontal lobe damage failed to reproduce from memory but if they were provided with a plan, they could then succeed in preserving the spatial relationships of the shape (Shallice, 1988). Such help did not generalize to new tasks as they could not solve the problem without a plan.

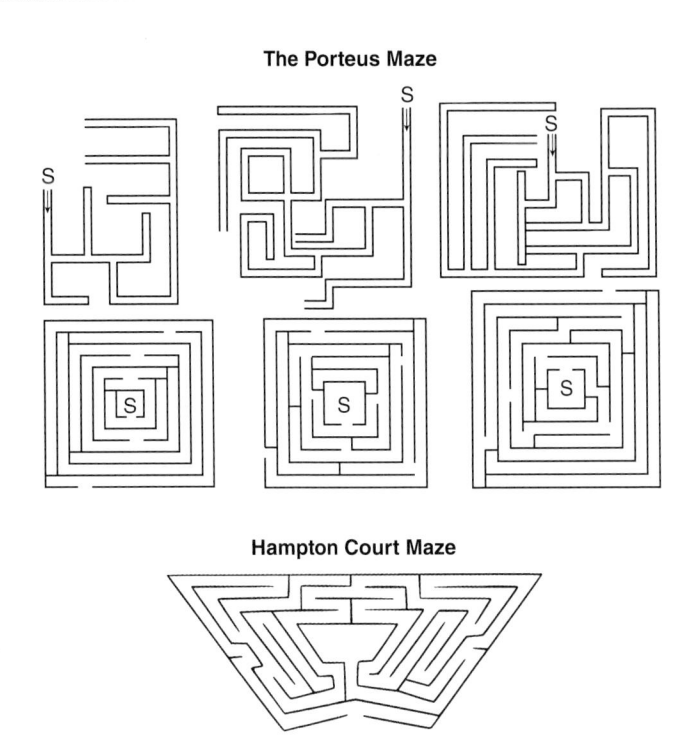

FIGURE 12.5 *The Porteus maze versus the Hampton Court maze. Porteus mazes have a start position(s) and an open exit. They are similar to the Hampton Court maze (in which the frontal lobes will be very important in order to escape).*

The **Tower of London** is a test of frontal lobe dysfunction (Shallice, 1982). The Tower of London requires the participant to solve novel problems in which the degrees of complexity can be adjusted and the patient has to organize goals and subgoals in order to find a solution. The task involves moving different coloured balls on a three-peg stand (Figure 12.7). The patient is provided with an initial position and they have to move the balls one at the time to adjacent pegs in order to get to the target goal. As can be seen in Figure 12.7, the goal position can be many moves from the initial position. This requires thinking ahead and planning a route to the goal position. Patients with unilateral or bilateral lesions of the frontal lobe took longer to complete the task and required more moves in order to reach the goal position (Owen et al., 1990).

Morris et al. (1993) scanned people with an intact frontal lobe and measured regional cerebral blood flow (rCBF) as an indicator of energy consumption in the brain whilst they performed a computerized version of the Tower of London task. They found that there was an increase in rCBF in the prefrontal cortex and that participants who spent more time planning and made the fewest moves

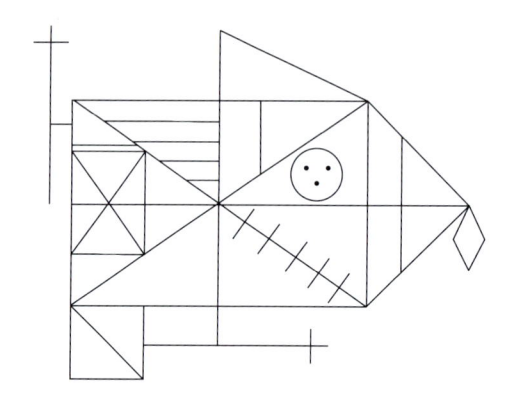

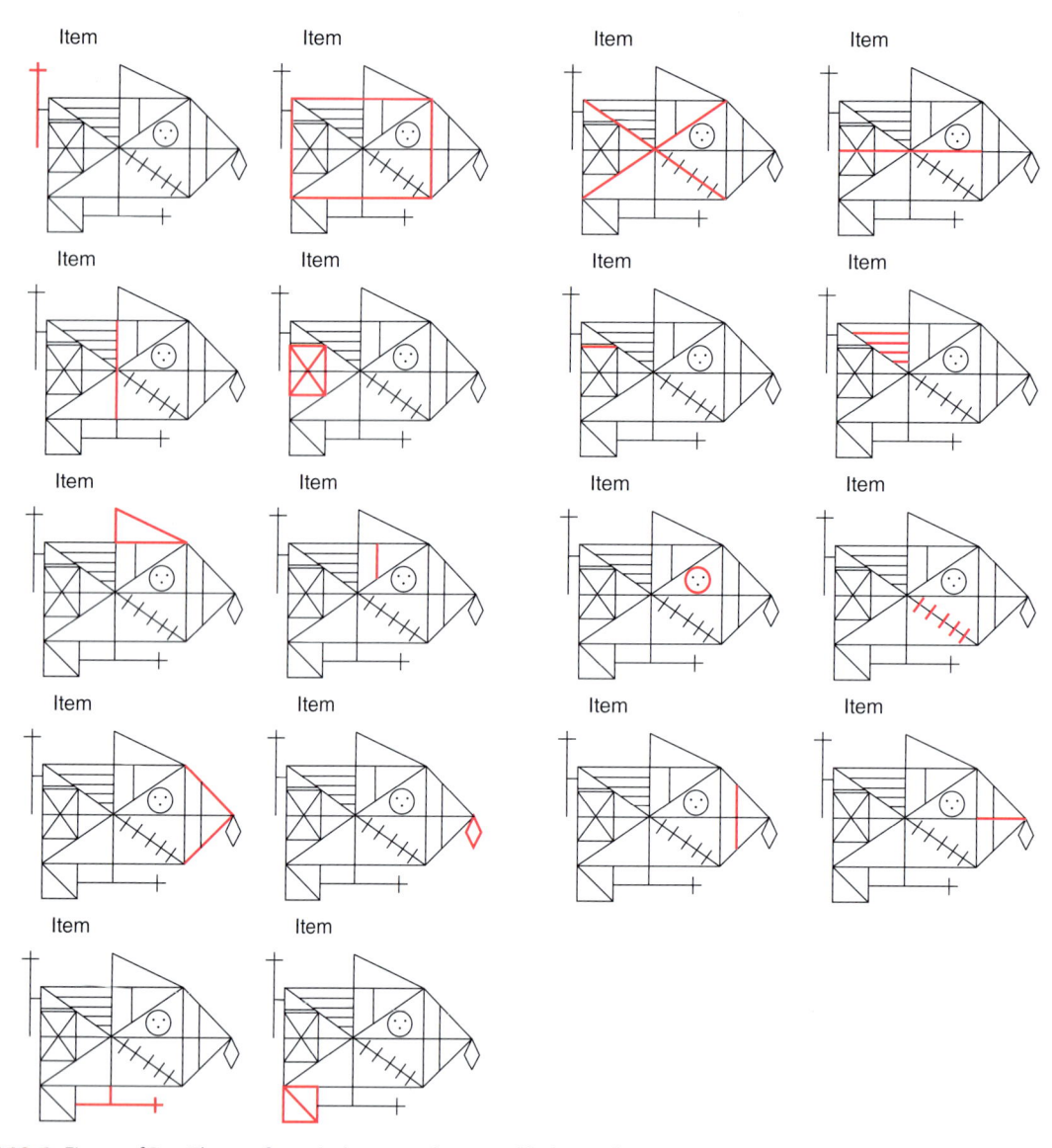

FIGURE 12.6 *Figure of Rey. The top figure is the target figure and below is the scoring and analysis of components.*

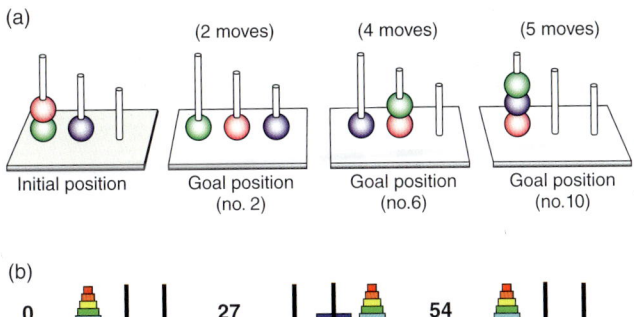

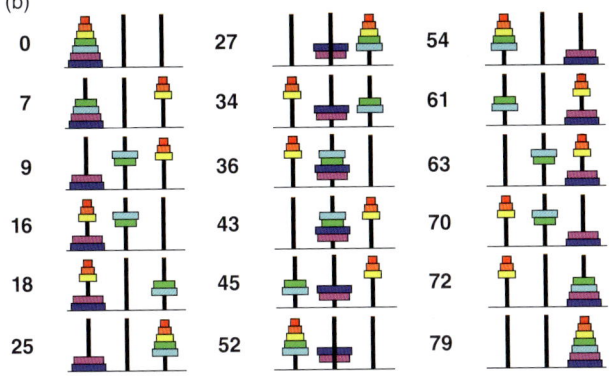

FIGURE 12.7 Towers of London and Hanoi. (a) Tower of London. The aim of the task is to get to a goal position by moving one ball at a time by only one peg. (b) Tower of Hanoi. The aim of the task is to get to a common goal position (0) from different starting points by moving one disc at a time and by only one peg. This task requires a different number of moves (7–79) and counterintuitive backward steps to get to the goal.
Sources: (a) Shallice, T. (1982). Specific impairments of planning. *Philosophical Transactions of the Royal Society B: Biological Sciences, 298*(1089), 199–209, by permission of the Royal Society. (b) Goel, V., & Grafman, J. (1995). Are the frontal lobes implicated in 'planning' functions? Interpreting data from the Tower of Hanoi. *Neuropsychologia, 33*(5), 623–642.

TABLE 12.1 The percentage of frontal lobe patients and control participants using clear (perceptual) methods or unclear (ambiguous) methods for solving the Tower of Hanoi in Goel and Grafman's (1995) study

	Perceptual (%)	Ambiguous (%)
Normal control	79	21
Patients	83	17

The perceptual strategy is the most obvious and natural method for solving the problem and is as follows (Goel & Grafman, 1995).

1. If all n discs are placed on the target peg, stop; else
2. Find the next disc (i) to be placed on the target peg.
3. If there are smaller discs on top of disc i, clear them.
4. Clear discs smaller than i off the target peg.
5. Move disc i to the target peg.
6. Go to 1.

The question remains as to why patients performed poorly despite using the same techniques as controls for solving the Tower of Hanoi. In order to complete the task successfully, there is a counterintuitive backward move, i.e. one that takes you away from the main goal (this is not required in the Tower of London). This results in a goal/subgoal conflict in which:

> ... the prepotent response is to satisfy the global goal, while the alternative response is to satisfy the local goal. In each case frontal patients have difficulty in inhibiting the prepotent (but inappropriate) response in favour of the (appropriate) alternative response. (Goel & Grafman, 1995, p.639)

The **Wisconsin Card Sorting Test** (WCST) (Grant & Berg, 1948) uses a deck of cards that have shapes on them. The cards differ by shape, the colour of the shapes and the number of shapes (Figure 12.8). The cards have to be sorted according to a category, which is decided secretly by the experimenter and not communicated to the participant, e.g. sort by colour. The participant has to go through a period of trial and error to determine the strategy for sorting. The only information they get is whether they are right or

to completion showed the greatest increase in rCBF. Using fMRI in healthy participants, the dorsolateral prefrontal cortex, and the anterior part of the cingulate cortex were seen to be active during planning and the parietal lobe and cerebellum were active when the person actually executed the action (Lazeron et al., 2000).

The **Tower of Hanoi** is similar to the Tower of London (Hinz et al., 2013). Patients with lesions to the prefrontal cortex (mixed aetiology) were compared with normal volunteers on the Tower of Hanoi (Goel & Grafman, 1995). The performance of patients was poor compared to normal volunteers and related to the task difficulty. When the strategies used were investigated, Goel and Grafman noted that patients and controls used the same method for solving the puzzle (Table 12.1).

FIGURE 12.8 The Wisconsin Card Sorting Test. Participants have to sort the cards according to a rule only known by the administrator of the task. The rule can be based on shape, colour or number. Once the participant gets it right, the administrator will change the rule and the participant then has to test for the new rule. The only feedback they get is whether something is right or wrong.

wrong. After the participant correctly sorts the cards a number of times, the experimenter then changes the rule (e.g. to shape). The participant then will generate errors by which they have to find the new correct sorting rule. Patients with frontal lobe damage failed to change to the new rule and perseverated with the old incorrect rule (Milner, 1963).

However, the advantages of having neuroimaging data have shown that there is considerable variability in the WCST, with some people with focal lesions of the frontal lobe performing within normal limits and other patients with damage to non-frontal regions performing poorly (Anderson et al., 1991). It has also been suggested that 'the concept of an anatomically *pure* test of prefrontal function is not only empirically unattainable, but also theoretically inaccurate' and that modifications may tap into the specific processes of the WCST (Nyhus & Barceló, 2009, p.427). Despite this assertion, the WCST is still used to assess frontal lobe function (Stuss et al., 2000). Similar to other tasks, patients benefited from explicit instruction on what was happening (Stuss et al., 2000). The lateral prefrontal cortex, anterior cingulate cortex and inferior parietal lobe have been shown to increase in activity during the WCST (Buchsbaum et al., 2005). When the WCST is broken down into subcomponents, the mid-dorsolateral prefrontal cortex was more active during feedback and a cortical-basal-ganglia loop comprising the mid-ventrolateral prefrontal cortex, caudate nucleus and mediodorsal thalamus was particularly active during negative feedback, indicating the necessity to change from the previous rule (Monchi et al., 2001). The anterior cingulate cortex and temporoparietal junction represented a network for error detection (Lie et al., 2006). Thus, the neuroimaging data support a role of the frontal lobe in the WCST but extend our knowledge to subcomponents of the task being mediated by specific regions of the brain.

BOX 12.3: ARITHMETIC PROBLEM SOLVING

1. There are 18 books on two shelves, and there are twice as many books on one as the other. How many books are on each shelf?
2. A son is five years old; in 15 years his father will be twice as old as he. How old is the father now?
3. A pedestrian takes 30 minutes to reach the station, while a cyclist goes three times as fast. How long does the cyclist take?

Christensen (1975) states that:

> The patient only grasps one particular fragment of the problem; he does not make any plans but starts to carry out disconnected arithmetic operations with this fragment. The whole process of solution may be transformed into a series of impulsive, fragmentary arithmetical operations, frequently unconnected with the ultimate goal.

Answers:

1. There are 6 books on one shelf and 12 books on the other.
   $(6 \times 2 = 12) + 6 = 18$
2. Child 5 ($+15$ years $= 20$)
   20×2 father 40 years old in 15 years time
   $40-15$ years $= 25$ years now
3. Walking takes 30 minutes
   Cycling is 3 time faster
   $30/3 = 10$ minutes

Error Utilization

Patients with frontal lobe damage are often aware of making an error but fail to use errors to guide future behaviour. In a case study of a patient with frontal lobe damage, Konow and Pribram (1970) noted that she gave clear indications of error, even when watching experimenters perform tasks, and that 'the patient usually had no difficulty in spotting our errors. This was true even when they were embedded in rather complex serial performances' (pp.490–491).

When it comes to problem solving, patients with frontal lobe damage have the mechanical ability but they do not have a full understanding of the problem. In tasks such as the Arithmetic Problem Solving Test, patients with frontal lobe dysfunction do not show deficits in arithmetic ability (e.g. subtraction), but they do when it is embedded in problem solving. In a suite of neuropsychological tests, Christensen (1975) was able to identify difficulties related to problem solving in which patients failed to generate and execute simple programmes (see Box 12.3).

Attention

One of the key elements of any task is attention. Frontal lobe patients' attention can easily wander. The **Stroop task** (Stroop, 1935) requires participants to either report the colour that word is printed in or report the word that is written. That seems quite straightforward but the difficulty lies in the fact that some of the words are colour nouns (Figure 12.9). The difficulty comes when you have to report the colour name of a word that is printed in a different colour. Typically, people are slower when there is interference between the name and the colour. The requirements for such selective attention have been located within the frontal lobe (Taylor et al., 1997) with a particular role for the dorsolateral prefrontal cortex (DLPFC) (Milham et al., 2003). The Stroop task is sensitive to frontal lobe damage in

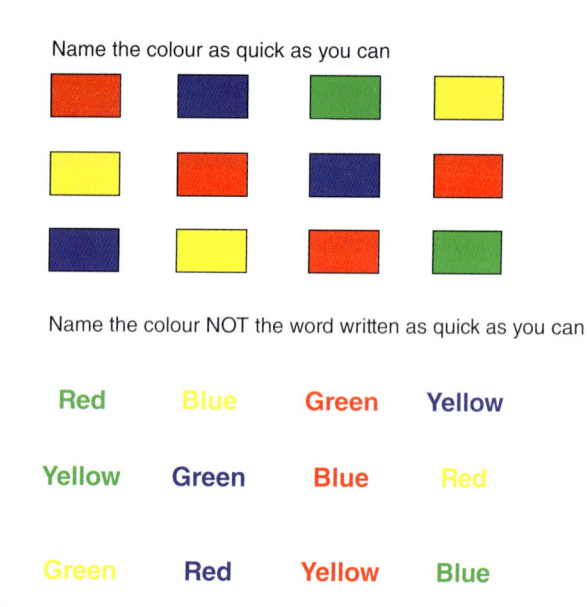

FIGURE 12.9 The Stroop task. Try naming the blocks of colour from left to right. Then name the colours of the words (DO NOT READ THE WORD). The second task is more difficult as there is a conflict of information between the written word and the colour it is printed in.

which patients perform poorly (Demakis, 2004). For example, Vendrell et al. (1995) compared 32 frontal patients with matched controls and found that errors increased in the frontal patients, but there was no effect on reaction time and the increase in errors was associated with the right frontal lobe.

THEORIES DESCRIBING FRONTAL LOBE FUNCTION

There are numerous theoretical perspectives that have aimed to provide a neuropsychological view of the frontal lobes. These range from social to cognitive neuroscientific explanations in which descriptors focus on the emotional/motivational component of EF or on the metacognitive EF of planning, etc.

Theory of Mind: Mind Reading (or Knowing Me, Knowing You (Aha!))

A theory of mind is uniquely human and 'mind reading is crucial to understanding what it means to be human' (Heyes & Frith, 2014). Not surprisingly, this unique gift is associated with the frontal lobes, the most recently evolved region of the cortex. **Theory of Mind** (ToM) is the phrase given to the ability to know that others have thoughts, ideas, beliefs and opinions separate from our own (see Doherty, 2008). ToM is essential for successful navigation of the social world – the ability to read minds or at least be able to adopt another person's perspective is a useful social tool. The importance of this social tool is most notable when it is compromised, e.g. in schizophrenia. ToM is a concept that develops through early childhood and is affected in some developmental disorders. Interestingly, whilst both autistic children and ADHD children have EF deficits, it is often only autistic children who fail ToM tasks (Charman et al., 2001; Perner et al., 2002) (see Chapter 20). ToM together with memory networks have been argued to allow individuals to project themselves into different scenarios with diverging perspectives, thereby supporting thinking about the future (Buckner & Carroll, 2007)

Theory of Mind can be acquired through experience rather than via pre-programmed genetic mechanisms. Twin studies have indicated a potential role for environmental influences on ToM as there was little difference between monozygotic and dizygotic twins (Hughes et al., 2005). The learning of a ToM can be derived from instruction or through hypothesis testing in which the child is seen as a scientist (Gopnik & Wellman, 2012; Kahneman & A, 1982). In a cross-cultural study of preschool children, individual differences in executive functioning predicted the development of ToM (Sabbagh et al., 2006).

The link between EF and ToM is not necessarily direct. It has been argued that 'domain-general executive functioning skills enable children to more fully capitalize on domain-specific experiential factors to foster the conceptual developments necessary for theory of mind' (Sabbagh et al., 2006, p.779), thereby highlighting the infrastructure required for learning. Heyes and Frith (2014) argue that the human child is born with mechanisms that are not necessarily intended for ToM, but through experience and the adaptive utility of having a ToM, mind-reading skills emerge. They use the analogy of learning to read in which we have the biological mechanisms that underpin this ability, but its development is determined by the environment. The mirror neuron system, which is shown to be active when watching somebody else perform a motor task, has been extended to a ToM. In the case of ToM, mirror neurons may allow individuals to detect and infer other people's mental states (Gallese & Goldman,

1998). If such a system were to exist then individuals possessing mirror neurons would have an advantage because their 'cortical motor system enables a direct appreciation of purpose without relying on explicit propositional inference' (mind reading) (Gallese, 2013, p.2955).

Abu-Akel and Shamay-Tsoory (2011) provide a detailed neuroanatomical and neurochemical basis for ToM in which there are two ToM circuits: cognitive and affective. They refer to the cognitive components of ToM as the cold dimensions and the effective components as hot dimensions. Not surprisingly, each of these dimensions has a distinct yet overlapping neuroanatomical basis. The cognitive dimension of ToM involves the dorsomedial prefrontal cortex, the dorsolateral anterior cingulate cortex and the dorsal striatum. The affective network involves the ventromedial and orbitofrontal cortices, the ventral anterior cingulate cortex, the amygdala and the ventral striatum (see Table 12.2 and Figure 12.10). Being able to distinguish between one's own conscious self and the inference of others is argued to occur at the temporoparietal junction (temporal and parietal lobe) and the anterior cingulate cortex. Connecting these regions and explicitly involved in ToM are dopamine and serotonin. The cognitive and affective networks related to ToM are schematically represented in Figure 12.11 in which dorsal and ventral regions process the thoughts and feelings of others and oneself. The evidence for the involvement of dopamine and serotonin in ToM stems from accounts of faulty ToM in known disorders where the modulation of serotonin and dopamine have been implicated (see Table 12.3).

Just Say No – The Case of Free Won't

Leading the study of **behavioural inhibition** (BI) is Professor Russell Barkley. Barkley has been extremely influential in conceptualizing ADHD as a disorder arising from a failure of the BI system (Barkley, 1997a, 1997b, 2005). The clinical manifestation of a BI deficit is most obvious in impulsivity; however, the effects of BI are thought to extend beyond just impulsivity.

Barkley's theory is one of executive function in general, but with a clear application to ADHD. Barkley sees a failure to inhibit responses to be the *cause* of all the other executive function deficits. In fact, Barkley sees deficits in BI as so well established in the ADHD population that it should be treated as a 'fact' (Barkley, 2006a). 'Fact' is not a word that is often used in the behavioural sciences. Whilst the use of the term 'fact' highlights the importance placed upon BI and the data supporting a deficit, BI should not be considered without question.

The necessity of BI in behaviour is argued to manifest in four EF domains: (1) non-verbal working memory; (2) internalization of speech (verbal working memory); (3) self-regulation of affect/motivation/arousal; and (4) reconstitution (planning) (Barkley, 2006b). Thus, Barkley sees BI as at the top of an EF hierarchy.

Behavioural inhibition consists of three main components: (1) inhibiting the initial prepotent or immediate/dominant response as determined by reinforcement history (to stop a response that has become already likely because of previous experience and learning); (2) stopping an ongoing response, therefore permitting a delay in deciding to respond; and (3) protection of this decision-making process during this delay from interference. This is all about thinking and decision making.

How does this affect a person? First, an inability to inhibit the prepotent response means that an individual will not be able to assess the task demands and the possible outcome of responding. Second, a failure to interrupt ongoing behaviour may lead to an individual following a well-learned behavioural pattern even when feedback is stating that this response is erroneous. The third process is all about avoiding being distracted when a response is required. In order to deal with the modern world, we have to delay our rewards, check that what we are doing is going to work and modify accordingly. For someone with BI difficulties, this has ramifications for the whole of the EF (Figure 12.12).

The question remains, 'Is a deficit in behavioural inhibition the same as impulsivity?'. At first, the answer appears to be obvious – YES! However, a more detailed investigation finds a debate within the literature.

What is impulsivity?

Impulsivity describes the inability to defer obtaining immediate access to a small reward rather than waiting for a larger but temporally more distant reward – a phenomenon tested in tasks such as delay discounting (Neef et al., 2001, 2005). Impulsivity is not a single unitary construct but a multidimensional entity (Evenden, 1999; Winstanley et al., 2006) and it is though that alterations in the

TABLE 12.2 *Theory of Mind brain regions*

Brain region	Brodmann's area
Posterior regions	
Temporoparietal junction (including the inferior parietal lobe) (IPL/pSTS or TPJ)	39/40
Posterior cingulate/precuneus (PCC/PCun)	31/7
Superior temporal sulcus (STS)	21/22
Limbic-paralimbic regions	
Orbitofrontal (OFC)	11/12/47
Ventral medial prefrontal cortex (vMPFC)	10/32
Anterior cingulate/paracingulate cortex (ACC/PrCC)	24/32
Temporal pole (TP)	38
Amygdala	Subcortical
Striatum	Subcortical
Frontal regions	
Dorsomedial prefrontal cortex (DMPFC)	8/9
Dorsolateral prefrontal cortex (DLPFC)	9/46
Inferior lateral frontal cortex (ILFC)	44/45/47

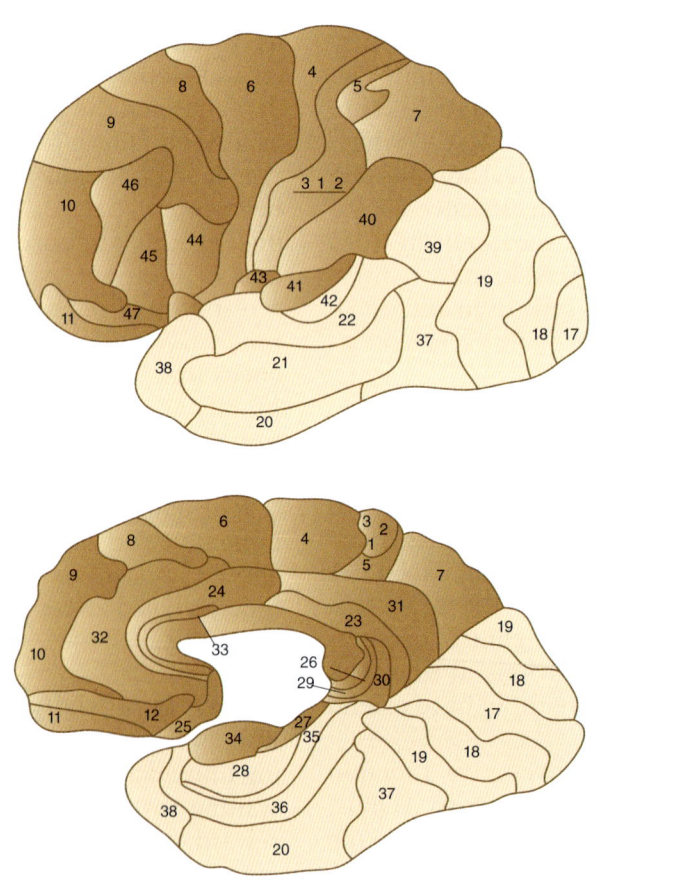

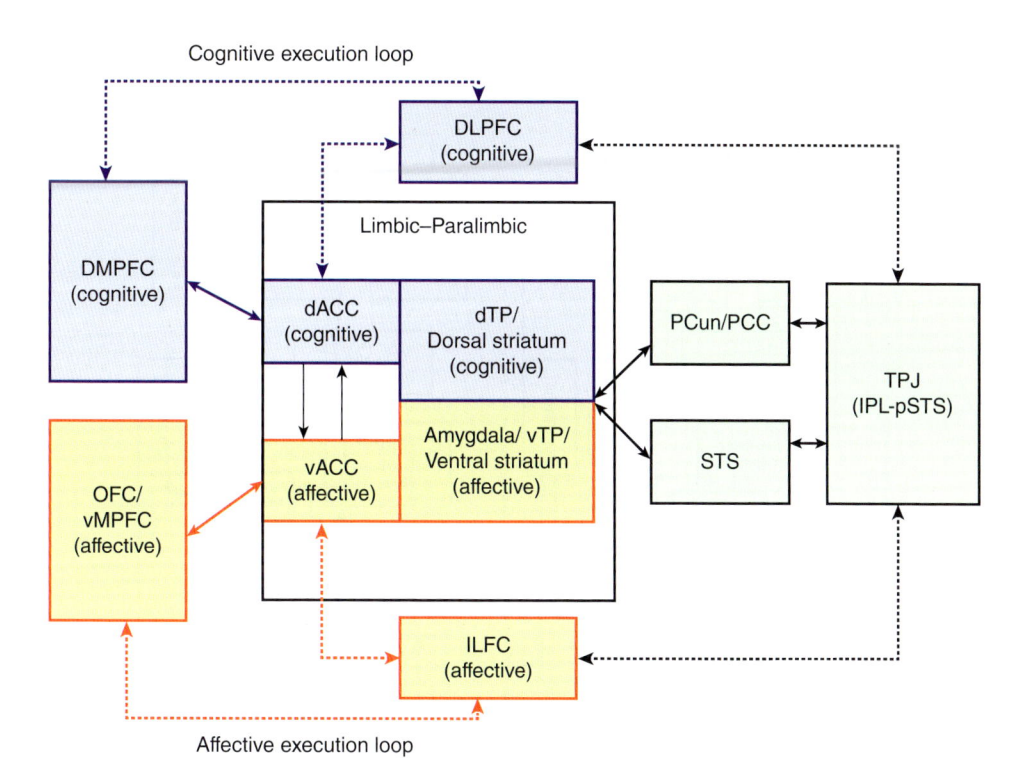

FIGURE 12.10 Neural network for processing affective and cognitive mental states. The arrows are bidirectional. Represented mental states are formed at the temporoparietal junction (TPJ) which is then relayed through the superior temporal sulcus (STS) or the precuneus/posterior cingulate complex (PCun/PCC) to limbic–paralimbic regions to be assigned cognitive or affective values. Affective ToM (hot – red boxes) is mediated by a network that engages the ventral striatum, amygdala, ventral temporal pole (vTP), ventral anterior cingulate cortex (vACC), orbitofrontal cortex (OFC), ventral medial prefrontal cortex (vMPFC) and inferolateral frontal cortex (ILFC). Cognitive ToM (cold – blue boxes), on the other hand, is mediated by a network that engages the dorsal striatum, dorsal temporal pole (dTP), dorsal anterior cingulate cortex (dACC), dorsal medial prefrontal cortex (DMPFC) and dorsal lateral prefrontal cortex (DLPFC). The ILFC and the DLPFC represent the execution/application structures of their respective affective and cognitive ToM networks. Interacting functions of the two networks could be mediated within the ACC.
Source: Abu-Akel, A., & Shamay-Tsoory, S. (2011). Neuroanatomical and neurochemical bases of theory of mind. *Neuropsychologia, 49*(11), 2971–2984.

different dimensions of impulsivity could account for the differing subtypes of ADHD (Nigg, 2003). Impulsivity has been associated with inattentive and hyperactive subtypes (Mathias et al., 2007; Rubia et al., 2007).

Impulsivity has been argued to fit into two broad domains: reward drive and rash impulsiveness (Dawe & Loxton, 2004; Dawe et al., 2004). Although these two facets of impulsivity have not been linked explicitly to ADHD, they have been linked to other impulse control problems such as addiction. Reward drive is a motivational component of impulsivity, whereas rash impulsiveness is the varying ability of being able to stop a response. In ADHD and addiction, this could translate as goals that are immediate and desired but cannot be delayed until a more appropriate time when such actions are warranted.

Behavioural inhibition may be the underlying neuropsychological construct that gives rise to impulsive behaviour. In fact, it is highly likely – but that is not to say we should accept it without criticism. BI deficits are certainly a phenomenon that is evident and measurable in neuropsychological tests; BI is, after all, what tests of BI measure (e.g. Go/No-go and the Stop-Signal Reaction Time tasks). Thus, BI is often operationally defined and serves as a reminder of the old saying about intelligence put forward by Professor Boring in 1923: intelligence is whatever it is that intelligence tests measure (see Sternberg et al., 2008).

Measures of behavioural inhibition

As I have emphasized the role of BI measures in defining BI, it is necessary to describe these tests for clarification. There are two tests that are frequently used:

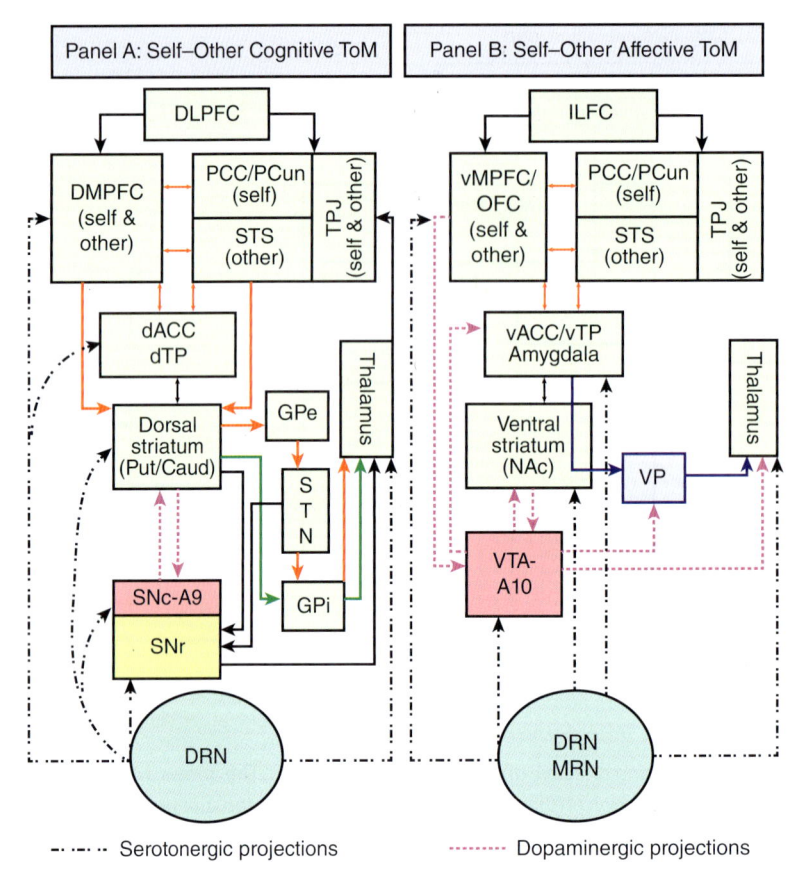

FIGURE 12.11 *Schematic representation of serotonin–dopamine interaction within the cognitive and affective networks. The cognitive and affective processing of other people in ToM is mediated via overlapping regions of the brain and connected via serotonin (yellow line) and dopamine (pink line). Other colours represent internal networks mediated by other transmitters, e.g. GABA and glutamate. ACC, anterior cingulate cortex; DMPFC, dorsal medial prefrontal cortex; DRN, dorsal raphe nucleus; DLPFC, dorsolateral prefrontal cortex; GPi, globus pallidus interna; GPe, globus pallidus externa; ILFC, inferolateral frontal cortex; MRN, median raphe nucleus; NAc, nucleus accumbens; OFC, orbitofrontal cortex; PCC/PCun, posterior cingulate/precuneus; STS, superior temporal cortex; SN, substantia nigra pars compacta; SNc, substantia nigra pars reticulata; STN, subthalamic nucleus; TPJ, temporoparietal junctions; vMPFC, ventral medial prefrontal cortex; VP, ventral pallidum; VTA, ventral tegmental area.*
Source: Abu-Akel, A., & Shamay-Tsoory, S. (2011). Neuroanatomical and neurochemical bases of theory of mind. *Neuropsychologia*, 49(11), 2971–2984.

the **Go/No-go** task and the **Stop Signal Reaction Time** test (SSRT). Both tasks require the suppression of a well-learned response and are thought to reflect motor BI (Ersche & Sahakian, 2007). In the Go/No-go task, individuals are told to respond quickly (e.g. press a button) to a particular stimulus on the Go trials, but to withhold responses when presented with a No-go stimulus, e.g. press Go for the digits 0–9 appearing randomly, except for the number 7 (No-go). The inclusion of more Go than No-go stimuli means that the Go responses become prepotent (learned). The number of inappropriate responses to No-go stimuli, pressing the button when you should not (an error of commission), measures BI. Thus, the Go/No-go task measures the ability, or in the case of psychopathologies the inability, to stop responding.

The SSRT task involves participants having to withhold a response to a Go signal whenever it is followed or accompanied by a Stop signal. The Stop signal can be an auditory beep during the presentation of visually displayed Go stimuli.

In Figure 12.12, we can see the probability of either responding or inhibiting a response as a function of time after the Stop signal. In a study by Alderson et al. (2008) three variants of the standard SSRT were performed: (1) a no tone condition, in which there was no Stop signal; (2) an ignore the tone condition, in which a tone was not associated with stopping; and (3) a second ignore that tone condition that presented a neutral auditory tone after a previous tone had been paired with a stopping tone. Using these variants, Alderson and colleagues noted

TABLE 12.3 *Pathologies and disorders that affect Theory of Mind functioning*

Psychiatric and personality disorders

Autism

Asperger's syndrome

Anorexia nervosa

Bipolar disorder

Psychopathy and antipersonality disorders

Schizophrenia

Social anxiety

Basal ganglia disorders

Attention deficit hyperactivity disorder

Huntington's disease

Parkinson's disease

Genetic disorders

22q11.2 deletion syndrome

Down's syndrome

Fragile X syndrome (Martin–Bell syndrome)

Phenylketonuria (PKU)

Prader–Willi syndrome

Sotos' syndrome (cerebral gigantism)

Spinocerebellar ataxia

Turner's syndrome (Ullrich–Turner syndrome)

Williams' syndrome

Neurological disorders

Frontotemporal dementia

Alzheimer's disease

Multiple sclerosis (MS)

Traumatic brain injury (TBI)

that it was the differences in the mean reaction time rather than the Stop signal delay that accounted for the variants seen in the SSRT. Slower SSRTs in cases of ADHD were considered to be a product of a generally slower processing of, and responding to, visually presented stimuli and additionally the slower processing of a second stimulus (the auditory tone). This prompted the authors to suggest that failure in the SSRT was not a result of deficient BI as it was a more general deficit.

A great deal has been written about these two paradigms in both healthy and psychiatric groups. However, the measurement of BI is not restricted to these tasks and interested readers are referred to a review by Joel Nigg (2001).

Numerous disorders such as obsessive-compulsive disorder (OCD), borderline personality disorder, ADHD and addiction exhibit deficits on BI measures (Chamberlain & Sahakian, 2007; Nigg et al., 2005, 2006; Schachar et al., 2004). Thus, BI tests are unable to discriminate between disorders. One study has demonstrated that BI deficits are associated with the prefrontal cortex in ADHD compared with the temporoparietal area in conduct disorder (Rubia et al., 2008). This study is important as it highlights that the deficits in BI can arise from different regions of the brain and may explain why different disorders can all have deficits in BI. Another issue in assessing BI is that it is not stable across the lifespan; there are developmental differences which mean that BI increases throughout childhood and into adulthood (Bedard et al., 2002; Mani et al., 2005; Williams et al., 1999).

Due to the reliance on the Go/No-go and SSRT tasks in dissecting BI, the very nature of these tasks becomes important, from both a theoretical and clinical perspective.

A review of the literature on impulsivity supports the importance of the notion of BI underlying the impulsivity in which 'the term "response [behavioural] inhibition" refers to the ability to inhibit or suppress simple motor responses that have been rendered prepotent … and deficits in this ability are implicated in impulsivity' (Chamberlain et al., 2006b). An important point to note here is that when discussing BI, most accounts are referring to the suppression of a motor response as in the Go/No-go or SSRT task. It has been argued that BI is only evident for motor responding and has been overextended to include cognitive control (Aron, 2007). This may be the case for some disorders where motor BI but not attentional inhibition was compromised (Carr et al., 2006), although these latter experiments did not use the Go/No-go or the SSRT task, but instead looked at saccadic eye movements and the attentional blink paradigm, thereby making direct comparisons difficult.

Aron (2007) claims that there are a number of reasons why BI cannot be used in the context of cognitive control.

- It is not economically viable for neural resources to be used for BI; instead amplification of stimuli would be a more suitable mechanism – a simple stimulus–response association being strengthened.

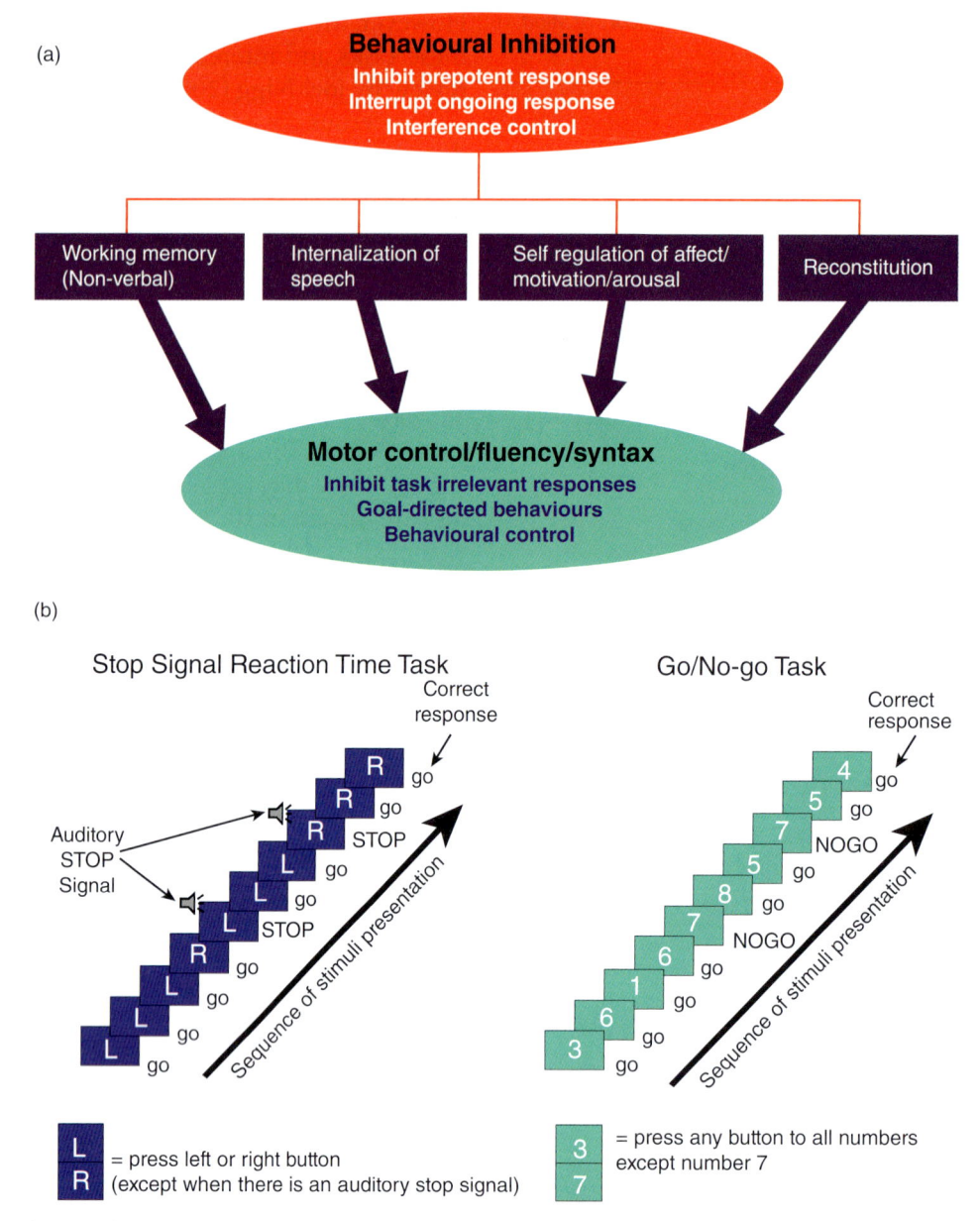

FIGURE 12.12 *Behavioural inhibition. (a) Barkley's model of behavioural inhibition. Being able or unable to inhibit responses has an effect on systems beneath the behavioural inhibition module. (b) Common measures of behavioural inhibition. (Left) The Stop Signal Reaction Time task based on Logan (1994) in which participants have to withhold a response upon hearing an auditory tone. (Right) The Go/No-go task after Ersche and Sahakian (2007) in which participants have to withhold a response when they see the number 7.*
Source: (b) Chandler, C. (2010). *The science of ADHD*. Wiley. Reproduced with permission.

- Lesions of the prefrontal cortex produce BI but that is not to say that the prefrontal cortex is the site of BI.
- There are better accounts of the performance deficits that are encountered, e.g. working memory (see below).

A general criticism of the Go/No-go and SSRT tasks is that obtaining baselines of behaviour is arbitrary and that the SSRT may influence following Go trials in terms of speed and accuracy; that is, there is a carry-over effect of one trial to another and when compared to their own baselines, there was little dysfunction (Rommelse et al., 2007). Differentiating higher order cognitive processes, such as EF, from lower level cognitive processes, such as encoding, perception and response organization, needs to be accomplished because it has been demonstrated that deficits are not only accounted for by disturbances in EF but could rather be explained as dysfunction of lower level cognitive processes (Rommelse et al., 2007).

In a study measuring the brain's activity using surface placed electrodes, Banaschewski et al. (2004) were able to detect neural events associated with motor preparation, motor response execution and motor **response inhibition** on a Go/No-go task. They investigated a particular set of brain waves called event-related potentials (ERP); the two that they specifically looked at are called N2 and P3 which are recorded in response to a stimulus at different sites on the scalp and therefore correspond to different brain regions (see McLoughlin et al. (2005) for review). The N2 ERP is associated with frontal areas of the brain and with BI, the P3 is associated more with central-frontal regions.

Another minor difficulty with the impulsivity/BI debate centres on the neurochemical basis of the construct. The neurochemical serotonin (5-HT) has long been associated with impulsivity (King et al., 2003; Soubrié, 1986). Others have argued that impulsivity can be subdivided into different types with different biological bases (Evenden, 1999). The Go/No-go task is possibly mediated by serotonin whereas the SSRT task may be mediated by noradrenaline (Eagle, Bari et al., 2008). At this point, we should note that serotonergic drugs have limited effects in BI paradigms (Chamberlain et al., 2007). Drugs that are effective in reversing deficits in BI, e.g. methylphenidate and atomoxetine, work on both dopamine and noradrenaline (see Chapters 7 and 9). The neurochemical that is frequently associated with BI is noradrenaline whereas the use of feedback is associated with serotonin (Chamberlain et al., 2006a). Thus, two systems may be in operation during BI tasks.

Impulsive behaviours may appear to be automatic and executed without thinking. They may appear to be quick, automatic responses that have little intention, attention, awareness or insight. Another hypothesis that may possibly account for BI could be automatic responding. According to Aron (2007), response amplification might be more economical than BI. The prepotent response, as in the Go/No-go task, is to have well-learned responses to Go stimuli that become overinclusive and are difficult to stop. Another way to describe the data is via the notion of automaticity; that is, participants have learned to respond in a particular way to stimuli. This response is automatic and does not deal with the constraints of the experimental situation. Thus, it appears that the person reacts impulsively, without consideration of the task.

Automaticity of responses is defined as a 'simple, elegant, efficient processing which takes advantage of assumed relationships . . .' (Saling & Phillips, 2007, p458). Therefore, impulsivity can be considered as a case of evolutionary adaptiveness (see Chapters 2 and 20). It is only when the assumed relationships of a stimulus and response cannot be upheld (that is, a prepotent response is no longer appropriate) that the problems arise, e.g. college work does not require impulsive actions, which may be somewhat disruptive to the status quo of the lecture theatre; however, impulsive reactions may be very useful in field sports). When automatic responses are no longer appropriate, conscious awareness of the changes in the environment becomes necessary and then BI may be required. The cortical-subcortical connections appear to be important in accounts of automaticity (Saling & Phillips, 2007), impulsivity (Chamberlain & Sahakian, 2007) and BI (Aron, 2007), although the exact nature and extent of overlap and differences remain uncertain.

Nigg (2001) elaborates further on the nature of the deficit in BI and states that, on the basis of the evidence, there are two distinct types of inhibition: (1) executive inhibition, consistent with Barkley, and (2) reactive or motivational inhibition, which is more reflexive and responsive to emotionally salient stimuli, e.g. reward and punishment, unexpected mismatches and social unfamiliarity. This latter view is perhaps more closely linked to what we think of as impulsivity. Which one of these accounts of BI is dominant, if indeed one of them can be, is uncertain.

Motivational inhibition

The concept of **motivational inhibition** (MI) is not new, but its application to psychopathologies has not yet been fully explored (Nigg, 2001). The use of MI can be traced back to the work of the late Professor Jeffery Gray (Gray 1982; Gray & McNaughton, 2003). Gray proposed two components of MI: a **behavioural inhibition system (BIS)** and a **behavioural approach system (BAS)**. The BIS and BAS of Gray's theory have been argued to fall under the concept of the reward drive component in impulsivity (Dawe & Loxton, 2004). The BAS is activated when the environment is indicating reward or punishment (and is dopaminergically mediated).

The BIS detects mismatches between the environment and expectations by stopping ongoing behaviour and directing cognitive resources to the mismatch. When the BIS is activated, the BAS is inhibited. Psychopathologies such as anxiety disorders are associated with a dysfunction in one or more of these systems which can account for impulsivity and anxiety (see Chapters 20 and 23), e.g. a weak BIS which allows approach behaviours to be maintained despite input to the contrary (Quay, 1997, 1998) or a strong BAS (Gorenstein & Newman, 1980).

The theoretical perspective developed by Swanson et al. (1998) starts with the idea that separate and distinct neural circuits work independently on alerting, orienting and executive control (Posner & Raichle, 1994). Alerting is when background neural activity (noise) is inhibited, thus removing the interference of other stimuli – this is the signal-to-noise ratio in which signals should gain strength over background noise derived from competing signals. Orienting activates appropriate resources favouring specialized processes to deal with the input stimuli whilst inhibiting unnecessary processes; thus a favourable response is selected (similar to the supervisory attentional system – see below). Executive control refers to overseeing the many specialized neural responses and directs behaviour towards achieving the goal. These three systems therefore work to produce an economic use of limited neural resources.

Working memory

Working memory (WM) has become a widely accepted and dominant neurocognitive construct since its first outing in the early 1970s (Baddeley & Hitch, 1974). Since then, it has evolved into a comprehensive theory of mental life with a huge body of literature supporting it (Baddeley, 2000). WM's endurance in the psychological literature demonstrates its powerful application to understanding behaviour (Baddeley, 2001). WM has been implicated and researched in the context of many disorders and ADHD is no exception.

But what is WM? Let us start with what it is *not*. It is not just memory. WM is much more to do with attentional mechanisms and allocation of resources for information processing. WM is not one entity but a set of processes that construct, maintain and manipulate the psychological representation of stimuli. WM is another way of discussing EFs.

Information within WM is stored temporarily and has a limited capacity. To use a computer analogy to describe working memory, we have two types of memory in a computer: the hard drive and RAM. The hard drive is like long-term memory. To access these memories (files) using the necessary software, we need RAM. RAM is like our WM; it is the fluid memory that holds the information whilst it is been

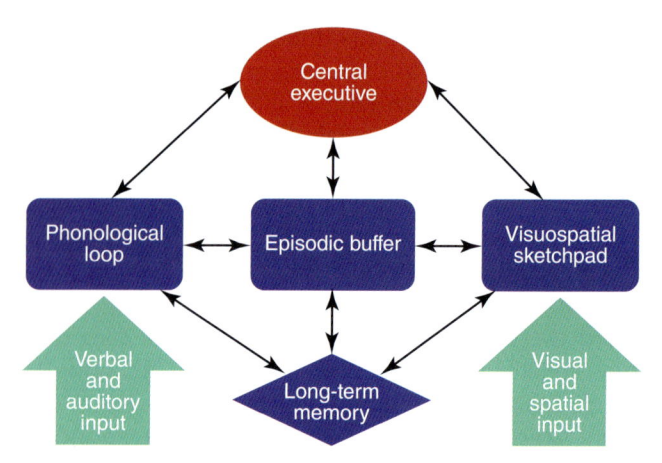

FIGURE 12.13 *Working memory. Baddely's working memory provides another theoretical explanation of the workings of the frontal lobe. The central executive is the manager of slave units that process auditory (phonological loop) and visual (visuospatial sketchpad) inputs. The episodic buffer integrates activity with past experience and current actions of working memory.*
Source: Chandler, C. (2010). *The science of ADHD*. Wiley. Reproduced with permission.

worked upon. Thus, WM provides temporary storage of psychological representations of stimuli for processing and permits higher order functions to occur, e.g. understanding language – we need to hold the words of a sentence together in order to gain the meaning of the sentence rather than have a series of disconnected words in list.

Working memory is made up of a number of separate but interconnected components (Figure 12.13). At the core of working memory is the central executive. Continuing with the computer analogy, the central executive is like the dual core processors, and the software works upon the information depending on the nature of that information; for example, iTunes™ works with music files whereas Photoshop™ works with picture files.

The central executive is an attentional control system similar to that outlined by Norman and Shallice (see below). Additional to the central executive are two slave systems: the visuospatial sketchpad and the phonological loop. The visuospatial sketchpad holds information that can be broken down into visual, spatial and kinaesthetic components, all of which are associated with areas in the right hemisphere of the brain. The phonological loop holds verbal and acoustic information. The WM model also includes an episodic buffer (Baddeley, 2000), which is a temporary storage system that can integrate information from different sources. The central executive controls and retrieves information from the episodic buffer in the form of conscious

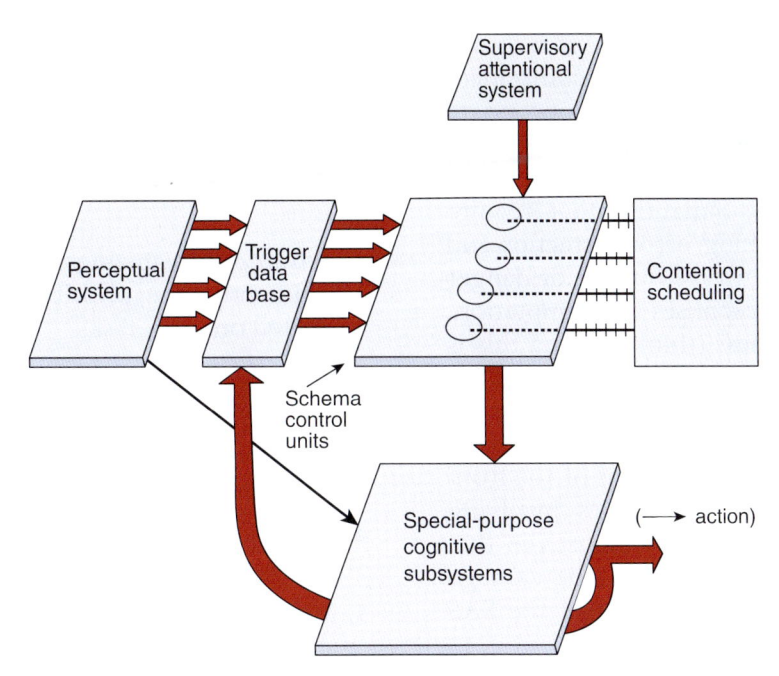

FIGURE 12.14 *The supervisory attentional system. The model of frontal lobe function presented by Shallice and Burgess shows the SAS participating in tasks that involve the frontal lobe when automatic process are not appropriate, e.g. novelty or error feedback.*
Source: Shallice, T. (1988). *From Neuropsychology to Mental Structure.* Cambridge, UK: Cambridge University Press.

awareness, which can then be worked upon in problem-solving activities.

The location of both the central executive and the episodic buffer is thought to be in the frontal lobes, with different cortical subregions being involved in different mental processes (Khan & Muly, 2011).

Thus, WM is not a box of tools with one identifiable function, but rather a set of theoretical processes that work on different information in different regions of the brain. We cannot put our finger on the exact location of WM because it is an emergent property of the functional interactions between the prefrontal cortex and other regions of the brain (D'Esposito, 2007).

Supervisory attentional system

Baddeley's notion of the central executive was not a lightning bolt of inspiration but rather a carefully studied reconceptualization of another theory (Baddeley, 1986, 2007; Baddeley & Hitch, 1974). This influential model of attentional control was provided by Donald Norman and Tim Shallice (1986). Central to their model of cognitive functioning is the **supervisory attentional system** (SAS) which unashamedly shares marked similarities with Baddeley's central executive. This is a theory of EF and how behaviour is controlled. The theory is based on two premises: (1) the routine selection of routine operations is automated (well learned), and (2) the selection of non-routine operations is qualitatively different from routine selection and involves a general-purpose supervisory system that oversees behaviour (Figure 12.14). There is also some similarity with what Wiers and Stacy have called implicit and explicit cognitions (Wiers & Stacy, 2005, 2006; Wiers, Bartholow et al., 2007; Wiers, Teachman, 2007).

In the Norman–Shallice model of executive control, there are two levels of response programmes: low-level and high-level processes. Low-level processes (or schemata as they are called) are activated when certain demands are created in the environment, e.g. driving a car activates schemata such as stopping at red lights.

Selection of a schema is dependent on the potential inputs that can act as a trigger; once a schema has been activated, other schemata are inhibited. The selection between routine actions is regarded as an automatic process without conscious awareness or allocation of attentional resources; it prevents conflict between potentially competing schemata. In this regard, when driving a car component schemata are primed, and if the environmental circumstances dictate, e.g. a red light shows, the schema of braking will be activated and the accelerating schema will be inhibited. The automaticity of this action depends on learning and experience. Schemata are well-learned response programmes. Clearly, our behaviour is not all automatic, but it does allow us to economically perform actions without recourse to the effort of thinking. However, circumstances might arise when routine selection is inappropriate and conscious awareness of the environmental context becomes necessary; thinking is required and thinking requires energy. Situations that require planning and decision making, error correction and troubleshooting, or that involve novelty or danger or overcoming habitual responses and temptation, require conscious awareness (thinking) and this is when the SAS is needed. The SAS modulates the schemata's activation level, thereby increasing the likelihood of the correct schema being triggered.

This theory accounts for the actions of the frontal lobe, using evidence from studies involving lesions of various subregions to support the theory (Shallice, 1988) in which frontal lobe damage is linked to dysfunctional components of the SAS (Shallice & Burgess, 1991).

Shallice argues that without the SAS and no triggering stimuli, patients exhibit utilization behaviour in which visual and tactile stimulation are grasped and manipulated by patients with frontal lobe damage (Lhermitte, 1983). Shallice and Evans (1978) used mini problems dealing with a novel situation in which patients had to think of a non-obvious approach and checked the plausibility of that approach, e.g. how fast does a racehorse gallop? One way of deriving a plausible answer despite not knowing the actual answer would be to consider the galloping horse as going faster than a man can run but slower than a car. People with frontal lobe deficits make bizarre suggestions, suggesting a breakdown in SAS. A similar effect was found when frontal lobe patients had to estimate the price of a toy as if it were the real thing, e.g. a toy Ferrari costs about £20, whereas the real thing is closer to £170,000 (Smith & Milner, 1984). Using a covered maze in which only a portion of the maze can be seen at any one time revealed that there were more rule-breaking errors in frontal lobe patients (Karnath et al., 1991). The same patients were unable to reverse a route that they had previously learned and deficits were more apparent when required to organize or plan their behaviour over longer periods of time or set priorities in the face of two or more competing tasks (Karnath & Wallesch, 1992).

Brown (2005) has taken a different approach to the development of a theoretical account of EF: he took a psychopathology and placed it in a new theoretical framework of EFs. One may consider this as fitting the data to your own theory, but it is not that different from the original concepts of the SAS and WM. Brown evaluated reports highlighting the EF problems experienced in psychopathologies and compared them with normal controls. His endeavours resulted in the identification of six clusters within the domain of executive functions.

1. *Activation*: organizing tasks and materials, estimating time, prioritizing tasks, and getting started on work tasks.
2. *Focus*: focusing, sustaining focus, and shifting focus to tasks.
3. *Effort*: regulating alertness, sustaining effort, and processing speed.
4. *Emotion*: managing frustration and modulating emotions.
5. *Memory*: utilizing working memory and accessing recall (see earlier).
6. *Action*: monitoring and regulating self-action; impulse control.

The six clusters are not mutually exclusive; they can overlap and influence each other. Brown does not ascribe any one particular deficit as being more important than another, and therefore this is more of a description of executive function rather than a theoretical attempt to understand the processes.

Impulsivity has been linked to numerous disorders, e.g. addiction, and in particular in disorders of the orbitofrontal cortex and cingulate (see Chapter 16) (Matsuo et al., 2009; Torregrossa et al., 2008; Volkow, Fowler et al., 2009) and ADHD (Barbelivien et al., 2001; Bush et al., 1999; Carmona et al., 2005; Hesslinger et al., 2002; Itami & Uno, 2002; Lee et al., 2005) (see Chapter 20). Animal studies of impulsivity point to differential actions of the orbitofrontal cortex depending on the task (Cardinal et al., 2004). However, linking the psychological substrate of impulsivity with a neuroanatomical site such as the frontal cortex and associated subregions (cingulate and orbitofrontal cortices) is not necessarily straightforward. The brain undergoes changes right up until early adulthood (Sowell, Thompson, Holmes, Jernigan et al., 1999; Sowell et al., 2007) and these neural changes are thought to be critical in generating psychopathologies (Andersen & Navalta, 2004; Chambers et al., 2003; Crews et al., 2007; O'Brien, 2007). Not surprisingly, adolescence is a period of development characterized by overemotional responses that have not been thought through in a cool, rational way – after all, the rational part of the brain is yet to be fully developed.

SUMMARY

The frontal lobes are the most recent region of our brain to evolve and are not surprisingly implicated in a vast array of behaviours and in particular higher cognitive functions. Damage to the frontal lobes can cause a disruption of normal behaviour along both cognitive and social dimensions. Much of our understanding of frontal lobe function has come from studies on brain damage, but also from neurosurgery in which a frontal lobotomy is performed (Strecker et al., 1942). See Jack Nicholson's portrait of a patient who has undergone a frontal lobotomy in the film One Flew Over the Cuckoo's Nest. This is a highly recommended film (from the book written by Ken Kesey) for the psychology student as it covers issues of enforced hospitalization/treatment, the sociopolitical environment of mental health, institutionalization and some of the more extreme forms of treatment.

Advances in neuroimaging have meant that we no longer have to rely on brain-damaged patients as the activity of the brain can be measured (albeit indirectly) in so-called normal people (I've yet to meet one).

BOX 12.4: EXAMS, EF AND THE FRONTAL LOBE

Presumably, you want to get a good mark for your exam. This will require you to use your brain – and not just memory. You will need to use the frontal lobes.

What is the role of the frontal lobe and its connections in the successful answering of an exam question?

In the tradition of neuropsychology, we might wish to consider the effect of damage to the frontal lobe and how that affects exam performance.

Some points to be considered.

- What is necessary to answer a question well?
- What is the role of the frontal lobes in facilitating this good answer?
- What experimental data support your view?
- What happens when thing go wrong?
- What would the exam answer look like if the frontal lobe had been lesioned?
- Is there a theoretical context to which we can apply our account of the frontal lobes in examination answers?
- Are there any other areas involved in successful examination answers, e.g. the temporal lobe or the hippocampus?

Frontal lobe function	Exam requirement	Possible lesion effect
Respond to novelty	The question is a novel situation that requires applying existing knowledge to a new question	Perseveration (like on the WCST). May not see the novelty of the question and revert back to the old past questions used for revision
Organize the meaning of the question and plan ahead	Need to read the question and see how the words join up to create meaning	May just look at key words and write everything you know about the topic and not answer the specific target of the question
Use feedback to modify behaviour	Need to constantly check that you are answering the question. Use error feedback to keep on task	Chance of drifting off the actual question. Need to be explicit about how it answers the question in every paragraph. Errors from the past not heeded
Planning	Essays need a plan and organization. It is not just what you know, it is how it all relates to the question	Lack of planning leads to disconnected paragraphs that do not aid comprehension and have no logical pathway
Attention	Sustained attention is required to achieve outcome	Distraction will result in going off task. Too much concern about changes in environment, e.g. not another trip to the toilet by the student in front or if they crunch their mints one more time I will explode (affective regulation needed)

Frontal lobe function	Exam requirement	Possible lesion effect
Goal formation	Answering the question and bigger goals, such as obtaining degree	Might not be able to operate on immediate goals which appear to take one away from the ultimate goal but are required for the successful completion of the task
Automaticity	Well-learned behaviours such as writing allow thought to be concentrated on the task rather than on the actual motor mechanics of writing	Cognitive effort put into online processing of the writing process itself leading to a lack of content
Deferred gratification	Overall goals require putting off immediate rewards for more distant goals	Out on the piss every night. No revision. The story of Chris and Carl! I want it all and I want it now!
Inhibitory control	This should be used to stop engaging in non-goal-oriented tasks and keep within the exam rule	Non-focused and rules broken, cheating, talking. Other rules such as answering the specified question
Temporal accountancy	Need to organize the time of question answering	Too much time spent on one question
Working memory	An account of EF. Especially the central executive	Unable to do two things at once. Write and think. Chew gum and walk …
Learning	Revision is just that … not new learning. Use the information once learned to answer any question	Information not consolidated and therefore not able to be used creatively
Theory of Mind	Need to have a concept of what the examiner wants to see	No ToM, then you may not be able to convey the information in an intelligible fashion, e.g. sentences that don't relate. Think what an essay by a schizophrenic would look like!

Other regions	Function
Hippocampus	Spatial learning and memory
Amygdala	Provokes fear and anxiety – best avoided by preparation
Temporal lobe	Memory/language – obviously
Occipital lobe	Visual processing of exam paper converted to verbal information
Basal ganglia	Automated motor processes – focus on the content rather than the mechanics of writing
Mesolimbic system	Motivation/reward – good marks are like stickers to a primary school child – everyone wants them and will work like a rat in an operant chamber to get them
Brainstem	Keeps you alive – very important
Cerebellum	Fine motor movements and timing – essential for writing
Thalamus	Sensory integration
Hypothalamus	Maintains nutritional state required for brain activity, reduction leads to reduced glucose and slow brain. Eat a Mars bar!
Pituitary gland	Master gland responsible for stress responses. Too much stress is debilitating, but too relaxed might also mean low motivation
Reticular formation	Consciousness – helps keep you awake, quite important in an exam

LEARNING OUTCOME QUESTIONS

You should be able to answer the following questions.

- Evaluate the main theoretical positions describing frontal lobe functions.
- How would you determine if a patient has frontal lobe deficits?
- Being able to inhibit behaviour is a fundamental process of the frontal lobes. Discuss.
- Know why it is important to have frontal lobes in an exam (see Box 12.4).

FURTHER READING

Baddeley, A. (2007). *Working memory, thought, and action.* Oxford, UK: Oxford University Press.

Barkley, R. A. (2001). The executive functions and self-regulation: An evolutionary neuropsychological perspective. *Neuropsychology Review, 11*(1), 1–29.

Driver, J., Haggard, P., & Shallice, T. (Eds.) (2007). *Mental processes in the human brain.* Oxford, UK: Oxford University Press.

Filevich, E., Kuhn, S., & Haggard, P. (2012). Intentional inhibition in human action: the power of 'no'. *Neuroscience and Biobehavioral Reviews, 36*(4), 1107–1118.

Jurado, M. B., & Rosselli, M. (2007). The elusive nature of executive functions: A review of our current understanding. *Neuropsychology Review, 17*(3), 213–233.

Macmillan, M. (2002). *An odd kind of fame: Stories of Phineas Gage.* Cambridge, MA: MIT Press.

Rolls, E. T., & Grabenhorst, F. (2008). The orbitofrontal cortex and beyond: From affect to decision-making. *Progress in Neurobiology, 86*(3), 216–244.

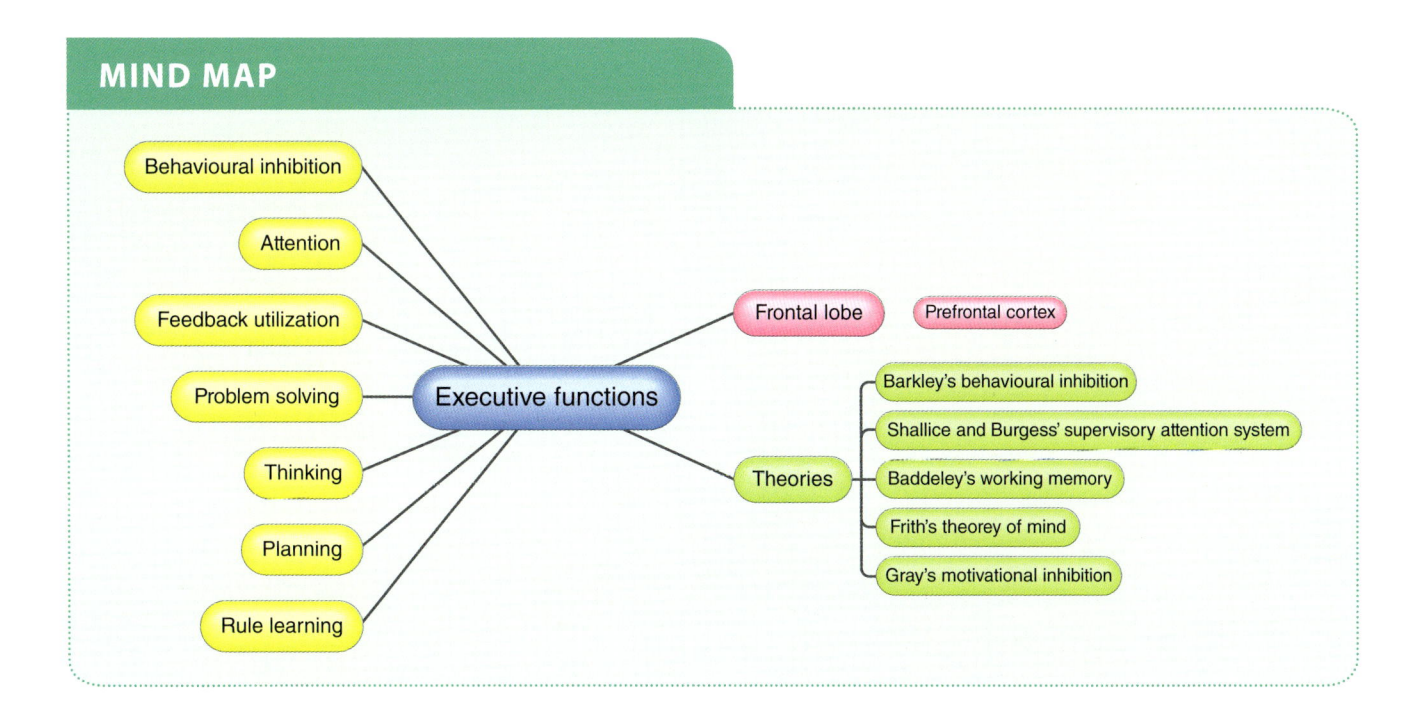

MIND MAP

13 Neural Plasticity and Memory

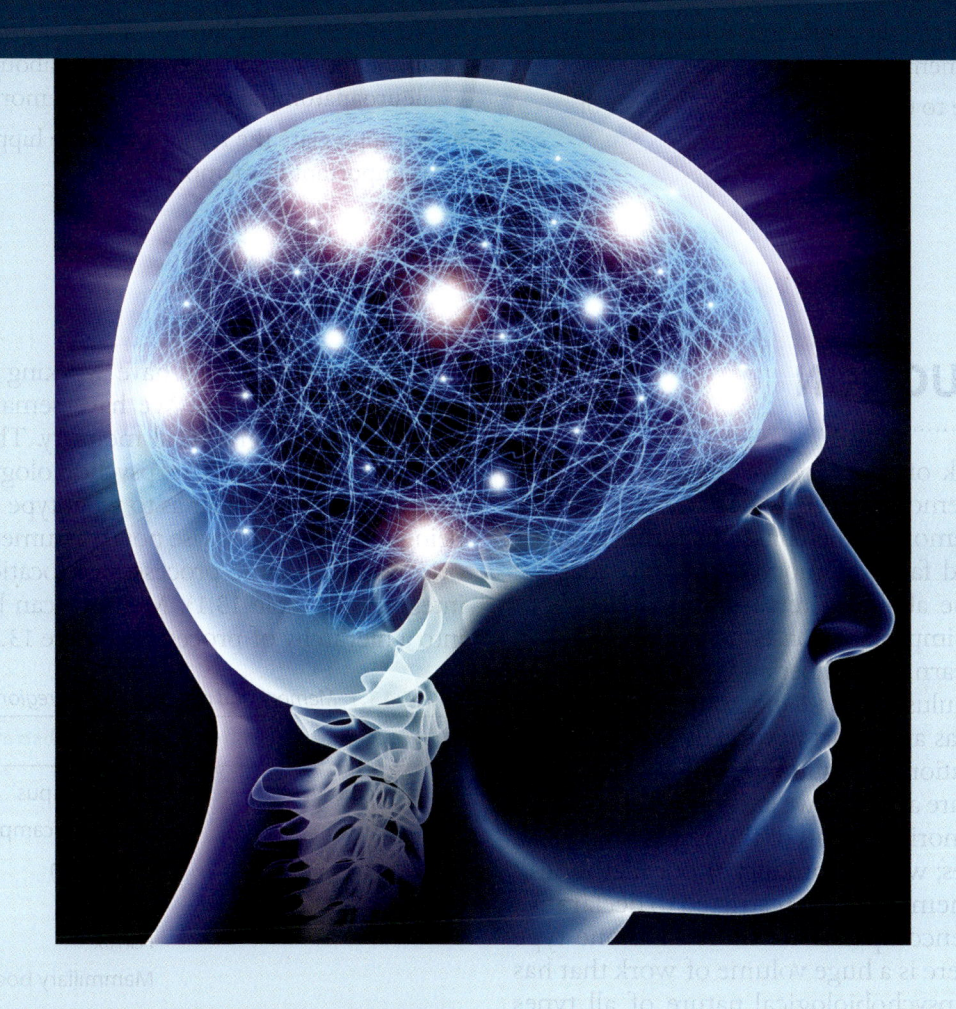

ANATOMY OF THE CHAPTER

This chapter will highlight the following.

- The divisions of memory and the difficulty of psychobiological studies.
- Amnesia.
- The regions of the brain involved in memory.
- The molecular processes underlying memory and neuroplasticity.

INTRODUCTION 344

MEMORY: WHAT IS IT AND WHERE IS IT? 344

AMNESIA 345

THE NEURAL BASIS OF MEMORY 353

WHAT HAPPENS AT THE NEURAL LEVEL? 353

NEUROPLASTICITY 355

SUMMARY 356

LEARNING OUTCOMES

1. To understand the limitations inherent in studying memory.
2. To be able to describe the molecular basis of memory.
3. To be able to evaluate the use of case studies in the formulation of hypotheses about the neuroanatomical substrates of memory.
4. To appreciate the reasons why the hippocampus is important in memory.

INTRODUCTION

When we think of memory, we think of a particular type of memory which is declarative memory. Declarative memory is the conscious recollection of experiences and facts. Memory clearly has adaptive functions as the ability to retain information about the world has important consequences for our survival, e.g. we learn, remember and recall information about the stimulus that is dangerous or important. But memory has an impact beyond the simple retention of information. Our autobiographical memories shape who we are and how we are going to respond in the future. Memories are part of the process that make up our identities; we are a product of our memories.

The word memory is not restricted to declarative memory and encompasses far more than one type of process. There is a huge volume of work that has addressed the psychobiological nature of all types of memory. Case studies of when memory fails and animal studies have been influential in increasing our understanding of memory and directing our search to areas such as the hippocampus. The question remains, though, what is the molecular basis of memory? How are conscious and non-conscious memories biologically stored?

MEMORY: WHAT IS IT AND WHERE IS IT?

More often than not, when we think of memory, it is the memory for events or shopping lists or anything that is conscious. However, memory as a broader definition includes declarative memory but also procedural memory. We have short-term memory and long-term memory. We have working memory. We have episodic memory. We have semantic memory. We have autobiographical memory. That is a lot of memory processes. The psychobiological study of memory has to be clear as to what type of memory is being measured. It is wise not to assume that all memories have the same processes or locations or neural integration (Table 13.1). Memory can be divided up into a hierarchy of processes (Figure 13.1).

TABLE 13.1 *Memory and associated brain regions*

Type of memory/learning	Neural substrate
Spatial memory	Hippocampus
	Parahippocampus
	Subiculum
	Cortex
	Fornix
	Mammillary bodies
Emotional memory	Amygdala
Semantic memory	Temporal lobe
	Prefrontal cortex
	Distributed networks
Episodic	Fornix
	Prefrontal cortex
Recognition memory	Hippocampus
	Temporal lobe
Working memory	Hippocampus
	Prefrontal cortex
Motor memory	Striatum
	Cerebellum
Sensory memory	Sensory cortices
Classical conditioning	Cerebellum
Habituation	Basal ganglia
Operant conditioning	Ventral/dorsal striatum

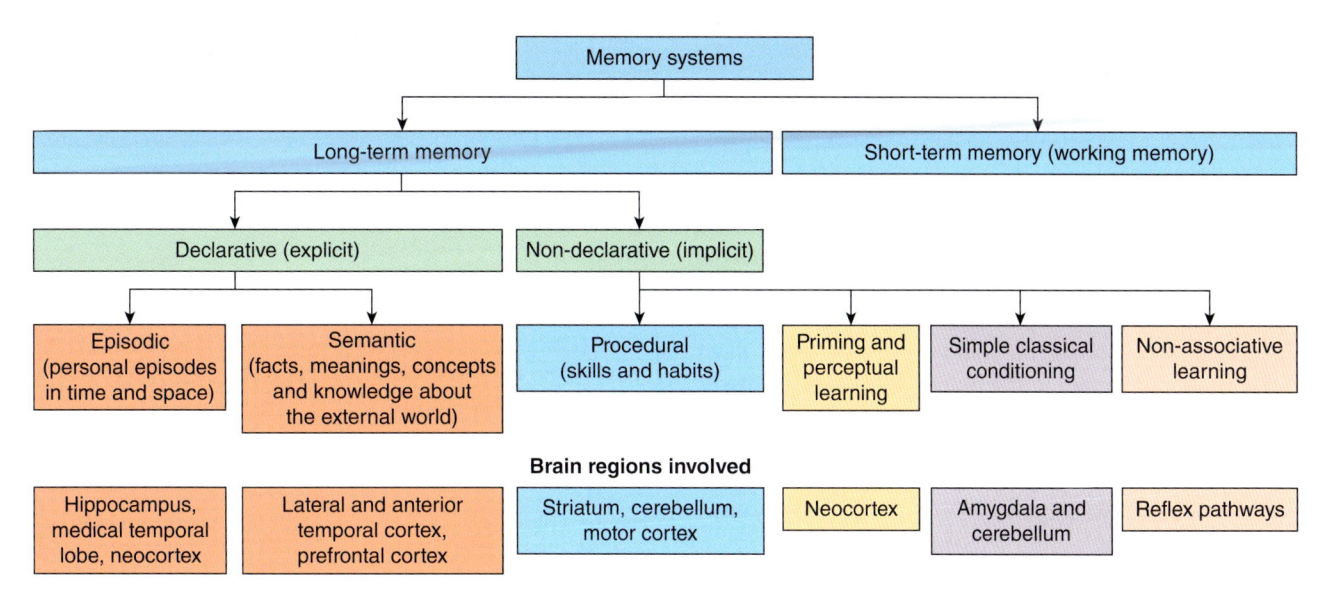

FIGURE 13.1 *Memory hierarchies.*

The study of memory is more than just the study of mere storage. To be able to remember something, the information must first be processed. Factors such as motivation, attention, executive function and perception are all important in allowing the material to be stored. Storage of information is what most people consider to be memory but as becomes evident when reading cognitive psychology textbooks, there are many types of memory and therefore possibly different types of storage. Storage involves learning (see Chapter 8 for the most simple of associative learning). Finally, how do we know that we have remembered something? This is assessed by retrieval. However, retrieval can be obtained via different mechanisms, e.g. free recall, recognition or cued recall.

Memory has been studied extensively by cognitive psychologists who have identified mechanisms and processes of learning, encoding, consolidation, and retrieval. They have provided models which generally consist of boxes and arrows. Although this is a simple schematic representation of the psychological processes of memory, we must not think that the boxes represent storage entities memory as actual discrete locations in the brain and that the arrows are the connecting neurons. The neurobiology is far more complex than the description and theorizing of processes that is evident in the early accounts of memory.

As with many areas, memory has been studied from a normal perspective and from the psychopathology perspective. There are many disorders that have a memory dysfunction, e.g. Alzheimer's disease (see Chapter 24). However, the initial psychopathological clues to memory arise from case studies of those with amnesia.

AMNESIA

Studies of amnesic patients, whether the amnesia is caused by surgery or accident, have provided the beginnings of the psychobiological accounts of memory. The most notable case study is that of HM who had profound anterograde amnesia (Box 13.1).

There are two types of amnesia: **anterograde amnesia** and **retrograde amnesia**. Anterograde amnesia is the inability to establish new memories following injury or trauma. Retrograde amnesia is the inability to remember events occurring before the trauma. Anterograde and retrograde amnesia can co-exist; they are not mutually exclusive. Indeed, anterograde amnesia has been hypothesized to be the main problem that influences retrograde amnesia in a group of alcoholic patients that have neurological damage as a result of alcohol consumption (Box 13.2). The case studies and group studies of **Korsakoff's syndrome** have generally

BOX 13.1: HENRY MOLAISON (AKA HM)

It is difficult to decide which case study is most famous in the neuropsychological literature: HM or Phineas Gage. The case of Phineas Gage, focused on executive functioning, is considered in Chapter 12. The case of HM expanded our knowledge of memory and HM became the most published participant in the history of neuropsychology. It became known that HM was Henry Molaison after his death in 2008 but we still use his initials to help protect his anonymity (Phineas Gage's name is always used because he died a long time ago, and the ethics of anonymity were perhaps less troublesome in the past).

HM suffered from epilepsy which was sufficiently severe to be debilitating. In order to try and control the epilepsy, the temporal lobes were removed from both sides of his brain. Included with the lesion of the temporal lobe were the entorhinal cortex, amygdala and hippocampus. Whilst the surgery was successful in containing the epileptic discharge from the temporal lobes, it also had some negative effects. HM had profound amnesia. He could not remember daily events but was otherwise cognitively intact (Scoville & Milner, 1957). The surgery took place on 1 September 1953 and the first psychological examination took place on 26 April 1955 in which:

> The memory defect was immediately apparent. The patient gave the date as March, 1953, and his age as 27. Just before coming into the examining room he had been talking to Dr. Karl Pribram, yet he had no recollection of this at all and denied that anyone had spoken to him. In conversation, he reverted constantly to boyhood events and seemed scarcely to realize that he had had an operation. (Scoville & Milner, 1957, p.16)

HM failed to remember any new information since the surgery.

The first paper on HM used in its title the phrase 'hippocampal lesions'. However, the specificity of the surgery could not be attributed solely to the hippocampus; modern technology was not available to scan the brain. According to Squire (2009), the case of HM provided the impetus to develop animal models of amnesia, which eventually identified the hippocampus, perirhinal, entorhinal and parahippocampal cortices, collectively known as the medial temporal lobe memory system (Squire & Zola-Morgan, 1991).

HM's participation in research spans many decades, and eventually imaging technology was used to assess the damage caused by the neurosurgery. Corkin et al. (1997), using MRI scans, found that HM's lesion was less extensive than had been described at the time of surgery. The lesion was:

> ... bilaterally symmetrical and included the medial temporal polar cortex, most of the amygdaloid complex, most or all of the entorhinal cortex, and approximately half of the rostrocaudal extent of the intraventricular portion of the hippocampal formation (dentate gyrus, hippocampus, and subicular complex). (Corkin et al., 1997, p.3964)

The parahippocampal gyrus was differentially affected, with the posterior gyrus relatively intact, whereas the anterior parahippocampal gyrus was related to the severity of the amnesia and not just the hippocampus itself. HM was aged 66 at the time of the first scan. In a ten-year follow-up, Salat et al. (2006) found that a number of changes had occurred over the ten-year period. These included cortical thinning, reduced volume of grey matter structures and abnormal white matter. These were regarded as a possible sign of ageing and related to his hypertension (increased blood pressure). These changes mean that caution needs to be exercised when reading the studies conducted in the decade prior to HM's death because the specificity of the neurological damage could no longer be maintained (Squire, 2009).

HM had pure amnesia and his deficits generalized all types of information arriving from different sensory modalities (Corkin, 2002). He was able to remember events prior to the surgery (Corkin, 1984).

Milner (1962) reported that HM's memory deficits were restricted to events and facts because his amnesia did not affect motor or cognitive skills (procedural memory). His procedural memory was demonstrated in a mirror drawing task in which he had to trace the outline of a five-pointed star when all he could see was the reflection. He performed well and learned the task but when asked to perform the task again, despite evidence of motor/skill learning, he was unable to recall doing the task previously. Therefore, memory was not just one system that was affected by the lesions but rather there were multiple systems of memory that were differentially affected. Skill learning involves other regions of the brain that were not included in the neurosurgery, e.g. the basal ganglia.

Another case study was that of NA who had an accident in which a fencing foil entered the right nostril and went upwards towards the brain. The result was anterograde amnesia similar to that seen in HM (Teuber et al., 1968). The deficits in acquiring new knowledge were argued to be a result of faulty encoding at the time of input (Squire, 1982).

In a subsequent neuroimaging study, NA's hippocampal formation appeared to be intact but other parts of the temporal lobe had abnormalities, indicating that amnesia can arise due to other structures that are damaged at the same time (Squire et al., 1989). The ability to remember events from the past, as both NA and HM could do, was verified in other case studies, leading Squire and colleagues to suggest that remote memories of an autobiographical nature involve cortical regions after learning and coding take place that are independent of the temporal lobes and hippocampus (Bayley et al., 2003).

These case studies indicate that memory is not located as a cognitive box within the brain, but are processes that can be uniquely disrupted, depending on the site and extent of a lesion. They have also told us that memory is more than one entity, that there are different processes and different types of memory, e.g. declarative and non-declarative (procedural).

BOX 13.2: ALCOHOL, ALCOHOLISM AND KORSAKOFF'S SYNDROME

Case studies of amnesia have been hugely influential in understanding memory. However, case studies are always limited by the fact that the damage inflicted to the brain is often unique and idiosyncratic to the individual being reviewed. In the world of neuropsychology, it is rare to find groups of people with brain damage that is unique to the disorder but not an individual. However, there is an exception to this. Chronic abuse of alcohol leading to alcoholism and neurological damage has provided research participants who can be grouped together.

Alcohol has many effects on the CNS. The main effects are to enhance GABAergic activity (i.e. inhibitory effects) and decrease glutamatergic effects (i.e. reduce excitation) (Davis & Wu, 2001). The net effect is CNS depression.

Alcohol intoxication has numerous effects on psychological functions.

- Acute alcohol-induced memory loss ('blackout').
- Tolerance, neuroadaptation and alcohol dependence syndrome.
- Alcohol withdrawal syndrome (tremor, hallucinations, seizures, delirium tremens).
- Alcoholic dementia.
- Hepatic encephalopathy.
- Alcohol amnesic disorder (Wernicke–Korsakoff syndrome).

It is the alcoholic amnesic disorder that has told us more about the processes of memory than the other effects of alcohol. Korsakoff's syndrome (sometimes called psychosis or amnesia or dementia) is the indirect result of long-term alcohol abuse. It sometimes is described as **Wernicke–Korsakoff syndrome** because of **Wernicke's encephalopathy** which is a life-threatening neurological disorder. Wernicke's encephalopathy can lead to Korsakoff's amnesia if untreated. The reason for these disorders is not alcohol *per se* but the loss of **thiamine** which is a vitamin (B1) that helps convert food into energy in the form of **adenosine triphosphate** (ATP) (Osiezagha et al., 2013). Because of their lifestyle and their intake of alcohol, alcoholics are at increased risk of thiamine deficiency (Lieber, 2003; Martin et al., 2003).

Thiamine deficiency can lead to reduced cerebral energy metabolism, NMDA receptor-mediated excitotoxicity and a breakdown of the blood–brain barrier (Leong & Butterworth, 1996). The result is that those cells that require more energy eventually die (Hazell et al., 1998). The areas that are more vulnerable to thiamine deficiency are the thalamic nuclei, oculomotor and vestibular nuclei, hippocampus, ventricles, cerebellum and cortex (Jung et al., 2012; Osiezagha et al., 2013).

Carl Wernicke in 1881 described a rapid onset of paralysis of eye movements, mental confusion and ataxia in patients who were alcoholic. Sergei Korsakoff during the period 1887–1891 further identified amnesic affect in alcoholics (Zubaran et al., 1997). The clinical picture of Korsakoff's syndrome includes:

- impaired recent memory (anterograde amnesia);
- relatively spared remote memory along a temporal gradient (retrograde amnesia);
- confabulation;
- reduced insight into illness;
- disorientation in time, place and person; and
- intact IQ.

By the time of diagnosis, Korsakoff's syndrome symptoms are usually so bad that the damage extends to the frontal lobes and there are also deficits in executive functioning (see Chapter 12) (Oscar-Berman, 2012; Oscar-Berman et al., 2004).

The most obvious feature of Korsakoff's syndrome is the profound amnesia. The retention span rapidly decayed in patients with Korsakoff's syndrome undergoing a short-term memory task (Cermak et al., 1971). They were more sensitive to the effects of proactive interference (by using an interpolated task to stop rehearsal, e.g. counting backwards) and did not utilize external cues provided by the experiments (Cermak & Butters, 1972). The nature of the proactive interference was primarily intrusion errors from prior lists of learning (Meudell et al., 1978). Performance was better when there was a reduction in proactive interference caused by a change in the type of information to be recalled from that of the previous list, e.g. numbers or letters (Warrington & Weiskrantz, 1970; Winocur et al., 1981).

In a series of experiments investigating the use of encoding strategies, Cermak et al. (1973) noted that those with Korsakoff's syndrome failed to use semantic processing and default to using acoustic (sounds) and associative encoding (see Chapter 8). Semantic processing was seen to be faulty in a study looking at the release of proactive interference. Participants were given lists that were either letters or numbers and when there was an alphanumeric shift to a new list (i.e. letters to numbers), the effect of proactive interference was not seen. However, when the lists comprised semantically related items in which there was a taxonomic shift to a new list, those with Korsakoff's syndrome demonstrated proactive interference effects (Cermak et al., 1974) (Figure 13.2.1).

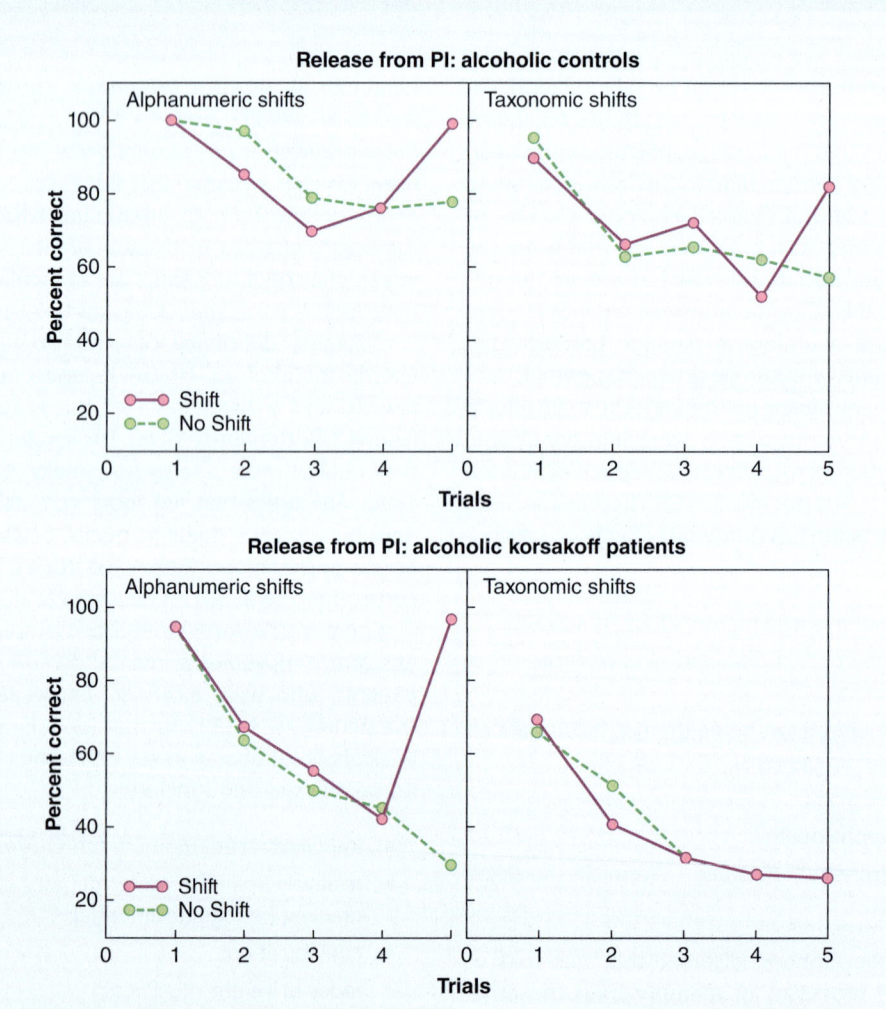

FIGURE 13.2.1 *Proactive interference in alcoholics and Korsakoff's syndrome. Korsakoff's syndrome patients were released from proactive interference when they had a taxonomic shift in items on a list. Alcoholics without Korsakoff's syndrome showed better performance in both alphanumeric shifts (letters to numbers) and taxonomic shifts.*
Source: Cermak, L. S., Butters, N., & Moreines, J. (1974). Some analyses of the verbal encoding deficit of alcoholic Korsakoff patients. *Brain and Language, 1*(2), 141–150.

Rather than the encoding deficit, others have argued that there is evidence to suggest that there is also a retrieval deficit (see Butters, 1985). Graf et al. (1984) demonstrated that when there is cued recall, those with Korsakoff's syndrome can perform at control levels. Korsakoff's syndrome can be differentiated from control groups during free recall tasks where there is no cue, an effect that diminishes if they are provided with the first three letters of the word to be recalled (Warrington & Weiskrantz, 1970).

In a task involving naming of remote historical events in photos, performance was related to posterior cortical white matter and sequencing was related to prefrontal volumes, and neither to hippocampal volumes (Fama et al., 2004). In the same study, anterograde memory for non-verbal visual material showed a relationship to hippocampal volume and not cortical. The retrograde amnesia following a temporal gradient can be explained in terms of the development of alcoholism and Korsakoff's syndrome over a period of time. During the history of alcoholism leading to Korsakoff's syndrome, anterograde amnesia could be responsible for the temporal gradient. The lifestyle of someone with alcoholism and the psychobiological effects of alcohol itself may be one explanation for the retrograde amnesia; as the disease continues, new information is unlikely to be retained.

The retrograde amnesia seen in Korsakoff's syndrome is far greater than one would expect if it were a function of long-term alcoholism. Butters and Brandt (1985) used a case study to illustrate the disassociation between anterograde amnesia and retrograde amnesia. Patient PZ was a university professor and scientist who had published his autobiography three years prior to a diagnosis of cortical syndrome at the age of 65. This was a valuable resource because it provided a temporal and detailed account of his life. Using this autobiography, Butters and Brandt were able to construct a bespoke neuropsychological test battery. The results indicated that there was a temporal gradient of retrograde amnesia (Figure 13.2.2). PZ was unable to remember things that were more recent and that he had previously had a good command over. The authors concluded that this was evidence, albeit from a case study, that anterograde amnesia does not entirely explain the temporal gradient of retrograde amnesia because he once had a good knowledge of his life at the point of writing the biography. Thus, the retrograde amnesia was not secondary to a deficiency to learn. The neuroanatomical basis of the retrograde amnesia has received less attention than that of the anterograde amnesia. In a review of the available data, Race and Verfaellie (2012) conclude that the retrograde amnesia arising in Korsakoff's syndrome is a function of decreased frontal lobe activity.

It is common for patients with Korsakoff's syndrome to be able to remember information from childhood and

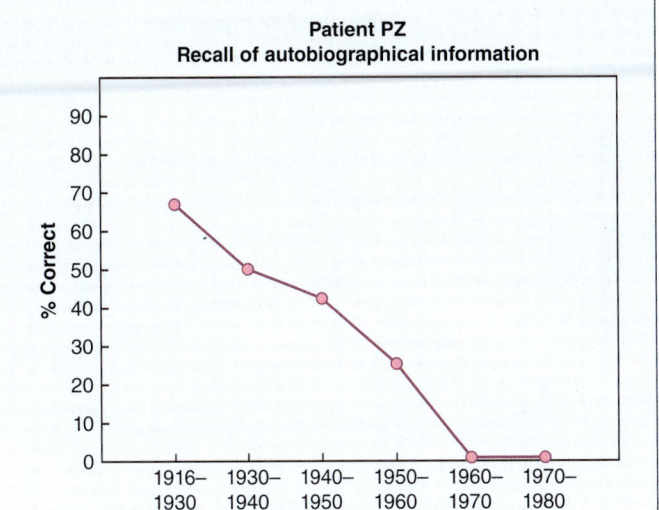

FIGURE 13.2.2 *Autobiographical recall of PZ's life. PZ demonstrated retrograde amnesia with a temporal gradient.* Source: Butters, N., & Brandt, J. (1985). The continuity hypothesis: The relationship of long-term alcoholism to the Wernicke–Korsakoff syndrome. *Recent Developments in Alcoholism, 3*, 207–226. With kind permission from Springer Science and Business Media.

early adulthood. However, studies have failed to show a sparing of remote memory and those that do find a deficit have been argued not to have controlled the task difficulty, e.g. old faces are easier to recall than recent faces (Sanders & Warrington, 1971) (Figure 13.2.3). This could simply be due to a rehearsal repetition effect, i.e. those faces from the distant past have more decades to be repeated than those from the recent past. Albert et al. (1979) gave the famous faces test to Korsakoff's patients and controlled for task difficulty, e.g. some people are more recognizably famous than others. The famous faces test involves remembering faces that were prominent during a particular decade. They noted that patients with Korsakoff's demonstrated a temporary graded retrograde amnesia in which recollection from the distant past was much better than the more recent past. They were also able to recognize 'hard' faces from the distant past more readily than easy faces from the more recent past (Butters & Albert, 1982).

The damage to the brain caused by alcohol, and its impact on thiamine metabolism have pronounced neurological effects which underlie the amnesia seen in Korsakoff's syndrome. However, teasing apart anterograde and retrograde amnesia in Korsakoff's syndrome and the effects of alcohol (and alcoholism) over the decades requires careful methodology. Ironically, the partial resolution of the involvement of anterograde amnesia in the temporal gradient retrograde amnesia came from a case study.

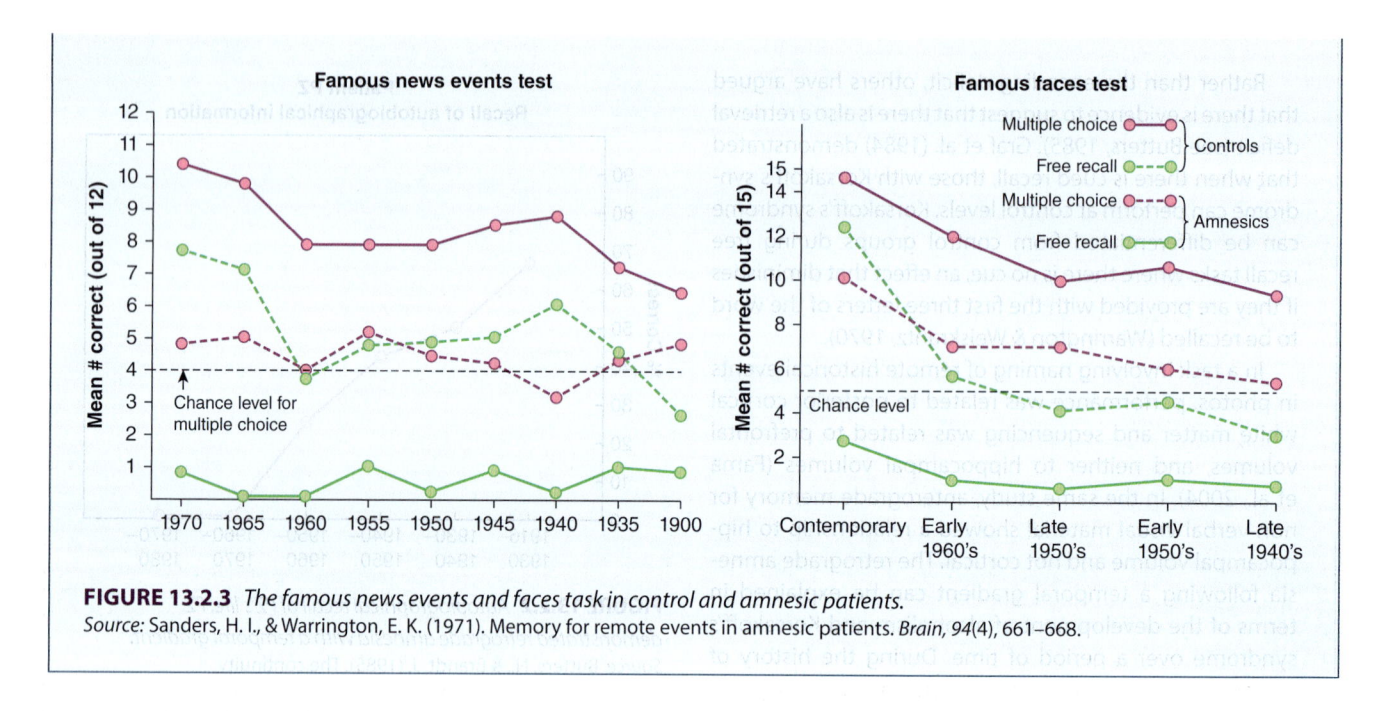

FIGURE 13.2.3 The famous news events and faces task in control and amnesic patients.
Source: Sanders, H. I., & Warrington, E. K. (1971). Memory for remote events in amnesic patients. *Brain*, 94(4), 661–668.

supported a role of memory located in the temporal lobe and diencephalon, including the hippocampus (Figure 13.2).

Amnesia can be the result of accidents, tumours, toxicity, neurosurgery, infections and metabolic diseases. One of the problems in trying to pinpoint a location of memory is that clinical populations often have extensive damage to large areas of the brain. Thus, it is difficult to draw conclusions as to specific neuroanatomical location and also, prelesion cognitive performance is rarely established. In cases of neurosurgery, in which the precision is somewhat greater than in an accident, the preoperative cognitive functioning can be assessed but is often found to be impaired due to the primary effect of the existing disorder or via secondary effects of drugs used in treatment prior to surgery. The same caveat applies to postoperative measurements, and the addition of test-retest effects, in which participants are repeatedly exposed to neuropsychological test batteries (e.g. HM and 40 years of evaluation; see Box 13.1).

With the identification that the temporal lobes may be critically important in memory, a left temporal lobe lobectomy affected verbal tasks such as storytelling, list recalling and unpaired associations (Powell et al., 1985). Lesions of the right temporal lobe affected spatial tasks, e.g. reproduction of complex drawings, recognition of visual patterns (e.g. delayed matching to sample – see Chapter 24), non-verbal paired associative learning and spatial location learning (Fedio & Buchsbaum, 1971; Kimura, 1963; Milner, 1968; Smith & Milner, 1981).

In some studies, there is an improvement in memory with temporal lobe lesions. Whilst this might seem contradictory, it can be explained by the treatment bringing about a cessation of abnormal electrical activity in the contralateral hemisphere to the site of epileptic discharge. Novelly et al. (1984) studied 23 patients both preoperatively and postoperatively up to one year. Prior to surgery, four patients were impaired on verbal memory but after right temporal lobe lobectomy there was a marked improvement in memory scores. Similarly, left temporal lobectomy produced an improvement in delayed recall of non-verbal material. The point here is that verbal information is processed by the

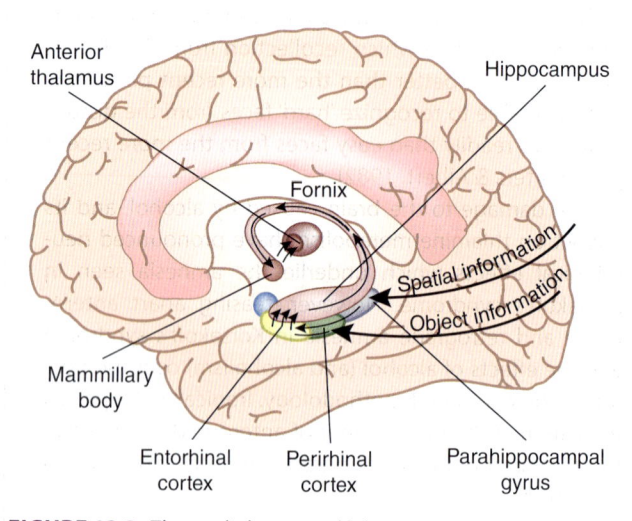

FIGURE 13.2 The medial temporal lobe memory system.

left hemisphere and the improvement seen after right temporal lobectomy was due to the containment of the epileptic discharge and the prevention of its spread to the left hemisphere and vice versa.

The removal of the temporal lobe involves some collateral damage to other structures. Perhaps the most notable is the hippocampus. Milner (1965) studied 79 patients with varied lesions on a visually guided maze task and found that bilateral hippocampal lesions resulted in the most severe deficits followed by right temporal lobe lesions. The same effect was found on tactile mazes (Corkin, 1965). The amount of hippocampal damage on the left side was also associated with impairments on short-term memory tasks as measured by the **Brown Peterson task** and for recall of items presented early in a list (Milner, 1970, 1978). Damage to the right temporal lobe including the hippocampus resulted in impaired visual memory, but this was not evident when the lesion was restricted to only the temporal lobe (Jones-Gotman, 1986a, 1986b).

The hippocampus has since been the focus of memory. The hippocampus has also benefited from attention because spatial memory and associative learning can be readily measured in animals and in taxi drivers (Box 13.3). There are numerous animal models of memory, e.g. the water maze (see Chapter 24). While animal models have been extremely important in

BOX 13.3: SPATIAL MEMORY, THE HIPPOCAMPUS AND LONDON TAXI DRIVERS

According to Biegler et al. (2001):

> Volumetric studies in a range of animals (London taxi-drivers, polygynous male voles, nest-parasitic female cowbirds, and a number of food-storing birds) have shown that the size of the hippocampus, a brain region essential to learning and memory, is correlated with tasks involving an extra demand for spatial learning and memory. (p.6941)

I like the fact that the London taxi driver is grouped with voles and parasitic cowbirds.

All the work on the London taxi driver stems from an original and captivating investigation by Professor Eleanor Maguire and her team. London taxi drivers have to pass the Knowledge before they are licensed, which consists of knowing many routes around London. Maguire et al. (1997) tested taxi drivers' knowledge whilst undergoing positron emission tomography (PET). A PET scan measures radioactivity. If you make oxygen radioactive, you can find out which parts of the brain are using the most.

The taxi drivers were given three tasks: (1) to provide the route between two locations (spatial task), (2) to describe landmarks not in London that they had not visited (non-spatial task), and (3) to recall the plot of a film (control task). A number of brain regions were activated during these tasks, but the one that differentiated the taxi drivers was the hippocampus which was only activated in the spatial task.

Further investigation by Maguire et al. (2000) using MRI scans indicated that the posterior hippocampus was larger in taxi drivers. Interestingly, this increase was a function of years as a taxi driver. Therefore, it is unlikely that taxi drivers are born with an increased posterior hippocampus. The increase occurs through learning and experience. Retired taxi drivers also were not so good at spatial tasks compared to current taxi drivers and there was a reduction in hippocampal volume, but this was not to the levels of non-taxi driver controls (Woollett et al., 2009).

This failure to find an association between hippocampal volume and navigational expertise thus suggests that structural differences in the human hippocampus reflect the detail and/or duration of use of the spatial representation acquired, and not innate navigational expertise *per se* (Maguire et al., 2003).

Another study compared taxi drivers with bus drivers because bus drivers had a similar job but were restricted to a particular route. Therefore, this experimental design removed the confounding variable of driving as an occupation. Compared with bus drivers, taxi drivers had greater grey matter volume in the mid-posterior hippocampi and less volume in the anterior hippocampi. Furthermore, years of navigation experience correlated with hippocampal grey matter volume only in taxi drivers, with right posterior grey matter volume increasing and anterior volume decreasing with more navigation experience (Maguire et al., 2006b) (Figure 13.3.1).

TT had bilateral damage to the hippocampus and was once a taxi driver with 40 years of experience. Using a virtual reality paradigm, TT was able to have a general orientation in London and a detailed topographical knowledge of landmarks and their postion (Maguire et al., 2006a). However, TT was only able to navigate with relative ease

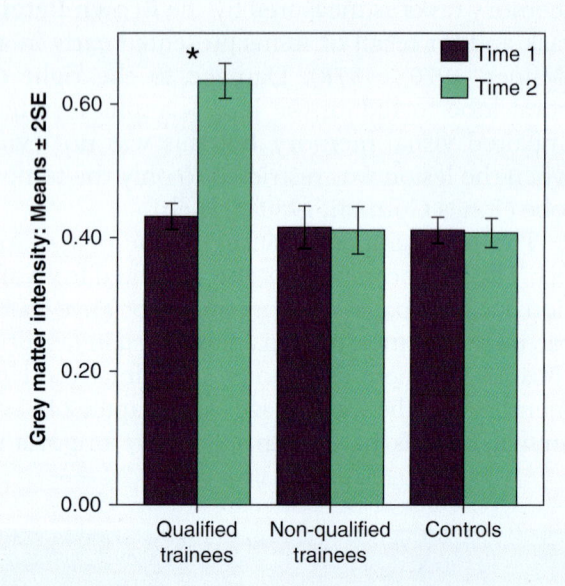

FIGURE 13.3.1 *The hippocampus in London taxi drivers. Before training and after training grey matter intensity in the hippocampus in taxi drivers who passed and failed the Knowledge in comparison to controls (public service employees).*
Source: Woollett, K., & Maguire, E. A. (2011). Acquiring 'the Knowledge' of London's layout drives structural brain changes. *Current Biology*, 21(24), 2109–2114.

Woollett and Maguire (2011) followed trainee London taxi drivers over their four-year training period. Those who successfully qualified after the four years had an increased volume of grey matter in their hippocampus that correlated with their spatial ability to navigate the maze of London. Interestingly, those who failed the Knowledge did not have the increase in hippocampal volume. Another feature about this acquired skill is that there is a trade-off. The taxi drivers are not so good at making new object-location associations (Woollett & Maguire, 2009, 2011) or at other neuropsychological tasks, e.g. the Figure of Rey (Maguire et al., 2006b). The argument put forward by Maguire and colleagues is that the taxi driver's hippocampus is too full of London-based information for anything new to be acquired. Acquiring new information with a spatial component (the object-location task) seems to be specifically constrained in the context of their navigational expertise rather than associative memory taken from the Weschler Memory III task (Woollett & Maguire, 2012).

In Helsinki, taxi drivers were found to be able to recall names of streets and routes better than non-taxi drivers and did so in a route-organized order (even when the items were randomly presented) and not alphabetically or using semantics (Kalakoski & Saariluoma, 2001). Thus, they were using the spatial representations to solve the task.

With advanced technology in our pockets, it would be interesting to see what the effects of satellite navigation systems (GPS) are on the hippocampus of taxi drivers. Looking at the benefits of GPS systems:

> People with a poor sense of direction experience daily problems with navigation, sometimes even in familiar environments. With the widespread use of GPS-based navigation aids, these problems become even more severe when the technology fails or is unavailable. (Wolbers & Hegarty, 2010)

when using the main arterial roads and would be lost when required to deviate off them. Maguire et al. (2006a) suggest that the hippocampus is essential for the fine detail of the spatial map that was learned many years ago.

Doctors have to learn a lot of information, and they were compared to taxi drivers to see if the changes seen in taxi drivers were a general learning phenomenon or specific to spatial learning. The analysis revealed that it was indeed restricted to spatial memory of complex designs (such as London) because there was no increase in the hippocampal grey volume in the medics (Woollett et al., 2008).

---

understanding memory, Thorpe et al. (2004) argue that because memory is accessed via indirect measures (e.g. maze performance), the measurement of memory may be potentially missed. One reason put forward is that there may be what Thorpe and colleagues refer to as 'silent associations' in which an animal may have learned an association but does not perform an act indicative of that learning. In their paper, they cite the example of Wilkie and Masson (1976) who trained pigeons to peck a compound stimulus (shape and colour) for reward. These pigeons were then tested on the individual components of the compound stimulus and it was found that the colour red was the guiding stimulus. One might assume that other shapes and other colours were redundant, i.e. that there had been no learning. However, when the same pigeons were retrained to associate shape with reward they were very quick to learn the association. Therefore they had retained the information in prior learning trials but they had not expressed it during the initial test; the memory was there but it was just not available. The other problem with animal measures of memory, according to Thorpe and colleagues, is the intrusion of species-typical behaviours. In this case, the animal's failure on the memory task might not be due to a failure in memory but rather its preference for engaging in species-typical behaviours. For example, a rat may not overtly demonstrate retention of information in a task because they naturally choose to explore. In an open field maze or a water maze, rats tend to gravitate towards the walls of the apparatus and not head directly to the reinforcer or platform.

Many of the tasks used in assessing memory in the animal have found a role for the hippocampus. The hippocampus also provides us with important insights into understanding the neural and molecular basis of memory.

THE NEURAL BASIS OF MEMORY

The neural basis of memory has been investigated, taking advantage of associative learning in animals (Chapter 8). Associative learning is comparatively simple in terms of its neurobiology. Identifying the neural substrates and molecular basis of declarative memory, however, is somewhat perplexing. How conscious memories emerge in a neural system is a constant question that eludes a definitive answer. Conscious memory, like other aspects of consciousness (see Chapter 18), rages as a philosophical debate and a neuroscientific exploration.

WHAT HAPPENS AT THE NEURAL LEVEL?

The above studies provide neural correlates of behaviour. The temporal lobes and the hippocampus are involved in learning and memory. Understanding the neuroanatomy is important but it does not tell us about the processes of learning and memory. Changes in hippocampal activity during associative learning have been identified (e.g. Wirth et al., 2003).

The Neural Bases of Learning: Long-Term Potentiation (LTP) and Long-Term Depression (LTD)

Sigmund Freud, best known for psychodynamic theories, was perhaps a neuroscientist at heart. Freud suggested concepts of neural plasticity (see Frank, 2008):

- the law of association, in which when two or more neurons fire simultaneously, associative learning is increased;
- critical periods of neuroplasticity (obviously Freud focused on sexual plasticity in later life);
- long-term memories can change according to circumstances and developmental processes; and
- memories can become conscious when provoked by a stimulus.

Richard Semon (1921), a biologist, coined the word 'engram' to refer to a memory trace. The engram had its physical base in the cells of the nervous system. In a series of experiments on rats, Karl Lashley (1950) found that the engram was distributed throughout the cortex and not restricted to one specific site. The larger the lesion of the rat brain, the greater the effect on memory. Therefore, memory exists somehow as networks throughout the brain.

Donald Hebb (1949) is credited with proposing the idea that neurons adapt during learning and create networks to become engrams. Hebb did not differentiate between different types of memory, but suggested that the neural networks that underpin memories, which he called cell assemblies, required reactivation in order to become conscious memories. The essence of Hebb's view is not that different from Freud's account. Hebb argued that it is through repetition and simultaneous activation of neurons that synapses became stronger; as he said, 'cells that fire together, wire together. Cells that fire out of sync, lose their link'.

Eric Kandel, who received the Nobel Prize for medicine for his work on memory, studied the sea slug (*Aplysia californica*) and habituation and sensitization (Carew et al., 1971; Castellucci et al., 1970; Kupfermann et al., 1970; Pinsker et al., 1970a, 1970b). The sea slug is comparatively simple with a small number of neurons (in the thousands) that are of sufficient size to be identified and their activity measured. Habituation, the most ubiquitous form of learning and memory, was studied by looking at the reflexive withdrawal when the siphon is touched (Figure 13.3). Habituation of this reflex resulted in the sea slug no longer withdrawing its gills. Sensitization, which is the opposite of habituation in which there is an increased response to stimulation, could be produced in the sea slug. This was done by pairing the tactile stimulus with an aversive stimulus such as shock. As can be seen in

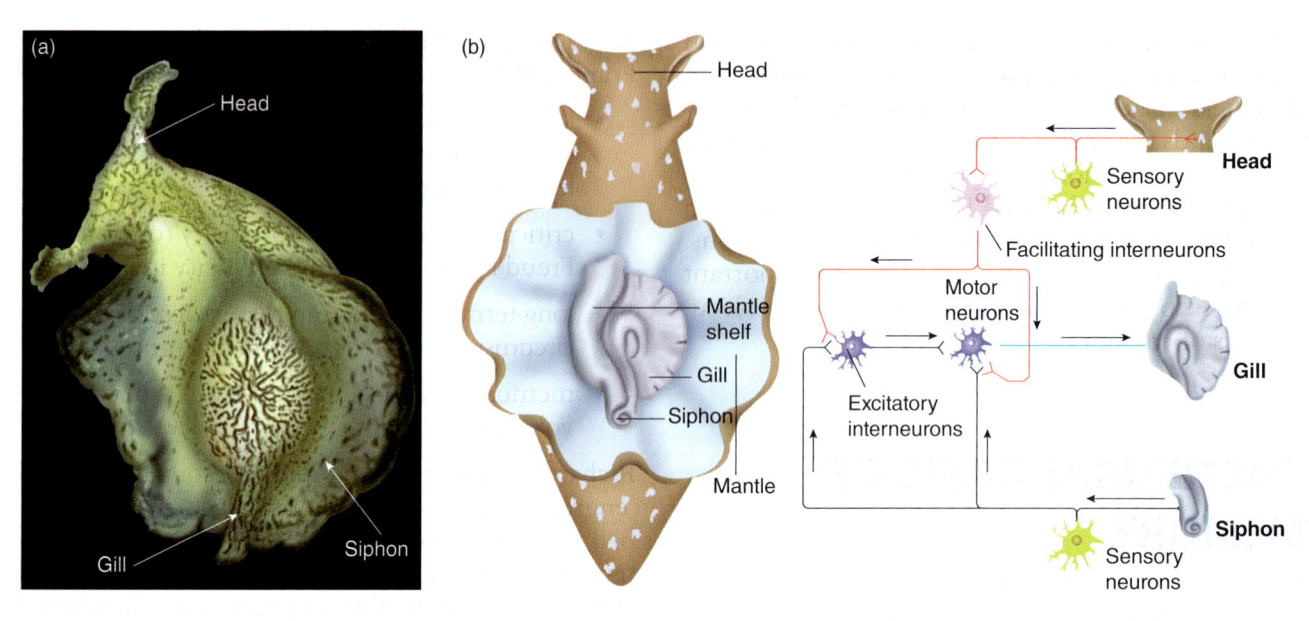

FIGURE 13.3 *The sea slug. (a) Anatomy. (b) Neurocircuitry.*

Figure 13.3, touching the siphon stimulates sensory neurons which activate interneurons and motor neurons which produce the reflex. Measuring the activity of neurons during habituation and sensitization revealed that habituation was the result of a decrease of neurotransmitter release, whereas sensitization correlates with an increase in neurotransmitter release (serotonin) (Brunelli et al., 1976). Such changes through repetitive exposure can produce long-term sensitization (Pinsker et al., 1973). Thus, studies of the sea slug have provided evidence for the Hebbian laws of memory.

Hebb's (1949) initial theory of changes in synaptic transmission has since been supported and refined by experimental evidence (Bliss & Lomo, 1973). Obviously, a good place to look is the hippocampus. With the induction of **long-term potentiation** (LTP), there is a facilitation of synaptic transmission. After a period of high-frequency electrical stimulation of the presynaptic neuron by an electrode, the response to low-frequency stimulation is potentiated. Long-lasting decrease in synaptic strength is known as **long-term depression** (LTD). LTP can last for a long time and requires the activation of both pre- and postsynaptic neurons (Bliss & Gardner-Medwin, 1973; Sastry et al., 1986). Iriki et al. (1989) found changes in the rat hippocampus after conditioning that are similar to LTP.

The search for the neural mechanisms underlying LTP has focused primarily on the **NMDA** and **AMPA receptors**, which are configured to receive messages from glutamate (an excitatory amino acid). The NMDA receptor and LTP share some similarities. Instead of high-frequency stimulation, the NMDA receptor can produce LTP from converging inputs (temporal and spatial summation). If the NMDA receptor is to respond fully, it requires glutamate to bind to the NMDA and AMPA receptors, and partial depolarization of the postsynaptic neuron. In the second requirement, partial depolarizations are produced by inputs to the AMPA receptor or other receptors nearby (Figure 13.4). Thus, naturally occurring LTP requires the convergence of two inputs.

The postsynaptic neuron responds to stimulation by producing a series of biochemical events. Without going into fine detail, these events increase both glutamate release and the number of AMPA receptors. Therefore, the initial stimulation results in synaptic changes that can be enduring. Supporting evidence for the involvement of the NMDA receptor comes from 'knockout mice', which do not express the receptor (Tsien et al., 1996), and psychopharmacological studies that use drugs to block the NMDA receptor (Morris et al., 1986).

With LTP, if it continues with persistent stimulation there is an increase in the strength of synaptic connections, but this cannot continue beyond asymptote. There is a point at which the storage mechanism of LTP becomes full. LTD weakens synapses, thereby making room for new learning. Like LTP, LTD requires NMDA receptors. LTP is

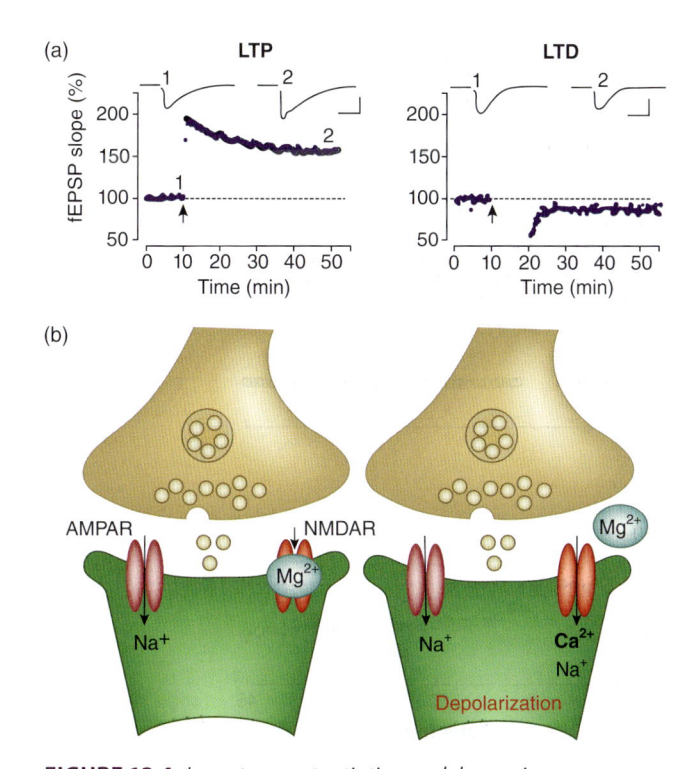

FIGURE 13.4 *Long-term potentiation and depression. (a) LTP and LTD in the CA1 region of the hippocampus. Synaptic strength, defined as the initial slope of the field excitatory postsynaptic potential (fEPSP; normalized to baseline), is plotted as a function of time. Left panel demonstrates LTP elicited by high-frequency stimulation. Right panel illustrates LTD elicited by low-frequency stimulation. Data traces were taken at the times indicated by the numbers on the graphs (scale bar: 0.5 mV; 10 ms). (b) Model of synaptic transmission at excitatory synapses. During basal synaptic transmission (left panel), synaptically released glutamate binds both the NMDA and AMPA receptors (R). Na$^+$ flows through the AMPAR channel but not through the NMDAR channel because of the Mg^{2+} block of this channel. Depolarization of the postsynaptic cell (right) relieves the Mg^{2+} block of the NMDAR channel and allows both Na$^+$ and Ca^{2+} to flow into the dendritic spine. The resultant increase in Ca^{2+} in the dendritic spine is necessary for triggering the subsequent events that drive synaptic plasticity.*
Source: Reprinted by permission of Macmillan Publishers Ltd. from Citri, A., & Malenka, R. C. (2008). Synaptic plasticity: Multiple forms, functions, and mechanisms. *Neuropsychopharmacology*, 33(1), 18–41. © 2008.

differentiated from LTD by calcium signals in the postsynaptic cell. Slow and small increases in calcium lead to LTD and large and fast increases produce LTP (Mulkey & Malenka, 1992; Sakurai, 1990).

While LTP offers great insight into putative neural mechanisms of memory, there is still a link to be made with the psychology of learning and memory.

Whilst LTP and LTD have informed us about the molecular nature of synaptic plasticity, there are other factors involved. The timing of presynaptic and postsynaptic activity in synaptic plasticity requires precision to determine the direction of the changes. If a presynaptic action potential happens after presynaptic activity, there is LTP, whereas if it occurs before, it produces LTD (Bi & Poo, 1998; Froemke & Dan, 2002; Markram et al., 1997). The timing of neural activity is also emphasized by Fell and Axmacher (2011) on a network scale. They state that:

> Neurons do not function in isolation. They are embedded in assemblies and networks, in which they influence each other through excitatory and inhibitory synaptic connections. As a result, the neurons in a network are rhythmically activated and inhibited. (Fell & Axmacher, 2011, p.105)

The synchronization of activity into areas can increase the likelihood of LTP and the connection between the regions.

There is still much to be learned when it comes to understanding the mechanisms of memory, but the knowledge of neural plasticity also has practical applications.

NEUROPLASTICITY

Plasticity is advantageous to the organism because (Møller, 2006):

- it underlies postnatal development. The immature nervous system is shaped and moulded according to experiences. We learn to see, hear, walk and talk;
- it allows for adaptation to changing demands, e.g. the reallocation and expansion of regions of the brain in Braille reading (Pascual-Leone & Torres, 1993; Sadato et al., 1998) or the neural adaptations to learning music (Seppanen et al., 2012);
- compensation for damage and injury in which self-repair facilitates recovery after, for example, stroke (Warraich & Kleim, 2010).

Neuroplasticity is the basis of neurorehabilitation in which either damaged regions can be repaired or the function once subserved by the damaged region is ascribed to a new region. It has been argued that the reuse of existing neural systems may have been an important contributory factor to the development of cognition in our species, with advanced cognitive

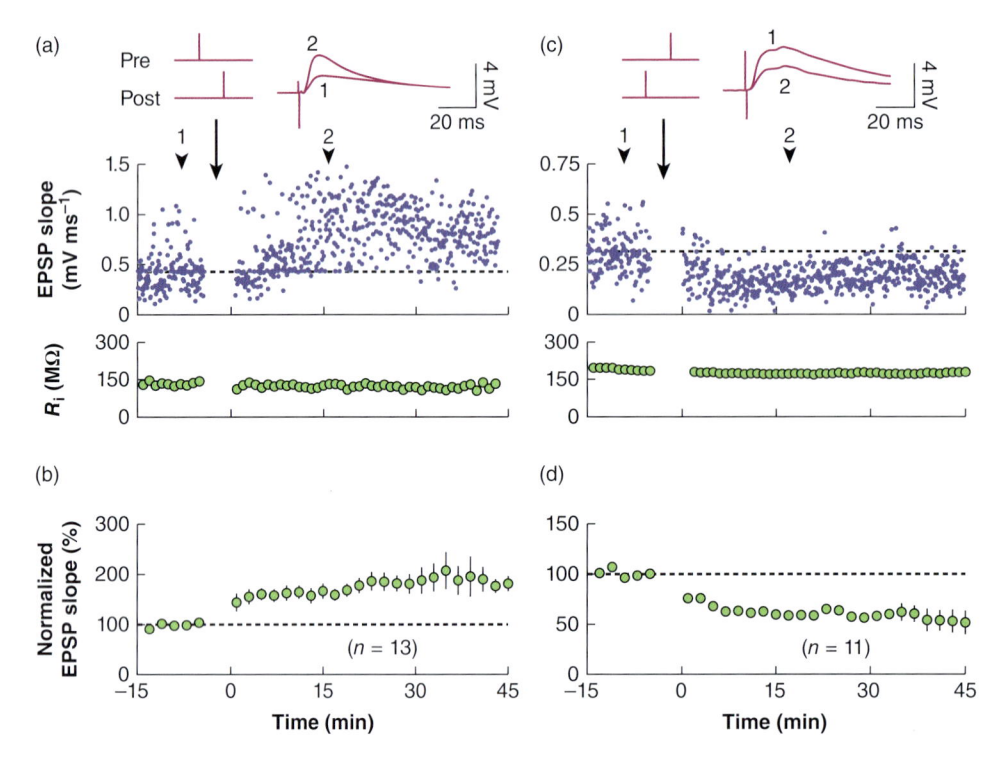

FIGURE 13.5 *Synaptic modification of L2/3 visual cortical connections induced by pre-/postsynaptic spike pairs.*
Source: Reprinted by permission from Macmillan Publishers Ltd: NATURE Froemke, R. C. & Dan, Y. (2002). Spike-timing-dependent synaptic modification induced by natural spike trains. *Nature, 416,* 433–438, copyright 2002.

functions using more regions scattered across the entire brain (Anderson, 2007).

There is a distinct disadvantage to neural plasticity inasmuch as it has been associated with pain (Coderre et al., 1993). For example, phantom limb pain is the experience of pain after amputation of the affected area (see Chapter 10) and can be accounted for in terms of long-term changes of the pain pathways (see Flor et al., 2006).

SUMMARY

The neuroscience of memory has progressed dramatically over the last 60 years, from case studies pointing in the direction of the temporal lobes and the hippocampus, and then to the identification of the molecular mechanisms that may underlie memory in the hippocampus. Memory has been considered as a mere storage mechanism, but it requires several other cognitive processes to be intact, e.g. attention and learning. When are our memories made? One hypothesis of the function of sleep was that it was for memory consolidation and neuroplasticity (Walker & Stickgold, 2006). Much of the work has looked at brain regions or single neurons but 'the neural basis of memory will require an approach that emphasizes the importance of the network of neurons that are activated during learning' (Neves et al., 2008).

The study of memory can also identify shortcomings in our understanding of being. We become aware of our memories when they enter our consciousness. Declarative memory is what most people think of when they are asked to describe memory. How memories embedded within the vast network of synapses of our brain emerge as conscious recollections remains to be determined. The answers to such questions are, I would imagine, a long way in the future.

LEARNING OUTCOME QUESTIONS

You should be able to answer the following questions.

- What is the role of the hippocampus in memory?
- To what extent have case studies been important in the formulation of hypotheses about the biological underpinning of memory?
- Describe the alleged molecular basis of memory.
- Critically evaluate the methodological approaches of studying memory.
- Why is it important that your taxi driver has the Knowledge?

FURTHER READING

Fields, R. D. (Ed.) (2008). *Beyond the synapses: cell-cell signalling in synaptic plasticity*. Cambridge, UK: Cambridge University Press.
Kandel, E. R., Dudai, Y., & Mayford, M. R. (2014). The molecular and systems biology of memory. *Cell, 157*(1), 163–186.
Kupers, R., & Ptito, M. (2014). Compensatory plasticity and cross-modal reorganization following early visual deprivation. *Neuroscience and Biobehavioral Review, 41*, 3652.
Møller, A. R. (2006). *Neural plasticity and disorders of the nervous system*. Cambridge, UK: Cambridge University Press.
Pascual-Leone, A., Amedi, A., Fregni, F., & Merabet, L. B. (2005). The plastic human brain cortex. *Annual Review of Neuroscience, 28*, 377–401.
Renier, L., de Volder, A. G., & Rauschecker, J. P. (2014). Cortical plasticity and preserved function in early blindness. *Neuroscience and Biobehavioral Review, 41*, 53–63.
Woollett, K., Spiers, H. J., & Maguire, E. A. (2009). Talent in the taxi: a model system for exploring expertise. *Philosophical Transactions of the Royal Society of London B: Biological Science, 364*(1522), 1407–1416.

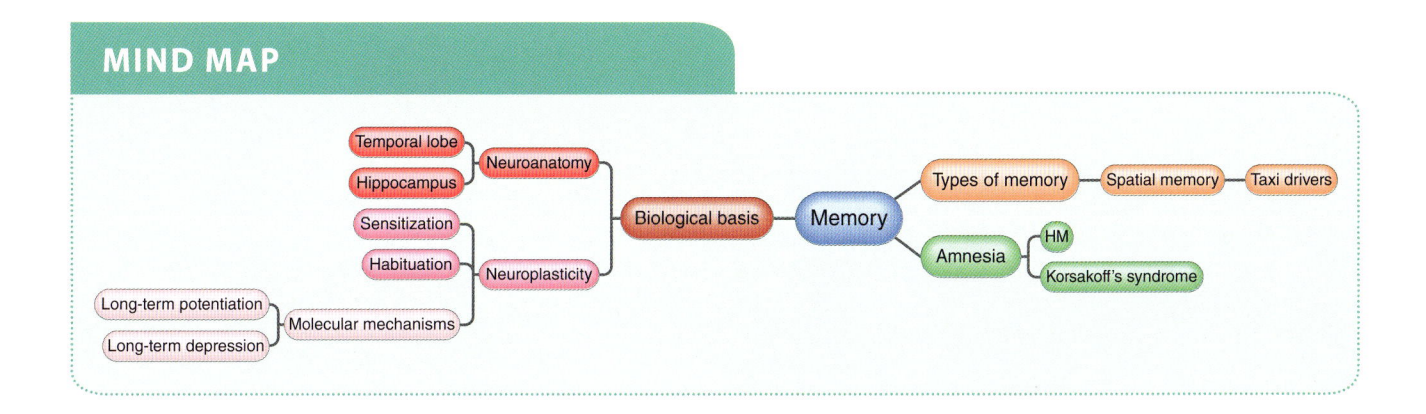

MIND MAP

14 Sex

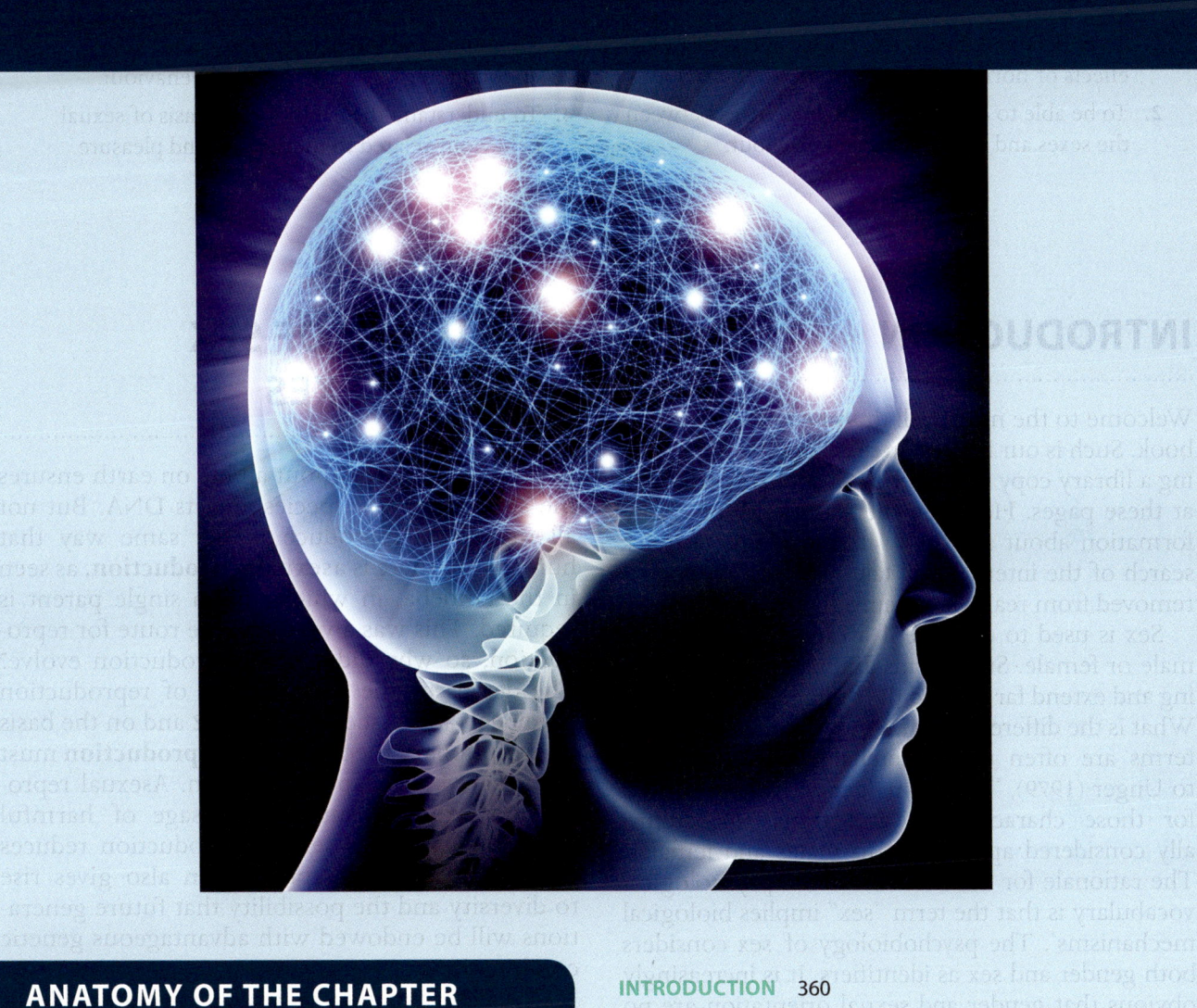

ANATOMY OF THE CHAPTER

This chapter will highlight the following.

- The biological differences between the sexes.
- Differentiation of the male and female brain.
- Neurobiology of sexual behaviour.

INTRODUCTION 360

EVOLUTION OF SEX AND THE SEXES 360

DIFFERENTIATION OF THE SEXES 361

SEX HORMONES 368

MENSTRUAL CYCLE AND OVULATION 369

SEXUAL DEVELOPMENT 373

WHAT REGIONS OF THE BRAIN ARE DIFFERENT IN THE SEXES? 377

WHAT HAPPENS DURING SEXUAL AROUSAL? 380

EVOLUTION OF PLEASURE 386

SEXUAL ORIENTATION 386

SUMMARY 388

LEARNING OUTCOMES

1. To understand the organizational and activational effects of hormones on the brain and behaviour.
2. To be able to evaluate neural differences between the sexes and their effects on behaviour.
3. To understand the neurobiology and endocrinology governing sexual behaviour.
4. To understand the evolutionary basis of sexual behaviour related to motivation and pleasure.

INTRODUCTION

Welcome to the most well-thumbed chapter in this book. Such is our interest in sex that if you are reading a library copy of this book, it probably fell open at these pages. However, there is plenty of misinformation about sex (in all its meanings); a quick search of the internet will take you into worlds far removed from reality and reproduction.

Sex is used to describe if an individual is either male or female. Such terms are loaded with meaning and extend far beyond the biological definitions. What is the difference between sex and gender? The terms are often used interchangeably. According to Unger (1979), 'The term "gender" is introduced for those characteristics and traits socioculturally considered appropriate to males and females. The rationale for this addition to the psychological vocabulary is that the term "sex" implies biological mechanisms'. The psychobiology of sex considers both gender and sex as identifiers. It is increasingly obvious that gender and sexual orientation are no longer dichotomous characteristics. Rather than being considered a man or a woman, sexual orientation and gender identity can be measured along a spectrum with characteristics that are traditionally considered more male or female (Savin-Williams, 2014). The question remains about what makes us male and female, and that is a much easier question to address than what makes us a man or a woman.

The act of sex ensures the survival of the species and the continuation of the individual's DNA. However, sex is far more complex than just a mere biological transmission of genetic material; after all, we engage in sexual activity for pleasure and not only reproduction. The motivation for sexual contact is evident throughout the internet, but also sex is the commodity in the oldest profession: prostitution.

EVOLUTION OF SEX AND THE SEXES

Reproduction throughout all life on earth ensures the survival of the species and its DNA. But not all organisms reproduce in the same way that humans do; there is **asexual reproduction**, as seen in the amoeba, in which only a single parent is required. This was a very sensible route for reproduction, so why did sexual reproduction evolve? The details of the cellular basis of reproduction have been addressed in Chapter 2 and on the basis of evolutionary theory, **sexual reproduction** must have served an adaptive function. Asexual reproduction would ensure the passage of harmful mutations, whereas sexual reproduction reduces this chance. Sexual reproduction also gives rise to diversity and the possibility that future generations will be endowed with advantageous genetic combinations.

The determination of whether we are male or female is based on our chromosomes. If the fertilized egg has two X chromosomes (XX) then a female should develop and if it has one X and one Y chromosome (XY) then a male should develop. Remember, it is the male that carries the Y chromosome, therefore it is the male's sperm that determines the genetic/biological sex of the offspring. Chromosomal variation in which there is no Y chromosome results in female development. Thus, on the Y chromosome there is a gene coding for sex, referred to as the **sex determining region of the Y chromosome** (SRY) (Sinclair et al., 1990) (Figure 14.1). The SRY is linked to a **testes determining factor** (TDF) which allows male gonads to develop (Gubbay et al., 1990; Koopman et al., 1990). Thus, there is a clear genetic basis by which sex is coded. How that code results in a male and a female

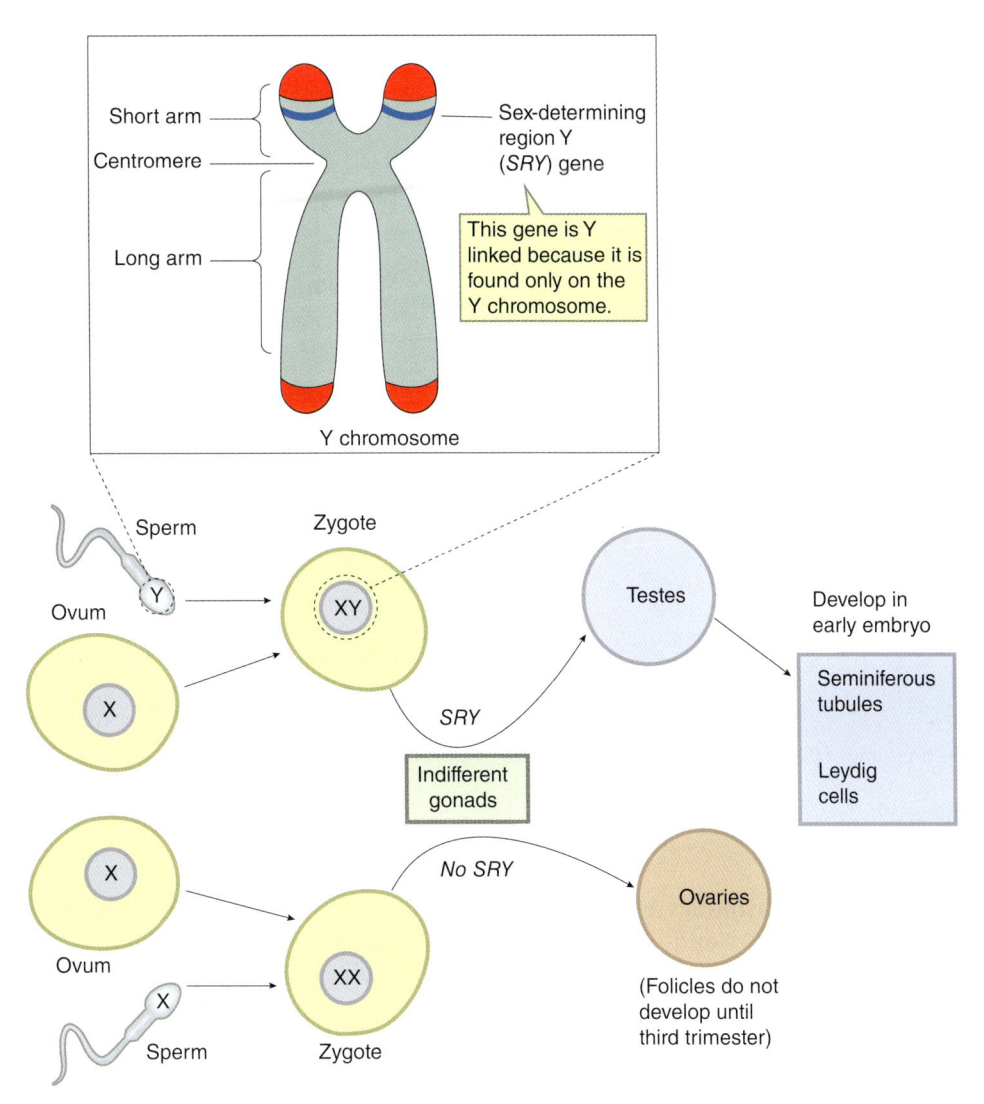

FIGURE 14.1 *SRY gene determines the male sex.*

is not as straightforward as one might think. Before we consider the developmental process of the two sexes (and there are never more than two), we need to consider the general differences between males and females.

DIFFERENTIATION OF THE SEXES

Males and females differ along a number of dimensions, e.g. distribution of hair, fat and muscle. The most notable difference between males and females is in their sexual and reproductive organs.

Female Genitalia

The complete external female genitalia is referred to as the **vulva** (Figure 14.2). First, there is the **mons veneris** which is an area of fatty tissue above which is a triangle of pubic hair. Pubic hair must serve some function despite the fact that many women try to remove it – in one study only just over 12% of female respondents aged 18–24 did not remove pubic hair (Herbenick et al., 2010). According to Bhutta (2007), 'The specific development of hair in these regions (in our otherwise largely naked bodies) is thought to aid the dispersal of odorants in sexually mature humans' (p.271). Such odorants refer to human apocrine glands which are like sweat glands that may give off pheromones (Bhutta, 2007). The rise in pubic hair removal has led to the

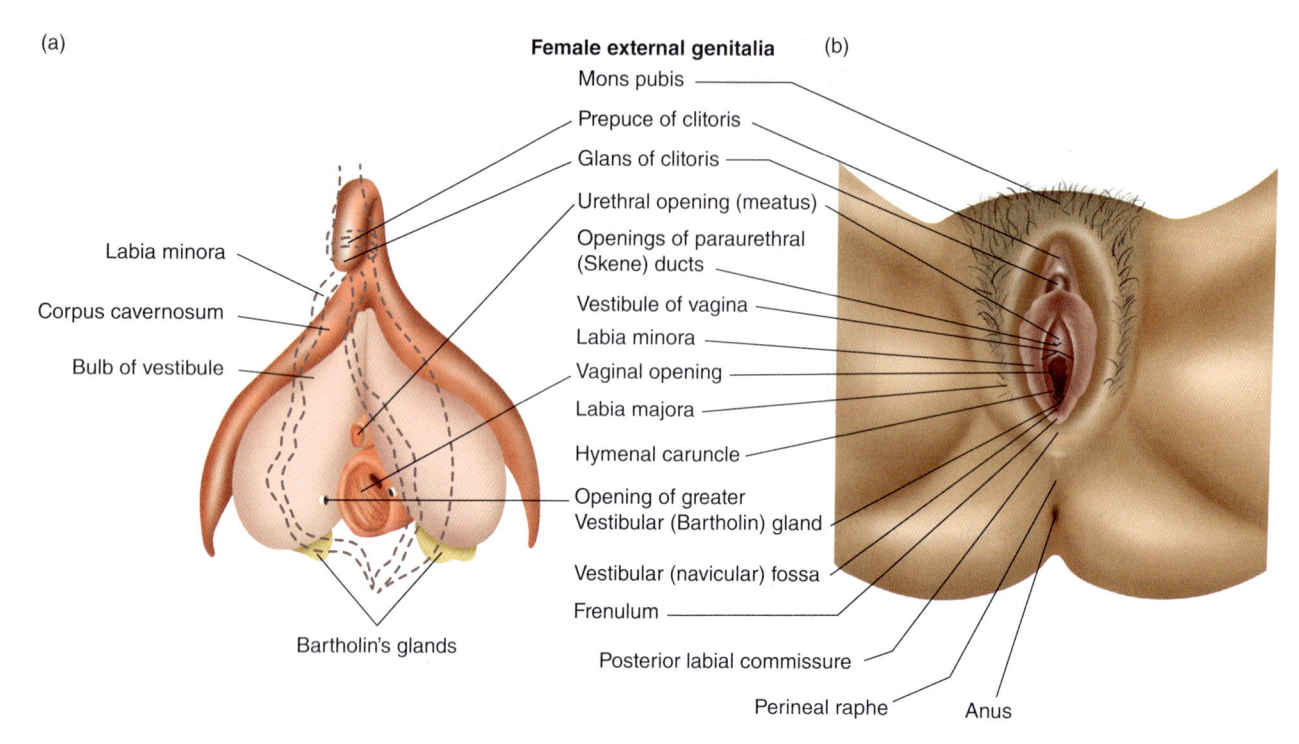

FIGURE 14.2 *(a) The anatomy of the clitoris and (b) the female genitals and clitoris.*

development of a new area of cosmetics, e.g. 'vulvar skincare treatments (vagacials) and decorative vulvar services (vajazzling)' (Iglesia, 2012), which also highlights the evolutionary and psychological importance of the region.

Extending down from the mons on either side of the vulva is the **labia majora** which are separated by the **pudendal cleft** (or the cleft of Venus, the Roman goddess of love; see also mons Venus (the mount of love)). The labia majora also carry hair follicles in the outer regions towards the side. The **labia minora** are hairless flaps of skin which are inside the labia majora (but can sometimes protrude) and surround the opening of the vagina. It is this region that is modified in labiaplasty (Goodman et al., 2010) and is of great aesthetic debate, with some women choosing to have surgical modification on the basis of appearance (Miklos & Moore, 2008). Pornography has been considered influential in cosmetic gynaecology; one woman was quoted as saying 'The only women I could compare myself to was women in pornographic movies' (Navarro, 2004) which is hardly a representative sample.

The area within the labia is referred to as the **vestibule** and at the top where the labia minora meet is the **clitoral hood**. Protruding from under the clitoral hood is the **clitoris**. Only part of the clitoris is visible – the glans. The glans is highly sensitive and is the terminal region of the shaft of the clitoris which extends upwards under the clitoral hood. The glans and the shaft of the clitoris are composed of erectile tissue.

The erectile tissue of the clitoral shaft is made of two **corpus cavernosum** which are blood-filled chambers. During clitoral erection, the corpus cavernosum fills with blood, leading to the extrusion of the glans clitoris (more blood enters than can leave hence the clitoral erection). A similar phenomenon occurs in the vestibular bulbs of the clitoris that lie below the labia minora. Erectile tissue of the glans consists of a single **corpus spongiosum** (Van Turnhout et al., 1995). The glands of the clitoris contain sensory receptors, e.g. **Pacini's corpuscles,** which provide 'deep sensation and sense vibration' (O'Connell et al., 2005, p.1191). The clitoris extends internally and downwards (the **crura**), surrounding the urethra and vagina and connecting to the vestibular bulbs of the clitoris (O'Connell & DeLancey, 2005). The clitoris is connected to the **sensory dorsal nerve of the clitoris** which originates from pudendal nerves and the inferior hypogastric plexus (Martin-Alguacil et al., 2008a, 2008b; Moszkowicz et al., 2011).

Motor neurons are located in **Onuf's nucleus** in the ventral horn in the lower lumbar and upper sacral regions of the spine. A similar organization is seen with the penis. The clitoris is therefore a complex structure that is highly sensitive but the only certain and unique function of the clitoris is to produce sexual pleasure (Puppo, 2013). The sensory input of the female genitalia and its cortical representation were not considered in Penfield's original homunculus. However, Di Noto et al. (2013) have attempted to put that right and provide sensory representation of the female, with what they amusingly refer to as the *hermunculus* (Figure 14.3). From an evolutionary psychologist's viewpoint, the induction of sexual pleasure provides the setting for sexual intercourse which thereby increases the chances of successful reproduction. The separate issue of female orgasm is addressed later.

Interest in the anatomy and function of the clitoris is surprisingly recent. In a BBC interview, Dr Margaret Davy, a gynaecologist, said, 'The original anatomists weren't interested in the clitoris. The penis was much more interesting. It was bigger and you didn't have to wear your spectacles to see it' (Mascall, 2006). In a world where big is often considered to be better, it is noteworthy that those women in possession of a comparatively small clitoris have improved sexual functions (Vaccaro et al., 2014).

Moving down from the glans clitoris is the meatus of the **urethral opening**. The urethra's main function is to allow urine to exit the bladder. Whilst the urethra does not have a prominent role in sex, it has been part of 'an erotic zone . . . On the anterior wall of the vagina along the course of the urethra' (Gräfenberg, 1950, p.146). This region was later to be known as the **G-spot** and its existence is debated (Hines, 2001). The urethra also is at the centre of the controversy over female ejaculation (see Box 14.4). Below the urethra and in the final part of the vestibule is the vaginal opening or **introitus**. Below the vagina is the **perineum** which is the sensitive area between the vagina and the anus.

In young girls the vagina is covered by the membrane of skin referred to as the **hymen**. The breaking of the hymen during sex has great significance in many cultures, indicating that the woman is no longer a virgin (Amy, 2008).

The **vagina** is a tube that connects the uterus to the external genitalia. Its function is to transport the male's sperm to the uterus for fertilization, and it is also the route via which the offspring is delivered to the outside world. The vagina is made up of three layers.

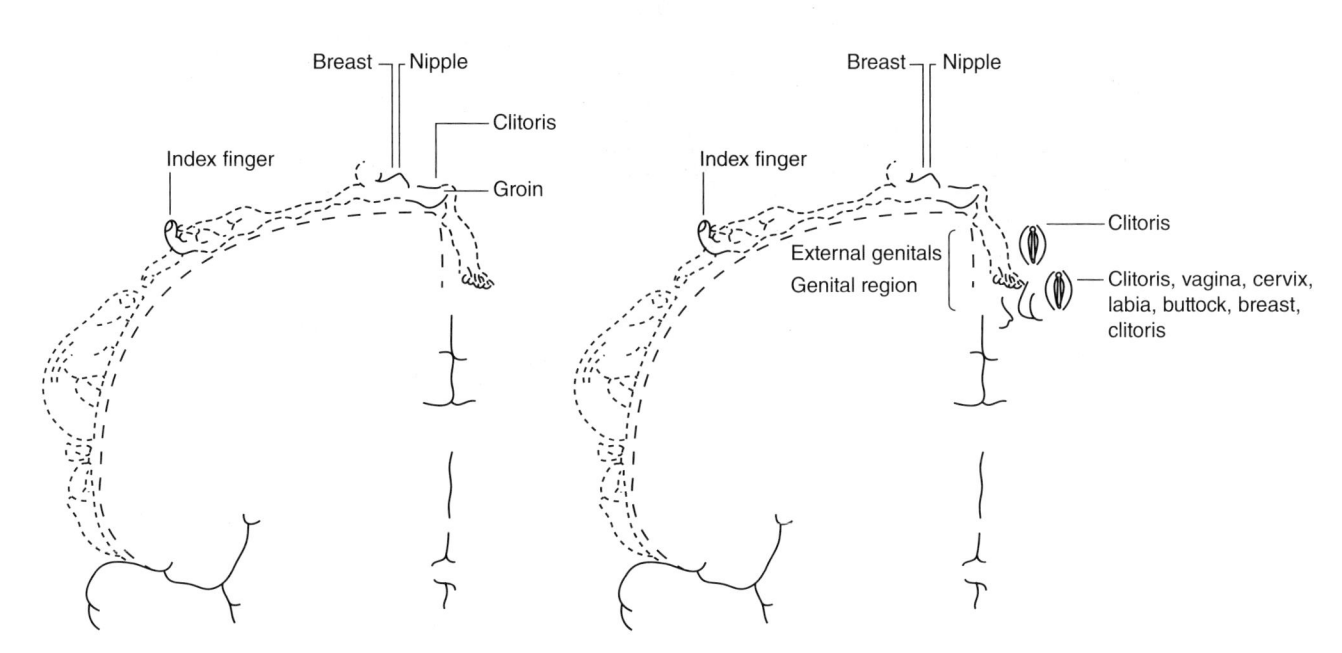

FIGURE 14.3 *Two versions of the somatosensory hermunculus, depicting findings from human female mapping studies and showing alternative localizations for the genitalia. Left depicts the genitalia mapped to the dorsal somatosensory cortex and right depicts the genital representation mapped along the medial wall. Penfield's homunculus (shown with a grey dashed outline) is included to provide context and to demonstrate how much of the female somatosensory system remains unmapped. These illustrations are conceptual: the extent and location of each representation are not precise.*
Source: Di Noto, P. M., Newman, L., Wall, S., & Einstein, G. (2013). The hermunculus: what is known about the representation of the female body in the brain? *Cerebral Cortex, 23*(5), 1005–1013, by permission of Oxford University Press.

- The **internal mucosal layer** – allows for increased surface area when expanded due to the elastic fibres present and the network of blood vessels. It is **transudate** from these blood vessels, combined with cervical mucus, that provides vaginal lubrication during sexual arousal (Wagner, 1979) and is thought to be controlled by vasoactive intestinal polypeptide producing increase blood flow (Ottesen et al., 1987).
- The **intermediate muscularis layer** – the muscular layer.
- The **external adventitial layer** – elastic tissue that provides structural support and allows for expansion.

At the top of the vagina is the **cervix** (Figure 14.4). The cervix has an aperture (**os**) that allows sperm to enter the uterine environment and menstrual fluid to leave. The cervix also contributes to the lubrication of the vagina. The purpose of this mucus is to aid the transport of sperm during ovulation and inhibit sperm transmission at the luteal phase (Carlstedt & Sheehan, 1988; Druart, 2012). On the other side of the cervix is the **uterus** which has three layers:

- the inner layer – the endometrium made of connective tissue;
- the middle layer – the myometrium made of smooth muscle; and
- the outer layer – the perimetrium made of connective tissue.

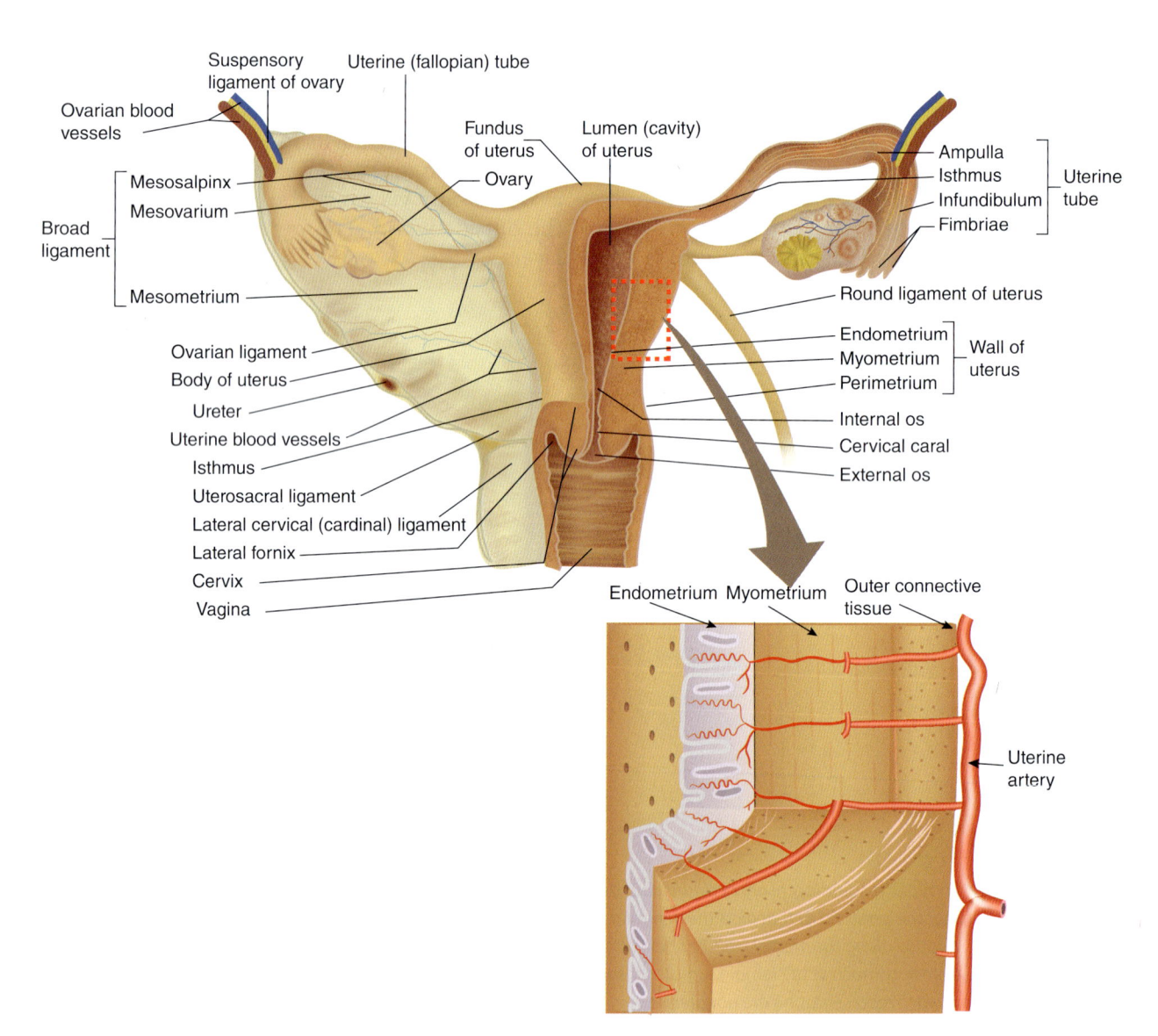

FIGURE 14.4 *The female reproductive system.*

It is the endometrium that facilitates the transport of sperm to the site of fertilization and also the implantation and support of an embryo. Because of the dual functionality of the endometrium, it undergoes changes over the menstrual cycle in which part of it is eliminated during menstruation (see below).

At the top end of the uterus is the **fallopian tube** which extends left and right. The fallopian tube delivers eggs from the ovaries to the uterus. At the end of the fallopian tubes, in a region called the **infundibulum,** are **fimbriae** which branch out to catch released eggs and guide them towards the tube. The fallopian tubes are lined with **cilia** (hair-like structures) which facilitate movement of the egg along the fallopian tube. Sperm that enters the uterus has to swim against the movement produced by the cilia. It is in the middle section of the fallopian tube, the ampulla, that fertilization is most likely to occur. The ovaries are the woman's gonads and produce sex hormones and ova (the eggs). The ovary contains a large number of follicles which consist of an **oocyte** which is a progenitor **ovum** (egg). The follicle also consists of supporting cells called **granulosa cells**. The ovaries contain a finite number of oocytes which declines over time. Whilst reproductively viable, the female will release only one mature ovum per menstrual cycle from either of the ovaries.

Male Genitalia

The external genitalia of males is the **penis** and **scrotum** (Figure 14.5). The scrotum contains the testicles which can be seen below the surface of the skin. Like their female counterparts, males have a similar distribution of pubic hair, which is also subject to grooming (especially in the world of pornography). The penis in developmental terms is the male equivalent of the clitoris. However, the functionality of the penis includes the clitoris, urethra and the vagina. The penis comprises a **glans**, **foreskin** and **shaft** (the size of which is discussed in Box 14.1).

The foreskin is a loose tube of skin that can cover the glans. It is the foreskin that is removed during male circumcision. Like the clitoris, the penis can become erect when sexually aroused. The change from the flaccid to the erect state allows for the potential of sexual intercourse. In the shaft of the penis are three erectile structures: two **corpora cavernosa** and a single **corpus spongiosum**. The corpora cavernosa, which span the shaft of the penis and extend into the pelvic area, provide the bulk of the erection. Around the corpora cavernosa is a capsule of connective tissue called the **tunica albuginea**. The corpus spongiosum runs along the midline of the undersurface of the penis around the urethra. It extends into the glans of the penis and fills its entire volume. The glans has a ridge that encircles the penis called the corona. On the underside of the corona is the **frenulum**, which is a loose strip of skin between the glans and the shaft of the penis. The shaft of the penis also contains nerves and blood vessels and, together with all the other structures, is enclosed in a fibrous sheath of connective tissue called **fascia**. The outer skin of the penis contains little hair and is loose to the internal structures. The loose skin allows for the movement of the penis without abrasive friction.

The corpora cavernosa diverge within the root of the penis (at the pelvis) forming the crura. There are two muscles associated with the root of the penis (which are larger than those serving the clitoris): the **ischiocavernosus muscle** and the **bulbospongiosus muscle**, both of which are involved in erection and ejaculation (see later).

Running down the centre of the penis is the **urethra** which allows for the passage of urine from the bladder but also provides the route via which sperm exits the penis at the **urethral meatus**.

The testes reside within the scrotum. The testes need to be kept 4–7°C below body temperature, hence they are outside the main core of the body. Under the skin is smooth muscle known as the **dartos** which contracts in response to cold (and sexual arousal), thus thickening the scrotal skin and providing warmth. The testes produce hormones and sperm. Behind the testes is the **epididymis** which sperm pass along after **spermatogenesis** (the making of sperm). Each testis is served by the **spermatic cord** that connects the testes with organs within the abdominal cavity. The spermatic cord has a muscular layer known as the **cremaster muscle** which responds to the cold by pulling the testes towards the body and helps the dartos muscle keep the testes at a regular temperature. Also within the spermatic cord is the **vas deferens** which carries sperm from the epididymis towards the prostate gland. On entry to the prostate gland, the vas deferens is joined with a duct that adds secretions from the seminal vesicles. After the union of the vas deferens and the seminal duct is the ejaculatory duct. Within the **prostate gland** the **ejaculatory ducts** join with the urethra. Contractions of the walls of the vas occur just before ejaculation, providing a small volume of sperm into the urethra. The seminal vesicles are small glands that add their secretions to semen. The **bulbourethral gland** is situated below the prostate gland and

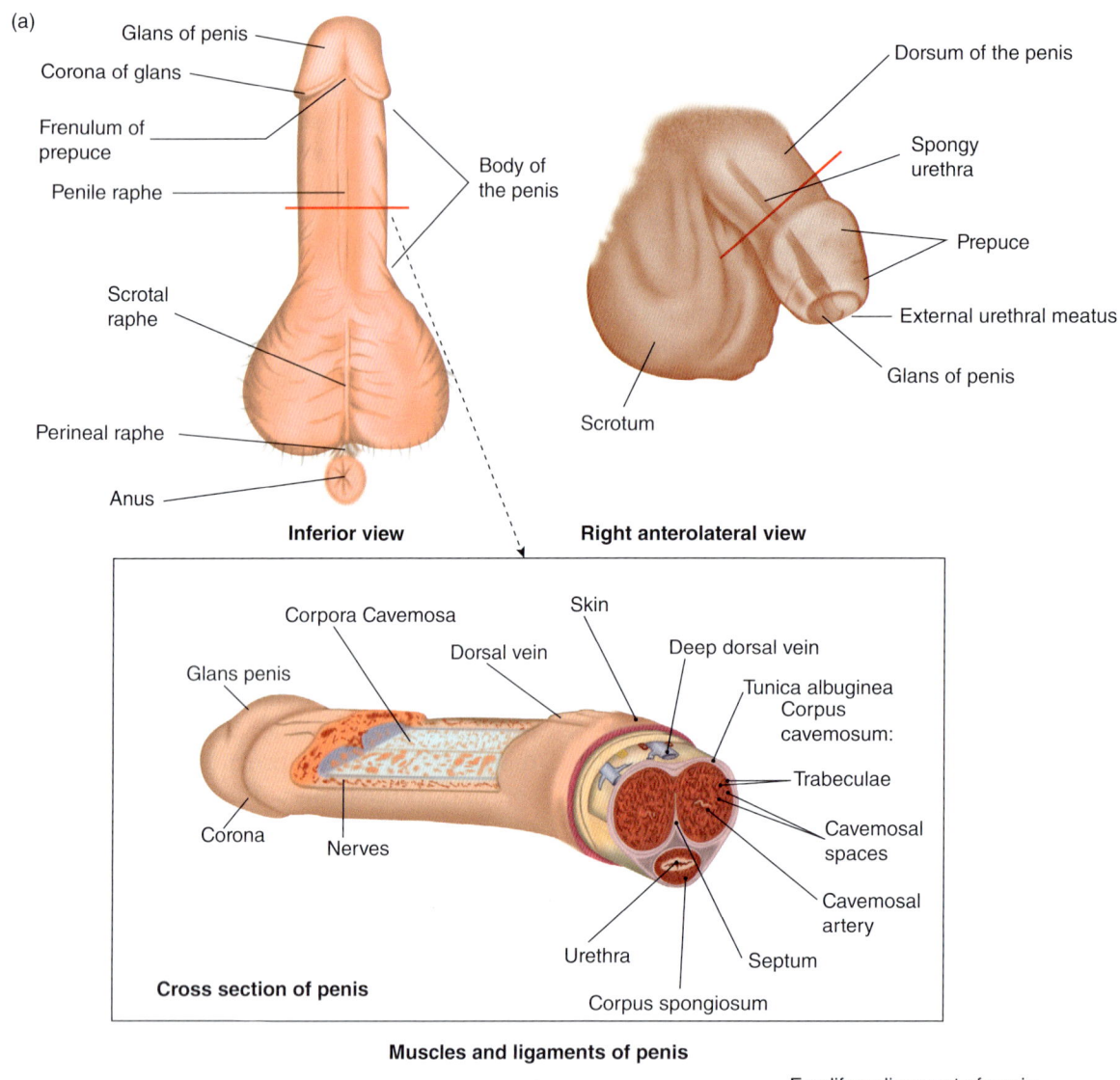

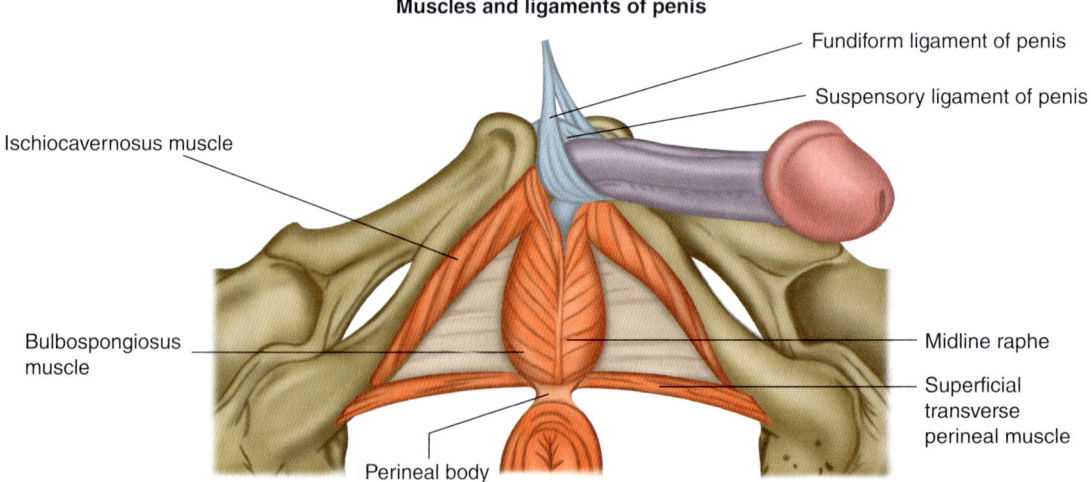

FIGURE 14.5 The penis and the muscles of the penis and the male reproductive system. (a) The surface detail of the penis and cross-section of the penis showing erectile tissue. (b) The male reproductive system.

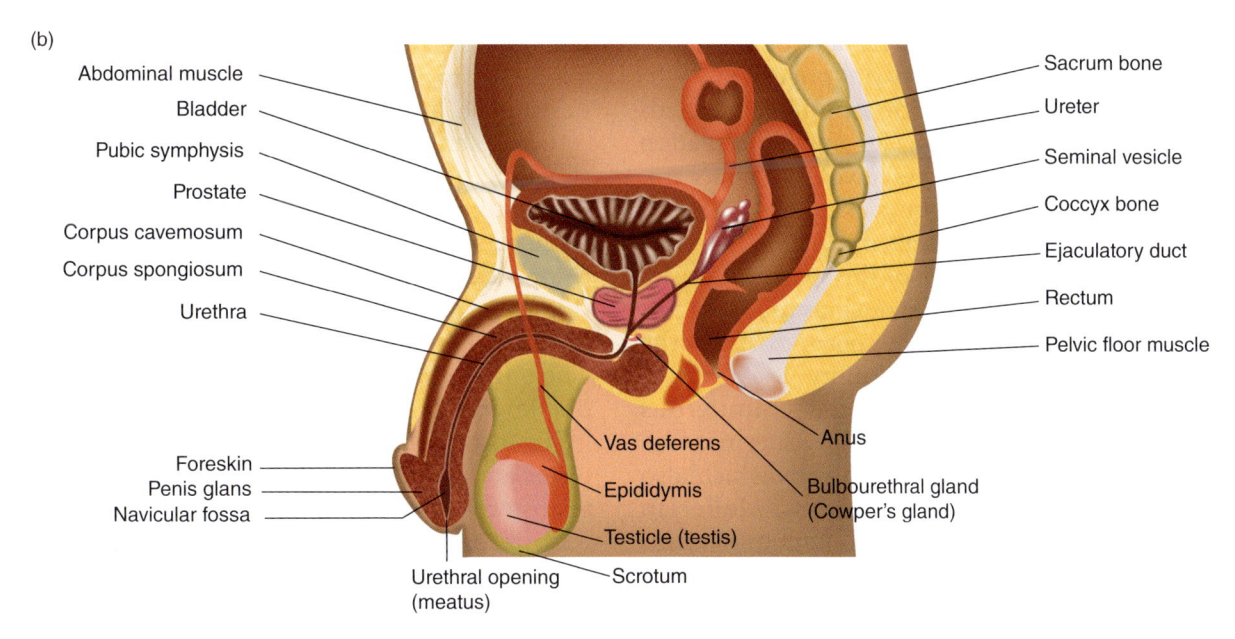

(b) Labels: Abdominal muscle, Bladder, Pubic symphysis, Prostate, Corpus cavernosum, Corpus spongiosum, Urethra, Foreskin, Penis glans, Navicular fossa, Urethral opening (meatus), Vas deferens, Epididymis, Testicle (testis), Scrotum, Sacrum bone, Ureter, Seminal vesicle, Coccyx bone, Ejaculatory duct, Rectum, Pelvic floor muscle, Anus, Bulbourethral gland (Cowper's gland)

FIGURE 14.5 *(Continued)*

BOX 14.1: HOW BIG IS BIG? THE SIZE OF THE HUMAN PENIS

No discussion of the penis would be complete without mention of size. Size is important, but mainly for the owner. Is it too big or is it too small? That question preoccupies many males – with huge (pun intended) psychological consequences. A flaccid penis has little relation to the size of an erect penis. However, when the flaccid penis is stretched and measured this provides a more reliable indication of the erect size (Chen et al., 2000). Templer (2002) stated the typical penis was approximately 8.9 cm long when flaccid and 15.2 cm long when erect. A review of several studies found average flaccid length to be 9–10 cm (3.5–3.9 in) (Wylie & Eardley, 2007). In a UK study measuring penile length along three dimensions, the average flaccid length was 8.7 cm, pinopubic (from the glans to the edge of the pubic bone) length was 10.2 cm and the stretched length was 14.3 cm (Khan et al., 2012). In a study of 3300 Italian males, the average stretched penile length was 12.5 cm and in the flaccid state 9 cm (Ponchietti et al., 2001). In the United States the average erect penile length was 14.15 cm (Herbenick et al., 2014). It is worth noting that this study in the United States required self-measurement and therefore may be biased towards having a large penis.

Does size matter to women? In a study in the United States, both male and female views on penis size were recorded. Satisfaction with penis size was different in males and females. Only 55% of males were satisfied with their penis size whereas 85% of females were satisfied (Lever et al., 2006). The study also noted that 45% of males wanted a larger penis and 0.2% wanted a smaller penis (who are these men?). Mautz et al. (2013) found that there was an inverted U-shaped curve for the preference of penis size. As the size of the flaccid penis increased from 7.6 cm, women began to find the size less attractive. A study looking at the erect penis found that nearly 30% of women in the sample claimed that penis size made no difference to whether they had an orgasm via penile-vaginal intercourse. Interestingly, 29% had never experienced an orgasm from penile-vaginal intercourse (Costa et al., 2012). The subject of the female orgasm is discussed in Box 14.4.

Where does the male dissatisfaction with penis size come from? It is most likely that viewing pornography has an impact on body satisfaction. According to Mondaini et al. (2002), 'Many young Western men seem to base their idea of normality on the images of penises seen in pornography. While we have not been able to construct a nomogram for the penis size of pornographic actors it is our anecdotal impression that men following this particular career are probably not representative of the average male in the genital area!' (p.285). Furthermore, camera angles, lighting and shaving pubic hair can all go some way to making your average porn star's penis look larger than it actually is. The only question remains why they measure this in centimetres when everybody knows that the unit of measure of the penis is inches!

secretes a clear fluid into the urethra prior to ejaculation which does not contain sperm (pre-cum).

Thus, sperm is mixed with a number of fluids which make up the semen. The single ejaculation produces semen with an average volume of 3.4 mL (Owen & Katz, 2005) and contains up to 15,000,000 sperm per millilitre (Cooper et al., 2010).

The morphological detail of the sperm is considered in Chapter 3 but it is the nucleus that contains the DNA; the remainder of the sperm exists for the penetration of the ovum and motility.

The testes' main component is the **seminiferous tubules** where sperm is produced. The sperm is supported during synthesis by **Sertoli cells** which also secrete a number of substances (e.g. **anti-Mullerian hormone** – see later). Also within the seminiferous tubules are the **Leydig cells** which secrete testosterone and peptide hormones controlling spermatogenesis. The manufactured sperm passes through a tubular network called the rete testis on its way to the epididymis.

The manufacture of sperms starts at the time of puberty and it is then continually manufactured.

SEX HORMONES

Much of our adolescent behaviour is attributed to the sex hormones which are made from cholesterol and fall into three categories.

- **Androgens**, e.g. **testosterone** and **5-alpha-dihydrotestosterone** (**DHT**).
- **Oestrogens**, e.g. **oestradiol**.
- **Progestins**, e.g. **progesterone**.

Do not consider these hormones to be uniquely female or male. Both sexes possess androgens and oestrogens, but just with varying concentrations.

Cholesterol undergoes several enzymatic steps before all the hormones are completed. Cholesterol is converted into progesterone which then gets converted into testosterone and testosterone can be converted into oestradiol or DHT (Figure 14.6). Testosterone is converted into oestradiol with the aid of the enzyme **aromatase**. The enzyme **5-alpha-reductase** converts testosterone into DHT.

Testosterone is secreted by the adrenal gland, the testes and also the ovaries. It is the large portion of testosterone produced in the testes that increases testosterone levels in males.

Oestradiol is traditionally considered the female hormone but it is synthesized using aromatase from testosterone. This occurs in the **granulosa cells** of the ovaries and also in the brain. Progesterone is the main female hormone.

The behavioural effects of the sex hormones are evident in neural development and also the fluctuations associated with the menstrual cycle.

Whilst the sex hormones have received considerable attention, this should not overshadow the fact that there are other hormones. Proteins and peptides can also influence sexual functioning.

- **Oxytocin** – pituitary hormone causing muscle contraction, involved in breastfeeding, childbirth and orgasm.
- **Gonadotrophin-releasing hormone** (GnRH) – hypothalamic hormone which facilitates the release of the gonadotrophins, **follicle-stimulating hormone** (FSH) and **luteinizing**

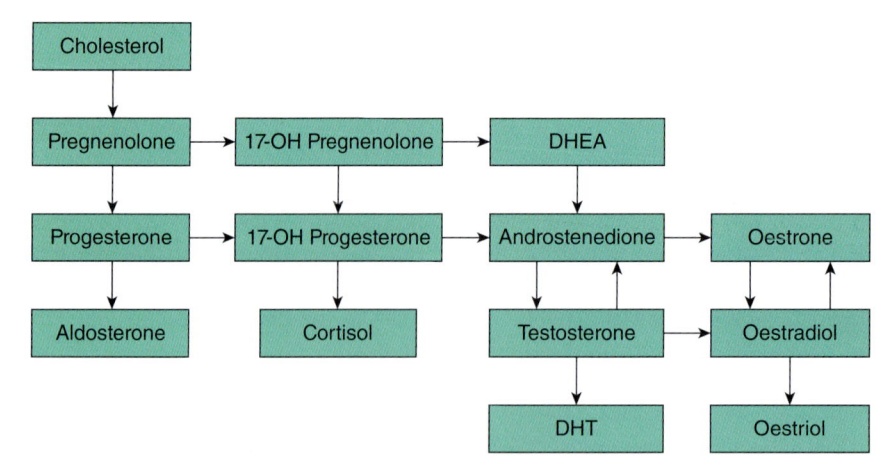

FIGURE 14.6 *The synthetic pathway of hormones. Hormones are synthesized from cholesterol. DHEA, dehydroepiandrosterone; DHT, dihydrotestosterone.*

hormone (LH), from the anterior pituitary gland.

- **FSH** – promotes maturation of gametes (ovum and sperm).
- **LH** – promotes the secretion of androgens and is involved in regulation of the menstrual cycle.
- **Prolactin** – involved in lactation.

MENSTRUAL CYCLE AND OVULATION

The **menstrual cycle** is composed of two interconnected cycles: the **ovarian cycle** and the **endometrial cycle** (Figure 14.7). The ovarian cycle is the interactions of the ovaries, the hypothalamus and the pituitary gland which impacts upon the endometrial

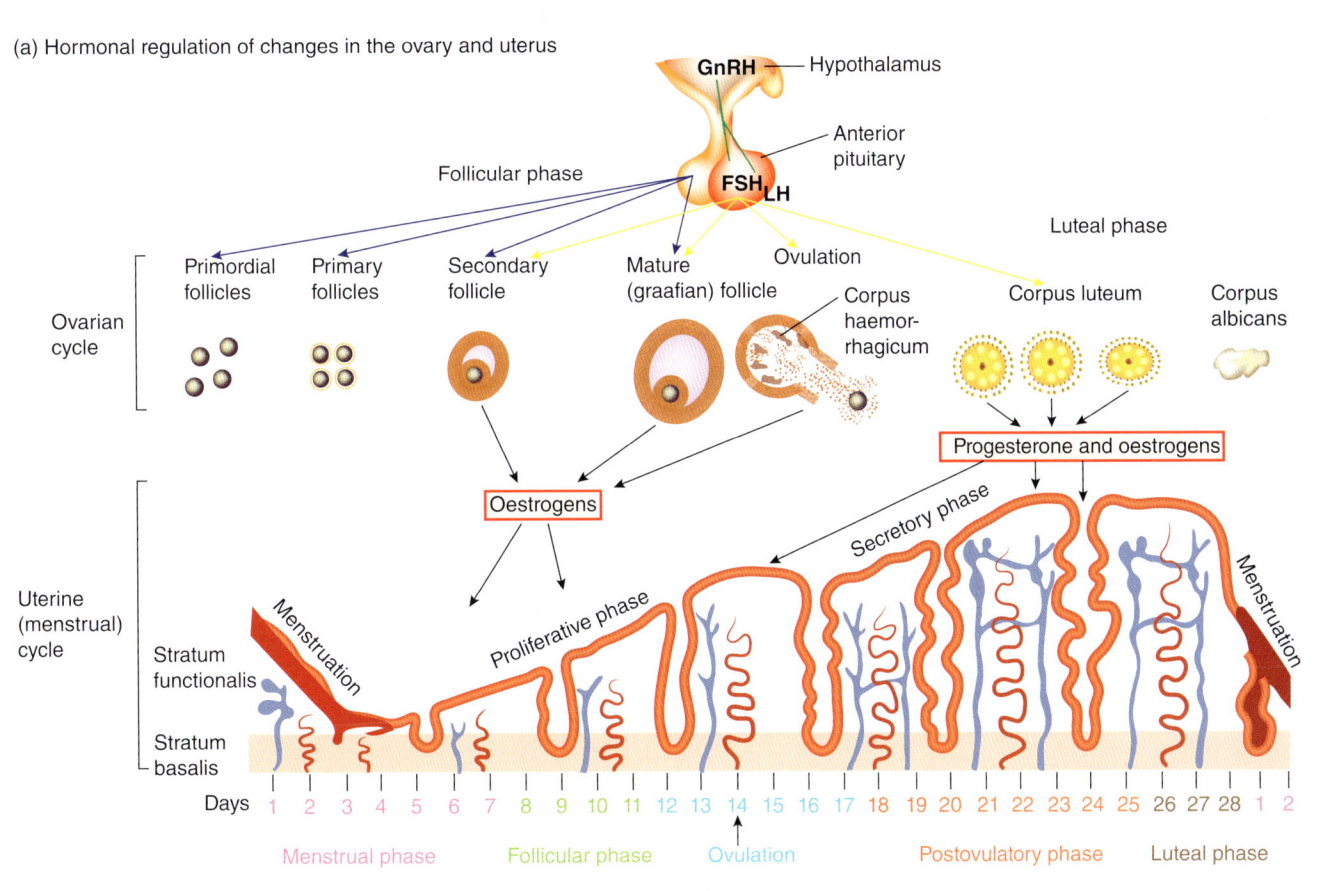

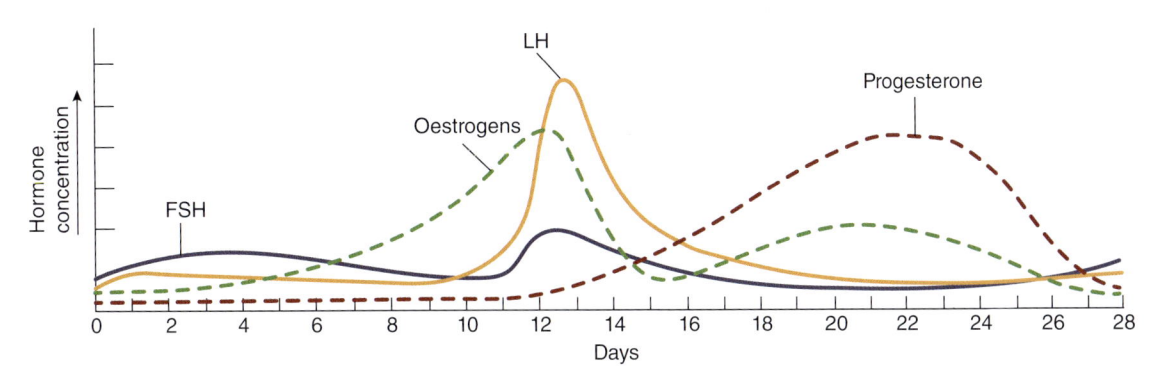

FIGURE 14.7 Changes throughout the menstrual cycle. (a) Hormonal regulation of the different phases. (b) Hormone levels during the menstrual cycle. (c) Schematic dial of the cycle. FSH, follicle-stimulating hormone; GnRH, gonadotrophin-releasing hormone; LH, luteinizing hormone.

FIGURE 14.7 *(Continued)*

cycle in which the endometrium of the uterus undergoes changes which result in partial removal during the 'period'. The natural cycle is calculated on a 28-day basis but there is a degree of variability across women and also within individual women.

The menstrual cycle can be divided into different phases: **menstrual**, **follicular** and **luteal phases**. During the cycle the significant event is **ovulation** in which an ovum is released from one of the ovaries (see Figure 14.7). Ovulation is the point in the cycle where the female is most fertile and is clearly identifiable in many species, but in humans it has become less obvious (Box 14.2).

Hormonal variation is responsible for the different phases of the menstrual cycle. A reduction in progesterone triggers the menstrual phase in which the endometrium breaks down and is removed. The reason for this is to change endometrium from a state in which it can support pregnancy into a state that facilitates the transportation of sperm. Progesterone is secreted by the **corpus luteum** which is a secretory structure in the ovary that comes from an ovarian follicle after ovulation. Oestrogen levels also drop and begin to rise at the follicular phase. The hormonal changes provide a negative feedback loop between the oestrogens and the gonadotrophins (LH and FSH) and provoke a reduction in GnRH. As oestrogen levels fall, LH and FSH rise. It is the increase of FSH that promotes the follicles in the ovaries to develop.

The ovary contains **primordial follicles** which have yet to mature. During follicular development, the primordial follicles leave storage and undergo a process of maturation before they are subject to hormonal influences (approximately three months) (Gougeon, 1986). After the initial stages of

BOX 14.2: MATE SELECTION – OVULATION

There is a great deal of interest in how we are attracted to each other; what are the characteristics that the opposite sex possesses that makes them attractive? There has been a great deal of work in evolutionary psychology to try and address such questions. After all, if it wasn't for the rules of attraction and the subsequent reproduction then the species would fail. Where would Richard Dawkins be then? Many studies have focused on the physical attributes of males and females, e.g. the waist to hip ratio (Singh, 1993), facial symmetry (Little & Jones, 2012) and masculinity (DeBruine et al., 2010).

If we take Dawkins' view that genes are everything and the whole point of life is the perpetuation of DNA, then the rules of attraction should be clear. However, they are far from clear. For many species of mammals, the period in which the female is fertile, just before ovulation (see Chapter 14), is correlated to increases in sexual behaviour and attractiveness. For example, chimpanzees, like humans, have sex throughout their ovulatory cycle and during their fertile period the genital swellings that coincide entice males to copulate more frequently, therefore increasing the likelihood of conception, pregnancy and eventually offspring. In humans these tell-tale signs of ovulation and fertility have been regarded as lost.

However, this has not stopped people looking for them. One hypothesis is that women's behavioural adaptations surrounding mating will take current ovulation into account. A second hypothesis is that men's behavioural adaptations surrounding mating will be responsive to ovulatory signals from women. During ovulation, women's social behaviours change, their body odours change (Gildersleeve et al., 2012), their voices change (Bryant & Haselton, 2009) and also their physical appearance (Durante et al., 2008; Haselton et al., 2007). It has been found that near ovulation, women are more likely to flirt with attractive men; they are more likely to say yes when asked to dance (Gueguen, 2009). They are also more likely to dress to impress, they are more likely to show skin (Haselton et al., 2007).

One study that went in search of hidden cues or signals looked at the earnings of lap dancers in Albuquerque, New Mexico (Miller et al., 2007). Miller and colleagues give a detailed account of their study:

> ... because academics may be unfamiliar with the gentlemen's club subculture, some background may be helpful to understand why this is an ideal setting for investigating real-world attractiveness effects of human female estrus. (p.376)

Who are they trying to kid? In this study, 18 lap dancers recorded their menstrual periods, their shifts and how much they earned from dances. They did this for 60 days and completed the information online. The women can be divided into two groups: those who were using hormone-based contraceptives and those who were not (ovulating normally). What the authors found was that those who were normally cycling earned US$335 in the oestrous phase compared to US$260 during the luteal phase. Those dancers who were using hormone-based contraceptive pills showed no oestrus peak earnings. An important methodological consideration here is to look at menstruation. In Miller and colleagues' study they did just that and found no differences between the two groups of women, thereby eliminating premenstrual syndrome as a confounding variable. Similarly, there was no difference at the luteal phase between the two groups of women; it was only during the fertile phase of the cycle that the normally cycling women increased their earnings.

In their discussion of the data, the authors suggest further directions for study. They suggest that they should try to distinguish between signals and leaked cues in females who are seeking extra pair copulation with good

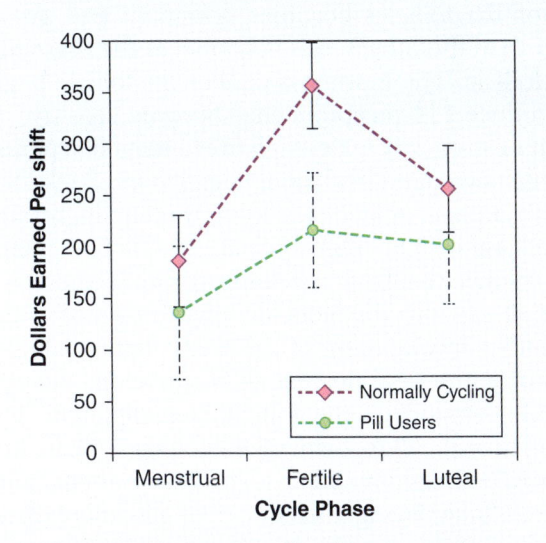

FIGURE 14.2.1 *The earnings of lap dancers according to ovulatory cycle. Dancers who were either on hormone contraceptives or not were asked about their cycle and earnings. Women in their fertile phase and not using hormone contraceptives earned more money.*
Source: Miller, G., Tybur, J. M., & Jordan, B. D. (2007). Ovulatory cycle effects on tip earnings by lap dancers: Economic evidence for human estrus? *Evolution and Human Behavior, 28*(6), 375–381.

> gene males (an affair). Indeed, in another study, during periods of high fertility women were shown to be attracted to other men rather than their romantic partner, depending on whether their romantic partner possessed characteristics conferring good genes (Larson et al., 2012). Furthermore, depending upon sexual desirability of the male partner, women during their high fertile phase rated their partners differently. Those male partners who were low in sexual desirability were perceived by their female partner to have more faults and they were more critical of them. Women with partners who were relatively high in sexual desirability were more satisfied with their relationship and felt closer to their partners (Larson et al., 2013).
>
> In their final sentence Miller et al. state:
>
> > In serially monogamous species such as ours, women's estrous signals may have evolved an extra degree of plausible deniability and tactical flexibility to maximize women's ability to attract high-quality extra-pair partners just before ovulation, while minimizing the primary partner's mate guarding and sexual jealousy. For these reasons, we suspect that human estrous cues are likely to be very flexible and stealthy – subtle behavioral signals that fly below the radar of conscious intention or perception, adaptively hugging the cost–benefit contours of opportunistic infidelity. (p. 380)
>
> Clearly more work needs to be done in this area.

development, the follicles become gonadotrophin dependent. Only those follicles that interact with LH and FSH will develop further; the remainder will die. LH and FSH levels rise during the follicular phase, thereby supporting the survival of 15–20 follicles.

As follicles develop, they produce a large amount of sex hormones. Testosterone from thecal cells is picked up by the granulosa cells and converted into oestrogen. Oestrogen in turn increases the number of granulosa cells which also increases oestrogen and so the cycle continues. During the follicular phase, one of the follicles becomes dominant and grows faster than the others: this is known as the preovulatory follicle. The granulosa cells of the follicle begin to produce LH receptors that become sensitive to LH. If oestrogen remains high over a sustained period of time (two days), the usual negative feedback loop flips to a positive feedback loop, thereby increasing the release of LH (Karsch et al., 1973). The switch to a positive feedback mechanism means there is a surge of LH into the bloodstream which pushes the continued development of the preovulatory follicle.

During the final process of maturation, the first meiotic division of the follicle is completed. The majority of the cytoplasm of the follicle is dedicated to a single daughter cell (a **secondary oocyte**) with the remainder being a small cell of discarded chromosomes (first polar body). The secondary oocyte goes through a second stage of meiotic division and simultaneously the secretion of oestrogens drops and progesterone takes over. Progesterone is the main sex hormone of the luteal phase.

Ovulation occurs when the follicle ruptures and releases the secondary oocyte to be transported in the fallopian tubes. The secondary oocyte is now referred to as the ovum (the egg). The ovum present in the fallopian tube is now available for fertilization.

If fertilization occurs then the egg will be implanted and pregnancy will commence (see Chapter 3). However, if it is not fertilized it will die within 24 hours. The fate of the ovum is unknown and the body works on the safe assumption that fertilization has occurred. Therefore, the uterus and endometrium enter a phase that will support pregnancy. Evolution has provided a mechanism that errs on the side of caution, favouring the transmission of DNA.

During the luteal phase, the dominant ovarian follicle transforms into the **corpus luteum** which secretes progesterone and oestrogen which help maintain a pregnancy for the fertilized ovum. The granulosa and **thecal cells** of the follicle convert into new cells that increase the levels of progesterone output. During the luteal phase, the endometrium of the uterus thickens due to progesterone. The cervix also changes and acts as a barrier to any sperm, providing protection should fertilization occur. At the end of the luteal phase, the corpus luteum begins to deteriorate and the levels of progesterone and oestrogen decline. Without the hormonal support, the endometrium breaks down and along with some blood from the innervating arteries, forms a menstrual flow. And then we are back at the beginning and the cycle continues until an egg is fertilized.

During the menstrual cycle, some women suffer from what is referred to as **premenstrual syndrome** (PMS) or in the *Diagnostic and statistical manual* (DSM) 5, **premenstrual dysphoric disorder** (PMDD). The symptoms of PMDD include:

- flattened affect and feelings of helplessness, or even thoughts of suicide;
- tension or anxiety;
- panic attacks;

- mood swings;
- lasting irritability or anger;
- lack of interest in daily activities;
- lack of concentration;
- lethargy;
- food cravings;
- insomnia;
- feeling out of control; and
- physical symptoms, e.g. bloating, breast tenderness, headaches and joint or muscle pain.

Such can be the severity of symptoms that PMS has been used in a court of law to explain even murder (see Chapter 25).

SEXUAL DEVELOPMENT

In Chapter 3 the development from conception through to old age was briefly addressed. However, one aspect of development that has not been considered is sexual differentiation. One might consider that sex is a genetically determined feature. However important the genetic contribution is, there are other factors involved in creating man and woman.

A good place to start is with the genes. As has already been mentioned, the X and Y chromosomes determine the genetic sex of the individual. The presence of the SRY region of the Y chromosome instructs the body to form a male.

Sexual differentiation as a result of either having or not having SRY affects the genitals, gonads, reproductive tract and brain. Although sexual differentiation at the molecular level occurs at conception, many of the differences between the sexes occur over a period of time that continues into puberty and a little bit beyond.

Six weeks after conception, the gonads begin to differentiate as ovaries and testes and two separate ducts develop from each gonad to the exterior of the embryonic body where the future genitalia will develop (Figure 14.8). These are the **Wolffian duct** and the **Mullerian duct**. The Wolffian duct is in direct contact with the gonads. The Mullerian duct runs alongside the gonads but without contact. Both ducts are precursors of the male and female reproductive tracts. The Mullerian duct will develop into the oviduct, the uterus and the innermost part of the vagina whereas the Wolffian duct will develop into the vas deferens.

Embryos at the outset contain both kinds of ducts – male and female. To develop into a female, nothing has to be done. Female is the essential blueprint. However, for a male to develop, the testes secrete anti-Mullerian hormone (AMH) which binds with receptors in the ducts and causes them to disappear early in development. The Leydig cells in the testes secrete androgens which peak around 12–16 weeks and prevent degeneration of the Wolffian ducts which continue to develop into the epididymis, vas deferens, ejaculatory ducts and seminal vesicles.

The external genitalia of males and females arises from the same embryonic structures. At four weeks, the embryo has a slick known as a **cloaca** which has two urethral folds alongside it. At the top of the cloaca is the **genital tubercle** that will develop into either the clitoris or the penis. By six weeks the urethral folds have separated to provide the anal fold which becomes the anus; the point of fusion between the two urethral folds is the perineum. In the absence of any hormonal influence, the female external genitalia is the default mode of development. In the male foetus, the presence of testosterone promotes the development of the male genitalia.

The urethral folds in the female develop into the labia minora, the outer regions of the vagina and the crura of the clitoris (see Figure 14.8). The genital tubercle develops into the glans of the clitoris.

Testosterone in the male foetus is converted into DHT, which is a more potent androgen. The action of DHT promotes the urethral folds to fuse along the midline, thereby creating the shaft of the penis around the urethra. The genital swellings fuse forming the scrotum and the genital tubercle forms the glans of the penis.

During development, the ovaries and testes enter the pelvic region and take different routes thereafter. The ovaries after birth descend to the pelvis and end up on either side of the uterus whereas the testes shortly before birth enter into the scrotum. The testes descend into the scrotum because of the **gubernacula**, which is a band of tissue that will not stretch and is attached to the testes and pubic bone. As the body grows, the tissue does not expand with it and pulls the testes and related structures into the scrotum.

If everything is normal then the mother gives birth to either a boy or a girl. However, the genitalia and reproductive organs will undergo further development on their way to sexual maturity. If there are genetic or hormonal problems then the difference is not always straightforward (Box 14.3).

The Male and Female Brain

In typically developing individuals sexual differentiation is clearly visible, but the central nervous system is also changing according to sex. Traditionally, it

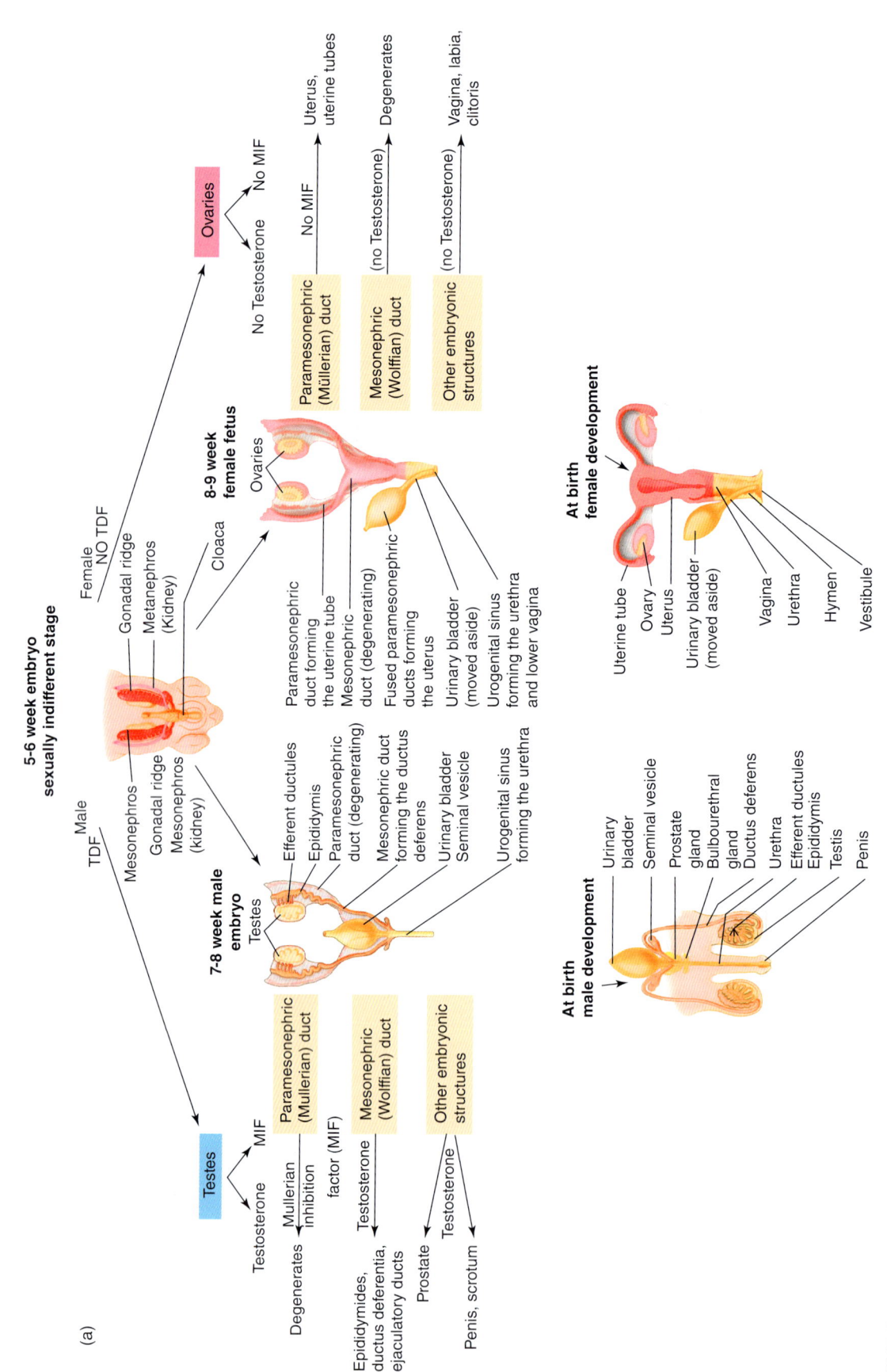

FIGURE 14.8 *Development in utero of male and females and external genitals. (a) Development in utero of male and female reproductive systems. MIF, Mullerian inhibiting factor; TDF, testes determining factor. (b) External genitalia.*

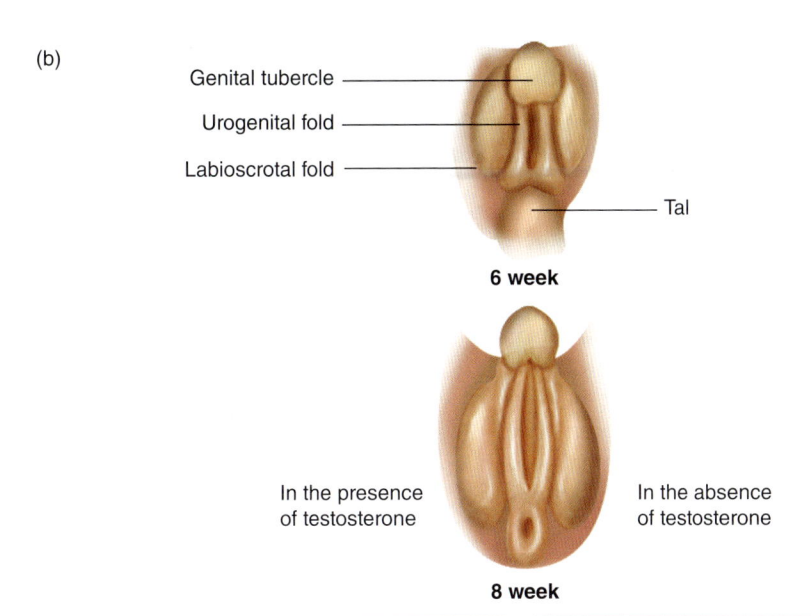

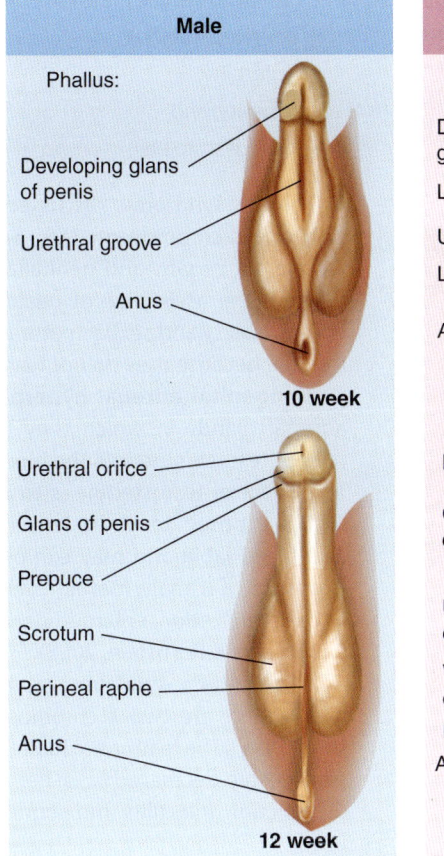

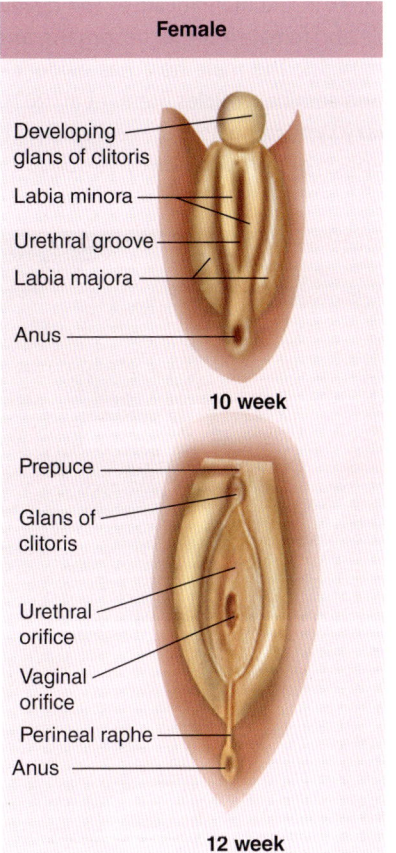

FIGURE 14.8 *(Continued)*

has been considered that there are two periods of sexual differentiation of the brain: **organizational** and **activational** periods.

The first insight into sex differences in the brain came from a paper published in 1959 by Phoenix and co-workers (Phoenix et al., 1959). In the experiments reported, pregnant guinea pigs were injected with testosterone. The offspring were evaluated for sex-appropriate behaviour when mating, e.g. **lordosis** in females (arching of the back) and mounting in males. In order to control the experiment further, the offspring had their gonads removed before

BOX 14.3: GENETIC AND HORMONAL ABNORMALITIES

Not everything always goes according to plan and there can be errors and external influences that affect sexual development.

Androgen insensitivity syndrome is where a person has XY chromosomes but they are phenotypically female (Hughes et al., 2012). The reason for this is that they lack androgen receptors and without those receptors their body cannot respond to testosterone. The external genitalia are female but their internal female organs failed to develop because AMH is still active.

Persistent Mullerian duct syndrome is a condition caused by a congenital lack of AMH or its receptors (Guerrier et al., 1989). In the male it causes the development of both male and female internal sex organs, as can be seen in Figure 14.3.1. The male here has evidence of both the vagina and seminal vesicles (Renu et al., 2010).

Polycystic ovary syndrome (PCOS) is a disorder characterized by disruption of the ovulation cycle due to cysts around the edge of the ovaries and excessive secretion of androgens resulting in **hyperandrogenism** (Norman et al., 2007). The symptoms of hyperandrogenism are:

- increased growth of body hair;
- acne;
- irregular menstrual cycles;
- deepening of voice;
- increased muscle bulk;
- virilization;
- reduced size of uterus;
- reduced female breast size;
- increased libido;
- infertility;
- obesity; and
- loss of scalp hair.

In Turner's syndrome, discussed in Chapter 2, there is only one X chromosome (X0). Such individuals develop female sex organs and genitalia but often lack ovaries. Without the assistance of oestrogen pills, they do not enter puberty and sexual maturation. Obviously, they are infertile because they do not have ovaries.

Congenital adrenal hyperplasia is a defect of the adrenal glands in which they are overstimulated and release testosterone into the bloodstream (Figure 14.3.2). The effect of testosterone is to masculinize so a female foetus exposed to androgens has an enlarged clitoris and fused labia and may exhibit tomboyish behaviour. Exposure of a male foetus to excess androgens results in early virilization, enlarged penis and increases in body hair (Merke & Bornstein, 2005).

Klinefelter's syndrome is a genetic condition in which there are two X chromosomes and a Y chromosome (XXY). The features of Klinefelter's syndrome include small testes, decreased facial hair, gynaecomastia, erectile dysfunction, infertility and cognitive deficits (Groth et al., 2012).

Males with an XYY genotype have normal sexual development but tend to be more physically active as children and delayed in emotional maturity. The idea that having two Y chromosomes makes you more male was typified by the 1970s TV show called The XYY Man in which the lead character has a net extra Y chromosome leading to his criminal recidivism. The reality, however, is not so clear and a stereotype of XYY males generally

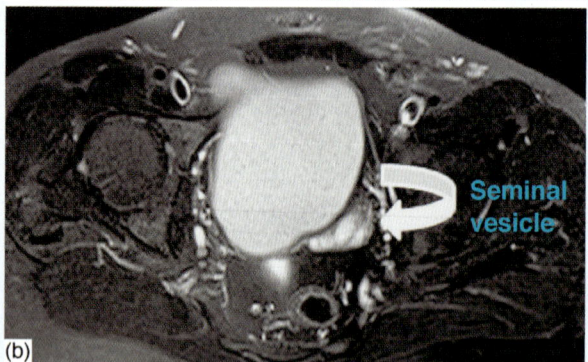

FIGURE 14.3.1 *Persistent Mullerian duct syndrome.*
Source: Renu, D., Rao, B. G., Ranganath, K., & Namitha. (2010). Persistent mullerian duct syndrome. *Indian Journal of Radiology and Imaging, 20*(1), 72–74.

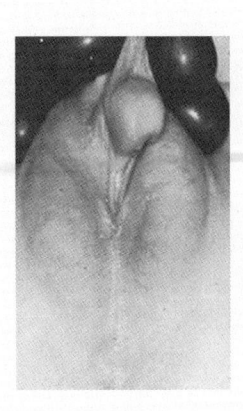

FIGURE 14.3.2 *Female with enlarged clitoris and fused labia.*
Source: Manipalviratn, S., Trivax, B., & Huang, A. (2005). Genetic disorders and sex chromosome abnormalities. In A. DeCherney, L. Nathan, T. M. Goodwin, N. Laufer & A. Roman (Eds.), *Current Diagnosis and Treatment: Obstetrics and Gynecology* (10th edn). The McGraw-Hill Companies, Inc. Figures 3-12.

had an effect rather than the genes themselves (Walzer et al., 1978). However, a recent study has associated the XYY genotype with committing more crimes (Stochholm et al., 2012). The increase in criminal behaviour may not be a direct consequence of the XYY genotype but rather the secondary effects of the genotype that actually leads to criminal behaviour, e.g. tallness and severe acne lead to them being considered more deviant or of low intelligence (Gotz et al., 1999; Hook, 1973).

Having three X chromosomes (XXX) could be the counterpoint to XYY man. These females are quite impassive as infants, they show delayed development in motor, speech and cognitive measures, but have normal physical development (Otter et al., 2010).

Sexual development is far from straightforward. From genetics through to hormones, a number of aberrations can occur that mean normal development is compromised.

puberty and received hormone replacements. The findings of the experiments indicated that:

- females treated prenatally with testosterone showed reduced lordosis and increased mounting (they were masculinized);
- the effects of prenatal testosterone were permanent when presented at critical periods of sensitivity;
- the effects of prenatal testosterone were considered to affect the organization of the sexual brain which then goes on to influence future adult behaviour; and
- hormones have different effects depending on the timing; prenatal hormones influence the organization of neural tissue, whereas later on at puberty hormones have an activating effect on the already established neural tissue.

After this paper was published, the **organizational-activational hypothesis** became the dominant theory of sex differences of the brain, organization being the influence of sex hormones on the developing brain (hardwired changes) and activation being the hormones influencing the activity of the hardwired brain, thereby influencing adult sexual behaviour. Many studies since the original Phoenix paper have supported and extended this paradigm to other behaviours (see Arnold (2009) for review).

If newborn female rats were treated with oestrogen they failed to show lordosis in adulthood, but would show mounting behaviour if administered androgens (Feder & Whalen, 1965). The conclusion from this study is that early oestrogen has a masculinizing effect on the brain and 'feminization is induced by lack of neonatal androgen rather than by the presence of estrogen' (Feder & Whalen, 1965, p.306). The reason for this finding is that oestradiol is a metabolite of testosterone and through aromatization, the enzyme aromatase changes testosterone into oestradiol (Figure 14.9). Thus, the increased levels of testosterone in the male can be converted into oestradiol, which masculinizes the neurons of the brain. Females' brains are protected from the masculinizing effects of oestradiol because the plasma protein called **alpha-fetoprotein** binds to oestrogens and stops it entering the brain. Testicular testosterone is not bound by alpha-fetoprotein and therefore enters the brain where it can then be aromatized into estradiol (Bakker et al., 2006). Therefore, in the absence of testosterone (and therefore oestradiol), the female foetus develops. The high levels of testosterone being converted into oestradiol allow for the male foetus to develop.

WHAT REGIONS OF THE BRAIN ARE DIFFERENT IN THE SEXES?

An obvious next step in understanding sex differences is to look at the brain. Early studies were only able to do this in animals that have undergone manipulations to alter their hormone levels. The key

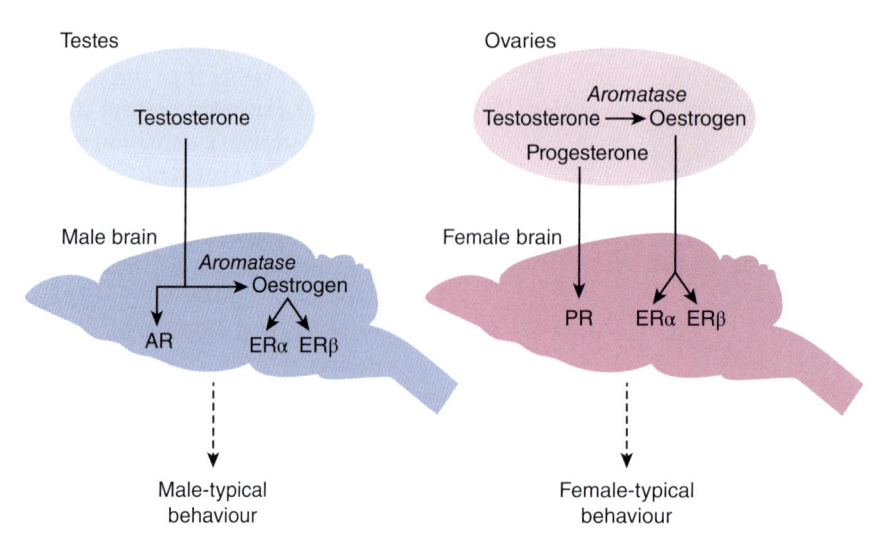

FIGURE 14.9 *Aromatization in the male (left) and female (right) rat brain.*

area of difference between male and female brains is in the **hypothalamus**, and in particular the preoptic area (Field & Raisman, 1971; Raisman & Field, 1971). The medial preoptic area of the hypothalamus was shown to be larger in male rats (Gorski et al., 1978) and humans (Swaab & Fliers, 1985). Due to the fact that the differences between the male and female hypothalamus were clearly identifiable, this region became known as the **sexually dimorphic nucleus** (SDN) (Figure 14.10). The equivalent area in humans is the third interstitial nucleus of the anterior hypothalamus (or the **bed nucleus of stria terminalis** (BDST)) which was 2.47 times bigger in males than females (Allen & Gorski, 1990).

In the rat at birth, the SDN was the same size in both males and females. However, during the first few postnatal days the SDN grew in the males. The growth of the SDN is initiated by aromatized oestradiol (Arnold & Gorski, 1984). However, the specific critical period during which the SDN is differentiated has been shown not to be as short as first thought. Male rats were castrated at different time points to see what the effects of a lack of endogenous steroids were on the SDN. What was found was a period of at least 29 days postnatally in which the SDN could be changed (Davis et al., 1995). How the presence or absence of sex hormones influences the growth of the SDN needs to be addressed. There is little effect of testosterone on the neurogenesis of cells within the SDN; however, the incidence of apoptosis in females was considerably higher and testosterone had an inhibitory effect on apoptosis in male castrated rats (Chung et al., 2000; Davis et al., 1996). Thus, the difference between male and female SDN is not due to a factor making cells grow, but rather a factor that stops them dying. Other factors then allow our cells to live (Arnold, 2009). How this translates to humans remains uncertain.

Whilst this SDN of the preoptic area has received considerable attention, it is noteworthy that the brain regions are also subject to hormonal influence. Oestradiol can influence cell proliferation in the hippocampus and the amygdala, promote cell death in the male ventral forebrain nucleus of the preoptic area, suppress synaptogenesis and astrocyte differentiation within the arcuate nucleus, and increase synaptogenesis and dendritic branching in the ventral medial nucleus of the hypothalamus (McCarthy & Arnold, 2011). On a more gross behavioural and anatomical view, there is evidence to suggest that the brain is more lateralized in the male than the female (see Chapter 19).

The neural mechanisms by which organization or activation occurs remain somewhat elusive. The search for one mechanism that fits all is limiting. However, a number of possibilities exist (see Arnold (2009) for review) in which sex hormones have an effect:

- they influence the growth of axons and dendrites;
- they influence the amount of cell death; and
- they regulate the number or type of synapses a cell makes.

Schwarz and McCarthy (2008) have revealed that masculinization and defeminization have different cellular mechanisms. They looked at the effects of NMDA antagonists and found that they blocked oestradiol-induced defeminization but not masculinization. What is the difference between masculinization and defeminization? Masculinization allows for the expression of male sex behaviour in adulthood, whereas defeminization suppresses

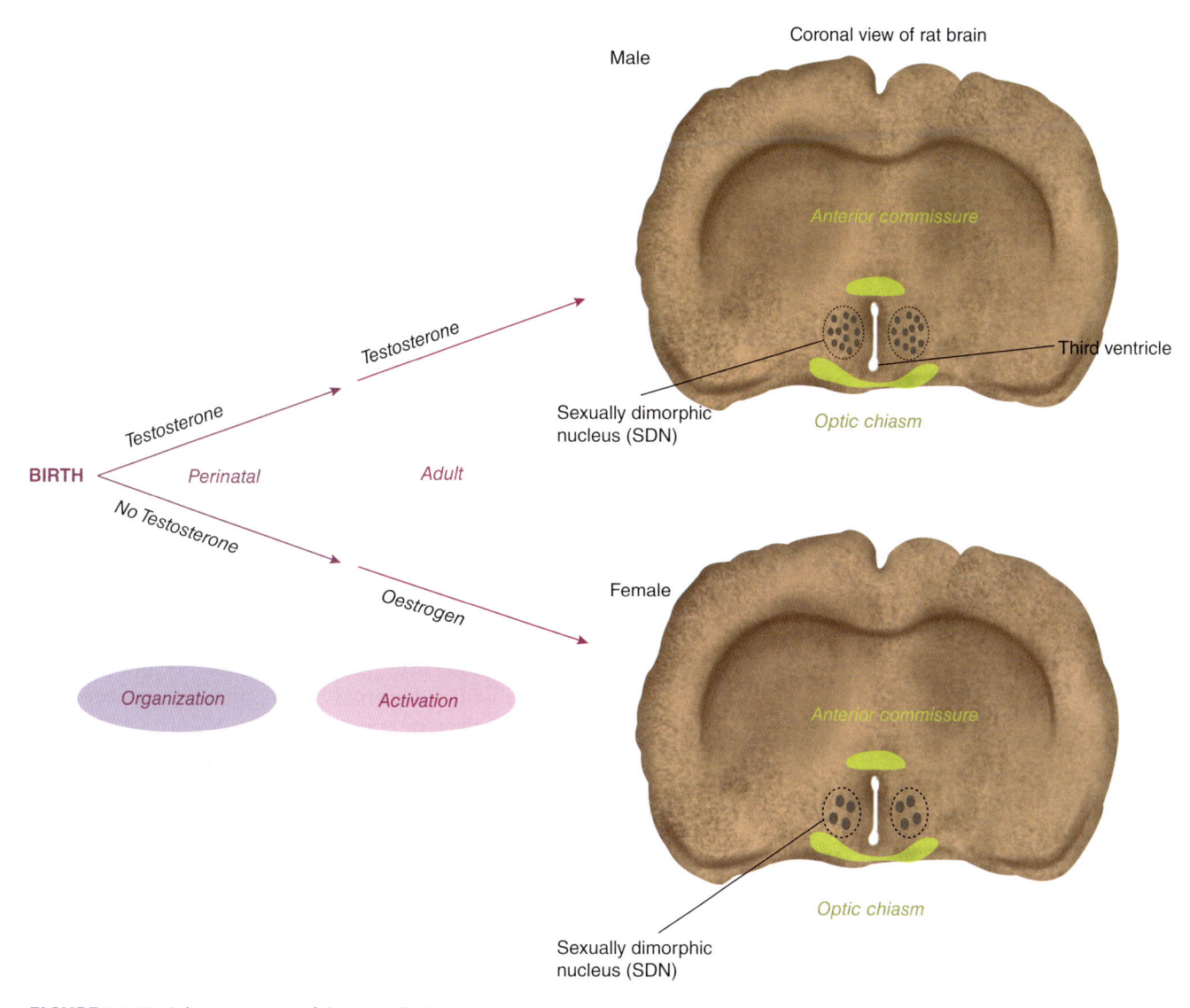

FIGURE 14.10 *Schematic view of the sexually dimorphic nucleus (SDN) of the hypothalamus.*

the capacity for female sex behaviour in adulthood (Schwarz & McCarthy, 2008).

The simplistic view that sex hormones have singular effects on the brain is somewhat incorrect.

> Importantly, however, when considering any one site of sex steroid action, or any one cellular or molecular event that is sexually dimorphic, the independence of masculinization and defeminization disappears. If only one sexually dimorphic phenotypic dependent variable is measured, it can vary only along a single continuum of masculine vs. feminine. (Arnold, 2009, p.573)

Such was the influence of the organizational-activational hypothesis of sexual differentiation that 'hormones became the only factors that were investigated or discussed as proximate signals causing sex differences in the brain' (Arnold, 2009, p.573).

Given that the only difference between the sexes in the human zygote is the sex chromosomes, genes come back into play in determining sexual differentiation. One of the main genes considered is the SRY gene. The SRY gene controls the development of the gonads and related hormones which in turn have organizational and activational effects. Therefore the SRY gene is the originator of sexual differentiation. Surprisingly, there is little information regarding the roles of the sex chromosomes in sex differences, but the advent of molecular biology and the utilization of mouse models have started to elucidate the underlying mechanisms. Studies using these mouse models have attempted to remove the SRY gene from the chromosome and in doing so have provided four core genotypes: XXSry, XX-SRY (deleted SRYgene), XX and XY. In a review of the literature using mouse models, McCarthy and Arnold

(2011) note that although SRY still remains important, other genetic factors coded on the X and Y chromosome have widespread effects on sexual differentiation of the brain but also behaviour.

Up to this point, sex and sex behaviour are determined by genes and their effects on hormonal activity. Environmental or experiential factors are also at play (Schulz et al., 2009). Much has been made within social psychology of the influence of parents, teachers, peers and the world in general on sex role stereotypes being adopted. Social psychology takes the nurture position whereas psychobiology has taken the nature position in this version of the nature–nurture debate. However, the polarized positions of the nature–nurture debate could be minimized by future epigenetic studies indicating that environments can modify the genome (McCarthy & Arnold, 2011).

The activational influence of hormones is most notable in puberty, but there is also the possibility that organizational effects of steroids are evident in adolescence (Schulz et al., 2009). The onset of puberty occurs when the hypothalamus starts secreting gonadotrophin-releasing hormone. This allows the anterior pituitary to produce LH and FSH which prompt the gonads to produce oestradiol and testosterone. Marshall and Tanner have identified five stages of puberty in males and females (Marshall & Tanner, 1969, 1970).

In females, breast enlargement (**thelarche**) is an early sign of puberty followed 2–3 years later by the onset of menstruation (**menarche**). As a result of the adrenal activity, pubic and axillary hair starts to grow and the apocrine glands produce sweat. During puberty, oestradiol levels fluctuate and the endometrium undergoes a cycle of proliferation and regression and when there is withdrawal of oestrogen, the first menstrual bleed occurs (period). There is no absolute age at which this occurs and evidence suggests that the age of menarche is reducing due to external factors, e.g. diet (Okasha et al., 2001).

In males, puberty is identified by enlargement of the scrotum and penis and the growth of pubic and facial hair. However, the first stage is an increase in the size of the testes which precedes other more obvious changes.

Puberty is often a very trying time for individuals. The hormones being secreted into the bloodstream are changing the body, and the brain is also changing independently of sexual puberty (see Chapter 3). Puberty marks the change from being a child to being an adult and is a biological marker point whereas the advent of adulthood is a sociopolitical/cultural concept. Clearly, puberty is a process in which sexual maturation is occurring. The question remains, when has it occurred? At what age do you become an adult? There is no absolute answer; for example, the age of consent for sex in the UK is 16, whereas in France and Poland it is 15, in Portugal 14 and in Spain 13 (although there are legal caveats that can make sex under 16 illegal). The age at which one can purchase alcohol in the UK is 18 whereas in the USA it is 21. Thus, the age of consent, or at least the age at which you can be considered individually responsible, is different across countries, different across behaviours and can change over time.

Regardless of the age of consent, sexual maturity is required for reproduction and the continuation of the species. For that to happen, we need to reproduce and that means sex (the verb rather than the noun that we have so far considered).

WHAT HAPPENS DURING SEXUAL AROUSAL?

The human sexual response undergoes several phases throughout a cycle. Notable descriptions of the human sexual cycle come from Masters and Johnson (1966) who identified four phases: **excitement**, **plateau**, **orgasm** and **resolution** (Figure 14.11).

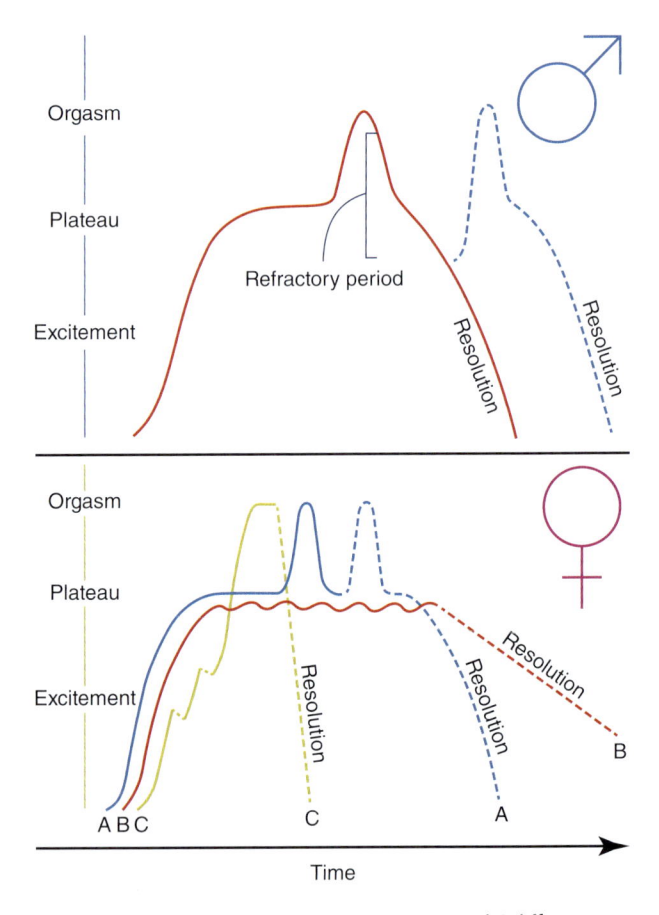

FIGURE 14.11 *Human sexual response. (A, B and C different female responses)*

During the excitement phase in women, the labia minora deepen in colour and open, lubrication in the vagina is increased, the clitoris and nipples of the breast become erect and the uterus elevates within the pelvis. In addition, heart rate and blood pressure rise. In men, the excitement phase is characterized by the erection of the penis and the testicles rising (Figure 14.12).

Erection of the penis and clitoris is mediated by spinal reflexes. The sensory free nerve endings of the penis are termed **genital end bulbs** and are highest in intensity in the area of the corona and near the frenulum (Halata & Munger, 1986). The nerve fibres of the genital end bulbs project towards the spine along the pudendal nerves. These sensory nerves enter the sacral regions of the spinal cord. Once in the spinal cord, they synapse with interneurons that are linked to the parasympathetic nervous system and via efferent fibres of the pelvic nerves and synapse with the erectile tissue in the penis.

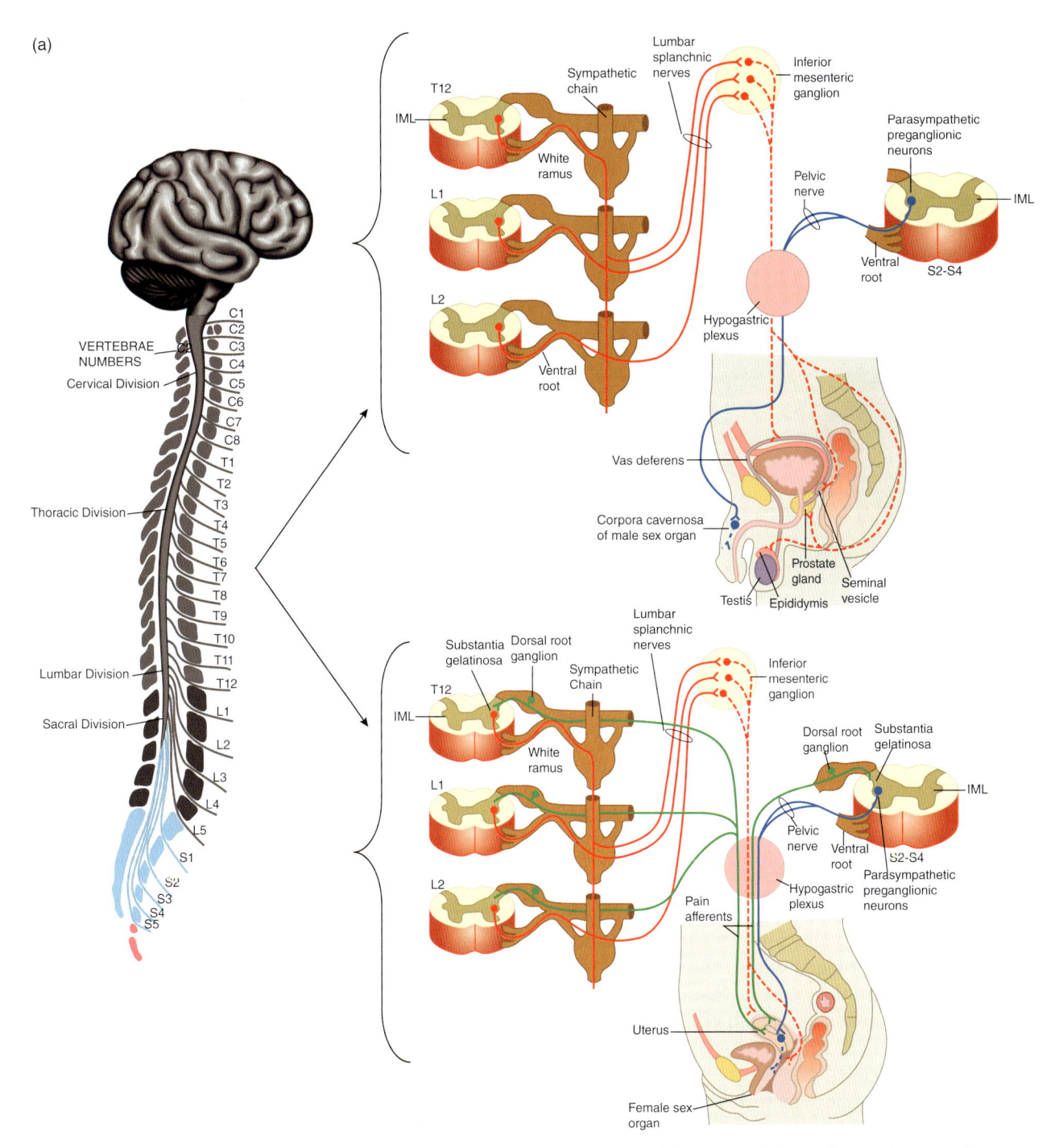

FIGURE 14.12 *Physical changes of the human sexual response. (a) The innervation of the penis and clitoris. (b) Females. (c) Males.*

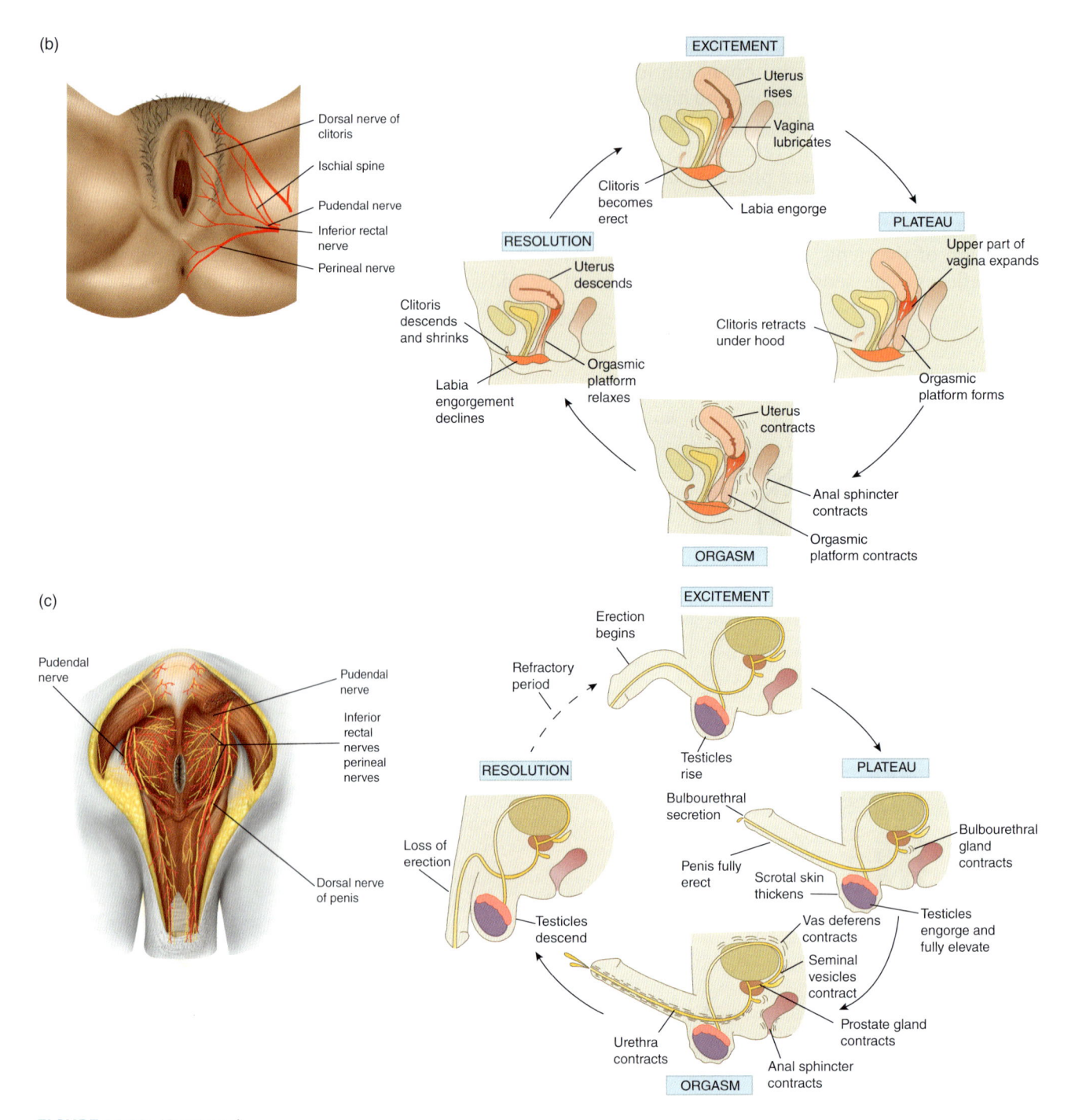

FIGURE 14.12 (Continued)

Interneurons also connect with efferent fibres, which are involved in the muscle contraction and stem from **Onuf's nucleus** within the spinal cord.

Within the penis the erectile tissue is made up of the corpus cavernosum which consists of a collapsible space called the sinusoids separated by connective tissue called trabeculae. The trabeculae contain smooth muscle which shrinks the sinusoid. Blood enters the sinusoids via the veins but this is limited by contractions of the arteries. It is interesting to note that the flaccid state of the penis is actively maintained by the sympathetic nerve fibres. Erection results because of a decrease in sympathetic activity and an increase in parasympathetic activity (Figure 14.13). Parasympathetic fibres release neurotransmitters into the erectile tissue. Nitric oxide relaxes the smooth muscle cells of the arteries and the trabecular wall, which in the flaccid state keeps

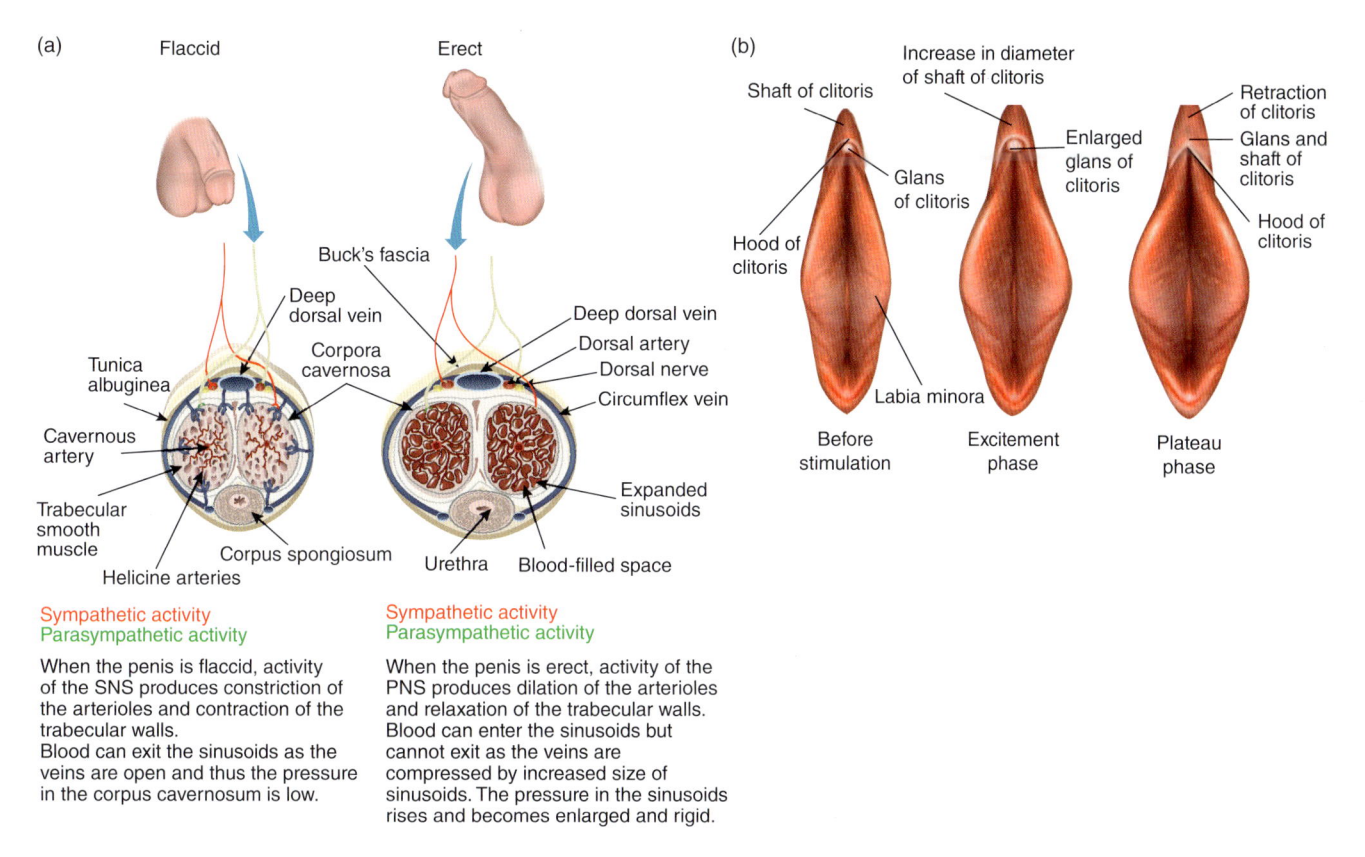

FIGURE 14.13 Genital erections. (a) The mechanism of a penile erection. (b) The observable erection of the clitoris.

blood flow low. Because of this relaxation, more blood flows into the sinusoids and the erectile tissue expands. The expansion of the erectile tissue compresses the veins that would allow the blood to exit. Blood therefore enters erectile tissue but has trouble escaping, thereby inducing distension and rigidity.

Viagra works for impotence by interfering with the nitric oxide metabolic pathway. Nitric oxide is released which then stimulates the enzymatic release of the second messenger **cyclic guanosine monophosphate** (cGMP) which acts as a vasodilator through relaxation of the smooth muscles in the blood vessels of the corpus cavernosum. cGMP is converted into an inactive form by an enzyme called PDE 5. Viagra binds with PDE 5, preventing it from converting cGMP. This allows cGMP to remain active for longer and hence so can the erection.

The signals involved in erections discussed so far have not involved the brain. The key region of the brain is the hypothalamus. It is hypothalamic nuclei that have been studied extensively and are referred to as the SDN. The hypothalamus communicates with the brainstem and sends signals via the autonomic nervous system down the spine, thereby either increasing or decreasing activity levels. Also active during an erection are the anterior cingulate, insula, amygdala and secondary somatosensory cortices (Ferretti et al., 2005).

A similar process occurs in females with the erection of the clitoris.

The next phase in the sexual response cycle is the plateau phase. This is a state of high arousal that may be maintained for a variable period of time. During the plateau phase the glans of the clitoris disappears under the hood and the outer part of the vagina tightens whereas the inner part expands to accommodate the penis. In males, erection becomes stronger and the bulbourethral glands secrete their clear viscous substance (pre-cum).

Next comes orgasm. Orgasm is comparatively straightforward in the male, but the purpose of orgasm in the female, and some of the features of the female orgasm, are a contentious issue (Box 14.4).

Orgasm is usually felt as a brief sequence of muscle contractions and the subjective experience of a release of sexual tension. In the male just prior to ejaculation, semen is expelled into the posterior part of the urethra. The mobilization of semen is caused by sympathetic nerve fibres producing contraction of smooth muscles in the prostate and seminal vesicles. The assembly of the ejaculate starts with secretions from the prostate gland followed by the

BOX 14.4: FEMALE ORGASM: G-SPOT, EJACULATION, SQUIRTING AND EVOLUTION

The purpose of the female orgasm remains unclear and is subject to debate within evolutionary psychology.

Masters and Johnson (1966) in their early studies identified the female orgasm as a single entity and for many researchers this continued to be the accepted school of thought (King & Belsky, 2012). There have been numerous types of orgasm identified in females ranging from clitoral to vaginal (Sayin, 2012). The subjective experiences varied and the physiological response has been well characterized (King & Belsky, 2012). An electrophysiological study using a vibrator on the clitoris indicated that vaginal, uterine and corpus cavernosum pressures diminished until a full clitoral erection and with continued clitoral stimulation at orgasm, the activity of ischio- and bulbocavernosus muscles intermittently increased (Shafik et al., 2009).

In the brain, self-stimulation of the clitoris, vagina or cervix activated regions of the medial cortex, but the location within the medial cortex was slightly different for each of the three self-stimulated areas (Komisaruk et al., 2011). Stimulation of the clitoris was associated with

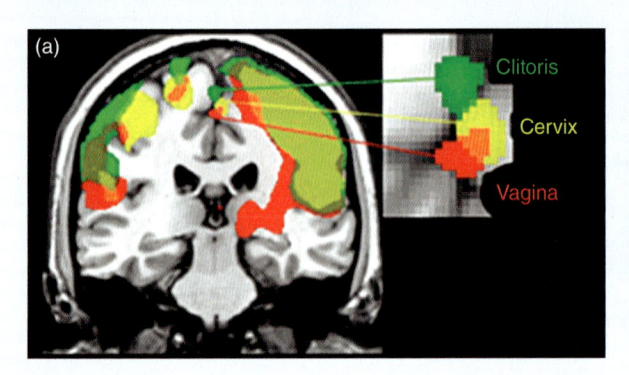

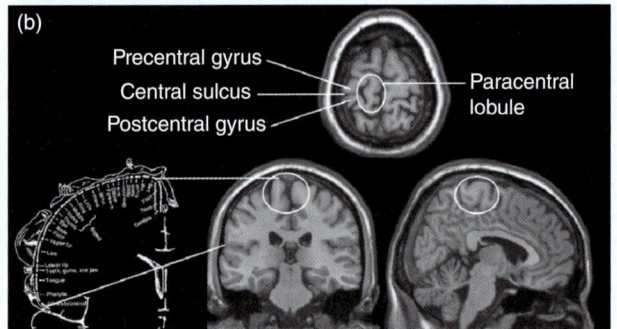

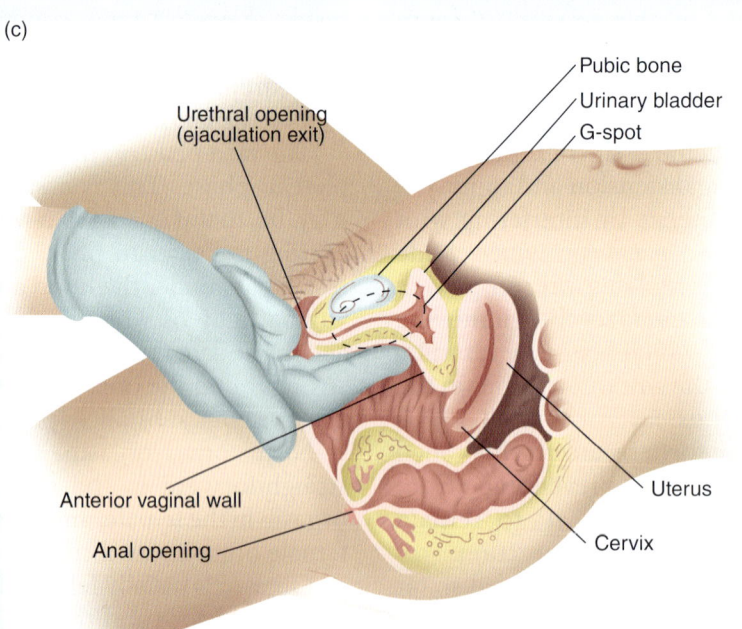

FIGURE 14.4.1 *Stimulation of the female genitalia. (a) Composite view of the brain's activation during stimulation of the clitoris, cervix and vagina. (b) Three views of the paracentral lobule, showing its relation to adjacent cortical regions (the relation of the paracentral lobule to the sensory cortical homunculus of Penfield and Rasmussen is shown by the connecting lines). (c) The G-spot and female orgasm.*
Source: (a) and (b) Komisaruk, B. R., Wise, N., Frangos, E., Liu, W. C., Allen, K., & Brody, S. (2011). Women's clitoris, vagina, and cervix mapped on the sensory cortex: fMRI evidence. *Journal of Sex Medicine*, 8(10), 2822–2830. Reproduced by permission of John Wiley & Sons.

activation of frontal regions and parietal regions and also the insula and putamen (Michels et al., 2010).

Given that the female orgasm is unquestionably a real phenomenon, the purpose of it needs clarification. The adaptive nature of the female orgasm has been theorized to exist for two reasons: that it is necessary for pair bonding or it is involved in mate selection, leading to increased quality of genetic material. Others have considered it to be an unnecessary evolutionary byproduct of the necessity of the male orgasm. The view that attracts the most evidence is its adaptive nature for harvesting sperm. Such a view is supported by the physiological data suggesting that female orgasms can create an insuck of deposited sperm (Fox et al., 1970). The insuck or upsuck is when the cervix dips into the deposited sperm and facilitates its journey to the site of fertilization. Upsuck is linked to the sperm competition hypothesis of female orgasm as a device equipping females with the ability to ensure the survival of the 'genetically strongest' sperm (Baker & Bellis, 1993).

One issue that interferes with a conclusive adaptive argument is that female orgasm is more likely to occur via masturbation rather than through sexual intercourse (Lloyd, 2005; Zietsch et al., 2011). Given the anatomy of the vulva, the clitoris may not receive much stimulation during penile-vaginal sex; thus Hite (2000) reports that simultaneous clitoral stimulation by hand 'is perhaps the best way for most women to orgasm during intercourse' (p.268).

Linked to orgasm is the G-spot or Gräfenberg spot located just inside the vagina on the anterior wall (Gräfenberg, 1950). The **paraurethral gland (Skene's gland)** has been identified as the most likely physiological substrate for the G-spot (see Dwyer, 2012). The significance of this is that the paraurethral gland stems from the same embryonic tissue as the male prostate gland (Zaviačič, 1985). However, a true anatomical identity of the G-spot has remained somewhat elusive (Kilchevsky et al., 2012; Puppo & Gruenwald, 2012).

Linked to the G-spot and also provoking great debate is female ejaculation. Female ejaculation may be considered a rare phenomenon, but 40% of respondents to a study in the USA and Canada reported ejaculation (Darling et al., 1990). Female ejaculation has been somewhat sensationalized by pornography which depicts women squirting an arc of liquid meters from the vulva. With males, there is a clear purpose of ejaculation as a delivery mechanism for sperm. With female ejaculation the purpose is uncertain.

The first aspect of female ejaculation to try and understand is the content of the ejaculation. That might seem a straightforward question, but there is the problem of determining what constitutes female ejaculation. Some have argued that female ejaculate is urine (Goldberg et al., 1983). Rubio-Casillas and Jannini (2011) were able to distinguish between 'squirting or gushing' and female ejaculation. In this case study, the participant, via stimulation of the anterior vaginal wall, released two fluids from the urethra. One fluid was thin and watery with little or no colour or smell and constituted squirting whereas after the squirt another fluid (the ejaculate) was released. The ejaculate was thick and milky and similar to male semen. The squirting fluid had low levels of prostate-specific antigen (PSA), uric acid, urea and creatinine. The ejaculate had high levels of PSA. The high levels of urinary markers in the squirting liquid indicated that the fluid came from the bladder. The second fluid is thought to come from the female equivalent of the prostate gland.

Schubach (2001) catheterized women with the tube passing above the paraurethral gland and measured emissions derived from masturbation. He found that the large quantity of liquid came via the catheter, indicating an origin in the bladder, whereas a small volume of liquid was released from outside the catheter and was consistent with other reports of female ejaculate. A review of the literature supports the case study reporting that female ejaculation is distinct from squirting which is a form of cortical incontinence (Pastor, 2013).

One might consider, with sexual liberation and a vast array of sex toys available to achieve orgasm, that these have enabled the discovery of female ejaculation. The literature is somewhat sparse on female ejaculation, but a historical review noted that Chinese Taoist literature contains references to female ejaculation, and enjoyed a renaissance with the discovery of the G-spot (Korda et al., 2010).

An evolutionary hypothesis on female ejaculation suggests that it has an adaptive function in protecting the female.

Moalem and Reidenberg (2009) speculate that antimicrobial elements of female ejaculate are adaptive because:

- women who ejaculate antimicrobial secretions into the urethra are less likely to suffer urinary tract infections (UTI) and therefore;
- women without UTIs were more likely to be sexually receptive which would lead to;
- frequent intercourse with the increased likelihood of becoming pregnant, and;
- pregnant women were more successful in reproduction.

Of course, one other consideration of the adaptive nature of the female orgasm and ejaculation is that it induces pleasure. Anything that induces pleasure is likely to be rewarding and the behaviour repeated. By inducing pleasure, humans engage in sex and that increases the likelihood of reproduction.

sperm and the secretion from the seminal vesicles providing a more jelly-like consistency after ejaculation. Spasmodic contractions of the smooth muscles in the urethral wall and in the muscles of the penis are responsible for ejaculation. The contractions stem from a burst of activity of motor neurons in the sacral region of the spinal cord. The muscles squeeze a semen-filled urethra and semen is propelled out of the penis in a series of decreasing spurts. The force of ejaculation may project the semen against the cervix.

Regardless of the biological necessity, sex and orgasm are pleasurable activities. Given the powerful motivating effects of sex, we engage in the behaviour because of the pleasurable reward and not because of reasons of pure reproduction (although that may well be the case at some points in life). We may engage in many sexual practices, e.g. masturbation, oral sex (fellatio and cunnilingus) and anal sex, all of which are independent of reproduction. Evolutionary psychologists have argued that oral sex serves an evolutionary purpose in partners being able to ascertain if the recipient of oral sex has had other sexual partners recently (Pham & Shackelford, 2013) or engaging in mate retention behaviour (Pham & Shackelford, 2013).

The resolution phase is when arousal subsides and the body relaxes again. Males have a refractory period in which further stimulation does not lead to erection or orgasm. Resolution is a time for rest, making a cup of tea and perhaps watching TV.

EVOLUTION OF PLEASURE

Such is the pleasure from sexual stimulation that it has been linked to death. A 30-year-old woman was found dead in the UK after watching a porn movie whilst using a vibrator. The high state of arousal that was produced gave rise to a sudden heart arrhythmia that killed her. Pornography is normally associated with male consumers and activated regions of the brain associated with sex (Box 14.5).

The seeking of sexual pleasure is powerfully motivating. Sex has been likened to feeding behaviour in which the cycle goes through stages of appetite, consumption and satiety (Georgiadis & Kortekaas, 2010). In sexual arousal a large number of cortical areas were active in response to visual stimulation alongside a number of subcortical regions (Stoleru et al., 2012); there were some differences in cortical activation between the sexes with genital stimulation but not during orgasm (Georgiadis et al., 2009).

At the heart of all motivation is dopamine. Animal studies have indicated that there is a rise in dopamine in the rat nucleus accumbens in response to sexual stimuli (Damsma et al., 1992; Pfaus et al., 1995). Dopamine has also been linked with human sexual behaviour (Kruger et al., 2005). Orgasm in males and females has been associated with increased activity in dopaminergic areas (Georgiadis et al., 2007; Holstege et al., 2003; Komisaruk and Whipple, 2005; Komisaruk et al., 2004). The activation of these areas is similar to the activation of areas seen in other rewarding behaviours, e.g. feeding and drug consumption (see Chapters 15 and 16). In particular, during orgasm, subcortical regions are more active, including the cerebellum, thalamus, PAG and midbrain (Georgiadis & Kortekaas, 2010). A number of areas are also deactivated, such as the orbitofrontal cortex which has been linked to the carefree state of mind during orgasm (Georgiadis & Kortekaas, 2010).

SEXUAL ORIENTATION

An evolutionary perspective on sex focuses on reproduction via coitus between males and females. However, sex is not exclusively an act that occurs between males and females. Both animals and humans have same-sex sexual interactions. There have been a number of hypotheses on the evolutionary background to same-sex sexual behaviour, e.g. it creates bonds that may be of benefit beyond the sex itself, maintains hierarchies and allows for practice, although it may be non-adaptive (Bailey & Zuk, 2009).

Sexual orientation, however, refers to sexual attraction towards persons of either the opposite or the same sex. Central to discussions on sexual orientation is the nature–nurture debate. Are people born with a particular sexual orientation which is therefore biologically hardwired? Or do people through socialization 'learn' to be gay? The complexity of sexual orientation has not found a strong home in biology (Rahman, 2005). Biological theories have focused on prenatal hormones and genes. The hormonal basis of sexual orientation in such theories derives from animal studies in which manipulations have either created an absence or extremely high levels of hormones (see Rahman, 2005). The genetic basis has been similarly elusive (McGuire, 1995).

BOX 14.5: MIRROR NEURONS AND PORNOGRAPHY

Pornography is a multi-billion pound industry that is often at the cutting edge of technology. The apparent appetite for pornography begs the question of what it is doing. There are many views about the damaging effects of pornography, particularly on the young child/adolescent, and it would be surprising if pornography did not have an impact on the sexual behaviours of the viewers. There are many genres of pornography ranging from the tame to the macabre and extreme. It is well known that males will have an erection when viewing pornographic images of their orientation (Bancroft et al., 1991). When viewing erotic stimulation, the occipital temporal area, anterior cingulate gyrus, insula, orbitofrontal cortex and caudate nucleus became active (surprisingly, neither the hypothalamus nor the thalamus is activated) (Kim et al., 2006).

Mirror neurons are activated when watching somebody else perform a task (Williams et al., 2001). It would not be inconceivable that a mirror neuron system is activated by viewing pornography, especially point of view pornography (POV) in which the view of the sexual scene is from the perspective of the recipient/voyeur.

Only one study has been conducted on mirror neurons and erotica (Mouras et al., 2008). In this study, 10 heterosexual males aged 18–60 were shown explicit films depicting heterosexual intercourse, a control clip of a humorous non-sexual nature that had emotional content, and a neutral film clip. The participants were placed in an MRI machine and a plethysmograph cuff was placed around their penis. Areas relevant to the mirror neuron system and the penile somatosensory system were identified by the scanner; these included frontal and parietal regions and the insula. The action of these brain regions was correlated with the amplitude of the penile erections (Table 14.5.1). The authors of the paper conclude that:

> There are similar perception-action coupling mechanism mediated by the mirror neuron system proxy observers to resonate with the motivational state of other individuals appearing in visual depictions of sexual interactions, with observers activating motor representations and erectile responses associated with the observed depictions. (Mouras et al., 2008, p.1149)

TABLE 14.5.1 *Plethysmographic and psychological responses to the three experimental conditions. The effect of different stimuli (film clips) on measures of penile volume and affect*

	Condition		
Responses	**Neutral**	**Humorous**	**Sexual**
Penile plethysmography**	−0.1 (0.1)	0.0 (0.1)	0.2** (0.1)
Perceived erection***	1.2 (0.1)	1.2 (0.1)	5.1*** (0.7)
Beauty***	1.4 (0.3)	1.7 (0.3)	6.6*** (0.3)
Pleasure***	2.2 (0.5)	4.1* (0.8)	6.6*** (0.4)
Displeasure**	4.1 (0.8)	1.7* (0.4)	1.3* (0.2)
Interest***	2.7 (0.4)	4.8** (0.6)	6.1*** (0.5)
Perceived humour***	1.9 (0.3)	5.0** (0.8)	1.3 (0.2)

The numbers are for comparisons across conditions (*not* within) and refer to the specific measure (penile volume changes and rating scales of 1–9) [*p < 0.05, **p < 0.01, ***p < 0.001].
Source: Mouras, H., Stoleru, S., Moulier, V., Pelegrini-Issac, M., Rouxel, R., Grandjean, B., et al. (2008). Activation of mirror-neuron system by erotic video clips predicts degree of induced erection: an fMRI study. *Neuroimage, 42*(3), 1142–1150.

Looking at the brain of homosexual and heterosexual men has revealed differences in the interstitial nucleus of the anterior hypothalamus (LeVay, 1991). This region of the hypothalamus was found to be smaller in homosexual men and heterosexual women when compared with heterosexual men. However, the functional impact of differences in the hypothalamus is yet to be determined. It is interesting to note that male-to-female transsexuals were not feminized across a number of brain regions (Savic & Arver, 2011).

SUMMARY

The strict dichotomy of male and female is perhaps a simple cultural heuristic. Studies of intersex have indicated that sexuality, orientation and identity exist along a continuum and that those born with ambiguous genitalia are a group in their own right (see Box 14.6 for the devastating effects of early gender reassignment). But that strict dichotomy of male and female serves a purpose for understanding the evolutionary basis of sex. Taking an evolutionary standpoint, the whole purpose of sex is to reproduce and continue the species. In order to do that, we have two sexes which are different, not only physiologically but also behaviourally. The behavioural and physiological differences serve a purpose in that they equip us for the act of sex. Sex is a highly motivating behaviour. Sexual arousal and orgasm are pleasurable endpoints in sexual consumption. The pleasure principle of sex is perhaps no different from other motivators and is a separate process from the pure evolutionary rationale of reproduction. We clearly have sex for pleasure. Contraception stops pregnancies so we can enjoy sex without pregnancy; masturbation, oral and anal sex and every other sexual fetish/behaviour are perpetuated by pleasure. But if pleasure guides us into sexual activities, as a byproduct the chances of pregnancy are increased, even with today's technology to prevent it. If that is all that is required, then pleasure promotes sex that promotes pregnancy and a new generation – job done.

BOX 14.6: THE JOHN/JOAN CASE

The early literature refers to this as the John/Joan case, but the identity of John/Joan was revealed and more information became available since the initial reports. This is the sad story of David Reimer (Colapinto (1997) provides a passionate account).

David Reimer was originally named Bruce and was one of monozygotic twins. Both boys had phimosis (the inability to pull the foreskin back over the glans penis, causing problems with urination). The medical recommendation was circumcision. The surgery went wrong and David Reimer's penis was destroyed. His parents took the boys to see John Money, a psychologist specializing in sexual identity. Money's position on sexual identity was based on how children were reared – that they were born gender neutral. Money's recommendation was gender reassignment. Reimer was to be brought up as a girl. He became Brenda and was dressed and treated as a girl. By the age of two years his testes had been removed and a vagina constructed.

Money published several papers on the success of what was referred to as the John/Joan case (Money, 1973, 1975; Money & Ehrhardt, 1972). This real-life psychological experiment fed into Money's view of sexual identity. Communication with Money ceased during Reimer's adolescence and nothing else was published by him. The success story remained unblemished and was influencing policy. Paediatric textbooks recommended surgery when the size of the stretched penis is less than about 2.0 cm (Kipnis & Diamond, 1998).

After the apparent disappearance of Reimer he was rediscovered and interviewed (Diamond & Sigmundson, 1997). The interview revealed that the original story was far from being a success. Interviews with his family indicated that Reimer was far from being a normal girl. And his brother claimed there was nothing feminine about him. During early adolescence, he rejected hormones and surgery for further construction of a vagina. At the age of 14, Reimer stopped living as a girl and became male (Diamond & Sigmundson, 1997). Shortly after the transition, Reimer's father informed him of what had happened, and this was a great relief to Reimer (Kipnis & Diamond, 1998a). Reimer went on to have further reassignment and hormone replacement to give him a male phenotype. At the age of 38 he committed suicide. The reasons were unspecified, but the psychological impact of his twin brother's overdose two years earlier and marital difficulties may have been contributing factors.

Milton Diamond is one of the leading experts on gender identity and in particular intersexuality. The final quote by Kipnis and Diamond (1998) provides a more educated and evidence-based view.

> The conceptual distinction between male and female persons . . . is standard cognitive equipment in culture, deeply implicated in self-identification and social ideology... Intersexuality – biologically variant sexuality – disturbs the conventional: both our institutional practices and our ways

of thinking and behaving. Though we are typically educated to think in binary terms, there are common medical conditions that move human beings away from the male and female norms. (p. 400)

Cheryl Chase was genetically female but was born with an enlarged clitoris that was considered to be a penis and was accordingly brought up to be a boy. At the age of 18 months, surgery revealed that she had a uterus and ovotestes and it was recommended that the enlarged clitoris be removed and she would be raised as a girl (Weil, 2006). In later life, Chase demanded access to her medical records. Unhappy with the decisions made for her, she went on to form the Intersex Society of North America (www.isna.org) whose mission statement is as follows.

The Intersex Society of North America (ISNA) is devoted to systemic change to end shame, secrecy, and unwanted genital surgeries for people born with an anatomy that someone decided is not standard for male or female.

We have learned from listening to individuals and families dealing with intersex that:

- Intersexuality is primarily a problem of stigma and trauma, not gender;
- Parents' distress must not be treated by surgery on the child;
- Professional mental health care is essential;
- Honest, complete disclosure is good medicine; and
- All children should be assigned as boy or girl, without early surgery.

LEARNING OUTCOME QUESTIONS

You should be able to answer the following questions.
- Describe the processes of sexual differentiation.
- Provide an evolutionary account of orgasm.
- Evaluate the role of biological sex in gender identity.
- Describe the neural mechanisms of sex.

FURTHER READING

Georgiadis, J. R., & Kortekaas, R. (2010). The sweetest taboo: functional neurobiology of human sexuality in relation to pleasure. In M. L. Kringelbach & K. C. Berridge (Eds.), *Pleasures of the Brain* (pp. 178–201). New York: Oxford University Press.
Lehmiller, J. J. (2014). *The psychology of human sexuality*. Chichester, UK: John Wiley & Sons.
LeVay, S., & Baldwin, J. (2012). *Human sexuality* (4th edn). Sunderland, MA: Sinauer Associates.
Rahman, Q. (2005). The neurodevelopment of human sexual orientation. *Neuroscience and Biobehavioral Reviews, 29*(7), 1057–1066.
Sayin, H. Ü. (2012). Doors of female orgasmic consciousness: New theories on the peak experience and mechanisms of female orgasm and expanded sexual response. *NeuroQuantology, 10*(4), 692–714.

MIND MAP

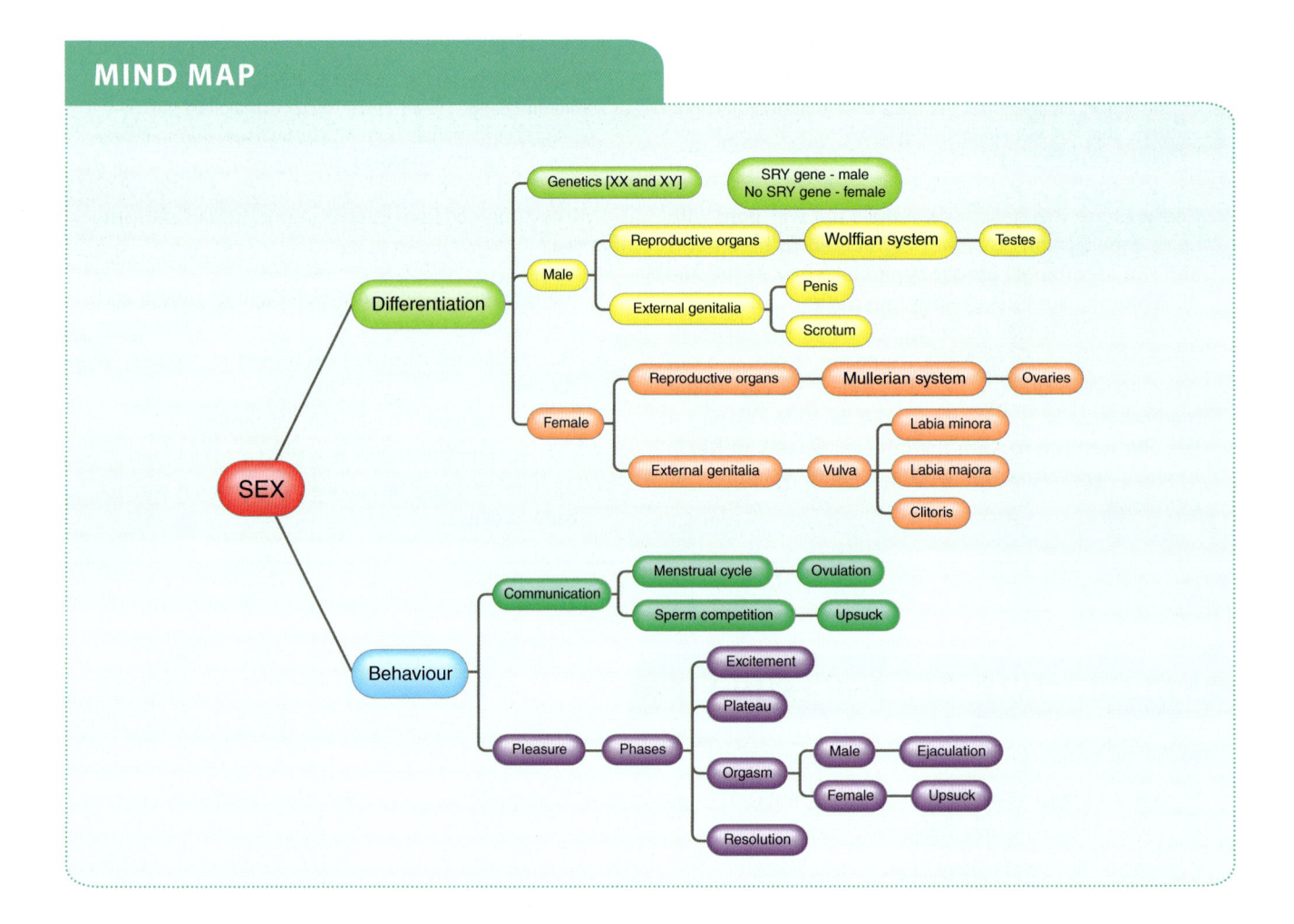

- **SEX**
  - **Differentiation**
    - Genetics [XX and XY]
      - SRY gene - male
      - No SRY gene - female
    - Male
      - Reproductive organs → Wolffian system → Testes
      - External genitalia
        - Penis
        - Scrotum
    - Female
      - Reproductive organs → Mullerian system → Ovaries
      - External genitalia → Vulva
        - Labia minora
        - Labia majora
        - Clitoris
  - **Behaviour**
    - Communication
      - Menstrual cycle → Ovulation
      - Sperm competition → Upsuck
    - Pleasure → Phases
      - Excitement
      - Plateau
      - Orgasm
        - Male → Ejaculation
        - Female → Upsuck
      - Resolution

15 The Neural Regulation of Homeostasis: Feeding and Drinking

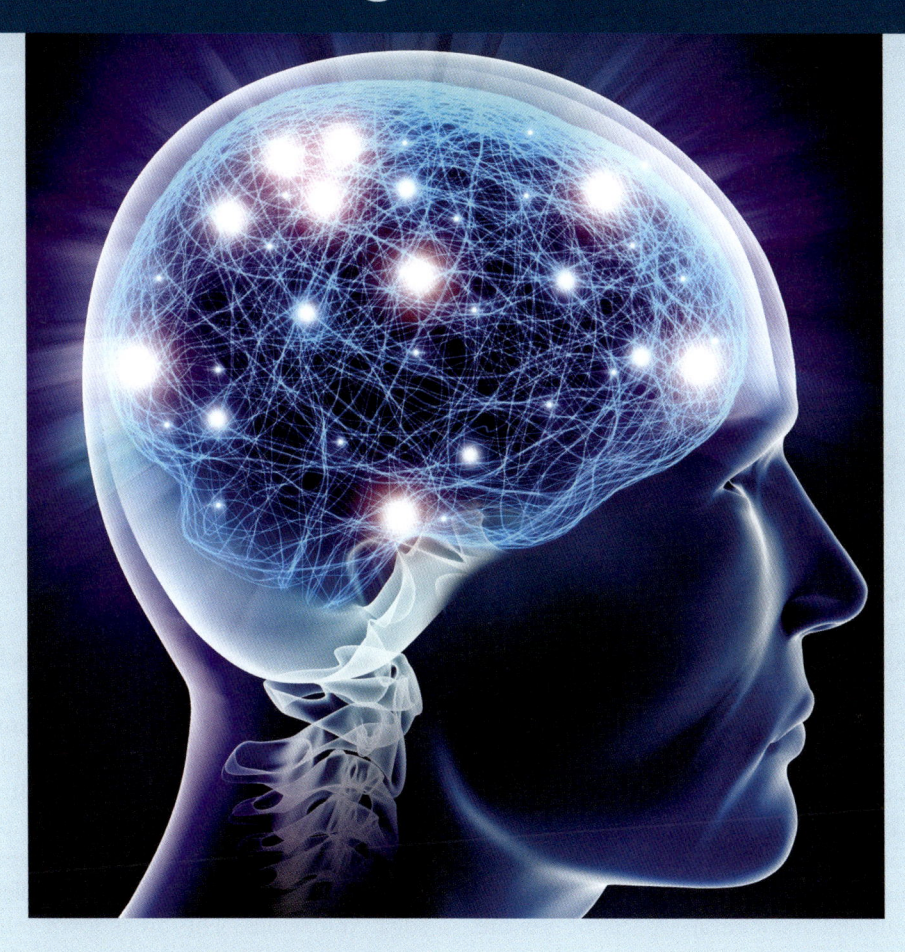

ANATOMY OF THE CHAPTER

This chapter will highlight the following.

- The importance of eating and drinking for survival.
- The digestive mechanisms required to retrieve energy.
- The role of the hypothalamus in energy regulation.
- The role of dopamine in motivation to eat.

INTRODUCTION   392

FEEDING BEHAVIOUR   392

DRINKING AND THIRST   406

SUMMARY   406

LEARNING OUTCOMES

1. To be able to evaluate experimental methodology leading to the hypothalamic hypothesis of eating behaviour.
2. To be able to integrate hypotheses of motivation and homeostatic regulation to promote feeding behaviour.
3. To be able to apply theoretical perspectives to real-world problems of eating disorders.

INTRODUCTION

There are four primary reinforcers: food, water, shelter and sex. The first three are all required by the organism to survive (Box 15.1). Sex is required to ensure the species survives. Balancing food and water intake is essential, as is finding shelter to regulate temperature. Eating food provides energy for the organs of the body and the brain is one of the more hungry organs. Fluid is required to ensure a balance between water and dissolved salts within the cells of the body. The composition of extracellular fluid appears to be a reflection of our early evolution, because most species have a similar concentration of sodium, potassium, urea and glucose (essentially an index of saltiness) in the intracellular and extracellular fluid (Figure 15.1) (Bourque, 2008).

Our optimal body temperature is within a narrow range of 36–38°C. Too cold or too hot can be dangerous for the survival of the organism and therefore being able to regulate one's temperature is an essential requirement. The motivational and neural aspects of sex are considered in Chapter 14.

A considerable amount of research is being conducted into the neural mechanisms underlying feeding behaviour, in part driven by scientific curiosity but also by the necessity to understand and treat eating disorders such as obesity.

FEEDING BEHAVIOUR

When we are hungry, we eat. This motivational state provides the impetus for obtaining nutrients to aid our survival. Although we are mainly concerned with the neural mechanisms underlying feeding behaviour, it is necessary to understand the basic elements of digestion, energy storage and energy release.

The **gastrointestinal tract** is the site of digestion in which food is broken down and absorbed so that the nutrients can be mobilized and delivered as sources of energy (Figure 15.2). Prior to the act of eating, the body begins the digestive process. Once food is in the mouth, with the aid of saliva, chewing breaks down the food ready to be swallowed. The saliva contains enzymes that facilitate the breakdown and also provide the lubrication needed to be able to swallow the food. Salivation has been shown to be initiated by conditioned stimuli associated with previous presentations of food (see Chapter 8).

In the mouth, the chewed food is made into a moist ball called a **bolus** and this is swallowed; it enters the oesophagus and is delivered into the stomach. The stomach is a storage area in which **hydrochloric acid** breaks food down into smaller particles. **Pepsin** initiates the breakdown of protein molecules into its constituent amino acids. Slowly, the stomach empties via the **pyloric sphincter** into the **duodenum**. In the duodenum, enzymes from the **gallbladder** and **pancreas** continue the metabolic degradation of proteins into amino acids, and starch and complex sugar molecules into simple sugar molecules. The breakdown into smaller components, e.g. simple sugars, means that the elements are sufficiently small to pass through the lining of the duodenum into the bloodstream. Once in the bloodstream, they are processed by the liver. Fats are broken down (or **emulsified**) by **bile** (which is made by the liver and stored in the gallbladder) which is released into the duodenum. Fat molecules will not pass through the wall of the duodenum and are therefore carried via small ducts into the lymphatic system. Water and electrolytes (e.g. sodium and potassium) are absorbed from the remaining waste material that is in the large intestine. The remaining waste products are eliminated via the anus.

This general process of digestion provides three forms of energy:

- **lipids** (fats);
- **amino acids**; and
- **glucose** (a simple sugar, broken down from carbohydrates).

BOX 15.1: EVOLUTIONARY EXPLANATION OF EATING DISORDERS

Evolutionary explanations of disorders are often hard to comprehend, e.g. what could possibly be the advantage of schizophrenia? Evolutionary accounts of eating disorders are to some extent a little more straightforward. After all, the consumption of food for energy is as old as life itself and is therefore a central and ubiquitous behaviour. Those organisms that have successfully adapted and survived to reproduce will pass on to the next generation the successful strategy of food consumption.

Obesity may arise as a result of a mismatch between evolutionary requirements and modern-day resources. In our distant past, resources were scarce. Food was not readily available and the next meal was uncertain. Today, in our resource-rich western world where food is easily available (austerity measures notwithstanding), the need to account for future food shortages no longer applies (Pinel et al., 2000). Therefore, obesity can be seen as a mismatch between an expectation of future resources and the reality of the environment. In addition to the mismatch that exists, the scarce resources that our ancestors had to accommodate meant that food would have a high positive incentive value (similar to drugs of abuse in the addict; see Chapter 16). Food therefore becomes reinforcing, and if something is reinforcing the organism is more likely to engage in that behaviour repetitively. Repetitive eating with low energy expenditure will result in weight gain. Modern life, with all its labour-saving devices and the abundance and variety of food, provides a perfect scene for obesity.

Anorexia nervosa and bulimia nervosa can also be accounted for via evolutionary psychology.

Wasser and Barash (1983) offer an explanation focusing on reproductive suppression. They argue that females can suppress their reproduction ability when the conditions are not suitable and wait for an environment that is more conducive. In anorexia nervosa, as a result of low bodyweight, ovulation stops. In a different version of the suppression hypothesis, Surbey (1987) claims that anorexia suppresses puberty (and therefore sexual maturation). Delaying sexual maturity reduces sexual fat such that the female body attracts fewer males and reduces the female's libido, leaving her free to pursue academic interests and careers that are valued by the family (Kardum et al., 2008). The reproductive suppression hypothesis does not explain why men and postmenopausal women sometimes have the condition (Kardum et al., 2008).

Using the same environment used to explain obesity, Guisinger (2003) suggests that the symptoms of anorexia nervosa are adaptive because they allow the individual to flee from famine. The symptoms of anorexia, e.g. restricted food intake, hyperactivity and denial of starvation, allow the individual to migrate in search of resources during times of famine. To facilitate this, exploration and sensation seeking have been associated with the dopamine **DRD4/7R receptor gene** which has been found to be increased in nomadic tribes in comparison with settled tribes (Chen et al., 1999; Eisenberg et al., 2008). Research in Kenya has concluded that individuals with the DRD4/7R gene who still live a nomadic life are better fit for their environment, but those who have adopted a more urban life show reduced fit. Those with the DRD4/7R gene who were still nomads were better nourished than those without the gene.

These represent the more parsimonious evolutionary accounts of eating disorders; there are other accounts about position in society and parental pressures (see Brüne (2005) for review).

The energy obtained via digestion is used to maintain body functions but not all of the energy is used immediately. Energy is stored as:

- fats (the main storage system, accounting for increased body fat);
- **glycogen** (which is converted into glucose); and
- proteins.

Fat is a physiologically economical way of storing energy compared to glycogen.

There are three processes or phases in energy metabolism (Figure 15.3):

- the **cephalic** or **reflex phase;**
- the **gastric** or **absorptive phase;**
- the **intestinal** or **fasting phase.**

The cephalic phase involves preparatory processes for feeding in which the sensory stimulus of food activates digestive systems. The cephalic phase stops when nutrients start being absorbed into the bloodstream. The gastric phase is when the immediate needs of the body are being attended to and nutrients are being absorbed into the bloodstream. The gastric phase lasts 3–4 hours. The physical distension created by food in the stomach activates stretch receptors

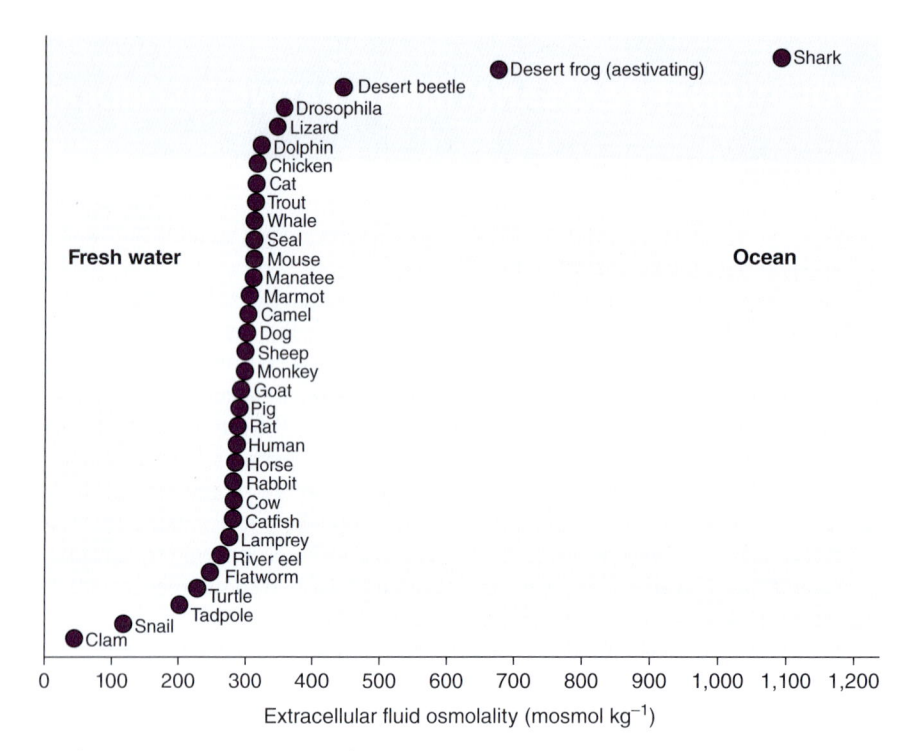

FIGURE 15.1 *Osmolality of many species. The amount of salt in different species is remarkably similar.*
Source: Reprinted by permission from Macmillan Publishers Ltd: NATURE REVIEWS NEUROSCIENCE, Bourque, C. W. (2008). Central mechanisms of osmosensation and systemic osmoregulation. *Nature Reviews Neuroscience, 9(7)*, 519–531. © 2008.

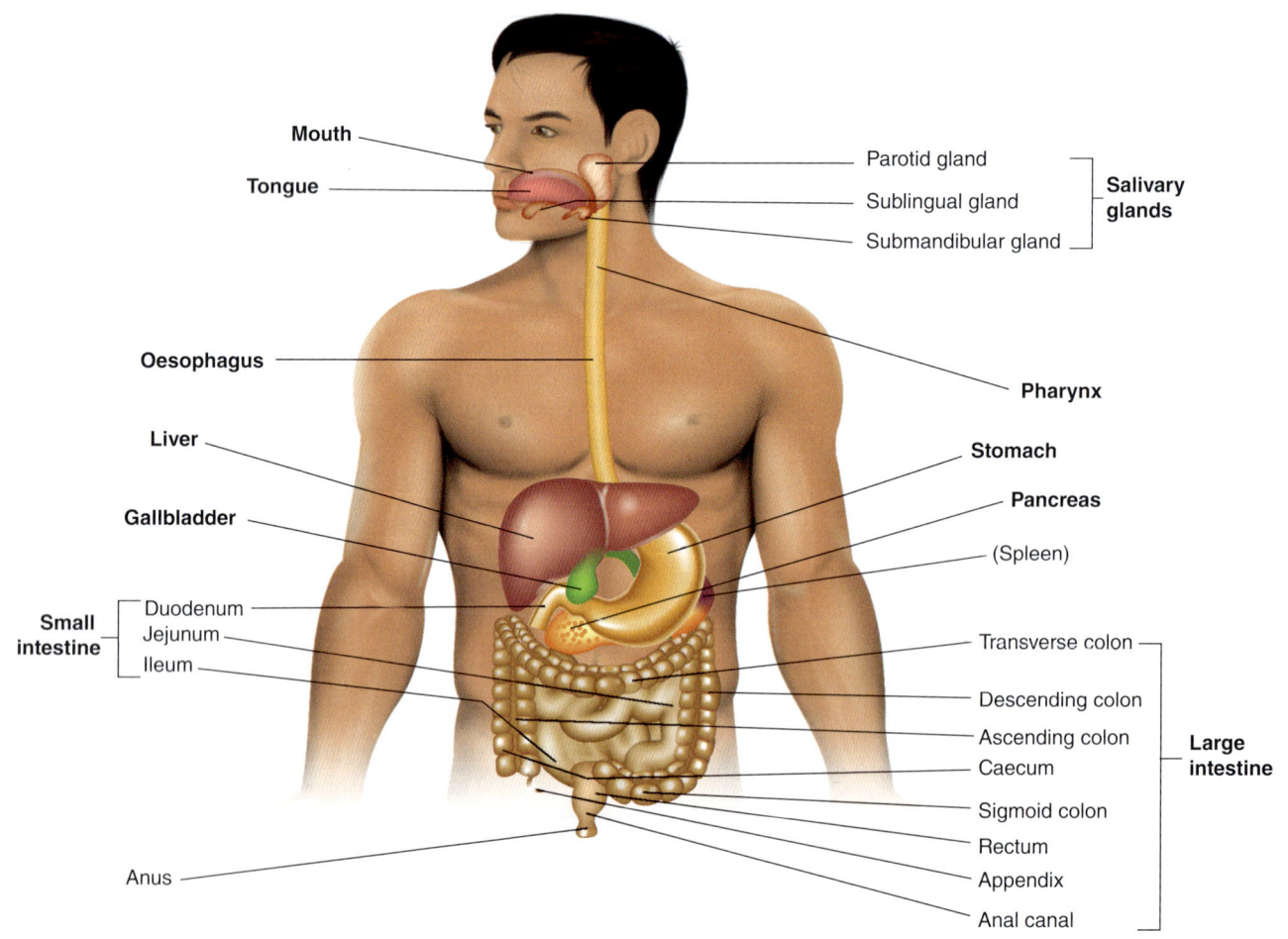

FIGURE 15.2 *The gastrointestinal tract.*

CHAPTER 15 THE NEURAL REGULATION OF HOMEOSTASIS: FEEDING AND DRINKING 395

Cephalic phase
- Sight / thought of food → Cerebral cortex → Conditioned reflex → Vagus nerve
- Stimulation of taste / smell receptors → Hypothalamus and medulla oblongata

Gastric phase
- Stomach distension activates stretch receptors → Vagovagal reflexes → Medulla → Vagus nerve
- Local reflexes
- Food chemicals and rising pH activate chemoreceptors → G cells secrete gastrin into blood

Intestinal phase
- Presence of low pH and partially digested foods in duodenum as stomach empties → Intestinal gastrin release into blood

Stimulates stomach secretory activity

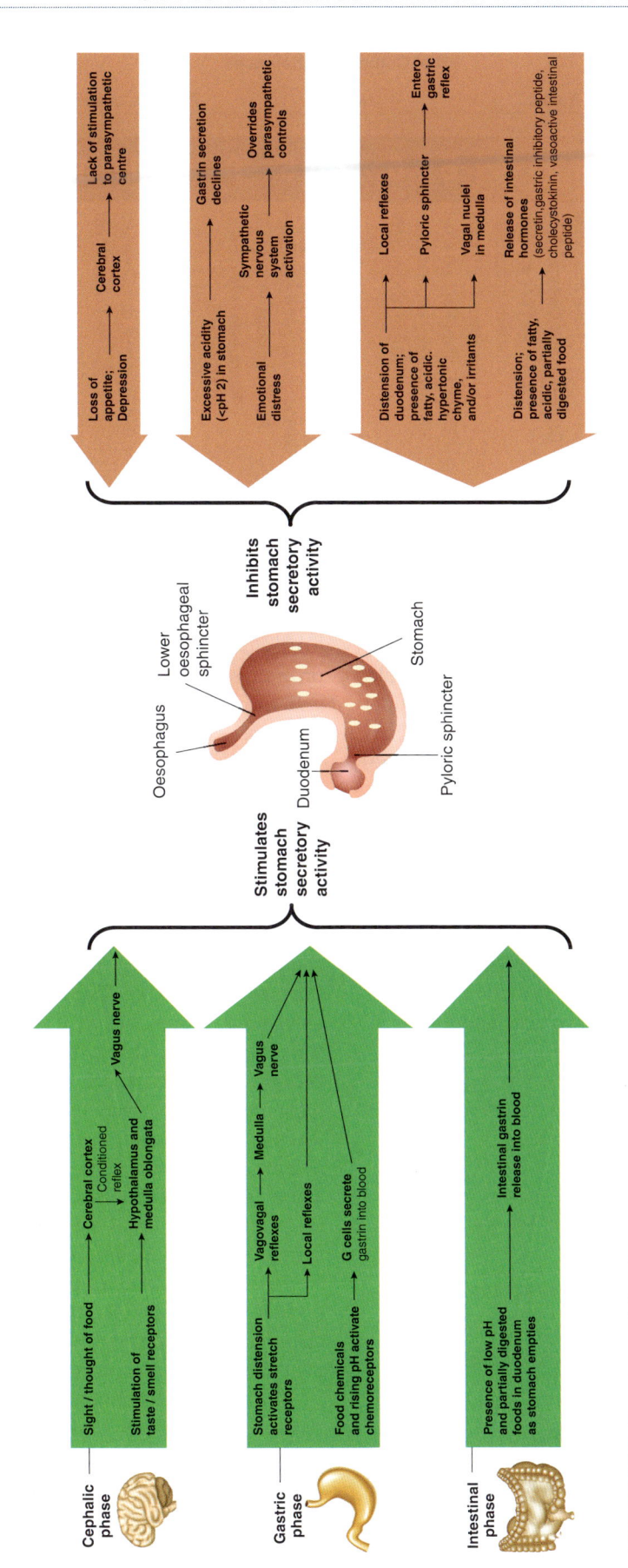

Oesophagus — Lower oesophageal sphincter — Stomach — Duodenum — Pyloric sphincter

Inhibits stomach secretory activity

- Loss of appetite; Depression → Cerebral cortex → Lack of stimulation to parasympathetic centre
- Excessive acidity (<pH 2) in stomach → Gastrin secretion declines
- Emotional distress → Sympathetic nervous system activation → Overrides parasympathetic controls
- Distension of duodenum; presence of fatty, acidic, hypertonic chyme, and/or irritants → Local reflexes → Pyloric sphincter → Entero gastric reflex
  → Vagal nuclei in medulla
- Distension; presence of fatty, acidic, partially digested food → Release of intestinal hormones (secretin, gastric inhibitory peptide, cholecystokinin, vasoactive intestinal peptide)

FIGURE 15.3 *The phases of digestion.*

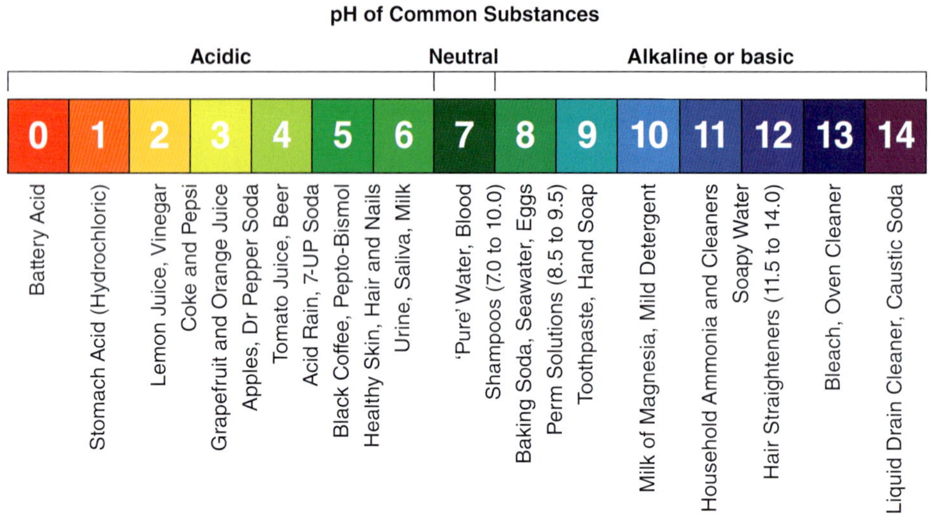

pH of Common Substances

| Acidic | Neutral | Alkaline or basic |

0 — Battery Acid
1 — Stomach Acid (Hydrochloric)
2 — Lemon Juice, Vinegar
3 — Coke and Pepsi
  — Grapefruit and Orange Juice
4 — Apples, Dr Pepper Soda
  — Tomato Juice, Beer
5 — Acid Rain, 7-UP Soda
  — Black Coffee, Pepto-Bismol
6 — Healthy Skin, Hair and Nails
  — Urine, Saliva, Milk
7 — 'Pure' Water, Blood
8 — Shampoos (7.0 to 10.0)
  — Baking Soda, Seawater, Eggs
9 — Perm Solutions (8.5 to 9.5)
  — Toothpaste, Hand Soap
10 — Milk of Magnesia, Mild Detergent
11 — Household Ammonia and Cleaners
12 — Soapy Water
  — Hair Straighteners (11.5 to 14.0)
13 — Bleach, Oven Cleaner
14 — Liquid Drain Cleaner, Caustic Soda

FIGURE 15.4 *pH values of common substances.*

which stimulate the parasympathetic release of acetylcholine (ACh). ACh increases the secretion of gastric juices. A rising pH (more alkaline) stimulates the release of **gastrin** from **enteroendocrine G** cells. These are specialized cells of the endocrine system situated in the gastrointestinal tract and pancreas and gastrin is a peptide hormone that goes on to stimulate hydrochloric acid (HCl). HCl creates an acidic environment for protein digestion (Figure 15.4). The low pH value also increases the firing rate of the vagus nerve (Davison, 1972).

Gastrin also activates smooth muscle contractions and the movement of food. The intestinal phase occurs when the nutrients no longer provide immediate energy and the body has to mobilize previously stored nutrients, e.g. fats. The end of the fasting phase precedes the onset of the cephalic phase, and the circle continues.

Insulin is an important hormone in the digestive process. During the gastric and cephalic phases, insulin is released from the pancreas and potentiates:

- the use of glucose;
- the conversion of glucose to glycogen and fat for storage;
- the conversion of amino acids to proteins for storage;
- the storage of glycogen in liver and muscle;
- the storage of fat in adipose tissue; and
- the storage of proteins in muscle.

Insulin therefore regulates the amount of blood-borne nutrients during the different phases.

During the intestinal phase there are high levels of glucagon and low levels of insulin. Glucagon is a peptide hormone released by the pancreas when glucose levels fall. It converts stored glycogen into glucose. Glucagon performs a task that is the opposite of insulin: it mobilizes glucose, whereas insulin stores glucose. Glucagon promotes the release of fatty acids from adipose tissue and stimulates the conversion of these fatty acids into ketones. Ketones are used by muscles as an energy source.

The purpose of the process of digestion is to ensure there is sufficient energy for survival. However, how this is balanced has been subject to much conjecture. Early theories focused on gastric distension leading to **satiety** (Anand & Pillai, 1967), which is clearly not true. Satiety is the feeling of being full. The idea that there are specific receptors in the duodenum that are sensitive to the chemical composition of food also appears not to be true (Ehman et al., 1971). This is not to say that they are not involved as factors, but they are not the most critical factor. The intuitive nature of the setpoint assumption of hunger posits that there is an optimal level of energy resources and that when that level declines, this promotes feeding. This is analogous to the thermostat on a central heating system and works on the process of maintaining a homeostatic equilibrium, using negative feedback loops, i.e. when energy levels are high, there is no need for consumption. The setpoint theories that were initially generated focus on the levels of glucose and fats (glucostatic and lipostatic theory) (Mayer, 1955). With the increase in eating disorders and psychological mechanisms influencing feeding behaviour, the setpoint theory is no longer justified.

The energy that the brain consumes differs from time to time, and with the brain's adaptive nature, a setpoint does not seem to be a realistic hypothesis. Furthermore, from an evolutionary perspective, this does not make sense. According to Pinel et al. (2000), our ancestors would benefit more from being able to store food than to respond to the moment-by-moment needs for food, when the environment is harsh and food is not in ready supply.

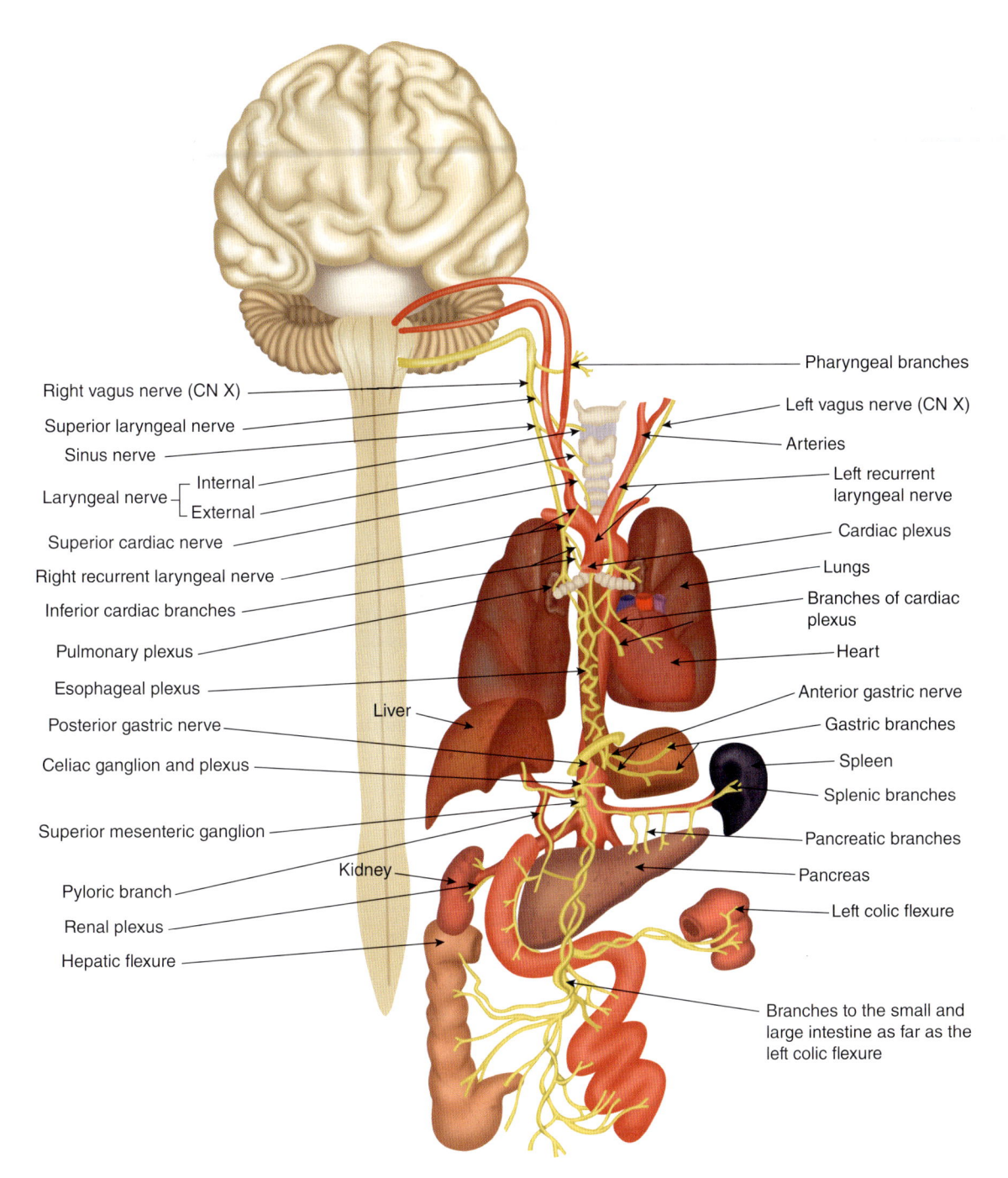

CHAPTER 15 THE NEURAL REGULATION OF HOMEOSTASIS: FEEDING AND DRINKING 397

FIGURE 15.5 *The vagus nerve.*

To some extent, the focus of feeding behaviour has been on the digestive system, but Figure 15.5 demonstrates that the regions of the digestive system are connected to neural systems in the brain via the vagus nerve. The focus of feeding behaviour can therefore be redirected towards the brain.

Brain Mechanisms for Eating

The brain is in control of feeding behaviour, but responds to the general environment of the body. The brain itself requires enormous amounts of energy, in the form of glucose (Mergenthaler et al., 2013). The brain's role in feeding has been determined through a number of adaptations that demonstrate the benefits of hindsight and the advantages of modern technology. At the centre of feeding behaviour, and other homeostatic processes, e.g. thermoregulation, is the hypothalamus.

The hypothalamus
The **hypothalamus** is made of separate nuclei (Figure 15.6). Two regions of the **hypothalamus** were initially emphasized

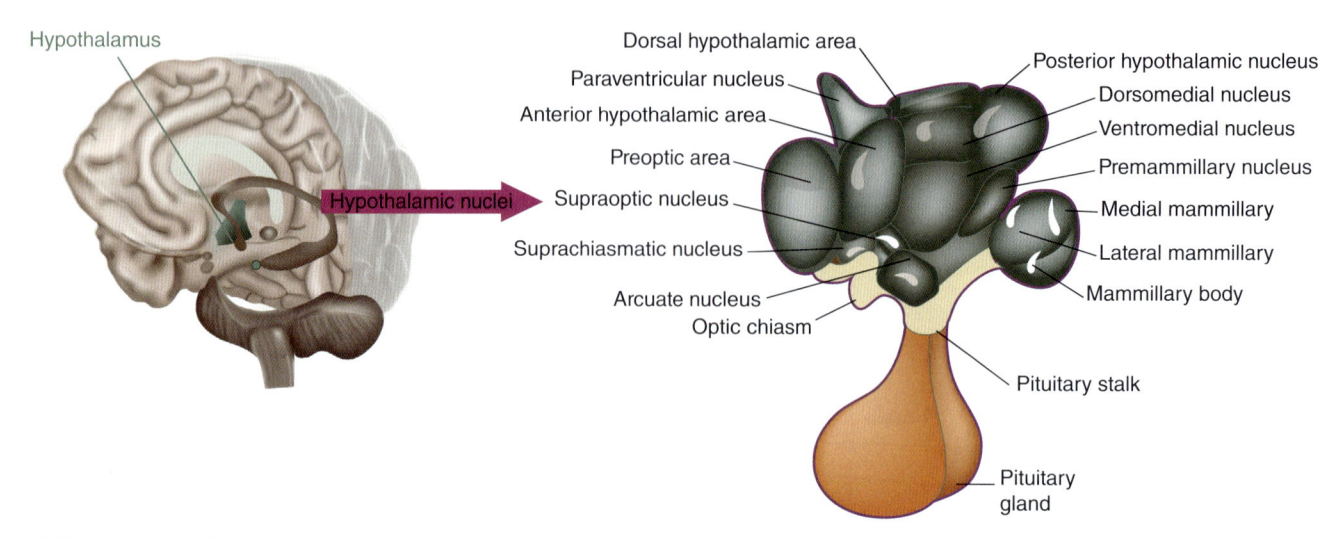

FIGURE 15.6 *The human hypothalamus.*

with regard to feeding behaviour: the **lateral hypothalamus** (LH) and the **ventromedial hypothalamus** (VMH) (Figure 15.7). The evidence implicating these regions in the brain was accumulated from physiological psychology experiments in which lesions of the hypothalamus were performed in rats. Lesions of the VMH led to **hyperphagia** (overeating) (Hetherington & Ranson, 1940) (Figure 15.8). There were two phases of hyperphagia: the dynamic phase, during which the rats gained the most weight, occurred immediately after surgery. During the following static phase, they ate enough to maintain obesity.

Lesions of the LH produced **aphagia** in rats and cats: they stopped eating (Anand & Brobeck, 1951). The aphagia was accompanied by **adipsia** (they stopped drinking); the animal could recover from both conditions with intensive care (Teitelbaum & Stellar, 1954).

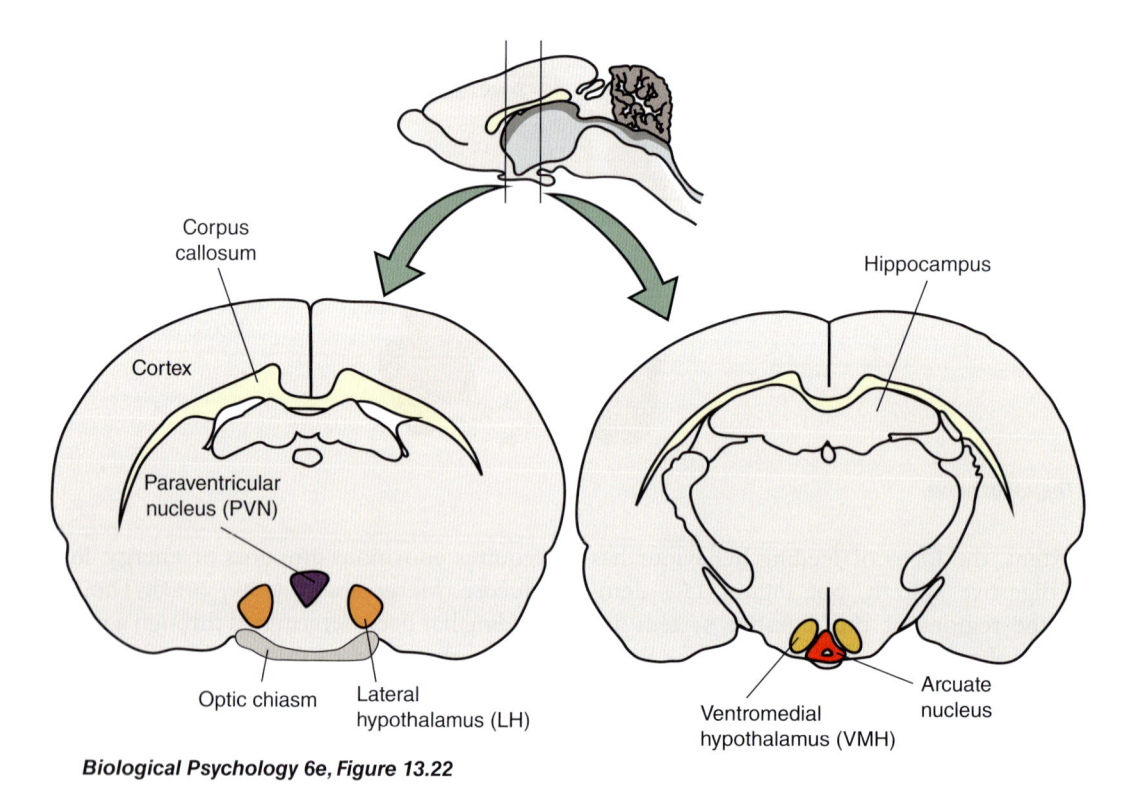

FIGURE 15.7 *Hypothalamic nuclei in the rat.*
Source: Breedlove, S. M., Watson, N. V., & Rosenzweig, M. R. (2010). *Biological psychology* (6th edn). Sunderland, MA: Sinauer Associates. Reproduced with permission.

FIGURE 15.8 *The effects of a VHM lesion on the rat* (left). Source: Reproduced with permission from Professor Philip Teitelbaum.

Thus, a hypothesis combining the LH and VMH emerged. The LH is regarded as the hunger centre and the VMH as the satiety centre. Satiety is the motivational state that terminates feeding. When the LH is stimulated, the state of hunger is induced and eating commences. The LH is under the inhibitory control of the VMH. There are receptors for glucose, called **glucoreceptors**, in the VMH (Routh, 2010; Vazirani et al., 2013), and when glucose is low the LH is released from inhibition by the VMH (Anand & Brobeck, 1951). Conversely, when glucose concentrations are high, the VMH inhibits the LH. Glucose is a simple type of sugar and provides energy for cells.

A reappraisal of the literature calls into question the absolute role of the hypothalamus. Unfortunately, but not surprisingly, the idea of the hypothalamus as the control centre of feeding is an oversimplification. Lesions of both the LH and VMH have behavioural consequences other than altering the regulation of feeding *per se*. Lesions of the LH produce non-specific deficits, most notably deterioration of motor behaviour. The hypothalamus has both intrinsic nuclei and neurons that pass through without synaptic contact. The **nigrostriatal pathway** is also lesioned during LH destruction.

Lesions of the nigrostriatal pathway can lead to extreme motor problems; after all, Parkinson's disease is a result of degeneration of this pathway (see Chapters 11 and 24). Selective lesions of the nigrostriatal pathway also induce aphagia (Marshall et al., 1974).

Does this mean that the LH has no role in feeding behaviour? Just because the methodology originally used was somewhat limited, this does not mean that the LH is devoid of function in terms of feeding. Since the initial studies, new research also points to a role for the LH. In the monkey, neurons of the LH fire in response to the sight of food (Burton et al., 1976). Lesions with **ibotenic acid**, which selectively destroys the LH while leaving the nigrostriatal pathway intact, also produce aphagia (Dunnett et al., 1985). Ibotenic acid is a neurotoxic agent that destroys glutamatergic neurons. Therefore, glutamate might be an interesting neurotransmitter to follow in the feeding saga. When placed directly in the LH, glutamate produces eating (Stanley, Willett et al., 1993), whereas antagonists of the glutamatergic NMDA receptor decrease eating (Stanley et al., 1996). The amygdala innervates and suppresses the activity of glutamate in neurons in the LH, thereby controlling food consumption (Jennings et al., 2013).

Thus, the hypothalamus remains an area of key interest, but attention is now diverted to the role of various chemicals in the LH. Chemical modulation of hypothalamic nuclei can operate with a degree of subtlety in modulating feeding behaviour, whereas lesions of either the LH or VMH are rather unsubtle techniques that clearly have a profound effect. Thus, the LH and VMH still have a role in feeding behaviour, but the interest now is in the detail.

There are two neuropeptides that are released by the LH that affect feeding: **melanin-concentrating hormone** (MCH) and **orexin**. Both of these induce eating, and when the animal is deprived of food, there is an increase in mRNA levels to manufacture MCH and orexin (Dube et al., 1999; Qu et al., 1996; Sakurai et al., 1998).

Neuropeptide Y (NPY) is a potent stimulator of food intake (Clark et al., 1984), and activates MCH and orexin (Broberger et al., 1998; Elias et al., 1998). When **leptin** (a hormone derived from fat tissue) is released, it inhibits NPY, reducing feeding (Wang et al., 1997). Leptin receptors have been identified in several regions including the hypothalamus (Hakansson et al., 1998). Animals that have defective genes for leptin receptors become obese (Al-Barazanji et al., 1997) (a subtle revisit of the lipostatic hypothesis).

Injection of NPY into the LH makes rats eat under aversive conditions (Flood & Morley, 1991; Jewett et al., 1992). NPY in the **paraventricular nucleus** (PVN) of the hypothalamus increases insulin levels (Stanley, Magdalin et al., 1993), and inhibition of NPY synthesis suppresses feeding and insulin (Akabayashi et al., 1994). Food deprivation increases NPY and eating (Sahu et al., 1988), an effect that can be blocked by NPY antagonism (Myers et al., 1995).

Deprivation of glucose leads to activation of NPY in the **arcuate nucleus** of the hypothalamus that projects to the PVN (Minami et al., 1995). This increases insulin, thus promoting hunger and preserving energy stores. The arcuate nucleus has become a centre of attention; it is a set of neurons with opposing effects on the feeding systems. The differentiation of these regions is based upon neurotransmitters and hormones: NPY and **agouti-related peptide** (AgRP) forming the **NYP/AgRP neurons**, and **pro-opiomelanocortin** (POMC) **and cocaine- and amphetamine-regulated transcript** (CART). CART is a peptide with similar effects to cocaine and amphetamine. The NPY/AgRP neurons stimulate appetite when activated and reduce metabolism, leading to weight gain (Luquet et al., 2005), and AgRP stimulates voracious feeding in its own right (Aponte et al., 2011). The POMC/CART neurons inhibit appetite and increase metabolism, promoting weight loss (Meister, 2007). Leptin activates the POMC/CART neurons of the arcuate nucleus, thereby enhancing appetite suppression, whereas leptin inhibits the NPY/AgRP neurons which reduces feeding (Elias et al., 1999).

The neurons of the arcuate nucleus project to other hypothalamic regions, thereby regulating feeding behaviour. Connections of the arcuate nucleus to the LH have been shown to have opposite effects depending on which neurons are activated in the arcuate nucleus (Elias et al., 1999). The arcuate nucleus been argued to be the site of integration of leptin signals in which projections of the POMC/CART and NPY/AgRP to the lateral hypothalamus in turn act on MCH and orexin cells which project to the cerebral cortex (where the conscious experience of hunger resides). Furthermore, AgRP neurons inhibit POMC neurons, promoting eating (Atasoy et al., 2012).

Input to the arcuate nucleus has been identified from the PVN, where stimulation of the PVN results in increased activity of AgRP neurons. The increased activity induced intense feeding in sated animals, and conversely inhibition in hungry mice decreased feeding (Krashes et al., 2014). A reciprocal connection shows when there is prolonged inhibition of the PVN by AgRP neurons. However, when suppression of PVN neurons is sufficient, it activates AgRP neurons and promotes eating (Atasoy et al., 2012).

The LH has also been shown to be connected to the **amygdala**. Lesions of the amygdala in the rat produced aphagia and adipsia which were similar to that observed with lesions of the LH (Box & Mogenson, 1975). Furthermore, stimulation of the amygdala increased feeding behaviour (Montgomery & Singer, 1975).

Lesions of the VMH result in more than a loss of inhibitory control of eating. Rats will not eat food that is made bitter – they become fussy eaters (Ferguson & Keesey, 1975). VMH lesions cause an increase in the parasympathetic activity of the vagus nerve, which stimulates insulin secretion and inhibits glucagon (Weingarten et al., 1985). VMH lesions increase insulin levels, promoting storage and therefore body fat production. They also decrease the breakdown of fat for utilization. Therefore, most of the energy is derived from the absorption of nutrients and not from the release of stored nutrients. If the vagus nerve is cut, thereby blocking communication between brain and pancreas, the effects of the VMH lesion are negated. Gold (1973) claimed that obesity produced by VMH lesions was a myth, and that it was other areas producing weight gain.

There are also anatomical consequences of VMH lesions. In VMH lesions, axons are destroyed that connect the PVN (and its functions) to other brain stem structures, e.g. the **ventral noradrenergic bundle** (Gold et al., 1977). Very specific lesions of the VMH did not produce increased weight gain (Joseph & Knigge, 1968). The arcuate nucleus is one of the regions that may have been lesioned in those early studies. The arcuate nucleus and POMC may be responsible for the lesion effect of the VMH (see King (2006) for review). Arcuate nucleus POMC neurons activate VMH **brain-derived neurotrophic factor** (BDNF), a protein promoting the survival of existing neurons and new neuronal growth. Removal of the BDNF gene results in obesity (Rios et al., 2001; Xu et al., 2003).

Serotonin (5-HT) in the VMH and PVN leads to inhibition of eating (Leibowitz et al., 1990). Food intake is increased by 5-HT destruction (Saller & Stricker, 1976), inhibition of 5-HT synthesis (Breisch et al., 1976) or 5-HT receptor blockade (Stallone & Nicolaidis, 1989). Serotonergic antagonism increases NPY secretion, which in turn leads to increased food intake (Dryden et al., 1995). Drugs that increase 5-HT can be used for obesity.

A further attack on the VMH came in the form of the irritative hypothesis (Reynolds, 1965). Simply stated, the argument was that VMH lesions left behind iron deposits that were irritating adjacent tissue. It was the adjacent tissue that was involved in feeding regulation, e.g. the LH.

The rise of **eating disorders**, and in particular **obesity**, has introduced a number of other regions of the brain to the neural circuitry controlling feeding behaviour. The areas that have received most attention are those that have been implicated most strongly in motivational behaviours. In Chapter 16, the general issue of motivation is discussed, in which two areas stand out: the **ventral tegmental area** (VTA) and the **nucleus accumbens** (NAcc). Dopamine (DA) is released from these regions when presented with primary reinforcers. Food, being a primary reinforcer and essential for survival, increases DA outflow from the NAcc (see Chapter 16). It is these areas of the brain that become problematic and overactive when drugs such as cocaine or amphetamine are consumed. Although not entirely accurate, the **mesolimbic dopamine pathway** (VTA to NAcc) is considered the reward pathway.

It is not surprising that these regions are connected to hypothalamic nuclei. The VTA receives direct input from the gastrointestinal tract in which dopamine neurons are activated in the VTA (Abizaid et al., 2006). Activation of the VTA increases dopamine output from the NAcc. **Ghrelin** is a peptide linked to hunger but when placed in the VTA, it increases the intake of palatable food in sated animals because of its reward value (Egecioglu et al., 2010). Leptin also has actions on the VTA and inhibits firing of neurons (Hommel et al., 2006; Trinko et al., 2011). Leptin is thought to suppress the incentive/motivational value of food and other rewards (Bruijnzeel et al., 2011). Neurons of the NAcc shell project to the LH. Inhibition of the shell promotes feeding (Frazier & Mrejeru, 2010). This effect is thought to derive from the activation of LH neurons by the NAcc shell (Baldo et al., 2004). Lesions of the LH blocked increases in feeding induced by activation of the NAcc shell, an effect that was seen when the lesion was ipsilateral to the side of stimulation and not contralateral (Stratford & Wirtshafter, 2012). The LH projects to the NAcc, regulating feeding behaviour via orexin (increased cue activation to food-related rewards) and MCH (increasing food intake) (Georgescu et al., 2005; Harris et al., 2005).

A complex network emerges that controls feeding, one mediated by the hypothalamus in order to maintain homeostatic balance of energy supplies, and connected to that the mesolimbic pathway that guides motivational behaviour (Figure 15.9).

Eating Disorders

One might consider, with all our knowledge regarding the functional neuroanatomy underlying feeding behaviour, that effective treatments for eating disorders might be aimed at the brain. Sadly, the treatment of eating disorders via neural mechanisms is lacking. The term **eating disorders** describes a broad range of

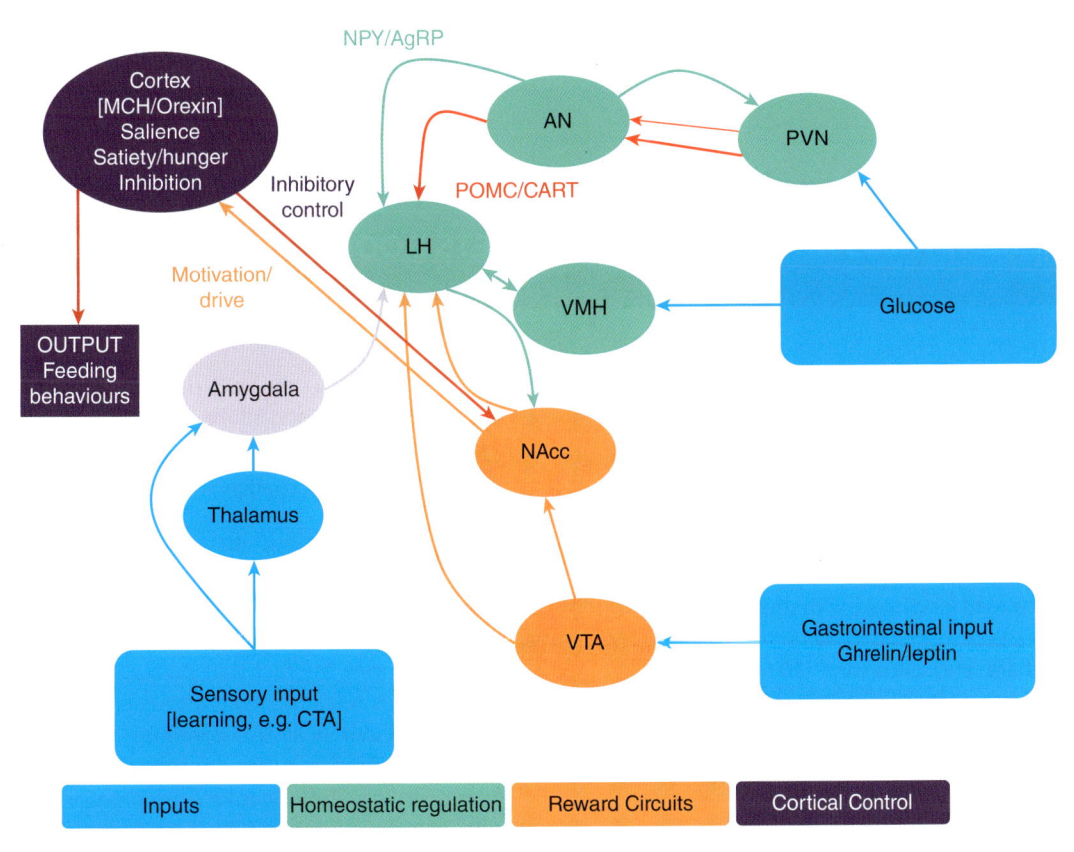

FIGURE 15.9 Circuits involved in feeding behaviour. Hypothalamic circuits modulate homeostasis and connect to the mesolimbic reward circuit. All the behaviour is controlled by cortical regions. The arrows represent connection and reciprocal connection of the circuits. AN, arcuate nucleus; CART, cocaine- and amphetamine-regulated transcript; CTA, conditioned taste aversion; LH, lateral hypothalamus; NAcc, nucleus accumbens; NPY/AgRP, neuropeptide Y/agouti-related peptide; POMC, pro-opiomelanocortin; PVN, paraventricular nucleus; VMH, ventromedial hypothalamus; VTA, ventral tegmental area.

diverging problems. However, there are three main eating disorders to be considered: obesity, anorexia nervosa and bulimia nervosa.

Obesity

The media love to print stories about an increasingly obese nation, and that the statistics paint a negative picture of the size of people in western countries. As testimony to the difficulties of dealing with obesity, the diet industry is extremely profitable. Even with our current understanding of feeding, the pharmaceutical industry has yet to deliver a drug alternative to the diet, although there are drugs to aid dieting that are focused on fat intake. Part of the problem in treating obesity is a lack of understanding surrounding the aetiology and pathogenesis of this behaviour. There are many reasons why someone may be obese, ranging from hormonal (Box 15.2) through to genetic and behavioural. Some drugs have been used, e.g. **fenfluramine**, which is a 5-HT agonist, but side-effects tend to limit this (Blundell & Halford, 1998). The majority of the drugs that target neural systems in the battle against obesity are noradrenergic and/or serotonergic. However, the need to treat obesity has meant a recapitulation of the theoretical underpinnings of the disorder. Rather than consider it a disorder of eating (albeit an obvious symptom), the view is changing towards obesity being similar to other motivational disorders such as addiction (Box 15.3).

Anorexia nervosa and bulimia nervosa

Anorexia nervosa is a disorder of restricted food intake leading to severe weight loss; **bulimia nervosa** has a similar endpoint in weight loss but is achieved through eating and purging. Anorexia nervosa has a lifetime prevalence rate of between 1.2% and 2.2% (Smink et al., 2012) and a 12-month prevalence rate of 0.4% in females (APA, 2013). It is associated predominantly with females and the aspiration to have a body image similar to the media portrayal of the ideal female body shape. A person with anorexia nervosa restricts their food intake, which leads to a dramatic decline in weight.

Anorexia nervosa, like obesity, has had several theories associated with it. The neuroscience suggests that NPY is high in anorexics and returns to normal levels when they gain more weight (Kaye et al., 1990). Although this may seem counterintuitive because NPY promotes eating in the animals, it has been suggested that this may account for the obsession with food and the increased knowledge about food because the anorexic is in a perpetual hunger state. Grey matter atrophy has been measured in the

---

BOX 15.2: STRESS AND OBESITY – ARE DIETS DOOMED TO FAIL?

Obesity would appear to be no different from many other psychiatric disorders because stress is a risk factor. Many of us will be familiar with comfort eating. Stress can both increase and decrease food consumption. However, it is noted that when food is highly palatable, there is generally an increase in intake (most likely linked to reward) (Sinha & Jastreboff, 2013). In a self-report study, 42% of students reported increased food intake with stress and 73% reported increased bouts of snacking (Oliver & Wardle, 1999).

Jauch-Chara and Oltmanns (2014) propose a neuropsychological model involving stress in obesity. The theory is based on four points.

- Chronic stress increases food intake, especially highly calorific palatable food which blunts the stress response (therefore a form of self-medication).
- Food consumption activates reward circuits of the brain (e.g. an increase in dopamine with palatable food).
- Stress stimulates the reward system which potentiates stress-induced food intake.
- Obesity is the result of a vicious circle between chronic stress circuitry activation and reward circuitry.

These authors continue to argue that during childhood, one way of appeasing stress is to consume food. Through classical conditioning, this becomes an automatic response in the face of stress. Incidental to the stress reaction is the fact that palatable, highly calorific food activates reward circuitry, thus ensuring repetition of the behaviour. If all this continues for too long, and to become obese requires considerable repetition, the dopaminergic systems invoke compensatory downregulation. Downregulation of dopaminergic neurons in the reward circuitry may lead to anhedonia and other undesirable affective states, which can be overcome by consumption of food.

BOX 15.3: OBESITY AS AN ADDICTION

The continual consumption of food, particularly that high in fat and sugar, extends the concept of food intake from mere energy consumption to that of a compulsive or addictive behaviour. It has been hypothesized that in addiction, dopamine is reduced as a predetermining factor (see Chapter 16). Similarly, data from imaging studies have demonstrated that obesity subjects had reduced striatal D2 recetors (Figure 15.3.1) which were inversely related to their weight (Figure 15.3.2) (Wang et al., 2001, 2002). Responsiveness of dopamine receptors in the striatum was also shown to be reduced in obese subjects when given palatable food (Stice et al., 2008) and was associated with weight gain (Stice et al., 2010). In an experiment looking at dopamine activity in the ventral striatum (an area studied in addiction that calculates the mismatch between expected and achieved goals), it was found that obese patients had reduced dopamine release with calorie consumption (the opposite is true for non-obese participants), and 'It is therefore more likely that a discrepancy between an enhanced expectation and a reduced response to the calories consumed in the obese person might trigger the drive to continue eating in order to compensate for this deficit' (Wang et al., 2014).

The reduction in D2 receptors in obese patients was argued to give rise to the decreased metabolism in the prefrontal cortex (PFC), leading to a lack of inhibitory control of eating (Volkow, Wang, Telang, Fowler, Thanos et al., 2008). In healthy individuals, increased Body Mass Index (BMI) correlated with lower activity in the PFC (Volkow, Wang et al., 2009). Like addiction, obesity can be seen as a disorder characterized by a lack of inhibitory control and an increase in subcortical motivational systems (Figure 15.3.3) (Appelhans, 2009).

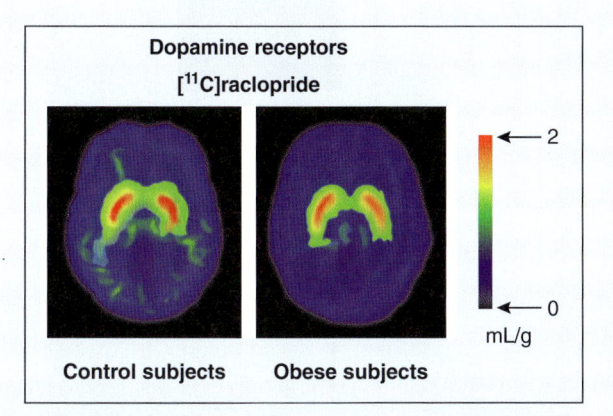

FIGURE 15.3.1 *Reduced DA receptors in obese participants.*
Source: Wang, G. J., Volkow, N. D., Logan, J., Pappas, N. R., Wong, C. T., Zhu, W., et al. (2001). Brain dopamine and obesity. *Lancet, 357*(9253), 354–357.

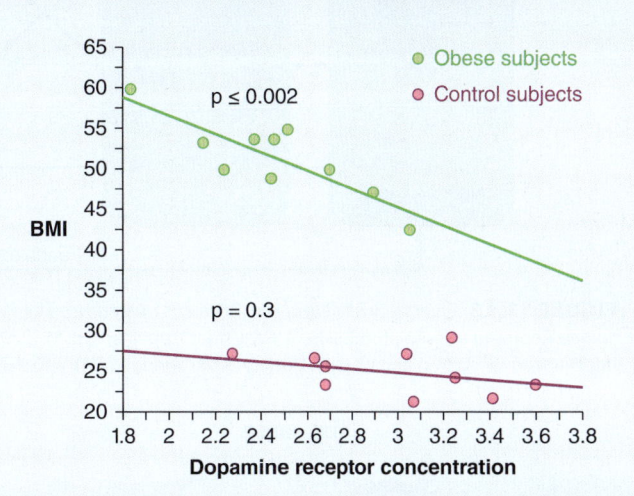

FIGURE 15.3.2 *Correlation between DA receptors and BMI.*
Source: Wang, G. J., Volkow, N. D., Logan, J., Pappas, N. R., Wong, C. T., Zhu, W., et al. (2001). Brain dopamine and obesity. *Lancet, 357*(9253), 354–357.

Food has been identified as similar to drugs in addiction in the incentive sensitization theory of addiction, in which obesity is tantamount to addiction and food acts like a drug (Berridge et al., 2010). In this model, food brings about pleasure and is reinforcing and via dopaminergic mechanismsm food-associated stimuli become powerful motivators for the consumption of food. The increased consumption of palatable food mediating the hedonic response overrides homeostatic mechanisms that would prevent obesity (Figure 15.3.4) (Egecioglu et al., 2011).

Numerous authors have viewed obesity along the addiction dimension (e.g. Volkow et al., 2011). Whilst this is a refreshing and potentially fruitful explanation of obesity, others have not been so convinced. Ziauddeen et al. (2012) argue that there are limitations with this view, as obesity is a highly heterogeneous disorder without a consistent region of the brain being identified. They take the DSM IV criteria of substance abuse and provide a proposed equivalent of food addiction, e.g. larger amount of drug taken than intended has an equivalent in larger amounts of food eaten than intended. However, withdrawal symptoms seen with discontinuation of drugs do not appear to have a food addiction equivalent. They continue throughout the diagnostic criteria to show many limitations with the addiction model of obesity. Their

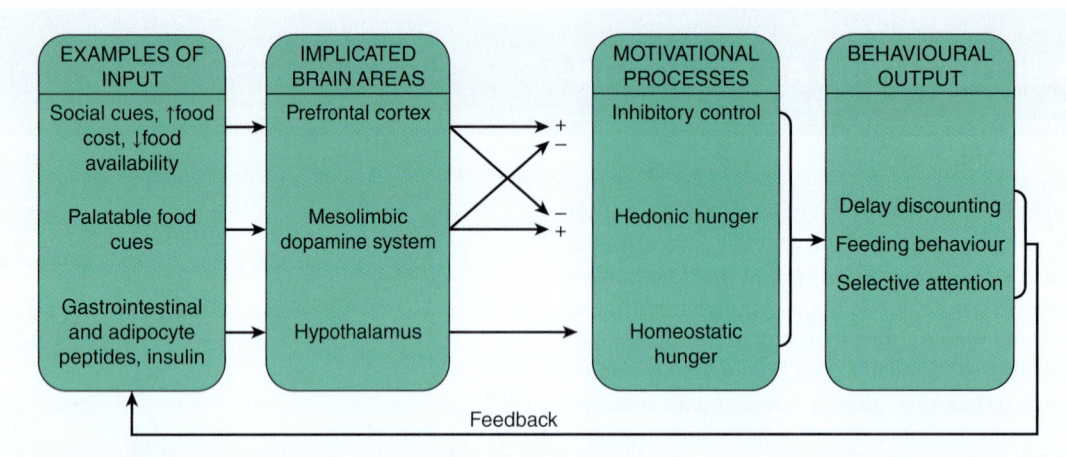

FIGURE 15.3.3 *Overview of neural mechanisms in feeding. The role of different brain systems in feeding behaviour.*
Source: Reproduced with permission of Wiley from Appelhans, B. M. (2009). Neurobehavioral inhibition of reward-driven feeding: Implications for dieting and obesity. *Obesity (Silver Spring), 17*(4), 640–647. Reproduced by permission of John Wiley & Sons.

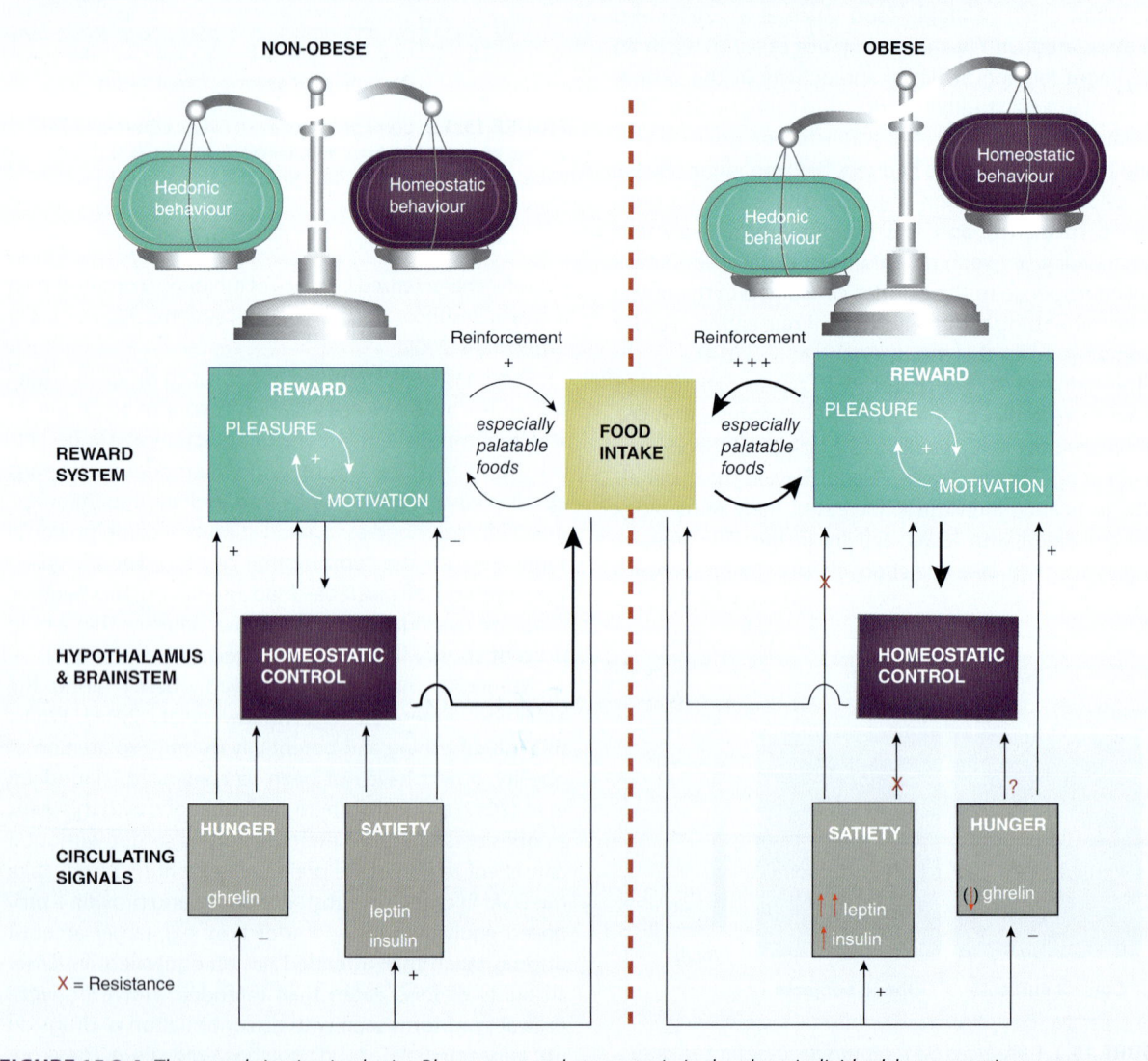

FIGURE 15.3.4 *The neural circuitry in obesity. Pleasure versus homeostasis. In the obese individual, homeostatic processes are ignored and hedonic behaviour dominates, leading to unnecessary increases in food intake.*
Source: Egecioglu, E., Skibicka, K. P., Hansson, C., Alvarez-Crespo, M., Friberg, P. A., Jerlhag, E., et al. (2011). Hedonic and incentive signals for body weight control. *Reviews in Endocrine and Metabolic Disorders, 12*(3), 141–151.

chief argument is that the model has been adopted with more enthusiasm than the scientific evidence would suggest. Animal models of eating as an addiction still require further consideration before they can be deemed to be valid (Hone-Blanchet & Fecteau, 2014).

Despite these criticisms, the addiction model of obesity has provided a new avenue of research in an area that is lacking in effective treatments. It is interesting to note that the vast majority of drugs used off label for obesity are reuptake inhibitors of dopamine, noradrenaline and serotonin (Adan et al., 2008) which will serve to enhance monoaminergic activity in their respective synapses. There are other potential sites that have been targeted, e.g. 5-HT receptor and cannabis receptors, all of which require further investigation and verification (Adan, 2013).

hypothalamus of patients with anorexia (Boghi et al., 2011). Co-morbidity in anorexia is commonplace, and no specific brain region has been identified as being the culprit for anorexia (Melotto, 2014). A further difficulty in measuring brain function in anorexia nervosa focuses on the issue of whether the changes that occur are a result of the condition or are due to the effects of starvation (Phillipou et al., 2014).

Of regions that have been identified as playing an important role, the **insula** and **cingulate cortex** have been found to differ in anorexia nervosa (Phillipou et al., 2014). The cingulate cortex underlies motivation, goal-directed behaviours and emotional processes whereas the insula is involved in the emotion of disgust. Disgust is an emotion that anorexics have difficulty with (Aharoni & Hertz, 2012; Pollatos et al., 2008) and they experience self-disgust/self-loathing which may maintain anorexic behaviour (Moncrieff-Boyd et al., 2013). The insula has been proposed as the central mechanism underlying anorexia nervosa (Nunn et al., 2011). The hypothesis is that the insula is the central communication hub of cortical and subcortical regions of the brain, e.g. frontal lobe, amygdala and striatum. A fault with the insula may trigger anorexia nervosa due to specific contextual conditions (e.g. genetic predispositions and sociocultural influences on body size) and general stressors (e.g. puberty). Others have argued that there is an overactivity of the prefrontal cortex leading to increased inhibition of subcortical motivational circuits that mediate reward mechanisms for palatable foods (Kaye et al., 2013). This is perhaps one of the few disorders that have been associated with *increased* inhibitory function, as the opposite has been said of obesity (see Box 15.3).

In terms of neurochemistry, serotonergic and dopaminergic systems have been identified as key candidates in anorexia nervosa. Low levels of serotonin have been found in anorexics (Kaye et al., 1988). Increased receptors have been identified for 5-HT1a and reduced binding for 5-HT2a, but the pattern is not consistent throughout the brain (Phillipou et al., 2014). Dopamine levels are also reduced in anorexia nervosa which may be linked to changes in motivation and reinforcement (Phillipou et al., 2014). Again, there is little pharmacological help at hand for the patient with anorexia nervosa. The main drugs used have been selective serotonin reuptake inhibitors (SSRIs) (see Chapters 7 and 22), typically employed in the treatment of depression. Unfortunately, the effect of SSRIs is limited, with many patients not recovering, and those who recover only do so after an increase in weight (Kaye et al., 1998; Yu et al., 2011).

Patients with bulimia nervosa binge-eat and then vomit or use laxatives to control their weight. Fluoxetine (Prozac) is a 5-HT agonist that has been used to treat bulimia nervosa (Kaye et al., 2001). This is contradictory to the actions of serotonergic drugs in the PVN. However, those with bulimia nervosa also suffer depression. Fluoxetine is an antidepressant and it may be that once the depression is treated, the eating disorder improves.

This highlights an important point in all disorders, not just eating disorders. The symptoms of eating disorders are focused on food intake. Food intake may be a secondary symptom of a psychiatric/psychological disorder (depression), rather than a primary symptom of an eating disorder in its own right.

Psychological Factors which Influence Eating

Eating is not merely about activation of hypothalamic nuclei and dopamine reward circuits. External factors such as advertising of food also influence consumption. Parental attitudes and learning influence food consumption. And in the resource-rich western countries, the great variety and availability of food can lead to increased intake. We are less likely to eat boring, repetitive, bland meals. In a restaurant, we are provided with a menu of choices. Even when we have completed our meal and are fully sated, the presentation of the dessert menu can promote another bout of eating. If the choice on the menu is different in its stimulus properties (e.g. expected taste), it can increase food intake even when full; thus sensory-specific factors are involved in controlling feeding. In the rat, a varied diet resulted in a dramatic increase of calories and nearly 50% increase in body weight after 120 days (Rogers & Blundell, 1980). In humans, the liking for food diminished after they had consumed a meal and they rated other food as more desirable (Rolls et al., 1981).

It is not just taste that is influential in eating. Shape and colour have also been linked to sensory specific satiety (Rolls, 1985). In a study by Rolls et al. (1982), they found that schoolchildren who were given the same coloured sweets (Smarties) noted that the pleasantness of that colour diminished in comparison to the others when they were offered a choice later on. Similarly, eating the same shaped pasta led to a decline in pleasantness for that shape when given a subsequent choice, and when participants were able to eat a mixture of shapes, consumption increased (Rolls et al., 1982).

DRINKING AND THIRST

The consequences of not eating for a short period of time are unpleasant but not necessarily life-threatening. To go without water is far more serious.

We have two fluid-filled compartments in the body: **intracellular fluid** (in the cytoplasm) and **extracellular fluid**, which includes **intravascular fluid** (blood plasma), **interstitial fluid** (between the cells) and cerebrospinal fluid (CSF). There is movement between the fluid compartments that allows cells to survive. The extracellular fluid acts in a supporting role to the cells and is controlled by brain mechanisms that monitor its levels. The brain does this by promoting thirst as the motivator for drinking.

There are two types of thirst: **osmotic thirst** and **hypovolaemic thirst**. Osmotic thirst occurs when the solute concentration of extracellular fluid increases (it becomes more salty) and takes water from the intracellular fluid (which may place the cells in danger of damage). Basically, salty food changes the constituents of the fluid. Such food increases thirst, and that's why some pubs and bars serve free salted peanuts as these enhance the fluid intake of their customers. **Osmoreceptors**, perhaps located in the anterior hypothalamus and other areas, detect changes in the concentration of the interstitial fluid.

Hypovolaemic thirst occurs when the intravascular fluid decreases. A loss of blood volume is detected by **baroreceptors**, which detect blood pressure, and also by receptors in the kidneys. The kidneys secrete **renin** at times of low blood flow. Renin aids the production of **angiotensin**, a hormone that increases drinking (Epstein et al., 1970). Angiotensin activates two other hormones: **aldosterone** and **vasopressin**. Aldosterone retains salt and water, plus it constricts the blood vessels. Vasopressin (or antidiuretic hormone) reduces the amount of fluid going to the bladder. Vasopressin conserves water, whereas aldosterone conserves salt until more is consumed.

Brain Mechanisms in Thirst

Signals from the baroreceptors located in the heart are sent to the nucleus of the solitary tract (in the medulla). Angiotensin levels are detected by neurons projecting to the **subfornical organ** which communicates with the **median preoptic nucleus** (**MPN**). According to Thrasher (1989), the MPN integrates hypovolaemic and osmotic signals. The MPN is therefore instrumental in initiating drinking behaviour.

SUMMARY

As an evolutionary behaviour, eating has provided living organisms with energy. The consumption of food for energy is subject to homeostasis and is regulated in part by the hypothalamus. The hypothalamus received early attention in experiments and theories about feeding behaviour. The early focus on the lateral and ventromedial hypothalamus gave way to more detailed accounts involving other hypothalamic nuclei and also their integration with other neural circuits, including cortical and mesolimbic circuits. The interaction of these overlapping circuits is mediated by a number of neurotransmitters and neuropeptides, which all interact in subtle ways to modify eating behaviour, that was perhaps not seen in the early studies involving lesions of the hypothalamus.

Eating disorders are stark and clear reminders of when the consumption of food becomes abnormal. The eating disorders have also provided further insight into the general mechanisms of feeding behaviour.

LEARNING OUTCOME QUESTIONS

You should be able to answer the following questions.

- To what extent is the hypothalamus the regulator of feeding behaviour?
- To what extent does our understanding of the psychobiology of feeding influence the treatment of eating disorders?
- Obesity is an addiction, not an eating disorder. Discuss.

FURTHER READING

Bourque, C. W. (2008). Central mechanisms of osmosensation and systemic osmoregulation. *Nature Reviews Neuroscience*, 9, 519–531.

Jauch-Chara, K., & Oltmanns, K. M. (2014). Obesity – a neuropsychological disease? Systematic review and neuropsychological model. *Progress in Neurobiology*, 114, 84–101.

King, B. M. (2006). The rise, fall, and resurrection of the ventromedial hypothalamus in the regulation of feeding behavior and body weight. *Physiology and Behavior*, 87(2), 221–244.

Phillipou, A., Rossell, S. L., & Castle, D. J. (2014). The neurobiology of anorexia nervosa: a systematic review. *Australia and New Zealand Journal of Psychiatry*, 48(2), 128–152.

Piqueras-Fiszman, B., & Spence, C. (2014). Colour, pleasantness, and consumption behaviour within a meal. *Appetite*, 75(0), 165–172.

Sohn, J. W., Elmquist, J. K., & Williams, K. W. (2013). Neuronal circuits that regulate feeding behavior and metabolism. *Trends in Neuroscience*, 36(9), 504–512.

Volkow, N. D., Wang, G. J., & Baler, R. D. (2011). Reward, dopamine and the control of food intake: implications for obesity. *Trends in Cognitive Science*, 15(1), 37–46.

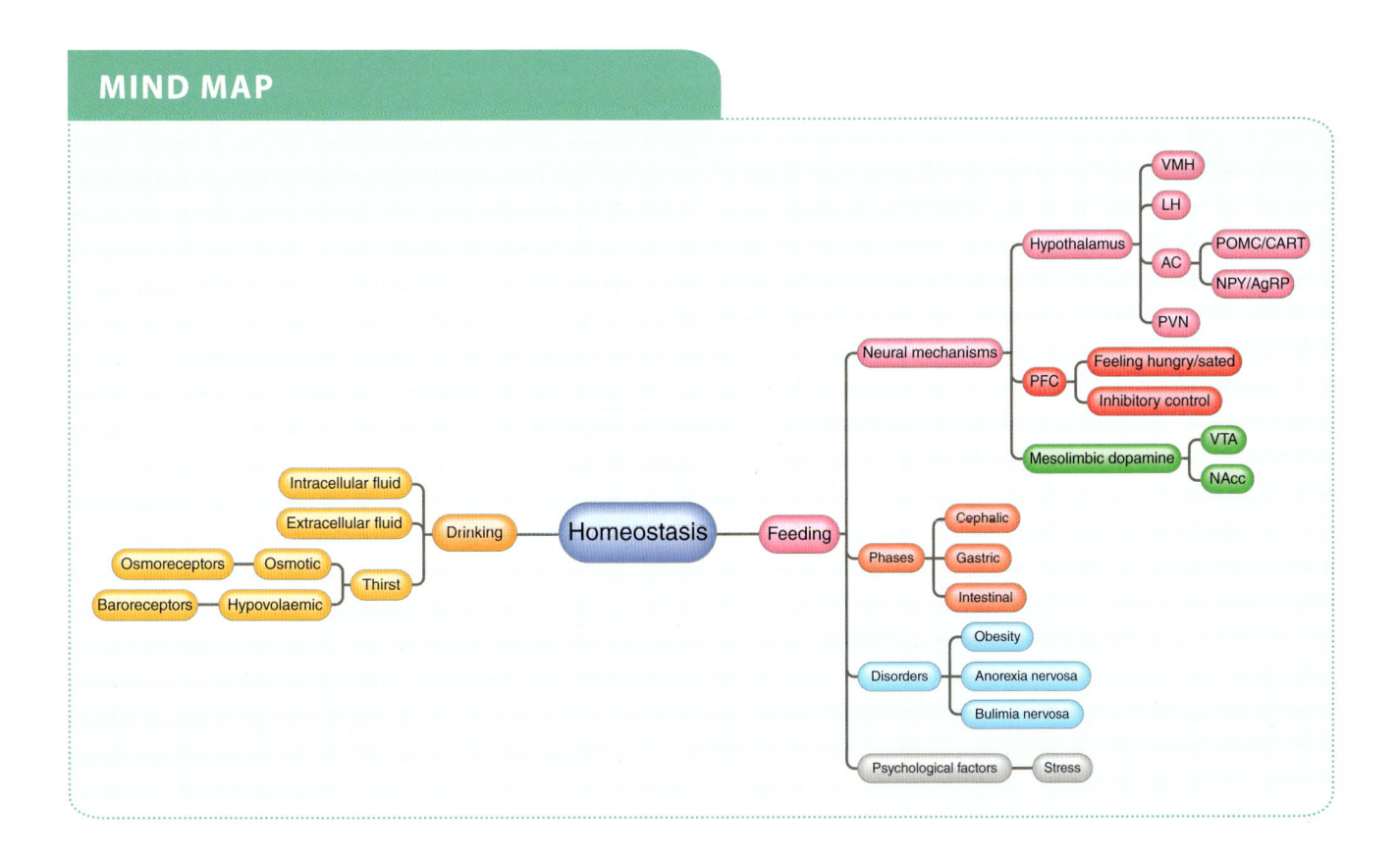

MIND MAP

16 Motivation

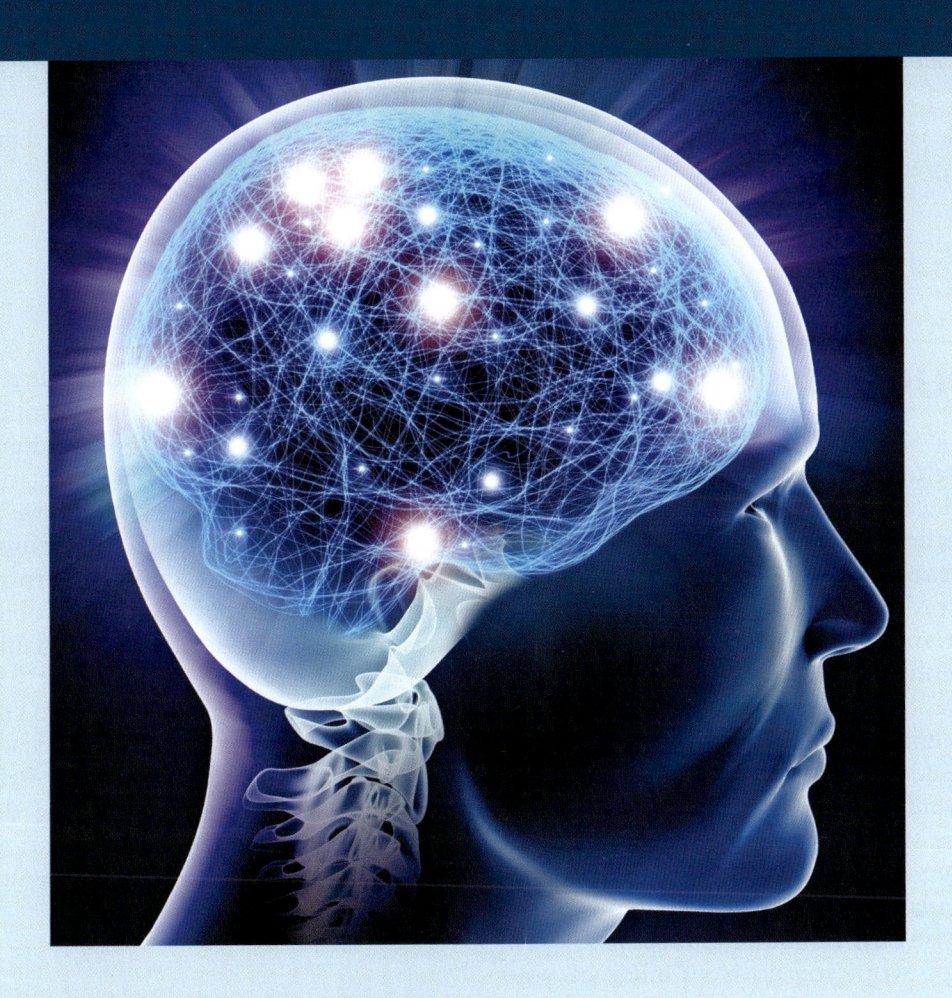

ANATOMY OF THE CHAPTER

This chapter will highlight the following.

- The role of dopamine in motivation.
- The importance of addiction as a form of reverse engineering to understanding motivation.
- The interaction of different brain regions in addiction.
- The theoretical accounts of specific aspects of the addiction process.

INTRODUCTION   410

DRUG ADDICTION: THE TRIUMPH OF MOTIVATION OVER REASON   410

WHAT IS ADDICTION?   412

A REWARD PATHWAY: A COMMON DENOMINATOR IN ADDICTION AND MOTIVATION   413

AMPHETAMINE, COCAINE AND NICOTINE   416

NATURAL REINFORCERS   419

THEORIES OF ADDICTION – THEORIES OF MOTIVATION   419

WHICH THEORY IS CORRECT?   430

SUMMARY   431

LEARNING OUTCOMES

1. To understand why addiction is an important psychopathology for understanding human motivation.
2. To be able to evaluate neural differences underlying addiction and therefore motivation.
3. To understand and evaluate the theoretical accounts of addiction and their limitations.
4. To understand the complex mechanisms of addiction and how to address the difficulty of treating addiction.

INTRODUCTION

What is motivation? Here is another word for which we have a collective understanding of its meaning, but when it comes to defining and studying motivation, it becomes a little less tangible and a little more complex. According to the German philosopher Schopenhauer, motivation means to be moved into action (Schopenhauer, 2005). This implies that there is an incentive behind the behaviour, the incentive being the anticipation of reward. Other words that may be used to describe motivation are 'drive', 'desire' and 'wanting'.

Much of the study of motivation is the study of goal acquisition. Behaviour is performed in order to access a particular goal, e.g. you study hard to pass exams so that you can become a clinical psychologist. The amount of work you do is an index of your motivation, i.e. the harder you work, the more highly motivated you are. This is closely aligned to the notion of reinforcement and reward discussed in Chapter 8. Animals will press a lever in order to obtain their goal (food). How hungry they are will determine how hard they will work to obtain the food – how motivated are they to obtain the food? Animal studies have been particularly important in understanding the neural basis of motivation. The use of operant techniques has been instrumental in evaluating the motivation and incentive value of rewards.

From an evolutionary perspective, it is clearly important to be motivated for food, drink, shelter and sex. Without engagement with these reinforcers, the individual themselves will die; without sex, reproduction will not occur and the species will become extinct (pandas should take note). In Chapter 15 the role of the hypothalamus was discussed in terms of homeostatic regulation and the motivation to consume food/water. The link was made between hypothalamic activation and motivational systems, most notably the dopamine system. Acquiring food and water is important, but there are other powerful reinforcers that have very little benefit in the long term – addictive drugs.

The motivation to consume drugs has provided considerable insight into the neurobiological mechanisms of motivation. The mechanisms by which drugs of abuse exert their effect have similarities with the primary reinforcers. The consumption of drugs becomes maladaptive and leads to addiction in some cases. Understanding motivation is almost synonymous with understanding drug addiction. Understanding abnormal motivation helps us to understand motivation *per se*; it is a type of reverse engineering.

DRUG ADDICTION: THE TRIUMPH OF MOTIVATION OVER REASON

Drug addiction is a surprisingly complex set of behaviours in which people consume drugs despite the negative consequences that long-term use can have (and also in the short term, e.g. death).

Drug misuse is a growing concern with many people using drugs for recreational purposes. Drug misuse is a concern because it is linked to a number of other problems: criminality, poverty, poor health and psychological problems. Drug addiction may therefore not be problem specifically for the individual but rather it is the impact that that individual has on society that leads to the pathological label. Understanding the science of motivation is essential to understanding drug addiction and why politicians and policymakers should remain open-minded about legislation. The refusal of the British Prime Minister in 2012 to consider a Royal Commission on drugs typifies the political landscape on drug use.

Why start taking drugs? There are a number of circumstances that could induce drug-taking behaviour, ranging from peer pressure to stress relief and genetic vulnerabilities. To understand the factors involved is a multidisciplinary task. Psychobiology has made advances in the understanding of the neural mechanisms involved once the drug has been consumed.

The continued consumption of a drug would appear to be illogical in view of the negative repercussions. It is the illogical nature of continued drug consumption that makes the study of addiction critically important to understanding motivational processes. Another question that arises is how evolution has promoted such destructive behaviours (Box 16.1).

BOX 16.1: THE EVOLUTION OF ADDICTION

Most of the drugs that we consume are secondary metabolites from plants.

Drug	Plant
Nicotine	Tobacco
Arecoline	Betel nut
Cocaine	Coca
Ephedrine (amphetamine like)	Khat
Caffeine	Coffee
Heroin/morphine	Opium poppy
Delta ^{9}-tetrahydrocannabinol (THC)	Cannabis
Alcohol	Fermenting fruits
Psilocybin	Magic mushrooms
Mescaline	Peyote cactus

Given that these drugs are derived from plants, it has been considered that the neurotoxic effects have evolved to deter eating by herbivores (Roberts & Wink, 1998). The notion is similar to the conditioned taste aversion experiments that have identified aversive properties of the likes of nicotine. This would fly in the face of reward-based accounts of drug abuse. The adaptive nature of reward mechanisms to steer behaviours towards survival has been regarded to be hijacked by drugs of abuse (Nesse & Berridge, 1997).

The systems which may have evolved to maintain drug-taking behaviour are most likely there for general motivational purposes. The system should be old and seen in a number of animal species. Indeed, a number of species readily consume psychoactive substances in both the natural and laboratory setting, e.g. self-administration of alcohol by elephants (Siegel & Brodie, 1984).

Sullivan et al. (2008) argue that drugs are not new features in evolution and that genetics has revealed that hepatic enzymes have arisen in human and animal history because of the exposure to plant toxins. The argument continues that if there is an evolutionary history of exposure to neurotoxins then humans should be avoiding drugs. The incompatibility of traditional reward-based models and the co-evolution of hepatic enzymes and plant toxins have led Sullivan and colleagues to refer to it as the paradox of drug reward.

Sullivan et al. (2008) provide five areas of research that could possibly help to answer the question of the paradox of drug reward. Research should:

- make a distinction between causality and the subsequent physiological and behavioural adaptations associated with chronic drug use;
- look for the ecologically salient factors affecting initial drug use;
- use measures that are ecologically plausible, for example conditioned taste aversion rather than intracranial self-stimulation;
- focus on the neurobiological target of the neurotoxin rather than its downstream effects on dopamine; and
- consider co-evolutionary processes, e.g. adaptations to counterexploit the neurotoxin.

The authors suggest that the neurotoxic properties of plant alkaloids may be an adaptation to combat bacterial infections of food. Furthermore, they may be used to self-medicate against gastrointestinal parasites. Thus, they serve to maintain nutritional balance and energy levels (Sullivan & Hagen, 2002).

What other mechanisms steer this motivation that higher-order control from the frontal cortex cannot manage? Addiction has been referred to as an impulse control disorder (Pattij & Vanderschuren, 2008) and has dopaminergic imbalances in subcortical regions as a core pathology which DSM V considers to be a common denominator (Di Chiara & Imperato, 1988; Di Chiara et al., 1999; Volkow et al., 1996a, 2007).

WHAT IS ADDICTION?

The word 'addiction' is often used interchangeably with 'dependence' and 'abuse'. DSM IV and V do not use the term 'drug addiction' *per se* but the same concept is described under **substance dependence disorder** and **substance use disorder** (SUD) (Box 16.2).

BOX 16.2: ADDICTION: DSM IV AND V

The *Diagnostic and statistical manual* of the American Psychiatric Association does not use the word 'addiction' (except with reference to gambling). DSM V combines the categories of substance abuse and substance dependence into a single disorder. Rather than having a generic set of criteria, DSM V has specific criteria for each individual drug. However, there is also a generic overarching set of criteria common to that entire stem from the predecessor DSM IV. Therefore, DSM IV criteria are illustrated below rather than accounting for individual drugs.

DSM IV substance abuse criteria

Substance abuse is defined as a maladaptive pattern of substance use leading to clinically significant impairment or distress as manifested by one (or more) of the following, occurring within a 12-month period.

- Recurrent substance use resulting in a failure to fulfil major role obligations at work, school or home (such as repeated absences or poor work performance related to substance use; substance-related absences, suspensions or expulsions from school; or neglect of children or household).
- Recurrent substance use in situations in which it is physically hazardous (such as driving an automobile or operating a machine when impaired by substance use).
- Recurrent substance-related legal problems (such as arrests for substance-related disorderly conduct).
- Continued substance use despite having persistent or recurrent social or interpersonal problems caused or exacerbated by the effects of the substance (for example, arguments with spouse about consequences of intoxication and physical fights).

DSM IV substance dependence criteria

Addiction (termed 'substance dependence' by the American Psychiatric Association) is defined as a maladaptive pattern of substance use leading to clinically significant impairment or distress, as manifested by three (or more) of the following, occurring any time in the same 12-month period.

- Tolerance, as defined by either of the following.
  - A need for markedly increased amounts of the substance to achieve intoxication or the desired effect.
  - Markedly diminished effect with continued use of the same amount of the substance.
- Withdrawal, as manifested by either of the following.
  - The characteristic withdrawal syndrome for the substance.
  - The same (or closely related) substance is taken to relieve or avoid withdrawal symptoms.
- The substance is often taken in larger amounts or over a longer period than intended.
- There is a persistent desire or unsuccessful efforts to cut down or control substance use.
- A great deal of time is spent in activities necessary to obtain the substance, use the substance or recover from its effects.
- Important social, occupational or recreational activities are given up or reduced because of substance use.
- The substance use is continued despite knowledge of having a persistent physical or psychological problem that is likely to have been caused or exacerbated by the substance.

By the end of this chapter you should be able to determine which aspects of the diagnostic criteria have successfully been addressed by the variety of theories on addiction.

Some of the problems associated with the SUD label are the concepts of addiction, abuse, misuse and dependence. Addiction, dependence and abuse are often used interchangeably, adding to the confusion. Dependence is no longer seen to be pathological but rather a normal adaptation in the process of addiction. Despite this change in DSM V, confusion will still reign due to the previous history. The terms should not be used interchangeably as they can reflect different problems and levels of severity. According to Altman et al., **addiction** is the extreme or psychopathological state where control over drug use is lost whereas **dependence** is the state of needing a drug to operate within normal limits; **abuse** is the use of drugs which leads to problems for the individual and use/**misuse** is any non-medical consumption (Altman et al., 1996).

A REWARD PATHWAY: A COMMON DENOMINATOR IN ADDICTION AND MOTIVATION

There is general agreement that there is a common mechanism in motivation and addiction. This view has been generated to a large extent by the analysis of human and animal behaviour. Early studies utilized animals to great effect and established the site of action on which more recent neuroimaging technologies are able to focus. A number of methods are used to determine the reward pathways in the brain and the site of action of drugs in animals (Stolerman, 1992):

- **intracranial self-stimulation** (ICSS);
- **drug self-administration**;
- **conditioned place preference** (CPP) (see Box 16.3).

Intracranial self-stimulation

The classic experiments by Olds and Milner (1954) demonstrated that rats would press a lever to receive electrical stimulation, via an implanted electrode, in specific regions of the brain; for a review see Wise (2005) (Figure 16.1). The rationale is that if the animal presses the lever to receive electrical stimulation, then it is motivated to do so presumably because of a positive reinforcing effect. In terms of methodology, it is important to distinguish motor behaviour from motivational behaviour. Electrical stimulation may just be stimulating motor neurons and therefore the animal presses the lever because it cannot do anything else. It is not because it wants to press the lever or is motivated to do so. To subtract this confounding variable, the use of two bars ascertains whether

BOX 16.3: CONDITIONED PLACE PREFERENCE

Conditioned place preference (CPP) is a non-invasive method for assessing the reinforcing properties of a drug (Figure 16.3.1) (Carr et al., 1989; Tzschentke, 2007). CPP looks at drug-seeking behaviour by using secondary conditioning, in which a drug becomes associated with a particular environment (see Figure 16.3.2 and also Chapter 8). Previously neutral stimuli become associated with the drug. The drug is the unconditioned stimulus (US) that produces pleasurable effects (the unconditioned response – UR), and the environment in which the drug is received becomes associated with the drug (the conditioned stimulus – CS). When tested drug free, the rat seeks out the drug-associated environment if it is reinforcing (conditioned response – CR).

In the simplest form of CPP, a rat is exposed to one compartment of a chamber comprising at least two distinct compartments. The chambers can differ along a number of sensory dimensions that tap into visual, tactile and olfactory modalities (or indeed a mix of them). If the animal is exposed to the drug in environment A and placebo in environment B, then the animal is more likely to spend time in environment A when tested drug free. Essentially, the animal associates the environment with the drug, presumably the pleasurable effects. CPP has been used to assess dopaminergic drugs such as **cocaine** and **amphetamine** which both produce robust data showing a preference for the drug-associated environment (Anderson & Pierce, 2005; Spyraki et al., 1982).

Clearly distinctive environments can trigger drug-taking behaviour, e.g. the bar and drinking. Embracing new technology, Astur et al. (2014) used virtual reality to induce a conditioned place preference in humans (which is much easier than putting them in a box). In this study,

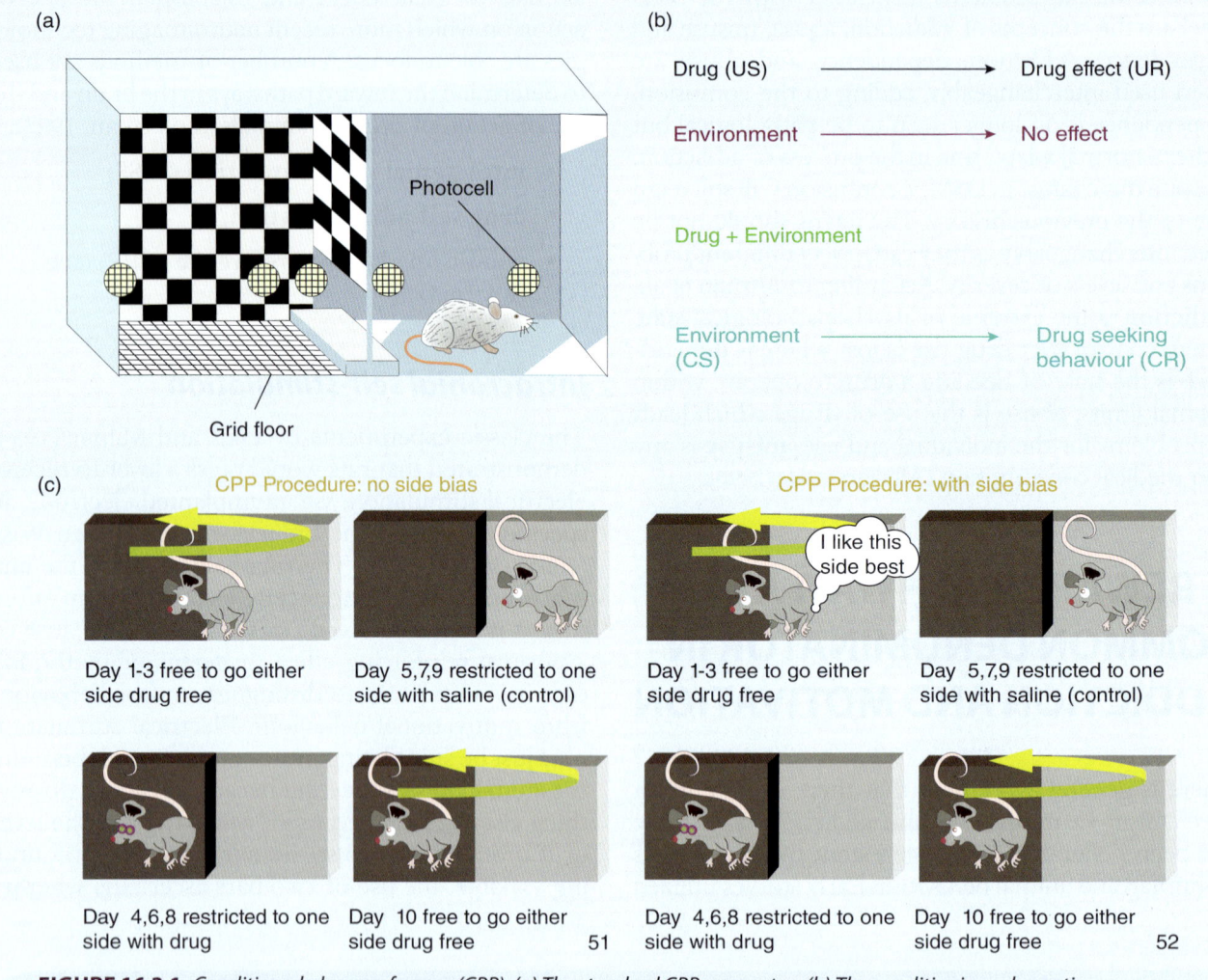

FIGURE 16.3.1 Conditioned place preference (CPP). (a) The standard CPP apparatus. (b) The conditioning schematic. (c) CPP without a side bias in which animals are randomly allocated to a drug side. (d) CPP with a side bias in which animals are allocated the drug to their least preferred side. UR, unconditioned response; US, unconditioned stimulus.

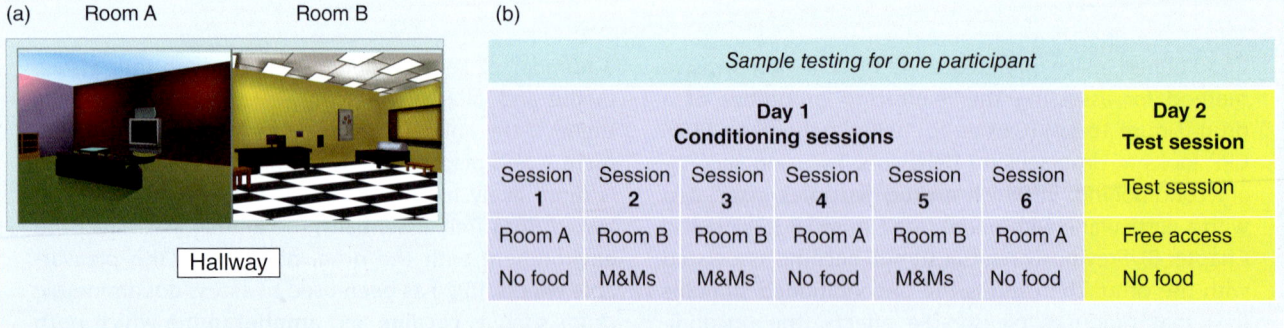

FIGURE 16.3.2 A virtual reality conditioned place preference. CPP can be assessed in humans using virtual reality technology.
Source: Astur, R. S., Carew, A. W., & Deaton, B. E. (2014). Conditioned place preferences in humans using virtual reality. *Behavioural Brain Research, 267,* 173–177.

they put undergraduate students into virtual environments. Because it is unethical to turn undergraduates into drug addicts, they used food reward (M&Ms). In one virtual environment, the undergraduates received the food reward and in a different virtual environment, they did not. When they were given free access to the whole of the virtual reality world, those students who had received food reward spent more time in the associated environment.

(a) Intracranial self stimulation

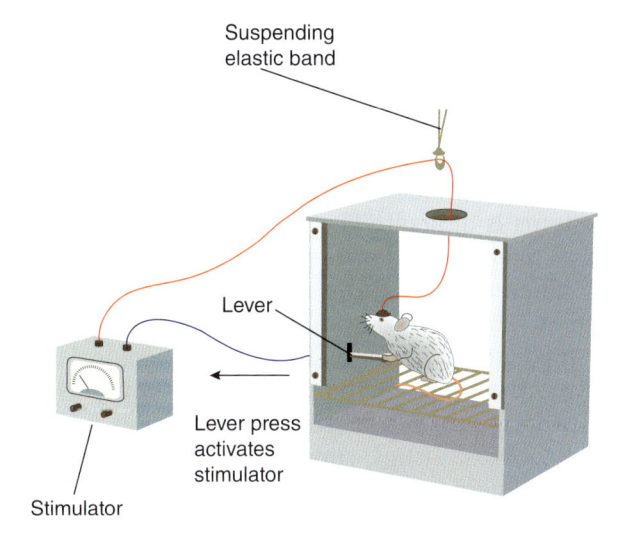

(b) Acquisition and extinction scores for all animals together with electrode placements and threshold voltages used during acquisition tests

Animal's no.	Locus of electrode	Stimulation voltage r.m.s.	Percentage of acquisition time spent responding	Percentage of extinction time spent responding
32	septal	2.2-2.8	75	18
34	septal	1.4	92	6
M-1	septal	1.7-4.8	85	21
M-4	septal	2.3-4.8	88	13
40	c.c.	.7-1.1	6	3
41	caudate	.9-1.2	4	4
31	cingulate	1.8	37	9
82	cingulate	.5-1.8	36	10
36	hip.	.8-2.8	11	14
3	m.l.	.5	0	4
A-5	m.t.	1.4	71	9
6	m.g.	.5	0	31
11	m.g.	.5	0	21
17	teg.	.7	2	1
9	teg.	.5	77	81

(c) The septal region and mesolimbic pathways in the human brain

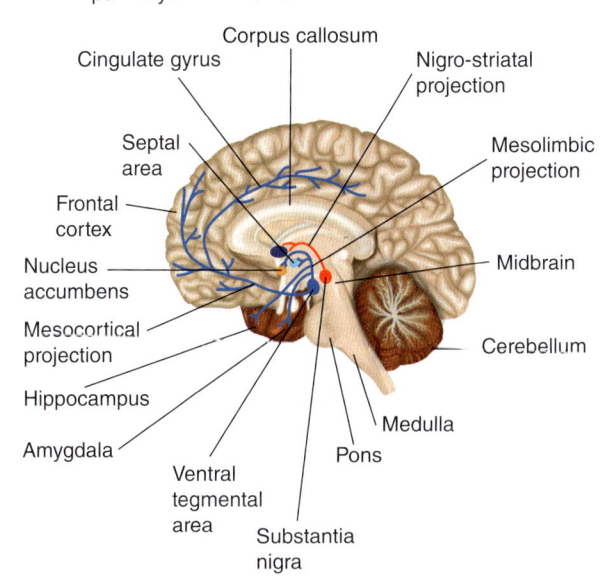

(d) The septal and mesolimbic system in the rat brain

retrorubral area (A8)
substantia nigra (SN, A9)
ventral tegmental area (VTA, A10)

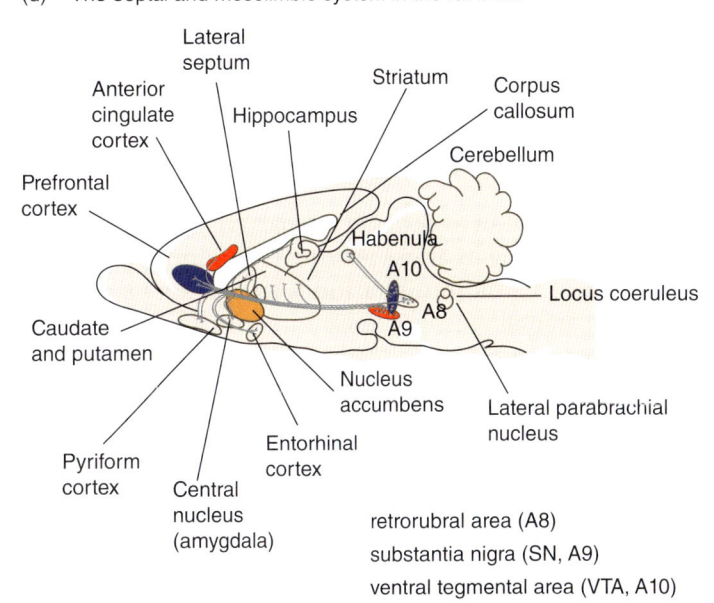

FIGURE 16.1 *Intracranial self-stimulation. (a) The ICSS apparatus. (b) Data from Olds and Milner identified the septal region as the main area mediating ICSS. (c) The septal and mesolimbic system in the human brain. (d) The septal and mesolimbic system in the rat brain.*
Source: (b) Data from Olds, J., & Milner, P. (1954). Positive reinforcement produced by electrical stimulation of septal area and other regions of rat brain. *Journal of Comparative and Physiological Psychology, 47*(6), 419–427.

the animal is merely activated or motivated. If activated, the animal will press on both bars with equal frequency but if motivated, it will focus its activity on the lever that delivers the electrical stimulation.

The areas of the brain that mediate electrical stimulation also contain high levels of dopamine (DA) (Corbett & Wise, 1980), in particular the **nucleus accumbens** (NAcc) (Phillips et al., 1975), the **striatum** (Phillips et al., 1976) and the prefrontal cortex (Mora et al., 1976).

This method of assessing the neural mechanisms of reward may seem a far cry from addiction, but it has been used to assess the addictive nature of drugs (Kenny, 2007; Wise, 1996). The electrical stimulation produced neural activity in the brain regions where the electrode is placed; thus action potentials and DA release occur. Using this method, the administration of cocaine and amphetamines has been shown to reduce responding for the electrical stimulation by presumably substituting for the rewarding effects of illogical stimulation (Leith & Barrett, 1981; Risner & Jones, 1975; Tyce, 1968).

The nucleus accumbens does not act alone and has some very important connections. The area of the brain that has received most attention as the neural substrate of addiction is the **mesolimbic pathway** (see Figure 16.1) which runs from the **ventral tegmental area** (VTA) to the NAcc. Destroying the mesolimbic pathway with a neurotoxin disrupted ICSS, especially when the electrodes were placed in the NAcc on the same side as the lesion (Fibiger et al., 1987; Phillips & Fibiger, 1978).

Drug self-administration

Self-administration of drugs in animals is an important step in identifying its abuse potential (O'Connor et al., 2011). **Drug self-administration** is an operant task in which an animal presses a lever to receive an infusion of a drug via an indwelling catheter in the jugular vein (but also into specific regions of the brain) (see Sanchis-Segura & Spanagel (2006) for review and Chapter 8).

The neurobiology of addiction has received extensive attention as there are now a number of tools (drugs) to probe this behaviour. Given that there are a number of substances to which one can become addicted, the question of a common mechanism needs to be addressed. By understanding how the drugs work, the neuroscientist can follow the route to their site of action and begin to understand the mechanisms of motivation.

The drugs that we choose to take, for whatever reason, differ considerably in their pharmacology (see Chapter 7). Nicotine works on acetylcholine (ACh) receptors; heroin is converted into morphine and interacts with opiate receptors; diazepam operates at the benzodiazepine complex of the GABA receptor; cannabis works within the endocannabinoid system; and cocaine works within the DA system. Perhaps the hardest drug to account for is alcohol because it does so much that identification of simple single neural systems is difficult. The different pharmacology of these drugs would at first suggest that there are many different mechanism that lead to reward and addiction. Their differing subjective effects are most likely mediated by their different pharmacology, but their motivational ability to produce compulsive drug seeking and intake shares a common neural substrate. Most drugs support self-administration but the hallucinogenic drugs, e.g. LSD and mescaline, are exceptions (see Box 16.4 and Table 16.1).

AMPHETAMINE, COCAINE AND NICOTINE

Amphetamine and cocaine are psychostimulants that act on the dopaminergic system. Both enhance DA transmission but they do this in different ways (see Chapter 7). Generally speaking, amphetamine releases DA from the vesicles without the need for an action potential, whereas cocaine blocks reuptake and does require an action potential (Carboni, Imperato et al., 1989).

A number of studies have been conducted to determine the effects of cocaine and amphetamine on ICSS. Using a rate free method, in which the rat presses a lever to obtain different frequencies of electrical stimulation, cocaine decreased the frequency administered by the rat (Maldonado-Irizarry et al., 1994). This is indicative of cocaine being a substitute for the rewarding properties of ICSS (i.e. the rat does not require as much electrical stimulation after cocaine).

Many experiments have verified that animals will self-administer cocaine and amphetamine (see Katz, 1989). It should be noted that the dose–response curve is critically important in establishing self-administration of a drug. Optimizing the dose ensures that the animal performs at a high level in order to receive an infusion. Increasing the dose does not necessarily mean that the animal will work harder. High doses of cocaine have been shown to reduce lever presses whilst maintaining high levels of cocaine within the brain (Figure 16.2) (Broadbear

BOX 16.4: LSD AND SELF-ADMINISTRATION

LSD is the exception to the rule when it comes to drug abuse and self-administration.

It has been claimed that the common denominator of addictive drugs is the mesolimbic DA pathway but there is a group of drugs that are not addictive, but misused. The psychedelics are typified by **D-lysergic acid diethylamide** (LSD), an extremely potent hallucinogen. LSD and other hallucinogens are not self-administered by animals. In fact, rhesus monkeys will press a lever to turn off a stimulus associated with LSD infusion (Hoffmeister & Wuttke, 1975). The reason for this is that LSD acts on serotonergic neurons and not on the mesolimbic pathway, as do cocaine, amphetamine and nicotine. However, MDMA (ecstasy), a mixed DA and 5-HT drug, is self-administered (Fantegrossi et al., 2002; Schenk et al., 2003) and produces a conditioned place preference (Meyer et al., 2002), thus pointing to the role of DA in mediating these behaviours rather than serotonin.

In contrast CPP experiments, LSD produces a CPP in the rat (Meehan & Schechter, 1998; Parker, 1996). Thus, a CPP may be acquired without exclusive activation of the mesolimbic DA pathway.

TABLE 16.1 *The self-administration of commonly used recreational drugs*

Self-administered drugs	Drugs which do not support self-administration
Heroin	LSD
Morphine	Mescaline
Amphetamine	
Cocaine	
Phencyclidine (PCP)	
Ketamine	
Ethanol	
Nicotine	
MDMA (ecstasy)	
Cannabis	

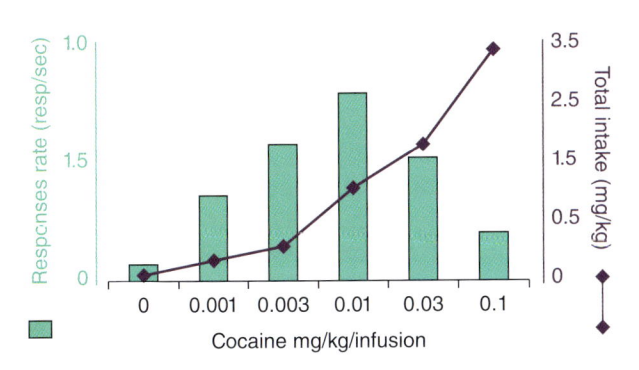

FIGURE 16.2 *Cocaine self-administration. Rhesus monkeys were reliably trained to self-administer cocaine. In test, they produced a high response rate at 0.01 mg/kg/infusion. As the dose increased, responding diminished but the levels of cocaine intake increased.*
Source: Broadbear, J. H., Winger, G., & Woods, J. H. (2004). Self-administration of fentanyl, cocaine and ketamine: Effects on the pituitary–adrenal axis in rhesus monkeys. *Psychopharmacology, 176*(3-4), 398–406. With kind permission from Springer Science and Business Media.

et al., 2004). Roberts and Ranaldi (1995) pointed out that DA antagonists increase responding for cocaine and amphetamine. This is a compensatory mechanism; the animal presses the lever even more to overcome the interruption of the drug effects. This is like the extinction burst in operant experiments (Figure 16.3).

Looking specifically at cocaine, we can see that its actions are mediated via postsynaptic DA receptors. There are two families of DA receptor: D1 and D2 (Kebabian & Calne, 1979). There are other receptors for DA and these can be classed according to the original categorization of D1 and D2 receptors.

One way of probing the receptor mechanisms of cocaine and amphetamine self-administration is to

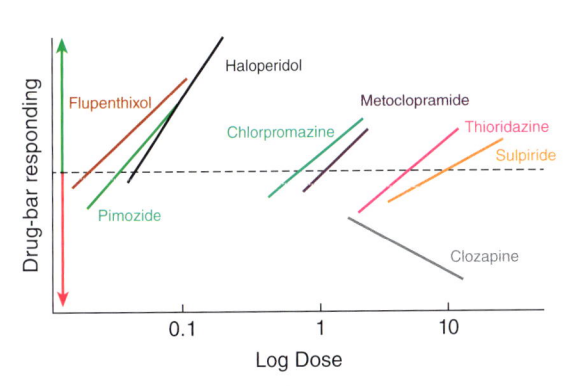

FIGURE 16.3 *The effects of dopamine antagonists on cocaine self-administration. All dopamine antagonists (antipsychotics) produced an extinction burst-like responding for cocaine, except clozapine.*
Source: Roberts, D. C. S., & Ranaldi, R. (1995). Effect of dopaminergic drugs on cocaine reinforcement. *Clinical Neuropharmacology, 18*(Suppl 1), S84–S95.

replace them with more specifically targeted drugs. Woolverton et al. (1984) found that the D2 agonists maintained responding for cocaine or amphetamine in rhesus monkeys. In contrast, D1 agonists failed to maintain responding. The increased responding seen with D2 antagonists was not evident with D1 antagonists. Thus, DA is important but more specifically, DA acting at the D2 receptor is important for drug self-administration.

If the NAcc and VTA are destroyed, cocaine and amphetamine responding stops in the rat (Roberts & Koob, 1982; Roberts et al., 1977). Furthermore, Koob et al. (1987), using a progressive ratio (PR) schedule, demonstrated that NAcc lesions decreased the number of drug infusions and produced an unwillingness to work for cocaine in rats. However, lesions of the NAcc are not a realistic treatment for addiction – after all, blockade of this area is achieved by a number of drugs that have not shown any therapeutic efficacy.

Both cocaine and amphetamine produce robust CPPs (Carr et al., 1989). The amphetamine-induced CPP can be blocked by DA antagonists (Leone & Di Chiara, 1987). Lesions of the NAcc also produce a reduction in amphetamine-induced CPP (Spyraki et al., 1982). Therefore, a DA mechanism.

Cocaine and amphetamine are both DA agonists and increase DA in the synapse. Their powerful addictive properties appear to be mediated by DA in the mesolimbic pathway. Nicotine is derived from tobacco, which is usually smoked, and there has been great debate about its addictive properties (Stolerman & Jarvis, 1995). Nicotine is an agonist at nicotinic ACh receptors. Nicotine acts at an ACh receptor and not at DA receptors, so how is it addictive if it does not act at DA directly?

Nicotine receptors can be found in the VTA and NAcc. A number of studies have shown that nicotine can also increase the levels of DA in the NAcc (e.g. Mirza et al., 1996). These studies have used *in vivo* microdialysis, a method of obtaining sample fluid from the synapse in the functioning animal (see Chapter 6). Imperato et al. (1986) found that nicotine increased DA in the NAcc by 100% and also increased the levels of the DA metabolites DOPAC and HVA – an effect that was blocked by nicotine antagonists (Mifsud et al., 1989).

Nicotine increases the levels of DA very quickly, but these then diminish (Figure 16.4). As the levels of DA diminish, the metabolites of DA increase. This is indicative of DA being used and eliminated by metabolic enzymes (e.g. monoamine oxidase – MAO). Thus, the DA neurons in the NAcc have been very busy after nicotine administration. Nicotine's ability to increase DA from the NAcc is something it shares with many other addictive drugs (e.g. the opiates, such as heroin) (Pontieri et al., 1996).

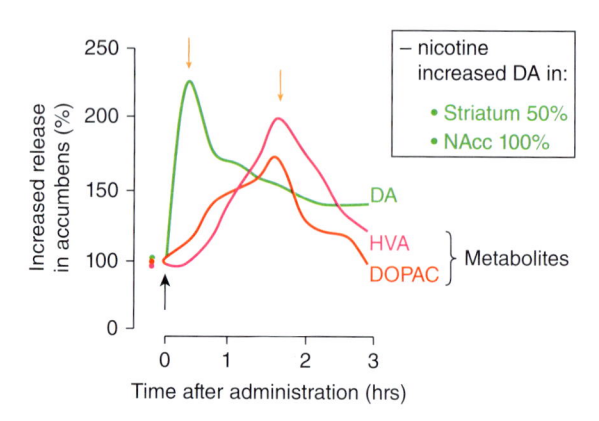

FIGURE 16.4 *The effects of nicotine on dopamine (DA) release. Nicotine increased the release of DA in the nucleus accumbens (NAcc) quickly. The drop in DA is followed by an increase in DA metabolites. The arrow pointing to DA is the first peak which gets metabolized into homovanillic acid (HVA) and dihydroxyphenylacetic acid (DOPAC) (second arrow).*
Source: Imperato, A., Mulas, A., & Di Chiara, G. (1986). Nicotine preferentially stimulates dopamine release in the limbic system of freely moving rats. *European Journal of Pharmacology, 132*(2-3), 337–338.

Nicotine has been shown to affect ICSS (Clarke & Kumar, 1984). Like amphetamine and cocaine, nicotine lowered the frequency of ICSS, indicating its rewarding properties (Huston-Lyons & Kornetsky, 1992). However, some of the scientific debate regarding nicotine's addictive qualities revolved around the experiments using nicotine self-administration.

Nicotine self-administration has been seen in primates (Goldberg et al., 1981) and, obviously, humans (Henningfield et al., 1983). Surprisingly, rats did not engage in nicotine self-administration. This was because the studies used a continuous reinforcement schedule, which produced low rates of responding. Thus, the early rat literature was not indicative of nicotine being a reinforcer.

Corrigall and Coen (1989) put rats on a fixed ratio schedule of five bar presses for each reinforcer (FR5) and found dose-dependent responding for nicotine (Figure 16.5). The schedule was critical to achieving nicotine self-administration. On continuous reinforcement (CRF) and FR2 schedules, responding was low (Donny et al., 1995, 2003); the rats needed to work harder for their reward so that a behaviour could be seen. Once obtained, nicotine antagonists blocked nicotine self-administration (Corrigall & Coen, 1989). As with cocaine and amphetamine, lesions of the NAcc also stopped nicotine self-administration (Corrigall et al., 1992).

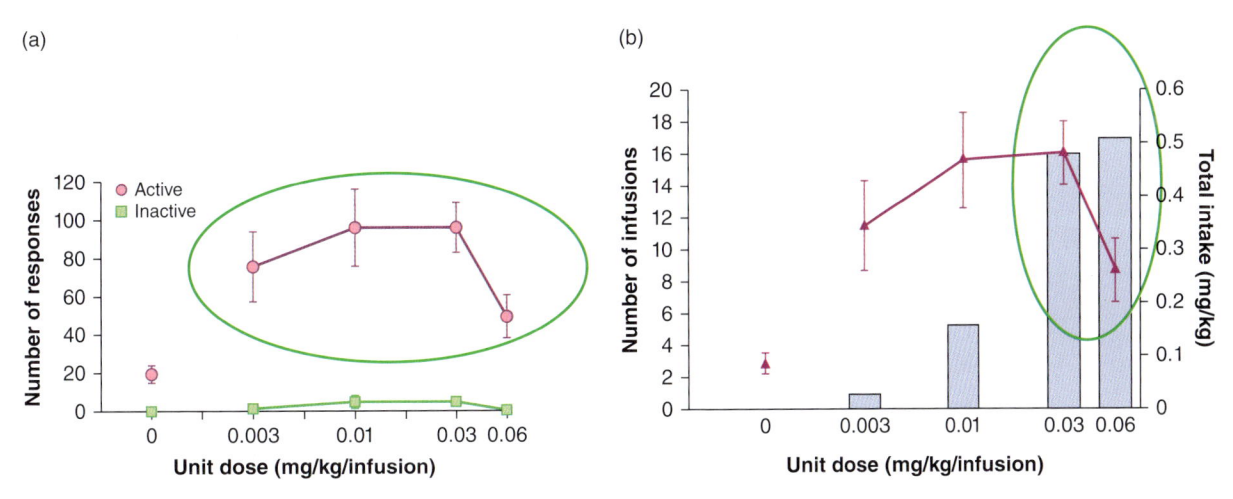

FIGURE 16.5 Nicotine self-administration. (a) Rats trained on nicotine produce a high level of responding on the active (nicotine-contingent) lever l (circled in green). (b) At 0.06 mg/kg/infusion, rat responding is reduced but the level of nicotine is maintained.
Source: Corrigall, W. A., & Coen, K. M. (1989). Nicotine maintains robust self-administration in rats on a limited-access schedule. *Psychopharmacology (Berlin), 99*(4), 473–478. With kind permission from Springer Science and Business Media.

Thus, nicotine also appears to mediate its reinforcing and motivating properties via mesolimbic DA.

The addictive properties of nicotine have not been entirely supported by studies using CPP. Some studies have found a CPP with nicotine (e.g. Fudala et al., 1985), others have not (e.g. Chandler et al., 1995). The reason for this is unclear, but for the majority of cases it is a methodological issue. However, when a CPP was found with nicotine, it could be blocked with both nicotine and DA antagonists (Carboni, Acquas et al., 1989; Iwamoto, 1990).

Nicotine acts at receptors for ACh and increases DA in the mesolimbic pathway. Detailed studies have shown that its addictive properties are mediated in a similar pattern to that of cocaine and amphetamine. This action of nicotine is not unique; a number of other drugs that are addictive also increase mesolimbic DA, and this pathway is regarded as the common denominator of drug addiction (see Wise & Bozarth, 1987).

The psychostimulants are not unique in their ability to enhance DA release. Opiates, alcohol, benzodiazepines and cannabinoids have all been shown to have dopaminergic activity, albeit indirectly (Di Chiara & Imperato, 1988).

NATURAL REINFORCERS

The use of drugs has suggested that the DAergic limbic system is the common denominator. Does this extend to non-drug reinforcers? Generally the answer is yes. Using food as a reinforcer, rats were shown to have elevated DA levels in the nucleus accumbens when either food was presented or stimuli associated with food were presented (Bassareo & Di Chiara, 1997, 1999). Similarly, DA is elevated in the NAcc when a male rat is exposed to a sexually receptive female rat (Damsma et al., 1992 (Figure 16.6); Fiorino & Phillips, 1999). Dopamine would also appear to be behind the Coolidge effect in sexually sated rats in which the presence of a novel receptive female initiates rising dopamine and copulatory behaviour (Fiorino et al., 1997). The increasing DA is not restricted to male sexual behaviour and is also evident in female rats (Pfaus et al., 1995) and in human responses to sex-related stimuli (Sylva et al., 2013).

THEORIES OF ADDICTION – THEORIES OF MOTIVATION

Having established that there is a physiological basis for addiction – mesolimbic DA – these physiological accounts can be placed within a theoretical framework to account for addiction specifically but also motivation in general. The main theoretical positions are based on associative learning (see Chapter 8). However, there is increasing evidence to suggest a genetic predisposition to addiction but how this informs motivation remains to be determined (Uhl et al., 2002).

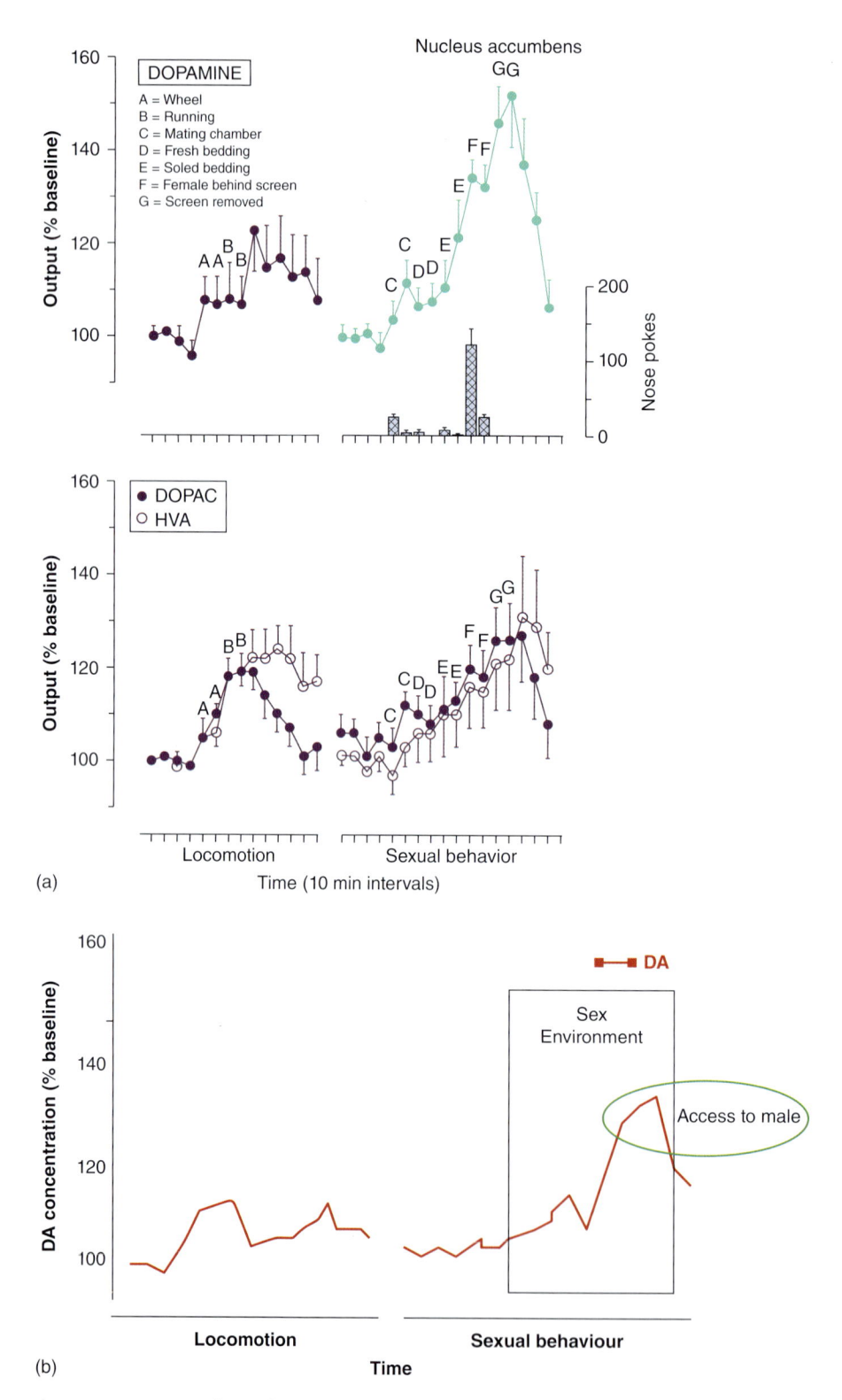

FIGURE 16.6 Dopamine response to sexual stimuli. (a) Increase in DA response in the male rat with access to a female rat. (b) Increase in DA response in the female rat with access to a male rat.
Sources: (a) Damsma, G., Pfaus, J. G., Wenkstern, D., Phillips, A. G. & Fibiger, H. C. (1992). Sexual behavior increases dopamine transmission in the nucleus accumbens and striatum of male rats: comparison with novelty and locomotion. *Behavioral Neuroscience, 106,* 181–191. (b) Pfaus, J., Damsma, G., Wenkstern, D., & Fibiger, H. (1995). Sexual activity increases dopamine transmission in the nucleus accumbens and striatum of female rats. *Brain Research, 693*(1), 21–30.

The theories of addiction fall into two main camps: positive reinforcement and negative reinforcement.

Positive reinforcement

In Chapter 8, a detailed description indicated that a rat will press a lever to obtain a reinforcer. In drug self-administration experiments, the drug is the reinforcer. If there is a good outcome from the behaviour, we are likely to engage in it again.

Taking the position of explaining addiction from the perspective of the psychostimulants, Wise and Bozarth (1987) provided an account of addiction that focused on the psychomotor properties of drugs in which 'The crux of the theory is that the reinforcing effects of the drugs, and thus their addiction liability, can be predicted from their ability to induce psychomotor activation' (Wise & Bozarth, 1987, p.474). There are three major assertions of the theory:

- all addictive drugs have psychomotor stimulant actions;
- the stimulant actions of these drugs share a biological mechanism; and
- this mechanism is homologous with the mechanism for positive reinforcement.

The theory stems from an earlier account in which reinforcement is explained in terms of approach behaviours (Glickman & Schiff, 1967). If you want something then you have got to move towards it. Thus, drugs, like all positive reinforcers, should elicit forward locomotion. The neural basis of the psychomotor stimulant theory places emphasis on the two dopamine systems: the mesolimbic system, in which low doses produce forward locomotion; and the nigrostriatal system in which high doses increase small localized movements, e.g. stereotypy.

The importance of these two systems is that they derive from the same embryological tissue. The ventral tegmental area has the equivalent of the substantia nigra and the nucleus accumbens with the nucleus caudate (striatum).

In their review of the evidence Wise and Bozarth account for numerous drugs, including the depressants. They point out that even the CNS depressants have psychomotor activating effects, depending upon time course and dose. For example, they point out that the opiates have a biphasic effect on locomotor activation where low doses stimulate activity and high doses inhibit it. The time course of action of opiate psychomotor activation indicates an effect early on after drug administration, which may be partially down to the pharmacokinetics of absorption and distribution.

The psychomotor stimulant theory of addiction places locomotor activity as an important measure of reinforcement. However, whilst the theory provided a clear account of a drug's effect on motor activity, it did not tell us about the adaptations that occur during the process of addiction. Neural adaptation as a result of repetitive drug taking is currently one of the most dominant theories in addiction and has been approached from a number of perspectives, e.g. sensitization and learning.

Sensitization

In the search for a common denominator, the sensitization of locomotor behaviour has received considerable attention. Sensitization is an increase in activity after repeated doses (see Chapter 9). Sensitization as a psychopharmacological phenomenon has been incorporated into a theory of addiction and motivation.

Sensitization of incentive salience: a theory of addiction

With continuing exposure to a drug, there is a heightened responsiveness to subsequent drug administrations; basically, there is a bigger effect. This is an effect that mesolimbic DA may mediate (Kalivas & Weber, 1988; Kolta et al., 1989).

Wise and Bozarth (1987) presented a view that the common denominator of reinforcing drugs is their psychomotor stimulant properties, which are mediated via mesolimbic DA. Robinson and Berridge's theory (Berridge & Robinson, 2003; Robinson & Berridge, 1993, 2000) has integrated learning and the physiological action of drugs: the incentive–sensitization theory of addiction (Figure 16.7). The theory of incentive sensitization has also been conceptualized as a computational model with successful predictions being made (Zhang et al., 2012).

In this theory there are three major features of addiction:

- there is craving for the drug;
- the drug craving is persistent and can reappear after abstinence; and
- as the craving for the drug increases (the wanting of the drug), the pleasure obtained from it decreases (the liking) (see Figure 16.7).

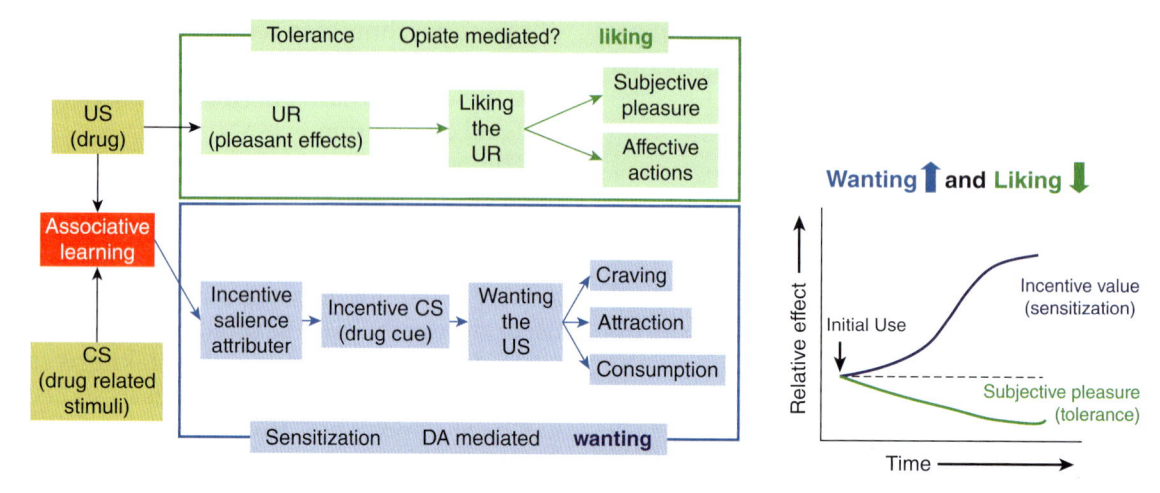

FIGURE 16.7 The incentive sensitization theory of addiction. Two processes are combined via learning to increase wanting and reduce liking. CS, conditioned stimulus; DA, dopamine; UR, unconditioned response; US, unconditioned stimulus.
Source: Robinson, T. E., & Berridge, K. C. (1993). The neural basis of drug craving: An incentive-sensitization theory of addiction. *Brain Research Reviews, 18*(3), 247–291.

The process of drug taking leads to sensitization of physiological and behavioural measures. The neural system that is sensitized is hypothesized to mediate a psychological function involved in incentive motivation. In the addict, the drug becomes a highly motivating reinforcer and is given **incentive salience** – the wanting of the drug. Sensitization, then, enhances incentive salience, a motivational state, which turns stimuli into desired must-have objects.

The theory states that, via conditioning, drug and associated stimuli become more salient (Figure 16.8). Thus, stimuli associated with the drug (e.g. drug paraphernalia, such as the syringe with intravenous heroin use) become able to control behaviour – that is, induce the wanting of the drug.

This increase in wanting the drug is due to the neural substrate, and the associative learning, becoming more sensitized. The bad news is that repeated exposure only sensitizes the wanting, not the liking. The pleasure derived from the drug is mediated by another system, perhaps an opiate system (see the interview with Kent Berridge in Phillips (2003)) and is subject to tolerance. Robbins and Everitt (2007) suggest that wanting is linked to appetitive behaviour (drug seeking) and liking to consummatory behaviour (taking the drug). They argue that wanting represents a stimulus response processing circuitry that may be beyond conscious control whereas liking may be mediated via opiate receptors in the nucleus accumbens (Berridge, 2000). A study by Lambert et al. (2006) supported the notion that liking decreases and wanting increases in a group of participants who had a previous history of stimulant medication and smoking (inducing sensitization) when they were subsequently asked to rate cocaine. In genetically modified, dopamine-deficient mice, the liking of sugar was not dopamine mediated whereas the motor behaviour of licking to obtain sugar was dopamine mediated (Cannon & Bseikri, 2004). Mice that were genetically modified to be hyperdopaminergic (DAT knockout – therefore preventing the reuptake of dopamine once released) ate more food, drank more water, ran faster for food in a runway and gained more weight than wild-type animals but they showed fewer liking responses to sugar (Pecina et al., 2003).

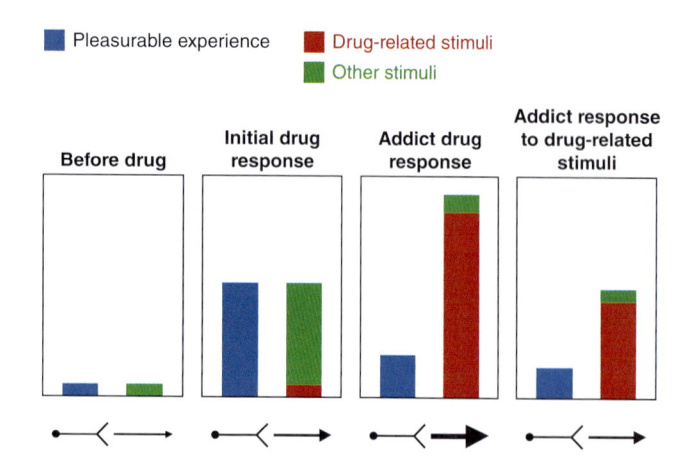

FIGURE 16.8 The affective experience of drugs and drug-associated stimuli.
Source: Robinson, T. E., & Berridge, K. C. (1993). The neural basis of drug craving: An incentive-sensitization theory of addiction. *Brain Research Reviews, 18*(3), 247–291.

Not all reports are consistent with wanting and liking being dissociated. Professor Paul Willner and colleagues evaluated wanting and liking in moderate to extreme alcohol drinkers (Willner et al., 2005). In their pseudo-dose response study, wanting increased with the level of drinking but in contrast to the predictions made by the incentive salience theory of addiction, liking also increased.

Sensitization remains for a long period of time, even after the drug taking has stopped; it may even be permanent. The endurance of sensitization has been demonstrated in human participants given amphetamine and tested a year later, when a greater dopamine response was obtained in extended regions of the mesolimbic system (Boileau et al., 2006). It is this that can lead to the reinstatement of drug taking (somewhat like spontaneous recovery). The conditioning of drug-related stimuli can precipitate relapse. Anecdotal accounts from detoxified drug users have indicated that returning to the drug-taking environment can lead to relapse.

Whilst the theory has generated a great deal of interest and debate, it does not hold out the prospect of an optimistic future for the drug addict. But of all the therapies available, cognitive-behavioural therapy is potentially the most effective intervention to help reduce the problem (Robinson & Berridge, 2000).

Physical dependence theories and negative reinforcement

Drugs clearly produce physiological effects. With positive reinforcement, this may be the euphoric nature of getting high. However, drugs often produce **withdrawal symptoms** in their absence. Given the extremely unpleasant nature of withdrawal symptoms, the addict is compelled to alleviate them by continuing to take the drug. Therefore, drug-taking behaviour is maintained by negative reinforcement: a response (drug taking) stops a negative consequence (withdrawal symptoms).

Withdrawal symptoms can be initiated by the absence of the drug; in **conditioned withdrawal** stimuli precipitate withdrawal symptoms in the absence of the drug and initiate opponent processes (similar to tolerance) (Eissenberg, 2004). The withdrawal symptoms are an aversive state induced by the addiction process itself but another aspect of negative reinforcement that maintains drug consumption is self-medication. With self-medication, the drug is consumed to avoid aversive states that exist prior to the drug-taking behaviour commencing, e.g. depression and/or anxiety (Khantzian, 1985). It is easy to see that a drink at the end of the day can help deal with all the day's stresses or that diazepam can calm anxiety on first waking. The fact that co-morbidity exists with addiction is a point highlighted by Professor Mike Gossop who argues that treating the addiction and not the pre-existing co-morbidities that may appear again post detoxification will lead to limited treatment success (Gossop, 2003) (see Box 16.5).

Perhaps the most influential theory focusing on negative reinforcement is that of Professor George Koob. The initial consumption of drugs leads to positive reinforcement (Koob, 1987). However, positive reinforcement diminishes and leads to negative motivational states in the chronic drug user (Koob

BOX 16.5: ADDICTION AND CO-MORBIDITY

Addiction in ADHD

Early reports suggest that many of those seeking treatment for drug addiction had a previous history of attention deficit hyperactivity disorder (ADHD) (Carroll & Rounsaville, 1993; DeMilio, 1989; Dennis et al., 2002; Eyre et al., 1982; Horner & Scheibe, 1997; Hovens et al., 1994; Ohlmeier et al., 2007, 2008; Wilens, 2007; Ziedonis et al., 1994). In one review of the evidence, an estimated 20% of substance abusers had symptoms consistent with ADHD (Wilens, 2007). These studies cannot be used as conclusive evidence supporting a causal role of ADHD in substance abuse; the methodologies used do not permit that (Looby, 2008; Lynskey & Hall, 2001). Asking people, especially drug users, to recall past events is not a sturdy basis for any study; drug users are notoriously difficult to study. These reports do, however, add some circumstantial evidence, which will require further careful study.

Longitudinal prospective studies have been conducted and indicate an increased likelihood of substance abuse amongst those with ADHD (Barkley et al., 1990; Gittelman et al., 1985; Mannuzza et al., 1991, 1998; Minde et al., 1972; Satterfield et al., 1982; Weiss et al., 1979). In a study of 1142 cases of ADHD, it was found that severity of childhood inattention symptoms predicted multiple substance use outcomes and also that childhood oppositional defiant disorder/conduct disorder (ODD/CD) symptoms predicted drug use. Persistence of ADHD and adolescent CD were associated with increased substance use behaviours relative to controls (Volkow et al., 2003).

In a 10-year follow up of ADHD cases, it was found that there was a greater risk of substance abuse as well as other co-morbidities (e.g. anxiety) (Biederman et al., 2006a). In this study, nicotine was found to be the main drug currently used, prompting the conclusion that smoking is a gateway drug to alcohol and illegal substances (Biederman et al., 2006b; Lai et al., 2000; Torabi et al., 1993). Starting with nicotine, the person with psychopathology may move next to alcohol, then to cannabis and finally to other illicit substances (Kuperman et al., 2001). Maintenance of smoking in those with ADHD may be increased because they experience more withdrawal symptoms than their non-ADHD counterparts (Pomerleau et al., 2003), suggesting that avoidance of withdrawal could maintain smoking behaviour, or that they are self-medicating.

Co-morbidity is also a problem that needs to be disentangled. Substance abuse was associated more with conduct problems (Lynskey & Fergusson, 1995) which indicates a possible influence of CD and ODD aetiology. According to one study, the vast majority also met the criteria for CD and ODD (Biederman et al., 1996), so it is difficult to ascribe causality to ADHD alone. Co-morbid CD has been demonstrated to increase the severity of substance abuse, with a greater variety of substances used (Barkley et al., 2004).

DSM IV identified three subtypes of ADHD. The question of which symptoms and subtype are more likely to give rise to substance abuse needs addressing. This is a separate issue from that of co-morbidity and is vulnerable to the validity of such distinctions within the ADHD diagnostic framework. For example, the ADHD HI subtype emphasizes impulsivity; substance abuse is also regarded as an impulse control problem (Volkow & Fowler, 2000; Volkow et al., 2004).

ADHD symptoms have been related to alcohol and marijuana consumption. ADHD I symptoms, but not ADHD HI symptoms, were associated with marijuana and nicotine dependence (Abrantes et al., 2005) and in another study many different drugs were consumed (Molina & Pelham, 2003). When it comes to smoking cigarettes, the same was true of the ADHD I symptoms and marijuana (Burke et al., 2001). In other studies it was the ADHD HI symptoms that predicted the initiation of drug taking (Elkins et al., 2007), of smoking (Kollins et al., 2005) and of substance abuse in general (Lee & Hinshaw, 2006). Symptom severity was also associated with choosing methylphenidate over placebo (Fredericks & Kollins, 2004).

In theoretical terms there is a meeting of a common neuropharmacological system subserving both ADHD and addiction. Sagvolden has indicated that there is deficient reward processing in animal models of ADHD (Johansen & Sagvolden, 2005a, 2005b) similar to that seen in ADHD cases where small immediate rewards are preferred (Johansen et al., 2002; Sagvolden et al., 1998). Furthermore, the all-important symptom (and endophenotype) impulsivity has been linked to addiction and the frontal cortex (Matsuo et al., 2009; Torregrossa et al., 2008; Volkow, Fowler et al., 2009). Changes in frontal areas are also seen in ADHD (Barbelivien et al., 2001; Bush et al., 1999; Carmona et al., 2005; Hesslinger et al., 2002; Itami & Uno, 2002; Lee et al., 2005) and are active in reward anticipation in males with ADHD (Strohle et al., 2008). Thus, the connection of ADHD with addiction is not merely a result of the symptoms making the person with ADHD more vulnerable to future substance abuse, but rather the manifestation of a common dysfunctional reward pathway.

Self-medication

One possible hypothesis is that those with ADHD are actually self-medicating their symptoms with nicotine, cocaine or amphetamines, etc. Are those with ADHD acting as patient and doctor and trying to treat their condition? The self-medication hypothesis is part of a negative reinforcement view, that the person is not trying to get high but is rather trying to avoid unpleasant experiences (Eissenberg, 2004). Individuals predisposed by biological or psychological vulnerabilities find that drug effects corresponding to their particular problems are powerfully reinforcing (Hall & Queener, 2007). Anecdotal evidence often supports a self-medication view; after all, cocaine is pharmacologically similar to methylphenidate, amphetamine is used in the treatment of ADHD and nicotine has also been evaluated in ADHD treatment. Thus, those with ADHD may use some drugs to calm down; to be able to think more clearly and to concentrate; to reduce anxiety or depression; and to relieve boredom. The drug of choice appears to be nicotine, with more of those with ADHD smoking compared to controls (Wilens et al., 2007). Even adults with ADHD will choose methylphenidate over placebo to control their symptoms, and this is independent of other measures of abuse (Fredericks & Kollins, 2004).

In a study comparing the motivation for taking drugs between ADHD individuals and controls, Wilens et al. (2007) noted that across both groups, 36% were using drugs for self-medication purposes. However, no difference emerged when this was analysed between groups and ADHD symptoms did not differ between self-medicators and those using drugs to get high.

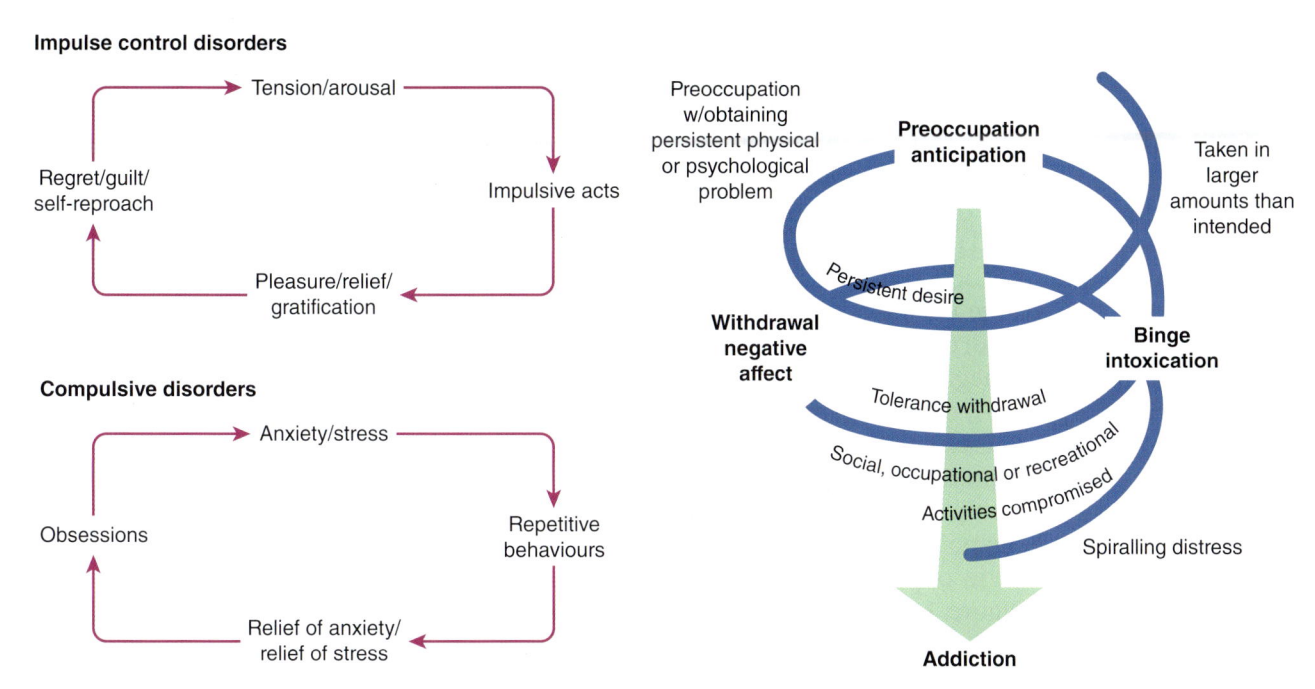

FIGURE 16.9 Koob's dynamic process of addiction. Addiction is conceptualized as starting as a impulse control problem that descends into a compulsive disorder or from positive to negative reinforcement. The spiral descent into addiction involves the vicious circle of intoxication, withdrawal and preoccupation with acquisition of the drug.
Source: Koob, G. F. (2003). Alcoholism: Allostasis and beyond. *Alcoholism: Clinical and Experimental Research*, 27(2), 232–243. Reproduced by permission of John Wiley & Sons.

& Le Moal, 2005). This theory sees addiction as a dynamic process that moves from positive reinforcement to negative reinforcement, typified by positive reinforcement being a problem of impulse control developing into a compulsive disorder, similar to Obsessive Compulsive Disorder (OCD) that is governed by negative reinforcement (see Figure 16.14). During positive reinforcement, there is pleasure, relief and gratification whereas in negative reinforcement it is the relief of anxiety and stress that is the goal. The process of addiction is seen as a spiralling descent of preoccupation anticipation leading to consumption and intoxication and then withdrawal which then leads to preoccupation anticipation again (Koob & Le Moal, 1997) (Figure 16.9).

The negative reinforcement theory introduces the **extended amygdala** which comprises the **central nucleus**, **bed nucleus of the stria terminalis** and the transition zone, in part of the NAcc (Figure 16.10). In great concentration in these regions are opioid and dopamine systems (Koob, 2003). Changes in the extended amygdala and brain stress systems provide the negative emotional state that drives addiction, in what Koob refers to as the *dark side* of motivation (Koob & Le Moal, 2005).

Chronic drug use results in opponent processes in which there is a functional downregulation of the brain reward mechanisms through overexposure and these reward systems do not reset themselves (Koob & Le Moal, 2001). The process by which the reward systems recalibrate themselves is not homeostasis, but rather **allostasis**. Allostasis is a term introduced by Sterling and Eyer (1988) as an alternative to homeostasis; allostasis is the ability to achieve 'stability through change' and in order 'to obtain stability, an organism must vary all of the

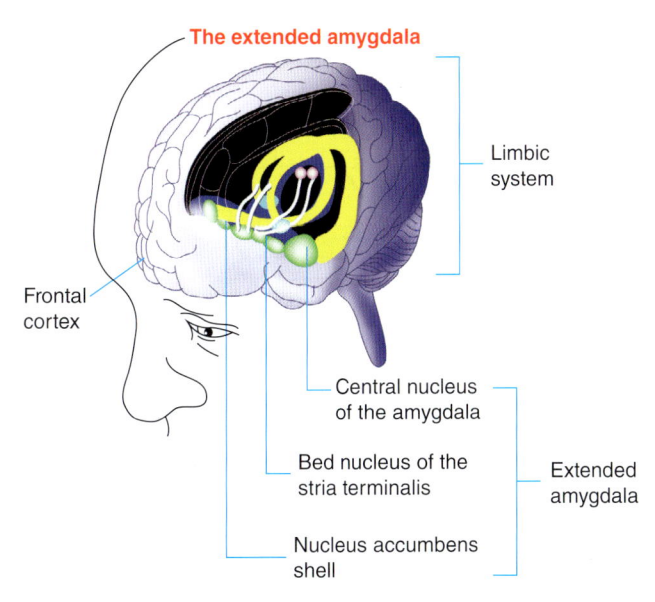

FIGURE 16.10 The extended amygdala.

parameters of its internal milieu and match them appropriately to environmental demands' (Sterling & Eyer, 1988, p.636). The application of allostasis to addiction involves stability of reward functioning being achieved by changes in the reward and stress neurocircuitry. These opponent processes are counteradaptations and lead to a deviation from the normal reward setpoints. Koob and Le Moal (2001) argue that there is a change in mood states associated with the transition to drug addiction. Elevated mood is countered by negative mood. Positive mood is mediated by GABA, opioids and dopamine whereas negative mood is a result of increased stress hormones, e.g. corticotrophin releasing factor (see Chapter 23). Due to the actions of drugs, there is a shift from a homeostatic point to a new setpoint (allostatic setpoint) that is in opposition to normal reward processing (see Figure 16.11). According to this theory of addiction, it becomes a vicious circle in which the negative affect is negated by drug consumption, but it is that very drug consumption that changes the brain to potentiate the negative affect. Thus, addiction is maintained by negative reinforcement.

Neuroadaptations of the DA system have been revealed in imaging studies of human addicts. The general pharmacological principle is that stimulation of receptors leads to a functional downregulation in terms of number and affinity (see Chapter 7). Studies conducted by Nora Volkow (Director of the National Institute on Drug Abuse (NIDA) in America) have shown reduced DA receptors in alcoholics and cocaine users (Volkow, Wang, Fowler, Logan et al., 1993, 1996b, 1997). Low levels of DA receptors have been linked with increased liking of the drug (Volkow et al., 1999). Thus, it is conceivable that the drug user is consuming drugs in order to counter the neuroadaptive effects that mean there are fewer DA receptors available for stimulation and therefore presumably a hyperactive reward pathway. What is needed is a prospective study of humans to determine if low DA receptors are a risk factor for later drug abuse rather than an artefact of drug administration.

The only ethical way to solve this conundrum is with animal studies. A study using cynomolgus macaques sought to understand the influence of DA receptor number on subsequent cocaine self-administration. In this study by Morgan et al. (2002), DA receptors were measured using a positron emission tomography (PET) scan. When the macaques were individually housed, they all had a similar number of DA D2 receptors but when they were put into group housing, there was a difference between dominant and subordinate animals (Figure 16.12). Those that became dominant were not stressed and the number of DA receptors increased, whereas those that remained subordinate within the group enclosure did not have a corresponding elevation in DA receptors. The significance of this finding arose when the animals were trained to self-administer cocaine. Those that were dominant were less likely

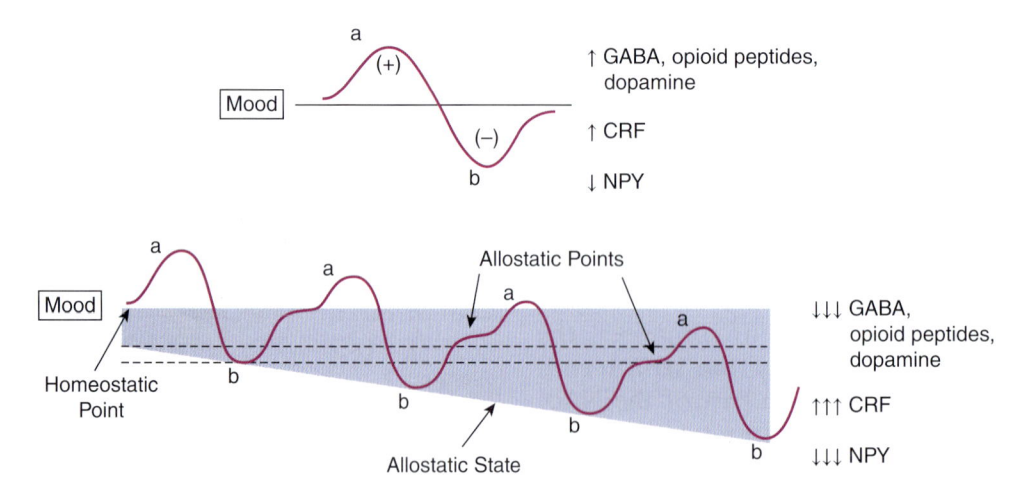

FIGURE 16.11 *Allostatic shift in addiction. Through increases in DA, GABA and opioids, mood increases which is followed by a depression of mood as a result of an increase in CRF (stress hormone). Through neuroadaptations to repeated drug use, the homeostatic balance shifts down and is reset to a new average (allostatic shift) of increased stress and lower reward thresholds. CRF, corticotrophin releasing factor; GABA, gamma-aminobutyric acid; NPY, neuropeptide Y.*
Source: Adapted by permission from Macmillan Publishers Ltd from Koob, G. F., & Le Moal, M. (2001). Drug addiction, dysregulation of reward, and allostasis. *Neuropsychopharmacology, 24*(2), 97–129, copyright 2001.

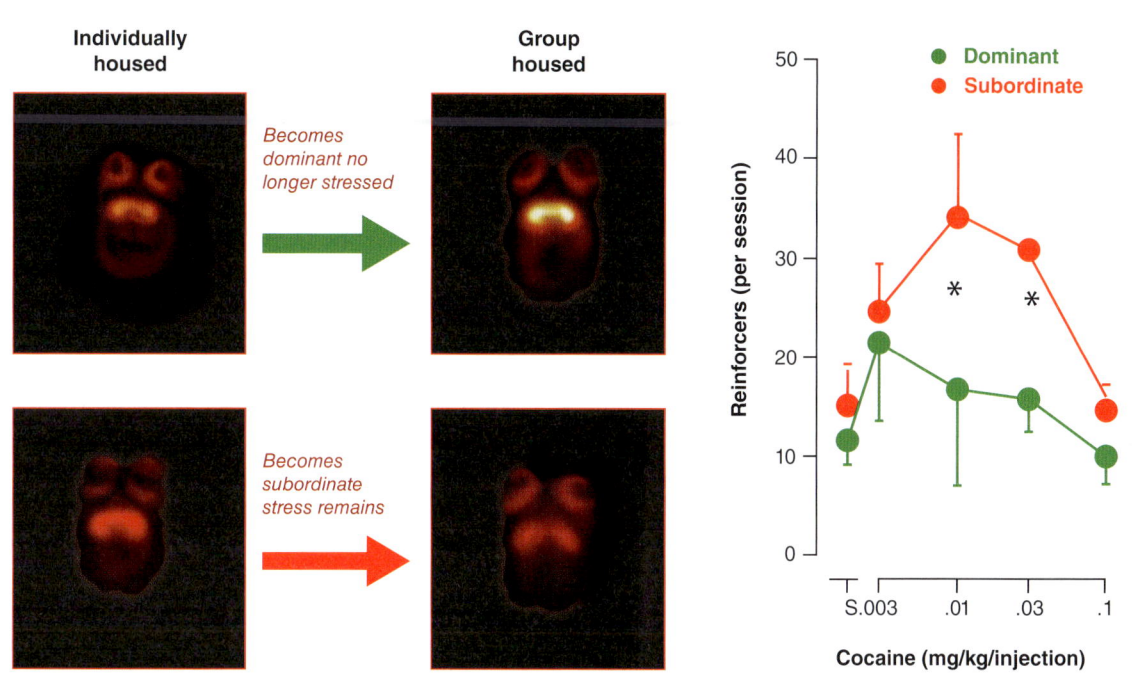

FIGURE 16.12 *Social status, DA receptors and cocaine self-administration.*
Source: Adapted by permission from Macmillan Publishers Ltd from Morgan, D., Grant, K. A., Gage, H. D., Mach, R. H., Kaplan, J. R., Prioleau, O., et al. (2002). Social dominance in monkeys: Dopamine D2 receptors and cocaine self-administration. *Nature Neuroscience*, 5(2), 169–174, copyright 2002.

to administer cocaine whereas the subordinate animals readily pressed the lever to receive an infusion. This study therefore suggests that environmental circumstances can lead to differences in DA receptor number which confer a vulnerability for drug addiction. Could the same be true of humans? Social status has been shown to correlate with DA receptor levels in the striatum (Martinez et al., 2010).

Just say no

If addiction is predominantly the by-product of a faulty reward system that is operating for positive and negative reinforcement, then the laws of associative learning would suggest that discontinuation of the drug would lead to extinction. When an animal trained to self-administer a drug has that drug removed, an extinction burst can be measured in which the animal rapidly responds in an attempt to acquire the drug (see Chapters 7 and 9). As time passes and the drug is no longer delivered, extinction occurs. However, the laws of associative learning also tell us that there is spontaneous recovery. Priming doses of the drug, conditioned stimuli that have become associated with the drug and life's stresses can all precipitate drug self-administration.

Animal learning theories have suggested some aspects of the addiction process but according to Miller (2003):

> Some years ago the eminent learning theorist, Frank Logan, gave the keynote address to the International Conference on Treatment of Addictive Behaviors. He offered a brilliant and encyclopedic review of research on animal self-administration of alcohol (including one ill-advised study of the effects of intoxication in elephants). He concluded that one needs nothing more than animal learning models to explain how people get trapped in addiction, but that there is no adequate animal model of recovery . . . Animal learning principles describe the dilemma but not its resolution . . . To understand how people escape from addiction – be it in treatment, in Alcoholics Anonymous, or in the natural course of life events – one must turn to that which is uniquely human, to the higher-order processes of the human mind (p.63).

The behaviour of addiction and even some of the theories would suggest that all we have to do is say no to drugs. The 'Just Say No' campaign launched by Nancy Reagan wanted people to decline drugs. History indicates that this was easier said than done. Saying no requires the individual to override the neuroadaptations that have occurred in subcortical regions of the brain. The area of the brain that could potentially override the automatic processes of addiction is the frontal lobe. It is the frontal lobe that is able to inhibit our behaviour, is able to say no. However, the frontal lobe might not be fully operational and therefore may not be able to override the powerfully motivating effects of drugs on the mesolimbic system. Indeed, the top-down processing of the frontal lobe to the subcortical regions has been shown not to be as effective with reductions in glutamatergic processes evident in addiction (Kalivas, 2009). Professor Trevor Robbins states: 'the notion that "pleasure" can be mediated by receptors in a sub-cortical nucleus is perhaps too simple. Activity in this circuitry is probably subject to further processing in cortical circuits' (Robbins et al., 2006, p.22).

There are a number of neuropsychological accounts of addiction that describe the processes at the cognitive level. Cognitive models tend to talk about automatic processes which are effortless and beyond consciousness (Tiffany, 1990; Wiers & Stacy, 2005; Wiers Bartholow et al., 2007). Being able to access subconscious processes would therefore be important in mitigating addiction (Jentsch & Pennington, 2014). Thus, the inability to inhibit drug taking has been considered by some to be fundamentally flawed in addiction (Volkow et al., 2004). The orbitofrontal cortex and the amygdala have also been identified as important regions linking reward to hedonic experiences (Kringelbach, 2005; Rothkirch et al., 2012; Schoenbaum et al., 1998). The orbitofrontal cortex therefore may be involved in some of the aspects of learning.

In the following section, the role of DA changes from being a big neurochemical of reward to the neurochemical of learning about reward.

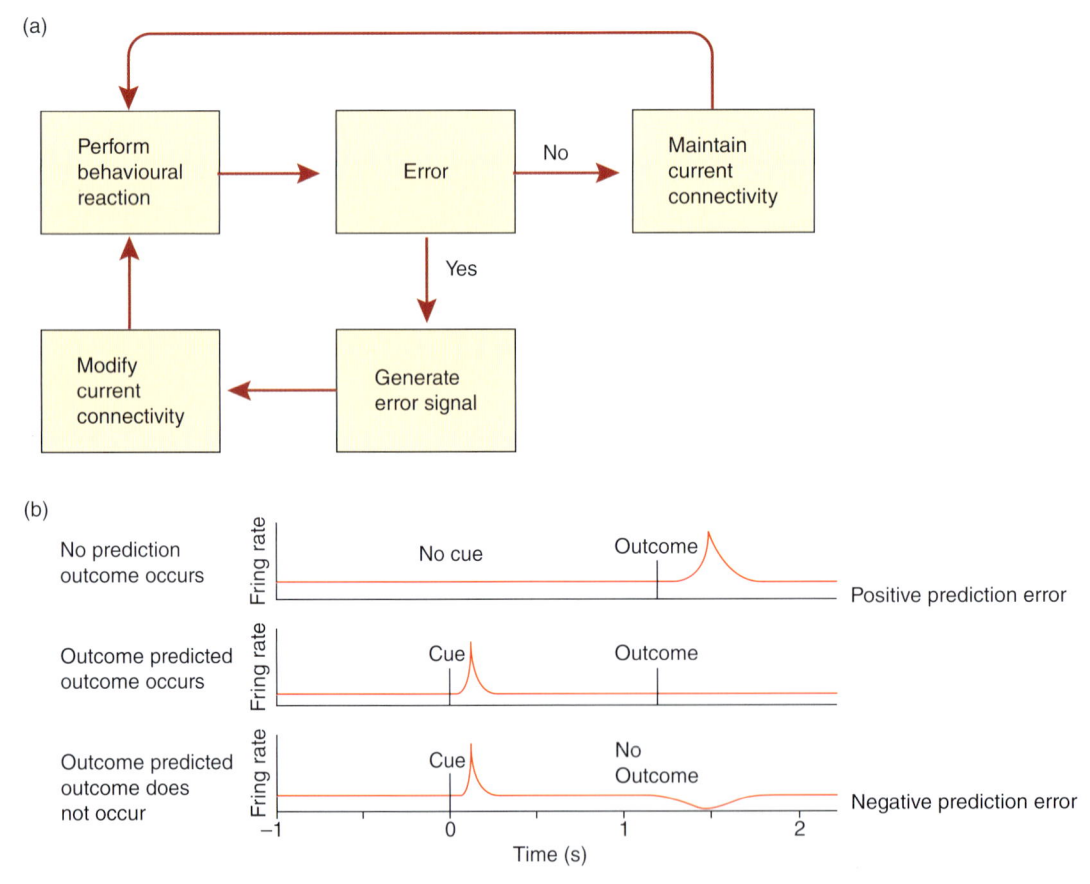

FIGURE 16.13 *(a) For a reward to be learned, it has to be surprising or unpredicted (see Chapter 8). If a reward occurs unpredictably, there is a positive prediction error in which learning about consequences and actions occurs. Once the association is acquired, the prediction error provides no new information on action and consequences (see Chapter 8). Once learned, if an expected reward is not received there is a negative prediction error and the action is stopped. (b) The firing rate of DA neurons in response to unexpected reward, learned reward and the omission of a learned reward.*
Sources: (a) Adapted by permission from Macmillan Publishers Ltd from Schultz, W. (2000). Multiple reward signals in the brain. *Nature Reviews Neuroscience*, *1*(3), 199–207, copyright 2000. (b) Adapted by permission from Macmillan Publishers Ltd from Schoenbaum, G., Esber, G. R., & Iordanova, M. D. (2013). Dopamine signals mimic reward prediction errors. *Nature Neuroscience*, *16*(7), 777–779, copyright 2013.

Motivation, addiction and learning

The accumulated evidence supports a DA-mediated reward pathway. The textbook case for mesolimbic DA being the reward pathway is appealing, as the early data from studies were supportive of such a stance. However, science has moved the argument on further. The NAcc and other areas of the mesolimbic system are no longer considered to be the reward pathway *per se*. The evidence now points to these regions being involved in the learning of associations between stimuli and reward, and the probability of reward.

Much of the work that contributes to our new understanding of dopamine and reward has been conducted on the phasic DA response (Schultz, 2006, 2007; Tobler et al., 2005). When an animal is presented with a primary reinforcer, e.g. food or water, DA cells respond, increasing DA release. The same is also true for stimuli associated with reward (Schultz, 1998; Schultz et al., 1997, 1998). These DA neurons are depressed when a signalled reward is omitted and by stimuli predicting the absence of reward (Tobler et al., 2003) (Figure 16.13). This phasic DA response is argued to be a teaching signal involved in the learning of associations (Schultz, 2007). DA neurons project to various brain regions including the **dorsal** and **ventral striatum** (NAcc) (which are thought to have independent actions on learning with transfer of new learning in the ventral regions to automated process in more dorsal regions (Everitt et al., 2008)) and subregions of the prefrontal cortex. Haber et al. (2000) have identified cascading loops (Figure 16.14) in which the striatal:

> ...shell influences the core, the core influences the central striatum, and the central striatum influences the dorsolateral striatum. This anatomical arrangement creates a hierarchy of information flow and provides an anatomical basis for the limbic/cognitive/motor interface via the ventral midbrain. (p.2369)

In human participants, the ventral striatum has been associated with learning and the dorsal striatum with the maintenance of information regarding reward outcomes (O'Doherty et al., 2004). Sensitization by an increase in DA may strengthen the learning that takes place within the dorsal striatum (Nelson & Killcross, 2006).

Within the wider theoretical context, the learning that takes place under the auspices of DA leads to capture of the habit, whereas the habit is maintained by the automated processes of wider brain regions of the basal ganglia and the cognitive expectations of the orbitofrontal cortex (Newlin & Strubler, 2007).

The prefrontal neurons carry signals related to the preparation of movement and goal achievement (Matsumoto et al., 2003) and the motivational value of rewards (Shaw & Rolls, 1976). Imaging studies have indicated that there is a dysfunction in cortical regions of the brain linked to drug compulsion and lack of behavioural inhibition – in the case of addiction, not being able to stop taking the drug (Volkow et al., 2004).

An interesting feature of the phasic response to stimuli is that it occurs when rewards are different from predictions; this is called the **reward prediction error** (Schultz, 1998). The phasic DA response differs if a reward is unpredicted or not available or delayed (Hollerman & Schultz, 1998). Thus, the following DA codes are available to the organism: (1) an unpredicted reward elicits an activation – a positive prediction error; (2) a predicted reward elicits no response; and (3) the omission or extended delay of a predicted reward induces a depression (Schultz, 2007). In the words of Professor Wolfgang Schultz, 'A "prediction error" message may constitute a powerful teaching signal for behavior and learning' and it 'may contribute to the self-organization of goal-directed behavior' (Schultz, 2001, p.293). Furthermore, the reward prediction error may act as an impulse to instigate neural changes that lead to subsequent changes in reward predictions and behavioural reactions, i.e. learning. The process continues until the behavioural outcomes match the reward predictions and then there is no prediction error with no DA activity. A variation on the role of phasic DA states that negative DA signal would mean that behaviour would be suppressed whereas positive signals increase repetition (Redgrave & Gurney, 2006; Redgrave et al., 2008).

This is all well and good for rats and monkeys, but does the reward prediction error occur in humans? It has been demonstrated that stimuli associated with drugs such as cocaine can in fact increase brain activation in their own right (Goldstein et al., 2007; Volkow et al., 2005, 2006; Wong et al., 2006). Such studies clearly demonstrate that we humans learn that a previously neutral stimulus can become associated with the drug itself. Indeed, recent studies indicate that an increase in DA alone does not produce drug craving, but requires cues associated with the drug (Volkow, Wang, Telang, Fowler, Logan et al., 2008), and in this study they used methylphenidate

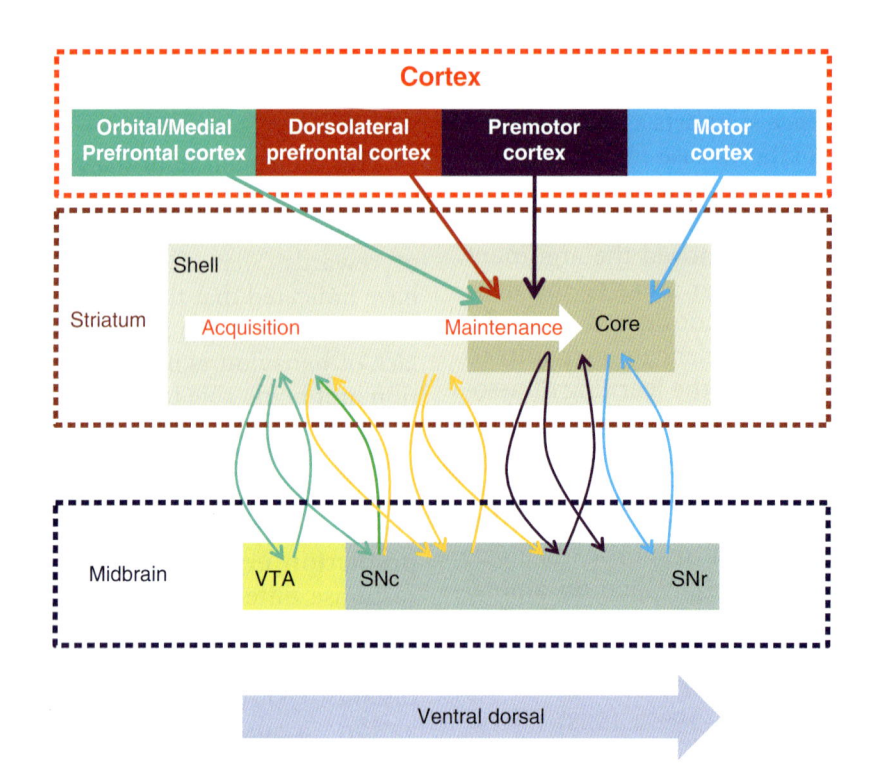

FIGURE 16.14 Cascading loops of striatonigrostriatal (SNS) projections maintaining habit. The shell of the striatum (in its biggest sense, including nucleus accumbens) is involved in acquisition and reinforcement. The core is involved in maintenance. Loops projection from shell to core to the substantia nigra and beyond. The core receives input from the cortex. Projections from the shell target both the ventral tegmental area (VTA) and substantia nigra pars compacta (SNc). Projections from the VTA to the shell form a reciprocal loop. Projections from the SN feed forward towards the core. Ventral striatal regions impact upon more dorsal regions via looping projections. SNr, substantia nigra pars reticulata.

Source: Based on Haber, S. N., Fudge, J. L., & McFarland, N. R. (2000). Striatonigrostriatal pathways in primates form an ascending spiral from the shell to the dorsolateral striatum. *Journal of Neuroscience, 20*(6), 2369–2382.

to increase DA levels. The use of neuroimaging techniques has revealed that there is also a case for the reward prediction error in humans (Kelly et al., 2007). The concept of a reward prediction error has been incorporated into a computational model of learning in which actions are evaluated through experience of a mismatch between expectancy and actual reward (Figure 16.15) (Daw & Doya, 2006).

WHICH THEORY IS CORRECT?

It is tempting to want to find one definitive theory of addiction and motivation. The theories above approach addiction from very specific starting points. The incentive salience theory presents a view of addiction in which craving becomes unmanageable and leads to the motivation to consume drugs. The incentive value of drugs and drug-related stimuli becomes heightened, steering the motivation to consume. The compulsive nature of addiction and involvement of stress systems in maintaining it have been addressed by Koob. Continual drug-taking behaviour results in adaptive changes in the reward and stress circuitry of the brain. These changes provide a new setpoint that is lower than normal and represents a shift from impulse control difficulties to more obsessive-compulsive behaviour regarding the drug. Beyond the subcortical regions, the cortex has substantial effects on cognition and control within addiction. The orbitofrontal cortex and the dopaminergic regions of the ventral striatum have been shown to be particularly important in learning about reward rather than reward itself. And once learnt, the events are remembered, but can become a maladaptive memory in addiction (Milton & Everitt, 2012).

Goldstein and Volkow (2002) acknowledge the extent of neuronal adaptations in addiction (Figure 16.16).

- Saliency/reward – NAcc, ventral pallidum.
- Motivation/drive – orbitofrontal cortex.

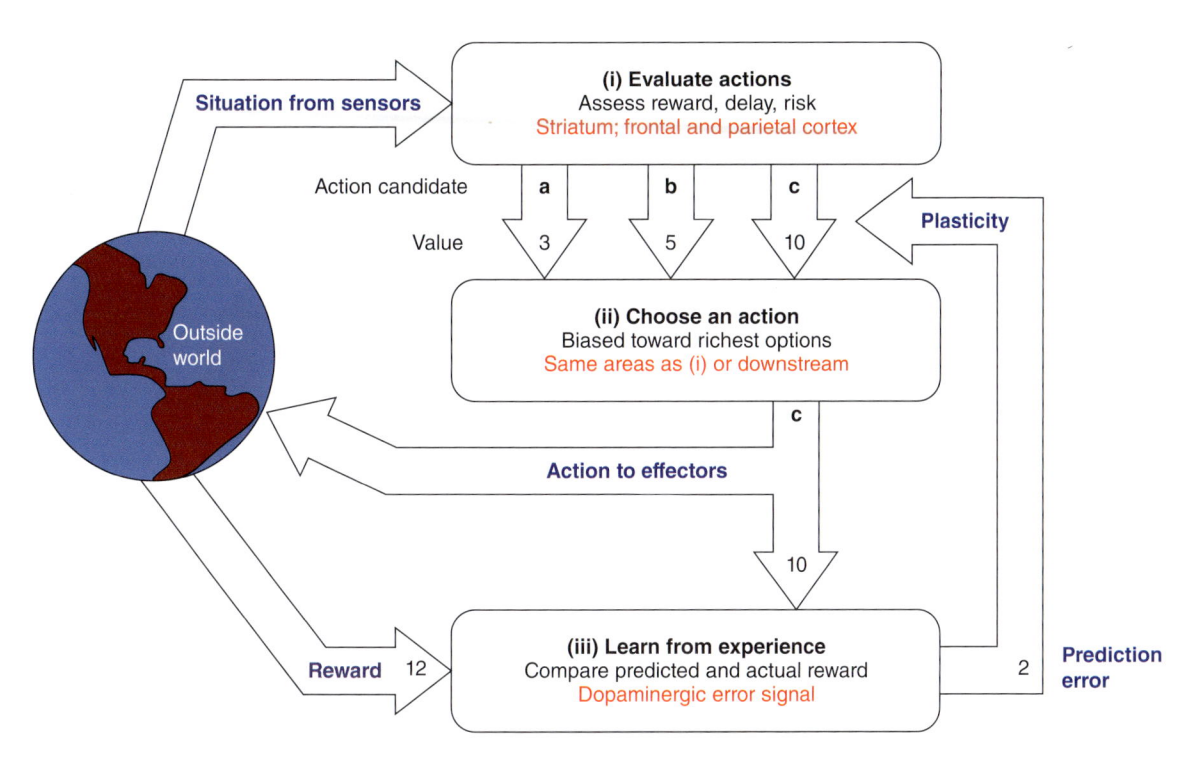

FIGURE 16.15 *The three basic stages of many reinforcement learning accounts of learned decision making. (i) Predict the rewards expected for candidate actions (here a, b, c) in the current situation. (ii) Choose and execute one by comparing the predicted rewards. (iii) Finally, learn from the reward prediction error to improve future decisions. Numbers indicate the predicted action values, the obtained reward and the resulting prediction error. Thus, if choice (c) with a value of 10 is selected and executed and the reward obtained has a value of 12, this leaves a discrepancy of 2 which is a positive prediction error leading to continued learning.*
Source: Daw, N. D., & Doya, K. (2006). The computational neurobiology of learning and reward. *Current Opinion in Neurobiology, 16*(2), 199–204.

- Memory/learning – amygdala, hippocampus and basal ganglia.
- Control/inhibition – prefrontal cortex and anterior cingulate cortex.

It is evident from the literature that the theories of addiction can all be a little right and a little wrong inasmuch as they are addressing specific aspects of the addictive process rather than addiction as a whole.

SUMMARY

The understanding of motivation owes a great debt to addiction. The general hypothesis that has driven the use of drug addiction in understanding motivation is that drugs are said to hijack our natural reward systems. To obtain rewards is highly motivating, and pleasure may be one of those rewards that we are so keen to seek. By probing addiction, we are probing a motivational system. Addiction has directed us to dopamine with its undisputed role in the process. Our understanding of dopamine's role within the addiction process has evolved over the last four decades. Dopamine has moved from a simplistic elevation in response to a reward to being involved in the learning of probabilities about obtaining a reward or not. But dopamine does not sit in isolation within subcortical regions of the brain. The rich connections that dopamine facilitates bring to light the role of cortical functioning and cognitive processes that maintain drug-taking behaviour. The neurobiological understanding of addiction has moved forward rapidly. As always, there is much more to learn, but sadly scientific endeavour has yet to find its place within treatment and policy.

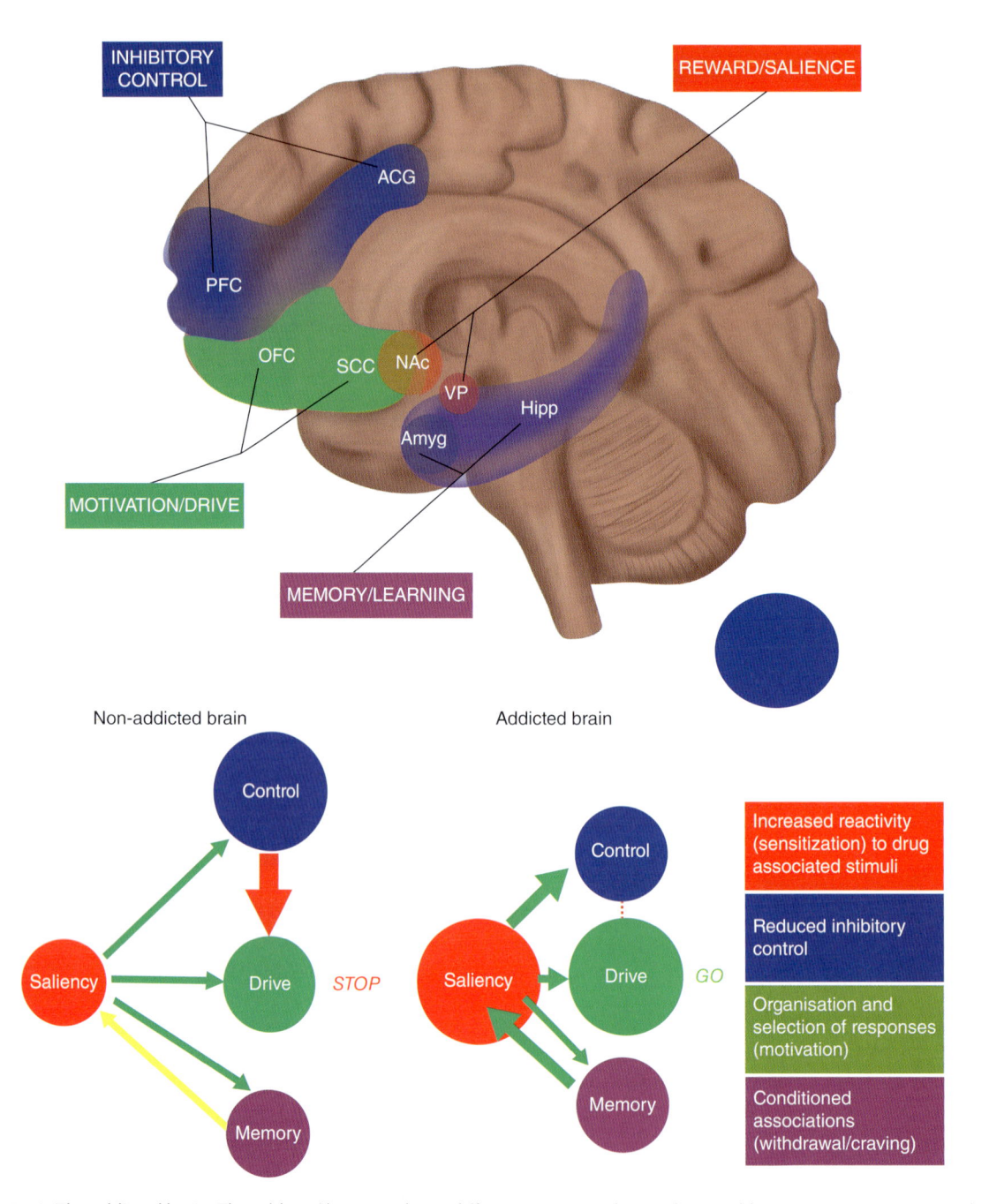

FIGURE 16.16 *The addicted brain. The addicted brain mediates different processes that make up addiction.* ACG, anterior cingulate gyrus; Amyg, amygdala; Hipp, hippocampus; NAcc, nucleus accumbens; OFC, orbitofrontal cortex; PFC, prefrontal cortex; SCC, subcallosal cortex; VP, ventral pallidum.
Source: Adapted from Volkow, N. D., Fowler, J. S., & Wang, G. J. (2004). The addicted human brain viewed in the light of imaging studies: Brain circuits and treatment strategies. *Neuropharmacology, 47*(Suppl 1), 3–13.

LEARNING OUTCOME QUESTIONS

You should be able to answer the following questions.
- Describe the purpose of studying addiction in relation to motivation.
- Provide an evolutionary account of addiction.
- Critically evaluate the role of dopamine in motivation.
- Compare and contrast the different theories of addiction.

FURTHER READING

Everitt, B. J., Belin, D., Economidou, D., Pelloux, Y., Dalley, J. W., & Robbins, T. W. (2008). Neural mechanisms underlying the vulnerability to develop compulsive drug-seeking habits and addiction. *Philosophical Transactions of the Royal Society of London B: Biological Sciences*, 363(1507), 3125–3135.

Haber, S. N., & Knutson, B. (2010). The reward circuit: linking primate anatomy and human imaging. *Neuropsychopharmacology*, 35(1), 4–26.

Koob, G. F., & Le Moal, M. (2006). *Neurobiology of addiction*. Amsterdam, Netherlands: Academic Press.

Munafo, M., & Albery, I. (Eds.). (2006). *Cognition and addiction*. Oxford, UK: Oxford University Press.

Nutt, D. J., Robbins, T. W., Stimson, G. V., Ince, M., & Jackson, A. (2006). *Drugs and the future: Brain science, addiction and society*. Burlington, MA: Academic Press.

Robinson, T. E., & Berridge, K. C. (2003). Addiction. *Annual Review of Psychology*, 54, 25–53.

Volkow, N. D., & Baler, R. D. (2014). Addiction science: Uncovering neurobiological complexity. *Neuropharmacology*, 76(Pt B), 235–249.

Volkow, N. D., Fowler, J. S., Wang, G. J., Baler, R., & Telang, F. (2009). Imaging dopamine's role in drug abuse and addiction. *Neuropharmacology*, 56(Suppl 1), 3–8.

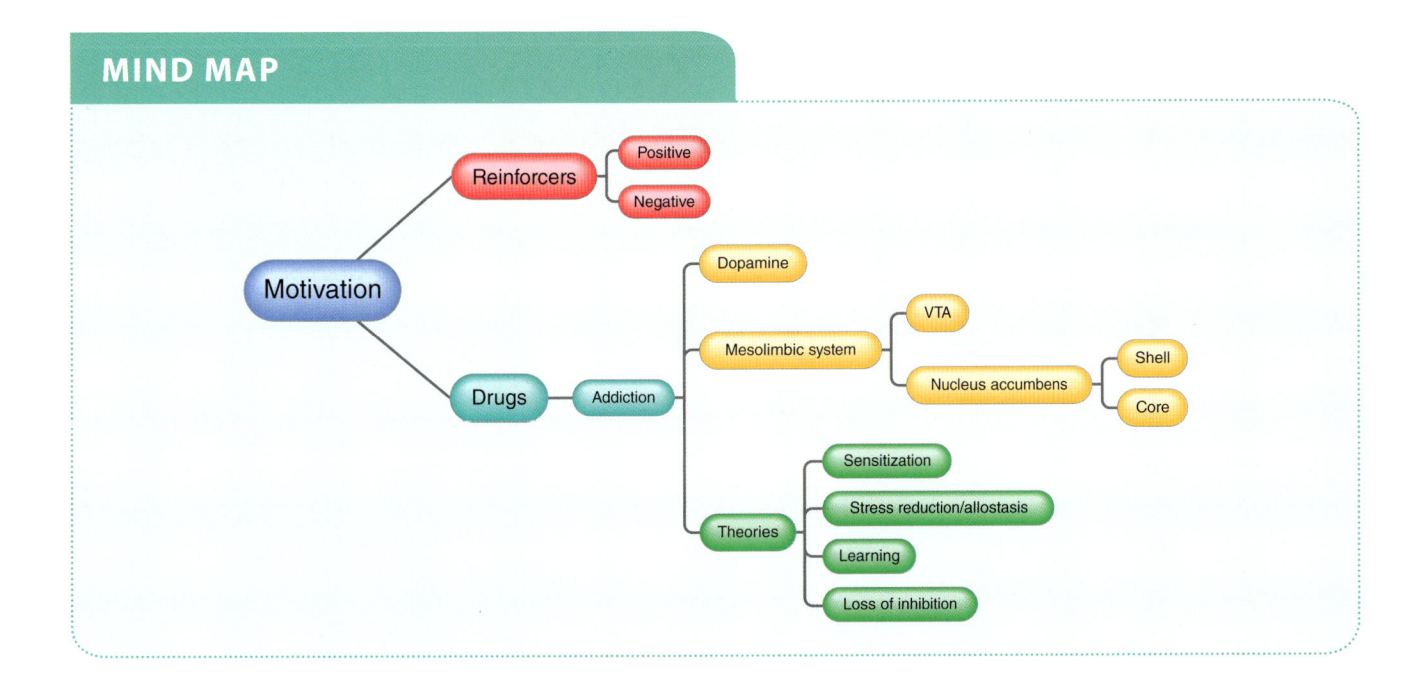

MIND MAP

- Motivation
  - Reinforcers
    - Positive
    - Negative
  - Drugs
    - Addiction
      - Dopamine
      - Mesolimbic system
        - VTA
        - Nucleus accumbens
          - Shell
          - Core
      - Theories
        - Sensitization
        - Stress reduction/allostasis
        - Learning
        - Loss of inhibition

17 Emotion

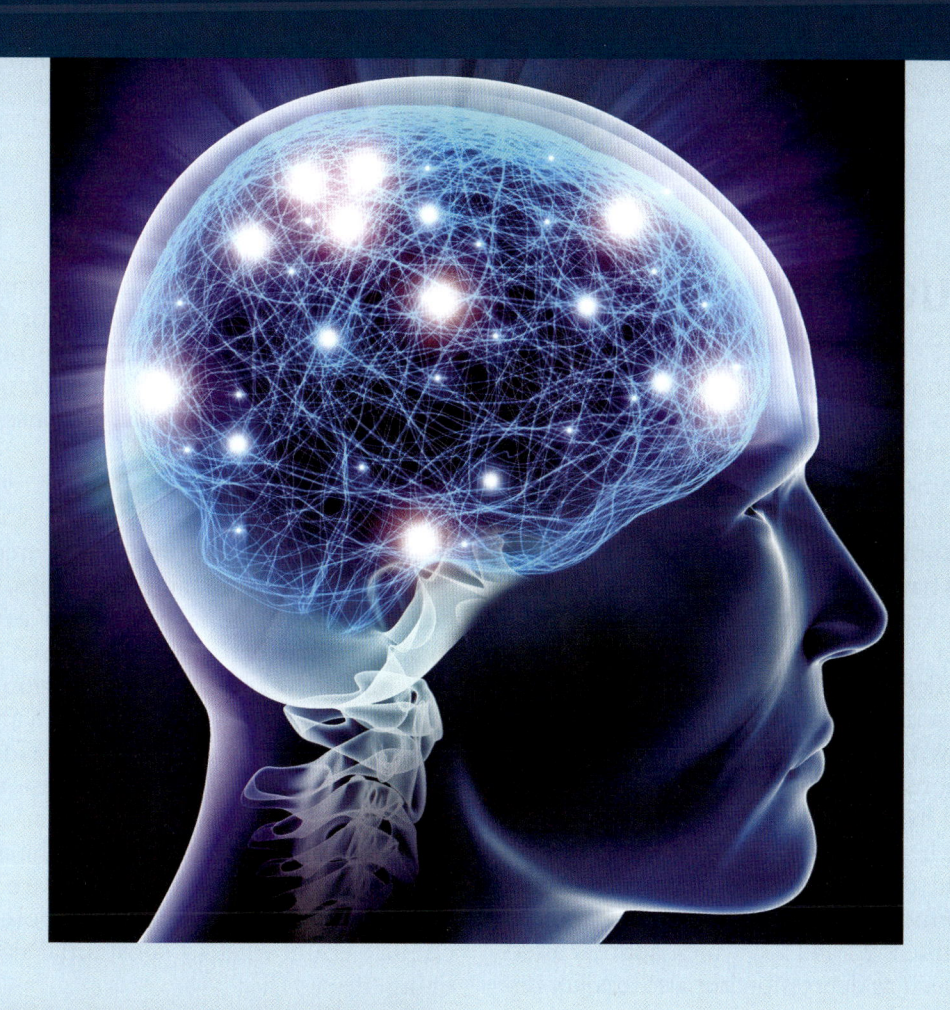

ANATOMY OF THE CHAPTER

This chapter will highlight the following.

- The evolutionary importance of emotions.
- The development of theories of emotion.
- The regions of the brain involved in emotions, especially fear.
- The consideration of love as a motivation and not an emotion.

INTRODUCTION   436

WHAT IS EMOTION?   436

FACIAL EXPRESSION   438

PHYSIOLOGICAL/PSYCHOLOGICAL THEORIES OF EMOTION   443

THE EMOTIONAL BRAIN   447

BEYOND FEAR   452

CONCEPTUAL ACT MODEL OF EMOTION   452

ROLLS' REINFORCEMENT MODEL OF EMOTION   454

THE SOMATIC MARKER HYPOTHESIS OF EMOTION   456

EMOTION: WHAT'S LOVE GOT TO DO WITH IT?   456

AGGRESSION AND VIOLENCE   458

STRESS   459

EMOTION AND MUSIC: BEYOND EMOTION AS AN EVOLUTIONARY ADAPTATION (OR NOT)   459

SUMMARY   461

LEARNING OUTCOMES

1. To understand why emotions have evolved and the adaptive functions they serve.
2. To be able to evaluate neural differences underlying emotion and the links with motivation.
3. To understand the theoretical positions that have been put forward to account for emotion.

INTRODUCTION

Our emotions make life a colourful experience; the ups and downs and the trials and tribulations of life can all be manifest in emotions. The conscious experience of emotion has troubled philosophers for centuries. Psychologists have attempted to provide theoretical accounts of emotions and more recently, neuroscientists have tried to ascertain the location of emotions. Although the subjective emotions reside in a single chapter within this textbook, emotion is far reaching and affects all aspects of life. Emotion can affect our decision making, it can guide motivation and it can go wrong. Emotion can be seen to have adaptive functions and helps us to survive, otherwise it would surely have been removed from the human genome. But when emotions go wrong, the effect is devastating and debilitating. Although the psychopathology of emotion is not key to this chapter, it underpins Chapters 22 and 23, which address affective disorders such as depression but also anxiety disorders, e.g. fear and stress.

When studying emotion, the first hurdle to overcome is defining what emotion actually is. This may seem simplistic because we are all familiar with emotional experiences, but is there a collective understanding of what love is, for example?

WHAT IS EMOTION?

We all have an idea of what love, anger, fear, etc. are. Emotions are complex experiences that involve cognition, affect and physiology. What happens when we are confronted by a fierce animal or a violent and aggressive human, for example? The cognitive part of the emotion identifies the stimulus as a fierce bear. The affective component of the emotion produces the feeling of fear and the physiological response is the activation of the sympathetic nervous system. This gets us ready for fight or flight. Although fight and flight are the behaviours that are typically addressed in discussion of the function of emotion, there are other responses: freeze, faint and/or flop (Box 17.1).

An evolutionary perspective was suggested by Charles Darwin (1872) as the same emotional responses tend to accompany particular emotions cross-culturally and across species. Darwin suggested that 'emotional expression' evolved in order to signal what behaviour an animal might engage in. Thus, the expression of emotions serves as an effective means of communication about intention and possible behaviour. When one looks at the animal world, the emotional expression of potential aggression is a valuable signal that can potentially avoid conflict if the recipient of the aggression has learned the signals and can therefore retreat. It also benefits the aggressor as any potential physical conflict could lead to substantial damage, threatening life.

Given that emotion is a cross-cultural phenomenon and that the expression of emotions via the somatic nervous system is universal, this chapter will focus on the neural mechanisms that underlie emotion.

Definitions of emotion are wide and varied but emotional responses have at least three components:

- subjective (e.g. the feeling);
- behavioural (e.g. facial expression); and
- physiological (e.g. autonomic responses including changes in heart rate, blood pressure and respiratory rate).

The latter two are more amenable to investigation in animals. The subjective nature of emotion, e.g. the feeling, is somewhat more difficult to ascertain and requires a degree of experimenter interpretation. Darwin (1872) noted that non-human primates had similar facial musculature and therefore are

BOX 17.1: FIGHT/FLIGHT/FREEZE/FAINT/FLOP

Lodrick (2007) provides evidence indicating that people respond in one (or more) of five ways when threatened (by a predator): fight, flight and freeze, plus 'friend' (e.g. seek help) and 'flop' (e.g. physical, but conscious collapse) (Ogden & Minton, 2000; Porges, 1995, 2004).

According to Porges' (2001) **polyvagal theory**, neural regulation of the autonomic nervous system (ANS) passes through three stages.

1. The primitive unmyelinated visceral vagus nerve mediates digestion and responds to threat by depressing metabolic activity. Behaviourally, the first stage is associated with immobilization behaviours.
2. The sympathetic nervous system (SNS) increases metabolic activity and inhibits the visceral vagus nerve to facilitate behaviours necessary for *fight* or *flight*.
3. In mammals, a myelinated vagus nerve can quickly alter cardiac activity to support engagement and disengagement with the environment. The mammalian vagus nerve is neuroanatomically linked to the cranial nerves that regulate social engagement via facial expression and vocalization.

Schauer and Elbert (2010) consider that responses to traumatic stress also go through a number of phases (see Figure 17.1.1).

- *Freeze.* Also referred to as attentive immobility in which an orienting response is exhibited and the animal/person stops what they are doing and searches the environment for the source of threat.
- *Flight.* If possible, the animal will flee so as to avoid conflict, but if this is not possible then one has to move to the next option
- *Fight.* Sympathetic activation mobilizes resources ready for combat when fleeing is not an option. However, there are circumstances in which fight will not be successful and the next option is required.
- *Fright.* Similar to freeze, fright is also called tonic immobility (or unresponsive immobility). It is different from freeze in that its purpose is not to gather information regarding the threat. Another phrase for tonic immobility is playing dead in which the animal is motionless but is receiving considerable sensory information about its situation (flop). This may have

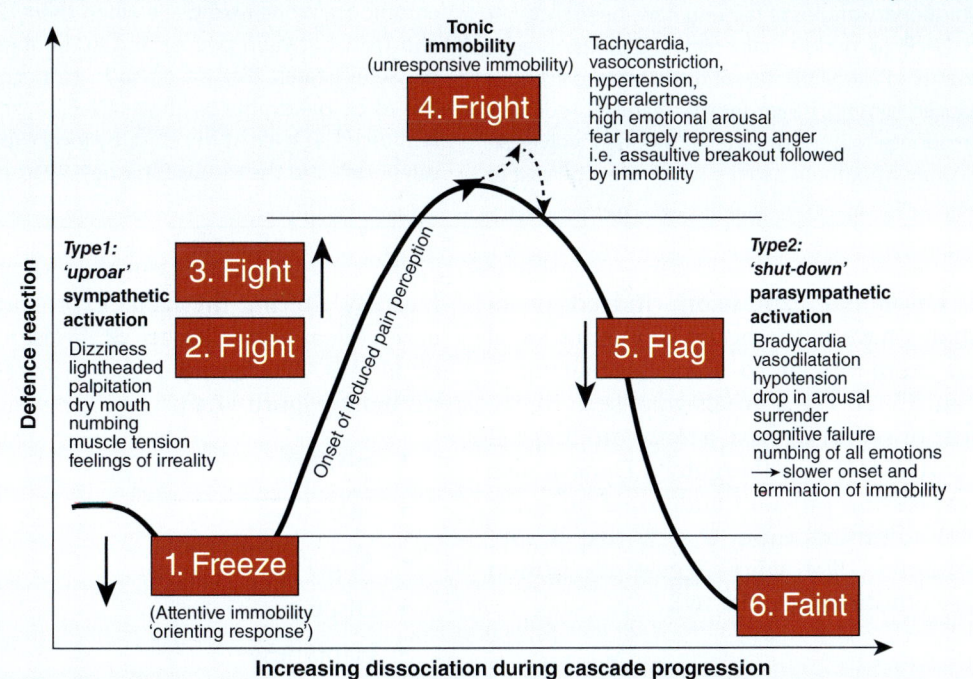

FIGURE 17.1.1 Schematic illustration of the defence cascade as it progresses. The 'uproar' sympathetic arousal reaches a maximum at the fright stage, eventually superseded by the onset of dissociative 'shutdown'.
Source: Schauer, M., & Elbert, T. (2010). Dissociation following traumatic stress. *Zeitschrift für Psychologie/Journal of Psychology*, 218(2), 109–127. Reproduced by permission from *Zeitschrift für Psychologie / Journal of Psychology* 2010; 218(2):109–127 ©2010 Hogrefe Publishing. www.hogrefe.com.

adaptive benefits as an animal feigning death may evade unwanted attention. Furthermore, by playing dead the predator may relax their grip, giving the victim the opportunity for escape.

- *Flag.* This occurs after fright and starts a 'shutdown' of activity via parasympathetic activation. Behaviourally, this will be seen as surrender and a numbing of emotions. There will be a drop in blood pressure and heart rate. An evolutionary argument for this is that hypertension and bradycardia lead to loss of consciousness as a result of global cerebrum hypoperfusion (Brignole et al., 2004) in which being horizontal ensures a blood supply to the brain (Schauer & Elbert, 2010).
- *Faint.* This is a loss of consciousness which is mediated through disgust (Curtis & Biran, 2001). It has been argued that disgust as an emotion evolved because it served a protective function from threats of infectious disease (Curtis et al., 2004). Fainting therefore protects the organism in advance from potentially infectious or noxious stimuli.

Early views that considered fainting as a defence mechanism to bloodletting have been found not to have credibility. The view had been that blood/injection/injury type phobias lead to fainting because they minimize blood loss (Engel, 1978). However, there has to be a 30% decrease in blood volume before fainting is experienced (Bracha, 2004).

The evolutionary origins of fainting have been thought to extend back to middle Palaeolithic periods. Bracha (2004) presents a Palaeolithic threat hypothesis to account for fear-induced fainting. He argues that fear-induced fainting was a response to human warfare. Fainting involves an increase in parasympathetic activity which is in contrast to what happens when involved in combat. If a person finds themselves on the losing side and sees approaching sharp objects, skin penetration or fresh blood, this signals the requirement for a new approach to survival. Increased sympathetic arousal is no longer effective. By fainting, the individual removes themselves as a potential threat, thereby sending a signal that they are not worth the fight. The survival value of this behaviour means that any genes conferring such an advantage get passed on to subsequent generations (Bracha, Bracha et al., 2005).

Continuing this evolutionary account of fainting, Bracha, Yoshioka et al. (2005) extend their hypothesis to pseudo-neurological symptoms (conversion symptoms) in which there is no real physical cause, e.g. limping, staggering, blindness, which all provide a visible sign of injury or disease. Such reactions to potential threats have been extended to account for the reactions seen in response to large-scale massacres. The phrase used is 'acute sociogenic illness' in which mass hysteria can lead to physical changes but without a physical origin (Bartholomew & Wessely, 2002). The changes that may occur in response to terrorism-like threats (or reports of flesh-eating bacteria) have been argued to be similar to the voodoo-like nocebo effect (see Chapter 9). According to Professor Simon Wessely (1987), acute hysterical reactions in mass hysteria occur all the time and vanish quickly once the truth about their cause has been discovered. However, chronic reactions take place when there is social trauma and trust between people and authorities is negligible. Wesseley states: 'For an episode to become chronic it has to be believable by those affected, and it has to be reinforced, at least at the start, by local experts, including physicians and the media' (Spinney, 2010, p.164).

capable of emotional expression. Indeed, non-human primates have been shown to exhibit facial patterns that seem similar to some human emotions (Redican, 1982). The animals were seen to grimace (e.g. fear or surprise), have a tense mouth (e.g. anger) and have a play face (laughter). Darwin also noted that expression provides additional information to verbal communication, a view that is supported by Fridlund (1994) who suggests the notion of six primary emotions (see below).

FACIAL EXPRESSION

A considerable amount of information about the emotional state of the organism is manifest in the face. By altering the facial expression, Paul Ekman and colleagues (Ekman & Friesen, 2003; Ekman et al., 1972) identified six 'primary emotions' in humans (Figure 17.1).

- Surprise
- Fear
- Anger
- Disgust
- Happiness
- Sadness

Additional emotions have also been considered.

- Contempt (Ekman & Friesen, 1986)
- Embarrassment/shame (Keltner, 1995; Keltner & Ekman, 2000)

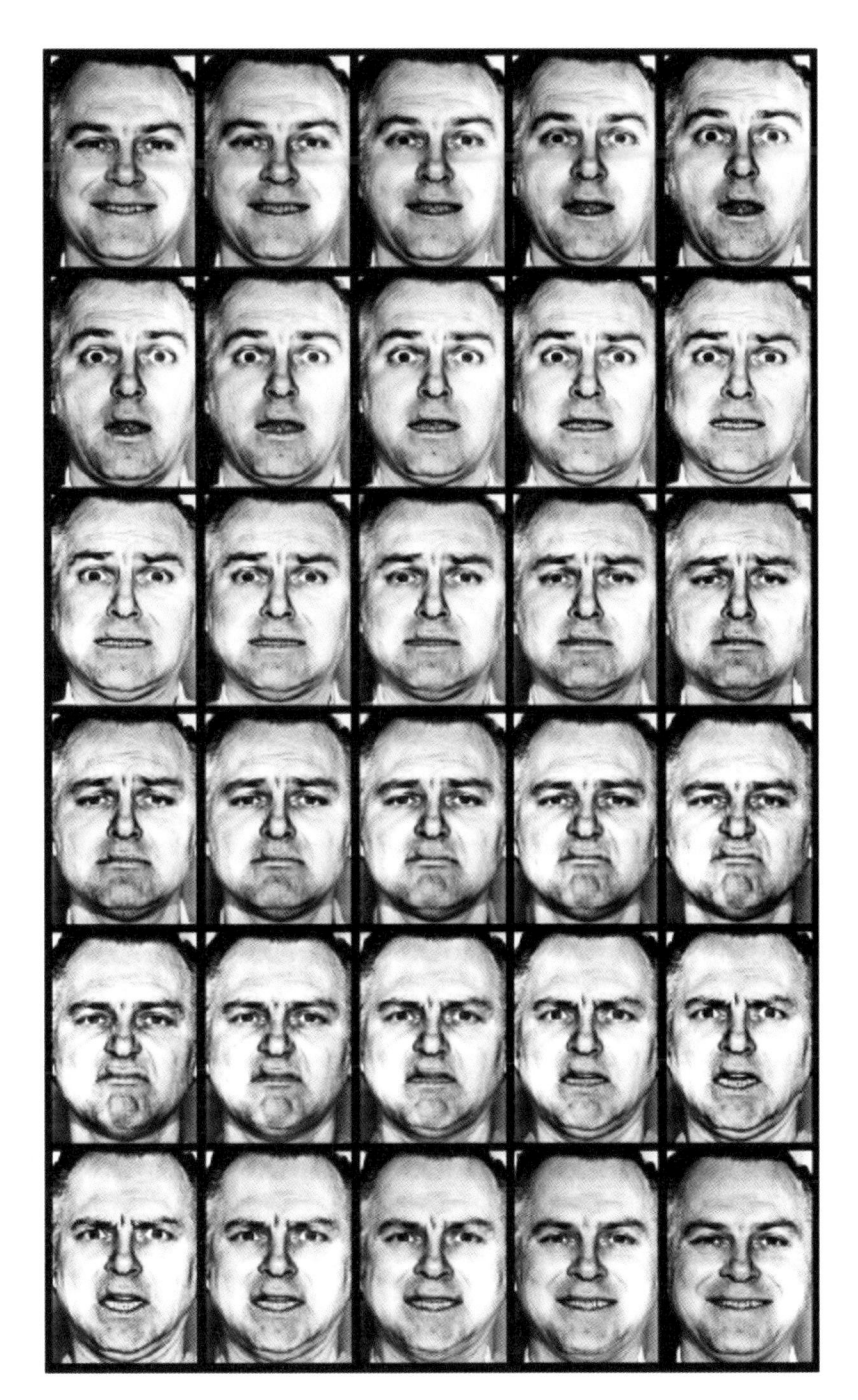

FIGURE 17.1 *Facial expression revealing emotions. The six rows of this illustration contain morphed (blended) continua ranging between the following six expression pairs. From top to bottom, the continua shown in each row are happiness–surprise (top row), surprise–fear (second row), fear–sadness (third row), sadness–disgust (fourth row), disgust–anger (fifth row), anger–happiness (bottom row). Going from left to right, the columns show 90%, 70%, 50%, 30% and 10% morphs along each continuum.*
Source: Reproduced by permission from Macmillan Publishers Ltd: NATURE REVIEWS NEUROSCIENCE Calder, A. J., Lawrence, A. D., & Young, A. W. (2001). Neuropsychology of fear and loathing. *Nature Reviews Neuroscience, 2*(5), 352-363 copyright 2001

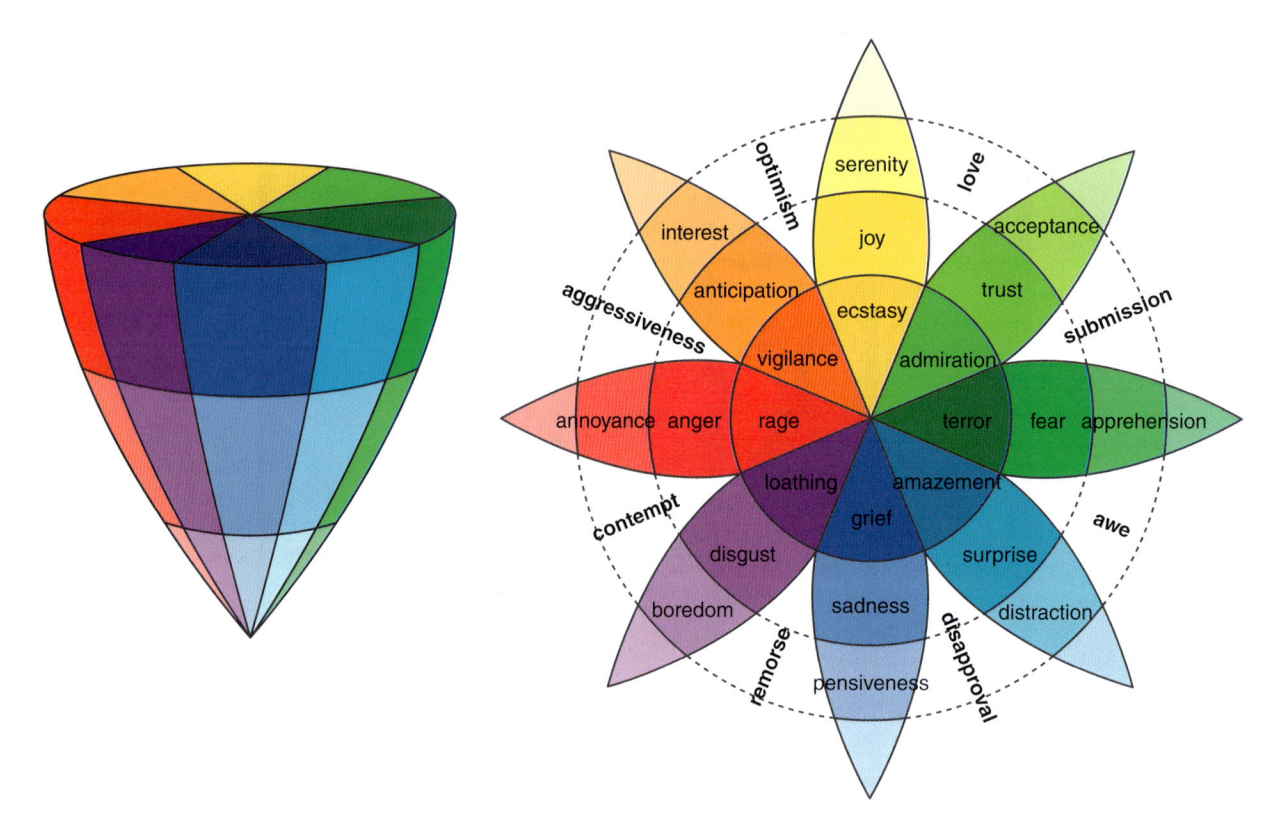

FIGURE 17.2 Plutchik's eight basic emotions with differing intensities (cone shape); the circles represent degrees of similarity between emotions.
Source: Plutchik, R. (2001). The nature of emotions. American Scientist, 89(4), 344–350.

These 6/8 primary emotions can make up the core of other more subtle emotions. The six primary emotions have been readily recognized in cross-cultural studies spanning western and Asian cultures (Ekman et al., 1987; Fridlund et al., 1987).

Plutchik (1994) provides a similar account but this view is one of emotions being on a continuum with extremes at either end. Plutchik (1994) argues that there are eight basic emotions that represent opposite-paired dimensions (e.g. joy being the opposite of sadness). All the different shades of emotion arise from combinations of these dimensional emotions (Figure 17.2).

The view of emotions as a dimension stems from early work by Wundt (1897) who suggested that emotional experience could be described along an effective continuum, e.g. pleasantness/unpleasantness, subdued/excited and relaxation/strain.

In a similar manner, Russell's (1980) circumplex model of affect viewed emotion on dimensions of pleasant/unpleasant and aroused/not aroused (Figure 17.3). Although there has been support for this model (Russell et al., 1989), the integrity of the dimensions has been called into

FIGURE 17.3 Russell's circumplex model of emotion.
Source: Based on Russell, J. A. (1980). A circumplex model of affect. Journal of Personality and Social Psychology, 39(6), 1161–1178.

CHAPTER 17 EMOTION   441

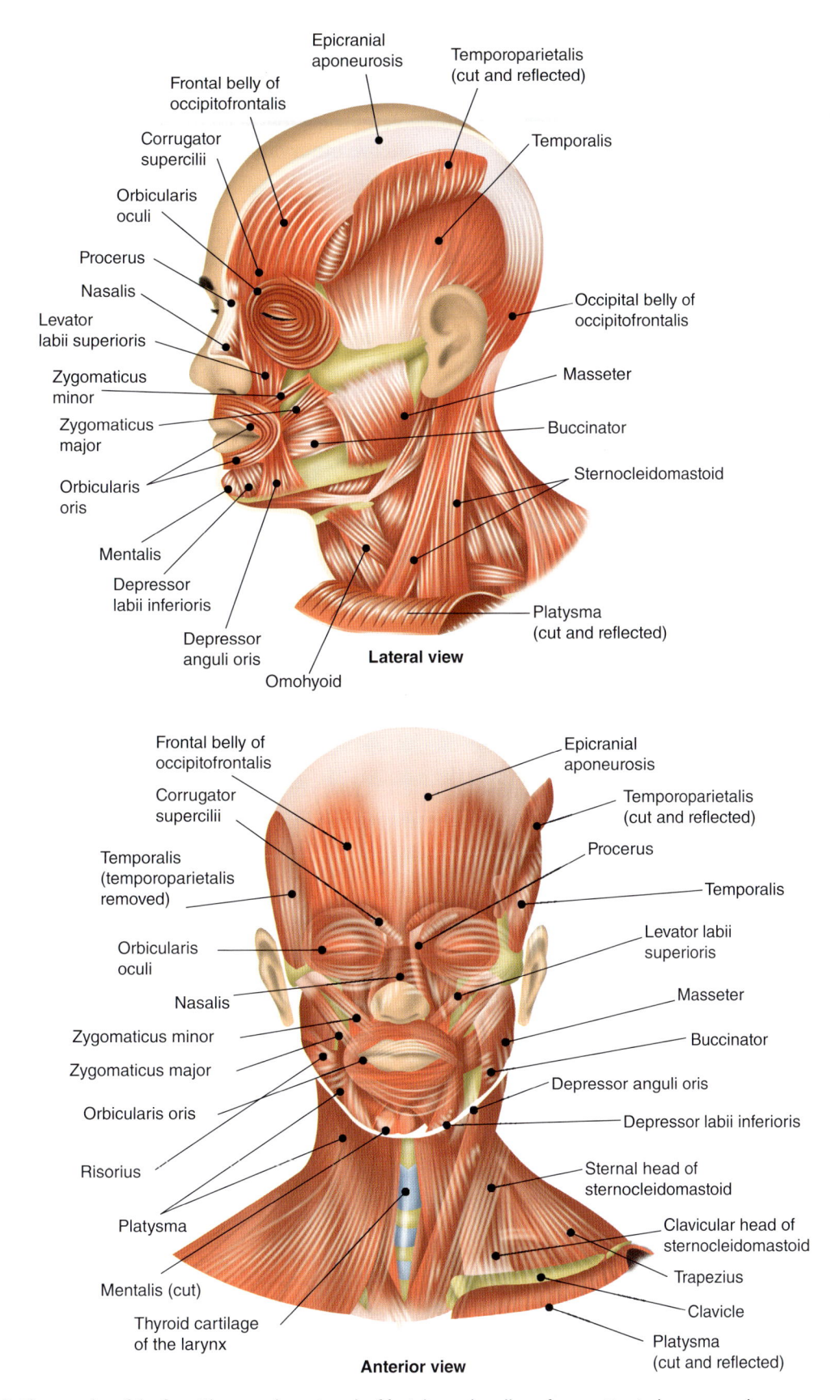

FIGURE 17.4 *The muscles of the face. The complex network of facial muscles allows for emotion to be expressed.*

question using statistical modelling which found substantial variability among opposing effective states, in which terms postulated to be in the positive-evaluation/high-arousal, no-evaluation/high-arousal, or no-evaluation/low-arousal areas failed to fall into their predicted regions (Remmington et al., 2000).

Changes in facial expression are brought about by a network of muscles. There are two types of facial muscles: superficial and deep. The **deep facial muscles** attach to bone and enable large movements such as chewing. **Superficial facial muscles** attach only to the skin and provide much of the subtlety in emotional expression and when they contract, they change the shape of the mouth, eyes and nose, etc. The numerous muscles of the face can be individually affected to bring about emotional expressions (Figure 17.4). For example, the **orbicularis oculi** and **zygomaticus muscles** are activated to produce a smile whereas the **corrugator muscle** is active during frowning in anger and the **levator labii superioris muscle** produces the grimace of disgust (Niedenthal, 2007). The muscles of the face are innervated by two cranial nerves: the facial nerve and the trigeminal nerve. The facial nerve innervates the superficial muscles whereas the trigeminal nerve innervates the deep facial muscles such as the temporalis.

The importance of facial expression in conveying emotion has given rise to the **facial feedback hypothesis** of emotion which states that feedback from facial expressions plays a causal role in the emotional experience (Buck, 1980; Zajonc et al., 1989). Being unable to recognize facial expressions, and therefore understand other people's perspective, leads to difficulties in prosocial behaviour. Such difficulties are seen in autistic spectrum disorders (Chapter 20) and alcoholism (Box 17.2).

Notions that emotion is a psychological expression of physiological changes have been pervasive in the literature on emotion. The very earliest theories posit a physiological basis of emotion.

BOX 17.2: ALCOHOL, ALCOHOLISM AND EMOTIONAL PROCESSING

Social processing, specifically emotional processing, is impaired in alcoholics. Emotional understanding (Philippot, Kornreich et al., 2003), emotional self-regulation (Khantzian, 2007) and emotional expression (Thorberg et al., 2009) are all believed to be linked to alcoholism. In general, social cognition is compromised due to brain damage caused through alcohol abuse, specifically in the right hemisphere (Oscar-Berman, 2000; Oscar-Berman & Marinkovic, 2003) and the frontal lobes (Moselhy et al., 2001; Uekermann et al., 2005). The right hemisphere plays a major role in social processing tasks and hence damage to this area is believed to be one reason why alcoholics (and drug users) may present with poor social skills (known as the right hemisphere hypothesis). The deficits in emotional processing are specific to the domain of emotion and not the results of general cognitive decline (Foisy et al., 2007), with alcohol having the greatest effect (Foisy et al., 2005).

There is evidence to suggest that some poor social processing may be the result of alcoholism. Research suggests alcoholism and poor social cognition may be explained by:

- *visuospatial deficits*: misidentification of emotions may arise because of poor cognitive processing which causes slow recognition and misidentification of facial expressions (Clark et al., 2007; Ellis & Oscar-Berman, 1989);

- *abnormal processing of social information*: as detected through slow response times and high rates of error in emotional processing tasks and a lack of inhibitory control. As frontal lobe function is compromised because of substance abuse, their ability to mediate activity from the amygdala is minimal and thus possibly relates to a bias in exaggerating emotions (Duka & Townshend, 2004); and

- *interpersonal feelings and stress*: linked with abnormal processing. For various reasons, one's own stress may not be dealt with well and may be compounded by subcortical damage, which may explain exaggerated or blunt responses to emotional stimuli (Philippot, Feldman et al., 2003).

Philippot et al. (1999) investigated whether alcoholics present a deficit in the processing of emotional expressions. Alcoholics made more errors, particularly in the case of identifying anger and disgust, which the authors describe as emotions of 'interpersonal interest' (emotions that are relevant to the alcoholic at the time and that they may be experiencing regularly) (Kornreich et al., 2002). Normally threatening faces are highly salient to the average person (Hansen & Hansen, 1988). Alcoholics rated the anger as more intense than control participants. Similarly, fearful faces were more prominent with alcoholics, who would rate neutral faces as expressing fear and difficulties in understanding other people's emotions (Cox et al., 2011, 2012). Duka and Townshend (2004) suggest that overestimates of facial emotions may be related to disruption with frontally mediated inhibition processes that would usually negate hyperemotional activity, thus resulting in an exaggerating bias.

Philippot et al. (1999) suggest that alcoholics overestimate the intensity of emotional expressions and this effect is most pronounced when the valence of the face is mild to moderate.

More recently, Kornreich et al. (2013) found that alcoholics have impaired ability to detect emotion in music compared with controls. Such research provides evidence that alcoholics show abnormal processing of emotions not only in facial stimuli tasks but also in other socially relevant domains. Kornreich et al. (2013) suggest that alcoholics exhibit a 'general' deficit in the processing of emotional information.

Maurage et al. (2007) studied the cross-modal relationship between alcoholism and emotional facial expression using visual and auditory stimuli. The expected result was that information presented cross-modally should enhance recognition of emotion as the information is enhanced by its volume and availability. Alcoholics made more errors than controls in the visual detection task, but not in the auditory task. Alcoholics were also slower overall compared to the control group. Moreover, results showed specifically that for controls only the cross-modal effect enhanced accuracy and speed of detection. Thus, for alcoholics the enhanced facilitation seen in normal controls had no effect or was detrimental in improving their performance.

Deficits in emotional face recognition have been shown to be persistent after a period of abstinence and therefore might represent a vulnerability factor for relapse (Kornreich et al., 2001). Increased activity of the anterior cingulate cortex (ACC) in alcoholics in response to aversive faces was seen to be a protective factor which enhanced therapeutic outcomes, leading the authors to suggest that emotional training might be a useful tool in the fight against relapse (Charlet et al., 2014).

PHYSIOLOGICAL/ PSYCHOLOGICAL THEORIES OF EMOTION

James–Lange Theory of Emotion

William James (1842–1910) and Carl Lange (1834–1900) both had a similar view on emotions. The theory that was to become known as the **James–Lange theory** is depicted in Figure 17.5a. Essentially, an emotionally salient stimulus is perceived (e.g. an aggressive male/bear/tiger, etc.); this leads to a set of physiological responses (e.g. increase in heart rate) that then determine the emotion experienced (e.g. fear).

Cannon–Bard Theory of Emotion

Walter Cannon (1927) criticized the James–Lange theory for several reasons.

- *Total separation of the viscera from the central nervous system (CNS) does not impair emotional behaviour observed in laboratory animals (therefore no feedback)*. Interruption of physiological feedback (e.g. after spinal injury) does not prevent emotions being experienced (Hohmann, 1966) but may limit the intensity felt (Lowe & Carroll, 1985). However, using more objective measures than self-rating of emotion, Cobos et al. (2002) found that there was no difference between participants with spinal cord injuries and control participants when rating emotional pictures. Furthermore, there was no difference in heart rate in both groups and no decrease in the emotional experience in the spinal cord injury group.

- *The same visceral changes occur in very different emotional states and also non-emotional states, e.g. fever* (therefore physiological changes are not specific to any one given emotion).

- *The viscera are somewhat insensitive structures* (therefore, it would be surprising if they were able to generate the subtleties of experienced emotion).

- *Visceral changes are too slow to be a source of emotional feeling* (does not make evolutionary sense – emotions need to be fast).

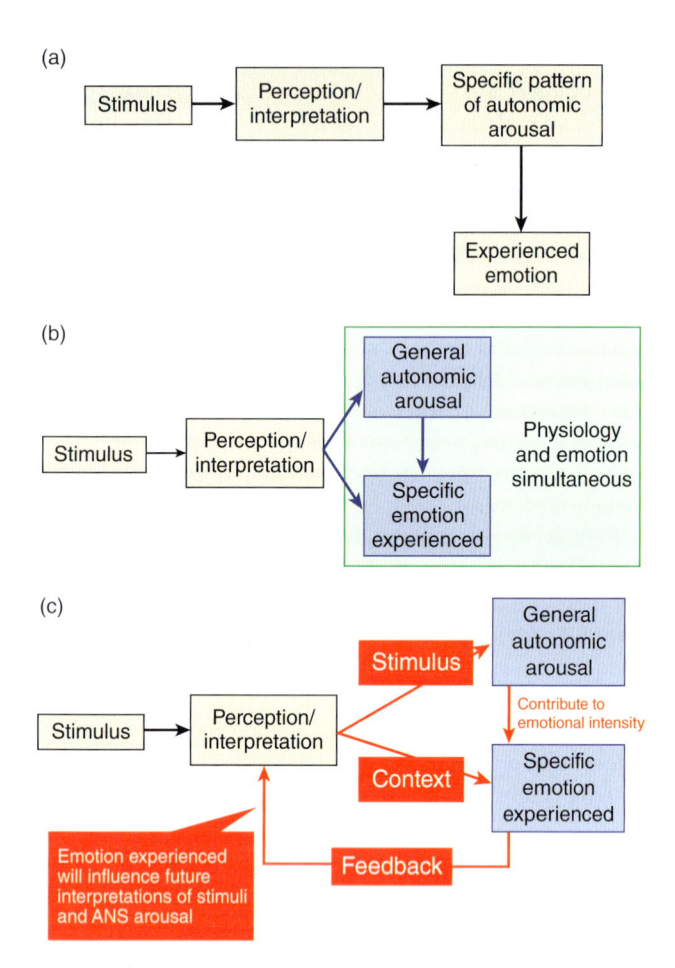

FIGURE 17.5 Psychological theories of emotion.
(a) James–Lange theory. (b) Cannon–Bard theory.
(c) Schachter's cognitive labelling theory. ANS, autonomic nervous system.

- *Artificial induction of the visceral changes typical of strong emotions does not actually produce emotional experience* (e.g. the majority of participants administered adrenaline only reported physical symptoms and those who did experience an affective change reported the emotions in terms of 'as if' emotions, i.e. they were not the real thing (Maranon, 1924).

Criticisms of the James–Lange theory provoked an alternative by Cannon (1927) and subsequently Philip Bard (1934). The **Cannon–Bard theory** uses the same 'boxes' as the James–Lange theory, but after the perception of the emotionally salient stimulus, both a physiological reaction and an emotional reaction occur simultaneously. This has clear implications for survival and can be seen as having an evolutionary advantage by increasing the speed of the fight or flight response.

The physiological change can adjust the intensity of the emotion felt, but not the affect. However, this theoretical position asserts the notion that physiological responses have no influence on the emotion being expressed. There is no evidence to support this. Cannon also subscribed to the view that the neuroanatomical basis of emotion resided in the thalamus. The thalamus is a structure that receives input from the sensory modalities and projects to cortical regions. It is easy to see why Cannon would suggest that the thalamus is involved, but the evidence does not support this. The independent processing stimuli with emotional valence by the cortex indicate that there is higher order processing in order to generate the experience of the emotion.

Not all of Cannon's criticisms remain valid. Some studies suggest that there are different physiological profiles for different emotional states, e.g. Ax (1953) showed that when comparing fear and anger, only half of the physiological measures were able to differentiate between the two emotional states (e.g. blood pressure, heart rate and skin conductance) (see Levenson (1992) for a review of differences in the ANS). In a review of 134 studies assessing the physiology of the ANS, Kreibig (2010) found support for the physiological specificity of emotion. The negative emotions were:

- anger;
- anxiety;
- disgust;
- embarrassment;
- fear; and
- sadness.

The positive emotions were:

- affection;
- amusement;
- contentment;
- happiness;
- joy;
- anticipatory pleasure;
- pride; and
- relief (safety).

The emotions without clear valence connotation were:

- surprise; and
- suspense.

The profile of the emotions is presented in Table 17.1. As can be seen, there are substantial differences

TABLE 17.1 *Profile of the emotions*

Physiological measure	Anger	Anxiety	Disgust	Embarrassment	Fear	Sadness	Affection	Amusement	Contentment	Happiness	Joy	Anticipatory pleasure	Pride	Relief	Surprise	Suspense
Heart rate	↑	↑	↑	↓	↑	↑↓	↑	↑↓	↓	↑	↑	↓	↑↓	↑	↑	↓
Heart rate variability	↓	↓	↑	↓	↓	↑↓		↑	↑↓	↓	↑	↑	–			
Left ventricular ejection time	↓		↓		↓	↑↓			↑	–	↓					
Finger pulse amplitude	↓	↓	↓	↓	↓	–		↓	–	↑↓	–			–		
Forehead temperature	↑↓	↑	↓		↑											
Finger temperature	↓	↓	↑↓		↓	↑↓	–				↑	↑			↑↓	
Stroke volume (the volume of blood pumped from one ventricle with each heart beat)	↑↓	–	↓	–	↓	↓		↓		–	↓					
Cardiac output	↑↓	↑↓	↓	–	↑	↑↓		↓		–	–		–			
Systolic blood pressure	↑	↑	↑	↑	↑	↑		↑		↑	↑					
Diastolic blood pressure	↑	↑	↑	↑	↑	↑		↑	↓	↑	–					
Mean arterial pressure		↑			↑	↑		↑	↓	↑						
Skin conductance response	↑	↑	↑	↑	↑	↓		↑	–				↑		↑	
Non-specific skin conductance response	↑	↑	↑	↑	↑			↑		↑	↑	↑			↓	↑
Skin conductance level	↑	↑	↑	↑	↑	↑↓	↑	↑	↓	↑	–	↑	↑	↓	↑	↑
Respiration rate	↑	↑	↑	↑	↑	↑↓	↑	↑	↑↓	↑	↑	↓	↑	↓	↓	↑
Expiratory time (time exhaling)	↓	↓	↓		↓	↓		↓	↓	↓		↓		↓		
Inspiratory time (time inhaling)	↓	↓	↑		↑	↓			↑	↓		↑↓		↑		↓
Tidal volume (the volume of air displaced between inhalation and exhalation)	↑↓	↓	↓		↑↓			↑↓	↑↓	↑↓		↓			↑	↑
Alpha-adrenergic activity	↑	↑	↑	↑	↑	↑		↑		↓						
Beta-adrenergic activity	↑	↑	↑	↑	↑	↑		↑	↓	↑						
Cholinergic activity	↑	↑	↑		↑	↓	↑	↑	↓	↑	↑		↑	↓	↑	↑
Vagal activity	↓	↓	↑	↓	↓	↑↓	↑	↑	↑↓	↓	↓	↑	–			

↑, increase in activity; ↓, decrease in activity; ↑↓, increase or decrease in activity depending upon methodology; – no change; **blank cell,** no data available.
Source: Based on Kreibig, S. D. (2010). Autonomic nervous system activity in emotion: A review. *Biological Psychology, 84*(3), 394–421.

across the emotions, depending on the measure being studied. With increasing sophistication in measuring ANS activity, a more detailed evaluation of physiological specificity to the emotions can be achieved.

Although the studies with spinal cord-injured individuals suggested that emotions could be experienced, albeit lacking intensity and linked to the height of the lesion, the participants talked about emotions 'as if' they had full intensity. They would report anger, for example, but lacking the drive or ferocity in that anger (Hohmann, 1966). Therefore, feedback is important to some parts of the emotional experience.

Schachter's Cognitive Labelling Theory of Emotion

Putting a contextual element, or cognitive appraisal, to emotional responses was demonstrated by a classic psychology experiment (Schachter & Singer, 1962).

The hypotheses of this study were that cognitive factors will determine emotional states, that physiological arousal that is explicable will not be attributed to the context or stimuli, and with the same cognitive context emotions will be described according to the physiological arousal. In order to do this, the authors manipulated three variables: physiological arousal, information about the physiological arousal, and the environment in which explanatory cognitions can be derived. The study was a case of deception in which participants were told that the authors were investigating the effects of a vitamin on vision when in fact they were not given a vitamin but rather were given adrenaline which increases arousal. Other participants received a placebo as a control drug. Information about the drugs that they were given was also manipulated in that they were either informed as to what the effects would be, misinformed about the drug effects or not informed at all. The third variable that was manipulated was the environment. To achieve this, the experiment involved a collaborator who was to act out one of two scenarios: anger inducing or euphoric environments.

Thus, in this experiment there were seven conditions.

1. A group given adrenaline and told of the effects (euphoria condition).
2. A group given adrenaline but not informed (euphoria condition).
3. A group given adrenaline and misinformed (euphoria condition).
4. A placebo group (euphoria condition).
5. A group given adrenaline and told of the effects (anger condition).
6. A group given adrenaline but not informed (anger condition).
7. A placebo group (anger condition).

The authors found that the groups who were informed about the drug were able to attribute the changes they experienced to the treatment. Those who were not provided information labelled the changes in terms of the cognitions available to them, either angry or euphoric. Thus, the emotion experienced is a product of the interpretation of the environment. In the placebo conditions, the level of emotion experienced was related to physiological arousal. Thus, according to the theory, there is a cognitive attribution of emotion in which the context is critical and physiological arousal increased the intensity of the emotion experienced.

In an experiment that took place on a suspension bridge that was fear arousing and compared to a suspension bridge that was not fear arousing, male passers-by were interviewed by an attractive female or a male (Dutton & Aron, 1974). The participants were asked to write stories and it was found that those participants interviewed by the attractive female on the fear-inducing suspension bridge produced stories with greater sexual content. They were also more likely to try and contact the interviewer after the experiment had finished. In contrast, there was no difference between the bridges when the passers-by were interviewed by a male. This study suggests that arousal (induced by the scary bridge) was misattributed to the female (an available cognition).

A study by Valins (1966) attempted to determine whether the labelling of emotional stimuli would be affected by biofeedback. In this study, male participants viewed slides of semi-nude females whilst hearing their own heart beat. However, the experiment manipulated heart rates to provide false feedback. The participants had to rate the slides according to the attractiveness of the females and those who received false feedback (either increased or decreased heart rate) rated the females as more attractive. Thus, false arousal can also be misattributed.

The cognitive appraisal model of emotion generated considerable interest and subsequent experimentation. However, a review by Reisenzein (1983) found there was little evidence to support the theory. The reviewed studies did not demonstrate that peripheral arousal was a necessary prerequisite for emotions, with reductions in arousal not leading to similar reductions in the intensity of the emotional state. Furthermore, there is no firm evidence to support the view that misattributed arousal to a neutral source was first considered as unexplained and then subsequently explained in terms of the available cognitions. However, there was some support for the view that misattributed arousal intensified emotional reactions.

All the theories of emotion have encompassed some bodily changes, but the emphasis was on processes and experience. They did not dwell on the involvement of the brain or which brain regions might be involved.

THE EMOTIONAL BRAIN

The psychological theories of emotion have supported a key role of physiological activity in determining or influencing the emotion. However, in general, the theories of emotion have not addressed a neural substrate of emotion. This is perhaps not surprising given the state of science during the period when the theories were constructed. Cannon did, however, provide a tentative suggestion that the thalamus was at the centre of the emotional experience. Perhaps this is not a bad guess, as the thalamus is a site of sensory integration in which emotionally provocative stimuli are processed (with the exception of olfaction – see Chapter 10). The thalamus clearly has a role in the circuitry of emotion, but that could be merely because it is involved in sensory perception of the world at large and not be specific to emotionally valent stimuli.

Shortly after Cannon's critique of William James and publication of his own theory, James Papez provided what could arguably be referred to as the first neuroscientific theory of emotion which identified specific regions of the brain. In summary, Papez states: 'Is emotion a magic product, or is it a physiologic process which depends on an anatomic mechanism?' (Papez, 1937, p.743). Although the question was asked in 1937, there is still some validity in asking it again even in the early 21st century.

There is still something magic about emotion (and absolutely everything else).

Papez Circuit

The initial proposal by Papez (1937) was a neural circuit for the expression of emotion. The route of information flow places the thalamus at the beginning of the chain of events. The thalamus receives the sensory input about the emotional stimulus. The thalamus then projects to the sensory cortices which process the emotionally valent stimulus further and communicate with the cingulate cortex. Simultaneously, the thalamus communicates with the hypothalamus (a nod to the Cannon–Bard theory) which implements the necessary mechanisms for the body's response but also projects to the anterior thalamus and then to the cingulate cortex.

The cingulate cortex provides output to the **hippocampus** and via the fornix back to the mammillary bodies of the hypothalamus. Thus, there are two routes of information flow in the **Papez circuit**: the cortical circuit and the thalamic circuit (Figure 17.6). The cortical circuit represents the thinking or perception of the emotion and a feeling circuit of the mamillothalamic tract.

Papez provided a framework for assessing the neuroanatomical basis of emotion. History dictates that although this was an important catalyst for subsequent research, the regions proposed have not all been as readily identified with emotional expression as originally considered (Dalgleish, 2004).

The Temporal Lobe and Limbic System in Emotion

After lesions of the medial temporal lobe, monkeys demonstrated a set of behaviours that became known as **Klüver–Bucy syndrome** (Klüver & Bucy, 1938). There are many behavioural consequences of such a lesion, e.g. hypersexuality and coprophagia (eating faeces). In the context of emotion, these monkeys did not demonstrate fear or hostility to humans. Prior to the surgery, they would act aggressively towards their keepers. However, now they were placid or tamed. The changes in the monkeys' emotional output were considered to be due to disruption of the Papez circuit.

With subsequent neuroanatomical investigation, other areas of the brain have been implicated, in

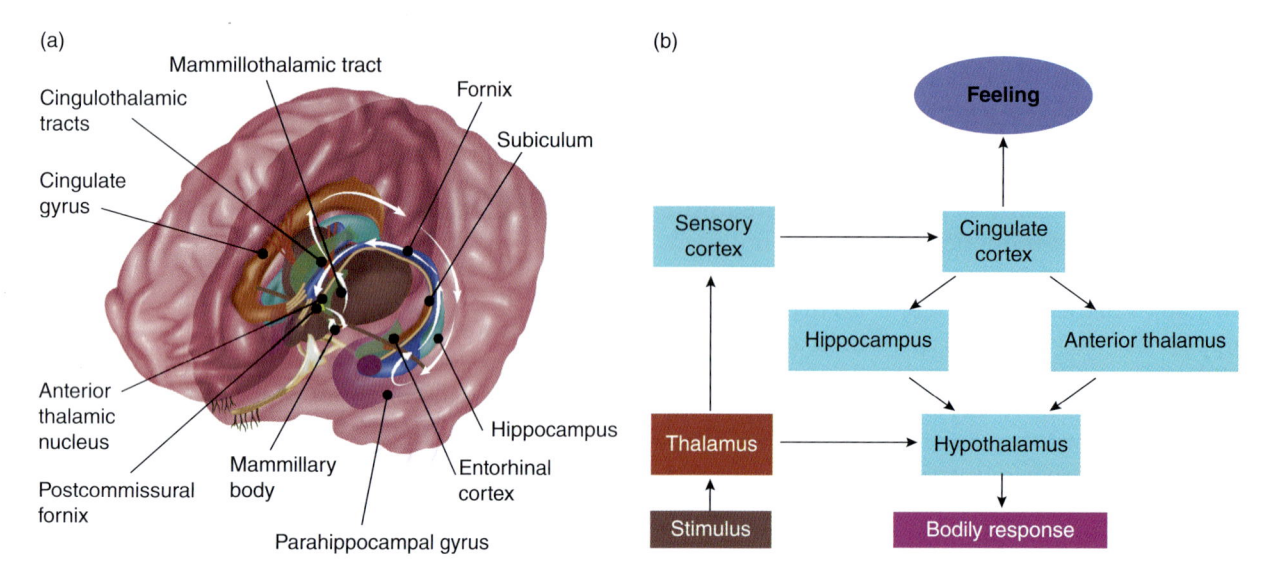

FIGURE 17.6 *Papez circuit. (a) Location in the brain. (b) Schematic representation of the circuit with input and output.*

particular the amygdala. Lesions, specifically to the amygdala, can account for the reduction in the fear response seen in Klüver–Bucy syndrome.

MacLean (1949) took the work of Papez, Cannon and Klüver–Bucy syndrome and extended it further. He saw primitive emotions (e.g. fear/aggression) as coming from the striatal regions and basal ganglia. Part of the brain was referred to by MacLean as the visceral brain, comprising the thalamus, hypothalamus, hippocampus, cingulate cortex, prefrontal cortex and the amygdala. The visceral brain enhances the primitive emotions. On top of all of these regions is the neocortex which integrates emotion with cognition, thus providing a controlling influence downstream to the other regions of the brain. The location of the visceral brain '. . . appears to be so strategically situated as to be able to correlate every form of internal and external perception' (MacLean, 1949, p.351). The visceral brain became known as the limbic system which is functionally identified as the emotional brain (MacLean, 1952).

Despite MacLean's assertion that '. . . one can no longer be content to think of dynamic psychologic phenomena as existing apart from the restrictions of ordered neural mechanisms' (1949, p.351), finding the evidence for specific regions of the brain is still ongoing.

The Amygdala

The **amygdala** is not one set of nuclei but rather a complex of different regions (see Chapter 5), and these different regions have different neuroanatomical connections. The medial nucleus receives input from the olfactory cortex and olfactory bulb. The **basolateral nuclei** receive input from the cortex, thalamus and hippocampus. The central nucleus receives input from the basolateral nuclei. The amygdala is the site of convergence for the integration of cortical and subcortical information. Thus, the amygdala receives a direct projection from the thalamus carrying the sensory information which can activate body systems without conscious awareness and a conscious route through the sensory cortex where magically the feeling of emotion is manifest (LeDoux, 2000).

The amygdala and fear

The amygdala's role in emotion has been championed by Joseph Ledoux at New York University. The central nucleus projects to a diverse set of brain regions (Figure 17.7) and unilateral removal of the amygdala in split-brain monkeys revealed the importance of this region (Downer, 1961). By cutting the communication of the hemispheres, stimuli presented to one eye could not be passed to the other hemisphere. Stimuli that would normally provoke an emotional reaction did not do so if they were presented to the side with the amygdala lesion. If the stimuli were presented to the intact side then an emotional response was seen.

In terms of neuroscientific exploration of emotion, one may consider that it is the exploration specifically of fear. Fear is seen in many species and clearly has an adaptive function in terms of flight/fight responses. In comparison to other emotions,

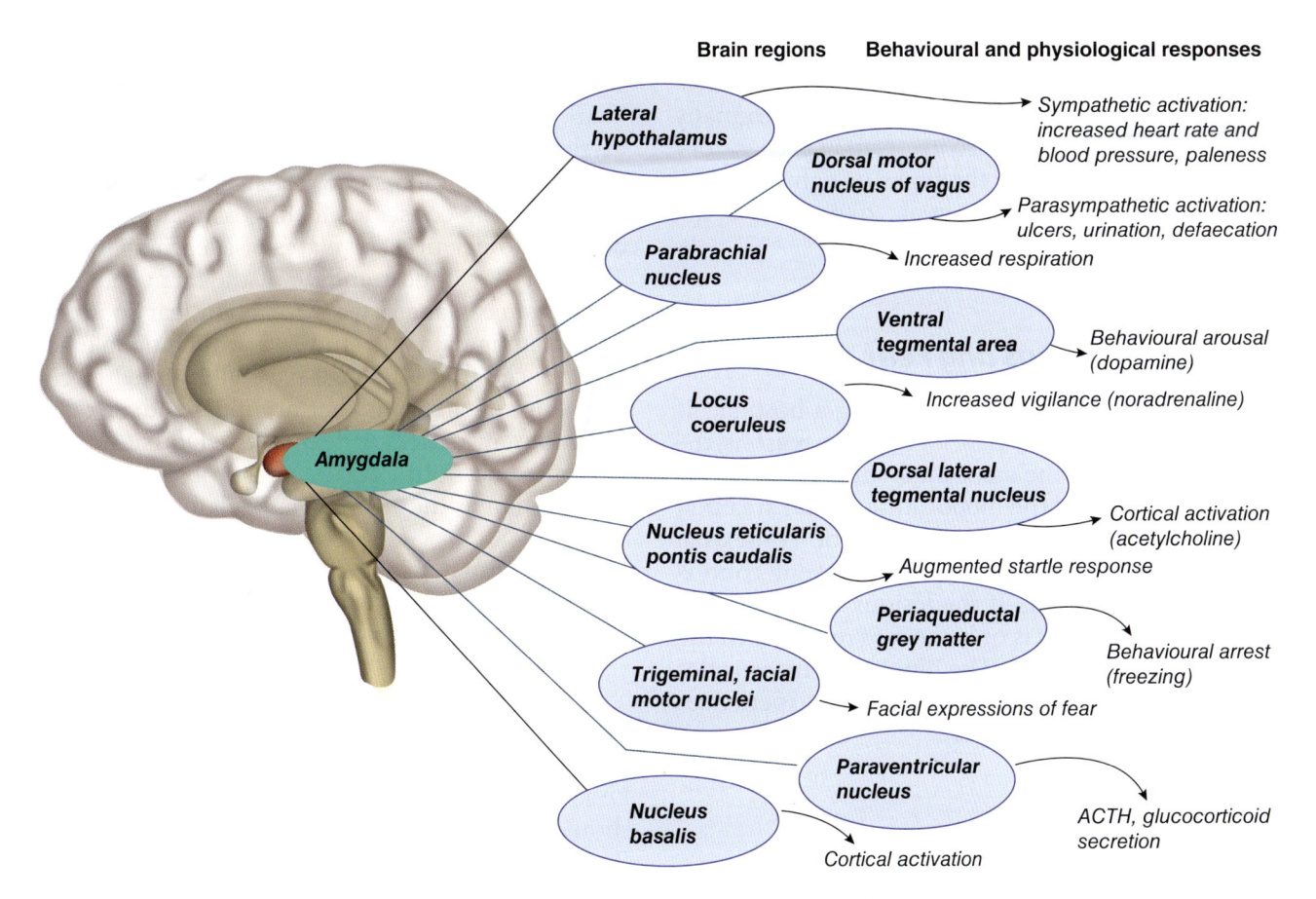

FIGURE 17.7 The amygdala and its connection and functions. ACTH=adrenocorticotrophic hormone.

fear is easily generated and is relatively unambiguous across species. A further advantage of studying fear is that it can be produced under controlled experimental conditions in animals, and therefore experiments can be performed that could not be undertaken in humans (LeDoux, 1998). Fear responses can be learned by animals (see the section in Chapter 8 on the conditioned emotional response (CER)). Using conditioning procedures to induce fear to an auditory stimulus, LeDoux's laboratory has been able to study the role of the amygdala. By systematically lesioning pathways within the brain that process auditory signals, the pathway that mediates the fear response can be traced. Lesions of the central amygdala prevent a CER developing, whereas lesions connecting cortical processing have no effect (LeDoux et al., 1988). Conversely, when the amygdala is stimulated, animals show signs of fear and agitation (Davis, 1992).

The lack of CER after damage to the amygdala can also be seen in humans (LaBar et al., 1995) and blood flow to the amygdala is increased when a cue associated with an aversive stimulus is presented (LaBar et al., 1998). Studies using functional magnetic resonance imaging (fMRI) have shown that the amygdala is activated in response to fear-inducing faces (Phillips et al., 1998) and during fear conditioning (Cheng et al., 2003). Lesions of the amygdala prevent negative facial expressions being rated as less favourable than positive facial expressions (Adolphs et al., 1998), and patients with lesions of the amygdala have trouble recognizing the emotional content of complex social scenes only when there is facial expression; they are not affected when the faces are erased (Adolphs & Tranel, 2003).

Positron emission tomography (PET) scans have revealed activation of the amygdala when participants have to recall the content of emotionally loaded films compared to neutral films (Cahill et al., 1996) or are shown threatening words (Isenberg et al., 1999). The experimental evidence supports a central role of the amygdala in emotion.

Despite the evidence for the role of the amygdala in negative emotions, such as fear, there is evidence to suggest that the earlier findings stating a reduction in amygdala activity in positive emotion were an artefact of experimental methodology using neuroimaging and lesions (Zald, 2003). Whilst activation of the amygdala is seen with input from many sensory modalities, it is also involved in preparatory responses that make up the flight or fight response (Cheng et al., 2006; Knight et al., 2005; Yaniv et al., 2004).

The Hippocampus and Fear

Many people feel fear when entering a hospital. If you have to attend a hospital for negative reasons, the hospital may become associated with fear. LeDoux (1998) has included the hippocampus as an area that is responsible for the conditioning of contextual fear. Lesions of the hippocampus prevent contextual fear conditioning. If the lesions are performed after conditioning, it is only the fear response to the context that is blocked. The hippocampus provides the memory for previous events and experiences (LeDoux, 1994) (Figure 17.8).

Fear or Fear Conditioning

The importance of fear conditioning in understanding the neuroanatomical regions and neural processes involved in the emotional experience of fear needs greater clarification (LeDoux, 2013). The question whether the animal in a conditioning experiment feels fear does not have an answer. Such introspective requirements are beyond non-human species. With fear conditioning, there is a procedure which brings about the behavioural change that can be readily quantified, measured and analysed.

LeDoux sees the problem as partly due to semantics and the general understanding of the term 'fear'. Fear conditioning represents the processes carried out by neural mechanisms in response to a conditioned stimulus (CS). Fear conditioning does not signal the conscious feeling of fear – it merely describes the neural correlates of a learning process. The everyday understanding of the term 'fear' then became an explanatory construct for fear conditioning. Imaging data and studies in which people have experienced brain damage have all pointed to conditioning mechanisms that are independent of the conscious awareness of fear (see LeDoux (2014) for a detailed account). Again, the problem with fear conditioning is the word 'fear' itself, but:

> The problem is not the terms but the way we use them. Specifically, problems arise when we conflate terms that refer to conscious experiences with those that refer to the processing of stimuli and control of responses and assume that the brain mechanisms that underlie the two kinds of processes are the same. (LeDoux, 2014, p.4)

Ledoux proposes that instead of using 'fear', he should have used the phrase 'threat conditioning'. Fear should be reserved for the conscious experience of feeling. Understanding of the conscious experience of fear becomes another question entirely. It is a question of consciousness in general and is referred to as the hard question (see Chapter 18). This hard question eludes an answer but provides fertile ground for philosophical discussions and neuroscientific endeavour.

Due to dissatisfaction with trying to understand emotion, LeDoux (2012) moved away from categorical accounts of emotion (e.g. fear) and their

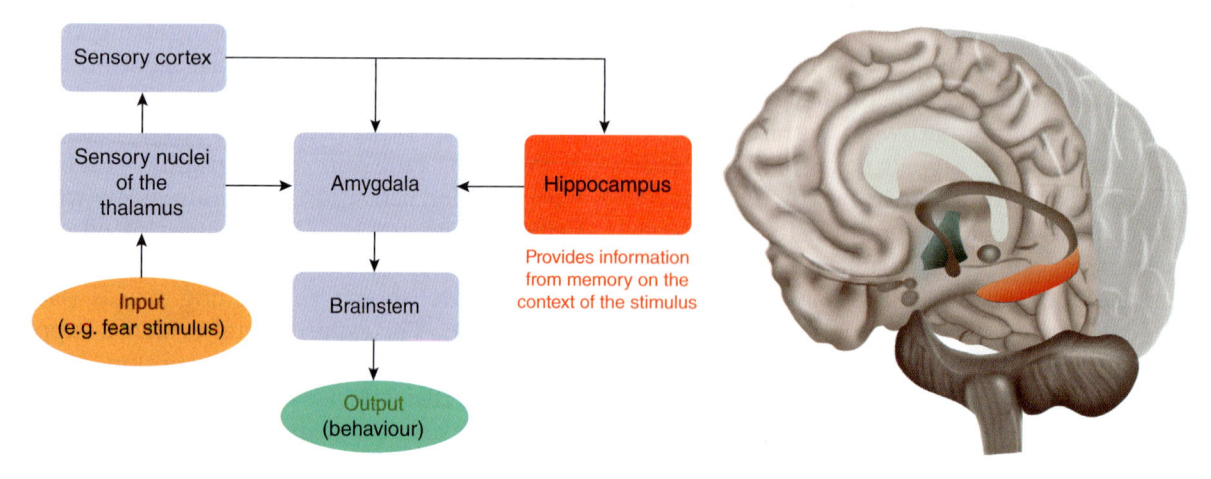

FIGURE 17.8 *The hippocampus and emotion.*

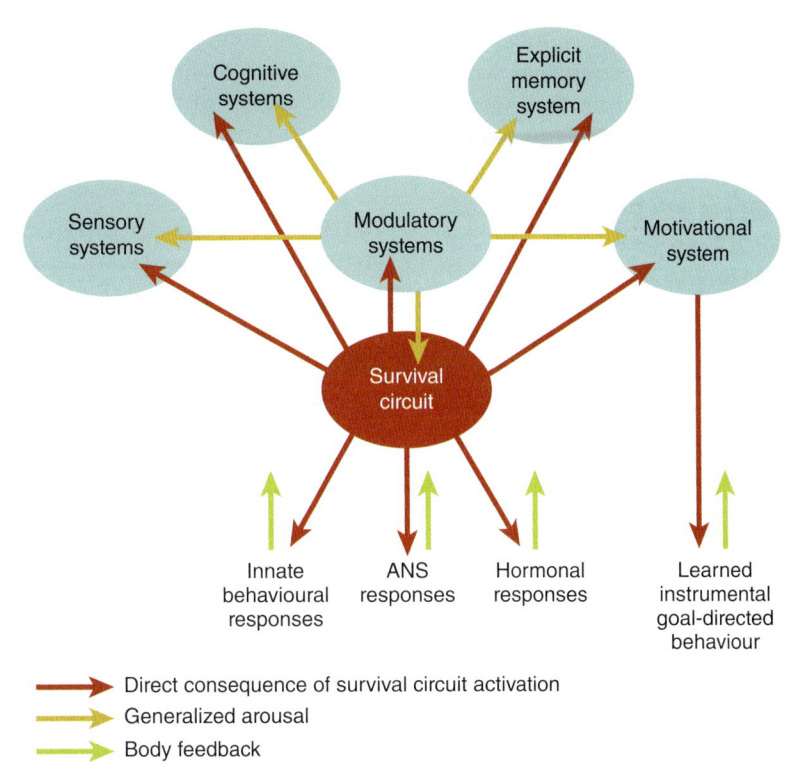

FIGURE 17.9 *LeDoux's survival circuit. When a trigger activates a survival circuit: (1) Innate behavioural, autonomic nervous system (ANS) and hormonal responses are activated, which generate feedback. (2) Neuromodulator systems are activated and regulate neurotransmission. (3) Goal-directed behaviour is initiated by the motivation system. (4) Sensory, cognitive and explicit memory systems are also affected, leading to enhanced attention to relevant stimuli and the formation of new explicit memories (the hippocampus and related cortical areas) and implicit memories (memories from the survival circuit).*
Source: LeDoux, J. (2012). Rethinking the emotional brain. *Neuron, 73*(4), 653–676.

specific location (the amygdala) towards a view of emotion that is derived from survival circuits (Figure 17.9). Survival circuits are evolutionary and include defence circuitry, reproductive circuitry and feeding circuitry.

According to LeDoux, survival circuitry has an indirect influence on emotions (feelings). It activates arousal systems within the central nervous system, autonomic nervous system and hormonal systems. Activation of survival circuits also initiates motivational systems which mediate goal-directed behaviour. Activation of the survival circuits and motivational circuits and the generalized increase in arousal produce a brain state that is purposeful in order to maintain survival. The brain therefore co-ordinates a diversity of resources that ensure survival. These brain states are referred to as global organismic states. When an animal is confronted with a dangerous situation, the global organismic state of fear will be activated; however, LeDoux referred to this as a defensive organismic state (LeDoux, 2014). Thus, a defensive organismic state is triggered by activity from survival circuits that detect threat.

Importantly, in this conceptualization of emotion, survival circuits can be either innate or learned. LeDoux elaborates on how survival circuits and global organismic states become conscious feelings. He does not consider that global organismic states are synonymous with feelings. He considers them to be part of the components of feelings but they can also exist in their own right without feelings. LeDoux argues that feelings occur in humans when 'consciousness (1) detects that survival circuits are active or witnesses the existence of a global organismic state initiated by the activation of a survival circuit in the presence of a particular kind of challenge or opportunity and (2) appraises and labels this state' (LeDoux, 2012, p.664).

As we shall see in Chapter 18, the neural correlates of consciousness are being evaluated, but how a neuron or a group of neurons produce conscious awareness is unknown. However, LeDoux gives a tentative account of how emotions become conscious experiences. He uses the concept of representation of experience in a cognitive workspace within cortical areas. Conscious feelings are therefore manifest when global organismic states are represented within the cognitive workspace. Thus, the global organismic state provides information about the stimulus, the environment, the survival circuit, arousal and memory (see Figure 17.9). The conscious experience of emotion is the bringing together of a considerable amount of information within the so-called cognitive workspace. There are clear similarities with the cognitive appraisal approach to emotion but without the overreliance on physiological arousal as a defining characteristic.

BEYOND FEAR

The relative ease with which fear can be produced in humans and non-humans has meant that this emotion has been the main focus of attention for researchers, and other emotions have not been as well studied. Despite the adaptive nature of fear and the tendency for a reductionistic perspective to suggest that it emanates from a phylogenetically old substrate, LeDoux (2014) concedes that 'the feeling of fear occurs in the same way as the feeling of compassion or pride – through cognitive processing of neural raw materials ' (p.6). Fear is easy to measure, but the measurement of positive emotions in animals also requires a behavioural output that is quantifiable. How do we assess whether the rat is happy? This question has occupied psychobiologists in an attempt to elucidate other emotions. It has been suggested that the ultrasonic vocalizations of rats (at 50 kHz) are indicative of social joy (Burgdorf & Panksepp, 2006; Panksepp, 2007). In future, this line of investigation may provide valuable insight into the neuroscience of other emotions.

CONCEPTUAL ACT MODEL OF EMOTION

According to Lisa Feldman Barrett:

> It is highly unlikely that each emotion emerged as its own mechanism, with its own selection pressures, along its own evolutionary path. It is inefficient to evolve a unique solution for every contingency. Instead, it is more likely that evolution produced a generative, multipurpose set of mechanisms that work together in each instance to produce a variety of emotional responses that are exquisitely tailored to each situation. (Barrett, 2011b, p.403)

Barrett continues to provide a psychological constructionist approach to understanding emotion: a conceptual act model (Barrett, 2005, 2006; Lindquist et al., 2012). This model sees emotion as a psychological phenomenon that requires socially shared conceptual knowledge to provide meaning about physiological changes.

The conceptual act model moves away from the Darwinian evolutionary account of specific emotions to a view that emotions as defined by words such as 'anger' correspond to mental events emerging from the interaction of basic psychological constructs. Barrett refers to the conceptual act model as having three general hypotheses.

- Emotions are mental events constructed, almost instantaneously, from psychological processes producing variations in 'core affect'. The core affect is the feeling of positive or negative affective states (pleasant or unpleasant). Core affect is therefore the mental representation of bodily sensations that inform the organism that something in the environment is important. Barrett sees that words of emotion, e.g. anger, can feel and look different between individuals and across cultures (Barrett, 2011a). The core affect consists of neurobiological states across the dimensions of pleasant to unpleasant (Figure 17.10). The importance of this dimension in Barrett's theory comes from the universal nature of this state. Core affect is the constant alteration in an organism's neurophysiology and somatovisceral state representing changing environmental events.

- Primitive psychological processes are not specific to emotion but are rather general processes for mental life. The combination of psychological primitive processes creates a variety of mental states which are commonly called emotions.

- Non-emotional factors such as concepts and language have an important role in determining emotion.

The changes in core affect as a result of incoming sensory information mean that the organism diverts

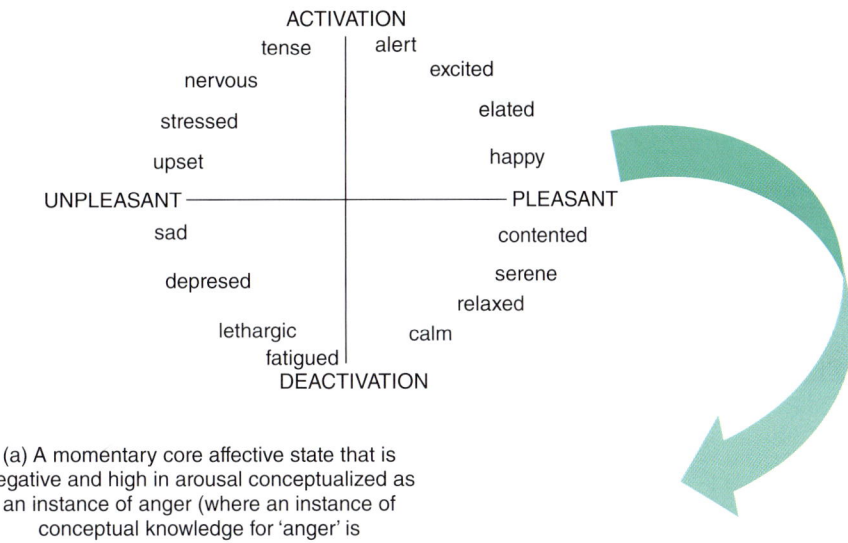

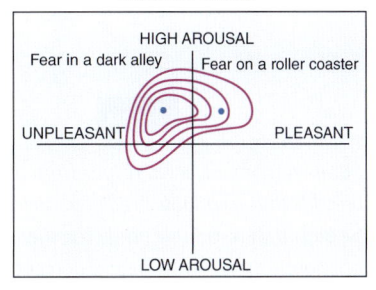

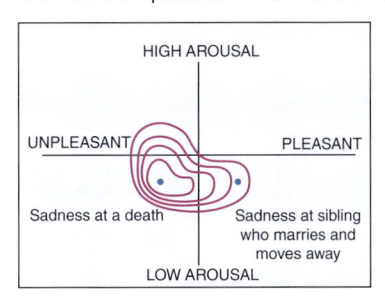

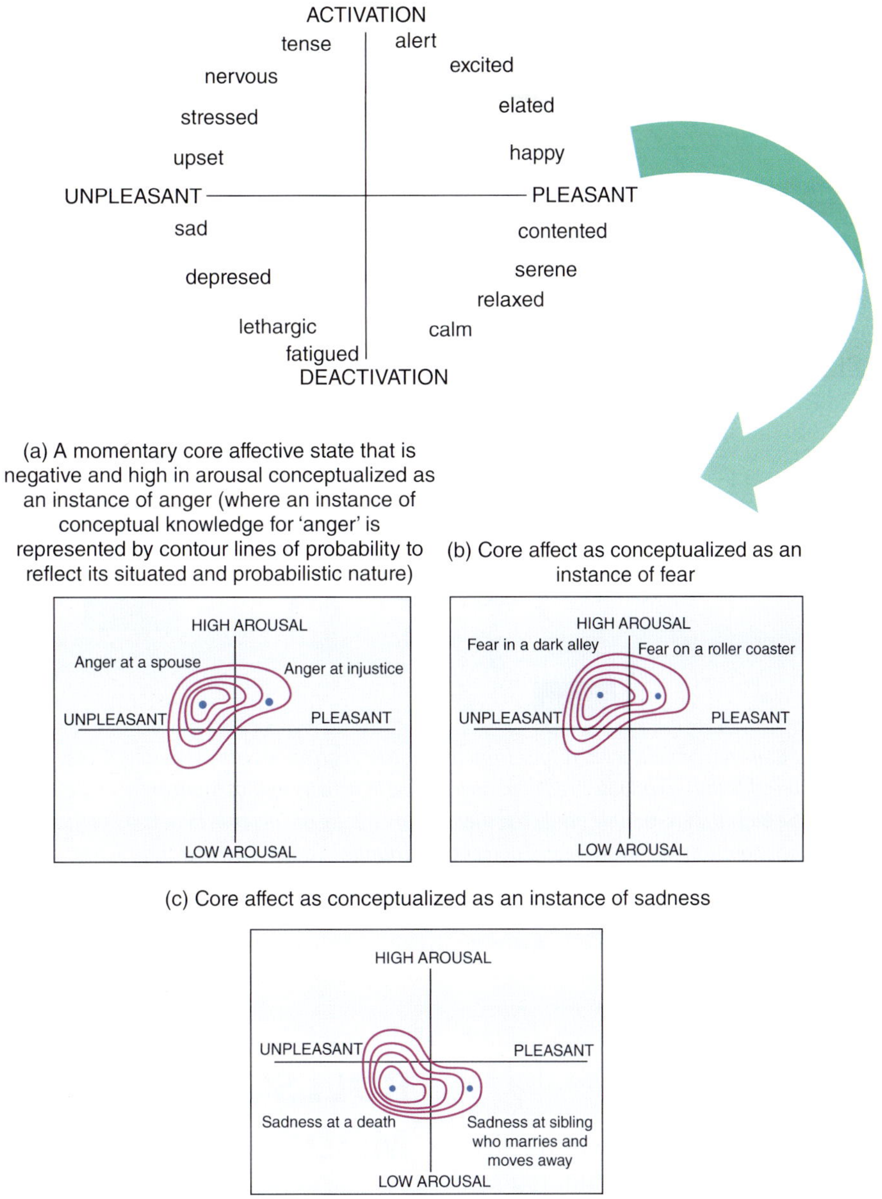

FIGURE 17.10 *Barrett's matrix of emotions. The basic matrix and its application to emotions.*
Source: Barrett, L. F. (2011). Constructing emotion. *Psychological Topics*, *20*, 359–380. Reproduced by permission of Faculty of Humanities and Sciences, University of Rijeka.

processing resources to the salient information and memories. The conceptual system of identifying emotion places categories of emotion onto changes in core affect. Thus, categorizing the emotions provides meaning to that conceptual experience. By categorization of the emotions, the individual provides meaning about their own world and can infer the intentions and views of other people's world. This clearly has an adaptive function in that understanding how other people see the world gives rise to our understanding of their intentions and possible behaviours. Barrett provides a figurative conceptualization of core affect along the dimensions of unpleasant to pleasant and high and low arousal (see Figure 17.10). These figures depicting anger, fear and sadness provide relief maps (as in geographical maps depicting altitude) for those individual emotions. The emotions described are therefore not discrete entities but are instead a collection of concepts for the emotion that can be combined in a number of diverse and flexible ways, e.g. different types of anger or different types of fear.

Barrett therefore sees emotion as the physiological changes brought about by perception of

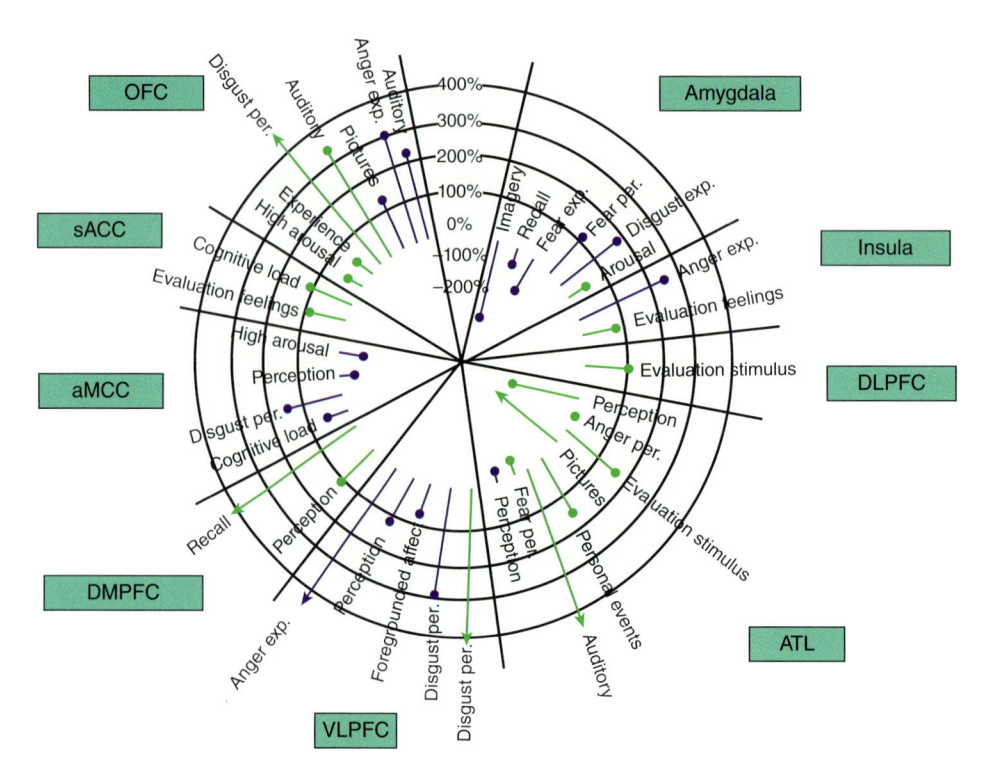

FIGURE 17.11 *Emotions and brain regions. Selected results from the logistic regressions are presented. Circles with positive values represent a 100% increase in the odds that a variable predicted an increase in activity in that brain area. Circles with negative values represent a 100% increase in the odds that a variable predicted there would not be an increase in activity in that brain area. Blue lines: left hemisphere. Green lines: right hemisphere. Arrow heads: percentage change in odds is greater than values represented in this figure. aMCC, anterior mid-cingulate cortex; ATL, anterior temporal lobe; DLPFC, dorsolateral prefrontal cortex; DMPFC, dorsomedial prefrontal cortex; OFC, orbitofrontal cortex; sACC, subgenual anterior cingulate cortex; VLPFC, ventrolateral prefrontal cortex.*
Source: Lindquist, K. A., Wager, T. D., Kober, H., Bliss-Moreau, E., & Barrett, L. F. (2012). The brain basis of emotion: A meta-analytic review. *Behavioral and Brain Sciences*, 35(3), 121–143, reproduced with permission.

stimuli along a dimension of pleasantness that are subsequently conceptualized as specific categorical emotions. A meta-analysis of neuroimaging data highlighted the importance of several brain regions being involved in different emotions (Lindquist et al., 2012). What is clear from this analysis is that a number of brain regions are altered during the expression of any one particular emotion (Figure 17.11). The conceptual act model therefore moves away from the idea of a specific location for each emotion towards a more complex network of connections.

Damasio et al. (2000) investigated the recall of happiness, sadness, anger and fear, and the number of brain regions that were activated during emotional experience differed from emotion to emotion. However, the mere identification of different regions of the brain does not necessarily give insight into how these regions are connected in emotion (Deshpande et al., 2012).

ROLLS' REINFORCEMENT MODEL OF EMOTION

Rolls provides an alternative account of emotion based on reinforcement and punishment. In order to understand Rolls' perspective, one first has to have his definition of emotion: 'Emotions are states elicited by rewards and punishers, that is, like instrumental reinforcers' (Rolls, 2005, p.11). Rolls sees emotions as states that are created along the same lines as the laws of operant learning (see Chapter 8). Many of the other theories of emotion have included learning but those theories, e.g. Ledoux's theory of fear, address the issues of classical conditioning. Rolls' theory does not discount the role of classical conditioning in the generation of emotion where the conditioned stimulus can provoke an emotional reaction. Rolls views emotion as a product of reward and punishment. In a similar vein to Barrett's view of pleasant and unpleasant emotions, Rolls considers pleasant emotions, e.g. happiness, to be rewarding. Conversely, we would seek to minimize and avoid stimuli that may provide aversive conditions and be punishers, e.g. fear.

The reinforcement model of emotion is depicted in Figure 17.12, in which positive emotions are associated with reward (S+) and negative emotions (e.g. fear) are associated with a punisher (S−). Along the horizontal axis are emotions associated with either the omission of reward or the omission of a punisher (S+ or S- respectively). The omission of a reward can lead to anger or frustration whereas the omission of a punisher results in the feeling of relief (signified as a ! in Figure 17.12). Although the studies of motivation and the coding of probability of reinforcement were not directly evaluating emotion, the underlying mechanisms of dopaminergic activity within the ventral striatum can be extrapolated to emotion (Rolls, 2005; Schultz et al., 1998, 2000; Spicer et al., 2007).

Rolls considers that different emotions are a product of different reinforcement contingencies and that the probabilities of reward affect the intensity of emotion experienced. The model also accounts for stimuli being able to produce different reinforcement associations, e.g. the presence of a stimulus indicates both reward and a punisher. When this occurs, states such as conflict or guilt can arise. For instance, an individual might experience positive reinforcing effects from the consumption of a chocolate bar but also the knowledge of the negative aspects of consumption leading to increased weight gain (especially when one is on a diet).

Different emotions will also arise because of the different primary reinforcers. For example, the positive reinforcing effects of food are different from the primary reinforcing effects of sex. Emotions can also be different because of the conditioned stimulus. Even if the reinforcement contingency and the unconditional reinforcer are identical emotions can still be different cognitions. This occurs if the conditioned stimuli are different, e.g. losing a bet might lead to frustration whereas being prevented from winning by somebody else may lead to anger. Thus, Rolls also has a role for cognitive appraisal. The expression of emotions can also be differentiated depending on the opportunities to express those emotions. The environmental conditions can therefore determine the emotion experienced, e.g. losing out on reward may lead to anger when the environment allows the behavioural response to be made whereas when that environment only allows for passive behaviour, the resultant emotion may be more akin to sadness or depression.

Rolls continues to elaborate on the theory, suggesting the following.

- The reinforcing stimuli that are relevant to a particular motivational state (e.g. taste and hunger) are not classified as emotional stimuli.

- Emotional states can be produced by remembered reinforcing stimuli.

- The stimulus that produces the emotional state only has to have reinforcing properties, i.e. it can be either a reward or a punisher. It is the association that is important.

- Cognitive processes are required to determine if the stimulus is a reward or punisher.

- The primary (and learned) reinforcers, e.g. pain, do not produce emotion but the secondary reinforcers (e.g. stimuli associated with pain) do produce emotion (e.g. fear). Thus, describing emotion in terms of reinforcement contingencies is more appropriate because the primary and secondary reinforcers produce affective emotional states.

- Emotional states have many functions and only some of those functions are associated with emotional feelings.

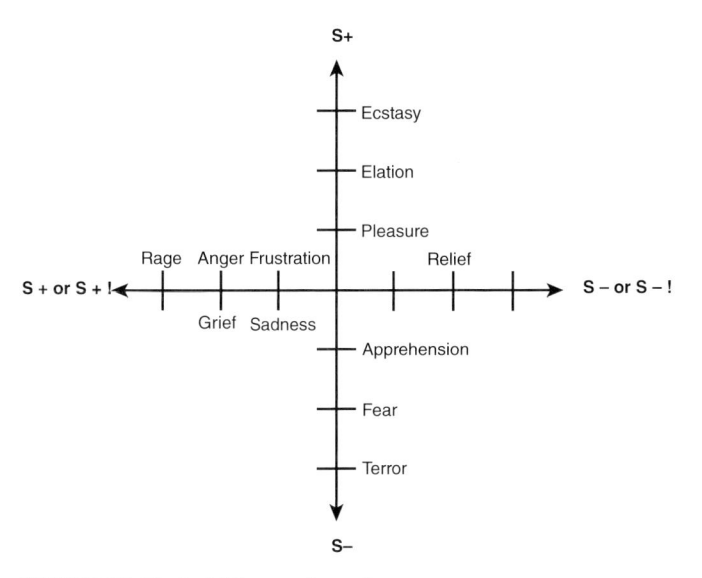

FIGURE 17.12 Rolls' theory of emotion.
Source: Rolls, E. T. (2005). *Emotion explained*. Oxford, UK: Oxford University Press.

- Learning is critically important as it is the association of a stimulus with the reinforcer that occurs when an emotional response is learned.
- Understanding the nature of emotions requires understanding of the function of emotions. Rolls argues that emotions can be explained according to gene-specified goals and that our use of language and symbolism as descriptors of emotional states might provide distance from those goals.

Rolls identifies the orbitofrontal cortex, amygdala and cingulate cortex as particularly important regions in processing emotion. The orbitofrontal cortex permits flexibility of emotional behaviour and is sensitive to changes in reinforcement. Within the orbitofrontal cortex there is a representation of cognitive inputs and the reinforcing states. The orbitofrontal cortex considers a representation of the different reinforcement values of stimuli. Action selection on the basis of the orbitofrontal cortex choice is initiated by the cingulate cortex. The cingulate cortex is argued to receive inputs about reward expectation and about actual rewards received from the orbitofrontal cortex and amygdala. The anterior cingulate cortex may then compare signals from the orbitofrontal cortex and amygdala in order to guide decision making.

The amygdala has less of a role in Rolls' theory of emotion. It may be involved in the conditioned associations between primary reinforcers and associated stimuli which can give rise to autonomic responses as described by LeDoux.

THE SOMATIC MARKER HYPOTHESIS OF EMOTION

Antonio Damasio (2008) distinguishes between emotions and feelings of emotions. He argues that the feeling of emotion or 'feelings' is a term that should only be used for the subjective mental experience of emotion, whereas the term 'emotion' should refer to all the processes involved in emotion, e.g. the physiological state (Damasio, 2002). Thus, a distinction is made between the measurable/observable and the introspective/non-observable. Damasio's theory of emotion is derived from his work looking at brain-damaged patients (prefrontal cortex) who were cognitively able but their personal decisions were ill judged and did not appear to make sense (Damasio, 1996). This theory also involves reinforcement; when a reinforcer is evaluated, the body responds according to the evaluation (the somatic marker). The change in the body leads to changing feelings that determine a course of action to be taken. Thus, emotional decision making is influenced by peripheral feedback from the body. Rolls (2012) is somewhat scathing of this theory and suggests it is just a re-emergence of the James–Lange theory, the criticisms of which remain valid.

EMOTION: WHAT'S LOVE GOT TO DO WITH IT?

Bartels and Zeki (2000) investigated the brain activation of people who claimed to be in love. When looking at pictures of their loved ones, there was an increase of activity in the anterior cingulate cortex and the striatum (Figure 17.13). This was accompanied by a reduction of activity in the amygdala. Subsequent studies investigating love have indicated that love is associated with activation of brain reward mechanisms (Aron et al., 2005; Bartels & Zeki, 2004). Regions such as the ventral tegmental area and the nucleus accumbens that have been considered central to motivational pathways of the brain have all been shown to light up in imaging studies assessing the neurocorrelates of love (Aron et al., 2005; Fisher et al., 2005). From the imaging data on love, Fisher argues that romantic love has similarities with attraction which has been considered to have evolved to direct mating energy at specific individuals (Fisher et al., 2005). Interestingly, no differences in the brain regions activated by love were found between heterosexual and homosexual men and women (Zeki & Romaya, 2010).

Such studies might lead us to question love as an emotion and instead consider it as a motivation akin to a positive reinforcer which aids the continuation of the species (Aron et al., 2005; Esch & Stefano, 2005; Fisher et al., 2005, 2006). Not surprisingly, the identification of a neuroanatomical site has provoked some degree of philosophical debate about the use of brain imaging and the definitions of constructs such as love (Fusar-Poli & Broome, 2006, 2007). After all, what is love?

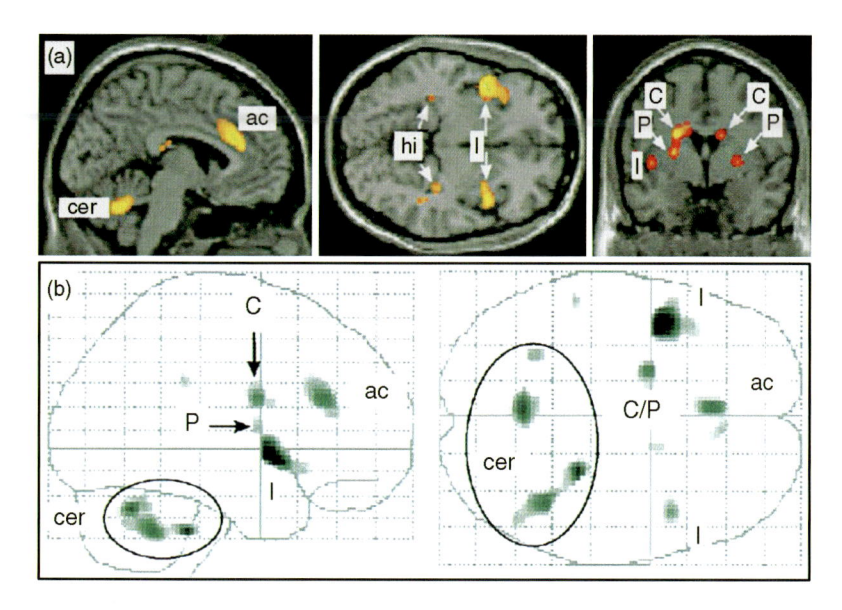

FIGURE 17.13 *Love regions of the brain. Activity when subjects viewed pictures of their loved partner versus pictures of friends. The activity, restricted to only a few areas, is shown in (a) sagittal, transverse and coronal sections and (b) in glassbrain projections. ac, anterior cingulate; cer, cerebellum; I, insula; hi, posterior hippocampus and the coronal section activity in caudate nucleus (C) and putamen (P).*
Source: Bartels, A., & Zeki, S. (2000). The neural basis of romantic love. Neuroreport, 11(17), 3829–3834.

In the neurochemistry of love, **cortisol** levels rise leading to an increase in arousal levels (Marazziti & Canale, 2004). In addition, **oxytocin** and **vasopressin** are released (Esch & Stefano, 2005). The effects of oxytocin and vasopressin on prosocial behaviours and love can be seen in Table 17.2. Testosterone also changes in those who are in love, with a decrease in males and an increase in females, which is thought to reduce the polarity of the sexes (Marazziti & Canale, 2004). **Endorphins** and **enkephalins** are also involved in the love response, as is dopamine (DA) (Esch & Stefano, 2005). The involvement of these neurotransmitters in love also suggests a role for motivation.

Love is the Drug

If we consider love not to be an emotion but rather a motivation, then a comparison with drugs of abuse appears more appropriate. There are some similarities between addiction and love (Burkett & Young, 2012).

- People in love feel protective of the one they love and will do anything for them. Addicts will do anything to get a drug.
- Motivation is centred around that person at the expense of other responsibilities, e.g. other friends are no longer as important as they once were. The drug addict's world shrinks as the focus on the drug increases.
- Obsessive thoughts concerning the loved one are common.
- The lover becomes salient in everyday occurrences. The drug addict is likely to see opportunities for drugs in the environment to a greater extent than anything else.
- Stimuli that one ordinarily would not attend to suddenly make one think of the loved one (e.g. a scent). Stimuli associated with the drug are powerful mediators of the addiction process.
- When one is in love, the pleasure parts of the brain are activated. Elevated levels of dopamine are seen within the mesolimbic system in response to the administration of the drug and its conditioned stimuli.
- The longer a couple are together, the more their brains become tolerant to the hormones being released, which causes the euphoric feeling not to be felt as strongly. Allostasis

TABLE 17.2 *The effects of oxytocin and vasopressin on prosocial behaviours and love*

Oxytocin		Vasopressin	
Social contact induction	↑	Positive social behaviours	↑
Formation of partner preferences	↑	Partner selection	↑
Parents' social bonding	↑	Formation of social attachments	↑
Aggression	↓	Territorial behaviours	↑
Relaxation and well-being	↑	Attraction	↑
Anxiety	↓	Anxiety	↓
HPA axis regulation	↓	Blood pressure	↑
Glucocorticoid release	↓		↓
Reproduction and sexual behaviours	↑	Sexual behaviours	↑
Sensory processing	↑	Reward and limbic activity	↑
Memory processes	↑	Attention, learning and memory	↑
Parasympathetic activity	↑	Sympathetic and parasympathetic regulation	↑

Adapted from Esch and Stefano (2005)
HPA, hypothalamic-pituitary-adrenal.

produces adjustments to the new state which is similar to tolerating drugs. However, the good news is that older married couples also had increased dopamine activity in the ventral tegmental area which was correlated with romantic love, activity in the globus pallidus was associated with friendship-based love, and the hypothalamus and hippocampus correlated with frequency of sex (Acevedo et al., 2012).

- Breaking up with a loved one can lead to a withdrawal phase characterized by depression, anxiety and possibly suicide (Fisher and Szreter, 2003; Fisher et al., 2010; Yaseen et al., 2012). Withdrawal is a prominent feature in addiction.

Love and hate have often been seen as extremes on a spectrum of liking. The neural signatures of love and hate have been shown to be different in imaging studies but there are some common areas activated in both love and hate, e.g. putamen and insula (Zeki & Romaya, 2008).

Rolls' account of emotion fits with Bartels and Zeki's studies on love, suggesting a motivational network, and with the role of dopamine in fear conditioning (Pezze & Feldon, 2004).

AGGRESSION AND VIOLENCE

Far removed from love is violence and aggression. Aggressive behaviour is a subject of great concern for many branches of our society, and the male of the species has been studied at great length to try and understand aggression and violence.

Neural Mechanisms and Aggression

In animal studies, the amygdala and hypothalamus have been shown to influence defence behaviours and attack behaviours (Siegel et al., 1999). The amygdala was activated in the brains of convicted murderers whose crime was impulsive and not premeditated, whereas those who were guilty of premeditated murder exhibited greater prefrontal activity (Raine et al., 1997, 1998).

Research suggests that the job of the prefrontal cortex is inhibiting the amygdala's response (Quirk et al., 2003). As the executive controlling mechanism of the brain, the frontal areas are involved in initiating, planning and execution of behaviours. The frontal lobes consider the implications of our actions and suppress them if necessary (see Chapter 12).

The potential of neuroimaging to predict violent and aggressive offenders is at present somewhat limited. However, the day may come when such technologies are predictive and the ethical implications of that are enormous (see Chapter 25). Questions of accountability and pre-emptive incarceration are frightening political concepts that require strong democratic leadership.

Hormones and Aggression

It is predominantly males who display aggression, and this has given rise to evolutionary and hormonal explanations for this behaviour.

The male hormones (in particular, the androgens such as testosterone) have been held responsible for male aggression and, consistent with this belief, castration in rats reduces aggression, while testosterone treatment reinstates it (Beeman, 1947). Early exposure to androgens during the organizational period of brain development results in less androgen being required to produce an aggressive response later in life (vom Saal, 1983).

Research into human aggression has not been entirely conclusive. Methodological limitations, such as the fact that experimenters cannot castrate males, mean that many experimental manipulations are not permitted. This leaves us with correlation studies, which have looked at the circulating levels of androgens and attempted to map them onto behaviour. The overall view is that there is a possibility that androgens are involved in human male aggression (Albert et al., 1993).

STRESS

One might consider stress to be a by-product of modern life but stress has a long history. Stress, like many concepts in psychology, means different things to different people. One person's stressor may be very different from another person's. Regardless of the stressor, our bodies' physiological reactions to stressors can give rise to many health problems. If there is a long-term stress reaction, these responses are harmful. The area of health psychology has focused on stress and its effects on, for example, heart disease and immunology and addiction (see Chapter 16). Stress responses are considered in more detail in Chapter 23.

EMOTION AND MUSIC: BEYOND EMOTION AS AN EVOLUTIONARY ADAPTATION (OR NOT)

Much of the consideration of emotion in this chapter has been concerned with emotions that have reasonably clear evolutionary adaptive purposes, but this is not so obvious for music, for example (Box 17.3). It has been long known that music can provoke emotional experiences (Hunter & Schellenberg, 2010). For example, I feel great pleasure/joy/happiness when I hear Mike McCready from Pearl Jam play a wailing guitar solo on a Gibson Les Paul. Others get an intense emotional experience from listening to Mozart, and some people even gain pleasure from listening to One Direction (or insert the latest offering from any recent talent show). The screaming fans greeting the Beatles at airports were perhaps less to do with music and more to do with the contents of Chapter 14. However, removing sex from the equation of teen adulation of musicians, how and why music produces such a powerful emotional reaction is an interesting question.

The experience of music is poorly defined in terms of psychology and neuroscience (Juslin et al., 2010). Music is often considered to be a cultural concept that serves no obvious adaptive purpose (see Box 17.3; Perlovsky, 2010). However, music activates large neural networks related to attention, semantic processing, memory, motor functions and emotional processing. Obviously music is processed initially by auditory pathways (but let's not forget somatosensory pathways that mediate the visceral feelings of the bass). The pathway by which music enters the brain is described in Chapter 10, but what happens when the neural impulses of sounds are processed by the brain is of greater interest. The brain processes music in numerous regions, including many that have been described in other emotional responses.

Increased activity levels in the ventral striatum have been recorded in response to music (Blood & Zatorre, 2001; Blood et al., 1999). Neural activation has also been recorded in fMRI studies highlighting the nucleus accumbens and ventral tegmental area (Menon & Levitin, 2005). In another fMRI study, pleasant music was shown to activate the

BOX 17.3: MUSIC: EMOTION, REWARD AND EVOLUTION

It is not entirely clear why we have adapted to have emotional responses to music. However, just because there is no clear link between natural selection and music does not mean there are no hypotheses regarding the evolution of music.

Huron (2001) suggests that there are eight theories on this topic.

- *Mate selection*. Making music may be seen as a courtship behaviour, e.g. singing suggesting good health.
- *Social cohesion*. Music may bring groups of individuals together as a collective against rival groups (although this theory probably considered tribal behaviours when it was conceived, think of the Bank Holiday fighting on Brighton beach between mods and rockers).
- *Group effort*. Music may facilitate co-ordination of group work (e.g. yo-heave-ho from sailors working together).
- *Perceptual development*. Music can be seen as a hearing exercise, which is beneficial for language.
- *Motor skill development*. Fine motor skills from playing instruments and singing may provide practice for co-ordinated motor acts such as speech.
- *Conflict reduction*. Music may reduce interpersonal conflict (and enhance social cohesion – see above).
- *Passing time safely*. As humans became efficient hunters, they also became rich with time. Music provides a harmless activity for the quiet moments between hunting (similar to sleep keeping an animal out of harm's way).
- *Transgenerational communication*. Music provides a channel of communication via which information can be passed on to successive generations (the folk song).

What is clear from this evolutionary account is that music has evolved not so much in its own right but rather in combination with information exchanges bestowed by language/symbolism.

The importance of language and symbolism within cognition and how we think has been well documented. Honing and Ploeger (2012) suggest that music is itself a cognitive adaptation and the evidence for that is in the cognitive mechanisms involved in music perception and production. From a similar perspective, Perlovsky (2010) concludes that music has a fundamental role in cognition, consciousness and culture. He considers the language vocalizations of human ancestry as split down two lines: a semantic and less emotional route, which evolves into language, and a more emotional route with semantic ambiguity, developing into music.

Music in its different forms communicates different emotions that may be a method of facilitating communication. For example, the minor third is a musical interval that is considered sad and is mirrored in speech reflecting sadness (Curtis & Bharucha, 2010). Other types of music produce different types of emotional reactions (Hunter & Schellenberg, 2010).

Despite the difficulty in describing an evolutionary function for music, one indisputable feature remains – it evokes emotions.

---

inferior frontal gyrus, anterior superior insula, ventral striatum, **Heschel's gyrus** and **rolandic operculum**. With unpleasant music, activation of the amygdala, hippocampus, parahippocampal gyrus and temporal lobes was increased (Koelsch et al., 2006), all of which are areas associated with negative emotions.

The role of DA has been reported during anticipation and the emotional peak experience of music (Salimpoor et al., 2011). In this study PET scans were combined with fMRI scans to provide temporal and spatial recordings of neural and dopamine activity in response to music. Music was found to trigger the release of dopamine in the dorsal and ventral striatum (nucleus accumbens). Comparisons can be made with theories of drug reward and pleasure (see Chapter 16), in which there is an anticipatory phase and a consummatory phase. The consummatory phase is upon hearing the desired music and is similar to the liking phase whereas the anticipatory phase provides signals of possibility and wanting. Differentiation of the two processes of music revealed that the nucleus accumbens increased activity during the experience and the caudate nucleus was more active during anticipation.

The neurochemical activity in response to music also reveals that there is (Chanda & Levitin, 2013):

- reduced or increased cortisol depending on the style of music (relaxing versus stimulating);
- reduced beta-endorphins;
- increased immunoglobulin A (an antibody enhancing immune response); and
- increased oxytocin when singing.

Like being in love, music is a powerful stimulus for the induction of emotions. The neuroscience demonstrates that similar to love, there is an underlying interaction with motivational systems. As students of psychology, you may be interested to note that music improves academic grades in what is known as the 'Mozart effect' (Perlovsky et al., 2013).

SUMMARY

Emotion is an intriguing human concept. How we feel has profound effects on cognition, physiology and overt behaviour. Emotion has troubled philosophers for centuries and continues to trouble psychobiologists and neuroscientists to this day. Evolutionary psychologists put forward accounts of the adaptive nature of emotions and suggest that they serve a purpose in terms of survival. Thus, those animals that utilize and experience emotions are able to survive and reproduce. Through reproduction, genes that confer the benefits of emotion are more likely to be passed on to subsequent generations.

Many theories have been presented to explain how emotions emerge. Most of those theories suffer from inadequacies that mean the search for a definitive neurobiology of emotion must continue. Considerable work has provided neural correlates of emotion but just because an area of the brain lights up during a particular emotion does not explain how that emotion becomes conscious. Emotion is also inextricably linked with motivation. We engage in behaviours because they induce the emotion of pleasure, or reduction of unpleasant experiences, e.g. fear. Emotions colour our decision making, but also make life an exciting rollercoaster.

LEARNING OUTCOME QUESTIONS

You should be able to answer the following questions.
- What is the role of physiological feedback in emotion?
- How can emotions be considered adaptive?
- To what extent is the study of emotion the study of fear?
- What is the role of the amygdala in emotion?

FURTHER READING

Barrett, L. F. (2011). Constructing emotion. *Psychological Topics, 20*, 359–380.
Dalgleish, T. (2004). The emotional brain. *Nature Reviews Neuroscience, 5*(7), 583–589.
Kreibig, S. D. (2010). Autonomic nervous system activity in emotion: A review. *Biological Psychology, 84*(3), 394–421.
LeDoux, J. (1998) *The emotional brain.* London: Phoenix.
LeDoux, J. (2012). Rethinking the emotional brain. *Neuron, 73*(4), 653–676.
Lindquist, K. A., Wager, T. D., Kober, H., Bliss-Moreau, E., & Barrett, L. F. (2012). The brain basis of emotion: A meta-analytic review. *Behavioral and Brain Sciences, 35*(3), 121–143.
Rolls, E. T. (2012). *Neuroculture: On the implications of brain science.* Oxford, UK: Oxford University Press.

462 PSYCHOBIOLOGY

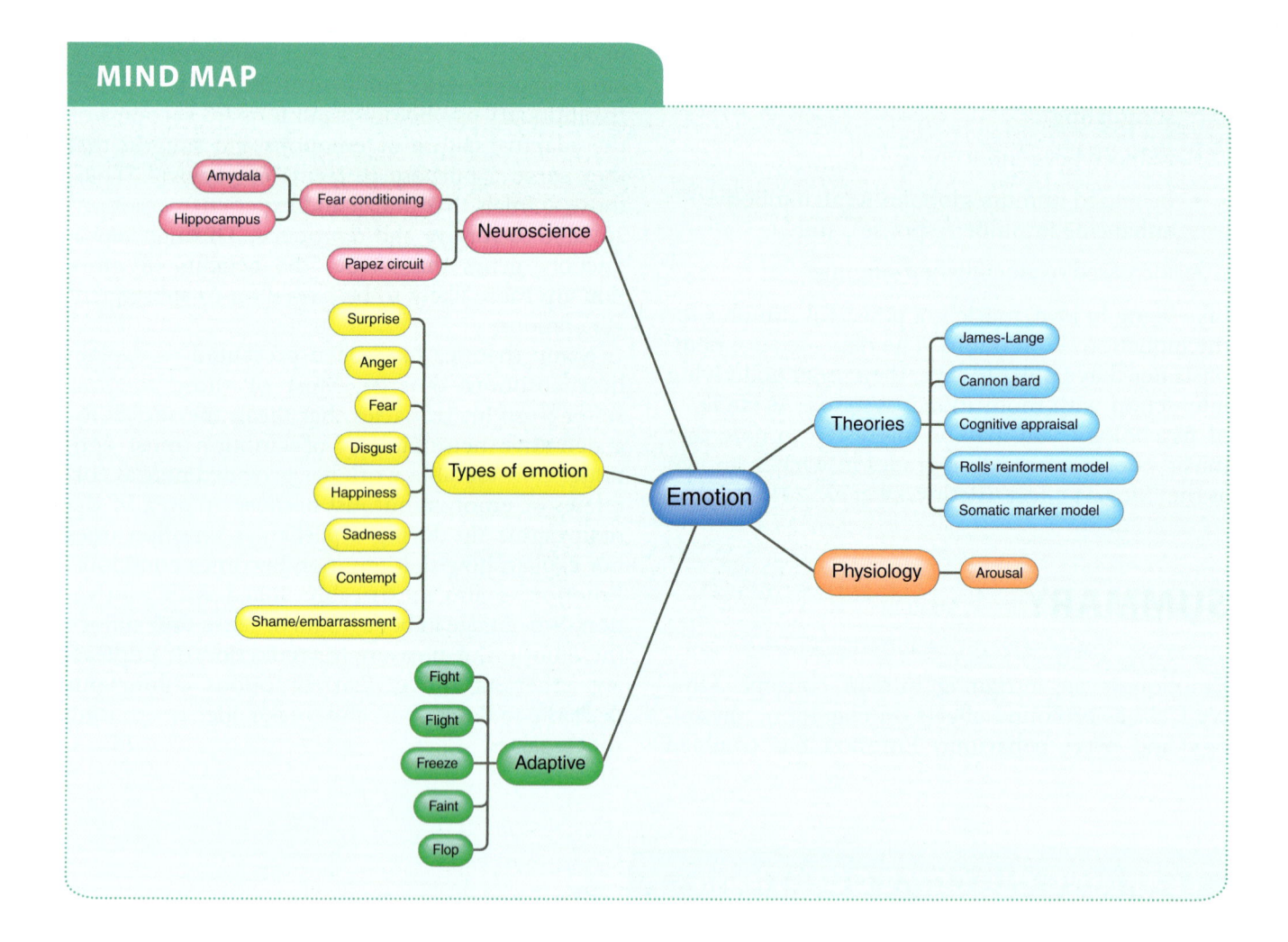

MIND MAP

- **Emotion**
  - **Neuroscience**
    - Fear conditioning
      - Amydala
      - Hippocampus
    - Papez circuit
  - **Types of emotion**
    - Surprise
    - Anger
    - Fear
    - Disgust
    - Happiness
    - Sadness
    - Contempt
    - Shame/embarrassment
  - **Theories**
    - James-Lange
    - Cannon bard
    - Cognitive appraisal
    - Rolls' reinforment model
    - Somatic marker model
  - **Physiology**
    - Arousal
  - **Adaptive**
    - Fight
    - Flight
    - Freeze
    - Faint
    - Flop

18 Sleep and Consciousness

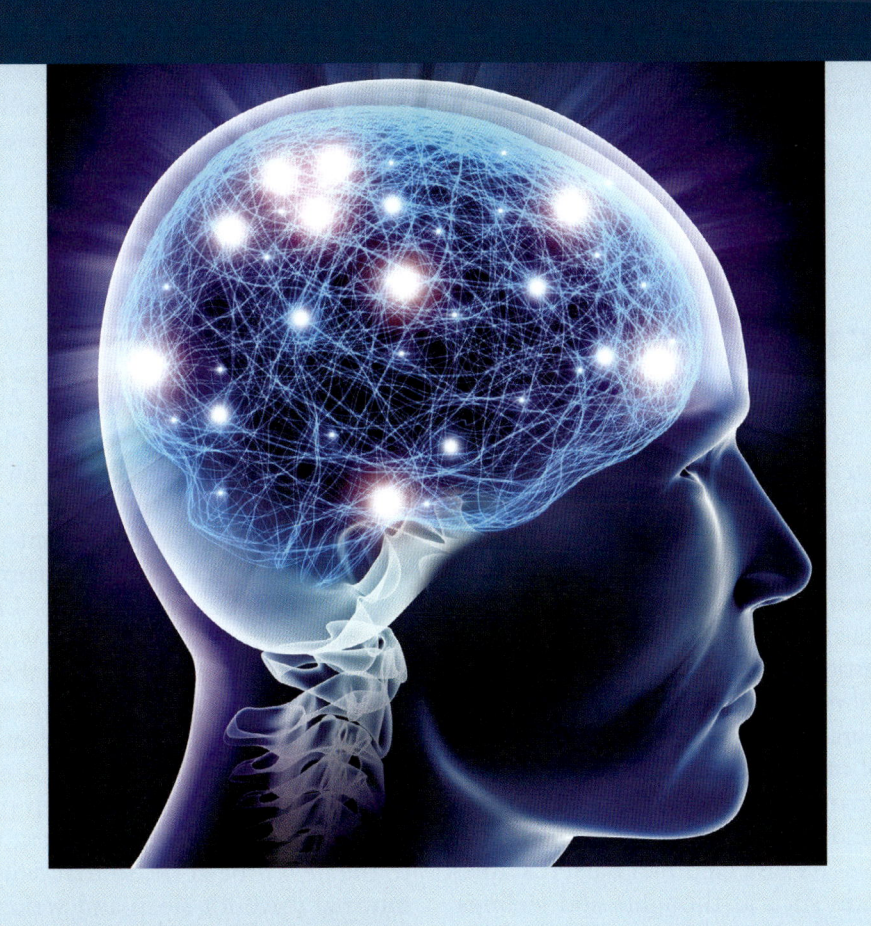

ANATOMY OF THE CHAPTER

This chapter will highlight the following.
- The circadian rhythm mediating sleep and wakefulness.
- The processes of sleep.
- The functions of sleep.
- The conceptual difficulties in understanding consciousness.

INTRODUCTION 464

CIRCADIAN RHYTHMS 464

SLEEP 465

SLEEP ARCHITECTURE 465

THEORIES OF SLEEP 470

CONSCIOUSNESS 472

SUMMARY 481

LEARNING OUTCOMES

1. To understand the mechanisms involved in response to the light/dark cycle.
2. To be able to differentiate the different stages of sleep.
3. To be able to identify the normal pattern of the stages of sleep.
4. To understand the difficulties of identifying a neural substrate of consciousness.

INTRODUCTION

On first reading, the title of this chapter may give you the impression that there are two states of consciousness. However, sleep is not the opposite of consciousness. Sleep is on a spectrum of conscious states. To say that sleep is being unconscious is perhaps misleading as it makes us think that nothing is going on, when that is far from true. Consciousness is the hard question. We know that we have thoughts, perceptions and feelings; we are agents of our own destiny and decide upon our actions; we have free will. All of these phenomena are important to being human. However, what is the origin of these feelings and how do brain states emerge as conscious thoughts? As Lisa Feldman Barrett states, 'Psychological states such as thoughts and feelings are real. Brain states are real. The problem is that the two are not real in the same way, creating the mind–brain correspondence problem' (Barrett, 2009, p.326).

CIRCADIAN RHYTHMS

The most obvious **circadian rhythm** is the sleep pattern. The circadian rhythms take place over a day. Many animals are **nocturnal** and are active during the dark periods of the day; humans and other primates are **diurnal**, as we are active during the day. Throughout these 24-hour cycles, body temperature, hormone levels and brain activity change.

Much of our understanding of the circadian cycle has come through studies of rodents and manipulation of the light/dark cycles. In a laboratory environment, the animal can be controlled and in the absence of an enriched environment, the placement of a running wheel provides a source of measurement of the animal's moment-by-moment activity. In normal circumstances, the circadian clock is adjusted by light. By manipulating exposure to light, the circadian cycle can be moved – a phase shift. Alternatively, the rhythm can be disrupted in a process called entrainment. Any environmental cue that alters the circadian cycle is referred to as a **zeitgeber** (time giver). Light is a powerful zeitgeber and in our modern world, the change in light is in part responsible for the jetlag experience when travelling east to west over several time zones. Symptoms of jetlag include decreased motivation, decreased concentration, increased fatigue and irritability and alterations in sleep pattern. The cause of jetlag is the 'slow adjustment of the body clock to the new time zone, so that daily rhythms and the internal drive for sleep and wakefulness are out of synchrony with the new environment' (Waterhouse et al., 2007, p.1118).

The functional significance of the circadian rhythm is that they harmonize the internal body states with that of the environment. The endogenous circadian clock allows for preparatory behaviours to be initiated prior to changes in light level.

As with many of the regulatory processes in which humans and other animals engage, the hypothalamus is the site receiving most attention. Lesions of the **suprachiasmatic nucleus** (SCN) of the hypothalamus disrupt normal circadian rhythms (Moore & Eichler, 1972; Stephan & Zucker, 1972) (Figure 18.1). Rats with lesions to the SCN had their circadian rhythm restored after transplants were performed (Drucker-Colín et al., 1984). Hamsters that had lesions of the SCN were given transplants from other hamsters that had short circadian rhythms and the recipient hamsters subsequently had a circadian rhythm similar to that of the donor (Ralph et al., 1990), thus indicating the importance of the SCN. However, the effects of transplants are

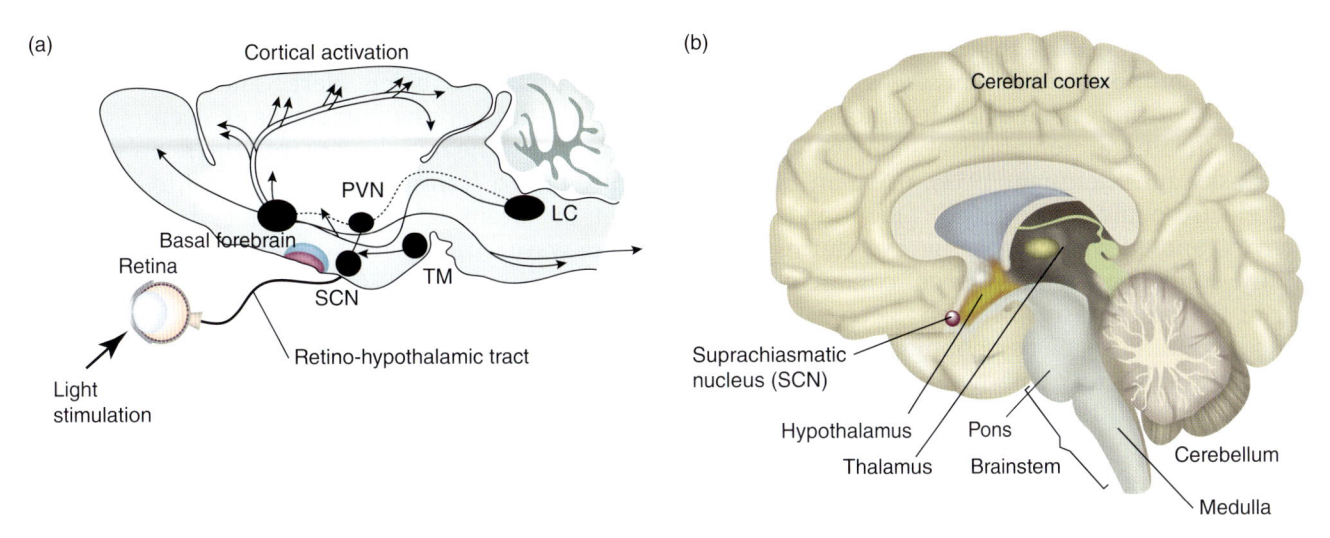

FIGURE 18.1 Suprachiasmatic nucleus (a) in the rat, (b) in the human. LC, locus coeruleus; PVN, paraventricular nucleus; SCN, suprachiasmatic nucleus; TM, hypothalamic tuberomammillary nucleus.

effective in behavioural measures, but there were few effects on the circadian rhythms of hormones in transplant recipients, suggesting that the network of SCN outputs is widespread and affected differentially (Meyer-Bernstein et al., 1999). In the isolated mouse SCN, a circadian rhythm of spontaneous neural firing was observed for weeks in tissue culture preparations (Herzog et al., 1997).

The SCN, referred to as the circadian pacemaker, is clearly important and must therefore receive information from the environment in order to synchronize circadian rhythms and make adjustments. An obvious place to look for input mechanisms is the visual system. Retinal ganglion cells are photosensitive and independent from the rods and cones (see Chapter 10). The retinal ganglion cells have been shown to project to the SCN and their activity matches that of the **entrainment** of the circadian cycle (Berson et al., 2002). These retinal ganglion cells contain **melanopsin** (Do et al., 2009) which is most sensitive to blue light (Gooley et al., 2010). Blue light is emitted from visual display screens (e.g. smartphones and computers) and adjusts the circadian rhythm, leading to sleep problems and other psychological deviations (Cajochen et al., 2011); hence the recommendation not to use such devices before bedtime.

The SCN also controls **melatonin**. Melatonin is a hormone synthesized from serotonin within the **pineal gland** and synthesis is reduced upon exposure to light in the rat (Wurtman et al., 1964). High levels of melatonin are associated with darkness and sleep (Vaughan et al., 1976) and it has therefore been considered as a potential agent for improving sleep (Waldhauser et al., 1990).

The circadian rhythm operates in the current discussion along a continuum of sleep and wakefulness. Much of the psychological literature focuses on what happens during the periods of the day when we are awake but sleep is a mysterious process in which we spend so much time.

SLEEP

Many of us are preoccupied with our emotions during our waking moments, and sometimes these emotions interfere with the respite of sleep. We spend a great deal of time asleep, and sleep takes us into a different state of consciousness. But what is sleep made of? And what is it for? (NB: to stop you being tired is not a useful answer.) Stenberg (2007) defines sleep as a 'reversible, physiological state with reduced motility and reduced responsiveness to sensory stimuli' (p.1187). The identification of a function of sleep is somewhat more difficult.

SLEEP ARCHITECTURE

The Stages of Sleep

The brain's activity can be measured by an **electroencephalogram** (EEG). Despite appearances to the contrary, the EEG reveals that the brain goes through a number of different stages of sleep. Sleep is actually a time of activity. It is not the equivalent of turning a metaphorical light switch to off. Aserinsky and Kleitman (1953), using an EEG and an electro-oculogram (EOG), identified neural activity and movement of the eye during sleep. Many studies have since been conducted looking at the mechanisms of sleep. Sleep is generally described in terms of psychophysiology. The three psychophysiological parameters that assess sleep architecture are the EEG, EOG and electromyogram (EMG), measuring electrical activity of brain, eye movements and muscle movements respectively (see Chapter 6).

The brainwaves present during the various stages of sleep can be seen in Figure 18.2. When we are awake, there are two types of brain activity (or waves): **alpha** and **beta**. Alpha activity predominates during rest and inactivity, whereas beta activity is associated with being alert. The brain's activity changes through the four stages of sleep.

Stage 1 is the initial entry into the sleep state and represents a transitional state. The EEG indicates that the brain activity has changed, producing a theta wave. After a short period, the person enters *stage 2* sleep. The EEG recording during stage 2 is irregular: there is theta activity, with a burst of activity called **sleep spindles**. Also within stage 2 are K-complexes which are negative potentials. *Stage 3* sleep is characterized by **delta waves**, and during stage 3 the number of spindles diminishes. The difference between stage 3 and *stage 4* is not clear-cut, but appears to be related to the number of delta waves. In stage 3 there are less than 50% delta waves, whereas in stage 4 there are more than 50%. These stages are called **slow-wave sleep (SWS)**.

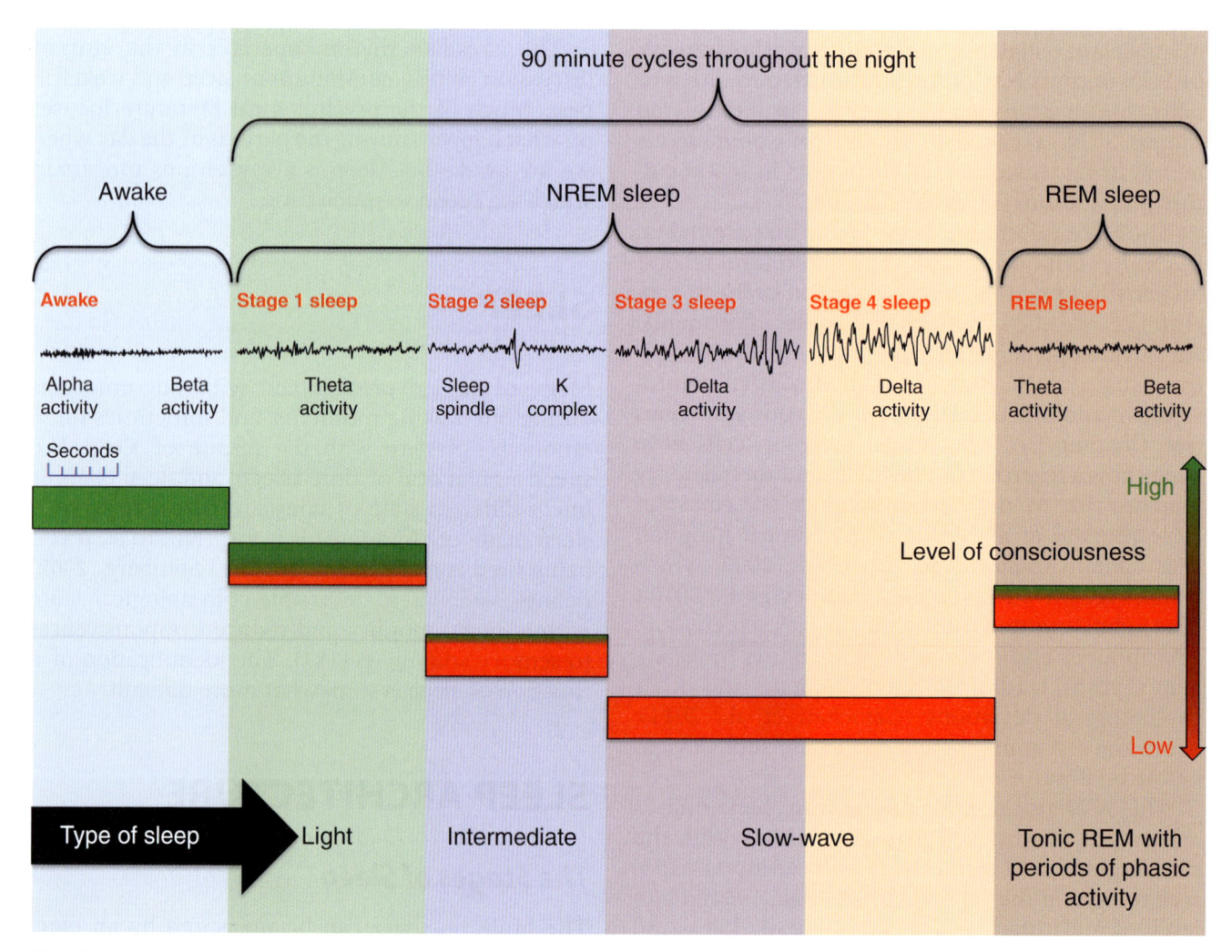

FIGURE 18.2 *Stages of sleep. Sleep is an active process as measured by the electroencephalogram (EEG). REM, rapid eye movement.*

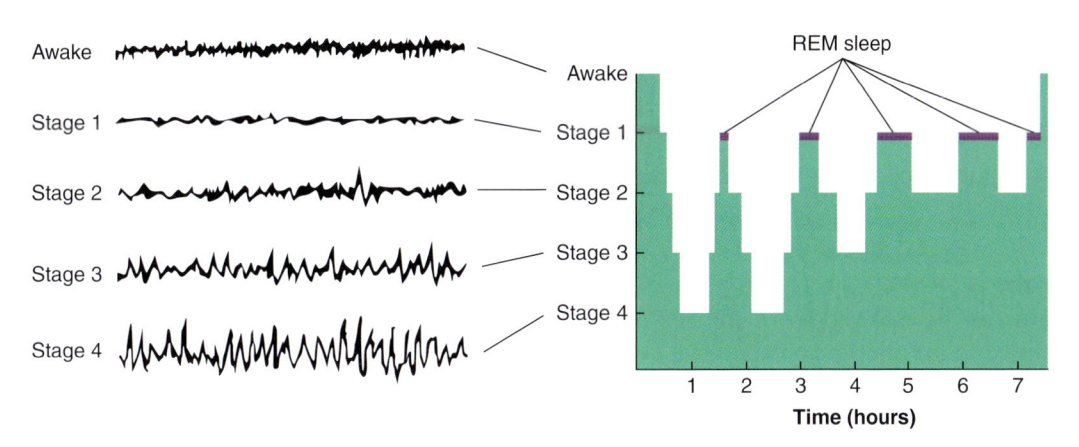

FIGURE 18.3 *The pattern of sleep over 8 hours. REM, rapid eye movement.*

It takes about an hour to go through stages 1–4, and these stages are referred to as non-rapid eye movement (**non-REM**) sleep. After about 45 minutes of stage 4 sleep, there is a change in the EEG recording. The brain activity is desynchronized, with some theta and beta activity. Electrodes attached to the muscles of the eye (EOG) indicate that the eyes are active. This is called **REM sleep**, and during this sleep phase the rest of the body is paralysed.

During a night's sleep, there is a cycle of non-REM and REM sleep. Each cycle lasts about 90 minutes, a third of which may be REM sleep (Figure 18.3). Figure 18.3 demonstrates the pattern of normal adult sleep. However, sleep changes throughout the lifespan (Figure 18.4). The sleep/wake cycle commences in the second trimester and can be differentiated up until the first few months of life into active and quiet sleep which eventually become REM and non-REM sleep (Ferrarelli & Benca, 2010). After about three months, a more adult-like pattern of sleeping emerges. Childhood sleep is characterized by reduced REM sleep and increased SWS. During this time, there is a high arousal threshold in which it is harder to wake the child up (Davis et al., 2004). Adolescence is characterized by a shift in the pattern of sleep. SWS (delta waves) decreases in adolescence and is associated with changes and reorganization within the brain (e.g. synaptic pruning – see Chapter 3) (Colrain & Baker, 2011). When entering old age, sleep becomes more difficult to initiate and maintain. Older people tend to nap during the day and get sleepy during the evening.

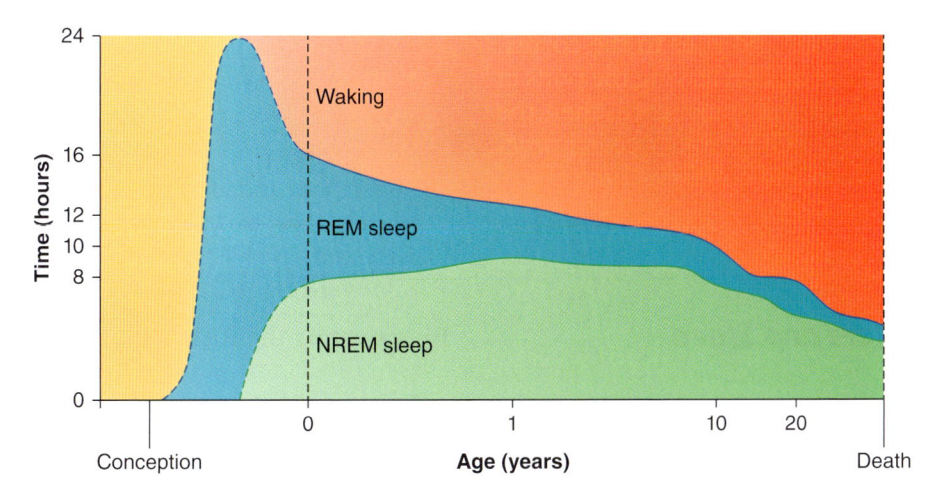

FIGURE 18.4 *Sleep across different ages. Prior to birth the foetus has more REM-like sleep which continues for the first year. As you get older, there is less REM and comparatively more non-REM sleep. NREM, non-rapid eye movement; REM, rapid eye movement.*
Source: Herman, M. D., Denlinger, S. L., Patarca, R., Katz, L. & Hobson J. A. (1991). Developmental phases of sleep and motor behaviour in a cat mother–infant system: A time-lapse video approach. *Canadian Journal of Psychology, 45,* 101–114.

The Neural Mechanisms of Sleep

There are many changes in brain activity during sleep (Maquet, 1999). Three neural systems are thought to produce sleep, and these communicate with each other.

The Forebrain
The forebrain can be isolated from the rest of the brain by surgery in an operation called the **cerveau isole**. The isolated forebrain can generate SWS, while lesions of the basal forebrain prevent SWS (Clemente & Sterman, 1963). During sleep, neurons became active, resulting in widespread inhibition of other brain regions (Gallopin et al., 2000).

The Reticular Formation
Stimulation of the **reticular formation** will wake a sleeping animal (Moruzzi & Magoun, 1995) and so the reticular formation appears to function as a wake-up call to the basal ganglia, thalamus and forebrain. Microinjections of acetylcholine (ACh) agonists into the reticular formation induce parasympathetic activity and increase the measures of sleep in the cat (George et al., 1964).

The Pons
The **pons** is the focus of REM sleep, and if various cuts are made to transect the brainstem, the action of the pons's ability to trigger REM sleep can be seen. If the transection is below the pons, the brain shows alternation between SWS and REM sleep. A particular waveform indicative of REM sleep is the **PGO wave** (pons, geniculate and occipital cortex) which arises from the pons and goes to the cortex. If the transection is made higher, leaving the pons in contact with the medulla and spinal cord, then the body shows REM sleep. PGO waves occur immediately before REM sleep and continue throughout (Ito et al., 2002; Jouvet, 1994).

Neurotransmitters and Sleep

Acetylcholine
Acetylcholine in the pons produces eye activity during REM sleep and PGO waves (Baghdoyan et al., 1984; Kodama & Honda, 1996). ACh is involved in vigilance and activation in wakefulness, in particular projections to the reticular activating system from the basal forebrain and tegmentum (Stenberg, 2007).

Serotonin and Noradrenaline
Serotonin and noradrenaline have both been implicated in the control of sleep. Serotonin is found in the **raphe nucleus** of the reticular formation, where activation produces arousal and inhibition of 5-HT synthesis reduces it (Peck & Vanderwolf, 1991). Sleep is disrupted in rats with lesions of the raphe nucleus (Jouvet, 1999). When aroused, the raphe nucleus is active; when in REM sleep, it is silent (Trulson & Jacobs, 1979).

The noradrenergic neurons of the **locus coeruleus** show increased firing during waking hours and decreased firing during sleep (Aston-Jones & Bloom, 1981). Noradrenaline release is associated with the change from sleep to wakefulness (Mendelson, 2001).

The different actions of neurotransmitters promote either sleep or waking. The fact that neurotransmission is altered during sleeping and waking states permits the modification of sleep. However, drugs that are used to induce sleep act elsewhere.

Dopamine
Dopamine (DA) has not received as much attention as the other neurotransmitters with regard to sleep. However, the activating effects of amphetamine, methylphenidate and cocaine may all be mediated by dopamine. Dopamine's involvement in reward mechanisms is well established and has now been extended to sleep and dreaming (Perogamvros & Schwartz, 2012). The reward activation model (RAM) states that the activation of mesolimbic dopamine during sleep serves several functions:

- facilitates memory consolidation by prioritizing emotional and/or motivational content;
- modulates REM sleep via projections to the pons; and
- contributes to dream generation via motivational and affective drives of what is being called the seeking system (a curiosity-driven system associated with appetitive craving and reward).

By activating the RAM, it has been argued that:

> Sleep creates an internal environment of high exploratory excitability and elevated novelty seeking (i.e. activation of the seeking system), which can bias dream content toward events that are of motivational relevance, or generate other forms of exploratory behaviours during sleep (e.g. instinctual and motivational behaviours in parasomnias, sniffing in rats). (Perogamvros & Schwartz, 2012, p.1946)

Dreams

The DA hypothesis of dreams is not the only psychobiological account of dreaming. We are in a different state of consciousness when we are asleep, but we are not unconscious. The fact that we dream indicates that the brain is active during sleep, and the visual cortex in particular is active during sleep (Madsen et al., 1991). This may account for REM sleep; indeed, the brain activity during REM sleep is similar to that of a person scanning a visual scene (Miyauchi et al., 1990).

The function of dreams and REM sleep is still to be determined. However, many theories have been put forward to account for dreams. For example, Freud suggested that dreams were revelations from the unconscious, more often than not alluding to some repressed sexual activity.

Hobson et al. (2000) provide an account of dreams in the AIM model. They argue that whether awake, in non-REM sleep or REM sleep, consciousness is governed by three factors.

- *Activation* (**A**) – the level of energy required by the brain (high during waking hours).
- *Input-output gating* (**I**) – the process that facilitates or inhibits access of sensory information to the brain, and motor signals from the brain to the musculature of the body.
- *Modulation* (**M**) – the chemical modulation of the brain via various neurotransmitters (high levels when awake).

Using these three parameters, Hobson and colleagues have placed consciousness in a three-dimensional space (Figure 18.5). Within this

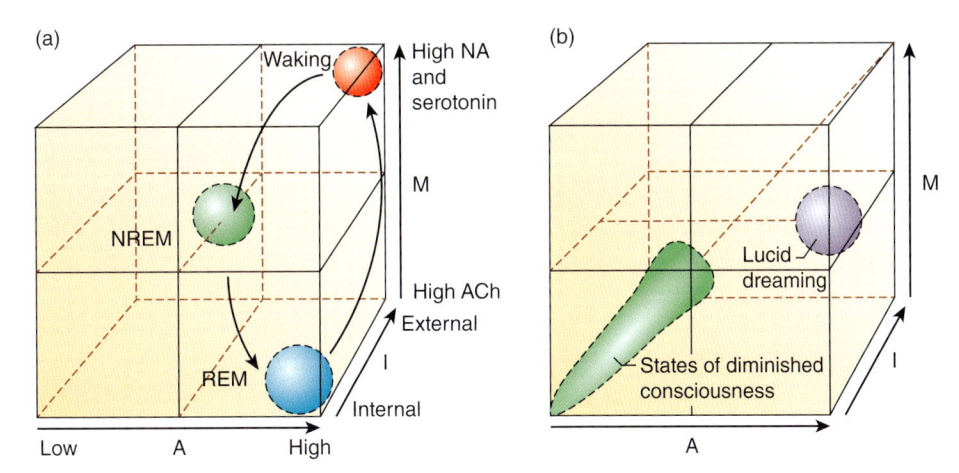

FIGURE 18.5 *The three-dimensional space of the AIM model of sleep, dreams and consciousness. (a) The three-dimensional AIM state-space model showing normal transitions within the AIM state space from waking to non-rapid eye movement (NREM) and then to rapid eye movement (REM) sleep. The x axis represents A (for activation), the y axis represents M (for modulation) and the z axis represents I (for input-output gating). The values of A, I and M can be derived from the neuronal data of animal experiments; factors A and I can also be estimated in human sleep laboratory data but there is currently no way of measuring factor M in humans. Waking, NREM sleep and REM sleep occupy distinct loci of this space. Waking and REM sleep are both in the right-hand segment of the space, owing to their high activation levels, but they have different I and M values. Thus, the activated, REM-sleeping brain-mind is both off-line and chemically differentiated compared with the waking brain-mind. NREM sleep is positioned in the centre of the space because it is intermediate in all quantitative respects between waking and REM sleep. The values of A, I and M change constantly, but the changes are constrained. Sleep and waking states alternate owing to circadian influences (not shown). During sleep, AIM values tend to follow elliptical trajectories through the space. As sleep advances in time, AIM values go less deeply into the NREM sleep domain and more deeply into the REM sleep domain. The normal, cardinal domains of waking, NREM and REM sleep occupy relatively limited zones of the space. (b) Diseases, such as those neurological conditions that produce coma and minimally conscious states, are arrayed in the left-hand segment of the space, owing to their low activation values. Lucid dreaming, which is a hybrid state with features of both waking and dreaming, is situated in the middle of the extreme right-hand side of the AIM state space between waking and REM, towards either of which lucid dreamers are drawn. Sleep and psychiatric disorders can also be placed in the schema. ACh, acetylcholine; NA, noradrenaline.*
Source: Reproduced by permission from Macmillan Publishers Ltd: NATURE REVIEWS NEUROSCIENCE Hobson, J. A. (2009). REM sleep and dreaming: towards a theory of protoconsciousness. *Nature Reviews Neuroscience, 10*(11), 803-813 copyright 2009

three-dimensional space, the different states of sleep and being awake occupy discrete separate areas. During REM sleep, sensory input gates (I) are closed but there are also PGO waves generating pseudo-sensorimotor stimulation which may be representative of the vivid sensory nature of dreaming (Hobson, 2009). Additionally during REM sleep, the activation (A) of the prefrontal cortex is suspended, whereas the amygdala and paralimbic cortex increase in activity and project to the parietal regions of the cortex, thus ensuring emotion and remote memory integrate with visuospatial imagery. Modulation (M) of brain activity is reduced with a decrease in aminergic and cholinergic neurons in the pons and subsequently a reduction in innervation of cortical regions (Figure 18.6).

Hobson (2009) sees dreaming as essential for the human experience of consciousness. He argues that dreaming acts as a virtual reality generator that performs a preparatory function for consciousness. During development, REM sleep may be linked to the generation of a proto-self in which one has agency over motor actions. Hobson argues that protoconscious REM sleep could:

> ... provide a virtual world model, complete with an emergent imaginary agent (the proto-self) that moves (via fixed action patterns) through a fictive space (the internally engendered environment) and experiences strong emotions as it does so. (Hobson, 2009, p.808)

Therefore, dreams represent a practice session for the neural mechanisms of consciousness.

THEORIES OF SLEEP

Why Do We Need to Sleep?

This may seem like a simple question with a straightforward answer: because we are tired! However, although there are several theories about the function of sleep, a definitive answer is elusive.

An evolutionary account of sleep involves animals conserving energy and avoiding danger (Meddis, 1975). Perhaps this is why we sleep best at night. Our visual system is not tuned for night vision and therefore we are vulnerable during the hours of darkness. The opposite is the case for nocturnal animals that function best at night.

When we are awake, we are busy. This requires energy and there is wear and tear on the body, so sleep has been considered to be a period in which restoration of the body can take place (Moruzzi, 1972). After a difficult day, you may feel like you could sleep for many hours. However, a strenuous day does not lead to an increase in sleep. The restorative powers of sleep for the brain have been demonstrated. Around the cells of the brain in the interstitial space are toxic waste products that are removed by the cerebrospinal fluid (CSF) (Xie et al., 2013). The importance of this can be seen in **beta-amyloid**, which is involved in Alzheimer's disease (see Chapter 24). During sleep, the clearance of beta-amyloid from the interstitial space is twice as fast as when awake (Xie et al., 2013).

Another view is that sleep is cognitively beneficial (Walker, 2009). Sleep aids the retention and consolidation of material learned during the day (Stickgold & Walker, 2005, 2007; Walker & Stickgold, 2006). REM sleep increases after learning, and brain activity during REM sleep has been shown to be similar to that when performing a task (Maquet et al., 2000). However, other studies have failed to show a specific effect with REM sleep, but have concluded that the density of sleep spindles in stage 2 sleep is correlated with recall performance on a learned task (Gais et al., 2002) and has been argued to be a physiological index of intelligence (Fogel & Smith, 2011).

In order to understand the function(s) of sleep, others have argued that this can only be achieved in an evolutionary context (Lee Kavanau, 2004). From such a perspective, Lee Kavanau has argued that sleep is required because of the development of complex vision. Essentially, the dual processes of the brain compete when awake, and sleep allows one of those processes (vision) to have little impact on other neural activities, e.g. memory consolidation (Lee Kavanau, 2005).

Sleep Disorders and Mental Health

Disorders of sleep – whether it is too much or too little – can have a profound effect on behaviour. Simply not getting enough sleep can produce a number of problems.

Insomnia

Insomnia is difficulty in falling asleep or staying asleep. However, there are large individual

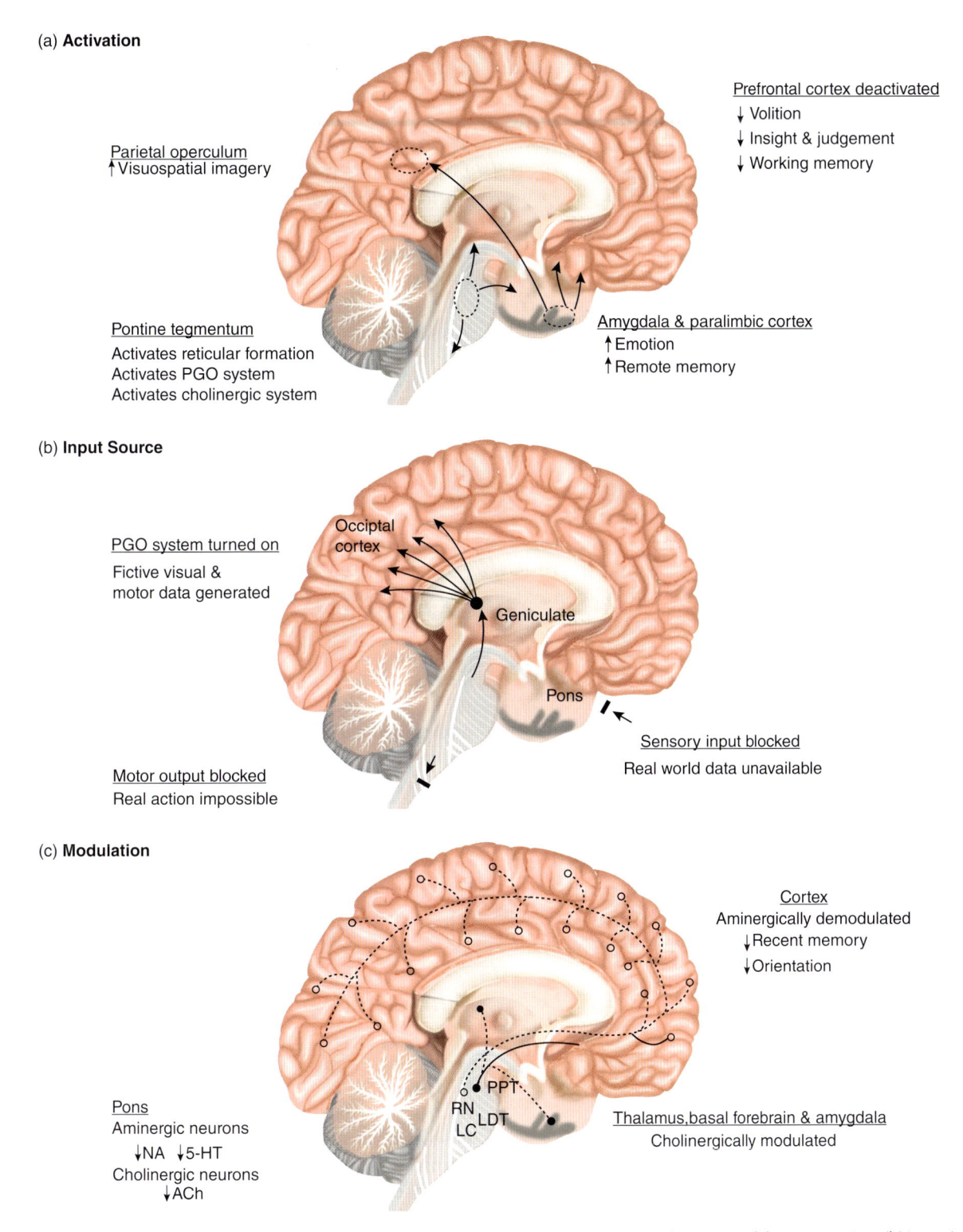

FIGURE 18.6 Physiological signs and regional brain mechanisms of REM sleep according to the AIM model. (a) Activation. (b) Input/output. (c) Modulation. 5-HT, 5-hydroxytryptamine; ACh, acetylcholine; LC, locus coeruleus; LDT, laterodorsal tegmental nucleus; NA, noradrenaline; PGO, ponto-geniculo-occipital; PPT, pedunculopontine tegmental nucleus; RN, raphe nuclei.

differences in the amount of sleep a person needs. Margaret Thatcher, for example, reputedly needed very little sleep when she was Prime Minister. Thus, insomnia is relative to an individual's needs. Some people may seek a medical solution to insomnia (see below). However, this can have rebound effects when drug treatment is discontinued.

Narcolepsy

People who cannot resist falling asleep at inappropriate times during the day have a condition called **narcolepsy**. However, if you were to fall asleep during a tedious lecture, this would be quite normal and not a symptom of narcolepsy!

There are specific symptoms of narcolepsy: **cataplexy**, **sleep paralysis** and **hypnogogic hallucinations**. Cataplexy happens when the person is awake, and during cataplexy there is a complete paralysis of the body – the person simply can't move. One view of cataplexy is that the muscle paralysis in REM sleep occurs out of context. Sleep paralysis is similar to cataplexy, but happens either just before or just after sleep. Hypnogogic hallucinations are dream-like states that happen prior to falling asleep, while still awake. They occur during sleep paralysis and are not that form of daydreaming you may also experience during a tedious lecture.

Narcolepsy is primarily a genetic disorder (Lin et al., 1999), and the gene that is dysfunctional in narcolepsy codes for the peptide **orexin** (Kilduff & Peyron, 2000). Orexin has been shown to be reduced in people with narcolepsy (Peyron et al., 2000) and general sleepiness (Martinez-Rodriguez et al., 2003).

A number of pharmacological treatments are available for narcolepsy, but none of these drugs directly influences orexin levels. They are stimulants that act on dopaminergic, serotonergic and noradrenergic systems (e.g. methylphenidate, aka Ritalin) (Chandler, 2010).

Sleep Deprivation

Sleep deprivation can have serious consequences. For example, sleep-deprived rats have reduced immunity, which can be fatal (Everson, 1993); this supports a restorative theory of sleep. In extreme cases, most humans with fatal familial insomnia die within two years of the insomnia starting (Manetto et al., 1992). Sleep deprivation in the short term can have pronounced cognitive effects, impairing academic performance (Boxes 18.1 and 18.2).

Sedatives/Sleeping Pills

Drugs can be used to aid sleep; these are called hypnotics. Barbiturates were once used to induce sleep, and they act at the GABA A receptor and influence such areas of the brain as the reticular formation. However, barbiturates are dangerous drugs with abuse liability. Another group of drugs, the benzodiazepines (such as diazepam (Valium)), are also effective hypnotics. The benzodiazepines act at a receptor complex on GABA neurons; they are anxiolytic and somewhat safer to use than barbiturates. However, benzodiazepines are also used to treat anxiety disorders and there is a high risk of dependence developing.

CONSCIOUSNESS

This should really have a whole book dedicated to it. In fact, there are many books on this subject, and none of them has anything close to an answer. However, just because there is no answer (yet) does not mean that it is a pointless pursuit.

The challenge of understanding consciousness embraces psychology, neuroscience and philosophy. The results could have profound effects on our perception of ourselves and our world (see Chapter 25).

Who are We and What Do We feel? What is It to Think?

Consciousness is hard to define. Searle (2013) points out that the problem of defining consciousness is the scientific definition coming after the common-sense definition. To illustrate this, he uses the concept of water, in which the common-sense definition is that it is clear, colourless and tasteless. The scientific definition is in reference to its molecular composition, e.g. H2O. Searle maintains that this study of consciousness remains at the common-sense level. He identifies features associated with consciousness.

- *Qualitativeness* – that there are different feelings to different conscious states.

BOX 18.1: THE EFFECTS OF SLEEP DEPRIVATION ON EDUCATIONAL PERFORMANCE

If you have very young children or very noisy neighbours, you will be familiar with the effects of sleep deprivation. The importance of a good night's sleep for children was highlighted by Randazzo et al. (1998). In this study, children aged 10–14 had their sleep restricted. These children performed poorly on complex cognitive tasks, whereas performance of simpler tasks remained the same as non-sleep-deprived children, thereby supporting every teacher's and parent's experience.

Being tired and irritable the next day is just part of the problem. A lack of sleep has detrimental effects on cognitive tasks, e.g. coursework and exams. Many students prior to an examination have difficulty sleeping or engage in last minute revision. Sleep quality and quantity are closely related to student learning capacity and academic achievement. Sleep loss was associated with poor learning in students and studies in which sleep was restricted showed a worsening in neurocognitive and academic performance. The authors of this report suggest the results may be related to the involvement of the prefrontal cortex (PFC) in sleep loss (Curcio et al., 2006). Experimental studies have shown the consequences of sleep deprivation to the frontal lobe (Jones & Harrison, 2001).

Sleep habits, especially wake-up times, accounted for the variance in results in which later wake-up times were associated with lower grades (Trockel et al., 2000). Poor sleep patterns were associated with weaker academic performance in medical students (medical students appear to be the favourite type of student to study) (Medeiros et al., 2001) and the effects of sleep were greatest prior to an exam rather than after the exam or during the semester (Ahrberg et al., 2012). However, the effect was really one based on stress that affected sleep quality. An early bedtime was associated with students who were high performing (BaHammam et al., 2012).

Staying up late to study might not be the best idea for a successful academic outcome. A study by Gillen-O'Neel et al. (2013) in adolescents demonstrated that if students sacrificed sleep time for study time, they had greater difficulties the next day.

In studies looking at numerous variables and performing regression analysis, having sufficient sleep and attendance at class were predictors of academic success in undergraduates (Gomes et al., 2011) and high scores on sleepiness during the day were, not surprisingly, correlated with poorer academic performance (Abdulghani et al., 2012). Attendance is critical to learning but physical attendance at a lecture is not the same as psychological attendance. If you are not cognitively equipped for the learning session because you are too tired, then your mere presence is not enough to override it (and just collecting the hand-out/reading list is not sufficient either).

On a more neurocognitive level, sleep deprivation has been shown to impair working memory (Smith et al., 2002), creative thinking and attention (Wimmer et al., 1992), all of which are essential for successful academic pursuit.

BOX 18.2: DANGER: DOCTORS WORK LONG HOURS WITH LITTLE SLEEP

Performance on many tasks can be impaired by sleep deprivation. There are a number of occupations in which sleep deprivation can have dramatic effects. Experimental evidence also suggests that partial sleep deprivation can affect driving (De Valck et al., 2003). The wars in Afghanistan and Iraq have required military personnel to go without sleep during stressful situations and such conditions could have dramatic effects on combat performance. Marksmanship deteriorated in elite soldiers after nearly 73 hours of partial sleep deprivation (Tharion et al., 2003), as did cognitive performance (Lieberman et al., 2002).

The one profession we hear the most about in relation to sleep deprivation is medicine. Hospital doctors have to work long hours with very little sleep. This is said to affect their judgements, which are sometimes critical to the well-being of their patients (Buysse et al., 2003). For example, the doctor needs to be attentive to giving the correct dose of a drug to a patient or vigilant in diagnosis of symptoms.

Research looking at sleep deprivation and fatigue in surgeons has indicated an increase in errors when sleep deprived (Eastridge et al., 2003).

- *Ontological subjectivity* – it exists only insofar as it is experienced.
- *Unity* – a single unified conscious state represents many subcomponents, e.g. sound and sight.
- *Intentionality* – the feature of the mind oriented at objects and internal affective states.
- *Intentional causation* – the conscious mind works to causally produce behaviour, e.g. the perception of a reinforcing stimulus, e.g. food, is experienced consciously and motivates approach behaviours.

Searle also has opinions on the evolutionary function of consciousness and argues that the traditional methods of evolutionary psychology and biology are somewhat redundant in the study of consciousness. He argues that evolutionary accounts arise from subtraction methods, e.g. what do we get if we remove a particular neural substrate, e.g. reflex? By removing the reflex/biological substrate, we can identify its function. However, Searle writes that 'the problem with trying to do this with consciousness is that, if you subtract consciousness, you subtract, roughly speaking, all of our life, except such basic unconscious processes as breathing' (Searle, 2013, p.10347). This is one subject that does not have an immediately compelling evolutionary explanation, although many have attributed it to language (see Arbib (2001) for example).

Another problem with studying consciousness is that we are dealing with people's subjective experiences. As objective scientists, it is impossible to determine if one person's subjective experience is the same as another person's. The subjective experience that is private to the individual is often referred to as the qualia. The qualia is the 'what is it like to see the colour red?' question, for example. My experience of red may be different from your experience of red although the physics of red remains stable. This links to thought experiments.

> Mary is a brilliant scientist who is, for whatever reason, forced to investigate the world from a black and white room via a black and white television monitor. She specializes in the neurophysiology of vision and acquires, let us suppose, all the physical information there is to obtain about what goes on when we see ripe tomatoes, or the sky, and use terms like 'red', 'blue', and so on. She discovers, for example, just which wave-length combinations from the sky stimulate the retina, and exactly how this produces via the central nervous system the contraction of the vocal chords and expulsion of air from the lungs that results in the uttering of the sentence 'The sky is blue' . . . What will happen when Mary is released from her black and white room or is given a colour television monitor? Will she learn anything or not? It seems just obvious that she will learn something about the world and our visual experience of it. But then it is inescapable that her previous knowledge was incomplete. But she had all the physical information.
> (Jackson, 1982, p.130)

Mary did not know what it was like to experience the colour red. There is something missing, but it is hard to know what it is, e.g. what is the experience and how is it manifest from the brain?

The study of consciousness is a real head-scratching, headache-inducing academic pursuit. A more practical application of the whole of consciousness extends from perception and enters into action and behaviour.

Free Will

Another aspect of consciousness is about making choices. The big question is, are we free to make those choices? Do we have free will? Are we agents of our own behaviour (hence the phrase 'agency')?

Free will is the ability to act freely; as David Hume said, freedom is 'a power of acting or of not acting, according to the determination of the will' (Hume, 1997).

Benjamin Libet performed neurosurgery whilst patients were conscious. Libet stimulated their brains and their hands with electrodes whilst timing their verbal responses and monitoring their brain activity. What he discovered was that consciousness of sensation lags behind the stimulation by about half a second (500 ms) (Libet, 1965; Libet et al., 1964). He argued that the timing of consciousness of the sensation was referred backward to the time of the stimulus, therefore the perception was not one of delay. In 1983 Libet and colleagues performed an experiment that generated a huge amount of discussion in neuroscience and philosophy. They measured the EEG recordings of participants undergoing a specifically designed experiment, which involved an oscilloscope set up to look like the dial of the clock. A spot of light would revolve around the face of the clock approximately 25 times per second (Figure 18.7). The participants were asked to generate a small movement with

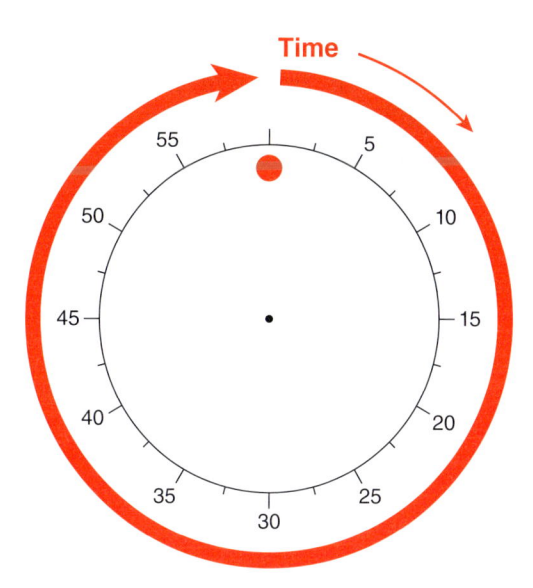

FIGURE 18.7 Libet's clock face.

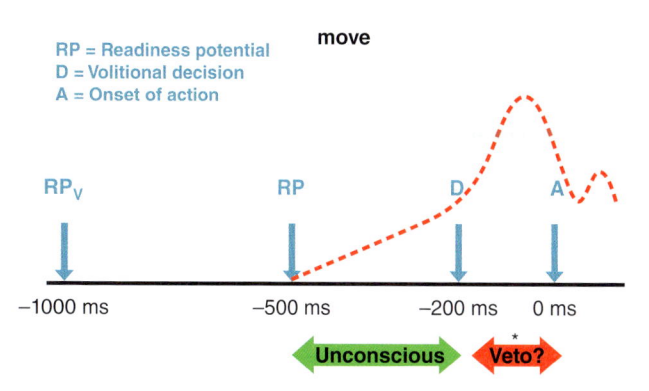

FIGURE 18.8 *The readiness potential. The readiness potential occurs prior to the conscious decision to act. In between the decision and the onset of action is a period of time in which a response can be inhibited (veto).*
Source: After Libet, B., Gleason, C. A., Wright, E. W., & Pearl, D. K. (1983). Time of conscious intention to act in relation to onset of cerebral activity (readiness-potential). The unconscious initiation of a freely voluntary act. *Brain, 106*(Pt 3), 623–642.
*Libet, B., Wright, E. W. Jr., & Gleason, C. A. (1983). Preparation- or intention-to-act, in relation to pre-event potentials recorded at the vertex. *Electroencephalography and Clinical Neurophysiology, 56*(4), 367–372. A, onset of action; D, volitional decisions; RP, readiness potential.

their hands spontaneously, e.g. flicking their wrists, whenever they felt like it (movements by their own free will). Whilst doing this, the participants had to watch the oscilloscope and report the exact position of the light revolving around the face of the dial when they first decided to make the movement.

Measurements from the EEG identified a readiness potential which preceded the conscious awareness of the decision to make the movement (Figure 18.8). The readiness potential was identified 500 ms before the action and about 300 ms before the volitional decision was made. Therefore, the conscious decision to make a movement came some 300 ms after neurons fired in the brain; activity in the brain preceded the decision to make the movement. Due to the fact that the conscious decision was preceded by unconscious processes in the brain, there is a challenge to the notion of free will. Decisions are not made consciously via deliberation but rather by unconscious activity of synapses. The conscious decision is therefore an artefact of neural activity and consciousness of one's decisions is an illusion.

Such experiments can fundamentally change how we view our own existence. As Banks and Pockett (2007) state:

> If conscious decisions are not the cause of actions, it follows that we do not have conscious free will. Even worse, because the ability consciously to initiate actions is an essential property of self, the denial of conscious, personal origination of action is a challenge to our sense of selfhood. The implication is that we, our conscious selves, are not free actors with control over our choices in life. We are only conduits for unconsciously made decisions. Libet's one simple experiment has slipped our entire self-concept from its moorings. (p.657)

Libet and colleagues did not throw out free will as a concept. Even though decisions become conscious approximately 200 ms before the movements are made, only 50 ms is needed for the activation of the nerves to result in the movement. That leaves 150 ms after a decision to act becomes conscious and before a motor command is sent. During this time a decision not to act can also be made, in what Libet referred to as *veto power* (Libet, Gleason et al., 1983). Libet states:

> Cerebral activity *initiates* this volitional process at least 350 msec before the conscious wish (W) to act appears. However, W appears about 200 msec before the muscles are activated. That [delay] retained the possibility that the conscious will could *control* the outcome of the volitional process; it could veto it and block the performance of the act. These discoveries have profound implications for the nature of free will, for individual responsibility and guilt. (Libet, 1999, p.339).

The role of conscious free will would be, then, not to initiate a voluntary act but rather to *control* whether the act takes place. We may view the unconscious initiatives for voluntary actions as 'bubbling up' in the brain. The conscious will then selects which of these initiatives may go forward to an action or which ones to veto and abort, with no act appearing. (Libet, 2010, p.7)

Thus, in our decision making, free will is perhaps not the right term; rather, it is *free won't*. It is what we choose *not* to do that is our decision.

Using the same paradigms as Libet, Lau et al. (2007) looked at the effects of transcranial magnetic stimulation (TMS) over the presupplementary motor area (preSMA). They had previously found that preSMA activity recorded in an earlier fMRI study reflected a site for the representation of intention (Lau et al., 2004). Now they:

> ... showed that there was a retrospective effect for TMS over the pre-SMA on the perceived onset of intention as well as for perceived timing of the movement itself. TMS shifted the perceived onset of intention backward in time and shifted the perceived timing of the movement forward in time (Lau et al., 2007, p.87)

and they concluded that 'the perceived onset of intention depends, at least in part, on neural activity that takes place after the execution of action'. They concede that the experiment challenges our beliefs about free will and that 'the commonsensical view is attractive when we assume that the main function of experience of intention is for the conscious control of action, but it cannot account for the data'. There is no room for common sense in the study of consciousness; it just gets in the way of creative thinking!

Further support comes from neuroimaging studies that have identified the frontal and parietal cortex in the decision-making machinery of the brain. Soon et al. (2008) used a slightly different task in which participants could freely decide if they wanted to press a button with their left or right hand but they had to remember when they made that decision. The outcome of the experiment demonstrated that:

> ... two specific regions in the frontal and parietal cortex of the human brain had considerable information that predicted the outcome of a motor decision the subject had not yet consciously made. This suggests that when the subject's decision reached awareness it had been influenced by unconscious brain activity for up to 10 s, which also provides a potential cortical origin for unconscious changes in skin conductance preceding risky decisions (Soon et al., 2008, p.545) (Figure 18.9).

Theories of Free Will

The tricky issue of free will has occupied the thoughts of philosophers for centuries, with many different views on the subject. The neuroscience is not so advanced as to be able to answer the question of free will. However, it is thought-provoking and the arguments should advance your critical thinking and logical deductions.

Determinism A deterministic point of view regards the universe and all the actions and all the behaviours seen within it as predetermined (thus **Determinism**). That is, behaviour can be predicted and is governed by the laws of physics. Thus, our behaviour is not the result of our decision-making processes, but rather a foregone conclusion due to the activity of atoms that can be traced back a long way in time. Clearly, with this perspective there is no free will, so it is referred to as **incompatiblism**; free will and determinism cannot both exist.

Many people have adopted this perspective and for the neuroscientist with a reductionistic viewpoint, it is perhaps the obvious conclusion. For example, Francis Crick states 'you, your joys and your sorrows, your memories and your ambitions, your sense of personal identity and free will, are in fact no more than the behavior of a vast assembly of nerve cells and associated molecules' (Crick, 1994, p.3). Joseph Ledoux signs off his book by saying 'You are your synapses. They are who you are' (LeDoux, 2002). On one level, this all seems very reasonable because we *are* just made up of cells, but intuitively our folk psychology tells us that this cannot possibly be true; we make decisions and we act on those decisions.

Determinism does not account for our sense of self and our inner subjective experiences; it leaves the **hard question** of consciousness unanswered. It cannot explain moral reasoning and social organization, or laws created by humans. Such phenomena cannot be predicted by mathematical modelling. With neuroimaging allowing a view of the brain, it is tempting to ascribe causality to the hotspots that can be identified during conscious experiences. But remember, neuroimaging provides neural correlates, it does not provide information beyond the fact that there might be increased energy consumption in a particular area. It does not tell us *how* that activity of the brain becomes conscious experience.

Compatabilism Compatabilists can be seen to occupy the middle ground between determinism and the classic libertarian views of free will. From this perspective, we have free will even though they acknowledge that thoughts are a product of the brain. The big question is how thoughts emerge as a product of the brain. Within **compatibilism**, free will is defined as having choices and the ability to have acted differently if you so choose.

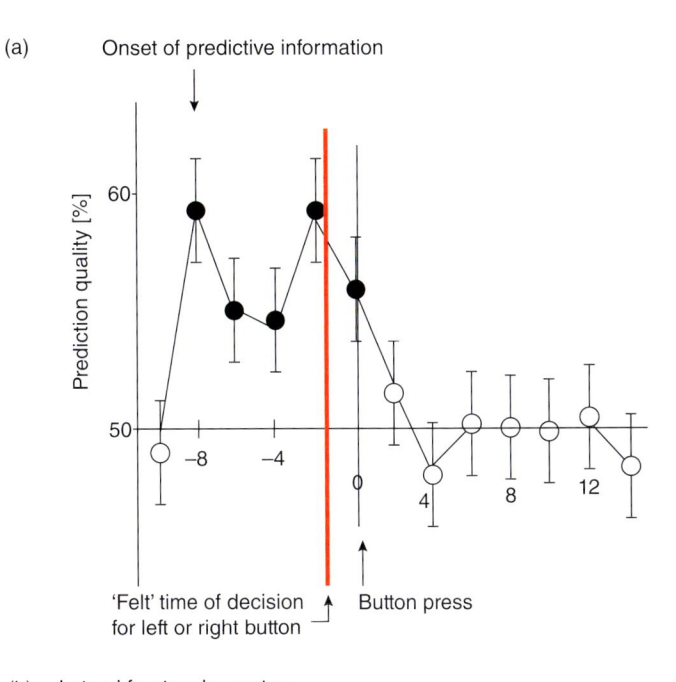

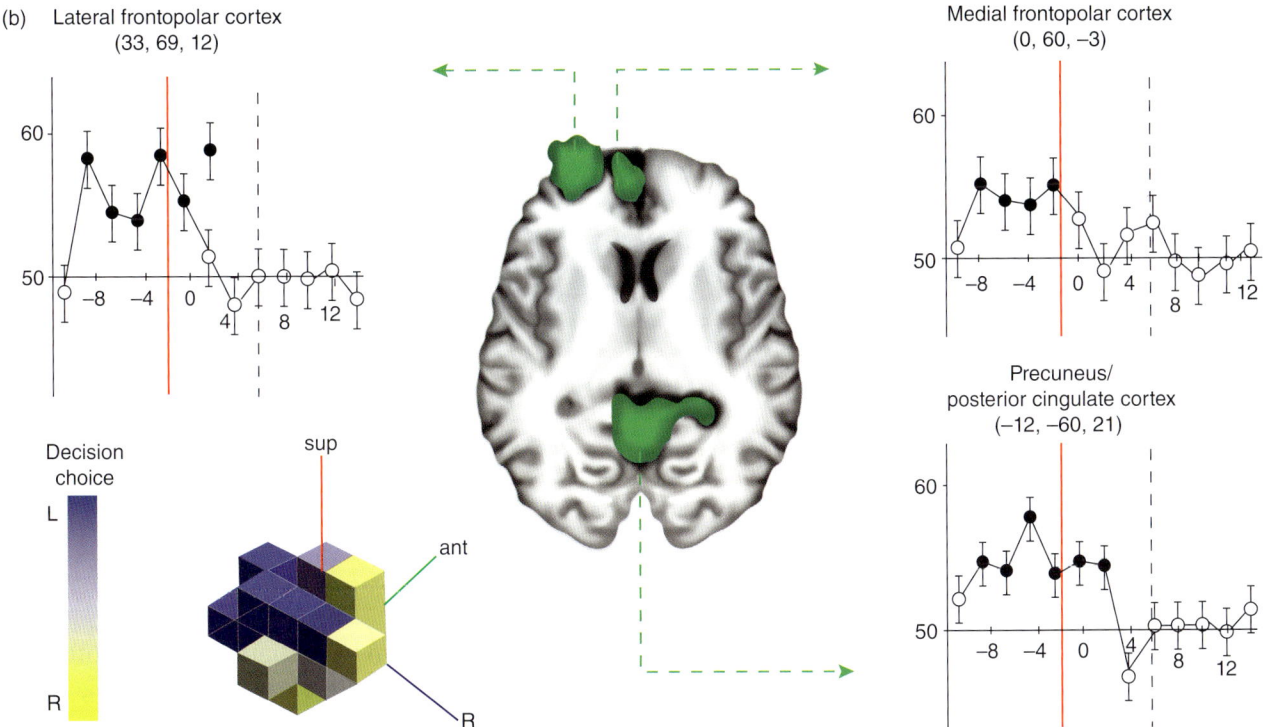

FIGURE 18.9 *Imaging data of the readiness potential. (a) The temporal relationship of Soon et al.'s experiment. (b) The outcome of a decision can be encoded in the brain activity of the prefrontal and parietal cortex up to 10 s before it enters awareness* (bottom panel). *The vertical red line shows the earliest time at which the subjects became aware of their choices. (c) The motor cortex and SMA activated for the motor response.*
Source: Reproduced by permission from Macmillan Publishers Ltd: NATURE NEUROSCIENCE Soon, C. S., Brass, M., Heinze, H. J., & Haynes, J. D. (2008). Unconscious determinants of free decisions in the human brain. Nature Neuroscience, 11(5), 543–545 copyright 2008.

(c)

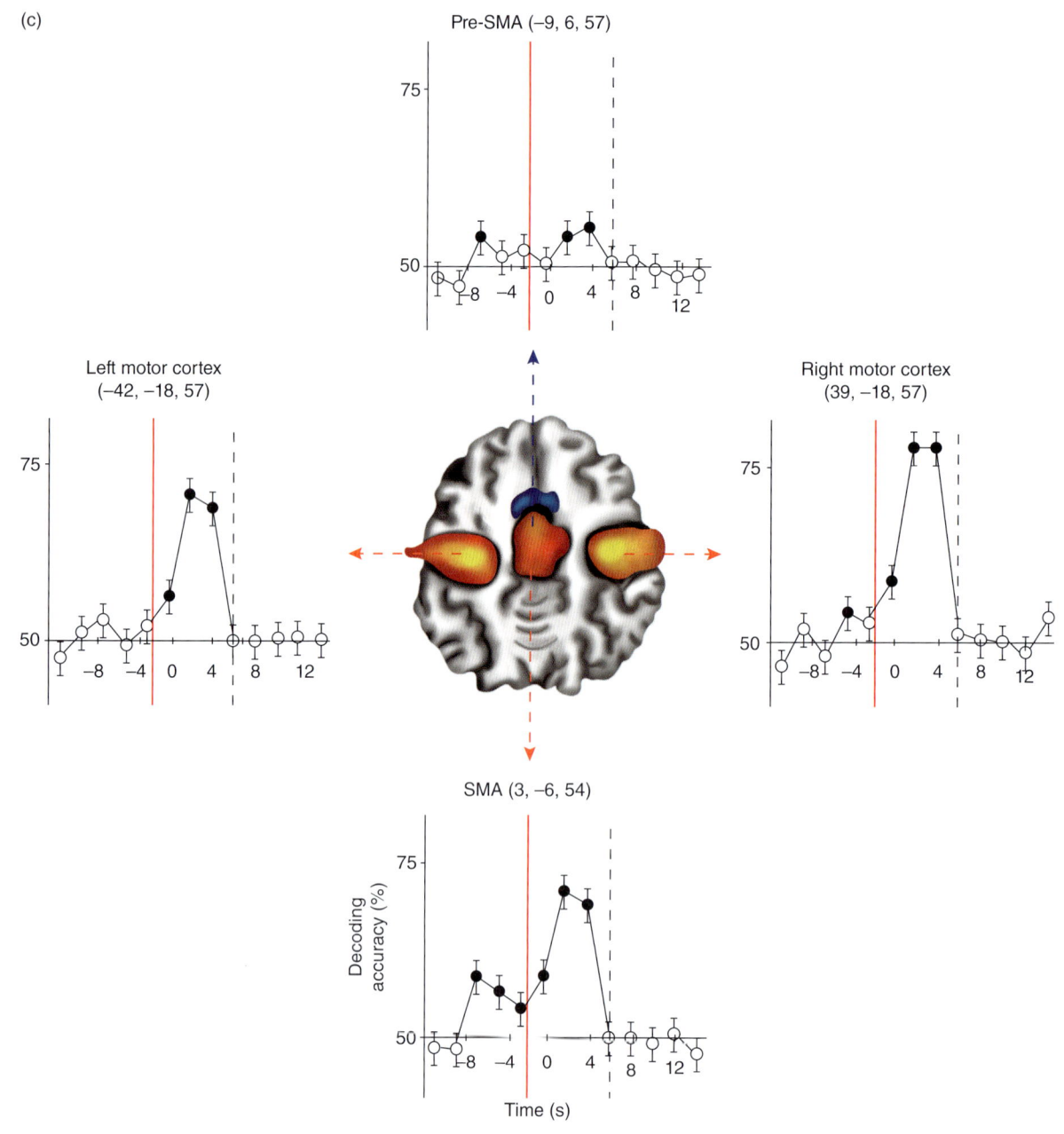

FIGURE 18.9 *(Continued)*

Tse (2013) states that a neural basis of free will is entirely possible. He argues that free will is based upon many systems and circuits of the brain that evoke procedures and subprocedures. Three criteria are proposed as a model of mental causation.

1. New physical/informational criteria are located in neural circuits and determined on the basis of preceding physical/mental processing at an earlier time (T1). This is achieved by rapid synaptic resetting (quicker than long-term potentiation; see Chapter 13) with glutamatergic systems that change the inputs to postsynaptic neurons.

2. At time T2, variable inputs are received by the postsynaptic neuron.

3. At time T3, physical/informational criteria are either met or not, resulting in neural firing of the postsynaptic neuron or not.

Tse suggests that randomness plays a role in the first two stages but not in the third stage, because neurons themselves generate random activity. Essentially, this theory views conscious decision making as the outcome of moment-by-moment changes in neural systems as a result of random activity and learning. Of course, we are still left trying to understand how all this neural activity becomes conscious thought. There is the view that conscious experience is the emergent properties of smaller subsystems, that they themselves are separate from the end product (consciousness/free will).

Free will: the grand illusion Daniel Wegner (2002) makes a bold claim suggesting that free will is an illusion. Wegner acknowledges the intuitive feeling of free will, when he writes:

> … it seems to each of us that we have conscious will. It seems we have selves. It seems we have minds. It seems we are agents. It seems we cause what we do. Although it is sobering and ultimately accurate to call all this an illusion, it is a mistake to conclude that the illusion is trivial. On the contrary, the illusions piled atop apparent mental causation are the building blocks of human psychology and social life. (Wegner, 2002, p.342)

Adopting a stance similar to Libet, Wegner acknowledges that 'the brain started first, followed by the experience of conscious will, and finally followed by action' (Wegner, 2002, p.55).

Wegner cites three ways in which our experience of conscious will can be incorrect:

- someone thinks they have not caused an action that they actually have caused;
- someone thinks they have caused an action that they actually have not caused; and
- confabulation, in which someone is mistaken about how they have caused an action.

The theory continues to suggest that unconscious thought produces conscious thought and that unconscious thought produces action. Therefore, conscious thoughts and actions have underlying unconscious mental process. These unconscious processes produce the feeling of having consciously willed an action but this is not the same as actually having willed an action – it is just a feeling; the feeling of free will is an illusion.

We therefore attribute actions to conscious thoughts, because conscious thoughts apparently precede actions and therefore we make a causal assumption. The causal assumption is not necessarily correct, e.g. if A follows B then B must have caused A, rather than A and B having a common causal pathway (see Figure 18.10).

In common with illusionists and magicians, the illusion of free will is subject to manipulation. Pronin et al. (2006) conducted a number of studies in which false causation was manipulated. In their studies they got college students to adopt the role of witchdoctor and perform a ritualistic curse on an experimental confederate. They introduced the participants to the confederate who was either neutral or offensive. They then had to stick voodoo pins into the voodoo doll, to which the confederate victim responded with the symptoms of a headache. To set the scene, the experimenters provided participants with Walter Cannon's paper on voodoo death (see Chapter 9 and the nocebo effect). Participants were assessed for their evil thinking or neutral thinking about the victim. Those participants who were ascribed to the evil thinking condition were more likely to believe that they had caused the headache. Two other experiments in the paper also supported the voodoo experiment. Thus, people perceived that they were in control of outcomes even when they were not.

In a study looking at depressed and non-depressed students, Alloy and Abramson (1979) assessed the probability/contingency of a response to an outcome. In depressed students they were found to be more accurate in assessing response-outcome probabilities in comparison to non-depressed students who were more likely to provide overestimations of the degree of control and causality they actually had. This illusion of control has been supported by others (Ackermann & DeRubeis, 1991; Benassi & Mahler, 1985) and perhaps fits with the theory of learned helplessness and depression (see Chapter 8) in which depressed individuals do not view that their actions are linked to outcomes (determinism) whereas non-depressed individuals would appear to have the illusion of control in which their actions bring about outcomes (libertarians).

Rigoni et al. (2012) performed an experiment in which participants underwent three phases.

1. Belief manipulation, in which participants read sets of sentences and were asked to think about their meaning; the statements were either deterministic or neutral.
2. Experimental tasks included an inhibition task that involved intentional inhibition (e.g. a type of go/no-go task; see Chapter 12).

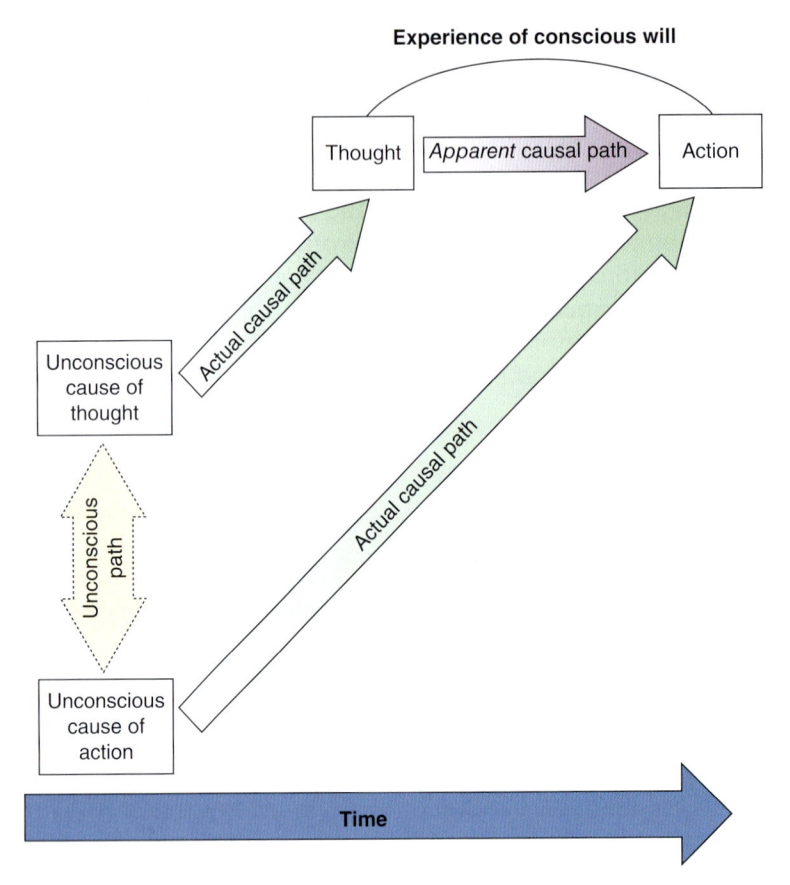

FIGURE 18.10 *Wegner's grand illusion of free will. Two pathways lead to action: a thought pathway and an action pathway.*
Source: Wegner, D. M. (2003). The mind's best trick: How we experience conscious will. *Trends in Cognitive Sciences*, 7(2), 65–69.

3. Self-report questionnaires were used to assess their beliefs in free will and self-control.

The results indicated that those who had been exposed to the no free will/deterministic condition reported feelings of less control and free will, but also that they performed poorly on cognitive tasks in which they had to intentionally inhibit a response.

On a large societal scale, the illusion of free will may have many benefits, e.g. prosocial behaviours such as honesty and helpfulness and reducing aggression (Baumeister et al., 2009; Vohs & Schooler, 2008). Furthermore, inducing disbelief in free will was shown to change brain activity with a reduction in the readiness potential, thus indicating a complex network of conscious and preconscious activity influencing neural activity and the illusion of free will (Rigoni et al., 2011).

The societal importance of free will is highlighted by Michael Gazzaniga (2005b) in his book *The ethical brain*. He argues that brains are automatic, rule governed and determined devices. Brains are distinct from people, who are personally responsible agents free to make their own decisions because responsibility is a public concept (reminiscent of Cartesian dualism). Concepts of responsibility, rules and ethics are created in the space in between individuals – societies. Thus, aspects of agency are not located in the brain, but rather exist within the relationships and interactions with other brains. This works in terms of a description, but it does not explain how the brain creates the perception of agency in the space between collective brains.

You cannot put your finger on consciousness. You cannot touch it, but you can remove it. Consciousness is something that we all recognize but have great difficulty understanding. Neuroscience has yet to identify causality of consciousness. Even with the modern technologies available, how neurons firing and communicating with each other provide the emergent properties of consciousness remains elusive. Central to consciousness are the notions of free will and agency in which we are in charge of our own decision-making processes. Again, the intuitive grasp on free will is distinct from the scientific basis of free will. If you are looking for a definitive answer, then forget it; if you are looking for an intellectual argument then you've come to the right place – consciousness divides philosophers and neuroscientists both within and between disciplines.

SUMMARY

Consciousness can be looked at across a dimensional range, from sleep to being awake. Sleep is far from a state of unconsciousness. Sleep is an active process that potentially serves some important functions in terms of memory and consciousness. The different stages of sleep undergo constant change throughout the lifespan. REM sleep has received the most attention and is thought to be of the most functional benefit to humans. Descriptions of sleep and wake states have focused on psychophysiological measures. However, consciousness itself has successfully evaded a neurobiological substrate. How do the neurons of the brain work to provide awareness, and meta-awareness (being aware of being aware)? The question remains, and is not surprisingly referred to as the hard question. If you ask me what is the answer to the hard question of the neurobiology of consciousness, I have a surprisingly simple answer – I do not know.

LEARNING OUTCOME QUESTIONS

You should be able to answer the following questions.

- To what extent is circadian rhythm under the control of sunlight?
- Sleep is an active process. Discuss.
- What is the function of sleep?
- Evaluate the ramifications of Benjamin Libet's experiments on consciousness.

FURTHER READING

Churchland, P. S. (2008). The impact of neuroscience on philosophy. *Neuron, 60*(3), 409–411.
Frank, M. G. (2006). The mystery of sleep function: Current perspectives and future directions. *Reviews of Neuroscience, 17*(4), 375–392.
Gottesmann, C. (1999). Neurophysiological support of consciousness during waking and sleeping. *Progress in Neurobiology, 59*, 469–508.
Hobson, J. A. (2009). REM sleep and dreaming: Towards a theory of protoconsciousness. *Nature Reviews Neuroscience, 10*(11), 803–813.
Lee Kavanau, J. (2002). REM and NREM sleep as natural accompaniments of the evolution of warm-bloodedness. *Neuroscience and Biobehavioral Reviews, 26*(8), 889–906.
Nicolau, M. C., Akaarir, M., Gamundi, A., Gonzalez, J., & Rial, R. V. (2000). Why we sleep: The evolutionary pathway to the mammalian sleep. *Progress in Neurobiology, 62*(4), 379–406.
Roskies, A. L. (2010). How does neuroscience affect our conception of volition? *Annual Review of Neuroscience, 33*, 109–130.
Roskies, A. L. (2012). How does the neuroscience of decision making bear on our understanding of moral responsibility and free will? *Current Opinion in Neurobiology, 22*(6), 1022–1026.
Stenberg, D. (2007). Neuroanatomy and neurochemistry of sleep. *Cellular and Molecular Life Sciences, 64*(10), 1187–1204.
Stickgold, R., & Walker, M. P. (2007). Sleep-dependent memory consolidation and reconsolidation. *Sleep Medicine, 8*(4), 331–343.
Wegner, D. M. (2003). The mind's best trick: How we experience conscious will. *Trends in Cognitive Science, 7*(2), 65–69.

MIND MAP

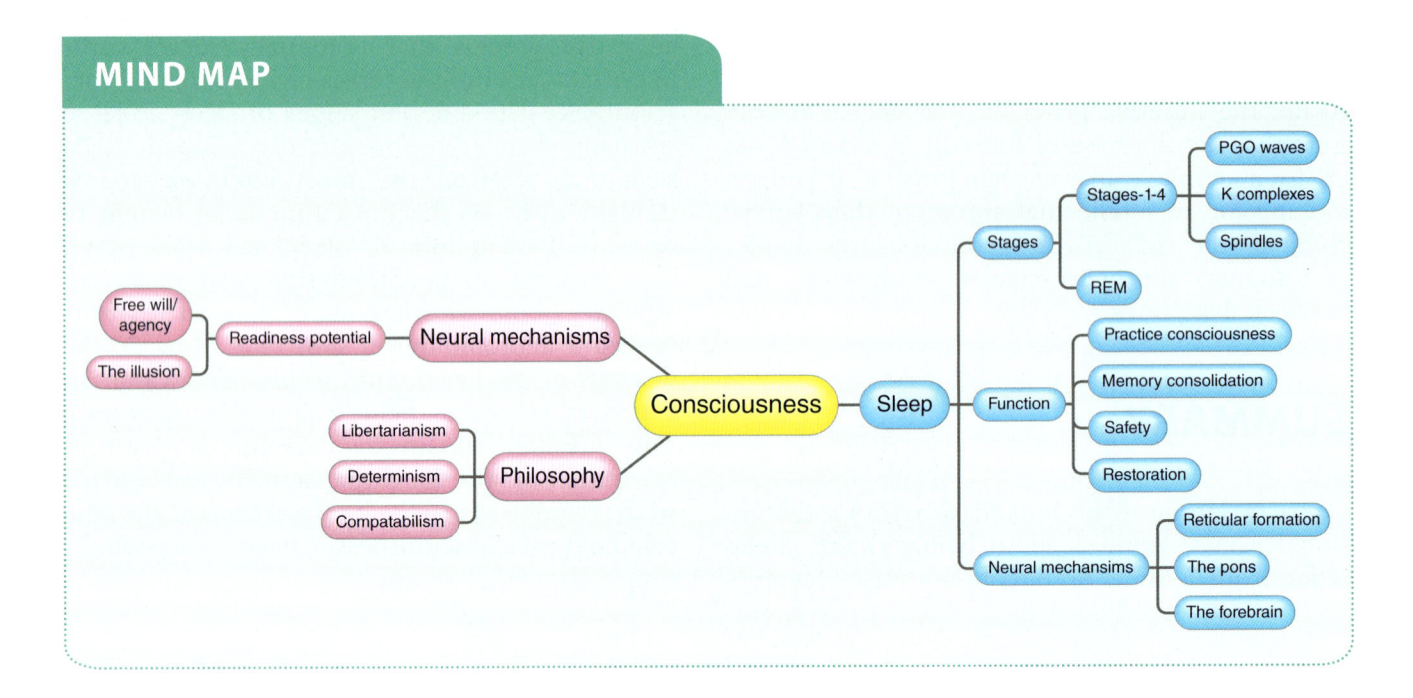

- **Consciousness**
  - Neural mechanisms
    - Readiness potential
      - Free will/agency
      - The illusion
  - Philosophy
    - Libertarianism
    - Determinism
    - Compatabilism
  - Sleep
    - Stages
      - Stages-1-4
        - PGO waves
        - K complexes
        - Spindles
      - REM
    - Function
      - Practice consciousness
      - Memory consolidation
      - Safety
      - Restoration
    - Neural mechansims
      - Reticular formation
      - The pons
      - The forebrain

19 Lateralization and Language

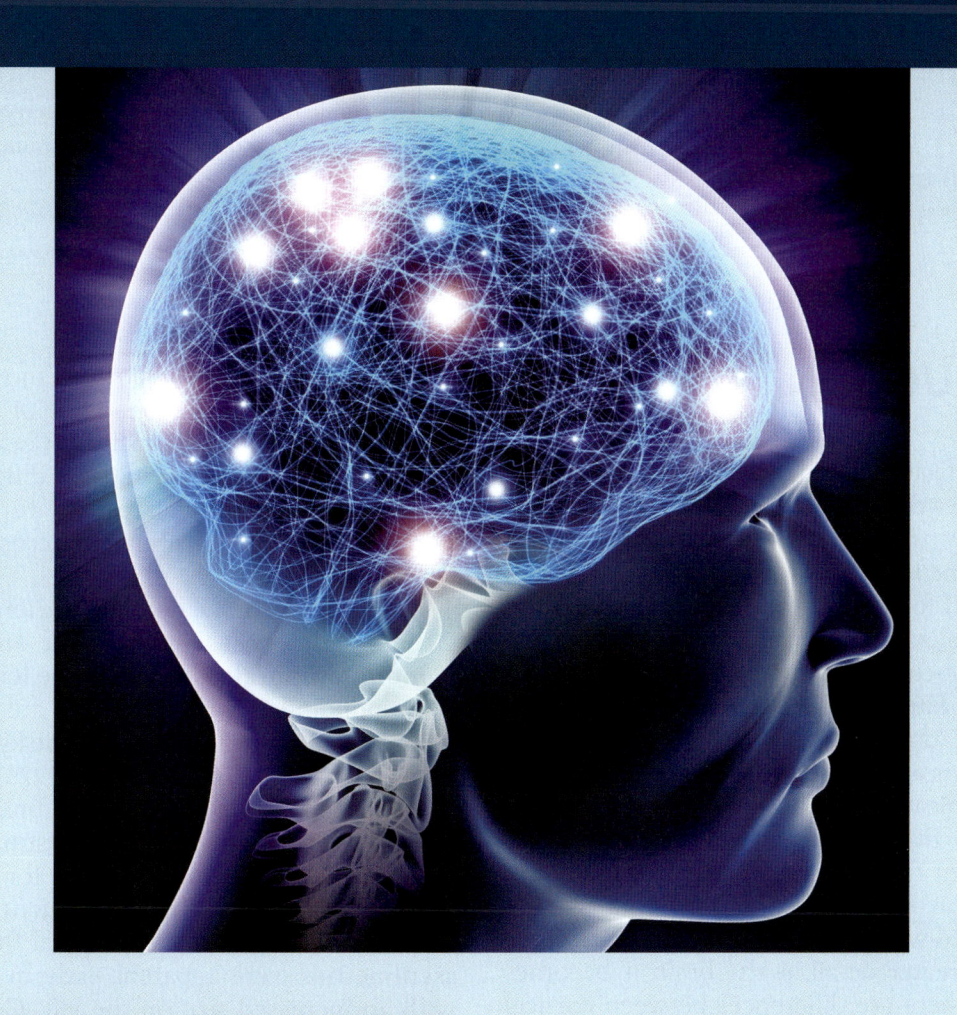

ANATOMY OF THE CHAPTER

This chapter will highlight the following.

- Asymmetry of the brain.
- Functional asymmetry of cognitive processes.
- The location of language-processing units in the brain.
- The evolution of asymmetry.

INTRODUCTION   484

LATERALIZATION: NEUROANATOMY   484

FUNCTIONAL LATERALIZATION   486

SUMMARY   496

LEARNING OUTCOMES

1. To understand the development of hypotheses regarding language.
2. To understand that the neuroanatomical asymmetry does not necessarily correlate with functional asymmetry.
3. To be able to account for changes in functional asymmetry across the lifespan.
4. To be able to explain the evolutionary rationale for cerebral asymmetries and lateralization of function.

INTRODUCTION

A quick surface examination of the exposed brain reveals two hemispheres that look identical. However, they are not identical in neuroanatomy or in their function. The notion that hemispheres are specialized for certain tasks is the basis of the study of lateralization, i.e. one side is more specialized for a particular task than another. Central to the theme of lateralization is language. Language is completely unique to humans. Do not forget that language is a form of communication and animals communicate, but not with the same degree of complexity that language allows. Although language has been the dominant behaviour in studies of lateralization, it is not the only behaviour that has been associated with a particular hemisphere. Once we look in greater detail at the brain it becomes evident that there are differences between cortical and subcortical areas. The big challenge has been to determine those neuroanatomical differences that underlie the functional lateralization that psychology experiments revealed. There is no denying that there is lateralization but how it emerges is still the subject of conjecture.

LATERALIZATION: NEUROANATOMY

Drawing a line down the centre of our body to bisect left and right does not reveal mirror images. The left and right feet, for example, are slightly different sizes. The same can be said for the brain. However, there are numerous sections of the brain, with some showing large differences between left and right and others showing minimal difference. Furthermore, the size of the regions is not the only factor to consider. The cellular composition of the regions may be different and the neurotransmitters that are used for communication have uneven distributions across the left and right hemispheres.

There are some notable regions that show distinct differences between left and right. The **planum temporale** is larger in the left hemisphere, corresponding with Wernicke's area (see below; Figure 19.1) (Geschwind & Levitsky, 1968; Wada et al., 1975; Witelson & Pallie, 1973). Asymmetry has been shown to exist in the brain as early as week 11–13 of gestation. Abu-Rustum et al. (2013) investigated 114 foetuses *in utero* for differences in the choroid plexus. This is a structure in the ventricles that produces cerebrospinal fluid (CSF) and asymmetries were apparent early in development, with an increased size on the left. Corballis (2013) suggests that there is good reason to think that this early asymmetry may give rise to the asymmetries seen in the planum temporale.

Behind the planum temporale is **Heschl's gyrus** containing auditory cortex, which is larger in the right hemisphere (Dorsaint-Pierre et al., 2006; Rademacher et al., 1993) (see Figure 19.1). The slope of the lateral fissure is gentler on the left hemisphere (Rubens et al., 1976) and there is a different organization of cells and increased size of the frontal operculum (Wada et al., 1975). The distribution of neurotransmitters is also asymmetrical (Glick et al., 1982). The anterior insular cortex was found to be greater in the right hemisphere (Watkins et al., 2001). The cortex is thicker in the left hemisphere than the right (Luders et al., 2006) and the right hemisphere extends further anteriorly whereas the left hemisphere extends further posteriorly (Toga & Thompson, 2003) (Figure 19.2). At the microscopic level, Scheibel et al. (1985) found

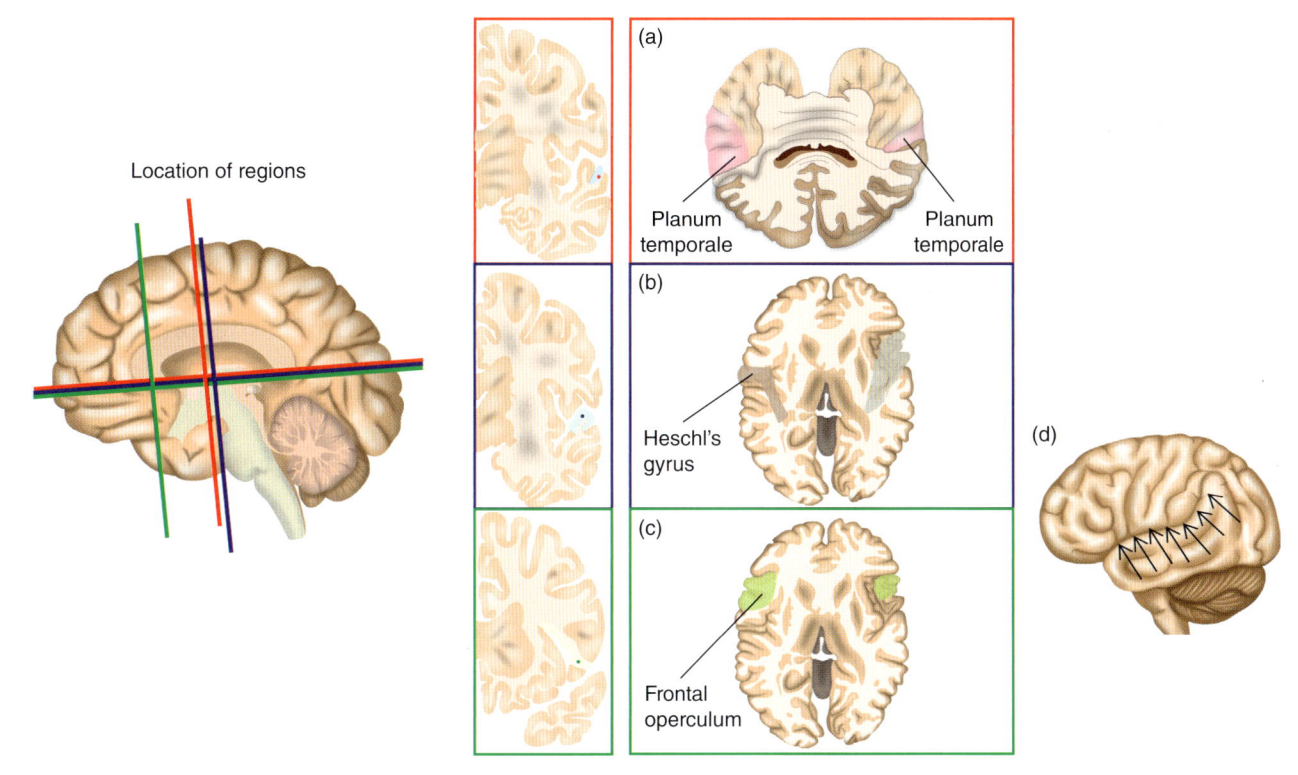

FIGURE 19.1 *Areas with asymmetry. (a) Planum temporale. (b) Heschl's gyrus. (c) Frontal operculum. (d) Lateral fissure.*

a difference in dendritic structure in the left hemisphere, with more higher order dendritic branches (thin branches that are distal to the soma) than on the right side. The left hemisphere was also found to contain an increased number of the largest pyramidal cells providing long-range connectivity within the cortex (Hutsler, 2003). Neurons in columns or units within the cortex are more interconnected in the right hemisphere and have become somewhat disentangled in the left hemisphere, thus potentially providing a greater capacity for differentiated responses in the left hemisphere (Seldon, 1982). The dendritic asymmetry seen in younger people has been shown to decrease with age, so the brain is not a static asymmetric organ (Jacobs & Scheibel, 1993).

It would be tempting to suggest that the neuroanatomical asymmetries give rise to functional asymmetries. However:

> The relationship of certain cytoarchitectonic features (presence of large pyramidal cells, laminar pattern, neuronal number, etc.) with brain function, and subsequently resulting complex human behaviour and language, has not been established for the vast majority of brain areas. (Keller et al., 2009, p.45) (Figure 19.3)

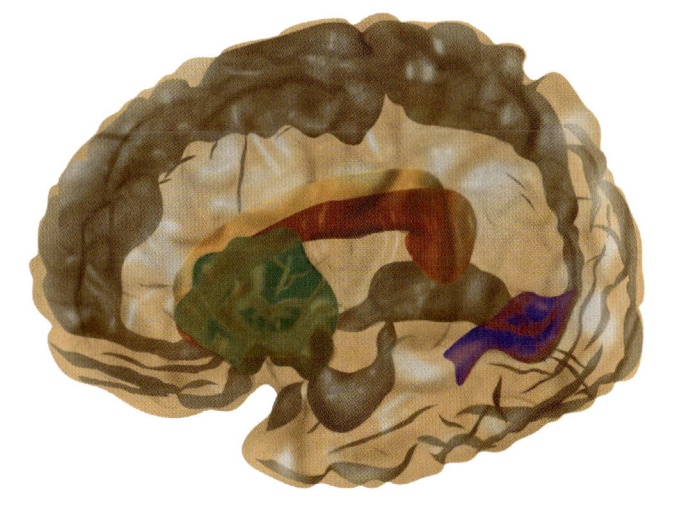

FIGURE 19.2 *Language areas with anatomical and functional asymmetries. Broca's speech area (green) and Wernicke's language comprehension area (blue) are identified on a transparent surface model of the human cerebral cortex. All cortical regions are heavily interconnected with corresponding systems in the opposite brain hemisphere, through the corpus callosum (yellow). The language areas show profound asymmetries, both structurally and functionally, the left hemisphere being dominant for language in most right-handed individuals.*

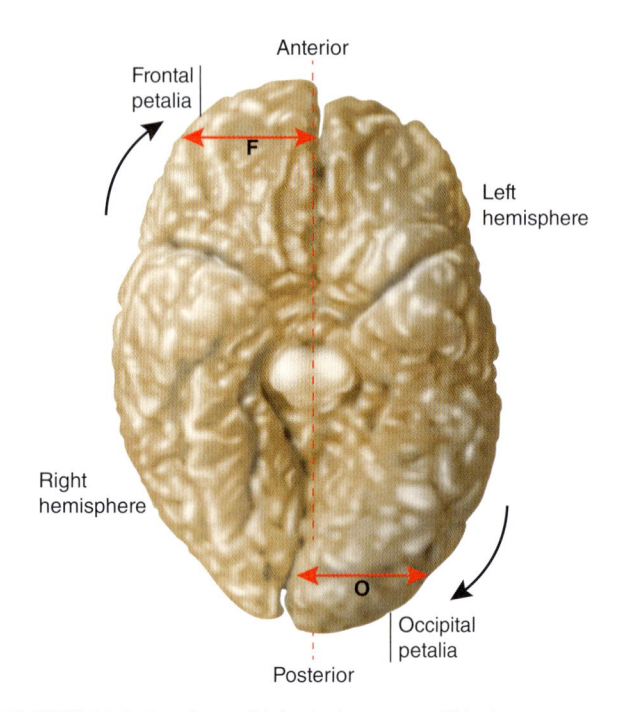

FIGURE 19.3 *Petalia and Yakovlevian torque. This three-dimensional rendering of the inferior surface of a human brain is derived from an in vivo MRI scan that has been exaggerated to illustrate prominent asymmetries found in the gross anatomy of the two brain hemispheres. Noticeable protrusions of the hemispheres, anteriorly and posteriorly, are observed, as well as differences in the widths of the frontal (F) and occipital (O) lobes. These protrusions produce imprints on the inner skull surface, known as petalia. A twisting effect is also observed, known as Yakovlevian torque, in which structures surrounding the right Sylvian fissure are 'torqued forward' relative to their counterparts on the left. The left occipital lobe is also splayed across the midline and skews the interhemispheric fissure in a rightward direction.*
Source: Reproduced by permission from Macmillan Publishers Ltd. NATURE REVIEWS NEUROSCIENCE Toga, A. W., & Thompson, P. M. (2003). Mapping brain asymmetry. Nature Reviews Neuroscience, 4(1), 37-48 copyright 2003.

FUNCTIONAL LATERALIZATION

The two cerebral hemispheres have been associated with many different functions (Springer & Deutsch, 1998). The neuroanatomical asymmetries are subject to a great deal of variation which is in contrast to the functional asymmetries seen in language (Keller et al., 2009). It is beyond the scope of this chapter to go into the details of language processing, but interested readers are guided to Ingram (2007).

The history of functional cerebral asymmetry begins with Marc Dax who in 1836 described neurological damage in the left hemisphere associated with paralysis on the right side of the body and aphasia. **Aphasia** is a dysfunction of language production. At the time of his report, the notion of functional lateralization was on a par with Darwin's theory of evolution; it was met with great scepticism.

However, Paul Broca is more widely credited as the originator of the view that language is located in the left hemisphere. In 1861, Broca reported a case study (patient Leborgne or 'Tan', the word that his speech was limited to) of damage to the anterior left hemisphere (Broca 1861a, 1861b)[1]. The lesion was discovered postmortem, but during his lifetime patient Tan had aphasia. From several case studies, Broca (1861a, 1863, 1865) developed an account of language being located in the left hemisphere. The area in question became known as **Broca's area** (Figure 19.4). Damage to Broca's area left the individual with normal comprehension, but with omissions of pronouns, prepositions, conjunctions, auxiliary verbs, tense and number endings during speech production. Their speech was understandable but disjointed and laboured. For example, someone with Broca's aphasia might say 'dinner now'

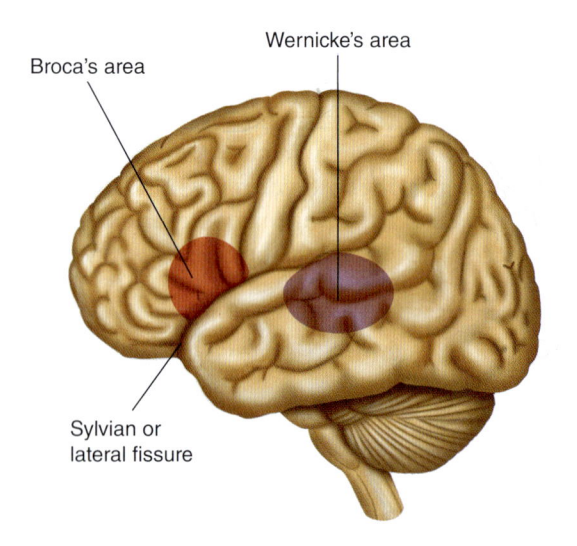

FIGURE 19.4 *Broca's and Wernicke's areas.*

[1] http://psychclassics.yorku.ca/Broca/ for translations

when they would mean to say 'it is the right time now for us all to have dinner'.

In addition to the aphasia, Broca described voluntary motor control deficits which were also associated with the left brain, as patients with lesions were apraxic. **Apraxia** is the inability to perform conscious motor movements. It is important to note that the postmortem evaluation of the brain came a number of years after damage was inflicted and the aphasia and motor problems were progressively deteriorating. Broca only evaluated the surface detail of the brain and did not investigate the subcortical structures that may also have had considerable damage. Therefore, the extent of the damage seen at postmortem may not be a true reflection of the actual damage that gave rise to the language difficulties.

Despite these caveats, one cannot overestimate the importance of these case studies which gave rise to the notion that the location of a function is predominantly in one hemisphere. This is lateralization with the left hemisphere being referred to as the dominant hemisphere. However, the dominance of the left hemisphere does not relegate the right hemisphere to a superfluous supporting role. The right hemisphere has been associated with spatial tasks (Witelson, 1976) and emotions (Schwartz et al., 1975).

Ascribing a function to a particular hemisphere does not provide it with a precise location; although described in detail by Broca, it was only the surface detail and the cytoarchitecture was not differentiated with other regions of the brain. Whereas Broca's area is associated with speech production, another area, **Wernicke's area**, is associated with language comprehension. As one might expect, Wernicke's area takes its name from a doctor who noted that a different aspect of speech could be affected by damage to a more posterior area than the one Broca described (see Wernicke (1977) for a collection of translated papers by Eggert). The result of damage to this part of the brain was to induce fluent aphasia or receptive aphasia (or Wernicke's aphasia). The symptoms of damage to Wernicke's area are poor comprehension, in which speech sounds normal but actually has no meaning. The wonderful phrase 'word salad' is used to describe Wernicke's aphasia where there is randomness of words and phrases with the addition of misspeaking words and making new words up, e.g. 'You know that smoodle pinkered and that I want to get him round and take care of him like you want before' (NIDCD, 2008).

Lichtheim (1885) integrated these two areas with a hypothetical concept centre (see Catani & Mesulam, 2008). This conceptual centre did not have a neuroanatomical basis.

It has been argued that the symptoms of brain damage may not necessarily be due to the primary site of damage but instead to distant 'hodological effects' (that is, connecting pathways further afield) (Catani & Ffytche, 2005).

Both areas produce their own type of aphasia. Dejerine in 1892 identified damage to an area that was posterior to Wernicke's area: the left angular gyrus. The consequence of such damage was **alexia** and **agraphia** (the inability to read and write respectively). The patient was able to speak and comprehend and the problem was restricted to language-related visual input from the left visual cortex.

Geschwind (1965a, 1965b, 1970) placed Broca's, Wernicke's and Dejerine's areas in a neural disconnectionist context within the left hemisphere (Figure 19.5). In general, incoming language is received by the auditory cortex and sent to Wernicke's area for comprehension. If a response is needed, a message is sent to Broca's area which then sends messages to the primary motor cortex. The motor cortex organizes the muscles to articulate the response. Visual words are sent to the angular gyrus, which codes the visual information for comprehension in Wernicke's area. This concept of language production and comprehension has been extremely influential, but is rather simplistic.

Whilst Broca's and Wernicke's areas appear far away, they are in fact connected by the arcuate fasciculus (Catani et al., 2005; Hong et al., 2009) (Figure 19.6). Catani et al. (2005) discovered a **perisylvian language network** comprising the **arcuate fasciculus** but also an indirect pathway that runs parallel and lateral to the arcuate fasciculus. This pathway connects areas of the parietal cortex

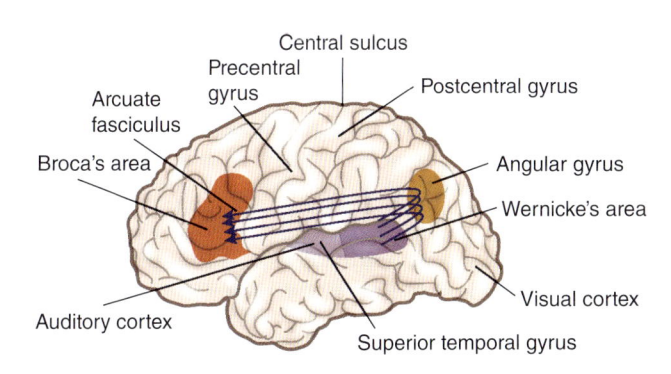

FIGURE 19.5 Wernicke–Geschwind model of language.

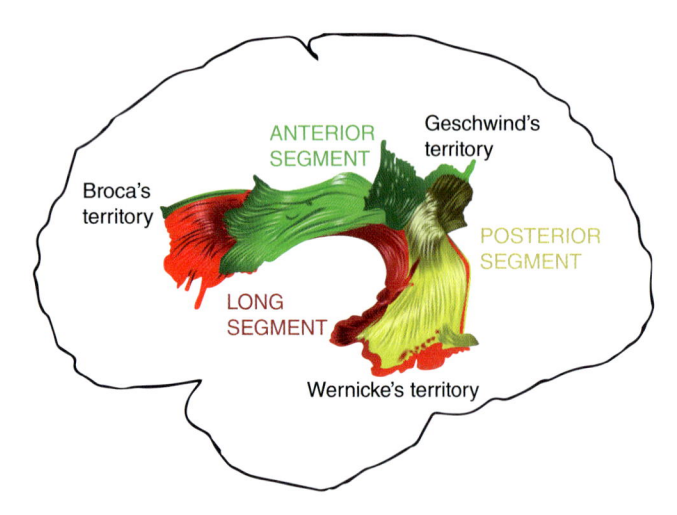

FIGURE 19.6 *Perisylvian language networks of the human brain.*
Source: Catani, M., Jones, D. K., & Ffytche, D. H. (2005). Perisylvian language networks of the human brain. *Annals of Neurology, 57*(1), 8–16. Reproduced by permission of John Wiley & Sons.

to the language areas. Since the days of Broca and Wernicke, aphasias have been differentiated further. The different types of aphasia have been attributed to different components of the pathway of the arcuate fasciculus (see Figure 19.6).

- **Classical conduction aphasia** – associated with a long segment lesion and a failure in automatic repetition.
- **Transcortical aphasia** – associated with an anterior segment lesion and a failure to vocalize semantic content.
- **Sensory aphasia** – associated with a posterior segment lesion and a failure of auditory semantic comprehension.

However, lesions specific to this region did not lead to permanent aphasia (Rasmussen & Milne, 1975).

Experimental evidence does not support all the assumptions of the Geschwind–Wernicke model (Catani & Mesulam, 2008). While the aphasias are evident, the lesions are often widespread and localization of function differs across individuals (remember, there are no specifically identified cells for Broca's and Wernicke's area and differentiation is functional). If a lesion is precisely targeted on these areas, there is little evidence for aphasia (Keller et al., 2009; Rasmussen & Milne, 1975). The Geschwind–Wernicke model hypothesizes that lesions anywhere along the projection of the arcuate fasciculus would produce identical aphasias. However, this is not the case with aphasias 'forming a heterogeneous group ranging from "Broca-like" to "Wernicke-like" deficits' (Catani & Mesulam, 2008, p.955).

In a large study of patients with left hemisphere damage, Hecaen and Angelergues (1964) noted that damage to Broca's or Wernicke's area did not always have long-lasting language effects. The lack of permanence should not necessarily be seen as confirming that these regions are not involved in language and aphasia. Recovery of function may represent neuroplasticity within the nervous system (see Chapter 13). However, the specificity of the lesions is more problematic. Language deficits tend to be associated with large-scale lesions, rather than surgically precise targeting. Effects of lesions are often widespread and, as we have already described, can have downstream knock-on effects. Although undertaken in patients with neurological problems, the studies by Penfield and Roberts (1959), in which they performed electrical stimulation of the cortex in awake patients, provided a refreshing outlook without the inherent problems of lesion studies. These studies demonstrated that disruptions of language traditionally ascribed to Broca's and Wernicke's areas were more widespread than originally thought.

Studies since then have also found that electrical stimulation has pronounced effects on language in the left hemispheres, but not confined to discrete areas (Ojemann et al., 1989) (Figure 19.7). Bavelier et al. (1997) used powerful functional

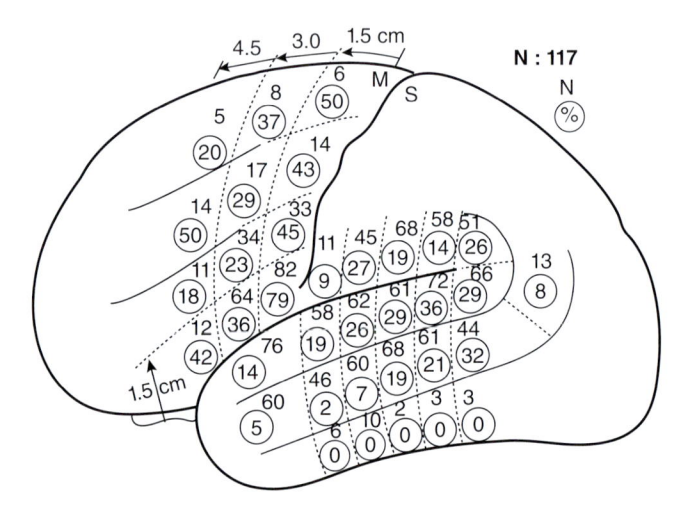

FIGURE 19.7 *Variability in localization of sites essential for naming, based on electrical stimulation mapping in left, language-dominant hemisphere of 117 patients.*
Source: Ojemann, G., Ojemann, J., Lettich, E., & Berger, M. (1989). Cortical language localization in left, dominant hemisphere. An electrical stimulation mapping investigation in 117 patients. *Journal of Neurosurgery, 71*(3), 316–326. Reproduced with permission.

magnetic resonance imaging (fMRI) machines and asked their participants to read sentences or consonants (as a control condition). There was a great deal of individual variability and variability across the hemispheres. However, in general, there was more activation in the left hemisphere and it was widespread beyond the boundaries of Broca's and Wenicke's area.

Neuroimaging data of grey matter volume was unable to detect a strong case for a neuroanatomical difference across the hemispheres that would explain the lateralization of language (Greve et al., 2013). Thus, we find ourselves with a neuroanatomical and functional dichotomy.

The **Wada test** involves injecting **amobarbital** (**sodium amytal**) into the carotid artery (Wada & Rasmussen, 2007). Amobarbital is a barbiturate derivative acting on GABA A receptors that leads to sedation and anaesthesia. When injected into the carotid artery in low doses, the effect is transient anaesthesia of the ipsilateral hemisphere (Figure 19.8). The effect is to render the patient momentarily mute and upon recovery, there are errors in components of speech. If the injection delivers the anaesthetic to the right hemisphere (non-speech) then there is little effect on language functions. Whilst the effect indicates which hemisphere is language dominant, it does not tell us anything more about the location of language processes. Binder et al. (1996) compared the Wada test with data obtained from fMRI scans and found a good correlation between the results. The use of neuroimaging has generally supported left lateralization of language (Binder et al., 1995; Hinke et al., 1993; Price, 2010, 2012).

The **dichotic listening test** is a wonderful experimental design by Kimura (1961). Using this test, Kimura was able to identify functional asymmetry without the use of any invasive procedures (Kimura, 1967). There are a number of variations on the methodology but the general procedure is as follows: using headphones, participants are simultaneously presented with a list of digits to each ear independently. The participant has to recall the digits and there is a tendency to recall more digits presented to the right ear than the left (Figure 19.9). The right ear dominance is translated as a left hemisphere advantage (contralateral to the ear) (Bryden, 1988). The more lateralization (left or right ear preference) was evident during the dichotomy listening tasks was related to increased accuracy during task performance (Hirnstein et al., 2014).

What is certain is that a more complicated language network is evident throughout the brain and is subject to individual variation, rather than the localized view of Broca and others (Amunts et al., 1999; Ojemann, 1979). Figure 19.10 from Price (2012) elegantly demonstrates the complexity and spread of language function throughout the hemisphere.

The right hemisphere is not devoid of language effect. It has been associated with prosody (Weintraub et al., 1981) which is the emotional emphasis in language and discourse (the meaning) (Beeman, 1993).

Asymmetry and Sex

An area of hot debate is the difference in cognitive abilities between the sexes (Weiss et al., 2003). Males are regarded as more right brain and more lateralized. Females are thought to be more left brain and have less lateralization. The stereotype is that women are better communicators and men are better at spatial tasks. A car insurance report points to this stereotype: women are more likely to claim for accidents in car parks whilst manoeuvring. Men on the other hand have far more serious (and costly) accidents involving high speeds. Thus, the myth about women drivers is perpetuated.

Why should there be a difference in lateralization between the sexes?

Numerous evolutionary theories have been presented to account for lateralization in general (Box 19.1). The case for spatial abilities has emphasized the male as hunter-gatherer. Therefore, spatial

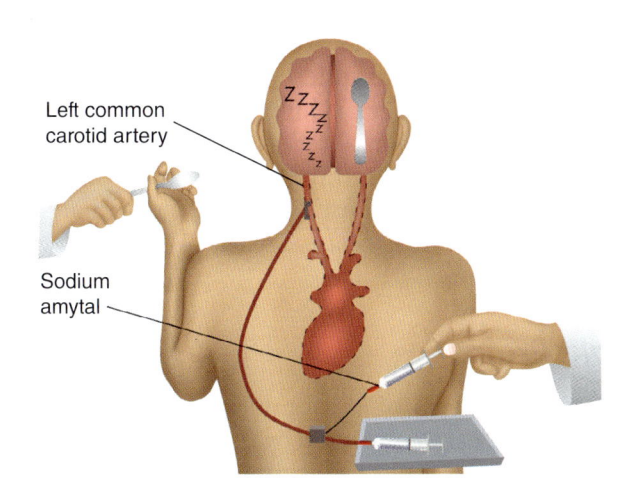

FIGURE 19.8 *The Wada test. Amobarbital is injected into one side of the brain (see Chapter 5 for vascular supplies).*

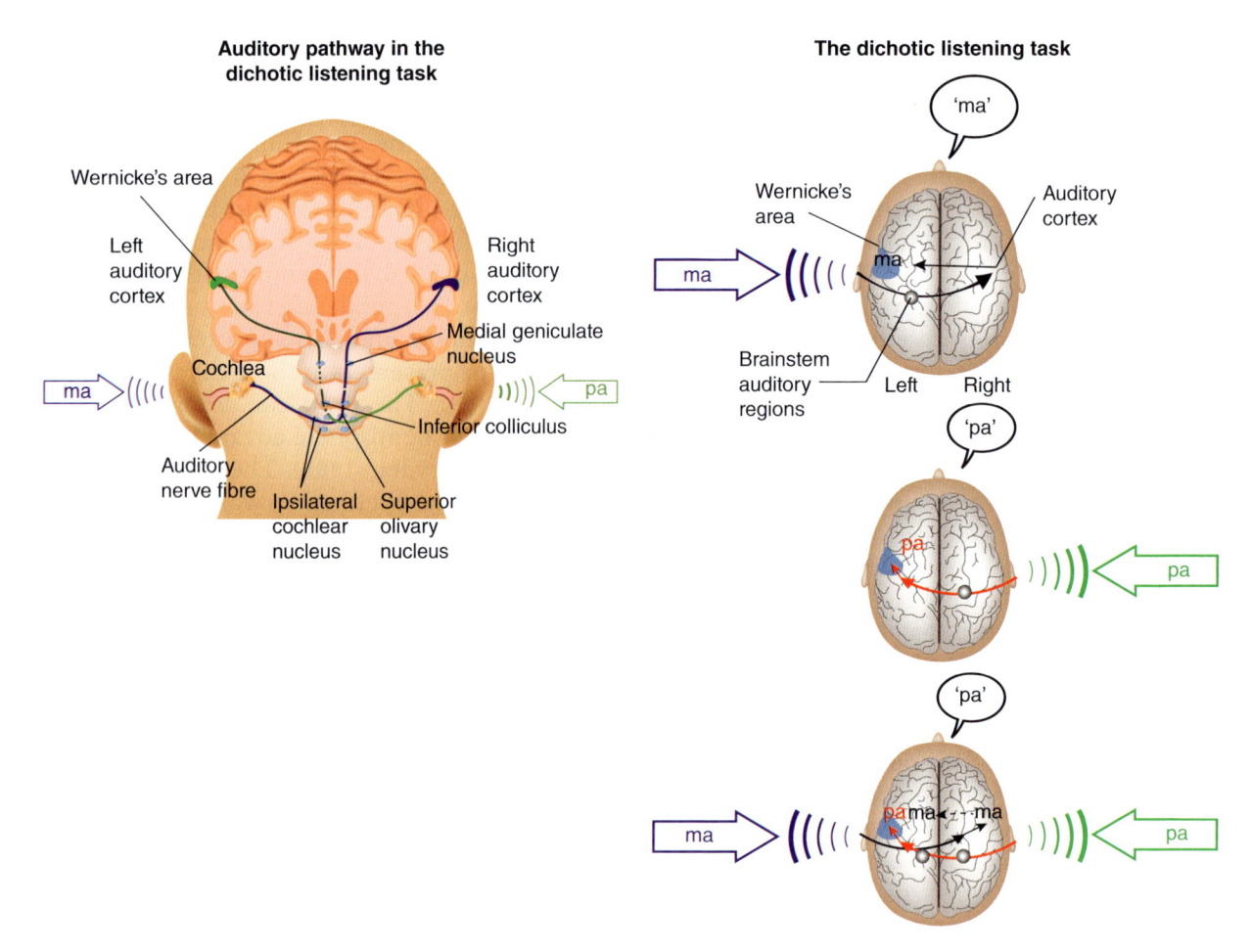

FIGURE 19.9 *The dichotic listening tasks.*

abilities have been perpetuated via natural selection (Jones et al., 2003).

Is Functional Lateralization Fixed?

Lateralization changes throughout development and subsequent ageing (Best, 1988). However, functional asymmetry can change in the short term. The functional asymmetry of the brain has been investigated during different phases of the menstrual cycle. Sanders and Wenmoth (1998) used a verbal and musical dichotic listening task to reveal the effects of the menstrual cycle on cerebral asymmetries. The verbal task is aimed at the left hemisphere, whereas the music task is for the right hemisphere. In the experiment by Sanders and Wenmoth, one dichotic listening task was to either identify consonants or vowels. The other task was to identify which of four musical chords had been presented. The listening tasks were conducted at different times during the menstrual cycle. The results of this study demonstrated that the women's ability at these tasks differed as a function of menstrual status. During menses, when oestrogen is low, there was a left ear advantage for the music task (right hemisphere). During the midluteal phase, when oestrogen is high, there was a right ear advantage for the verbal task (left hemisphere). The functional cerebral asymmetry was greatest for the music task during menses, and for the verbal task during the midluteal phase.

Split Brains

The hemispheres of the brain appear to be separate but they are connected by the corpus callosum. Lesions of the corpus callosum have been important

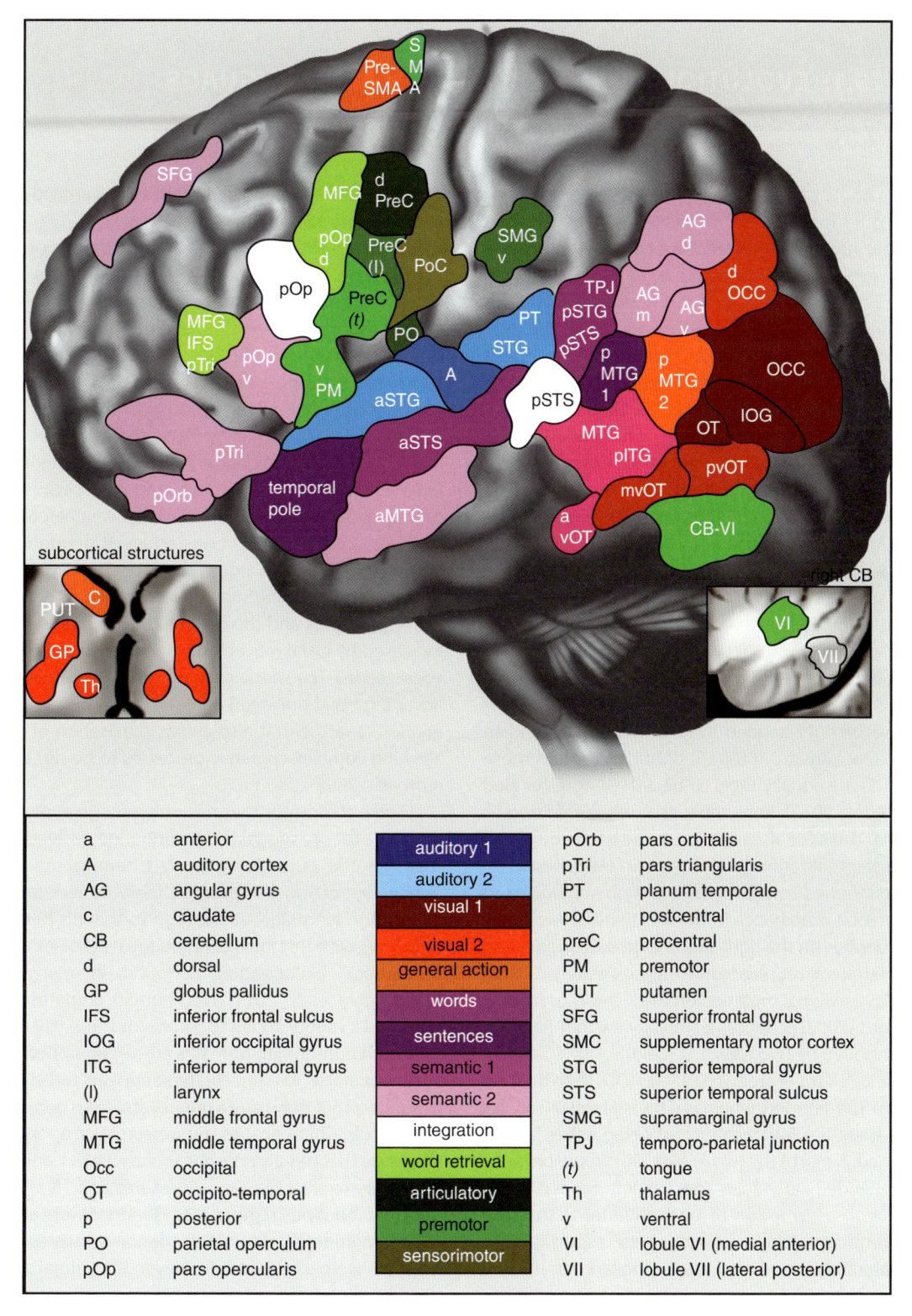

FIGURE 19.10 *Left hemisphere areas activated by spoken and written language tasks.*
Source: Price, C. J. (2012). A review and synthesis of the first 20 years of PET and fMRI studies of heard speech, spoken language and reading. *Neuroimage, 62*(2), 816–847.

BOX 19.1: EVOLUTION OF LATERALIZATION AND LANGUAGE

The vast majority of people show lateralization in certain tasks. The question is, why? The evolutionary accounts of why lateralization was selected adopt different positions. Within the evolutionary conjecture is the rise of language. Language is unique to humans and is an advanced form of communication. Many of the theories about the evolution of cerebral asymmetry join language with motor co-ordination.

One of the clearly demonstrable functional lateralizations is handedness. Most of us are right-handed with a minority preferring to use the left hand (Coren & Porac, 1977). Unlike many other lateralized functions, handedness is easy to evaluate. Annett (2002) proposed that there was a right shift (RS) gene for handedness that had two alleles: RS- and RS+. The function of the RS gene is to impair the control of speech systems in the right hemisphere, thereby permitting language to develop in the left side. The RS+ allele promotes this right shift whereas the RS- has no effect and does not cause a left shift. The interaction of these genes is additive. If there are two RS+ alleles then the vast majority will be right-handed. In those with an RS+ and an RS- allele, approximately 68% are right-handed and those with two RS- are equally likely to be left- or right-handed (Corballis et al., 2012). Remember that when referring to the right hand, we are also referring to the left hemisphere. In this conceptualization of the genetic transmission of handedness, Annett considers the selection not for a hand but for cerebral dominance in the left hemisphere. Crow (2010) elaborates on the right shift hypothesis, suggesting that cerebral lateralization occurred approximately 200,000 years ago as a result of mutation on the X chromosome.

McManus (2002) proposes a similar view that handedness is controlled by two alleles: D (dextral, right-handed) and C (chance). If there are two D alleles (DD) then the person will be right-handed, whereas if there are two C alleles (CC) then there is a 50/50 chance of being either left- or right-handed. A mix of the two alleles (DC) would produce 75% right-handed individuals and 25% left-handed.

A common assumption of both theories is that the gene responsible for handedness is also responsible for cerebral lateralization and language. The left hemisphere dominance is evident in nearly 95% of people who are right-handed (Knecht et al., 2000) whereas only 76% of left-handed people had left hemisphere dominance (Pujol et al., 1999; Warrington & Pratt, 1973). Thus, being left-handed does not mean that language dominance is in the right hemisphere. Milner (1974) reported important results of using the Wada test, finding that 92% of right-handed individuals were left hemisphere dominant and 69% of left-handed or ambidextrous individuals were left hemisphere dominant.

Kimura (1979) proposed a motor theory of cerebral asymmetry in which the left hemisphere was not specifically specialized for speech but for the control of fine motor movements which speech requires, e.g. oral and brachial movements (Kimura, 1982). Studies of the aphasia indirectly support such a view, as the condition affects not only language but also motor control.

Corballis (2012) similarly views the evolution of asymmetry as a motor artefact and argues that there is a link between physical actions and language because of the nature of language gestures themselves. Before spoken language, communication was achieved through gestures and actions. Corballis argues that at some point in evolution, making grasping movements turned into communicative processes and the benefits of communication were increased by facial movements and eventually turned into vocalizations. The specialization in one hemisphere has the advantage that unilateral processing can be carried out at greater speeds and it also avoids duplication of function, allowing complex cognitive processes to be run efficiently (Corballis, 2009).

Unlike the motor theories of language evolution, the linguistic theory suggests that language evolved because that was the purpose of the left hemisphere. The evidence supporting a linguistic theory derives from studies on sign language, as damage to the left hemisphere interferes with this form of language (Hickok et al., 1996).

Cerebral lateralization is found in many species (Vallortigara et al., 2011). Non-human primates use gestures and a variety of calls to communicate with each other. Although non-human primates are not equipped with the vocal apparatus for speech, there appears to be evidence to suggest that they have a greater ability for comprehending sounds. Chimpanzees use gestures, i.e. a form of sign language that has a subtle vocabulary. Pollick and de Waal (2007) discovered 31 manual gestures and 18 facial/vocal signals in bonobo chimpanzees. Bonobos were also found to use multimodal communication in which all types of gestures were integrated. However, the primates seldom used symbols in creative or original combinations. For a critique of a ape language research, see Hixson (1998).

Is there a genetic basis for lateralization?

If there is an evolutionary case for lateralization and language development then it should be evident somewhere in the human genome. Behavioural genetics has demonstrated a familial transmission. However, in a twin study spanning Australia and the Netherlands comprising over 54,000 participants, Medland et al. (2009) found no difference between monozygotic and dizygotic twins or their non-twin siblings, with genetics contributing 23.64% of the variance in handedness. Twins were also used to assess language abilities, with prevalence towards a genetic contribution to variance in the left hemisphere (Badzakova-Trajkov et al., 2010).

In terms of structural changes, the genetic influence on brain volume and cortical thickness was found to be more prevalent in the left hemisphere (78% of the variance) compared with the right hemisphere (51% of variance) (Yoon et al., 2010) (Figure 19.1.1).

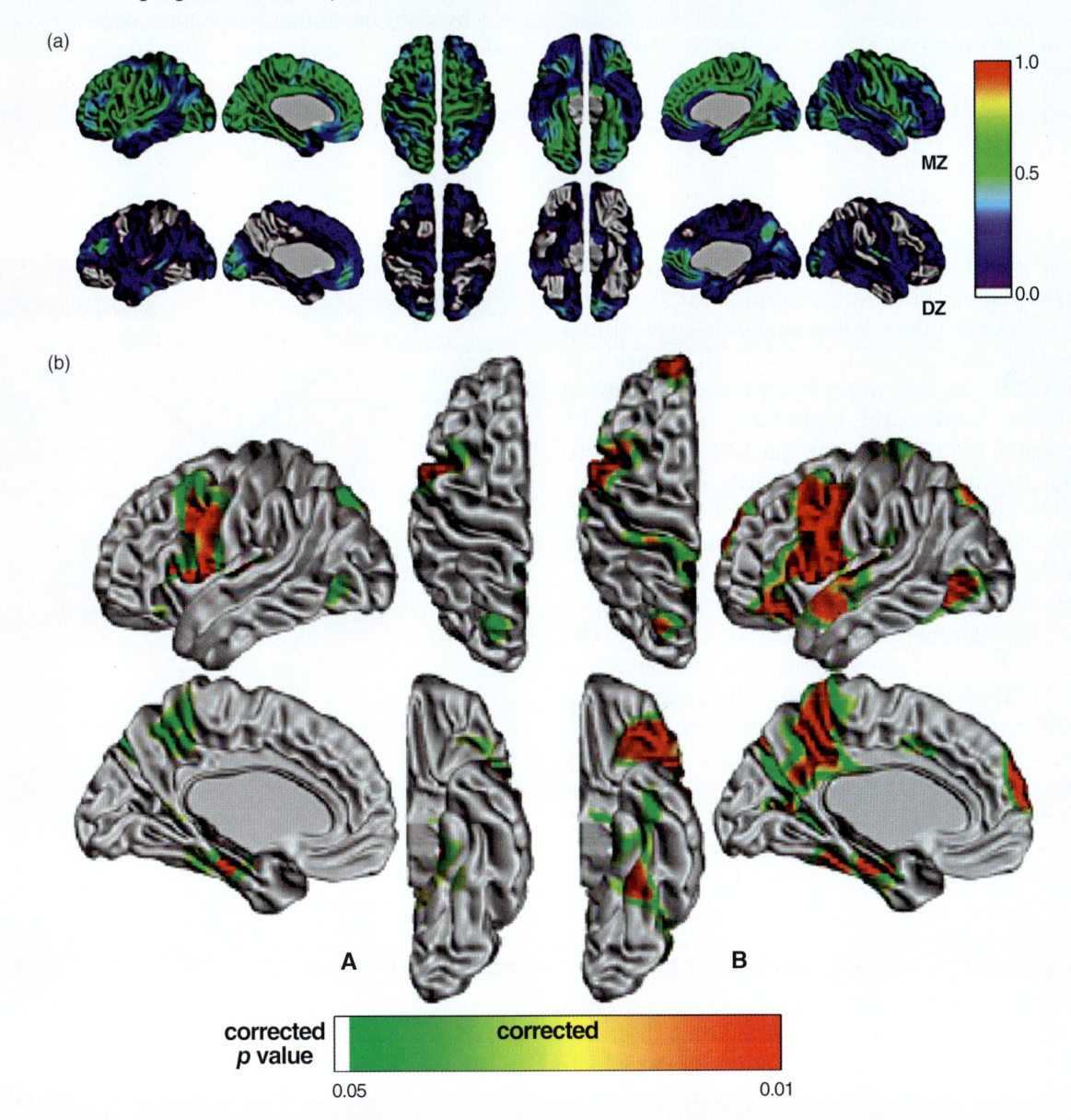

FIGURE 19.1.1 *(a) Intraclass correlation map for cortical thickness. Colour bar displays the scale of the correlation value. MZ correlations were significantly higher than those for DZ at most vertices in both hemispheres. (b) Brain regions with significant genetic effects on cortical thickness (A) and its hemispheric asymmetry (B). Each vertex is colour-mapped for level of significance following the application of a false discovery rate (FDR) threshold. Since there is no region with a significant genetic effect in the right hemisphere, only the left hemispheric cortical surface is displayed. In particular, Broca's area (BA 44), parahippocampal gyri (BA 34) and the medial region of the primary somatosensory cortex (BA 1, 2, 3) showed a statistically significant heritability of cortical thickness (A). These areas were included in regions of significantly heritable hemispheric asymmetry (B).*
Source: Yoon, U., Fahim, C., Perusse, D., & Evans, A. C. (2010). Lateralized genetic and environmental influences on human brain morphology of 8-year-old twins. *Neuroimage, 53*(3), 1117-1125.

If there is an evolutionary benefit of lateralization, can this be traced back to the molecular level? Three molecular mechanisms have been proposed:

- the addition or removal of genes between species;
- alterations in the genetic sequence; and
- changes in the pattern or level of gene expression.

An obvious place to look for the molecular basis of asymmetries is the language-dominant areas of the left hemisphere. Sun et al. (2005) investigated gene expression in the perisylvian region of the cortex in the tissue of foetuses at 12, 14 and 19 weeks. They found differential expression across the hemispheres that may underlie the developing cerebral asymmetry. With something so complex as language and lateralization, the identification of a single gene is unlikely as there may be many genes that support language (Graham & Fisher, 2013).

---

in understanding the functional specialization of the hemispheres and how the hemispheres communicate with each other. Some studies have exploited the visual system (see Chapter 10). Each hemisphere of the brain receives input from the contralateral half of the visual world. Light from the right half of the visual field falls on the left half of both retinas (the left and right eye) and light from the left visual field falls onto the right half of both retinas. Note that the discussion is about visual fields and not about the eyes themselves being left or right. The left half of each retina connects to the left hemisphere; the right half of each retina connects to the right hemisphere. Such organization of the visual system requires a cross-over so that the left visual field of the right retina is projecting to the left hemisphere. The point of cross-over is called the **optic chiasm** (Figure 19.11). Clearly, there is integration of information with both the left and right occipital lobes processing the visual fields. Information is passed across the hemispheres via the corpus callosum. By lesioning the corpus callosum, transfer of information is prevented.

Myers and Sperry (1953) performed lesions of the corpus callosum and the optic chiasm in cats (Figure 19.12). The cats were trained on a discrimination task (square versus circle stimulus) in which choosing the correct shape lead to food reward. The authors isolated the information being sent to the hemispheres by covering one eye up. The cats were quick to learn the discrimination task even with only one eye operational. However, if the cover was taken off the eye during training and then placed on to the other eye, the cat had to learn the whole discrimination process again, whereas those cats whose cover remained on the original eye demonstrated retention of learning (Figure 19.13). Numerous studies have supported these original findings (see Gazzaniga, 2005a).

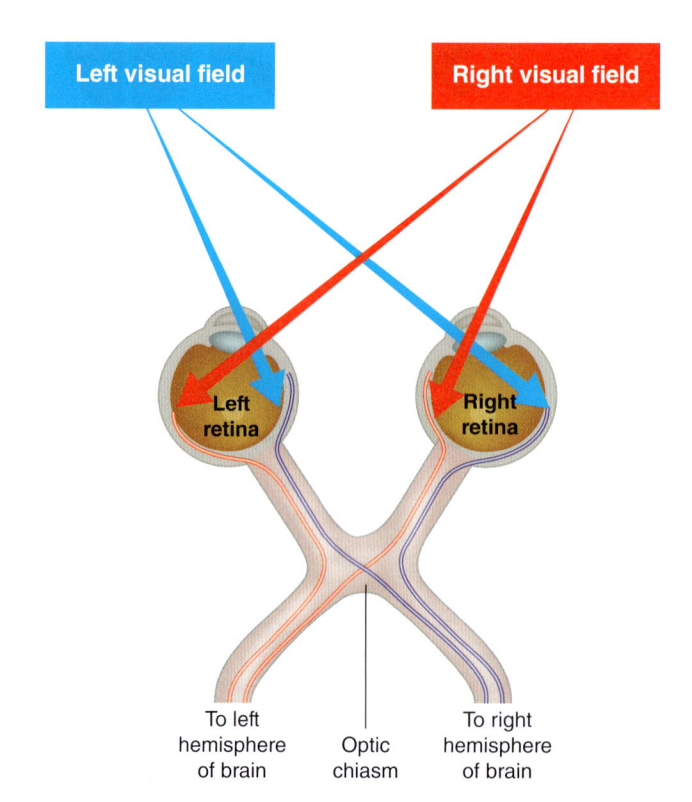

FIGURE 19.11 *Visual fields.*

Split-brain phenomena extend to humans. Lesions of the corpus callosum may be undertaken to contain the epileptic discharge from one hemisphere spreading to the other (Figure 19.14). Michael Gazzaniga and colleagues studied split-brain surgery in epileptic patients (Bogen & Gazzaniga, 1965; Gazzaniga et al., 1965; Springer & Gazzaniga, 1975). In order to determine the effects of split-brain

CHAPTER 19 LATERALIZATION AND LANGUAGE 495

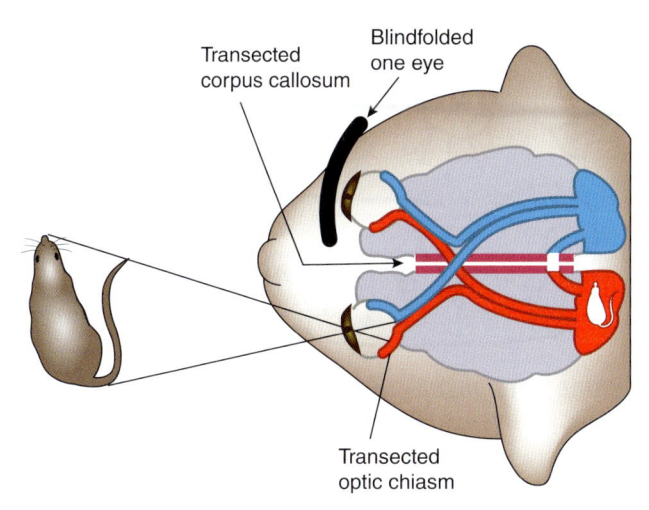

FIGURE 19.12 *Split-brain cat.*
Source: PINEL, JOHN P.J., BIOPSYCHOLOGY, 6th Edition, © 2006. Reprinted by permission of Pearson Education, Inc., Upper Saddle River, NJ.

surgery, the studies exploited the architecture of the visual system and designed experimental methodology to direct visually presented material independently to each hemisphere. The result was that when a word was presented on the screen, a person with split-brain surgery could only report what was seen in the left hemisphere but could point to the physical object that the word represented with the right hemisphere. For example, the word 'skyscraper' can be divided into 'sky' and 'scraper'. The word 'skyscraper' is processed as two words separately by each hemisphere (due to the experimental control) (Figure 19.15). The same can be seen in drawings (Figure 19.16) (Kingstone & Gazzaniga, 1995). One of the important experimental features was the speed of presentation. Long presentations would allow for hemispheric transfer via different routes.

Zaidel (1975) developed the Z lens which restricted visual input to one hemisphere. The Z lens allows information of the complex scene that involved scanning with the eyes to be restricted to a limited part of the visual field. It does this by focusing the entire visual field on to one half of the retina (Figure 19.17). In split-brain patients, emotionally evocative images were projected to the right hemisphere and they behaved in an emotionally appropriate way and were able to articulate this in their speech. This led Sperry et al. (1979) to conclude that emotional reactions are readily passed across hemispheres whereas visual information was not.

How the corpus callosum produces interhemispheric communication is still to be determined.

There were four groups

1. Control group—only the optic chiasm transected
2. Control group—only the corpus chiasm transected
3. Control group—unlesioned
4. Experimental group—the optic chiasm and corpus callosum transected

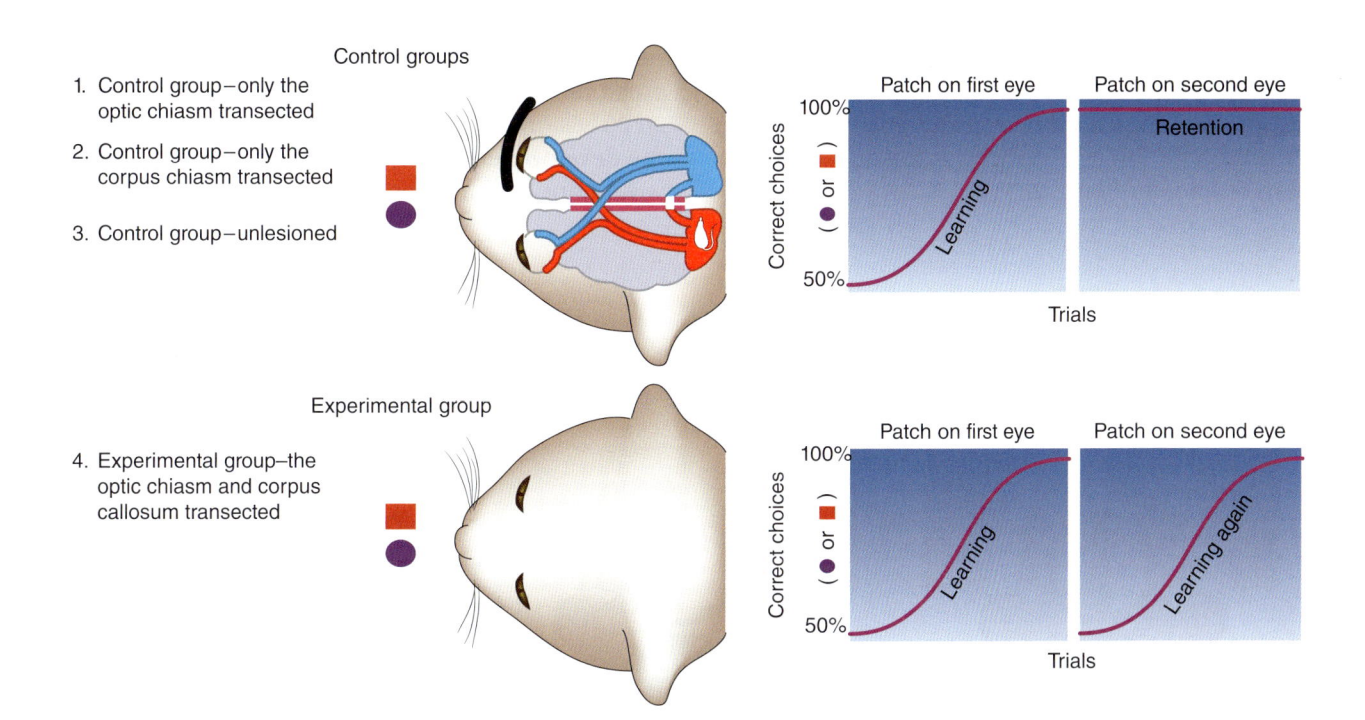

FIGURE 19.13 *Myers and Sperry's experiment.*
Source: PINEL, JOHN P.J., BIOPSYCHOLOGY, 6th Edition, © 2006. Reprinted by permission of Pearson Education, Inc., Upper Saddle River, NJ.

496 PSYCHOBIOLOGY

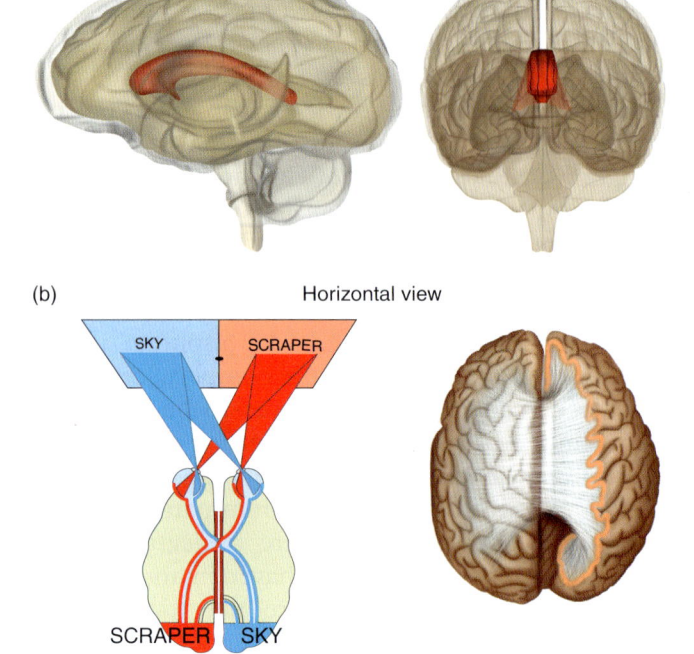

FIGURE 19.14 *The corpus callosum and split brains. (a) Corpus callosum. (b) The projection of information to the visual fields.*

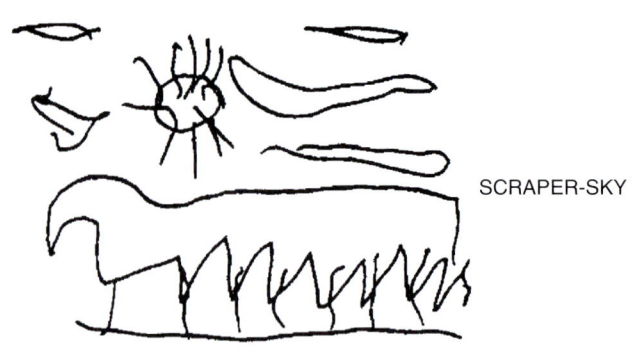

FIGURE 19.16 *The transfer of information across hemispheres. Patients are unable to process the word 'skyscraper' as one word, but instead draw a picture of the sky and a picture of a scraping tool.*
Source: Kingstone, A., & Gazzaniga, M. S. (1995). Subcortical transfer of higher order information: More illusory than real? *Neuropsychology, 9*, 321-328.

However, it has been argued that it is an interaction of excitatory and inhibitory influences on the hemispheres. Inhibitory influences from the corpus callosum mean that the dominant hemisphere can be left to get on with its tasks, depending upon task demands. The excitatory theory posits that cross-hemispheric information transfer and integration are reinforced by the corpus callosum (Van der Knaap & Van der Ham, 2011).

SUMMARY

Lateralization exists, but the detail requires greater evaluation. Broad brush strokes that identified the left hemisphere as dominant in language probably remain the most accurate. Largely, the left hemisphere is the language dominance hemisphere in the majority of people (and may be responsible for learning difficulties, e.g. **dyslexia**) (Box 19.2). Trying to identify the detail of the left hemisphere has proved to be somewhat more difficult. In part this is due to the early studies relating aphasia to brain damage in portions of the left temporal lobe. Hindsight is always 20:20 vision and without those studies and views, the development of the psychobiology of language would not have advanced. Broca and Wernicke gave

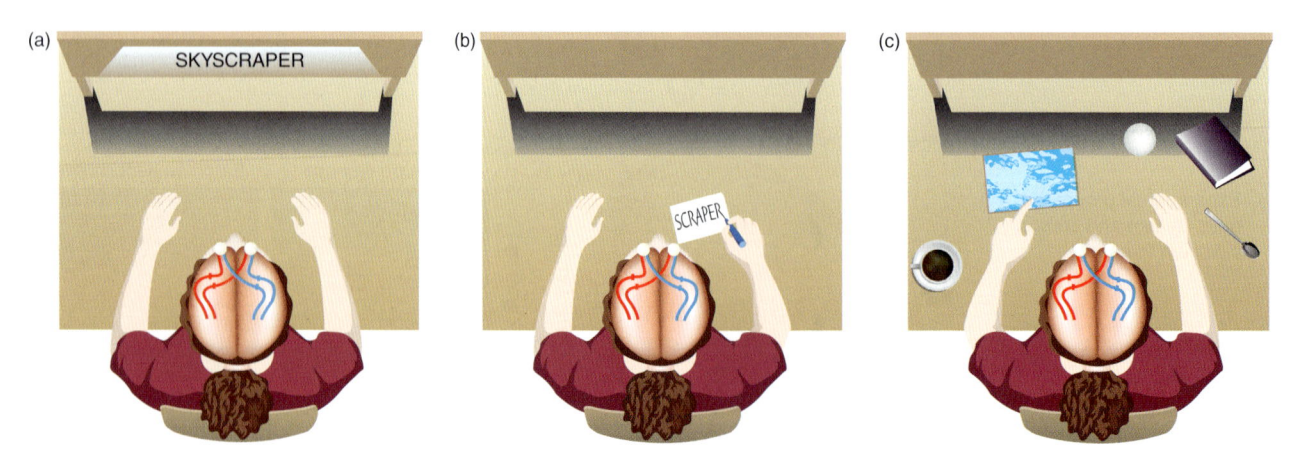

FIGURE 19.15 *(a) The word 'skyscraper' is flashed on the screen. (b) This split-brain patient can only report what the left hemisphere saw (scraper). (c) Same patient can point to the representation of the rest of the word (picture of the sky).*

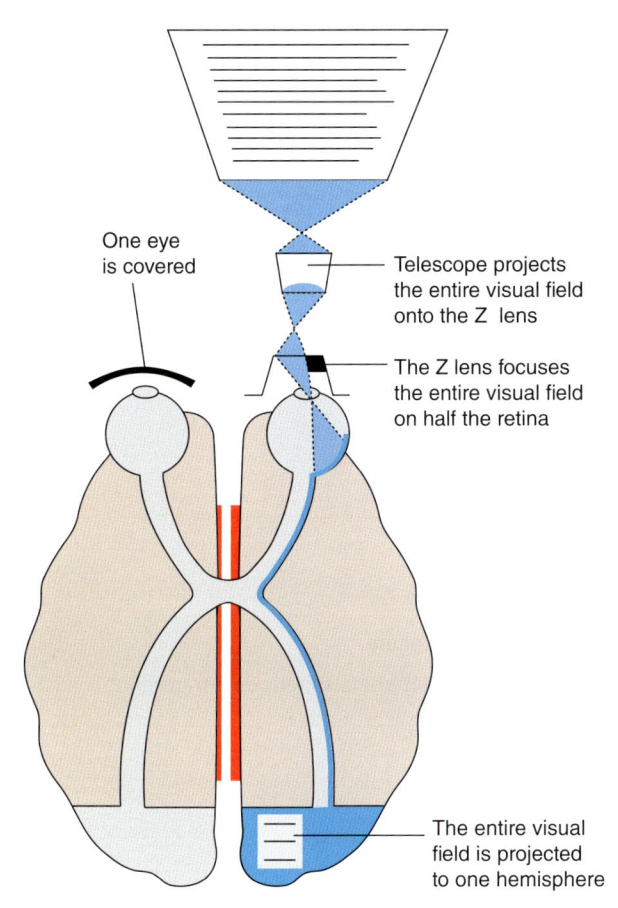

FIGURE 19.17 *The Z lens.*
Source: PINEL, JOHN P.J., BIOPSYCHOLOGY, 6th Edition, © 2006. Reprinted by permission of Pearson Education, Inc., Upper Saddle River, NJ.

their names to specific regions of the brain involved in language processing. In the absence of clear architectural differences within the cortex, these regions have functionally defined boundaries. These boundaries should not be confused with the neuroanatomical boundaries suggested by Brodmann. Identifying areas with boundaries that have discrete functions is appealing (after all, it is reminiscent of the boxes and arrows of cognitive psychology). However, over time it has become clear that these areas are not discrete entities of language production and comprehension as had previously been thought. Many regions of the left hemisphere (and also some in the right) are involved in language.

Lateralization of function is often misinterpreted as the person being *either* language based or spatially oriented (e.g. the stereotype that exists for the sexes). The truth is that it is not the broad cognitive categories that are lateralized but rather the constituents of cognitive processes. The individual elements that are necessary in cognition may reside in specialized units. The process of language exists in both hemispheres (albeit with dominance in the left hemisphere) and spatial tasks can be differentiated across the hemispheres. As always, the detail reveals incredible complexity that the summaries do not necessarily allude to. Lateralization of function is about statistical averages and not about the absolutes of individuals.

BOX 19.2: DYSLEXIA

Dyslexia is a neurocognitive disorder leading to difficulty in reading. There are generally two types of dyslexia: developmental and acquired. Acquired dyslexia is the result of neural damage whereas developmental dyslexia is the type that is all too prevalent in children. Trying to determine the prevalence of dyslexia is somewhat difficult because according to Miles (2004), dyslexia may emerge differentially depending on the language, the variation in the types of dyslexia and economic considerations of mass testing. However, despite the limitations, it would seem that approximately 9% of 10 year olds in the UK have this dyslexia in the mild-to-severe range (Miles, 2004).

Given the detailed account of language being a left hemisphere phenomenon, it might be expected that dyslexic symptoms and putative neuroanatomical differences would be located in these language regions. Deficits in the middle temporal gyrus of the left hemisphere were found in dyslexics during a reading task (Paulesu et al., 2001). The left temporoparietal and frontal areas and the arcuate fasciculus showed reduced innervation in a neuroimaging study amongst dyslexic readers. However, many newer imaging studies have found differences leading to widespread regions of the brain being correlated with different patterns of neural activity and volume (Eden & Zeffiro, 1998). In a recent review of the neuroimaging studies, Richlan (2012) found little evidence to support the left temporoparietal region in dyslexia but instead there was a disruption in the left hemisphere reading network consisting of the occipitotemporal region and the inferior frontal and parietal regions.

Looking at the whole brain to see what emerges during reading tasks revealed that dyslexics had differences in neural connectivity. There was increased connectivity within the right hemisphere and reduced connectivity in the left hemisphere, leading the authors to suggest that dyslexics rely more on the phonological components of the word rather than the visual properties of the word that non-dyslexic participants used (Finn et al., 2014). Changes in the left hemisphere appear to be a prerequisite rather than a consequence of dyslexia because the alterations predate reading ability (Raschle et al., 2012).

The cause, consequence and neurobiology of dyslexia are heterogeneous. Such diversity always makes scientific study difficult but more importantly, it has not yielded a consistent intervention or treatment for dyslexia, which can lead to a debilitating life.

LEARNING OUTCOME QUESTIONS

You should be able to answer the following questions.
- To what extent does being right-handed mean that the left brain is dominant?
- Critically evaluate the notion that language is a dominant function of the left hemisphere.
- Describe how lesions of the corpus callosum have enhanced our understanding of interhemispheric data transfer.

FURTHER READING

Catani, M., & Mesulam, M. (2008). The arcuate fasciculus and the disconnection theme in language and aphasia: history and current state. *Cortex, 44*(8), 953–961.

Corballis, M. C. (2009). The evolution and genetics of cerebral asymmetry. *Philosophical Transactions of the Royal Society of London B: Biological Sciences, 364*(1519), 867–879.

Corballis, M. C. (2010). Mirror neurons and the evolution of language. *Brain and Language, 112*(1), 25–35.

Corballis, P. M., Funnell, M. G., & Gazzaniga, M. S. (2000). An evolutionary perspective on hemispheric asymmetries. *Brain and Cognition, 43*(1-3), 112–117.

Friederici, A. D. (2011). The brain basis of language processing: From structure to function. *Physiology Review, 91*(4), 1357–1392.

Herve, P. Y., Zago, L., Petit, L., Mazoyer, B., & Tzourio-Mazoyer, N. (2013). Revisiting human hemispheric specialization with neuroimaging. *Trends in Cognitive Science, 17*(2), 69–80.

Ingram, J. C. (2007). *Neurolinguistics: An introduction to spoken language processing and its disorders*. Cambridge, UK: Cambridge University Press.

Springer, S.P & Deutsch, G, (1998). *Left brain – right brain* (5th edn). New York: Freeman-Worth.

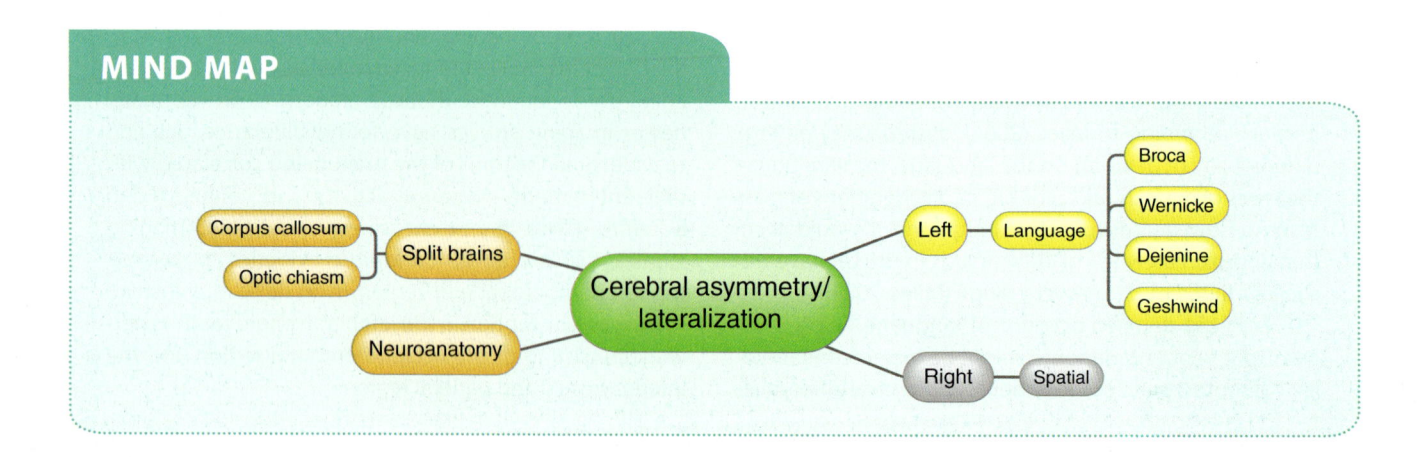

MIND MAP

Part III
The Psychobiology of Psychopathology

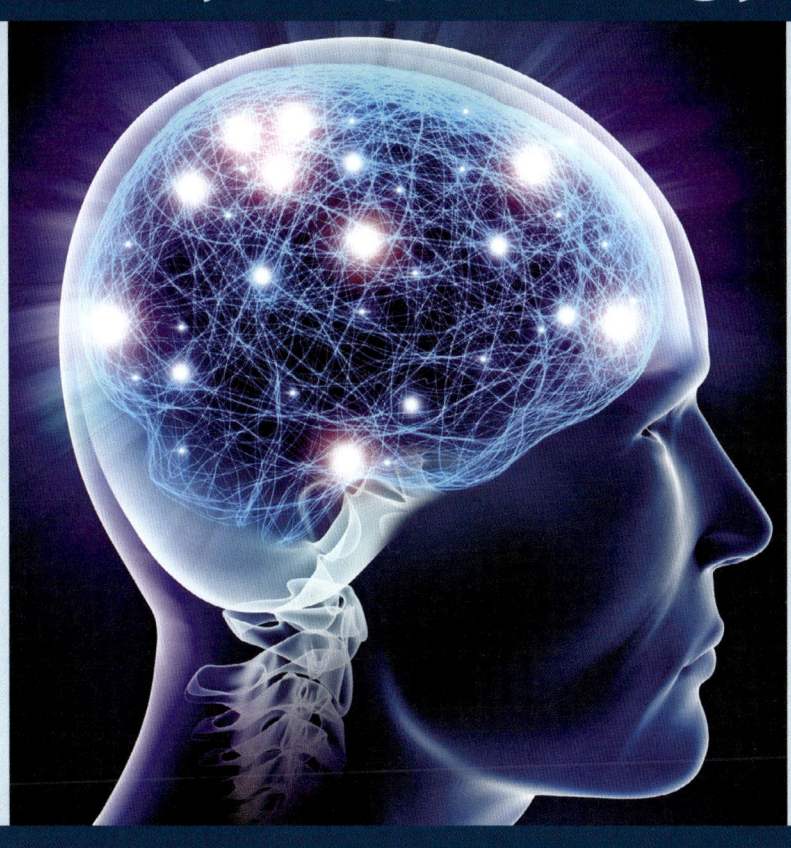

20. Developmental Disorders
21. Schizophrenia Spectrum and Other Psychotic Disorders
22. Affective Disorders
23. Anxiety and Stress
24. Neurodegeneration
25. Psychobiology: Implications for the Brave New World

Psychiatry is unlike other areas of medicine, e.g. oncology (cancer) and cardiology (heart). Diagnosis in psychiatry is somewhat open to interpretation, much as the law is about interpretation. Symptoms are observed, assessed and evaluated against manuals containing descriptions of disorders and lists of symptoms; previous experience and cases are used as guides. In neurology, the brain can be assessed with sophisticated imaging equipment. In oncology, we can detect a cancer. In psychiatry, we have behaviours, and the interpretation of behaviours. We have tests for assessing all sorts of health-related problems; blood tests can reveal a multitude of diseases, but psychiatry does not possess such diagnostic tools.

The diagnosis of psychiatric conditions is open to variation and interpretation, both between individuals and across cultures. In fact, the cultural context of psychiatry is of great importance. The discussions presented by Timimi and others (e.g. Timimi, 2005) highlight the cross-cultural differences in diagnosis. The whole area of psychiatry is a minefield (or should that be a mind-field?) full of interpretation and philosophical debate, e.g. what is a disorder (Bolton, 2008)? And some even consider mental illness to be a myth (Szasz, 1997). Whilst such a position is somewhat controversial, it remains an important position that one has to take account of.

The aetiology of a psychiatric condition is something of a holy grail. Due to the problematic nature of ascribing a cause within psychiatry, even at the genetic level, a number of theories have emerged. The big diagnostic manual used by the American Psychiatric Association – DSM 5 – is keen to avoid issues of causality, but rather focuses entirely on description (and that description is somewhat controversial).

There is a symbiotic relationship between diagnosis and research: increased diagnostic accuracy influences research, which in turn influences diagnosis and so the cycle continues. We are co-dependent upon each other, scientist and clinician alike.

Causality

Finding causality in some sciences is an easy academic exercise. In the behavioural sciences it is a considerable challenge. In fact, the word 'cause' is often avoided, with tentative words like 'association' or 'link' being used instead of grandiose statements reflecting causality. Furthermore, the search for a single cause may be futile; there is every chance that psychiatric disorders stem from multiple aetiologies.

The accuracy of diagnosis is paramount in searching for aetiology. If we have poor measures of diagnosis then the scientist's job becomes all the more difficult; how can you find the cause of something when you do not even know what it is in the first place! Although this is a somewhat extreme position, we have to accept the limitations of past and present accounts because of the changing nature of the diagnosis.

Given that we cannot experiment on individuals by attempting to inflict psychiatric conditions on them, we have to find alternatives; the questions are too important not to be answered. To get around this problem, scientists are able to use animals – especially, but not exclusively, the rat. Whether we like it or not, animals are used experimentally (see Chapter 1). However, the results obtained from animal studies need to be addressed. The data from such animal studies require close scrutiny, but the information obtained can be invaluable and should not be discounted if credible. Such experiments allow direct manipulation of the animal's biology to determine the behavioural effects.

Case studies of individuals are often the first reports to identify a problem. Eventually, when more people are identified with a similar problem, the problems raised in the case studies come under systematic scrutiny using scientific methods. Thus, the only way we can gain knowledge of the psychiatric condition is through research. Research in psychiatry can be approached from the different directions of the contributing disciplines. Geneticists investigate the role of DNA; neuropsychologists investigate cognitive functioning and thought processes; and psychopharmacologists investigate the neurochemistry of the brain via drug action.

All of the disciplines *try* to bring scientific rigour to the study of psychobiology. However, human behaviour does not always obey true scientific rules. In physics and chemistry there are absolutes – the freezing point of water is 0°C and the boiling point is 100°C. In the behavioural sciences there are no such absolutes. When conducting an experiment in chemistry, if you follow exactly the same procedure you will get the exact same results. In behavioural sciences, this is not always the case. People (and animals) have all sorts of different experiences and histories that can affect their behaviour. One person will not necessarily react in the same way as another person, even when the experimental conditions are the same.

Proof

When watching television advertisements for cosmetics, health products or foods, the viewer is confronted with statements of authority such as 'clinically proven' or 'scientifically proven'. The manufacturers present their product as having clinical powers that are a FACT. But is it a fact? The word 'fact' is rarely used in behavioural sciences. A fact tends to lead the reader into assuming that the information is an absolute irrefutable truth; research can do a lot to change that truth – even in chemistry!

To obtain reliable information on human behaviour, groups of people are studied. We often look for differences that are statistically significant between our target disorder and a control group.

The word 'significant' requires some clarification. The use of this word in the sentence above refers to a mathematically supported difference – a group of numbers are truly different from another group of numbers. The lay use of the word 'significance' means there is an *important* difference that sets those with the disorder apart from others.

The statistically significant effect is open to considerable confusion amongst not only the lay population but also professionals. The ramifications of this 'statistical illiteracy' are seen in health care and policy making, which can be exacerbated by the media (Monahan, 2007) consider the effects of a press release to the media that starts off with a portrayal of information that maximizes an effect. The journalist, who is also not adept at statistics, goes on to report this with their usual sensationalism. Suddenly something becomes a fact and not a tentative suggestion as originally published. The lack of transparency in a report can be seriously misleading. It has been argued that:

> Statistical literacy is a necessary precondition for an educated citizenship in a technological democracy. Understanding risks and asking critical questions can also shape the emotional climate in a society so that hopes and anxieties are no longer as easily manipulated from outside and citizens can develop a better-informed and more relaxed attitude toward their health. (Gigerenzer et al., 2007, p.53)

A statistically significant effect on a measure in people with a disorder does not necessarily translate into a clinically significant or important difference in that disorder, e.g. those with depression may have a slightly longer thumb than autistic children, but is this really an important difference between the two disorders?

There are many mathematical tests that can be used on data to determine statistical significance. On the whole, these tests give what is called a p-value. Although 5% is used, and is now almost a holy division within science, it does not necessarily have to be the case. As Everitt and Wessley (2004) state, the dichotomy of significance remains appealing to clinicians, students and scientists who are pleased when $p=0.049$, but are disappointed when $p=0.051$. With such a small difference, the study will report either a positive or a negative effect.

Remember also that non-significance is very different from insignificance (which is a common mistake students make when discussing their own data). Non-significant data are as interesting and important as significant data, but due to a bias for publishing positive results, it is harder to find examples of no effect in the literature. Just because they do not prove something is significant, the data are still important.

The media's portrayal of science is often misleading. Good journalism is valuable and informative, bringing complex ideas to a non-expert audience. Bad journalism is often ignorant and full of misinterpretation and prejudice – which in turn may appeal to the reader's own prejudices. Thus, the media can sometimes be guilty of sensationalizing research in a non-critical and authoritative way. A recent example is the reporting of the MMR vaccine for mumps, measles and rubella and its so-called link to autism, in which the poor science was broadcast via the media without critical awareness. The reporting led to a decrease in the number of parents having their young infants vaccinated, thus exposing them to the potentially harmful outcomes of these diseases. The fact that the original article on which the subsequent reports were based got published in the first place is worrying. Furthermore, the impartiality of the scientists had also been queried as they received funding from pharmaceutical companies that they failed to disclose. This is a problem as the companies have a financial interest in the direction of the results. It is commonplace for scientists to disclose information about potential conflicts of interest, e.g. a hypothetical cigarette company may not wish the results of a study they fund to link nicotine with addiction – this bias is not conducive to good science.

Psychological Cadavers

Our attitudes, our understanding and our use of language surrounding mental health issues have changed over the years. In the 21st century, we are far more enlightened with regard to mental illness but we still have a long way to go. In our language, we have now started to use the nomenclature of psychiatry to describe our behaviours along a spectrum, e.g. when one is feeling a little blue or sad one is depressed or when one likes to have things in order we are a little OCD or when we do not bow down to the social niceties of life, we describe ourselves as being a little autistic. Whilst it is good to have these disorders acknowledged by the general population, the use of these terms as adjectives does not do justice to the severity of the disorder and the impact it has upon the sufferer's life.

The cost of brain disorders in Europe was calculated at €798 billion for 2010 (Gustavsson et al., 2011). This is a large sum of money, a sum that governments would like to reduce. Considerable time, effort, blood, sweat and tears go into trying to understand the nature of psychopathologies and psychiatric disorders. The diagnostic criteria are rather cold descriptions; as students and researchers/teachers, we pick over the neural 'bones' of people with disorders. In psychiatry, we would wish to understand how the behaviours emerge from a dysfunctional brain. It may seem somewhat like the medical student picking over the cadaver in order to understand human anatomy. However, within psychology and psychiatry, we are not picking over the deceased; we are picking over the lives of severely distressed and disabled living humans and we should all remember that despite their illness, they are feeling individuals. When one looks at the prevalence rate of psychiatric disorders in a class of 100 people, the epidemiologists would tell us that approximately 5% may have schizophrenia, 20% may have depression, 1% may have eating disorders and the list can continue. When we discuss psychopathology, we should always consider that those around us may be directly, or indirectly as carers and relatives, affected by psychopathology.

The human cost of psychopathology, whilst it cannot be measured in euros, is high. Quality of life can be severely compromised by such disorders. This is the most important reason for trying to understand psychopathology – to improve the human condition, but to do so from a compassionate, ethical and scientifically rigorous position.

20 Developmental Disorders

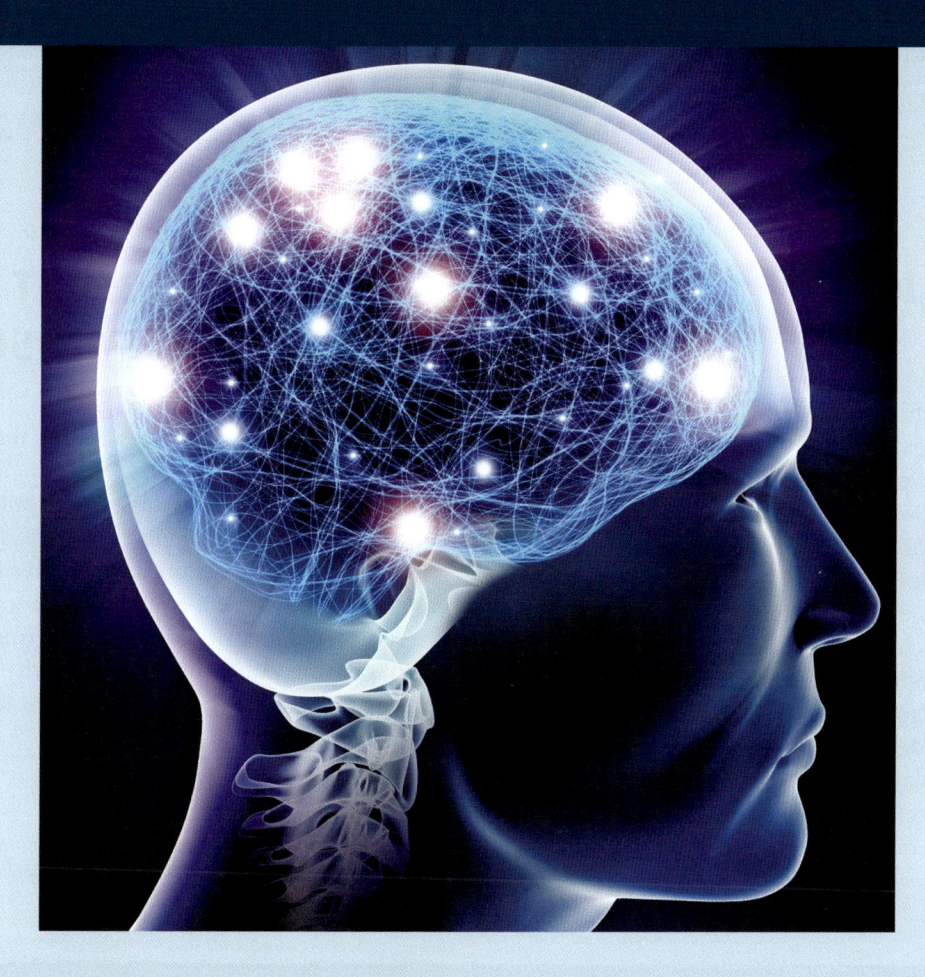

ANATOMY OF THE CHAPTER

This chapter will highlight the following.

- Attention deficit hyperactivity disorder (ADHD).
- Autism spectrum disorder (ASD).
- Neuropsychological and psychopharmacological accounts of abnormal behaviours.

INTRODUCTION 504

ATTENTION DEFICIT HYPERACTIVITY DISORDER 504

AUTISM SPECTRUM DISORDER 515

SUMMARY 520

LEARNING OUTCOMES

1. To understand the neuropsychopharmacology of the developmental disorders: ADHD and ASD.
2. To understand the scientific basis of theoretical accounts of ADHD and ASD.
3. To understand neuropsychological theories of ADHD and ASD.

INTRODUCTION

Much can go wrong in development from conception and throughout life. As we have seen in Chapter 3, there are critical or sensitive periods that can change the course of development. In this chapter, we consider developmental disorders to be those disorders that manifest themselves during development and affect the normal course of development. In Chapter 2 we saw that there are many genes that contribute to developmental disorders. This chapter will address two of the most common developmental disorders: **attention deficit hyperactivity disorder** (ADHD) and **autism** (or **autistic spectrum disorder, ASD**). That is not to say that the paediatric population does not suffer from anxiety, depression, Tourette's or addiction; they clearly do, and more often than not they are combined.

ATTENTION DEFICIT HYPERACTIVITY DISORDER

In the early 20th century, behaviours that now constitute the central symptoms of ADHD were identified and systematically documented (Still, 1902). Still described symptoms of overactivity, aggression, little inhibitory volition (impulsivity) and passion, but also resistance to punishment. ADHD is not a new phenomenon and should not be considered a fabrication of North America and a malevolent pharmaceutical industry, but rather a UK export that has been repackaged in the USA and sold back to the UK.

Diagnostic Criteria

Looking at the DSM 5 and ICD-10 criteria, you will notice similarities (Box 20.1). Clearly, the DSM 5 is

---

BOX 20.1: DSM DIAGNOSTIC CRITERIA FOR ADHD

I. Either A or B:

A. **Six or more of the following symptoms of inattention have been present for at least 6 months to a point that is disruptive and inappropriate for developmental level.**

Inattention

1. Often does not give close attention to details or makes careless mistakes in schoolwork, work, or other activities.
2. Often has trouble keeping attention on tasks or play activities.
3. Often does not seem to listen when spoken to directly.
4. Often does not follow instructions and fails to finish schoolwork, chores, or duties in the workplace (not due to oppositional behavior or failure to understand instructions).
5. Often has trouble organizing activities.
6. Often avoids, dislikes, or doesn't want to do things that take a lot of mental effort for a long period of time (such as schoolwork or homework).
7. Often loses things needed for tasks and activities (e.g. toys, school assignments, pencils, books, or tools).
8. Is often easily distracted.
9. Is often forgetful in daily activities.

B. Six or more of the following symptoms of hyperactivity-impulsivity have been present for at least 6 months to an extent that is disruptive and inappropriate for developmental level.

Hyperactivity

1. Often fidgets with hands or feet or squirms in seat.
2. Often gets up from seat when remaining in seat is expected.
3. Often runs about or climbs when and where it is not appropriate (adolescents or adults may feel very restless).
4. Often has trouble playing or enjoying leisure activities quietly.
5. Is often 'on the go' or often acts as if 'driven by a motor'.
6. Often talks excessively.

Impulsivity

1. Often blurts out answers before questions have been finished.
2. Often has trouble waiting one's turn.
3. Often interrupts or intrudes on others (e.g. butts into conversations or games).

II. Some symptoms that cause impairment were present before age 7 years.
III. Some impairment from the symptoms is present in two or more settings (e.g. at school/work and at home).
IV. There must be clear evidence of significant impairment in social, school, or work functioning.
V. The symptoms do not happen only during the course of a Pervasive Developmental Disorder, Schizophrenia, or other Psychotic Disorder. The symptoms are not better accounted for by another mental disorder (e.g. Mood Disorder, Anxiety Disorder, Dissociative Disorder, or a Personality Disorder).

Based on these criteria, three types of ADHD are identified:

1. ADHD, *Combined Type*: if both criteria 1A and 1B are met for the past 6 months (ADHD-C).
2. ADHD, *Predominantly Inattentive Type*: if criterion 1A is met but criterion 1B is not met for the past 6 months (ADHD-I).
3. ADHD, *Predominantly Hyperactive-Impulsive Type*: if criterion 1B is met but criterion 1A is not met for the past 6 months (ADHD-H).

Changes in DSM 5

- Examples have been added to the criterion items to facilitate application across the life span.
- The cross-situational requirement has been strengthened to 'several' symptoms in each setting.
- The onset criterion has been changed from 'symptoms that caused impairment were present before age 7 years' to 'several inattentive or hyperactive-impulsive symptoms were present prior to age 12'.
- Subtypes have been replaced with presentation specifiers that map directly to the prior subtypes.
- A co-morbid diagnosis with autism spectrum disorder is now allowed.
- A symptom threshold change has been made for adults, to reflect their substantial evidence of clinically significant ADHD impairment, with the cut-off for ADHD of five symptoms, instead of six required for younger persons, both for inattention and for hyperactivity and impulsivity.
- ADHD was placed in the neurodevelopmental disorders chapter to reflect brain developmental correlates with ADHD and the DSM 5 decision to eliminate the DSM IV chapter that includes all diagnoses usually first made in infancy, childhood, or adolescence.

With DSM IV/5, patients must have six (or more) symptoms of inattention **AND/OR** hyperactivity-impulsivity. However, the more stringent ICD-10 must have (Buitelaar et al., 2003):

– at least six symptoms of inattention **AND**
– at least three symptoms of hyperactivity **AND**
– at least one symptom of impulsivity.

The two important words are '*and*' and '*or*'. They make a big difference!

ICD-10 (hyperkinetic disorder)	DSM 4 (ADHD)
Symptoms required in all domains (inattention, hyperactivity, impulsivity)	Symptoms required in only one domain (inattention, hyperactivity/impulsivity)
Anxiety and mood disorders are exclusion criteria	Allows co-morbid disorders to be present
Special provision for conduct disorder	No special provision for conduct disorder

American based, whereas the ICD-10 is used outside the USA.

There are important differences between the two classification systems which give rise to some of the discrepancies in the prevalence of ADHD. A study comparing the two diagnostic systems over a six-year period found that only 26% of those diagnosed with ADHD (DSM 4) also met the criteria for HKD in the ICD-10 (Lahey et al., 2006). Thus, if the epidemiological studies are using ICD-10 they may underrepresent the prevalence of ADHD; conversely, those studies using DSM 4 may overestimate cases. In the UK it has been argued that there is underdiagnosis of ADHD.

Structural Changes in the Brain

In general, the volume of the brain is reduced in ADHD (Carmona et al., 2005). A number of studies have looked more closely at specific brain regions and composition of the brain in ADHD, measuring structure against function (McAlonan et al., 2009). Such studies are somewhat more informative than the global changes in brain volume; after all, there is a great deal of variability in brain size across individuals and it is uncertain how, for example, a 3.4% reduction (Castellanos & Acosta, 2004) translates clinically.

Both grey and white matter change over the lifespan (Krain & Castellanos, 2006), especially in the prefrontal cortex (Filipek et al., 1997; Kates et al., 2002; McAlonan et al., 2007; Mostofsky et al., 2002; Overmeyer et al., 2001). Other regions of interest were the right putamen/globus pallidus (Ellison-Wright et al., 2008) and the corpus callosum (Hill et al., 2003). These area are all connected, mainly by dopamine (DA), and therefore deficits in white and grey matter may be indicative of a dysfunctional DA system (Ellison-Wright et al., 2008).

The neuropsychological literature points to a dysfunction in the cortex, most notably the frontal lobe. The cortex in cases of ADHD has been shown to have reductions in cortical volume and the sulci (Li et al., 2007; Wolosin et al., 2009), with an average cerebral reduction of 8.3% (Mostofsky et al., 2002) in the right prefrontal cortex (PFC) (Krain & Castellanos, 2006), left PFC (Ranta et al., 2009) and anterior cingulate cortex (Makris et al., 2010).

The basal ganglia have been argued to be smaller in ADHD (Qiu et al., 2009). A study by Silk et al. (2009) found that normal development is seen in the **caudate** (region of the striatum) between the ages of 8 and 18 years and was delayed in ADHD. Whereas the caudate is more frequently associated with cognitive functioning, the **putamen** (another region of the striatum) is associated with the physical motor symptoms of ADHD, although the data are conflicting (Krain & Castellanos, 2006). In adults who had not received medication for more than one month, it was also shown that DA activity was reduced in the caudate (Volkow et al., 2007).

The cerebellum, like the putaman, is associated with movement, but it is also associated with cognitive functioning (Baldacara et al., 2008; Krain & Castellanos, 2006). Magnetic resonance imaging (MRI) studies indicate a smaller volume of tissue in this area in ADHD (Berquin et al., 1998; Durston et al., 2004) which was linked to the DRD4 7R genotype (Monuteaux et al., 2008). Reduction in the **cerebellar vermis** of the cerebellum is seen in ADHD (Mackie et al., 2007) and is normalized by treatment (Bledsoe et al., 2009).

An understanding of how structural changes are converted into functional significance has been attempted. Numerous studies have linked the above regions with symptom severity and test scores on rating scales and neuropsychological tests (Krain & Castellanos, 2006).

Functional Neuroimaging of ADHD

Using functional MRI (fMRI), the anterior cingulate cortex (ACC) has been demonstrated by many to be dysfunctional in ADHD, especially when using tasks such as the **Go/No-go task** (Bush et al., 2005; Pliszka et al., 2006). In the striatum, lower levels of activity were seen in ADHD during task performance (Durston et al., 2003; Rubia et al., 1999; Teicher et al., 2000; Vaidya et al., 2005).

Many researchers have used **behavioural inhibition** as a key theoretical neuropsychological construct and looked for differences in neural processing in ADHD. Such studies typically find reduced activation in such tasks as the Go/No-go task (Aron & Poldrack, 2006) and the **Stop Signal Reaction Time task** (SSRT) (Eagle, Baunez et al., 2008).

Drugs such as methylphenidate can have long-lasting effects on the structure and function of the brain (Silveri et al., 2004). Numerous animal studies have shown neural changes in response to medications such as antipsychotics and psychostimulants which block DA receptors or stimulate DA respectively (Hall et al., 1984; Jenner et al., 1983, 1985; Kerwin et al., 1984) which fits with our pharmacological understanding of up- and downregulation, (Creese et al., 1981). However, we have to be careful that we are not in fact measuring drug-induced brain changes in neuroimaging studies.

Psychophysiological Studies

Electroencephalogram (EEG) studies have generally found differences in cortical activity in ADHD (Chabot &

Serfontein, 1996; Chabot et al., 1996; Clarke et al., 1998; El-Sayed et al., 2002; Mann et al., 1992). Such studies have claimed to be able to differentiate between subtypes (Clarke et al., 1998) and potential positive responses to treatment (Chabot et al., 1999).

Event-related potentials (ERP) studies look at responses to tasks or stimuli. Such studies have found differences in ADHD groups with a slowing of activity during cognitive tasks (Johnstone et al., 2009).

Frontostriatal Circuits

The term 'frontostriatal circuit' is a general term that includes numerous circuits that link the frontal cortex and the striatum. Bradshaw (2001) identified five circuits: (1) motor circuit, (2) oculomotor circuit, (3) dorsolateral prefrontal cortical circuit, (4) lateral orbitofrontal cortical circuit, and (5) anterior cingulate circuit (Figure 20.1). All have been implicated in ADHD, with the latter four being associated with the cognitive dysfunction that is pervasive (Itami & Uno, 2002; Mahone et al., 2009; Seidman et al., 2006; Van der Stigchel et al., 2007). The differing effects of dysfunction in each circuit may contribute to the heterogeneous nature of ADHD: different severities in the anterior cingulate may reflect more on inhibition, whereas the oculomotor circuit may malfunction in preparing to make a response.

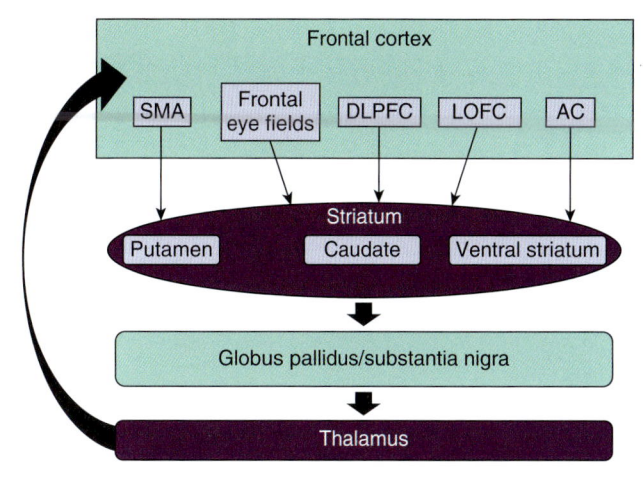

FIGURE 20.1 *Frontostriatal circuits. The regions of the frontal cortex communicate with striatal regions which go on to communicate with other regions of the basal ganglia and the thalamus. The thalamus communicates back with the cortex. This provides five distinct cortico-striatal-thalamic loops. AC, anterior cingulate; DLPFC, dorsolateral prefontal cortex; LOFC, lateral orbitofrontal cortex; SMA, supplementary motor area.*
Source: Chandler, C. (2010). *The science of ADHD*. Wiley. Reproduced with permission.

Pharmacology and Efficacy of Psychostimulants used in treating ADHD

Both **methylphenidate** and **amphetamine** are dopamine-enhancing drugs or agonists and are the main drugs used in the treatment of ADHD. Both have the potential to inform us about the neuropathology of ADHD.

Methylphenidate comes in a number of different preparations. The nature of these different preparations is based upon their duration of action. Methylphenidate shares a great deal in common with cocaine. It blocks the **dopamine transporter** (DAT), which recovers released DA from the synapse, thereby deactivating it. The effect of such a blockade is the accumulation of DA in the synapse (Figure 20.2).

Amphetamine works by increasing dopamine release from the presynaptic neuron. Amphetamine mimics DA and enters the presynaptic terminal via the DAT. This has two effects: (1) it competes with DA for reuptake and thus less DA can be removed from the synapse, and (2) it causes a release of DA that is independent of action potentials. This release of DA is via reversing the reuptake processes (Sulzer et al., 2005) (see Chapter 7 and Figure 20.2).

Numerous studies have looked at the effectiveness of the drugs across many domains ranging from cognitive functions to parental reports, but not everyone benefits from the treatment. According to Mary Solanto (Solanto, 2001), up to 25% of ADHD cases may not respond. These cases represent an interesting group to treat but are also interesting from a scientific perspective, given that the hypotheses generated about the pathological changes of ADHD stem from successful treatment strategies. Why are they different? This question remains unanswered, but some may benefit from a change of medication.

A set of studies has shown that parental interactions with a child with ADHD were more directive and critical when the child was unmedicated (Cunningham & Barkley, 1979), whereas upon treatment the parents were less critical and directive and expressed greater warmth (Barkley & Cunningham, 1979; Schachar et al., 1997). Such data have been used to suggest that the parent's interaction with the ADHD child is a response to the condition and not a cause of the condition.

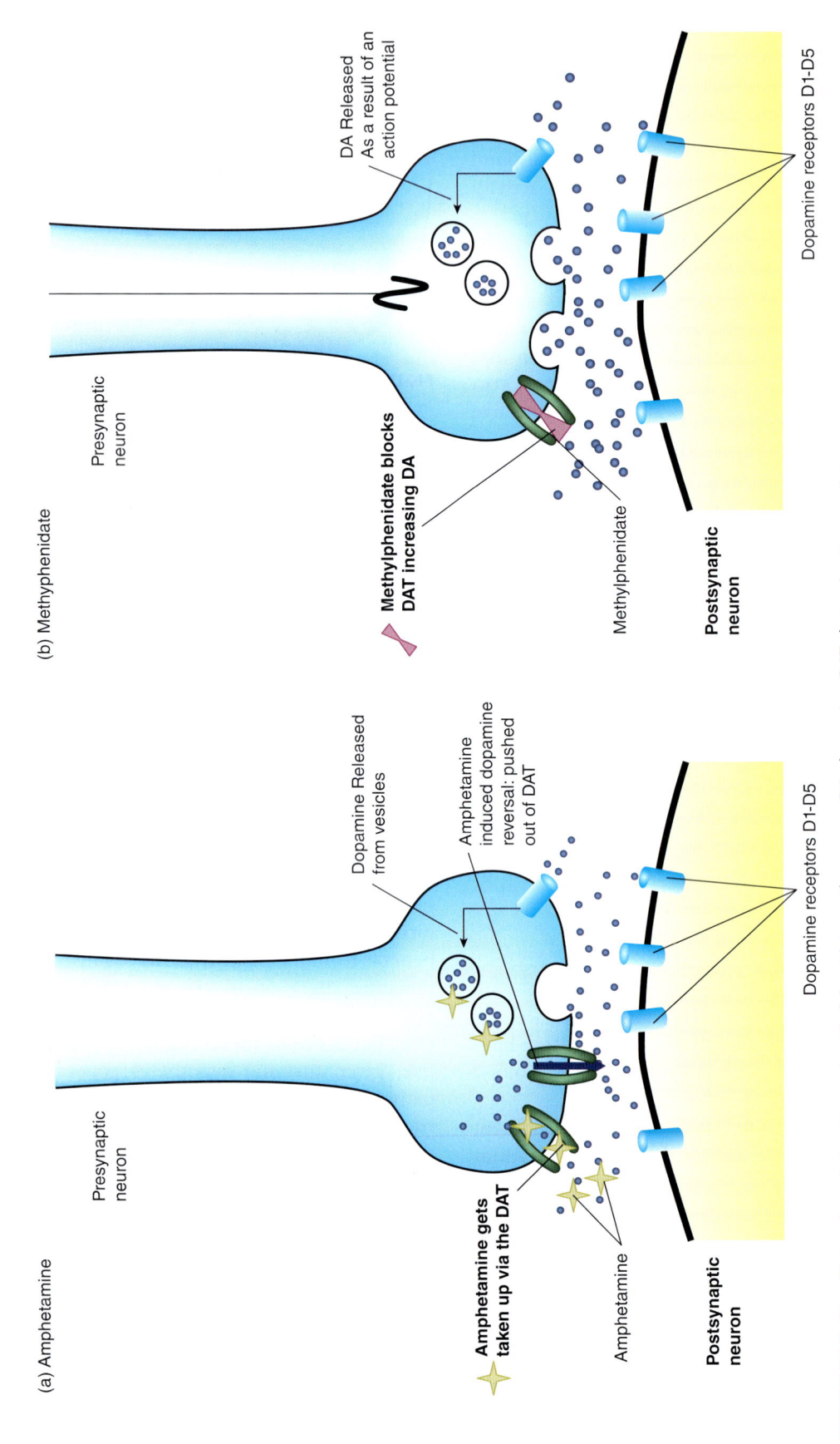

FIGURE 20.2 *The effects of amphetamine and methylphenidate on the neuron. DA, dopamine; DAT, dopamine transporter.*
Source: Chandler, C. (2010). *The science of ADHD.* Wiley. Reproduced with permission.

Psychopharmacology: From Treatment to Theory

Neurochemical theories of ADHD predominantly address a DA dysfunction. Such theories have evolved primarily from the use of methylphenidate in treatment. Methylphenidate is therefore the search engine for looking at the brain in ADHD. However, this approach is only as good as the drug itself. If we have many drugs to use we can look for their common features which may pinpoint the underlying problems. Unfortunately we are limited to only three main drugs: **methylphenidate**, **amphetamine** and **atomoxetine**.

Hypo/hyperfunctioning DA in ADHD

The logic is simple: methylphenidate increases DA, therefore ADHD is a result of too little DA (Wender, 1971). In fact, much of the support comes from animal studies where lesions of the DA system are used as a model of ADHD (Ferguson, 2001) using genetically modified animals that are DA hypoactive (Sagvolden, 2001; Sagvolden, Russell et al., 2005). Given that methylphenidate acts on the DAT, perhaps this is also the faulty mechanisms in ADHD. Early studies indicated that the DAT was increased by as much as 70% in the human striatum (Dougherty et al., 1999). However, the human data obtained from positron emission tomography (PET) scans are not consistent (Solanto, 2001). One of the main problems is that stimulation of the DAT with a drug can have an upregulating effect in animals and humans (Koff et al., 1994; Little et al., 1999), increasing the number of DATs.

Flying in face of the hypoactive argument are DA metabolite studies looking at **homovanillic acid** (HVA). Increased levels of HVA in children were associated with increased DA and increased severity of ADHD (Castellanos et al., 1994, 1996).

Solanto (1984) speculated that ADHD was a consequence of hyperdopaminergic activity and that methylphenidate was working not to increase DA levels postsynaptically, but rather to stimulate autoreceptors to provide feedback, thereby stopping DA activity. Autoreceptors are approximately 10 times more sensitive than their postsynaptic counterparts and therefore small doses can preferentially activate them (Seeman, 1980). Thus, low doses stimulate the autoreceptor, turning off DA activity and associated behaviour in animals (Pinsky et al., 1988) and reducing activity in children with a subclinical dose of methylphenidate (Solanto, 1986).

According to Seeman and Madras (1998, 2002), during normal neural activity, tonic DA levels transiently rise. Psychostimulants raise tonic levels of DA several-fold, but reduce the extent to which dopamine is released with action potentials (phasic release). Thus, the signals from stimuli are smaller and result in less activation of postsynaptic DA receptors. In addition, the elevated tonic DA reduces the number of DA receptors. At high dose, the stimulants activate the nervous system due to the very high concentrations of tonic DA and the increased release of phasic DA. These high levels of DA stimulate postsynaptic DA receptors, thereby negating presynaptic inhibition.

Grace's tonic and phasic account of ADHD

Professor Anthony Grace provides an elaborate account of methylphenidate's action and ADHD itself (Grace, 2001) (Figure 20.3). His account focuses on the presynaptic autoreceptor which regulates DA in the synapse. Accordingly, three types of DA autoreceptors are involved: (1) firing rate inhibiting autoreceptors (stop the action potentials and the signal), (2) synthesis inhibiting autoreceptors (stop the DA being made), and (3) release inhibiting autoreceptors (stop the DA being released). All have the net effect of reducing DA transmission using negative feedback loops when activated. Furthermore, Grace describes two types of DA release: tonic and phasic. Tonic DA release is the low constant background level of DA in the synapse, which is modulated by glutamatergic projections from the cortex. In contrast, phasic release consists of a large and transient discharge of DA from the synapse as a result of an action potential (Grace & Bunney, 1984).

Grace (2001) proposes that methylphenidate has a two-stage action to its therapeutic efficacy: (1) a short-term effect due to the immediate blockade of the DAT with the resultant accumulation of DA after phasic release, and (2) a methylphenidate induced increase in DA which is unable to escape via the DAT which then goes on to elevate tonic levels of DA. This activates autoreceptors, leading to feedback inhibition and a decrease in phasic DA release. This is the synapse responding to maintain an equilibrium or homeostasis.

The symptoms of ADHD are a direct result of an abnormally low level of tonic DA within the striatum and nucleus accumbens which leads to increased phasic responses. The variability in tonic release and consequential changes in phasic release are arguably linked to symptom severity, so much so that methylphenidate works best when the severity of the symptoms is more pronounced (Robbins & Sahakian, 1979; Sahakian & Robbins, 1977). Grace argues that this may explain the rate dependency hypothesis of amphetamine's and methylphenidate's paradoxical effect in ADHD in which high levels of activity are depressed and low levels of activity are increased (see Chapter 9).

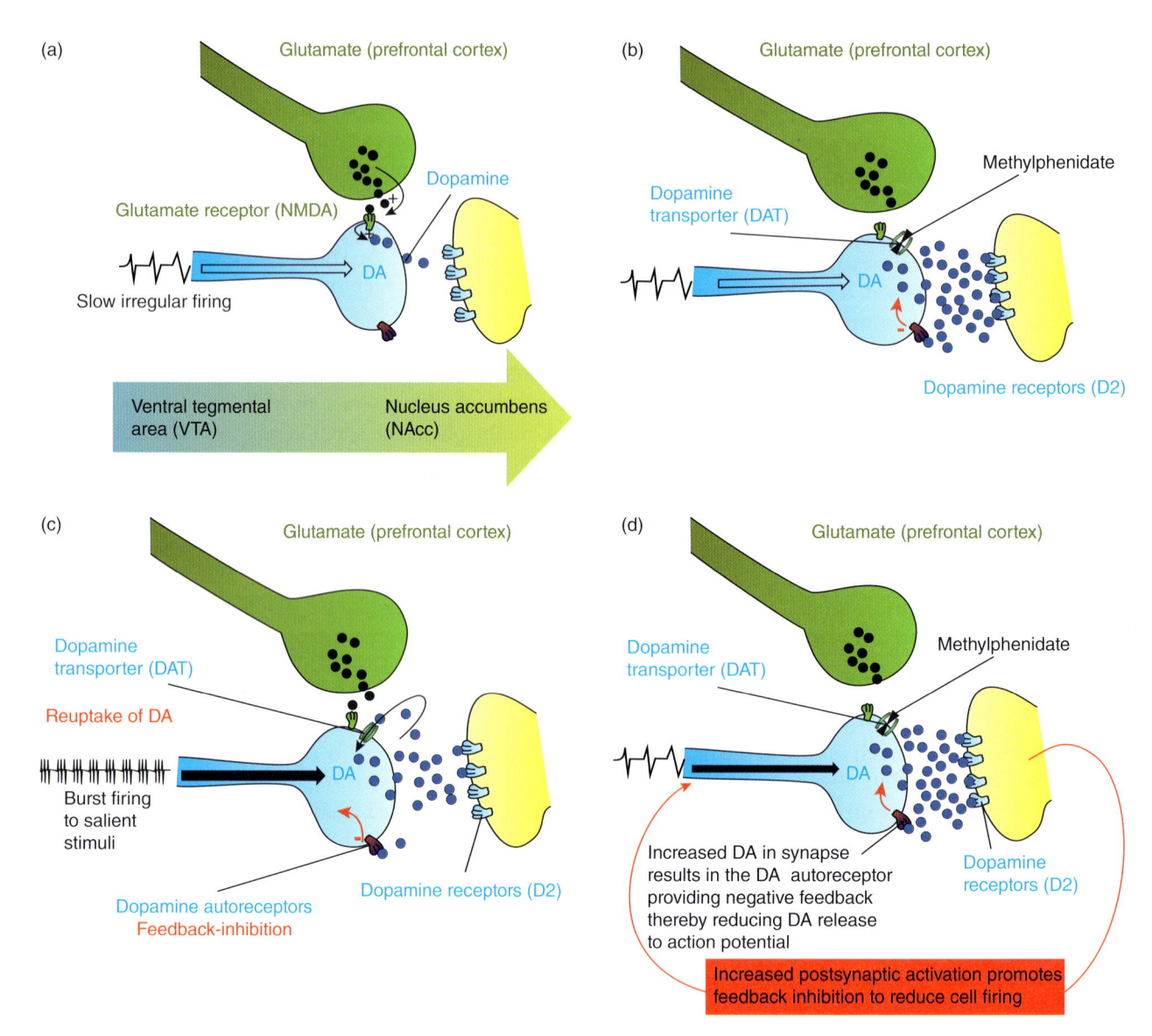

FIGURE 20.3 *Grace's tonic and phasic DA in ADHD. Grace (2001) proposes that methylphenidate has a two-stage action to its therapeutic efficacy: (1) a short-term effect due to the immediate blockade of the dopamine transporter (DAT) with the resultant accumulation of DA after phasic release; (2) a methylphenidate-induced increase in DA which is unable to escape via the DAT which then goes on to elevate tonic levels of DA. This activates autoreceptors, leading to feedback inhibition and a decrease in phasic DA release.*

A dynamic developmental theory of ADHD

This theory stems from rat models and was pioneered by Sagvolden, Johansen and colleagues (2005). The view is of a general underactivity or hypofunctioning of DA circuits and a failure to modulate other neurotransmitters such as GABA and glutamate. These circuits are the mesolimbic, mesocortical and nigrostriatal DA pathways. They have all had particular behaviours associated with them and can be differentially affected in ADHD. A dysfunctioning mesolimbic dopamine circuit will alter reinforcement of behaviour and produce deficient extinction of previously reinforced behaviour. This will manifest as delay aversion, hyperactivity impulsiveness, inattention, and a failure in behavioural inhibition – all cardinal symptoms of ADHD. Dysfunction in the mesocortical dopamine circuit will cause attentional problems such as poor orienting responses, impaired saccadic eye movements and poor executive functions. A dysfunctioning nigrostriatal dopamine circuit will cause impaired modulation of motor functions and deficient habit learning and memory, which will be clinically manifest as clumsiness and a failure to inhibit responses when quick reactions are required. All of these circuits are discussed by others in the context of the cortical regions to which they connect.

According to the theory, ADHD is a manifestation of differential dysfunction in these circuits. Central to the theory is the disruption of reinforcement in ADHD. From the developmental perspective, Sagvolden et al. suggest that early in development overactivity of mesolimbic dopamine neurons could activate DA receptors and have the knock-on effects of increasing glutamate receptors in the mesolimbic circuit. Increased glutamatergic activity could result in compensatory changes that would lead to deactivation of dopamine neurons and hypoactivity of the mesolimbic dopaminergic system. This shares some similarities with Grace's theory above.

Atomoxetine is the first non-stimulant approved for ADHD. It is a highly selective noradrenergic reuptake inhibitor (Bymaster et al., 2002; Wong et al., 1982). Amphetamine and methylphenidate both have effects on noradrenergic reuptake, but also affect DA reuptake. It has been suggested that the noradrenergic component may be the critical therapeutic target and the underlying substrate of pathology (Oades, 2005, 2006).

Reward deficiency in ADHD

Reward deficiency is where there is reduced efficacy of the reward pathways in the brain (see Chapter 16). Taylor and Jentsch (2001) have reviewed the data on reward function in ADHD and suggest that the reward system is dysfunctional and treatment with methylphenidate corrective. Again, at the heart of this is DA, which has been incorporated into several theoretical accounts of ADHD (Blum et al., 2000; Castellanos & Tannock, 2002; Douglas & Parry, 1983; Haenlein & Caul, 1987; Sagvolden et al., 1998; Sagvolden, Johansen et al., 2005; Sonuga-Barke, 2002, 2005). In general, children with ADHD have been shown to choose small immediate rewards rather than larger delayed rewards which are chosen by healthy controls (Barkley et al., 2001; Kuntsi et al., 2001; Rapport et al., 1986; Schweitzer & Sulzer-Azaroff, 1995; Solanto et al., 2001; Sonuga-Barke et al., 1992; Tripp & Alsop, 2001). Children with ADHD want frequent rewards immediately even if it means they get a smaller reward (Luman et al., 2005).

The **reward deficiency syndrome**, as described by Blum and colleagues (2000), postulates that a common mechanism in ADHD, and other disorders, is a reduction in D2 receptors. Some support exists for this in addiction, with imaging studies showing a reduction of D2 receptors (Martinez et al., 2004; Volkow et al., 1993; Volkow, Fowler & Wang, 1999). In unmedicated adults with ADHD, there are reduced striatal D2 and D3 receptors which were associated with inattention (Volkow et al., 2007).

Kelly and colleagues (2007) have argued that the evidence base for ADHD and reward deficiency is not on a solid foundation; there are numerous facets of reward, e.g. size, speed of delivery and chance of getting the reward, that need to be looked at in ADHD before firm conclusions can be made.

Barkley's Neuropsychological Account – Behavioural Inhibition

Of all the neuropsychological deficits that can be seen in ADHD, behavioural inhibition (BI) (or response inhibition) stands out (Figure 20.4). BI is a neuropsychological concept that is considered central to the symptoms of ADHD. BI can be defined as the ability to stop a particular response when signalled to do so. BI is akin to self-control and is the process that stops us responding to stimuli; BI is not a case of *free will*, but rather *free won't*! A deficit in BI has been described as the bedrock of the impulsivity seen in ADHD.

In addition to the myriad cognitive deficits that appear to plague those with ADHD, early studies have demonstrated that children with ADHD have problems with BI (Schachar et al., 1995, 2000).

Leading the study of BI is Professor Russell Barkley who has been extremely influential in conceptualizing ADHD as a disorder arising from a failure of the BI system (Barkley, 1997a, 1997b, 2005).

The necessity of BI in normal functioning behaviour is argued to manifest itself in four executive function (EF) domains: (1) non-verbal working memory; (2) internalization of speech (verbal working memory); (3) self-regulation of affect/motivation/arousal; and (4) reconstitution (planning) (Barkley, 2006b). Thus, Barkley sees BI as being at the top of an EF hierarchy.

Behavioural inhibition consists of three main components: (1) inhibiting the initial prepotent or immediate/dominant response as determined by reinforcement history (to stop a response that has already become likely because of previous experience and learning); (2) stopping an ongoing response, therefore permitting a delay in deciding to respond; and (3) protection of the decision-making process during this delay from interference. This is all about thinking and decision making.

This affects ADHD in three ways.

- An inability to inhibit the prepotent response means that an individual will not be able to assess the task demands and the possible outcome of responding.
- A failure to interrupt ongoing behaviour may lead to an individual following a well-learned

Behavioural inhibition/response inhibition

The ability to stop well learnt responses or ongoing responses and prevent interference from external stimuli
Measures: Go/no-go and stop signal reaction time tasks
(ADHD symptoms characterized by faulty inhibitory processes resulting in the dysfunction of systems below)

Working memory also influences behavioural inhibition

Working memory
Limited capacity allows manipulation and organization of events in the mind

Self regulation
Self control, regulation of emotions and arousal

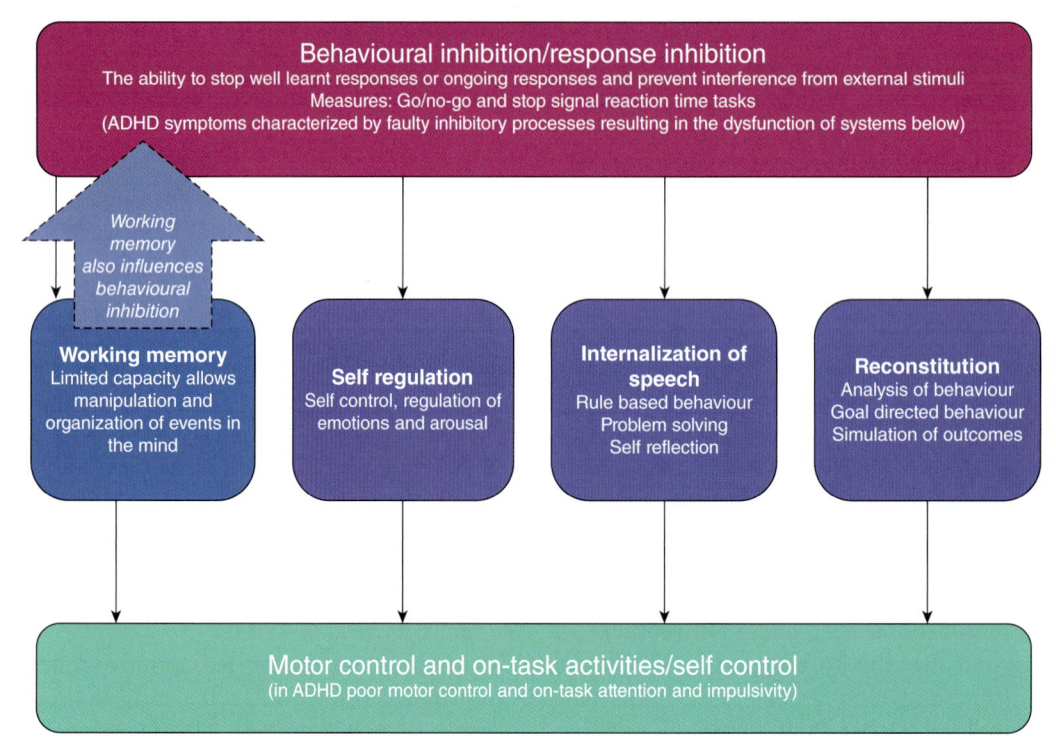

Internalization of speech
Rule based behaviour
Problem solving
Self reflection

Reconstitution
Analysis of behaviour
Goal directed behaviour
Simulation of outcomes

Motor control and on-task activities/self control
(in ADHD poor motor control and on-task attention and impulsivity)

FIGURE 20.4 *Behavioural inhibition. BI is considered to have effects on working memory, self-regulation, internalization of speech and reconstitution. Because of a fault in BI, these can all be dysfunctional in ADHD, leading to changes in the behaviour of those with ADHD. This view, based on Barkley's model (Barkley, 1997), has been argued to be a result of a working memory deficit that feeds into a dysfunctional BI system (Rapport, et al., 2008).*
Source: Chandler, C. (2010). *The science of ADHD.* Oxford, UK: Wiley.

behavioural pattern even when feedback is stating that the response is erroneous.

- Avoiding being distracted when a response is required is normally necessary.

For someone with ADHD, BI is difficult and has ramifications for the whole of the EF (see Figure 20.4).

There are two tests that are frequently used in BI research: the Go/No-go task and the Stop Signal Reaction Time test (SSRT) (see Chapter 12). Both require the suppression of a well-learned response and are thought to reflect motor BI (Ersche & Sahakian, 2007)

In the Go/No-go task, individuals are told to respond quickly (e.g. press a button) to a particular stimulus on the Go trials, but to withhold responses when presented with a No-go stimulus, e.g. press go for the digits 0–9 appearing randomly, except for the number 7 (No-go). The inclusion of more Go than No-go stimuli means that the Go responses become prepotent (learned). The number of inappropriate responses to No-go stimuli, pressing the button when you should not (an error of commission), measures BI. Thus, the Go/No-go task measures the ability, or in the case of ADHD the inability, to stop responding.

The SSRT task involves participants having to withhold a response to a Go signal whenever it is followed by a Stop signal. The Stop signal can be an auditory beep during the presentation of visually displayed Go stimuli.

Due to reliance on the Go/No-go and SSRT tasks in dissecting BI, the very nature of these tasks becomes important, from both a theoretical and clinical perspective. Recent reviews on these tasks have questioned their application to explaining ADHD symptoms.

A breakdown in BI occurs when there are competing options and the strongest (prepotent) yet incorrect response is selected over the correct response. This quick reaction to stimuli presentation has been argued to be the basis of impulsivity. Impulsivity itself is a phenomenon that needs further elucidation in this context; not surprisingly, agreement about the nature of impulsivity is limited in the literature.

If Barkley's BI is the same as impulsivity (i.e. a neuropsychological measure of impulsivity) then this is the cardinal symptom of ADHD, which affects all other symptoms. However, Barkley makes it clear that deficits in working memory (for which there is extensive evidence) may be separate and distinct from BI but they may also co-arise (Barkley, 2006b).

A review of the literature on impulsivity supports the notion of BI underlying impulsivity in which 'the term "response [behavioural] inhibition" refers to the ability to inhibit or suppress simple motor responses that have been rendered prepotent... and deficits in this ability are implicated in impulsivity' (Chamberlain, Muller, Robbins et al., 2006, p.608). An important point to note here is that when discussing BI, most accounts are referring to the suppression of a motor response as in the Go/No-go or the SSRT task. It has been argued that BI is only evident for motor responding and has been overextended to the inclusion of cognitive control (Aron, 2007).

Aron (2007) claims that there are a number of reasons why BI cannot be used in the context of cognitive control:

- it is not economically viable for neural resources to be occupied on BI; instead, amplification of stimuli would be a more suitable mechanism – a simple stimulus–response association being strengthened;
- lesions of the prefrontal cortex produce BI, but that is not to say that the prefrontal cortex is the site of BI; the prefrontal cortex has been reported to be involved in ADHD and BI;
- there are better accounts of the performance deficits that are encountered, e.g. working memory (see next column).

Working Memory

Working memory (WM) has become a widely accepted and dominant neurocognitive construct since its first outing in the early 1970s (Baddeley & Hitch, 1974). Since then it has evolved into a comprehensive theory of mental life with a huge body of supporting literature (Baddeley, 2000). WM's endurance in the psychological literature demonstrates its powerful application to understanding behaviour (Baddeley, 2001). WM has been implicated and researched in the context of many disorders and ADHD is no exception.

Deficits in WM have been identified in ADHD (e.g. Barkley's account and neurochemical accounts) (Levy & Farrow, 2001), in experimental studies (Karatekin & Asarnow, 1998; Martinussen & Tannock, 2006; Martinussen et al., 2005) and within subsections of intelligence tests (Marusiak & Janzen, 2005). A meta-analysis of WM in ADHD indicates that there are widespread deficits across systems, but the spatial slave system and spatial wing of the central executive were the most affected (Martinussen et al., 2005).

Rapport and colleagues (2001) have modified the WM concept to account for the symptoms of ADHD including hyperactivity (Figure 20.5). Hyperactivity is somewhat neglected. In this model the central executive is compromised, resulting in haphazard and disorganized responding to input stimuli which can be seen in ADHD.

In addition to the disorganization in ADHD, and because of failures within WM and the associated cortical underarousal, motivation to irrelevant stimuli is

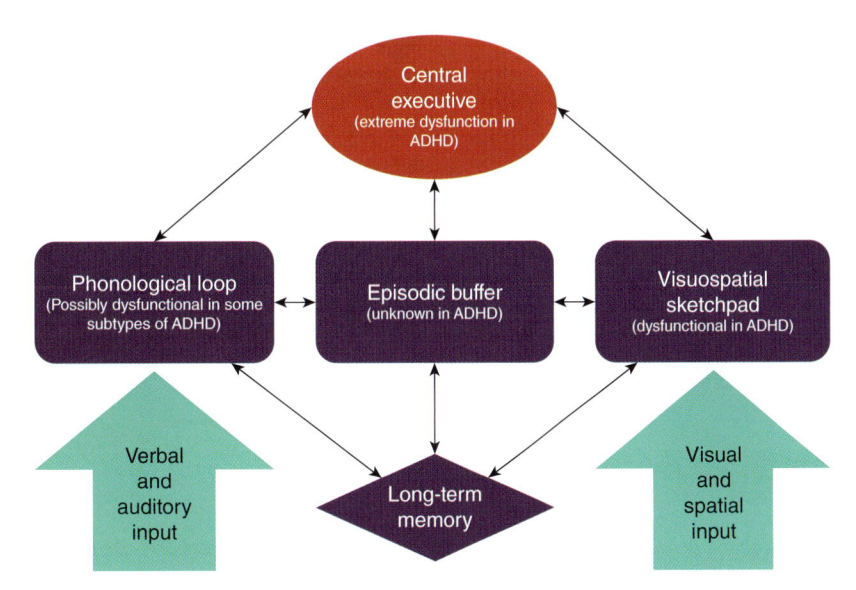

FIGURE 20.5 *Working memory in ADHD. The central executive and the visuospatial sketchpad are dysfunctional in ADHD.*
Source: Chandler, C. (2010). *The science of ADHD*. Wiley. Reproduced with permission.

increased and is not beneficial! Input to the slave systems of WM will induce increased activity levels to compensate for cortical underarousal. Although Rapport et al. (2001) are careful not to place WM in a specific neuroanatomical location, they find support for cortical underactivity from psychophysiological studies (Clarke et al., 1998; El-Sayed et al., 2002; Mann et al., 1992). As the representations within WM fade rapidly, their loss is compensated for by increased input to working memory. Thus, in this conceptualization of ADHD, WM becomes overloaded by incoming environmental stimuli. When WM is overloaded, those with ADHD will seek to escape (and eventually avoid) situations associated with this aversive state. As Rapport et al. note, redirecting attention to other stimuli can alleviate monotonous or difficult tasks (academic work!) which can be manifest as impulsivity and/or hyperactivity, i.e. the child gets out of his seat at school. In an elegant study by Rapport, Timko, Kofler and Alderson (2005; reported in Rapport et al., 2007), all children who were given WM tasks demonstrated increased concurrent motor activity; however, those children with ADHD engaged in escape/avoidance behaviour when the task was made more difficult. This has led to the suggestion that arousal facilitates cognitive functioning in all. However, ADHD children engage in more activity to compensate for the loss of cortical arousal.

Behavioural inhibition addresses a single behaviour – stopping a response; WM deals with a vast array of information processing. Rapport et al. (2007, p.375) suggest that:

> . . . working memory processes must be invoked to evaluate stimuli (including situational cues) prior to the initiation of the inhibition process . . .This suggests that behavioural inhibition is downstream of working memory processes.

The vast array of data deals with specific aspects of ADHD at different levels. These differing inputs can be synthesized into an overall model involving genetics, pharmacology and psychology, all within a psychosocial context (Figure 20.6).

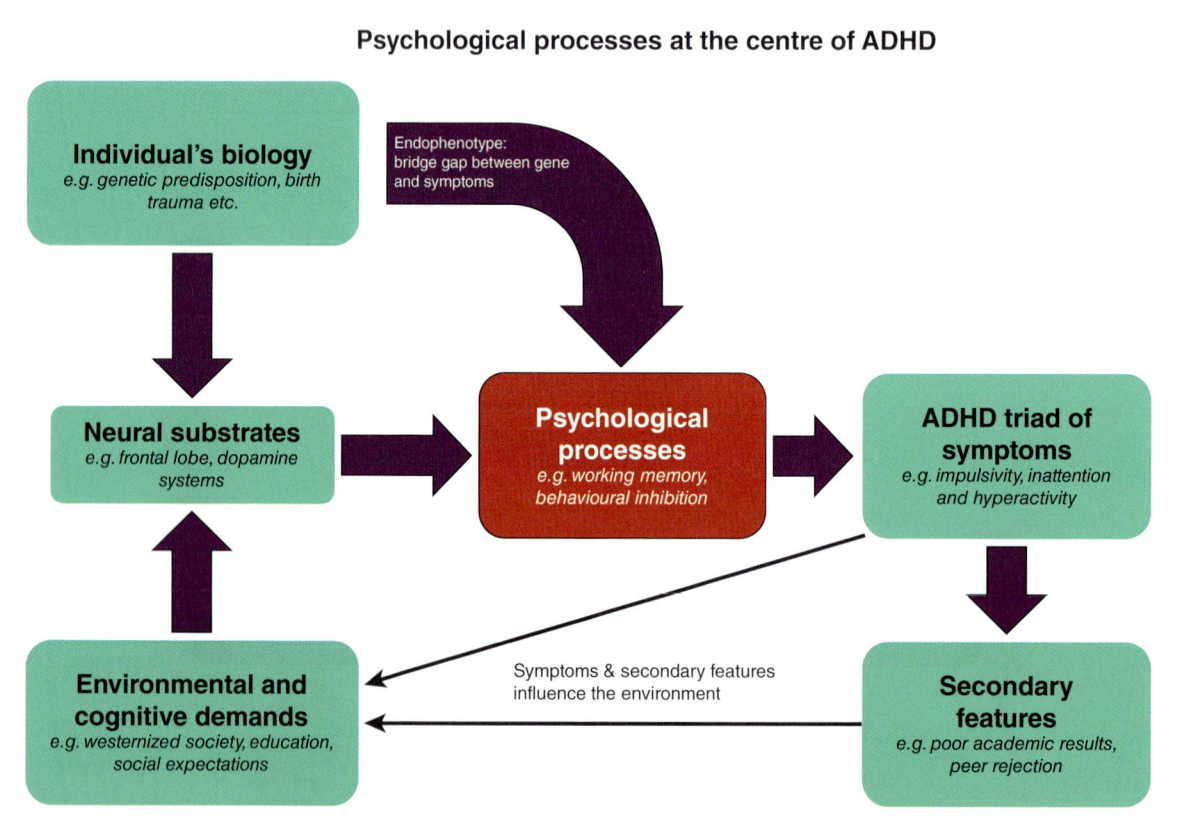

Psychological processes at the centre of ADHD

FIGURE 20.6 *The role of biological, social and psychological factors in ADHD. Numerous factors give rise to ADHD and the symptoms also feed back into the biological mechanisms and potentially exacerbate the symptoms.*
Source: Based on Rapport, M. D., Kofler, M. J., Alderson, R. M., & Raiker, J. (2007). Attention-deficit/hyperactivity disorder. In M. Hersen, & D. Reitman (Eds.), *Handbook of psychological assessment, case conceptualization and treatment (Vol. 2: Children and Adolescents)*. New York: Wiley & Sons.

AUTISM SPECTRUM DISORDER

Although I have chosen to use the phrase autistic spectrum disorder, autism and related disorders are referred to as **pervasive developmental disorders** in the DSM 4 criteria. ASD is characterized by individuals having difficulty with social interaction and communication and also for some with behavioural impairments. Of the ASDs, the two most notable are autism and **Asperger's syndrome**.

Kanner (1943) was the first to describe autism in children in a paper called 'Autistic disturbances of affective contact'. In this report similarities are drawn between the symptoms of autism and those of schizophrenia (see Chapter 21). Having discussed the children's backgrounds and family life, Kanner concludes that:

> ... these children have come into the world with innate inability to form the usual, biologically provided affective contact with people, just as other children come into the world with innate physical or intellectual handicaps. (p.250)

The view that there are similarities with schizophrenia is no longer supported. Professor Sir Michael Rutter (1978) enhanced Kanner's original description by highlighting the early onset of autism and the pervasive nature of the social and language problems. He emphasized the behavioural rigidity and insistence on things remaining the same.

To fall into the trap of ascribing autistic traits to individuals, an illustration is Sheldon Cooper from the US television series *The Big Bang Theory*. Cooper fails to understand social communication and is a creature of habit. He also fails to understand that other people may have their own worldview. Note also that Cooper's extreme intellect also suggests the stereotype of the *idiot savant*.

The condition is often noticed in the first few months of life, but can also take a number of years to manifest. This is in part due to the spectrum of severity within ASD. ASD has also been shown to be more prevalent in males which has lead to the notion of the disorder being an extreme variant of the male brain (Box 20.2).

Diagnostic Criteria

The first official recognition of autism by the American Psychiatric Association was in 1987 (APA, 1987). In DSM 5 it is now autism spectrum disorder (Box 20.3) in which communication deficits and restricted repetitive patterns of behaviour are highlighted. The behavioural features of the person with ASD suggest an individual who is somewhat self-contained. For example, they prefer their own company when engaged in play. Communication is compromised and this has a huge impact on functioning. Speech may be delayed and may include echolalia and neologisms. If speech is well developed, there are usually still problems in communication as the person with ASD has difficulty in taking the other person's perspective in a conversation. They can appear rude and insensitive but this is not deliberate, it is a statement of facts, albeit unpalatable facts sometimes. Most children like structure in their lives but this is more marked in ASD. Children with ASD are resistant to change and become distressed when they are required to do something different. Whereas typically developing children become attached to their cuddly toys, children with ASD are more likely to become attached to unusual objects that are not cuddly at all, e.g. a set of keys.

As with ADHD, ASD is not a new disorder. We should, however, note that our precision and understanding of diagnosis has increased over the years, as indicated by the DSM criteria, and this may be in part a reason for an increase in prevalence.

The question remains, why is there such a thing as ASD?

The Genetics of ASD

The quest to find the genetic basis of ASD is an ongoing pursuit. Many genes have been associated with ASD but the actual single mutant gene for ASD remains elusive – that's because it does not exist.

Twin studies have revealed heritability estimates of about 70–80% (Bailey et al., 1995), with one study showing that the concordance rates were 31% for dizygotic twins and 88% for monozygotic twins (Rosenberg et al., 2009) (see Chapter 2 for a critique of twin studies). In further support, first-degree relatives of ASD cases have an increase in features associated with ASD, although these features are not so pronounced, when compared with the general population (Geschwind, 2011). However, Hallmayer et al. (2011), in a study of 192 twin pairs, noted that there was only a moderate effect of genetic heritability whereas there was an increased contribution of the shared twin environment.

The real challenge is trying to find the genes that contribute to ASD. Structural changes in chromosomes or **copy number variants** (CNV) have large effect sizes and thus are thought sufficient to cause ASD in 10% of cases (Geschwind, 2011). However, there are those who have a CNV but are unaffected (Bucan et al., 2009). Such mutations are rare and should follow Mendelian inheritance patterns. However, 'few such variants cause autism alone but instead could cause a wide variety

BOX 20.2: THE MALE BRAIN IN ASD

Professor Simon Baron-Cohen of Cambridge University has suggested that autism is the result of having an extreme male brain (Baron-Cohen, 2002). Although early reports by Hans Asperger (1944) claimed that autism is an extreme variant of male intelligence, Baron-Cohen takes the view further and provides an elaborate account of empathizing and systematizing. Empathizing maps onto a female brain whereas systematizing maps onto the male brain. Empathizing is where one can respond to other people's affective states; it also includes the Theory of Mind or mentalizing. Empathy is something at which generally females excel, in comparison with males. Empathizing is an important way of being able to understand the complexities of the social world. The systematizing (or male) brain tends to understand the world according to laws and rules. For example, the rules of physics and chemistry allow one to predict how an independent variable may affect a dependent variable (within physics there are many rules and laws that govern the physical world).

According to Baron-Cohen, there are six types of systematizing:

- technical systems, e.g. a computer;
- natural systems, e.g. weather systems;
- abstract systems, e.g. the computer program;
- social systems, e.g. legal system;
- organizable systems, e.g. having your CDs in alphabetical order; and
- motoric systems, e.g. a skilled technique required in sport.

All these rule-based systems can be ascertained by the collection of data and examples in the real world.

Baron-Cohen divides the brain into types depending on the degree of systematizing or empathizing. In doing so, he arrives at five main brain types:

- an empathizing brain, in which there is more empathy (E) than systematizing (S) (E > S). This is the female brain;
- systematizing brain (S > E) or male brain;
- a balanced brain in which both systematizing and empathy are equal (S = E);
- a brain that is extremely systematizing (S >> E); this is the extreme male brain (or ASD brain); and
- a brain that is extremely empathizing (E >> S); an extreme female brain in which systematization is negligible.

In terms of trying to understand ASD, the male systematizing brain can be seen throughout the lifespan in a number of features.

- Toy choices, in which construction toys and vehicles are preferred.
- Occupation, e.g. builder or engineer.
- Academic choices, e.g. maths, physics and engineering are male-dominated degree subjects.
- Constructional ability, in which males can work in 3-D, e.g. with building bricks.
- Map reading.
- Motoric systems, e.g. sports that involve targets.
- Organizable systems, e.g. males have more subcategories of classification (just look at how iTunes can organize your music catalogue).
- There are a number of psychological tasks that are sensitive to the male brain.

How does this all relate to ASD? According to Baron-Cohen, the individual with ASD is impaired in empathy but superior in systematizing. The fact that more males are diagnosed with ASD than females lends some support to this notion. In Chapter 14 there is a more detailed account of the differences between the sexes; when it comes to ASD, their finger length ratio is larger and they show signs of early puberty. Baron-Cohen suggests that one of the biological mechanisms that may be at play in the aetiology of ASD is overexposure *in utero* to testosterone (Baron-Cohen et al., 2011). Female-to-male transsexuals have a higher ASD quotient than typical males and females, leading to the suggestion that these individuals had difficulty socializing with females and found a greater coherence with male peer group identity (Jones et al., 2012).

Females with ASD were shown to have some degree of neural masculinization (Lai et al., 2013) and a difference in brain activity on verbal fluency and mental rotation tasks (Beacher, Radulescu et al., 2012). Typical sexual dimorphism was also found to be absent or attenuated in participants with ASD but this did not equate with a more masculinized brain (Beacher, Minati et al., 2012).

Whilst it is an appealing theory and on the surface a reasonably accurate description of ASD, the search for a conclusive neurobiological correlate goes on.

BOX 20.3: DIAGNOSTIC CRITERIA OF ASD (DSM IV-TR)

(I) A total of six (or more) items from (A), (B), and (C), with at least two from (A), and one each from (B) and (C).

(A) Qualitative impairment in social interaction, as manifested by at least two of the following:
   1. Marked impairments in the use of multiple nonverbal behaviors such as eye-to-eye gaze, facial expression, body posture, and gestures to regulate social interaction.
   2. Failure to develop peer relationships appropriate to developmental level.
   3. A lack of spontaneous seeking to share enjoyment, interests, or achievements with other people, (e.g. by a lack of showing, bringing, or pointing out objects of interest to other people).
   4. Lack of social or emotional reciprocity (note: in the description, it gives the following as examples: not actively participating in simple social play or games, preferring solitary activities, or involving others in activities only as tools or 'mechanical' aids).

(B) Qualitative impairments in communication as manifested by at least one of the following:
   1. Delay in, or total lack of, the development of spoken language (not accompanied by an attempt to compensate through alternative modes of communication such as gesture or mime).
   2. In individuals with adequate speech, marked impairment in the ability to initiate or sustain a conversation with others.
   3. Stereotyped and repetitive use of language or idiosyncratic language.
   4. Lack of varied, spontaneous make-believe play or social imitative play appropriate to developmental level.

(C) Restricted repetitive and stereotyped patterns of behaviour, interests and activities, as manifested by at least two of the following:
   1. Encompassing preoccupation with one or more stereotyped and restricted patterns of interest that is abnormal either in intensity or focus.
   2. Apparently inflexible adherence to specific, nonfunctional routines or rituals.
   3. Stereotyped and repetitive motor mannerisms (e.g. hand or finger flapping or twisting, or complex whole-body movements).
   4. Persistent preoccupation with parts of objects.

(II) Delays or abnormal functioning in at least one of the following areas, with onset prior to age 3 years:
   (A) Social interaction.
   (B) Language as used in social communication.
   (C) Symbolic or imaginative play.

(III) The disturbance is not better accounted for by Rett's Disorder or Childhood Disintegrative Disorder.

And now in the DSM 5:

Autism Spectrum Disorder – neurodevelopmental disorder

(A) Persistent deficits in social communication and social interaction across multiple contexts, as manifested by the following:
   1. Deficits in social-emotional reciprocity, ranging, for example, from abnormal social approach and failure of normal back-and-forth conversation.
   2. Deficits in nonverbal communication behaviours used for social interaction, ranging, for example, from poorly integrated verbal and non verbal communication; to abnormalities in eye contact and body language or deficits in understanding and use of gestures; to a lack of facial expressions and non verbal communication.
   3. Deficits in developing, maintaining and understanding relationships, ranging, for example, from difficulties adjusting behaviour to suit various social contexts; to difficulties in sharing imaginative play or making friends; to absence of interest in peers.

(B) Restricted, repetitive patterns of behaviour, interests or activities, as manifested by at least 2 of the following, currently or by history.
   1. Stereotyped or repetitive motor movements, use of objects, or speech.
   2. Insistence on sameness, inflexible adherence to routines, or ritualised patterns of verbal and non verbal communication.
   3. Highly restricted, fixated interests that are abnormal in intensity or focus.
   4. Hyper- or hyporeactivity to sensory input or unusual interest in sensory aspects of the environment.

of phenotypes (variable expressivity) with or without autism' (Geschwind, 2011). Furthermore, many of the CNVs are not unique to ASD.

When one is looking for the genes involved in ASD, one is actually looking for a large catalogue of genes that may be involved. These genes are wide and varied and have differential effects in terms of neural architecture and psychological functioning (Persico & Napolioni, 2013). According to Krumm et al. (2014), the genetic variations identified in ASD influence three functional pathways: (1) wnt signalling in development, which is signalling from outside of a cell to the inside; (2) chromatin remodelling (chromatin being the contents of a cell's nucleus); and (3) synaptic functioning.

Whilst one should not stop the search just because it is difficult and the findings are inconclusive, the position with regard to the genetics of ASD can be summed up as follows: 'There are still about 70–80% of patients for whom an autism-related genetic change cannot be identified' (Guo et al., 2011, p.703).

Structural Neuroimaging in the Brain

When one looks at the brains of people with ASD, the most notable finding is increased brain size. Clearly, this is a case of bigger is not always better. In a study measuring head circumference in ASD, Courchesne et al. (2003) stated that:

> The clinical onset of autism appears to be preceded by two phases of brain growth abnormality: a reduced head size at birth and a sudden and excessive increase in head size between 1 to 2 months and 6 to 14 months. (p.337)

Magnetic resonance imaging studies suggest that very young children with ASD have increased total brain volume (see Amaral et al. (2008) for review). The nature of the increased brain volume has been argued to be a result of an increase in white matter rather than grey matter. In a study looking at the ASD brain, it was noted that the diencephalon, cerebral white matter, cerebellum and globus pallidus-putamen were significantly larger, with white matter being a main factor in this analysis (Herbert et al., 2003). Whilst the increase in white matter in early childhood has been replicated (Hoppenbrouwers et al., 2014), it has also been noted that grey matter increases occur later in life (Amaral et al., 2008). Although one might expect that, the white matter changes correspond with the time course of ASD. Although changes have been identified throughout the cortex, it is the frontal lobe that has been found to have the most consistent enlargement of grey and white matter. Other areas that have been associated with an increase in size include the cerebellum, hippocampus and amygdala (Polleux

& Lauder, 2004). An increase in the striatum has also been measured in ASD and this has been associated with repetitive behaviours (Hollander et al., 2005); this is a large dopaminergic area in which stimulation via drugs such as amphetamine produces stereotyped behaviour in humans and animals (Ridley & Baker, 1982).

The increase in brain volume may be derived from a number of mechanisms such as an increased number of neurons, the size or myelination of neuroglia, increased elaboration of dendrites or decreased pruning (Parellada et al., 2014).

Functional Neuroimaging of ASD

The world of social neuroscience seeks an understanding of brain activity during tasks that require social processing which may be illuminating in the pursuit of further increasing our knowledge of ASD. The **default mode network** (DMN) is a network of brain regions that are active when the individual is not focused on the external environment. It is made up of the medial prefrontal cortex and its connection with different subsystems, e.g. medial temporal lobe, cingulate cortex and temporo-parietal junction (Li et al., 2014). Activity of the DMN is recorded in participants when they are involved in internally focused tasks such as autobiographical memory retrieval, imagining the future and conceiving the perspectives of others (Buckner et al., 2008). The DMN is involved in emotion perception, empathy, Theory of Mind (ToM), and morality. Participants with ASD in an fMRI study had lower activation of the temporo-parietal junction, which was associated with ToM (Kana et al., 2014) and social functioning (von dem Hagen et al., 2013).

Research has suggested that these regions of the brain that are advanced in human evolution and involved in higher order social processing may be disconnected in ASD: this is the disconnection syndrome (Geschwind & Levitt, 2007; Maximo et al., 2014). From a developmental perspective, disconnection of frontotemporal, frontolimbic and frontoparietal pathways would change the developmental course of experience-dependent processes that refine and strengthen connections (Geschwind & Levitt, 2007). To account for some of the clinical features of ASD, it has been suggested that there is a disconnection of the long-distance connections and an overconnectivity of short-range or local connections (Belmonte et al., 2004; Just et al., 2004). The reduction in long-range connectivity may be responsible for difficulties in social processing whereas the increase in short-range connectivity might underlie superior performance in some cognitive domains, e.g. mathematical abilities.

Such a complex set of symptoms means that ultimately the neurobiology of ASD is going to consist of multiple cortical regions and reciprocal connections (Ecker et al., 2010).

Neurochemistry and Psychopharmacology of ASD

Unlike ADHD which has hypotheses and treatments grounded in dopamine, ASD is not associated with one specific neurotransmitter. There is also a lack of pharmaceuticals that target the social and communication aspects of ASD; treatments are restricted to behavioural management. There is no specific pharmacological treatment available for ASD. Whilst this is a problem for those who suffer with ASD, it is also detrimental to furthering our understanding of the neurochemistry of ASD; from treatment often comes hypothesis.

Three main candidate neurotransmitter systems emerge in connection with ASD: GABA, serotonin and glutamate. Neurotransmitters are not only involved in synaptic communication but they are also involved in brain development and cortical organization.

Serotonin has been shown to be elevated in blood platelets in those with ASD (Anderson, 2002; Cook & Leventhal, 1996). However, such peripheral measures of serotonin are not necessarily reflective of serotonin in the brain. Some studies have, however, looked at serotonin in the brain using PET scans, and have found reductions in synthesis (Chandana et al., 2005; Chugani, 2004, 2012; Chugani et al., 1997, 1999), serotonin transporters (Nakamura et al., 2010) and receptors (Oblak et al., 2013).

Given that we have a large number of drugs that target certain allergic systems, e.g. selective serotonin reuptake inhibitors used in the treatment of depression and anxiety, one might expect these to be effective in ASD. However, these drugs have shown limited efficacy in ASD in which there is a decrease in repetitive behaviours and aggression (Canitano & Scandurra, 2011).

Decreased GABA has also been associated with ASD (Blatt & Fatemi, 2011) and this may be linked to some of the behaviours seen in ASD (Polleux & Lauder, 2004). Drugs that target the GABA system such as antiepileptic drugs have also been shown to have limited efficacy in stabilizing mood (Canitano & Scandurra, 2011). Again, these drugs are not specifically targeting the core symptoms seen in ASD.

Whereas GABA is an inhibitory amino acid and is potentially reduced in ASD, thereby removing the inhibitory actions of GABA, glutamate – the excitatory amino acid – is overactive in ASD (Fatemi, 2008), which means that there is a large excitatory input. Taken together, the imbalance of activity between GABA and glutamate has been hypothesized to be the pathological mechanism in ASD (Rubenstein & Merzenich, 2003). Acamprosate, a GABA A agonist and excitatory glutamate antagonist which is typically used in the treatment of alcoholism, was shown to improve measures of social withdrawal, hyperactivity and social responsiveness (Erickson et al., 2011, 2014).

Other drugs are also used in the treatment of ASD but these do not necessarily have a clear indication of the rationale for their limited efficacy. Atypical antipsychotics have been used in ASD with some effectiveness and these drugs are antagonists within the dopamine system (Canitano & Scandurra, 2011); however, the dopamine system does not appear to have a unique role in ASD. Drugs used to treat ADHD have also been used to manage inattention in ASD patients. These drugs are dopaminergic agonists and more influential in furthering our understanding of ADHD rather than ASD.

Theories of ASD

In the absence of conclusive genetic and neurobiological underpinnings, a number of theories have been advanced to explain ASD. One of the most well established is that of a **'Theory of Mind'** (ToM) which has been applied to many disorders, including schizophrenia (see Chapter 21). Central to this work is Professor Uta Frith. Frith and colleagues (Baron-Cohen et al., 1985) assert that the main problem in ASD can be attributed to a deficit in ToM. ToM is the ability to understand that other people have their own thoughts and intentions, that they have different mental states from you. A failure in ToM leads to social deficits typified by the Sally–Anne task in which two dolls are the protagonists in a false belief task. In this task the doll Sally takes a marble and hides it in her basket. Sally then leaves the room and whilst she is away, Anne takes the marble out of Sally's basket and puts it in her box. Upon Sally's return, the child is asked 'Where will Sally look for her marble?'. Typically developing children correctly assume the position of Sally and state that she will think it is in the basket even though the child knows it is not. A child with ASD will answer that Sally will go to the box where Anne put the marble despite Sally not knowing such information.

Other tasks that require ToM also reveal deficits in ASD (Perner et al., 1989; White et al., 2009, 2011). The left medial prefrontal cortex was shown to be a region of interest in ASD during ToM tasks (Happe et al., 1996). In an fMRI study, ASD adolescents who did not have a history of ToM deficits showed the same atypical neurophysiological response as children who did have such a history (White et al., 2014). The authors suggest that the differences in ToM deficits map onto a similar neurocognitive dysfunction; alternatively it might mean that the regions of interest in this study were not sensitive to ToM. Furthermore, given that some individuals with

> **BOX 20.4: MIRROR NEURONS**
>
> Mirror neurons are active when an individual executes a motor act or when they observe somebody else performing the same motor act. The mirror neuron system has been argued to be important in understanding goals and intentions, and to be involved in the development of movement, emotions and language (Rizzolatti & Fabbri-Destro, 2008). It has been associated with a lack of empathy in psychopaths and their failure to understand the pain of others (Fecteau et al., 2008). Given the importance of social processing, it is not surprising that mirror neurons have been linked to ASD (Williams et al., 2001): the broken mirror theory of autism. A breakdown of the mirror neurons has an impact on empathy, ToM, and language and communication.
>
> However, the mirror neuron theory of autism does not remain unchallenged, as when no difference was found between EEG recordings in ASD and control subjects (Fan et al., 2010). An alternative explanation has been provided to account for the limitations of the broken mirror neuron theory: the social top-down response modulation model (Hamilton, 2013). In this model there are two components: visual to motor mapping, and a top-down modulating system. The visuomotor mapping is mediated via the higher order regions of the visual system to the motor cortex. The visuomotor mapping is subject to social evaluation and higher order top-down control mechanisms. Thus, a failure of the mirror neuron system in ASD can also be accounted for by the failure in social and emotional cues to modulate the mirror neuron system. Hamilton's account acknowledges the existence of the mirror neuron system but suggests that the mirror neuron system is itself controlled by top-down processes that evaluate the social context.
>
> What can we deduce from the many studies of mirror neurons in ASD? We can deduce that autism is an extremely complex disorder. Perhaps this is the only true fact.

ASD do not show the typical deficits in ToM then one might consider this a weakness in the overall argument. However, one has to remember that whilst the diagnosis of ASD has improved, it could be that the diagnostic category of ASD is overinclusive and represents a group with heterogeneous aetiologies.

Frith and Happe (1994) acknowledge that there are some limitations with the ToM account of ASD. They note that some ASD cases can actually pass the false belief tasks and in addition, not all aspects of ASD are captured by an impaired ToM. In acknowledging this, Frith and Happe (1994) present a model of ASD referred to as the weak central coherence model (WCC). The central premise of the WCC model is that there is a bias towards local processing rather than global processing. Those with ASD do not use context to support their understanding of their environment. They are more likely to be interested in the subcomponents of an object rather than the whole. Ascribing a neural location was not considered to be a suitable pursuit in the WCC model; rather it was considered to be a problem of reduced connectivity of cortical and subcortical regions (Happe & Frith, 2006).

A more neural-based ToM account of autism is evident in the **mirror neuron** theory (Box 20.4). Mirror neurons are activated when an observer sees an action being performed. This was first noted by Rizzolatti et al. (1996), who observed the activation of neurons in the premotor cortex of monkeys when they performed an action or when they watched the action. A more detailed account of the mirror neuron hypothesis is given in Box 20.4.

There is a lot of theoretical conjecture and uncertainty about the aetiology, neuropathology and psychopathology of ASD. It has been stated that:

> If different features of autism are caused by different genes, associated with different brain regions and related to different core cognitive impairments, it seems likely they will respond to different types of treatment. Abandoning the search for a single cause for a single entity of autism may also mean abandoning the search for a single 'cure' or intervention'. (Happe et al., 2006, p.1220)

Despite this being said in 2006, the sentiment remains the same.

SUMMARY

Attention deficit hyperactivity disorder and ASD both emerge early in childhood with very different symptoms, all of which can be severely debilitating. Furthermore, both disorders can be mapped along a spectrum of severity (Box 20.5). The known neuropathological differences

BOX 20.5: SPECTRUMS

Both ADHD and ASD can be considered spectrum disorders (Figure 20.5.1). In a categorical world, one either has or does not have the condition. In these categorical views of disorder, the person who receives a diagnosis is seen as being qualitatively different from normal. However, under a spectrum analysis the behaviours that contribute to a disorder can be seen along a continuum. An example of this could be attention, in which the normal population has an average attention span; let us call it an attention quotient (AQ). Some people might have enhanced attention and a large AQ, whilst others have deficits in attention and would have a low AQ. We could map this on to the disorders we have been discussing.

If we accept the systematizing male brain view of Baron-Cohen (2002), we might see ASD as having focused attention on small details, and indeed this would fit with the weak central coherence (WCC) theory (Frith & Happe, 1994). At the other end of the spectrum is inattention, as exhibited in many cases of ADHD.

If the whole population falls along a spectrum, the question becomes, at which point on that spectrum does functional impairment occur? Furthermore, how do the spectrums of all symptoms contribute and overlap to produce a syndrome/disorder? For example, if you have a low AQ, at what cut-off point does this lead to a diagnosis of ADHD? Clearly, if one establishes a strict percentile range then that job is easier, but when one looks at functional impairment then how does a person who just makes the diagnosis differ from one who just misses out on diagnosis? If the percentile range is 5%, what is the difference between 4% and 6% in real terms? This does have important ramifications for the individual because it may be the difference between receiving support or not. This is often seen in the education sector where children who fall short of the cut-off point, but are also functionally impaired, do not get access to services that could make the condition better. Why might this be the case? From a cynical perspective, it is down to the finite pot of money.

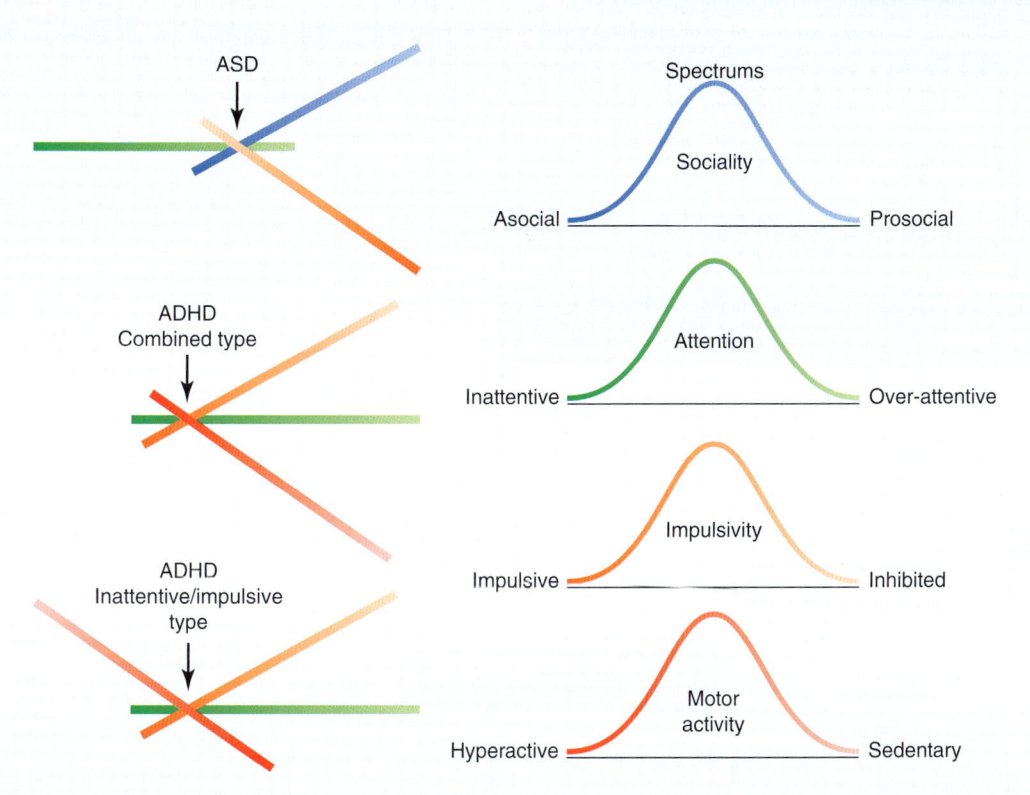

FIGURE 20.5.1 *ADHD and ASD spectrum disorders. The symptoms of both ADHD and ASD can be considered as extremes of normal behaviour. However, both disorders can be mapped onto a normal distribution curve, and each individual symptom can also be mapped on to the neural distribution. How each symptom contributes to a disorder will depend upon how those symptoms overlap to create a functional impairment.*

in both disorders have been placed onto psychological processes in order to provide theories and levels of explanation of how the symptoms/behaviours emerge. The search for the actual cause of these disorders may in fact find multiple locations or causal routes and therefore implicate ASD, etc. as disorders of many aetiologies, e.g. genetic, neurological and environmental. In addition, risk/vulnerability factors need to be determined in order to understand the aetiology and its developmental process.

LEARNING OUTCOME QUESTIONS

You should be able to answer the following questions.
- Describe how important diagnosis is to the scientific understanding of ADHD and ASD.
- Account for ADHD and ASD in a theoretical framework.
- Critically evaluate the role of drug treatments in the understanding of ADHD.

FURTHER READING

Chandler, C. (2010). *The Science of ADHD: A guide for parents and professionals*. Oxford, UK: Wiley-Blackwell.
Frith, U., & Hill, E. (2003). *Autism: Mind and brain*. Oxford, UK: Oxford University Press.
Romer, D., & Walker, E. F. (2007). *Adolescent psychopathology and the developing brain: Integrating brain and prevention science*. New York: Oxford University Press.
Turk, J., Graham, P. J., & Verhulst, F. C. (2007). *Child and adolescent psychiatry: A developmental approach*. Oxford, UK: Oxford University Press.
Wolfe, D. A., & Mash, E. J. (2006). *Behavioral and emotional disorders in adolescents: Nature, assessment, and treatment*. New York: Guilford Press.

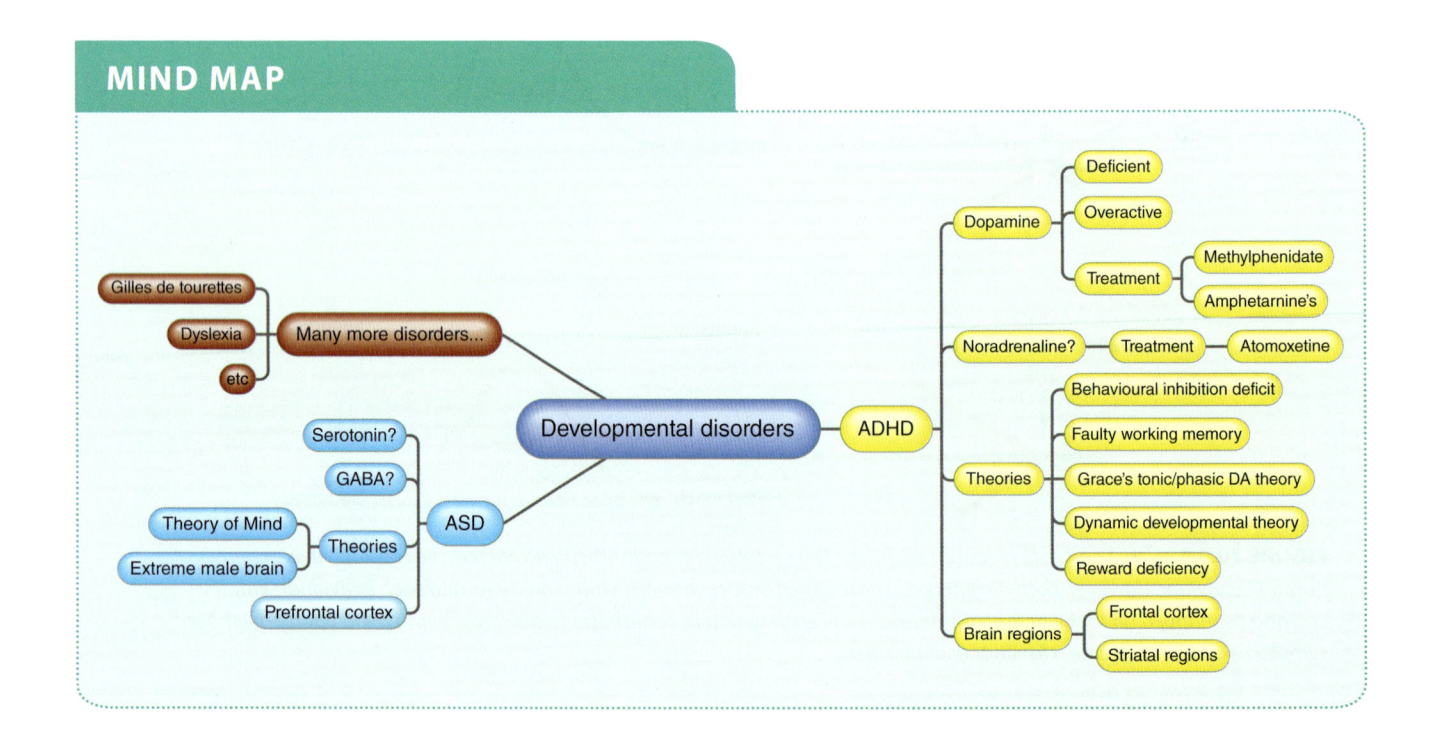

MIND MAP

21 Schizophrenia Spectrum and Other Psychotic Disorders

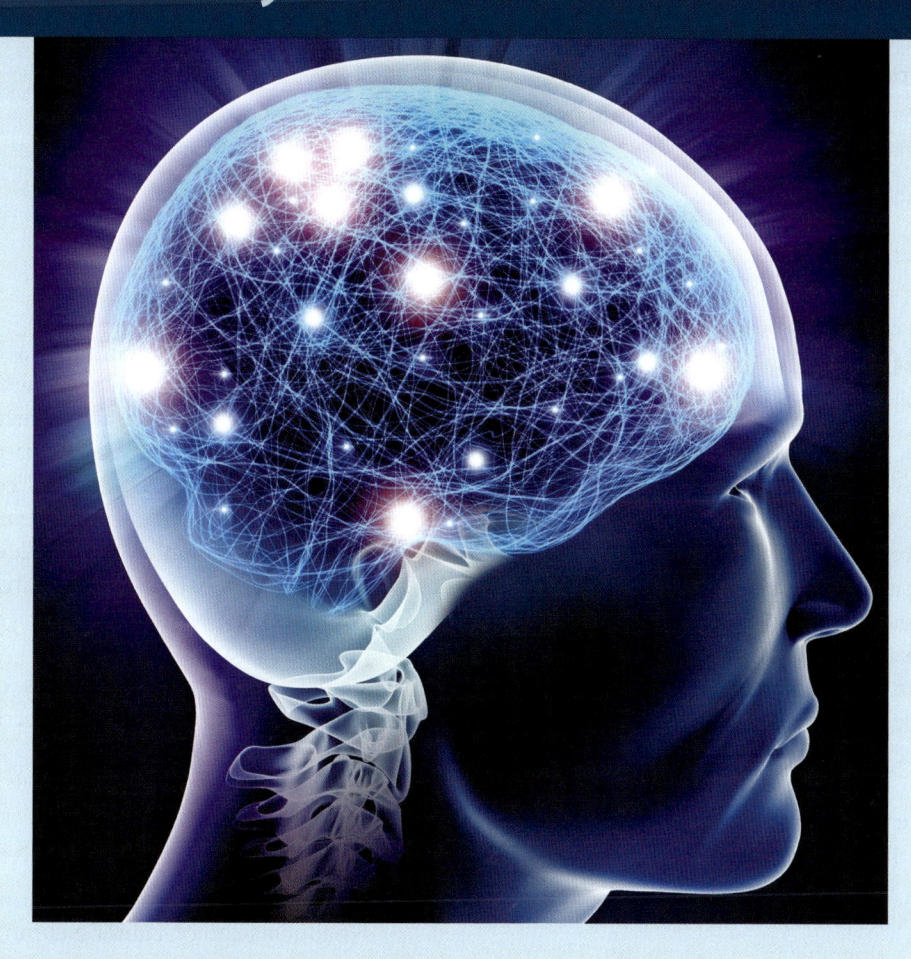

THE ANATOMY OF THE CHAPTER

This chapter will highlight the following.

- The genetic basis of schizophrenia.
- The neurochemistry of schizophrenia.
- The neuropsychological and neuropathological aspects of schizophrenia.
- The evolutionary psychology of schizophrenia.
- Animal models of schizophrenia.

INTRODUCTION   524

GENETICS OF SCHIZOPHRENIA   525

NEUROCHEMISTRY OF SCHIZOPHRENIA   529

NEUROBIOLOGICAL THEORIES   534

NEUROPSYCHOLOGICAL THEORIES   535

LIMITATIONS OF MANY STUDIES IN SCHIZOPHRENIA   537

SUMMARY   537

LEARNING OUTCOMES

1. To understand the development of hypotheses regarding the neuropsychopharmacological basis of schizophrenia.
2. To be aware of the limitations when studying schizophrenia.
3. To be able to provide a neuropsychological explanation of schizophrenia.

INTRODUCTION

Schizophrenia is a disorder that is generally envisaged when one refers to 'the insane'. It is a type of psychotic disorder (see below). There is an estimated lifetime prevalence of schizophrenia of 1% (Stilo & Murray, 2010). In real terms, that is quite a lot of people. It was estimated that in 2010 in the UK, there were 586,840 people diagnosed with psychotic disorders and 5 million in Europe (Gustavsson et al., 2011). However, the incidence of schizophrenia varies across nations, time and the sexes (McGrath, 2006).

Males are more likely to suffer from schizophrenia, especially between 20 and 24 years old (Kirkbride et al., 2006). One of the potential reasons for this might be the vulnerability of the male brain during development (Castle & Murray, 1991). In an article entitled *'The fragile male'*, Kraemer (2000) reviews the literature that points to males being more vulnerable from conception. The male embryo is more vulnerable to insult and trauma with more resultant deaths (Mizuno, 2000). At birth the female child is 4–6 weeks more physiologically advanced than her male counterpart (Gualtieri & Hicks, 1985). Stilo and Murray (2010) also note that the incidence of schizophrenia across the sexes depends on diagnostic criteria and the severity of presenting symptoms, with females exhibiting at a later age and males exhibiting with more severe symptoms.

Schizophrenia is the main grouping under the umbrella term **psychosis**. Psychosis is thought disorder characterized by disturbances of reality and perception, impaired cognition functioning and inappropriate or diminished affect.

Whilst there is a considerable amount of research investigating schizophrenia, its pathogenesis is not known. The likelihood is that there are a number of genes of modest effect involved that interact with environmental triggers to bring about a comparatively late onset.

Schizophrenia can be seen in the literature over many centuries. However, Emil Kraepelin (1856–1926) popularized the term 'dementia praecox' ('premature dementia' or 'precocious madness') which encapsulated the disparate categories of insanity prevailing at the time. Much of the description of dementia praecox involved emotional weakening and a loss of cognitive abilities. However, the actual term 'schizophrenia' was suggested by Bleuler in 1911 (Bleuler, 1950). Bleuler's conception of schizophrenia was that of a syndrome of disorders that have a similar psychopathology. This consideration is still pertinent today.

Schneider's first rank symptoms of schizophrenia provide a simple but informative description of the disorder (Schneider, 1959).

- Auditory hallucinations:
  – hearing voices conversing with one another;
  – voices heard commenting on one's actions (hallucination of running commentary); and
  – thought echo (a form of auditory hallucination in which the patient hears their thoughts spoken aloud).
- Somatic hallucinations.
- Passivity experiences, e.g. thoughts, sensations and actions are under external control (delusional).
- Thought withdrawal.
- Thought insertion (thoughts are ascribed to other people who are intruding into the patient's mind).
- Thought broadcasting (also called thought diffusion).
- Delusional perception (linking a normal sensory perception to a bizarre conclusion, e.g. seeing an aeroplane means the patient is the president).

Classifications dividing schizophrenia into simple, hebephrenic, paranoid and catatonic share some similarities but are also distinct from each other.

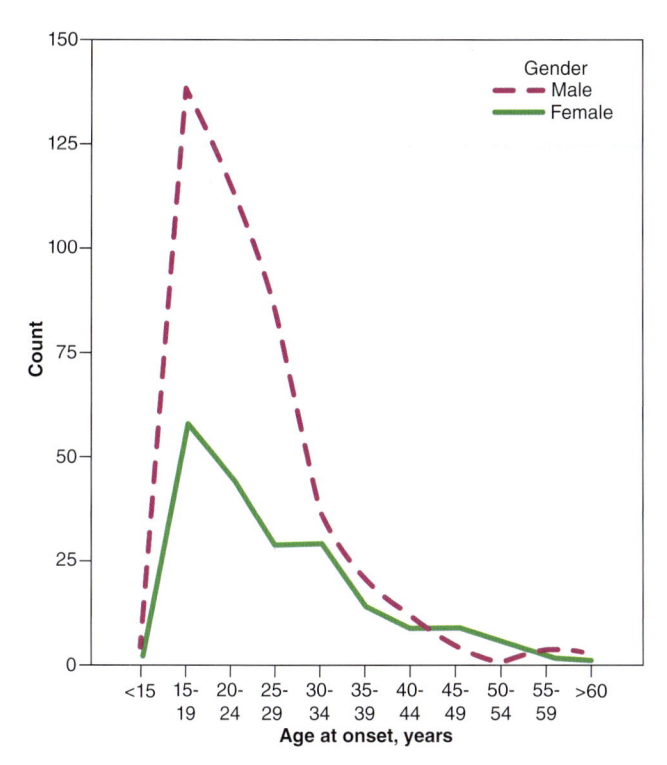

FIGURE 21.1 *The incidence by age and sex in a sample (n=537) of first episode schizophrenia.*
Source: Abel, K. M., Drake, R. & Goldstein, J. M. 2010. Sex differences in schizophrenia. *International Review of Psychiatry, 22,* 417–28.

Crow (1980) divided the symptoms of schizophrenia into positive and negative. The **positive symptoms** represent acute schizophrenia (or type I) whereas the **negative symptoms** are indicative of chronic schizophrenia (or type II). The first thing to remember in discussing the positive and negative symptoms of schizophrenia is that they are not quality judgements. Positive symptoms refer to behaviours that are in addition to normal behaviours (add-ons, e.g. hallucinations). Negative symptoms refer to deficits in normal behaviour (e.g. anhedonia). This division is depicted in Figure 21.2.

Diagnosis of schizophrenia has changed over the years and this has had an impact on research and ultimately the quest for a biological underpinning of the disorder. The most recent categorization of schizophrenia is given in Box 21.1.

GENETICS OF SCHIZOPHRENIA

A family history of schizophrenia provides a risk factor in first-degree relatives (Tsuang, 2000). Twin and adoption studies indicate that the extra risk is more probably due to genetic factors and not environmental factors, with a mean heritability estimate of 80–85% (Cardno et al., 1999; Sullivan et al., 2003). Candidate gene studies have looked at serotonin and dopamine (DA) receptors (Pal et al., 2009; Virgos et al., 2001). In a meta-analysis of candidate genes, seven were identified as being associated with schizophrenia, including the dopamine DRD4 gene (which has also been associated with addiction, ADHD and personality characteristics such as sensation seeking; see Lusher et al. (2001) and Shi et al. (2008) Genome-wide scans have found numerous sites in which there are single nucleotide polymorphisms (SNPs) associated with schizophrenia (Schizophrenia Psychiatric Genome-Wide Association Study, 2011). Although a gene for schizophrenia remains elusive, familial studies indicate a large heritable component. How this translates into schizophrenia is another question and if it is genetic, can the evolutionary psychologist find an adaptive purpose of the disorder (Box 21.2)? Schizophrenia is considered a neurodevelopmental disorder that expresses itself in early adulthood. Many have considered that the genetic component of schizophrenia interferes with the normal neurodevelopment of the brain (Klempan et al., 2004).

There are numerous other factors that may affect the incidence of schizophrenia.

- *Obstetric complications* – pregnancy, development *in utero* and delivery (Cannon et al., 2002).

- *season of birth* – higher incidence in winter/spring births (McGrath & Welham, 1999), which might be linked to white matter development (Giezendanner et al., 2013). Why this should be the case is a matter for speculation. Some have argued that it might be caused by geomagnetic storms (Kay, 2004) and rainfall (Messias et al., 2006). However, in a retrospective study of 376 schizophrenia patients, there was a pattern favouring winter/spring births (Demler, 2011).

- *Parental age* – a higher incidence of schizophrenia is found in the children of older fathers (Kong et al., 2012) and is thought to be mediated by sperm mutations (Goriely & Wilkie, 2012)

- *Drug abuse* – amphetamines have been linked with the symptoms of paranoid schizophrenia (Chen et al., 2003, 2005). However, the drug that has received most attention in connection with schizophrenia is cannabis (McGuire et al., 1993, 1994). The debate about cannabis has also influenced policy with changes of drug classification (see Chapter 7). This is in part due to high potency cannabis having a greater effect and potentially leading to an early onset of psychotic behaviour (Di Forti et al., 2014) with an underlying dopaminergic component (Murray et al., 2014).

Positive symptoms

- **Delusions**
  - Firmly held beliefs
  - Against reality
  - Resistant to reality
- **Persecutory delusions** common
  - 'The VC is out to get me'
- **Other common forms:**
  - Thought insertion
  - Thought broadcasting
- **Hallucinations**
  - Sensory experiences in the absence of sensory stimulation
    - Audible thoughts
    - Voices commenting
    - Voices arguing
- **Incongruity of affect**
- **Incoherence of speech**
- Respond well to antipsychotic medication
- Represents acute stage of disease
- Good prognosis
- Pathophysiology DAergic

Positive symptoms *in addition to normal behaviours*

Normality

Negative symptoms *deficits in normal behaviours*

Negative symptoms

- **Avolition**
  - Lack of interest; apathy
- **Alogia**
  - Reduction in speech
- **Anhedonia**
  - Inability to experience pleasure
    - Consummatory pleasure
    - Anticipatory pleasure
- **Flat affect**
  - Exhibits little or no affect in face or voice
- **Asociality**
  - Inability to form close personal relationships
- **Attentional impairment**
- Poor response to traditional pharmacotherapy
- Poor prognosis
- Pathology centred on structural brain changes (enlarged ventricles)

FIGURE 21.2 *The positive and negative symptoms of schizophrenia.*

BOX 21.1: DIAGNOSTIC CRITERIA OF SCHIZOPHRENIA (DSM)

DSM IV

A. Two (or more) of the following symptoms, each present for a significant portion of time during a 1-month period (or less if successfully treated).

1. Delusions.
2. Hallucinations.
3. Disorganized speech (e.g. frequent derailment or incoherence).
4. Grossly disorganized or catatonic behaviour.
5. Negative symptoms, i.e. affective flattening, alogia, or avolition.

Note: Only one Criterion A symptom is required if delusions are bizarre or hallucinations consist of a voice keeping up a running commentary on the person's behaviour or thoughts, or two or more voices conversing with each other.

B. Social/occupational dysfunction:
For a significant portion of the time since the onset of the disturbance, one or more major areas of functioning such as work, interpersonal relations, or self-care are markedly below the level achieved prior to the onset (or when the onset is in childhood or adolescence, failure to achieve expected level of interpersonal, academic, or occupational achievement).

C. Duration:
Continuous signs of the disturbance persist for at least 6 months. This 6-month period must include at least 1 month of symptoms (or less if successfully treated) that meet Criterion A (i.e. active-phase symptoms) and may include periods of prodromal or residual symptoms.
  – During these prodromal or residual periods, the signs of the disturbance may be manifested by only negative symptoms or two or more symptoms listed in Criterion A present in an attenuated form (e.g. odd beliefs, unusual perceptual experiences).

D. Schizoaffective and mood disorder exclusion.

E. Substance/general medical condition exclusion: The disturbance is not due to the direct physiological effects of a substance (e.g. a drug of abuse, a medication) or a general medical condition.

F. Relationship to a pervasive developmental disorder. If there is a history of autistic disorder or another pervasive developmental disorder, the additional diagnosis of schizophrenia is made only if prominent delusion, or hallucinations are also present for at least a month (or less if successfully treated).

DSM 5

A. Two (or more) of the following, each present for a significant portion of time during a 1 month period (or less if successfully treated). At least one of these must be (1), (2) or (3).

1. Delusions.
2. Hallucinations.
3. Disorganized speech.
4. Grossly disorganized or catatonic behaviour.
5. Negative symptoms.

B. For a significant portion of the time since the onset of the disturbance, level of functioning in one or more major areas, such as work, interpersonal relations, or self-care, is markedly below the level achieved prior to the onset.

C. Continuous signs of the disturbance persist for at least 6 months.

Types of schizophrenia and related diagnosis

Paranoid schizophrenia
Disorganized
Catatonic
Undifferentiated and residual
Schizophrenia spectrum
Schizophrenia
Schizotypal (personality) disorder
Other psychotic disorders

Abnormalities in one or more of the following five domains

Disorganized speech and/or thinking
Hallucinations
Delusions
Grossly disorganized or abnormal motor behaviour
Negative symptoms

BOX 21.2: EVOLUTIONARY PSYCHOLOGY OF SCHIZOPHRENIA

It is hard to imagine how schizophrenia could possibly have any evolutionary advantage. Brune (2008) claims that the number and diversity of hypotheses of the evolution of schizophrenia are greater than for any other psychopathology. Some have argued that schizophrenia confers an advantage with creativity and genius, i.e. those with schizophrenia think differently. However, the predominant evolutionary theories suggest that schizophrenia is an unfortunate artefact of evolutionary specialization of the brain.

One of the major hypotheses focuses on language and cerebral dominance. Professor Tim Crow (1997a, 1997b, 2000) argues that schizophrenia is a failure in lateralization and dominance of the left hemisphere for language. In particular:

> The symptoms of schizophrenia can be understood as a failure to establish dominance for a key component – the phonological sequence – of language in the dominant hemisphere, with consequent disruption of the mechanism of indexicality that allows the speaker to distinguish his thoughts from the speech output that he generates and that which he receives from others. (Crow, 2000, p.126)

A failure in phonological tasks and a reduction in the cerebral dominance, as measured by electroencephalogram (EEG), has been seen in schizophrenic patients (Angrilli et al., 2009), thus providing some support for Crow's theory (Figure 21.2.1).

Burns (2004) argues that schizophrenia is a disorder of abnormal connectivity and is the result of an evolutionary trade-off at two periods of time.

- Through evolution with increasing neural complexity underlying cognitive processes, the brain was more vulnerable to genetic variation and environmental insults.
- About 150,000 years ago, before the migration out of Africa, slow changes in the brain were promoted under genetic control, and the changes in brain architecture were most notable in the frontal circuitry. When the symptoms of schizophrenia are considered along a spectrum of severity, only the most severe would die out because the genes were coding for the more advantageous social communication.

Central to the social brain is the Theory of Mind which is thought to reside in the frontal lobes (see Chapter 12)

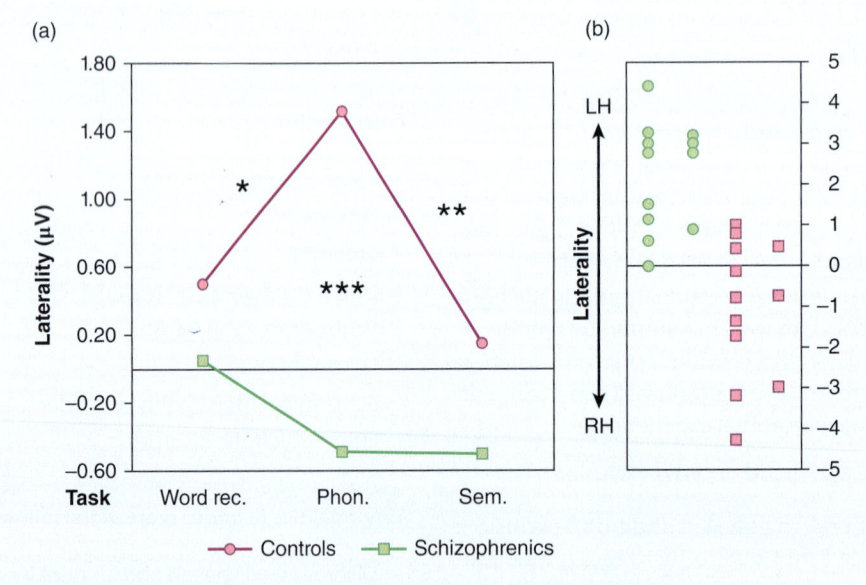

FIGURE 21.2.1 Lateralization in schizophrenia. (a) Lateralization scores (right minus left hemisphere electrical activity). (b) Distribution of individual laterality scores from anterior sites in the phonological task. Word rec, word recognition task; Phon, phonological task; Sem, semantic task.
Source: Angrilli, A., Spironelli, C., Elbert, T., Crow, T. J., Marano, G., & Stegagno, L. (2009). Schizophrenia as failure of left hemispheric dominance for the phonological component of language. PLoS ONE, 4(2), e4507.

and is also central to theories of autistic spectrum disorder (ASD) (see Chapter 20).

Both theories suggest that schizophrenia is a non-adaptive by-product of brain specialization. However, according to Brune (2008), evolutionary theories are inadequate because they only address specific components of schizophrenia rather than the syndrome itself.

- *Urban residence* – living in urban compared to suburban areas has been linked with a higher prevalence of schizophrenia (Kirkbride et al., 2006). However, other factors such as poverty may be more important.
- *Migration* – moving to another country has also been associated with schizophrenia, seen in first- and second-generation offspring (Selten et al., 2007). At first, a biological mechanism appears elusive but a link with DA has been suggested in which animal models of defeat demonstrate sensitization of dopamine (Covington & Miczek, 2001) which may be similar to the lower status of new migrant populations (Selten & Cantor-Graae, 2005).
- *Childhood adversity* – parental loss, child abuse and bullying are all factors that are overrepresented in schizophrenic probands (Matheson et al., 2013). Children may have a heightened stress response after such life events and it has been argued that there may be dopamine sensitization as a result (Murray et al., 2002).
- *Adult adversity* – life events in adulthood have also been linked with schizophrenia (Schwartz & Myers, 1977a, 1977b). However, it has been argued that it is not the number of life events *per se* that matters but rather the reaction to life events (Norman & Malla, 1993).

Structural differences and functional impairment have been associated with numerous brain regions in schizophrenia (Lawrie et al., 2004), but it would appear that all roads lead to dopamine. However, the reason DA is so prominent in the research literature is that early studies indicated a faulty DA mechanism. The DA hypothesis has therefore guided much research into understanding the neurobiological basis of schizophrenia. However, the adherence to a DA deficit in schizophrenia has been a case in which the philosophical standpoint is to extend the paradigm. Therefore, it is not surprising that research finds that there are effects of DA in schizophrenia. Nevertheless, the DA hypothesis still remains a hypothesis and is not an established fact.

NEUROCHEMISTRY OF SCHIZOPHRENIA

The DA hypothesis of schizophrenia has been remarkably persistent in neuropsychopharmacology. Simply put, schizophrenia is the result of an excess of DA in the brain. The evidence to support this hypothesis comes from drugs that treat schizophrenia, which have provided a route of investigation to trace their mode of action. Furthermore, drugs such as amphetamine have also provided insight into schizophrenia as they potentially exacerbate or mimic schizophrenia in non-schizophrenic population. Case studies have included amphetamine-induced psychosis (Wallis et al., 1949). The administration of amphetamine to people suffering with narcolepsy resulted in amphetamine-induced psychosis with symptoms resembling paranoid schizophrenia (Young & Scoville, 1938). Others regarded amphetamine psychosis as being indistinguishable from paranoid schizophrenia (Connell, 1958). Such was the similarity that amphetamine psychosis was once considered a model of schizophrenia based on its ability to increase catecholamines (Snyder, 1972, 1973). Further support was derived from animal models of schizophrenia (Box 21.3).

Amphetamine works by increasing the amount of dopamine in the synapses (see Chapters 7 and 16). The logic is that if amphetamine increases schizophrenic symptoms and amphetamine increases dopamine, then schizophrenia is possibly due to an increase in dopamine (as mimicked by amphetamine).

Psychiatry was revolutionized in 1955 with the introduction of the first antipsychotic medication, **chlorpromazine** (Delay & Deniker, 1955). Although not intended for schizophrenia, chlorpromazine was seen to be effective at quietening the florid symptoms of schizophrenia. There has been much criticism of chlorpromazine since its first introduction but one must remember that prior to its use, treatments for schizophrenia were somewhat limited and torturous, e.g. hydrotherapy in which cold water was poured from a height onto the forehead, lobotomies (see Chapter 12) and other forms of shock therapy. Chlorpromazine can provide some improvement in the treatment of schizophrenia, but perhaps its real value is in the increased understanding of schizophrenia that has come from its use.

Chlorpromazine is an antipsychotic and is sometimes referred to as a **neuroleptic**. It is of the class **phenothiazines**. 'Neuroleptic' refers to the neurological side-effects, in particular those affecting the motor system that can produce a syndrome resembling Parkinson's disease. It is important to realize that these drugs are only effective whilst they remain in the brain. There is no cure

BOX 21.3: ANIMAL MODELS OF SCHIZOPHRENIA

With reports of amphetamine psychosis in the human population, the next logical step is to investigate the effects of amphetamine in animals in which controlled and systematic studies can be conducted.

Ellenbroek and Cools (1990) identified the components of an animal model of schizophrenia.

Predictive validity

- Neuroleptics of various chemical classes should be effective, e.g. chlorpromazine, clozapine, haloperidol, respiridone, olanzapine, thioridazine, sulpiride, etc.
- There should be a relationship between the clinical potency of neuroleptics and their potency in the model, e.g. compare *in vitro* techniques with behavioural measures.
- No false negatives/positives.
- Anticholinergic drugs should not reduce the effects of neuroleptics (many drugs have anticholinergic activity).
- Chronic treatments should not reduce the effect of the treatments (often long term).

Criteria for assessing the face validity of animal models of schizophrenia

- The model should resemble schizophrenia in a number of respects, but how do you evaluate hallucination in an animal? Lyon and Nielsen (1979) identify three criteria of an animal model of hallucination: (1) a clear orienting to a stimulus that is not visible or audible to a human observer, (2) clear signs of a strong emotional reaction to a stimulus point (e.g. stiffening of muscles, piloerection, pupillary dilation, etc.), and (3) a definite co-ordinated sequence of responses oriented with respect to the given point in space (e.g. striking or fleeing from the point).
- These similarities should be specific to schizophrenia, and not be related to mania, dementia, depression, organic brain damage or drug abuse.
- These similarities should co-exist in a specific subtype of schizophrenia (e.g. positive or negative symptoms).
- The model should not show features unrelated to schizophrenia.

Criteria for assessing the construct validity of animal models of schizophrenia

- The essential feature(s) in the model of schizophrenia should be unambiguously interpretable (e.g. thought disorder).
- The feature(s) being modelled should stand in an established empirical relationship to schizophrenia (e.g. amphetamine-induced hyperactivity).
- The feature(s) being modelled should stand in an established theoretical relationship to schizophrenia (e.g. hypofrontality).

Ellinwood and Escalante (1977) noted that as the dose of amphetamine increased in the rat, so did motor activity and eventually stereotyped behaviour would emerge. They argued that this represented dyssynchrony in which one body part or body segment would move without proper relation to the other parts. As time progressed, the animals demonstrated the degeneration of object relations in which they could not interact with stimuli in the environment in a typical manner. Stereotyped behaviour is argued to represent a level of perception that deteriorates and was analogous to the disturbances and thought processes seen in schizophrenia (Ellinwood & Kilbey, 1975). Using slow-release amphetamine, rats showed an initial increase in activity followed by social isolation. After some 24 hours of socialization, the animals would re-emerge into the rat community and engage in abnormal social behaviours such as antagonizing the dominant rat and being attacked for doing so (Ellison et al., 1978).

Pharmacologically induced models of schizophrenia have since moved to the use of **phencyclidine** (PCP) which also models the negative symptoms of schizophrenia (Mouri et al., 2007).

for schizophrenia; all that is on offer is long-term maintenance treatment to alleviate some of the symptoms.

In a similar vein to amphetamine, the use of antipsychotic medication opens up a line of research in which scientists can investigate the mechanisms underlying successful treatment and thereby generate hypotheses about the disease process itself. The antipsychotics also provide some experimental symmetry to the studies conducted using amphetamine. Where amphetamine exacerbated schizophrenic symptoms, the antipsychotics treated the symptoms; the drugs had opposite effects. The common denominator of the vast majority of antipsychotics that were initially available was the blockade of DA. This provides complementary symmetry to the work with amphetamine: amphetamine increases dopamine – antipsychotics decrease dopamine.

Antipsychotics have numerous mechanisms that interact with dopamine. They may, counterintuitively, increase the levels of DA (which is the last thing you might want to do). They do this by blocking autoreceptors on the presynaptic terminal of dopaminergic neurons (Carlsson & Lindqvist, 1963). This blockade leads to compensatory effects which increase the firing rate of subcortical dopaminergic neurons in the nigrostriatal and mesolimbic pathways. Such false feedback promotes an increasing DA synthesis, metabolism and release. However, the putative therapeutic effects of antipsychotic medication are thought to be exerted via the presynaptic receptors in which blockade prevents dopaminergic signals from being transmitted. Therefore, any increase by autoreceptor feedback is offset by the presynaptic blockade. Antipsychotic medication produces a depolarization blockade in which subsequent action potentials cannot be initiated, thereby inactivating nigrostriatal and mesolimbic dopaminergic neurons.

The evidence is further supported by biochemical studies in which chlorpromazine is able to block DA-stimulated **adenylate cyclase** and the increase in **cyclic AMP**.

Once chlorpromazine had been found to be an effective agent in schizophrenia, other drugs were discovered. **Haloperidol** is a different class of antipsychotic drug to chlorpromazine (haloperidol is a **butyrophenone**) and is clinically efficacious in schizophrenia. However, the biochemical evidence supporting a dopamine system and mode of action in treating schizophrenia was challenged by haloperidol. Haloperidol did not have a pronounced effect on DA-sensitive adenylate cyclase (Clement-Cormier et al., 1974). However, there was a high correlation between inhibition of haloperidol binding and clinical efficacy and the ability to block stereotyped behaviour in animals (Burt et al., 1976; Creese et al., 1975). The difference in biochemical measures was reconciled by the

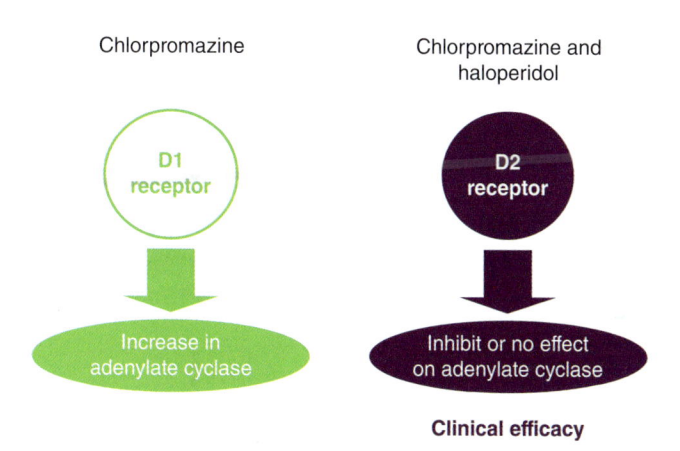

FIGURE 21.3 *Dopamine D1 and D2 receptors. The D1 receptor has little effect in schizophrenia. The D2 receptor is linked with clinical efficacy.*

identification of two dopamine receptors, the D1 and D2 receptors (Kebabian & Calne, 1979). The D1 receptor was linked with adenylate cyclase, whereas the D2 receptor was not linked to adenylate cyclase nor could it inhibit adenylate cyclase. Through a process of elimination, the D2 receptor was regarded as the mechanism underlying antipsychotic activity (Figure 21.3). With the identification of D1 and D2 receptors (now referred to as D1 and D2 receptor families, including the D3, D4 and D5 receptors), a new avenue of research opened up.

Radiolabelled D2 binding was associated with clinical efficacy and blockade of DA agonist-induced behaviours (Seeman & Lee, 1975; Seeman et al., 1975, 1976). This was specific to DA receptors and not histamine, adrenaline or serotonin receptors (Peroutka & Synder, 1980b). If the D2 receptor is the location of therapeutic efficacy, then it is reasonable to investigate the D2 receptor in schizophrenia. Owen et al. (1978) found an increase in D2 receptor binding using [^{3}H]-**spiperone** (like haloperidol) in the schizophrenic brain (Figure 21.4). There was no evidence of alterations in D1 binding in schizophrenia (Cross et al., 1981). The increase in DA receptors was associated with positive symptoms and not negative symptoms (Owen et al., 1983). However, the increase in D2 receptors in the schizophrenic brain may be an artefact of antipsychotic medication rather than the disease itself, as only those who had being on the long-term medication showed such increases (Mackay et al., 1980). Animal studies have shown that chronic administration of antipsychotics increases the number of D2 receptors in the rat brain, due to a compensatory reaction to the decrease of dopaminergic activity (Rupniak et al., 1983). Changes in the sensitivity of DA receptors

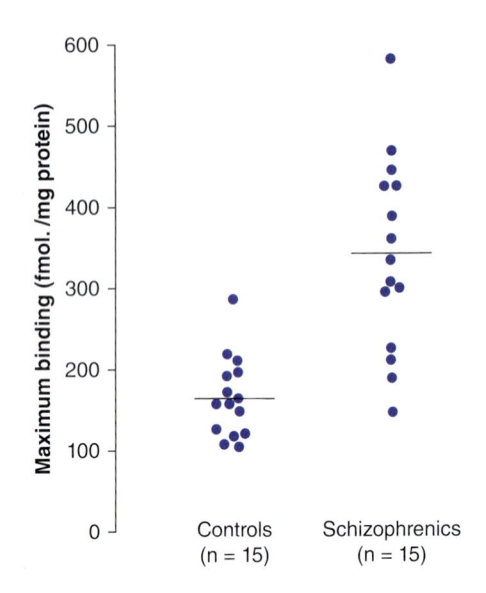

FIGURE 21.4 The number of dopamine D2 receptors in schizophrenia. Schizophrenic patients had more dopamine D2 receptors in the brain.
Source: Owen, F., Cross, A. J., Crow, T. J., Longden, A., Poulter, M., & Riley, G. J. (1978). Increased dopamine-receptor sensitivity in schizophrenia. *Lancet, 312*(8083), 223–226.

have been argued to be one of the core problems in schizophrenia.

In the account of schizophrenia provided by Philip Seeman (2013), DA D2 receptors were said to exist in two states: D2low and D2high, referring to low and high sensitivity. In schizophrenia, the D2 receptors move from low sensitivity to high sensitivity (an effect also seen with amphetamine). Seeman suggests that haloperidol works by reducing the number of D2high receptors.

Despite the clinical efficacy of antipsychotics, side-effects can sometimes be prohibitive. The main side-effect of antipsychotic medication is impaired movement. Antipsychotics produce **extrapyramidal side-effects** (EPSE) and symptoms similar to Parkinson's disease, e.g. **akathisia** (motor restlessness), **dystonia** (abnormal movements of the facial musculature) and **tardive dyskinesia** (TD, orofacial dystonia). The reason for these side-effects is the blockade of DA receptors in the nigrostriatal pathway which is similar to the effects of degeneration in Parkinson's disease.

These debilitating side-effects were once considered to be essential if the antipsychotic medication was going to work (Bishop et al., 1965). Fortunately, such dogmatic perspectives were not adhered to and new improved drugs were later developed. Of all the side-effects, TD affected 20–40% of patients and appeared from two months to some years after the start of medication (Khot et al., 1992). Alarmingly, TD is not readily reversible upon withdrawal. More rare than TD is neuroleptic malignant syndrome which is lethal and due to the rapid blockade of DA receptors interfering with homeostatic mechanisms and the hypothalamus (Henderson & Wooten, 1981). However, side-effects are also informative and provide more impetus to the DA hypothesis of schizophrenia, because the side-effects are a result of DA blockade in regions of the brain that are not the target for clinical efficacy.

Typical and Atypical Antipsychotics

The generation of new agents to treat schizophrenia was not only looking to improve symptom management, but also to reduce potential side-effects. To this end, antipsychotics can be designated as either:

- *typical* – high incidence of side-effects (e.g. haloperidol); or
- *atypical* – reduced risk of side-effects (e.g. clozapine).

What makes an antipsychotic atypical? Kinon and Lieberman (1996) suggest three criteria that define an atypical antipsychotic:

- decrease or absence of acute EPSE and TD;
- increased efficacy of positive, negative or cognitive symptoms; and
- decrease/absence of ability to elevate prolactin (this is pure biochemistry).

Thus, the atypical antipsychotic has a broader treatment efficacy and reduced side-effect profile. There are numerous atypical antipsychotics available, e.g. **clozapine**. Following how the atypical and typical drugs work has identified specific behaviours reflecting their clinical efficacy. In animal models, inhibition of locomotor activity is more reflective of antipsychotic activity (which is common to both atypical and typical), whereas blockade of stereotypy is more indicative of potential motor side-effects (and is characteristic of typical antipsychotics). Calderon et al. (1988) suggest that neuroleptic-induced catalepsy requires blockade of the postsynaptic DA receptor in the striatum. DA-induced stereotypy was reflective of increased striatal activity and locomotor hyperactivity in the nucleus accumbens (Woodruff, Kelly et al., 1976; Woodruff, Mccarthy et al., 1976). Thus, the mesolimbic DA system would appear to be the target for antipsychotic activity and the side-effects are due to blockade of the nigrostriatal pathway.

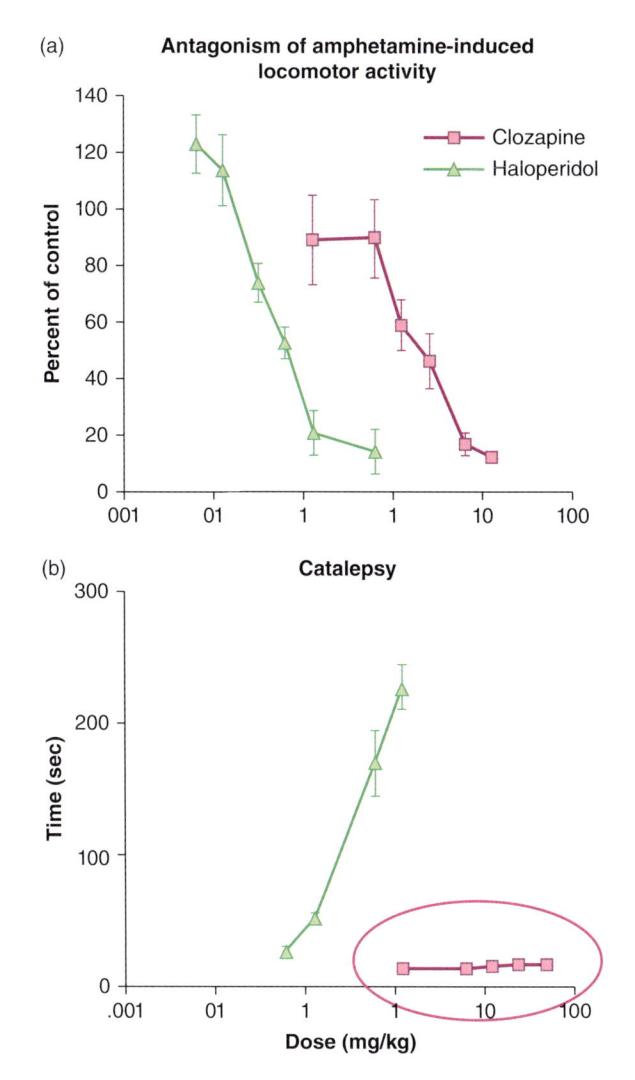

FIGURE 21.5 The effects of clozapine and haloperidol in the rat. (a) Both haloperidol and clozapine antagonize amphetamine-induced locomotor activity. (b) Only haloperidol induces catalepsy.
Source: Hoffman, D. C., & Donovan, H. (1995). Catalepsy as a rodent model for detecting antipsychotic drugs with extrapyramidal side effect liability. *Psychopharmacology (Berlin), 120*(2), 128–133. With kind permission from Springer Science and Business Media.

Clozapine has been an interesting drug to study as it has changed some of our understanding of the processes in schizophrenia and its treatment. Using *in vivo* microdialysis, dopamine was seen to increase in the nucleus accumbens with clozapine, whereas haloperidol increased dopamine in both the nucleus accumbens and the striatum (hence the increased side-effects) (Chen et al., 1991). In similar studies clozapine was found to increase dopamine in the prefrontal cortex (PFC), therefore pointing to a new region of interest (Moghaddam & Bunney, 1990). Interestingly, lesions of the DA terminals of the medial prefrontal cortex enhanced activity of postsynaptic and presynaptic receptors downstream in striatal and limbic regions (Pycock et al., 1980). Thus, projections from the medial prefrontal cortex provide inhibitory control of striatum and limbic regions; when there is a lesion of the prefrontal cortex or reduced activity, as seen in schizophrenia, this releases subcortical regions from inhibitory control, thereby producing an increase in dopamine. These data suggest that schizophrenia is a disorder primarily of cortical aberrations that have a knock-on effect subcortically; treatment with antipsychotics is at the subcortical level and not at the primary site. Again, clozapine has been an interesting drug to follow as it provides support for a dysfunctional prefrontal cortex.

Because clozapine is useful in treating the negative symptoms of schizophrenia, which had previously been thought to be beyond the reach of pharmacotherapy, and has reduced propensity for side-effects (the potentially fatal agranulocytosis [blood poisoning] notwithstanding), it has provided new directions of research. The identification of the DA D4 receptor provided a new site for clozapine binding (Van Tol et al., 1991). Some authors have reported elevated D4 receptors in schizophrenia (Seeman et al., 1993), while others have not found such an elevation (Reynolds & Mason, 1994). The therapeutic potential of the D4 receptor has not proved to be a fruitful avenue to follow (Tarazi et al., 2004).

Interestingly, clozapine occupies fewer D2 receptors in comparison to other antipsychotic drugs (Nordstrom et al., 1995) and the clinical efficacy was associated with a reduced D2 occupancy (Pilowsky et al., 1992). A reduction in side-effects with clozapine can also be attributed to reduced activity in striatal regions in comparison to haloperidol (Kasper et al., 1998). A lack of DA D2-mediated clozapine effect was also supported by studies in rats in which there was no regulation of striatum or nucleus accumbens D2 receptors after prolonged treatment (Rupniak et al., 1984) whereas there was an increase in the DA D1 receptor (Jenner et al., 1985). The DA D1 receptor has increased clozapine

One of the attractions of clozapine is that it is devoid of cataleptic (Burki et al., 1975) and dystonic effects (Casey, 1996). Hoffman and Donovan (1995) noted that catalepsy in a rodent model of EPSE was able to distinguish between haloperidol and clozapine; both haloperidol and clozapine were able to block the amphetamine-induced locomotor behaviour but clozapine was devoid of cataleptic effects (Figure 21.5). Other atypical drugs were able to induce catalepsy but at doses that would never be required for clinical efficacy (Chakrabarti et al., 1980).

binding in positron emission tomography (PET) studies (Nordstrom et al., 1995). DA D1 receptors in the prefrontal cortex have also been associated with the cognitive deficits seen in schizophrenia (Goldman-Rakic et al., 2004). Clozapine has also guided the search for other neurotransmitters in this region, e.g. glutamate and serotonin. Serotonergic mechanisms have long been associated with schizophrenia but have not received the same attention as DA (Meltzer, 1999). Atypical antipsychotics have been shown to target serotonin receptors in the PFC, with an increased ratio of serotonin/DA receptor occupancy (Meltzer & Massey, 2011). The therapeutic efficacy of atypical antipsychotics has been argued to derive from enhanced D2 and D3 DA receptor binding affinity and increased binding affinity to serotonin 5-HT2C and 5-HT2A receptors (Richtand et al., 2008).

The action of atypical antipsychotics involves not only 5-HT receptors and DA but also the other transmitter associated with clozapine's action – glutamate. Cortical 5-HT2A receptors facilitate glutamatergic neurotransmission in the nucleus accumbens, and atypical antipsychotics blocking 5-HT2A receptors facilitate D2 blockade (Mocci et al., 2014).

Clozapine was seen to increase glutamate within the nucleus accumbens whereas haloperidol did not have such an effect (Yamamoto & Cooperman, 1994). Phencyclidine (PCP or angel dust) is an antagonist of the glutamatergic **N-methyl-D-aspartate** (**NMDA**) **receptor**. Allen and Young (1978) reported a syndrome of phencyclidine-induced psychosis in nine patients. Ketamine, which has a similar pharmacology to phencyclidine, also induced psychosis in normal volunteers and increased psychotic episodes in schizophrenic volunteers (Lahti et al., 2001). Clozapine was able to block the hyperactivity induced by a drug similar to PCP called MK 801 which is in keeping with other atypical antipsychotics (Hoffman, 1992). Clozapine also regulates the PCP binding site on the NMDA receptor (Lang et al., 1992). The identification of glutamate as a potential focus in schizophrenia has given rise to a greater understanding of dopamine systems in general.

NEUROBIOLOGICAL THEORIES

The DA hypothesis of schizophrenia has evolved over time, beginning with a simple elevation of DA in schizophrenia. Embracing the notion of elevated DA activity, Davis et al. (1991) provided a more detailed account involving hypodopaminergic activity in the PFC. Reduced activity in the PFC fits with the neuroimaging data and neuropsychological profile of schizophrenia. The neuropsychological hypothesis of hypofrontality in schizophrenia may account for many of the symptoms because of the diverse connections of the frontal cortex.

Grace's account focuses on the autoreceptors which are presynaptic and regulate the presence of DA in the synapse. According to Grace, three types of dopaminergic autoreceptors are involved: (1) firing rate inhibiting autoreceptors (stop the action potentials and the signal), (2) synthesis inhibiting autoreceptors (stop the DA being made), and (3) release inhibiting autoreceptors (stop the DA being released). All have the net effect of reducing dopaminergic transmission using negative feedback loops when activated. Furthermore, Grace describes two types of DA release: tonic and phasic. Tonic DA release is the low constant background level of DA in the synapse, which is modulated by glutamatergic projections from the cortex. In contrast, phasic release consists of a large and transient discharge of DA from the synapse as the result of an action potential (Grace & Bunney, 1984). According to Grace (1991), in schizophrenia, there is a decrease in tonic dopamine in which homeostatic processes eventually regulate dopamine activity (a similar effect is seen with lesions of the medial prefrontal cortex) (Figure 21.6). Phasic dopaminergic responses to stimulation would produce larger than normal peaks due to the homeostatic mechanisms put in place due to the decrease in tonic dopamine. The negative symptoms of schizophrenia are associated with the decrease of tonic dopamine whereas the positive symptoms are thought to be reflective of the overactivity of dopamine at the receptor in response to stimuli.

Antipsychotics work by blocking the dopamine receptors and therefore operate predominantly on the positive symptoms. Via mechanisms mediated by dopamine D1 receptors and glutamate, clozapine may elevate tonic dopamine, thereby improving negative symptoms (Figure 21.7).

Within this theoretical context of glutamate and dopamine interactions in which NMDA antagonists exacerbate symptoms, the logical step is to treat schizophrenia with NMDA agonists (Kantrowitz & Javitt, 2012). Initial studies have indicated a positive potential of NMDA agonists in the treatment of schizophrenia, but full clinical trials are yet to demonstrate full efficacy (Javitt, 2010).

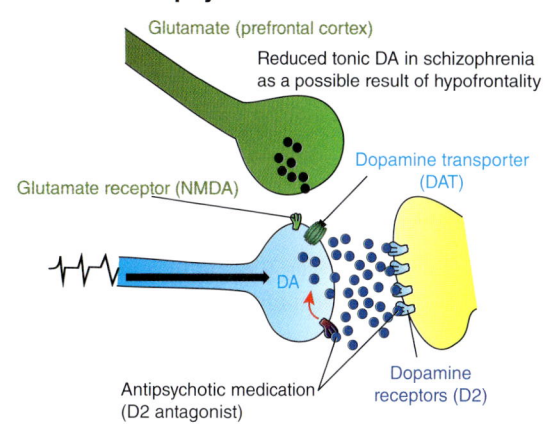

FIGURE 21.6 Grace's theory of tonic and phasic DA in schizophrenia. (a) Tonic DA is released in the background (basal DA) and is under the control of glutamatergic projection from the prefrontal cortex. (b) Phasic DA is released in response to stimuli. (c) Phasic and tonic DA signals in schizophrenia. A loss of glutamatergic influence on subcortical DA results in homeostatic changes that amplify phasic DA responses. (d) Antipsychotics block the effect of DA at the D2 receptor. DA, dopamine; GLU, glutamate; NMDA, N-methyl-D-aspartate.
Source: Grace, A. A. (1991). Phasic versus tonic dopamine release and the modulation of dopamine system responsivity: A hypothesis for the etiology of schizophrenia. *Neuroscience*, 41(1), 1–24.

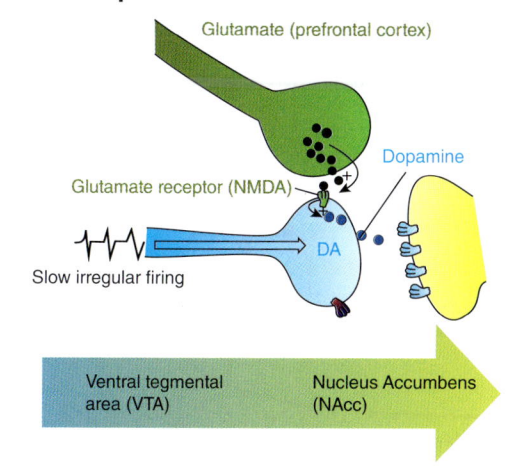

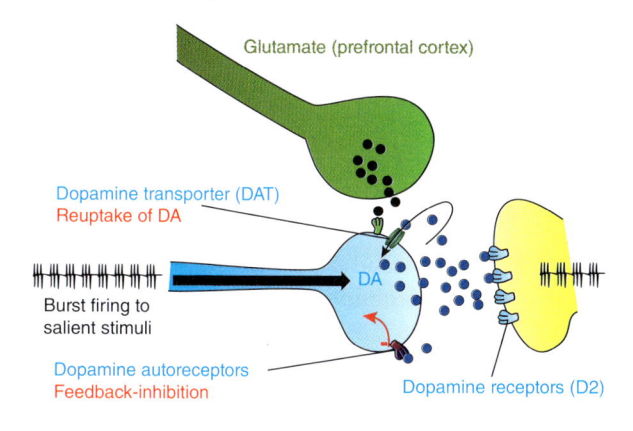

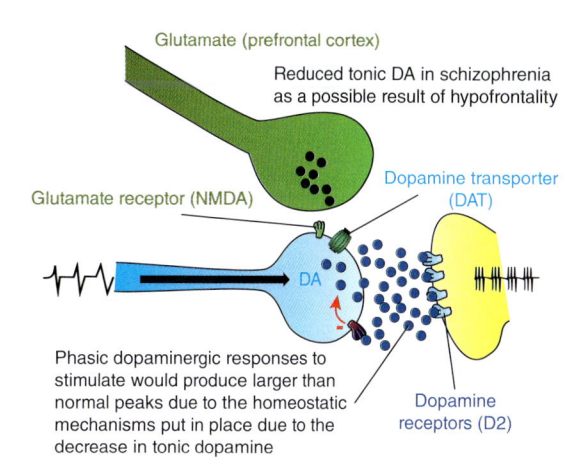

NEUROPSYCHOLOGICAL THEORIES

Rubin et al. (1995) found deficits on a number of neuropsychological tasks which were correlated with measures on computed tomography (CT) scans, e.g. decreased brain volume and increased ventricular volume. In a barrage of neuropsychology tasks, Morrison-Stewart et al. (1992) found neuropsychological deficits in schizophrenia, particularly relating to neuropsychological tasks that were sensitive to frontal lobe activity. Furthermore, deficits seen on frontal lobe tasks correlated with the positive symptoms of schizophrenia (Zakzanis, 1998). Reduced activation of the left frontal cortex was recorded in schizophrenics whilst performing the Tower of London task (Andreasen et al., 1992). Using the same task, Morris et al. (1995) found that schizophrenics required more moves, took longer and that the overall slowness might be related to the negative symptoms of schizophrenia. Using a more ecologically valid version of the Tower of London indicated that there was inefficient planning in both tasks but the poor performance was only evident in the Tower of London, and not evidence in the real-life analogue task after IQ was taken into account (Greenwood et al., 2011). Such studies are important as they reveal that the artificial nature of the

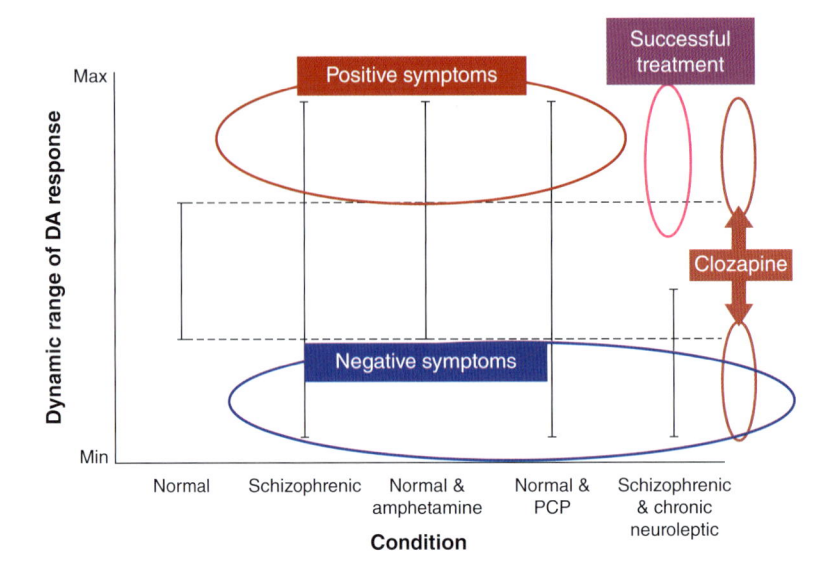

FIGURE 21.7 *The range of dopaminergic response. Fluctuating levels of DA are linked to different components of schizophrenia and its treatment. DA, dopamine; PCP, phencyclidine.*
Source: Grace, A. A. (1991). Phasic versus tonic dopamine release and the modulation of dopamine system responsivity: A hypothesis for the etiology of schizophrenia. *Neuroscience, 41*(1), 1–24.

neuropsychological test can yield different results from those that have a more real-life feel.

The plethora of data indicating reduced neuropsychological functioning with neural correlates of frontal lobe dysfunction can be placed into the theoretical perspective of hypofunctioning leading to increased dopamine activity in subcortical regions.

Given that ASD has a long association with the faulty development of a Theory of Mind (ToM), and that it has been considered by some to be an early-onset version of schizophrenia (see Crespi et al., 2010), can the same be said about schizophrenia?

Frith (1992) provides a theoretical account of schizophrenia based on frontal disconnections with posterior regions of the brain and the disruption of ToM. He argues that schizophrenics assume that their understanding of a situation is shared by everyone else, and have an inadequate ToM. In a task involving descriptions of photographs of people, schizophrenics were more likely to describe physical dimensions rather than the emotional state, with failure to attend to the mental states of others associated with the negative symptoms of schizophrenia (Allen, 1984; Pilowsky & Bassett, 1980). The incoherence of speech in schizophrenia has been demonstrated by Cohen (1978), who noted that everyone was able to understand control participants' description of a stimulus whereas no one was able to understand the descriptions generated by schizophrenic patients.

Hallucinations and **delusions** have been argued to arise through a decoupling of propositions and their content (Leslie, 1987). A belief is different from the truth about something, e.g. a belief is not a statement of fact. Frith argues that in schizophrenics there is confusion between beliefs and reality. Divorced or free-floating representations may therefore give rise to third-party hallucinations. In a variant of Frith's example, 'Diane thinks that *Chris drinks too much*', decoupling the proposition 'Diane thinks' from the content leads to the statement '*Chris drinks too much*' coming from outside the mind, i.e. it is either a fact or a demand, not a belief or opinion. Similarly, different propositions may lead to different experiences (Table 21.1). Frith continues to suggest that central monitoring defects are evident in schizophrenia. A distinction between internally and externally generated actions is maintained by a central monitoring system. The system monitors three aspects of action: (1) the action appropriate to current external stimulation, (2) the action appropriate to current goals (e.g. will), and (3) the action which was actually selected (Frith, 1987). Thus, central monitoring requires intentions to be known before a response is made. In schizophrenia, central monitoring can only be obtained from peripheral feedback, e.g. we know what we are going to say before we say it. According to Frith, developmental study suggests that there are three stages in which we become (1) aware of our goals, (2) aware of our attentions and other mental states, and (3) aware of other

TABLE 21.1 Abnormalities of awareness at various levels and some associated signs and symptoms

Loss of awareness of...	Positive features	Negative features
Own goals	Grandiose ability	Depersonalization Lack of will
Own intentions	Delusions of control Thought insertion	Poverty of thought Loss of affect
Others' intentions	Delusions of persecution Third-person hallucinations	Derealization Social withdrawal

Source: Based on Frith, C. (1992). *The cognitive neuropsychology of schizophrenia.* Hove, UK: LEA.

people's mental states. The effects of a breakdown in the system can be seen in Table 21.2.

LIMITATIONS OF MANY STUDIES IN SCHIZOPHRENIA

Studying schizophrenia is a hard task. Research and treatment may be in conflict as there are medication effects that can influence results. Most cases of schizophrenia have received medication, and anticholinergic activity may have an impact upon cognitive functioning. The symptoms themselves may influence the results of neuropsychological tests rather than being a primary deficit in schizophrenia (e.g. a failure in a memory task may be due to hallucinations). Due to the severity of schizophrenia, some patients may experience long-term hospitalization and institutionalization. However, in terms of cognitive assessment, the decline over time was no different from those who were not hospitalized (Goldstein et al., 1991). The tragedy is that the nature of schizophrenia also provides a source of 'noise' in understanding the neuropathological genetic basis of the disorder. The question remains: is it one disease, or is it many similar diseases.

Some even argue that schizophrenia is a social construct manufactured by psychiatry. For example, Thomas Szasz (1973) claims: 'If you talk to God, you are praying; if God talks to you, you have schizophrenia. If you talk to the dead, you are a spiritualist; if the dead talk to you, you are a schizophrenic'.

SUMMARY

Schizophrenia is the archetypal psychiatric illness. Even with the enormous amount of research undertaken, there is little in the way of established facts about the cause of schizophrenia. The most parsimonious accounts of schizophrenia involve reduced cortical activity in the frontal lobe which has a downstream effect on increasing dopamine in subcortical regions. Also impinging upon this are genetic and environmental factors (Figure 21.8). The treatments for schizophrenia have been instrumental in shaping our understanding of the biochemical abnormalities underlying symptoms. However, it should be noted that the drugs do not address the root cause of schizophrenia, but rather manage the symptoms. Causality, as with all other aspects of psychiatry, is not clear-cut in schizophrenia. Multiple aetiologies and interacting elements may be responsible.

TABLE 21.2 The abnormal experiences that occur when the content of a proposition becomes 'detached'

Normal proposition	Detached content	Abnormal experience
I know that 'my car is faulty'	My car is faulty	Thought insertion
I intend to 'make a cup of tea'	Make a cup of tea	Delusion of control
Diane thinks 'Chris drinks too much'	Chris drinks too much	Third-person hallucination

Source: Based on Frith, C. (1992). *The cognitive neuropsychology of schizophrenia.* Hove, UK: LEA.

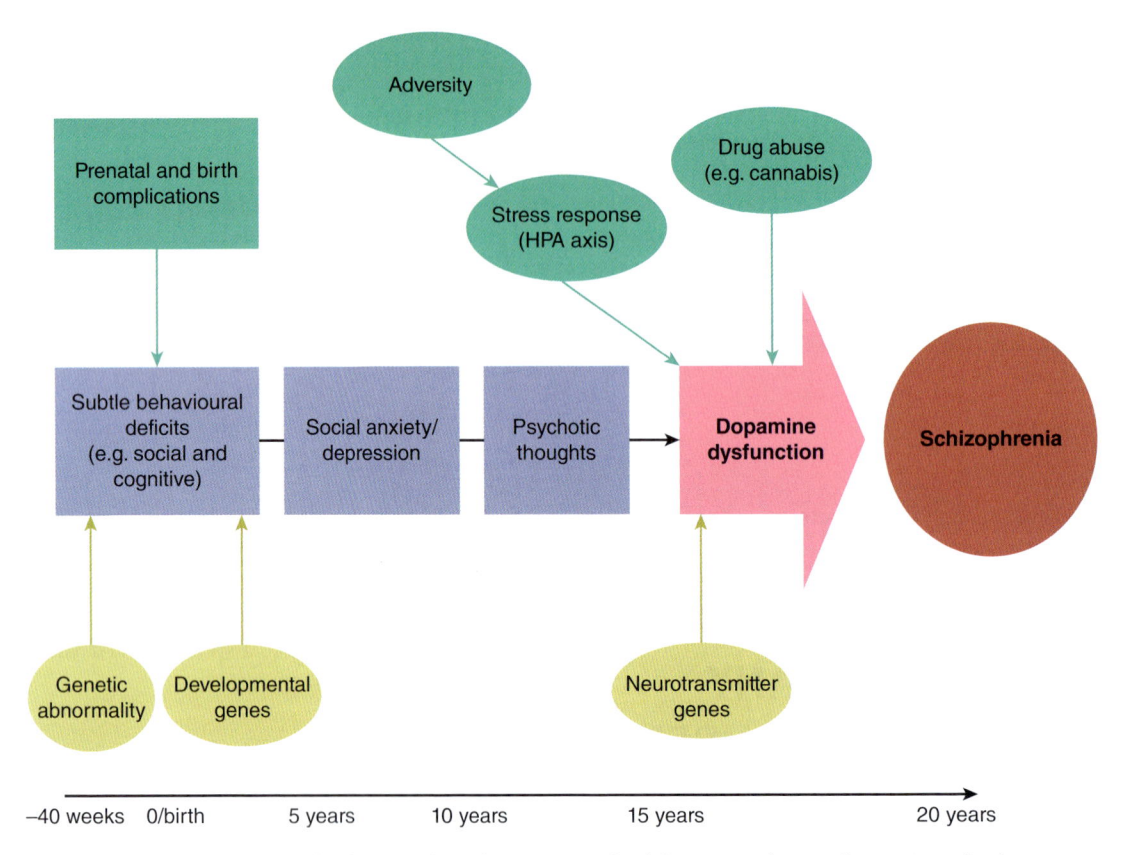

FIGURE 21.8 *The contributory pathways leading to schizophrenia. Several risk factors combine with genetics to lead to schizophrenia. HPA, hypothalamic-pituitary-adrenal.*
Source: Adapted from Stilo, S. A., & Murray, R. M. (2010). The epidemiology of schizophrenia: Replacing dogma with knowledge. *Dialogues in Clinical Neuroscience, 12*(3), 305–315 by permission of Servier International.

LEARNING OUTCOME QUESTIONS

You should be able to answer the following questions.

- What evidence contributed to the initial development of the dopamine hypothesis of schizophrenia?
- How can glutamate and serotonin contribute to the understanding of schizophrenia?
- Hypofrontality in schizophrenia leads to faulty Theory of Mind. Discuss.
- What makes an atypical antipsychotic atypical?

FURTHER READING

Brüne, M. (2005). 'Theory of mind' in schizophrenia: a review of the literature. *Schizophrenia Bulletin, 31*(1), 21–42.

Kendler, K. S., & Schaffner, K. F. (2011). The dopamine hypothesis of schizophrenia: An historical and philosophical analysis. *Philosophy, Psychiatry, & Psychology, 18*(1), 41–63.

Laruelle, M. (2014). Schizophrenia: From dopaminergic to glutamatergic interventions. *Current Opinion in Pharmacology, 14*, 97–102.

Moghaddam, B., & Javitt, D. (2011). From revolution to evolution: The glutamate hypothesis of schizophrenia and its implication for treatment. *Neuropsychopharmacology, 37*(1), 4–15.

Pickup, G. J., & Frith, C. D. (2001). Theory of mind impairments in schizophrenia: Symptomatology, severity and specificity. *Psychological Medicine, 31*(2), 207–220.

MIND MAP

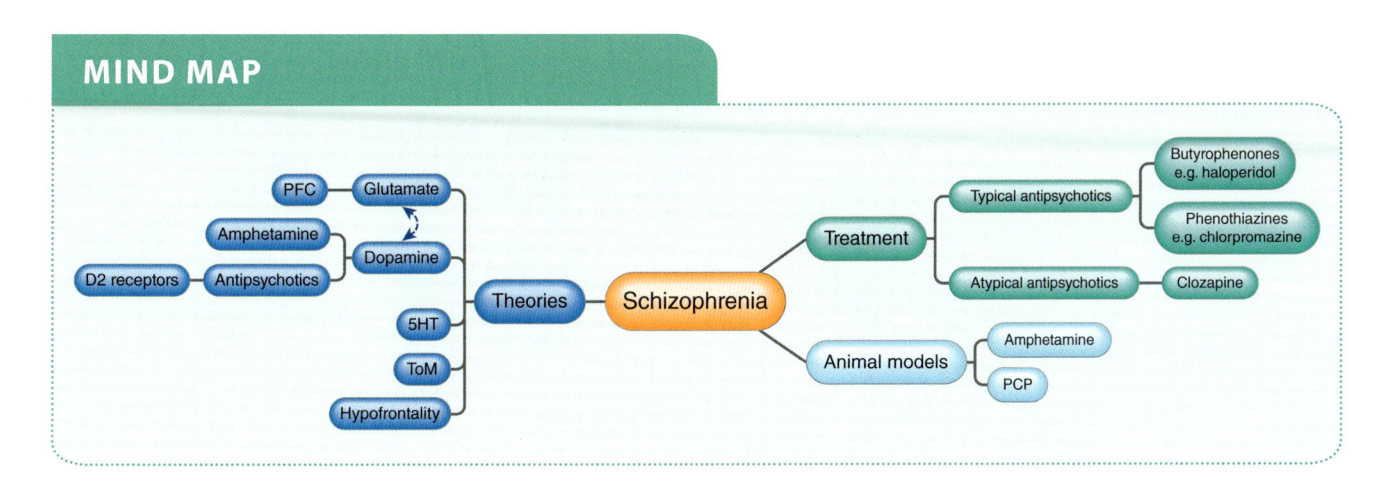

Schizophrenia

- Theories
  - Glutamate — PFC
  - Dopamine
    - Amphetamine
    - Antipsychotics — D2 receptors
  - 5HT
  - ToM
  - Hypofrontality
- Treatment
  - Typical antipsychotics
    - Butyrophenones e.g. haloperidol
    - Phenothiazines e.g. chlorpromazine
  - Atypical antipsychotics
    - Clozapine
- Animal models
  - Amphetamine
  - PCP

22 Affective Disorders

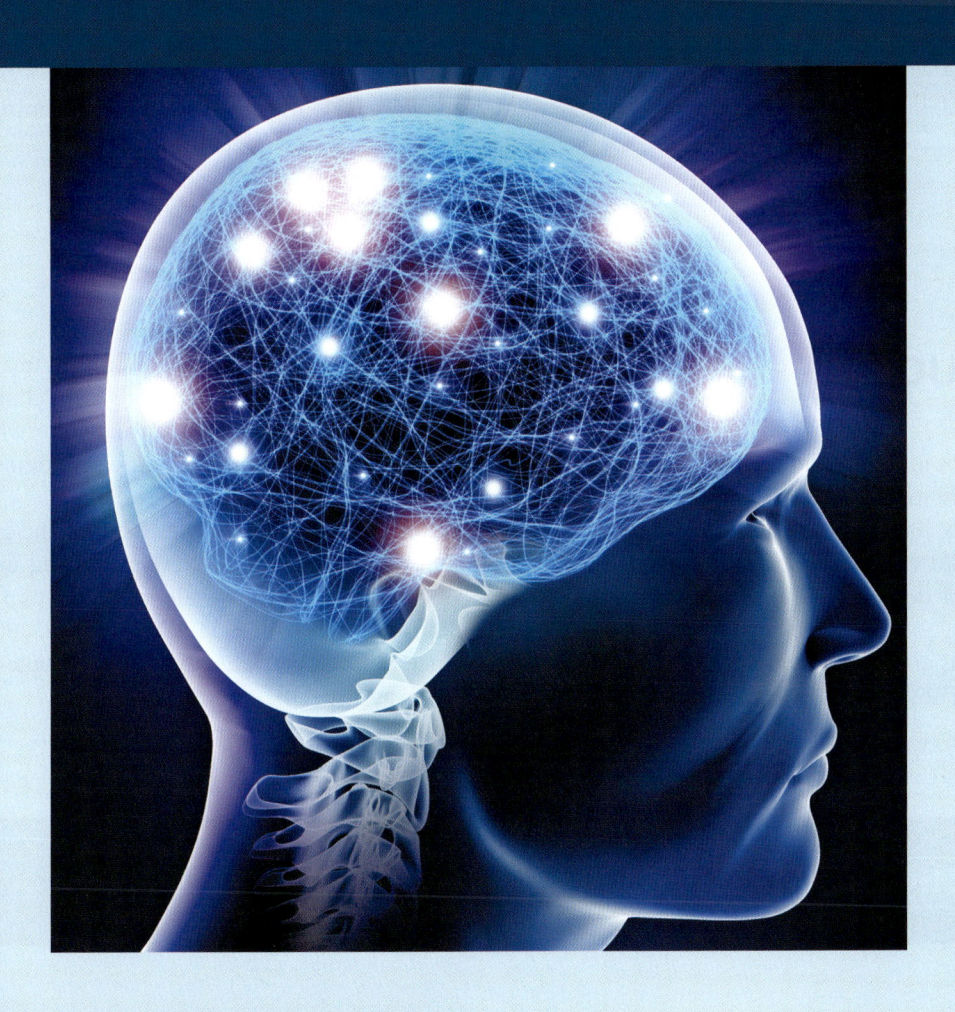

ANATOMY OF THE CHAPTER

This chapter will highlight the following.

- The genetic basis of depression.
- The neurochemistry of depression.
- The neuropsychological and neuropathological aspects of depression.
- The evolutionary psychology of depression.

INTRODUCTION 542

GENETICS OF DEPRESSION 545

NEUROCHEMISTRY OF DEPRESSION 548

TREATMENTS FOR DEPRESSION 552

NEUROANATOMY OF DEPRESSION 553

IS THERE A COMMON DENOMINATOR IN ALL THE TREATMENTS FOR DEPRESSION? 554

SUMMARY 556

LEARNING OUTCOMES

1. To understand the development of hypotheses regarding the neuropsychopharmacological basis of depression.
2. To be aware of the limitations when studying depression.
3. To be able to provide a neuropsychological explanation of depression.

INTRODUCTION

Depression is not merely feeling a little bit sad for a long time. It is a debilitating disorder that functionally impairs individuals who have it, but also affects family and friends. The DSM criteria in Box 22.1 do not do justice to the feelings of despair and hopelessness that pervade depression.

Depression as a clinical term is far removed from its colloquial use. Those of us who say we are feeling a little bit depressed today are not depressed but may be suffering from a lowering of mood. Real clinical depression is almost incomprehensible to anyone who has not suffered from it. Of all the psychopathologies listed in DSM 5, depression is the most prevalent.

In a sample of 6694 members of the general population of California and New York aged between 18 and 96, the one-month prevalence rate was 5.2% for **major depressive disorder** (MDD) (Ohayon, 2007). The prevalence rate refers to the number of people having the disorder at a specific point in time or over a specified time

BOX 22.1: DSM IV TR AND DSM 5 MAJOR DEPRESSIVE DISORDER

DSM IV TR

A. At least five of the following symptoms have been present during the same 2-week period and represent a change from previous functioning: at least one of the symptoms is either (1) depressed mood or (2) loss of interest or pleasure.

1. Depressed mood most of the day, nearly every day, as indicated either by subjective report (e.g. feels sad or empty) or observation made by others (e.g. appears tearful).
2. Markedly diminished interest or pleasure in all, or almost all, activities most of the day, nearly every day (as indicated either by subjective account or observation made by others).
3. Significant weight loss when not dieting or weight gain (e.g. a change of more than 5% of body weight in a month), or decrease or increase in appetite nearly every day.
4. Insomnia or hypersomnia nearly every day.
5. Psychomotor agitation or retardation nearly every day (observable by others, not merely subjective feelings of restlessness or being slowed down).
6. Fatigue or loss of energy nearly every day.
7. Feelings of worthlessness or excessive or inappropriate guilt (which may be delusional) nearly every day (not merely self-reproach or guilt about being sick).
8. Diminished ability to think or concentrate, or indecisiveness, nearly every day (either by subjective account or as observed by others).
9. Recurrent thoughts of death (not just fear of dying), recurrent suicidal ideation without a specific plan, or a suicide attempt or specific plan for committing suicide.

> B. The symptoms do not meet criteria for a mixed episode.
> C. The symptoms cause clinically significant distress or impairment in social, occupational, or other important areas of functioning.
> D. The symptoms are not due to the direct physiological effects of a substance (e.g. a drug of abuse, a medication) or a general medical condition (e.g. hypothyroidism).
> E. The symptoms are not better accounted for by bereavement, i.e. after the loss of a loved one, the symptoms persist for longer than 2 months or are characterized by marked functional impairment, morbid preoccupation with worthlessness, suicidal ideation, psychotic symptoms, or psychomotor retardation.
>
> **Major Depressive Disorder, Single Episode**
>
> A. Presence of a single Major Depressive Episode.
> B. The Major Depressive Episode is not better accounted for by Schizoaffective Disorder and is not superimposed on Schizophrenia, Schizophreniform Disorder, Delusional Disorder, or Psychotic Disorder Not Otherwise Specified.
> C. There has never been a Manic Episode, a Mixed Episode, or a Hypomanic Episode.
>
> **Note:** This exclusion does not apply if all of the manic-like, mixed-like, or hypomanic-like episodes are substance or treatment induced or are due to the direct physiological effects of a general medical condition.
>
> **Major Depressive Disorder, Recurrent**
>
> A. Presence of two or more Major Depressive Episodes.
>
> **Note:** To be considered separate episodes, there must be an interval of at least 2 consecutive months in which criteria are not met for a Major Depressive Episode.
>
> B. The Major Depressive Episodes are not better accounted for by Schizoaffective Disorder and are not superimposed on Schizophrenia, Schizophreniform Disorder, Delusional Disorder, or Psychotic Disorder Not Otherwise Specified.
> C. There has never been a Manic Episode, a Mixed Episode, or a Hypomanic Episode.
>
> **Note:** This exclusion does not apply if all of the manic-like, mixed-like, or hypomanic-like episodes are substance or treatment induced or are due to the direct physiological effects of a general medical condition.
>
> **DSM 5**
>
> Little has changed in the DSM 5 criteria for major depressive disorder. However, there are new disorders, e.g. disruptive mood dysregulation disorder and premenstrual dysphoric disorder.
>
> Under DSM 5 category depressive disorders, in addition to the above are:
>
> - Persistent Depressive Disorder (Dysthymia);
> - Substance/Medication-Induced Depressive Disorder;
> - Depressive Disorder Due To Another Medical Condition;
> - Other Specified Depressive Disorders, e.g. recurrent brief depression, short duration depressive episodes (4 to 13 days) and depressive episodes with insufficient symptoms.

period. In American adults, the 12-month prevalence rate of an MDD episode was 8.3%, and the lifetime prevalence rate was 19.2% (Kessler et al., 2010). One in five people is a lot of people. Nearly 4 million people in the UK have mood disorders including MDD and in Europe it is over 33 million (Gustavsson et al., 2011).

The time course of the disease suggests that 54% of patients will probably recover from MDD within six months and 81% within two years (Keller et al., 1992). For those lucky enough to recover, relapse is highly likely – 58% relapse over the following 10 years (Fichter et al., 2008).

The diagnostic criteria are shown in Box 22.1. Evaluating whether somebody has MDD or other variants of depressive disorders requires assessment of whether they have unipolar or bipolar depression (Box 22.2). Unipolar depression is a purely depressive disorder whereas bipolar patients have depression alternating with periods of mania (once called manic depression). Depressed patients may not initially present with manic or hypomanic symptoms but during follow-up it may become evident that there is bipolar disorder. Other elements of differentiation between subtypes of depression include endogenous versus reactive (exogenous). Endogenous depression arises for no apparent reason whereas reactive can be seen as a consequence of a stressful life events. Endogenous depression tends to respond well to pharmacotherapy with perhaps an underlying neurochemical imbalance as the critical neuropathology. Reactive depressions may respond better to psychological interventions, e.g. cognitive behavioural therapy (CBT).

BOX 22.2: DSM IV TR AND DSM 5 BIPOLAR DISORDER

In DSM 5 bipolar related disorders are removed from depressive disorders as was previously the case in DSM IV and occupy the pages between schizophrenia spectrum and other psychotic disorders and depressive disorders. What might seem an arbitrary placement within DSM 5 is actually a deliberate act in recognition of the fact that bipolar disorders span schizophrenia and depression.

Bipolar I disorder is the classic manic depression. In bipolar II disorder, depression is the most prevalent symptom, and has been considered a milder form of bipolar I.

For a diagnosis of bipolar I disorder, it is necessary to meet the following criteria for a manic episode. The manic episode may have been preceded by and may be followed by hypomanic or major depressive episodes.

Manic episode

A. A distinct period of abnormality and persistently elevated, expansive, or irritable mood and abnormally and persistently increased goal-directed activity or energy, lasting at least one week and present most of the day, nearly every day (or any duration if hospitalisation is necessary).

B. During the period of mood disturbance and increased energy or activity, three (or more) of the following symptoms (for if the mood is only irritable) are persistent to a significant degree and represent a noticeable change from usual behaviour:

1. Inflated self-esteem or grandiosity.
2. Decreased need for sleep (e.g. feels rested after only 3 hours sleep).
3. More talkative than usual or pressure to keep talking.
4. Flight of ideas or subjective experience that thoughts are racing.
5. Distractibility (i.e. attention easily drawn to unimportant or irrelevant external stimuli), as reported or observed.
6. Increase in goal directed activity (either socially, at work or school, or sexually) or psychomotor agitation (i.e. purposeless non-goal-directed activity).
7. Excessive involvement in activities that have a high potential for painful consequences (e.g. engaging in unrestrained buying sprees, sexual indiscretions, or foolish business investments).

C. The mood disturbance is sufficiently severe to cause marked impairment in social or occupational function or to necessitate hospitalization to prevent harm to self or others, or there are psychotic features.

D. The episode is not attributable to the physiological effects of a substance (e.g. a drug of abuse, and medication, other treatment) or to another medical condition.

Note: a full manic episode that emerges during antidepressant treatment (e.g. medication, electroconvulsive therapy) but persists at a fully syndromal level beyond the physiological effect of that treatment is sufficient evidence for a manic episode and, therefore, a bipolar I disorder.

Note: criteria A–D constitute a manic episode. At least one lifetime manic episode is required for the diagnosis of bipolar I disorder.

Hypomanic episode

A. A distinct period of abnormally and persistently elevated, expansive or irritable mood and abnormally and persistently increased activity or energy, lasting at least 4 consecutive days and present most of the day, nearly every day.

B. During the period of mood disturbance and increased energy and activity, 3 (or more) of the following symptoms (four if the mood is only irritable) have persistently represented a noticeable change from usual behaviour, and have been present to a significant degree: items 1 to 7 as above.

C. The episode is associated with an unequivocal change in functioning that is uncharacteristic of the individual when not symptomatic.

D. The disturbance in mood and the change in functioning are observable by others.

E. The episode is not severe enough to cause marked impairment in social or occupational functioning or to necessitate hospitalization. If there are psychotic features, the episode is, by definition, manic.

F. The episode is not attributable to the physiological effects of the substance (e.g. a drug of abuse, and medication, other treatments).

Note: criteria A–F constitute a hypomanic episode.

Major depressive episode
See Box 22.1.

Note: criteria A–C constitute a major depressive episode.

BOX 22.3: STRESS AND DEPRESSION

Stress is an important feature precipitating and exacerbating numerous conditions, and depression is no exception. Stress is considered in more detail in Chapter 23, but activation of stress systems has been consistently demonstrated in depression (Pariante & Lightman, 2008). The activation of the hypothalamic-pituitary-adrenal (HPA) axis in depression has received considerable attention. In response to stress, noradrenaline, acetylcholine (ACh), serotonin and gamma-aminobutyric acid (GABA) are mobilized. The net effect is activation of cortisol (a stress hormone) (Gibbons, 1964). Furthermore, the secretion of cortisol, whilst elevated, follows an abnormal circadian pattern (Linkowski et al., 1985). Depressed patients also failed to respond to the dexamethasone suppression test in which a synthetic glucocorticoid would provide negative feedback, reducing cortisol secretion. This effect is generally absent in depression (Coppen et al., 1983).

The effects of stress are integrated in the stress diathesis model of depression (Monroe & Simons, 1991).

This model integrates environmental experiences, e.g. stressors such as abuse or neglect, with genetic predisposition (diathesis). Low serotonin levels conspire with increased reactivity of stress systems to produce MDD. Reducing stress would therefore be critical to enhancing any antidepressant therapy. It has already been noted that the stresses of the day can lead to increased alcohol consumption, and alcohol consumption may be a form of self-medication for depression. When alcoholism and depression co-exist, the chances are that the destructive behaviours associated with alcoholism are more salient than the causal factors of depression. However, when detoxified, expression of depressive symptoms may be more apparent.

Although stress is an important variable in the stress diathesis model of depression, other factors need to be considered, e.g. the context of stressors and personal resilience (Hammen, 2005). Being retrained to manage stressful situations and have increased resolve may be a very useful adjunct to antidepressant therapy.

What causes depression?

- Family history.
- Abuse.
- Trauma and stress (see Box 22.3).
- Death or other loss.
- Pessimistic personality.
- Major events.
- Physical conditions.
- Social isolation.
- Lack of exposure to sunlight.
- Hormones.
- Other psychological disorders.
- Substance abuse. Nearly 30% of people with substance abuse problems also have depression (Regier et al., 1990; Sullivan et al., 2005). In particular, alcohol is associated with depression, but the link is still ambiguous. Alcohol can be used as self-medication for depression, but also it can be a contributing factor in depression (Boden & Fergusson, 2011).

GENETICS OF DEPRESSION

Twin studies report a heritability estimate of 40–50% in depression (Kendler et al., 2006; Levinson, 2006). In one early study the concordance ratio for depression in monozygotic twins was 54% whereas in dizygotic twins it was 19% (Bertelsen, 1978; Bertelsen et al., 1977). A genetic component to depression is also evident in adoption studies (Mendlewicz & Rainer, 1977; Wender et al., 1986). In first-degree relatives of MDD patients, the risk of also having MDD is increased three-fold (Sullivan et al., 2000).

The prevalence of depression is higher in females (Blazer et al., 1994) with women being 1.7 times more likely to be diagnosed than males (Kessler et al., 1993). Thus, some of the genes contributing to depression may be sex specific, e.g. females have a small difference in serotonergic genes, resulting in changes in whole blood serotonin levels, which have been linked with depression (Weiss et al., 2005).

However, the pursuit of the genetic loci for MDD has been disappointing.

Despite convincing evidence for a genetic contribution to disease susceptibility, there has been a dearth of substantive molecular genetic findings. Nevertheless, there is an impressive quantity of relevant literature. Does it amount to anything? Yes, because negative findings impart important lessons. (Flint & Kendler, 2014, p.497)

The final sentence is important; one should always remember that any findings derived from methodologically rigorous experimentation are valuable regardless of the direction of effect. Flint and Kendler (2014) suggest that the heterogeneous nature of MDD means that there might be genetically differentiated subtypes of MDD and that 'the picture is consistent with a fairly undifferentiated phenotype emerging as the final common outcome of diverse processes, a process called equifinality* in the developmental literature. The list of possible pathways is large' (Flint & Kendler, 2014) (*a given phenotype can be reached by many potential means).

Despite the fact that an actual gene (or even a group of genes with moderate effect) has not been found, this has not curtailed speculation about the evolutionary psychology of depression (see Box 22.4).

BOX 22.4: THE EVOLUTIONARY PSYCHOLOGY OF DEPRESSION

As with many of the psychopathologies, it is hard to see any advantage or adaptive function that the symptoms of depression may confer. However, with a high prevalence rate of MDD and behavioural geneticists demonstrating a high likelihood of an inheritable factor, an evolutionary explanation is warranted. From the outset, one has to remember that:

> Evolutionary theories do not suggest that all depressions or anxieties are necessarily adaptive in all environments. In fact phenotypes can operate outside their adaptive range when they are: too easily triggered, too intense, frequent or long lasting. Understanding which depressions are adaptive in which contexts is complex, for much depends on the associated reproductive costs and benefits, and frequency dependent selection. (Gilbert, 2006, p.293).

Many of the evolutionary theories of MDD focus on low mood. Mood can be seen as a continuum (high to low) with MDD occupying the far end of the distribution. According to Nesse (2009), the adaptive nature of mood can be seen in progress towards valuable resources, in which fast progress elicits positive mood and slow progress low mood. When failing to obtain resources or a goal, the low mood that is generated is motivating, utilizing the conservation of energy and reappraisal of options (Klinger, 1975). Continued persistence in attempting to obtain an unachievable goal leads to a negative affect which can culminate in MDD.

Watt and Panksepp (2009) consider the adaptive function giving rise to depression as the failure to terminate separation distress. They argue that separation distress is an early mammalian emotional state that arises when infant mammals are separated from their carers. Long-term distress is damaging to the organism and therefore the normal reaction is time-limited. In those with vulnerabilities, genetic or otherwise, the shutdown mechanisms on separation distress continue beyond infancy and in depression may result in negative reactions to any stressor.

Andrews and Thomson (2009) put forward an analytic ruminations hypothesis in which MDD is the response to complex problems. From the anecdotal evidence suggesting that depressed people benefit from their ruminations which give them insight into their problems, Andrews and Thompson propose that depression is an evolutionary artefact of being able to direct attention and resources towards complex problem-solving tasks.

- Complex problems trigger depression.
- Depression co-ordinates changes in body systems that promote sustained attention and analysis.
- Depressive rumination helps people solve problems.
- Depression reduces cognitive performance in the laboratory due to the elimination taking up cognitive resources.

All of these claims can be placed within a complex framework permitting engagement in problem solving (Figure 22.4.1).

In order to understand the evolutionary psychology of MDD, the dividing line between normal and pathological has been considered. In terms of the response to

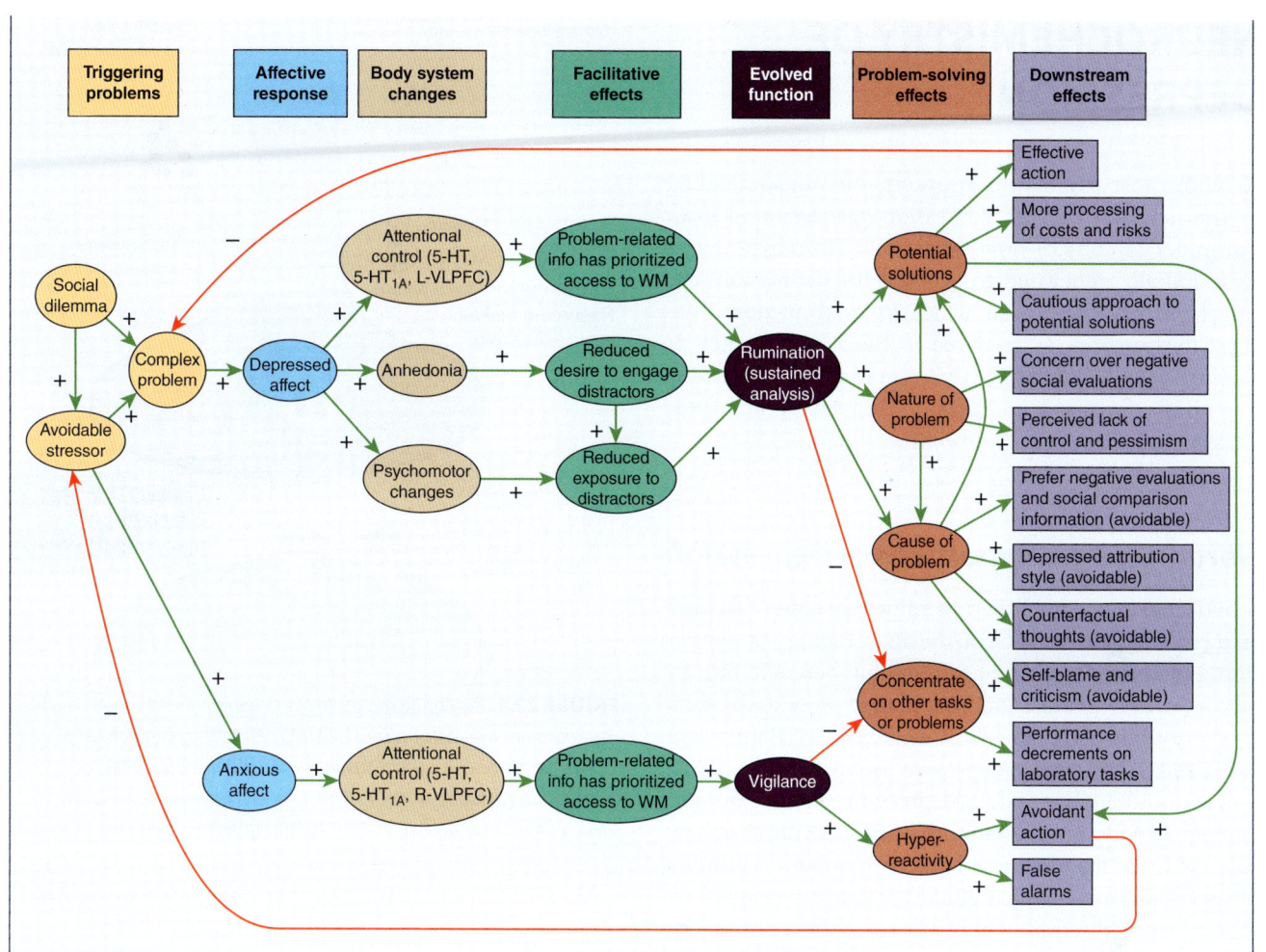

FIGURE 22.4.1 *The proposed causal relationships between the variables and constructs that are prominent in the analytical rumination hypothesis. Circles represent latent constructs, rectangles represent manifest behaviour/constructs, and arrows denote the hypothesized direction of causation. L-VLPFC, left ventrolateral prefrontal cortex; R-VLPFC; right ventrolateral prefrontal cortex; WM, working memory.*
Source: Andrews, P. W., & Thomson Jr, J. A. (2009). The bright side of being blue: Depression as an adaptation for analyzing complex problems. *Psychological Review, 116*(3), 620–654.

adversity, MDD might actually be a healthy response but when it becomes severe, its adaptive nature and rationality disappear (Hagen, 2011) (Figure 22.4.2).

Alternatively, MDD has communication advantages that convey cries for help (even suicide) (Hagen, 2011). Those that are in need of help under conditions of adversity may use their depressive symptoms (MDD, self-harm) in order to get help.

However, Hagen (2011), summing up a critique of evolutionary theories of depression, states that:

> The primary weakness of these hypotheses is that although remission of MDD is associated with important life improvements, there is as yet no evidence that depressive symptoms themselves bring about life improvements, as these hypotheses require. (p.722)

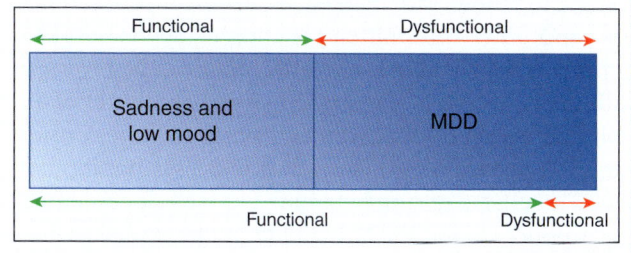

FIGURE 22.4.2 *All evolutionary theorists agree that sadness and low mood are probably adaptations. Most see major depressive disorder (MDD) as a dysfunction of sadness and low mood (top). Some, however, argue that much MDD is also functional (bottom). Because all mechanisms can dysfunction, all agree, though, that at least some MDD is dysfunctional.*
Source: Hagen, E. H. (2011). Evolutionary theories of depression: A critical review. *Canadian Journal of Psychiatry, 56*(12), 716–726. Reproduced by permission of the Canadian Psychiatric Association.

NEUROCHEMISTRY OF DEPRESSION

As with most psychiatric disorders, our understanding of the neurobiology of depression has stemmed from our understanding of how drugs work. Two hypotheses were initially generated to account for depression: the catecholamine hypothesis which focused on noradrenergic dysfunction, as favoured in the USA (Bunney & Davis, 1965; Schildkraut, 1965), and the indoleamine hypothesis favoured in Europe (Coppen et al., 1963; Glassman, 1969; Lapin & Oxenkrug, 1969).

Noradrenergic Hypothesis of Depression

Schildkraut (1965) published an influential paper that initiated considerable research on the neurobiology of depression. However, the ideas of Schildkraut were not entirely new as in 1959 Everett and Tolman had presented a similar theory but with less robust evidence (see Baumeister et al., 2003). Put simply, depression is a result of a reduction in noradrenaline and antidepressants increase noradrenergic activity and therefore that must be the problem. The evidence for this hypothesis comes from a number of psychopharmacological studies. It is worth remembering that many discoveries about drugs in the treatment of depression came about by chance (Ban, 2006).

Reserpine is a drug that depletes the brain of monoamines by making the vesicles 'leaky' so that noradrenaline passes out into the cytoplasm and is deactivated by the metabolic enzyme **monoamine oxidase** (MAO). In doing this, there is a marked reduction in noradrenaline (and other transmitters) leading to depression-like symptoms in the animal – an effect that can be reversed with antidepressants (Figure 22.1) (see Baumeister et al. (2003) for review). Amphetamine, which we have considered as a dopaminergic drug, also increases noradrenaline. The effects of amphetamine are well documented and produce a euphoric high and therefore it was used as a treatment for depression (albeit not that successfully) (Guttmann & Sargant, 1937). Amphetamine works in this context by increasing monoamines, but more specifically noradrenaline. A successful pharmaceutical for depression was the **monoamine oxidase inhibitor** (MAOI) iproniazid. This and similar drugs were therapeutic for depression (Crane, 1956) and worked by blocking the effects of MAO and therefore stopping the enzymatic degradation of noradrenaline. By preventing this degradation, the MAOIs increase the amount of noradrenaline available at the synapses (Figure 22.2), the hypothesis

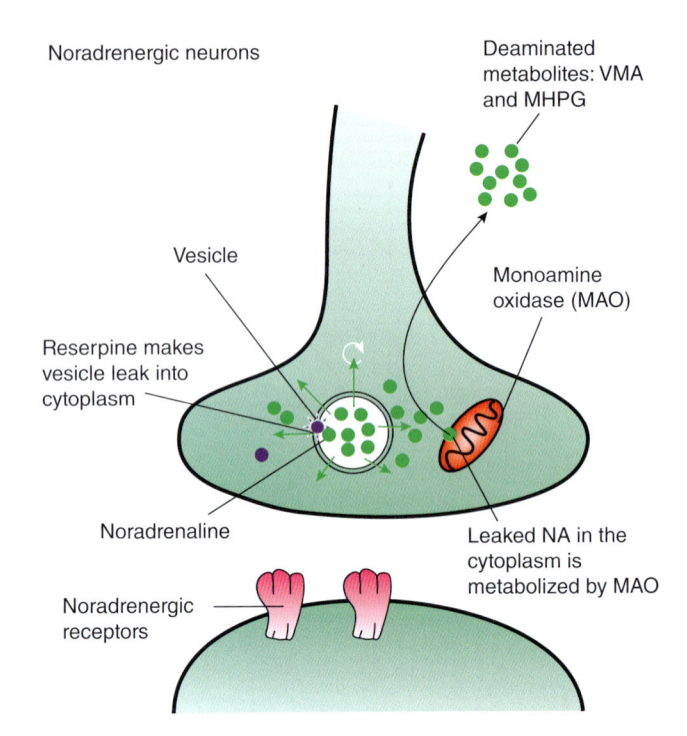

FIGURE 22.1 *Reserpine makes the vesicles leaky and monoamines are metabolized by MAO before they can act. COMT, catechol-O-methyltransferase; DA, dopamine; MAO, monoamine oxidase; MHPG, 3-Methoxy-4-hydroxyphenylglycol; VMA, Vanillyl mandelic acid; NA, Noradrenaline.*

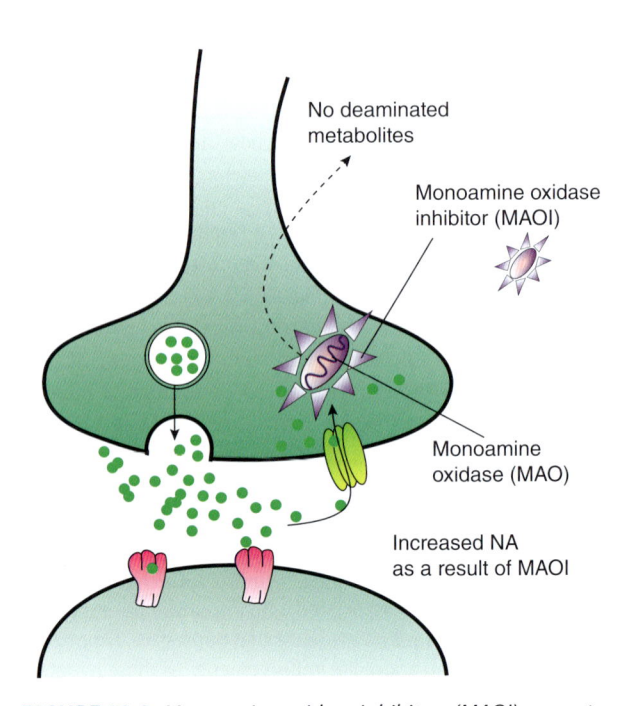

FIGURE 22.2 *Monoamine oxidase inhibitors (MAOI) prevent the degradation of noradrenaline (and dopamine and serotonin). MAO, monoamine oxidase; NA, noradrenaline.*

being that if the clinically efficacious drug works by increasing noradrenaline, then it must be noradrenaline that needs to be fixed.

Tricyclic antidepressants (TCAs) were introduced in 1957 to treat depression after Kuhn had reported successful alterations in mood with the drug imipramine (Ban, 2006). In general, the TCAs inhibit or block reuptake of released noradrenaline (Figure 22.3). By preventing noradrenaline from being retrieved by the presynaptic neuron, levels of noradrenaline within the synapses increase; if a TCA works by preventing the escape of noradrenaline, then depression is a result of having too little noradrenaline.

Though not the most reliable measure of brain activity, measuring peripheral metabolites of noradrenaline has shown that those suffering from depression have lower levels of noradrenergic metabolites, e.g. 3-methoxy-4-hydroxyphenylglycol (MHPG), in the urine (Maas et al., 1968). Reduced metabolites are argued to be indicative of a reduction of noradrenaline, and therefore that must be the problem in depression.

On the surface, the evidence builds up a reasonably convincing case for noradrenaline being involved in depression. However, there were problems with the noradrenergic hypothesis of depression as stated in the 1960s. Reserpine was re-evaluated and it was noted that the majority of research was in induced depressions, not true depressions (Baumeister et al., 2003; Goodwin & Bunney, 1971).

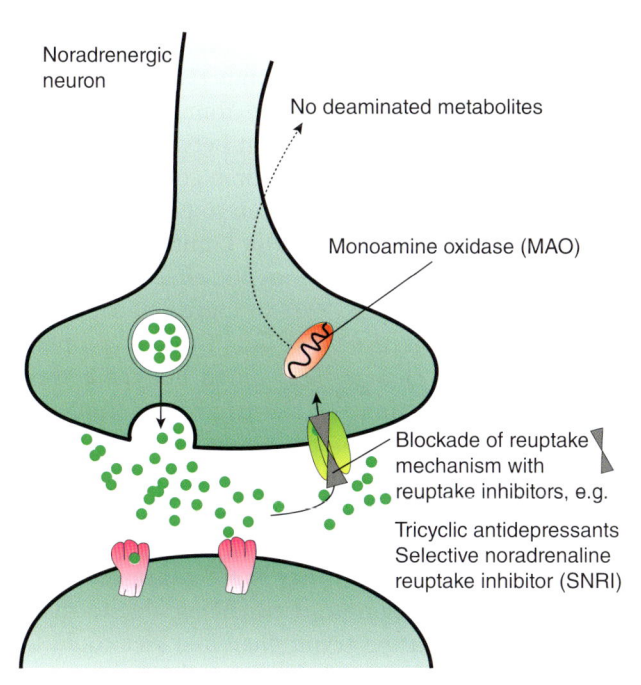

Amphetamine improves mood in normal people, but is not as effective as noradrenergic drugs. One of the big drawbacks of using amphetamine is its abuse potential. Furthermore, the precursor of noradrenaline is dopamine and before that is DOPA. DOPA as a replacement medication (e.g. Parkinson's disease) should theoretically work as an antidepressant; however, it leads to psychomotor activating effects but does not affect mood (Goodwin et al., 1970), i.e. the person may be more active but they do not feel better.

The glaringly obvious problem with this hypothesis (hindsight is always 20:20 vision) was that the TCAs would boost noradrenergic levels very quickly after administration, but there was a time lag of approximately 21 days before any clinical effect was seen. Therefore, the initial elevation of noradrenaline was not directly linked to the antidepressant effect. The delay in clinical action may reflect neural changes that occur after long-term administration (long term being 21 days).

The obvious experiment is to see what happens to the brain when antidepressants are given chronically. Numerous studies have been conducted to try to account for the time delay in clinical efficacy. Most hypotheses focus on up- and downregulation of noradrenergic receptors.

There are three kinds of receptors to consider in this scenario: presynaptic receptors (alpha-2) that inhibit noradrenergic cells, alpha- and beta-postsynaptic receptors. The alpha-2 autoreceptor is located on the presynaptic terminal of noradrenergic cells in the locus coeruleus and activation reduces cell firing and synthesis (Figure 22.4).

The use of **clonidine** as a alpha-2 autoreceptor agonist enables specific probing of this receptor's function. Clonidine produces change in cell firing and after chronic administration of antidepressants produces a reduction in the response to the alpha-2 autoreceptor (Eriksson et al., 1982; U'Prichard, 1984). Thus, they are subsensitive leading to a gradual increase in firing and increasing synthesis (McMillen et al., 1980; Murphy et al., 1987). However, not all drugs that are antidepressants act in the same way. In animal models, the number of antipsychotics increase noradrenaline turnover but after chronic administration there is no change in activity (Willner, 1985b). The search continued for a site of action.

Presynaptic alpha-1 receptors have not yielded a site of action although there is some evidence to suggest chronic administration of antidepressants leads to

FIGURE 22.3 *Tricyclic antidepressants (TCAs) work by blocking the reuptake of noradrenaline into the presynaptic neuron. MAO, monoamine oxidase; MAOI, monoamine oxidase inhibitor; NA, noradrenaline.*

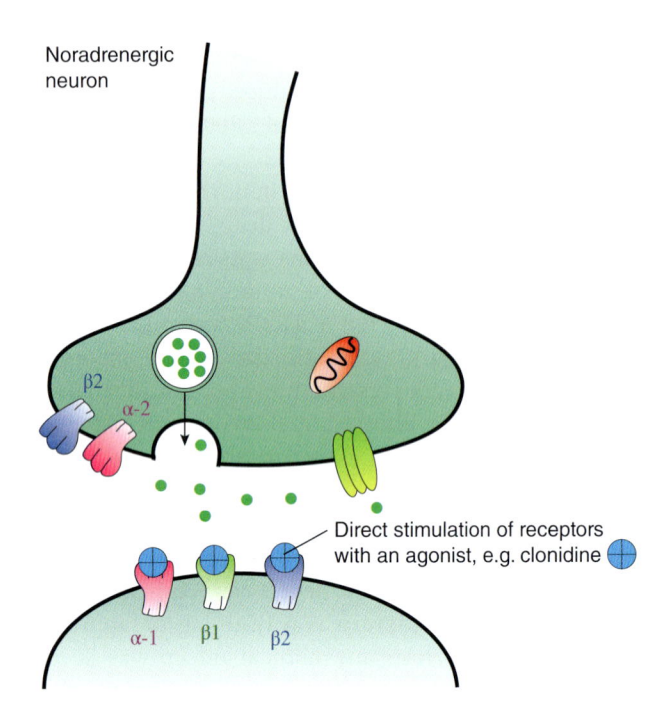

FIGURE 22.4 *Noradrenergic receptors. Alpha-1, alpha-2, beta-1 and beta-2 noradrenergic receptors on the pre- and postsynaptic membrane of noradrenergic synapses.*

increased receptor sensitivity (Menkes & Aghajanian, 1981). However, other studies found no increase in the number of receptors in the rat brain (Stockmeier et al., 1987). The beta receptor has also received attention in order to explain long-term effects of antidepressants. Biochemically, beta receptors activate second messengers and the accumulation of cyclic AMP and antagonists of beta receptors block the effect (Madison & Nicoll, 1986). Deprivation of noradrenaline within the synapses induced by reserpine produced supersensitivity of the cAMP response (Williams & Pirch, 1974). The opposite position exists in which chronic imipramine, and other antidepressant treatments, produced a subsensitivity to noradrenergic activity and the activation of cAMP (Sulser, 1983; Vetulani et al., 1976). This biochemical action may be mediated by changes in the receptor number, as long-term treatment reduces the number of beta receptors (Peroutka & Snyder, 1980a). Such long-term changes prompted a revision of the mode of action in which it was suggested that depression may be a disorder resulting from hypersensitive receptors and antidepressant drugs reverse the sensitivity (Sulser et al., 1978). All of this evidence fits with the time course of action with antidepressants (Caldecott-Hazard et al., 1991). However, just because it fits does not necessarily mean that it is the direct mechanism of action.

Reformulation by Segal et al. (1974) and Sulser et al. (1978) of the catecholamine hypothesis provides a *prima facie* case for antidepressant action and therefore a possible aetiological mechanism in depression. It is unlikely that this biochemical change is the direct mediator of antidepressant effects. There are too many diverging actions of the drugs, with some drugs that are effective not producing the biochemical change and other drugs that produce the biochemical change but are without clinical efficacy, e.g. chlorpromazine has similar pharmacological effects to imipramine.

Serotonin Hypothesis of Depression

A similar viewpoint to the noradrenergic hypothesis was put forward by Coppen et al. (1967) and Lapin and Oxenkrug (1969) but instead focusing on serotonin. Tryptophan, which is the precursor of serotonin, was shown to potentiate the antidepressant properties of MAOIs, suggesting that depression may have a serotonergic component (Coppen et al., 1967). The hypothesis suggested that serotonin levels are low in people with depression. However, inconclusive findings that serotonin levels are different in depression have made it difficult to uphold such a view.

Supporting the role of serotonin in mood (and therefore the logical extension of depression) are studies using a tryptophan-free diet. Because tryptophan is found in food, meals can be contrived to be free of tryptophan. If they are free of tryptophan then the vital ingredient for making serotonin is gone, thereby producing a reduction in serotonin (Figure 22.5). In a group of non-depressed males, Young et al. (1985) noted that there was a correlation between serotonin levels and mood; if levels of serotonin go up mood also improves. Such a diet was also seen to provoke relapse in patients who were in remission (Smith et al., 1997) and negated some of the therapeutic effects of antidepressants (Delgado et al., 1990). In untreated depressed patients, Delgado et al. (1994) found that tryptophan depletion did not change their mood but there were changes on the day after the diet had been completed. The fact that there was not a potentiated depression upon tryptophan depletion was cited as a reason for not accepting a simplistic serotonergic hypothesis. One may wish to consider the baseline levels of depression in these patients; as they were untreated, they were more severely symptomatic. Being able to make patients worse with the tryptophan-free diet could be a harder phenomenon to measure as the patients are already at a low baseline and therefore any changes may not be detected by the psychometric measures. Similar support of the serotonergic hypothesis comes from the ability of the 5-HT synthesis inhibitor PCPA to block the therapeutic effects of TCAs and MAOIs (Delgado

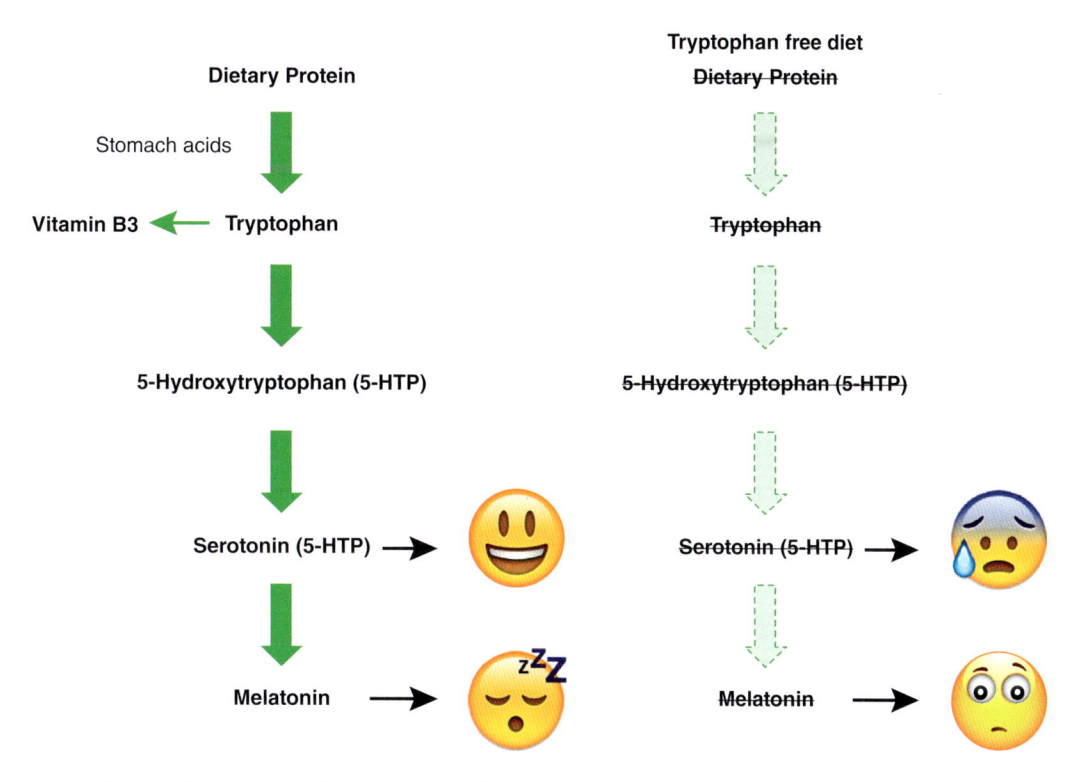

FIGURE 22.5 *The basis and effects of a tryptophan-free diet.*

et al., 1994). Conversely, tryptophan supplements elevate mood, but also improve the quality of social interactions. Thus, enhancing serotonin not only improves mood directly but indirectly mood is improved because of better social interactions (Young, 2013).

Many of the drugs used to treat depression have effects on both noradrenaline and serotonin systems. And again the time difference between the initial biochemical effects and clinical efficacy remains an enigma. Chronic antidepressants have been shown to increase levels of 5-HT2 receptors (Willner, 1985a) whereas in depression they are upregulated (Hrdina et al., 1993; Owens & Nemeroff, 1994). Electrophysiological studies assessing the firing pattern of serotonergic neurons after antidepressant treatment show that initial administration resulted in no change but after 15 days there was increased sensitivity to serotonin (de Montigny, 1981). Again this correlation fits with the clinical time course.

Animal models of depression have targeted serotonergic systems, e.g. the **olfactory bulbectomy** and social isolation procedures. In olfactory bulbectomy, rats have bilateral lesions of the olfactory bulbs and are seen to be hyperactive and irritable with increased levels of cortisol and deficient in **passive avoidance learning**. Passive avoidance is sensitive to antidepressants of numerous classes (Broekkamp et al., 1980). In passive avoidance, the animals are exposed to an apparatus that has a light and a dark side. One side of the compartment delivers an electrical shock and the rats were quick to learn which side that was. Passive avoidance involves the animal moving from the shock side to the non-shock side (see learned helplessness in Chapter 8). Whilst the olfactory bulbectomy lacks construct validity, it is particularly effective in identifying antidepressant agents (Cryan et al., 2002). The olfactory bulbectomy (Figure 22.6) has been associated with decreased levels of serotonin (Song & Leonard, 2005) and hyperinnervation of the serotonergic system within the frontal cortex as a compensatory response (Zhou et al., 1998) which might be analogous to depression in which the volume and sensitivity of the olfactory bulb were reduced (Negoias et al., 2010). Similar effects were found by the selective serotonergic neurotoxin **5,7-DHT** in the olfactory bulb (Cairncross et al., 1978).

The social isolation procedure is based on the premise that isolated housing results in rats having lower levels of serotonin than those in group housing (Grippo et al., 2007). Such studies use experiments involving procedures that require social co-operation or persistence, as in the forced swim test, and rats can only do this if they lived with one another. Impairments of the forced swim test are reversed by antidepressants (Heritch et al., 1990) and social co-operation can be improved by chronic antidepressant treatment, an effect which was blocked by the 5-HT antagonist **metergoline** (Willner et al., 1989).

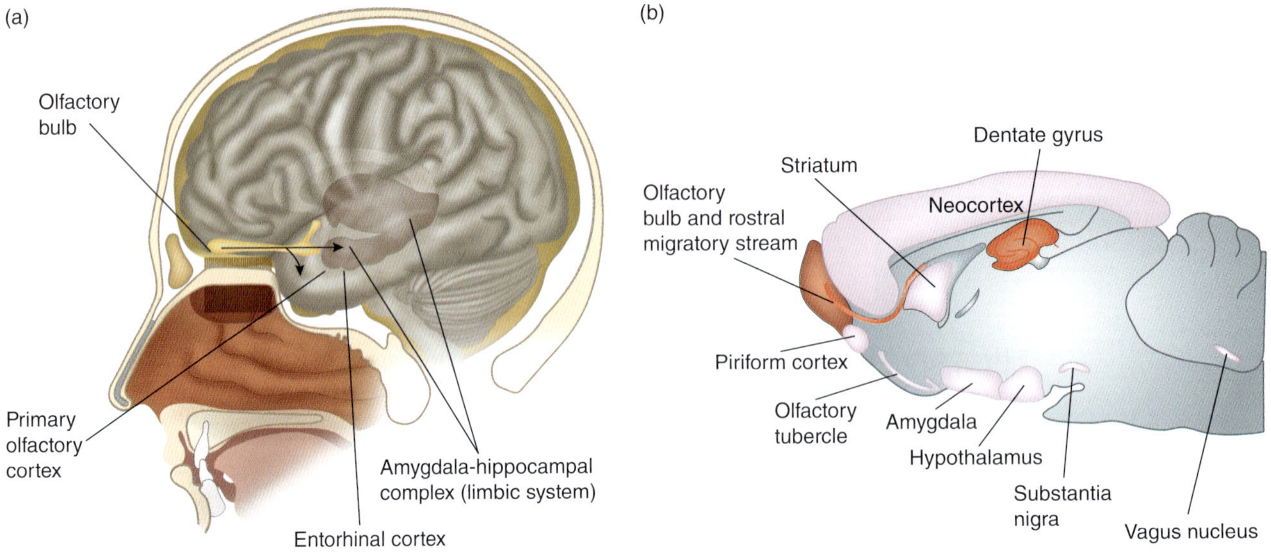

FIGURE 22.6 *The olfactory bulb in (a) the human and (b) the rat.*

TREATMENTS FOR DEPRESSION

Early drug treatments for depression were the catalysts for the noradrenergic and serotonergic hypotheses. Many of the early drugs had both noradrenergic and serotonergic activity. However, more recent drugs available for the treatment of depression are either specific to one system or mixed.

Selective Serotonin Reuptake Inhibitors

Selective serotonin reuptake inhibitors (SSRIs) are clinically efficacious drugs that do exactly what the name suggests (Anderson, 2000) – they selectively block the reuptake of serotonin into the presynaptic neuron (Figure 22.7). By doing this, serotonin is released in response to a stimulus and it remains in the synapses where it is available to stimulate postsynaptic receptors. Thus, one might expect the hypothesis to suggest that depression is due to a deficit in serotonin. Perhaps the most infamous mood-altering drug fits into this class – **fluoxetine**, better known as Prozac. Indeed, deficits have been found in the various components of the serotonin system (Owens & Nemeroff, 1994), as have polymorphisms of the serotonin transporter in MDD (Ogilvie et al., 1996).

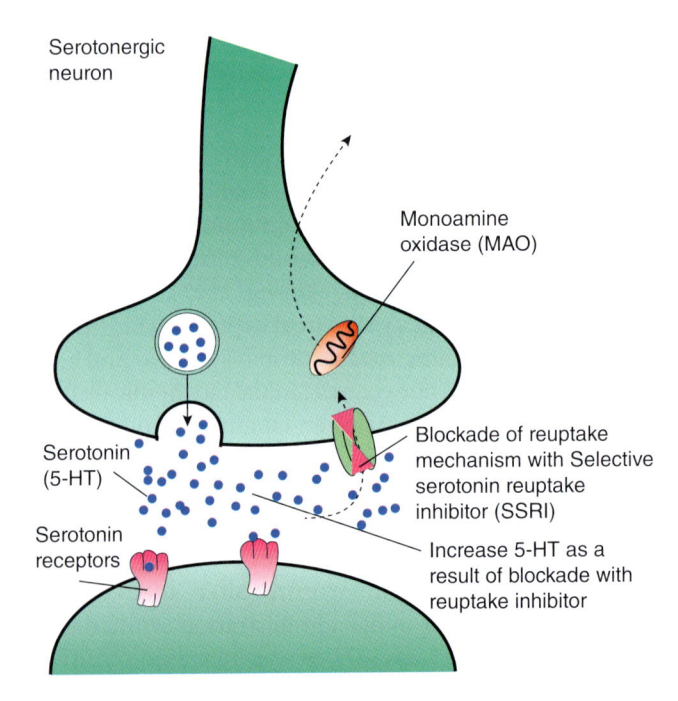

FIGURE 22.7 *Selective serotonin reuptake inhibitors (SSRIs) block the reuptake of serotonin into the presynaptic serotonergic neuron.*

Atypical Antidepressants

The atypical antidepressants are a mixed group of pharmaceuticals that were generated to minimize side-effects and increase efficacy. Many have mixed effects on noradrenaline and serotonin and are often similar to TCAs. Each one needs to be considered individually (interested readers are directed to Advokat et al. (2014)). Of interest is **bupropion** (Wellbutrin or Zyban) which is a reuptake inhibitor of both DA and noradrenaline. This is a good example of a drug that was deployed for the treatment of depression, but was subsequently discovered to be effective for another purpose – as an aid to smoking cessation (Hurt et al., 1997).

Selective Noradrenergic Reuptake Inhibitors

Like their serotonergic counterparts, the selective noradrenergic reuptake inhibitors (SNRIs) block the noradrenergic transporter, thereby increasing levels of noradrenaline in the synapse. Although genes had been found for the noradrenergic transporter, they have not been considered to be major determinants in MDD (Owen et al., 1999; Zill et al., 2002).

Dual Action Antidepressants

Specificity is required in psychopharmacological studies in order to locate mechanisms of action. However, widespread effects may be more conducive to the therapeutic response. For example, mirtazapine is an alpha-2 antagonist, a 5-HT2 antagonist, a 5-HT3 antagonist and a 5-HT1 agonist, all of which provide a unique contribution to the therapeutic effect (Figure 22.8) (de Boer, 1995). Understanding the interactions between the multiple sites of action is necessary to explain the effects of mirtazapine.

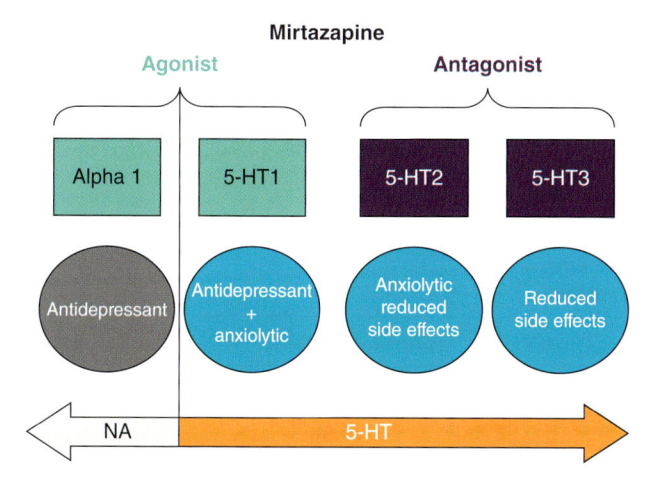

FIGURE 22.8 *Mirtazapine. An example of a drug with mixed agonist and antagonist actions on different neurotransmitter systems potentiating clinical efficacy. NA, noradrenaline.*

Electroconvulsive Therapy

Electroconvulsive therapy (ECT) involves placing electrodes on the skull and passing an electrical charge through the brain, inducing a seizure. This highly controversial treatment is used occasionally for the treatment of depression. Unlike drug therapy, ECT is rapid. The effects of ECT on neurotransmitters have shown an increasing function of noradrenaline, serotonin, dopamine and GABA (Mann, 1998). Noradrenergic activity has been shown to be reduced following ECT which was similar to antidepressants (MAOIs, TCAs and SSRIs) (Linnoila et al., 1983). Increased levels of DA and the DA response have been recorded following ECT (Costain et al., 1982; McGarvey et al., 1993). Similarly, elevation of GABA in response to ECT is thought to underlie the therapeutic effect in a subgroup of depressed patients (Devanand et al., 1995; Sanacora et al., 2003). Reductions have been measured in 5-HT1a receptors after ECT in patients with MDD in the anterior cingulate cortex, orbitofrontal cortex, amygdala, hippocampus and insula (all areas considered dysfunctional in depression) (Lanzenberger et al., 2013). Thus, because of its non-specific targeting of neurotransmitters in the brain, ECT has differential effects that may be key to its therapeutic effects. Increases in dopamine and GABA may facilitate motivation/learning and reduction in fear respectively. Changes in the serotonergic and noradrenergic systems may reverse deficits seen in depression that are linked to alterations of mood.

Lithium

The drugs that we have considered so far have been used in the treatment of unipolar depression. **Bipolar disorder** responds more favourably to **lithium carbonate**. It is particularly effective at calming the manic episodes (Geddes et al., 2004) but this is not matched with an ability to address the depression and therefore it may be used in conjunction with TCA medication. Lithium's mode of action is centred round serotonin. Lithium elevates tryptophan, serotonin and 5-HIAA levels and serotonin release targeting pre- and postsynaptic mechanisms (Price et al., 1990).

NEUROANATOMY OF DEPRESSION

Drugs acting successfully to treat depression via mechanisms centred on serotonin and/or noradrenaline provide another route of investigation to determine the location of differences within the brain between depressed and non-depressed patients. Primary candidates include the prefrontal cortex, amygdala and hippocampus (Papez circuit). Neuroimaging studies have shown changes in regional cerebral blood flow in depression indicative of changes in activity. Hamilton et al. (2012) performed a meta-analysis of 14 studies assessing the activity of brain regions in MDD using PET (comprising 299 patients). They found an effect of increased regional cerebral blood flow being greater in depressed patients than in comparison groups in the pulvinar nucleus of the thalamus when assessed at baseline. Regions of the brain that were identified responding to negative valence included the following.

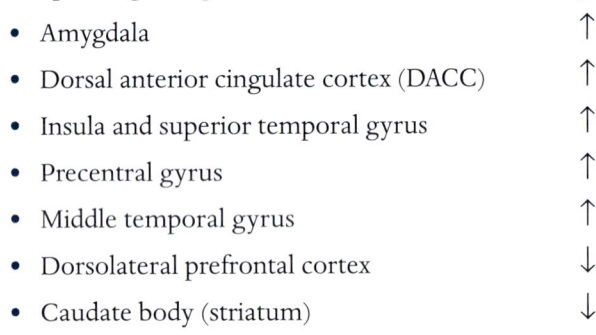

- Amygdala ↑
- Dorsal anterior cingulate cortex (DACC) ↑
- Insula and superior temporal gyrus ↑
- Precentral gyrus ↑
- Middle temporal gyrus ↑
- Dorsolateral prefrontal cortex ↓
- Caudate body (striatum) ↓

Many of these areas are targeted with antidepressant treatments, e.g. prefrontal cortex and amygdala (Bellani et al., 2011).

IS THERE A COMMON DENOMINATOR IN ALL THE TREATMENTS FOR DEPRESSION?

The neuropharmacological explanation of why antidepressants take so long to work has remained unsatisfactory. Current views suggest that the delay in improvement of mood is due to learning mechanisms (Harmer, Goodwin et al., 2009) which may or may not be mediated via reductions in neuroplasticity in the cortex (Nissen et al., 2010; Normann et al., 2007). At the heart of these accounts is the notion that depressed patients have cognitive processing deficits that are sensitive to a negative bias and affect memory, emotion recognition and salience. Emotional processing may be improved rapidly following SSRIs or SNRIs in both non-clinical and clinical populations (Harmer, Bhagwagar et al., 2003; Harmer, Hill et al., 2003; Harmer, O'sullivan et al., 2009).

In a review of the literature, Harmer, Goodwin et al. (2009) assessed the effects of depression and subsequent antidepressant treatment on the processing of negative and positive emotions (e.g. facial expressions and self-descriptors) (Table 22.1). **Citalopram** is an SSRI and **reboxetine** is an SNRI, both of which reduced the deficits seen in depression favouring negative affective bias. Mediating this process might be the amygdala where initial elevations of serotonin lead to anxiety, but dissipates with prolonged treatment (di Simplicio et al., 2014; Harmer et al., 2004, 2006). Depressed patients

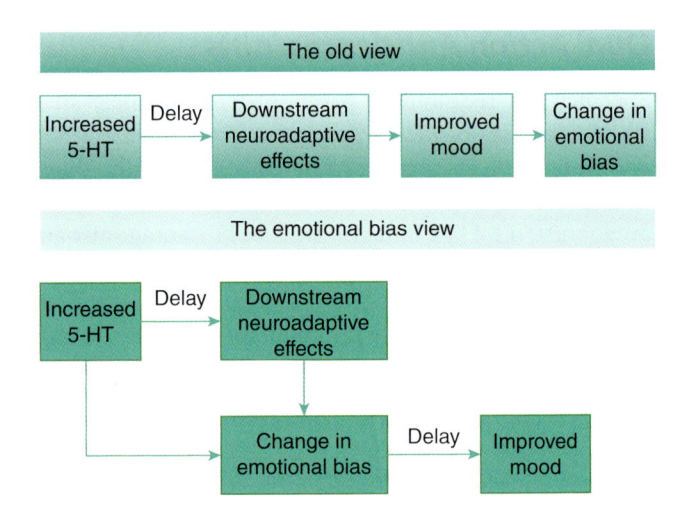

FIGURE 22.9 *The shift from old adaption theories of antidepressant to an emotional bias view.*
Source: Adapted from Harmer, C. J., Goodwin, G. M., & Cowen, P. J. (2009). Why do antidepressants take so long to work? A cognitive neuropsychological model of antidepressant drug action. *British Journal of Psychiatry,* 195(2), 102–108 by permission of the Royal College of Psychiatrists.

TABLE 22.1 *The effect of antidepressants on positive (+) and negative (−) salience*

Test	Depression	Citalopram (SSRI)	Reboxetine (SNRI)
Recognition of negative versus positive facial expressions	↑	↓	↓
Speed to name positive versus negative self-descriptors	↓	↑	↑
Number of positive versus negative descriptors named	↓	↑	↑
Amygdala response to masked fear-inducing faces	↑	↓	↓

SNRI, selective noradrenaline reuptake inhibitor; SSRI, selective serotonin reuptake inhibitor.

demonstrated a negative bias in future forecasts of events in a study that looked at their predictions for Valentine's Day (Hoerger et al., 2012) (although not depressed, I have a feeling that they are accurate).

Furthermore, **tryptophan depletion** induces a negative information-processing bias, and negative biases become associated with low mood (Harmer, 2008).

Thus, Harmer and colleagues shift away from a delay account of antidepressants solely on the basis of downstream neuroadaptations, and move towards a position in which increased serotonin, which will undoubtedly have downstream neuroadaptive effects, produces a change in emotional bias which then leads to improved mood and antidepressants effects (Figure 22.9).

Increased activity in the pulvinar nucleus of the thalamus at baseline has been argued to potentiate responses in the amygdala, anterior cingulate cortex and insula that maintains activation of salience networks tuned to negative information (see Figure 22.9). Furthermore, a failure of dopaminergic mechanisms to communicate with the dorsolateral prefrontal cortex means patients are 'unable to evoke emotionally attenuating appraisals and contextual information to the viscerally overcharged data from limbic structures' (Hamilton et al., 2012, p.699). Thus, the negative bias of depression is a failure of cortical regions to negate or even manage incoming stimuli.

Disner et al. (2011) provide a similar account of bias processing in depression. In their conceptualization of the regions involved in negative bias, they modularize for attention, processing, memory and rumination (Figure 22.10).

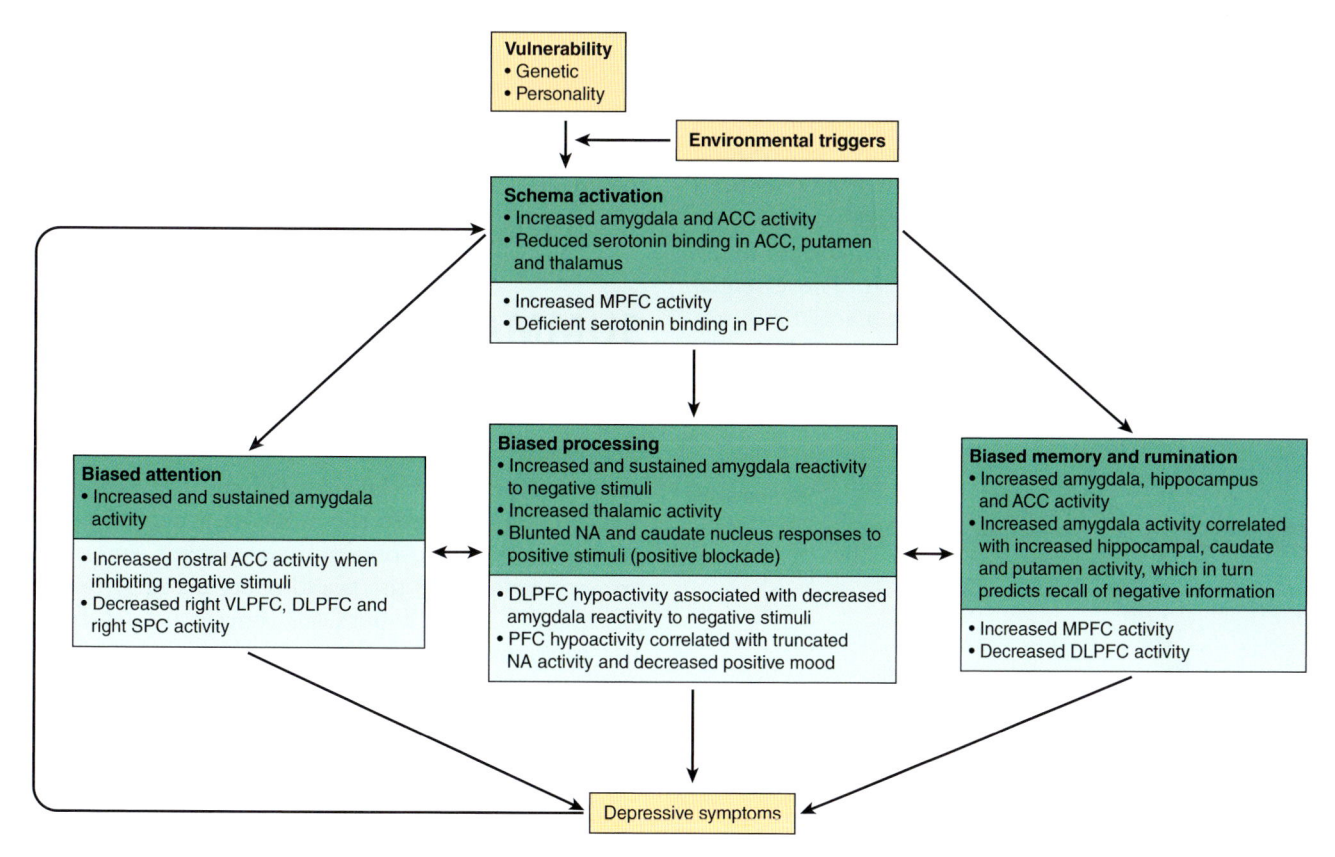

FIGURE 22.10 *Disner et al.'s integrated cognitive neurobiological model of depression. This flowchart shows the sequence of events proposed to be involved in the development of depression, beginning with depression vulnerability factors and environmental stressors, and resulting in depressive symptoms. The figure outlines the neurobiological events associated with each step of the cognitive model: schema activation, biased attention, biased processing, and biased memory and rumination. The brain regions in this flowchart are divided into two groups: regions associated with bottom-up, limbic system influences (blue boxes) and regions that maintain bottom-up influences through altered top-down, cognitive control (grey boxes). Note that all elements contribute directly to depressive symptoms, and that depressive symptoms also feed back into the system, thus exacerbating schema activation. ACC, anterior cingulate cortex; DLPFC, dorsolateral prefrontal cortex; MPFC, medial prefrontal cortex; NA, nucleus accumbens; PFC, prefrontal cortex; SPC, superior parietal cortex.*
Source: Reproduced by permission from Macmillan Publishers Ltd: NATURE REVIEWS NEUROSCIENCE Disner, S. G., Beevers, C. G., Haigh, E. A., & Beck, A. T. (2011). Neural mechanisms of the cognitive model of depression. *Nature Reviews Neuroscience*, 12(8), 467-477 copyright 2011.

The theory has important ramifications for treatment and some authors suggest that a reprogramming from negative to positive bias would be a useful adjunct in the treatment of depression (Blaut et al., 2013; Lang et al., 2012) or as a preventive inoculation against depression (Browning et al., 2012). The effects of reprogramming towards positive processing were correlated with changes in the prefrontal cortex (Browning et al., 2010; di Simplicio et al., 2012). Psychotherapy in general has been shown to result in normalization of the frontal limbic circuitry in depression (Barsaglini et al., 2014) which gives further support for the negative bias hypothesis. The vast majority of psychotherapeutic interventions involve learning new associations. The different effects of psychotherapy and medication have been argued to reflect different processes converging on the same construct. Psychotherapy operates a top-down modification of behaviour using frontal cortical limbic projections, whereas pharmacotherapy involves bottom-up changes of the ventral limbic regions that mediate cognitive mechanisms towards emotionally salient stimuli (Goldapple et al., 2004). Thus, cognitive behavioural therapy (CBT) and even psychodynamic interventions have biological mechanisms (Figure 22.11).

Willner et al. (2013) identified two weaknesses to the negative bias hypothesis of depression. The essential requirements for relearning of positive associations prohibit a rapid onset of antidepressant action (which is in keeping with a number of drugs). However, there are a number of interventions that do have rapid onset, e.g. deep brain stimulation, ECT and intravenous ketamine. Although the effects of a positive bias in these treatments remain to be determined, the theory focuses on long-term neuroadaptations. The rapid antidepressant actions of ketamine are beginning to provide further understanding of the mechanisms involved in antidepressants and depression. Ketamine has been argued to initiate a rapid elevation of glutamate activity leading to increased synaptic connectivity in the PFC (Duman, 2014). Whilst there are no data on cognitive bias with ECT, it is well known that ECT produces cognitive deficits and that ECT-induced amnesia is a common occurrence (Lisanby et al., 2000). The implication of this is that ECT erases memories, and that by erasing memories one can learn new positive associations.

Secondly, later episodes of depression should be easier to treat than first episodes because the drugs provided during the first episode should have established the positive associations that could be rekindled in later episodes. However, later episodes are not easier to treat (Willner et al., 2013). No theory is ever perfect . . . or even close to perfect.

SUMMARY

Depression is most likely a heterogeneous disorder with many pathways leading to symptoms. Numerous hypotheses exist to explain not only the symptoms of depression, but also the mode of action of antidepressants. Two neurotransmitter systems emerge as primary candidates: the noradrenergic and serotonergic systems. Initial hypotheses concerning depression and antidepressants were simple, emanating from the view that 'if drug A changes neurotransmitter B and is clinically efficacious, then the disorder in question must be due to neurotransmitter B'. Such logic has not reconciled the neurobiology of depression. More recent accounts that have tried to integrate the time delay of clinical effect after commencing antidepressant treatment have focused on the relearning of positive associations.

Many factors will contribute to depression, including genetics, personality characteristics, past experiences and stress reactivity. It is no small exercise attempting to understand the interaction of all the variables.

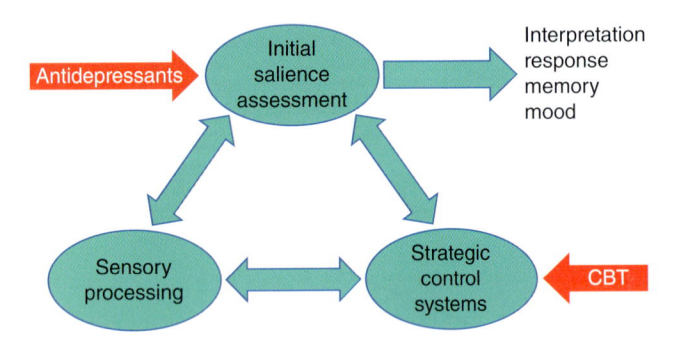

FIGURE 22.11 *The point of action of different antidepressant therapies. The negative bias that is seen as an increase in salience is targeted by antidepressants and the control systems of the cortex targeted in cognitive behavioural therapy (CBT) and other directive therapies.*
Source: Adapted from Harmer, C. J., Goodwin, G. M., & Cowen, P. J. (2009). Why do antidepressants take so long to work? A cognitive neuropsychological model of antidepressant drug action. *British Journal of Psychiatry, 195*(2), 102–108 by permission of the Royal College of Psychiatrists.

LEARNING OUTCOME QUESTIONS

You should be able to answer the following questions.
- To what extent is there a genetic basis of MDD and how is it adaptive?
- What evidence supports a monoamine hypothesis of depression?
- Antidepressant medication works because it refocuses the individual on positive thoughts. Discuss.

FURTHER READING

Berton, O., & Nestler, E. J. (2006). New approaches to antidepressant drug discovery: beyond monoamines. *Nature Reviews Neuroscience*, 7(2), 137–151.

Harmer, C. J., & Cowen, P. J. (2013). 'It's the way that you look at it' – a cognitive neuropsychological account of SSRI action in depression. *Philosophical Transactions of the Royal Society of London B: Biological Sciences*, 368(1615), 20120407.

Willner, P., Scheel-Kruger, J., & Belzung, C. (2013). The neurobiology of depression and antidepressant action. *Neuroscience and Biobehavioral Reviews*, 37(10 Pt 1), 2331–2371.

Young, S. N. (2013). The effect of raising and lowering tryptophan levels on human mood and social behaviour. *Philosophical Transactions of the Royal Society of London B: Biological Sciences*, 368(1615), 20110375.

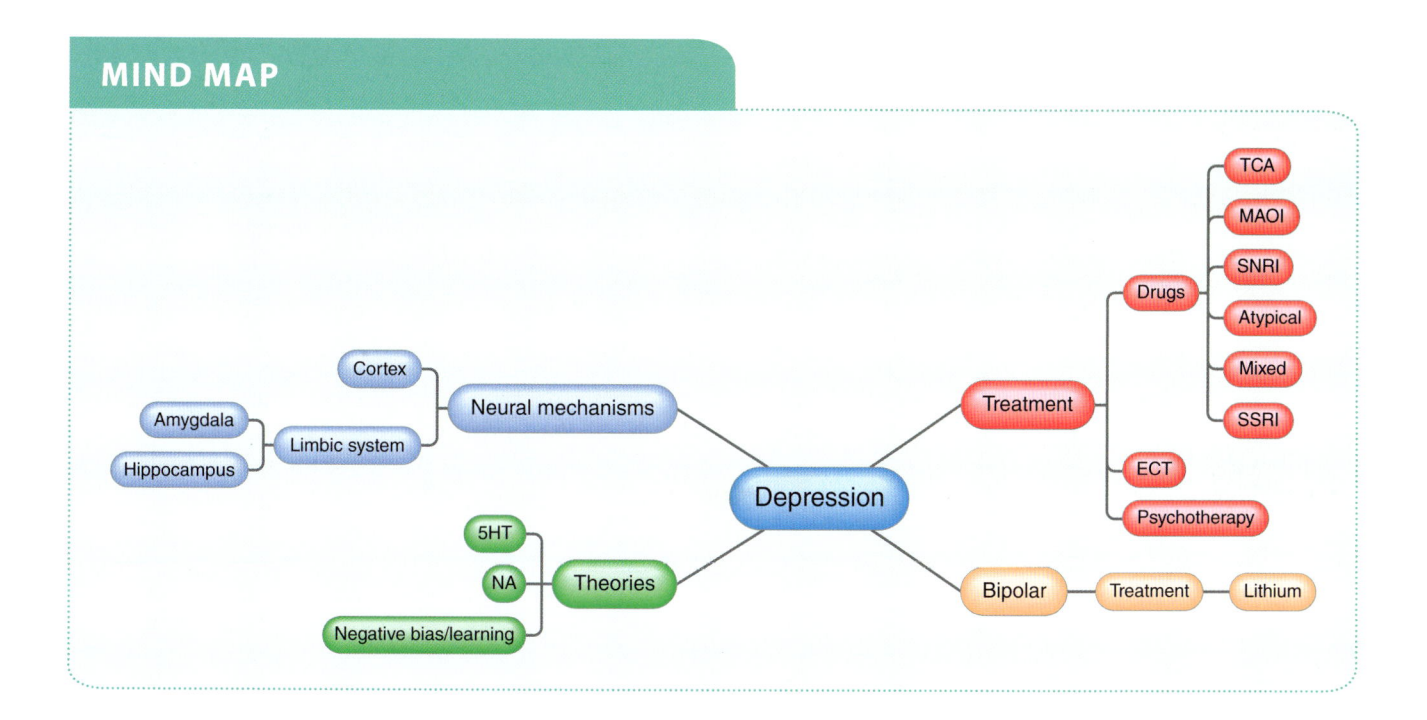

MIND MAP

23 Stress and Anxiety

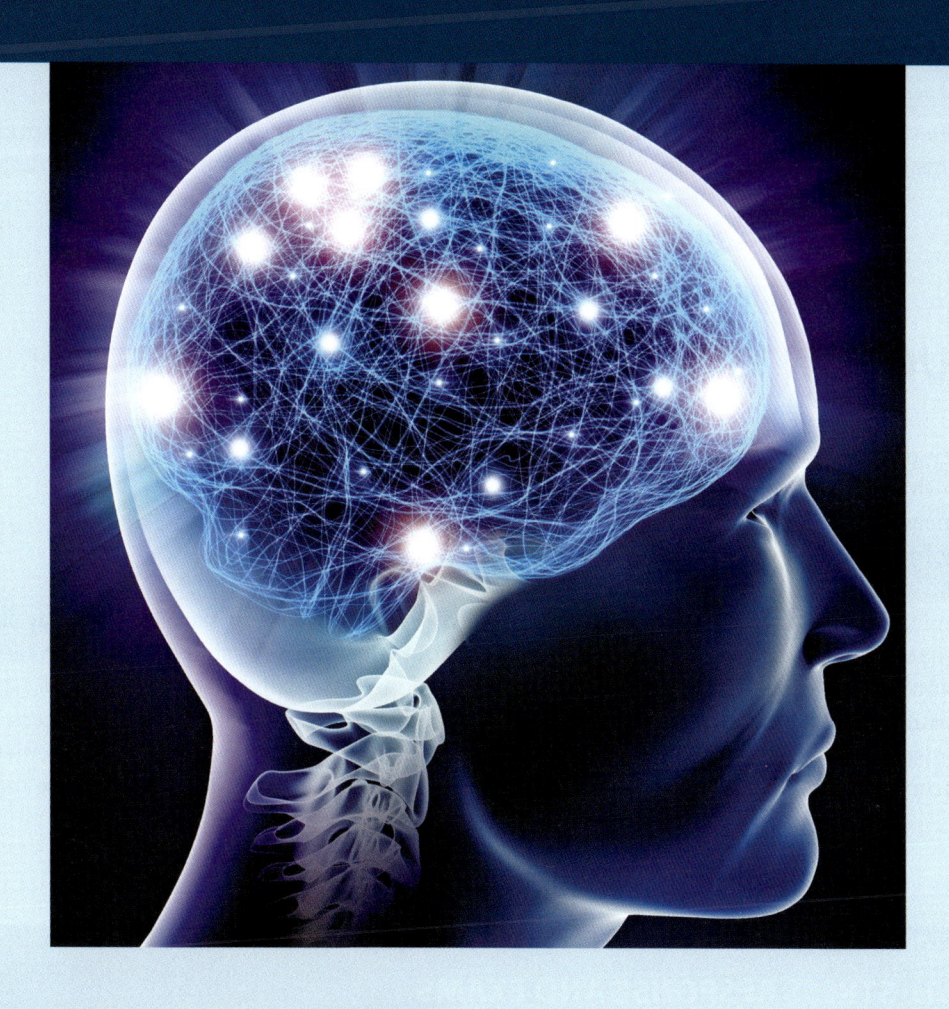

ANATOMY OF THE CHAPTER

This chapter will highlight the following.

- The physiology of stress reactions.
- The adaptive/non-adaptive nature of stress.
- The pathological conditions of anxiety.
- The neural mechanisms of anxiety.
- Treatment of anxiety disorders.

INTRODUCTION 560

STRESS 560

ANXIETY 571

SUMMARY 582

LEARNING OUTCOMES

1. To understand the physiological mechanisms that have evolved to produce stress.
2. To evaluate the different physiological mechanisms involved in producing anxiety.
3. To be able to place stress and anxiety in an evolutionary framework.
4. To understand the role of anxiolytics in the development of hypotheses regarding the pathogenesis of anxiety.

INTRODUCTION

Stress and anxiety are two states of being that we are most familiar with. Both stress and anxiety confer an adaptive function that means we survive. However, stress and anxiety can become maladaptive. The maladaptive versions of stress and anxiety lead to psychological reactions which may seem far removed from having any beneficial function. Stress itself may produce wear and tear on the body, that if prolonged can lead to changes in physiology that may be detrimental to the individual. For example, health psychologists may seek to reduce stress levels in patients with coronary heart disease. Stress also hinders immune responses which are studied in the subdiscipline of psychoneuroimmunology.

STRESS

Stress is a common part of everyday life. You will no doubt feel considerable stress when faced with examinations, especially when ill-prepared (Box 23.1). There are many events that can lead to stress, e.g. death of a spouse, moving house or even retirement. Stress is big business – there is much money to be made in the stress

BOX 23.1: STRESS RESPONSE AND EXAMS

For many students the exam is a stressful event. During exam stress, urinary cortisol, adrenaline, noradrenaline and **3-methoxy-4-hydroxyphenylglycol** (MHPG) have all been shown to be elevated (Frankenhaeuser et al., 1978). The dopamine metabolite homovanillic acid (HVA) and the noradrenaline metabolite MHPG were elevated in healthy students after an examination compared with a day of ordinary school work, indicating an increased turnover of dopamine and noradrenaline (Frankenhaeuser et al., 1986). Cortisol levels have been shown to be elevated in the hour preceding an exam and are linked to feelings of stress (Shamsdin et al., 2010). However, other studies have not shown such a link between cortisol and perceived exam stress, but they have found changes in immunosuppression (Gilbert et al., 1996; Loft et al., 2007).

In a study measuring cortisol in the saliva of students undergoing exams and oral presentations (another student favourite which induces considerable stress), the levels of cortisol increased prior to the exam but reverted to control levels afterwards (Preuss et al., 2010). However, for the oral presentation, cortisol levels were elevated before and after the presentation, thus indicating that oral presentations produce a stronger stress response than written examinations, leading the authors to identify the social/evaluative nature of the oral presentation as a factor in the stress response.

Stress can produce immunosuppression in which there is suppression of natural killer cell cytotoxicity, thus compromising the immune system and leaving it vulnerable to attack. Of particular importance in the immune response are a group of proteins called cytokines, which

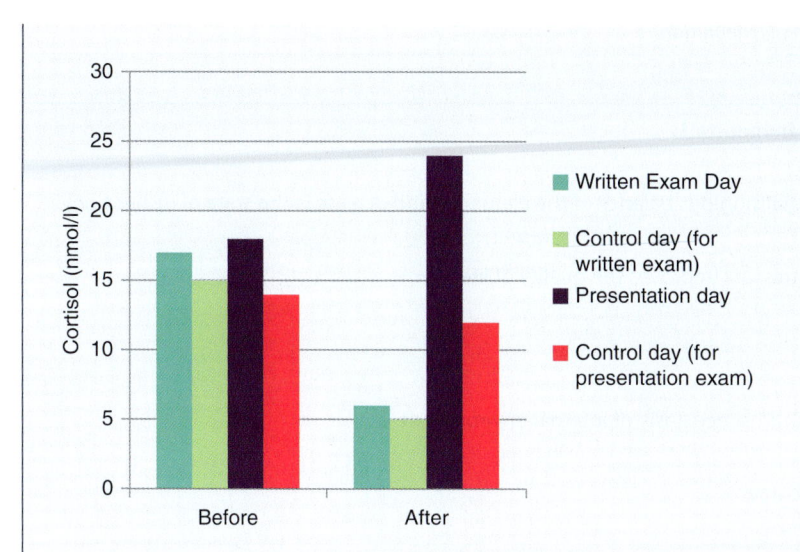

FIGURE 23.1.1 *Salivary cortisol concentrations before and after a written examination and a control day and an oral presentation and on a control day. Cortisol concentrations were significantly elevated on the examination day. Cortisol concentrations were significantly elevated before (Pre) and after (Post) the oral presentation.*
Source: Based on data from Preuss, D., Schoofs, D., Schlotz, W., & Wolf, O. T. (2010). The stressed student: Influence of written examinations and oral presentations on salivary cortisol concentrations in university students. *Stress, 13*(3), 221–229.

are modulators of humoral and cell-mediated immune responses. Type 1 cytokines mediate cellular immunity, e.g. phagocytes that ingest harmful particles, and type 2 cytokines mediate antibody immune responses within the blood system. A study by Marshall et al. (1998) measured cytokine activity in medical students undergoing a stressful academic examination. They found a decrease in type 1 immune responses and an increase in type 2 immune responses as a result of the exam stress. Marshall et al. (1998) suggest that psychologically stressful situations move the type 1/type 2 cytokine balance in favour of the type 2 response which results in an immune dysregulation that may increase viral infections, allergic/asthmatic reactions and autoimmunity responses reported during periods of high stress.

This may go some way to explain why after the exam, when arousal drops, the immune system is compromised and therefore is vulnerable to surrounding viruses and bacteria.

Clearly, examinations and oral presentations have a psychological and physiological impact, but they remain firmly established in most universities as a mode of assessment. Looking on the bright side, taking exams under pressure is a feature of your degree which demonstrates how well you can deal with stressful situations. This may be valuable to future employers. Think of it as a transferable skill.

Many other methods are used to assess anxiety levels, with varying degrees of success (Haller & Alicki, 2012).

marketplace, e.g. litigation as a result of stress in the workplace or stress management courses.

What is Stress?

Stress has been recognized for centuries (Table 23.1) but despite its longevity, stress is a tricky concept to pin down in terms of a definition.

> Everybody knows what stress is and nobody knows what it is. The word stress, like success, failure or happiness, means different things to different people and, except for a few specialised scientists, no one has really tried to define it although it has become part of our daily vocabulary. (Selye, 1973, p.692)

Whilst this is an accurate statement, it is not entirely helpful, but it does highlight the contrast between folk understanding of terms and the scientific necessity for a specific definition. Thus, stress is the state produced by a stressor, and a stressor is what produces stress. This is somewhat circular and reminiscent of the quote about intelligence being what intelligence tests measure.

TABLE 23.1 *Stress and homeostasis: the slow evolution of a definition*

Author	Definition
Empedocles (500–430 BC)	First written reference to homeostasis
Hippocrates (460–375 BC)	Health is the state of the harmonious balance of the elements, and disease is the state of disharmony
Epicurus (341–270 BC)	Coping with emotional stressors improves the quality of life
Claude Bernard (1813–1878)	*Milieu interieur*
Walter Cannon (1871–1945)	'Fight or flight' reaction and 'homeostasis' of internal environment
Hans Selye (1907–1982)	General adaptation syndrome

Source: Johnson, E. O., Kamilaris, T. C., Chrousos, G. P., & Gold, P. W. (1992). Mechanisms of stress: A dynamic overview of hormonal and behavioral homeostasis. *Neuroscience and Biobehavioral Reviews, 16*(2), 115–130.

Definitions trying to identify stress also identify the stress response. In describing the stress response, definitions are hypothesizing about the function of the stress response. Therefore stress as a small word encompasses the stressor, the response and its adaptive nature. Cannon (1929) was the first to use the term 'hom(o)eostasis' in 1925 at the Congress of American Physicians and Surgeons.

The definition of **homeostasis** is somewhat clearer than that of stress.

> The highly developed living being is an open system having many relations to its surroundings – in the respiratory and alimentary tracts and through surface receptors, neuromuscular organs and bony levers . . . Changes in the surroundings excite reactions in this system, or affect it directly, so that internal disturbances of the system are produced. Such disturbances are normally kept within narrow limits, because automatic adjustments within the system are brought into action, and thereby wide oscillations are prevented and the internal conditions are held fairly constant. The term 'equilibrium' might be used to designate these constant conditions. (Cannon, 1929, p.400)

Indeed, the father of the academic study of stress, Hans Selye, discussed many areas in which there was confusion about the stress concept (Selye, 1976). According to Selye (1974), stress was not . . .

- . . . simply nervous tension; it can occur in organisms without nervous systems;
- an emergency discharge of hormones from the adrenal medulla; even though catecholamines are a part of the stress reaction, they are not the only hormones activated;
- . . . everything that causes a secretion of the adrenal gland, e.g. adrenocorticotrophic hormone (ACTH) can stimulate the release of corticoids without producing a stress response;
- . . . always the non-specific result of damage; normal activities can produce a stress response without damage;
- . . . the same as a deviation from homeostasis; reactions, e.g. to loud noises, may cause deviations from the resting state without a generalized stress reaction;
- . . . anything that causes an alarm reaction; it is the stressor that is the stimulus, not the stress itself;
- . . . identical with the alarm reaction; these reactions are characterized by certain end-organ changes caused by stress and, hence, cannot be stress;
- . . . a non-specific reaction; the stress response itself is specific but the causes and effects may vary;
- . . . necessarily bad; the stress of success, challenge and creativity is positive, whereas that of failure, anxiety and infection can be negative;
- . . . to be avoided: stress is ubiquitous and unavoidable.

Selye defined stress as 'the non-specific response of the body to any demand. A stressor is an agent that

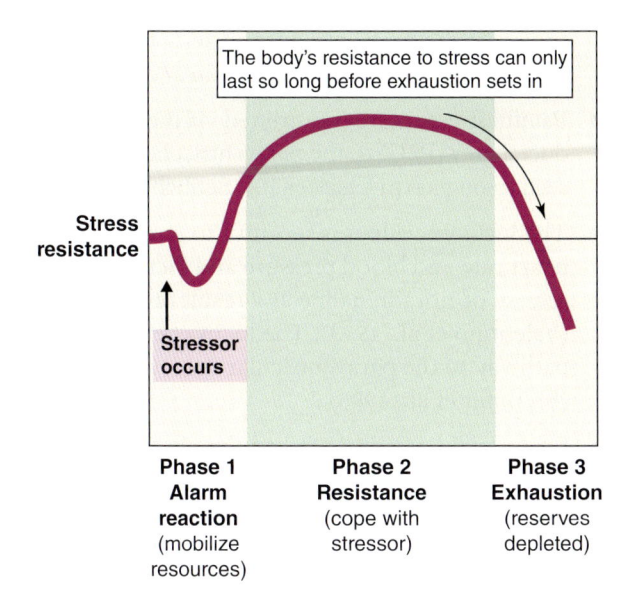

FIGURE 23.1 *Selye's general adaptation syndrome. There are three consecutive phases to the stress response.*
Source: Based on Selye, H. (1950). Stress and the general adaptation syndrome. *British Medical Journal*, 1(4667), 1383–1392.

produces stress at any time' (Selye, 1976, p.53). Selye was the first to identify the psychobiological impact of stress. In 1936 he identified a non-specific response to noxious agents (later referred to as stressors). He called this the **general adaptation syndrome**. The stressors, e.g. cold or excessive muscular exercise, lead to a three-stage process (Figure 23.1).

1. The general alarm reaction which occurs in the first 6–48 hours and is characterized by numerous physiological changes (flight/fight physiology).
2. Resistance, which occurs from approximately 48 hours after the stressor and if continued in a mild form, the body adapts to a point where there is no discernible difference.
3. If the stress continues, this leads to exhaustion and there is no longer any resistance and therefore the initial stress response is evident. Continuation of this stage leads to stress as a pathological state.

With the identification of these three stages, Selye (1936) states:

> Since the syndrome, as a whole, seems to represent a generalized effort of the organism to adapt itself to new conditions, it might be termed the general adaptation syndrome. It might be compared to other general defence reactions such as inflammation or the formation of immune bodies, (p.32)

thus highlighting the evolutionary importance of this response.

Other definitions include identification of stressors and a series of physiological changes that make up the stress response leading to a return of homeostasis.

> Stress can be defined as a state of threatened homeostasis or disharmony. An intricate repertoire of physiologic and behavioral responses is mobilized under stressful situations forming the adaptive stress response that aims to re-establish the challenged body equilibrium. (Kyrou & Tsigos, 2007, p.430).

Kim and Diamond (2002) provide a three-point definition of stress.

1. Stress requires heightened excitability or arousal, which can be operationally measured using an electroencephalogram (EEG), behavioural activity or neurochemicals (thus it can be objectively measured).
2. Stress must also be perceived as aversive. Arousal *per se* can increase under either pleasurable or aversive conditions.
3. Controllability. Control over an aversive experience has a profound mitigating influence on how stressful the experience feels; if one feels in control than one is less likely to experience stress.

Control and the perception of the threat are interrelated with unpredictability and uncontrollability in the face of life-threatening stressors being regarded as the real definition of stress (Figure 23.2) (Koolhaas et al., 2011).

The Stress Response

Stress can be produced by external or internal events (see Table 23.2). Sensory pathways transmit information regarding the stressor to the brain. At the centre of the body's response to stress is the hypothalamus because it is responsible for restoring homeostatic balance. The **paraventricular nucleus** of the hypothalamus is particularly important in mediating the stress response as this is a point of convergence of sensory information regarding stressors and co-ordinates endocrine and autonomic responses (Benarroch, 2005; Swanson & Sawchenko, 1980) (Table 23.2).

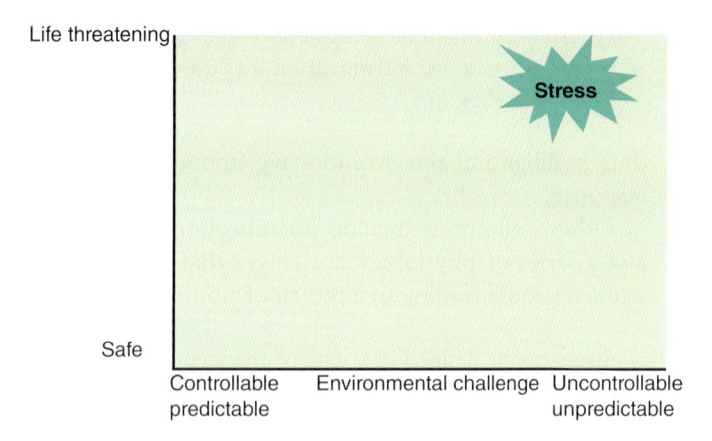

FIGURE 23.2 Graphic presentation of the relationship between the controllability and predictability of environmental challenges and the life-threatening nature of these challenges.
Source: Koolhaas, J. M., Bartolomucci, A., Buwalda, B., de Boer, S. F., et al. (2011). Stress revisited: A critical evaluation of the stress concept. *Neuroscience & Biobehavioral Reviews*, 35(5), 1291–1301.

Input of the Stress Response

Different stressors enter sensory processes via different pathways.

- The vagus nerve provides information about internal stressors to the nucleus of the solitary tract in the medulla which transmits information regarding stress to the periventricular nucleus (Larsen & Mikkelsen, 1995).

- Somatosensory stressors are mediated via the tegmentum and the reticular formation which also project to the paraventricular nucleus, thus sending sensory information about the skin and the muscles.

- Painful stressors are transmitted via the periaqueductal grey (PAG) to the paraventricular nucleus (see section on pain in Chapter 10) (Behbehani, 1995).

- The locus coeruleus is sensitive to changes in heart rate and blood pressure and increases the release of noradrenaline as a result of stressors (Valentino et al., 1993). The locus coeruleus has a pathway to the paraventricular nucleus (Bremner et al., 1996).

- Emotional stressors, e.g. handling in the rat and forced swimming, can be mediated via the raphe system that projects to the paraventricular nucleus (Abrams et al., 2004; Adell et al., 1997).

- The hippocampus, septum and amygdala are also involved in stress responses to emotional and cognitive input (Herman et al., 2005). The amygdala releases **corticotrophin-releasing hormone** (CRH), which activates the autonomic and endocrine systems (Merali et al., 1998). The activation of these systems mobilizes energy for a fight or flight response. The route of information from the limbic system to the paraventricular nucleus is thought to be via the **bed nucleus of the stria terminalis** (Cullinan et al., 1993; Herman et al., 1994). However, the involvement of the bed nucleus of the stria terminalis is thought to mediate slower onset responses to prolonged threat rather than the acute reaction (Walker et al., 2003).

TABLE 23.2 Behavioural and physical adaptation during acute stress

Behavioural adaptation – adaptive redirection of behaviour	Physical adaptation – adaptive redirection of energy
Increased arousal and alertness	Oxygen and nutrients directed to the central nervous system and stressed body site(s)
Increased cognition, vigilance and focused attention	Altered cardiovascular tone, increased blood pressure and heart rate
Euphoria or dysphoria	Increased respiratory rate
Suppression of appetite and feeding behaviour	Increased gluconeogenesis and lipolysis
Suppression of reproductive behaviour	Detoxification from endogenous or exogenous toxic products
Containment of the stress response	Inhibition of growth and reproductive systems
	Inhibition of digestion and stimulation of colonic motility
	Containment of the inflammatory/immmune response Containment of the stress response

Source: Chrousos, G. P. (1998). Stressors, stress, and neuroendocrine integration of the adaptive response: The 1997 Hans Selye Memorial Lecture. *Annals of the New York Academy of Sciences*, 851, 311–335. Reproduced by permission of John Wiley & Sons.

Thus, the paraventricular nucleus receives information about stressors presenting an immediate physiological threat via brainstem catecholamine projections, and stressors requiring more cognitive processing arrive through limbic circuits passing through the bed nucleus of the stria terminalis to connect with the paraventricular nucleus (Herman & Cullinan, 1997).

The stressor evokes a response via the sympathetic adrenomedullary axis and the **hypothalamic-pituitary-adrenocortical axis** (HPA axis) (Figure 23.3).

Sympathetic-adrenomedullary axis (SAM)

Activation of the locus coeruleus in response to a stressor is rapid and leads to activation of the sympathetic nervous system (SNS), producing a release of adrenaline, noradrenaline (NA) and stress hormones. Adrenaline interacts with glucose, allowing more energy to be released, and adrenaline and NA increase blood flow and heart rate. Behaviourally, activation of the locus

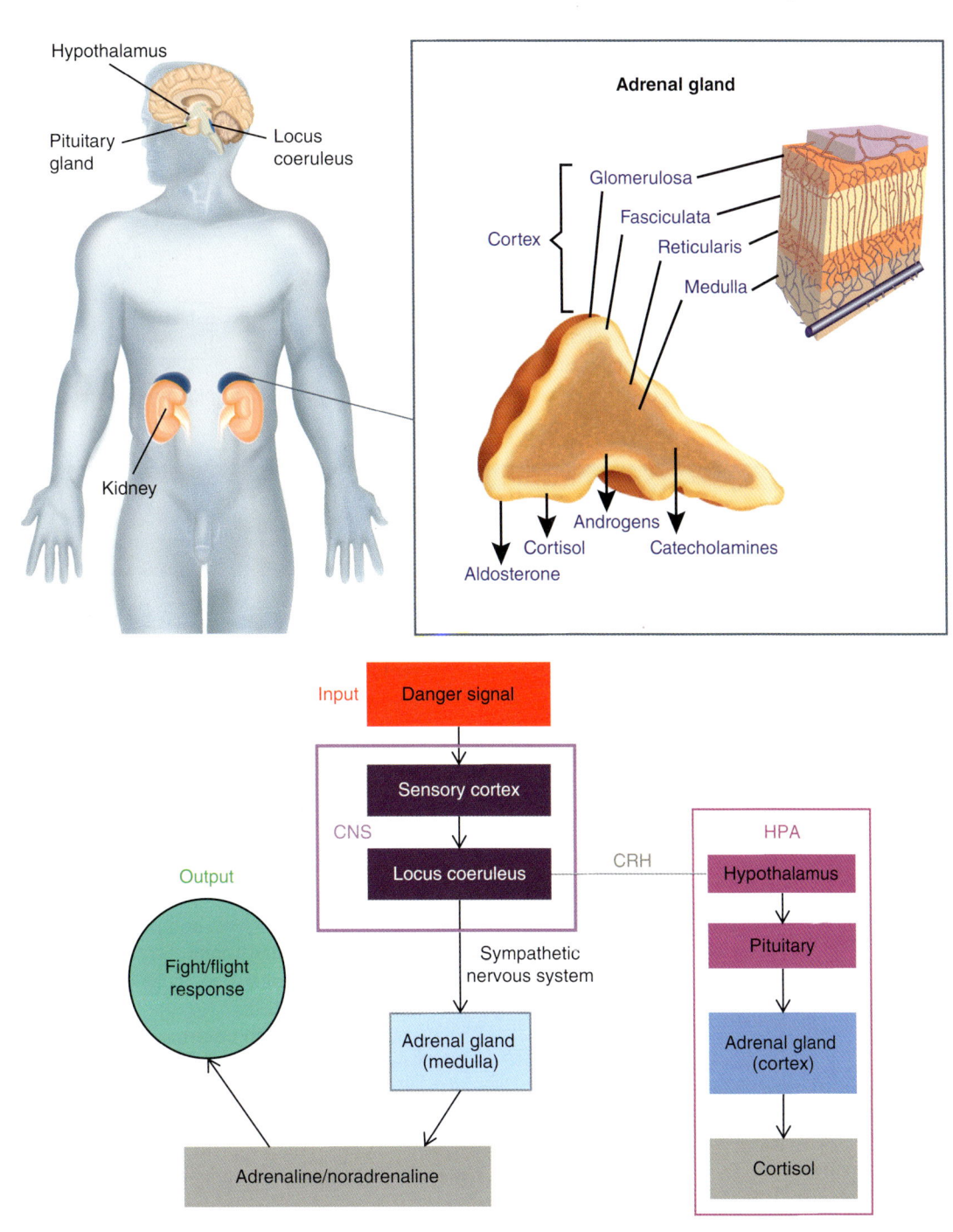

FIGURE 23.3 *Sympathetic-adrenomedullary axis.*

coeruleus results in an increase in arousal and vigilance (Aston-Jones et al., 1999). Thus, the organism is prepared to respond rapidly and effectively to the stressor.

Hypothalamic-pituitary-adrenocortical axis

The paraventricular nucleus activates the HPA axis (Figure 23.4). When excited, it releases CRH, which then enters the pituitary gland and is transported to the anterior portion of the pituitary gland where it stimulates ACTH. ACTH stimulates the cortex of the adrenal gland (sitting above the kidney), leading to the synthesis and release of glucocorticoids. In the rat, the main glucocorticoid is corticosteroid and in the human it is cortisol. Cortisol is readily measured in saliva. The glucocorticoids increase the availability of blood glucose, providing the energy required during stress. Furthermore, they inhibit resource-hungry systems such as the immune system. The glucocorticoids target various sites of action because of the long-distance effects of the endocrine system. The effects of CRH in the brain are widespread, facilitating the response to the stressor (Box 23.2). The presence of CRH

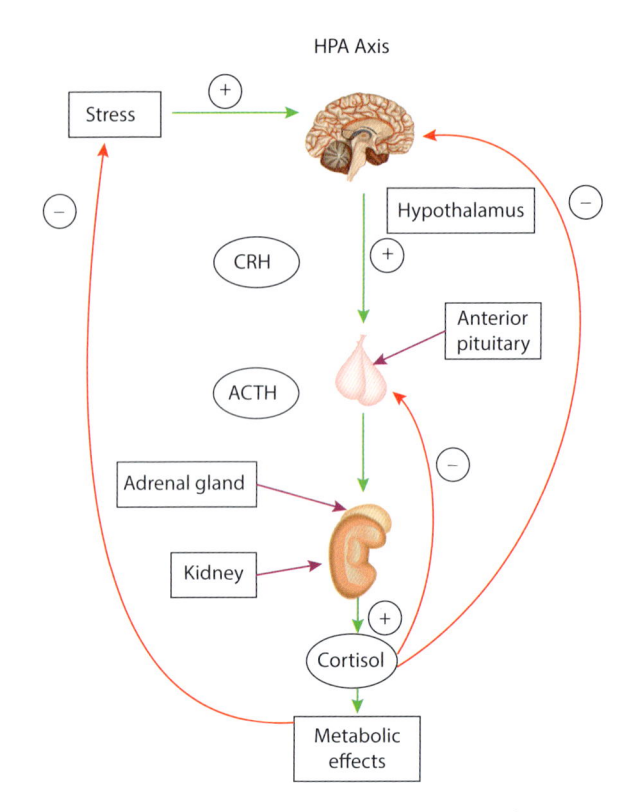

FIGURE 23.4 *Hypothalamic-pituitary-adrenocortical axis.*

BOX 23.2: STRESS AND THE HPA AXIS: CO-CONSPIRATORS IN THE ADDICTION PROCESS

Stress is an adaptive system that evolution has provided to ensure survival. However, stress can become maladaptive and lead to serious pathological and psychopathological problems. This is the arena in which health psychologists mostly work.

Stress is a word we use without having a full appreciation of the underlying mechanisms and damage that it can do. According to Rushen (1986):

> Stress is one of those terms that we use to shield us from our ignorances. We would be better off without it. It survives because it is a convenient term to indicate a general topic under discussion. Attempts to provide such a vague concept with a precise physiological and psychological definition engender confusion and misunderstanding. (p.359)

The stress response involves mobilizing resources or conserving energy in an attempt to deal with the stressor.

- Increased immediate availability of energy.
- Increased oxygen intake.
- Decreased blood flow to areas not necessary for movement.
- Inhibition of digestion, growth, immune function, reproduction and pain perception.
- Enhancement of memory and sensory fluctuation.

The endocrine mechanism at the core of the stress response is the HPA axis. This involves the hypothalamus releasing CRH, which activates CRh R1 receptors of the anterior pituitary gland, which then releases ACTH which in turn acts on the adrenal glands to secrete cortisol. Cortisol spreads throughout the body, communicating with multiple organs, and prepares the organism to respond to potential threat. Stress increases cortisol release, as can be measured by salivary cortisol levels (Kirschbaum et al., 1995).

Combat veterans with **post-traumatic stress disorder (PTSD)** have been shown to have higher levels of substance abuse (Helzer, 1984; Jelinek & Williams, 1984; McFall et al., 1992). Therefore, it is reasonable to consider that stress is involved in the different processes of addiction. Indeed, stress is an important component in a number of theoretical accounts of addiction (Koob & Le Moal, 2006). Stress and the HPA axis have both been shown to be involved in cocaine

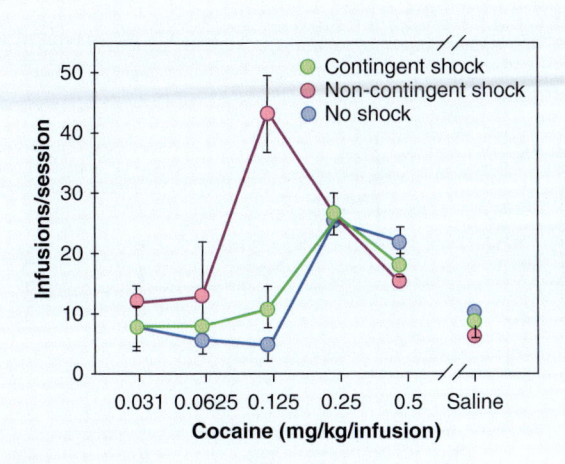

FIGURE 23.2.1 The effects of contingent and non-contingent shock.
Source: Adapted from Goeders, N. E., & Guerin, G. F. (1994). Non-contingent electric footshock facilitates the acquisition of intravenous cocaine self-administration in rats. *Psychopharmacology (Berlin), 114*(1), 63–70. With kind permission from Springer Science and Business Media.

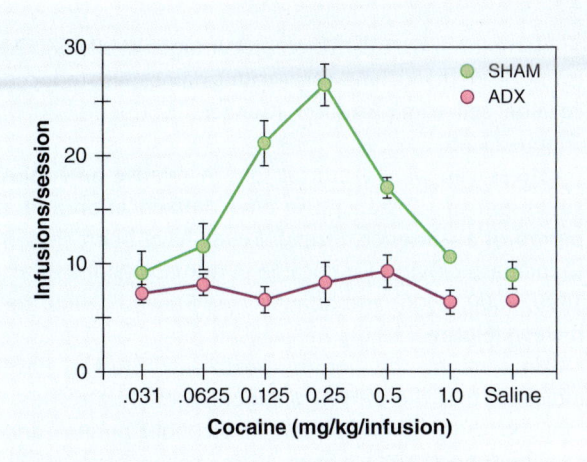

FIGURE 23.2.3 The effects of adrenalectomy on cocaine self-administration. ADX, adrenalectomized; SHAM, sham control surgery.
Source: Goeders, N. E., & Guerin, G. F. (1996). Effects of surgical and pharmacological adrenalectomy on the initiation and maintenance of intravenous cocaine self-administration in rats. *Brain Research, 722*(1-2), 145–152.

self-administration in the rat. Cocaine self-administration is an operant technique in which the rat performs a task in order to get an infusion of cocaine (see Chapter 8).

Goeders and Guerin (1994) demonstrated that the stressful delivery of an electric shock increased the acquisition of cocaine self-administration in the rat (Figure 23.2.1). Furthermore, the administration of corticosteroid to the rat also enhanced the acquisition of cocaine self-administration (Goeders & Guerin, 1996b) (Figure 23.2.2) although this was not found for metamphetamine (Moffett & Goeders, 2005), which warrants further investigation. Rather than promote the acquisition of cocaine self-administration by enhancing the stress system, Goeders and Guerin (1996a) performed an adrenalectomy (the removal of the adrenal glands) on the rats and found that it inhibited the acquisition of cocaine self-administration (Figure 23.2.3). Thus, we have data suggesting that stress affects the acquisition of drug taking, or at least cocaine.

Once the habit (or task) of cocaine self-administration has been learned, stress also conspires to maintain drug consumption. Using a benzodiazepine agonist which is used to treat anxiety and therefore stress, Goeders (1997) demonstrated a dose-dependent reduction in cocaine self-administration. By inhibiting corticosterone synthesis, ketoconazole reduces cocaine self-administration in rats (Goeders et al., 1998) (Figure 23.2.4). In a

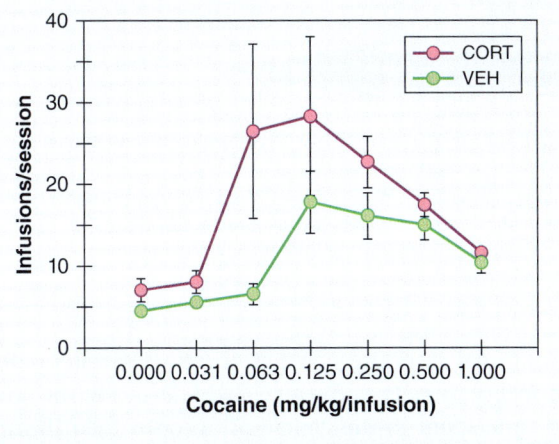

FIGURE 23.2.2 The effects of corticosterone on cocaine self-administration. CORT, corticosterone; VEH, vehicle.
Source: Goeders, N. E., & Guerin, G. F. (1996). Role of corticosterone in intravenous cocaine self-administration in rats. *Neuroendocrinology, 64*(5), 337–348. Copyright © 1996 Karger Publishers, Basel, Switzerland.

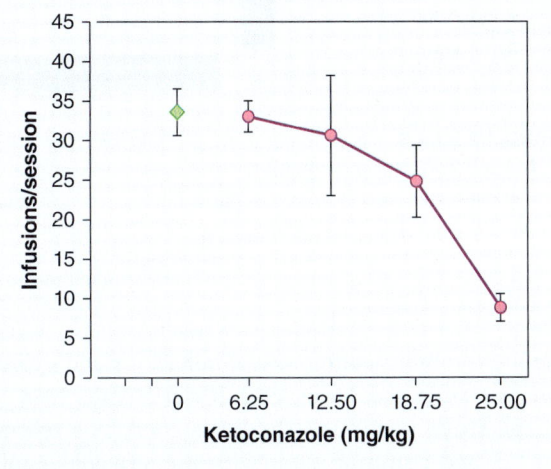

FIGURE 23.2.4 The effects of the corticosterone synthesis inhibitor ketoconazole on cocaine self-administration.
Source: Goeders, N. E., Peltier, R. L., & Guerin, G. F. (1998). Ketoconazole reduces low dose cocaine self-administration in rats. *Drug and Alcohol Dependence, 53*(1), 67–77.

similar manner, the CRH R1 receptor antagonist CP-154,526 (some drugs do not have very exciting names) also reduced cocaine self-administration (Goeders & Guerin, 2000) (Figure 23.2.5).

Stress can play a crucial role in relapse and reinstatement of substance use after detoxification and a period of abstinence. Stressful cues have been shown to increase craving for cocaine in humans (Sinha et al., 1999, 2000, 2006) and animals (see Stewart (2000) for review) (Figure 23.2.6).

How might this inform treatment? Studies have indicated that the CRH R1 antagonists attenuate stress-induced drug administration in alcohol-, heroin- and cocaine-trained rats (Le et al., 2000; Shaham et al., 1998). Arguably, the science indicates that in order to be successful at abstinence, one needs to be taught effective stress management.

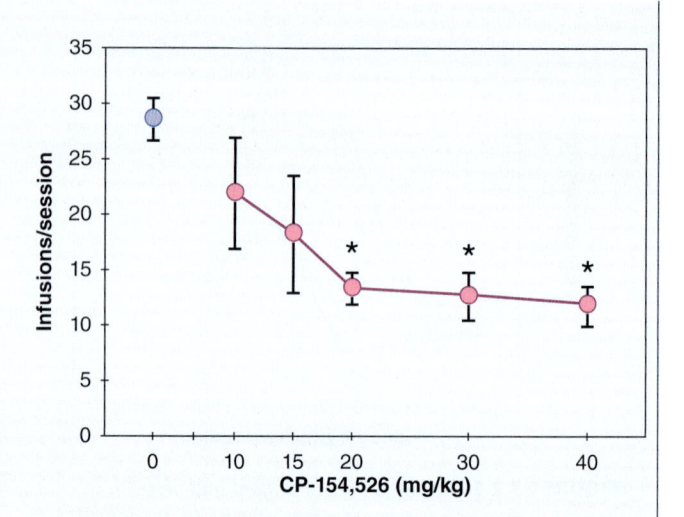

FIGURE 23.2.5 *The effects of the CRH antagonist CP154,526 on cocaine self-administration.*
Source: Reproduced by permission from Macmillan Publishers Ltd: NEUROPSYCHOPHARMACOLOGY Goeders, N. E., & Guerin, G. F. (2000). Effects of the CRH receptor antagonist CP-154,526 on intravenous cocaine self-administration in rats. Neuropsychopharmacology, 23(5), 577-586 copyright 2000.

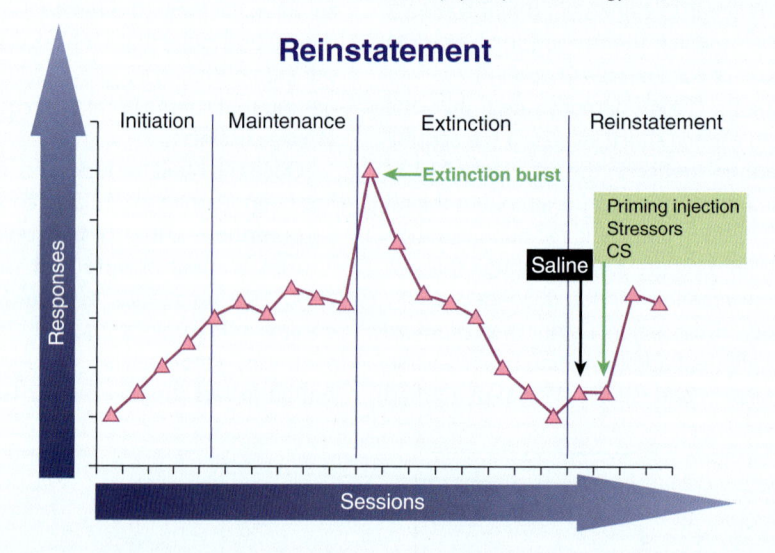

FIGURE 23.2.6 *The effects of stress, priming injections and conditioned stimuli on response rate in drug self installation studies. CS, conditioned stimulus.*
Source: Adapted from Stewart, J. (2000). Pathways to relapse: the neurobiology of drug- and stress-induced relapse to drug-taking. Journal of Psychiatry & Neuroscience, 25(2), 125-136. © Canadian Medical Association 2000. This work is protected by copyright and the making of this copy was with the permission of Access Copyright. Any alteration of its content or further copying in any form whatsoever is strictly prohibited unless otherwise permitted by law.

in the brain inhibits eating, sexual behaviour and growth (Ferin, 1995; Olster & Ferin, 1987; Rivier & Vale, 1984).

If the stress continues, the locus coeruleus releases more NA and communicates with the amygdala, causing more CRH to be released, and a vicious circle begins (Sapolsky, 2003). The behavioural response to administration of CRH is consistent with the brain's reaction to aversive stimuli, where CRH enhances a conditioned emotional response (Cole & Koob, 1988). In an animal model of anxiety and stress, CRH decreases the amount of time spent in the centre of an open field (Britton et al., 1982). To provide symmetry to the data, blockade of CRH prevented stress in rats (Heinrichs et al., 1992).

The paraventricular nucleus and the locus coeruleus work together in a positive feedback loop facilitating the stress response. Activation of the paraventricular nucleus and the release of CRH increases activity in the locus coeruleus; similarly, activation of the locus coeruleus and the release of noradrenaline activates the paraventricular nucleus (Calogero et al., 1988; Valentino et al., 1993).

Regulation of the HPA after a stress response is via a negative feedback loop. Released glucocorticoids bind with receptors within the pituitary gland, producing activation. The activation of these neurons produces inhibition of the paraventricular nucleus which normally produces CRH and the release of ACTH which should bring the levels back to normal.

To evaluate the responsiveness of the HPA system, the **dexamethasone** suppression test can be used. Dexamethasone is a synthetic glucocorticoid mimicking the endogenous ligands, thereby inhibiting the release of glucocorticoids. In a healthy individual, cortisol is suppressed following the administration of dexamethasone (hence dexamethasone suppression test). However, patients with depression and schizophrenia, for example, show an impaired response to dexamethasone with increasing cortisol (Heuser et al., 1994).

After the stressor is removed, the systems revert to normal. However, stress can continue for a period of time beyond the acute response. Chronic stress, like the exposure to chronic drug administration, leads to adaptations in the stress regulating systems. Exposure to chronic stress in the rat leads to changes in the responsiveness of the locus coeruleus. Through repetitive exposure to the stressor, the locus coeruleus becomes habituated as measured by a decrease in the firing rate and release of noradrenaline (Pavcovich et al., 1990). In contrast, others have found an increased sensitized response to chronic stress in which the locus coeruleus is more active (Melia et al., 1992; Nisenbaum et al., 1991). These results can be reconciled as a decrease in activity of the locus coeruleus can lead to long-term adaptations resulting in increased sensitivity to subsequent exposures. Furthermore, habituation may occur to the same stressor whereas sensitization can occur to a novel stressor. According to Bremner et al. (1996):

> Exposure to chronic stress results in long-term alterations in locus coeruleus firing and norepinephrine [noradrenaline] release in target brain regions of the locus coeruleus. Norepinephrine is also involved in neural mechanisms such as sensitization and fear conditioning, which are associated with stress. These findings are relevant to an understanding of psychiatric disorders, such as panic disorder and post-traumatic stress disorder (PTSD), the symptoms of which have been hypothesized to be related to alterations in noradrenergic function. (p.28)

Within the HPA axis the negative feedback loop can become impaired. Interruption of the feedback loop results in glucocorticoid circulating in the bloodstream and not turning off the neurons of the paraventricular nucleus. With inhibition of the paraventricular nucleus, CRH and ACTH are released, leading to high levels of stress hormones being maintained for a long period of time.

The impact of elevated concentrations of glucocorticoids is most notable in the hippocampus. Chronic stress leads to atrophy of the dendritic projections of the pyramidal neurons in the hippocampus. In humans, Cushing's syndrome is characterized by an overproduction of cortisol due to a tumour in the pituitary gland. If cortisol levels are high then it should follow that there will be damage to the hippocampus. Indeed, magnetic resonance imaging (MRI) studies have demonstrated hippocampal damage in this patient group (Starkman et al., 1999). Continuing investigations of the hippocampus also demonstrate that people with PTSD have reduced hippocampal volume, although direct causality of cortisol cannot be verified (Villarreal et al., 2002). Reduced hippocampal volume was also predictive of a poor response to stress (Gilbertson et al., 2002).

Damage to the hippocampus further alters glucocorticoid feedback mechanisms via disinhibition of the paraventricular nucleus (Herman et al., 1992). Disinhibition of the paraventricular nucleus permits CRH to be released and continues the vicious cycle of the chronic stress response.

Homeostasis Versus Allostasis (Acute Versus Chronic Stress)

Cannon (1929) introduced the idea of homeostasis to describe the process of ensuring stability within biological systems. The short-term goal of homeostasis to bring about equilibrium within biological systems was integrated into Selye's (1950) account of stress. For many systems, homeostasis works, e.g. temperature. However, according to Selye (1956):

> Natural homeostatic mechanisms are usually sufficient to maintain a normal state of resistance. When faced with unusually heavy demands, however, ordinary homeostasis is not enough. The 'thermostat of defense' must be raised to a higher level. For this process, Selye proposed the term 'heterostasis' (from the Greek *heteros* = other) as the establishment of a new steady state by treatment with agents which stimulate the physiological adaptive mechanisms through the development of normally dormant defensive tissue reactions. Both homeostasis and heterostasis, the milieu interior participates actively. (p.85)

Thus, for long-term survival it is essential to reset the homeostatic systems. Moore-Ede (1986) used the

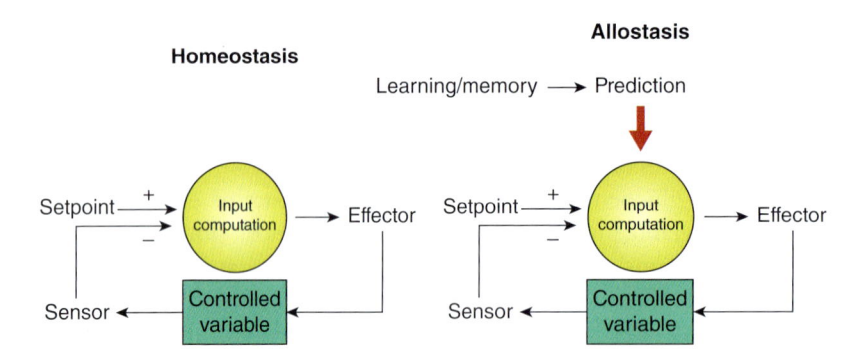

FIGURE 23.5 Homeostasis and allostasis. Homeostasis maintains a setpoint by adjusting variables when there is a mismatch of input computation. Allostasis changes the control variable by prediction of requirements and overriding local feedback to meet future demands.
Source: Sterling, P. (2003). Principles of allostasis: Optimal design, predictive regulation, pathophysiology, and rational therapeutics. In J. Schulkin (Ed.), *Allostasis, Homeostasis, and the costs of physiological adaptation.* Cambridge: Cambridge University Press.

term **'predictive homeostasis'** to account for anticipatory adaptations as opposed to the simple **reactive homeostasis** in which there is no anticipation of future demands.

The idea of **allostasis** was introduced by Sterling and Eyer (1988) to account for changes in physiology and adaptation to future events (see Figure 23.5 and Table 23.3 for a comparison with homeostasis). Greek *allo* means variable and *stasis* means stability, therefore allostasis is about achieving stability through physiological or behavioural change. Allostasis takes into account that:

- setpoints can be variable;
- there are individual differences;
- behaviour and physiological responses can be anticipatory (but they need not be); and
- there is a vulnerability to overloading physiological systems.

According to Sterling and Eyer (1988), there are three distinguishable meanings associated with allostasis.

- Allostasis – the process by which an organism achieves stability through bodily change.

- **Allostatic state** – the chronic overactivation of systems and the alteration of setpoints.
- **Allostatic load** – the expression of pathophysiology by long-term chronic overactivation of systems (Figure 23.6).

Allostasis is linked to the neural regulation of behaviour and systemic physiological systems. Thus, demands upon physiological systems guide behaviour. Key to allostasis is the anticipatory regulation which serves an adaptive function for the long-term viability of the organism. Being able to adapt to the demands of the environment is essential for survival. Those demands by far exceed normal setpoints as suggested by the concept of homeostasis.

The pathophysiology of allostatic load represents the wear and tear of the organism. Perceived or real threats to homeostasis initiate the SAM axis and HPA axis in order to respond to the threat. The acute activation of these systems is adaptive but chronic overactivation in response to long-term stressors leads to biological systems overcompensating to the point at which they eventually collapse. When this occurs the organism is susceptible to stress-related diseases (Juster et al., 2010).

TABLE 23.3 *Homeostasis versus allostasis*

Homeostasis	Allostasis
Normal setpoint	Changing setpoint
Physiological equilibrium	Compensated equilibrium
No anticipation of demand	Anticipation of demand
No adjustments based on physiological history	Adjustment based on physiological history
Adjustment carries no additional price	Adjustment and accommodation carry an additional price
No pathology	Pathology

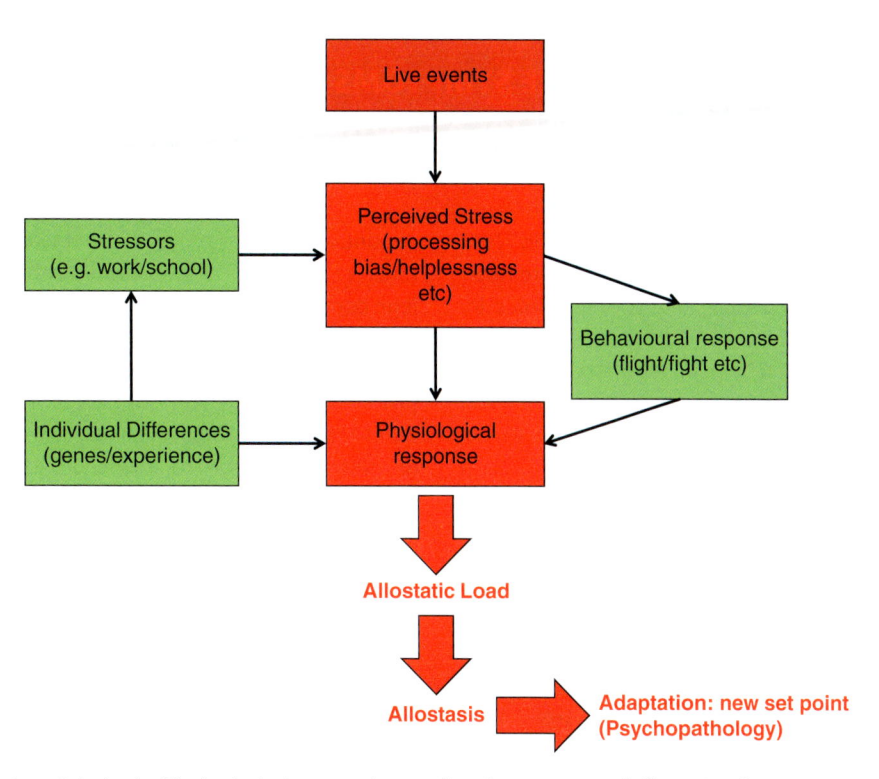

```
                    ┌─────────────┐
                    │ Live events │
                    └──────┬──────┘
                           ↓
   ┌──────────────┐   ┌─────────────┐
   │  Stressors   │──→│Perceived Stress│
   │(e.g. work/   │   │(processing  │
   │  school)     │   │bias/helplessness│──┐
   └──────┬───────┘   │    etc)     │  │
          ↑           └──────┬──────┘  ↓
          │                  │    ┌─────────────┐
   ┌──────┴───────┐          │    │Behavioural response│
   │Individual Differences│  │    │(flight/fight etc)│
   │(genes/experience)│───→┌─┴──────────┐←┘
   └──────────────┘        │Physiological│
                           │  response  │
                           └──────┬─────┘
                                  ↓
                          Allostatic Load
                                  ↓
                     Allostasis →  Adaptation: new set point
                                   (Psychopathology)
```

FIGURE 23.6 *Allostasis and the brain. The brain is the central controller of responses and allostatic adaptations to stress.*

Allostatic overload is argued to reflect four types of allodynamic and physiological responses arising from:

- repetitive hits of the stressor;
- reduced adaptation;
- prolonged stress response with little recovery; and
- inadequate response leading to compensatory hyperactivity of other systems (McEwen & Gianaros, 2011).

Additionally, neural changes as a result of chronic stress and the impact of allostatic load reduce the cognitive processing and physiological responses to stressors (McEwen, 2000). The changes lead to an allostatic state that is a substantial deviation from the original normal state. The systems have essentially recalibrated. The hippocampus, amygdala and prefrontal cortex have all been shown to be adaptive in the face of chronic stress (McEwen & Gianaros, 2011). Chronic stress remodels the structure of the hippocampus which affects memory systems and the activity of the HPA axis. The hippocampus is no longer able to turn off the HPA axis response and therefore heightened levels of glucocorticoids remain in the system. In the amygdala changes are different from those of the hippocampus; chronic stress increases dendritic growth and remodelling in the amygdala, leading to the emotional reaction (Vyas et al., 2002). The prefrontal cortex when chronically exposed to glucocorticoids has been shown to have reduced volume which may be linked to impairments in cognition (McEwen & Gianaros, 2011).

Neuronal adaptations in response to chronic stress and communication with other physiological systems mediating the stress response lead to a recalibration of stress systems, making individuals more susceptible to future stressors and other ailments. Under conditions of normal stress, e.g. fear, changes in physiology are adaptive but if these adaptations continue they can manifest as chronic anxiety. The effect of overload is metabolically expensive because the organism is in a constant state of expectation of adversity (Rosen & Schulkin, 2003).

ANXIETY

Extreme stress can lead to anxiety disorders. PTSD was once considered under the banner of anxiety disorders within DSM IV but is now considered within DSM 5 in a chapter entitled 'Trauma- and stressor-related disorders' (Box 23.3). Anxiety disorders are the most prevalent psychiatric conditions in the population (Andlin-Sobocki et al., 2005). The epidemiology of anxiety disorders is not straightforward due to the splitting of the diagnostic criteria into subgroups. Lifetime prevalence of anxiety disorders in general and specific phobias is in the 6–12% range (Kessler et al., 2010). Across nations the prevalence

BOX 23.3: VICARIOUS PTSD-LIKE SYMPTOMS: 9/11 NEW YORK'S WORLD TRADE CENTRE ATTACKS AND 7 JULY ATTACKS, LONDON 2005

The terrorist attacks on the World Trade Center in New York and the Pentagon in Washington on 11 September 2001, killing thousands of people, are firmly imprinted in my memory. I was not in New York at the time; I was not even in America, I was watching TV reports in Brighton, UK. The news reports and television footage were constantly replayed to the entire world. The images made harrowing and distressing viewing.

Elevated levels of cortisol were measured in high-exposure 9/11 survivors (Dekel et al., 2013; Pfeffer et al., 2009). Children who lost a parent in the attacks showed increased levels of PTSD and cortisol (Pfeffer et al., 2007). Genetic expression was altered in the HPA axis, signal transduction or in brain and immune cell function (Sarapas et al., 2011; Yehuda et al., 2009).

Not surprisingly, those living in Manhattan had increased likelihood of suffering from PTSD and depression with an increase in cases the closer they were to the World Trade Center (Galea et al., 2002a). Two to three years after the attacks, 95.6% of survivors reported at least one current symptom of PTSD (DiGrande et al., 2011). The effects of PTSD and depression in the aftermath of 9/11 lead to an increase in the use of tobacco, alcohol and cannabis, perhaps as a form of self-medication (Vlahov et al., 2002). However, six months later, the rate of PTSD and depression declined without a concomitant decline in substance misuse (Vlahov et al., 2004). One might consider that the consumption of drugs in the aftermath was serving a function in terms of self-medication, or that substance misuse becomes a problem in its own right after the natural decline in PTSD and depression.

Many more people suffered from intrusive thoughts and insomnia that may lead to PTSD and depression (Galea et al., 2002b). Increased TV viewing was associated with more symptoms of PTSD, e.g. the bigger the dose of television, the higher the probability of PTSD (Ahern et al., 2004).

The role of the media has been implicated in the development of PTSD and depression in those who viewed the repetitive broadcasts of the attacks, in particular the frequent viewing of people falling or jumping from the World Trade Center towers (Ahern et al., 2002). At the one-year anniversary, increased TV viewing of the events was associated with a 3.4-fold increased risk of PTSD (Bernstein et al., 2007).

Across the United States between 14 and 16 September 2001, 44% of sampled Americans reported substantial stress symptoms and 90% had one or more symptoms of less severity (Schuster et al., 2001). For many, the symptoms continued with symptoms evident two months post 9/11 (Stein et al., 2004). Far away from Manhattan, an entire college community was assessed for the stress post 9/11. Of those responding to the survey, 76% exhibited substantial symptoms of stress indicating a vicarious stress reaction (Swenson & Henkel-Johnson, 2003). The closer a college was to New York, the more likely individuals were to suffer from stress disorders (Blanchard et al., 2004) and this continued one year later (Blanchard et al., 2005). Suvak et al. (2008) performed a factor analysis and identified four stress symptoms similar to PTSD in those with vicarious exposure to 9/11: re-experiencing, strategic avoidance, emotional numbing and hyperarousal symptoms.

Veterans with pre-existing PTSD were evaluated for changes in symptoms following 9/11 due to vicarious exposure to media. The effects of 9/11 increased some of their symptom impact upon their functioning; however, the authors argued that vicarious exposure to 9/11 events did not alter the course of their PTSD despite the patients' perceptions (Rosen et al., 2005).

A study looking at refugees from war-torn countries indicated a transient increase in the symptoms of PTSD in those with an earlier diagnosis. However, if the diagnosis was schizophrenia then there was no increase in symptoms (Kinzie et al., 2002). Thus, pre-exposure to trauma may lead to a transient increase in the stress reaction, but this does not last more than a few months.

During 2004–2005 the rates of PTSD in individuals who had indirect experience of 9/11 were diminished (Breslau et al., 2010). When assessing the distance from the attacks, 9/11-related stress responses were mild and transitory (Matt & Vazquez, 2008).

In London on 7 July 2005, terrorist attacks were conducted on London transport, killing 52 people and injuring hundreds more. The terrorist attacks on London, like those in New York, were witnessed by many via constant replay of television footage.

Rubin et al. (2005) found in an interview with Londoners that 31% experienced substantial stress relating to the attacks 11–13 days after the bombings. In a follow-up study interviewing Londoners over the telephone seven months later, 11% of those questioned reported substantial stress and 43% perceived a threat to themselves (Rubin et al., 2007).

The effects of the media have been evaluated in a study looking at national threat and terrorism in Israel (Slone, 2000). In this study participants were divided into two groups: one exposed to terrorist threat newsreels and the other exposed to newsreels that did not have terrorist threat material. In keeping with the studies on terrorism, those participants who were exposed to the terrorist threat newsreels displayed increased levels of anxiety.

The importance of the media in providing misinformation and increasing stress levels cannot be overestimated.

However, if government agencies use the media correctly by providing accurate and consistent information via different routes then anxiety levels may be somewhat reduced (Pearce et al., 2013; Rubin et al., 2012). Providing such information can offset the chance of mass hysteria developing (Wessely, 1987).

of PTSD differs widely, depending upon the level of violence experienced within a particular country, with those at war experiencing greater levels (Kessler et al., 2010). Anxiety and anxiety disorders (Boxes 23.4 and 23.5) are a maladaptive response to stress and fear leading to an unpleasant state of anticipation, apprehension, fear and dread. The maladaptive nature of anxiety disorders can be illustrated with arachnophobia (fear of spiders). In the UK the indigenous spider population is generally benign and therefore a phobia or extreme fear of spiders in the UK is

BOX 23.4: DSM IV-TR TO DSM 5 GENERALIZED ANXIETY DISORDER

The new DSM 5 has evolved from DSM IV-TR. It is important to see the changes as the literature currently reviewed rests on DSM IV-TR and earlier. Future research will use the DSM 5, but it may take some time for these papers to materialize. Differences in results over time may be explained by subtle changes in diagnostic criteria (the diagnostic criteria for DSM 5 are highlighted in italics).

DSM IV-TR

A. *Excessive anxiety and worry (apprehensive expectation), occurring more days than not for at least 6 months, about a number of events or activities (such as work or school performance).*
B. *The person finds it difficult to control the worry.*
C. The anxiety and worry are associated with three (or more) of the following six symptoms (with at least some symptoms present for more days than not for the past 6 months).

Note: *Only one item is required in children.*

  (1) *restlessness or feeling keyed up or on edge*
  (2) *being easily fatigued*
  (3) *difficulty concentrating or mind going blank*
  (4) *irritability*
  (5) *muscle tension*
  (6) *sleep disturbance (difficulty falling or staying asleep, or restless unsatisfying sleep)*

D. The focus of the anxiety and worry is not confined to features of an Axis I disorder, e.g. the anxiety or worry is not about having a Panic Attack (as in Panic Disorder), being embarrassed in public (as in Social Phobia), being contaminated (as in Obsessive-Compulsive Disorder), being away from home or close relatives (as in Separation Anxiety Disorder), gaining weight (as in Anorexia Nervosa), having multiple physical complaints (as in Somatization Disorder), or having a serious illness (as in Hypochondriasis), and the anxiety and worry do not occur exclusively during Post-traumatic Stress Disorder.
E. The anxiety, worry, or physical symptoms cause clinically significant distress or impairment in social, occupational, or other important areas of functioning.
F. The disturbance is not due to the direct physiological effects of a substance (e.g. a drug of abuse, a medication) or a general medical condition (e.g. hyperthyroidism) and does not occur exclusively during a Mood Disorder, a Psychotic Disorder, or a Pervasive Developmental Disorder.

Change for DSM 5

D. *The anxiety, worry, or physical symptoms cause clinically significant distress or impairment in social, occupational, or other important areas of functioning.*
E. *The disturbance is not attributable to the physiological effects of a substance (e.g. a drug of abuse, and medication) or another medical condition (e.g. hyperthyroidism).*

F. The disturbance is not better explained by another mental disorder (e.g. anxiety or worry about having panic attacks in Panic Disorder, negative evaluation in Social Anxiety Disorder [Social Phobia], contamination or other obsessions in Obsessive-Compulsive Disorder, separation from attachment figures in Separation Anxiety Disorder, reminders of traumatic events in Post-Traumatic Stress Disorder, gaining weight in Anorexia Nervosa, physical complaints in Somatic Symptoms Disorder, perceived appearance flaws in Body Dysmorphic Disorder, having a serious illness in Illness Anxiety Disorder, or the content of delusional beliefs in Schizophrenia or Delusional Disorder).

---

maladaptive. However, if you live in Australia, a fear of spiders has clear adaptive benefits for the population. Not all spiders in Australia are venomous, but there are some that can cause pain and damage so they are best avoided. A fear of spiders is therefore a useful survival mechanism in Australia. Similarly, hand washing is an important hygienic behaviour, but when it is excessive and involves scrubbing and damaging the tissue of the hands, leading to potential lesions of the skin that render the individual vulnerable to bacteria and infection, that is maladaptive (see Box 23.6 for an evolutionary account of anxiety).

The maladaptive response may be to real or imagined stresses or threats in which:

- responses are disproportionate to stress or threat;
- the stress or threat is non-existent, imaginary or misinterpreted;
- the symptoms interfere with adaptation or response to stress or threat; and
- the symptoms interfere with other life functions.

BOX 23.5: DSM 5 ANXIETY DISORDERS

Anxiety disorders

Separation Anxiety Disorder
Selective Mutism
Specific Phobia
Social Anxiety Disorder (Social Phobia)
Panic Disorder
Panic Attack (Specifier)
Agoraphobia
Generalized Anxiety Disorder
Substance/Medication-Induced Anxiety Disorder
Anxiety Disorder Due to Another Medical Condition
Other Specified Anxiety Disorder
Unspecified Anxiety Disorder

Obsessive-Compulsive and Related Disorders

Obsessive-Compulsive Disorder
Body Dysmorphic Disorder
Hoarding Disorder
Trichotillomania (Hair-Pulling Disorder)
Excoriation (Skin-Picking) Disorder
Substance/Medication-Induced Obsessive-Compulsive and Related Disorder
Obsessive-Compulsive and Related Disorder Due to Another Medical Condition
Other Specified Obsessive-Compulsive and Related Disorder
Unspecified Obsessive-Compulsive and Related Disorder

Trauma- and Stressor-Related Disorders

Reactive Attachment Disorder
Disinhibited Social Engagement Disorder
Post-traumatic Stress Disorder
Acute Stress Disorder
Adjustment Disorders
Other Specified Trauma- and Stressor-Related Disorder
Unspecified Trauma- and Stressor-Related Disorder

BOX 23.6: EVOLUTIONARY ACCOUNTS OF ANXIETY

Given the high prevalence of anxiety disorders in the population, one might consider that this is a maladaptive response to a once advantageous set of behaviours going back to our evolutionary past.

- Phobias may stem from an adaptive behaviour because they provoke fear reactions which may serve as a protective measure. Phobias can be acquired through direct conditioning and vicarious witnessing of phobic reactions in others.
- Panic disorder may arise from a false suffocation alarm.
- Agoraphobia can be seen as an exaggerated response to avoid open spaces in which there may be dangers.
- Obsessive-compulsive disorders, for example hand washing and checking, may be maladaptive harm-avoidance behaviours.

Bateson et al. (2011) describe the evolutionary functions of anxiety like responses (see Table 23.6.1), suggesting:

> It is also possible that some cases [of anxiety] represent appropriate adaptive responses to the situation in which the person currently finds him or herself. As a corollary, insufficient anxiety-proneness may be a commonly occurring dysfunction. However, as it is not associated with subjective distress, presumably the people affected do not present for treatment. (p.708)

Bateson et al. see anxiety as a shift in the signal detection problem. People with anxiety are considered to have unusually low thresholds for threat responses, thereby responding to many more false alarms (see Table 23.6.1).

In terms of being adaptive, anxiety-like responses should have been shaped by evolution for the following characteristics.

- Initiation of anxiety responses would not be fixed but instead modulated, depending on the individual's environment and current state.
- It would be more easily activated in environments where threats are more common.
- It would be more easily activated when individuals are vulnerable to undetected threats and do not have the resources to address potential threats.
- It will consist of a series of physiological, cognitive and behavioural changes that divert resources facilitating the detection of and response to threats.
- Even when functioning optimally, the system will produce many more false alarms than hits, and the greater the probability and vulnerability, the greater the ratio of false alarms to hits will be.

TABLE 23.6.1 *Symptoms of anxiety and their adaptive functions*

Symptom	Functional significance
Easily startled, hypersensitive to noise	Response to threat easily evoked
Insomnia	Constant alertness
Restlessness, increased heart rate	Body prepared for action
Attention diverted to cues related to threat	Notice threats earlier
Ambiguous information interpreted as threatening	Reduced likelihood of making a false-negative assessment and missing a possible threat
Ambiguity averse	Avoidance of situations where threat is uncertain

Source: Adapted from Bateson, M., Brilot, B., & Nettle, D. (2011). Anxiety: An evolutionary approach. *Canadian Journal of Psychiatry,* 56(12), 707–715. Reproduced by permission of the Canadian Psychiatric Association.

The physiological symptoms include the following.

- Diaphoresis (sweating)
- Diarrhoea
- Dizziness
- Flushing or chills
- Muscle tension

- Pupil dilation
- Restlessness
- Shortness of breath
- Syncope (fainting)
- Tachycardia
- Hyperventilation
- Lightheadedness
- Numbness
- Palpitations (pounding heart)
- Tingling
- Tremor
- Upset stomach ('butterflies')
- Urinary frequency

Psychological symptoms include the following.

- Fear
- Apprehension
- Dread
- Sense of impending doom
- Worry
- Rumination
- Obsession
- Nervousness
- Uneasiness
- Distress
- Feeling of helplessness
- Difficulty in concentrating
- Irritability and insomnia

Given the huge numbers of people who suffer from anxiety disorders, our increased understanding of the cause, mechanisms and treatment is extremely valuable.

Neurobiology

The neuropathological basis of anxiety has three neurotransmitter systems that are implicated mainly through the use of clinically efficacious agents.

- GABA, especially the benzodiazepine receptor complex.
- Noradrenaline – especially within the locus coeruleus.
- Serotonin – in the amygdala and dorsal raphe nuclei.

Animal models have been used to increase the understanding of how these systems operate in anxiety (Box 23.7).

GABA and Anxiety

Gamma-aminobutyric acid (GABA) is an inhibitory amino acid found throughout the central nervous system. The GABAergic synapses comprise the reuptake transporter to retrieve released GABA and GABA A and GABA B receptors on the postsynaptic terminal (Figure 23.7). The GABA A receptor has received most attention with regard to anxiety as it is the mechanism by which barbiturates and benzodiazepines exert their anxiolytic effect.

Barbiturates

Diethylbarbituric acid (barbital), synthesized by Fischer & von Mering in 1903, was found to have sedative and hypnotic effects. Since then a number of other barbiturates have been synthesized, most notably **phenobarbital** in 1912. All the barbiturates were able to induce sleep and at moderate doses they were also anxiolytic. Barbiturates are classed as central nervous system (CNS) depressants. The barbiturate's mode of action is to suppress excitatory postsynaptic potentials (EPSPs) (Barker & Gainer, 1973).

Barbiturates potentiate GABA-induced increases in chloride conductance due to an increase in affinity of GABA at the GABA A receptor. At high doses, barbiturates can mimic GABA, opening chloride conductance even in the absence of GABA (Nicoll & Wojtowicz, 1980). Furthermore, they block glutamate and sodium channels, thereby enhancing the inhibitory actions of GABA (Nicoll & Wojtowicz, 1980).

The GABA A receptor is a complex in which there is a barbiturates site, a GABA site and a benzodiazepine site (see Figure 23.7). The reticular formation has been highlighted as a region mediating the effects of barbiturates (Bradley, 1958). Within the reticular formation, the pontine region activates cortical areas whereas the medulla suppresses them, which may be further mediated by acetylcholine release within the regions (Baghdoyan et al., 1984). The action of barbiturates within the pontine region of the reticular formation may lead to relaxation, drowsiness and sleep, whereas barbiturates acting in the medulla lead to activation and euphoria (Feldman et al., 1997).

Although barbiturates can act as relaxants and anxiolytics, these very properties give the barbiturates the potential for abuse (Glatt, 1962). The abuse potential is obvious when one considers that the early stages of acute intoxication with barbiturates are similar to being

BOX 23.7: ANIMAL MODELS OF ANXIETY

Much of our understanding about anxiety stems from the study of animals. The use of animals is also instrumental in identifying potential therapeutic agents. The question remains, how do you identify anxiety in an animal or how do you provoke anxiety in an animal?

Similar to the conditioned emotional response (see Chapters 8 and 17), a number of methods have been used to detect anxiolytics, e.g. the Geller Seifter test (Geller & Seifter, 1960). This is a conflict test in which the animal is placed in an operant chamber and responds on a lever for reward (food). The availability of the reward is interrupted when a signal indicates that the reward would be more frequently obtained under conditions in which they would also receive a low-intensity electrical shock. An anxiolytic (anti-anxiety drug) should only have an effect on the suppression of responding during conflict periods.

The elevated plus maze has two open runways and two enclosed runways (Figure 23.7.1). Rats tend to remain in the enclosed runways due to the safety that the walls provide. An anxiolytic increases the amount of time spent in the exposed runways (Pellow et al., 1985).

There are many other animal models of anxiety that have been used with varying degrees of success (Haller and Alicki, 2012).

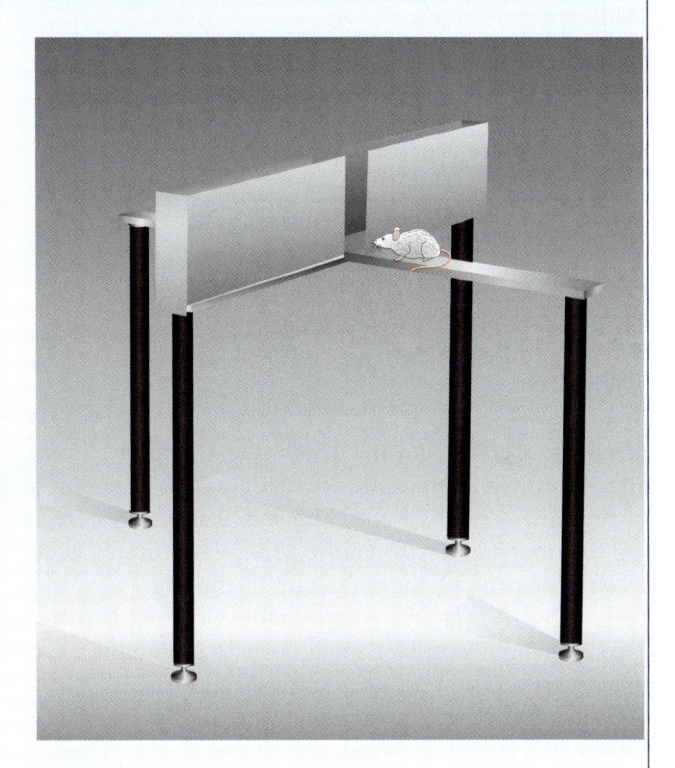

FIGURE 23.7.1 *Elevated plus maze. After an anxiolytic, rats will spend more time in the open walkways.*

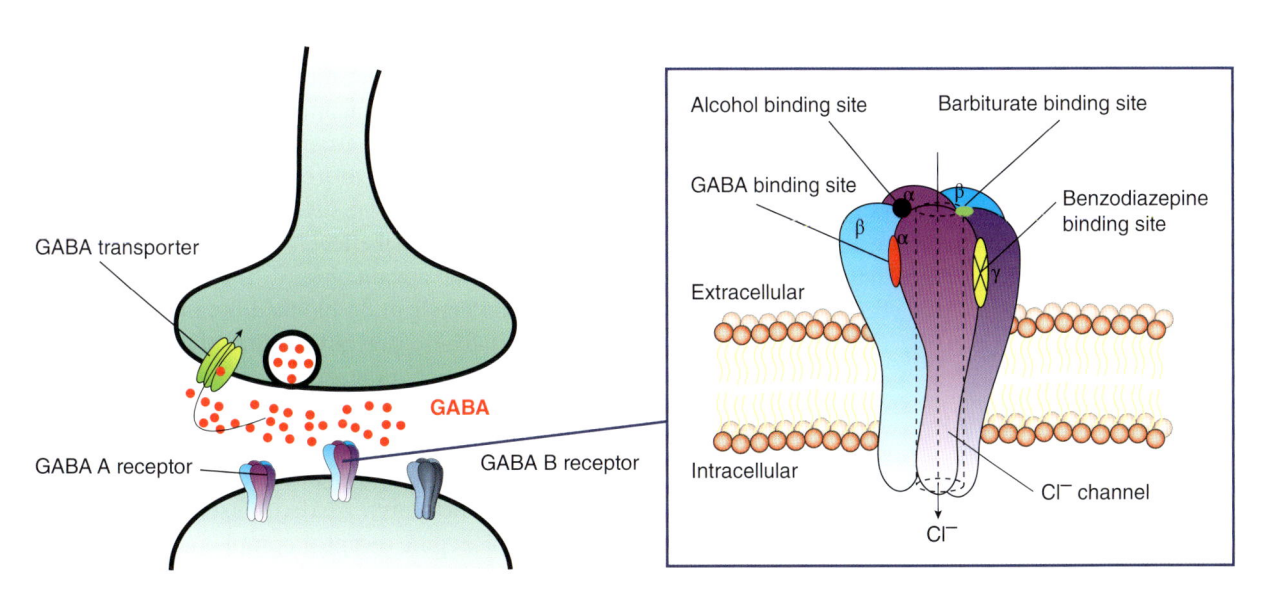

FIGURE 23.7 *GABA A receptor. BZ, benzodiazepine; GABA, gamma-aminobutyric acid; GAD, glutamic acid decarboxylase.*

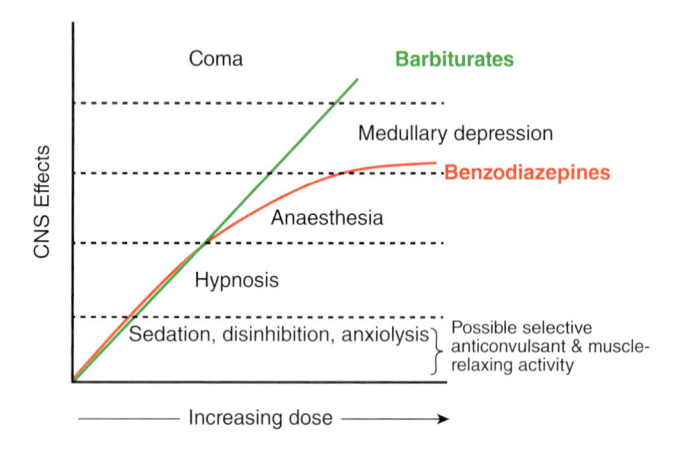

FIGURE 23.8 The effects of barbiturates and benzodiazepines on the CNS as a function of dose. CNS, central nervous system.

drunk on alcohol and the latter stages similar to opiates. However, barbiturate toxicity leads to depression of reflexes, respiratory and cardiovascular systems, leading to coma and death (Figure 23.8). Barbiturates were a favourite drug of the rock stars of the late 1960s and early 1970s. Perhaps the most notable victim of barbiturates was Jimi Hendrix, who died on 21 September 1970 in his London flat. Postmortem verification revealed barbiturates and other drugs in his system, with a coroner returning a verdict of 'inhalation of vomit due to barbiturate intoxication'.

The effects of barbiturates are not readily reversible which increases their danger as a drug to treat anxiety, with potential overdose implications. Barbiturates have been further implicated in drug-induced automatism, in which the amnesic properties of a drug such as phenobarbital lead individuals to take more drugs because they forget that they have already taken them (Good, 1976; Richards, 1934). Therefore the individual unintentionally takes an overdose because they have forgotten taking earlier doses and this can lead to fatalities being recorded as suicide.

The clinical utility of barbiturates is somewhat overshadowed by their potential for abuse and overdose. The result was the big market for drugs that can treat anxiety without having the unwanted side-effects that came with barbiturates.

Benzodiazepines

Randall et al. (1960) reported the effects of the drug **chlordiazepoxide** (marketed as Librium) which has sedative, muscle relaxant, anxiolytic and anticonvulsant activity. Shortly after, **diazepam** (marketed as Valium) was developed as a more potent version of chlordiazepoxide (Randall et al., 1961). Since then many drugs have been added to the list of anxiolytics (e.g. **lorazepam** (Ativan) and **nitrazepam** (Mogadon)).

All of these drugs are classified as **benzodiazepines**, reflecting their chemical structure. The benzodiazepines can treat anxiety-related disorders without the dangerous side-effects typified by the barbiturates. Therefore, the benzodiazepines represent a new search tool for understanding anxiety (both normal and pathological).

The GABA A receptor is made up of subunits (alpha, beta and gamma) (see Figure 23.7). Benzodiazepines require the gamma subunit alongside alpha and beta subunits for high-affinity binding (Pritchett et al., 1989). It has been suggested that there is a benzodiazepine receptor complex on the GABA A receptor. Benzodiazepines act on the GABA A receptor to increase the affinity for GABA, thereby facilitating GABA neurotransmission. A benzodiazepine alone has little effect as GABA is always required. The presence of GABA at the GABA A receptor plus a benzodiazepine at the benzodiazepine receptor complex leads to an amplification of GABA's ability to increase chloride conductance. GABA alone can produce a modest increase in chloride conductance, but to maximize conductance there has to be activation of the benzodiazepine receptor complex.

This gives rise to a little equation:

$$GABA + BZ (1 + 0) = 2 \text{ NOT } 1$$

where GABA alone has a modest effect and the benzodiazepine alone has no effect but together they provide a large synergistic effect.

The binding of GABA and benzodiazepines is allosterically regulated. **Allosteric modulation** refers to the binding of a drug at an adjacent site to the active site (Figure 23.9). Allosteric modulation can be either positive or negative, i.e. it facilitates or inhibits activity at the receptor. With GABA attached to the receptor, benzodiazepines will attach more tightly and vice versa, thus indicating how the two sites work together in order to produce the maximal effect.

One of the advantages of the benzodiazepines is that their effects can be blocked by antagonists such as **flumazenil**. Therefore, any detrimental effects caused by overdosing on benzodiazepines could be reversed.

Just as the opiates provoked a search for endogenous compounds that are similar in their *modus operandi* to morphine, the benzodiazepines lead to a search for their equivalent. The search yielded substances that bound to the benzodiazepine receptor complex and had functional similarities to the benzodiazepines (de Blas & Sotelo, 1987; de Blas et al., 1987; Sangameswaran et al., 1986).

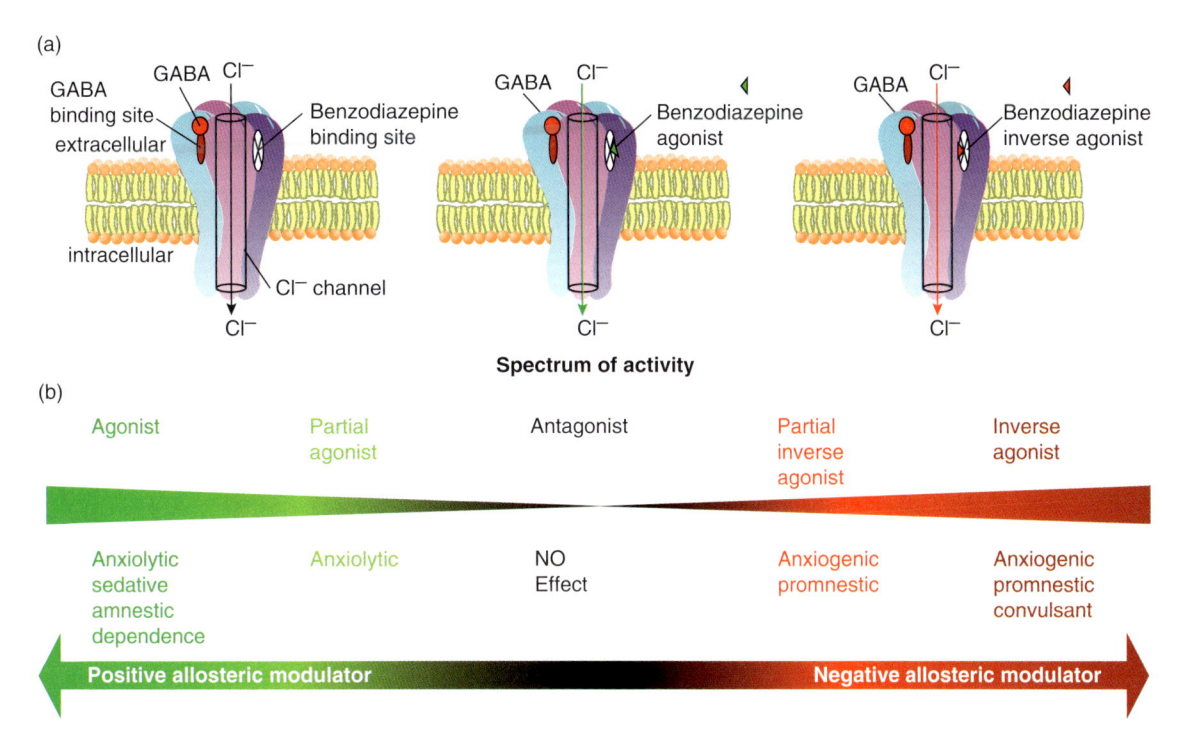

FIGURE 23.9 *Allosteric modulation at the GABA A receptor. (a) The GABA A receptor is subject to either positive or negative allosteric modulation by agonists and inverse agonists at the benzodiazepine site. (b) The effects of the spectrum of drug activity in anxiety.*

These were then referred to as endogenous benzodiazepines. One of the first to be identified was the metabolite of diazepam – **N-desmethyldiazepam** (DDZ). In an attempt to confirm that DDZ was indeed an endogenous ligand and not an artefact of exposure to diazepam, the brains of humans that had been stored since 1940 indicated that DDZ was endogenous (de Blas et al., 1987). These brains were used because they came from people who died before the advent of benzodiazepines, so the results were not an artefact of previous exposures to benzodiazepines.

Another class of drugs which act at the benzodiazepine receptor are called the **beta-carbolines**. These drugs are particularly interesting as they have a high affinity for the benzodiazepine receptor complex but have a mixed pharmacodynamic profile as some are anxiolytic whilst others are anxiogenic. All of the effects could be blocked by the benzodiazepine antagonist flumazenil. Thus, the benzodiazepine receptor complex can mediate anxiety along its full spectrum (increased to decreased) (Insel et al., 1984; Ninan et al., 1982).

In terms of evolutionary adaptation, the presence of the benzodiazepine receptor complex mediating anxiety makes sense. To provoke anxiety is to provoke fear and fear is an adaptive emotion to ensure survival. The drugs that produce an opposite response to diazepam (e.g. anxiogenic) are referred to as inverse agonists. A schematic representation of the GABA A receptor with the benzodiazepine receptor complex is depicted in Figure 23.10. The benzodiazepine receptor site is uniquely configured to receive agonists and inverse agonists, both of which can be interrupted by antagonists. Additionally, there may be a barbiturates site, alcohol site, steroid site and a picrotoxin site (which mediates convulsions).

Whereas the benzodiazepines such as diazepam are full agonists at the benzodiazepine receptor complex and confer positive allosteric modulation, the inverse agonist which has the opposite action is a negative allosteric modulator. An inverse agonist produces an action that is opposite to the agonist at the GABA A, thereby reducing the conduction of chloride through the chloride channel. Inverse agonists are anxiogenic, proconvulsant, activating and promnestic, which is essentially the opposite to a full agonist at the benzodiazepine receptor site.

So far we have addressed how we can manipulate the GABA receptor with pharmaceuticals, but what are the changes due to stress? In a number of studies looking at stress in the rat, the GABA receptor has shown reduced binding of ligands by 'releasing an endogenous ligand for benzodiazepine receptors possessing similar properties to β-carbolines' (Biggio et al., 1981, 1984).

Benzodiazepines are not without their problems. They are known to produce abuse, dependence and addiction (Lader, 1994). They can also produce a withdrawal syndrome in which abrupt cessation of treatment

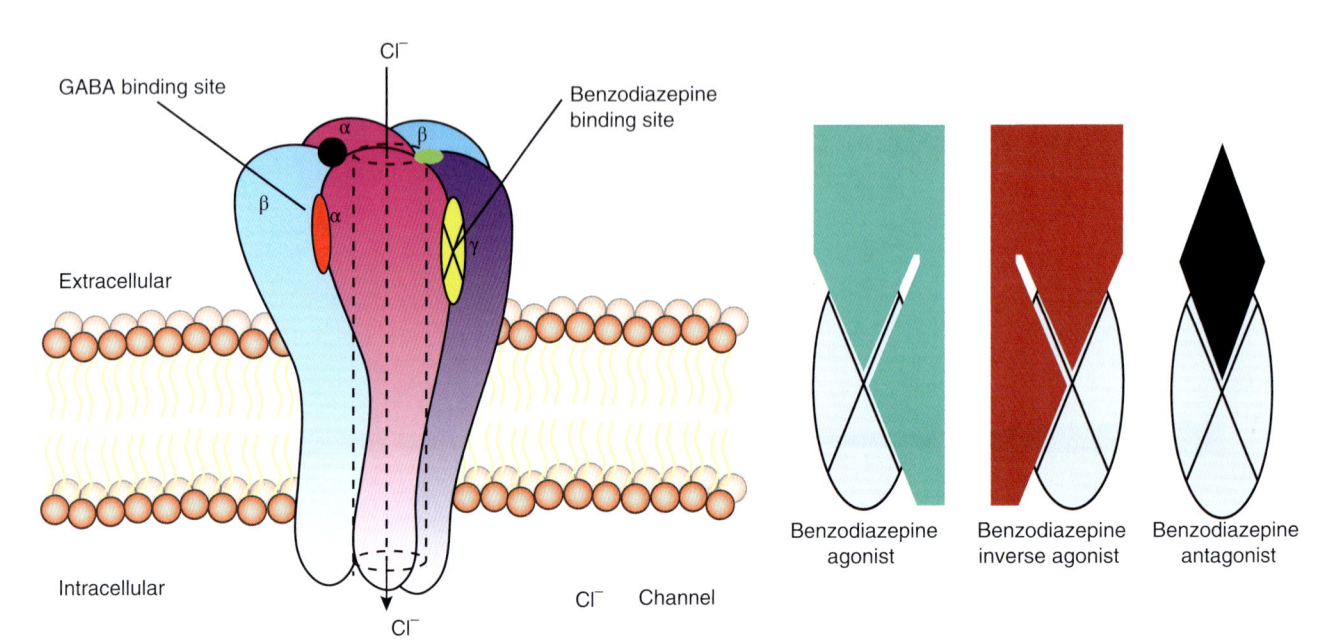

GABA A receptor and benzodiazepine receptor complex

FIGURE 23.10 *The GABA A receptor with the benzodiazepine receptor complex. BZ, benzodiazepine; GABA, gamma-aminobutyric acid.*

leads to rebound anxiety, often worse than the original anxiety (Fontaine et al., 1984). In order to come off benzodiazepines, it is necessary to deploy a tapering method in which the dose is gradually reduced, thereby avoiding withdrawal effects and rebound anxiety.

Noradrenaline

Noradrenaline has also been indicated in anxiety. In particular, the noradrenergic region of the brain, the locus coeruleus, has been shown to produce anxiety when stimulated and may increase arousal and vigilance to threat (Aston-Jones et al., 1991; Redmond & Huang, 1979; Tanaka et al., 2000). In the locus coeruleus, alpha-2 adrenoceptors are also receptors in which blockade increases the release of noradrenaline and stimulation decreases the release of noradrenaline. Handley and Mithani (1984) observed in the rat undergoing an elevated plus maze that alpha-2 adrenoceptor antagonists are anxiogenic whereas alpha-2 adrenoceptor agonists are anxiolytic (e.g. clonidine (Hoehn-Saric et al., 1981)). Clonidine is an antihypertensive agent that has been used for the treatment of panic attacks (Uhde et al., 1989) and suppressing the symptoms of anxiety during withdrawal from nicotine (Glassman et al., 1988) and opiates (Gold et al., 1978).

Beta adrenoceptors are postsynaptic receptors in which blockade is anxiolytic (conversely agonists are anxiogenic), the effects of which appear to be mediated by peripheral receptors (Bonn et al., 1972). Peripheral beta adrenoceptors mediate the peripheral autonomic effects of anxiety (such as increased heart rate, tremor and sweatiness), but do not directly relate to the conscious experience of anxiety. They may contribute to the conscious feeling of anxiety indirectly as autonomic activation provides feedback which may be interpreted negatively. Propranolol is a beta adrenoceptor antagonist that is able to treat some of the symptoms of anxiety, particularly the autonomic symptoms such as sweating, tremor and tachycardia. Whilst beta adrenoceptor antagonists are able to block the peripheral effects of anxiety, they do not block the conscious experience of anxiety. However, by calming autonomic activity, feedback becomes normalized and a vicious cycle of increased heart rate, etc. feeding the experience of anxiety can be interrupted.

Serotonin

Enhancement of serotonergic neurotransmission increases anxiety whereas a reduction in serotonergic activity reduces anxiety (Durant et al., 2010). Serotonin is also central to the neurobiological theories of depression (see Chapter 22). Depression can be seen as the opposite of anxiety in terms of a neurobiological spectrum where anxiety is seen in response to elevated serotonin levels and depression is seen when serotonin levels are greatly reduced. Comparing anxiety and depression is not a straightforward task. As a rule of thumb, depression is a reaction to events in the past whereas anxiety relates to events happening in the future.

The challenge to the hypothesis that serotonergic neurotransmission is increased in anxiety comes from studies looking at serotonergic reductions using tryptophan-free diets (a diet without tryptophan means that serotonin cannot be synthesized). Acute reductions in tryptophan have been shown to block the effects of selective serotonin reuptake inhibitors (SSRIs) in some anxiety disorders (Argyropoulos et al., 2004; Bell et al., 2002; Schruers & Griez, 2004). This supports the view that serotonin is necessary at high levels for the SSRIs to work. Similar to the theories of depression, these data lead to a different hypothesis suggesting that anxiety is the result of serotonin deficiencies. In this theory, SSRIs increase serotonin but their effect is delayed (SSRIs take three weeks to work) because of changes of the 5-HT1a autoreceptor. The initial impact of an SSRI on the 5-HT1a autoreceptor is to increase stimulation, providing feedback resulting in decreased firing of neurons. After three weeks of exposure to the SSRI, the 5-HT1a autoreceptors are downregulated and serotoninergic activity is normalized (Blier et al., 1990).

Partial agonists for serotonin receptors may be useful for both disorders due to the different baseline states. In anxiety, when serotonin levels are high, partial agonists will occupy serotonergic receptors, preventing endogenous serotonin from interacting with that receptor but only allowing a moderate amount of stimulation. Therefore, when serotonin levels are high, partial agonists will reduce activity at the serotonin receptor and may appear somewhat like an antagonist (however, the partial agonist is providing some stimulation of the receptor unlike an antagonist which would completely prevent stimulation). Buspirone is a 5-HT1a partial agonist and is effective in the treatment of generalized anxiety disorder (Davidson et al., 1999; Eison & Temple, 1986). In patients with panic disorder and social anxiety, the levels of 5-HT1a receptors are reduced (Lanzenberger et al., 2007; Nash et al., 2008; Neumeister et al., 2004).

In depression, there is the opposite case. Low levels of serotonin have been argued to be the culprit in depression. The same partial agonist in a system of low serotonin interacts with the receptor to produce a biological response and therefore reveals its agonist properties. The partial agonist is neither a full agonist nor an antagonist. It operates in the grey area in between the agonists and antagonists. It is somewhat like a dimmer switch by which the ambient lighting can be adjusted rather than merely being on or off.

Following treatment with SSRIs, postsynaptic 5-HT2c receptors are downregulated (Millan, 2005; van Oekelen et al., 2003), and 5-HT2c receptor antagonists have been shown to be anxiolytic in the rat (Kennett et al., 1994). Clinical trials with agomelatine (a 5-HT2c receptor antagonist) have shown it to be effective in the treatment of generalized anxiety (Stein et al., 2014), but despite promising results, there is a need for more double-blind placebo-controlled trials (de Berardis et al., 2013).

A Neuropsychological Theory of Anxiety

In Chapter 12 we considered the frontal lobes and behavioural inhibition. One of the many theories proposed was that of Jeffrey Gray (Gray, 1982; Gray & McNaughton, 2003). According to Gray's neuropsychological theory of anxiety, activation of a hypothetical **behavioural inhibition system** (BIS) is responsible for anxiety due to increased sensitivity to conditioned aversive stimuli. The BIS is activated in terms of punishment and negative stimuli. Signals that suggest punishment or a negative outcome are likely to lead to engagement of the BIS system, resulting in avoidance. Increased activity of the BIS leads to heightened sensitivity to non-reward and punishment cues. This higher level of sensitivity to these cues results in avoidance in order to negate negative experiences such as fear and anxiety.

The physiological basis of the BIS is the septo-hippocampal system utilizing GABA, serotonin and noradrenaline. Gray later suggested that the BIS is involved in goal conflict resolution. Gray makes a distinction between fear and anxiety: fear is mainly controlled by the amygdala response to immediate threat and anxiety is mediated through the septohippocampal system that deals with possible future threats. Anxiety is created by competition between goals requiring resolution. Conflicting goals create the uncertainty and, according to Gray, the hippocampus tries to reduce the uncertainty by inhibiting prepotent responses, e.g. approach behaviours for food even when there is a chance of threat. The question the organism has to evaluate is: should one get more information on the environment and assess the risk, and if the threat is imminent then it's time to mobilise the flight/fight responses.

Thus, the BIS generates anxiety, which entails the inhibition of conflicting behaviours, whilst assessing risk and the scanning of memory and the environment to facilitate goal conflict resolution. The BIS resolves conflicts by increasing the negative valence of stimuli with the associated subjective experience of worry. Thus, the individual is more sensitive to negative stimuli which creates activity in the BIS, which in turn increases the sensitivity to negative stimuli.

SUMMARY

Stress and anxiety affect all of us in some way. Stress is necessary for survival, but it can become a maladaptive and prolonged problem which has a detrimental effect on mind and body. Taken to the extreme, the anxiety disorders represent an affective reaction to possible threats. There are numerous anxiety disorders that have been grouped together. As a whole, anxiety has been associated with changes in the GABA system, but also the serotonergic and noradrenergic systems. Many drugs have been deployed in order to counter the symptoms of anxiety, but these have come with a price – addiction and death. The anxiety disorders represent big business, with an estimated 61.3 million people in Europe suffering from them in 2010 (Gustavsson et al., 2011). Considering the anxiety disorders as a homogenous group may not reveal the different pathways that each individual anxiety disorder may take. Future research will elucidate the individual nature of the anxiety disorders with the hope of finding specific treatments for them.

LEARNING OUTCOME QUESTIONS

You should be able to answer the following questions.
- Describe the homeostatic and allostatic mechanisms of stress.
- How is stress adaptive?
- What are the main neurobiological theories of anxiety?
- How have inverse agonists informed theories of anxiety?

FURTHER READING

Durant, C., Christmas, D., & Nutt, D. (2010). The pharmacology of anxiety. In W. B. Stein & T. Strecker (Eds.), *Behavioral Neurobiology of Anxiety and Its Treatment* (pp. 303-330). Berlin: Springer-Verlag.

Lovallo, W. R. (2005). *Stress and health: Biological and psychological interactions* (2nd ed.). Thousand Oaks, CA: Sage Publications, Inc.

McEwen, B. S., & Gianaros, P. J. (2011). Stress- and allostasis-induced brain plasticity. *Annu Rev Med, 62,* 431-445.

Schulkin, J. (Ed.) (2003). *Rethinking homeostasis: Allostatic regulation in physiology and pathophysiology.* Cambridge, MA: MIT press.

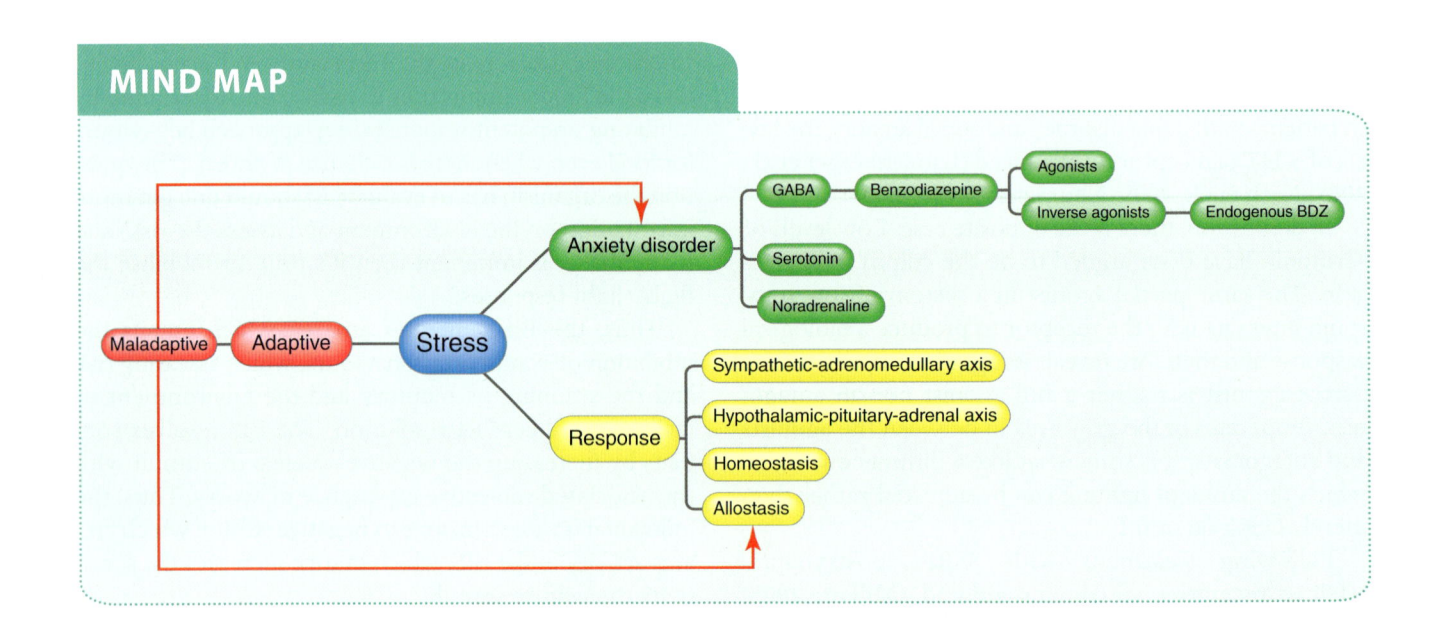

MIND MAP

Maladaptive — Adaptive — Stress
- Anxiety disorder
  - GABA — Benzodiazepine
    - Agonists
    - Inverse agonists — Endogenous BDZ
  - Serotonin
  - Noradrenaline
- Response
  - Sympathetic-adrenomedullary axis
  - Hypothalamic-pituitary-adrenal axis
  - Homeostasis
  - Allostasis

24 Neurodegeneration

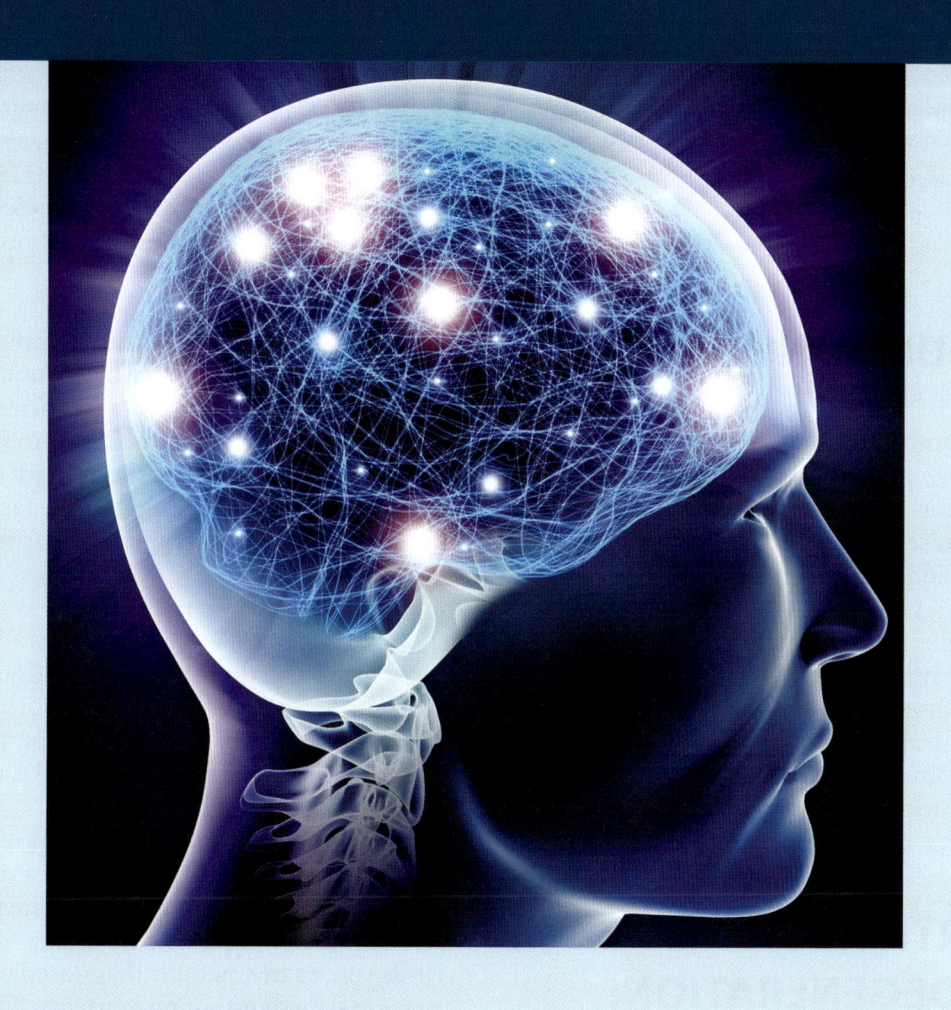

ANATOMY OF THE CHAPTER

This chapter will highlight the following.

- The role of the basal ganglia in motor behaviour and cognition.
- The neuropathology of Parkinson's disease.
- Manipulation of the basal ganglia circuitry in the treatment of Parkinson's disease.
- Large-scale neuropathy in Alzheimer's disease.
- Potential treatments for Alzheimer's disease.

INTRODUCTION   584

SUBCORTICAL NEURODEGENERATION: PARKINSON'S DISEASE   584

CORTICAL NEURODEGENERATION: ALZHEIMER'S DISEASE   593

SUMMARY   600

LEARNING OUTCOMES

1. To understand the neural circuitry involved in Parkinson's disease.
2. To understand how manipulation with drugs and surgery can manage the symptoms of Parkinson's disease.
3. To be able to evaluate the differences between cortical and subcortical neurodegeneration.
4. To appreciate the difficulties in understanding and therefore treating Alzheimer's disease.

INTRODUCTION

There are numerous neurodegenerative diseases that can have pronounced effects on humans. Throughout the book we have used examples of Huntington's disease, multiple sclerosis, Alzheimer's disease (AD) and Parkinson's disease (PD). In this chapter the focus is on AD and PD. Parkinson's disease is a neurodegenerative disorder that primarily affects motor behaviour. It is a subcortical degenerative disorder, unlike AD which has widespread cortical abnormalities. Therefore, AD and PD provide common and contrasting examples of neurodegeneration.

SUBCORTICAL NEURODEGENERATION: PARKINSON'S DISEASE

Parkinson's disease is a neurodegenerative disorder that primarily affects motor behaviour. However, in some cases of PD there is a cognitive decline that is linked to the disease itself, and not to any co-morbidities, e.g. depression.

In 1817 James Parkinson identified what was to become known as Parkinson's disease as the shaking palsy (paralysis agitans) which he described as 'involuntary tremulous motion, with a lessened muscular power, in parts not in action and even when supported; with a propensity to bend the trunk forwards, and to pass from walking to a running pace: the senses and intellect being uninjured'.

Parkinson's disease in most cases has a slow onset and progresses slowly throughout the course of the disease. It is characterized by **hypokinesia**, **bradykinesia** and **akinesia**, which refer to the impairment, slowness and loss of fine motor movements respectively. The muscles of the face, mouth and tongue and the skilful actions of the arms and legs are affected by PD. The hypokinesia in PD contributes to the expressionless face seen in some patients. As was illustrated in Chapter 17, facial expressions require considerable input and convey a great deal of information.

The gait of someone with PD is referred to as a stalling gait; there is slowness in walking, they take short steps and their feet do not lift off the ground. There is a fear of falling, with forward flexion of the body, and they hesitate before avoiding obstacles, having to plan a route around rather than move with a smooth flowing vector.

When discussing the symptoms of PD, it is noteworthy that people often get the wrong impression of what the true symptoms are. The true symptoms are of motor impairment (a loss of movement). However, many people diagnosed with PD show abnormal involuntary movements. They may writhe and engage in jerky movements of the arms and legs. This is not a symptom of PD, but rather a response to the medication that is used to enable them to move.

The prevalence of PD increases with age (Pringsheim et al., 2014) (Figure 24.1) and there is a difference in prevalence rates across countries, with North America, Europe and Australia having higher rates than Asia. However, this is a factor of survival rates in different nations, i.e. populations which generally do not live long enough to exhibit PD (Muangpaisan et al., 2011). In general, PD is rare in young people; the actor Michael J. Fox is an exception to this rule. In the UK, the prevalence rate in 2009 was 27.4 per 10,000, with males being more likely to have PD (Parkinson's UK, 2010).

Despite our clear neuropathological understanding of PD, the cause of the changes in the brain remain to be determined. Searching for one aetiology for PD is probably a mistake, as there are several routes to the degeneration. For example, the

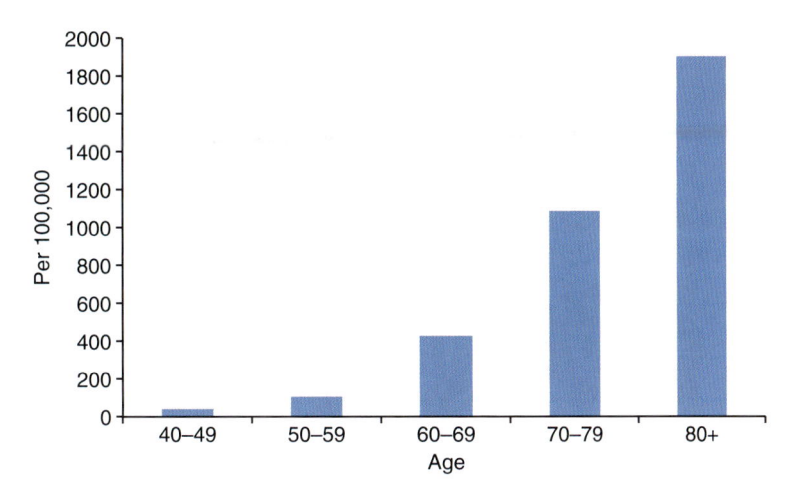

FIGURE 24.1 *The increasing prevalence of Parkinson's disease by age.*
Source: Data from Pringsheim, T., Jette, N., Frolkis, A., & Steeves, T. D. L. (2014). The prevalence of Parkinson's disease: A systematic review and meta-analysis. *Movement Disorders, 29,* 1583–1590.

encephalitis epidemic of the early 1900s gave rise to a rapid increase in PD. This was illustrated elegantly in Oliver Sacks' book *Awakenings*, which was later made into a film starring Robert de Niro and Robin Williams. Interestingly, PD was the result of the encephalitis epidemic in adults, whereas in children the resultant symptoms were more commensurate with attention deficit hyperactivity disorder (ADHD) (see Chapter 20). There is evidence to suggest that PD is a genetic disorder (Hardy et al., 2009) in which a meta-analysis identified 11 loci associated with PD (Lill et al., 2012). Another causal route is via the neurotoxin **MPTP** that was accidentally synthesized in the search for a new recreational drug (Box 24.1).

BOX 24.1: MPTP: SEARCHING FOR A HIGH AND FINDING PARKINSON'S DISEASE

In San Francisco, California, during the late 1970s and early 1980s the search for new ways of getting high ended up providing the predominant model of PD. A chemistry graduate was synthesizing new opiate-like compounds and in the spirit of self-experimentation induced a type of PD (see Langston and Palfreman (1995) for review).

Langston et al. (1983) identified a group of drug addicts who presented with PD, but were much younger than typically associated with its onset. Upon further investigation, it was found that these drug abusers were taking a synthetic pethidine derivative (MPPP). Evaluation of the synthetic opiate revealed that it contained another compound called **1-methyl-4-phenyl-1,2,3,6-tetrahydropyridine** (MPTP).

The discovery led researchers to consider MPTP as a possible animal model of PD, the rationale being that understanding how MPTP operated could provide some insight into the pathological process, but also a mechanism to evaluate potential therapeutic drugs.

MPTP itself is benign, and readily crosses the blood–brain barrier and is converted into other substances. Monoamine oxidase (MAO) B is the main mechanism for metabolism of MPTP (Chiba et al., 1984; Fritz et al., 1985; Glover et al., 1986). It is the metabolism of MPTP into **1-methyl-4-phenyl-pyridinium** (MPP+) that provides the neurotoxicity seen with MPTP in the mitochondria of the dopamine transporter. The neurotoxicity is, in general, uniquely specific to the substantia nigra (Burns et al., 1983). The effects of MPTP are seen in mammals and mice but rats are less sensitive to its neurotoxic effects (Przedborski et al., 2001). The reason for this difference across species is a relatively low level of MAO B in the rat substantia nigra (Willoughby et al., 1988).

While the MPTP model of PD provided important insights into the disease and treatment, it was not without problems. For example, PD is of insidious onset; an individual may experience low levels of neurodegeneration for many years before recognizable symptoms emerge, but the MPTP model has a rapid onset. Furthermore, it does not address aetiological mechanisms or the slow neuroadaptations seen with the natural time course of the disease. However, despite some limitations, the MPTP model of PD is currently used to great effect.

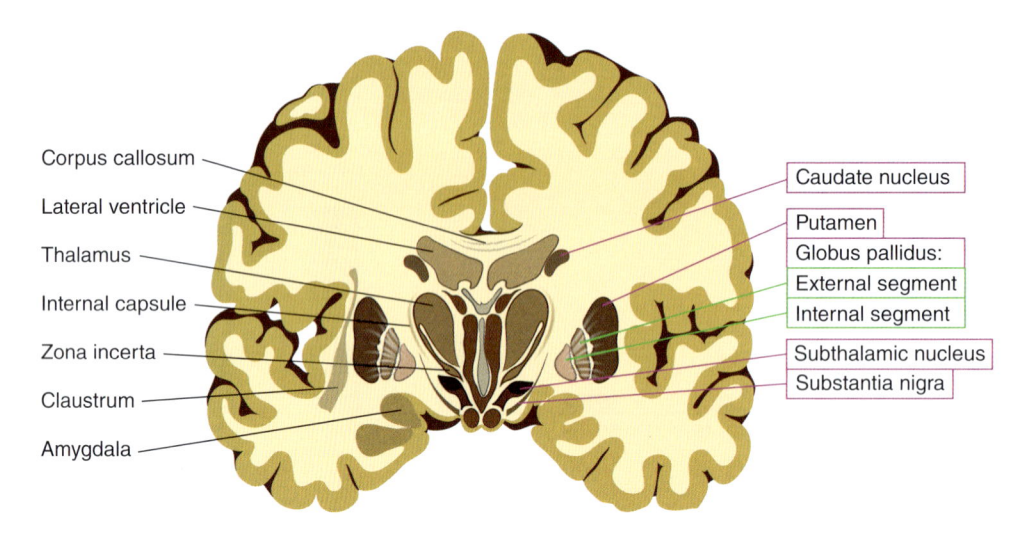

FIGURE 24.2 *The basal ganglia.*

Neuropathology

Parkinsons' disease is a severe motor disorder caused by a reduction of dopamine (DA) in basal ganglia (Ehringer & Hornykiewicz, 1960) (Figure 24.2). Specifically, there is an 80–90% reduction of DA in the substantia nigra and striatum (Bernheimer et al., 1973) (Figure 24.3). The rate-limiting step in the synthesis of DA is tyrosine hydroxylase and this has been found to be reduced in activity in PD (McGeer and McGeer, 1976), as is the next step in synthesis – DOPA (Lloyd et al., 1975). The net effect is a substantial loss of neural connectivity within the nigrostriatal pathway. The mesolimbic pathway which runs alongside the nigrostriatal pathway remains relatively intact. The loss of nigrostriatal dopamine is the common denominator in PD which may arise from multiple aetiologies.

The degenerative nature of PD means that as the neurons die, those that remain have to work harder. Although the levels of DA metabolites are low in PD (Bernheimer & Hornykiewicz, 1965), there is an increase in the homovanillic acid (HVA):DA ratio in favour of HVA, indicating increased activity of the remaining neurons (Bernheimer et al., 1966). A similar effect is seen in the rat after lesions of the nigrostriatal pathway (Hefti et al., 1985). The increase in dopaminergic activity was also accompanied by another compensatory mechanism which was the increasing DA receptors (Bokobza et al., 1984). Despite the adaptive plasticity of the nigrostriatal pathway in response to substantial loss of neurons, the compensatory effect is suboptimal (Hefti et al., 1985).

Postsynaptic receptors are not subject to the neurodegenerative process in PD (if they were, then current pharmacotherapy would be ineffective). When there is chronic degeneration, there is an increase in DA receptors which is reversed after treatment (Rinne et al., 1981). However, the symptoms of PD emerge when there is no more capacity in the compensatory mechanisms. According to Riederer and Wuketich (1976), when the reduction in dopaminergic activity is less than 70%, the compensatory mechanisms of increased release of DA are sufficient to maintain neurotransmission. When the dopamine degeneration exceeds 70%, hyperactivity of the DA terminals is no longer sufficient and symptoms begin to emerge. As the neurogeneration continues and exceeds 90%, the increasing dopamine is no longer effective and dopamine receptors increase in number. It is at this point that the severe symptoms emerge. With prolonged reduction in DA and the initial compensatory mechanisms failing, the remaining receptors become supersensitive (Figure 24.4).

The degree of motor akinesia is correlated with the level of destruction of the nigrostriatal pathway (Bernheimer et al., 1973) and a similar effect was seen in animal studies in which lesions of the nigrostriatal pathway were induced with MPTP (Elsworth et al., 1999). The severity of the lesion is manifest on the contralateral side of the lesion (Langston et al., 1984).

Neuropharmacology

As DA is the prime deficit in PD, then the logical solution is to treat the deficit. The first treatment tried for PD is still used to this day and is based on synthesis. By providing the immediate precursor

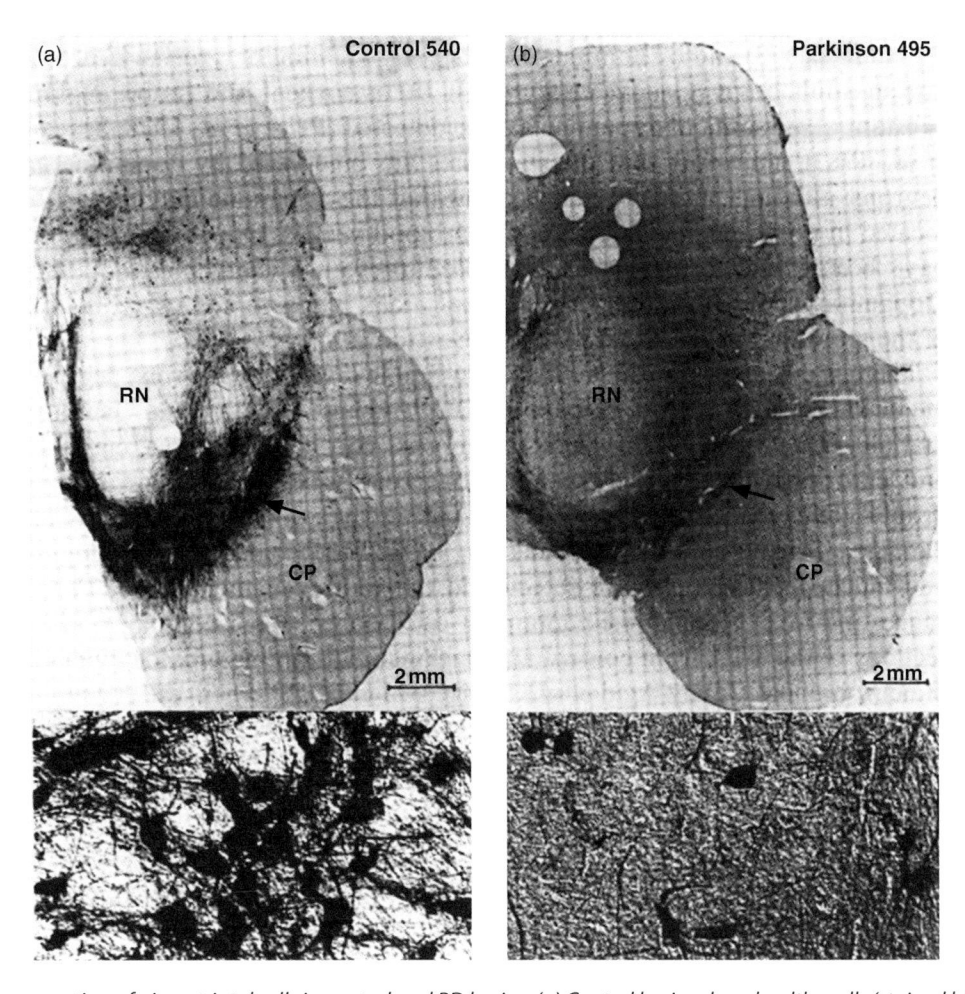

FIGURE 24.3 *Degeneration of nigrostriatal cells in control and PD brains. (a) Control brains show healthy cells (stained black) whereas (b) PD brains have few cells when stained to reveal their presence.*
Source: Agid, Y., Javoy-Agid, F., Ruberg, M., & Hirsch, E. (1989). Dopaminergic systems in Parkinson's disease. In N. P. Quinn, & P. G. Jenner (Eds.), *Disorders of movement: Clinical, pharmacological and physiological aspects* (pp. 85–114). London, UK: Academic Press.

to DA, L-DOPA can be converted into DA in the remaining neurons (Birkmayer & Hornykiewicz, 1961). However, as the disease progresses the drug needs to be given more frequently and in larger doses. Whilst L-DOPA provides much-needed dopaminergic support, it has considerable problems.

L-DOPA has a short duration of action so patients can go from being able to move normally to akinetic in a very short space of time. As the disease progresses, it is hard to adjust the dose optimally (with doses that are too high, dyskinesia and psychosis can emerge). The quick switch to being akinetic can only be reversed by another dose of the drug. This means that as the disease progresses, the patient has to take more of the drug more frequently, leading to the 'on-off' phenomenon (on being able to move; off being akinetic). One of the pronounced side-effects that can fill the whole 'on' time is L-DOPA-induced dyskinesia. Clozapine (see below) is an atypical antipsychotic which has been shown to be effective in treating L-DOPA-induced dyskinesia (Fox et al., 2011). It has been argued that L-DOPA-induced dyskinesia is a result of dopamine agonists acting in the putamen of the striatum which is supersensitive after chronic deprivation (Crossman, 1990).

L-DOPA is converted into DA in the periphery and not just the site where it is needed. In order to maximize the effect of L-DOPA at the nigrostriatal pathway, a peripheral decarboxylase inhibitor is used in combination (Boshes, 1981). The peripheral decarboxylase inhibitor blocks the metabolism of L-DOPA into DA in the periphery, thereby ensuring that it is the brain that gets the support. Furthermore, this avoids some of the side-effects of L-DOPA, e.g. nausea and vomiting due to the stimulation of D2 receptors in the area postrema of

Dopamine denervation	Dopamine nerve terminal	Striatal neurons	Neurotransmission status and symptoms
<70%			Compensatory mechanisms of increased pre-synaptic DA are sufficient to maintain adequate transmission. No symptoms
70%<90%			Hyperactivity of the DA terminal is not sufficient and symptoms emerge. No DA receptor supersensitivity
>90%			Increase in DA no longer effective and the D2 receptors increase in number. Severe symptoms emerge
>90% Add L-DOPA			DA transmission re-established with L-DOPA. Symptoms managed. The loss of capacity of the presynaptic neuron results in the 'on-off' phenomenon. Supersensitive receptors lead to dyskinesia

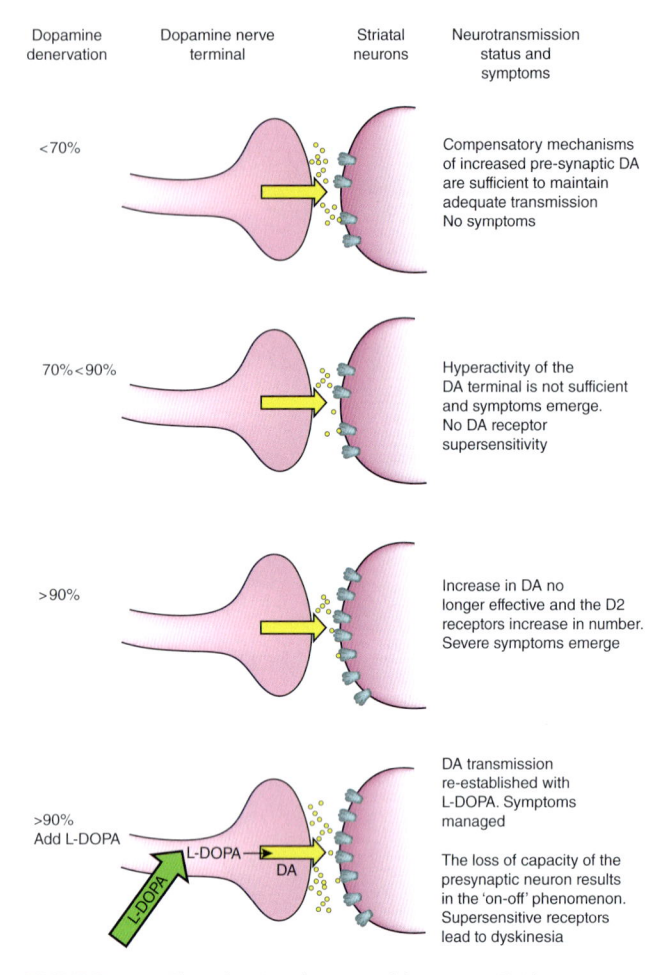

FIGURE 24.4 *The adaptive changes of dopamine (DA) neurons in PD.*

the brainstem (Parkes, 1986). L-DOPA-induced dyskinesia can be as distressing as PD itself. After six months of treatment with L-DOPA, 37% of patients will show some dyskinesia which rises to 70% after two years (Boshes, 1981). The L-DOPA-induced dyskinesia is the direct result of the degeneration of the nigrostriatal pathway (Agid et al., 1985).

Another method of enhancing dopamine within the synapses is to block its metabolism. This is the same principle as seen with depression and the MAO inhibitors (MAOIs). Instead of increasing levels of noradrenaline, as is therapeutic in depression, the MAOIs can block the enzymatic degradation of dopamine by MAO. A specific MAO-B inhibitor, **deprenyl**, was shown many years ago to facilitate L-DOPA therapy. The co-administration improves the symptoms of PD (Birkmayer & Riederer, 1984; Birkmayer et al., 1982). A further advantage of deprenyl is that it was shown to retard the progression of the dopaminergic neurodegeneration in the nigrostriatal pathway (Tetrud & Langston, 1987, 1992). A similar profile can be seen with other MAO-B inhibitors, therefore indicating a potential therapeutic method for slowing down the disease progress (Schapira, 2011).

All the above treatments require some integrity of DA neurons and the use of dopamine itself. An alternative mechanism is to mimic DA by acting directly at the dopamine receptors. The DA D2 receptor family is the mediator of clinical efficacy of antiparkinsonian drugs. Thus, targeting the postsynaptic DA receptors avoids the need for some integrity in a degenerating nigrostriatal pathway. Apomorphine is a direct DA receptor agonist which has been used in the treatment of PD but the side-effects (e.g. nausea and vomiting) make it an unsuitable therapy (Schwab et al., 1951).

Bromocriptine has been used successfully in the treatment of PD for a number of years. Bromocriptine is a DA receptor agonist, similar to apomorphine, and acts predominantly on the D2 receptor. The side-effect problems associated with apomorphine can be managed successfully with bromocriptine via the combination of the peripheral D2 antagonist which stops bromocriptine acting in the brainstem (Quinn et al., 1981). Bromocriptine has now been joined by numerous other receptor agonists.

As we have seen in numerous other disorders, turning a system on or off may have therapeutic benefits, but the side-effects can be sufficiently severe to be prohibitive. A possible strategy to avoid prohibitive side-effects and increase clinical efficacy is to use partial agonists. **Transdihydrolisuride (terguride)** is such a partial agonist at the D2 receptor and is effective in treating PD whilst minimizing the side-effect profile (Brucke et al., 1987). In lesioned animals terguride presents as an agonist because the baseline activity is extremely low (Kehr, 1984).

Although not a pharmacotherapy, neurosurgery has been put forward as an option in the treatment of PD. The neural transplant is an option because of the very specific nature of the neurodegeneration. Like L-DOPA therapy, the rationale behind the neural transplant is to replace the damaged or dying nigrostriatal pathway with new tissue. Transplants have had mixed results. Many of the problems with transplants have not been about the science, but more about where the transplanted tissue is harvested. Tissue derived from the adrenal medulla of the patient has been shown to have some effect (Porena et al., 1996) but the use of foetal tissue (obtained from aborted foetuses) has provoked extreme controversy (Vogel, 2001).

In the animal, neural transplants have been shown to have some beneficial effect on motor behaviour in animals that have received lesions of the nigrostriatal pathway. Schmidt et al. (1981) found that DA levels increased after transplant but not to the same extent as prior to the lesion, but DA turnover and synthesis were greatly increased. With unilateral lesions of the nigrostriatal pathway with a neurotoxin, **6-OHDA**, rats move towards the side of the lesion (ipsilateral) (Ungerstedt, 1971). This effect is exacerbated by amphetamine, but the opposite effect (e.g. contralateral turning) is produced with low doses of apomorphine (Ungerstedt, 1971). Why should this happen given that both are dopamine agonists? The answer lies in two mechanisms. First, apomorphine is a direct receptor agonist whereas amphetamine operates to enhance dopamine output. Second, the lesion of the nigrostriatal pathway invokes compensatory changes in receptor sensitivity. Thus, amphetamine only works on the side of the brain that has not been lesioned, because it needs to have a substrate in order to release dopamine. Apomorphine works on both sides of the brain because it does not require the presynaptic neuron and just stimulates postsynaptic receptors. However, the contralateral turning is generated by the lesion side, in which the receptors are more sensitive to those in the intact side due to compensatory changes. Therefore, the effect of apomorphine is predominant in the lesion side promoting contralateral turning (Figure 24.5).

Despite the scientific data in animals supporting the role of the neural transplant, the ethical objections required a different strategy in replacement therapy. Stem cells offer an alternative to the transplant, and there is some evidence that stem cells derived from the umbilical cord (rather than the foetus) alleviate the symptoms of PD (Shetty et al., 2013).

Whilst the focus of treatments in PD has remained on the nigrostriatal pathway and DA, an alternative strategy is to manipulate the wider network within the basal ganglia. Another site that can be targeted in treating PD is the globus pallidus which is illustrated in Box 24.2.

A further side-effect that can develop in the treatment of PD with DA agonists is psychosis. In Chapter 21, the evidence that supported a DA hypothesis of schizophrenia was generated in part by the fact that the antipsychotic medication used could induce parkinsonian side-effects. Underlying schizophrenia is an increase in the DA mesolimbic system. When DA agonists are given to negate the effects of DA loss in the nigrostriatal pathway, they also act at other DA sites. One of those sites is the mesolimbic DA system, which in PD is relatively spared. However, antiparkinsonian therapy elevates DA in this region with the potential to induce psychotic episodes.

The simple solution would be to provide an antipsychotic to stop the psychotic episodes. However, many antipsychotic agents induce parkinsonian side-effects and therefore are not practical. Clozapine is the exception. Clozapine has been shown to effectively manage the psychotic symptoms in parkinsonian patients as a result of L-DOPA therapy without exacerbating the motor symptoms (Jalenques & Coudert, 1994; Scholz & Dichgans, 1985). A literature review of studies comprising 200 patients indicated that clozapine was effective in reducing 90% of the psychotic symptoms in response to L-DOPA (Auzou et al., 1996).

Another consequence of DA agonists acting beyond the nigrostriatal pathway is the increased prevalence of problematic gambling in people being treated for PD, possibly due to an increase in DA in the nucleus accumbens (Gallagher et al., 2007) (see Chapter 16).

Neuropsychology

The neuropsychological perspective on PD addresses both motor and cognitive functioning. The basal ganglia have been argued to act as an autopilot controlling at a subconscious level different motor programs selected from higher cortical regions (Steg & Johnels, 1993). Brotchie, Mitchell et al. (1991) suggested that phasic activity is generated by the basal ganglia in which well-learned, internally generated movements provide a cue to signal switch between components in a motor sequence. Just before a motor movement is made, the activity in the **supplementary motor area** (SMA) is terminated. In the MPTP model of PD there is no abrupt cessation of SMA activity.

The direct and indirect pathways of the basal ganglia serve different functions (see Chapter 11). The direct pathway provides feedback for sustaining or facilitating an ongoing action and damage to this pathway results in the akinesia seen in PD. The indirect pathway suppresses unwanted movements and in PD is overactive which means PD patients cannot switch programs and exhibit dyskinesia (DeLong & Wichmann, 2007).

The destruction of the nigrostriatal pathway in PD differentially affects the direct and indirect pathways, the direct pathway becoming underactive whereas

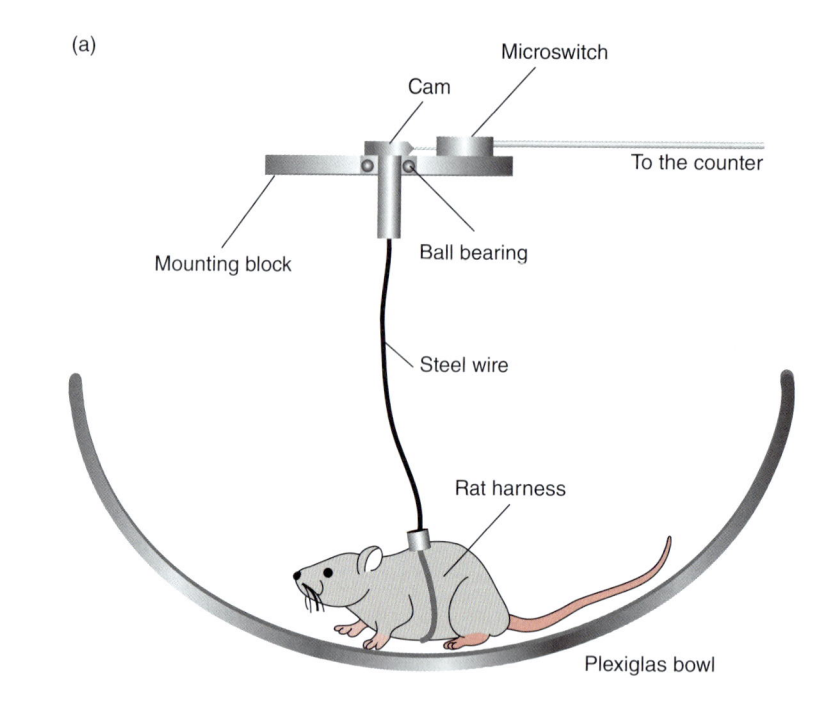

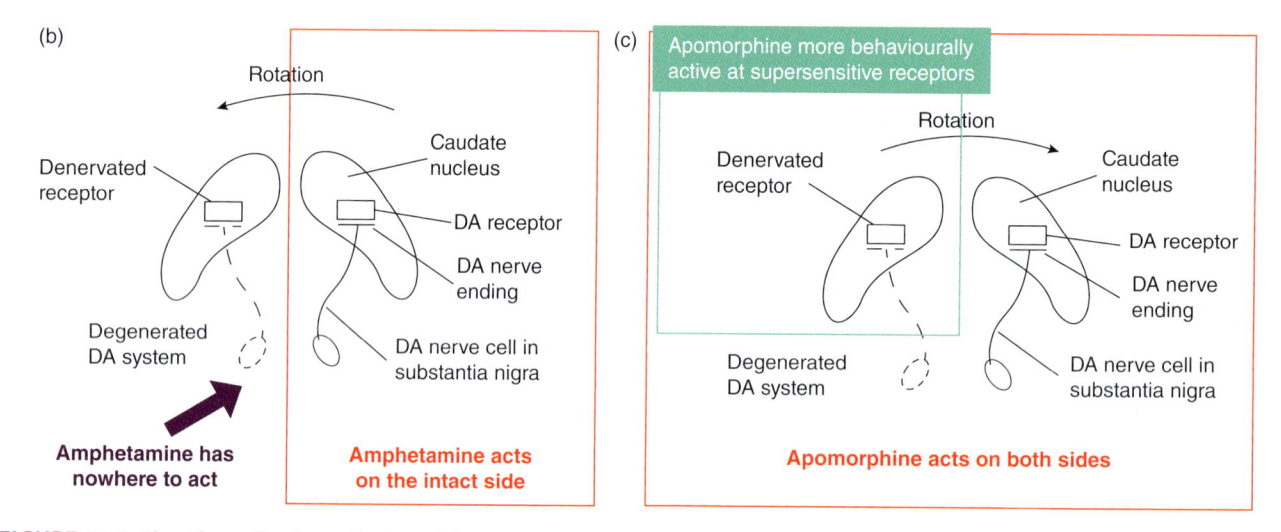

FIGURE 24.5 The effects of unilateral lesions of the nigrostriatal pathway in rats and the response to amphetamine and apomorphine. (a) A rotometer to measure the turning of rats. (b) Amphetamine releases dopamine (DA) on the intact side of the brain, promoting turning to the contralateral side. (c) Apomorphine works directly on DA receptors, but promotes ipsilateral turning due to supersensitive receptors on the side of the lesion.
Source: Adapted from Ungerstedt, U. (1971). Striatal dopamine release after amphetamine or nerve degeneration revealed by rotational behaviour. *Acta Physiologica Scandinavica, 367,* 49–68.

the indirect pathway is overactive (Wichmann & DeLong, 1996). This leads to increased activity of the globus pallidus and therefore suppressed thalamic and cortical activity leading to difficulties in the initiation of movements.

Some of the motor deficits seen in PD have similarities with the dysexecutive syndrome (see Chapter 12) (Kudlicka et al., 2011). Similar to those with damage to the frontal lobe, patients with PD had problems using internalized cues due to faulty information being sent to the SMA from the basal ganglia (Georgiou et al., 1994). The faulty internalized cues resulted in difficulty in generating rapid sequential movements that are impaired in PD (Georgiou et al., 1993). Dick et al. (1989) found that there was a reduced **Bereitschaftspotential** (readiness potential) in PD in the SMA due to a lack of afferent input from the basal ganglia. Thus, the

BOX 24.2: LESIONS OF THE GLOBUS PALLIDUS AS A TREATMENT FOR PARKINSON'S DISEASE

Parkinson's disease is a severe motor disorder caused by a reduction of DA in basal ganglia (Ehringer & Hornykiewicz, 1960). However, loss of DA in the nigrostriatal pathway has knock-on effects in other areas of the brain. The knock-on effects are mediated by two amino acid neurotransmitters. GABA is an inhibitory transmitter and glutamate is excitatory. Think of them as instructions. GABA is saying be quiet, whereas glutamate wants to make some noise.

In Figure 24.2.1a, the basal ganglia is in harmony because there is no loss of nigrostriatal DA. In Figure 24.2.1b, the loss of nigrostriatal DA has profound effects and produces the symptoms of PD.

The DA deficiency fails to inhibit the subthalamic nucleus (STN) because not enough GABA is received from the globus pallidus external section. This is called disinhibition. A lack of STN inhibition means that it sends excitatory glutamate messages to the globus pallidus internal (GPi) section. The GPi is then overactive and sends its inhibitory GABAergic message to the thalamus. The thalamus is effectively told to be quiet by the GABA and therefore does not talk to the cortex.

From this example, it can be seen how both excitatory and inhibitory neurotransmitters affect groups of cells. Due to one deficiency the effects are seen throughout the motor system. Most therapies for PD have sought to replace the deficit.

Would you consider destroying another part of the brain as a treatment? Your probable answer would be no. It is counterintuitive to treat neurodegeneration with further destruction. However, this is exactly what happens when a patient receives a pallidotomy. A **pallidotomy** is the destruction of the globus pallidus.

Why should this work?

Gerfen (1995) states that there is an increase in activity in the striatopallidal system (striatum to globus pallidus) in relation to the striatonigral system (striatum to substantia nigra) in PD.

If the globus pallidus is overactive in PD, then damping down its activity may be clinically effective. A lesion of the globus pallidus is a dramatic way of achieving silence from the globus pallidus. After pallidotomy, 81% had relief from tremor and improvement of gait (Laitinen et al., 1992). Ten years after surgery there was still a marked improvement (Hariz & Bergenheim, 2001). The improvements seen after pallidotomy may arise because the patient can tolerate higher doses of therapeutic drugs due to a reduction of side-effects (Dogali et al., 1995). Even with this consideration that the pallidotomy is not a cure, the benefits remain for at least one year (Baron et al., 1996). In a randomized trial in which PD patients were given either medical therapy or unilateral pallidotomy, those who received the surgery showed marked improvements that were sustained at two-year follow-up (Vitek et al., 2003).

Positron emission tomography (PET) measures of regional cerebral blood flow before and 17 weeks after pallidotomy show increased activity in the supplementary

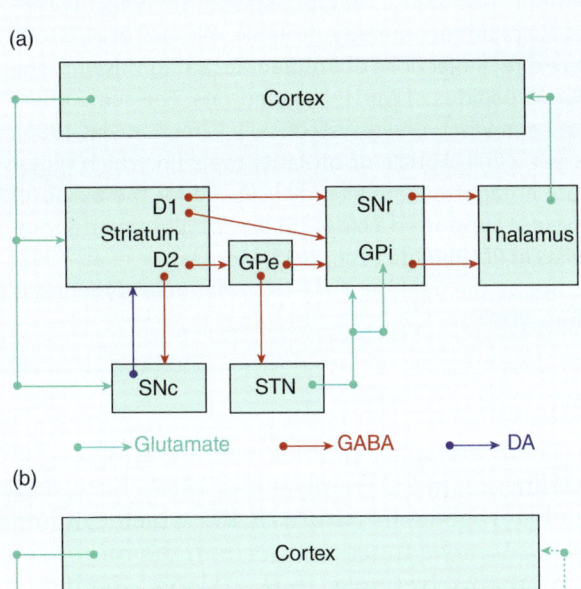

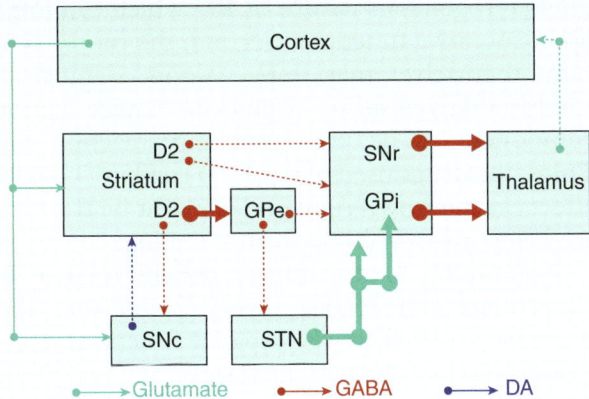

FIGURE 24.2.1 *Basal ganglia circuitry. (a) Normal circuitry. (b) Parkinson's disease circuitry (pallidotomy removes the GPi). DA, dopamine; GABA, gamma-aminobutyric acid; GPe, globus pallidus external segment; GPi, globus pallidus internal segment; SNc, substantia nigra pars compacta; SNr, substantia nigra pars reticulata; STN, subthalamic nucleus.*

motor area and the premotor cortex (Grafton et al., 1995). This indicates that the motor circuits of the basal ganglia are being reactivated to some extent because they are seen to be busy once again.

The majority of studies have assessed motor behaviour, but some have looked for the consequences of the pallidotomy on cognition; there was an improvement in sustained attention but a decline in working memory and executive functioning (Trepanier et al., 2000). Others found deficits in verbal fluency but the benefit far outweighed the cost (Gray et al., 2002; Scott et al., 1998). The decline in verbal fluency was evident mainly when the lesion was on the left side (language-dominant hemisphere) (Cahn et al., 1998).

Lesions of the STN have also been shown to be effective in treating PD and L-DOPA-induced dyskinesia (Jourdain et al., 2014; Munhoz et al., 2014). From the neural circuitry depicted in Figure 24.2.1 the STN can be seen projecting to the globus pallidus.

An alternative to the pallidotomy is **deep brain stimulation** (DBS). DBS involves the insertion of a microelectrode into a specified region of the brain, e.g. globus pallidus, which acts like a pacemaker to stimulate that region. Using high-frequency stimulation, improvements in the symptoms of PD can be measured (Bronstein et al., 2011).

In a very small study involving five patients, the effects of pallidotomy and DBS indicated that lesions were not only cheaper but also more effective in treating PD (Blomstedt et al., 2006; Hariz & Hariz, 2013). However, DBS is safer than pallidotomy, which is, after all, further damage to the brain (Kumar et al., 1998). DBS can also be performed bilaterally and adjusted. Stimulation of the GPi excites the axon terminals of striatal and/or external pallidal neurons, causing release of GABA and inhibition of GPi neurons, a similar effect to pallidotomy (Dostrovsky et al., 2000), and also by depolarization block as evidenced in animal models (Benazzouz & Hallett, 2000). The effect of DBS is therefore to reinstate a normal pattern of neural activity within the basal ganglia circuitry. The greatest effect is derived from placement in regions that have the greatest reach within that circuitry, e.g. STN and globus pallidus (Hammond et al., 2008).

Given the dangerous nature of neurosurgery, not to mention the expense, the globus pallidus may also be a target for pharmacotherapy. Brotchie, Mitchell et al. (1991) gave direct injections of a glutamate antagonist into the globus pallidus of MPTP-lesioned rats. The same effect was seen when given systemically (Greenamyre, 1996). As yet, clinical trials or off-label trials (in which glutamate antagonists are already licensed for the purpose) have not supported a clear-cut use for glutamate antagonists in PD (Brichta et al., 2013; Montastruc et al., 1997) except for the treatment of L-DOPA-induced dyskinesias (Duty, 2012).

---

patient with PD has to control their movements with full attention monitoring using visual feedback, which makes movements slow and laboured (Roy et al., 1993).

As the frontal lobes and the basal ganglia are involved in the operation of motor plans or schemata, they use interoceptive and exteroceptive cues to update schemata. In PD, the ability to rapidly adapt schemata was much slower than in control participants (Soliveri et al., 1992). Therefore, the execution of motor plans is slower and more cognitively effortful, requiring the external generation of plans consciously.

The vast majority of research in PD has focused, understandably, on motor behaviour but there are also cognitive symptoms similar to those of the frontal lobe syndrome. The motor behaviours are associated with nigrostriatal degeneration, most notably in the putamen region of the striatum (Ma et al., 2002). In contrast, the cognitive symptoms sometimes seen in PD are related to degeneration of the nigrostriatal pathway extending towards the caudate nucleus of the striatum (Jokinen et al., 2009).

There are some problems in assessing cognitive dysfunction in PD (Karayanidis, 1989). First, there is the heterogeneous nature of PD which can impact upon cognitive functions. Second, the motor symptoms themselves may impact upon cognitive test results; many tests of cognition require a motor component to be measured, e.g. reaction time. Third, the drugs used to treat PD can have cognitive effects in their own right and it might be those that are being measured in cognitive testing.

Accounting for the motor deficits seen in PD, Cummings and Huber (1992) found that there was also a deficit in visuospatial functions, e.g. in a discrimination task. Ransmayr et al. (1987) found that PD patients performed poorly in a task involving drawing an angular figure in which they had to divide the shape into two to form a square, whereas in a mental rotation task, in which a cube with faces on the sides had to be matched with another cube in a different orientation, they were able to perform as well as controls. The difference was that the first task required a self-generated solution whereas the second task only required the matching of two different orientations.

Brown and Marsden (1986) suggested that the deficit in being able to change a mental set reflects the reduction in projections from the basal ganglia to the frontal cortex. PD patients were slower to change a particular set on the Stroop task (Taylor et al., 1987) and on visuospatial tasks requiring a shift between two mental perspectives (Brown & Marsden, 1986, 1988b). On the Wisconsin card sorting test, PD patients show high levels of perseveration (Brown & Marsden, 1988b). Using a battery of neuropsychological tests, Cools et al. (1984) found a notable deficit in PD when the task was divided into two processes that required a set shift. Brown and Marsden (1990) state that there is a differentiation between tasks that require sensory input and those that do not and that PD patients were 'impaired in switching set where they had to rely on internal cues and strategies for performing the task, but that performance was normal where external cues were provided' (p.27). In the Stroop test, PD patients had to identify the meaning of the word or the colour in which it was printed. In addition, they were either given a visual cue as to which category to focus on or just a warning signal (with no information other than that a change was about to occur) and patients were impaired when the task did not have an external cue (i.e. they needed to be told what to do exactly) (Brown & Marsden, 1988a).

Parkinson's disease patients had longer latencies of making the first move in the Tower of London task, but once the plan was made, they continued as normal (Morris et al., 1988). Using the same task, Owen et al. (1998) found an increase in blood flow in the right globus pallidus in normal controls, whereas in PD patients there was a decrease.

Using the picture arrangement test on the Wechsler Adult Intelligence Scale (WAIS), PD patients were impaired in providing a logical storyline, but this was not due to any deficits in short-term memory (Sullivan et al., 1989).

Thus, in some cases of PD the cognitive disturbances seen are reflective of frontal lobe dysfunction (see Chapter 12) due to the disconnection of afferent input from the basal ganglia, with difficulties in generating internal cues for both motor and cognitive behaviours.

CORTICAL NEURODEGENERATION: ALZHEIMER'S DISEASE

There are many forms of dementia, with an estimated global prevalence rate of 24.3 million people in 2006 and a forecast of double that in 2040 (Ferri et al., 2005). Of all the dementias, the one that is most commonly heard of is Alzheimer's disease (AD).

Diagnosis tends to be retrospective with confirmation of AD dependent on postmortem findings. **Senile dementia of Alzheimer's type (SDAT)** is a more cautious label for a group of patients that display similar symptomatology to those with confirmed AD. With this in mind, DSM 5 makes an attempt to recognize such symptoms (Box 24.3). A diagnosis of AD is gained from clinical examination and neuropsychological tests. As AD is a progressive

---

BOX 24.3: DSM 5: NEUROCOGNITIVE DISORDERS – ALZHEIMER'S DISEASE

Alzheimer's disease comes under neurocognitive disorders in the DSM 5.

Major neurocognitive disorders

Diagnostic criteria

A. Evidence of significant cognitive decline from previous level of performance in one or more cognitive domains (complex attention, executive function, learning and memory, language, perceptual-motor, or social cognition) based on:

1. concern of the individual, a knowledgeable informant, or the clinician that there has been a significant decline in cognitive function; and
2. a substantial impairment in cognitive performance, preferably documented by standardized neuropsychological testing or, in its absence, another quantified clinical assessment.

B. The cognitive deficits interfere with independence in everyday activities (i.e. at a minimum, requiring assistance with complex instrumental activities of daily living such as paying bills or managing medications).

> C. The cognitive deficits do not occur exclusively in the context of a delirium.
> D. The cognitive deficits are not better explained by another mental disorder (e.g. major depressive disorder, schizophrenia).
>
> **Major to mild neurocognitive disorder due to Alzheimer's disease**
>
> *Diagnostic criteria*
>
> A. The criteria are met for a major or mild neurocognitive disorder.
> B. There is insidious onset and gradual progression of impairment in one or more cognitive domains (for major neurocognitive disorder, at least two domains must be impaired).
> C. Criteria are met for either probable or possible Alzheimer's disease as follows:
>
> **For major neurocognitive disorder**
>
> *Probable Alzheimer's disease* is diagnosed if either of the following is present; otherwise *possible Alzheimer's disease* should be diagnosed.
>
> 1. Evidence of the causative Alzheimer's disease genetic mutation from family history or genetic testing.
> 2. All three of the following are present:
>   a. clear evidence of declining memory and learning and at least one other cognitive domain (based on detailed history or serial neuropsychological testing);
>   b. steadily progressive, gradual decline in cognition, without extended plateaus; and
>   c. no evidence of mixed aetiology (i.e., absence of other neurodegenerative or cerebrovascular disease, or another neurological, mental, or systemic disease or condition likely contributing to cognitive decline).
>
> **For mild neurocognitive disorder**
>
> *Probable Alzheimer's disease* is diagnosed if there is evidence of a causative Alzheimer's disease genetic mutation from either genetic testing or family history.
> *Possible Alzheimer's disease* is diagnosed if there is no evidence of the causative Alzheimer's disease genetic mutation from either genetic testing or family history, and all three of the following are present (see as major neurocognitive disorder).
>
> D. The disturbance is not better explained by cerebrovascular disease, another neurodegenerative disease, the effects of a substance, or another mental, neurological, or systemic disorder.

condition, symptoms vary across the individual's lifespan.

The early stages of AD start with small changes in a person's abilities or behaviour that can often be misattributed to distress or normal ageing. Memory decline for recent events is an early sign of AD and includes:

- forgetting recent conversations or events;
- repetition of behaviour or conversation;
- losing the thread of the conversation;
- occasional confusion; and
- impaired decision making.

In moderate AD the symptoms become more obvious and there is an increased functional impact in day-to-day living. The person may need help with daily activities and may be increasingly forgetful.

In the severe stages of AD the person may become totally dependent on others for care and the memory loss is pronounced. They may not be able to remember familiar objects or people and their personality may appear to change to the extent that family members do not recognize them as the person that they once knew.

Neuropathology

Auguste D was a 51-year-old woman with a five-year history of progressive cognitive impairment, hallucinations, delusions and impaired social functioning. After her death, Alois Alzheimer (1906) found on postmortem examination what were to become the hallmark characteristics that define the disease that takes his name: **amyloid-beta plaques** and **neurofibrillary tangles** (Alzheimer, 1907) (see Alzheimer et al. (1995) for an English translation of the 1906 and 1907 papers; Alzheimer et al., 1991). The plaques and tangles are microscopic changes in the brain of AD patients, but more gross changes are visible

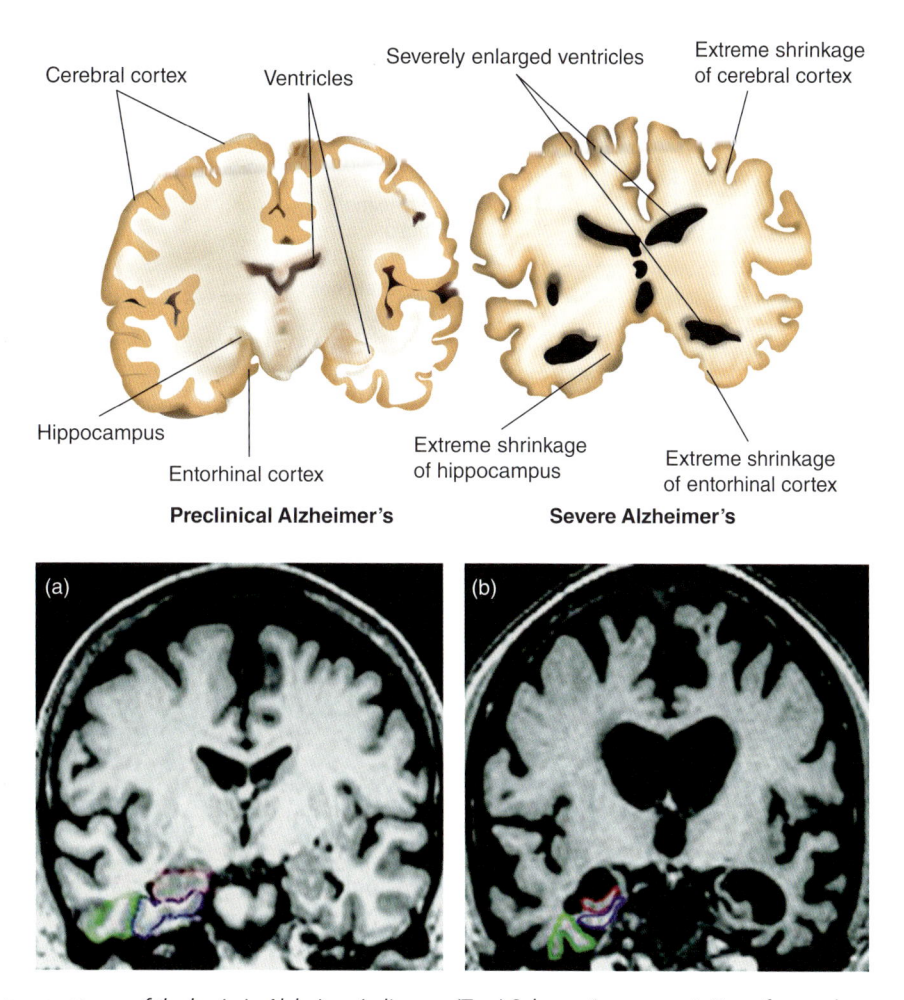

FIGURE 24.6 *The gross anatomy of the brain in Alzheimer's disease. (Top) Schematic representation of gross degeneration. (Bottom) MRI scans showing (a) no dementia and (b) dementia in AD. Hippocampus (outlined in red) responsible for forming, storing and organizing memory. Entorhinal cortex (outlined in blue) responsible for memory and navigation. Perirhinal cortex (outlined in green) responsible for object perception, memory and associations.*

without the use of the microscope. The cortex shows signs of atrophy and this is particularly pronounced in the hippocampus (Frisoni et al., 2010), which has become a valid biomarker for improving diagnosis (Albert et al., 2011; McKhann et al., 2011; Sperling et al., 2011). In addition to the shrinkage of the cortex and hippocampus, the ventricles increase in size (Apostolova et al., 2012). Therefore, in AD, cortical tissue shrinks and ventricles enlarge, leading to less brain tissue (Figure 24.6).

Generally beyond the reach of neuroimaging techniques, amyloid-beta plaques and neurofibrillary tangles are features that are considered to underlie the symptoms of Alzheimer's disease (Figure 24.7). Amyloid-beta plaques are abnormal extracellular clusters of amyloid-beta proteins. It is the build-up of amyloid-beta in the brain that is thought to give rise to all the problems with AD. Amyloid-beta has been shown to alter neurotransmission and inhibit synaptic plasticity, thereby reducing the functional effectiveness of the synapse and learning (Snyder et al., 2005). Furthermore, amyloid-beta proteins are implicated in abnormal dendritic processes in AD, which includes reduced dendritic complexity and loss of dendritic spines, therefore limiting neural communication (Cochran et al., 2014).

The neurofibrillary tangles and neuronal cell death are thought to be a downstream result of the accumulation and slowing of clearance of amyloid-beta (Caccamo et al., 2005; Hardy & Selkoe, 2002; Mawuenyega et al., 2010). The critical importance of amyloid-beta plaque formation in AD means that it is now a potential target for treatments that can focus on the causal pathway rather than symptom management once the disease process is firmly established.

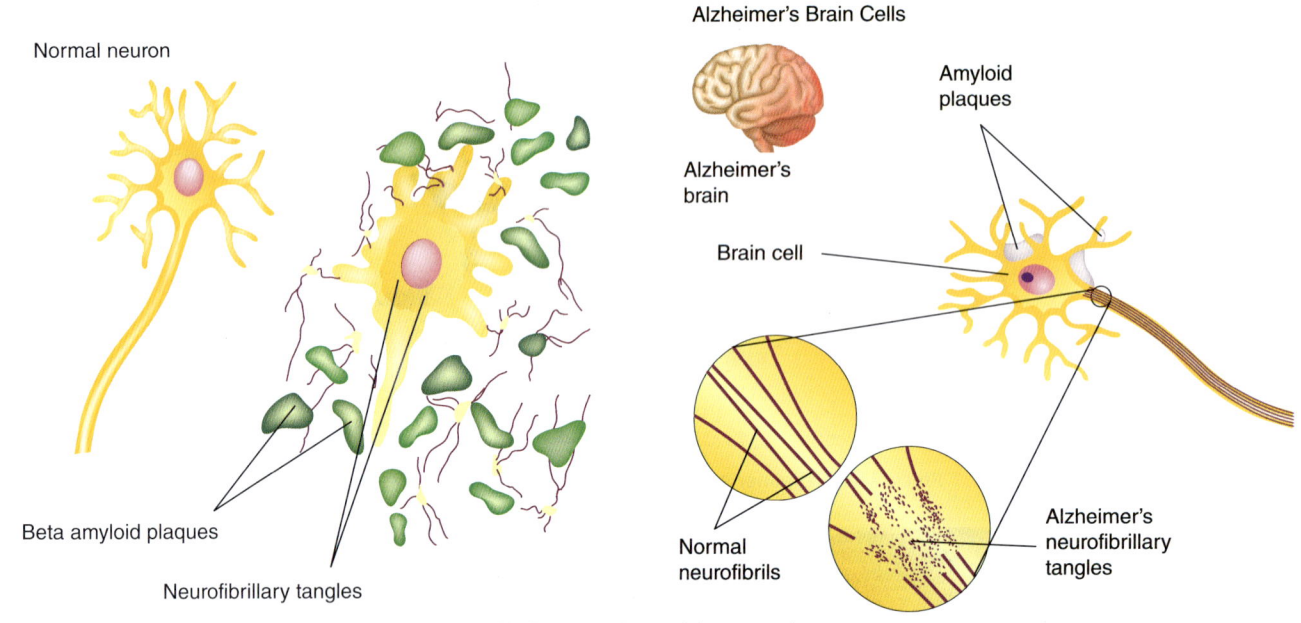

FIGURE 24.7 The beta-amyloid plaques and neurofibrillary tangles in Alzheimer's disease.

Neurofibrillary tangles (NFT) can be found early in the entorhinal cortex and then progresses to the hippocampus and other regions of the cortex (Braak & Braak, 1991). NFTs are formed by the hyperphosphorylated **tau proteins** which are involved in the stability of microtubules in the neuron. Phosphorylation detaches tau proteins from the microtubules, thereby affecting axon structure and communication. Tau proteins become hyperphosphorylated (phosphorylation is a biochemical action altering the function of a protein). These tau proteins begin to pair with the threads of other tau proteins, forming tangles within the neuron which correlate with dementia symptoms (Dickson et al., 1995).

The widespread destruction and abnormalities in the brain of AD patients lead to global cognitive changes that are difficult to target and treat. The symptoms are extensive and similar to frontal lobe syndrome and amnesias.

Neuropharmacology

Despite the global significance of AD and dementia, there is little in the way of drug therapy. Indeed, drug therapy in the UK has remained controversial with the National Institute for Health and Care Excellence (NICE) in 2005 finding little evidence to warrant the expense of treatment (NICE, 2005). However, after pressure from the Alzheimer's Disease Society, drugs became available again in 2011.

Underlying many of the drug therapies is the cholinergic hypothesis of AD and cognition in general. The main premise is that there is a reduction in acetylcholine (ACh) in AD leading to the cognitive deficits, especially of memory. Perry et al. (1978) first identified alterations in ACh in AD and stated:

> Choline acetyltransferase and acetylcholinesterase activities decreased significantly as the mean plaque count rose, and in depressed and demented subjects the reduction in choline acetyltransferase activity correlated with the extent of intellectual impairment as measured by a memory information test. (p.1457)

Given that there are numerous drugs that target cholinergic neurotransmission, the scope for investigation and treatment is greater than for targeting the neuropathological biomarkers. Scopolamine and atropine are muscarinic receptor antagonists and have been used as animal models of the memory deficits associated with AD (Box 24.4).

The data from animal studies and human studies support a cholinergic hypothesis whereby deficits are inflicted using scopolamine. Arising from the hypotheses are potential treatment strategies. In a similar vein to the treatment of PD by providing the precursors of dopamine, perhaps the precursor for ACh may have promise. Whilst this is intuitively appealing, evidence is not in support (Bartus et al., 1982). **Physostigmine** and **tacrine** are **acetylcholinesterase inhibitors** (AChEI) which act similarly to MAOIs and depression, increasing the availability of ACh at the synapses

BOX 24.4: ANIMAL MODELS OF ALZHEIMER'S DISEASE

With the widespread cognitive deficits seen in AD, animal models fall somewhat short in mimicking the condition. However, animal models of memory have been used in conjunction with drugs that can impair memory in order to understand the mechanisms involved in AD and memory generally.

The use of anticholinergic drugs to induce memory deficits has to be controlled carefully as otherwise there are problems with misinterpretation of the data. There are indirect effects of the drugs which may primarily affect perception and attention, but also have a downstream effect on memory. Therefore, experiments have to be carefully designed in order to manipulate memory and not another cognitive process. Furthermore, cholinergic drugs have effects on motivation and affect that can impact on cognitive psychopharmacological measures, and to add to the complexity, the effects of the drugs can be task dependent rather than construct dependent.

Questions that need to be asked include, what sort of memory are you measuring? There are many types of memory, for example, episodic, long term, semantic and working memory.

What else might you be measuring as well as memory? Memory is made up of different processes, e.g. attention, learning, encoding, storage and retrieval – not every component will be equally impaired.

Scopolamine has been shown to produce marked impairments in passive avoidance tasks in which animals learn to associate the dark side of a two-box compartment with electrical shock (Elrod & Buccafusco, 1988); this is attributed to both acquisition and consolidation of information (Rush, 1988). Whilst this type of memory is not readily recognizable as a problem in AD, spatial memory is identifiable. Morris (1984) developed the water maze as a method for investigating spatial learning in rodents. Using the water maze Smith et al. (1994) found that scopolamine induced impairments in rats' navigation. The maze consists of a pool of water (circumference circa 2 meters) that a rat cannot escape from. The water is coloured to obscure a platform just below the surface. The rat is placed in the pool and to get out has to find the platform. Initially the rat just swims about until, by accident, it finds the platform. After a number of trials, the rat is able to find the platform relatively easily. The rat uses spatial cues in the environment to locate the platform.

There are a number of measures that can be used to determine spatial learning in the water maze.

- Latency (time taken to find the platform).
- Path length (distance they swim to find the platform).
- Average speed (speed of swimming).
- Side wall proximity (distance from the walls of the pool).
- Directionality (the direction in which the rat swims when placed in the pool).
- Quadrant times (the amount of time spent in a particular quadrant).

Continuing with mazes, the eight-arm radial maze investigates the amount of re-entry to an arm after bait has been removed. Eckerman et al. (1980) found that scopolamine reduced accuracy with animals revisiting arms from which they had previously removed the bait.

Delayed matching to sample (and also delayed non-matching to sample) involves a stimulus being presented followed by an interval before the presentation of a novel stimulus. In delayed matching to sample, the previous stimulus is the correct choice whereas in delayed non-matching to sample, it is the novel stimulus that is the correct choice. The task can be made more difficult by increasing the inter-stimulus interval. This memory task can be readily used in rodents, monkeys and humans and is sensitive to anticholinergic drugs. Dunnett (1985) found that scopolamine impaired performance on delayed matching to sample tasks and this effect was reversed by physostigmine (a cholinesterase inhibitor, i.e. increases ACh via blockade of metabolism).

---

through metabolic inhibition and both have effects in improving deficits in AD (Eagger et al., 1992; Sahakian et al., 1987). However, the effects are limited because of potential liver toxicity (Watkins et al., 1994).

There are four AChEIs licensed by the American Food and Drug Administration for AD: tacrine, **donepezil**, rivastigmine and galantamine Galantamine also has agonist activity at the nicotine receptor which may contribute to its clinical efficacy (Coyle & Kershaw, 2001). Animal studies have supported a role for nicotine in attention (e.g. Mirza & Stolerman, 2000) and memory (e.g. Levin et al., 1996). In humans, Sahakian et al. (1989) administered nicotine to young, aged and AD patients and gave them all a neuropsychological test battery. They found improvements in attention and information processing, reaction times to visual information processing and delayed matching to location.

The drug that has received most media attention is **donepezil** (**Aricept**) which is used for mild to moderate AD (Birks, 2012). In animal models, donepezil was able to reverse the scopolamine-induced deficit in passive avoidance (Suzuki et al., 1995) the eight-arm radial maze (Braida et al., 1996) and delayed matching to sample (Dawson & Iversen, 1993). In AD patients improvements were seen on rating scales of symptoms (Rogers & Friedhoff, 1996). Donepezil did not prevent the decline in AD, but it did delay the process (Rogers & Friedhoff, 1998) (Figure 24.8). The clinical effects of donepezil were correlated with its ability to inhibit AChE (Rogers et al., 1998) (Figure 24.9).

With the huge impact of AD on individuals and society, other therapeutic targets are being investigated, e.g. tau and amyloid-beta (Anand et al., 2014).

Neuropsychology

It should be clear by now that widespread neural changes in AD are going to have similarly widespread effects on neuropsychological constructs.

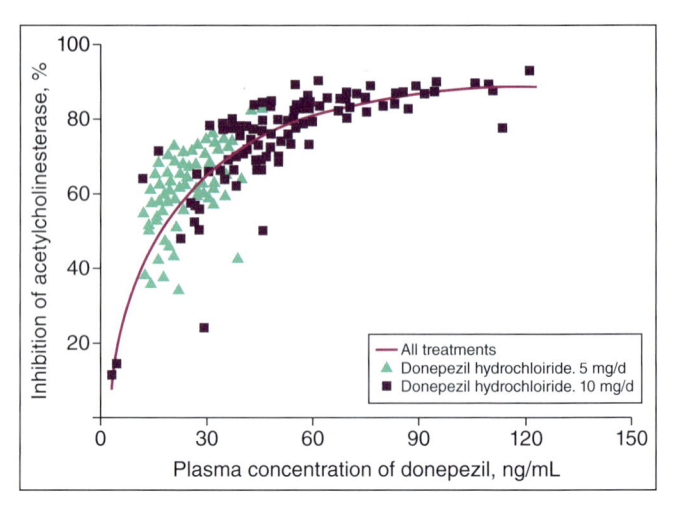

FIGURE 24.9 *Inhibition of AChE correlates with the concentration of donepezil.*
Source: Rogers, S. L., & Friedhoff, L. T. (1998). Long-term efficacy and safety of donepezil in the treatment of Alzheimer's disease: An interim analysis of the results of a US multicentre open label extension study. *European Neuropsychopharmacology*, 8(1), 67–75.

Using the framework of working memory, AD deficits can be seen in different systems. Morris (1987) argued that the articulatory loop system was not affected in AD. However, other systems within working memory were affected in AD (Morris & Baddeley, 1988) (Figure 24.10). Using

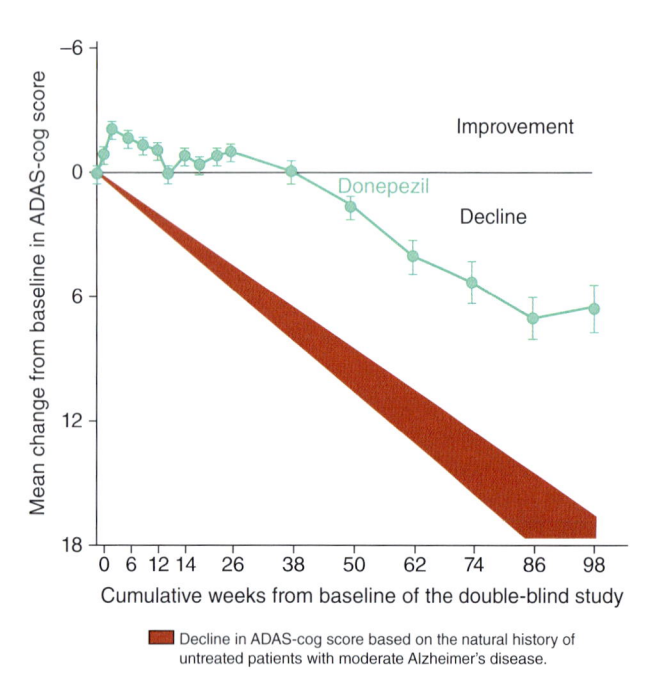

FIGURE 24.8 *The hypothetical decline in AD with and without donepezil. The decline in AD as measured by the Alzheimer's Disease Assessment Scale (ADAS) cognitive subscale is reduced in AD following donepezil.*
Source: Rogers, S. L., & Friedhoff, L. T. (1998). Long-term efficacy and safety of donepezil in the treatment of Alzheimer's disease: An interim analysis of the results of a US multicentre open label extension study. *European Neuropsychopharmacology*, 8(1), 67–75.

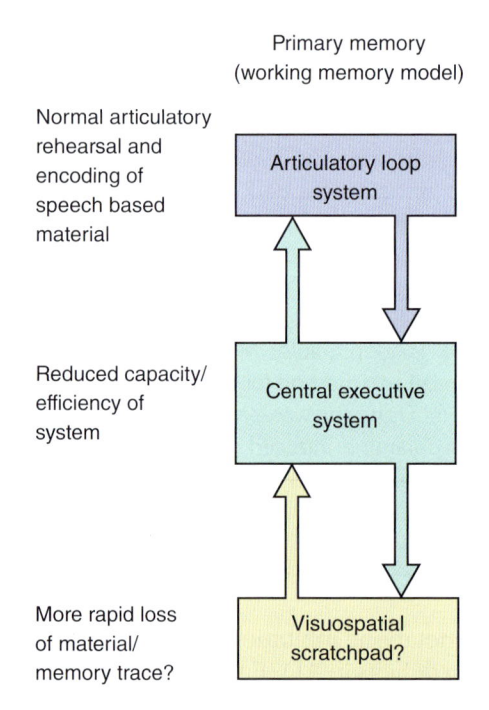

FIGURE 24.10 *Working memory deficits in Alzheimer's disease. Both the central executive and the visuospatial scratchpad are affected in AD.*
Source: Morris, R. G., & Baddeley, A. D. (1988). Primary and working memory functioning in Alzheimer-type dementia. *Journal of Clinical and Experimental Neuropsychology*, 10(2), 279–296.

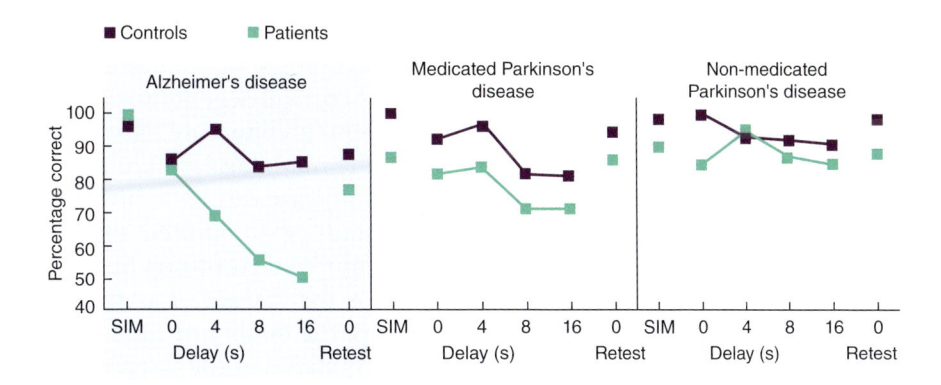

FIGURE 24.11 The effects of stimulus interval on a delayed matching to sample task. Alzheimer's patients performed poorly on a delayed matching to sample task as a function of delay of target stimulus (left panel) whereas medicated and non-medicated patients with Parkinson's disease did not show a progressive impairment. SIM, simultaneous matching-to-sample.
Source: Adapted from Sahakian, B. J., Morris, R. G., Evenden, J. L., Heald, A., Levy, R., Philpot, M., & Robbins, T. W. (1988). A comparative study of visuospatial memory and learning in Alzheimer-type dementia and Parkinson's disease. *Brain, 111*(Pt 3), 695–718.

a delayed matching to sample task to assess visuospatial memory, Sahakian et al. (1988) compared AD with PD and found that as the inter-stimulus interval increased, AD patients performed less well whereas PD patients were relatively unaffected (Figure 24.11). Baddeley et al. (1986) found that there was a deficit in the central executive system in AD. Using dual task performance, AD patients had to perform a pursuit tracking task with a subsidiary task that was (A) counting from 1 to 5, (B) a tone detection task or (C) a digital recall task. The effects of having to engage in two tasks at once impacted far more on the performance of AD patients (Figure 24.12).

Many other cognitive and memory tasks in particular are affected by AD. For more information, read Albert (2008) and Morris and Becker (2004).

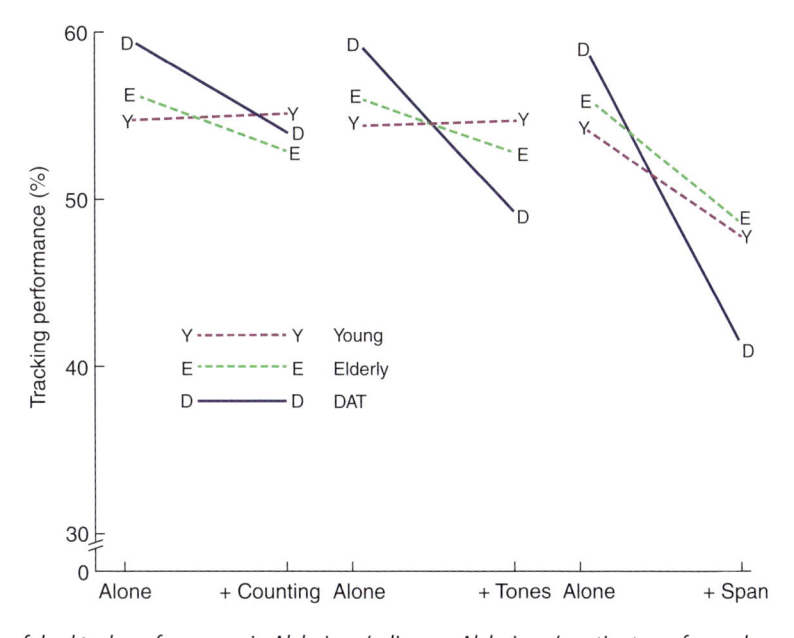

FIGURE 24.12 The effects of dual task performance in Alzheimer's disease. Alzheimer's patients performed more poorly on dual tasks that were combined compared to elderly and young participants. The effect was greatest with tasks requiring greater access to the central executive system as seen in the middle and right-hand panels. DAT, dementia of Alzheimer's type.
Source: Baddeley, A., Logie, R., Bressi, S., Della Sala, S., & Spinnler, H. (1986). Dementia and working memory. *Quarterly Journal of Experimental Psychology Section A: Human Experimental Psychology, 38*(4), 603–618.

SUMMARY

There are many neurodegenerative disorders and Alzheimer's disease and Parkinson's disease are two common types. Neurodegeneration is often of slow and insidious onset. The neuropathological changes occur long before symptoms emerge, as the brain tries to compensate for the loss of neural activity. Symptoms become evident after the brain loses its capacity to compensate. Parkinson's disease is considered mainly as a motor disorder caused by neurodegeneration of the nigrostriatal pathway. However, the extent of the neurodegeneration can extend to other regions of the brain, thereby giving rise to cognitive changes. Cognitive changes are the primary symptom in Alzheimer's disease. Unlike Parkinson's disease, Alzheimer's disease is a non-specific cortical degeneration and disorganization of the neural architecture. Not surprisingly, the effects of Alzheimer's disease are pronounced and extensive. Both diseases have no cure, but they do have treatments with limited efficacy. The treatments may improve symptoms but will not stop the progress of the disease. The treatments therefore can improve the quality of life for patients, especially in the early stages of the diseases, but they do very little to affect the disease process itself. Research is pushing forward to find better treatments, and advanced technologies, stem cells for example, may offer the patient an alternative that exceeds the effectiveness of current treatments.

LEARNING OUTCOME QUESTIONS

You should be able to answer the following questions.

- To what extent is Parkinson's disease merely a disorder of DA?
- What are the neuropsychological deficits associated with Parkinson's disease and what are their origins?
- What is the rationale behind pharmacological and surgical treatments for Parkinson's disease?
- Why is Alzheimer's disease so difficult to treat?

FURTHER READING

Anand, R., Gill, K. D., & Mahdi, A. A. (2014). Therapeutics of Alzheimer's disease: Past, present and future. *Neuropharmacology, 76*(Pt A), 27–50.

Fox, S. H., Katzenschlager, R., Lim, S.Y., Ravina, B., Seppi, K., Coelho, M., et al. (2011). The Movement Disorder Society evidence-based medicine review update: Treatments for the motor symptoms of Parkinson's disease. *Movement Disorders, 26*(S3), S2–S41.

Hariz, M. I., & Hariz, G. M. (2013). Therapeutic stimulation versus ablation. *Handbook of Clinical Neurology, 116*, 63–71.

Kudlicka, A., Clare, L., & Hindle, J. V. (2011). Executive functions in Parkinson's disease: Systematic review and meta-analysis. *Movement Disorders, 26*(13), 2305–2315.

Perl, D. P. (2010). Neuropathology of Alzheimer's disease. *Mount Sinai Journal of Medicine, 77*(1), 32–42.

Sarter, M., Hagan, J., & Dudchenko, P. (1992). Behavioral screening for cognition enhancers: From indiscriminate to valid testing: Part I. *Psychopharmacology (Berlin), 107*(2–3), 144–159.

Sarter, M., Hagan, J., & Dudchenko, P. (1992). Behavioral screening for cognition enhancers: From indiscriminate to valid testing: Part II. *Psychopharmacology (Berlin), 107*(4), 461–473.

Schapira, A. H. (2011). Monoamine oxidase B inhibitors for the treatment of Parkinson's disease: A review of symptomatic and potential disease-modifying effects. *CNS Drugs, 25*(12), 1061–1071.

MIND MAP

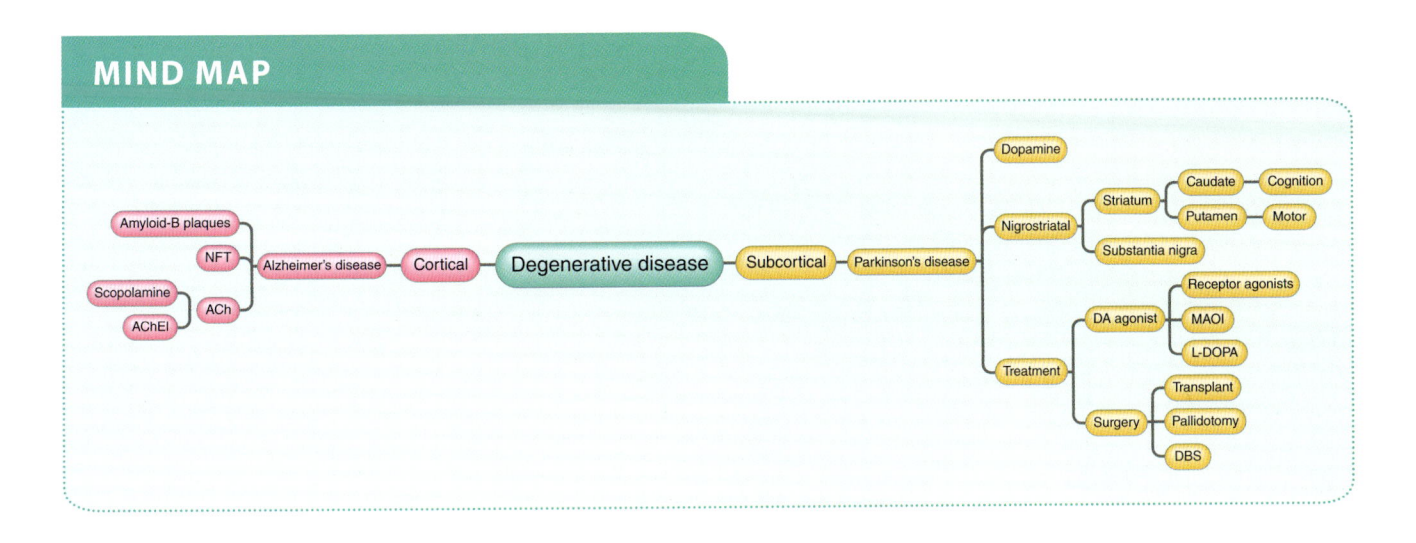

- Degenerative disease
  - Cortical — Alzheimer's disease
    - Amyloid-β plaques
    - NFT
    - ACh
      - Scopolamine
      - AChEI
  - Subcortical — Parkinson's disease
    - Dopamine
    - Nigrostriatal
      - Striatum
        - Caudate — Cognition
        - Putamen — Motor
      - Substantia nigra
    - Treatment
      - DA agonist
        - Receptor agonists
        - MAOI
        - L-DOPA
      - Surgery
        - Transplant
        - Pallidotomy
        - DBS

25 Psychobiology: Implications for the Brave New World

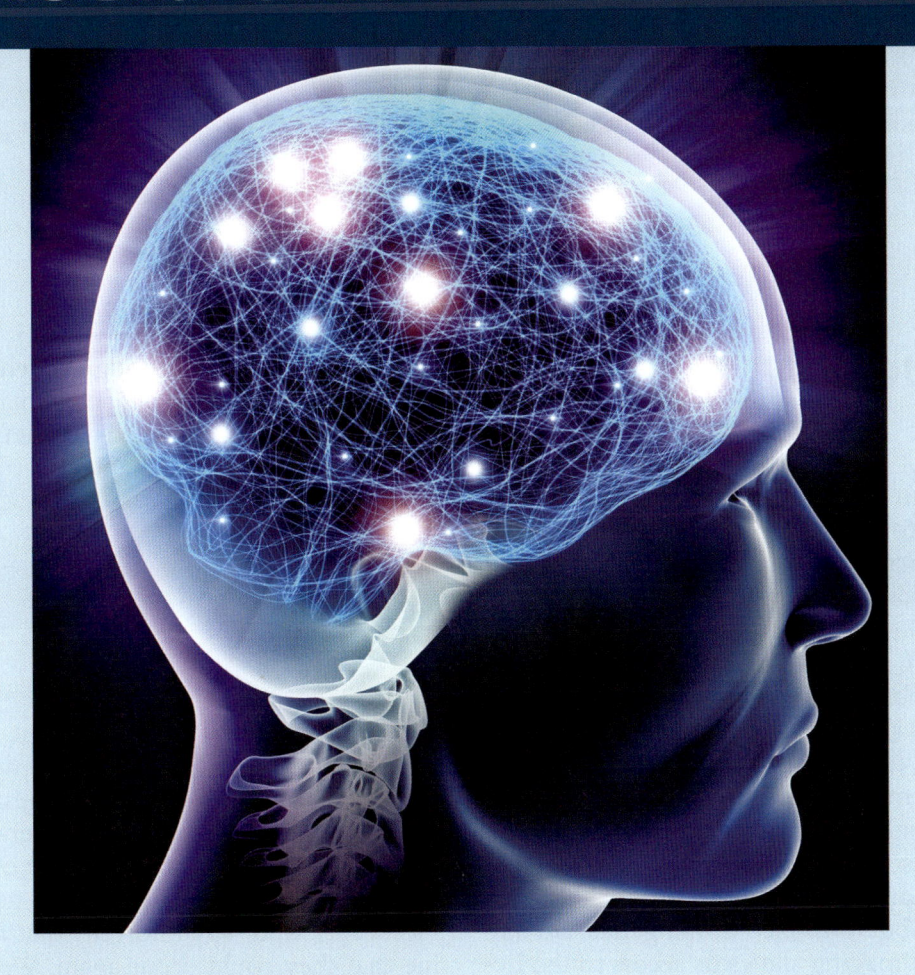

ANATOMY OF THE CHAPTER

This chapter will highlight the following.

- The importance of neuroscience and psychobiology to the real world.
- The dangers associated with unquestioning acceptance of scientific data.
- The importance of neuroethics and bioethics as the psychobiological subdisciplines make new discoveries.

INTRODUCTION   604

POLICY   604

DIAGNOSIS   606

TREATMENT   606

EDUCATION   607

LAW   608

SUMMARY   610

LEARNING OBJECTIVES

1. To understand the far-reaching implications of psychobiology.
2. To be able to evaluate psychobiology and neurotechnology/biotechnology in the court room.
3. To understand the limitations of psychobiology.

INTRODUCTION

The potential of psychobiology and neuroscience to influence our world takes them to relatively uncharted territories of society in its widest context. There is increasing impact of the science and research on medicine, education, law and on how we see ourselves in society. Psychobiology and neuroscience are not just about the individual, the owner of the brain. Knowledge obtained from these disciplines should shape our collective future. Understanding how biology and environments interact to determine behaviour will have important consequences for how we organize our societies and how we see ourselves within society. Technological breakthroughs are making the unthinkable not only thinkable but possible. Cloning has already occurred, neuroimaging allows us access to the living brain and psychopharmacology changes our behaviour for both good and bad, but how far can such developments go?

The answer is, potentially a long way. In reality, we have only just started, although it might seem that this is all new and that developments have been rapid. It is useful to suspend the concrete reality that is now and consider where technology and understanding can take us in the future. In such conjecture, we can take extreme positions and extreme examples and debate the relative merits of such a course of action. Ethical and moral consideration of psychobiology and neuroscience needs to take place at every stage of development. The possibility of enhancing our world and our lives is clearly apparent, but that is all dependent upon who is in power. Psychobiology and neuroscience are not just disciplines for understanding the brain and behaviour, they are also disciplines that address our freedom, liberty and agency. Although much of what is discussed below focuses on neuroimaging, the same arguments can be extended to genetics. I would also suggest you read this chapter in conjunction with Chapter 18.

POLICY

Science should inform policy, but it is politicians who determine policy. There are numerous examples in the literature which suggest that laws and policies have not always used science as the scientists would hope. Darwin's theory of evolution was the backbone of eugenics. The atrocities of the Holocaust were so abhorrent that one can't imagine that they could occur again. We often attribute it to a specific set of people during a specific period of time. Sadly, this is not the case. Wars and genocide still remain on the basis of people being different. Homosexuality was once illegal in the UK and remains so in other regions of the world (sometimes as a capital offence). Psychobiology has given us a neural account of sexual orientation (albeit not definitive). The heart of the argument is the nature/nurture debate: is it predetermined or is it a choice? Policies have changed over time, but we still have arguments about the sanctity of marriage and whether same-sex marriage should be allowed (Figure 25.1).

The drink-drive laws are also influenced by psychobiological research. Despite the fact that alcohol units are not consistent across nations, they do provide us with a way of standardizing and measuring our consumption. Surprisingly, the decision on what constitutes safe drinking is not evidence

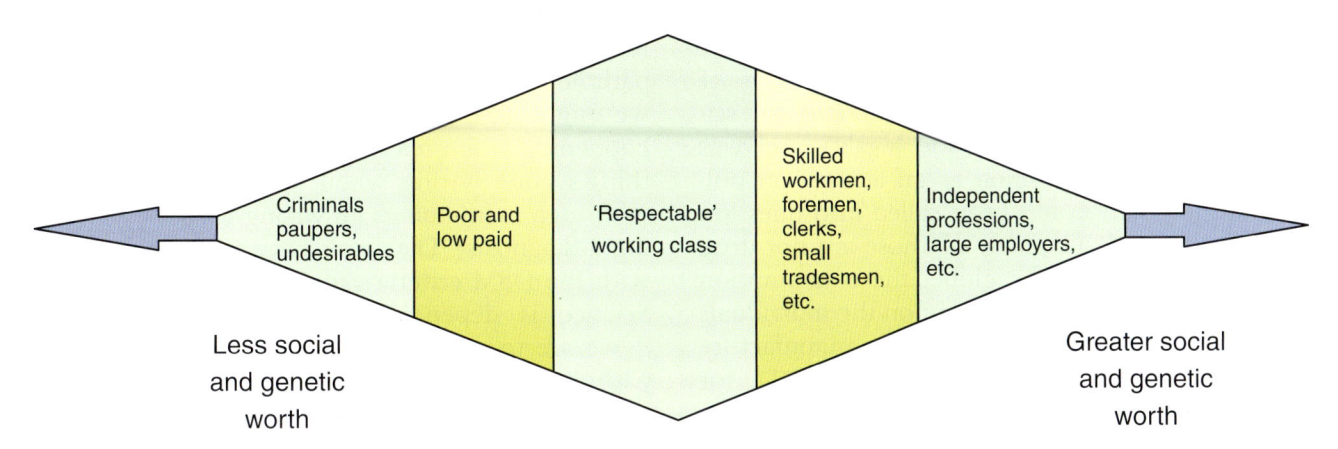

FIGURE 25.1 *Francis Galton's view of social and genetic worth of members of the British population*
Source: http://en.wikipedia.org/wiki/History_of_eugenics#/media/File:Galton_class_eugenics.svg. Attribution: D666D at the English language Wikipedia.

based. It is a political number. That is not to say that we are free to go and drink as much as we like without consequences. Alcohol is clearly a very damaging drug to the individual, but the cost to society is also enormous. Different countries have different legal limits of blood alcohol concentrations for driving. There is a call to change the blood alcohol concentration for driving in the UK from 0.08 to 0.05. A review of the effects of such a change, as occurred in the United States, suggests that lowering the limit means that people are less likely to have car crashes with potential fatalities (Fell & Voas, 2014).

Alcohol is not the only drug that affects behaviour, cognition and perception. Many of our illegal drugs also have effects that can affect driving performance. Albery et al. (2000) noted that nearly 82% of drug users in one study admitted to driving immediately after consuming either heroin or cannabis. Accidents were rife in this group. Where will policy take drug driving? Drugs are illegal; therefore, you should not have taken them (Figure 25.2). However, in California, for example, you are able to get a prescription for medicinal marijuana. Perhaps we need to consider what levels are appropriate for cannabis. Methylphenidate, which is a controlled substance, also has an impact on driving; for those with attention deficit hyperactivity disorder (ADHD), it improves their performance (Verster & Cox, 2008). Diazepam is used to treat anxiety but has a sedative effect and it has been suggested that:

> . . . diazepam adversely affects the ability of a patient to drive a car. It is preferable for anxious, aggressive, or depressed patients not to drive. Since diazepam tends to relieve these symptoms, this particular medication should not lead to an automatic prohibition of car driving. (Landauer, 1981, p.624)

Thus, the drug may be a problem, but so might not having the drug be a problem for such people.

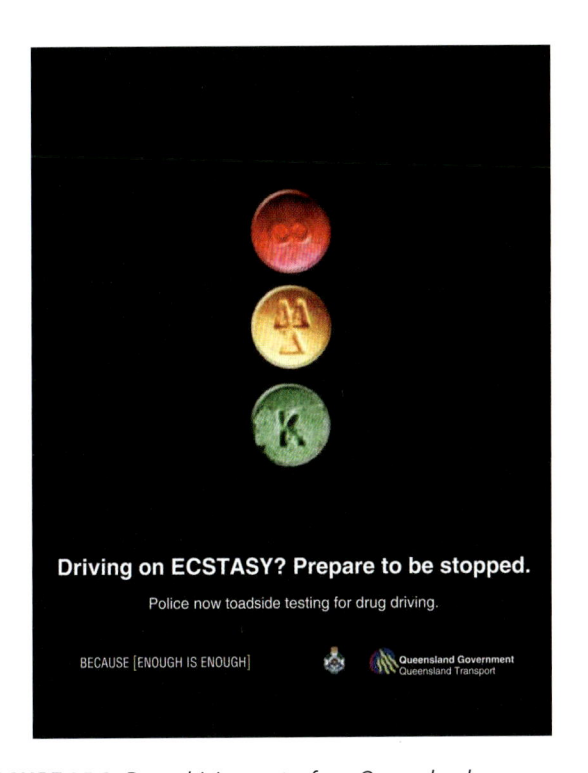

FIGURE 25.2 *Drug-driving poster from Queensland.*
Source: Reproduced with permission of State of Queensland (Department of Transport and Main Roads) (2007), Driving on ecstasy poster.

Continuing the theme of drug policy, Chapter 7 addressed how drugs were classified in terms of dangers and legality. David Nutt addressed the scientific validation of danger and legality and was dismissed from his position as an adviser on policy. Drug legislation has been called into question by many groups (and many of those are not drug user groups). Across the globe, the consumption of drugs has a profound effect upon the individuals who consume them, the people who manufacture them and the wider societies (see Pryce (2012) for an excellent review).

Drug policy and law are intimately entwined. The legal position is that drug users have a choice in their behaviour; the psychobiological evidence and even the diagnostic criteria suggest that control is lost in most drug users. Opening up the dialogue between politicians and all stakeholders in the 'war on drugs' is necessary. Questions remain as to why people take drugs in the first place. There may be pre-existing brain abnormalities or abnormalities may arise as a result of consuming drugs. Either way, for many drug users their lifestyle becomes problematic.

Currently, in the UK, access to drug services is often facilitated by the judge. However, there are alternatives that would benefit from further exploration. In 2001 Portugal changed its drug laws so that possession and acquisition of all types of drugs for personal use were decriminalized. Growing and distribution are still criminal acts. This has led drug users into treatment rather than making them criminals (Hughes & Stevens, 2010, 2012).

It would be a brave politician who opens up the debate on drug laws. It is a politically controversial arena. The potential benefits in terms of crime allied to drug use (organized crime) and health might be offset by an increase in drug use due to a permissive state. However, in the UK, we do not know what would happen and furthermore, the success or failure of a policy that effectively decriminalized drugs might not be known for many years. And politicians want answers quickly – in time for the next election.

DIAGNOSIS

There is an uncomfortable relationship between diagnosis and science. In order to understand the neurobiological basis of behaviour, one of the methods used is to see what goes wrong in psychopathologies. If we know what's gone wrong then we might have a chance of understanding what is happening when it's going right. We know something's gone wrong when it has been diagnosed (although many things go wrong without warranting a diagnosis). Diagnosis changes over the years with the DSM criteria growing with each edition. Science is dependent upon accurate diagnosis if we are to gain an understanding of the neuropathological basis of many of the psychological disorders. Without accurate diagnosis, we might be measuring the wrong constructs. Diagnosis similarly is dependent upon science, and this is probably most notable in DSM 5 where neurobiological causes are presented that have been informed by the most recent research. The symbiotic relationship between diagnosis and science means that diagnosis will become more refined and with that more refined and accurate diagnosis, scientists will be able to study psychopathology with more confidence. As research continues, diagnosis can be further refined (Figure 25.3).

In terms of psychopathologies, there is a lack of biomarkers for identifying disorders. Even brain imaging studies only give us a limited amount of information. They tell us about structure and activity, but not how the structure and activity manifest as abnormal behaviours. It is conceivable that such biomarkers will become available and these will clearly be of benefit to patients and scientists. There is a potential that treatments can be tailor-made to the individual's specific needs (e.g. pharmacogenetics).

TREATMENT

New treatments are constantly being sought. Psychobiology and neuroscience are at the forefront of finding new ways of treating pathology. Furthermore, understanding the placebo effect will be important for their use in clinical trials (see Chapter 7).

Few would dispute the valuable contribution of new treatment discoveries, but what about treating normality? What about engineering a better brain? Cognitive enhancers and cosmetic neurology provide fertile ground for neuroethical discussions. Cognitive enhancers or smart drugs do exactly

Science needed for accurate diagnosis

Diagnosis ⟷ Science

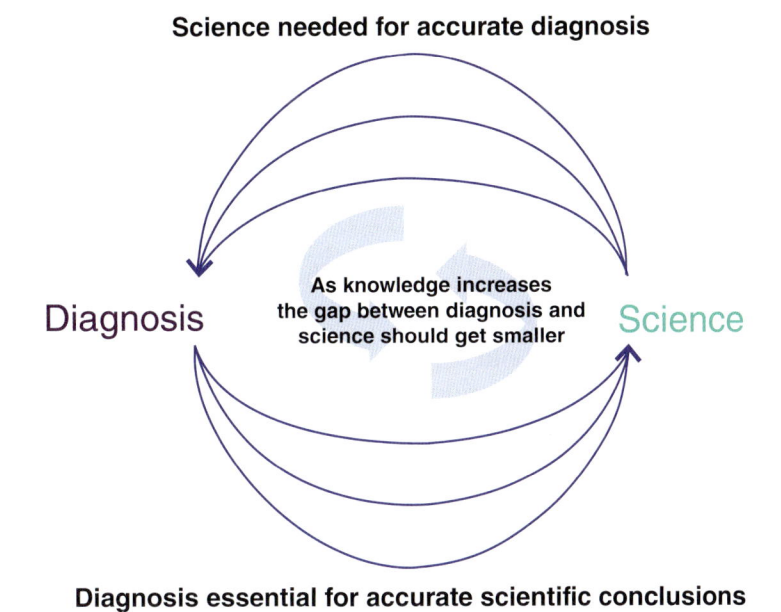

As knowledge increases the gap between diagnosis and science should get smaller

Diagnosis essential for accurate scientific conclusions

FIGURE 25.3 *The relationship between diagnosis and science.*
Source: Chandler, C. (2010). *The Science of ADHD: A guide for parents and professionals*. Chichester: Wiley. Reproduced by permission of John Wiley & Sons Ltd.

what they say they are going to do – they improve attention and memory, but questions remain about whether this should be sanctioned or controlled (Cakic, 2009). The debate takes us from treating illness through to treating normality. There is no easy answer.

Cosmetic neurology is a term that has been used to draw parallels with cosmetic surgery (Chatterjee, 2004). Changes in mood and affect can be brought about by pharmaceuticals, learning can be enhanced and perhaps personalities can be changed, but should they? A move to treating the healthy changes the whole ethos of medicine. No longer would it be just about disease. But the move towards cosmetic neurology does have ethical considerations, e.g. safety, equality (is it only the province of the wealthy?), coercion/pressure to conform (Chatterjee, 2004). All of this is somewhat reminiscent of Aldous Huxley's 'brave new world' in which a fictional drug, 'soma', provides a calming effect (and feelings of bliss and happiness) without withdrawal or adverse effects such as a hangover. In the brave new world, the state has conditioned citizens to desire the drug and escape from the trials and tribulations of life. Thus, we have a state-controlled politicopsychopharmacology – a new opiate of the masses which can sedate individuals or make them compliant.

EDUCATION

The adolescent is a work in progress. Sexual maturity and the activation of hormonal influences take place against a backdrop of neural reorganization. Adolescents like to sleep a lot (for some reason parents don't like this, whereas only a few years earlier they would have been grateful for their toddler staying in bed beyond 5.30 in the morning). The circadian rhythms of adolescence show changes in sleep patterns (Crowley et al., 2007). In a review of the literature on sleep in adolescence, Carskadon (2011) recommends that the authorities should start the school day later through adolescence. Such advice has been heeded, for example by Jon Barker, headteacher of Hugh Christie Technology College in Tonbridge, Kent, with an overall view that there are positive benefits of a late start.

It is not all about sleep – exercise is also important. It has been suggested that the concentration of children with ADHD is greatly improved by a walk in the park (Taylor & Kuo, 2009). Schools often require children to sit still, be quiet and concentrate, all of which seems entirely reasonable. However, all children who were given working memory tasks demonstrated increased motor activity (Rapport et al.,

2007, Rapport et al., 2009). This has led to the suggestion that arousal facilitates cognitive functioning in all individuals. To illustrate this point, look at people when they are engaged in cognitive tasks in everyday life; when people try to solve crossword puzzles, for example, they may rock their legs or tap their pencil on their heads (or is that just me?). The lesson from this report would suggest that some activity is beneficial for learning.

Neuroscientists have stepped out of the laboratory and started to inform teachers about the psychobiology of behaviours such as attention, learning and memory, as well as dealing with the brain of an adolescent and children with dyslexia (Dommett et al., 2011). Neuroscience can also dispel common myths about the brain – I am always surprised that the layperson is often willing to engage in discussion about the product of brain activity (behaviour), but would not dream of discussing the intricacies of cardiology (that would require expert knowledge).

The expertise of the psychobiologist and neuroscientist needs to be accessed in order to dispel many myths. Goswami (2006) reports that at a conference at the University of Cambridge, teachers received a considerable volume of information from businesses encouraging them to adopt brain-based practices. This is all well and good if there is a sound evidence-based reason for using some of these technologies. However, Goswami points out that many of the claims of the sales literature are unfounded and lack strong scientific principles but disguise the fact by using psychobabble and neuro- prefixes (putting 'neuro' in front of a word apparently gives it more credibility, e.g. neurolinguistic programming has a limited evidence base) (Witkowski, 2010).

Advertisements for cosmetics, health products or foods present statements of authority such as 'clinically proven' or 'scientifically proven' often surrounded by pseudo-scientific jargon. Manufacturers present their product as having clinical powers that are a fact. But is it a fact? The word 'fact' is rarely used in the behavioural sciences. A fact tends to lead the reader into assuming that the information is an absolute irrefutable truth; research can do a lot to change that truth – even in chemistry! (Chandler, 2010).

The overall view was that:

> . . . the teachers were amazed by how little was known. Although there was enthusiasm for and appreciation of getting first-hand information, this was coupled with frustration at hearing that many of the brain-based programmes currently in schools had no scientific basis. (Goswami, 2006, p.410).

LAW

Psychobiology and the neurosciences are increasingly being brought into courts of law. Expert witnesses can provide general information about psychology and the brain which may act as a defence for the accused. With the increasing use of neuroimaging technologies, being able to rely on scientific data is particularly appealing to defence lawyers. However, neuroimaging has yet to be a defining piece of evidence. A magnetic resonance imaging (MRI) scan may tell the judge and jury that the defendant has a brain abnormality. However, there are many people with brain abnormalities who do not commit crimes. Imaging studies cannot currently show intent. There is a growing body of research that is using neuroimaging to determine whether someone is telling the truth or not, although the accuracy is somewhat limited (Spence et al., 2004). This is just a very expensive version of the polygraph, to some extent (Figure 25.4).

At the heart of legal systems is the concept of *mens rea*, which is criminal responsibility, e.g. a guilty mind. It is a guilty mind that tells us if there was intent to commit the crime.

In the UK there are a number of defences that can be used in criminal law that have a direct link with neuroscience (Eastman & Campbell, 2006).

- *Automatism*: the mind did not initiate the action. There is no intended will, e.g. someone who physically strikes someone else

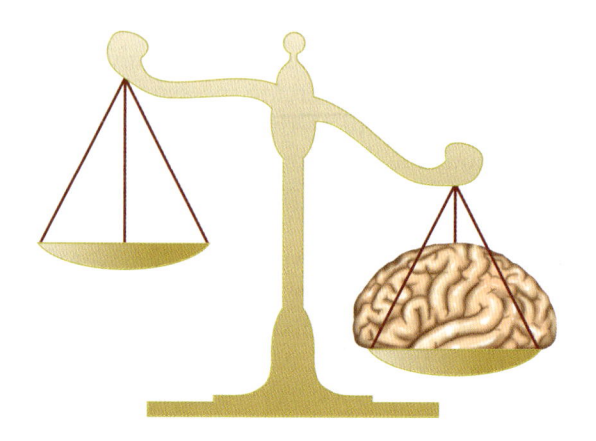

FIGURE 25.4 *Neuroscientific knowledge of the brain is becoming increasingly weighty evidence in law and justice.*

during an epileptic seizure is not responsible for their actions despite being the person who committed the act.

- *Insanity*: a defect of reason or mental illness of such a severe nature that a person cannot distinguish fantasy from reality; they have a psychosis; or are subject to uncontrollable and impulsive behaviour.

- *Diminished responsibility*: used for downgrading murder to manslaughter. There is a substantial impairment in mental responsibility for action.

- *Provocation*: in this defence, a *reasonable* man may 'lose mastery over mind' in response to provocation, e.g. the Lorena Bobbitt case in which a woman who suffered years of abuse finally snapped and cut off her husband's penis (Margolick, 1994).

Indeed, many claims have been made for *diminished responsibility* on neuropsychological grounds. Other criminal acts which are morally repugnant such as paedophilia also fall into the neuro-legal dimension. For example, a man had what doctors referred to as acquired paedophilia as a consequence of a tumour on the right orbitofrontal cortex. Removal of the tumour resulted in him being considered safe again. The tumour grew again and so did the sexual behaviour (Burns & Swerdlow, 2003). The question is, how accountable was he for his behaviour?

In the UK, premenstrual syndrome (PMS) has been used as a mitigating plea in some legal cases, including murder. As far back as 1845, a woman was acquitted of shoplifting due to menstruation and in 1851 two women were found not guilty of murder. Mothers who killed their children were seldom punished because they were seen as not responsible for their actions (Sommer, 1984). They were all considered to have temporary insanity as a consequence of 'suppression of menstruation' (Spitz, 1987).

Shockingly, Lombroso and Ferrero (1898), in a very early book called *The Female Offender*, wrote:

> One peculiarity of the female criminal lunatic which is, however, only an exaggeration of her normal state, is that her madness becomes more acute at particular periods, such as menstruation, menopause, and pregnancy. (p.294)

Clearly, such statements are now seen as outrageous but we should remember that history has a habit of repeating itself. In an editorial in the *New Statesman*, Cox and Ince (2012) state: 'As the past becomes hazy, we start to believe that there can be no other sort of world'. Thus, we should not become complacent in our more enlightened world as there may be challenges ahead.

Lombroso and Ferrero continue their dissection of the female criminal and associate tattoos with criminal activity and prostitution – in my home town of Brighton, such a view would be met with disdain (to say the least). Lombroso and Ferrero provide an interesting review of brain differences in the female criminal compared to the non-criminal. The interesting feature is that whilst the list may not be accurate, the criticisms of the search for brain abnormalities that can be levelled at them are still in play to this day. Changes in the brain may or may not affect behaviour and the differences are small. How differences are operationalized in terms of behaviour remains elusive. Times change and we should remember that the past influenced the present and will influence the future.

In 1980–81, two British women escaped murder convictions by arguing that PMS resulted in diminished responsibility (Boorse, 1987). How can this happen? The answer lies in the philosophical and legal view of being in control.

In law, at the core of jurisprudence is the **M'Naghten Rule**, which has the following features.

- The presumption that the defendant is sane and responsible for their criminal acts.

- That the defendant must have been suffering 'under a defect of reason' or 'from disease of the mind' to be found not guilty.

- That the defendant must 'not know the nature and quality of the act he was doing, or if he did know it that he did not know what he was doing was wrong'.

Knowing the difference between right and wrong does not necessarily mean that the individual is capable of regulating behaviour according to those principles, even with abnormalities of the frontal cortex (Sapolsky, 2004).

Looking at the M'Naghten Rule, it becomes clear that changes to our understanding of personal responsibility are far reaching. Greene and Cohen (2004) claim that the law itself is unlikely to change its assumptions because of neuroscience; the change that neuroscience may bring about is considered to be how people view themselves as free agents. They assert that neuroscience will change people's perceptions of agency, guiding law from a system based on retribution to a consequentialist perspective of promoting future social welfare.

Use of brain scans in the courtroom to determine the potential mental state of the defendant is perhaps more common in the United States than in the UK. But the use of neuroimaging can be said to be questionable at best in a court of law, especially where the death penalty may be the final sentence.

Steven Hyman is quoted as saying about brain scans in court:

> I believe that our behaviour is a production of activity in our brain circuits, but I would never tell a parole board to decide whether to release somebody or hold onto somebody based on their brain scan as an individual, because I can't tell what are the causal factors in that individual. (Stix, 2014, p.14)

A large amount of money is being spent by the US military and security services on cognitive neuroscience research for warfare and detecting deception and lies (Tennison & Moreno, 2012). Lie detectors are not new. The use of MRI scans to detect different types of lies has met with some success (Ganis et al., 2003), but this is experimental work in a laboratory; it is not yet sophisticated enough to be the defining word in a court of law.

The use of brain scans in the court room has also been criticized because of the powerful impact it can have on information being presented. The impact of neuroscientific evidence, albeit inaccurate, has been shown to have a detrimental effect on people's reasoning, with people giving more credence to neuroscientific explanations (Weisberg et al., 2008). Such spurious evidence can be referred to as 'neurobabble'. Using colourful pictures of brains also gives people a false impression of increased credibility of the evidence (McCabe & Castel, 2008). In a simulated court setting, jurors were more likely to find a defendant not guilty by reason of insanity if the diagnosis was supported with brain images (Gurley & Marcus, 2008). Not all studies have found a similar bias towards brain images (Schweitzer et al., 2011). However, jurors who were not provided with a neuroimage indicated that they believed neuroimagery would have been helpful in their evaluations of the defendant (Schweitzer & Saks, 2011). In a challenge to the seductive allure of neuroimaging, Farah and Hook (2013) have suggested that there is little effect of such images and that the original reports have not been replicated.

The different agendas that science and the legal system have is exemplified in a statement by Schauer (2010): 'Science must inform the legal system about reliability rates and degrees of validity, but whether some rate or degree is good enough for some legal purpose is a question of law and not of science' (p.102). The reliability of neuroimages was called into question in a study suggesting that fMRI-based deception detection measures were vulnerable to countermeasures to avoid such detection (Ganis et al., 2011). Before we place too much emphasis on the importance of technology, we have to understand its limitations.

And then there are also the differing agendas of science and policy linked to the deployment of law. What is the possible extreme position arising from the knowledge that the prefrontal cortex is involved in moral and rational decision making and that damage to this area leads to psychopathic behaviour, especially when linked with damage to the amygdala (Mobbs et al., 2007)? Are we to start engaging in pre-emptive imprisonment on the basis of a 'just in case' scenario?

Brain imaging may not be restricted to the defendant; what about the jurors? Knowledge about how we make moral decisions is increasing rapidly. In a study in which participants were given either an impersonal or a personal dilemma, different regions of the brain were shown to be activated. In this study, the choice was to divert a runaway train by flicking a switch that could send the train down a track that would kill one person or down a track that would kill several people. The personal dilemma involved a decision being made on a bridge over the railway track and the only way to save the threatened people was to push a stranger off the bridge onto the tracks below, thereby killing the stranger but stopping the train and saving the other people (Figure 25.5). Greene et al. (2001) were able to differentiate between the personal and impersonal dilemmas using fMRI. In the future, will all jurors need to be screened for their ability in such decision making?

SUMMARY

Psychobiology and the modern technologies used to investigate brain and behaviour have an impact far greater than just being academic pursuits. The

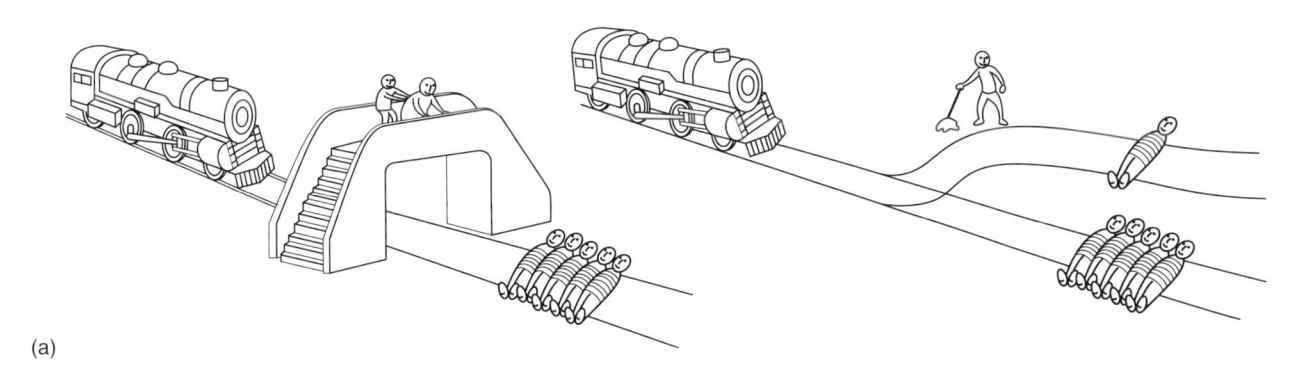

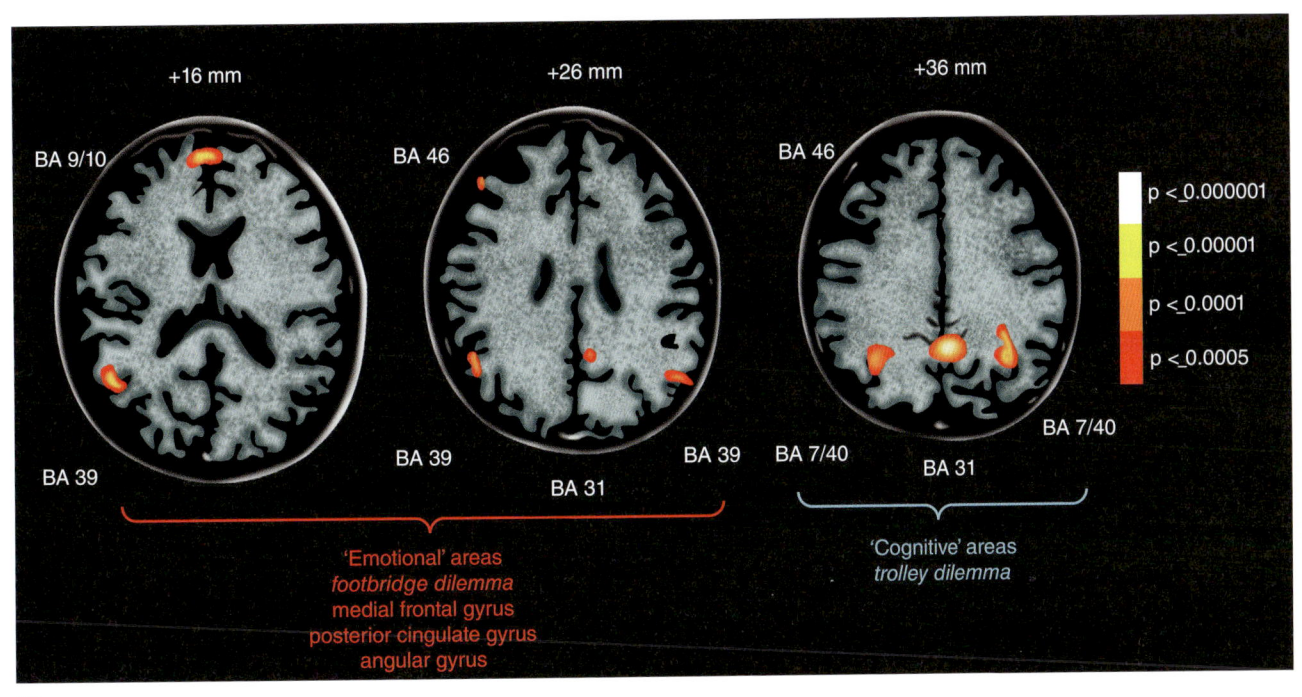

FIGURE 25.5 (a) Do you push one person of the bridge to save four people (personal)? Do you change the path of a train to avoid killing four people and killing only one (impersonal)? (b) The neural correlates of the dilemma identify different regions of the brain.
Source: (b) From Greene J. D. et al (2001). An fMRI investigation of emotional engagement in moral judgment. *Science, 14*, 293(5537), 2105–2108. Reprinted with permission from AAAS.

necessity of evaluating and steering the impact of this newly acquired knowledge has given birth to neuroethics. This is a fascinating and stimulating new branch of philosophy, as what was once considered impossible is now happening, and today's impossible is probable. However, there are no answers. We have to look at history and how thought has changed over the decades and centuries. We have to be adaptable, open to new ideas and possibilities.

And finally, as a physicist and a comedian write:

> Science is a framework with only one absolute: all opinions, theories and 'laws' are open to revision in the face of evidence. It should not be seen or presented, therefore, as a body of inviolate knowledge against which policy should be judged; the effect of this would be to replace one priesthood with another. Rather, science is a process, a series of structures that allow us, in as unbiased a way as possible, to test our assertions against Nature ... Elected politicians are free to disregard its findings and recommendations. Indeed, there may be good reasons for doing so. But they must understand in detail what they are disregarding, and be prepared to explain with precision why they chose to do so. (Cox & Ince, 2012).

LEARNING OUTCOME QUESTIONS

You should be able to answer the following questions.
- What are the pros and cons of using brain images in law?
- To what extent should drug policy be informed by science?
- Are we responsible for our own actions?

FURTHER READING

Farah, M. J. (2012). Neuroethics: The ethical, legal, and societal impact of neuroscience. *Annual Review of Psychology, 63,* 571–591.
Farahany, N. A. (Ed.) (2009). *The impact of behavioural sciences on criminal law.* Oxford, UK: Oxford University Press.
Giordano, J. J., & Gordijn, B. (2010). *Scientific and philosophical perspectives in neuroethics.* Cambridge, UK: Cambridge University Press.
Glannon, W. (2006). Neuroethics. *Bioethics, 20*(1), 37–52.
Glannon, W. (Ed.) (2007). *Defining right and wrong in brain science: Essential readings in neuroethics.* New York: Dana Press.
Illes, J., & Sahakian, B. J. (Eds.) (2011). *The Oxford handbook of neuroethics.* Oxford, UK: Oxford University Press.
Pryce, S. (2012). *Fixing drugs: The politics of drug prohibition.* Basingstoke, UK: Palgrave Macmillan.
Schacter, D. L., & Loftus, E. F. (2013). Memory and law: What can cognitive neuroscience contribute? *Nature Neuroscience, 16*(2), 119–123.
Seymour, B., & Vlaev, I. (2012). Can, and should, behavioural neuroscience influence public policy? *Trends in Cognitive Science, 16*(9), 449–451.
Zeki, S., & Goodenough, O. R. (2004). *Law and the brain.* Oxford, UK: Oxford University Press.

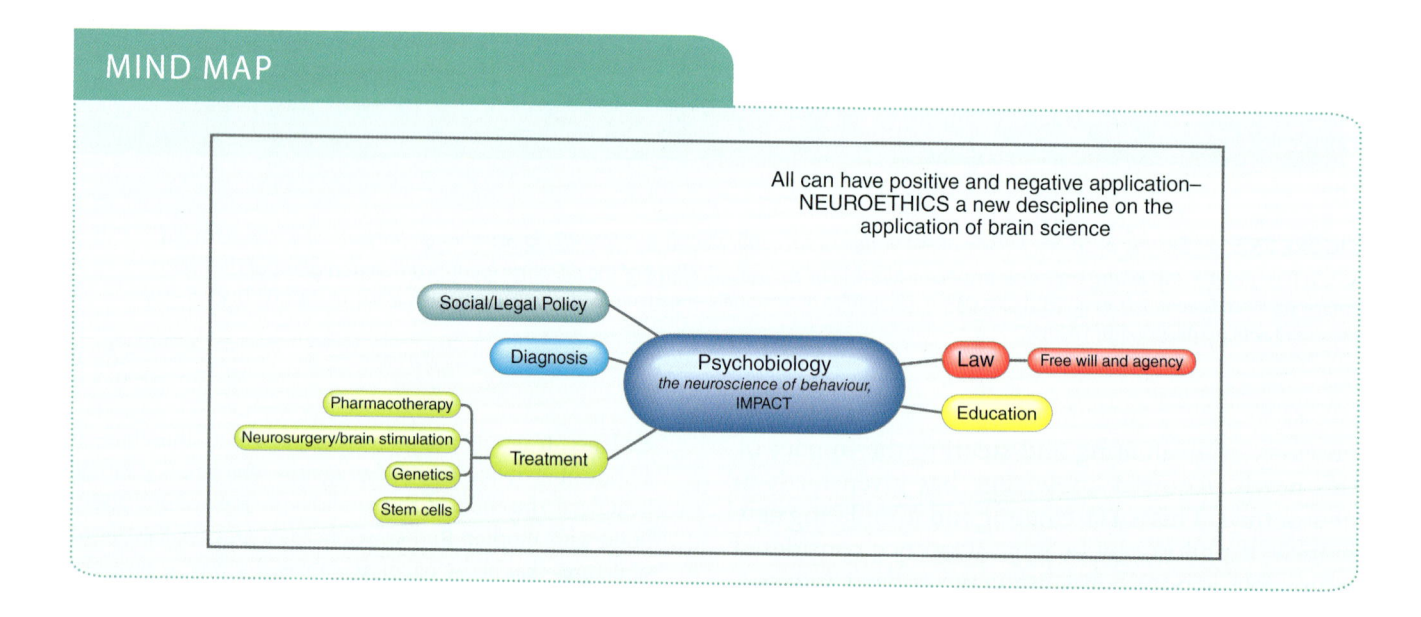

MIND MAP

Glossary

3-methoxy-4-hydroxyphenylglycol A metabolite of noradrenaline

5,7-DHT A selective serotonergic neurotoxin

5-alpha-reductase An enzyme which converts testosterone into DHT

6-hydroxydopamine A neurotoxin

6-OHDA See 6-hydroxydopamine

Abducens nerve (CN VI) A cranial nerve

Absolute refractory period The period immediately following the firing of a nerve fibre when it cannot be stimulated no matter how great a stimulus is applied

Abuse The use of drugs which leads to problems for the individual

Acetylcholine A neurotransmitter

Acetylcholinesterase inhibitor A drug which prevents the degradation of acetylcholine

Acrosome The tip of a sperm that contains enzymes which break down the outer part of the ovum

Actin A protein involved in muscle contraction and the structure of cells

Action potential The depolarization of the membrane potential that sends a signal down the axon of a neuron. This is the neuron firing or creating a spike on a graphic representation of the action potential (on an oscilloscope)

Activational period The time when the effect of a hormone occurs in the fully developed organism

Addiction Compulsive engagement in rewarding stimuli, despite adverse consequences, e.g. drugs, gambling etc.

Aδ fibres Fibres that send fast pain messages

Adenine A nucleotide base. Part of the genetic code

Adenosine triphosphate A nucleotide compound that provides the storage of energy within cells

Adenylate cyclase An enzyme that creates the formation of cyclic AMP

Adipsia Cessation of drinking

Adolescence A period of development characterized by the onset of puberty and finishing in adulthood (i.e. starts with a biological marker and ends with a social construct)

Adoption studies Studies using adopted individuals to determine the genetic contribution to a behaviour or trait. The assumption is that adopted children share the genes but not the environment with their biological parents

Adrenal glands Endocrine glands that sit above the kidney. Release cortisol and adrenaline

Adrenaline/epinephrine A neurotransmitter (UK/USA name respectively)

Adrenocorticotrophic hormone A hormone of the anterior pituitary that stimulates the production of steroids in the cortex of the adrenal glands

Advisory Council on the Misuse of Drugs A statutory and non-executive non-departmental public body that makes recommendations to government on the control of dangerous or otherwise harmful drugs

Affective neuroscience A branch of neuroscience looking at emotion and affect

Afferent pathway Sensory pathway (input to the brain)

Affinity The strength of binding of a single molecule to its ligand

Agarose gel block A tool used in molecular genetics during electrophoresis

Agnosia Difficulty with recognizing or inability to recognize objects

Agonist A substance which initiates a physiological response when combined with a receptor

Agouti-related peptide A neuropeptide involved in feeding

Agraphia Inability to write

Akathisia Motor restlessness

Akinesia Loss of movement

Alcohol The intoxicating constituent of wine, beer, spirits and other drinks

Alcohol unit A measure of the alcohol content in various drinks of different volumes. Differs across countries

Aldosterone A corticosteroid hormone which stimulates ab-sorption of sodium by the kidneys, thereby regulating water and salt balance

Alexia Inability to read

Alleles The two alternative forms of a gene found at the same place on a chromosome

All-or-nothing law An action potential is either present or not present

Allostasis The process of achieving stability through physiological or behavioural change

Allostatic load The expression of pathophysiology by long-term chronic overactivation of systems

Allostatic state The chronic overactivation of systems and the alteration of setpoints

Allosteric modulation The binding of a drug at a site adjacent to the active site

Alpha-fetoprotein A plasma protein that binds to oestrogens and stops them entering the brain

Alpha motor neurons Lower motor neurons of the brainstem and spinal cord innervating muscle fibres of skeletal muscle

Alpha waves The normal electrical activity of the brain when conscious and relaxed

Alveoli Air sacs in the lung

Alzheimer's disease Progressive mental deterioration that can occur in middle or old age, due to generalized degeneration of the brain

Amacrine cell A type of neuron in the retina. Most amacrine cells lack axons and work laterally, affecting the output from bipolar cells

American Psychological Association The professional association for US psychologists. APA guidelines for writing are, in general, favoured by UK universities

Amino acids Simple organic compounds that when assembled in long chains create proteins

Amobarbital (sodium amytal) A barbiturate

AMPA receptor A glutamate receptor

Amphetamine A psychostimulant that facilitates the release of dopamine into the synapse

Amphibian A cold-blooded vertebrate animal, e.g. frog

Ampulla The second portion of the fallopian tube and the location of fertilization

Amygdala Two almond-shaped groups of nuclei located deep and medially within the temporal lobes of the brain

Amyloid-beta plaque Abnormal extracellular cluster of amyloid-beta proteins

Analgesia Pain relief

Androgen insensitivity syndrome A person has XY chromosomes but they are phenotypically female due to a lack of androgen receptors

Androgens Typically male sex hormones (but females also possess them)

Angiotensin A protein that promotes aldosterone secretion and tends to raise blood pressure

Animals (Scientific Procedures) UK legislation that governs animal experiments
Act (1986)

Anion A negatively charged ion

Anorexia nervosa A disorder of restricted food intake leading to severe weight loss

Antagonist Drug that blocks or dampens agonist-mediated responses rather than provoking a biological response itself upon binding to a receptor

Anterior nucleus of the hypothalamus A part of the hypothalamus

Anterograde amnesia The inability to establish new memories following injury or trauma

Antidepressant A drug used to treat depression

Anti-Mullerian hormone A hormone which inhibits the development of the Mullerian ducts

Antipsychotic A drug used to treat the symptoms of schizophrenia (psychosis)

Anvil (incus) One of the bones within the ear

Anxiolytic A drug used to treat anxiety disorders

Aphagia Cessation of feeding

Aphasia A dysfunction of language production

Apoptosis Programmed cell death

Apraxia The inability to perform conscious motor movements

Aqueous humour The clear fluid filling the space in the front of the eyeball between the lens and the cornea

Arachnoid mater One of the three meninges that form the protective membranes that cover the brain and spinal cord

Arborization The growth of dendrites

Arcuate fasciculus A bundle of fibres around the lateral sulcus connecting Broca's area to Wernicke's area

Arcuate nucleus of the hypothalamus A part of the hypothalamus

Aromatase An enzyme which converts testosterone into oestradiol

Arteries The blood vessels that deliver oxygen-rich blood from the heart to the tissues of the body

Asexual reproduction Reproduction in which only a single parent is required

Asperger's syndrome A developmental disorder related to autism and characterized by awkwardness in social interaction, pedantry in speech and preoccupation with very narrow interests

Aspiration lesion Removal of tissue by suction

Astrocyte A star-shaped glial cell of the central nervous system

Asymptote The maximal performance associated with any behaviour

Ataxia A lack of voluntary motor control

Atom The smallest particle of a chemical element that can exist

Atomoxetine A noradrenaline reuptake inhibitor

Atropine An anticholinergic (from deadly nightshade/belladona)

Attention deficit hyperactivity disorder A neurodevelopmental disorder with key symptoms of hyperactivity, inattention and impulsivity

Auditory canal The tube passing from the outer ear to the eardrum

Autism (or autism/autistic spectrum disorder) A pervasive developmental disorder characterized by individuals having difficulty with social interaction and communication

Autocrine feedback A form of feedback in which a cell secretes a hormone that binds to autocrine receptors on that same cell, leading to changes in that cell

Autonomic nervous system Part of the nervous system responsible for control of the bodily functions

Autoreceptors Presynaptic receptors that regulate the release of neurotransmitters

Autosomes The first 22 chromosomes (not the sex chromosome)

Axoaxonic synapse A synapse connecting two axons

Axodendritic synapse A synapse connecting an axon and dendrite

Axon A projection of a neuron, that typically conducts electrical impulses away from the neuron's cell body towards the synapse

Axon hillock A specialized part of the soma of a neuron that connects to the axon where membrane potentials are integrated before an action potential travels down the axon

Axonal elaboration Occurs during arborization when learning increases dendritic innervation

Axosomatic synapse A synapse connecting an axon and soma

Axosynaptic synapse Where the presynaptic terminal of one axon synapses with the presynaptic terminal of another neuron

Backward conditioning A procedure in which an unconditioned stimulus is consistently presented before a neutral stimulus

Baroreceptors Receptors that detect blood pressure

Basal ganglia A collection of subcortical structures involved in movement and other behaviours. Includes the striatum, substantia nigra, globus pallidus and subthalamic nucleus

Basolateral nuclei A region of the amygdala

Bed nucleus of the stria terminalis A part of the septum and the extended amygdala

Behavioural approach system In Gray's theory, a system which is activated when the environment is indicating reward or punishment

Behavioural bioassay A way of assessing the effect of a drug/chemical in an animal. Confirms bioavailability of a drug in the brain

Behavioural genetics A branch of psychobiology that investigates the genetic and environmental contributions to behaviour. A key argument is the nature–nurture debate

Behavioural inhibition The ability to stop a response. Thought to be analogous to impulsivity

Behavioural inhibition system In Gray's theory, a system which detects mismatches between the environment and the person's expectations by stopping ongoing behaviour and directing cognitive resources to the mismatch

Behavioural tolerance The reduction of the effectiveness of a drug due to associative learning. Opponent process are evoked to stimuli associated with the drug and counteract the drug effect

Behaviourism The theory that human and animal behaviour can be explained in terms of conditioning, without appeal to thoughts or feelings

Benzodiazepine receptor A receptor complex on a GABA receptor. Sensitive to benzodiazepines, e.g. diazepam (Valium)

Benzodiazepines A group of compounds acting at the benzodiazepine receptor complex

Bereitschaftspotential The readiness potential

Beta-amyloid See Amyloid-beta plaques

Beta carbolines Endogenous benzodiazepines

Beta motor neurons Motor neurons connecting muscle spindles

Beta waves The normal electrical activity of the brain when conscious and alert

Bile A fluid that aids digestion and is secreted by the liver and stored in the gallbladder

Binocular vision Vision using two eyes with overlapping fields of view, allowing good perception of depth

Bioethics A specialized branch of ethics looking at the impact of biological technologies on humanity

Bipolar cells These cells are found in the retina and transmit signals from the photoreceptors to the ganglion cells

Bipolar disorder An affective disorder characterized as having increases and decreases in mood

Bipolar neurons Neurons which have two extensions

Blastocyst An embryo that has developed for 4–6 days after fertilization

Blastomere A cell produced by cellular division of the zygote after fertilization

Blind spot The point of the retina at which cells converge on the optic nerve

Blood–brain barrier A semi-permeable membrane separating the blood from the cerebrospinal fluid, thereby constituting a barrier to the passage of cells, particles and large molecules

Blood oxygen level dependent A method used in functional magnetic resonance imaging to observe different areas of the brain which are active and consuming oxygen

Bolus A moist ball of food

Bowman's layer A layer of the cornea

Bradykinesia Slowness in movement

Brain-derived neurotrophic factor A protein promoting the survival of existing neurons and new neuronal growth

Brainstem Part of the brain composed of the midbrain, pons and medulla oblongata connecting the spinal cord with the forebrain and cerebrum

Bregma The area where the front of the skull is fused with the two lateral parts. Used as a surface landmark in stereotaxic surgery

British National Formulary A book detailing the prescribing, dispensing and administering of medicines

British Psychological Society The professional association for UK psychologists. The BPS's ethics must be adhered to by all those collecting psychological data in the UK

Broca's area An area of the left hemisphere associated with language Named after Paul Broca

Brodmann's areas A region of the cortex as mapped by Korbinian Brodmann

Bromocriptine A dopamine receptor agonist

Brown Peterson task A cognitive exercise for testing the limits of working memory capacity in which syllables have to be recalled after a period of time. Rehearsal is prevented by an interpolated task (e.g. counting backwards)

Brown-Séquard syndrome An incomplete spinal cord lesion

Bulbospongiosus muscle Muscle at the root of the penis involved in erection and ejaculation

Bulbourethral gland Provides a component of semen

Bulimia nervosa A disorder of weight loss consisting of eating and purging

Bupropion A reuptake inhibitor of dopamine and noradrenaline

Butyrophenone A chemical class of antipsychotics, e.g. haloperidol

Caffeine A psychostimulant compound found in tea and coffee plants. An adenosine receptor

Calcium A chemical element

Calorie Unit of energy in food

Candidate gene Any gene thought likely to cause a disease

Cannabinoid A class of diverse chemical compounds that act on cannabinoid receptors

Cannabis A plant with psychoactive properties

Cannon–Bard theory A theory of emotion that postulates that physiological changes are simultaneous with affect

Carbon monoxide A colourless, odourless, tasteless gas produced in normal animal metabolism

Carotid artery Major blood vessel in the neck that supplies blood to the brain, neck and face

Cataplexy Complete paralysis of the body

Catecholamines A family of neurotransmitters: dopamine, noradrenaline and adrenaline

Cation A positively charged ion
Caudate nucleus A part of the striatum
Cell adhesion molecules Molecules that can cross-link pre- and postsynaptic membranes; these act like scaffolding around the synapse
Cell membrane The lipid structure surrounding a cell
Central nervous system The brain and spinal column/cord
Central nucleus of amygdala A component of the amygdala
Centromere Structure on the chromosome, appearing during cell division as the constricted central region and the point at which the two chromatids are joined together
Cephalic or reflex phase The preparatory processes for feeding
Cerebellar vermis A region of the cerebellum
Cerebellum The portion of the brain in the back of the head involved in the control of voluntary and involuntary movement as well as balance
Cerebral hemispheres The two parts of the cerebrum
Cerebral palsy A group of disorders affecting a person's ability to move caused by damage to the brain and neurons
Cerebral ventricles Fluid-filled cavities in the brain
Cerebrospinal fluid A fluid that is continuously produced that flows in the ventricles of the brain and around the surface of the brain and spinal cord
Cerebrovascular stroke Loss of brain function due to a disturbance in the blood supply to the brain
Cerveau isole Surgery disconnecting the forebrain
Cervix The lower, narrow portion of the uterus at the top of the vagina
C fibres Fibres that send slow pain messages
Chemistry A science that investigates the composition, structure, properties and change of substances
Chlordiazepoxide A benzodiazepine. Anti-anxiety agent (anxioloytic)
Chlorpromazine A phenothiazine and the first antipsychotic medication
Chromatid One copy of a duplicated chromosome
Chromosome The thread-like strand of DNA that contains the genetic code
Cilia Hair-like structures
Ciliary muscle A muscle of the eye that relaxes or tightens to change the shape of the lens, enabling focusing
Cingulate cortex Part of the cortex including the cingulate gyrus and sulcus
Cingulate gyrus A medial gyrus of each cerebral hemisphere that partly surrounds the corpus callosum
Cingulate motor area Supplementary motor area
Circadian rhythm A 24-hour cycle that regulates many physiological processes
Circle of Willis A network of blood vessels that receives all the blood that is pumped up the two internal carotid arteries that come up the front of the neck
Citalopram A selective serotonin reuptake inhibitor
Classical conduction aphasia Poor speech repetition
Classical conditioning (Pavlovian) A learning process that occurs when two stimuli are repeatedly paired

Clinical trial A study to assess the efficacy of a drug in the target population
Clitoral hood Where the labia minora meet; protects/surrounds the glans clitoris
Clitoris A female sex organ and erogenous zone
Cloaca A structure in the development of the urinary and reproductive organs
Clonidine An alpha-2 autoreceptor agonist
Clozapine An atypical antipsychotic drug
Cocaine A psychostimulant that increases the amount of dopamine available in the synapse by blocking reuptake via the dopamine transporter
Cocaine- and amphetamine-regulated A protein involved in feeding transcript
Cochlea Part of the inner ear that converts vibrations into nerve impulses
Codons A sequence of three nucleotides which together form a unit of genetic code in a DNA or RNA molecule. A sequence begins with a start codon and ends with a stop codon
Cognitive neuroscience A branch of neuroscience looking at cognition and information processing
Cognitive reserve The resistance to the behavioural effects of brain damage
Colour vision The ability to perceive objects as giving off different wavelengths of light, thereby being interpreted as colour
Comparative psychology A branch of psychobiology that compares human behaviour to animal behaviour. See also evolutionary psychology. Central to the rationale for this is the theory of evolution
Compatibilism The belief that free will and determinism are compatible ideas
Competitive antagonist A receptor antagonist that binds to a receptor and competes with the agonist for receptor binding sites on the same receptor
Complex cells Cells of the visual cortex that respond to straight lines of a particular orientation and their receptive field cannot be divided
Computational neuroscience A branch of psychobiology that models brain function in machines and computer programs
Computed tomography A series of X-ray views taken from many different angles processed to make an image using a computer
Concentration gradient Particles move from an area of high concentration to an area of low concentration
Concordance rate In twins studies, the probability that a pair of individuals will both have a certain characteristic, given that one of the pair has the characteristic
Conditioned emotional response An emotional response that results from classical conditioning, usually from the association of a relatively neutral stimulus with a painful or fear-inducing experience
Conditioned place preference A method for assessing drug-seeking behaviour in an animal by conditioning the animal to associate a particular environment with the presence of a drug
Conditioned response In classical conditioning, an automatic response to a neutral stimulus established via learning

Conditioned stimulus In classical conditioning, a previously neutral stimulus that comes to elicit the conditioned response
Conditioned taste aversion The tendency to develop aversions to types of food that resemble the foods which cause us illness
Conditioned withdrawal The provocation of withdrawal symptoms in response to stimuli associated with the delivery of the drug
Conditioning by successive approximations The process of rewarding responses that are increasingly closer to the ultimate goal
Cones Photoreceptors with high acuity and able to process colour
Congenital adrenal hyperplasia A defect of the adrenal glands in which they are overstimulated and release testosterone into the bloodstream
Consciousness The state of being conscious; awareness of one's own existence, sensations, thoughts, surroundings
Conspecific A member of the same species
Construct validity The theoretical rationale for an animal model
Contiguity Close together in time, e.g. the conditioned stimulus and unconditioned stimulus need to be close together for effective learning to take place
Contingency One being dependent upon the other
Continuous reinforcement When an animal/person receives a reinforcer for every operant behaviour made
Contralateral Opposite side of the body
Convergence The process by which several rods/comes connect with the neurons (bipolar cells) in the next layer of the retina
Copy number variants A form of structural variation when the number of copies of a particular gene varies from one individual to the next
Cornea The clear outermost layer of the eye covering the pupil and iris
Coronal plane A vertical plane at right angles to a sagittal plane, dividing the body into anterior and posterior portions. Also called frontal plane
Corona radiata A layer surrounding the ovum
Corpus callosum A band of nerve fibres joining the two hemispheres of the brain
Corpus cavernosum Blood-filled chambers of the penis and clitoris
Corpus luteum Secretory structure in the ovary producing progesterone
Corpus spongiosum A mass of erectile tissue alongside the corpora cavernosa of the penis and clitoris terminating in the glans
Corrugator muscle A muscle of the face
Corticobulbar tract White matter motor pathway connecting the cerebral cortex to the brainstem, primarily involved in carrying the motor function of the trigeminal and hypoglossal cranial nerves
Corticospinal tract Columns of motor fibres of which two run on each side of the spinal cord and which are continuations of the pyramids of the medulla oblongata
Corticosterone A hormone secreted by the adrenal cortex
Corticotrophin-releasing hormone A hormone made by the hypothalamus that stimulates the or corticotrophin-releasing factor release of corticotrophin by the anterior pituitary gland

Cortisol Stress hormone released by adrenal gland
Cranial nerves The 12 pairs of nerves that emerge from or enter the brain
Cremaster muscle A muscle that pulls the testes towards the body
Crossing over The exchange of genes between homologous chromosomes (the crossing over of chromatids), resulting in a mixture of parental characteristics in offspring
Crura Internal and downward projections of the clitoris
Cryogenic lesion A reversible lesion caused by lowering the temperature at the tip of a probe
Cryoprobe A probe inserted into a specific area of the brain to produce a temporary lesion by means of temperature reduction
Cyclic AMP A second messenger
Cyclic guanosine monophosphate (cGMP) A second messenger
Cyclophosphamide An immunosuppressive agent
Cyclotron A machine that makes radioactive isotopes. Used in positron emission tomography scans
Cytoarchitecture The arrangement of cells in a tissue
Cytogenetic bands The transverse bands that appear to stripe the chromosome in light and dark cycles after being stained for viability
Cytoplasm The contents of a cell, except for the nucleus
Cytosine A nucleotide base. Part of the genetic code
Dartos muscle A smooth muscle which contracts in response to cold (and sexual arousal), thickening the scrotal skin and providing warmth
Darwinian The central theory of evolution as proposed by Charles Darwin
Declaration of Helsinki A set of ethical guidelines for human experimentation
Decussation The point of crossing over of neurons from one side of the central nervous system to the other
Deep brain stimulation Stimulation via an eletrode placed in discrete subcortical areas of the brain
Deep facial muscles Muscles of the face that enable gross movements
Default mode network A network of brain regions that are active when the individual is not focused on the external environment
Dehydroepiandrosterone An androgen
Delay conditioning In classical conditioning, the conditioned stimulus is presented before the unconditioned stimulus
Delta receptors Receptors for endorphins and enkephalins that mediate pain and other behaviours
Delta^9-tetrahydrocannabinol The active ingredient isolated from cannabis
Delta wave A slow brain wave associated with sleep
Delusion A belief or impression maintained despite being contradicted by reality or rational argument
Dendrites The tree-like branches emanating from the neuronal cell body that receive messages from other neurons via synaptic communication
Dendrodendritic synapse A synapse between two dendrites
Dentate gyrus A part of the cerebral cortex, belonging to the hippocampus

Dependence The state of needing a drug to operate within normal limits

Depolarizing The reduction in the membrane potential

Deprenyl A monoamine oxidase inhibitor

Descemet's membrane A layer of the cornea

Descending pathways Nerve pathways that go down the spinal cord and allow the brain to control movement

Determinism The philosophical stance that all events are predetermined and we are not free agents

Dexamethasone A synthetic glucocorticoid

Diastolic blood pressure The minimum arterial pressure during relaxation. The diastolic pressure is typically the second number recorded

Diazepam (N-desmethyldiazepam) An endogenous benzodiazepine

Diazepam (Valium) A benzodiazepine anxiolytic

Dichotic listening An experimental procedure involving the simultaneous presentation of stimuli independently to the ears

Dichotomous traits In Mendelian genetics, characteristics that occur in an either/or form but not both, e.g. green or yellow seeds

Diencephalon The posterior part of the forebrain comprising the hypothalamus, thalamus, metathalamus, epithalamus and subthalamus

Diethylbarbituric acid (barbital) A barbiturate/anxiolytic

Diffusion tensor imaging A magnetic resonance imaging technique that allows the mapping of the diffusion process of water molecules. Other molecules get in the way of the diffusion and therefore change the pattern which is measured in diffusion tensor imaging

Dihydrotestosterone From the male hormone testosterone responsible for the formation of male primary sex characteristics during embryonic life

Diploid A cell or nucleus containing two complete sets of chromosomes

Dishabituation The recovery of a response that has undergone habituation

Disulfiram (Antabuse) A synthetic compound used in the treatment of alcoholics to make drinking alcohol produce unpleasant after-effects. It is an aldehyde dehydrogenase inhibitor that causes an excess build-up of acetaldehyde

Diurnal Active during the day

Dizygotic twin A non-identical twin

D-lysergic diethylamide (LSD) A hallucinogen

DNA (deoxyribonucleic acid) A nucleic acid that encodes the genetic instructions used in the development and functioning of all known living organisms

Dominant trait In genetics, a trait that will appear in the offspring if only one of the parents contributes it

Donepezil Acetylcholinesterase inhibitor

Dopamine A catecholamine neurotransmitter

Dopamine transporter The reuptake protein of a dopamine synapse

Dorsal column of the spinal cord Area of white matter in the middle to posterior side of the spinal cord

Dorsal horn Grey matter in the dorsal part of each lateral half of the spinal cord that receives terminals from some afferent fibres of the dorsal roots of the spinal nerves

Dorsal striatum Part of the striatum

Dorsomedial nucleus A region of the hypothalamus

Double blind Information which may influence the behaviour of the tester or the subject is withheld

Double-blind, randomised, placebo-controlled trial Considered to be the gold standard of clinical trials. The participant is assigned at random to a condition by the investigator and neither knows if they are getting the drug or placebo

Double helix The coiled structure of double-stranded DNA in which strands linked by hydrogen bonds form a spiral configuration

DRD4/7R receptor gene A dopamine receptor gene

Drug classification The legal categorization of drugs

Drug discrimination The ability of animals or humans to differentiate the stimulus properties of a drug

Drug Enforcement Agency The American government agency which upholds drug laws

Drug self-administration An animal model of addiction, in which the animal receives an infusion of drug on performing an operant behaviour (lever pressing)

Duodenum First part of the small intestine immediately beyond the stomach

Duplication (genetic) Any duplication of a region of DNA that contains a gene

Dura mater The outermost membrane enveloping the brain and spinal cord, forming the meninges

Dysexecutive syndrome A failure of executive functioning. Often due to a fault in the frontal lobe

Dyslexia A neurocognitive disorder leading to difficulty in reading

Dystonia Abnormal movements of the facial musculature

Eating disorders A number psychological disorders characterized by abnormal or disturbed eating habits

Ectoderm The outermost layer of cells or tissue of an embryo in early development

ED$_{50}$ The median effective dose that produces an effect in 50% of the population

Edinger–Westphal nucleus Parasympathetic preganglionic neurons that originate the oculomotor nerve

Efferent pathways Motor pathways (output from the brain) reaching to neuromuscular junctions)

Efficacy The ability to produce a desired or intended result

Ejaculation The ejection of semen from the penis

Ejaculatory ducts A canal through which semen is ejaculated

Electroconvulsive therapy A therapy involving the induction of seizures via electrodes placed on the skull

Electrodermal activity The measurement of the electrical activity in the skin using surface-placed electrodes

Electroencephalogram The measurement of the electrical activity of the brain using surface-placed electrodes on the scalp

Electrolytic lesion A technique that destroys brain tissue using an electrode placed in a particular region

Electromyography The recording of the electrical activity of muscle tissue

Electron A subatomic particle with a negative charge found in all atoms

Electro-oculogram The measurement of the electrical activity in the muscles of the eye using surface-placed electrodes

Electrophoresis A method used for separating molecules according to their size and electrical charge

Electrostatic pressure Electrostatic pressure occurs when particles with different charges are attracted to each other, in that positively charged ions are attracted to negatively charged ones and vice versa (i.e. opposites attract and like repels)

Embryonic stem cells Stem cells that are obtained from the undifferentiated mass cells of a human embryo

Emulsification The process of breaking down fats

Enantiomers Pair of molecules that are mirror images of each other

Endocannabinoid An endogenous system that interact with cannabis

Endocrine system A collection of glands that secrete hormones directly into the circulatory system to be carried towards a distant target organ

Endocrinology A branch of medicine that addresses the function and dysfunction of hormones

Endocytosis A process by which cells absorb molecules by invaginating them

Endoderm The innermost layer of cells or tissue of an embryo in early development

Endometrial cycle Part of the menstrual cycle in which the endometrium of the uterus undergoes changes which result in its partial removal during the 'period'

Endophenotype Any hereditary characteristic that is normally associated with some condition but is not a direct symptom of that condition

Endoplasmic reticulum An interconnected network of membrane vesicles, or small containers used by cells to transport or hold materials

Endorphins Endogenous morphine. A naturally occurring substance with effects similar to that of morphine. An analgesic (painkiller)

Endothelium Tissue which forms a single layer of cells lining various organs and cavities of the body

Enkephalins Endogenous peptides related to the endorphins and having similar physiological effects

Enteroendocrine G cells Specialized cells of the endocrine system situated in the gastrointestinal tract and pancreas

Entorhinal cortex An area of the brain located in the medial temporal lobe

Entrainment The synchronization or alignment of the internal biological clock rhythm, including its phase and period, to external time cues

Enzymes Proteins that speed up the rate of a chemical reaction in living organisms. An enzyme acts as a catalyst for specific chemical reactions producing an end product

Ependymal cells Cells that line the fluid-filled ventricles in the brain and the central canal of the spinal cord

Epididymis The coiled segment behind the testes connecting to the vas deferens

Epidural An injection into the space around the dura mater of the spinal cord

Epigenetics External modifications to DNA that turn genes on or off

Epithalamus Part of the dorsal forebrain

Equal environment assumption In twin studies, the view that the environment remains a constant for both twins

Ethology The study of animal behaviour in the natural habitat

Eukaryote cell Any cell that possesses a clearly defined nucleus

Event-related potential The change in electroencephalogram signal in response to an event

Evolution The change in inherited characteristics over successive generations

Evolutionary psychology A branch of psychology that seeks to explain behaviour in terms of previous adaptive behaviours in early humans and animals

Excitatory postsynaptic potential A temporary depolarization of postsynaptic membrane potential caused by the flow of positively charged ions into the postsynaptic cell creating an action potential

Excitement phase Part of the human sexual response cycle

Executive functions A collection of high-level cognitive processes that control and regulate other lower-level processes

Exocytosis The release of a neurotransmitter contained within a vesicle by fusion of the vesicular membrane with the cell membrane

Exon A segment of a DNA or RNA molecule containing information coding for a protein or peptide sequence

Extended amygdala A collection of regions described by Kooc to account for addiction

External adventitial layer A layer of the vaginal wall

External validity An assessment of the generalizability of experimental findings obtained from animals

Extinction The cessation of responding after the termination of a reinforcer

Extracellular Outside the cell

Extracellular fluid Body fluid outside the cells

Extrafusal muscle fibres Skeletal standard muscle fibres that are innervated by alpha motor neurons, allowing for skeletal movement

Extrapyramidal side-effects The effects of blocking the dopamine receptors of the extrapyramidal system

Extrapyramidal system A motor system that receives input from the primary motor cortex and the supplementary motor area, and communicates with a diverse set of structures to control gross motor movements

Face validity The level of similarity between the model and the behaviour/symptom to be modelled

Facial feedback hypothesis A view that feedback from facial expressions plays a causal role in the emotional experience

Facial nerve (CN VII) A cranial nerve
Fallopian tubes A pair of tubes along which ova travel from the ovaries to the uterus
Familial studies Genetic studies investigating the heritability of a trait or behaviour
Fascia Fibrous sheath of connective tissue that surrounds the three erectile bodies of the penis
Fenfluramine A 5-HT agonist
Figure of Rey A spatial task
Fimbriae Finger-like projections at the end of the fallopian tube near the ovary which branch out to catch released eggs and guide them towards the fallopian tube
Fissures Deep folds in the cerebral cortex
Five prime (5′) An area designating the end of a DNA/RNA strand
Fixed interval schedule When reinforcement is provided after a specified period of time and only if the subject has responded correctly
Fixed ratio schedule When reinforcement occurs after a specified amount of responses
Flooding A form of behavioural intervention in which a phobic stimulus is repeatedly presented
Flumazenil Benzodiazepine receptor antagonist
Fluoxetine Prozac; a selective serotonin reuptake inhibitor
Foetus An unborn offspring of a mammal, in particular more than eight weeks after conception
Follicle-stimulating hormone A hormone secreted by the anterior pituitary gland which promotes the formation of ova or sperm
Follicular phase A phase of the menstrual cycle in which follicle-stimulating hormone stimulates the growth of ovarian follicles and oestrogen causes the endometrium to develop in order to receive a fertilized egg
Foreskin The retractable roll of skin covering the end of the penis
Fovea An area of high density of cones in a central area of the retina
Frenulum A loose strip of skin on the underside of the penis between the glans and the shaft
Frontal eye field A region located in the frontal cortex used for voluntary eye movements
Frontal lobe The most anterior portion of the cerebral cortex (in front of the central sulcus)
Full fusion (exocytosis) During exocytosis where the vesicle collapses fully into the plasma membrane
Functional magnetic resonance imaging A variant of magnetic resonance imaging that measures brain activity by detecting associated changes in blood flow
Galatea effect When people believe in themselves and succeed as a result
Gallbladder The storage area for bile
Gamete A mature haploid male or female germ cell (ovum/sperm)
Gamma-aminobutyric acid The most prevalent inhibitory amino acid
Gamma motor neurons Motor neurons of the brainstem and spinal cord connecting to muscle spindles

Ganglion A structure containing a number of nerve cell bodies, typically linked by synapses, and often forming a swelling on a nerve fibre
Gap junctions/electrical synapse Direct connections between the cytoplasm of two cells allowing various molecules, ions and electrical impulses to directly pass through a regulated pore between cells
Gastric or absorptive phase A phase when nutrients are being absorbed into the bloodstream
Gastrin A peptide hormone that stimulates hydrochloric acid
Gastrointestinal tract A system responsible for consuming and digesting foodstuffs, absorbing nutrients and expelling waste
Gastrulation An early phase in embryonic development, when the single-layered blastula is reorganized into a three-layered structure called the gastrula
Gate control theory Melzack and Wall's theory of pain
General adaptation syndrome A non-specific response to noxious agents
Mutation (genetic) A permanent change in the DNA sequence that makes up a gene
Genetics The branch of science that studies genes and the inheritance of physical and behavioural characteristics
Genital end bulbs Sensory free nerve endings of the penis/clitoris
Genital tubercle Tissue of the cloaca that will develop into the clitoris or penis
Genome An organism's complete set of DNA
Genotype The genetic constitution of an individual organism
Ghrelin A peptide linked to hunger
Glans The rounded part forming the end of the penis or clitoris
Glial cells Support cells of the nervous system, consisting of several different types of cell associated with neurons
Globus pallidus A subcortical structure of the brain. Part of the basal ganglia
Globus pallidus internal segment Part of the globus pallidus and in contrast to the external segment
Glossopharyngeal nerve (CN IX) A cranial nerve
Glucocorticoid An adrenocortical hormone
Glucoreceptors Receptors sensitive to glucose
Glucose A sugar and source of energy
Glutamate An excitatory amino acid. Ubiquitous neurotransmitter
Glycine An amino acid
Glycogen A substance deposited in bodily tissues as a store of carbohydrates. When released from storage forms glucose
Golgi apparatus/body A cell organelle that helps process and package proteins and lipid molecules, especially proteins destined to be exported from the cell
Golgi cell A neuron in the cerebral cortex with short dendrites
Golgi tendon organs Receptors located between the muscle and the tendon that respond to being stretched
Gollum effect Low expectations lead to poor performance
Gonadotrophin-releasing hormone A hypothalamic hormone responsible for the release of follicle-stimulating hormone and luteinizing hormone from the anterior pituitary
Go/No-go task A test of behavioural inhibition where the participant has to withhold a response in response to a stimulus

Granulosa cells Cells that provide nutrients to the oocyte
G-proteins Proteins involved in transmitting signals from a variety of stimuli outside a cell into the inside of the cell
Grey matter The darker tissue of the brain and spinal cord, consisting mainly of nerve cell bodies and branching dendrites (see also white matter)
G-spot An erogenous zone on the anterior wall of the vagina
Guanine A nucleotide base. Part of the genetic code
Guanosine diphosphate A regulator of G-proteins, turning them off
Guanosine triphosphate A regulator of G proteins, turning them on
Gubernaculum A band of non-stretchable tissue that is attached to the testes and pubic bone, pulling the testes down into the scrotum during development
Gyri (s. gyrus) Convolutions on the surface of a cerebral hemisphere caused by the infolding of the cerebral cortex
Habenula Part of the epithalamus
Habituation Learning not to respond to irrelevant stimuli. The most basic form of associative learning
Haemoglobin A protein responsible for transporting oxygen in the blood
Haemorrhage An escape of blood from a ruptured blood vessel
Hallucination The apparent perception of something not present
Hallucinogen A drug that causes hallucinations
Halo effect Behaviour changes as a result of the novelty of the situation
Haloperidol A typical antipsychotic (D2 antagonist)
Hammer (malleus) One of the bones within the ear
Haploid A cell or nucleus having a single set of unpaired chromosomes
Hard question Philosophical question about the nature of consciousness and free will
Hawthorne effect Changes in behaviour due to being paid attention
Hepatic biotransformation The chemical modification or alteration of compounds via enzymatic activity, which takes place in the liver
Heritability The proportion of observed differences in a trait among individuals of a population that are due to genetic differences
Heroin (diacetylmorphine) An analgesic drug derived from morphine
Heschl's gyrus A convolution of the temporal lobe that is the cortical centre for hearing
Heterochromia iridis (iridium) A difference in colour between the irises of the two eyes or between parts of one iris
Heteroreceptor A receptor regulating the synthesis and/or release of another neurotransmitter
Hippocampus An area along the edge of the cortex that regulates many behaviours. Associated with memory
Histamine A neurotransmitter involved in immune responses
Holism The philosophical view that considers the organism as a whole entity and distinct from the sum of the parts
Homeostasis Maintenance of metabolic equilibrium within an animal by a tendency to compensate for disrupting changes

Homo sapiens The primate species to which modern humans belong
Homovanillic acid A dopamine metabolite
Homunculus A pictorial representation of the anatomical divisions of the primary motor cortex and primary somatosensory cortex
Horizontal cells Cells of the retina that are inhibitory interneurons that release GABA upon depolarization
Horizontal plane A view of the brain looking down from the top
Hormone A substance, usually a peptide or steroid, produced by one tissue and conveyed by the bloodstream to another to effect physiological activity
Human Genome Project An international research effort to determine the DNA sequence of the entire human genome
Huntingtin The gene responsible for Huntington's disease and the protein encoded by that gene
Huntington's disease A motor disorder of the basal ganglia that is transmitted as a dominant allele along Mendelian principles
Hydrochloric acid An acid that breaks down food into chemical components
Hydrophilic Having an affinity for water; readily absorbing or dissolving in water
Hymen Membrane of skin covering the vagina
Hyperandrogenism Increased masculinization
Hypercolumns The organization of cells of the visual cortex into columns
Hypercomplex cell A neuron of the visual cortex which is sensitive to stimulus length (detects ends) and orientation
Hyperphagia Increased eating
Hyperpolarization A change in a cell's membrane potential that makes it more negative
Hypnogogic hallucinations Dream-like states that happen prior to falling asleep
Hypoglossal nerve (CN XII) A cranial nerve
Hypokinesia Impaired movement
Hypothalamic-pituitary-adrenal axis A set of direct influences and feedback among the hypothalamus, pituitary gland and adrenal glands. Involved in the stress response
Hypothalamus A forebrain region below (hypo) the thalamus which controls the autonomic nervous system and the activity of the pituitary gland
Hypothyroidism Low activity of the thyroid gland
Hypovolaemic thirst Occurs when the intravascular fluid decreases
Ibotenic acid A selective neurotoxin of glutamate
Immunosuppression Suppression of the immune system
Incentive salience A motivational state, which turns stimuli into desired must-have objects
Incompatiblism The view that a deterministic universe is contradictory with the possession of free will
Indolamines A family of neurotransmitters that share a common molecular structure. Serotonin is the chief example of an indolamine
Infarction Obstruction of the blood supply
Inferior colliculus Midbrain nucleus of the auditory pathway which receives input from several peripheral brainstem nuclei in the auditory pathway

Inferior olive   A large nucleus situated in the medulla and involved in motor control
Infundibulum   An area at the end of the fallopian tubes
Inhibitory postsynaptic potential   A postsynaptic potential that makes a neuron less likely to generate an action potential
Insertion   The point of tendon connection furthest from the midline
Insertion (genetic)   A type of mutation involving the addition of genetic material
In situ   In its natural position
Insomnia   Difficulty in falling or staying asleep
Insula   A portion of the cerebral cortex folded deep within the lateral sulcus
Insulin   A pancreatic hormone involved in digestion
Intermediate muscularis layer   A layer of the vaginal wall
Internal mucosal layer   A layer of the vaginal wall
Internal validity   The consideration of the integrity of an experiment, e.g. controlled
Interneuron   A neuron which transmits impulses between other neurons, especially as part of a reflex arc
Interoception   The sense of the physiological condition of the body
Interstitial fluid   Fluid between the cells
Interventricular foramina   Channels that connect the paired lateral ventricles with the third ventricle
Intestinal or fasting phase   This phase occurs when the nutrients no longer provide immediate energy and the body has to mobilize previously stored nutrients
Intracellular   Inside of the cell
Intracellular fluid   Fluid in the cytoplasm of a cell
Intracerebroventricular   An injection into the cerebral ventricles
Intracranial self-stimulation   The delivery of an electrical stimulus in discrete areas of the brain via an electrode when an animal performs an operant task
Intrafusal muscle fibres   Skeletal muscle fibres that serve as specialized sensory organs (proprioceptors) that detect the amount and rate of change in length of a muscle
Intramuscular   An injection into muscle
Intraperitoneal   An injection into the peritoneal cavity
Intrathecal   Injection into the fluid surrounding the brain and spinal cord
Intravascular fluid   Blood plasma
Intravenous   An injection into the blood system
Introitus   The vaginal opening
Intron   A segment of a gene situated between exons that is removed before translation of messenger RNA and does not function in coding for protein synthesis
In utero   In the uterus. During pregnancy
Invagination   To fold over, to make a pocket
Inverse agonist   An agent that binds to the same receptor as an agonist but induces a pharmacological response opposite to that agonist
Inversion (genetic)   A chromosomal rearrangement in which a segment of genetic material is broken away from the chromosome, inverted from end to end, and reinserted into the chromosome at the same breakage site

In vitro   In the glass, test tube. See also *in vivo*
In vitro **fertilization (IVF)**   Fertilization of the ovum outside the body in a test tube
In vivo   Taking place in a living organism
Ion   An atom or molecule with a net electric charge due to the loss or gain of one or more electrons
Ion channel   Pores in the membrane of a cell that can allow the flow of ions across the membrane, e.g. during an action potential
Ionotropic receptor   A receptor that forms part of a ligand-gated ion channel, so that binding of a ligand (neurotransmitter) causes the opening of the channel, permitting ions to flow through it
Ipsilateral   Same side of the body
Iris   The colour part of the eye which acts as an aperture allowing light to enter
Ischaemia   An inadequate blood supply
Ischiocavernosus muscle   Muscles at the root of the penis that are involved in erection and ejaculation
James–Lange theory   A theory of emotion postulating that physiological changes precede affect
John Henry effect   When a control group compares themselves to the experimental group and by virtue of effort gets the same results
Kappa receptors   Receptors for endorphins and enkephalins that mediate pain and other behaviours
Karyotype   The number and visual appearance of the chromosomes in the cell nuclei of an organism or species
Ketamine   An anaesthetic and analgesic drug. An NMDA antagonist
Kiss-and-run fusion (exocytosis)   In exocytosis when vesicles release the transmitter through a transient fusion pore in the cell membrane and retain its shape, preventing full integration into the cell membrane
Klinefelter's syndrome   A genetic condition in which there are two X chromosomes and a Y chromosome (XXY)
Klüver–Bucy syndrome   Lesions of the amygdala producing a lack of fear
Knock-in/knock-out models   A genetic manipulation in an animal (normally a mouse) in which a gene is inserted (knock-in) or deleted (knock-out)
Koh block design test   A spatial task
Koniocellular layer   A layer of the lateral geniculate nucleus
Korsakoff's syndrome   A set of symptoms, especially amnesia, arising as a result of chronic alcoholism
Labia majora   The larger outer folds of the vulva
Labia minora   Hairless flaps of skin that are inside the labia majora and surround the opening of the vagina
Lambda waves   Electroencephalogram patterns from the visual cortex
Laminae of the dorsal horn   The distribution of cells and fibres within the grey matter of the spinal cord based upon the cytoarchitecture of neurons as characterized by Bror Rexed (referred to as Rexed laminae)
Latent inhibition   A process in which a familiar stimulus takes longer to become a conditioned stimulus than a new, comparatively unfamiliar stimulus

Latent learning A form of learning that is not immediately expressed in an overt response, but may be expressed at a later time under new conditions

Lateral corticospinal tract Fibres of the corticospinal tract that cross over to the other side of the spinal column

Lateral geniculate nucleus Sensory (visual) relay area of the thalamus

Lateral hypothalamus Part of the hypothalamus

Lateral inhibition When one neuron inhibits its neighbouring neurons

Lateral nucleus Part of the hypothalamus

Law of effect Behaviour strengthened by its relationship with reward

Learned helplessness The phenomenon in which one learns that one has little control over the environment

Leptin A protein produced by fatty tissue regulating fat storage

Lesion The destruction of neural tissue

Levator labii superioris muscle A muscle of the face

Leydig cells Cells which secrete testosterone and peptide hormones controlling spermatogenesis

Ligand A chemical/drug/neurotransmitter that attaches to a receptor

Limbic system Set of structures that forms the inner border of the cortex and consists of the parahippocampus, cingulate, subcallosal gyrus, hippocampus and dentate gyrus. The deep-lying structures include the hippocampus, amygdala, mammillary body, habenula, anterior thalamic nuclei and olfactory bulb

Linkage The tendency for alleles located on a chromosome to be inherited together

Lipids Fatty acids or their derivatives, insoluble in water

Lithium carbonate A drug used for bipolar disorder

Locus coeruleus Part of the brain located in the posterior area of the rostral pons. Releases noradrenaline

Longitudinal study A study that follows the participants for a relatively long period of a time. Has high attrition rates

Long-term depression Inhibition of synaptic transmission after successive stimulation of the neuron

Long-term potentiation Facilitation of synaptic transmission after successive stimulation of the neuron

Lorazepam A benzodiazepine anxiolytic

Lordosis A posture assumed by some female mammals during mating, in which the back is arched downward

Luteal phase The latter phase of the menstrual cycle in which there is the formation of the corpus luteum

Luteinizing hormone A hormone secreted by the anterior pituitary gland that stimulates ovulation in females and the synthesis of androgen in males

Lysosome Vesicular structure that contains enzymes which can break down and metabolize many biomolecules

Magnetic resonance imaging A neuroimaging technique that measures the response of the atomic nuclei of the brain to high-frequency radio waves when placed in a strong magnetic field

Magnetic resonance spectroscopy A magnetic resonance imaging technique measuring body chemistry

Magnetoencephalography A technique that detects and records the magnetic field associated with electrical activity in the brain

Magnocellular layer A layer of the lateral geniculate nucleus

Major depressive disorder A mental disorder characterized by a pervasive and persistent low mood

Mammal A warm-blooded vertebrate animal that usually has hair/fur and the females produce milk

Mammillary body Part of the hypothalamus

Mammillothalamic tract Nerve fibres extending from the mammillary body to the anterior nucleus of the thalamus

Martinotti cells Small multipolar neurons with short branching dendrites

MDMA 3,4-methylenedioxy-methamphetamine is a psychoactive drug. A dopamine, noradrenaline and 5-HT agonist. Also known as ecstasy

Mechanoreceptors A cell that responds to mechanical stimuli, e.g. touch/sound

Medial geniculate nucleus Sensory (auditory) relay area of the thalamus

Medial lemniscus Ascending bundle of myelinated axons carrying sensory signals

Median preoptic nucleus A hypothalamic structure

Medulla (oblongata) The lower half of the brainstem

Medullary pyramids Ridges spanning the length of the medulla

Meiosis The process of cell division in sexually reproducing organisms that reduces the number of chromosomes in reproductive cells from diploid to haploid

Melanin-concentrating hormone A hypothalamic neuropeptide

Melanopsin A light-sensitive substance

Melatonin A hormone secreted by the pineal gland which inhibits melanin formation. Regulates sleep

Membrane The outer surface of the cell that encloses the cytoplasm

Menarche Onset of menstruation

Mendelian inheritance An inheritance pattern proposed by Gregor Mendel in which a genetic trait is passed from parent to offspring and is either dominant or recessive

Meninges The three membranes that cover the brain and spinal cord

Meningitis A disease resulting in a swelling of the meninges of the brain. Can be fatal

Menstrual cycle The process of ovulation and menstruation in women

Menstrual phases A woman's monthly bleeding

Mescaline A hallucinogen and dopamine/5-HT agonist

Mesencephalon The midbrain

Mesoderm The middle layer of cells or tissues of an embryo

Mesolimbic-dopamine pathway A dopamine pathway arising in the ventral tegmental area (VTA) and projecting to the nucleus accumbens (NAcc). Often considered the reward pathway

Mesolimbic system A dopamine pathway connecting the ventral tegmental area with the nucleus accumbens

Mesopic vision Vision at light levels at which both retinal cones and retinal rods are stimulated

Messenger ribonucleic acid (mRNA) A type of RNA molecule that transports genetic information from DNA to the ribosome, where it specifies the sequence of amino acids to form a protein

Metabolites   Intermediates and end products of metabolism

Metabotropic receptor   A receptor that acts through the release of a second messenger

Metachromatic leukodystrophy   A disorder inherited in an autosomal recessive pattern

Metencephalon   The anterior segment of the developing vertebrate hindbrain

Metergoline   A 5-HT antagonist

Methyl-4-phenyl-1,2,3,6-   A dopamine neurotoxin and model of Parkinson's disease tetrahydropyridine

Methyl-4-phenyl-pyridium   A neurotoxic metabolite of methyl-4-phenyl-1,2,3,6- tetrahydropyridine

Methylphenidate   A dopamine transporter blocker used for the treatment of attention deficit hyperactivity disorder and narcolepsy

Microdialysis   A technique for measuring extracellular concentrations of substances in tissues, usually in vivo

Microglia   Small glial cells that scavenge and remove debris from the brain

Microtubule   A hollow cylindrical structure in the cytoplasm of most cells, involved in intracellular shape and transport

Migraine headache   A chronic neurological disease characterized by recurrent severe headaches

Minisatellite DNA   A section of DNA that consists of a short series of nucleotide bases, also called a variable number tandem repeat

Mirror neuron   A hypothetical construct accounting for neurons which activate in response to the actions of another agent (actor)

Misuse   Any non-medical consumption of a drug

Misuse of Drugs Act (1971)   Legislation that governs the use of drugs

Mitochondrial DNA   The DNA containing 37 genes essential for normal mitochondrial function

Mitochondrion(a)   A structure in cells which provides respiration and energy production

Mitosis   Cellular division that results in two daughter cells each having the same number and kind of chromosomes as the parent cell

M'Naghten Rule   A test applied to determine whether a person accused of a crime was sane at the time of its commission and, therefore, criminally responsible

Monoamine oxidase   Enzyme which degrades and metabolizes monoamines

Monoamine oxidase inhibitor   An antidepressant that blocks the enzymatic degradation of catecholamines and indolamines by monoamine oxidase

Monosomy   A genetic condition in which one chromosome lacks its homologous partner

Monozygotic twins   Twins developed from the fertilization of a single oocyte and are genetically identical

Mons veneris   An area of fatty tissue above which a triangle of pubic hair can be seen

Morphine   An opiate analgesic that acts on opiate receptors

Mosaicism   A condition in which cells within the same person have a different genetic make-up

Motivational inhibition   The inhibition of a response to emotionally salient stimuli, e.g. reward and punishment

Motor cortex   Part of the cerebral cortex in the brain in which originate the nerve impulses that initiate voluntary muscular activity

Motor endplate   Postjunctional sarcolemma of muscle that has acetylcholine receptors

Motor unit   The assembly of a motor neuron and several muscles fibres

Mullerian duct   Duct giving rise to the fallopian tubes, uterus, cervix and upper portion of the vagina in the female

Multiple sclerosis   A disorder of demyelination

Multipotent stem cell   A cell that possesses the ability to differentiate into related cell types

Mu receptors   Receptors for endorphins and enkephalins that mediate pain and other behaviours

Muscarinic receptors   A type of acetylcholine receptor (see also Nicotine receptor)

Muscle spindles   Sensory receptors in the muscle that detect changes inmuscle length

Myelencephalon   The posterior part of the developing vertebrate hindbrain

Myelin   A lipid-based sheath around the axon on a neuron. Contributes to the colour characteristic of white matter

Myelination   The development of a myelin sheath around the axon, the opposite of demyelination, which is the reduction in myelin that underlies multiple sclerosis

Myofibril   A small component of the muscle fibre

Myosin   A fibrous protein which forms the contractile filaments of muscle

Naloxone   An opiate receptor antagonist

Narcolepsy   A condition in which the person keeps falling asleep

Natural selection   The process by which any characteristic of an individual that allows it to survive to produce more offspring will continue in the species

Nature–nurture debate   The classic debate of behaviour arising because of nature (biology) or nurture (experience/learning/environment)

N-desmethyldiazepam   An active metabolite of diazepam

Negative reinforcement   The increase in behaviour in response to the removal of an aversive stimulus

Negative symptoms   Symptoms of schizophrenia that are a loss of function, e.g. anhedonia

Nerve growth factor   A protein that is important for the growth, maintenance and survival of certain target neurons

Nervous system   The system of nerves in the body that send signals

Neural crest   A group of ectodermal cells that develop into tissue of the spinal and autonomic ganglia and connective tissue around the central nervous system

Neural plasticity (neuroplasticity)   Changes in neural pathways and synapses due to changes in behaviour, environment, neural processes, thinking, emotions and damage

Neural plate A key developmental structure that serves as the basis for the nervous system. It is a thickened plate of ectoderm along the dorsal midline of the early vertebrate embryo that gives rise to the neural tube and neural crests

Neural proliferation Cell division of neuronal progenitor cells in the ventricular layer of the vertebrate neural tube

Neural tube A tube formed by the closure of ectodermal tissue (neural plate) in the early embryonic development that later develops into the brain, spinal cord, nerves and ganglia

Neuroanatomy A branch of medicine that addresses the structure and organization of the nervous system

Neuroethics A specialized branch of ethics looking at the impact of neuroscientific technologies and advances on humanity, e.g. the concept of free will. A narrower focus than bioethics

Neurofibrillary tangles Twisted masses of protein inside nerve cells

Neurofilaments Thread-like structures which make up the cytoskeleton

Neuroleptic Typically an antipsychotic drug and refers to the neurological side effects produced

Neuromuscular junction A synapse between a motor neuron and the muscle

Neuron A nerve cell

Neuropeptides Small protein-like molecules used as neurotransmitters

Neuropeptide Y Neuropeptide that acts as a neurotransmitter in the brain and autonomic nervous system; a potent stimulator of food intake

Neuroprotection The salvage, recovery or regeneration of the nervous system

Neuropsychology A branch of psychobiology that studies the structure and function of the brain and the relationship to psychological processes. Frequently studies investigate the aftermath of brain damage

Neuroscience A branch of the life sciences that studies the anatomy, physiology and biochemistry of the nervous system and especially in relation to behaviour and learning

Neurotoxic lesion The chemical destruction of a discrete area of the brain

Neurotransmitters Chemicals which send out signals across a synapse from one neuron to another

Neurulation The process that turns the neural plate into the neural tube

Neutron A subatomic particle of about the same mass as a proton but without an electric charge

Nicotine An acetylcholine agonist

Nicotinic receptors Receptors identified using nicotine but are responsive to the endogenous neurotransmitter acetylcholine

Nigrostriatal pathway A dopamine pathway projecting from the substantia nigra to the striatum

Nitrazepam A benzodiazepine anxiolytic

Nitric oxide A gas that acts as a mediator of intracellular and intercellular communication

NMDA A type of receptor for glutamate

N-methyl-D-aspartate (NMDA) receptor A glutamate receptor (not to be confused with MDMA!)

Nocebo The opposite of placebo meaning 'I shall harm'

Nociceptive The sensation of pain

Nocturnal Active at night

Nodes of Ranvier Gaps in the myelin along a neuron's axon in which an action potential can be measured

Non-competitive antagonist An antagonist that binds to a receptor but does not occupy the same position as the agonist

Non-REM sleep Stage 1–4 in the sleep cycle

Noradrenaline/norepinephrine A catecholamine neurotransmitter (UK/USA name respectively)

Notochord A cylinder-like structure in the mesoderm. Progenitor of the spine

Nuclear imaging A method of producing images by detecting radiation from parts of the brain

Nucleotide bases Nucleotides are molecules that make up DNA and RNA

Nucleus accumbens Part of the mesolimbic dopamine system

Nucleus (atom) A region consisting of protons and neutrons at the centre of an atom

Nucleus (cell) The DNA-containing unit of every cell

Nuremberg Code A set of ethical principles for human experimentation derived after the Nuremberg Trials

NYP/AgRP neurons Neurons producing neuropeptide Y (NPY) and agouti-related peptide in the arcuate nucleus of the hypothalamus and involved in regulating feeding behaviour

Obesity A medical condition characterized by excess body fat

Occipital eye field An area located near the junction of the occipital lobes with the posterior parietal and temporal lobes

Occipital lobe The cortical lobe at the anterior of the brain. Also called the visual cortex

Oculomotor nerve (CN III) A cranial nerve

Oedema An excess of watery fluid collecting in the cavities or tissues of the body

Oestrogen, oestradiol Reproductive hormones

Olfaction The act of smelling

Olfactory bulbectomy Removal of the olfactory bulb

Olfactory epithelium A membrane of the nose sensitive to smell

Olfactory nerve (CN I) A cranial nerve

Olfactory receptor Receptor of the nose sensitive to olfactory stimuli

Oligodendrocytes Cells which provide a myelin sheath around the axon

Oligopotent stem cells Stem cells with the ability to differentiate into only a few types of cells

Olivary nucleus (inferior olive) Part of the medulla oblongata, involved in motor control and sensory processing

Onuf's nucleus An area of motor neurons in the ventral horn which controls the ischiocavernosus and bulbocavernosus muscles involved in penile erection and ejaculation in males

Oocyte A progenitor ovum

Ootid In embryology, the cell produced by meiotic cellular division of an oocyte that continues to develop into an ovum

Operant conditioning A method of learning that occurs through rewards and punishments for behaviour

Opioid A compound resembling opium

Opsin Light-sensitive structure of photoreceptors that convert light into an electrical impulse

Optic chiasm The point of cross-over of visual signals travelling along the optic nerve

Optical imaging An imaging technique that uses light to obtain detailed images of cells and molecules

Optic nerve (CN II) A cranial nerve

Optic nerves Cranial nerves of each eye transmitting impulses from the retina to the lateral geniculate nucleus and visual cortex

Oral administration Delivery of a drug by consuming it via the mouth (per os, PO) in tablet or liquid form. The drug travels into the digestive system where it is absorbed into the bloodstream

Orbicularis oculi A muscle of the face

Orbitofrontal cortex Part of the frontal lobe involved in executive functioning

Orexin (hypocretin) A neurotransmitter that regulates appetite and wakefulness

Organizational-activational hypothesis The view of how hormones affect development

Organizational period The time when the effect of a hormone is permanent on tissue differentiation and development

Organ of Corti A structure in the cochlea of the inner ear which produces nerve impulses in response to sound vibrations

Orgasm phase Part of the human sexual response cycle

Os The aperture in the cervix

Osmoreceptors Receptors that detect changes in the concentration of the interstitial fluid

Osmotic thirst Thirst occurs when the solute concentration of extracellular fluid increases

Ossicles Small bones of the inner ear

Out of Africa hypothesis The view that humans descended from ancestors originating in Africa and then ventured further in the search for resources

Ovarian cycle Development of an ovarian follicle, rupture of the follicle, discharge of the ovum, and formation and regression of a corpus luteum

Ovulation The part of the menstrual cycle when an ovum is released from one of the ovaries and the female is most fertile

Ovum/egg The female gamete. Progenitor cell of new organism (see also Sperm)

Oxytocin A peptide hormone produced by the hypothalamus and stored and secreted by the posterior pituitary gland

Pacini's corpuscles Sensory receptors of the clitoris

Pain The perception of a noxious sensation

Pain asymbolia A condition in which pain is experienced without unpleasantness

Pallidotomy A lesion of the globus pallidus for the symptomatic treatment of Parkinson's disease

Pancreas A gland that secretes enzymes into the duodenum. In the pancreas are the islets, which secrete insulin and glucagon into the blood

Papez circuit A neural circuit for the expression of emotion

Parahippocampal gyrus A cortical region of the brain that surrounds the hippocampus and is part of the limbic system

Paraphilia A condition in which a person's sexual arousal and gratification depend on fantasizing about and engaging in sexual behaviour that is atypical and extreme

Parasympathetic nervous system A division of the autonomic nervous system responsible for controlling the bodily processes that are not undervoluntary control

Paraurethral gland (Skene's gland) The most likely physiological substrate for the G spot that stems from the same embryonic tissue as the male prostate gland

Paraventricular nucleus A neuronal nucleus in the hypothalamus

Parenteral Administration of a drug via injection

Parietal lobes The middle part of each cerebral hemisphere behind the central sulcus

Parkinson's disease A neurodegenerative disorder of the nigrostriatal pathway affecting movement. After James Parkinson

Partial agonist A drug with low efficacy at the receptor

Parvocellular layer A layer of the lateral geniculate nucleus

Passive avoidance learning A task in which an organism learns not to emit a certain response in order to avoid punishment

Pathology The scientific investigation of the causes of disease

Penis An external male sex organ

Pepsin A digestive enzyme which initiates the breakdown of protein molecules into its constituent amino acids

Periaqueductal grey The grey matter located around the cerebral aqueduct of the spinal column containing descending autonomic tracts

Perineum The area between the vagina and the anus

Peripheral nervous system Part of the nervous system that consists of the nerves and ganglia outside the brain and spinal cord

Perisylvian language network A network of structures involved in language comprising the arcuate fasciculus

Periventricular nucleus a region of the hypothalamus located along the third ventricle

Persistent Müllerian duct syndrome A condition caused by a congenital lack of anti-Mullerian hormone or its receptors

Pervasive developmental disorders A group of disorders, e.g. autism, in the DSM IV

PGO waves Waveforms indicative of rapid eye movement sleep coming from the pons, geniculate and occipital cortex

Phagocytosis The engulfing of micro-organisms or other cells and foreign particles by phagocytes

Phantom limb An amputated limb that is perceived as being present

Pharmacodynamics The effect of a drug at its target

Pharmacodynamic tolerance The diminishing of a drug's effect due to adaptations in the brain after exposure to the drug

Pharmacokinetics The movement of a drug to its target and also its elimination

Pharmacokinetic tolerance The diminishing of a drug's effect due to metabolism of a drug after exposure

Pharmacology The discipline that addresses the mechanism of action and effects of drugs

Phencyclidine (PCP) An NMDA antagonist (street name angel dust). Used in animals to model schizophrenia. Controlled substance

Phenobarbital A barbiturate/anxiolytic

Phenocopy An individual showing features characteristic of a genotype other than its own, but produced environmentally rather than genetically

Phenothiazines A chemical class of antipsychotic that is typified by chlorpromazine

Phenotype The observable characteristics of an individual. Compare with genotype

Phenylketonuria An inherited recessive disorder

Phobia An irrational fear. Can be debilitating

Phospholipid layers A two-layered arrangement of phosphate and lipid molecules that form a cell membrane, the hydrophobic lipid ends facing inward and the hydrophilic phosphate ends facing outward

Photoreceptors Light-sensitive receptors in the eye. See Rods and Cones

Physics The branch of science concerned with the nature and properties of matter and energy. Most relevant in the current context to biotechnologies such as neuroimaging

Physiological psychology The subdivision of psychobiology that studies the neural mechanisms of behaviour via direct manipulation of the brain during controlled animal experiments

Physiology The branch of biology that addresses the functions and processes of living organisms and their constituent parts

Physostigmine Acetylcholinesterase inhibitor

Pia mater The innermost membrane covering and protecting the brain and spinal cord

Pineal gland A gland in the brain which secretes melatonin

Pinna The outer visible cup of the ear. Catches sound

Pinocytosis A mechanism by which cells ingest extracellular fluid and its contents

Pituitary gland The major endocrine gland. The master gland. Divided into anterior and posterior regions. Secretes hormones

Placebo An inert substance devoid of pharmacological effect. Means 'I shall please'. Used as a control agent in clinical trials

Placental barrier A semi-permeable membrane made up of placental tissues limiting the kind and amount of material exchanged between mother and foetus

Planum temporale Cortical area just posterior to the auditory cortex

Plateau phase Part of the human sexual response cycle

Plethysmography The measuring of blood flow in regions of the body, e.g. blood flow in the penis/clitoris during sexual arousal

Pluripotent stem cell Stem cell having the ability to differentiate into more than one cell type

Polycystic ovary syndrome A disorder characterized by disruption of the ovulation cycle due to cysts around the edge of the ovaries and excessive secretion of androgens

Polygenetic disorder A disorder with multiple genetic contributions

Polymerase chain reaction A method of making many copies of a DNA sequence, thereby amplifying it so it is more readily studied

Polymorphisms Variations in a gene, DNA sequence or chromosome that have no adverse effects on the individual and occur with fairly high frequency in the general population

Polyploidy Having one or more extra sets of chromosomes

Polyvagal theory A theory of the flight/fight response

Pons Part of the brainstem that links the medulla oblongata and thalamus

Positive reinforcement The increase in behaviour following an appetitive stimulus (e.g. food)

Positive symptoms Symptoms of schizophrenia that are in addition to normal behaviour, e.g. hallucinations

Positron emission tomography A brain imaging technique that uses radioactive isotopes to map the brain

Postsynaptic membrane The membrane of the cell on the receiving side of a synapse

Postsynaptic neuron The neuron on the receiving side of a synapse

Post-traumatic stress disorder A disorder following a trauma

Potassium The major positive ion found inside cells

Potency The amount of drug needed to get the effect

Predictive homeostasis Anticipatory homeostatic adaptations

Predictive validity In animal models, the ability of a test to predict the results of the manipulation/model

Prefrontal cortex The front part of the frontal lobe

Preganglionic neuron A cell body located in the brain or spinal cord and a myelinated axon that travels out of the central nervous system as part of a cranial or spinal nerve

Premenstrual dysphoric disorder A severe form of premenstrual syndrome

Premenstrual syndrome A collection of emotional and/or physical symptoms related to a woman's menstrual cycle

Premotor cortex A part of the motor cortex

Preoptic nucleus Part of the hypothalamus

Pre-supplementary motor area Anterior part of the supplementary motor area and part of the motor cortex

Presynaptic terminal The end part of a neuron prior to the synapse

Primary motor cortex (M1) A part of the motor cortex

Primitive streak During embryonic development, the primitive streak is an elongated band of cells that defines bilateral symmetry

Primordial follicles Cells yet to develop into oocytes

Pro-creationism The view that evolution is untrue and that humans and the world were created by a superior being (a god)

Progenitor cell A cell that is able to differentiate into a specific type of cell, but is already more specific than a stem cell

Progesterone Female hormone

Progestin Female hormone

Prolactin A hormone involved in lactation

Pro-opiomelanocortin A protein cut into peptides, e.g. MCH

Proprioception Being able to perceive where one's body is in space

Prosencephalon The forebrain

Prosopagnosia The inability to recognize faces

Prostate gland The gland producing semen

Proteins Large molecules composed of one or more chains of amino acids in a specific order determined by the base sequence of nucleotides in the DNA

Proton A subatomic particle in atomic nuclei with a positive electric charge

Psilocybin Hallucinogen. Controlled substance. Interacts with serotonergic systems

Psychiatry A branch of medicine concerned with abnormalities of the mind

Psychobiology The branch of psychology concerned with the biological processes underlying behaviour

Psychopathology The scientific study of mental disorders

Psychopharmacology The branch of psychobiology that studies the behavioural effects of drugs

Psychophysiology The branch of psychobiology that studies the relationship between physiological and psychological processes. Not to be confused with physiological psychology

Psychosexual development The Freudian view of human psychological development

Psychosis A mental disorder in which thought and emotions are impaired and contact with external reality is lost

Pudendal cleft Part of the vulva, the channel at the base of the mons pubis where it divides to form the labia majora

Punishment An aversive event intended to suppress behaviour (not the same as negative reinforcement)

Pupil The black dot in the centre of the eye, which is actually a hole allowing the passage of light to the retina

Purkinje cell A cell of the cerebellum

Putamen Part of the striatum

Pygmalion effect When there is greater expectation placed upon individuals, they will perform better

Pyloric sphincter Valve that controls the movement of stomach contents

Pyramidal cells Pyramid-shaped cells of the cortex, hippocampus and amygdala

Pyramidal motor system Part of the motor system that starts in the primary motor cortex, which is responsible for fine motor programmes

Qualitative trait A trait that you either have or don't have. Without the gene you will not have the trait

Quantitative trait Rather than all or none, quantitative traits are about how much of the trait one has

Quantitative trait loci Sequences of DNA linked to the genes that underlie a quantitative trait

Radial glia Cells that provide a network of guidewires and support structures that the migrating neuron wraps around and follows

Radioactive isotope An element emitting radiation

Randomized controlled trial A clinical trial to evaluate the efficacy of a new treatment in participants who have been randomly assigned to either an experimental group or a control group

Raphe nucleus Part of the reticular formation

Rate dependency The effects of a drug on behaviour are a function of the baseline level of behaviour

Reactive homeostasis Responses to changes in physiological variables which have already occurred (compared to predictive homeostasis)

Reboxetine A selective noradrenaline reuptake inhibitor

Receptive fields Areas of a cell sensitive to light

Receptor-mediated endocytosis Receptor-based ingestion of specific molecules into the cell

Receptors Proteins which are configured to receive a particular endogenous chemical

Recessive trait A trait that must be contributed by both parents in order to appear in the offspring, e.g. phenylketonuria

Red nucleus A structure in the midbrain involved in motor co-ordination

Reductionism The philosophical point of view that describes a complex phenomenon in terms of its smaller constituent parts

Reflex An automatic response that is not under conscious control

Region of interest A portion of an image to be studied for a particular purpose

Reinforcement The process of strengthening a behaviour

Relative refractory period The period shortly after the firing of a nerve fibre when partial repolarization has occurred and a greater than normal stimulus can stimulate a second response

Reliability The consistency of a research study or measuring tool

Remifentanil An opiate receptor antagonist

REM sleep Sleep characterized by rapid eye movement

Renin An enzyme secreted by and stored in the kidneys which promotes the production of the protein angiotensin

Replicability The ability to obtain the same result when one conducts an experiment under the same conditions

Replication The process of copying DNA

Reproduction The production of offspring by a sexual or asexual process

Rescorla–Wagner model A mathematical model with predictive explanatory power of classical conditioning

Reserpine A drug that depletes the brain of monoamines by rendering the vesicles leaky

Resolution phase Part of the human sexual response cycle

Response inhibition The ability to stop a motor behaviour

Resting potential The potential difference between the two sides of the membrane of a nerve cell; when the cell is not conducting an impulse, the membrane potential is said to be polarized

Reticular formation A brainstem region connecting the spinal cord, cerebrum and cerebellum, and mediating the overall level of consciousness

Retina Multilayered region of the eye that transforms light into neural impulses

Retinotopic map The spatial arrangement of the retina that is maintained throughout the visual pathway

Retrograde amnesia The inability to remember events occurring before the trauma

Retrograde signalling A process in which the postsynaptic neuron communicates with the presynaptic neuron which may inhibit further release

Reward deficiency syndrome A reduction in the ability to experience and respond to rewards

Reward prediction error The phasic dopamine response that occurs if a reward is unpredicted, not available or delayed

Rhodopsin Photosensitive pigment in the retinal rods

Rhombencephalon The hindbrain

Ribosome A structure within the cytoplasm of a cell that is composed of RNA and protein and is the site of protein synthesis

Rod Light-sensitive receptor in the eye. Active in low light. Providing low-acuity and black-and-white vision

Rolandic operculum A region of the precentral and postcentral gyri

Saccadic eye movements The simultaneous movements of both eyes in the same direction

Saccule Part of the vestibular system that translates head movements into neural impulses

Sagittal plane A vertical plane dividing the body into right and left halves

Saltatory conduction Propagation of action potentials along myelinated axons from one node of Ranvier to the next

Sarcolemma Membrane of the muscle cell

Sarin Acetylcholinesterase inhibitor. A toxic nerve agent

Satiety The feeling of being full

Scheduled drugs A legal classification of drugs

Schedules of reinforcement Different forms of partial reinforcement

Schizophrenia A psychiatric disorder characterized by a breakdown in information processing leading to symptoms such as a dissociation from reality and hallucination and delusions

Schwann cells Provide myelin

Sclera The white outer layer of the eyeball

Scotopic vision Vision of the eye under low light conditions

Screening test The use of animals for finding new effective drugs

Scrotum A bag of skin containing the testicles

Secondary motor cortex motor areas outside of the primary motor cortex (M1) including: parietal cortex, the premotor cortex, and the supplementary motor area (SMA)

Secondary oocyte An oocyte that is produced by division of a primary oocyte in the first meiotic division

Selective breeding The breeding of animals and plants specifically to display a particular trait

Selective noradrenergic reuptake A drug that blocks the reuptake of released noradrenaline. inhibitor Used as an antidepressant

Selective serotonin reuptake A drug that blocks the reuptake of released 5-HT. Used as inhibitor an antidepressant

Semicircular canals Three fluid-filled channels in the inner ear that provide information about orientation to the brain to help maintain balance

Seminiferous tubules Part of the testes where sperms are produced

Senile dementia of Alzheimer's type A cautionary label for symptoms commensurate with Alzheimer's dementia

Sensation seeking A personality characteristic in which individuals are looking for new experiences/thrills

Sensitive periods Time points in neurodevelopment that are critical for normal development and are sensitive to environmental influences

Sensitization The increased effect after repeated exposure to a drug. Sometimes called reverse tolerance.

Sensorimotor loop The process of receiving sensory input and acting upon it

Sensory aphasia Poor auditory comprehension

Sensory dorsal nerve The sensory nerve of the clitoris originating from the pudendal nerves

Sensory modalities Sensory input from the sensory organs

Septum Part of the limbic system

Serotonin (5-HT) An indolamine neurotransmitter

Sertoli cells Support cells for sperms during development

Sex chromosomes The chromosomes concerned with determining the sex of the offspring (XX = female; XY = male)

Sex determining region of the Y chromosome Gene coding for sex on the Y chromosome

Sexually dimorphic nucleus An area of the hypothalamus that is different in males and females

Sexual reproduction Form of reproduction in which two parents are required

Shaft The area of the penis/clitoris below the glans

Shaping The gradual training of an operant behaviour

Sickle cell disease A genetic blood disorder caused by the presence of an abnormal form of haemoglobin

Simple cells Cells of the visual cortex with defined receptive fields

Simulation The true animal model of behaviour that seeks to mimic human behaviour in the animal. More often than not it is abnormal behaviour that is modelled

Simultaneous conditioning When both the onset and offset of the conditioned stimulus and unconditioned stimulus occur at the same time

Single-blind A clinical trial in which only the participant is not informed whether they are in a placebo or drug group

Single nucleotide polymorphism A variation at a single position in a DNA sequence among individuals

Single photon emission computed Neuroimaging technique using gamma rays tomography

Sinus A cavity within a bone or other tissue

Skin conductance The electrical conductance of the skin

Skin conductance level The tonic skin conductance

Skin conductance response The transient changes in skin conductance in response to an event

Sleep paralysis Similar to cataplexy, but happens either just before or just after sleep

Sleep spindles A burst of electroencephalogram activity during Stage 2 sleep

Slow-wave sleep Stage 1–4 in the sleep cycle

Social neuroscience The scientific investigation of the neural processing of emotional information. See also Affective neuroscience

Sodium The main cation of extracellular body fluids

Sodium–potassium pump A membrane-bound transporter found in nearly all mammalian cells that transports potassium ions into the cytoplasm from the extracellular fluid while simultaneously transporting sodium ions out of the cytoplasm to the extracellular fluid

Soluble gases Transient gases that act as neurotransmitters

Soma Another name for the cell body

Somatic nervous system Part of the peripheral nervous system associated with the voluntary control of body movements via skeletal muscles

Somatosensation The process of communicating information from regions of the body to areas of the brain

Somatosensory cortex Two regions in the postcentral gyrus that receive and process somatosensory stimuli

Somatotopic map A representation of the body in the cortex

Somites A bilateral segmental mass of mesoderm in the embryo

Sonic hedgehog gene A gene that makes a protein called Sonic Hedgehog that plays a role in cell growth and specialization

Spatial frequency The measure of fine detail in an optical image in terms of light waves of cycles measured in hertz

Spatial summation The integration of information coming in from different sites/dendrites at the axon hillock

Sperm The male gamete and progenitor cell for a new organism. See also Ovum

Spermatic cord Connects the testes with organs within the abdominal cavity

Spermatogenesis The production or development of mature spermatozoa

Sphygmomanometer An instrument for measuring blood pressure

Spina bifida A congenital defect of the spine in which part of the spinal cord and its meninges are exposed through a gap in the backbone

Spinal accessory nerve (CN XI) A cranial nerve

Spinal nerve A nerve that carries motor, sensory and autonomic signals between the spinal cord and the body

Spinoreticular pathway A pathway from the spine to the reticular formation

Spinotectal pathway A pathway from the spine to the tectum

Spinothalamic pathway A pathway from the spine to the thalamus

Spiperone A typical antipsychotic (D2 antagonist)

Spontaneous recovery The re-emergence of a previously extinguished conditioned response after a delay

Stem cells Unspecialized cells that have the ability to differentiate into other cells and to self-regenerate

Stereotaxic frame The apparatus used to hold the head in position during neurosurgery or to hold a surgical instrument in a stable position

Steroid hormone A steroid that acts as a hormone synthesized from cholesterol in the gonads and adrenal glands

Stirrup (stapes) One of the bones of the inner ear

Stop Signal Reaction Time test A neuropsychological test assessing the ability to stop a response when given a signal

Striatum Subcortical structure of the basal ganglia

Stroma A layer of the cornea

Stroop task A neuropsychological test of attention and conflict. Uses the presentation of colour nouns in different printed colours where the participant has to name the colour noun

Subarachnoid space The space between the arachnoid membrane and pia mater

Subcutaneous An injection under the skin

Subfornical organ A region of the brain not protected by the blood–brain barrier, involved in osmoregulation

Substance dependence disorder A DSM IV definition of drug abuse problems

Substance use disorder A DSM IV definition of drug abuse problems

Substantia gelatinosa Grey matter of the dorsal horn that extends the entire length of the spinal cord involved in pain transmission

Substantia nigra Midbrain structure (subcortical), part of the basal ganglia

Substantia nigra pars reticulata/pars Regions of the substantia nigra compacta

Subthalamus Part of the basal ganglia situated below the thalamus

Sulci (s. sulcus) The grooves seen in the surface of the brain

Superficial facial muscles Muscles of the face that enable fine movements

Superior colliculus Part of the midbrain processing visual signals

Superior olivary nuclei Part of the olivary nuclei

Supervisory attentional system A theoretical construct similar to working memory which offers an explanation of executive functioning

Supplementary motor area A part of the motor cortex

Suprachiasmatic nucleus Part of the hypothalamus

Supraoptic nucleus Part of the hypothalamus

Survival of the fittest The continuation of an organism that has successfully adapted to the environment which means they live long enough to reproduce

Sympathetic chain Groups of ganglia running along each side of the spinal column

Sympathetic nervous system Part of the autonomic nervous system

Synaesthesia A neurological phenomenon in which stimulation of one sensory pathway leads to experiences in a second sensory pathway

Synapse A junction between two neurons, consisting of a small gap across which a neurotransmitter crosses

Synaptic consolidation A mechanism strengthening the synapses with cell adhesion molecules

Synaptic elimination The pruning/elimination of neurons

Synaptogenesis The creation of new synapses

Synovial joints Skeletal joints that allow movement

Systematic desensitization The gradual exposure to different grades of a phobic stimulus whilst engaging in stress management exercises

Systolic blood pressure The peak pressure in the arteries

Tacrine Acetylcholinesterase inhibitor

Tandem repeat (satellite DNA) A sequence of two or more nucleotide base pairs that is repeated and lie adjacent to each other on the chromosome

Tardive dyskinesia Orofacial dystonia

Tau proteins Proteins that stabilize microtubules

Tectum The uppermost part of the midbrain

Tegmentum A general area within the brainstem. A region of grey matter on either side of the cerebral aqueduct

Telencephalon The most anterior part of the forebrain, including the cerebral hemispheres and olfactory lobes

Telomere The end of a chromosome

Temporal conditioning A fixed passage of time serves as a conditioned stimulus

Temporal lobes Cortical regions located beneath the lateral fissure on both cerebral hemispheres of the brain

Temporal summation The integration of information coming in at a similar time thereby increasing the probability of an action potential

Tendon Connecting tissue between bone and muscle

Teratogen An agent that affects the organism's development

Teratology The study of teratogens

Tesla The unit of measure of the power of a magnet, e.g. a 4 T MRI machine – very powerful

Testes-determining factor A sex-determining region Y-linked factor that allows testes to develop

Testosterone Male sex hormone (androgen)

Tetrabenazine A presynaptic monoamine transporter inhibitor which reduces the amount of catecholamine that can be released

Thalamic retrograde degeneration The measurable response of cells in the thalamus as a consequence of a cortical lesion

Thalamus A forebrain structure which processes sensory and motor signals to and from the cortex

Thalidomide A teratogen that was given during pregnancy to alleviate morning sickness that lead to babies with malformed or missing limbs

The 3Rs The goal of UK legislation on animal experimentation: Reduce, Replace and Refine

Thecal cell Androgen-producing cell of the ovarian follicle

Thelarche Onset of breast enlargement

Theory of Mind The ability to attribute mental states, e.g. beliefs, intents, desires, thoughts, etc., to oneself and others and to understand that others have beliefs, desires and intentions that are different from one's own

Theta waves Brain waves produced when relaxed and drowsy

Thiamine A vitamin

Three prime (3') An area designating the start of a DNA/RNA strand

Thymine A nucleotide base. Part of the genetic code

Thyroid gland A gland in the neck which secretes hormones regulating growth and development through the rate of metabolism

Thyroid hormone A chemical substance made by the thyroid gland for export into the bloodstream, e.g. thyroxine

Tinnitus A condition characterized by noise or ringing in the ears

Tolerance The diminishing effectiveness of a drug after previous administration

Tonotopic map The arrangement of auditory input that is maintained throughout the auditory pathway

Totipotent stem cells Stem cells with the ability to differentiate into all possible cell types

Tower of Hanoi A neuropsychological test of planning

Tower of London A neuropsychological test of planning

Trace conditioning The conditioned stimulus is presented and then there is a gap in time before the unconditioned stimulus is presented

Tract A large bundle of nerve fibres

Transcortical aphasia Poor auditory comprehension

Transcranial magnetic stimulation The stimulation of neurons below the skull (cranium) using magnetic pulses

Transcription The process by which the information in a strand of DNA is copied into a new molecule of messenger RNA (mTNA)

Transdermal Drug administration across the skin, e.g. nicotine patches

Transdihydrolisuride (terguride) A partial agonist at dopamine receptors

Transfer ribonucleic acid (tRNA) A type of RNA molecule that helps decode a messenger RNA (mRNA) sequence into a protein

Transgenic mouse A genetically manipulated mouse

Transient ischaemic attack A brief episode of neurological dysfunction resulting from an interruption in the blood supply to the brain

Translocation (genetic) A chromosome alteration in which a whole chromosome or segment of a chromosome becomes attached to or interchanged with another whole chromosome or segment

Transmucosal Absorption across the mucous membranes of the nose, rectum, vagina, mouth or eye

Transporter/reuptake proteins Proteins spanning the cell membrane that promote the reabsorption of the released neurotransmitter into the presynaptic cytoplasm

Transudate A fluid that passes through a membrane

Tricyclic antidepressant A type of antidepressant based on structure

Trigeminal nerve (CN V) A cranial nerve

Trimester The division of pregnancy into three time periods

Trisomy A condition in which an extra copy of a chromosome is present in the cell nuclei

Trisomy 21 Also known as Down's syndrome, caused by an extra copy of chromosome number 21

Trochlear nerve (CN IV) A cranial nerve

Tryptophan depletion The reduction of tryptophan and therefore 5-HT

Tunica albuginea Connective tissue that surrounds the corpora cavernosa of the penis that helps to trap the blood in the corpora cavernosa

Turner's syndrome A condition that affects females when a sex chromosome is missing or partially missing

Twin studies A method used in behavioural genetics to determine the genetic basis of a trait/disorder (see also Monozygotic twins and Dizygotic twins)

Unconditioned response The unlearned reaction to a stimulus

Unconditioned stimulus Something that elicits a natural and automatic reaction

Unipolar neuron A neuron whose cell body emits a single axonal process

Unipotent stem cells Cells with the ability to produce cells of only their own type

Uracil A nucleotide base. Part of the genetic code

Urethra The tube allowing the passage of urine from the bladder (also semen in males)

Urethral meatus The point at which urine exits the urethra

Urethral opening The exit area of the urethra allowing the passing of urine

Uterus A muscular organ of the female in which the foetus develops during gestation

Utricle Part of the vestibular system that provides information on the orientation of the head

Vagina A tube that connects the uterus to the external genitalia
Vagus nerve (CN X) A cranial nerve
Varenicline A nicotinic receptor partial agonist used to aid smoking cessation
Variable interval schedules When reinforcement is provided after an average period of time and only if the subject has responded correctly
Variable ratio schedule When reinforcement occurs after a variable amount of responses
Vas deferens Carries sperm from the epididymis towards the ejaculatory duct
Vasopressin A hormone secreted by cells of the hypothalamic nuclei and stored in the posterior pituitary for release that increases blood pressure and decreases urine flow (also called antidiuretic hormone)
Veins Veins are part of the circulatory system, which return blood to the heart
Ventral corticospinal tract Fibres of the corticospinal tract that do not cross over to the other side of the spinal column
Ventral noradrenergic bundle A collection of fibres containing noradrenaline
Ventral pallidum A region of the basal ganglia
Ventral striatum Part of the striatum
Ventral tegmental area A region of the mesolimbic dopamine system
Ventromedial hypothalamus Part of the hypothalamus
Ventromedial nucleus Part of the hypothalamus
Vertebral artery An artery located in the back of the neck that carries blood from the heart to the brain, spine and neck muscles
Vesicle A small spherical neurotransmitter-filled container
Vesicular monoamine transporter A protein integrated into the membrane of synaptic vesicles of presynaptic neurons that facilitates the packaging of monoamine into vesicles
Vestibular system A series of structures in the inner ear responsible for balance
Vestibule The area within the labia
Vestibulocochlear nerve (CN VIII) A cranial nerve
Viagra A drug used for impotence
Vitreous humour A large chamber behind the lens filled with fluid similar to that of the aqueous humour
Vulva Complete external female genitalia
Wada test The anaesthetizing of one side of the brain
Wechsler Intelligence Scale An IQ test
Wernicke's area An area in the left hemisphere associated with language comprehension
Wernicke's encephalopathy The presence of neurological symptoms caused by biochemical lesions of the central nervous system due to a reduction of thiamine, seen in chronic alcoholics
Wernicke–Korsakoff syndrome Korsakoff's syndrome with added Wernicke's encephalopathy
White matter Pale tissue of the brain and spinal cord, consisting mainly of nerve fibres with their myelin sheaths
Williams–Beuren syndrome A neurodevelopmental disorder caused by a deletion of genes on chromosome 7
Wisconsin Card Sorting Task A neuropsychological test of set-shifting and hypothesis testing
Withdrawal symptoms A collection of negative effects of not having a drug after a period of consumption
Wolffian duct The embryonic duct of the mesonephros, which becomes the vas deferens of the male
Working memory A system that holds multiple pieces of transitory information in the mind enabling conscious processing. An explanation of executive functions
Zeitgeber An environmental cue that alters the circadian cycle
Zona incerta Part of the subthalamus
Zona pellucida A layer around the ovum
Zonules of Zinn Fibres connecting the ciliary muscles to the lens of the eye
Zygomaticus muscle A muscle of the face
Zygote A fertilized ovum

Index

Note: *Italic* page numbers indicate figures and tables (where these are on a different page from the text).
Abbreviations used: AD for Alzheimer's disease; ADHD for attention deficit hyperactivity disorder; ASD for autism spectrum disorder; CR for conditioned response; CS for conditioned stimulus; PD for Parkinson's disease; UR for unconditioned response; US for unconditioned stimulus.

1-methyl-4-phenyl-1,2,3,6-tetrahydro-pyridine (MPTP) 585
1-methyl-4-phenyl-pyridinium (MPP+) 585
2-deoxyglucose (2-DG) 158
3-methoxy-4-hydroxyphenylglycol (MHPG) 560
5,7-DHT 551
5-alpha-reductase 368
5-HT *see* serotonin
6-OHDA, neurotoxin 589

abducens nerve 119, *121*
   disorders of 121
absolute refractory period 95
absorption of a drug 177, 178, 179, *184*
'abstract attitude', features of 322
abuse of drugs 412–13
   see also addiction
acetylcholine (ACh) 101, *102*, *103*, *104*, 126
   and Alzheimer's disease 596
   vigilance during wakefulness 468
acetylcholinesterase inhibitors (AChEIs) 597
   donepezil (Aricept) 598
acoustic agnosia 138
acquisition of learning
   classical conditioning 209
   and the law of effect 217
   operant conditioning 221, *222*
   Rescorla-Wagner equation 216
acrosome *62*, *63*
actin 100, 306
action potentials 95–8
activational period, hormones 375, 380
acute stress 564
   vs. chronic stress 569–71
addiction 412–13
   adolescents' vulnerability to 73–4
   animal model 219
   evolutionary perspective 411
   motivation theories 419–30

neuronal adaptations in 430–2
obesity model 403–5
reward pathway 413–16
and speed of drug entry 179–81
stress and the HPA axis 566–8
Adelta fibres, pain 281, 282, 283, 288, *289*
adenine 38, 43, 49
adenosine triphosphate (ATP) 85–6, 347
adenylate cyclase 531
ADHD (attention deficit hyperactivity disorder) 32–5, 504–14
   addiction and co-morbidity 423–4
   behavioural inhibition (BI) 329, 333, 511–13
   birth trauma and teratogens 66–7
   brain structure 506
   diagnostic criteria 504–6
   dynamic developmental theory 510–11
   frontostriatal circuits 507
   functional neuroimaging 506
   Grace's tonic and phasic DA 509–10
   hypo/hyperfunctioning DA 509
   and impulsivity 331
   methylphenidate 507–11
   pharmacology 507–8
   psychophysiological studies 506–7
   rate-dependent hypothesis & effects of amphetamines 231
   reward deficiency 511
   working memory 513–14
adipsia 398, 400
adolescents, neural development 71–5
adoption studies 54
adrenal cortex *110*, 112
adrenal gland 109, *110*, 111, *565*, 566
adrenal medulla *110*, 112
adrenaline 101, *102*, *103*, *104*, 109
   release in response to stress 565–6
adrenocorticotrophic hormone (ACTH) 109, 112, *113*, *141*, 566, 569
adults, neural development 75–6
adversity, link to schizophrenia 529

Advisory Council on the Misuse of drugs (ACMD) 175, 176
affective disorders 542–57
affective networks related to ToM *331*
affective neuroscience 10
afferent nerves 118
afferent pathways 90
affinity (Kd), drug-receptor *191*, 192
agarose gel block 49
ageing
   neuroscience of 75–6
   role of mitochondria 87
agency
   in movement, loss of 310–11
   see also free will
aggression
   and hormones 459
   neural mechanisms 458–9
agnosia 138
agonists, benzodiazepine receptor complex 579–80
agouti-related peptide (AgRP) 400, *401*
agraphia 487
AIM model of sleep, Hobson 469–70
akathisia 532
akinesia 584, 586, 589
alcohol 195
   counter-conditioning 216
   and placebo response 243
alcohol consumption
   in adolescence 73–4
   alcohol units 183, 604
   breathalyser test 183
   foetal alcohol syndrome 79–80
   and link to ADHD 66
   liver damage, blood test for 184
alcoholism
   and emotional processing 442–3
   familial studies 52
   Korsakoff's syndrome 347–9
   reduced DA receptors 426
   treatment using disulfiram 190

INDEX

aldosterone 112–13, 406
alexia 487
alien hand syndrome 310
all-or-nothing event 95
alleles 31, 36
   dominant 37–8
   recessive 39
allostasis 120, 425, 426
   vs. homeostasis 569–71
allostatic load 570–71, 571
allostatic state 570, 571
allosteric antagonism 185
allosteric modulation 578, 579
alpha-2 adrenoceptors 580
alpha activity 466
alpha-fetoprotein 377
alpha motor neurons 306
alpha waves 158, 159
alveoli 183
Alzheimer's disease (AD) 593–9
   and abnormalities in mitochondrial genes 87
   animal models 597
   anticholinesterase inhibitors 190
   diagnostic criteria 593–4
   negation of placebo effect 240, 241
   neuropathology 594–6
   neuropharmacology 596–8
   neuropsychology 598–9
amacrine cells, retina 256, 261
American Psychological Association (APA)
   animal research guidelines 15–16
amino acid hormones 109
amino acids 39, 101
   and digestion 392, 395
   protein synthesis 44–5
   see also GABA; glutamate
amnesia
   HM case study 346–7
   Korsakoff's syndrome 347–9
amobarbital (sodium amytal) 489
AMPA receptor 354, 355
amphetamine 175, 188, 192, 194, 548, 549
   ADHD treatment 507, 508, 509
   conditioned place preference (CPP) 413, 418
   effects in ADHD 231
   endurance of sensitization 422
   locomotor activity 533
   psychosis 529–31
   schedules of reinforcement 229–30
   schizophrenia symptoms 232, 528
   self-administration 416–19
   sensitization, effects of time and repetition 233, 235

amphibians, evolution of 27–8
ampulla 62, 364, 365
amygdala 141–2, 143, 448
   children from care homes 78
   chronic stress 571
   connections & functions 449
   defence & attack behaviours 458
   and depression 552, 553, 554, 554, 555
   emotion processing 276, 456
   extended 425
   and fear 448–50
   fear controlled by 581
   role in eating/feeding 399, 400
   stress response 564
amyloid-beta plaque formation in AD 594–6
amyotrophic lateral sclerosis (ALS) 120
analgesia
   behavioural tolerance 232–3
   congenital 290
   endogenous 286
   and PAG response 287
   studies of placebo effects 240–3
analytic ruminations hypothesis 546, 547
anarchic hand syndrome 310–11
androgen insensitivity syndrome 376
androgens 110, 111, 368, 373
   abnormalities 376
   and aggression 458
   lack of neonatal 377
angel dust, phencyclidine (PCP) 534
angiotensin 406
animal learning 204–25
   classical conditioning 208–16
   cognition 224–5
   habituation 205–7
   learning theory 205
   operant conditioning 216–24
   reflexes 207–8
   theories of and addiction 427
animal models
   memory deficits in AD 596–7
   in psychobiology 18
   schizophrenia 530
   stress and anxiety 577
   validity of 16–20
animal research/studies 13–20
   the 3Rs, UK legislation 14
   genetics 56–7
   professional bodies' guidelines 15–16
   species-typical behaviours 352–3
   US legislation 14–15
animals, physiological psychology 154–7
Animals (Scientific Procedures) Act (1986) 14

anions 92
anorexia nervosa (AN) 393, 402, 405
antagonists (blockers) 185–6, 188–9
anterior commissure 133
anterograde amnesia 345, 349
anti-Mullerian hormone (AMH) 368, 373
anticholinesterase inhibitors 190
antidepressants 197
   classification issues 174, 177
   medication 552–3
   neurochemistry of 548–52
   point of action 555–6
   theoretical shift 554–5
antidiuretic hormone (ADH) 140
antipsychotics 197, 532–4
   for Huntington's disease 300–1
anvil (incus) 273, 274
anxiety 571–81
   adaptive function of 575
   animal studies 577
   barbiturates 578–9
   benzodiazepines 578–80
   diagnostic criteria 573
   neurobiology 576
   neuropsychological theory of 581
   noradrenaline 580
   physiological symptoms 573, 575
   psychological symptoms 576
   role of GABA 576–8
   serotonin 580–81
anxiolytics 195–6, 577–8
aphagia 398, 399, 400
aphasia 486, 487, 488
apomorphine
   autoreceptor stimulation 189–90
   PD treatment 588, 589
apomorphine, PD treatment 590
apoptosis (cell death) 71
appetite, stimulation of 400
apraxia 138, 487
aqueous humour, the eye 255
arachnoid mater 127, 128
   infection of 129
arachnoid trabeculae 127, 128
arborization 68, 77, 88
arcuate fasciculus 487, 488
arcuate nucleus, hypothalamus 398, 399–400
arithmetic problem solving 327
aromatase 368, 377, 378
aromatization, sex differences 377, 378
arousal, misattribution of 446–7
arteries 147
   blood supply to brain 148
   cerebral arterial circle 149

INDEX

supply of oxygenated blood to brain 148–9
asexual reproduction 360
Asperger's syndrome 515
aspiration lesions 156
associative learning 350, 353
associative learning *see* conditioning
London taxi drivers 351–2
'silent associations', animal studies 352
associative learning and addiction 413, 419, 422, 426–7, 428–9, 430
astrocytes 88, 89
asymmetry of the brain 484–98
asymptote/plateau in learning 209, 215, 216
ataxia 301
atherosclerosis 146
atlas of rat brain 156
atomic structure 84, 85
atomoxetin, ADHD treatment 511
atropine 198, 596
attention deficit hyperactivity disorder *see* ADHD
attention quotient (AQ) 521
attention, role of frontal lobe 327–8, 340
atypical antidepressants 552–3
atypical antipsychotics 532–4
auditory canal 273
auditory nerve and cortex 274–5
auditory perception 272–5
auditory nerve and cortex 274–5
the ear 273–4
plasticity of auditory cortex 272–3
tinnitus 275
aura, migraines 147
autistic spectrum disorder (ASD) 515–20
diagnostic criteria 515, 517
function neuroimaging 518–19
genetics of 515, 518
male brain 516
neurochemistry & psychopharmacology 519
structural neuroimaging 518
theories of 519–20
autocrine feedback 114
autoimmune diseases/disorders 91, 111
automatic processes, and addiction 427–8, 429
automaticity of responses, behavioural inhibition 335, 337–8, 340
autonomic ganglia 120, 123
autonomic nervous system (ANS) 119, 120, 123–6
control of 126–7
development of 71

neural regulation of during threat 437
physiological specificity of emotion 444–6
autoradiography 158
autoreceptors 101, 105
alpha-2, clonadine as 549
dopaminergic 509, 510, 534
regulation 105, 106
serotonergic 581
stimulation and antagonism 189–90
autosomes 40
awareness abnormalities, schizophrenia 537
axoaxonic synapses 107, 108
axodendritic synapses 105, 108
axon hillock 86, 88
axon, neurons 85, 86, 88
giant axon of the squid 93
axonal elaboration 77
axosomatic synapses 105, 108
axosynaptic synapses 107, 108

backward conditioning 213–14
bacterial meningitis 129
barbiturates 195, 578–9
baroreceptors 406
basal ganglia 142, 143, 297, 305, 586
deep brain stimulation 592
Huntington's disease 300–1
pallidotomy effects in PD 591
role in cognition 593
role in motor behaviour 297–9, 589, 592
basal vein of Rosenthal 148, 149
basilar artery 148, 149
basolateral nuclei, amygdala 448
bed nucleus of the stria terminalis 142, 143, 564, 565
extended amygdala 424, 425
larger in male than female brain 378–9
behavioural approach system (BAS) 335–6
behavioural bioassays 16
behavioural genetics 11, 50–7
biotechnology 56–7
endophenotypes 56
methodological issues 55
nature-nurture debate 50–1
sensation seeking 55–6
three laws of 53–4
behavioural inhibition (BI) 329, 334
and ADHD 506, 511–13
and anxiety 335–6, 581
and impulsivity 329, 331
measures of 331–5

behavioural tolerance 232–3
behaviourism 217–18
belief-reality confusion, schizophrenia 536
benzodiazepine receptor 195–6, 576, 578–80
benzodiazepines 472, 578–80
bereitschaftspotential (readiness potential), reduced in PD 590, 592
beta activity, alertness 466, 467
beta adrenoceptors 580
beta-amyloid plaques
and Alzheimer's disease 594–6
clearance during sleep 470
beta-carbolines 579
beta motor neurons 306
beta waves 158, 159
bias
experimenter 200
processing in depression 554–6
publication 201
bilateral lesions 158
bile 7, 392
binding of ligands to receptors 185–6, 191, 531–2, 534
binocular vision 261, 264, 270–1
bioethics 12–13
biogeography 25
bioterrorism 198–9
biotransformation, phase 2 metabolism 184
bipolar cells, retina 256, 258, 259, 260, 261
bipolar disorder 543–4, 553
bipolar neurons 90
birth trauma, ADHD 66–7
BIS (behavioural inhibition system), Gray 335–6, 581
blastocyst 62, 64, 65
blastomere 62, 65
blind skier case study 266
blind spot, retina 257
blocking, conditioning 215
blood alcohol concentration (BAC) 183, 605
blood-brain barrier (BBB) 89, 129–31, 182–3
blood oxygen level dependent (BOLD) 164, 166
blood pressure changes, measurement of 160
blood supply to the brain 146–50
Bmax (maximum binding), receptors 191
body mass index (BMI) 403
body membranes 181–3
bolus 392
Bowman's layer, cornea 254–5
bradykinesia, Parkinson's disease 584

brain-derived neurotrophic factor (BDNF) 400
brain differences between the sexes 377–80
brain evolution 29, 30
brain regions 132–45
brain scans/imaging *see* neuroimaging
brain volume increase in ASD 518
'brain waves', EEG 158, 159
brainstem 131, 134, 135, 143, 144
　motor neurons in 302
breathalyser test 183
bregma 155, 156
British National Formulary 174
British Psychological Society (BPS)
　animal research guidelines 15–16
　areas within psychobiology 9–12
　ethics in research 12
Broca, Paul 8, 486–7
Broca's area 297, 485, 486
Brodmann areas 134, 135, 330
　names and functions 136–7
bromocriptine 588
Brown Peterson task, short-term memory 351
Brown-Séquard syndrome 120
bulbospongiosus muscle 365, 366
bulbourethal gland 365, 367, 374
bulimia nervosa 402, 405
bupropion 553
butyrophenones 531

C fibres, pain 281, 282, 283, 286, 288
caffeine 194
CAG (cytosine, adenine and guanine) repeats, Huntington's disease 38, 49
Calcium (Ca^{++}) ions 93, 108
calibration of drug dose 181
calorie intake
　benefits of reduced 76
　effect of varied diet 406
　and obesity 403
candidate genes 55
cannabinoids/cannabis 196–7
　active ingredient 411
　pain modulation role 286
　retrograde signalling 108
　and schizophrenia 528
Cannon-Bard theory of emotion 443–6
capsaicin (chili pepper) receptor 281
carbon monoxide (CO) 101, 102
cardiovascular measures 160
carotid arteries 148, 149
catalepsy 533
cataplexy 472
catecholamines 101, 109

cations 92
caudate nucleus 143, 586, 590
　active during anticipation 460
caudate, striatum 143, 506, 507
causal model of behaviour 4
causality 500
　and consciousness 474, 478–80
cell adhesion molecules (CAMs) 77
cell division 40–2
　abnormal 31, 48
　deletions and inversions 47
cell membrane 84–5
　drug penetration 181–2
　uneven distribution of ions across 93
central monitoring deficits, schizophrenia 536–7
central nervous system (CNS) 120, 127–31
central nucleus, extended amygdala 424, 425
centromeres 40
cephalic/reflex phase, digestion 393, 395, 396
cerebellar vermis 506
cerebellum 144
　and cognitive functioning 506
　motor behaviour 301–2
cerebral arterial circle 149
cerebral asymmetry 484–98
cerebral cortex/hemispheres 132
　fissures and gyri 133
cerebral ischaemia (stroke) 146–7
cerebral lateralization 132
cerebral palsy 97
cerebral ventricles 127–8
cerebrocerebellar tract 302, 303
cerebrocerebellum 301, 302
cerebrospinal fluid (CSF) 65, 89, 127
　four main functions of 128–9
cerebrovascular disease 146–7
cerebrum 132, 133, 143
cerveau isole 468
cervical nerves 120, 124, 127
cervical vertebrae 122
　areas connected to 123
　effect of lesions to 124
cervix 364, 384, 385
cGMP (cyclic guanosine monophosphate) 383
chemical pain, receptors for 281, 282
chimpanzees 27, 28
chlordiazepoxide (Librium) 578
chlorpromazine 322, 530
cholecystokinine (CCK), negative expectations and nocebo effect 245
cholinergic hypothesis of AD 596

choroid plexus 128, 484
chromatids 39
chromosomes 39–42
　abnormalities 376–7
　sex differentiation 360–1, 373, 379
ciliary body, the eye 253, 255
ciliary muscles, the eye 254, 255
cingulate cortex 136, 143
　anorexia 405
　and depression 553
　dysfunctional in ADHD 506
　emotion processing 456
　motor area 297
　Papez circuit, emotion 447, 448
　and theory of mind 329, 330
cingulate gyrus 137, 147, 275, 283, 387, 415, 448
circadian rhythms 464–5
circle of Willis 148, 149–50
circumplex model of emotion 440, 442
citalopram 554
classical conditioning 208–16
　acquisition 209
　applications of 215–16
　backward conditioning 213–14
　and behavioural tolerance 232, 233
　blocking 215
　delay conditioning 212
　differences in CR and UR 210–11
　discrimination & generalization 210
　extinction 209
　latent inhibition 215
　measuring the CR 209
　and the nocebo effect 244–5
　overdose effect 234–5
　placebo response 241–2
　relationship between CS and US 211–12
　Rescorla-Wagner model 215, 216
　simultaneous conditioning 212
　spontaneous recovery 209–10
　temporal conditioning 214
　trace conditioning 214
classical conduction aphasia 488
clinical trials 199–201
　ethics in use of placebos 236
clitoral hood 362
clitoris 362, 363, 373, 377
　erection 362, 381–3
　orgasm 383
cloaca, embryo 373, 374
clonidine 549
cloning 56
clozapine 532–4, 536, 589
co-morbidities, addiction 423–4
cocaine 194

conditioned place preference
  (CPP) 413–14, 418
  legal classification 175, 176
  modulation of neurotransmission 189
  self-administration in animals 219, 416–18
  self-administration & stress 567–8
  social dominance in monkeys 426, 427
  speed of entry and addiction 178, 179–81
cocaine- and amphetamine-regulated transcript (CART) 400, 401
coccygeal nerves, spinal column 119–20
cochlea, the ear 273–4
codons 44, 45, 46
cognition in animals 224–5
cognitive enhancers 606
cognitive labelling theory of emotion 446–7
cognitive maps, rat learning 224
cognitive models
  depression 554–6
  drug addiction 427–8
cognitive networks related to ToM 331
cognitive neuroscience 10
cognitive reserve 76
cold receptors 281, 282
collagen 127
colour perception 266–70, 271
column organization of visual cortex 266, 270
comparative anatomy 26
comparative psychology 10–11
compatabilism 476–7
competitive (orthosteric) antagonist 185–6
complex cells, visual cortex 263, 268
compulsive disorders and drug addiction 424, 425
computational neuroscience 11–12
computed tomography (CT) 162
concentration gradient 92, 94, 95
conceptual act model of emotion 452–4
concordance rate 53, 515, 545
concrete thinking, frontal lobotomy patients 321–2
conditioned emotional response (CER) 210–11
  lesions of amygdala preventing 449
conditioned place preference (CPP) 413–14
conditioned response (CR) 208
  acquisition of, Rescorla-Wagner equation 216
  measurement of 209
  vs. unconditioned response (UR) 210–11
  see also classical conditioning

conditioned stimulus (CS) 208
  relationship with US 211–12
  see also classical conditioning
conditioned suppression 211
conditioned taste aversion (CTA) 204, 205, 214, 411
conditioned withdrawal 423
conditioning
  classical 208–16
  operant 216–24
conduct disorder (CD), and drug use 423–4
cones, retina 257–8
  colour perception 267–70
congenital adrenal hyperplasia 376, 377
conscious processes, placebo effect 238–41
consciousness 472–81
consent, Neuremberg Code 197–8
conspecifics 35
construct validity 17–18, 530
contiguity, conditioning 212
contingency, conditioning 212, 221, 223
continuous reinforcement (CRF) schedule 220
control groups, clinical trials 200
control, illusion of 479
Controlled Substance Act (1970), USA 176
convergence, rods and conces 258
convergence, rods and cones 260
Coolidge effect, role of DA 419, 420
copy number variants (CNV) 515, 518
cornea of the eye 254–5
corona radiata 62, 63
coronal plane of the brain 132
corpus callosum 132–3
  foetal alcohol syndrome 79
  and split brains 492, 494–6
corpus cavernosum 362, 382, 383, 384
corpus luteum 369, 370, 372
corpus spongiosum 362, 365, 366, 367, 383
corrugator muscle 442
cortical cells 135
cortical layers 134, 135
  of the cerebellum 145
cortical spreading depression (CSD) 147
corticobulbar tract 294, 296
corticocollicar pathway 275
corticofugal projections 275
corticospinal tracts 294, 296, 304, 305
corticosterone 111, 567
corticotrophin-releasing hormone (CRH) 112, 564, 566, 568–9
cortisol levels
  hippocampal damage 569
  and love 457

  and music 461
  and stress 111, 113, 545, 560–61, 566, 569, 573
cosmetic neurology 606
counter-conditioning 216
cranial epidural space 127, 128
cranial nerves 119
  disorders of 121–2
craving for a drug, neural basis of 421–2
cremaster muscle 365
criminal law, links with neuro science 608
critical/sensitive periods 76–8
crossing over 42
crura 362, 365, 373
cryogenic lesions 156
cryoprobe 156
CT/CAT (computed tomography) scans 162
Cushing's syndrome 569
cyclic AMP (cAMP) 104, 531, 550
cyclic GMP (cGMP) 257, 383
cyclophosphamide 241, 242
cyclotron 162
cytoarchitecture 134
cytogenetic bands 40
cytokines 560–61
cytoplasm 44
cytosine 38, 43, 47, 49

D-lysergic diethylamide (LSD) 196, 417
'dark side' of motivation, chronic drug use 425–6
dark side of psychopharmacology
  motivation & drug addiction 425–6
  nerve agents and bioterrorism 198–9
  Nuremberg Code 197–8
dartos muscle 365
Darwin, Charles 24–5
  animal learning 204
  evolution of the eye 252–3
  evolution of emotion 436, 438
  neural Darwinism 70
  theory of evolution 25–6
decisions, unconscious determinants of 475–6
Declaration of Helsinki 197–8, 236
declarative (explicit) memory 344, 345
decussation (crossing) in medulla 296, 305
deep brain stimulation (DBS), PD treatment 238, 239, 246, 592
deep cerebral veins 149
deep facial muscles 442
default mode network (DMN) 518
defeminization 378, 379
defensive organismic state 451

INDEX

degenerative diseases 120
dehydroepiandrosterone (DHEA) 110, 368
Dejerine's area 487
delay conditioning 212
deletions, chromosome 47
delta-9-tetrahydrocannabinol (THC) 196, 411
delta receptors, opiates 286
delta waves 158, *159*, 466, 467
delusions 524, *526*, 527, 536, *537*
demyelination, multiple schlerosis 91
dendrites 85, *86*, 88, 90, 134
dendrodendritic synapse 105, *108*
dentate gyrus 141, *142*
dependence on drugs 412–13
depolarization *93*, 95, 96, 97, *98*
  and ischaemic cell death 146
deprenyl, L-DOPA therapy 588
depressants 194–6
depression
  cortical spreading 147
  and learned helplessness 213
  long-term 353–6
  response-outcomes assessment 479
  see also major depressive disorder (MDD)
dermatome 279
Descemet's membrane 255
descending pathways
  motor behaviour 302–5
  pain 284–6
determinism 476
developmental disorders 504–22
  attention deficit hyperactivity disorder (ADHD) 504–14
  autistic spectrum disorder (ASD) 515–20
dexamethasone, cortisol suppression 569
diagnosis 500, 606
  ADHD 504–6
  ASD 515, 517
  schizophrenia 525, 527
diamorphine *see* heroin
diastolic blood pressure 160
diazepam (Valium) 578
  N-desmethyldiazepam (DDZ) 579
dichotic listening test 489, *490*
dichotomous traits 35
diencephalon 138–41
  epithalamus 140
  hypothalamus 139–40
  subthalamus 140
  thalamus 138–9
diethylbarbituric acid (barbital) 576
differentiation of the sexes 361–8

diffusion tensor imaging (DTI) 164–5, *167*
digestion, phases of 393, *395*
dihydrotestosterone (DHT) 110, 368, 373
diminished responsibility issues 13, 609, 613
diploid set of chromosomes 39
disconnection syndrome, ASD 518
discriminative stimuli (SD) 221
dishabituation 206–7
distribution of a drug 181, *182*
disulfiram (Antabuse) 216
  alcoholism treatment 190
diurnal, humans 464
dizygotic twins (DZ) 53, 54
DNA (deoxyribonucleic acid) 42–9
  function of 44–6
  genetic variation 47
  and psychology 55–6
  variable number tandem repeats 47–8
dominant traits 35, 36
  Huntington's disease (HD) 37–8
donepezil (Aricept) 597–8
dopamine (DA) *101*, *102*, *103*
  ADHD, dysfunction in 32, 33, 506, 509–11
  and amphetamines 188, 232
  anorexia, reduced levels in 405
  antipsychotics, effects of 530—5, *535*
  autoreceptor regulation 105, *106*
  conversion to metabolites 104–5
  effects of nicotine on release of 418
  food increasing release of 400–1, *402*
  and Huntington's disease 300, *301*
  increased by natural reinforcers 419, *420*
  L-DOPA therapy for PD 588
  in mesolimbic system 418
  neuroadaptations of DA system 426
  nocebo and placebo effects 245
  Parkinson's disease 238–41, 586, *587*
  phasic DA response and reward learning 428–9, *430*
  and psychostimulant efficacy 507, *508*
  receptors for 104
  reuptake 105, *107*
  role in neurotoxicity 192–3
  schizophrenia 528, 534, *535*
  and sexual behaviour 386
  sleep and dreaming 468
  stimulants 194
  and ToM (Theory of Mind) 329, *332*
dopamine (DA) receptors
  agonists, PD treatment 588, 589
  antagonists, cocaine self-administration 417–18
  D2 receptors and schizophrenia 531–3

  D2 reduction in obesity 403
  level linked to social status 426, *427*
  low levels linked with drug use 426
dopamine receptor gene (DRD4-7R)
  and ADHD 34, 506
  fitting nomadic life 393
  and sensation seeking 55, 56
dopamine transporter (DAT) 107, 507, *508*, 509, *510*
  knockout mice study 422
dorsal column, spinal cord 279
dorsal horn laminae 282, 283, 284, 286
  gate control theory of pain 287, 288, 289
dorsal striatum 429
dorsolateral prefrontal cortex (DLPFC) *322*
  and executive functions 325–7
  role in placebo effect 240, *241*
dose-response curves 191, 229, 230
double blind, randomized, placebo-controlled trials 200
double helix 43–4
Down's syndrome 48–9
DRD4-7R receptor gene 34, 55–6, 393, 506
dreams 469–70
drink-drive laws 604–5
drinking and thirst 406
drive *see* motivation
drug abuse
  DSM IV diagnostic criteria 412
  and schizophrenia 528, 529
drug action 177–93
  pharmacodynamics 185–93
  pharmacokinetics 177–85
drug addiction 410–32
  conditioned place preference (CPP) 413–14
  drug self-administration 416–19, 426–7
  evolution of 411
  intracranial self-stimulation 413, *415*, 416
  neuronal adaptations in 430–2
  reward pathway 413–19
drug administration routes 177–81
drug classification 174–7
drug discrimination studies, operant conditioning 222–4
drug distribution 181, *182*
drug-driving 605
drug-elicited behaviour, schedules as determinants of 228–30
Drug Enforcement Agency (DEA), USA 176
drug laws 175, 606

drug metabolism and termination of
    action 183–5
drug-receptor affinity 192
    oral (per os,PO), drug administration
        route 178
drug self-administration, animal studies of
    addiction 219, 223, 416–19, 426–7
drug taking, age of onset 73
drug trials 199–201
drug types 193–7
    antidepressants 197
    antipsychotics 197
    depressants 194–6
    mind-altering drugs 196–7
    stimulants 194
dual action antidepressants 553
dual process theory, habituation 207
dual task performance, AD 599
duodenum 392, 394, 395
duplication, chromosome 41, 42
dura mater 127, 128
dynamic developmental theory,
    ADHD 510–11
dysexecutive syndrome, frontal lobe
    damage 322–8
dyskinesia, L-DOPA-induced 588, 592
dyslexia 497–8
dystonia 532

the ear 273–4
eating
    brain mechanisms for 398–401
    psychological factors influencing 405–6
eating disorders 400, 401–5
    anorexia 393, 402, 405
    evolutionary explanation 393
    obesity 400, 402–5
ecstacy (MDMA), long-term effects
    of 192–3
ectoderm 64
ED50 191
Edinger–Westphal nucleus 255
educational implications 607
educational performance, effect of sleep
    deprivation 473
efferent pathways 90
efficacy of a drug 191
ejaculation 62
    female 384, 385
    male 368, 383, 386
    sympathetic action 126
ejaculatory duct, penis 365, 367
electrical communication, neurons 90–2
electrical synapses 108–9
electro-oculogram (EOG) 160

electrode placement 161
    neural activity during sleep 466
electrocardiogram (ECG) 160
electroconvulsive therapy (ECT) 553
electrodermal activity (EDA) 160–1
electroencephalogram (EEG) 158
    ADHD 506–7
    brain waves from 159
    consciousness studies 474–5
    electrode placement 159
    sleep stages 465–6
electrolytic lesions 156
electromyography (EMG) 160, 466
electrons 84
electrophoresis 49
electrostatic pressure 92, 94, 95
elements 84, 85
embryology 26
embryonic stem cells 63–4
emotion 436–8
    and aggression 458–9
    Cannon-Bard theory 443–6
    conceptual act model 452–4
    facial expression 438–42
    James-Lange theory 443
    and love 456–8
    and music 459–61
    neural substrates 447–52, 454
    physiological profile of 444–6
    Rolls' reinforcement model 455–6
    Schachter's cognitive labelling
        theory 446–7
    somatic market hypothesis 456
    and stress 459
emotion processing see affective
    neuroscience
emulsification 392
enantiomers 192
endocannabinoid system 196, 291, 416
endocrine glands 110, 111–12, 114
endocrine system 109–15
    actions of hormones at their
        target 113–14
    hypo- and hyperthyroidism 111
    negative feedback mechanisms 114
    regulation 114
endocytosis 100, 105, 107
endoderm 64
endogenous analgesia 286
endometrial cycle 369–70
endophenotype(s) 56
endoplasmic reticulum 85
endorphins 101, 102, 104, 457
endothelial cells 130
endothelium, cornea 255

energy from digestion, storage of 393
engram (memory trace) 353
enkephalins 102, 457
enteroendocrine G cells 396
entorhinal cortex 141
entrainment 464
environment 4
    triggering drug-taking, virtual reality
        experiments 413, 414
environment-gene interaction 26–7, 50–5
enzymes 88, 103
    degradation of neurotransmitter 101,
        104–5
ependymal cells 89
epididymis 365, 367, 373, 374, 381
epidural injection 179
epigenetics 50
epilepsy
    split-brain surgery 494–5
    temporal lobe lobectomy and
        memory 346, 350–1
epinephrine see adrenaline
episodic buffer, working memory 336–7
epithalamus 140
epithelium, corneal 254
Equal Environment Assumption (EEA) 54
erection, genital 381, 383, 386
ethics
    and free will 480
    placebo use in clinical trials 236
    and psychopharmacology 197–8
    in research 12–13
eukaryote cells 85
event-related potentials (ERPs) 158,
    159–60, 335
evidence-based approach 24–5
evolution 24–5
    and conditioning 217–18
    Darwin's theory of 25–6
    frontal lobe 316–17
    of humans 27–9
    importance of environment 26–7
    and learning theory 204–5
    of the sense organs 252–3, 257, 291
    of sex/the sexes 360–1
evolutionary explanations
    addiction 411
    ageing 76
    anxiety 575–8
    consciousness 474
    eating disorders 393
    emotion 436, 438
    fainting 438
    function of pain 281, 286
    lateralization and language 492

evolutionary explanations (continued)
   of music 460
   placebo effect 242–3
   sleep function 470
evolutionary psychology 29
   and ADHD 32–5
   and comparative psychology 10–11
   of depression 546–7
   eating disorders 393
   ovulation 371–2
   schizophrenia 527–9
examinations
   brain regions needed for 339–40
   and stress 560–61
excitatory postsynaptic potential (EPSP) 96, 98, 99, 100, 101
executive functions (EFs) 74, 316
   and ADHD 33
   frontal lobe damage, effects of 322–8
   frontal lobe evolution 316–17
   lesion & imaging studies 317–22
   needed for passing exams 339–40
   six clusters 338
   theories of frontal lobe function 328–38
exocytosis 100
exons 44, 46
expectancy, classical & operant conditioning 224
expectations
   mediated via DLPFC 240–1
   negative, nocebo effect 244–6
   positive, placebo effect 238–40
experimental groups, clinical trials 200
experimenter bias/effect 200, 237
extended amygdala 424–5
external adventitial layer 364
external validity 18
exteroceptive & interoceptive stimuli 221
extinction of learning
   classical conditioning 209
   operant conditioning 221, 222
   and spontaneous recovery 209
extracellular 85
extracellular fluid 406
   osmolality of salt in different species 394
extrafusal muscle fibres 306, 307, 310
extrapyramidal side-effects (EPSE) 532
extrapyramidal system 305
extreme male brain and ASD 516
the eye 253–5
eye colour, inheritance of 36–7
eye movement
   frontal eye fields 297
   measures 160, 161

face validity 17, 530
facial expression
   effect of amygdala lesions 449
   and emotion 438–42
   recognition deficits in alcoholism 443
facial feedback hypothesis 442
facial muscles 441
facial nerve 119, 121
   disorders of 121
fainting 438
fallopian tubes 112, 364, 365, 372
familial studies 51–2
famous faces task, amnesia 349, 350
fascia, penis 365, 383
FAST acronym, stoke identification 146
fasting/intestinal phase 396
fear 573, 575, 581, 584
   and amygdala 448–50
   conditioning 450–2
   olfactory system 276
   and punishment 219–20
feedback loops, endocrynology 114
feedback utilization, frontal lobe function 326, 341
feeding behaviour 392–7
   brain mechanisms 398
   eating disorders 401–5
   external factors influencing 405–6
'feelings', subjective experience of emotion 455
female criminals, mitigating pleas 609
female genitalia 361–5
female reproductive system 62, 364
fertilization 62, 63
fetishes, conditioning 211
fibroblasts 127
Figure of Rey 323, 324
filopodium 86
fimbriae, fallopian tube 62, 364
fissures, cerebral cortex 133
five prime (5') 44
fixed interval (FI) schedule 220–1
   and drug response 229–30
fixed ratio (FR) schedule 220
   and drug effects 229–30
flight or fight responses, role of sympathetic nervous system 124
flooding technique 215
fluid-filled compartments in the body 406
flumazenil, antagonist 579, 580
fluoxetine (Prozac) 177, 190, 405, 552
fMRI (functional MRI) 164
foetus 373, 376, 377
   foetal alcohol syndrome (FAS) 79–80
   foetal period 62

placental barrier 183
   REM-like sleep 467
follicle-stimulating hormone (FSH) 112, 113, 141, 368, 369, 370, 372, 380
follicular phase, menstrual cycle 369–70, 372
food addiction 403–5
forebrain 132–41
   diencephalon 138–41
   role in sleep 468
   telencephalon 132–8
foreskin 365, 367
fossil records supporting theory of evolution 25–6
Fourier analysis 266
fovea 253, 257
free will 474–6
   theories of 476–81
frenulum 365, 366
Friedreich's ataxia 87
frontal eye fields 297
frontal lobe
   in different hominoids 318
   evolution 316–17
   subregions 322
frontal lobe damage 322–8
   arithmetic problem solving 327
   attention problems 327–8
   error utilization 326
   rule learning, planning and problem solving 323–6
   thinking 322–3
frontal lobe, effects of drug addiction 427
frontal lobe, executive functioning 74
frontal lobe function
   early studies 317
   theories of 328–38
frontal lobes 134, 137
frontal lobotomy 318, 321–2
frontostriatal circuits, ADHD 507
full agonists 185
full fusion 100
functional lateralization 486–96
functional magnetic resonance imaging (fMRI) 164

G-proteins 104
   and cannabinoid receptors 196–7
   G-protein-coupled receptors (GPCR) 186
G-spot 363, 384, 385
GABA A receptors
   alcohol 195
   and amobarbital 489
   anxiolytics 195–6

barbiturates 472, 576, *577*
benzodiazepines 578–80
and caffeine 194
GABA (gamma-aminobutyric acid) 101, 102, *103*, 104, *106*, 107
 and anxiety 576–80
 decreased in ASD 519
 and Parkinson's disease 591
Gage, Phineas 7, 319–20
Galatea effect 237
gametes (ovum and sperm) 31, 36, 39, 40, *41*
gamma motor neurons 306
gamma waves *159*
ganglion cells, retina 256, *258*, 259, *260*, 261, 269
gap junctions 108–9, 261
gastric/absorptive phase, digestion 393, 395–6
gastrin 395–6
gastrointestinal tract 126, 392, *394*, 401
gastrulation 64
gate control theory of pain 286–8, *290*
gender identity 360, 388
gender reassignment 388
gene-environment interaction 4
gene therapy 57–8
general adaptation syndrome, Selye 563
generalization of conditioned stimulus (CS) 210, 221
generalized anxiety disorder, diagnostic criteria 574
generic and brand names, drugs 177
genetic abnormalities, sexual development 376–7
genetic engineering 13, 51, 58
genetic mutation 31, 44, 47
 Alzheimer's disease 594
 and Huntington's disease 38
 mitochondrial disorders 87
genetic similarities, humans and closest relatives 27
genetic variation 47
 and crossing over 42
genetics
 ageing 76
 autism spectrum disorder 515, 518
 depression 545–6
 lateralization 492–4
 schizophrenia 525, 528
 sexual differentiation 360–1, 373, 379
 see also behavioural genetics
genital end bulbs 381
genital tubercle 373
genitalia
 female 361–5
 male 365–8
 in utero development *375*
genome 29
genotype 35–6
Geschwind-Wernicke model 487, *488*
ghrelin 401, *404*
glans 362, *362*, 365, 366, *373*, *375*, 383
glial cells 89–90
globus pallidus 143, *586*
 external segment (GPe) *299*, 300, *301*
 internal segment (GPi) 298, *299*, *301*
 lesions of, PD treatment 591–2
glossopharyngeal nerve 119, *121*
 disorders of 122
glucocorticoids 111, 112, 566, 569, 571
 activation of in adolescence 74
glucoreceptors 399
glucose 392, 396, 399
 effects of deprivation 399–400
glutamate 101, *102*, *103*, 104, *106*
 and eating 399
 Parkinson's disease 591
 reduction in response to light 257, 259–60, 261
 and schizophrenia 534, *535*
glutamate receptor (NMDA)
 action of alcohol 195
 cones in the eye 260
 and ischaemic cell death 146
 long-term potentiation & depression 354–5
 overactive in ADHD & ASD 511, 519
 psychodelic drugs 196
glycine 102
glycogen 393
Go/No-go task 332, *334*, 506, 512
goal formation, role of frontal lobe 323, 325, 340
Golgi apparatus 85
Golgi cells 134
Golgi tendon organs 309–10
Gollum effect 237
gonadotrophin-releasing hormone (GnRH) 112, 368, *369*, 370
gonads 110
good science 20
 clinical trials 199–201
Grace's theory of tonic and phasic DA
 and ADHD 509–10
 in schizophrenia 534, *535*
grand illusion of free will, Wegner 479, *480*
granule cells, cerebral cortex 134
granulosa cells, ovaries 368, *372*

Graves' disease 111
Gray, Jeffrey, neuropsychological theory of anxiety 581
gray matter 128
great cerebral vein of Galen 148, *149*
grey matter 128, *131*, 132
 development of 72
 increased volume in taxi drivers 351, 352
 pruning of 69–70, 72
 reduction with age 75
 thalamus 138–9
 volume and ASD 518
growth hormone (GH) 112, *141*
guanine 38, 43, 49
guanosine diphosphate (GDP) 104
guanosine monophosphate (GMP) 383
guanosine triphosphate (GTP) 104
gubernaculum 373
gyri, cerebral cortex 132, *133*

habenular 140, *141*
habit maintenance, drug addiction 429
habituation 237
 animal learning 205–7, 353–4
 partial agonists 187
 to stressors 569
haemoglobin 46, *47*
haemorrhagic stroke 146–7
half-life of drugs 184, *185*
hallucinations 524, *526*, *527*, 536
hallucinogens 196, 417
Halo effect 237
haloperidol 531, 532, 533, *533*, 534
hammer (malleus) 273, *274*
handedness, functional lateralization 492
haploid (of chromosomes) 39, 40
harm score for drugs 176–7
Hawthorne effect 237
headache stage, migraine attack 147
hearing, auditory perception 272–5
heart rate measurement 160
heat-sensitive receptors 281
hedonic response in obesity 403, *404*
Helsinki Declaration 197–8, 236
hepatic biotransformation 184
hepatic enzymes, evolution of 411
hepatic metabolism 184
heritability 51–2, 53
Hermann grid, receptive fields 259–60
heroin 175, 194–5
 outcome measures 200–1
 and the overdose effect 234–5
Heschl's gyrus 484, *485*
heterochromia iridis/iridium 36

heteroreceptors 100, 105, *106*
hindbrain 143–5
hippocampal cells *135*
hippocampal commissure 133
hippocampal formation 141, *142*
hippocampus 141, *142*, 564
    anxiety mediated via 581
    atrophy in Alzheimer patients 595
    conditioning of contextual fear 450
    damage from high cortisol 569
    effect of lesions on memory 346, 351–2
    increased grey matter volume in London taxi drivers 352
    memory substrate *345*, *350*
    remodelled by chronic stress 569, 571
    spatial learning and memory 351
    synaptic transmission 354–5, *355*
histamine 102, *104*
historical perspective 6–8
HM (Henry Molaison) case study, memory deficits 346–7
holism 6
homeostasis 120, 562
    role of hypothalamus 127
    and stress 562
    vs. allostasis 569–71
homeostasis in eating behaviour
    hedonic response overriding 403, *404*
    neural circuits regulating 397–401, *401*
homo sapiens 28, *317*
homonymous hemianopia 139
homovanillic acid (HVA) 509
homunculus *137*, *139*, 295
    'hermunculus' 363
horizontal cells, retina *256*, 261
horizontal plane of the brain *132*
hormones 109–13
    action at target organs 113–14
    and aggression 459
    during menstrual cycle 369, *370*, 372
    effects in puberty 380
    insulin 396
    regulation 114
    released by hypothalamus, effect on pituitary hormones 140, *141*
    sex hormones 368–9
HTT gene mutation, Huntington's disease 38
human brain 29, *30*
Human Brain Project 12
human evolution 27–9
Human Genome Project 24, 57–8
'Humphrey effect', immune response 243
hunger 399, 400, 401, *404*
    setpoint theory 396

huntingtin 38
Huntington's disease (HD) 37–8, 300–1
hydrochloric acid 392, 396
hydrophillic 184
hymen 363
hyperactivity, ADHD 505, 513–14
hyperandrogenism 376
hypercolumns, visual cortex 266, *270*
hypercomplex cells, visual cortex 266
hyperkinetic disorder (HKD) 505
hyperphagia (overeating) 398
hyperpolarization 95
hyperthyroidism 111
hypnogogic hallucinations 472
hypnotics 472
hypofrontality 317–18
hypoglossal nerve 119, *121*
    disorders of 122
hypokinesia, Parkinson's disease 584
hypomanic episode, bipolar disorder 544
hypothalamic-pituitary-adrenal (HPA) axis 111
    activated by anxiety 245
    activation in depression 545
    effects of chronic overactivation 570–71
    stress 565, 566–9
hypothalamus 139–40
    active during erections 383
    and circadian rhythms 464–5
    controlling ANS 136–7
    endocrine gland 111, *112*, *114*
    feeding behaviour 396–401
    hormones produced by *141*
    and ovarian cycle 369
    puberty onset 380
    sexual differences 378–9
    sexual orientation 386–7
    stress response 563, *565*, 566
hypothyroidism 111
hypovolaemic thirst 406

ibotenic acid, lesions 399
ICH, clinical trial guidelines 200
illusion of free will 479–80
immunosuppression 241
    and evolution of placebo effect 242–3
    and exam stress 560–61
imprinting 204
impulse control problem, addiction as 424, *425*
impulsivity 329, 331
    ADHD 505, 512–13, 514
    animal studies 338
    and behavioural inhibition 333, 335

    evolutionary adaptiveness 335
    link to disorders 338
inattention 504, 521
incentive salience theory of addiction 421–2
incentive sensitization theory of addiction 403
Independent Scientific Committee on Drugs (ISCD) 176
indolamines *101*, 109
infarction 146
inferior anastomotic vein 149
inferior colliculus 144, *273*, *274*
information-processing theory, habituation 207
infundibulum 62, *364*, *365*
inhalation, drug administration route 178
inheritance, Mendelian 31, 35–42
inhibitory control
    loss of in addiction 427, 431
    see also behavioural inhibition (BI)
inhibitory postsynaptic potential (IPSP) *96*, 98, 99, 100, *101*
injury to brain (infarction), following ischaemic attack 146–7
insomnia 470, 472
Institutional Animal Care and Use Committee (IACUC) 14, 15
instrumental conditioning *see* operant conditioning
insula, mechanism in anorexia 405
insulin 396, 399–400
intentionality 474, 476
    intentional inhibition 479–80
intermediate muscularis layer *364*
internal cerebral vein *148*, 149
internal mucosal layer *364*
internal validity 19
interneurons and reflexes 207
interoception 279
intersexuality 388
interstitial fluid 406
interventricular foramina 127
intestinal/fasting phase of digestion 393, *395*, 396
intracellular 85
intracellular fluid 406
intracerebroventricular 179
intracranial self-stimulation (ICSS) 413, *415*, 416
    cocaine & amphetamine effects 416
    nicotine effects 418
intrafusal muscle fibres 307
intramuscular (IM) 179

intraperitoneal (IP) 179
intrathecal (IT) injection 179
intravascular fluid 406
intravenous (IV) injection 178
introitus 363
introns 44, 46
invagination 64
inverse agonists 186, 188
    anxiogenic properties 580
inversions, chromosome 47
ion channel 93, 101, 102, 104, 108–9
ionotropic receptors 102, 104
ions 84
iris of the eye 255
ischaemic stroke 146
ischiocavernosus muscle 365, 366
IVF (in vitro fertilization) 63–4

James-Lange theory of emotion 443, 444
jetlag 464
John Henry effect 237
John/Joan case, intersexuality 388
'Just Say No' campaign, drugs 427

K complexes, stage 2 sleep 465
kappa receptors, opiate analgesia 286
karyotype 39, 40
    abnormal 32, 48
Kearns-Sayre syndrome 87
ketamine 196, 556
kiss-and-run fusion 100
Klinefelter's syndrome 376
Klüver-Bucy syndrome 447, 448
knock-in/knock-out models 57
Koh Block design test 323
koniocellular layer, visual cortex 261–3, 264
Korsakoff's syndrome 347–9

L-DOPA therapy 238–9, 587
labia majora 362, 375
labia minora 362, 373, 375, 381, 383
Laboratory Animal Welfare Act (AWA) 14
lambda 155, 156
lambda waves 158
laminae of the dorsal horn 284
language and lateralization 484, 486–9
    evolutionary accounts 492
    genetic basis 492–4
latent inhibition 215
latent learning 224
lateral corticospinal tract 294, 296, 304
lateral geniculate nucleus (LGN) 138, 139, 261–3, 264
    simple cells 263, 267

lateral hypothalamus (LH) 398, 399, 400, 401
lateral inhibition 261, 262
lateralization
    of function 486–99
    neuroanatomy 484–6
    in schizophrenia 528
law of effect, Thorndike 217
learned helplessness and depression 213
learned immune response 241
    evolutionary accounts of placebo effect 242–3
learning and addiction 427
    incentive-sensitization theory 421–2
    probabilities of obtaining rewards 428–30
learning theories 205
    see also classical conditioning; operant conditioning
LeDoux's survival circuit 451
left hemisphere
    areas activated by spoken and written language tasks 491
    dominance of language, reduced in schizophrenia 528
legal implications 604–12
legislation
    animal research 14–15
    drink-driving 604–5
    drugs 174–7, 605
    M'Naghten Rule 13
Leigh syndrome 87
lens of the eye 255
leptin 399, 400, 401
lesion studies 154–7, 317–22
    limitations of 321–2
levator labii superioris muscle 441, 442
Leydig cells 368, 373
Leydig vells 361
lie detectors 610
ligand-gated ion channels 104
ligands 102, 104
light/dark cycle, manipulation of 464
light, retinal cells sensitive to blue light 465
liking and wanting, drug addiction 421–2
limbic system 141–3
    role in emotion 447–8
linkage, genetic variation 42
lipid solubility, drugs 178, 181–2, 184
lipids 84–5
lithium carbonate 553
Little Albert study, phobias 210, 211
liver damage and alcohol consumption 184

lobes of the brain 133–4
lobotomies 321–2
locus coeruleus 468, 564
    activated by stress 565–6, 568–9
    anxiety production 580–1
long-term depression (LTD) 353, 354–5, 355
long-term memory 345, 353
long-term potentiation (LTP), synaptic transmission 353, 354–5, 355
lorazepam (Ativan) 578
lordosis 375, 377
love
    as a motivation 457–8
    brain regions 456–7
    neurochemistry 457
low mood, adaptive nature of 546
LSD (D-lysergic diethylamide) 196
lumbar vertebrae 122
    areas connected to 123
    effect of lesions to 124
luteal phase, menstrual cycle 370–1, 372
luteinizing hormone (LH) 112, 113, 141, 368–9, 370, 372
lysosomes 88

mach bands, lateral inhibition 262
magic mushrooms 196
magnetic resonance imaging (MRI) 164–6
magnetic resonance spectroscopy (MRS) 164
magnetoencephalography (MEG) 158–9
magnocellular layer, lateral geniculate nucleus 261, 264
major depressive disorder (MDD) 542–53
    causes of 545
    diagnostic criteria 542–3
    evolutionary theories 546–7
    genetics of 545–6
    neuroanatomy 553–4
    neurochemistry 548–52
    serotonin hypothesis 550–52
    and stress 545
    treatments for 552–3
male brain in ASD 516
male genitalia 365–8
male reproductive system 367
mammals, evolution of 28
mammillary bodies, hypothalamus 140
manic episode, bipolar disorder 544
Martinotti cells, cerbral cortex 134
masculinization 379
masochism 290–1
mate selection 371–2

matrix of emotions, conceptual act model 452–3
matrix of placebo effect methodology 237
mature synapse 70
maximum binding (Bmax) 191
maze tasks 323, 338
MDMA (ecstacy), long-term effects of 192–3
mechanical pain 281
  receptors 281, 282
mechanoreceptors 274, 279
media portrayal of science 20, 501
medial geniculate nucleus (MGN) 274
medial lemniscus 279, 304
medial temporal lobe memory system 346, 350
median preoptic nucleus (MPN) 406
medication, as confounding variable in imaging studies 168
Medicines and Healthcare products Regulatory Agency (MHRA) 200
medulla oblongata 144, 144
  medullary arteries 149
medullary pyramids 294
meiosis 40–1
  crossing over 42
melanin-concentrating hormone (MCH) 399
melanopsin and circadian cycle 465
melatonin 112, 465
membrane see cell membrane
memory 344–5
  amnesia 345–53
  deficits in Alzheimer's disease 594, 597, 598
  neural basis of 353–5
  spatial, taxi drivers 351–2
menarche 380
Mendelian genetics/inheritance 35–42
  chromosomes 39–42
  eye colour 36–7
  Huntington's disease (HD) 37–8
  pea plants 35–6
  phenylketonuria (PKU) 39
meninges 127, 128
  inflammation of 147
meningitis 129
menstrual cycle 369–73
  effect on cerebral asymmetries 490
menstrual phase 369
mental causation model, Tse 478–9
mescaline 196, 411, 416, 417
mesencephalon (midbrain) 68, 143
mesoderm 64
mesolimbic DA pathway 415, 416

cocaine and amphetamine addiction 418
  incentive-sensitization theory 421
  learning of stimulus-reward associations 428
  nicotine addiction 419
mesolimbic dopamine pathway 401, 404
mesopic vision 257
messenger ribonucleic acid (mRNA) 44, 45, 46
meta-analysis 201
metabolic inhibition 190
metabolism 104–5
metabolism of drugs 183–5
metabolites 104–5
metabotropic receptors 102, 104
metachromatic leukodystrophy (MLD), gene therapy for 57–8
metencephalon 143–4
metergoline 551
methodology
  issues in brain imaging 161
  see also neuroscience methods
methylphenidate (Ritalin)
  addiction and speed of entry 179–81
  and ADHD 507–11
  effect on developing brain 73
  rate-dependent effect, ADHD 231
MHPG (3-methoxy-4-hydroxyphenylglycol) 560
micro-dialysis 157–8
microglia 88, 89, 105, 107
microtubules 85, 88, 99, 102, 596
midbrain 144
middle cerebral artery 149
migraine headache 147
migration (of brain cells) 68, 69, 77
mind-altering drugs 196–7
mind reading see Theory of Mind (ToM)
minisatellites (tandem repeats) 47
mirror neuron theory of ASD 520
mirror neurons 288, 296
  and pornography 387
  and ToM 328–9
mirror therapy, phantom limb pain 288
mirtazapine 553
Misuse of Drugs Act (1971) 175–6
mitochondria 85–6, 87
mitochondrial disorders (MCDs) 87
mitochondrial DNA (mtDNA) 86, 87
mitochondrion 86, 88
mitosis 42
  replication of DNA 44
M'Naghten Rule 13, 609

Molaison, Henry, memory deficits case study 346–7
molecular biology 26, 55, 56
molecular biotechnology 56–7
molecular genetics see DNA
molecular mechanisms underlying memory in hippocampus 354–5, 356
monoamine oxidase inhibitors (MAOIs) 548–9
monoamine oxidase (MAO) 548, 549, 552
monoamine oxidase (MAO)-B inhibitors, PD treatment 585, 588
monoamines 101, 109
monosomy 31, 48
monozygotic (MZ) twins 50, 53, 54
mons veneris 361
mood changes and vestibular system 279
mood states, negative reinforcement maintaining addiction 425–6
morphine 195, 286
  behavioural tolerance to effects of 232–3
mosaicism 31
motion detection, vestibular system 277–9
motivation 410
  and love 457–8
  theories of addiction 419–30
motivational inhibition (MI) 335–6
motor behaviour and control 294–313
  brain regions associated with 149, 294–302
  control and agency 309
  descending pathways 302–5
  feedback 309
  transmission of information to muscles 305–8
motor cortex (M1) 294–5, 298, 305
motor endplate 307
motor impairment, Parkinson's disease 584, 586, 589, 590–6
motor neurons 86, 90
motor pathways 312
motor unit 307
movement perception deficits 138
MPP+ (1-methyl-4-phenyl-pyridinium) 585
MPTP (1-methyl-4-phenyl-1,2,3,6-tetrahydropyridine), Parkinson's disease 585, 589
mu receptors, opiates 286
Mullerian duct 373
multiple sclerosis (MS) 91, 97, 120
multipolar interneurons 86
multipotent stem cells 64

muscarinic receptors 307
muscle fibres, intrafusal and
    extrafusal 307
muscle measures 160
muscle spindles 309
muscles 306–7
    of the face 441–2
    feedback from 309
    neurochemical activation of 307–8
music and emotion 459–61
mutations, genetic 31, 38, 44, 47
myelencephalon 143
myelin sheath 86, 89–90, 93, 97, 98
myelinated axons 88, 98
myelination 68, 69, 77
myofibrils 306, 308
myosin 306

N-methyl-D-aspartate (NMDA) 534, 535
    see also glutamate receptor
naloxone 240, 241
naming of locations of the brain 131, 132
    veins 145
        cerebral 149
        sinuses 150–51
narcolepsy 472
    methylphenidate for 231
nasal hemiretina 261, 263
nasal membrane 275–6
National Treatment Outcome Research
    Study (NTORS) 201
natural reinforcers 419
natural selection 25–6
nature-nurture debate 50–1, 53–4
near infrared spectroscopy (NIRS) 166
negative bias hypothesis of depression 556
negative feedback mechanisms, endocrine
    system 114
negative reinforcement 218
    and drug addiction 423–6
negative symptoms, schizophrenia 525,
    526, 527, 534, 536, 537
neglect, effect on brain development 78
nerve agents, actions and effects of 198–9
nerve growth factor (NGF) 70
nervous system 118
    autonomic nervous system
        (ANS) 120–7
    central nervous system (CNS) 127–31
    interaction with endocrine system 150
    peripheral nervous system
        (PNS) 118–20
neural crest 64, 65, 67, 71
neural development 62
    adolescents 71–5

adults 75–6
autonomic nervous system (ANS) 71
critical periods 76–8
foetal alcohol syndrome 79–80
'in utero' 64–70
male and female brains 71
over the lifespan 62–4
peripheral nervous system (PNS) 71
stem cells 63–4
teratogens in ADHD 66–7
neural groove 65, 67
neural maps from neuroimaging 168
neural plasticity 76, 77
neural plate 64–5, 67
neural proliferation 68
neural tube 64–5, 67, 68
neuroanatomical labels and associated
    locations of the brain 131
neuroanatomy 131–2
    brain regions 132–45
    naming of locations of the brain 131,
        132
    white and grey matter 131–2
neurodegeneration 87, 584–600
    Alzheimer's disease 593–9
    Parkinson's disease 584–97
neuroethics 12–13
neurofibrillary tangles (NFTs), AD 592–6
neurofilaments 90
neuroimaging 161–8
    combined with psychophysiology 168
    executive function evaluation 318, 323,
        325–6
    limitations of 166–8
    magnetic resonance imaging 164–6
    mind maps from 168
    nuclear imaging 161–3
    optical imaging 166
    used as evidence in court 606, 608, 610
neuroleptic malignant syndrome 532
neuroleptics 530, 532
neuromatrix and body sensation 288–90
neuromuscular junction (NMJ) 199,
    307, 308
neuronal adaptations in addiction 431–2
neurons
    action potentials 95–8
    at the atomic level 84
    communication & signalling
        between 99–109
    communication & signalling
        within 90–9
    electrical communication 90–2
    gap junctions 108–9
    glial cells supporting 89–90

postsynaptic potentials 98–9
resting potential 92–5
structure and function 84–8
synaptic transmission 99–108
types of 90
neuropeptide Y (NPY) 399–400, 401, 402
neuropeptides 102
neuroplasticity
    advantages 355, 356
    Freud's views 353
neuroprotection 76
neuropsychology 10
neuropsychopharmacology 157–8
neuroscience, history of 6–8
neuroscience methods 154–70
    neuroimaging 161–8
    neuropsychopharmacology 157–8
    physiological psychology 154–7
    psychophysiology 158–61
    transcranial magnetic stimulation
        (TMS) 169
neurosurgery for PD treatment 588–9
neurotoxic lesions 156
neurotransmission 101–8
    modulation by drugs 186, 188–9
neurotransmitters 101–2, 109
    and autism spectrum disorder 519
    heteroreceptors 105, 106
    metabolism 104–5
    receptors 102, 104
    regulation 105, 106
    reuptake 105
    and sleep 468
    synthesis and metabolism 103
neurulation 64–5
neutrons 84
nicotine 194
    drug discrimination experiments 223–4
    role in attention & memory 597
nicotine addiction/dependence
    in ADHD individuals 423, 424
    mechanism of 418–19
    partial agonists in treatment of 187
nicotinic receptors 307
nigrostriatal pathway 298
    degeneration in PD 586, 587, 588, 592
    effects of lesions 399, 589, 590
    loss of DA in, knock-on effects 591
nitrazepam (Mogadon) 578
nitric oxide (NO) 101, 102
NMDA receptor see glutamate receptor
nocebo effect 243, 244–6
nocioception 279–91
nocturnal animals 464
nodes of Ranvier 86, 88, 90, 93, 97, 98

noise-induced hearing loss 272–3
non-competitive (allosteric) antagonist 185–6
non-declarative (implicit) memory 345
non-drug reinforcers 419, 420
non-REM sleep 467
'non-shared environment' 53
noradrenaline (NA) 101, 102, 103, 104, 109
 and anxiety 580–3
 conversion to metabolites 104–5
 and sleep control 468
 and stress 560, 564, 565–6, 569
noradrenergic hypothesis of depression 548–50
norepinephrine *see* noradrenaline (NA)
the nose, olfactory system 275–6
notochord 64
novelty, dealing with/responding to 338, 339
nuclear imaging 161–3
nucleotide bases 43, 44, 45, 47, 57
nucleus of the solitary tract 277
nucleus accumbens (NAcc) 142, 400–1, 415, 416
 DA elevated in
  nicotine producing 418
  non-drug reinforcers 419, 420
 effect of lesions 418, 419
 extended amygdala 425
 shell and core 429
nucleus, neurons 85
Nuremberg Code of medical ethics 197–8
Nutt, David 175, 176
NYP/AgRP neurons 400
nystagmoid eye movements 160

obesity 400, 402–5
 as an addiction 403–5
 evolutionary explanation 393
 neural circuitry in 404
 and stress 402
occipital eye field 138
occipital lobe 138
 see also visual cortex
oculomotor nerve 119, 121
oedema 129
oestrogens 111, 368, 369
 and lateralization 490
 masculinizing effect on brain 377, 378
 menstrual cycle & ovulation 370, 372
 oestradiol 368, 377, 378, 380
olfactory bulb 139, 142
olfactory bulbectomy 551
olfactory cortex 276
olfactory epithelium 275, 276

olfactory nerve 119, 121
 disorders of 121
olfactory receptor 29, 275, 276
olfactory system 275–6
oligodendrocytes 88, 89
oligopotent stem cells 64
olivary nucleus (inferior olive) 255
'on-centre' & 'off-centre' cells, receptive fields 258–60
ontogeny recapitulates phylogeny (ORP) theory 26
Onuf's nucleus, spinal cord 362–3, 382
oocyte 63, 365, 372
ootid 62
operant conditioning 216–24
 acquisition 221
 applications of 224, 228–30
 behaviourism 217–18
 discrimination & generalization 221
 and drug discrimination 222–4
 exteroceptive & interoceptive stimuli 221
 extinction 221
 law of effect 217
 reinforcement & punishment 218–21
 shaping 221
 spontaneous recovery 221
opiate analgesia 286
opioids 194–5
oppositional defiant disorder (ODD), co-morbidity with drug use 423
opsins 257
optic chiasm 494, 495
optic nerve 119, 253–4, 256, 261, 263
 disorders of 121
optical illusions 259–60, 262
optical imaging 166, 168
oral administration route 178
orbicularis oculi 441, 442
orbitofrontal cortex 73
 and emotion processing 454, 456
 and impulsivity 338
 and maintenance of drug habit 429
 placebo effect mediated by 240
 and reward learning 428, 431
 and theory of mind 329, 331
orexin 399, 400, 401
 reduced in narcolepsy 472
organizational-activational hypothesis 377, 378
organizational period, hormones 459
orgasm 380, 382, 383–6
orthosteric antagonism 185
osmolality of salt 394
osmoreceptors 406

osmotic thirst 406
ossicles, middle ear 273, 274
'Out of Africa' hypothesis 28
ovarian cycle 369
ovaries 113, 364, 365, 368, 370, 374
 abnormalities 376
 hormones released by 111, 369, 372
 sexual development 373
overdose effect 234–5
overshadowing 212
ovulation 369–72
ovum 361
oxidation, phase 1 metabolism 184
oxytocin 109, 112, 113, 140, 368
 and prosocial behaviours/love 458

p-value 501
Pacini's corpuscles 362
PAG *see* periaqueductal grey
pain asymbolia 290
pain control 286–7
pain disorders 290
pain mechanisms in migraines 147
pain pathways 282–6
pain perception 279–91
pallidotomy, PD treatment 591–2
pancreas 110, 111, 112
panic attacks 574, 575, 580
Papez circuit 447, 448
papillae on the tongue 276–7
parahippocampal gyrus 141, 142
paralysis 120
paraphilias 215
paraplegia 120
parasympathetic ganglia 124
parasympathetic nervous system 71, 124–5
paraurethral gland (Skene's gland) 362, 385
paraventricular nucleus (PVN) 140, 398, 399, 400, 401, 563, 564–5, 568–9
paravertebral ganglia 123, 126
parenteral (injections), drug administration route 178–9
parietal lobe 134, 137–8
Parkinson's disease (PD) 87, 584–93
 MPTP model 585
 neuropathology 586
 neuropharmacology 586–9
 neuropsychology 589–7
 placebo treatment 238–40
partial agonists 185, 186, 188
 serotonin receptors 581
 treatment of nicotine dependence 187
partial reinforcement 220

INDEX

passive avoidance learning 551
penis 363, 365, 366, 373, 375
   erection 381–3
   size 367
pentobarbital effects, schedules of reinforcement 229
penumbra 146
peptide hormones 109, 113
perceptual systems 252
   auditory perception 272–5
   gustatory system 276–7
   nocioception 279–91
   olfactory perception 275–6
   sensory integration 291
   somatosensation 279
   vestibular system 277–9
   visual perception 252–72
periaqueductal grey (PAG) 140, 144
   pain 238, 284, 286, 287, 288
   vocalization 297–8
perineum 363, 373
peripheral nervous system (PNS) 118–27
   autonomic 120, 123
      control of 126–7
      parasympathetic 124–6
      sympathetic 123–4, 125–6
   somatic 118–20, 121–2
peripheral nervous system (PNS), development of 71
perisylvian language network 487
perisylvian language networks 488
periventricular nucleus (PVN) 112
perseveration, frontal lobe patients 322–3
persistent Mullerian duct syndrome 376
pervasive developmental disorders 515
PGO waves, REM sleep 468, 470
pH values of common substances 396
phagocytosis 105, 107
phantom auditory perception 275
phantom limb pain 287–8
pharmacodynamic tolerance 231–3
pharmacodynamics 185–93
   drug-receptor affinity 192
   modulation of neurotransmission by drugs 186, 188–91
   multiple sites of drug action 192–3
   types of drug action 185–6, 187–8
pharmacokinetic tolerance 230–2
pharmacokinetics 177–85
   body membranes 181–3
   drug administration routes 177–81
   drug distribution 181
   drug metabolism and termination of action 183–5
Phases (I to IV), clinical trials 199–200

phencyclidine (PCP) 196, 530, 534, *536*
phenobarbital 576
phenocopies 31, 35
phenothiazines 530
phenotypes 31, 35–6
   atypical 47
   endophenotype 56
   epigenetics 50
phenylketonuria (PKU), Mendelian inheritance *38*, 39
philosophical perspectives
   bioethics 13
   history of neuroscience 6–7
   in practice of good science 20
   reductionism 4–6
phobias 571, 575
   classically conditioned 210
phonological loop, working memory 336
phospholipid cell membrane 181
phospholipid layers 85
photopic vision 257
photoreceptive retinal ganglion 255
photoreceptors 257, 258
physiological effects of drugs 423
physiological psychology 9, 154–7
physostigmine 596, 597
pia mater 127, *128*
pineal gland 110, 112, 140, *141*, 465
pinna 273
pinocytosis 105, *107*
pituitary gland 110, 111, 112, *113*, 114, 140, 150
placebo-controlled trials 200
placebo effect/response 199, 233, 235–43
   conscious processes 238–41
   research methodology 237–8
   unconscious processes 241–2
placebos 233, 235
   critique of research 235, 236–7
   evolution of response 242–3
   use in clinical trials 236
placental barrier 183
planning, role of frontal lobe areas 323, 341
planum temporale 484, *485*
plasticity 76, 77
   of auditory cortex 272–3
plateau/asymptote in learning 209, 215, 216
plateau phase, sexual response cycle 383
pleasure
   from drugs, wanting vs. liking 422
   evolution of 385, 386
plethysmography 160
pluripotent stem cells 64

policy implications 604–6
politics and drugs 176–7
polycystic ovary syndrome (PCOS) 376
polygenetic disorders 31, 35, 56
polygraphs, lie detection 608
polymerase chain reaction (PCR) 49
polymodal receptors, pain 281
polymorphisms 47, 49
polyploidy 48
polyvagal theory 437
pons 144, *144*
pons, REM sleep 468
pornography 367, 387
Porteus maze 323
positive reinforcement 218
   and drug addiction 420–1
   intracranial self-stimulation 413, *415*, 416
   Koob's dynamic process of addiction 424–5
positive symptoms, schizophrenia 525, *526*, 535, *536*, *537*
positron emission tomography (PET) 162–3
postdrome, following migraine attack 147
postganglionic neurons 123
postsynaptic membrane 100, 101, 102
   retrograde signalling 107, *108*
postsynaptic neuron 98, *99*, 102, 109
postsynaptic potentials 98–9
posttraumatic stress disorder (PTSD) 569
   and addiction 566–7
   vicarious symptoms of following 9/11 attacks 572
potassium ions (K$^+$) 84
   role in action potential 95–7
   role in resting potential 93–5
potency of a drug 191
potency of stem cells 64
pre-SMA *see* presupplementary motor area
precursor preloading drugs 186, 188
prediction errors and reward learning 428, 429–30
predictive homeostasis 570
predictive validity 17, 530
prefrontal cortex
   adaptive in chronic stress 571
   antipsychotic effects 533
   and bias processing in depression 555
   expectation processing 240
   inhibiting amygdala response 458
   involved in behavioural inhibition and ADHD 333, 334, 513
   involvement in sleep loss 473
   lobotomy 321–2
   methylphenidate action *510*
   role in abstract thinking 322

preganglionic autonomic neurons 123
premenstrual dysphoric disorder (PMDD) 372–3
premenstrual syndrome (PMS) 609
premotor cortex 295–7
preoccupation anticipation, addiction 424, 425
presupplementary motor area (preSMA) 295, 297
  and intention 476
presynaptic terminal 88
primary emotions 438–40
primary motor cortex (M1) 294–5, 305
primates 28
primitive streak 64, 67
primordial follicles 369, 371
pro-creationism 24
pro-opiomelanocortin (POMC) 400, 401
proactive interference 348
problem solving, effects of frontal lobe damage 327
procedural (non-declarative) memory 345, 346
prodrome, preceding migraine attack 147
progenitor cells 62, 65
progesterone 111, 368, 369, 370, 372
progestins 368
prolactin 112, 113, 369
prolactin-inhibiting hormone 141
proof 500–1
proprioception 279, 309
  loss of 120
prosencephalon (forebrain) 68, 132–41
prosopagnosia 138
prostate gland 365, 374, 381, 383, 385
protein synthesis 44–6
protons 84
  structural MRI 164, 165
psilocybin 196
psychobiology 4
  areas of expertise 9
  levels of analysis 5
  subdisciplines of 9–12
psychomotor stimulant theory of addiction 420–1
psychopathology
  affective disorders 542–57
  anxiety & stress 560–83
  developmental disorders 504–22
  neurodegeneration 584–99
  schizophrenia spectrum 524–41
psychopharmacology 6, 10, 174
  behavioural effect of drugs 228–30
  clinical trials 199–201
  dark side 197–9

drug action 177–93
drug classification 174–7
drug types 193–7
psychophysiology 9–10, 158–61
  sleep assessment 465–6
psychosexual development 9
psychosis 524
  in PD after treatment with DA agonists 589
  schizophrenia 524–40
psychosocial context, placebos 233, 238
  negative in the case of nocebos 244
psychostimulants 194
psychotherapy for depression 556
puberty, hormonal changes 380
publication bias 20, 201
pudendal cleft 362
punishment 218–20
pupil of the eye 255
Purkinje cell layer, cerebellum 145
putamen 143, 506, 586, 592
Pygmalion effect 237
pyloric sphincter 392, 395
pyramidal cells, cerebral cortex 134, 135, 141
pyramidal motor system 302, 305

quadriplegia 120
qualia, subjective experience 474
qualitative traits, inheritance of 29, 31
quantitative trait loci (QTL) 35
quantitative traits, inheritance of 31, 35

radial glia 68, 69
radioactive isotopes 191
  use in nuclear imaging 161–3
randomized controlled trial (RCT) 200
raphe nuclei 144, 468
rash impulsiveness 331
rat brain, atlas of 156
rate-dependent hypothesis, drug effects 231
reactive homeostasis 570
readiness potential 475, 480
  imaging data 477
reboxetine 554
receptive fields, visual system 258–60, 263, 267, 268, 269
receptor-mediated endocytosis 105, 107
receptors 98, 104
recessive traits 35–6
  phenylketonuria (PKU) 38, 39
rectal administration route 178
red nucleus 294, 302, 304, 305
  motor area 143, 144

Reduce, Replace and Refine, 3Rs of animal research legislation 14
reductionism 4–6
reflexes 207–8
region of interest (ROI) 164
regulation, endocrine system 114
reinforcement 218
  conditioned place preference 413–14
  and drug addiction 219, 420–6
  model of emotion 455–6
  schedules 220–1
reinforcers, natural/non-drug 419, 420
relapse, drug-taking, stress-induced 568
relatedness, degrees of 52
relative refractory period 95
reliability 18
REM sleep 466–7
  AIM model 469–70, 471
  role of the pons 468
remifentanil 238, 245
renal system 184
renin 406
replicability 18
replication, DNA 43, 44
reproductive suppression hypothesis, anorexia 393
reproductive system 361–8
  female 62, 364
  male 366
  in utero development 374
Rescorla-Wagner model 215, 216
research methodology 20
reserpine 548
resolution phase, sexual response cycle 380, 382, 386
response inhibition see behavioural inhibition (BI)
resting potential 92–5
reticular formation 144, 294, 302
  wakefulness 468
retina of the eye 255–61
retinorecipient olivary nucleus 255
retinotopic map/organization 263, 272
retrograde amnesia 345, 349
retrograde signalling 107–8, 108
retrograde thalamic degeneration 139
retroviruses 58
reuptake 105, 107
  drugs that block 190
reverse tolerance (sensitization) 233, 235
reverse transcription 58
reward
  and learning 224–5
  Rolls' model of emotion 454–6
reward activation model (RAM) 468

INDEX

reward circuits, feeding behaviour *401, 404*
   activated by stress 402
reward deficiency syndrome, ADHD 511
reward drive, impulsivity 331
reward pathway, DA-mediated 413–19, 428
reward prediction error, learning of associations 428–30
reward system calibration via allostasis 425–6
rhodopsin 257
rhombencephalon (hindbrain) 68, 143–5
ribosomes 44, *45*
right-handedness and left-hemisphere dominance for language 492
right shift (RS) gene for handedness 492
rods and cones, retina 257–8
rolandic operculum, activated by pleasant music 460
rubrospinal tract *304*, 305
rule learning, role of frontal lobe 322–6

saccadic eye movements 160
saccule, vestibular system 277, *278*
sacral nerves 120, *124*
sacral vertebrae 122
   areas connected to *123*
sagittal plane, the brain 132
saliency and addiction 421–2, 431
saltatory conduction 97, 98
saltiness 392, 394, 406
same-sex sexual behaviour 386
sarcolemma 307
sarin, action and effects of 198, *199*
satiety 396, 399, 404
scalp *128*
scanners
   MRI scanner 164, *165*
   PET scanner 162, *163*
Schachter's cognitive labelling theory of emotion *444*, 446–7
scheduled drugs 175–6
schedules of reinforcement 220–1
   determinants of behavioural response to drugs 228–30
   nicotine self-administration in rats 418–19
schemata 337–8
schizophrenia 524–5
   age of onset 525
   amphetamine 232
   animal models 530
   antipsychotic treatment 531–6
   diagnosis 525, 527
   evolutionary theories 528–9
   factors affecting incidence of 525, 529
   genetics 525
   limitations of studies 537
   neurobiological theories 534–5
   neurochemistry 529–36
   neuropsychological theories 535–7
   pathways contributing to 537–8
   symptoms 524–5, *526*, 527
Schwann cells 69, 71, 89
sclera, the eye 253–4
scopolamine, animal models of AD 596–7
scotopic vision 257
screening tests 16
scrotum 365, *366, 367*, 373, *375*, 380
sea slug, habituation & sensitization 353–4
secondary motor cortex 305
secondary oocyte 372
secondary oocyte, ovulation 372
sedatives 472
seeing *see* visual perception
selective breeding 25
selective noradrenergic reuptake inhibitors (SNRIs) 553, 554
selective serotonin reuptake inhibitors (SSRIs) 553, 554
   treatment for anorexia 405
self-administration of drugs, animal studies 219
self-medication 423
   ADHD individuals 424
semantic memory 344, *344*
semicircular canals 273, 277, *278*
seminiferous tubules *361*, 368
senile dementia of Alzheimer's type (SDAT) 593
sensation seeking (SS), genetics of 55–6
sensitive/critical periods 76–7
sensitivity, heightened, to conditioned aversive stimuli 581
sensitization 207, 353–4
   to chronic stress 569
   of drug effects 233, *235*
   to drugs 421–2
sensorimotor loop 309
sensory aphasia 488
sensory cells 71
sensory dorsal nerve, clitoris 362
sensory inputs, parietal lobe 137–8
sensory integration 291
sensory modalities 252
sensory neurons 86, 90
separation distress and depression 546
septohippocampal system & anxiety 581
septum/septal area 141, *142*

serotonin (5-HT) 101, 102, *104*, 112
   anorexia, low levels in 405
   and anxiety 581
   and ASD 519
   and depression 545, 548–52
   eating inhibition 400
   and impulsivity 335
   involvement in ToM 329, *332*
   MDMA neurotoxicity 193
   and schizophrenia 525, 532, 534
   and sleep 468
Sertoli cells 368
sex 360–89
   brain differences 377–80
   differentiation of the sexes 361–8
   and evolution of pleasure 386, 387
   evolution of sex/the sexes 360–1
   hormones 368–9
   human sexual response 380–6
   intersexuality 388
   menstrual cycle and ovulation 369–73
   sexual development 373–7
   sexual orientation 386
sex chromosomes 40
sex determining region of the Y chromosome (SRY) 360–1, 373, 379
sex differences 361–8
   of the brain 71, 373, 375, 377–80
   endocrine glands 110
   genes contributing to depression 545
   in lateralization 489–90
sex hormones 109–11, 368–9
sexual development 373–7
sexual fetish 211
sexual masochism 290–1
sexual orientation 386
sexual pleasure 386
sexual reproduction, adaptive function 360
sexual response cycle, humans 380–6
sexual stimuli, DA response to 419, *420*
sexually dimorphic nucleus (SDN) 378, 379
shaping 221
short-term memory 345, 351
sickle cell disease 44, 46, 47
simple cells, visual cortex 263, 265, 267, 268
simulations 16
simultaneous conditioning 212
sine waves 266, *269*
single-blind experiments 200
single nucleotide polymorphisms (SNPs) 47, 49
single photon emission computed tomography (SPECT) 162–3

sinuses, cranial venous 148, 149
skeleton 306
skin conductance level (SCL) 160
skin conductance response (SCR) 160–1
skin receptors 280
skin, touch sensation 279
skull 128
    damage to, Phineas Gage 319–20
    evolution of 316–17
sleep 465–72
    disorders of 470–2
    dreams 469–70
    functions 470
    neural mechanisms 468
    and neurotransmitters 468
    stages of 465–7
    theories of 470–2
sleep deprivation 472
    effects on educational performance 473
    and impaired performance at work 473
sleep paralysis 472
sleep spindles 466, 470
sleeping pills 472
slow-wave sleep (SWS) 466, 467, 468
smell, olfactory perception 275–6
smoking during pregnancy, effects of 66, 67
social neuroscience 10
social processing deficits and alcoholism 442–3
social status, DA receptor levels and 426, 427
sodium amytal (amobarbital) 489
sodium ions (NA+) 84
    role in action potential 95–7
    role in resting potential 93–5
sodium-potassium pump 93–5
soluble gases 101, 102
soma (cell body), neurons 85, 86, 88, 98
somatic association area, parietal lobe 137
somatic market hypothesis of emotion 456
somatic nervous system (SNS) 118–20
    cranial nerves 119, 121–2
    spinal nerves 119–20
somatic sensory cortices, parietal lobe 137
somatosensation 279
somatosensory cortex 280
somatosensory pathway 280
somatotopic maps 295
somites 65
sonic hedgehog gene 68
sound detection and location 273–5
spandrels 34
spatial abilities, male/right-brain 489–90, 497

spatial frequency, vision 265–6, 269
spatial learning, Alzheimer's disease 596
spatial memory
    neural substrate 345
    taxi drivers 351–2
spatial orientation 277–9
spatial summation 98, 99
spatial terms for the brain 132
spectrums 521
speech
    incoherent in schizophrenia 536
    motor control of 297–8
sperm 361, 365, 368, 385
spermatic cord 365
spermatogenesis 365, 368
sphygmomanometer 160
spina bifida 65, 68
spinal accessory nerve 119
    disorders of 122
spinal cord 120, 128, 208
    effect of lesions of 120
    effects of lesions of 124
    motor tracts 296, 303–4
    regions 122, 123, 125
spinal dura mater 127, 128
spinal meninges 128
spinal nerves 119–20, 124
spinocerebellar tract 303
spinocerebellum 301, 302
spinoreticular pathway 282–3, 285
spinotectal pathway 282, 283, 285
spinothalamic pathway 282–3, 285
spiperone 531
split-brain studies 490, 494–6
spontaneous recovery 209–10, 221
squid axon 90, 93
SRY gene, sex determination 360, 361, 373, 379
startle response, habituation to 205–6, 207
statistical literacy 501
stem cells 62, 63–4
stereopsis 271
stereotaxic frames, rat and human 155
steroid hormones 109–10, 368–9
    glucocorticoids 566, 569, 571
    receptor interaction 113–14
stimulants 194
stirrup (stapes) 273, 274
stomach secretory activity, factors stimulating & inhibiting 395
Stop Signal Reaction Time (SSRT) task 332–4, 334, 335
    and behavioural inhibition 506, 512, 513
stress 459, 560–71
    acute vs. chronic 569–71

    adaptive nature 560, 563, 564, 570
    animal studies 564, 567–8, 569
    definitions 561–3, 564
    effect on brain 74, 77
    and exams 560–61
    maladaptive nature of 566–8
    and obesity 402
    resistance, link to restricted diet 76
    stressors 563
stress diathesis model of depression 545
stress response 563–4
    input pathways 564–5
striatum 143, 416, 429
    abnormality in Huntington's disease 301
    and learning of new skills 299
stroke (cerebral ischaemia) 146–7
stroma 255
Stroop task 327–8
structural MRI 164
subarachnoid space 127, 128
subcutaneous (SC) 179
subdural space 127, 128
subfornical organ 130, 406
subjective experiences (qualia) 474
substance dependence disorder 412
substance use disorder (SUD) 412
substantia gelatinosa 282, 287, 288, 289
substantia nigra (SN) 143, 144, 305, 415
    Parkinson's disease 585, 586, 591
    pars compacta (SNc) 143, 299, 301, 429
    pars reticulata (SNr) 143, 298, 299, 301, 429
subthalamic nucleus (STN) 299, 301, 302
    inhibition, lack of in PD 591
    lesions of, PD treatment 592
subthalamus 140
sulci in cerebral cortex 132, 133
superficial facial muscles 442
superficial middle cerebral vein 149
superheroes, nature-nurture debate 50–1
superior anastomotic vein 149
superior colliculus 143, 261, 285, 304
superior olivary nuclei 273, 274, 490
supervisory attentional system (SAS) 337–8
supplementary motor area (SMA) 295, 297, 298, 305, 311, 312, 589
    reduced readiness potential in PD 590, 592
suprachiasmatic nucleus (SCN), circadian pacemaker 464–5
supraoptic nucleus 113, 140
Surgical Papyrus 6
'survival of the fittest' 25

survival circuits and emotion 451–2
sweating, electrodermal activity 160–1
switched twins 54–5
sympathetic-adrenomedullary axis (SAM) 565–6
sympathetic chain, spinal column 123
sympathetic nervous system 71, 123–5
synaesthesia 280
synapses 99–101
synaptic connections 108
synaptic consolidation 77
synaptic elimination 77
synaptic plasticity 355
synaptic transmission 99–101
   in the hippocampus 354–5, 356
   neurotransmitters 101–2
   receptors 102–4
   retrograde signalling 107–8
   synaptic and cellular regulation 104–7
synaptogenesis 68–70, 77
synovial joints 306
synthesis inhibition 188
   autoreceptors 509, 534
systematic desensitization 215
systematizing, male brain of ASD 516, 521
systolic blood pressure 160

tacrine 596
tactile stimuli, transmission to brain 279
tandem repeat (satellite DNA) 47–8
tardive dyskinesia (TD) 532
taste 276–7
   aversion learning 205
   influencing eating behaviour 405–6
tau proteins 596
taxi drivers, spatial memory 351–2
tectospinal tract 304, 305
tectum, midbrain 143
tegmentum, midbrain 143
telencephalon 132–8
   Brodmann areas 134, 135–7
   cells of the cortex 134, 135
   cerebral hemispheres 132, 133
   corpus callosum 132–3
   frontal lobes 134, 137
   lobes 133–4
   occipital lobe 138
   parietal lobe 137–8
   temporal lobe 138
telomeres 40
temporal conditioning 214
temporal gradient, retrograde amnesia 349
temporal hemiretina 261, 263
temporal lobe 134, 138

lobectomy, effects on memory 350–1
   role in memory 345, 350
temporal lobe, role in emotion 447–8
temporal lobes 72, 79
temporal summation 99
tendons 306, 309–10
teratogens in ADHD 66–7
teratology 78
terrorist attacks, vicarious PTSD-like symptoms 572
tesla (T) 164
testes 110–11, 361, 365, 368, 373, 374, 378
testes determining factor (TDF) 360, 374
testosterone 110, 111, 113, 368, 373, 374, 375, 376, 378
   and aggression 459
   effects of prenatal 377
   and love 457
tetrabenazine 300, 301
tetraplegia 120
thalamic retrograde degeneration 265, 321
thalamus 138–9
   olfactory signals bypassing 252, 275–6
   pain pathways 282–3, 285
thalidomide 78
thecal cells 372
thelarche 380
Theory of Mind (ToM) 328–9
   and ASD 519–20
   brain regions 330
   cognitive and affective networks related to 329, 331
   disorders implicated in 333
   dopamine and serotonin 332
   schizophrenia 536
thermal pain 281
thermal receptors 281, 282
theta activity, sleep 466, 467
theta waves 158, 159
thiamine deficiency, Korsakoff's amnesia 347
thinking
   abstract attitude 322
   in ADHD 511–12
   PET scan 163
   supervisory attentional system (SAS) 337–8
thirst 406
thoracic nerves 120, 124
thoracic vertebrae 122
   areas connected to 123
   effect of lesions to 124
threat conditioning, Ledoux 450
threats, response to 437–8
three prime (3') 44

three Rs of animal research 14
thrill seeking, vestibular system 279
thymine 43, 44, 47
thyroid gland 110, 111
thyroid hormones 109, 111
thyroid-stimulating hormone (TSH) 112, 113
thyrotrophin-releasing hormone 112
thyroxine 109, 111
tinnitus 275
token reinforcers 224
tolerance 230–3, 412, 421, 423
   and the paradoxical overdose 234–5
the tongue, taste buds 276–7
tonotopic map, auditory system 275
totipotent stem cells 64
touch/feeling, somatosensory system 279
Tower of Hanoi test 325, 325
Tower of London test 325, 325
trace conditioning 214
transcortical aphasia 488
transcranial magnetic stimulation (TMS) 169, 476
transcription 44, 47
   reverse 58
transdermal (TD) 178
transdihydrolisuride (terguride) 588
transfer ribonucleic acid (tRNA) 44, 45
transgenic mice 57
transient ischaemic attack (TIA) 146
translocation (genetic) 47–8
transmucosal (TM) 178
transplants, neural, Parkinson's disease 588–9
transporter proteins 101
traumatic stress, response to 437–8
treatment implications 604–10
trepanning of skulls 6
tricyclic antidepressants (TCAs) 549, 549
trigeminal nerve 119, 121, 127, 147
   disorders of 121
trimester 78
trisomy 31, 48
trisomy 21 (Down's syndrome) 48–9
trochlear nerve 119, 121
trochlear nerve, disorders of 121
tryptophan depletion 550, 555
tryptophan-free diets and reduced serotonin 581
tunica albuginea 365
Turner's syndrome 31–2, 376
twin studies 50, 52–5
   critique of 54
   switched twins 54–5
   virtual twins 54
typical antipsychotics 532

uncinate fasciculus 78
unconditioned response (UR) 208
    see also classical conditioning
unconditioned stimulus (US) 208
    see also classical conditioning
unconscious mechanisms, placebo effect 238, 241–3
unilateral lesions 158
unipolar neurons 90
unipotent stem cells 64
unmyelinated axons 98
uracil 44
urethra 363, 365, 374, 375, 383
urethral meatus 365, 366
urethral opening 362, 363, 367, 384
uterus 62, 363, 364, 365, 372, 373, 374, 384
utilization behaviour patients 311
utricle, vestibular system 277, 278

vagina 362, 363–4, 384, 385
vagus nerve 119, 121, 395, 396, 397, 400
    disorders of 122
validity
    animal models 16–20, 530
    construct validity 17–18, 530
    external validity 18
    face validity 17
    internal validity 19
    predictive validity 17, 530
varenicline, partial agonist, effect on nicotine receptor 187
variable interval (VI) schedule 221
variable ratio (VR) schedule 220
vas deferens 365, 367, 373, 381, 382
vasopressin 109, 112, 113, 140, 406
    effect on prosocial behaviour and love 458
vehicle, drug delivery agent 181
veins 145
    cerebral 149
    sinuses 149–50
ventral corticospinal tract 294
ventral noradrenergic bundle 400
ventral pallidum 142
ventral striatum 429
    learning about reward 431
ventral tegmental area (VTA) 142, 400, 401, 415, 416, 421, 429
    effect of lesions 418
    nicotine receptors 418
ventricles 129
ventromedial hypothalamus (VMH) 397–8, 398, 401
    effect of lesions of 398, 399, 400
ventromedial nucleus (VMA) 112, 140, 398

ventromedial prefrontal area, effect of damage to 319
vertebral artery 148, 149
vesicles, synaptic transmission 99–101, 107
vesicular monoamine transporter (VMAT) 300, 301
vestibular system 277–9
vestibule 362, 374
vestibulocerebellum 301, 302
vestibulocochlear nerve 71, 119, 121, 278
vestibulospinal tract 304, 305
veto power, decision not to act 475–6
Viagra 383
vicarious PTSD-like symptoms following terrorist attacks 572
violence see aggression
virtual lesions 169
virtual reality conditioned place preference 413–14
virtual twins 54
viruses and gene therapy 58
visceral brain 448
visceral pain 281
visual cortex 138, 263–6
    active during sleep 469
    complex cells 263, 265
    hypercolumns 266
    hypercomplex cells 266
    PET scan 163
    simple cells 263
    spatial frequency 265–6
visual deprivation, effects of 265
visual perception 252–72
    aqueous humour 255
    binocular vision 270–1
    bipolar cells and receptive fields 258–60
    colour perception 266–70
    deprivation effects 265
    the eye 253
    horizontal cells, retina 261
    iris and pupil 255
    lateral geniculate nucleus 261–3
    lateral inhibition 261, 262
    the lens 255
    optic nerve 261
    the retina 255–61
    rods and cones 257–8
    sclera and cornea 253–5
    visual cortex 263–6
    vitreous humour 255
visuospatial deficits, PD 592–3
visuospatial sketchpad, working memory 336
vitreous humour, the eye 255
vocalization, motor control of 297

volitional decisions, preceded by readiness potential 475–6
voluntary movement, control of 309
voodoo death 244
voodoo experiment, manipulation of free will 479
vulva 361–2

Wada test 489
wakefulness, circadian rhythms 464–5
wanting and liking, drug addiction 421–2
water, atomic structure of 84, 85
water maze, spatial learning in rodents 597
weak central coherence model (WCC) 520, 521
Wechsler Intelligence Scale 323
Wegner, Daniel, grand illusion of free will 479, 480
Wernicke-Geschwind model of language 487, 488
Wernicke's area 485, 486, 487, 488, 490
Wernicke's encephalopathy 347
white matter 72, 75, 78, 128, 131–2, 145
wide dynamic range (WDR) receptors, pain 288, 289
Williams-Beuren syndrome 47
winter/spring births and schizophrenia 525
Wisconsin Card Sorting Test (WCST) 325–6
withdrawal symptoms, drugs 412, 423, 425
Wolffian duct 373
working memory 336–7
    basal ganglia as filter for 299
    brain regions 345
    deficits in ADHD 513–14
    deficits in Alzheimer's disease 598

X-inactivation gene (XIST) 49
X-rays, CT/CAT scans 162
XYY genotype 376–7

Yellow Card system 200

Z lens 495, 497
zeitgeber (time giver) 464
zona incerta, subthalamus 140
zona pellucida 62, 63, 65
zonules of Zinn 255
zygomaticus muscles 441, 442
zygote 62
    development of 65